Physiology of Behavior

Sixth Edition

Physiology of Behavior

Neil R. Carlson   *University of Massachusetts*

Allyn and Bacon

Boston   London   Toronto   Sydney   Tokyo   Singapore

Vice-President and Editor-in-Chief, Social Sciences: *Sean W. Wakely*
Senior Editor: *Carolyn Merrill*
Series Editorial Assistant: *Amy Goldmacher*
Marketing Manager: *Joyce Nilsen*
Composition and Prepress Buyer: *Linda Cox*
Manufacturing Buyer: *Megan Cochran*
Cover Administrator: *Linda Knowles*
Photo Researcher: *Anne M. Barnard*
Production Administrator: *Mary Beth Finch*
Editorial Production Service: *Barbara Gracia*
Text Designer: *Glenna Collett*
Illustrator: *Jay Alexander*
Electronic Composition: *Omegatype Typography, Inc.*

Copyright © 1998, 1994, 1991, 1986, 1981, 1977 by Allyn and Bacon
A Viacom Company
Needham Heights, MA 02194

Internet: www.abacon.com
America Online: keyword: College Online

Library of Congress Cataloging-in-Publication Data
Carlson, Neil R., 1942–
    Physiology of behavior / Neil R. Carlson.—6th ed.
        p.   cm.
    Includes bibliographical references and index.
    ISBN 0-205-27340-8
    1. Psychophysiology.   I. Title.
    [DNLM: 1. Nervous System—physiology.   2. Behavior—physiology.
3. Nervous System—anatomy & histology.   4. Psychophysiology.   WL
102 C284p 1998]
QP360.C35 1998
612.8--dc21
DNLM/DLC
for Library of Congress   97–41384
                                                                    CIP

Printed in the United States of America
10 9 8 7 6 5 4 3 2 1   RRD 02 01 00 99 98 97

Chapter Opener Art Credits

Chapter 1: *The Birth of Venus* by Mercedes Nuñez. Courtesy of the artist.

Chapter 2: *The Port* by Joan Miro. © 1998 Artists Rights Society (ARS), New York/ADAGP, Paris. Private Collection/Art Resource, New York.

Chapter 3: *Double Metamorphosis* by Yaacov Agam. © 1998 Artists Rights Society (ARS), New York/ADAGP, Paris. Musée National d'Art Moderne, Paris, France/Art Resource, New York.

Chapter 4: *Accent Rose* by Wassily Kandinsky. Musée National d'Art Moderne, Centre Georges Pompidou, Paris. © Vaga, New York.

Credits continue on page 701 which should be considered an extension of the copyright page.

For Mary

Brief Contents

Contents

Preface

I wrote the first edition of *Physiology of Behavior* a little over twenty years ago. The interesting work coming out of my colleagues' laboratories—a result of their creativity and hard work—has given me something new to say with each edition. Because there was so much for me to learn, I enjoyed writing this edition just as much as the first one. That is what makes writing new editions interesting—learning something new and then trying to find a way to convey the information to the reader.

In the preface to each of the previous editions I mentioned some of the new research methods that had recently been developed. Investigators are continuing to develop new methods—for example, new staining techniques for specific substances, new imaging methods, new recording methods, and the means for analyzing the release of neurotransmitters and neuromodulators in restricted regions of the brains of freely moving animals. The research reported in this edition reflects the enormous advances made in staining methods: new anterograde and retrograde tracers, dye-coupled antibodies for just about everything, in situ hybridization methods to localize messenger RNA, stains for Fos, single-photon and multiphoton laser scanning microscopy, targeted mutations ("knockouts") of just about any gene—and the list continues. Nowadays, as soon as a new method is developed in one laboratory, it is adopted by other laboratories and applied to a wide range of problems. And more and more, researchers are combining techniques that converge upon the solution to a problem. In the past, individuals tended to apply their particular research method to a problem; now they are more likely to use many methods, sometimes in collaboration with other laboratories.

You will notice that the book has a different look. Jay Alexander and I have worked together to redraw almost all of the anatomical art. Jay, an artist who also works as a technician in the Psychology Department at the University of Massachusetts, supplied the artistic talent. I think the result of our collaboration is a set of clear, consistent, and attractive illustrations.

In this edition, as in the previous ones, I have made some changes to the outline of the book, as a reader familiar with the previous edition will discover. Some of these changes were made in response to new directions in research efforts, and some were made in response to suggestions of students and colleagues concerning pedagogy. The two most frequent requests were to include full chapters on psychopharmacology and on the physiology of drug abuse, which I have done. Psychopharmacological methods have become increasingly important in recent years, and the identification of specific subclasses of receptors and the development of drugs that interact with them have contributed much to our understanding of neural mechanisms of behavior. The new chapter on the physiology of drug abuse complements the two chapters on mental disorders and with them illustrates the important role that the methods of neuroscience have come to play in the field of mental health.

The first part of the book is concerned with foundations: the history of the field, the structure and functions of neurons, neuroanatomy, psychopharmacology, and research methods. The second part is concerned with inputs and outputs: the sensory systems and the motor system. The third part deals with classes of species-typical behavior: sleep, reproduction, emotional behavior, and ingestion. The chapter on reproductive behavior includes maternal behavior as well as mating. The chapter on emotion includes a discussion of emotional reactions, communication of emotions, feelings of emotions, and aggression. As in the previous edition, ingestive behavior is covered in two chapters—one on drinking and one on eating.

The fourth part of the book deals with learning. The first learning chapter discusses research on synaptic plasticity and the neural mechanisms responsible for perceptual learning and stimulus–response learning (including classical and operant conditioning). The second learning chapter discusses human amnesia and the role of the hippocampal formation in relational learning. The final part of the book deals with verbal communication and mental and behavioral disorders. The latter topic is now covered in three chapters; the first discusses schizophrenia and the affective disorders; the second discusses the anxiety disorders, autism, and stress; and, as I already mentioned, the third discusses drug abuse.

Besides updating my discussion of research, I have updated my writing. Writing is a difficult, time-consuming endeavor, and I find that I am still learning how to do it well. I have said this in the preface of every edition of this book, and it is still true. I have worked with copy editors who have ruthlessly marked up my manuscript, showing me how to do it better the next time. I keep thinking, "This time there will be nothing for the copy editor to do," but I am always proved wrong: each page contains notes showing me how to improve my prose. But I do think that each time the writing is better organized, smoother, and more coherent.

Good writing means including all steps of a logical discourse. My teaching experience has taught me that an entire lecture can be wasted if the students do not understand all of the "obvious" conclusions of a particular experiment before the next one is described. Unfortunately, puzzled students sometimes write notes feverishly, in an attempt to get the facts down so they can study them—and understand them—later. A roomful of busy, attentive students tends to reinforce the lecturer's behavior. I am sure all my colleagues have been dismayed by a question from a student that reveals a lack of understanding of details long since passed, accompanied by quizzical looks from other students that confirm that they too have the same question. Painful experiences such as these have taught me to examine the logical steps between the discussion of one experiment and the next and to make sure they are explicitly stated. A textbook writer must address the students who will read the book, not simply colleagues who are already acquainted with much of what he or she will say.

Because research on the physiology of behavior is an interdisciplinary effort, a textbook must provide the student with the background necessary for understanding a variety of approaches. I have been careful to provide enough biological background early in the book that students without a background in physiology can understand what is said later, while students with such a background can benefit from details that are familiar to them.

I designed this text for serious students who are willing to work. In return for their effort, I have endeavored to provide a solid foundation for further study. Those students who will not take subsequent courses in this or related fields should receive the satisfaction of a much better understanding of their own behavior. Also, they will have a greater appreciation for the forthcoming advances in med-

ical practices related to disorders that affect a person's perception, mood, or behavior. I hope that students who carefully read this book will henceforth perceive human behavior in a new light.

ACKNOWLEDGMENTS

Although I must accept the blame for any shortcomings of the book, I want to thank colleagues who helped me by sending reprints of their work, suggesting topics that I should cover, sending photographs that have been reproduced in this book, and pointing out deficiencies in the previous edition. I thank:

Peter Arnett, Gary Aston-Jones, Jeffrey Blaustein, Gemma Calvert, Edna Cohen, Geert DeVries, Nina Dronkers, Guinevere Eden, Mark George, Eugenia Gurevich, Marc Hauser, A.J. Hudspeth, Sarah Leibowitz, Deborah Mash, Julian Mercer, Jerrold Meyer, Shiro Minami, Mitchell Nobler, Steven Reppert, Randall Sakai, Dick Swaab, Simon Thornton, and Joe Tsien.

Before I began work on the book, my publisher sent a questionnaire to colleagues who were familiar with the previous edition. Their responses to this questionnaire helped me decide what changes to make in the revision. I thank:

A. Michael Anch, Anne Powell Anderson, Joyce Bishop, Joshua E. Blustein, John Broida, Edward Castaneda, Jess F. Deegun II, Linda Enloe, Paul Haerich, Jeremy Hall, Fred Heimstetter, Sandra Kelly, Michael Leon, Raymond Martinetti, June E. Millet, Antonio Nuñez, William Overman, Todd Schachtman, Ronald See, Rhea Steinpreis, Meg Waraczynski, Robert Webb, Frank Webbe, N. M. Weinberger, Margaret H. White, and Nancy J. Wolf.

Several colleagues have reviewed the manuscript of parts of this book and made suggestions for improving the final drafts. I thank:

Robin Bowers, Joshua E. Blustein, Nancy Woolf, B. Glenn Stanley, Linda M. Noble, Antonio A. Nuñez, Jeffrey W. Grimm, Meg Waraczynski, Frank Webbe, Beth Powell, John Broida, Eric Nisenbaum, and Karen Luh.

I also want to thank the people at Allyn and Bacon. Carolyn Merrill, my editor, provided assistance, support, and encouragement. Jennifer Normandin and Amy Goldmacher, editorial assistants, helped gather comments and suggestions from colleagues who have read the book. Mary Beth Finch, the production editor, assembled the team that designed and produced the book. Barbara Gracia, of Woodstock Publisher's Services, demonstrated her masterful skills of organization in managing the book's production. She got everything done on time, despite an extremely tight schedule. Few people realize what a difficult, demanding, and time-consuming job a production editor has with a project such as this, with hundreds of illustrations and an author who tends to procrastinate, but I do, and I thank her for all she has done. Joyce Grandy and Barbara Willette served as copy editors. Their attention to detail surprised me again and again; they found inconsistencies in my terminology, awkwardness in my prose, and disjunctions in my logical discourse and gave me a chance to fix them before anyone else saw them in print.

I must also thank my wife Mary for her support. Writing is a lonely pursuit, because one must be alone with one's thoughts for many hours of the day. I thank her for giving me the time to read, reflect, and write without feeling that I was neglecting her too much. I also thank her and my daughter, Kerstin Carlson Le Floch, for the superb job they did preparing the study guide.

I was delighted to hear from many students and colleagues who read previous editions of my book, and I hope that the dialogue will continue. Please write to me and tell me what you like and dislike about the book. My address is: Department of Psychology, Tobin Hall, University of Massachusetts, Amherst, Massachusetts 01003. My e-mail is *nrc@psych.umass.edu*. When I write, I like to imagine that I am talking with you, the reader. If you write to me, we can make the conversation a two-way exchange.

CHAPTER 1

Introduction

The Birth of Venus by Mercedes Nuñez. Courtesy of the artist.

The last frontier in this world—and perhaps the greatest one—lies within us. The human nervous system makes possible all that we can do, all that we can know, and all that we can experience. Its complexity is immense, and the task of studying it and understanding it dwarfs all previous explorations our species has undertaken.

One of the most universal of all human characteristics is curiosity. We want to explain what makes things happen. In ancient times, people believed that natural phenomena were caused by animating spirits. All moving objects—animals, the wind and tides, the sun, moon, and stars—were assumed to have spirits that caused them to move. For example, stones fell when they were dropped because their animating spirits wanted to be reunited with Mother Earth. As our ancestors became more sophisticated and learned more about nature, they abandoned this approach (which we call *animism*) in favor of physical explanations for inanimate moving objects. But they still used spirits to explain human behavior.

From the earliest historical times people have believed they possessed something intangible that animated them—a mind, or a soul, or a spirit. This belief stems from the fact that each of us is aware of his or her own existence. When we think or act, we feel as though something inside us is thinking or deciding to act. But what is the nature of the human mind? We have physical bodies, with muscles that move it and sensory organs such as eyes and ears that perceive information about the world around us. Within our bodies the nervous system plays a central role, receiving information from the sensory organs and controlling the movements of the muscles. But what role does the mind play? Does it *control* the nervous system? Is it a *part of* the nervous system? Is it physical and tangible, like the rest of the body, or is it a spirit that will always remain hidden?

This puzzle has historically been called the *mind–body question*. Philosophers have been trying to answer it for many centuries, and more recently scientists have taken up

the task. Basically, people have followed two different approaches: dualism and monism. **Dualism** is a belief in the dual nature of reality. Mind and body are separate; the body is made of ordinary matter, but the mind is not. **Monism** is a belief that everything in the universe consists of matter and energy and that the mind is a phenomenon produced by the workings of the nervous system.

Mere speculation about the nature of the mind is futile. If we could answer the mind–body question simply by thinking about it, philosophers would have done so long ago. Physiological psychologists take an empirical, practical, and monistic approach to the study of human nature. Most of us believe that once we understand the workings of the human body—and, in particular, the workings of the nervous system—the mind–body problem will have been solved. We will be able to explain how we perceive, how we think, how we remember, and how we act. We will even be able to explain the nature of our own self-awareness. Of course, we are far from understanding the workings of the nervous system, so only time will tell whether this belief is justified.

UNDERSTANDING HUMAN CONSCIOUSNESS: A PHYSIOLOGICAL APPROACH

As you will learn from subsequent chapters, scientists have discovered much about the physiology of behavior: of perception, motivation, memory, and control of specific movements. But before addressing these problems, I want

dualism The belief that the body is physical but the mind (or soul) is not.

monism (*mahn* ism) The belief that the world consists only of matter and energy and the mind is part of it.

to show you how physiological psychologists have attempted to understand perhaps the most complex phenomenon of all: human consciousness.

The term *consciousness* can be used to refer to a variety of concepts, including simple wakefulness. Thus, a researcher may write about an experiment using "conscious rats," referring to the fact that the rats were awake and not anesthetized. By *consciousness,* I am referring to the fact that we humans are aware of—and can tell others about—our thoughts, perceptions, memories, and feelings.

We know that consciousness can be altered by changes in the structure or chemistry of the brain; therefore, we may hypothesize that consciousness is a physiological function, just like behavior. We can even speculate about the origins of this self-awareness. Consciousness and the ability to communicate seem to go hand in hand. Our species, with its complex social structure and enormous capacity for learning, is well served by our ability to communicate: to express intentions to one another and to make requests of one another. Verbal communication makes cooperation possible and permits us to establish customs and laws of behavior. Perhaps the evolution of this ability is what has given rise to the phenomenon of consciousness. That is, our ability to send and receive messages with other people enables us to send and receive our own messages—in other words, to think and to be aware of our own existence. (See *Figure 1.1.*)

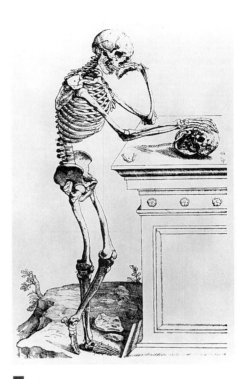

Figure 1.1
From a sixteenth-century anatomy woodcut by Andreas Vesalius.
(Courtesy, National Library of Medicine.)

● Blindsight

A particularly interesting phenomenon has some implications for our understanding of consciousness. It suggests that the common belief that perceptions must enter consciousness in order to affect our behavior is incorrect. The brain contains not one but several mechanisms involved in vision. To simplify matters somewhat, I will discuss two systems that evolved at different times. The simpler one, which resembles the visual system of animals such as fish and frogs, evolved first. The more complex one, which is possessed only by mammals, evolved later. This second, "mammalian" system seems to be the one that is responsible for our ability to perceive the world around us. The first, the "primitive" visual system, is mainly devoted to controlling eye movements and bringing our attention to sudden movements that occur off to the side of our field of vision.

Neurologists have long recognized that damage to the mammalian visual system on one side of a person's brain produces blindness in the visual field of the opposite side of the body. That is, if the right side of the brain is damaged, the patient will be blind to everything located to the

left when he or she looks straight ahead. However, Weiskrantz et al. (1974) reported a puzzling phenomenon that they called **blindsight:** If someone places an object in the patient's blind field and asks the patient to reach for it, he or she will be able to do so rather accurately. The patients are surprised to find their hands repeatedly coming in contact with an object in what appears to them as darkness; they say that they see nothing there.

The blindsight phenomenon shows that visual information can control behavior without producing a conscious sensation. Just as rats can learn to turn toward a particular visual stimulus after their mammalian visual system is damaged, humans apparently can use the primitive visual system of their brains to guide hand movements toward an object. The phenomenon of blindsight suggests that *consciousness is not a general property of all parts of the brain;* some parts of the brain, but not others, appear to

blindsight The ability of a person who cannot see objects in his or her blind field to accurately reach for them while remaining unconscious of perceiving them; caused by damage to the "mammalian" visual system of the brain.

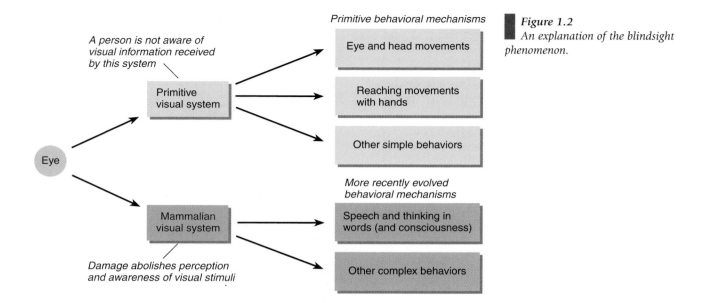

Primitive behavioral mechanisms

A person is not aware of visual information received by this system

Primitive visual system

Eye and head movements

Reaching movements with hands

Other simple behaviors

More recently evolved behavioral mechanisms

Eye

Mammalian visual system

Speech and thinking in words (and consciousness)

Damage abolishes perception and awareness of visual stimuli

Other complex behaviors

Figure 1.2
An explanation of the blindsight phenomenon.

play a special role in consciousness. Only the mammalian visual system communicates with those parts of the brain responsible for consciousness. The primitive system, which evolved before the development of consciousness, does not have direct connections with these parts of the brain. It *does* have connections with those parts of the brain responsible for controlling hand movements. (See *Figure 1.2.*)

● Split Brains

Studies of humans who have undergone a particular surgical procedure demonstrate dramatically how disconnecting parts of the brain involved with perceptions from parts that are involved with verbal behavior also disconnects them from consciousness. These results suggest that the parts of the brain involved in verbal behavior may be the ones responsible for consciousness.

The surgical procedure is one that has been used for people with very severe epilepsy that cannot be controlled by drugs. In these people, nerve cells in one side of the brain become overactive, and the overactivity is transmitted to the other side of the brain by the corpus callosum. The **corpus callosum** is a large bundle of nerve fibers that connect corresponding parts of one side of the brain with those of the other. Both sides of the brain then engage in wild activity and stimulate each other, causing a generalized epileptic seizure. These seizures can occur many times each day, preventing the patient from leading a normal life. Neurosurgeons discovered that cutting the corpus callosum (the **split-brain operation**) greatly reduced the frequency of the epileptic seizures.

Figure 1.3 shows a drawing of the split-brain operation. We see the brain being sliced down the middle, from front to back, dividing it into its two symmetrical halves. A "window" has been opened in the left side of the brain so that we can see the corpus callosum being cut by the neurosurgeon's special knife. (See *Figure 1.3.*)

Sperry (1966) and Gazzaniga and his associates (Gazzaniga, 1970; Gazzaniga and LeDoux, 1978) have studied these patients extensively. The largest part of the brain consists of two symmetrical parts, called the **cerebral hemispheres,** which receive sensory information from the opposite sides of the body. They also control movements of the opposite sides. The corpus callosum permits the two hemispheres to share information, so that each side knows what the other side is perceiving and doing. After the split-brain operation is performed, the two hemispheres are disconnected and operate independently; their sensory mechanisms, memories, and motor systems can no longer exchange information. The effects of these disconnections are not obvious to the casual observer, for the simple reason that only one hemisphere—in most people, the left—

corpus callosum *(core pus ka low sum)*   The largest commissure of the brain, interconnecting the areas of neocortex on each side of the brain.

split-brain operation   Brain surgery occasionally performed to treat a form of epilepsy; surgeon cuts the corpus callosum, which connects the two hemispheres of the brain.

cerebral hemispheres   The two symmetrical halves of the brain; constitute the major part of the brain.

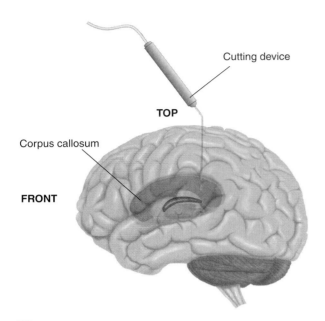

Figure 1.3
The split-brain operation. A "window" has been opened in the side of the brain so that we can see the corpus callosum being cut at the midline.

controls speech. The right hemisphere of an epileptic person with a split brain appears able to understand verbal instructions reasonably well, but it is totally incapable of producing speech.

Because only one side of the brain can talk about what it is experiencing, people speaking with a person with a split brain are conversing with only one hemisphere—the left. The operations of the right hemisphere are more difficult to detect. Even the patient's left hemisphere has to learn about the independent existence of the right hemisphere. One of the first things that these patients say they notice after the operation is that their left hand seems to have a "mind of its own." For example, patients may find themselves putting down a book held in the left hand, even if they have been reading it with great interest. This conflict occurs because the right hemisphere, which controls the left hand, cannot read and therefore finds the book boring. At other times, these patients surprise themselves by making obscene gestures (with the left hand) when they had not intended to. A psychologist once reported that a man with a split brain attempted to beat his wife with one hand and protect her with the other. Did he *really* want to hurt her? Yes and no, I guess.

One exception to the crossed representation of sensory information is the olfactory system. That is, when a person sniffs a flower through the left nostril, only the left brain receives a sensation of the odor. Thus, if the right nostril of a patient with a split brain is closed, leaving only the left nostril open, the patient will be able to tell us what the odors are (Gordon and Sperry, 1969). However, if the odor enters the right nostril, the patient will say that he or she smells nothing. But, in fact, the right brain *has* perceived the odor and *can* identify it. To show that this is so, we ask the patient to smell an odor with the right nostril and then reach for some objects that are hidden from view by a partition. If asked to use the left hand, controlled by the hemisphere that detected the smell, the patient will select the object that corresponds to the odor—a plastic flower for a floral odor, a toy fish for a fishy odor, a model tree for the odor of pine, and so forth. But if asked to use the right hand, the patient fails the test because the right hand is connected to the left hemisphere, which did not smell the odor. (See *Figure 1.4.*)

The effects of cutting the corpus callosum reinforce the conclusion that we become conscious of something only if information about it is able to reach the parts of the brain responsible for verbal communication, which are located in the left hemisphere. If the information does not reach these parts of the brain, then that information does not reach consciousness. We still know very little about the physiology of consciousness, but studies of people with brain damage are beginning to provide us with some useful insights. This issue is discussed in later chapters.

Interim Summary

The mind–body question has puzzled philosophers for many centuries. Modern science has adopted a monistic position—the belief that the world consists of matter and energy and that nonmaterial entities such as minds are not a part of the universe. Studies of the functions of the human nervous system tend to support this position, as two specific examples show. Both phenomena show that brain damage, by damaging conscious brain functions or disconnecting them from the speech mechanisms in the left hemisphere, can reveal the presence of other functions, of which the person is *not* conscious.

Blindsight is a phenomenon seen after partial damage to the "mammalian" visual system on one side of the brain. Although the person is, in the normal meaning of the word, blind to anything presented to part of the visual field, the person can nevertheless reach out and point to objects whose presence he or she is not conscious of. Similarly, when sensory information about a particular object is presented to the right hemisphere of a person who has had a split-brain operation, the person is not aware of the object but can, nevertheless, indicate by movements of the

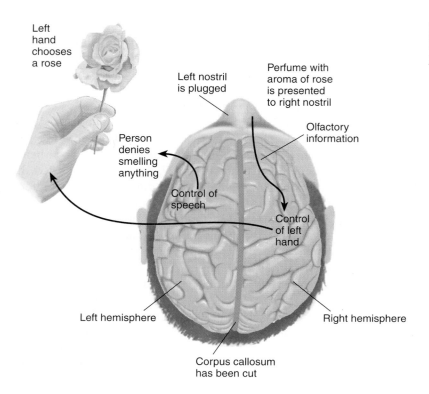

Figure 1.4
Indentification of an object in response to an olfactory stimulus by a person with a split brain.

Left hand chooses a rose

Left nostril is plugged

Perfume with aroma of rose is presented to right nostril

Olfactory information

Person denies smelling anything

Control of speech

Control of left hand

Left hemisphere

Right hemisphere

Corpus callosum has been cut

left hand that the object has been perceived. These phenomena suggest that consciousness involves operations of the verbal mechanisms of the left hemisphere. Indeed, consciousness may be, in large part, a matter of our "talking to ourselves." Thus, once we understand the language functions of the brain, we may have gone a long way to understanding how the brain can be conscious of its own existence.

THE NATURE OF PHYSIOLOGICAL PSYCHOLOGY

The field of physiological psychology grew out of psychology. Indeed, the first textbook of psychology, written by Wilhelm Wundt in the late nineteenth century, was titled *Principles of Physiological Psychology.* In recent years, with the explosion of information in experimental biology, scientists from other disciplines have become prominent contributors to the investigation of the physiology of behavior. The united effort of physiological psychologists, physiologists, and other neuroscientists is due to the realization that the ultimate function of the nervous system is behavior.

When I ask my students what they think the ultimate function of the brain is, they often say "thinking," or "logical reasoning," or "perceiving," or "remembering things."

Certainly, the nervous system performs these functions, but they support the primary one: control of movement. The basic function of perception is to inform us of what is happening in our environment so that our behaviors will be adaptive and useful: Perception without the ability to act would be useless. Of course, once perceptual abilities have evolved, they can be used for purposes other than guiding behavior. For example, we can enjoy a beautiful sunset or a great work of art without the perception causing us to do anything in particular. And thinking can often take place without causing any overt behavior. However, the *ability to think* evolved because it permits us to perform complex behaviors that accomplish useful goals. And whereas reminiscing about things that happened in our past can be an enjoyable pastime, the ability to learn and remember evolved—again—because it permitted our ancestors to profit from experience and perform behaviors that were useful to them.

The modern history of investigating the physiology of behavior has been written by psychologists who have combined the experimental methods of psychology with those of physiology and have applied them to the issues that concern all psychologists. Thus, we have studied perceptual processes, control of movement, sleep and waking, reproductive behaviors, ingestive behaviors, emotional behaviors, learning, and language. In recent years we have begun to study the physiology of human pathological conditions, such as addictions and mental disorders. All of these topics are discussed in subsequent chapters of this book.

● The Goals of Research

The goal of all scientists is to explain the phenomena they study. But what do we mean by *explain*? Scientific explanation takes two forms: generalization and reduction. Most psychologists deal with **generalization.** They explain particular instances of behavior as examples of general laws, which they deduce from their experiments. For instance, most psychologists would explain a pathologically strong fear of dogs as an example of a particular form of learning called *classical conditioning*. Presumably, the person was frightened earlier in life by a dog. An unpleasant stimulus was paired with the sight of the animal (perhaps the person was knocked down by an exuberant dog or was attacked by a vicious one), and the subsequent sight of dogs evokes the earlier response—fear.

Most physiologists deal with **reduction.** They explain complex phenomena in terms of simpler ones. For example, they may explain the movement of a muscle in terms of the changes in the membranes of muscle cells, the entry of particular chemicals, and the interactions among protein molecules within these cells. By contrast, a molecular biologist would explain these events in terms of forces that bind various molecules together and cause various parts of the molecules to be attracted to one another. In turn, the job of an atomic physicist is to describe matter and energy themselves and to account for the various forces found in nature. Practitioners of each branch of science use reduction to call on sets of more elementary generalizations to explain the phenomena they study.

The task of the physiological psychologist is to explain behavior in physiological terms. But physiological psychologists cannot simply be reductionists. It is not enough to observe behaviors and correlate them with physiological events that occur at the same time. Identical behaviors may occur for different reasons and thus may be initiated by different physiological mechanisms. Therefore, we must understand "psychologically" why a particular behavior occurs before we can understand what physiological events made it occur.

Let me provide a specific example: Mice, like many other mammals, often build nests. Behavioral observations show that mice will build nests under two conditions: when the air temperature is low and when the animal is pregnant. A nonpregnant mouse will build a nest only if the weather is cool, whereas a pregnant mouse will build one regardless of the temperature. The same behavior occurs for different reasons. In fact, nest-building behavior is controlled by two different physiological mechanisms. Nest building can be studied as a behavior related to the process of temperature regulation, or it can be studied in the context of parental behavior.

Sometimes, physiological mechanisms can tell us something about psychological processes. This relationship is particularly true of complex phenomena such as language, memory, and mood, which are poorly understood psychologically. For example, damage to a specific part of the brain can cause very specific impairments in a person's language abilities. The nature of these impairments suggests how these abilities are organized. When the damage involves a brain region that is important in analyzing speech sounds, it also produces deficits in spelling. This finding suggests that the ability to recognize a spoken word and the ability to spell it call on related brain mechanisms. Damage to another region of the brain can produce extreme difficulty in reading unfamiliar words by sounding them out, but it does not impair the person's ability to read words with which he or she is already familiar. This finding suggests that reading comprehension can take two routes: one that is related to speech sounds, and another that is primarily a matter of visual recognition of whole words.

In practice, the research efforts of physiological psychologists involve both forms of explanation—generalization and reduction. Ideas for experiments are stimulated by the investigator's knowledge both of psychological generalizations about behavior and of physiological mechanisms. A good physiological psychologist must therefore be both a good psychologist *and* a good physiologist.

● Biological Roots of Physiological Psychology

René Descartes, a seventeenth-century French philosopher and mathematician, has been called the father of modern philosophy. Although he was not a biologist, his speculations concerning the roles of the mind and brain in the control of behavior provide a good starting point in the history of physiological psychology. Descartes assumed that the world was a purely mechanical entity that, having once been set in motion by God, ran its course without divine interference. Thus, to understand the world, one had

generalization   Type of scientific explanation; a general conclusion based on many observations of similar phenomena.

reduction   Type of scientific explanation; a phenomenon is described in terms of the more elementary processes that underlie it.

only to understand how it was constructed. To Descartes, animals were mechanical devices; their behavior was controlled by environmental stimuli. His view of the human body was much the same: It was a machine. As Descartes observed, some movements of the human body were automatic and involuntary. For example, if a person's finger touched a hot object, the arm would immediately withdraw from the source of stimulation. Reactions like this did not require participation of the mind; they occurred automatically. Descartes called these actions **reflexes** (from the Latin *reflectere*, "to bend back upon itself"). Energy coming from the outside source would be reflected back through the nervous system to the muscles, which would contract. The term is still in use today, but, of course, we explain the operation of a reflex differently. (See *Figure 1.5.*)

Like most philosophers of his time, Descartes was a dualist; he believed that each person possessed a mind—a uniquely human attribute that was not subject to the laws of the universe. But his thinking differed from that of his predecessors in one important way: He was the first to suggest that a link exists between the human mind and its purely physical housing, the brain. He believed that the mind controlled the movements of the body, while the body, through its sense organs, supplied the mind with information about what was happening in the environment. In particular, he hypothesized that this interaction took

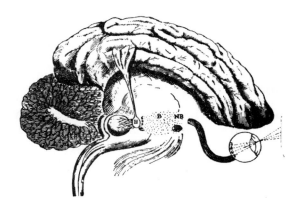

Figure 1.6
Descartes's theory. Descartes believed that the "soul" (what we would today call the mind) *controlled the movements of the muscles through its influence on the pineal body. His explanation is modeled on the mechanism that animated statues in the Royal Gardens.* (Courtesy of Historical Pictures Service, Chicago.)

place in the pineal body, a small organ situated on top of the brain stem, buried beneath the cerebral hemispheres. He noted that the brain contained hollow chambers (the *ventricles*) that were filled with fluid, and he hypothesized that this fluid was under pressure. When the mind decided to perform an action, it tilted the pineal body in a particular direction like a little joystick, causing fluid to flow from the brain into the appropriate set of nerves. This flow of fluid caused the same muscles to inflate and move. (See *Figure 1.6.*)

As a young man, René Descartes was greatly impressed by the moving statues in the grottoes of the Royal Gardens, just west of Paris (Jaynes, 1970). He was fascinated by the hidden mechanisms that caused the statues to move when visitors stepped on hidden plates. For example, as a visitor approached a bronze statue of Diana, bathing in a pool of water, she would flee and hide behind a bronze rose bush. If the visitor pursued her, an imposing statue of Neptune would rise up and bar the way with his trident.

These devices served as models for Descartes in theorizing about how the body worked. The pressurized water of the moving statues was replaced by pressurized fluid in the ventricles; the pipes were replaced by nerves; the cylinders by muscles; and finally, the hidden valves by the pineal body. This story illustrates one of the first times that a technological device was used as a model for explaining how

Figure 1.5
Descartes's explanation of a reflex action to a painful stimulus.

reflex   An automatic, stereotyped movement produced as the direct result of a stimulus.

the nervous system works. In science, a **model** is a relatively simple system that works on known principles and is able to do at least some of the things that a more complex system can do. For example, when scientists discovered that elements of the nervous system communicate by means of electrical impulses, researchers developed models of the brain based on telephone switchboards and, more recently, computers. Abstract models, which are completely mathematical in their properties, have also been developed.

Descartes's model was useful because, unlike purely philosophical speculations, it could be tested experimentally. In fact, it did not take long for biologists to prove that Descartes was wrong. For example, Luigi Galvani, a seventeenth-century Italian physiologist, found that electrical stimulation of a frog's nerve caused contraction of the muscle to which it was attached. Contraction occurred even when the nerve and muscle were detached from the rest of the body, so the ability of the muscle to contract and the ability of the nerve to send a message to the muscle were characteristics of these tissues themselves. Thus, the brain did not inflate muscles by directing pressurized fluid through the nerve. Galvani's experiment prompted others to study the nature of the message transmitted by the nerve and the means by which muscles contracted. The results of these efforts gave rise to an accumulation of knowledge about the physiology of behavior.

One of the most important figures in the development of experimental physiology was Johannes Müller, a nineteenth-century German physiologist. Müller was a forceful advocate of the application of experimental techniques to physiology. Previously, the activities of most natural scientists were limited to observation and classification. Although these activities are essential, Müller insisted that major advances in our understanding of the workings of the body would be achieved only by experimentally removing or isolating animals' organs, testing their responses to various chemicals, and otherwise altering the environment to see how the organs responded. (See *Figure 1.7.*) His most important contribution to the study of the physiology of behavior was his **doctrine of specific nerve energies.** Müller observed that although all nerves carry the same basic message—an electrical impulse—we perceive the messages of different nerves in different ways. For example, messages carried by the optic nerves produce sensations of visual images, and those carried by the auditory nerves produce sensations of sounds. How can different sensations arise from the same basic message?

The answer is that the messages occur in different channels. The portion of the brain that receives messages from the optic nerves interprets the activity as visual stimulation, even if the nerves are actually stimulated mechanically. (For

Figure 1.7
Johannes Müller (1801–1858).
(Courtesy of National Library of Medicine.)

example, when we rub our eyes, we see flashes of light.) Because different parts of the brain receive messages from different nerves, the brain must be functionally divided: Some parts perform some functions, while other parts perform others.

Müller's advocacy of experimentation and the logical deductions from his doctrine of specific nerve energies set the stage for performing experiments directly on the brain. Indeed, Pierre Flourens, a nineteenth-century French physiologist, did just that. Flourens removed various parts of animals' brains and observed their behavior. By seeing what the animal could no longer do, he could infer the function of the missing portion of the brain. This method is called **experimental ablation** (from the Latin *ablatus,* "carried away"). Flourens claimed to have discovered the regions of the brain that control heart rate and breathing, purposeful movements, and visual and auditory reflexes.

model A mathematical or physical analogy for a physiological process; for example, computers have been used as models for various functions of the brain.

doctrine of specific nerve energies Müller's conclusion that because all nerve fibers carry the same type of message, sensory information must be specified by the particular nerve fibers that are active.

experimental ablation The research method in which the function of a part of the brain is inferred by observing the behaviors an animal can no longer perform after that part is damaged.

Soon after Flourens performed his experiments, Paul Broca, a French surgeon, applied the principle of experimental ablation to the human brain. Of course, he did not intentionally remove parts of human brains to see how they worked, but instead observed the behavior of people whose brains had been damaged by strokes. In 1861 he performed an autopsy on the brain of a man who had had a stroke that resulted in the loss of the ability to speak. Broca's observations led him to conclude that a portion of the cerebral cortex on the left side of the brain performs functions necessary for speech. (See *Figure 1.8.*) Other physicians soon obtained evidence supporting his conclusions. As you will learn in Chapter 16, the control of speech is not localized in a particular region of the brain. Indeed, speech requires many different functions, which are organized throughout the brain. Nonetheless, the method of experimental ablation remains important to our understanding of the brains of both humans and laboratory animals.

As I mentioned earlier, Luigi Galvani used electricity to demonstrate that muscles contain the source of the energy that powers their contractions. In 1870, German physiologists Gustav Fritsch and Eduard Hitzig used electrical stimulation as a tool for understanding the physiology of the brain. They applied weak electrical current to the exposed surface of a dog's brain and observed the effects of the stimulation. They found that stimulation of different portions of a specific region of the brain caused contraction of specific muscles on the opposite side of the body. We now refer to this region as the *primary motor cortex,* and we know that nerve cells there communicate directly with those that cause muscular contractions. We also know that other re-

gions of the brain communicate with the primary motor cortex and thus control behaviors. For example, the region that Broca found necessary for speech communicates with, and controls, the portion of the primary motor cortex that controls the muscles of the lips, tongue, and throat, which we use to speak.

One of the most brilliant contributors to nineteenth-century science was the German physicist and physiologist Hermann von Helmholtz. Helmholtz devised a mathematical formulation of the law of conservation of energy, invented the ophthalmoscope (used to examine the retina of the eye), devised an important and influential theory of color vision and color blindness, and studied audition, music, and many physiological processes. Although Helmholtz had studied under Müller, he opposed Müller's belief that human organs are endowed with a vital nonmaterial force that coordinates their operations. Helmholtz believed that all aspects of physiology are mechanistic, subject to experimental investigation.

Helmholtz was also the first scientist to attempt to measure the speed of conduction through nerves. Scientists had previously believed that such conduction was identical to the conduction that occurs in wires, traveling at approximately the speed of light. But Helmholtz found that neural conduction was much slower—only about 90 feet per second. This measurement proved that neural conduction was more than a simple electrical message, as we will see in Chapter 2.

Twentieth-century developments in experimental physiology include many important inventions, such as sensitive amplifiers to detect weak electrical signals, neurochemical techniques to analyze chemical changes within and between cells, and histological techniques to see cells and their constituents. Because these developments belong to the modern era, they are discussed in detail in subsequent chapters.

● Functionalism: Natural Selection and Evolution

Müller's insistence that biology must be an experimental science provided the starting point for an important tradition. However, other biologists continued to observe, classify, and think about what they saw, and some of them arrived at valuable conclusions. The most important of these biologists was Charles Darwin. (See *Figure 1.9.*) Darwin formulated the principles of *evolution* and *natural selection,* which revolutionized biology. He noted that across succeeding generations, individual members of a species spontaneously undergo structural changes. If these changes produce favorable effects that permit the individual to re-

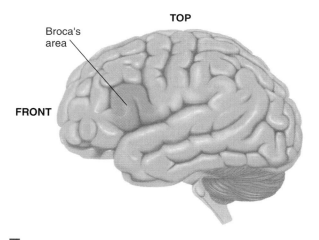

Figure 1.8
Broca's area, a region of the brain named for French surgeon Paul Broca. Broca discovered that damage to a part of the left side of the brain disrupted a person's ability to speak.

Figure 1.9
Charles Darwin (1809–1882). His theory of evolution revolutionized biology and strongly influenced early psychologists.
(North Wind Picture Archives.)

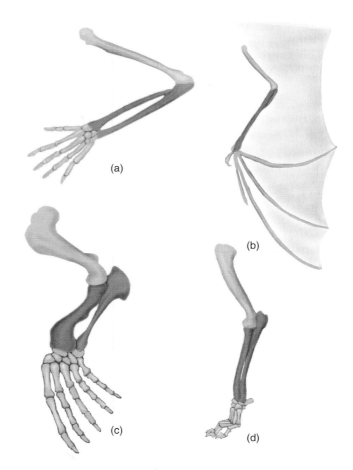

Figure 1.10
Bones of the forelimb: (a) human, (b) bat, (c) whale, (d) dog. Through the process of natural selection, these bones have been adapted to suit many different functions.

produce more successfully, some of the individual's offspring will inherit the favorable characteristics and will themselves produce more offspring.

Darwin's theory emphasized that all of an organism's characteristics—its structure, its coloration, its behavior—have functional significance. For example, the strong talons and sharp beaks that eagles possess permit the birds to catch and eat prey. Caterpillars that eat green leaves are themselves green, and their color makes it difficult for birds to see them against their usual background. Mother mice construct nests, which keep their offspring warm and out of harm's way. Obviously, the behavior itself is not inherited—how can it be? What *is* inherited is a brain that causes the behavior to occur. Thus, Darwin's theory gave rise to **functionalism,** a belief that characteristics of living organisms perform useful functions. So, to understand the physiological basis of various behaviors, we must first understand what these behaviors accomplish. We must therefore understand something about the natural history of the species being studied so that the behaviors can be seen in context.

To understand the workings of a complex piece of machinery, we should know what its functions are. This principle is just as true for a living organism as it is for a me-

chanical device. However, an important difference exists between machines and organisms: Machines have inventors who had a purpose when they designed them, whereas organisms are the result of a long series of accidents. Thus, strictly speaking, we cannot say that any physiological mechanisms of living organisms have a *purpose.* But they do have *functions,* and these we can try to determine. For example, the forelimbs shown in Figure 1.10 are adapted for different uses in different species of animals. (See *Figure 1.10.*)

A good example of the functional analysis of an adaptive trait was demonstrated in an experiment by Blest

functionalism The principle that the best way to understand a biological phenomenon (a behavior or a physiological structure) is to try to understand its useful functions for the organism.

(1957). Certain species of moths and butterflies have spots on their wings that resemble eyes—particularly the eyes of predators such as owls. (See *Figure 1.11.*) These insects normally rely on camouflage for protection; the backs of their wings, when folded, are colored like the bark of a tree. However, when a bird approaches, the insect's wings flip open, and the hidden eyespots are suddenly displayed. The bird then tends to fly away, rather than eat the insect. Blest performed an experiment to see whether the eyespots on a moth's or butterfly's wings really disturbed birds that saw them. He placed mealworms on different backgrounds and counted how many worms the birds ate. Indeed, when the worms were placed on a background that contained eyespots, the birds tended to avoid them.

Darwin formulated his theory of evolution in an attempt to explain the means by which species acquired their adaptive characteristics. The cornerstone of this theory is the principle of **natural selection.** Briefly, here is how the process works: Every sexually reproducing multicellular organism consists of a large number of cells, each of which contains chromosomes. Chromosomes are large, complex molecules that contain the recipes for producing the proteins that cells need to grow and to perform their functions. In essence, the chromosomes contain the blueprints for the construction (that is, the embryological development) of a particular member of a particular species. If the plans are altered, a different organism is produced.

The plans do get altered; mutations occur from time to time. **Mutations** are accidental changes in the chromosomes of sperms or eggs that join together and develop

Figure 1.12
An example of a maladaptive trait. Most mutations do not produce selective advantages, but those that do are passed on to future generations.
(J.H. Robinson/Animals Animals.)

into new organisms. For example, cosmic radiation might strike a chromosome in a cell of an animal's testis or ovary, thus producing a mutation that affects that animal's offspring. Most mutations are deleterious; the offspring either fails to survive or survives with some sort of deficit. (See *Figure 1.12.*) However, a small percentage of mutations are beneficial and confer a **selective advantage** to the organism that possesses them. That is, the animal is more likely than other members of its species to live long enough to reproduce and hence to pass on its chromosomes to its own offspring. Many different kinds of traits can confer a selective advantage: resistance to a particular disease, the ability to digest new kinds of food, more effective weapons for defense or for procurement of prey, and even a more attractive appearance to members of the opposite sex (after all, one must reproduce in order to pass on one's chromosomes).

Naturally, the traits that can be altered by mutations are physical ones; chromosomes make proteins, which affect

Figure 1.11
The owl butterfly. This butterfly displays its eyespots when approached by a bird. The bird usually will fly away.
(Cosmos/Photo Researchers Inc.)

natural selection   The process by which inherited traits that confer a selective advantage (increase an animal's likelihood to live and reproduce) become more prevalent in the population.

mutation   A change in the genetic information contained in the chromosomes of sperms or eggs, which can be passed on to an organism's offspring; provides genetic variability.

selective advantage   A characteristic of an organism that permits it to produce more than the average number of offspring of its species.

the structure and chemistry of cells. But the *effects* of these physical alterations can be seen in an animal's behavior. Thus, the process of natural selection can act on behavior indirectly. For example, if a particular mutation results in changes in the brain that cause a small animal to stop moving and freeze when it perceives a novel stimulus, that animal is more likely to escape undetected when a predator passes nearby. This tendency makes the animal more likely to survive and produce offspring, thus passing on its genes to future generations.

Other mutations are not immediately favorable, but because they do not put their possessors at a disadvantage, they are inherited by at least some members of the species. As a result of thousands of such mutations, the members of a particular species possess a variety of genes and are all at least somewhat different from one another. Variety is a definite advantage for a species. Different environments provide optimal habitats for different kinds of organisms. When the environment changes, species must adapt or run the risk of becoming extinct. If some members of the species possess assortments of genes that provide characteristics permitting them to adapt to the new environment, their offspring will survive and the species will continue.

An understanding of the principle of natural selection plays some role in the thinking of every person who undertakes research in physiological psychology. Some researchers explicitly consider the genetic mechanisms of various behaviors and the physiological processes on which these behaviors depend. Others are concerned with comparative aspects of behavior and its physiological basis; they compare the nervous systems of animals from a variety of species in order to make hypotheses about the evolution of brain structure and the behavioral capacities that correspond to this evolutionary development. But even though many researchers are not directly involved with the problem of evolution, the principle of natural selection guides the thinking of physiological psychologists. We ask ourselves what the selective advantage of a particular trait might be. We think about how nature might have used a physiological mechanism that already existed in order to perform more complex functions in more complex organisms. When we entertain hypotheses, we ask ourselves whether a particular explanation makes sense in an evolutionary perspective.

Interim Summary

All scientists hope to explain natural phenomena. In this context, the term *explanation* has two basic meanings: generalization and reduction. Generalization refers to the clas-

sification of phenomena according to their essential features so that general laws can be formulated. For example, observing that gravitational attraction is related to the mass of two bodies and to the distance between them helps explain the movement of planets. Reduction refers to the description of phenomena in terms of more basic physical processes. For example, gravitation can be explained in terms of forces and subatomic particles.

Physiological psychologists use both generalization and reduction to explain behavior. In large part, generalizations use the traditional methods of psychology. Reduction explains behaviors in terms of physiological events within the body—primarily within the nervous system. Thus, physiological psychology builds on the tradition of both experimental psychology and experimental physiology.

A dualist, René Descartes, proposed a model of the brain on the basis of hydraulically actuated statues. His model stimulated observations that produced important discoveries. The results of Galvani's experiments eventually led to an understanding of the nature of the message transmitted by nerves between the brain and the sensory organs and the muscles. Müller's doctrine of specific nerve energies paved the way for study of the functions of specific parts of the brain, through the methods of experimental ablation and electrical stimulation.

Darwin's theory of evolution, which was based on the concept of natural selection, provided an important contribution to modern physiological psychology. The theory asserts that we must understand the functions performed by an organ or body part, or by a behavior. Through random mutations, changes in an individual's genetic material cause different proteins to be produced, which results in the alteration of some physical characteristics. If the changes confer a selective advantage to the individual, the new genes will be transmitted to more and more members of the species. Even behaviors can evolve, through the selective advantage of alterations in the structure of the nervous system.

ETHICAL ISSUES IN RESEARCH WITH ANIMALS

Most of the research described in this book involves experimentation on living animals. Any time we use another species of animals for our own purposes, we should be sure that what we are doing is both humane and worthwhile. I believe that a good case can be made that research on the physiology of behavior qualifies on both counts. Humane treatment is a matter of procedure. We know how to maintain laboratory animals in good health in comfortable, sanitary conditions. We know how to administer anesthetics and analgesics so that animals do not suffer during or after surgery, and we know how to prevent infections with proper surgical procedures and the use of antibiotics. Most industrially developed societies have very strict regulations about the care of animals and require approval of the experimental procedures used on them. There is no excuse for mistreating animals in our care. In fact, the vast majority of laboratory animals *are* treated humanely.

Whether an experiment is *worthwhile* can be difficult to say. We use animals for many purposes. We eat their meat and eggs, and we drink their milk; we turn their hides into leather; we extract insulin and other hormones from their organs to treat people's diseases; we train them to do useful work on farms or to entertain us. Even having a pet is a form of exploitation; it is we—not they—who decide that they will live in our homes. The fact is, we have been using other animals throughout the history of our species.

Pet-owning causes much more suffering among animals than scientific research does. As Miller (1983) notes, pet owners are not required to receive permission from a board of experts that includes a veterinarian to house their pets, nor are they subject to periodic inspections to be sure that their home is clean and sanitary, that their pets have enough space to exercise properly, that their pets' diets are appropriate. Scientific researchers are. Miller also notes that fifty times more dogs and cats are killed by humane societies each year because they have been abandoned by former pet owners than are used in scientific research.

If a person believes that it is wrong to use another animal in any way, regardless of the benefits to humans, there is nothing anyone can say to convince him or her of the value of scientific research with animals. For this person, the issue is closed from the very beginning. Moral absolutes cannot be settled logically; like religious beliefs, they can be accepted or rejected, but they cannot be proved or disproved. My arguments in support of scientific research with animals are based on an evaluation of the benefits the research has to humans. (We should also remember that research with animals often helps *other animals*; procedures used by veterinarians, as well as those used by physicians, come from such research.)

Before describing the advantages of research with animals, let me point out that the use of animals in research and teaching is a special target of animal rights activists. Nicholl and Russell (1990) examined twenty-one books written by such activists and counted the number of pages devoted to concern for different uses of animals. Next, they compared the relative concern the authors showed for these uses to the numbers of animals actually involved in each of these categories. The results indicate that the authors showed relatively little concern for animals used for food, hunting, or furs, or for those killed in pounds; but although only 0.3 percent of the animals are used for research and education, 63.3 percent of the pages were devoted to this use. In terms of pages per million animals used, the authors devoted 0.08 to food, 0.23 to hunting, 1.27 to furs, 1.44 to killing in pounds—and 53.2 to research and education. The authors showed 665 times more concern for research and education compared with food, and 231 times compared with hunting. Even the use of animals for furs (which consumes two-thirds as many animals as research and education) attracted 41.9 times less attention per animal.

The disproportionate amount of concern that animal rights activists show toward the use of animals in research and education is puzzling, particularly because this is the one *indispensable* use of animals. We *can* survive without eating animals, we *can* live without hunting, we *can* do without furs, but without using animals for research and for training future researchers, we *cannot* make progress in understanding and treating diseases. In not too many years, our scientists will probably have developed a vaccine that will prevent the further spread of AIDS. Some animal rights activists believe that preventing the deaths of laboratory animals in the pursuit of such a vaccine is a more worthy goal than preventing the deaths of millions of humans that will occur as a result of the disease if a vaccine is not found. Even diseases we have already conquered would take new victims if drug companies could no longer use animals. If they were deprived of animals, these companies could no longer extract hormones used to treat human diseases, and they could not prepare many of the vaccines we now use to prevent them.

Our species is beset by medical, mental, and behavioral problems, many of which can be solved only through biological research. Let us consider some of the major neurological disorders. Strokes, caused by bleeding or occlusion of a blood vessel within the brain, often leave people partly paralyzed, unable to read, write, or converse with their friends and family. Basic research on the means by which nerve cells communicate with each other has led to important discoveries about the causes of the death of brain cells. This research was not directed toward a specific practical goal; the potential benefits actually came as a surprise to the investigators.

Experiments based on these results have shown that if a blood vessel leading to the brain is blocked for a few minutes, the part of the brain that is nourished by that vessel will die. However, the brain damage can be prevented by first administering a drug that interferes with a particular kind of neural communication. This research is important, because it may lead to medical treatments that can help reduce the brain damage caused by strokes. But it involves operating on a laboratory animal such as a rat, and pinching off a blood vessel. (The animals are anesthetized, of course.) Some of the animals will sustain brain damage, and all will be killed so that their brains can be examined. However, you will probably agree that research like this is just as legitimate as using animals for food.

As you will learn later in this book, research with laboratory animals has produced important discoveries about the possible causes or potential treatments of neurological and mental disorders, including Parkinson's disease, schizophrenia, manic-depressive illness, anxiety disorders, obsessive-compulsive disorders, anorexia nervosa, obesity, and drug addictions. Although much progress has been made, these problems are still with us, and they cause much human suffering. Unless we continue our research with laboratory animals, they will not be solved. Some people have suggested that instead of using laboratory animals in our research, we could use tissue cultures or computers. Unfortunately, tissue cultures or computers are not substitutes for living organisms. We have no way to study behavioral problems such as addictions in tissue cultures, nor can we program a computer to simulate the workings of an animal's nervous system. (If we could, that would mean we already had all the answers.)

This book will discuss some of the many important discoveries that have helped reduce human suffering. For example, the discovery of a vaccine for polio, a serious disease of the nervous system, involved the use of rhesus monkeys. As you will learn in Chapter 3, Parkinson's disease, an incurable, progressive neurological disorder, has been treated for years with a drug called L-DOPA, discovered through animal research. Now, because of research with rats, mice, rabbits, and monkeys stimulated by the accidental poisoning of several young people with a contaminated batch of synthetic heroin, patients are being treated with a drug that actually slows down the rate of brain degeneration. Researchers have hopes that a drug will be found to prevent the degeneration altogether.

The easiest way to justify research with animals is to point to actual and potential benefits to human health, as I have just done. However, we can also justify this research with a less practical, but perhaps equally important, argument. One of the things that characterizes our species is a quest for an understanding of our world. For example, astronomers study the universe and try to uncover its mysteries. Even if their discoveries never lead to practical benefits such as better drugs or faster methods of transportation, the fact that they enrich our understanding of the beginning and the fate of our universe justifies their efforts. The pursuit of knowledge is itself a worthwhile endeavor. Surely the attempt to understand the universe within us—our nervous system, which is responsible for all that we are or can be—is also valuable.

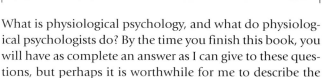

CAREERS IN NEUROSCIENCE

What is physiological psychology, and what do physiological psychologists do? By the time you finish this book, you will have as complete an answer as I can give to these questions, but perhaps it is worthwhile for me to describe the field—and careers open to those who specialize in it—before we begin our study in earnest.

Physiological psychologists study all behavioral phenomena that can be observed in nonhuman animals. They attempt to understand the physiology of behavior: the role of the nervous system, interacting with the rest of the body (especially the endocrine system, which secretes hormones), in controlling behavior. They study such topics as sensory processes, sleep, emotional behavior, ingestive behavior, aggressive behavior, sexual behavior, parental behavior, and learning and memory. They also study animal models of disorders that afflict humans, such as anxiety, depression, obsessions and compulsions, phobias, psychosomatic illnesses, and schizophrenia.

Although physiological psychology is the original name for this field, several other terms are now in general use, such as *biological psychology, biopsychology, psychobiology,* and *behavioral neuroscience.* Most professional physiological psychologists have received a Ph.D. from a graduate program in psychology or from an interdisciplinary program. (My own university awards a Ph.D. in Neuroscience and Behavior. The program includes faculty members from the departments of psychology, biology, biochemistry, and computer science.)

Physiological psychology belongs to the larger field of *neuroscience.* Neuroscientists concern themselves with all aspects of the nervous system: its anatomy, chemistry, physiology, development, and functioning. The research of neuroscientists ranges from the study of molecular genetics to the study of social behavior. The field has grown enormously in the last few years; the most recent meeting of the Society for Neuroscience was attended by over twenty thousand members and graduate students.

physiological psychologist   A scientist who studies the physiology of behavior, primarily by performing physiological and behavioral experiments with laboratory animals.

Most professional physiological psychologists are employed by colleges and universities, where they are engaged in teaching and research. Others are employed by institutions devoted to research—for example, in laboratories owned and operated by national governments or by private philanthropic organizations. A few work in industry, usually for pharmaceutical companies interested in assessing the effects of drugs on behavior. To become a professor or independent researcher, one must receive a doctorate—usually a Ph.D., although some people turn to research after receiving an M.D. Nowadays, most physiological psychologists spend two years in a temporary postdoctoral position, working in the laboratory of a senior scientist to gain more research experience. During this time, they write articles describing their research findings and submit them for publication in scientific journals. These publications are an important factor in obtaining a permanent position.

Two other fields often overlap with that of physiological psychology: *neurology* and *experimental neuropsychology.* Neurologists are physicians involved in the diagnosis and treatment of diseases of the nervous system. Most neurologists are solely involved in the practice of medicine, but a few engage in research devoted to advancing our understanding of the physiology of behavior. They study the behavior of people whose brains have been damaged by natural causes, using advanced brain-scanning devices to study the activity of various regions of the brain as a subject participates in various behaviors. This research is also carried out by experimental neuropsychologists—scientists with a Ph.D. in psychology and specialized training in the principles and procedures of neurology.

Not all people engaged in neuroscience research have doctoral degrees. Many research technicians perform essential—and intellectually rewarding—services for the scientists with whom they work. Some of these technicians gain enough experience and education on the job to enable them to collaborate with their employers on their research projects, rather than simply work for them.

▌Interim Summary

Research on the physiology of behavior necessarily involves the use of laboratory animals. It is incumbent on all scientists using these animals to see that they are housed comfortably and treated humanely, and laws have been enacted to ensure that they are. Such research has already produced many benefits to humankind and promises to continue to do so.

Physiological psychology (also called biological psychology, biopsychology, psychobiology, and behavioral neuroscience) is a field devoted to our understanding of the physiology of behavior. Physiological psychologists are allied with other scientists in the broader field of neuroscience. To pursue a career in physiological psychology (or in the sister field of experimental neuropsychology), one must obtain a graduate degree and (usually) serve two years or more as a "postdoc"—a junior scientist.

▌STRATEGIES FOR LEARNING

The brain is a complicated organ. After all, it is responsible for all our abilities and all our complexities. Scientists have been studying this organ for a good many years and (especially in recent years) have been learning a lot about how it works. It is impossible to summarize this progress in a few simple sentences; thus, this book contains a lot of information. I have tried to organize this information logically, telling you what you need to know in the order you need to know it. (After all, to understand some things, you sometimes need to understand other things first.) I have also tried to write as clearly as possible, making my examples as simple and as vivid as I can. But still, you cannot expect to master the information in this book by simply giving it a passive read; you will have to do some work.

Learning about the physiology of behavior involves much more than memorizing facts. Of course, there *are* facts to be memorized: names of parts of the nervous system, names of chemicals and drugs, scientific terms for particular phenomena and procedures used to investigate them, and so on. But the quest for information is nowhere near completed; we know only a small fraction of what we have to learn. And almost certainly, many of the "facts" that we now accept will some day be shown to be incorrect. If all you do is learn facts, where will you be when these facts are revised?

The antidote to obsolescence is knowledge of the process by which facts are obtained. In science, facts are the conclusions scientists make about their observations. If you learn only the conclusions, obsolescence is almost guaranteed. You will have to remember which conclusions are overturned, and what the new conclusions are—and that kind of rote learning is hard to do. But if you learn about the research strategies the scientists use, the observations they make, and the reasoning that leads to the conclusions, you will develop an understanding that is easily revised when new observations (and new "facts") emerge. If you understand what lies behind the conclusions, then you can incorporate new information into what you already know and revise these conclusions yourself.

In recognition of these realities about learning, knowledge, and the scientific method, this book presents not just a collection of facts, but a description of the procedures, experiments, and logical reasoning that scientists have used in their attempt to understand the physiology of behavior. If, in the interest of expediency, you focus on the conclusions and ignore the process that leads to them, you run the risk of acquiring information that will quickly become obsolete. On the other hand, if you try to understand the experiments and see how the conclusions follow from the results, you will acquire knowledge that lives and grows.

Enough said. Now, let me offer some practical advice about studying. You have been studying throughout your academic career, and you have undoubtedly learned some useful strategies along the way. Even if you have developed efficient and effective study skills, at least consider the possibility that there might be some ways to improve them.

If possible, the first reading of the assignment should be as uninterrupted as you can make it; that is, read the chapter without worrying much about remembering details. Next, after the first class meeting devoted to the topic, read the assignment again in earnest. Use a pen or pencil as you go, making notes. *Don't use a highlighter.* Sweeping the felt tip of a highlighter across some words on a page provides some instant gratification; you can even imagine that the highlighted words are somehow being transferred to your knowledge base. You have selected what is important, and when you review the reading assignment you have only to read the highlighted words. But this is an illusion.

Be active, not passive. Force yourself to write down whole words and phrases. The act of putting the information into your own words will not only give you something to study shortly before the next exam but also put something into your head (which is helpful at exam time). Using a highlighter puts off the learning until a later date; rephrasing the information in your own words starts the learning process *right then.*

A good way to get yourself to put the information into your own words (and thus into your own brain) is to answer the questions in the study guide. If you cannot answer a question, look up the answer in the book, *close the book,* and write the answer down. The phrase *close the book* is important. If you *copy* the answer, you will get very little out of the exercise. However, if you make yourself remember the information long enough to write it down, you have a good chance of remembering it later. The importance of the study guide is *not* to have a set of short answers in your own handwriting that you can study before the quiz. The behaviors that lead to long-term learning are doing enough thinking about the material to summarize it in your own words, then going through the mechanics of writing those words down.

Before you begin reading the first chapter, let me say a few things about the design of the book that may help you with your studies. The text and illustrations are integrated as closely as possible. In my experience, one of the most annoying aspects of reading some books is not knowing when to look at an illustration. Therefore, in this book you will find figure references in boldfaced italics (like this: *Figure 5.6*), which means "stop reading and look at the figure." These references appear in those locations I think will be optimal. If you look away from the text then, you will be assured that you will not be interrupting a line of reasoning in a crucial place and will not have to reread several sentences to get going again. You will find sections like this: "Figure 4.1 shows an alligator and a human. This alligator is certainly laid out in a linear fashion; we can draw a straight line that starts between its eyes and continues down the center of its spinal cord. (See *Figure 4.1.*)" This particular example is a trivial one and will give you no problems no matter when you look at the figure. But in other cases the material is more complex, and you will have less trouble if you know what to look for before you stop reading and examine the illustration.

You will notice that some words in the text are *italicized* and others are printed in **boldface.** Italics mean one of two things: either the word is being stressed for emphasis and is not a new term, or I am pointing out a new term that is not necessary for you to learn. On the other hand, a word in boldface is a new term that you should try to learn. Most of the boldfaced terms in the text are part of the vocabulary of the physiological psychologist. Often, they will be used again in a later chapter. As an aid to your studying, definitions of these terms are printed at the bottom of the page, along with pronunciation guides for those terms whose pronunciation is not obvious. In addition, a comprehensive index at the end of the book provides a list of terms and topics, with page references.

At the end of each major section (there are usually three to five of them in a chapter), you will find an *Interim Summary*, which provides a place for you to stop and think again about what you have just read, in order to make sure that you understand the direction the discussion has gone. Taken together, these sections provide a detailed summary of the information introduced in the chapter. My students tell me that they review the interim summaries just before taking a test.

Okay, the preliminaries are over. The next chapter starts with something you can sink your (metaphorical) teeth into: the structure and functions of neurons, the most important elements of the nervous system.

SUGGESTED READINGS

Butterfield, H. *The Origins of Modern Science: 1300–1800.* New York: Macmillan, 1959.

Damasio, A. R. *Descartes's Error: Emotion, Reason, and the Human Brain.* New York: G. P. Putnam, 1994.

Sacks, O. *The Man Who Mistook His Wife for a Hat and Other Clinical Tales.* New York: Harper & Row, 1987.

Schultz, D., and Schultz, S. E. *A History of Modern Psychology*, 4th ed. New York: Academic Press, 1987.

Structure and Functions of Cells of the Nervous System

The Port by Joan Miro.

T he brain is the organ that moves the muscles. That may sound a bit simplistic, but ultimately, movement—or more accurately, behavior—is the primary function of the nervous system. To make useful movements, the brain must know what is happening outside, in the environment. Thus, the body contains cells that are specialized for detecting environmental events and other cells that are specialized for producing movements. Of course, complex animals such as we do not react automatically to events in our environment; our brains are flexible enough so that we behave in different ways, according to present circumstances and those we experienced in the past. Besides perceiving and acting, we can remember and decide. All these abilities are made possible by the billions of cells found in the nervous system.

This chapter describes the structure and functions of the most important cells of the nervous system. Information, in the form of light, sound waves, odors, tastes, or contact with objects, is gathered from the environment by specialized cells called **sensory neurons.** Movements are accomplished by the contraction of muscles, which are controlled by **motor neurons.** (The term *motor* is used here in its original sense to refer to movement, not to a mechanical engine.) And in between sensory neurons and motor neurons come the **interneurons**—neurons that lie entirely within the central nervous system. Circuits of interneurons (primarily those in the brain) are responsible for perceiving, learning, remembering, deciding, and controlling of complex behaviors. How many neurons are there in the human nervous system? I have seen estimates of between 100 and 1000 billion—but no one has counted them yet.

To understand how the nervous system controls behavior, we must first understand its parts—the cells that compose it. Because this chapter deals with cells, you need not be familiar with the structure of the nervous system, which is presented in Chapter 3. However, you need to know that the nervous system consists of two basic divisions, the central nervous system and the peripheral nervous system. The **central nervous system (CNS)** consists of the parts that are encased by the bones of the skull and spinal column: the brain and the spinal cord. The **peripheral nervous system (PNS)** is found outside these bones and consists of the nerves and some of the sensory organs.

sensory neuron   A neuron that detects changes in the external or internal environment and sends information about these changes to the central nervous system.

motor neuron   A neuron located within the central nervous system that controls the contraction of a muscle or the secretion of a gland.

interneuron   A neuron located entirely within the central nervous system.

central nervous system (CNS)   The brain and spinal cord.

peripheral nervous system (PNS)   That part of the nervous system outside the brain and spinal cord, including the nerves attached to the brain and spinal cord.

CELLS OF THE NERVOUS SYSTEM

The first part of this chapter is devoted to a description of the most important cells of the nervous system—neurons and their supporting cells—and to the blood–brain barrier, which provides them with chemical isolation from the rest of the body.

Neurons

Basic Structure

The neuron (nerve cell) is the information-processing and information-transmitting element of the nervous system. Neurons come in many shapes and varieties, according to the specialized jobs they perform. Neurons usually have, in one form or another, the following four structures or regions: (1) cell body, or soma; (2) dendrites; (3) axon; and (4) terminal buttons.

Soma.   The **soma** (cell body) contains the nucleus and much of the machinery that provides for the life processes of the cell. (See *Figure 2.1.*) Its shape varies considerably in different kinds of neurons.

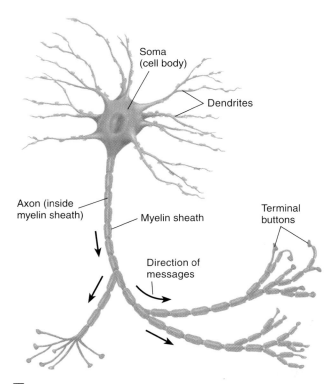

Figure 2.1
The principal parts of a multipolar neuron.

Dendrites.   *Dendron* is the Greek word for tree, and the **dendrites** of the neuron look very much like trees. (See *Figure 2.1.*) Neurons "converse" with one another, and dendrites serve as important recipients of these messages. The messages that pass from neuron to neuron are transmitted across the **synapse,** a junction between the terminal buttons (described later) of the sending cell and a portion of the somatic or dendritic membrane of the receiving cell. (The word *synapse* derives from the Greek *sunaptein,* "to join together.") Communication at a synapse proceeds in one direction: from the terminal button to the membrane of the other cell. (Like many general rules, this one has some exceptions. As we will see in Chapter 4, some synapses pass information in both directions.)

Axon.   The **axon** is a long, slender tube, often covered by a *myelin sheath.* (The myelin sheath is described later.) The axon carries information from the cell body to the terminal buttons. (See *Figure 2.1.*) The basic message it carries is called an *action potential.* This function is an important one and will be described in more detail later in the chapter. For now, it suffices to say that it is a brief electrical/chemical event that starts at the end of the axon next to the cell body and travels toward the terminal buttons. The action potential is like a brief pulse; in a given axon, the action potential is always the same size and duration. When it reaches a point where the axon branches, it splits but does not diminish in size. Each branch receives a *full-strength* action potential.

Like dendrites, axons and their branches come in different shapes. In fact, the three principal types of neurons are classified according to the way in which their axons and dendrites leave the soma. The neuron depicted in Figure 2.1 is the most common type found in the central nervous system; it is a **multipolar neuron.** In this type of neuron the somatic membrane gives rise to one axon but to the trunks

soma   The cell body of a neuron, which contains the nucleus.

dendrite   A branched, treelike structure attached to the soma of a neuron; receives information from the terminal buttons of other neurons.

synapse   A junction between the terminal button of an axon and the membrane of another neuron.

axon   The long, thin, cylindrical structure that conveys information from the soma of a neuron to its terminal buttons.

multipolar neuron   A neuron with one axon and many dendrites attached to its soma.

of many dendritic trees. **Bipolar neurons** give rise to one axon and one dendritic tree, at opposite ends of the soma. (See *Figure 2.2a.*) These neurons are usually sensory; that is, their dendrites detect events occurring in the environment and communicate information about these events to the central nervous system.

The third type of nerve cell is the **unipolar neuron.** It has only one stalk, which leaves the soma and divides into two branches a short distance away. (See *Figure 2.2b.*) Unipolar neurons, like bipolar neurons, transmit sensory information from the environment to the CNS. The arborizations (treelike branches) farther from the CNS are dendrites; the arborizations within the CNS end in terminal buttons. The dendrites of most unipolar neurons detect touch, temperature changes, and other sensory events that affect the skin. Other unipolar neurons detect events in our joints, muscles, and internal organs.

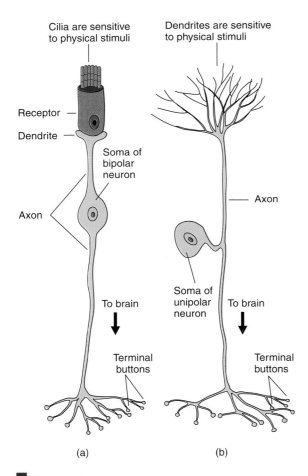

Figure 2.2
Neurons. (a) A bipolar neuron, primarily found in sensory systems (for example, vision and audition). (b) A unipolar neuron, found in the somatosensory system (touch, pain, and the like).

Terminal Buttons.   Most axons divide and branch many times. At the ends of the twigs are found little knobs called **terminal buttons.** (Some neuroscientists prefer the original French word *bouton.*) Terminal buttons have a very special function: When an action potential traveling down the axon reaches them, they secrete a chemical called a **transmitter substance,** also known as a **neurotransmitter.** This chemical (there are many different ones in the CNS) either excites or inhibits the receiving cell and thus helps determine whether an action potential occurs in its axon. Details of this process will be described later in this chapter.

An individual neuron receives information from the terminal buttons of axons of other neurons—and the terminal buttons of *its* axons form synapses with other neurons. A neuron may receive information from dozens or even hundreds of other neurons, each of which can form a large number of synaptic connections with it. Figure 2.3 illustrates the nature of these connections. As you can see, terminal buttons can form synapses on the membrane of the dendrites or the soma. (See *Figure 2.3.*)

Internal Structure

Figure 2.4 illustrates the internal structure of a typical multipolar neuron. (See *Figure 2.4* on page 24.) The **membrane** defines the boundary of the cell. It consists of a double layer of lipid (fatlike) molecules. Floating in it are a variety of protein molecules that have special functions. Some proteins detect substances outside the cell (such as hormones) and pass information about the presence of these substances to the interior of the cell. Other proteins control access to the interior of the cell, permitting some substances to enter but barring others. Still other proteins act as transporters, actively carrying certain molecules into or out of the cell. Because the membrane of the neuron is especially important in the transmission of information,

bipolar neuron   A neuron with one axon and one dendrite attached to its soma.

unipolar neuron   A neuron with one axon attached to its soma; the axon divides, with one branch receiving sensory information and the other sending the information into the central nervous system.

terminal button   The bud at the end of a branch of an axon; forms synapses with another neuron; sends information to that neuron.

transmitter substance/neurotransmitter   A chemical that is released by a terminal button; has an excitatory or inhibitory effect on another neuron.

membrane   A structure consisting principally of lipid molecules that defines the outer boundaries of a cell and also constitutes many of the cell organelles, such as the Golgi apparatus.

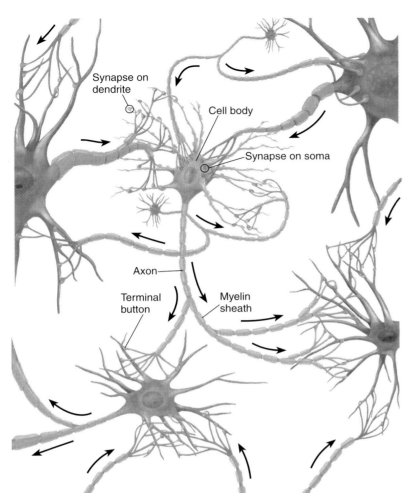

Synapse on dendrite

Cell body

Synapse on soma

Axon

Terminal button

Myelin sheath

Figure 2.3
An overview of the synaptic connections between neurons. The arrows represent the directions of the flow of information.

that cells actually do produce depend primarily on the particular enzymes that are present. Furthermore, there are enzymes that break molecules apart as well as put them together; the enzymes present in a particular region of a cell thus determine which molecules remain intact. For example,

$$A + B \overset{X}{\underset{Y}{\rightleftharpoons}} AB$$

In this reversible reaction the relative concentrations of enzymes X and Y determine whether the complex substance AB or its constituents, A and B, will predominate. Enzyme X makes A and B join together; enzyme Y splits AB apart. (Energy may also be required to make the reactions proceed.)

The bulk of the cell consists of cytoplasm. **Cytoplasm** is complex and varies considerably across types of cells, but it can be most easily characterized as a jellylike, semiliquid substance that fills the space outlined by the mem-

its characteristics will be discussed in more detail later in this chapter.

The **nucleus** ("nut") of the cell is round or oval and is covered by the nuclear membrane. The nucleolus and the chromosomes reside here. The **nucleolus** manufactures **ribosomes,** small structures that are involved in protein synthesis. The **chromosomes,** which consist of long strands of **deoxyribonucleic acid (DNA),** contain the organism's genetic information. When they are active, portions of the chromosomes (**genes**) cause production of another complex molecule, **messenger ribonucleic acid (mRNA),** which receives a copy of the information stored at that location. The mRNA leaves the nuclear membrane and attaches to ribosomes, where it causes the production of a particular protein. (See *Figure 2.5* on page 25.)

Proteins are important in cell functions. As well as providing structure, proteins serve as **enzymes,** which direct the chemical processes of a cell by controlling chemical reactions. Enzymes are special protein molecules that act as catalysts; that is, they cause a chemical reaction to take place without becoming a part of the final product themselves. Because cells contain the constituents needed to synthesize an enormous variety of compounds, the ones

nucleus   A structure in the central region of a cell, containing the nucleolus and chromosomes.

nucleolus (*new clee o lus*)   A structure within the nucleus of a cell that produces the ribosomes.

ribosome (*ry bo soam*)   A cytoplasmic structure, made of protein, that serves as the site of production of proteins translated from mRNA.

chromosome   A strand of DNA, with associated proteins, found in the nucleus; carries genetic information.

deoxyribonucleic acid (DNA) (*dee ox ee ry bo new clay ik*)   A long, complex macromolecule consisting of two interconnected helical strands; along with associated proteins, strands of DNA constitute the chromosomes.

gene   The functional unit of the chromosome, which directs synthesis of one or more proteins.

messenger ribonucleic acid (mRNA)   A macromolecule that delivers genetic information concerning the synthesis of a protein from a portion of a chromosome to a ribosome.

enzyme   A molecule that controls a chemical reaction, combining two substances or breaking a substance into two parts.

cytoplasm   The viscous, semiliquid substance contained in the interior of a cell.

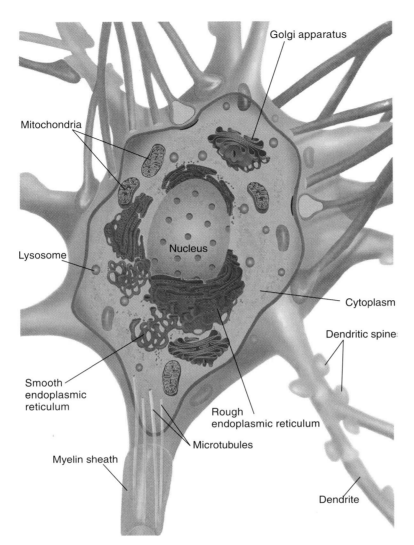

Figure 2.4
The principal internal structures of a multipolar neuron.

tochondria provide the cell with a special molecule—**adenosine triphosphate (ATP)**—that it uses as its immediate source of energy.

Endoplasmic reticulum, which serves as a storage reservoir and as a channel for transporting chemicals through the cytoplasm, appears in two forms: rough and smooth. Both types consist of parallel layers of membrane, arranged in pairs, of the sort that encloses the cell. Rough endoplasmic reticulum contains ribosomes. The protein produced by the ribosomes that are attached to the rough endoplasmic reticulum is destined to be transported out of the cell or used in the membrane. Unattached ribosomes are also distributed around the cytoplasm; the unattached variety appears to produce protein for use within the neuron. The smooth endoplasmic reticulum provides channels for the segregation of molecules involved in various cellular processes. Lipid (fatlike) molecules are produced here.

The **Golgi apparatus** is a special form of smooth endoplasmic reticulum. Some complex molecules, made up of simpler individual molecules, are assembled here. The Golgi apparatus also serves as a wrapping or packaging agent. For example, secretory cells (such as those that release hormones) wrap their product in a membrane produced by the Golgi apparatus. When the cell secretes its products, it uses a process called **exocytosis** (*exo,* "outside"; *cyto,* "cell"; *-osis,* "process"). Briefly stated, the container migrates to the outer membrane of the cell, fuses with it, and bursts, spilling the product into the fluid sur-

brane. It contains small, specialized structures, just as the body contains specialized organs. The most important of these are described next.

Mitochondria (singular: mitochondrion) are shaped like oval beads and are formed of a double membrane. The inner membrane is wrinkled, and the wrinkles make up a set of shelves (*cristae*) that fill the inside of the bead. Mitochondria perform a vital role in the economy of the cell; many of the biochemical steps involved in the extraction of energy from the breakdown of nutrients take place on the cristae. Most cell biologists believe that many eons ago mitochondria were free-living organisms that came to "infect" larger cells. Because the mitochondria could extract energy more efficiently than the larger cells, they became useful to them and eventually became a permanent part of the cells. The cell provides mitochondria with nutrients, and the mi-

mitochondria   An organelle responsible for extracting energy from nutrients.

adenosine triphosphate (ATP) *(ah **den** o seen)*   A molecule of prime importance to cellular energy metabolism; its breakdown liberates energy.

endoplasmic reticulum   Parallel layers of membrane found within the cytoplasm of a cell. Rough endoplasmic reticulum contains ribosomes and is involved with production of proteins that are secreted by the cell. Smooth endoplasmic reticulum is the site of synthesis of lipids and provides channels for the segregation of molecules involved in various cellular processes.

Golgi apparatus *(**goal** jee)*   A complex of parallel membranes in the cytoplasm that wraps the products of a secretory cell.

exocytosis *(**ex** o sy **toe** sis)*   The secretion of a substance by a cell through means of vesicles; the process by which neurotransmitters are secreted.

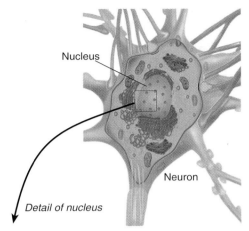

Nucleus

Neuron

Detail of nucleus

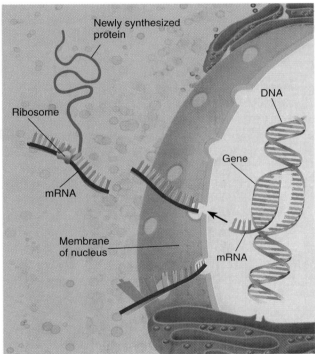

Newly synthesized protein

Ribosome

mRNA

Membrane of nucleus

DNA

Gene

mRNA

Figure 2.5
Protein synthesis. When a gene is active, a copy of the information is made onto a molecule of messenger RNA. The mRNA leaves the nucleus and attaches to a ribosome, where the protein is produced.

rounding the cell. As we will see, neurons are secretory cells; they communicate with one another by secreting chemicals by this means. Thus, I will describe the process of exocytosis in more detail later in this chapter. The Golgi apparatus also produces **lysosomes,** small sacs that contain enzymes that break down substances no longer needed by the cell. These products are then recycled or excreted from the cell.

If a neuron grown in a tissue culture is exposed to a detergent, the lipid membrane and much of the interior of

the cell dissolve away, leaving a matrix of insoluble strands of protein. This matrix, called the **cytoskeleton,** gives the neuron its shape. The cytoskeleton is made of three kinds of protein strands, linked to each other and forming a cohesive mass. The thickest of these strands, **microtubules,** are bundles of thirteen filaments arranged around a hollow core. Each filament consists of long chains of beads of a protein called *tubulin.* **Neurofilaments** are made of long, continuous strands of protein similar to those found in hair. **Microfilaments,** the thinnest fibers found in the cytoskeleton, consist of a double strand of *actin,* one of the proteins responsible for muscular contractions. Microfilaments form a meshwork just inside the membrane that holds membrane-bound proteins in place.

Axons can be extremely long, relative to their diameter and the size of the soma. For example, the longest axon in a human stretches from the foot to a region located in the base of the brain. Because terminal buttons need some items that can be produced only in the soma, there must be a system that can transport these items rapidly and efficiently through the axoplasm (that is, the cytoplasm of the axon). This system is referred to as **axoplasmic transport,** an active process by which substances are propelled along microtubules that run the length of the axon. Movement from the soma to the terminal buttons is called **anterograde** axoplasmic transport. (*Antero-* means "toward the front.") This form of transport is accomplished by molecules of a protein called *kinesin.* In the cell body, kinesin molecules, which resemble a pair of legs and feet, attach to the item being transported down the axon. The kinesin molecule then walks down a microtubule, carrying the cargo to its destination.

lysosome (*lye* so soam)   An organelle surrounded by membrane; contains enzymes that break down waste products.

cytoskeleton   Formed of microtubules, neurofilaments, and microfilaments, linked to each other and forming a cohesive mass that gives a cell its shape.

microtubule (*my kro too bule*)   A long strand of bundles of protein filaments arranged around a hollow core; part of the cytoskeleton and involved in transporting substances from place to place within the cell.

neurofilament   One of the fibers of the cytoskeleton, made of long, continuous strands of protein similar to those found in hair.

microfilament   The thinnest of the fibers of the cytoskeleton; forms a meshwork just inside the membrane that holds membrane-bound proteins in place.

axoplasmic transport   An active process by which substances are propelled along microtubules that run the length of the axon.

anterograde   In a direction along an axon from the cell body toward the terminal buttons.

Energy is supplied by ATP molecules produced by the mitochondria. (See *Figure 2.6.*) Another protein, *dynein*, carries substances from the terminal buttons to the soma, a process known as **retrograde** axoplasmic transport. Anterograde axoplasmic transport is remarkably fast: up to 500 mm per day. Retrograde axoplasmic transport is about half as fast as anterograde transport.

Neural Communication: An Overview

The central nervous system communicates with the rest of the body through nerves attached to the brain and to the spinal cord. Nerves are bundles of many thousands of individual fibers, all wrapped in a tough, protective membrane. Under a microscope, nerves look something like telephone cables, with their bundles of wires. (See *Figure 2.7.*) Like the

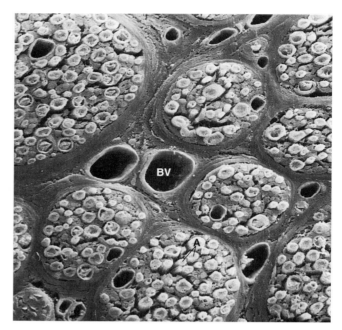

Figure 2.7
Nerves. A nerve consists of a sheath of tissue that encases a bundle of individual nerve fibers (also known as axons). BV = blood vessel; A = individual axons.
(From *Tissues and Organs: A Text-Atlas of Scanning Electron Microscopy,* by Richard G. Kessel and Randy H. Kardon. Copyright © 1979 by W.H. Freeman and Co. Reprinted by permission.)

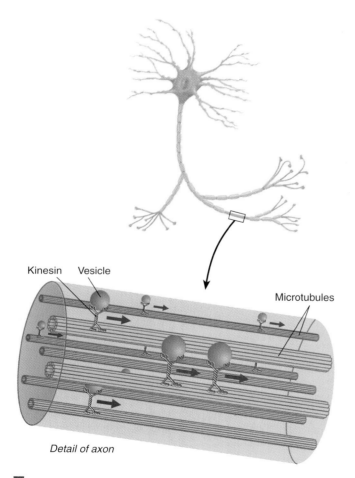

Detail of axon

Figure 2.6
Fast axoplasmic transport. Kinesin molecules "walk" down a microtubule, carrying their cargo from the soma to the terminal buttons. Another protein, dynein, carries substances from the terminal buttons to the soma.

individual wires in a telephone cable, nerve fibers transmit messages through the nerve, from a sense organ to the brain or from the brain to a muscle or gland.

Now that we have looked at the structure of neurons, let's see how they can interact to produce a useful behavior. We begin by examining a simple assembly of three neurons and a muscle that control a withdrawal reflex. In the next two figures (and in subsequent figures that illustrate simple neural circuits) neurons are depicted in shorthand fashion as several-sided stars. The points of these stars represent dendrites, and only one or two terminal buttons are shown at the end of the axon. The sensory neuron in this example detects painful stimuli. When its dendrites are stimulated by a noxious stimulus (such as contact with a hot object), it sends messages down the axon to the terminal buttons, which are located in the spinal cord. (You will recognize this cell as a unipolar neuron; see *Figure 2.8.*) The terminal buttons of the sensory

retrograde In a direction along an axon from the terminal buttons toward the cell body.

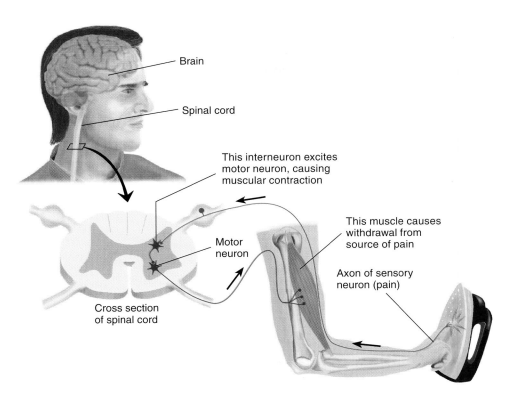

Figure 2.8
A withdrawal reflex, a simple example of a useful function of the nervous system. The painful stimulus causes the hand to pull away from the hot iron.

Brain

Spinal cord

This interneuron excites motor neuron, causing muscular contraction

Motor neuron

Cross section of spinal cord

This muscle causes withdrawal from source of pain

Axon of sensory neuron (pain)

neuron release a transmitter substance that excites the interneuron, causing it to send messages down its axon. The terminal buttons of the interneuron release a transmitter substance that excites the motor neuron, which sends messages down its axon. The axon of the motor neuron joins a nerve and travels to a muscle. When the terminal buttons of the motor neuron release their transmitter substance, the muscle cells contract, causing the hand to move away from the hot object. (See *Figure 2.8.*)

So far, all of the synapses have had excitatory effects. Now let us complicate matters a bit to see the effect of inhibitory synapses. Suppose you have removed a hot casserole from the oven. As you start over to the table to put it down, the heat begins to penetrate the rather thin potholders you are using. The pain caused by the hot casserole triggers a withdrawal reflex that tends to make you drop it. And yet you manage to keep hold of it long enough to get to the table and put it down. What prevented your withdrawal reflex from making you drop the casserole on the floor?

The pain from the hot casserole increases the activity of excitatory synapses on the motor neurons, which tends to cause the hand to pull away from the casserole. However, this excitation is counteracted by *inhibition*, supplied by another source—the brain. The brain contains neural circuits that recognize what a disaster it would be if you dropped

the casserole on the floor. These neural circuits send information to the spinal cord that prevents the withdrawal reflex from making you drop the dish.

Figure 2.9 shows how this information reaches the spinal cord. As you can see, an axon from a neuron in the brain reaches the spinal cord, where its terminal buttons form synapses with an inhibitory interneuron. When the neuron in the brain becomes active, it excites this inhibitory interneuron. The interneuron releases an inhibitory transmitter substance, which *decreases* the activity of the motor neuron, blocking the withdrawal reflex. This circuit provides an example of a contest between two competing tendencies: to drop the casserole and to hold on to it. (See *Figure 2.9.*)

Of course, reflexes are more complicated than this description, and the mechanisms that inhibit them are even more so. And thousands of neurons are involved in this process. The five neurons shown in Figure 2.9 represent many others: Dozens of sensory neurons detect the hot object, hundreds of interneurons are stimulated by their activity, hundreds of motor neurons produce the contraction—and thousands of neurons in the brain must become active if the reflex is to be inhibited. Yet this simple model provides an overview of the process of neural communication, which is described in more detail later in this chapter.

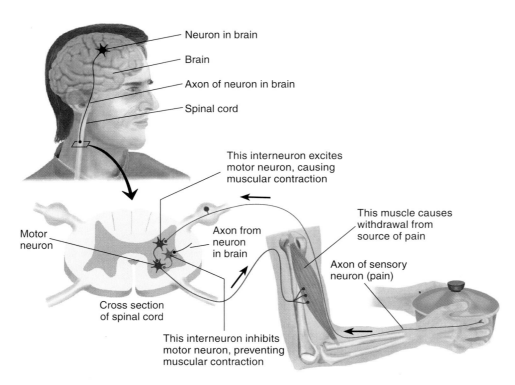

Neuron in brain

Brain

Axon of neuron in brain

Spinal cord

This interneuron excites
motor neuron, causing
muscular contraction

This muscle causes
withdrawal from
source of pain

Motor
neuron

Axon from
neuron
in brain

Axon of sensory
neuron (pain)

Cross section
of spinal cord

This interneuron inhibits
motor neuron, preventing
muscular contraction

Figure 2.9
*The role of inhibition. Inhibitory
signals arising from the brain can
prevent the withdrawal reflex from
causing the person to drop the
casserole.*

● Supporting Cells

Neurons constitute only about half the volume of the CNS. The rest consists of a variety of supporting cells. Because neurons have a very high rate of metabolism but have no means of storing nutrients, they must constantly be supplied with nutrients and oxygen or they will quickly die. Unlike most other cells of the body, neurons cannot be replaced when they die. Thus, the role played by the cells that support and protect neurons is very important to our existence.

Glia

The most important supporting cells of the central nervous system are the *neuroglia*, or "nerve glue." **Glia** (also called *glial cells*) do indeed glue the CNS together, but they do much more than that. Neurons lead a very sheltered existence; they are buffered physically and chemically from the rest of the body by the glial cells. Glial cells surround neurons and hold them in place, controlling their supply of some of the chemicals they need to exchange messages with other neurons; they insulate neurons from one another so that neural messages do not get scrambled; and they even act as housekeepers, destroying and removing the carcasses of neurons that are killed by injury or that die as a result of old age.

There are several types of glial cells, each of which plays a special role in the CNS. The two most important types are *astrocytes* and *oligodendrocytes.* **Astrocyte** means "star cell," and this name accurately describes the shape of these cells. Astrocytes (or *astroglia*) provide physical support to neurons and clean up debris within the brain. They produce some chemicals that neurons need to fulfill their functions. They help control the chemical composition of the fluid surrounding neurons by actively taking up or releasing substances whose concentrations must be kept within critical levels. Finally, astrocytes are involved in providing nourishment to neurons.

Some of the astrocyte's processes (the arms of the star) are wrapped around blood vessels; other processes are wrapped around parts of neurons, so that the somatic and dendritic membranes of neurons are largely surrounded by astrocytes. This arrangement suggested to the Italian histologist Camillo Golgi (1844–1926) that astrocytes sup-

glia (*glee* ah)   The supporting cells of the central nervous system.

astrocyte   A glial cell that provides support for neurons of the central nervous system, provides nutrients and other substances, and regulates the chemical composition of the extracellular fluid.

plied neurons with nutrients from the capillaries and disposed of their waste products (Golgi, 1903). He thought that nutrients passed from capillaries to the cytoplasm of the astrocytes and then through the cytoplasm to the neurons. Recent evidence suggests that Golgi was right. A review of the current literature (Tsacopoulos and Magistretti, 1996) suggests that astrocytes do more than pass glucose on to neurons: They receive glucose from capillaries and break it down to *lactate*, the chemical produced during the first step of glucose metabolism. They then release lactate into the extracellular fluid that surrounds neurons, and neurons take up the lactate, transport it to their mitochondria, and use it for energy. Presumably, this process provides neurons with a fuel that they can metabolize even more rapidly than glucose. (See *Figure 2.10.*) In addition,

astrocytes store a small amount of a carbohydrate called *glycogen* that can be broken down to glucose and then to lactate when the metabolic rate of neurons in their vicinity is especially high.

Besides having a possible role in transporting chemicals to neurons, astrocytes serve as the matrix that holds neurons in place. These cells also surround and isolate synapses, limiting the dispersion of transmitter substances that are released by the terminal buttons.

Neurons occasionally die for unknown reasons or are killed by head injury or stroke. Certain kinds of astrocytes then take up the task of cleaning away the debris. These cells are able to travel around the CNS; they extend and retract their processes (*pseudopodia*, or "false feet") and glide about the way amoebas do. When these astrocytes contact a piece of debris from a dead neuron, they push themselves against it, finally engulfing and digesting it. We call this process **phagocytosis** (*phagein*, "to eat"; *kutos*, "cell"). If there is a considerable amount of injured tissue to be cleaned up, astrocytes will divide and produce enough new cells to do the task. Once the dead tissue is broken down, a framework of astrocytes will be left to fill in the vacant area, and a specialized kind of astrocyte will form scar tissue, walling off the area.

Oligodendrocytes are residents of the CNS, and their principal function is to provide support to axons and to produce the **myelin sheath,** which insulates most axons from one another. (Some axons are not myelinated and lack this sheath.) Myelin, 80 percent lipid and 20 percent protein, is produced by the oligodendrocytes in the form of a tube surrounding the axon. This tube does not form a continuous sheath; rather, it consists of a series of segments, each approximately 1 mm long, with a small (1–2 µm) portion of uncoated axon between the segments. (A *micrometer*, abbreviated µm, is one-millionth of a meter, or one-thousandth of a millimeter.) The bare portion of axon is called a **node of Ranvier,** after its discoverer. The myelinated axon, then, resembles a string of elongated beads.

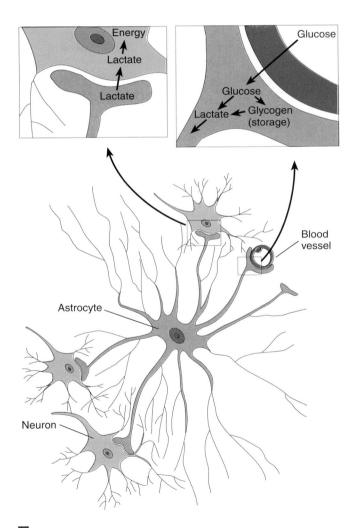

Figure 2.10
Structure and location of astrocytes, whose processes surround capillaries and neurons of the central nervous system.

phagocytosis (*fagg o sy **toe** sis*) The process by which cells engulf and digest other cells or debris caused by cellular degeneration.

oligodendrocyte (*oh li go **den** droh site*) A type of glial cell in the central nervous system that forms myelin sheaths.

myelin sheath (***my** a lin*) A sheath that surrounds axons and insulates them, preventing messages from spreading between adjacent axons.

node of Ranvier (***raw** vee ay*) A naked portion of a myelinated axon, between adjacent oligodendroglia or Schwann cells.

(Actually, the beads are *very much* elongated—their length is approximately 80 times their width.)

A given oligodendrocyte produces several segments of myelin. During the development of the CNS, oligodendrocytes form processes shaped something like canoe paddles. Each of these paddle-shaped processes then wraps itself many times around a segment of an axon and, while doing so, produces layers of myelin. Each paddle thus becomes a segment of an axon's myelin sheath. (See *Figure 2.11.*)

As their name indicates, **microglia** are the smallest of the glial cells. Like some types of astrocytes, they act as phagocytes, engulfing and breaking down dead and dying neurons. But in addition, they serve as one of the representatives of the immune system in the brain, protecting the brain from invading microorganisms. They are primarily responsible for the inflammatory reaction in response to brain damage.

Schwann Cells

In the CNS the oligodendrocytes support axons and produce myelin. In the PNS the **Schwann cells** perform the same functions. Most axons in the PNS are myelinated. The myelin sheath occurs in segments, as it does in the CNS; each segment consists of a single Schwann cell, wrapped many times around the axon. In the CNS the oligodendrocytes grow a number of paddle-shaped processes that wrap around a number of axons. In the PNS a Schwann cell provides myelin for only one axon, and the entire

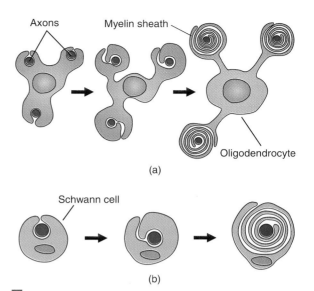

(a)

(b)

Figure 2.12
Formation of myelin. During development, a process of an oligodendrocyte or an entire Schwann cell tightly wraps itself many times around an individual axon and forms one segment of the myelin sheath. (a) Oligodendrocyte. (b) Schwann cell.

Schwann cell—not merely a part of it—surrounds the axon. (See *Figure 2.12.*)

Schwann cells also differ from their CNS counterparts, the oligodendrocytes, in an important way. As we saw, a nerve consists of a bundle of many myelinated axons, all covered in a sheath of tough, elastic connective tissue. If damage occurs to such a nerve, Schwann cells aid in the digestion of the dead and dying axons. Then the Schwann cells arrange themselves in a series of cylinders that act as guides for regrowth of the axons. The distal portions of the severed axons die, but the stump of each severed axon grows sprouts, which then spread in all directions. If one of these sprouts encounters a cylinder provided by a Schwann cell, the sprout will grow through the tube quickly (at a rate of up to 3–4 mm a day), while the other, nonproductive sprouts wither away. If the cut ends of the nerve are still located close enough to each other, the axons will reestablish connections with the muscles and sense organs they previously served.

On the other hand, if a section of the nerve is damaged beyond repair, the axons will not be able to find their way

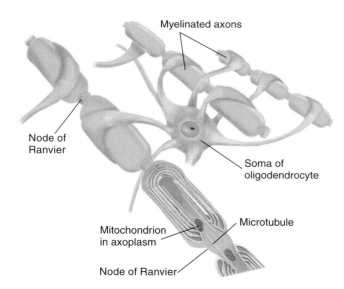

Figure 2.11
An oligodendrocyte, which forms the myelin that surrounds many axons in the central nervous system. Each cell forms one segment of myelin for several adjacent axons.

---

microglia The smallest of glial cells; act as phagocytes and protect the brain from invading microorganisms.

Schwann cell A cell in the peripheral nervous system that is wrapped around a myelinated axon, providing one segment of its myelin sheath.

to the original sites of innervation. In such cases neurosurgeons can sew the cut ends of the nerve together, if not too much of the nerve has been damaged. (Nerves are flexible and can be stretched a bit.) If too long a section has been lost, and if the nerve was an important one (controlling hand muscles, for example), a piece of nerve about the same size as the lost section can be taken from another part of the body. Because many nerves overlap in the area of tissue they innervate, neurosurgeons have no trouble finding a branch of a nerve that the patient can lose without ill effect. The surgeon, using a special microscope and very delicate instruments, grafts this piece of nerve to the damaged one. Of course, the axons in the excised and transplanted piece of nerve die away, but the tubes produced by the Schwann cells guide the sprouts of the damaged nerve and help them find their way back to the affected muscles—in this case, to the hand muscles.

Unfortunately, the glial cells of the CNS are not as cooperative as the supporting cells of the PNS. If axons in the brain or spinal cord are damaged, new sprouts will form, as in the PNS. However, the budding axons encounter scar tissue produced by the astrocytes, and they cannot penetrate this barrier. Even if the sprouts could get through, the axons would not reestablish their original connections without guidance similar to that provided by the Schwann cells of the PNS. During development, axons have two modes of growth. The first mode causes them to elongate so that they reach their target, which could be as far away as the other end of the brain or spinal cord. Schwann cells provide this signal to injured axons. The second mode causes axons to stop elongating and begin sprouting terminal buttons, because they have reached their target. Liuzzi and Lasek (1987) found that even when astrocytes do not produce scar tissue, they appear to produce a chemical signal that instructs regenerating axons to begin the second mode of growth: to stop elongating and start sprouting terminal buttons. Thus, the difference in the regenerative properties of the CNS and the PNS results from differences in the characteristics of the supporting cells, not from differences in the neurons.

● The Blood–Brain Barrier

Over one hundred years ago, Paul Ehrlich discovered that if a blue dye is injected into an animal's bloodstream, all tissues except the brain and spinal cord will be tinted blue. However, if the same dye is injected into the ventricles of the brain, the blue color will spread throughout the CNS (Bradbury, 1979). This experiment demonstrates that a barrier exists between the blood and the fluid that surrounds the cells of the brain—the **blood–brain barrier.**

Some substances can cross the blood-brain barrier; others cannot. Thus, it is *selectively permeable* (*per*, "through"; *meare*, "to pass"). In most of the body the cells that line the capillaries do not fit together absolutely tightly. Small gaps are found between them that permit the free exchange of most substances between the blood plasma and the fluid outside the blood vessels that surrounds the cells. In the central nervous system the capillaries lack these gaps, and thus, many substances cannot leave the blood. Other substances, such as glucose (the primary fuel of the central nervous system), must be actively transported through the capillary walls, carried by special proteins. (See *Figure 2.13*.)

The messages that are conveyed from place to place in the nervous system involve movements of substances through the membranes of neurons. If the composition of

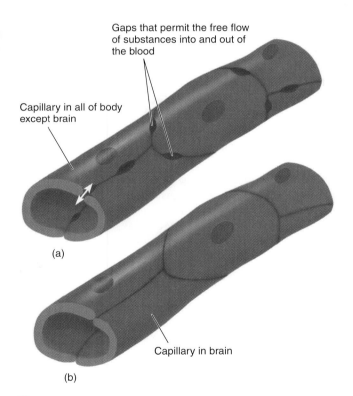

Gaps that permit the free flow of substances into and out of the blood

Capillary in all of body except brain

(a)

Capillary in brain

(b)

Figure 2.13
The blood–brain barrier. (a) The cells that form the walls of the capillaries in the body outside the brain have gaps that permit the free passage of substances into and out of the blood. (b) The cells that form the walls of the capillaries in the brain are tightly joined.

blood–brain barrier   A semipermeable barrier produced by the cells in the walls of the capillaries in the brain.

the fluid that bathes neurons is changed even slightly, the transmission of these messages will be disrupted. Thus, if this fluid is not closely regulated, the brain cannot function normally. The presence of the blood-brain barrier makes it easier to regulate the composition of this fluid.

The blood-brain barrier is not uniform throughout the nervous system. In several places the barrier is relatively permeable, allowing substances excluded elsewhere to cross freely. For example, the **area postrema** is a part of the brain that controls vomiting. The blood-brain barrier is much weaker there, permitting neurons in this region to detect the presence of toxic substances in the blood. A poison that enters the circulatory system from the stomach can thus stimulate this area to initiate vomiting. If the organism is lucky, the poison can be expelled from the stomach before it causes too much damage.

Interim Summary

Neurons are the most important cells of the nervous system. The central nervous system (CNS) includes the brain and spinal cord; the peripheral nervous system (PNS) includes nerves and some sensory organs.

Neurons have four principal parts: dendrites, soma (cell body), axon, and terminal buttons. They communicate by means of synapses, located at the ends of the axons. When an action potential travels down an axon, the terminal buttons secrete a chemical that has either an excitatory or an inhibitory effect on the neuron with which it communicates. Ultimately, the effects of these excitatory and inhibitory synapses cause behavior, in the form of muscular contraction.

Neurons contain a quantity of clear cytoplasm, enclosed in a membrane. Embedded in the membrane are protein molecules that have special functions, such as the transport of particular substances into and out of the cell. The cytoplasm contains the nucleus, which contains the genetic information; the nucleolus (located in the nucleus), which manufactures ribosomes; the ribosomes, which serve as sites of protein synthesis; the endoplasmic reticulum, which serves as a storage reservoir and as a channel for transportation of chemicals through the cytoplasm; the Golgi apparatus, which wraps substances that the cell secretes in a membrane; the lysosomes, which contain enzymes that destroy waste products; microtubules, neurofilaments, and microfilaments, which compose the cytoskeleton and help transport chemicals from place to place; and the mitochondria, which serve as the location for most of the chemical reactions through which the cell extracts energy from nutrients.

The withdrawal reflex illustrates how neurons can be connected to accomplish useful behaviors. The circuit responsible for this reflex consists of three sets of neurons: sensory neurons, interneurons, and motor neurons. The reflex can be suppressed when neurons in the brain activate inhibitory interneurons that form synapses with the motor neurons.

Neurons are supported by the glial cells of the central nervous system and the satellite cells of the peripheral nervous system. Within the CNS, astrocytes provide the primary support and also remove debris and form scar tissue in the event of tissue damage. Microglia are phagocytes that serve as the representatives of the immune system. Oligodendrocytes form myelin, the substance that insulates axons, and also support unmyelinated axons. Within the PNS, support and myelin are provided by the Schwann cells.

In most organs, molecules freely diffuse between the blood within the capillaries that serve them and the extracellular fluid that bathes their cells. The molecules pass through gaps between the cells that line the capillaries. The walls of the capillaries of the CNS lack these gaps; consequently, fewer substances can enter or leave the brain across the blood-brain barrier.

COMMUNICATION WITHIN A NEURON

This section describes the nature of communication *within* a neuron—the way an action potential is sent from the cell body down the axon to the terminal buttons, informing them to release some transmitter substance. The details of synaptic transmission—the communication between neurons—will be described in the next section. As we shall see in this section, an action potential consists of a series of alterations in the membrane of the axon that permit various chemicals to move between the interior of the axon and the fluid surrounding it. These exchanges produce electrical currents.

● Measuring Electrical Potentials of Axons

Let's examine the nature of the message that is conducted along the axon. To do so, we obtain an axon that is large enough to work with. Fortunately, nature has provided the neuroscientist with the giant squid axon (the giant axon of

area postrema (*poss **tree** ma*)   A region of the medulla where the blood–brain barrier is weak; poisons can be detected there and can initiate vomiting.

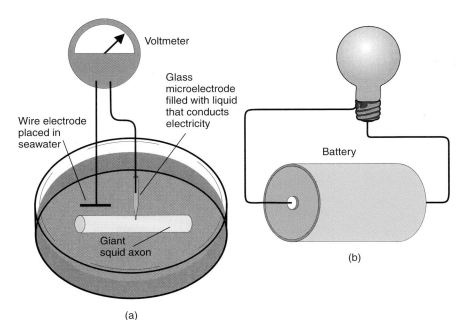

Figure 2.14
Measuring electrical charge. (a) A voltmeter detecting the charge across a membrane of an axon. (b) A light bulb detecting the charge across the terminals of a battery.

Voltmeter

Glass microelectrode filled with liquid that conducts electricity

Wire electrode placed in seawater

Battery

Giant squid axon

(a)

(b)

a squid, not the axon of a giant squid!). This axon is about 0.5 mm in diameter, which is hundreds of times larger than the largest mammalian axon. (This large axon controls an emergency response: sudden contraction of the mantle, which squirts water through a jet and propels the squid away from a source of danger.) We place an isolated giant squid axon in a dish of seawater, in which it can exist for a day or two.

To measure the electrical charges generated by an axon, we will need to use a pair of electrodes. **Electrodes** are electrical conductors that provide a path for electricity to enter or leave a medium. One of the electrodes is a simple wire that we place in the seawater. The other one, which we use to record the message from the axon, has to be special. Because even a giant squid axon is rather small, we must use a tiny electrode that will record the membrane potential without damaging the axon. To do so, we use a microelectrode.

A **microelectrode** is simply a very small electrode, which can be made of metal or glass. In this case we will use one made of thin glass tubing, which is heated and drawn down to an exceedingly fine point, less than a thousandth of a millimeter in diameter. Because glass will not conduct electricity, the glass microelectrode is filled with a liquid that conducts electricity, such as a solution of potassium chloride.

We place the wire electrode in the seawater and insert the microelectrode into the axon. (See *Figure 2.14a*.) As

soon as we do so, we discover that the inside of the axon is negatively charged with respect to the outside; the difference in charge being 70 mV (millivolts, or thousandths of a volt). Thus, the inside of the membrane is –70 mV. This electrical charge is called the **membrane potential.** The term *potential* refers to a stored-up source of energy—in this case, electrical energy. For example, a flashlight battery that is not connected to an electrical circuit has a *potential* charge of 1.5 V between its terminals. If we connect a light bulb to the terminals, the potential energy is tapped and converted into radiant energy (light). (See *Figure 2.14b*.) Similarly, if we connect our electrodes—one inside the axon and one outside it—to a very sensitive voltmeter, we will convert the potential energy to movement of the meter's needle. Of course, the potential electrical energy of the axonal membrane is very weak, compared with that of a flashlight battery.

As we shall see, the message that is conducted down the axon consists of a brief change in the membrane potential.

electrode   A conductive medium that can be used to apply electrical stimulation or to record electrical potentials.

microelectrode   A very fine electrode, generally used to record activity of individual neurons.

membrane potential   The electrical charge across a cell membrane; the difference in electrical potential inside and outside the cell.

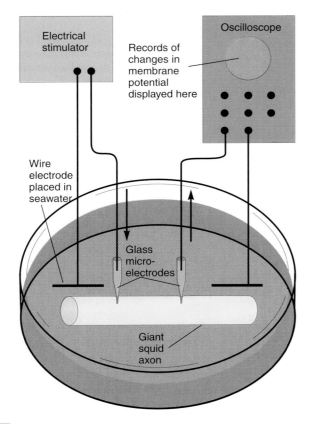

Figure 2.15
The means by which an axon can be stimulated while its membrane potential is being recorded.

However, this change occurs very rapidly—too rapidly for us to see if we were using a voltmeter. Thus, to study the message, we will use an **oscilloscope.** This device, like a voltmeter, measures voltages, but it also produces a record of these voltages, graphing them as a function of time. These graphs are displayed on a screen, much like the one found in a television. The vertical axis represents voltage, and the horizontal axis represents time, going from left to right.

Once we insert our microelectrode into the axon, the oscilloscope draws a straight horizontal line at –70 mV, as long as the axon is not disturbed. This electrical charge across the membrane is called, quite appropriately, the **resting potential.** Now let us disturb the resting potential and see what happens. To do so, we will use another device—an electrical stimulator that allows us to alter the membrane potential at a specific location. (See *Figure 2.15.*) The stimulator can pass current through another microelectrode that we have inserted into the axon. Because the inside of the axon is negative, a positive charge applied to the inside of the membrane produces a **depolarization.** That is, it takes away some of the electrical

charge across the membrane near the electrode, reducing the membrane potential.

Let us see what happens to an axon when we artificially change the membrane potential at one point. Figure 2.16 shows a graph drawn by an oscilloscope that has been monitoring the effects of brief depolarizing stimuli. The graphs of the effects of these separate stimuli are superimposed on the same drawing so that we can compare them. We deliver a series of depolarizing stimuli, starting with a very weak stimulus (number 1) and gradually increasing their strength. Each stimulus briefly depolarizes the membrane potential a little more. Finally, after we present depolarization number 4, the membrane potential suddenly reverses itself, so that the inside becomes *positive* (and the outside becomes negative). The membrane potential quickly returns to normal, but first it overshoots the resting potential, becoming **hyperpolarized**—more polarized than normal—for a short time. The whole process takes about 2 msec (milliseconds). (See *Figure 2.16.*)

This phenomenon, a very rapid reversal of the membrane potential, is called the **action potential.** It constitutes the message carried by the axon from the cell body to the terminal buttons. The voltage level that triggers an action potential—which was achieved only by depolarizing shock number 4—is called the **threshold of excitation.**

● The Membrane Potential: Balance of Two Forces

To understand what causes the action potential to occur, we must first understand the reasons for the existence of the membrane potential. As we will see, this electrical charge is the result of a balance between two opposing forces: diffusion and electrostatic pressure.

oscilloscope A laboratory instrument capable of displaying a graph of voltage as a function of time on the face of a cathode ray tube.

resting potential The membrane potential of a neuron when it is not being altered by excitatory or inhibitory postsynaptic potentials; approximately –70 mV in the giant squid axon.

depolarization Reduction (toward zero) of the membrane potential of a cell from its normal resting potential.

hyperpolarization An increase in the membrane potential of a cell, relative to the normal resting potential.

action potential The brief electrical impulse that provides the basis for conduction of information along an axon.

threshold of excitation The value of the membrane potential that must be reached in order to produce an action potential.

The Force of Diffusion

When a spoonful of sugar is carefully poured into a container of water, it settles to the bottom. After a time the sugar dissolves, but it remains close to the bottom of the container. After a much longer time (probably several days), the molecules of sugar distribute themselves evenly throughout the water, even if no one stirs the liquid. The process whereby molecules distribute themselves evenly throughout the medium in which they are dissolved is called **diffusion.**

When there are no forces or barriers to prevent diffusion, molecules diffuse from regions of high concentration to regions of low concentration. Molecules are constantly in motion, and their rate of movement is proportional to the temperature. Only at absolute zero [0 K (kelvin) = −273.15 C = −459.7 F] do molecules cease their random movement. At all other temperatures they move about, colliding and veering off in different directions, thus pushing one another away. The result of these collisions in the example of sugar and water is to force sugar molecules upward (and to force water molecules downward), away from the regions in which they are most concentrated.

The Force of Electrostatic Pressure

When some substances are dissolved in water, they split into two parts, each with an opposing electrical charge. Substances with this property are called **electrolytes;** the charged particles into which they decompose are called **ions.** Ions are of two basic types: *Cations* have a positive charge, and *anions* have a negative charge. For example, when sodium chloride (NaCl, table salt) is dissolved in water, many of the molecules split into sodium cations (Na^+) and chloride anions (Cl^-). (I find that the easiest way to keep the terms *cation* and *anion* straight is to think of the cation's plus sign as a cross, and remember the superstition of a black *cat* crossing your path.)

As you have undoubtedly learned, particles with the same kind of charge repel each other (+ repels +, and − repels −), but particles with different charges are attracted to each other (+ and − attract). Thus, anions repel anions, cations repel cations, but anions and cations attract each other. The force exerted by this attraction or repulsion is called **electrostatic pressure.** Just as the force of diffusion moves molecules from regions of high concentration to regions of low concentration, electrostatic pressure moves ions from place to place: Cations are pushed away from regions with an excess of cations, and anions are pushed away from regions with an excess of anions.

Ions in the Extracellular and Intracellular Fluid

The fluid within cells (**intracellular fluid**) and the fluid surrounding them (**extracellular fluid**) contain different ions.

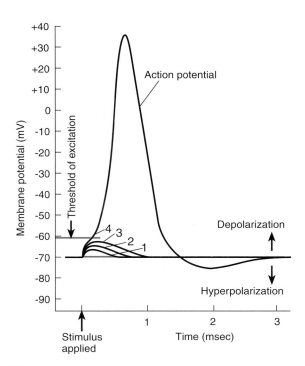

Figure 2.16
An action potential. These results would be seen on an oscilloscope screen if depolarizing stimuli of varying intensities were delivered to the axon shown in Figure 2.15.

The forces of diffusion and electrostatic pressure contributed by these ions give rise to the membrane potential. Because the membrane potential is produced by a balance between the forces of diffusion and electrostatic pressures, understanding what produces this potential requires that we know the concentration of the various ions in the extracellular and intracellular fluids.

There are several important ions in these fluids. I will discuss four of them here: organic anions (symbolized by A^-), chloride ions (Cl^-), sodium ions (Na^+), and potassium ions (K^+). The Latin words for sodium and potassium are *natrium* and *kalium;* hence, they are abbreviated *Na* and *K*, respectively. Organic anions—negatively charged proteins and intermediate products of the cell's metabolic

---

diffusion   Movement of molecules from regions of high concentration to regions of low concentration.

electrolyte   An aqueous solution of a material that ionizes—namely, a soluble acid, base, or salt.

ion   A charged molecule. *Cations* are positively charged, and *anions* are negatively charged.

electrostatic pressure   The attractive force between atomic particles charged with opposite signs, or the repulsive force between atomic particles charged with the same sign.

intracellular fluid   The fluid contained within cells.

extracellular fluid   Body fluids located outside of cells.

35

processes—are found only in the intracellular fluid. Although the other three ions are found in both the intracellular and extracellular fluids, K^+ is found predominantly in the intracellular fluid, whereas Na^+ and Cl^- are found predominantly in the extracellular fluid. The sizes of the boxes in Figure 2.17 indicate the relative concentrations of these four ions. (See *Figure 2.17.*) The easiest way to remember which ion is found where is to recall that the fluid that surrounds our cells is similar to seawater, which is predominantly a solution of salt, NaCl. The primitive ancestors of our cells lived in the ocean; thus, the seawater was their extracellular fluid. Our extracellular fluid thus resembles seawater, produced and maintained by regulatory mechanisms that are described in Chapter 12.

Let us consider the ions in Figure 2.17, examining the forces of diffusion and electrostatic pressure exerted on each and reasoning why each is located where it is. A^-, the organic anion, is unable to pass through the membrane of the axon; therefore, although the presence of this ion within the cell affects the other ions, it is located where it is because the membrane is impermeable to it.

The potassium ion K^+ is concentrated within the axon; thus, the force of diffusion tends to push it out of the cell. However, the outside of the cell is charged positively with respect to the inside, so electrostatic pressure tends to force the cation inside. Thus, the two opposing forces balance. (See *Figure 2.17.*)

The chloride ion Cl^- is in greatest concentration outside the axon. The force of diffusion pushes this ion inward. However, because the inside of the axon is negatively charged, electrostatic pressure pushes the anion outward.

Again, two opposing forces balance each other. (See *Figure 2.17.*)

The sodium ion Na^+ is also in greatest concentration outside the axon, so it, like Cl^-, is pushed into the cell by the force of diffusion. But unlike chloride, the sodium ion is *positively* charged. Therefore, electrostatic pressure does *not* prevent Na^+ from entering the cell; indeed, the negative charge inside the axon *attracts* Na^+. (See *Figure 2.17.*)

How can Na^+ remain in greatest concentration in the extracellular fluid, despite the fact that both forces (diffusion and electrostatic pressure) tend to push it inside? The simplest explanation would be that the membrane is impermeable to Na^+, as it is to A^-, the organic anion. This possibility can be tested with the following experiment. A giant squid axon is placed in a dish of seawater containing some radioactive Na^+, is allowed to sit a while, and is then removed and washed off. The axon is now found to be radioactive, which shows that Na^+ *can* pass through the membrane, because some of the radioactive Na^+ in the seawater found its way into the axon.

Although the axon contains radioactive Na^+, analysis of its cytoplasm (which can be squeezed out like toothpaste from a tube) shows that the concentration of Na^+ is unchanged. This analysis indicates that although some molecules of Na^+ entered the axon, an equal number left again, keeping the concentration constant. But as we know, the forces of diffusion and electrostatic pressure tend to push Na^+ into the cell. It is easy to understand why the axon became radioactive—these forces pushed some radioactive sodium ions in. But what pushed an equal number of Na^+ ions out again, against these two forces?

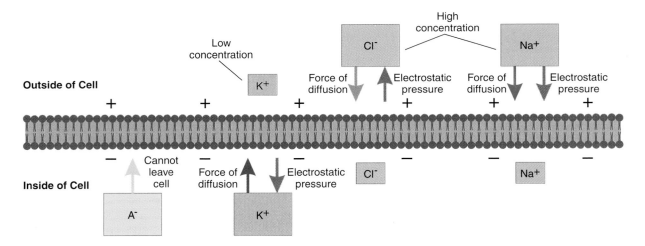

Figure 2.17
The relative concentration of some important ions inside and outside the neuron and the forces acting on them.

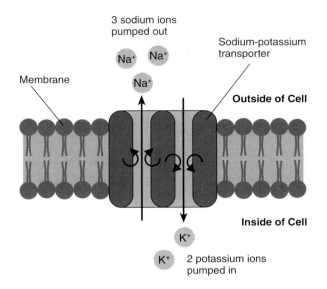

3 sodium ions
pumped out

Sodium-potassium
transporter

Membrane

Na⁺ Na⁺

Na⁺

Outside of Cell

Inside of Cell

K⁺

K⁺ 2 potassium ions
pumped in

Figure 2.18
A sodium-potassium transporter, situated in the cell membrane.

The answer is this: Another force, provided by the *sodium-potassium pump*, continuously pushes Na⁺ out of the axon. The sodium-potassium pump consists of a large number of individual protein molecules situated in the membrane, driven by energy provided by the mitochondria as they metabolize the cell's nutrients. These molecules, known as **sodium-potassium transporters,** exchange Na⁺ for K⁺, pushing three sodium ions out for every two potassium ions they push in. (See *Figure 2.18.*)

Because the membrane is not very permeable to Na⁺, sodium-potassium transporters very effectively keep the intracellular concentration of Na⁺ low. By transporting K⁺ into the cell, they also increase the intracellular concentration of K⁺ somewhat. The membrane is approximately 100 times more permeable to K⁺ than to Na⁺, so the increase is slight; but as we will see when we study the process of neural inhibition later in this chapter, it is very important. The transporters that make up the sodium-potassium pump use considerable energy: Up to 40 percent of a neuron's metabolic resources are used to operate them. Neurons, muscle cells, glia—in fact, most cells of the body—have sodium-potassium transporters in their membrane.

● The Action Potential

As we saw, the forces of both diffusion and electrostatic pressure tend to push Na⁺ into the cell. However, the membrane is not very permeable to this ion, and sodium-potassium transporters continuously pump out Na⁺, keep-

ing the intracellular level of Na⁺ low. But imagine what would happen if the membrane suddenly became permeable to Na⁺. The forces of diffusion and electrostatic pressure would cause Na⁺ to rush into the cell. This sudden influx (inflow) of positively charged ions would drastically change the membrane potential. Indeed, experiments have shown that this mechanism is precisely what causes the action potential: A brief drop in the membrane resistance to Na⁺ (allowing these ions to rush into the cell) is immediately followed by a transient drop in the membrane resistance to K⁺ (allowing these ions to rush out of the cell).

I said earlier that the membrane consists of a double layer of lipid molecules in which are floating many different kinds of protein molecules. One class of protein molecules provides a way for ions to enter or leave the cells. These molecules constitute **ion channels,** which contain passages ("pores") that can open or close. When an ion channel is open, a particular type of ion can flow through the pore and thus can enter or leave the cell. (See *Figure 2.19.*) Neural membranes contain many thousands of ion channels. For example, the giant squid axon contains from 100 to 600 sodium channels in each square micrometer of membrane. (There are one million square micrometers in a square millimeter; thus, a patch of axonal membrane the size of a lowercase letter "o" in this book would contain several hundred million sodium channels.) Each open sodium channel can admit up to 100 million ions per second. The permeability of a membrane to a particular ion at a given moment is determined by the number of ion channels that are open. (By the way, cell biologists have discovered approximately 75 different types of ion channels, and more will undoubtedly be discovered.)

The following numbered paragraphs describe the movements of ions through the membrane during the action potential. The numbers on the figure correspond to the numbers of the paragraphs that follow. (See *Figure 2.20.*)

1. As soon as the threshold of excitation is reached, the sodium channels in the membrane open and Na⁺ rushes in, propelled by the forces of diffusion and electrostatic pressure. The opening of these channels is triggered by the depolarization of the membrane potential; they open at the threshold of excitation. Because these

sodium-potassium transporter   A protein found in the membrane of all cells that extrudes sodium ions from and transports potassium ions into the cell.

ion channel   A specialized protein molecule that permits specific ions to enter or leave cells.

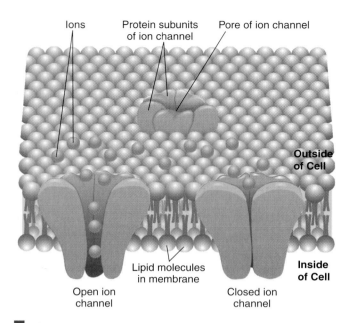

Figure 2.19
Ion channels. When they are open, ions can pass through them, entering or leaving the cell.

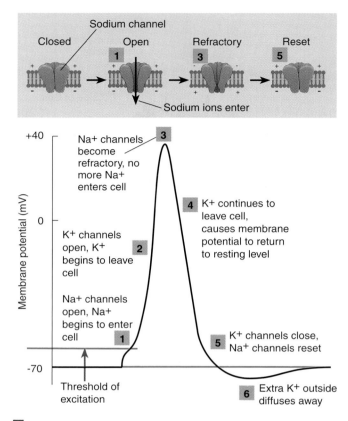

Figure 2.20
The movements of ions during the action potential.

channels are opened by changes in the membrane potential, they are called **voltage-dependent ion channels.** The influx of positively charged sodium ions produces a rapid change in the membrane potential, from –70 to +40 mV.

2. The membrane of the axon contains voltage-dependent potassium channels, but these channels are less sensitive than voltage-dependent sodium channels. That is, they require a greater level of depolarization before they begin to open. Thus, they begin to open later than the sodium channels.

3. At about the time the action potential reaches its peak (in approximately 1 msec), the sodium channels become *refractory*—they cannot open again until the membrane once more reaches the resting potential. At this time, then, no more Na+ can enter the cell.

4. By now, the voltage-dependent potassium channels in the membrane are open, letting K+ ions move freely through the membrane. At this time, the inside of the axon is now *positively* charged, so K+ is driven out of the cell by diffusion and by electrostatic pressure. This outflow of cations causes the membrane potential to return toward its normal value. As it does so, the potassium channels begin to close again.

5. As the membrane potential returns to normal, the potassium channels close, and no more potassium leaves the cell.

6. The membrane actually overshoots its resting value (–70 mV) and only gradually returns to normal. The accumulation of K+ ions outside the membrane causes it to become temporarily hyperpolarized. These extra ions soon diffuse away, and the membrane potential returns to –70 mV. Eventually, sodium-potassium transporters remove the Na+ that leaked in and retrieve the K+ that leaked out.

Figure 2.21 summarizes the changes in permeability of the membrane to sodium and potassium ions during the action potential. (See *Figure 2.21.*)

How much ionic flow is there? The drop in membrane resistance to Na+ is brief, and diffusion over any appreciable distance takes some time. Thus, when I say "Na+ rushes in," I do not mean that the axoplasm becomes flooded with Na+. At the peak of the action potential a very thin

voltage-dependent ion channel   An ion channel that opens or closes according to the value of the membrane potential.

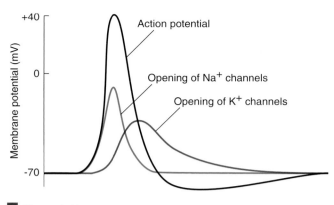

Figure 2.21
Changes in the permeability of the membrane to Na+ and K+ during the action potential.

layer of fluid immediately inside the axon becomes full of newly arrived Na+ ions; this amount is indeed enough to reverse the membrane potential. However, not enough time has elapsed for these ions to fill the entire axon. Before that event can take place, the Na+ channels close and K+ starts flowing out.

Experiments have shown that an action potential temporarily increases the number of Na+ ions inside the giant squid axon by 0.0003 percent. Although the concentration just inside the membrane is high, the total number of ions entering the cell is very small, relative to the number already there. On a short-term basis, sodium-potassium transporters are not very important. The few Na+ ions that manage to leak in diffuse into the rest of the axoplasm, and the slight increase in Na+ concentration is hardly noticeable. However, sodium-potassium transporters are important on a long-term basis, because in many axons action potentials occur at a very high rate. Without the activity of sodium-potassium transporters, the concentration of sodium ions in the axoplasm would increase enough so that the axon would no longer be able to function.

● Conduction of the Action Potential

Now that we have a basic understanding of the resting membrane potential and the production of the action potential, we can consider the movement of the message down the axon, or *conduction of the action potential*. To study this phenomenon, we again make use of the giant squid axon. We attach an electrical stimulator to an electrode at one end of the axon and place recording electrodes, attached to oscilloscopes, at different distances from the stimulating electrode. Then we apply a depolarizing stimulus to the end of the axon and trigger an action potential.

We record the action potential from each of the electrodes, one after the other. Thus, we see that the action potential is conducted down the axon. As the action potential travels, it remains constant in size. (See *Figure 2.22*.)

This experiment establishes a basic law of axonal conduction: the **all-or-none law.** This law states that an action potential either occurs or does not occur; once triggered, it is transmitted down the axon to its end. An action potential always remains the same size, without growing or diminishing. In fact, the axon will transmit an action potential in either direction, or even in both directions, if it is started in the middle of the axon's length. However, because action potentials in living animals always start at the end attached to the soma, axons normally carry one-way traffic.

As you know, the strength of a muscular contraction can vary from very weak to very forceful, and the strength of a stimulus can vary from barely detectable to very intense. We know that the occurrence of action potentials in axons controls the strength of muscular contractions and represents the intensity of a physical stimulus. But if the action potential is an all-or-none event, how can it represent information that can vary in a continuous fashion? The answer is simple: A single action potential is not the basic element of information; rather, variable information is represented by an axon's *rate of firing*. (In this context, *firing* refers to the production of action potentials.) A high rate of firing causes a strong muscular contraction, and a strong stimulus (such as a bright light) causes a high rate of firing in axons that serve the eyes. Thus, the all-or-none law is supplemented by the **rate law.** (See *Figure 2.23*.)

Action potentials are not the only kind of electrical signals that occur in neurons. As we shall see in the last section of this chapter, when a message is sent across a synapse, a small electrical signal is produced in the membrane of the neuron that receives the message. To understand this process, and to understand the way that action potentials are conducted in myelinated axons (described later in this section), we must see how such signals other than action potentials are conducted. To do so, we produce a subthreshold depolarization (too small to produce an action potential) at one end of an axon and record its effects from electrodes placed along the axon. We find that the

all-or-none law   The principle that once an action potential is triggered in an axon, it is propagated, without decrement, to the end of the fiber.

rate law   The principle that variations in the intensity of a stimulus or other information being transmitted in an axon are represented by variations in the rate at which that axon fires.

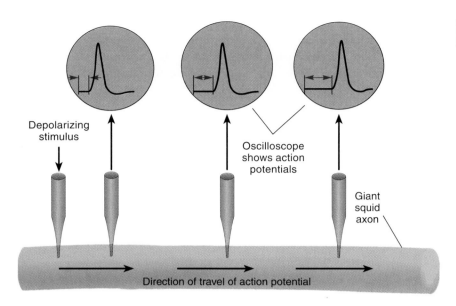

Depolarizing stimulus

Oscilloscope shows action potentials

Giant squid axon

Direction of travel of action potential

Figure 2.22
Conduction of the action potential. When an action potential is triggered, its size remains undiminished as it travels down the axon. The speed of conduction can be calculated from the delay between the stimulus and the action potential.

stimulus produces a disturbance in the membrane potential that becomes smaller as it moves away from the point of stimulation. (See *Figure 2.24.*)

The transmission of the small, subthreshold depolarization is *passive*. Neither sodium channels nor potassium channels are opening or closing. The axon is acting like an electrical cable, carrying along the current started at one end. This property of the axon follows laws discovered in the nineteenth century that describe the conduction of electricity through telegraph cables laid along the ocean floor. As a signal passes through an undersea cable, the signal gets smaller because of the electrical characteristics of the cable,

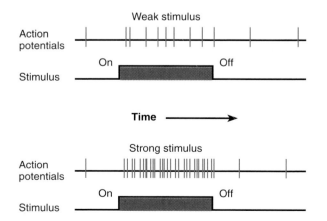

Weak stimulus

Action potentials

On   Off

Stimulus

Time

Strong stimulus

Action potentials

On   Off

Stimulus

Figure 2.23
The rate law. The strength of a stimulus is represented by the rate of firing of an axon. The size of each action potential is always constant.

including leakage through the insulator and resistance in the wire. Because the signal decreases in size (decrements), it is referred to as *decremental conduction*. We say that the conduction of a small depolarization by the axon follows the laws that describe the **cable properties** of the axon—the same laws that describe the electrical properties of an undersea cable. And because hyperpolarizations never trigger action potentials, these disturbances, too, are transmitted by means of the passive cable properties of an axon.

Recall that all but the smallest axons in mammalian nervous systems are myelinated; segments of the axons are covered by a myelin sheath produced by the oligodendrocytes of the CNS or the Schwann cells of the PNS. These segments are separated by portions of naked axon, the nodes of Ranvier. Conduction of an action potential in a myelinated axon is somewhat different from conduction in an unmyelinated axon.

Schwann cells (and the oligodendrocytes of the CNS) wrap tightly around the axon, leaving no measurable extracellular fluid between them and the axon. The only place where a myelinated axon comes in contact with the extracellular fluid is at a node of Ranvier, where the axon is naked. In the myelinated areas there can be no inward flow of Na^+ when the sodium channels open, because there *is* no extracellular sodium. How, then, does the "action potential" travel along the area of axonal membrane

cable properties The passive conduction of electrical current, in a decremental fashion, down the length of an axon.

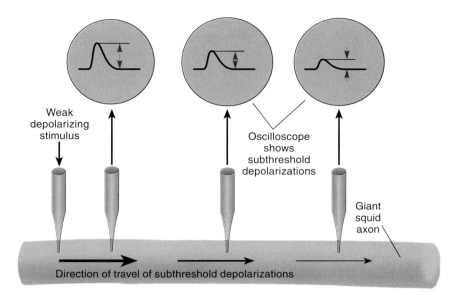

Weak depolarizing stimulus

Oscilloscope shows subthreshold depolarizations

Giant squid axon

Direction of travel of subthreshold depolarizations

Figure 2.24
Decremental conduction. When a sub-threshold depolarization is applied to the axon, the disturbance in the membrane potential is largest near the stimulating electrode and gets progressively smaller at distances farther along the axon.

covered by myelin sheath? You guessed it—by cable properties. The axon passively conducts the electrical disturbance from the action potential to the next node of Ranvier. The disturbance gets smaller, but it is still large enough to trigger an action potential at the node. The action potential gets retriggered, or repeated, at each node of Ranvier and is passed, by means of cable properties of the axon, along the myelinated area to the next node. Such conduction, hopping from node to node, is called **saltatory conduction,** from the Latin *saltare,* "to dance." (See *Figure 2.25.*)

Saltatory conduction confers two advantages. The first is economic. Energy must be expended by sodium- potassium transporters to get rid of the excess Na⁺ that enters the axon during the action potential. Sodium-potassium transporters must be located along an unmyelinated axon because Na⁺ enters everywhere. However, because Na⁺ can enter a myelinated axon only at the nodes of Ranvier, much less gets in and, consequently, much less has to be pumped out again. Therefore, a myelinated axon expends much less energy to maintain its sodium balance.

The second advantage to myelin is speed. Conduction of an action potential is faster in a myelinated axon because the transmission between the nodes, which occurs by means of the axon's cable properties, is very fast. Increased speed enables an animal to react faster and (undoubtedly) to think faster. One of the ways to increase the speed of conduction is to increase size. Because it is so large, the unmyelinated squid axon, with a diameter of 500 µm, achieves a conduction velocity of approximately 35 m/sec (meters per second). However, the same speed is achieved

by a myelinated cat axon with a diameter of a mere 6 µm. The fastest myelinated axon, 20 µm in diameter, can conduct action potentials at a speedy 120 m/sec, or 432 km/h. At that speed a signal can get from one end of an axon to the other without much delay.

Interim Summary

The message conducted down an axon is called an action potential. The membranes of all cells of the body are electrically charged, but only axons can produce action potentials. The resting membrane potential occurs because various ions are located in different concentrations in the fluid inside and outside the cell. The extracellular fluid (like seawater) is rich in Na⁺ and Cl⁻, and the intracellular fluid is rich in K⁺ and various organic anions, designated as A⁻.

The cell membrane is freely permeable to water, but its permeability to various ions—in particular, Na⁺ and K⁺—is regulated by ion channels. When the membrane potential is at its resting value (–70 mV), the gates of the voltage-dependent sodium and potassium channels are closed. The experiment with radioactive seawater showed us that some Na⁺ continuously leaks into the axon but is promptly forced out of the cell again by the sodium-potassium transporters (which also pump potassium *into* the

---

saltatory conduction Conduction of action potentials by myelinated axons. The action potential "jumps" from one node of Ranvier to the next.

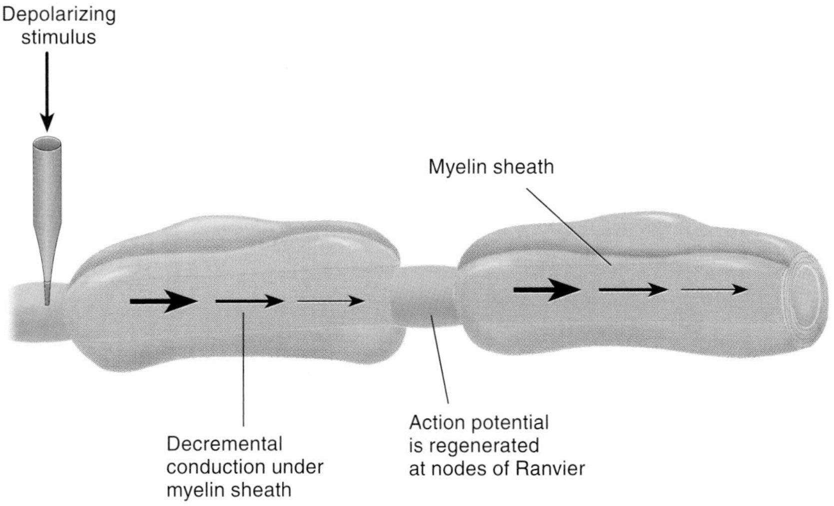

Depolarizing
stimulus

Myelin sheath

Figure 2.25
Saltatory conduction, showing propagation of
an action potential down a myelinated axon.

Decremental
conduction under
myelin sheath

Action potential
is regenerated
at nodes of Ranvier

axon). When an electrical stimulator depolarizes the membrane potential of the axon so that it reaches the threshold of excitation, voltage-dependent sodium channels open and Na^+ rushes into the cell, driven by the force of diffusion and by electrostatic pressure. The entry of the positively charged ions further reduces the membrane potential and, indeed, causes it to reverse, so that the inside becomes positive. The opening of the sodium channels is temporary; they soon close again. The depolarization of the membrane potential caused by the influx of Na^+ activates voltage-dependent potassium channels, and K^+ leaves the axon, traveling down its concentration gradient. This efflux (outflow) of K^+ quickly brings the membrane potential back to its resting value.

Because an action potential of a given axon is an all-or-none phenomenon, neurons represent intensity by their rate of firing. The action potential normally begins at one end of the axon, where the axon attaches to the soma. The action potential travels continuously down unmyelinated axons, remaining constant in size, until it reaches the terminal buttons. (When the axon divides, the action potential continues down each branch.) In myelinated axons, ions can flow through the membrane only at the nodes of Ranvier, because the axons are covered everywhere else with myelin, which isolates them from the extracellular fluid. Thus, the action potential is conducted from one node of Ranvier to the next by means of passive cable properties. When the electrical message reaches a node, voltage-dependent sodium channels open, and the action potential reaches full strength again. This mechanism saves a considerable amount of energy because sodium-potassium transporters are not needed along the myelinated portions of the axons, and saltatory conduction is faster.

COMMUNICATION BETWEEN NEURONS

Now that you know about the basic structure of neurons and the nature of the action potential, it is time to describe the ways that neurons can interact, gathering sensory information and initiating a behavior. As we have seen, neurons communicate by means of synapses, and the medium used for these messages is the chemical released by terminal buttons. These chemicals, called *transmitter substances* (or *neurotransmitters*), diffuse across the fluid-filled gap between the terminal buttons and the membranes of the neurons with which they form synapses. As we will see in this section, the transmitter substances produce **postsynaptic potentials**—brief depolarizations or hyperpolarizations—that increase or decrease the rate of firing of the axon of the postsynaptic neuron.

● The Concept of Chemical Transmission

Chemicals are used to transmit information between cells. These chemicals—transmitter substances, neuromodulators, and hormones—control the behavior of cells or organs. All these methods of transmission require the presence of cells that release the chemical and specialized protein molecules (receptors) that detect their presence. These methods differ

postsynaptic potential   Alterations in the membrane potential of a postsynaptic neuron, produced by liberation of transmitter substance at the synapse.

primarily in the distance between the cell that secretes the chemical and the receptors that detect its presence.

Transmitter substances (often called *neurotransmitters*) are released by terminal buttons of neurons and are detected by receptors in the membrane of another cell located a very short distance away. The communication at each synapse is private. Neuromodulators travel farther and are dispersed more widely than are neurotransmitters. **Neuromodulators,** too, are released by terminal buttons but are secreted in larger amounts and diffuse for longer distances, modulating the activity of many neurons in a particular part of the brain. Most neuromodulators are composed of proteinlike molecules called *peptides*, which are described later in this chapter.

Most hormones are produced in cells located in the **endocrine glands** (from the Greek *endo-*, "within," and *krinein*, "to secrete"). Others are produced by specialized cells located in various organs, such as the stomach, the intestines, the kidneys, and the brain. Cells that secrete hormones release these chemicals into the extracellular fluid. The hormones are then distributed to the rest of the body through the bloodstream. Hormones affect the activity of cells (including neurons) that contain specialized receptors located either on the surface of their membrane or deep within their nuclei. (Both types are described later in this chapter.) Cells that contain receptors for a particular hormone are referred to as **target cells** for that hormone; only these cells respond to its presence. Many neurons contain hormone receptors, and hormones are able to affect behavior by stimulating the receptors and changing the activity of these neurons. For example, a sex hormone, testosterone, increases the aggressiveness of most male mammals.

Neurotransmitters, neuromodulators, and hormones exert their effects on cells by attaching to a particular region of a receptor molecule called the **binding site.** A molecule of the chemical fits into the binding site the way a key fits into a lock; the shape of the binding site and the shape of the molecule of the transmitter substance are complementary. (A chemical that attaches to a binding site is called a **ligand,** from *ligare*, "to bind.") Neurotransmitters, neuromodulators, or hormones are natural ligands, produced by cells of the body. But other chemicals found in nature (primarily in plants or in the poisonous venoms of animals) can serve as ligands, too. In addition, artificial ligands can be produced in the laboratory. These chemicals are discussed in Chapter 4, which deals with drugs and their effects.

● Structure of Synapses

As you have already learned, synapses are junctions between the terminal buttons at the ends of the axonal branches of one neuron and the membrane of another. Synapses can occur in three places: on dendrites, on the soma, and on other axons. These synapses are referred to as *axodendritic, axosomatic,* and *axoaxonic.* Axodendritic synapses can occur on the smooth surface of a dendrite or on **dendritic spines**—small protrusions that stud the dendrites of several types of large neurons in the brain. (See *Figure 2.26.*)

Figure 2.27 illustrates a synapse. The **presynaptic membrane,** located at the end of the terminal button, faces the **postsynaptic membrane,** located on the neuron that receives the message (the *postsynaptic* neuron). These two membranes face each other across the **synaptic cleft,** a gap that varies in size from synapse to synapse but is usually around 200 Å wide. (An ångström, Å, is one ten-millionth of a millimeter.) The synaptic cleft contains extracellular fluid, through which the transmitter substance diffuses. (See *Figure 2.27* on page 45.)

As you may have noticed in Figure 2.27, three prominent structures are located in the cytoplasm of the terminal button: mitochondria, synaptic vesicles, and a cisterna. We also see microtubules, which are responsible for transporting material between the soma and terminal button. The presence of mitochondria implies that the terminal

---

neuromodulator   A naturally secreted substance that acts like a neurotransmitter except that it is not restricted to the synaptic cleft but diffuses through the extracellular fluid.

endocrine gland   A gland that liberates its secretions into the extracellular fluid around capillaries and hence into the bloodstream.

target cell   The type of cell that is directly affected by a hormone or nerve fiber.

binding site   The location on a receptor protein to which a ligand binds.

ligand (*ligh* gand or *ligg* and)   A chemical that binds with the binding site of a receptor.

dendritic spine   A small bud on the surface of a dendrite, with which a terminal button from another neuron forms a synapse.

presynaptic membrane   The membrane of a terminal button that lies adjacent to the postsynaptic membrane.

postsynaptic membrane   The cell membrane opposite the terminal button in a synapse; the membrane of the cell that receives the message.

synaptic cleft   The space between the presynaptic membrane and the postsynaptic membrane.

synaptic vesicle (*vess* i kul)   A small, hollow, beadlike structure found in terminal buttons; contains molecules of a neurotransmitter.

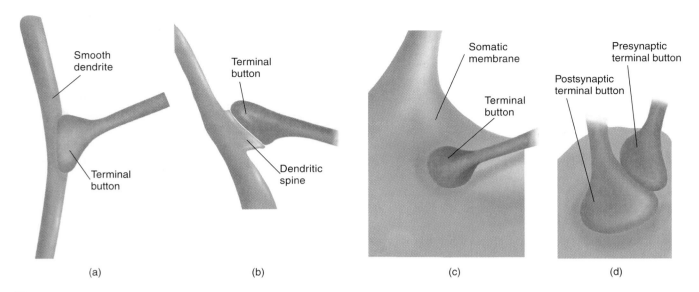

Figure 2.26
Types of synapses. Axodendritic synapses can occur on the smooth surface of a dendrite (a) or on dendritic spines (b). Axosomatic synapses occur on somatic membrane (c). Axoaxonic synapses consist of synapses between two terminal buttons (d).

button needs energy to perform its functions. **Synaptic vesicles** are small, rounded objects in the shape of spheres or ovoids. (The term *vesicle* means "little bladder.") Many terminal buttons contain two types of synaptic vesicles, large and small. Small synaptic vesicles (found in all terminal buttons) contain molecules of the transmitter substance. These vesicles are found in greatest numbers around the part of the presynaptic membrane that faces the synaptic cleft—next to the **release zone,** the region from which transmitter substance is released. In many terminal buttons, we see a scattering of large synaptic vesicles. These vesicles contain one of a number of different neuropeptides, the functions of which are described later in this chapter. (See *Figure 2.27.*)

Small synaptic vesicles are produced in the Golgi apparatus located in the soma and are carried by fast axoplasmic transport to the terminal button. As we will see, they are also produced from recycled material in the terminal button by the **cisternae,** collections of membrane similar to the Golgi apparatus. Large synaptic vesicles are produced in the soma and transported through the axoplasm to the terminal buttons.

In an electron micrograph the postsynaptic membrane under the terminal button appears somewhat thicker and more dense than the membrane elsewhere. This postsynaptic density is caused by the presence of receptors—specialized protein molecules that detect the presence of transmitter substances in the synaptic cleft. (See *Figure 2.27.*)

● Release of Transmitter Substance

When action potentials are conducted down an axon (and down all of its branches), something happens inside all of the terminal buttons: A number of small synaptic vesicles located just inside the postsynaptic membrane fuse with the membrane and then break open, spilling their contents into the synaptic cleft.

Heuser and colleagues (Heuser, 1977; Heuser et al., 1979) obtained photomicrographs that illustrate this process. Because the release of transmitter substance is a very rapid event, taking only a few msec to occur, special procedures are needed to stop the action so that the details can be studied. The experimenters electrically stimulated the nerve attached to an isolated frog muscle and then dropped the muscle against a block of pure copper that had been cooled to 4 K (approximately –453° F). Contact with the supercooled metal froze the outer layer of tissue in 2 msec or less. The ice held the components of the terminal buttons in place until they could be chemically stabilized and examined with an electron microscope. Figure 2.28 shows a por-

release zone   A region of the interior of the postsynaptic membrane of a synapse to which synaptic vesicles attach and release their neurotransmitter into the synaptic cleft.

cisterna   A part of the Golgi apparatus; through the process of pinocytosis, it receives portions of the presynaptic membrane and recycles them into synaptic vesicles.

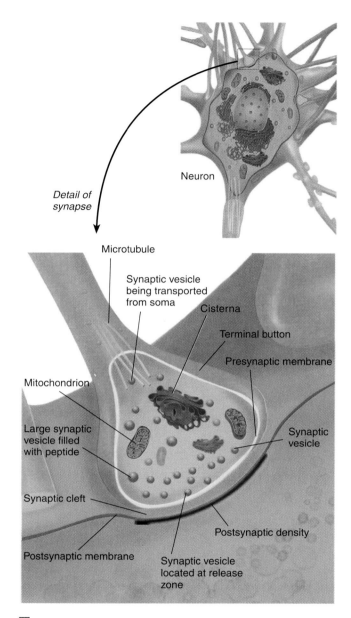

Figure 2.27
Details of a synapse.

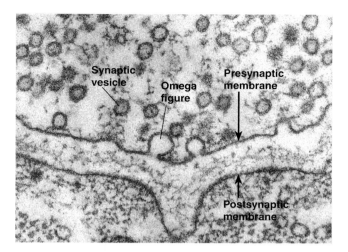

Figure 2.28
A photograph from an electron microscope, showing a cross section of a synapse. The omega-shaped figures are synaptic vesicles fusing with the presynaptic membranes of terminal buttons that form synapses with frog muscle.
(From Heuser, J.E., in *Society for Neuroscience Symposia, Vol. II*, edited by W.M. Cowan and J.A. Ferrendelli. Bethesda, MD: Society for Neuroscience, 1977.)

tion of the synapse in cross section; note the vesicles that appear to be fused with the presynaptic membrane, forming the shape of an omega (Ω). (See *Figure 2.28*.)

How does an action potential cause synaptic vesicles to release the transmitter substance? Based on experiments with secretory cells in a variety of different species, Almers (1990) suggested the following model. Some synaptic vesicles are "docked" against the presynaptic membrane, ready to release their transmitter substance into the synaptic cleft. Docking is accomplished when clusters of protein mole-

cules attach to protein molecules located in the presynaptic membrane. (See *Figure 2.29*.)

The release zone of the presynaptic membrane contains voltage-dependent calcium channels. When the membrane of the terminal button is depolarized by an arriving action potential, the calcium channels open. Like sodium ions, calcium ions (Ca^{2+}) are located in highest concentration in the extracellular fluid. Thus, when the voltage-dependent calcium channels open, Ca^{2+} flows into the cell, propelled by electrostatic pressure and the force of diffusion. The entry of Ca^{2+} is an essential step; if neurons are placed in a solution that contains no calcium ions, an action potential no longer causes the release of the transmitter substance. (Calcium transporters, similar in operation to sodium-potassium transporters, later remove the intracellular Ca^{2+}.)

As we will see later in this chapter and in subsequent chapters of this book, the calcium ion plays many important roles in biological processes within cells. The calcium ion can bind with various types of proteins, changing their characteristics. According to Almers (1990), the calcium that enters the terminal button binds with the clusters of protein molecules that join the membrane of the synaptic vesicles with the presynaptic membrane. This event makes the segments of the clusters of protein molecules move apart, producing a *fusion pore*—a hole through both membranes that enables them to fuse together. (See *Figure 2.29*.)

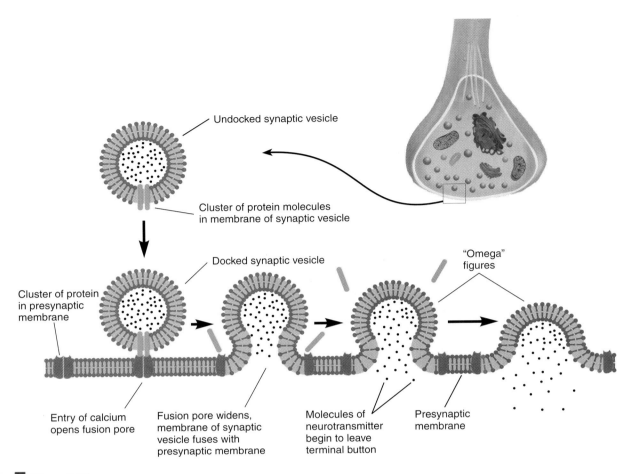

Undocked synaptic vesicle

Cluster of protein molecules
in membrane of synaptic vesicle

Docked synaptic vesicle

"Omega"
figures

Cluster of protein
in presynaptic
membrane

Entry of calcium
opens fusion pore

Fusion pore widens,
membrane of synaptic
vesicle fuses with
presynaptic membrane

Molecules of
neurotransmitter
begin to leave
terminal button

Presynaptic
membrane

Figure 2.29
Release of neurotransmitter. An action potential opens calcium channels. Calcium ions enter and bind with the protein embedded in the membrane of synaptic vesicles docked at the release zone. The fusion pores open and the transmitter substance is released into the synaptic cleft. The membrane of the vesicles fuses with that of the terminal button.

Figure 2.30 shows two photomicrographs of the presynaptic membrane, before and after the fusion pores have opened. We see the face of the presynaptic membrane as it would be viewed from the postsynaptic membrane. As you can see, the synaptic vesicles are aligned in a row along the release zone. The small bumps arranged in lines on each side of the synaptic vesicles appear to be voltage-dependent calcium channels. (See *Figure 2.30.*)

What happens to the membrane of the synaptic vesicles after they have broken open and released the transmitter substance they contain? Every time some transmitter substance is released the membrane of the terminal button gains the membrane of the synaptic vesicles that fuse with it and becomes slightly larger. Obviously, this process cannot go on indefinitely, or else the terminal buttons would get enormously big. The answer is that the membrane is recycled. Heuser and Reese (1973) proposed that as the synaptic vesicles fuse with the presynaptic membrane and burst open, their membrane becomes incorporated into that of the terminal button, which consequently becomes larger. Therefore, if the proper size of the terminal button is to be maintained, some membrane must be removed. Heuser and Reese obtained evidence that suggested that at the point of junction between the axon and the terminal button, little buds of membrane pinch off into the cytoplasm, in a process called **pinocytosis.** The buds of membrane migrate to the cisternae and fuse with them, pooling the lipid molecules in their membrane with that of the cisternae. Then new synaptic vesicles are produced as beads of membrane break off from the cisternae. These vesicles are

pinocytosis *(pee no sy **toh** sis)*   The pinching off of a bud of cell membrane, which travels to the interior of the cell.

Calcium channels—when open,
cause release of neurotransmitter

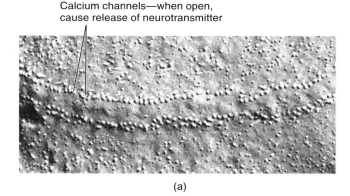

(a)

Synaptic vesicles fused with the presynaptic
membrane, releasing the neurotransmitter

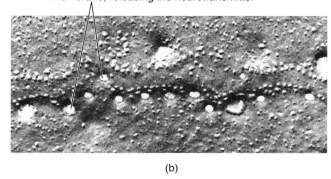

(b)

Figure 2.30
Photomicrographs of the release of neurotransmitter by a terminal button that forms a synapse with a frog muscle. The views are of the surface of the fusion zone of the terminal button. (a) Just prior to release. The two rows of dots are probably calcium channels. (b) During release. The larger circles are holes in the presynaptic membrane, revealing the contents of the synaptic vesicles that have fused with it.
(From Heuser, J., and Reese, T. *Journal of Cell Biology*, 1981, 88, 564–580.)

Pinocytosis–piece of
membrane buds off,
travels to cisterna

Cisterna–membrane
is recycled into new synaptic
vesicles, filled with neurotransmitter

Synaptic vesicles break away
from cisterna

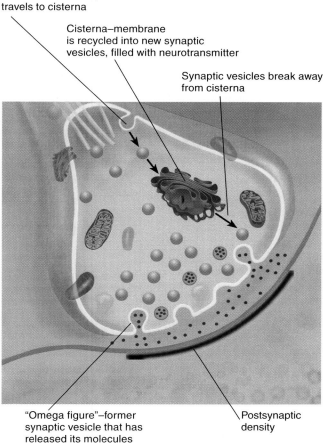

"Omega figure"–former
synaptic vesicle that has
released its molecules
of neurotransmitter

Postsynaptic
density

Figure 2.31
Recycling of the membrane of synaptic vesicles that have released neurotransmitter into the synaptic cleft.

then filled with molecules of transmitter substance, the appropriate proteins are inserted into the membrane, and they are transported toward the presynaptic membrane. (See *Figure 2.31.*)

● Activation of Receptors

How do molecules of the transmitter substance produce a depolarization or hyperpolarization in the postsynaptic membrane? They do so by diffusing across the synaptic cleft and attaching to the binding sites of special protein molecules attached to the postsynaptic membrane, called **postsynaptic receptors.** Once binding occurs, the postsynaptic receptors open **neurotransmitter-dependent ion**

channels, which permit the passage of specific ions into or out of the cell. Thus, the presence of the transmitter substance in the synaptic cleft allows particular ions to pass through the membrane, changing the local membrane potential.

Neurotransmitters open ion channels by at least two different methods, direct and indirect. The direct method is simpler, so I shall describe it first. Figure 2.32 illustrates

postsynaptic receptor   A receptor molecule in the postsynaptic membrane of a synapse that contains a binding site for a neurotransmitter.

neurotransmitter-dependent ion channel   An ion channel that opens when a molecule of a neurotransmitter binds with a postsynaptic receptor.

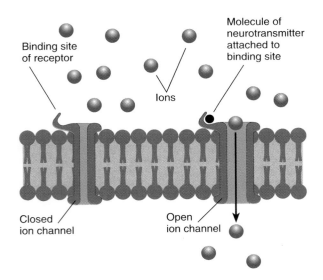

Figure 2.32
Ionotropic receptors. The ion channel opens when a molecule of neurotransmitter attaches to the binding site. For purposes of clarity, the drawing is schematic; molecules of neurotransmitter are actually much larger than individual ions.

a neurotransmitter-dependent ion channel that is equipped with its own binding site. When a molecule of the appropriate neurotransmitter attaches to it, the ion channel opens. The formal name for this combination receptor/ion channel is an **ionotropic receptor.** (See *Figure 2.32.*)

The ionotropic receptor was first discovered in the organ that produces electrical current in *Torpedo*, the electric ray, where it occurs in great number. (The electric ray is a fish that generates a powerful electrical current, not some kind of Star Wars weapon.) These receptors, which are sensitive to a transmitter substance called *acetylcholine*, contain sodium channels. When these channels are open, sodium ions enter the cell.

The indirect method is more complicated. Most receptors do not open ion channels directly but instead start a chain of chemical events. These receptors are called **metabotropic receptors** because they involve steps that require that the cell expend energy. Metabotropic receptors are located in close proximity to another protein attached to the membrane—a **G protein.** Figure 2.33(a) shows the simplest type of metabotropic receptor. (See *Figure 2.33*, and note that the numbers in the color squares correspond to the step numbers in the description that follows.) When a molecule of the transmitter substance binds with the receptor (step 1), the receptor activates a G protein situated nearby (step 2). An inactive G protein consists of three subunits. When activated, the α subunit breaks away from the others and attaches to a special binding site of an ion chan-

nel (step 3). The ion channel now opens (step 4), permitting ions to pass through the channel and thus producing a postsynaptic potential.

Figure 2.33(b) shows a more complicated system by which metabotropic receptors open ion channels. The first two steps are the same as in the simpler system. However, instead of binding directly with an ion channel, the α subunit of the G protein attaches to—and activates—an enzyme situated in the membrane (step 3). The activated enzyme causes the production of one of several different chemicals in the cytoplasm of the cell. Generically, these chemicals are called **second messengers** (the neurotransmitter being the first messenger). The second messenger then initiates another series of chemical steps that causes the ion channel to open. (See steps 1–6, *Figure 2.33b.*)

The first second messenger to be discovered was *cyclic AMP*, a chemical that is synthesized from ATP. Since then, several other second messengers have been discovered. As you will see in later chapters, second messengers play an important role in both synaptic and nonsynaptic communication. And they can do more than open ion channels; for example, they can travel to the nucleus or other parts of the cell and initiate biochemical changes.

● Postsynaptic Potentials

As we saw, postsynaptic potentials can be either depolarizing (excitatory) or hyperpolarizing (inhibitory). What determines the nature of the postsynaptic potential at a particular synapse is not the neurotransmitter itself. Instead, it is determined by the characteristics of the postsynaptic receptors—in particular, *by the particular type of ion channel they open.*

ionotropic receptor *(eye on oh **trow** pik)* A receptor that contains a binding site for a neurotransmitter and an ion channel that opens when a molecule of the neurotransmitter attaches to the binding site.

metabotropic receptor *(meh tab oh **trow** pik)* A receptor that contains a binding site for a neurotransmitter; activates an enzyme that begins a series of events that opens an ion channel elsewhere in the membrane of the cell when a molecule of the neurotransmitter attaches to the binding site.

G protein A protein coupled to a metabotropic receptor; conveys messages to other molecules when a ligand binds with and activates the receptor.

second messenger A chemical produced when a G protein activates an enzyme; carries a signal that results in the opening of the ion channel or causes other events to occur in the cell.

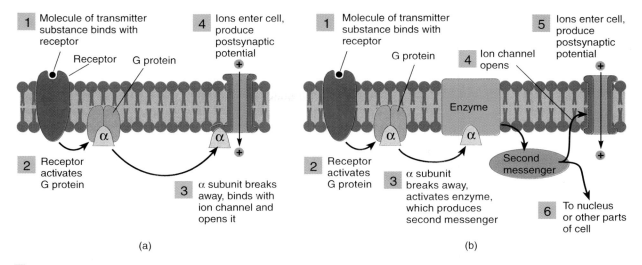

Figure 2.33
Metabotropic receptors. (a) The ion channel is opened directly by the α subunit of an activated G protein. (b) The α subunit of the G protein activates an enzyme, which produces a second messenger that opens the ion channel.

As Figure 2.34 shows, there are four major types of neurotransmitter-dependent ion channels found in the postsynaptic membrane: sodium (Na^+), potassium (K^+), chloride (Cl^-), and calcium (Ca^{2+}). Although the figure depicts only directly activated (ionotropic) ion channels, you should realize that many ion channels are activated indirectly, by metabotropic receptors coupled to G proteins.

The neurotransmitter-dependent sodium channel is the most important source of excitatory postsynaptic potentials. As we saw, sodium-potassium transporters keep sodium outside the cell, waiting for the forces of diffusion and electrostatic pressure to push it in. Obviously, when sodium channels are opened, the result is a depolarization—an *excitatory postsynaptic potential (EPSP)*. (See *Figure 2.34a.*)

We also saw that sodium-potassium transporters maintain a small surplus of potassium ions inside the cell. If potassium channels open, some of these cations will follow this gradient and leave the cell. Because K^+ is positively charged, its efflux will hyperpolarize the membrane, pro-

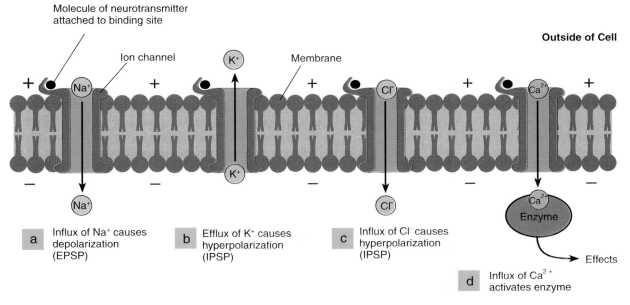

Figure 2.34
Ionic movements during postsynaptic potentials.

ducing an *inhibitory postsynaptic potential* (IPSP). (See *Figure 2.34b.*)

At many synapses, inhibitory transmitter substances open the chloride channels, instead of (or in addition to) potassium channels. The effect of opening chloride channels depends on the membrane potential of the neuron. If the membrane is at the resting potential, nothing happens, because (as we saw earlier) the forces of diffusion and electrostatic pressure balance perfectly for the chloride ion. However, if the membrane potential has already been depolarized by the activity of excitatory synapses located nearby, then the opening of chloride channels will permit Cl^- to enter the cell. The influx of anions will bring the membrane potential back to its normal resting condition. Thus, the opening of chloride channels serves to neutralize EPSPs. (See *Figure 2.34c.*)

The fourth type of neurotransmitter-dependent ion channel is the calcium channel. Calcium ions (Ca^{2+}), being positively charged and being located in highest concentration outside the cell, act like sodium ions; that is, the opening of calcium channels depolarizes the membrane, producing EPSPs. But calcium does even more. As we saw earlier in this chapter, the entry of calcium into the terminal button triggers the migration of synaptic vesicles and the release of the transmitter substance. In the dendrites of the postsynaptic cell, calcium binds with and activates special enzymes. These enzymes have a variety of effects, including the production of biochemical and structural changes in the postsynaptic neuron. As we will see in Chapter 14, one of the ways that learning affects the connections between neurons involves changes in dendritic spines initiated by the opening of calcium channels. (See *Figure 2.34d.*)

● Termination of Postsynaptic Potentials

Postsynaptic potentials are brief depolarizations or hyperpolarizations caused by the activation of postsynaptic receptors with molecules of a transmitter substance. They are kept brief by two mechanisms: reuptake and enzymatic deactivation.

The postsynaptic potentials produced by almost all transmitter substances are terminated by **reuptake.** This process is simply an extremely rapid removal of transmitter substance from the synaptic cleft by the terminal button. The transmitter substance does not return in the vesicles that get pinched off the membrane of the terminal button. Instead, the membrane contains special transporter molecules that draw on the cell's energy reserves to force molecules of the transmitter substance from the synaptic cleft directly into the cytoplasm—just as sodium-potassium transporters move Na^+ and K^+ across the mem-

brane. When an action potential arrives, the terminal button releases a small amount of transmitter substance into the synaptic cleft and then takes it back, giving the postsynaptic receptors only a brief exposure to the transmitter substance. (See *Figure 2.35.*)

Enzymatic deactivation is accomplished by an enzyme that destroys the transmitter molecule. As far as we know, postsynaptic potentials are terminated in this way for only one transmitter substance—**acetylcholine (ACh).** Transmission at synapses on muscle fibers and at some synapses between neurons is mediated by ACh. Postsynaptic potentials produced by ACh are short-lived because the postsynaptic membrane at these synapses contains an enzyme called **acetylcholinesterase (AChE).** AChE destroys ACh by cleaving it into its constituents—choline and acetate. Because neither of these substances is capable of activating postsynaptic receptors, the postsynaptic potential is terminated once the molecules of ACh are broken apart. AChE is an extremely energetic destroyer of ACh; one molecule of AChE will chop apart more that five thousand molecules of ACh each second.

● Effects of Postsynaptic Potentials: Neural Integration

We have seen how neurons are interconnected by means of synapses, how action potentials trigger the release of transmitter substances, and how these chemicals initiate excitatory or inhibitory postsynaptic potentials. Excitatory postsynaptic potentials increase the likelihood that the postsynaptic neuron will fire; inhibitory postsynaptic potentials decrease this likelihood. (In this context, "firing" refers to the occurrence of an action potential.) Thus, the rate at which an axon fires is determined by the relative activity of the excitatory and inhibitory synapses on the soma and dendrites of that cell.

reuptake The reentry of a transmitter substance just liberated by a terminal button back through its membrane, thus terminating the postsynaptic potential.

enzymatic deactivation The destruction of a transmitter substance by an enzyme after its release—for example, the destruction of acetylcholine by acetylcholinesterase.

acetylcholine (ACh) *(a see tul koh leen)* A neurotransmitter found in the brain, spinal cord, and parts of the peripheral nervous system; responsible for muscular contraction.

acetylcholinesterase (AChE) *(a see tul koh lin ess ter ace)* The enzyme that destroys acetylcholine soon after it is liberated by the terminal buttons, thus terminating the postsynaptic potential.

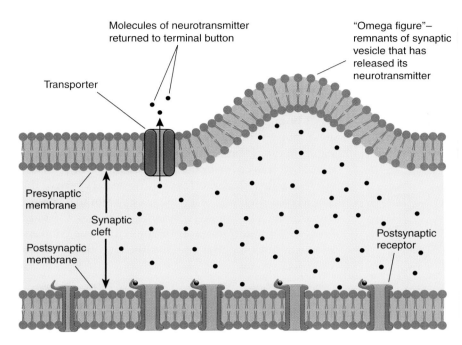

Molecules of neurotransmitter returned to terminal button

Transporter

"Omega figure"– remnants of synaptic vesicle that has released its neurotransmitter

Presynaptic membrane

Synaptic cleft

Postsynaptic membrane

Postsynaptic receptor

Figure 2.35
Reuptake. Molecules of a neurotransmitter that has been released into the synaptic cleft are transported back into the terminal button.

Let us look at the elements of this process. The interaction of the effects of excitatory and inhibitory synapses on a particular neuron is called **neural integration.** (*Integration* means "to make whole," in the sense of combining two or more functions.) Figure 2.36 illustrates the effects of excitatory and inhibitory synapses. The top panel shows what happens when several excitatory synapses become active. The release of the transmitter substance produces depolarizing EPSPs in the dendrites of neuron A. These EPSPs (represented in red) are then transmitted, by means of passive cable properties, down the dendrites, across the soma, to the base of the axon. If the depolarization is still strong enough when it reaches this point, the axon will fire. (See *Figure 2.36a.*)

Now let's consider what would happen if, at the same time, inhibitory synapses also become active. Inhibitory postsynaptic potentials are hyperpolarizing—they bring the membrane potential away from the threshold of excitation. Thus, they tend to cancel the effects of excitatory postsynaptic potentials. (See *Figure 2.36b.*)

The rate at which a neuron fires is controlled by the relative activity of the excitatory and inhibitory synapses on its dendrites and soma. If the activity of excitatory synapses goes up, the rate of firing will go up. If the rate of inhibitory synapses goes up, the rate of firing will go down.

Note that *neural* inhibition (that is, an inhibitory postsynaptic potential) does not always produce *behavioral* inhibition. For example, suppose a group of neurons inhibits a particular movement. If these neurons are inhibited, they

will no longer suppress the behavior. Thus, inhibition of the inhibitory neurons makes the behavior more likely to occur. Of course, the same is true for neural excitation. Neural *excitation* of neurons that *inhibit* a behavior suppresses that behavior. For example, when we are dreaming, a particular set of inhibitory neurons in the brain becomes active and prevents us from getting up and acting out our dreams. (As we will see in Chapter 9, if these neurons are destroyed, people *will* act out their dreams.) Neurons are elements in complex circuits; without knowing the details of these circuits, one cannot predict the effects of the excitation or inhibition of one set of neurons on an organism's behavior.

● Autoreceptors

Postsynaptic receptors detect the presence of a transmitter substance in the synaptic cleft and initiate excitatory or inhibitory postsynaptic potentials. But the postsynaptic membrane is not the only location of receptors that respond to transmitter substances. Many neurons also possess receptors that respond to the transmitter substance that *they* release, called **autoreceptors.**

neural integration The process by which inhibitory and excitatory postsynaptic potentials summate and control the rate of firing of a neuron.

autoreceptor A receptor molecule located on a neuron that responds to the neurotransmitter released by that neuron.

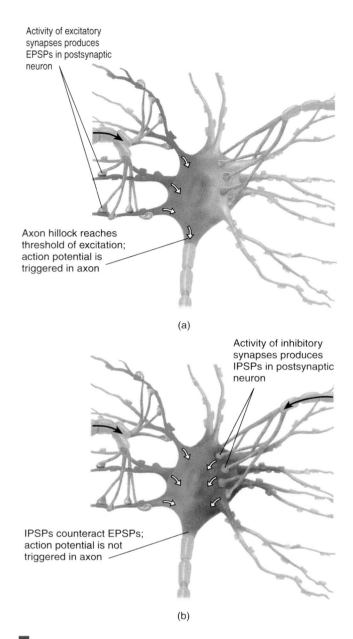

Activity of excitatory synapses produces EPSPs in postsynaptic neuron

Axon hillock reaches threshold of excitation; action potential is triggered in axon

(a)

Activity of inhibitory synapses produces IPSPs in postsynaptic neuron

IPSPs counteract EPSPs; action potential is not triggered in axon

(b)

Figure 2.36
Neural integration. (a) If several excitatory synapses are active at the same time, the EPSPs they produce (shown in red) summate as they travel toward the axon, and the axon fires. (b) If several inhibitory synapses are active at the same time, the IPSPs they produce (shown in blue) diminish the size of the EPSPs and prevent the axon from firing.

Autoreceptors can be located on the membrane of any part of the cell, but in this discussion we will consider those located on the terminal button. As far as we know, autoreceptors do not control ion channels. Thus, when stimulated by a molecule of the appropriate transmitter

substance, autoreceptors do not produce changes in the membrane potential. Instead, they regulate internal processes, including the synthesis and release of the transmitter substance. (As you may have guessed, autoreceptors are metabotropic; the control they exert on these processes is accomplished through G proteins and second messengers.) In most cases the effects of autoreceptor activation are inhibitory; that is, the presence of the transmitter substance in the extracellular fluid in the vicinity of the neuron causes a decrease in the rate of synthesis or release of the transmitter substance. Most investigators believe that autoreceptors are part of a regulatory system that controls the amount of transmitter substance released. If too much is released, the autoreceptors inhibit both production and release; if not enough is released, the rates of production and release go up.

● Other Types of Synapses

So far, the discussion of synaptic activity has referred only to the effects of postsynaptic excitation or inhibition. These effects occur at axosomatic or axodendritic synapses. Axoaxonic synapses work differently. Axoaxonic synapses do not contribute directly to neural integration. Instead, axoaxonic synapses alter the amount of transmitter substance released by the terminal buttons of the postsynaptic axon. They can produce presynaptic modulation: presynaptic inhibition or presynaptic facilitation.

As you know, the release of a transmitter substance by a terminal button is initiated by an action potential. Normally, a particular terminal button releases a fixed amount of transmitter substance each time an action potential arrives. However, the release of transmitter substance can be modulated by the activity of axoaxonic synapses. If the activity of the axoaxonic synapse decreases the release of the transmitter substance, the effect is called **presynaptic inhibition.** If it increases the release, it is called **presynaptic facilitation.** (See *Figure 2.37.*)

Many very small neurons have extremely short processes and apparently lack axons. These neurons form *dendrodendritic synapses,* or synapses between dendrites. Because these

presynaptic inhibition   The action of a presynaptic terminal button in an axoaxonic synapse; reduces the amount of neurotransmitter released by the postsynaptic terminal button.

presynaptic facilitation   The action of a presynaptic terminal button in an axoaxonic synapse; increases the amount of neurotransmitter released by the postsynaptic terminal button.

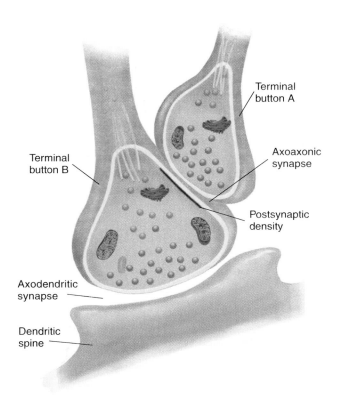

Figure 2.37
An axoaxonic synapse. The activity of terminal button A can in-crease or decrease the amount of neurotransmitter released by ter-minal button B.

neurons lack long axonal processes, they do not transmit information from place to place within the brain. Most investigators believe that they perform regulatory functions, perhaps helping to organize the activity of groups of neurons. Because these neurons are so small, they are difficult to study; thus, little is known about their function.

Some larger neurons, as well, form dendrodendritic synapses. Some of these synapses are chemical, indicated by the presence of synaptic vesicles in one of the juxtaposed dendrites and a postsynaptic thickening in the membrane of the other. Other synapses are *electrical*; the membranes meet and almost touch, forming a **gap junction.** The membranes on both sides of a gap junction contain channels that permit ions to diffuse from one cell to another. Thus, changes in the membrane potential of one neuron induce changes in the membrane of the other. (See *Figure 2.38.*) Although most gap junctions in vertebrate synapses are dendrodendritic, axosomatic and axodendritic gap junctions also occur. Gap junctions are common in invertebrates; their function in the vertebrate nervous system is not known.

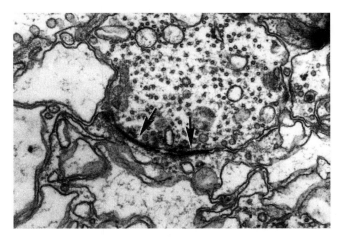

Figure 2.38
A gap junction, which permits direct electrical coupling between the membranes of adjacent neurons.
(From Bennett, M.V.L., and Pappas, G.D. *The Journal of Neuroscience,* 1983, *3,* 748–761.)

● Nonsynaptic Chemical Communication

Not all chemical communication takes place at synapses. Neurons possess receptors for a variety of substances in the membrane of all parts of the cell—and even in their nucleus. These receptors are sensitive to neuromodulators and to hormones.

Some of these receptors are ionotropic in nature and contain binding sites for several different molecules, including both neurotransmitters and neuromodulators. (The best known example, the GABA$_A$ receptor, is described in Chapter 4.) But most of the receptors found in the membrane are metabotropic—coupled to a G protein that generates a second messenger that produces changes in the cell's physiological processes.

First, let us consider receptors for hormones. Endocrine glands produce two classes of hormones: peptides and steroids. **Peptides** are chains of amino acids that are linked together by special chemical links called *peptide bonds* (hence their name). For example, insulin and the hormones of the pituitary gland are peptides. Peptides exert their effects on target cells by stimulating metabotropic receptors located in the membrane. The second messenger that is generated travels to the nucleus of the cell, where it initiates changes in the cell's physiological processes.

gap junction   A special junction between cells that permits direct communication by means of electrical coupling.

peptide   A chain of amino acids joined together by peptide bonds.

Steroids consist of very small fat-soluble molecules. (*Steroid* derives from *stereos,* "solid," and *oleum,* "oil." They are synthesized from chole*sterol.*) Examples of steroid hormones include the sex hormones secreted by the ovaries and testes and the hormones secreted by the adrenal cortex. Because steroid hormones are soluble in lipids, they pass easily through the cell membrane. They travel to the nucleus, where they attach themselves to receptors located there. The receptors, stimulated by the hormone, then direct the machinery of the cell to alter its protein production. (See *Figure 2.39.*)

In the past few years, investigators have discovered the presence of steroid receptors in terminal buttons and around the postsynaptic membrane of some neurons. These steroid receptors influence synaptic transmission, and they do so rapidly. Exactly how these steroid receptors work is still not known.

Interim Summary

Synapses consist of junctions between the terminal buttons of one neuron and the membrane—usually the somatic or dendritic membrane—of another. When an action potential is transmitted down an axon, the terminal buttons at the end release a transmitter substance, a chemical that produces either depolarizations (EPSPs) or hyperpolarizations (IPSPs) of the postsynaptic membrane. The rate of firing of the axon of the postsynaptic cell is determined by the relative activity of the excitatory and inhibitory synapses on the membrane of its dendrites and soma—a phenomenon known as *neural integration.*

Chemical communication takes place between a cell that secretes a chemical and one that contains receptors for that chemical. The communication can involve neurotransmitters, neuromodulators, or hormones; the distance varies from the space that separates the presynaptic and postsynaptic membrane to the space that separates cells at different locations in the body. Neurotransmitters, neuromodulators, and hormones act on cells by attaching to the binding sites of receptors and initiating chemical changes in these cells.

Synapses consist of junctions between the terminal buttons of one neuron and the membrane—usually the somatic or dendritic membrane—of another. The terminal button contains synaptic vesicles. Most terminal buttons contain two sizes of vesicles, the smaller of which are found in greatest numbers around the release zone of the presynaptic membrane. When an action potential is transmitted down an axon, the depolarization opens voltage-dependent calcium channels, which permit Ca^{2+} to enter. The calcium ions bind with the clusters of protein mole-

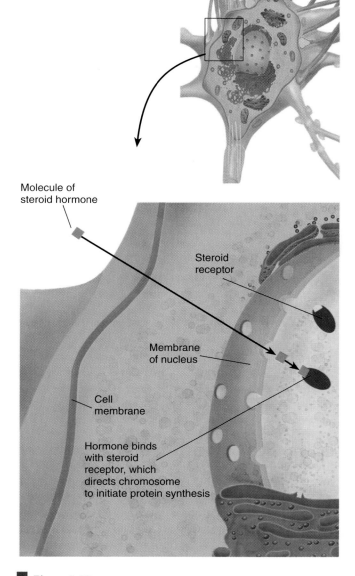

Figure 2.39
Action of steroid hormones. Steroid hormones affect their target cells by means of specialized receptors in the nucleus. Once a receptor binds with a molecule of a steroid hormone, it causes genetic mechanisms to initiate protein synthesis.

cules in the membranes of synaptic vesicles already docked at the release zone. The protein clusters spread apart, causing the vesicles to break open and fuse their membrane with that of the terminal button, thus releasing the trans-

steroid   A chemical of low molecular weight, derived from cholesterol. Steroid hormones affect their target cells by attaching to receptors found within the cell.

mitter substance. The extra membrane pinches off into the cytoplasm and travels to the cisternae, where it is recycled in the production of new vesicles.

The activation of postsynaptic receptors by molecules of a transmitter substance causes neurotransmitter-dependent ion channels to open, resulting in postsynaptic potentials. Ionotropic receptors contain ion channels, which are directly opened when a ligand attaches to the binding site. Metabotropic receptors are linked to G proteins, which, when activated, open ion channels—usually by producing a member of a category of chemicals called second messengers.

The nature of the postsynaptic potential depends on the type of ion channel that is opened by the postsynaptic receptors at a particular synapse. Excitatory postsynaptic potentials occur when Na^+ enters the cell. Inhibitory postsynaptic potentials are produced by the opening of K^+ channels or Cl^- channels. The entry of Ca^{2+} produces EPSPs, but even more importantly, it activates special enzymes that cause physiological changes in the postsynaptic cell.

Postsynaptic potentials normally are brief. They are terminated by two means. Acetylcholine is deactivated by the enzyme acetylcholinesterase. In all other cases (as far as we know) molecules of the transmitter substance are removed from the synaptic cleft by means of transporters located in the presynaptic membrane, which transport the molecules back into the cytoplasm. This retrieval process is called reuptake.

The presynaptic membrane, as well as the postsynaptic membrane, contains receptors that detect the presence of a transmitter substance. Presynaptic receptors, also called autoreceptors, monitor the quantity of transmitter substance that a neuron releases and, apparently, regulate the amount that is synthesized or released.

Axosomatic and axodendritic synapses are not the only kinds found in the nervous system. Axoaxonic synapses produce presynaptic inhibition or presynaptic facilitation by blocking or promoting the opening of calcium channels in the terminal button, thus reducing or enhancing the amount of transmitter substance that is liberated. Dendrodendritic synapses also exist, but their role in neural communication is not yet understood.

Nonsynaptic chemical transmission is similar to synaptic transmission. Peptide neuromodulators and hormones activate metabotropic peptide receptors located in the membrane; their effects are mediated through the production of second messengers. Steroid hormones enter the nucleus, where they bind with receptors capable of altering the synthesis of proteins that regulate the cell's physiological processes. These hormones also bind with receptors located outside the nucleus, but less is known about their functions.

SUGGESTED READINGS

Hall, A. *An Introduction to Molecular Neurobiology.* Sunderland, MA: Sinauer, 1992.

Kandel, E. R., Schwartz, J. H., and Jessell, T. M. *Principles of Neural Science*, 3rd ed. Norwalk, CT: Appleton & Lange, 1992.

Nicholls, J. G., Martin, A. R., Wallace, B. G., and Kuffler, S. W. *From Neuron to Brain*, 3rd ed. Sunderland, MA: Sinauer, 1992.

CHAPTER 3

Structure of the Nervous System

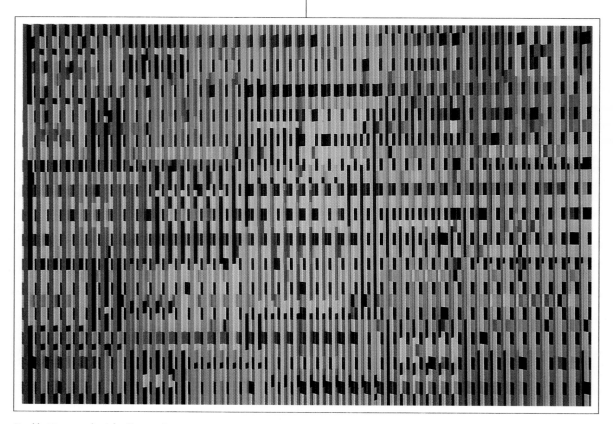

Double Metamorphosis by Yaacov Agam.

he goal of neuroscience research is to understand how the brain works. To understand the results of this research, you must be acquainted with the basic structure of the nervous system. The number of terms introduced in this chapter is kept to a minimum (but as you will see, the minimum is still a rather large number). With the framework you will receive from this chapter, you should have no trouble learning the material presented in subsequent chapters.

BASIC FEATURES OF THE NERVOUS SYSTEM

Before beginning a description of the nervous system, I want to discuss the terms used to describe it. The gross anatomy of the brain was described long ago, and everything that could be seen without the aid of a microscope was given a name. Early anatomists named most brain structures according to their similarity to commonplace objects: amygdala, or "almond-shaped object"; hippocampus, or "sea horse"; genu, or "knee"; cortex, or "bark"; pons, or "bridge"; uncus, or "hook," to give a few examples. Throughout this book I will translate the names of anatomical terms as I introduce them, because the translation makes the terms more memorable. For example, knowing that *cortex* means "bark" (like the bark of a tree) will help you remember that the cortex is the outer layer of the brain.

When describing features of a structure as complex as the brain, we need to use terms denoting directions. Directions in the nervous system are normally described relative to the **neuraxis,** an imaginary line drawn through the spinal cord up to the front of the brain. For simplicity's

sake, let us consider an animal with a straight neuraxis. Figure 3.1 shows an alligator and a human. This alligator is certainly laid out in a linear fashion; we can draw a straight line that starts between its eyes and continues down the center of its spinal cord. (See *Figure 3.1.*) The front end is **anterior,** and the tail is **posterior.** The terms **rostral** (toward the beak) and **caudal** (toward the tail) are also employed, especially when referring specifically to the brain. The top of the head and the back are part of the **dorsal** surface, while the **ventral** (front) surface faces the ground. These directions are somewhat more complicated in the human; because we stand upright, our neuraxis bends, so that the top of the head is perpendicular to the back. The frontal views of the alligator and the human il-

neuraxis   An imaginary line drawn through the center of the length of the central nervous system, from the bottom of the spinal cord to the front of the forebrain.

anterior   With respect to the central nervous system, located near or toward the head.

posterior   With respect to the central nervous system, located near or toward the tail.

rostral   "Toward the beak"; with respect to the central nervous system, in a direction along the neuraxis toward the front of the face.

caudal   "Toward the tail"; with respect to the central nervous system, in a direction along the neuraxis away from the front of the face.

dorsal   "Toward the back"; with respect to the central nervous system, in a direction perpendicular to the neuraxis toward the top of the head or the back.

ventral   "Toward the belly"; with respect to the central nervous system, in a direction perpendicular to the neuraxis toward the bottom of the skull or the front surface of the body.

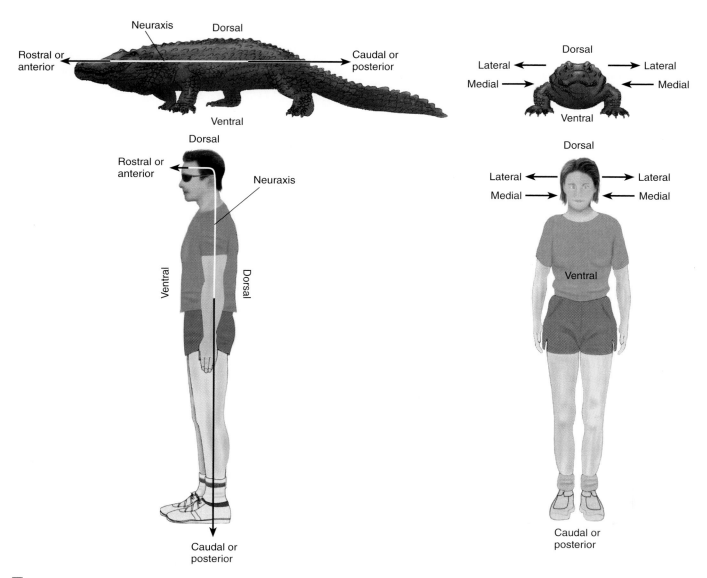

Figure 3.1
Side and frontal views of an alligator and a human, showing the terms used to denote anatomical directions.

lustrate the terms **lateral** and **medial,** toward the side and toward the midline, respectively. (See *Figure 3.1.*)

Two other useful terms are *ipsilateral* and *contralateral.* **Ipsilateral** refers to structures on the same side of the body. Thus, if we say that the olfactory bulb sends axons to the *ipsilateral* hemisphere, we mean that the left olfactory bulb sends axons to the left hemisphere and the right olfactory bulb sends axons to the right hemisphere. **Contralateral** refers to structures on opposite sides of the body. If we say that a particular region of the left cerebral cortex controls movements of the *contralateral* hand, we mean that the region controls movements of the right hand.

To see what is in the nervous system, we have to cut it open; to be able to convey information about what we find, we slice it in a standard way. Figure 3.2 shows a hu-

lateral   Toward the side of the body, in a direction at right angles with the neuraxis and away from it.

medial   Toward the neuraxis, away from the side of the body.

ipsilateral   Located on the same side of the body.

contralateral   Located on the opposite side of the body.

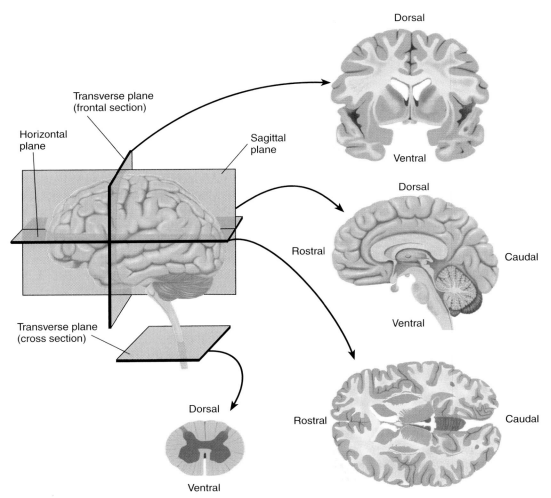

Figure 3.2
Planes of section as they pertain to the human central nervous system.

man nervous system. We can slice the nervous system in three ways:

1. Transversely, like a salami, giving us **cross sections** (also known as **frontal sections,** referring to the brain)
2. Parallel to the ground, giving us **horizontal sections**
3. Perpendicular to the ground and parallel to the neuraxis, giving us **sagittal sections.** The **midsagittal plane** divides the brain into two symmetrical halves. The sagittal section in Figure 3.2 lies in the midsagittal plane.

Note that because of our upright posture, cross sections of the spinal cord are actually parallel to the ground. (See *Figure 3.2.*)

● An Overview

The nervous system consists of the brain and spinal cord, which make up the *central nervous system* (CNS), and the cranial nerves, spinal nerves, and peripheral ganglia, which constitute the *peripheral nervous system* (PNS). The CNS is encased in bone: The brain is covered by the skull, and the spinal cord is encased by the vertebral column. (See *Table 3.1.*)

cross section   With respect to the central nervous system, a slice taken at right angles to the neuraxis.

frontal section   A slice through the brain parallel to the forehead.

horizontal section   A slice through the brain parallel to the ground.

sagittal section *(sadj i tul)*   A slice through the brain parallel to the neuraxis and perpendicular to the ground.

midsagittal plane   The plane through the neuraxis perpendicular to the ground; divides the brain into two symmetrical halves.

Table 3.1
The Major Divisions of the Nervous System

Central nervous system (CNS)	Peripheral nervous system (PNS)
Brain	Nerves
Spinal cord	Peripheral ganglia

Figure 3.3 illustrates the relation of the brain and spinal cord to the rest of the body. Do not be concerned with unfamiliar labels on this figure; these structures will be described later. (See *Figure 3.3.*) The brain is a large mass of neurons, glia, and other supporting cells. It is the most protected organ of the body, encased in a tough, bony skull and floating in a pool of cerebrospinal fluid. The brain receives a copious supply of blood and is chemically guarded by the blood–brain barrier.

● Blood Supply

The brain receives approximately 20 percent of the blood flow from the heart, and it receives it continuously. Other parts of the body, such as the skeletal muscles or digestive system, receive varying quantities of blood, depending on their needs, relative to those of other regions. But the brain always receives its share. The brain cannot store its fuel (primarily glucose), nor can it temporarily extract energy without oxygen, as the muscles can; therefore, a consistent blood supply is essential. A 1-second interruption of the blood flow to the brain uses up much of the dissolved oxygen; a 6-second interruption produces unconsciousness. Permanent damage occurs within a few minutes.

Circulation of blood in the body proceeds from large arteries to small arteries to capillaries. The capillaries then drain into small veins and then to large veins, which travel back to the heart, where the process begins again. Figure 3.4 shows a bottom view of the brain and its major arterial supply. (The spinal cord has been cut off, as have the left half of the cerebellum and the left temporal lobe.) Two major sets of arteries serve the brain: the **vertebral arteries,** which serve the caudal portion of the brain, and the **internal carotid arteries,** which serve the rostral portion. (See *Figure 3.4* on page 62.) You can see that the blood supply is rather peculiar; major arteries join together and then separate again. Normally, there is a little mixing of blood from the rostral and caudal arterial supplies and, in the case of the rostral supply, from that of the right and left sides of the brain. But if a blood vessel becomes blocked (for example, by a blood clot), blood flow can follow al-ternative routes, reducing the probability of loss of blood supply and subsequent destruction of brain tissue.

● Meninges

The entire nervous system—brain, spinal cord, cranial and spinal nerves, and peripheral ganglia—is covered by tough connective tissue. The protective sheaths around the brain and spinal cord are referred to as the **meninges** (singular: *meninx*). The meninges consist of three layers, which are shown in Figure 3.3. The outer layer is thick, tough, and flexible but unstretchable; its name, **dura mater,** means "hard mother." The middle layer of the meninges, the **arachnoid membrane,** gets its name from the weblike appearance of the *arachnoid trabeculae* that protrude from it (from the Greek *arachne*, meaning "spider"; *trabecula* means "track"). The arachnoid membrane, soft and spongy, lies beneath the dura mater. Closely attached to the brain and spinal cord, and following every surface convolution, is the **pia mater** ("pious mother"). The smaller surface blood vessels of the brain and spinal cord are contained within this layer. Between the pia mater and arachnoid membrane is a gap called the **subarachnoid space.** This space is filled with a liquid called **cerebrospinal fluid (CSF).** (Refer to *Figure 3.3.*)

central nervous system (CNS)   The brain and spinal cord.

peripheral nervous system (PNS)   The nerves and ganglia located outside the central nervous system.

vertebral artery *(ver **tee** brul)*   An artery whose branches serve the posterior region of the brain.

internal carotid artery   An artery whose branches serve the rostral and lateral portions of the brain.

meninges (singular: meninx) *(men **in** jees)*   The three layers of tissue that encase the central nervous system: the dura mater, arachnoid membrane, and pia mater.

dura mater   The outermost of the meninges; tough, flexible, unstretchable.

arachnoid membrane *(a **rak** noyd)*   The middle layer of the meninges, between the outer dura mater and inner pia mater. The subarachnoid space beneath the arachnoid membrane is filled with cerebrospinal fluid, which cushions the brain.

pia mater   The layer of the meninges adjacent to the surface of the brain.

subarachnoid space   The fluid-filled space between the arachnoid membrane and the pia mater.

cerebrospinal fluid (CSF)   A clear fluid, similar to blood plasma, that fills the ventricular system of the brain and the subarachnoid space surrounding the brain and spinal cord.

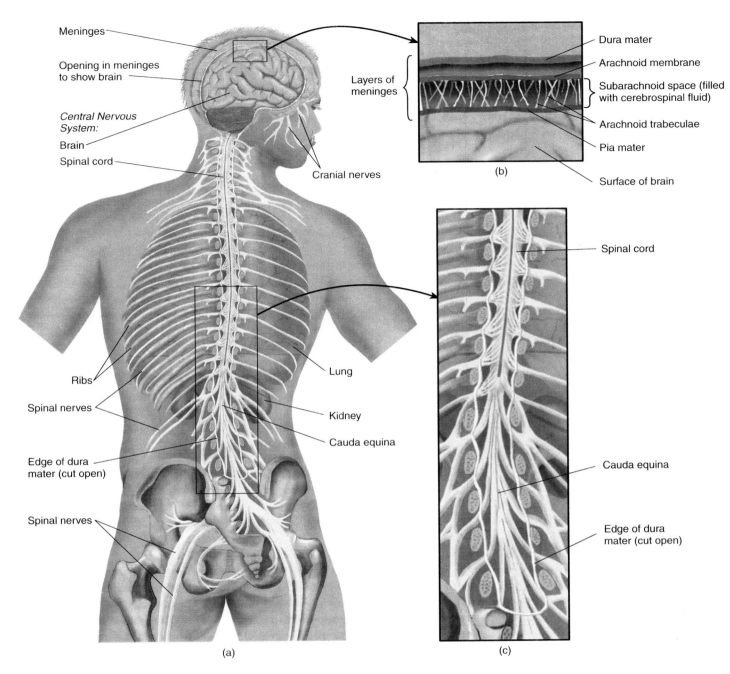

Figure 3.3
(a) The relation of the nervous system to the rest of the body. (b) Detail of the meninges that cover the central nervous system. (c) A closer view of the lower spinal cord and cauda equina.

The peripheral nervous system (PNS) is covered with two layers of meninges. The middle layer (arachnoid membrane), with its associated pool of CSF, covers only the brain and spinal cord. Outside the central nervous system, the outer and inner layers (dura mater and pia mater) fuse and form a sheath that covers the spinal and cranial nerves and the peripheral ganglia.

In the first edition of this book I said that I did not know why the outer and inner layers of the meninges were referred to as "mothers." I received a letter from medical historians at the Department of Anatomy at UCLA that explained the name. (Sometimes, it pays to proclaim one's ignorance.) A tenth-century Persian physician, Ali ibn Abbas, used the Arabic term *al umm* to refer to the meninges. The term literally means "mother" but was used to designate any swaddling material, because Arabic lacked a specific term for the word *membrane*. The tough outer membrane was called *al umm al djafiya*, and the soft inner one was

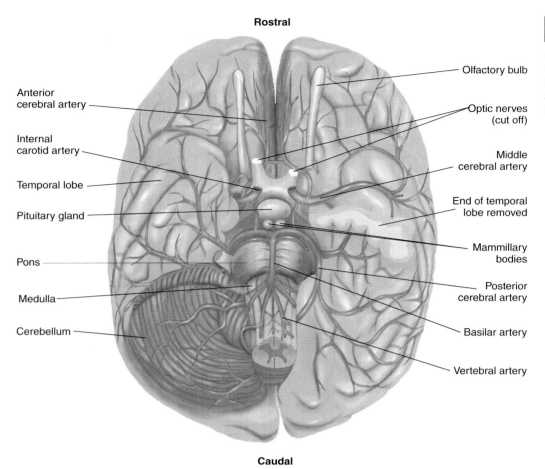

Rostral

Anterior
cerebral artery

Internal
carotid artery

Temporal lobe

Pituitary gland

Pons

Medulla

Cerebellum

Olfactory bulb

Optic nerves
(cut off)

Middle
cerebral artery

End of temporal
lobe removed

Mammillary
bodies

Posterior
cerebral artery

Basilar artery

Vertebral artery

Caudal

Figure 3.4
Arterial blood supply to the brain, viewed from beneath. Parts of the brain have been removed to show some arteries that would otherwise be hidden.

called *al umm al rigiga.* When the writings of Ali ibn Abbas were translated into Latin during the eleventh century, the translator, who was probably not familiar with the structure of the meninges, made a literal translation of *al umm.* He referred to the membranes as the "hard mother" and the "pious mother" (*pious* in the sense of "delicate"), rather than use a more appropriate Latin word.

● The Ventricular System and Production of CSF

The brain is very soft and jellylike. The considerable weight of a human brain (approximately 1400 g), along with its delicate construction, necessitates that it be protected from shock. A human brain cannot even support its own weight well; it is difficult to remove and handle a fresh brain from a recently deceased human without damaging it.

Fortunately, the intact brain within a living human is well protected. It floats in a bath of CSF contained within the subarachnoid space. Because the brain is completely immersed in liquid, its net weight is reduced to approximately 80 g; thus, pressure on the base of the brain is considerably diminished. The CSF surrounding the brain and spinal cord also reduces the shock to the central nervous system that would be caused by sudden head movement.

The brain contains a series of hollow, interconnected chambers called **ventricles,** which are filled with CSF. (See *Figure 3.5.*) The largest chambers are the **lateral ventricles,** which are connected to the **third ventricle.** The third ventricle is located at the midline of the brain; its walls divide the surrounding part of the brain into symmetrical

ventricle *(ven trik ul)*   One of the hollow spaces within the brain, filled with cerebrospinal fluid.

lateral ventricle   One of the two ventricles located in the center of the telencephalon.

third ventricle   The ventricle located in the center of the diencephalon.

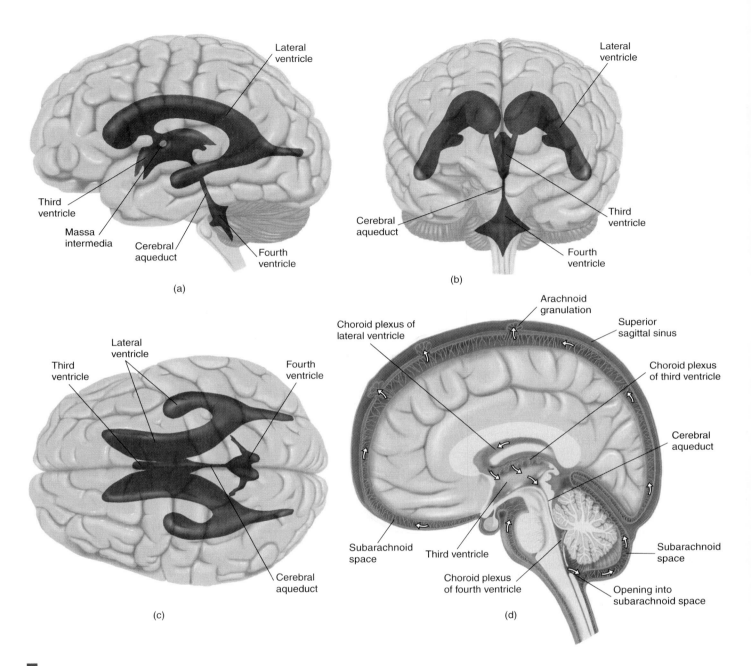

Figure 3.5
The ventricular system of the brain. (a) Lateral view of the left side of the brain. (b) Frontal view. (c) Dorsal view. (d) The production, circulation, and reabsorption of cerebrospinal fluid.

halves. A bridge of neural tissue called the *massa intermedia* crosses through the middle of the third ventricle and serves as a convenient reference point. The **cerebral aqueduct,** a long tube, connects the third ventricle to the **fourth ventricle.** The lateral ventricles constitute the first and second ventricles, but they are never referred to as such. (See *Figure 3.5.*)

cerebral aqueduct   A narrow tube interconnecting the third and fourth ventricles of the brain, located in the center of the mesencephalon.

fourth ventricle   The ventricle located between the cerebellum and the dorsal pons, in the center of the metencephalon.

Cerebrospinal fluid is extracted from the blood and re-sembles blood plasma in its composition. CSF is manu-factured by special tissue with an especially rich blood supply called the **choroid plexus,** which protrudes into all four of the ventricles. CSF is produced continuously; the total volume of CSF is approximately 125 ml, and the half-life (the time it takes for half of the CSF present in the ven-tricular system to be replaced by fresh fluid) is about 3 hours. Therefore, several times this amount is produced by the choroid plexus each day. The continuous production of CSF means that there must be a mechanism for its re-moval. The production, circulation, and reabsorption of CSF is illustrated in *Figure 3.5d.*

This figure shows a slightly rotated midsagittal view of the central nervous system, which shows only the right lat-eral ventricle (because the left hemisphere has been re-moved). Cerebrospinal fluid is produced by the choroid plexus of the lateral ventricles, and it flows into the third ventricle. More CSF is produced in this ventricle, which then flows through the cerebral aqueduct to the fourth ven-tricle, where still more CSF is produced. The CSF leaves the fourth ventricle through small openings that connect with the subarachnoid space surrounding the brain. The CSF then flows through the subarachnoid space around the central nervous system, where it is reabsorbed into the blood supply through the **arachnoid granulations.** These pouch-shaped structures protrude into the **superior sagit-tal sinus,** a blood vessel that drains into the veins serving the brain. (See *Figure 3.5d.*)

Occasionally, the flow of CSF is interrupted at some point in its route of passage. For example, a brain tumor growing in the midbrain may push against the cerebral aqueduct, blocking its flow, or an infant may be born with a cerebral aqueduct too small to accommodate a normal flow of CSF. This occlusion results in greatly increased pressure within the ventricles, because the choroid plexus continues to produce CSF. The walls of the ventricles then expand and produce a condition known as **obstructive hydrocephalus** (*hydrocephalus* literally means "water-head"). If the obstruction remains, and if nothing is done to reverse the increased intracerebral pressure, blood ves-sels will be occluded and permanent—perhaps fatal—brain damage will occur. Fortunately, a surgeon can usu-ally operate on the person, drilling a hole through the skull and inserting a plastic tube into one of the ventricles. The tube is then placed beneath the skin and connected to a pressure relief valve that is implanted in the abdominal cavity. When the pressure in the ventricles becomes exces-sive, the valve permits the CSF to escape into the ab-domen, where eventually it is reabsorbed into the blood supply. (See *Figure 3.6.*)

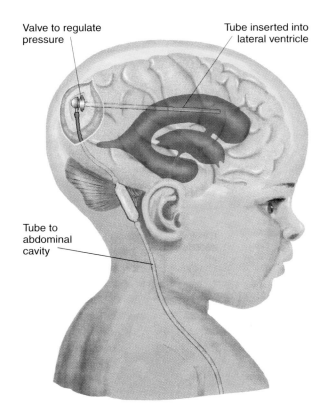

Valve to regulate pressure

Tube inserted into lateral ventricle

Tube to abdominal cavity

Figure 3.6
Hydrocephalus in an infant. A surgeon places a shunt in a lat-eral ventricle, which permits cerebrospinal fluid to escape to the ab-dominal cavity, where it is absorbed into the blood supply. A pressure valve regulates the flow of CSF through the shunt.

Interim Summary

Anatomists have adopted a set of terms to describe the lo-cations of parts of the body. *Anterior* is toward the head, *posterior* is toward the tail, *lateral* is toward the side, *medial*

choroid plexus   The highly vascular tissue that pro-trudes into the ventricles and produces cerebrospinal fluid.

arachnoid granulation   Small projections of the arach-noid membrane through the dura mater into the supe-rior sagittal sinus; CSF flows through them to be reabsorbed into the blood supply.

superior sagittal sinus   A venous sinus located in the midline just dorsal to the brain, between the two cere-bral hemispheres.

obstructive hydrocephalus   A condition in which all or some of the brain's ventricles are enlarged; caused by an obstruction that impedes the normal flow of CSF.

is toward the middle, *dorsal* is toward the back, and *ventral* is toward the front surface of the body. In the special case of the nervous system, *rostral* means toward the beak (or nose) and *caudal* means toward the tail. *Ipsilateral* means "same side," and *contralateral* means "other side." A cross section (or, in the case of the brain, a frontal section) slices the nervous system at right angles to the neuraxis, a horizontal section slices the brain parallel to the ground, and a sagittal section slices it perpendicular to the ground, parallel to the neuraxis.

The central nervous system consists of the brain and spinal cord, and the peripheral nervous system consists of the spinal and cranial nerves and peripheral ganglia. The CNS is covered with the meninges: dura mater, arachnoid membrane, and pia mater. The space under the arachnoid membrane is filled with cerebrospinal fluid, in which the brain floats. The PNS is covered with only the dura mater and pia mater. Cerebrospinal fluid is produced in the choroid plexus of the lateral, third, and fourth ventricles. It flows from the two lateral ventricles into the third ventricle, through the cerebral aqueduct into the fourth ventricle, then into the subarachnoid space, and finally back into the blood supply through the arachnoid granulations. If the flow of CSF is blocked by a tumor or other obstruction, the result is hydrocephalus: enlargement of the ventricles and subsequent brain damage.

THE CENTRAL NERVOUS SYSTEM

Although the brain is exceedingly complicated, an understanding of the basic features of brain development makes it easier to learn and remember the location of the most important structures. With that end in mind, I introduce these features here in the context of development of the central nervous system.

● Development of the Central Nervous System

The central nervous system begins its existence early in embryonic life as a hollow tube, and it maintains this basic shape even after it is fully developed. During development, parts of the tube elongate, pockets and folds form, and the tissue around the tube thickens. The cells that give rise to neurons are found on the inner surface of the tube. These cells divide and produce neurons, which then migrate in a radial direction, away from the center. Their final location is guided by both physical and chemical factors. Physical guidance is provided by radially oriented glial cells; the newly born neurons migrate along the processes of these cells. Chemical guidance attracts particular types of neurons to particular locations, where they come to rest. (See *Figure 3.7.*)

Early in development the central nervous system contains three interconnected chambers. These chambers become ventricles, and the tissue that surrounds them becomes the three major parts of the brain: the forebrain, the midbrain, and the hindbrain. (See *Figures 3.8a* and *3.8c.*) As development progresses, the rostral chamber divides into three separate chambers, which become the two lateral ventricles and the third ventricle. The region around the lateral ventricles becomes the telencephalon ("end brain"), and the region around the third ventricle becomes

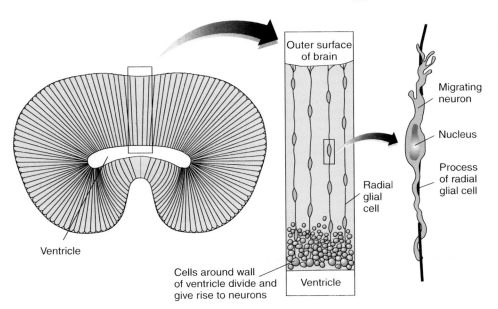

Figure 3.7
A cross section through the nervous system early in its development. Radially oriented glial cells help guide the migration of newly formed neurons.
(Adapted from Bloom, F.E., and Lazerson, A. *Brain, Mind, and Behavior,* 2nd ed. New York: W.H. Freeman, 1988.)

Outer surface of brain

Migrating neuron

Nucleus

Process of radial glial cell

Radial glial cell

Ventricle

Cells around wall of ventricle divide and give rise to neurons

Ventricle

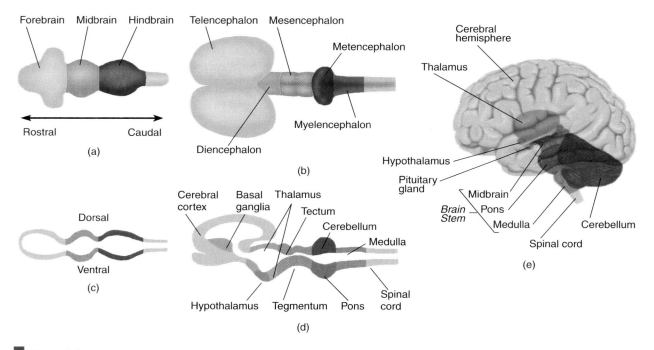

Figure 3.8
A schematic outline of brain development, showing its relation to the ventricles. (a) and (c) Early development. (b) and (d) Later in development. (e) A lateral view of the left side of a semitransparent human brain, showing the brain stem "ghosted in." The colors of all figures denote corresponding regions.

the diencephalon ("interbrain"). (See **Figures 3.8b** and **3.8d.**) In its final form the chamber inside the midbrain (mesencephalon) becomes narrow, forming the cerebral aqueduct, and two structures develop in the hindbrain: the metencephalon ("afterbrain") and the myelencephalon ("marrowbrain"). (See **Figure 3.8e.**)

Table 3.2 summarizes the terms I have introduced here and mentions some of the major structures found in each part of the brain. The colors in the table match those in Figure 3.8. These structures will be described in the remainder of the chapter. (See **Table 3.2.**)

Once neurons have migrated to their final locations where they collect in groups, they begin forming connections with other groups of neurons. They grow dendrites, which receive the terminal buttons from the axons of other neurons, and they grow axons of their own. Like neural migration, axonal growth is guided by physical and chemical factors. Once the growing ends of the axons (the *growth cones*) reach their targets, they form numerous branches. Each of these branches finds a vacant place on the membrane of the appropriate type of postsynaptic cell, grows a terminal button, and establishes a synaptic connection. (Apparently, different types of cells secrete different chemicals, which attract different types of axons.) Of course, the

establishment of a synaptic connection also requires efforts on the part of the postsynaptic cell; this cell must contribute its parts of the synapse, including the postsynaptic receptors. The chemical signals that the cells exchange in order to tell one another to establish these connections are not yet known.

The layer of cells surrounding the neural tube gives rise to many more neurons than are needed. In fact, the neurons that are produced must compete in order to survive. The axons of approximately 50 percent of these neurons do not find vacant postsynaptic cells of the right type with which to form synaptic connections—so they die. This phenomenon, too, involves a chemical signal; when a presynaptic neuron establishes synaptic connections, it receives a signal from the postsynaptic cell that permits it to survive. Those neurons that come too late do not find any available space and thus do not receive this life-sustaining signal. This scheme may seem wasteful, but apparently the evolutionary process found that the safest strategy was to produce too many neurons and let them fight to establish synaptic connections, rather than try to produce exactly the right number of each type of neuron.

During development, thousands of different pathways develop in the brain. These pathways—groups of axons

Table 3.2
Anatomical Subdivisions of the Brain

Major division	Ventricle	Subdivision	Principal structures
Forebrain	Lateral	Telencephalon	Cerebral cortex
			Basal ganglia
			Limbic system
	Third	Diencephalon	Thalamus
			Hypothalamus
Midbrain	Cerebral aqueduct	Mesencephalon	Tectum Tegmentum
Hindbrain	Fourth	Metencephalon	Cerebellum
			Pons
		Myelencephalon	Medulla oblongata

that connect one brain region with another—seem to be specified genetically. And within many of these pathways, the connections are orderly and systematic. For example, the axons of sensory neurons from the skin form orderly connections in the brain; axons from the little finger form synapses in one region, those of the ring finger form synapses in a neighboring region, and so on. In fact, the surface of the body is "mapped" on the surface of the brain. Similarly, the surface of the retina of the eye is "mapped" on another region of the surface of the brain.

● The Forebrain

As we saw, the **forebrain** surrounds the rostral end of the neural tube. Its two major components are the telencephalon and the diencephalon.

Telencephalon

The telencephalon includes most of the two symmetrical **cerebral hemispheres** that comprise the cerebrum. The cerebral hemispheres are covered by the cerebral cortex and contain the limbic system and the basal ganglia. The latter two sets of structures are primarily in the **subcortical regions** of the brain—those located deep within it, beneath the cerebral cortex.

Cerebral Cortex.   *Cortex* means "bark," and the **cerebral cortex** surrounds the cerebral hemispheres like the bark of

a tree. In humans the cerebral cortex is greatly convoluted; these convolutions, consisting of **sulci** (small grooves), **fissures** (large grooves), and **gyri** (bulges between adjacent sulci or fissures), greatly enlarge the surface area of the cortex, compared with a smooth brain of the same size. In fact, two-thirds of the surface of the cortex is hidden in the grooves; thus, the presence of gyri and sulci triples the area of the cerebral cortex. The total surface area is approximately 2360 cm^2 (2.5 ft^2), and the thickness is approxi-

forebrain   The most rostral of the three major divisions of the brain; includes the telencephalon and diencephalon.

cerebral hemisphere *(sa **ree** brul)*   One of the two major portions of the forebrain, covered by the cerebral cortex.

subcortical region   The region located within the brain, beneath the cortical surface.

cerebral cortex   The outermost layer of gray matter of the cerebral hemispheres.

sulcus (plural: sulci) *(**sul** kus, **sul** sigh)*   A groove in the surface of the cerebral hemisphere, smaller than a fissure.

fissure   A major groove in the surface of the brain, larger than a sulcus.

gyrus (plural: gyri) *(**jye** russ, **jye** rye)*   A convolution of the cortex of the cerebral hemispheres, separated by sulci or fissures.

mately 3 mm. The cerebral cortex consists mostly of glia and the cell bodies, dendrites, and interconnecting axons of neurons. Because cells predominate, giving the cerebral cortex a grayish brown appearance, it is referred to as *gray matter*. (See *Figure 3.9.*) Beneath the cerebral cortex run millions of axons that connect the neurons of the cerebral cortex with those located elsewhere in the brain. The large concentration of myelin gives this tissue an opaque white appearance—hence the term *white matter*.

Three areas of the cerebral cortex receive information from the sensory organs. The **primary visual cortex,** which receives visual information, is located at the back of the brain, on the inner surfaces of the cerebral hemispheres— primarily, on the upper and lower banks of the **calcarine**

fissure. (*Calcarine* means "spur-shaped." See *Figure 3.10.*) The **primary auditory cortex,** which receives auditory information, is located on the upper surface of a deep fissure in the side of the brain—the **lateral fissure.** (See inset, *Figure 3.10.*) The **primary somatosensory cortex,** a vertical strip of cortex just caudal to the **central sulcus,** receives information from the body senses. As Figure 3.10 shows, different regions of the primary somatosensory cortex receive information from different regions of the body. In addition, the base of the somatosensory cortex receives information concerning taste. (See *Figure 3.10.*)

With the exception of olfaction, sensory information from the body or the environment is sent to the primary sensory cortex of the contralateral hemisphere. Thus, the primary somatosensory cortex of the left hemisphere learns what the right hand is holding, the left primary visual cortex learns what is happening toward the person's right, and so on.

The region of the cerebral cortex most directly involved in the control of movement is the **primary motor cortex,** located just in front of the primary somatosensory cortex. Neurons in different parts of the primary motor cortex are connected to muscles in different parts of the body. The connections, like those of the sensory regions of the cerebral cortex, are contralateral; the left primary motor cortex controls the right side of the body and vice versa. Thus, if a surgeon places an electrode on the surface of the primary motor cortex and stimulates the neurons there with a weak electrical current, the result will be movement of a particular part of the body. Moving the electrode to a different spot will cause a different part of the body to move. (See *Figure 3.10.*) I like to think of the strip of primary motor cortex as the keyboard of a piano, with each key control-

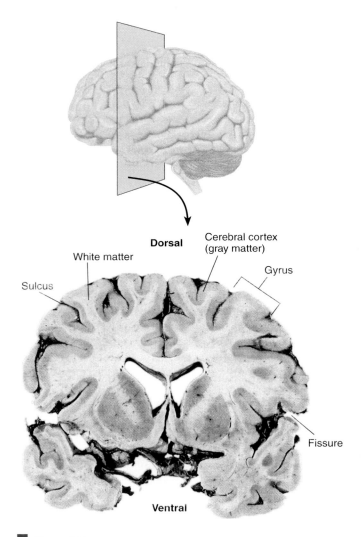

Figure 3.9
A slice of a human brain showing fissures and gyri and the layer of cerebral cortex that follows these convolutions.

primary visual cortex The region of the cerebral cortex whose primary input is from the visual system.

calcarine fissure (*kal ka rine*) A fissure located in the occipital lobe on the medial surface of the brain; contains most of the primary visual cortex.

primary auditory cortex The region of the cerebral cortex whose primary input is from the auditory system.

lateral fissure The fissure that separates the temporal lobe from the overlying frontal and parietal lobes.

primary somatosensory cortex The region of the cerebral cortex whose primary input is from the somatosensory system.

central sulcus (*sul kus*) The sulcus that separates the frontal lobe from the parietal lobe.

primary motor cortex The region of the cerebral cortex that contains neurons that control movements of skeletal muscles.

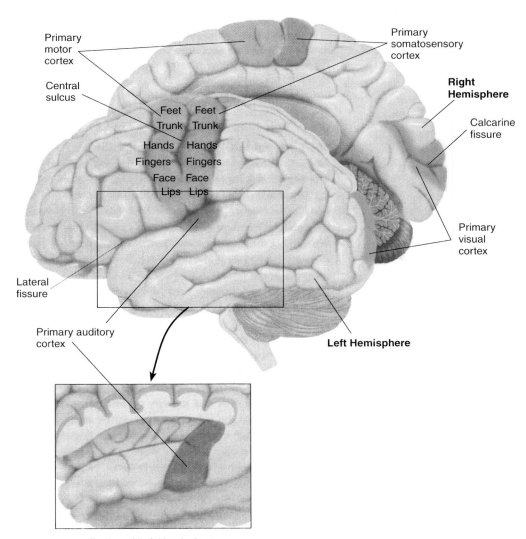

Primary
motor
cortex

Central
sulcus

Feet Feet
Trunk Trunk
Hands Hands
Fingers Fingers
Face Face
Lips Lips

Lateral
fissure

Primary auditory
cortex

Primary
somatosensory
cortex

**Right
Hemisphere**

Calcarine
fissure

Primary
visual
cortex

Left Hemisphere

Portion of Left Hemisphere

Figure 3.10
A lateral view of the left side of a human brain and part of the inner surface of the right side. The inset shows a cutaway of part of the frontal lobe of the left hemisphere, permitting us to see the primary auditory cortex on the dorsal surface of the temporal lobe.

ling a different movement. (We will see shortly who the "player" of this piano is.)

The regions of primary sensory and motor cortex occupy only a small part of the cerebral cortex. The rest of the cerebral cortex accomplishes what is done between sensation and action: perceiving, learning and remembering, planning, and acting. These processes take place in the *association areas* of the cerebral cortex. The central sulcus provides an important dividing line between the anterior and posterior regions of the cerebral cortex. (See *Figure 3.10.*) The anterior region is involved in movement-related activities, such as planning and executing behaviors. The posterior part is involved in perceiving and learning.

Discussing the various regions of the cerebral cortex is easier if we have names for them. In fact, the cerebral cor-

tex is divided into four areas, or *lobes,* named for the bones of the skull that cover them: the frontal lobe, parietal lobe, temporal lobe, and occipital lobe. (See *Figure 3.11.*) Of course, the brain contains two of each lobe, one in each hemisphere. The **frontal lobe** (the "front") includes everything in front of the central fissure. The **parietal lobe** (the "wall") is located on the side of the cerebral hemisphere, just behind the central sulcus, caudal to the frontal lobe.

frontal lobe   The anterior portion of the cerebral cortex, rostral to the parietal lobe and dorsal to the temporal lobe.
parietal lobe *(pa rye i tul)*   The region of the cerebral cortex caudal to the frontal lobe and dorsal to the temporal lobe.

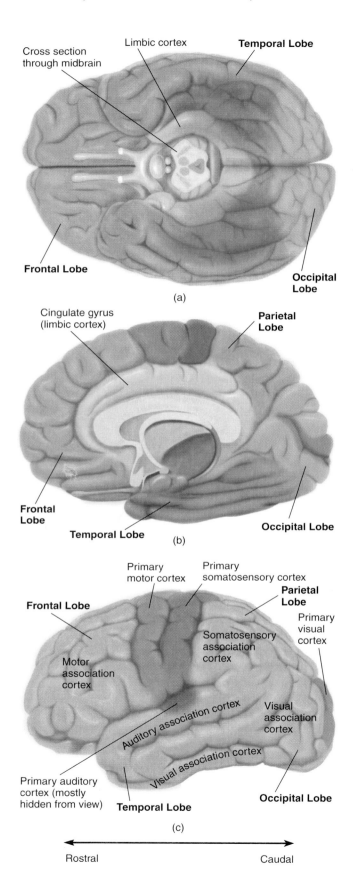

Cross section through midbrain

Limbic cortex

Temporal Lobe

Frontal Lobe

Occipital Lobe

(a)

Cingulate gyrus (limbic cortex)

Parietal Lobe

Frontal Lobe

Temporal Lobe

Occipital Lobe

(b)

Primary motor cortex

Primary somatosensory cortex

Parietal Lobe

Frontal Lobe

Primary visual cortex

Somatosensory association cortex

Motor association cortex

Auditory association cortex

Visual association cortex

Visual association cortex

Primary auditory cortex (mostly hidden from view)

Temporal Lobe

Occipital Lobe

(c)

Rostral ⟷ Caudal

Figure 3.11
The four lobes of the cerebral cortex, the primary sensory and motor cortex, and the association cortex. (a) View from the base of the brain. (b) Midsagittal view, with the cerebellum and brain stem removed. (c) Lateral view.

The **temporal lobe** (the "temple") juts forward from the base of the brain, ventral to the frontal and parietal lobes. The **occipital lobe** (*ob*, "in back of"; *caput*, "head") lies at the very back of the brain, caudal to the parietal and temporal lobes. Figure 3.11 shows three lobes in three views of the cerebral hemispheres: a ventral view (a view from the bottom), a midsagittal view (a view of the inner surface of the right hemisphere after the left hemisphere has been removed), and a lateral view. (See *Figure 3.11*.)

Each primary sensory area of the cerebral cortex sends information to adjacent regions, called the **sensory association cortex.** Circuits of neurons in the sensory association cortex analyze the information received from the primary sensory cortex; perception takes place there, and memories are stored there. The regions of the sensory association cortex located closest to the primary sensory areas receive information from only one sensory system. For example, the region closest to the primary visual cortex analyzes visual information and stores visual memories. Regions of the sensory association cortex located far from the primary sensory areas receive information from more than one sensory system; thus, they are involved in several kinds of perceptions and memories. These regions make it possible to integrate information from more than one sensory system. For example, we can learn the connection between the sight of a particular face and the sound of a particular voice. (See *Figure 3.11*.)

If people sustain damage to the somatosensory association cortex, their deficits are related to somatosensation and to the environment in general; for example, they may have difficulty perceiving the shapes of objects that they can touch but not see, they may be unable to name parts of their bodies, or they may have trouble drawing maps or following them. Destruction of the primary visual cortex

temporal lobe (*tem por ul*)   The region of the cerebral cortex rostral to the occipital lobe and ventral to the parietal and frontal lobes.

occipital lobe (*ok sip i tul*)   The region of the cerebral cortex caudal to the parietal and temporal lobes.

sensory association cortex   Those regions of the cerebral cortex that receive information from the regions of primary sensory cortex.

causes blindness. However, although people who sustain damage to the visual association cortex will not become blind, they may be unable to recognize objects by sight. People who sustain damage to the auditory association cortex may have difficulty perceiving speech or even producing meaningful speech of their own. People who sustain damage to regions of the association cortex at the junction of the three posterior lobes, where the somatosensory, visual, and auditory functions overlap, may have difficulty reading or writing.

Just as regions of the sensory association cortex of the posterior part of the brain are involved in perceiving and remembering, the frontal association cortex is involved in the planning and execution of movements. The **motor association cortex** is located just rostral to the primary motor cortex. This region controls the primary motor cortex; thus, it directly controls behavior. If the primary motor cortex is the keyboard of the piano, then the motor association cortex is the piano player. The rest of the frontal lobe, rostral to the motor association cortex, is known as the **prefrontal cortex.** This region of the brain is less involved with the control of movement and more involved in formulating plans and strategies.

Although the two cerebral hemispheres cooperate with each other, they do not perform identical functions. Some functions are *lateralized*—located primarily on one side of the brain. In general, the left hemisphere participates in the *analysis* of information—the extraction of the elements that make up the whole of an experience. This ability makes the left hemisphere particularly good at recognizing *serial events*—events whose elements occur one after the other. The left hemisphere is also involved in controlling serial behaviors. (In a few people the functions of the left and right hemispheres are reversed.) The serial functions performed by the left hemisphere include verbal activities, such as talking, understanding the speech of other people, reading, and writing. These abilities are disrupted by damage to the various regions of the left hemisphere. (I will say more about language and the brain in Chapter 16.)

In contrast, the right hemisphere is specialized for *synthesis*; it is particularly good at putting isolated elements together to perceive things as a whole. For example, our ability to draw sketches (especially of three-dimensional objects), read maps, and construct complex objects out of smaller elements depends heavily on circuits of neurons located in the right hemisphere. Damage to the right hemisphere disrupts these abilities.

We are not aware of the fact that each hemisphere perceives the world differently. Although the two cerebral hemispheres perform somewhat different functions, our perceptions and our memories are unified. This unity is accomplished by the **corpus callosum,** a large band of axons that connects the two cerebral hemispheres. The corpus callosum connects corresponding parts of the left and right hemispheres: The left and right temporal lobes are connected, the left and right parietal lobes are connected, and so on. Because of the corpus callosum, each region of the association cortex knows what is happening in the corresponding region of the opposite side of the brain.

Figure 3.12 shows a *midsagittal* view of the brain. The brain (and part of the spinal cord) has been sliced down the middle, dividing it into its two symmetrical halves. The left half has been removed, so we see the inner surface of the right half. The cerebral cortex that covers most of the surface of the cerebral hemispheres (including the frontal, parietal, occipital, and temporal lobes) is called the **neocortex** ("new" cortex, because it is of relatively recent evolutionary origin). Another form of cerebral cortex, the **limbic cortex,** is located around the medial edge of the cerebral hemispheres (*limbus* means "border"). The **cingulate gyrus,** an important region of the limbic cortex, can be seen in this figure. (See *Figure 3.12.*) In addition, if you look back at the top two drawings of Figure 3.11, you will see that the limbic cortex occupies the regions that have not been colored in. (Refer to *Figure 3.11.*)

Figure 3.12 also shows the corpus callosum, largest **commissure** (cross-hemisphere connection) in the brain. To slice the brain into its two symmetrical halves, one must slice through the middle of the corpus callosum. (Recall that I described the split-brain operation, in which the corpus callosum is severed, in Chapter 1.) (See *Figure 3.12.*)

motor association cortex   The region of the frontal lobe rostral to the primary motor cortex.

prefrontal cortex   The region of the frontal lobe rostral to the motor association cortex.

corpus callosum (*ka loh sum*)   The largest commissure of the brain, interconnecting the areas of neocortex on each side of the brain.

neocortex   The phylogenetically newest cortex, including the primary sensory cortex, primary motor cortex, and association cortex.

limbic cortex   Phylogenetically old cortex, located at the edge ("limbus") of the cerebral hemispheres; part of the limbic system.

cingulate gyrus (*sing yew lett*)   A strip of limbic cortex lying along the lateral walls of the groove separating the cerebral hemispheres, just above the corpus callosum.

commissure (*kahm i sher*)   A fiber bundle that interconnects corresponding regions on each side of the brain.

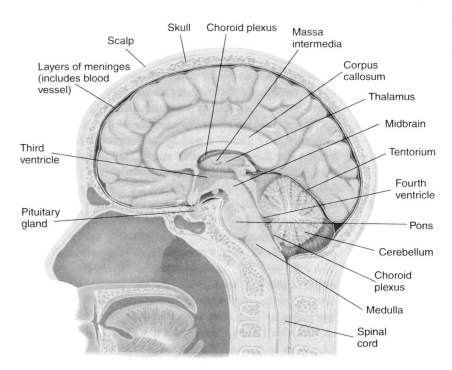

Scalp
Skull
Choroid plexus
Massa intermedia
Layers of meninges (includes blood vessel)
Corpus callosum
Thalamus
Midbrain
Third ventricle
Tentorium
Fourth ventricle
Pituitary gland
Pons
Cerebellum
Choroid plexus
Medulla
Spinal cord

Figure 3.12
A midsagittal view of the brain and part of the spinal cord.

Limbic System. A neuroanatomist, Papez (1937), suggested that a set of interconnected brain structures formed a circuit whose primary function was motivation and emotion. This system included several regions of the limbic cortex (already described) and a set of interconnected structures surrounding the core of the forebrain. A physiologist, MacLean (1949), expanded the system to include other structures and coined the term **limbic system.** Besides the limbic cortex, the most important parts of the limbic system are the **hippocampus** ("sea horse") and the **amygdala** ("almond"), located next to the lateral ventricle in the temporal lobe. The **fornix** is a bundle of axons that connects the hippocampus with other regions of the brain, including the **mammillary bodies,** protrusions on the base of the brain that contain some hypothalamic nuclei. (See *Figure 3.13.*)

MacLean noted that the evolution of this system, which includes the first and simplest form of cerebral cortex, appears to have coincided with the development of emotional responses. As you will see in Chapter 15, we now know that parts of the limbic system (notably, the hippocampal formation and the region of limbic cortex that surrounds it) are involved in learning and memory rather than emotional behavior. Only part of the limbic system—the amygdala—is specifically involved in emotions.

Basal Ganglia. The **basal ganglia** are a collection of subcortical nuclei in the forebrain, which lie beneath the an-

terior portion of the lateral ventricles. The major parts of the basal ganglia are the *caudate nucleus,* the *putamen,* and the *globus pallidus* (the "nucleus with a tail," the "shell," and the "pale globe." See *Figure 3.14*). The basal ganglia are involved in the control of movement. For example, Parkinson's disease is caused by degeneration of certain neurons located in the midbrain that send axons to the

limbic system   A group of brain regions including the anterior thalamic nuclei, amygdala, hippocampus, limbic cortex, and parts of the hypothalamus, as well as their interconnecting fiber bundles.

hippocampus   A forebrain structure of the temporal lobe, constituting an important part of the limbic system.

amygdala *(a **mig** da la)*   A structure in the interior of the rostral temporal lobe, containing a set of nuclei; part of the limbic system.

fornix   A fiber bundle that connects the hippocampus with other parts of the brain, including the mammillary bodies of the hypothalamus.

mammillary bodies *(**mam** i lair ee)*   A protrusion of the bottom of the brain at the posterior end of the hypothalamus, containing some hypothalamic nuclei.

basal ganglia   A group of subcortical nuclei in the telencephalon, the caudate nucleus, the globus pallidus, and the putamen; important parts of the motor system.

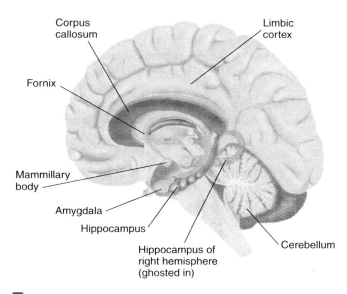

Figure 3.13
The major components of the limbic system. All of the left hemisphere except for the limbic system has been removed.

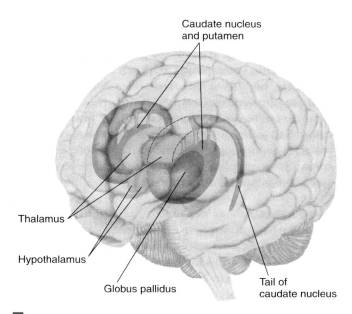

Figure 3.14
The location of the basal ganglia and diencephalon, "ghosted in" to a semitransparent brain.

caudate nucleus and the putamen. This disease consists of weakness, tremors, rigidity of the limbs, poor balance, and difficulty in initiating movements.

Diencephalon

The second major division of the forebrain, the **diencephalon,** is situated between the telencephalon and the mesencephalon; it surrounds the third ventricle. Its two most important structures are the thalamus and the hypothalamus. (See *Figure 3.14.*)

Thalamus.   The **thalamus** (from the Greek *thalamos,* "inner chamber") comprises the dorsal part of the diencephalon. It is situated near the middle of the cerebral hemispheres, immediately medial and caudal to the basal ganglia. The thalamus has two lobes, connected by a bridge of gray matter called the *massa intermedia,* which pierces the middle of the third ventricle. (See *Figure 3.14.*) The massa intermedia is probably not an important structure, because it is absent in the brains of many people. However, it serves as a useful reference point when looking at diagrams of the brain; it appears in Figures 3.5, 3.12, 3.14, and 3.15.

Most neural input to the cerebral cortex is received from the thalamus; indeed, much of the cortical surface can be divided into regions that receive projections from specific parts of the thalamus. **Projection fibers** are sets of axons that arise from cell bodies located in one region of the

brain and synapse on neurons located within another region (that is, they *project to* these regions).

The thalamus is divided into several **nuclei,** which are groups of neurons of similar shape. (The word *nucleus,* from the Greek "nut," can refer to the inner portion of an atom, to the structure of a cell that contains the chromosomes, and—as in this case—to a collection of neurons located within the brain.) Some thalamic nuclei receive sensory information from the sensory systems. The neurons in these nuclei then relay the sensory information to specific sensory projection areas of the cerebral cortex. For example, the **lateral geniculate nucleus** receives information from the

diencephalon *(dy en **seff** a lahn)*   A region of the forebrain surrounding the third ventricle; includes the thalamus and the hypothalamus.

thalamus   The largest portion of the diencephalon, located above the hypothalamus; contains nuclei that project information to specific regions of the cerebral cortex and receive information from it.

projection fiber   An axon of a neuron in one region of the brain whose terminals form synapses with neurons in another region.

nucleus (plural: nuclei)   An identifiable group of neural cell bodies in the central nervous system.

lateral geniculate nucleus   A group of cell bodies within the lateral geniculate body of the thalamus that receives fibers from the retina and projects fibers to the primary visual cortex.

eye and sends axons to the primary visual cortex, and the **medial geniculate nucleus** receives information from the inner ear and sends axons to the primary auditory cortex. Other thalamic nuclei project to specific regions of the cerebral cortex, but they do not relay sensory information. For example, the **ventrolateral nucleus** receives information from the cerebellum and projects it to the primary motor cortex. And as we will see in Chapter 9, several nuclei are involved in controlling the general excitability of the cerebral cortex. To accomplish this task, these nuclei have widespread projections to all cortical regions.

Hypothalamus.   As its name implies, the **hypothalamus** lies at the base of the brain, under the thalamus. Although the hypothalamus is a relatively small structure, it is an important one. It controls the autonomic nervous system and the endocrine system and organizes behaviors related to survival of the species—the so-called four F's: fighting, feeding, fleeing, and mating.

The hypothalamus is situated on both sides of the inferior portion of the third ventricle. The hypothalamus is a complex structure, containing many nuclei and fiber tracts. Figure 3.15 indicates its location and size. Note that the pituitary gland is attached to the base of the hypothalamus via the pituitary stalk. Just in front of the pituitary stalk is the **optic chiasm,** where half of the axons in the optic nerves (from the eyes) cross from one side of the brain to the other. (See *Figure 3.15.*) The role of the hypothalamus in the control of the four F's (and other behaviors, such as drinking and sleeping) will be considered in several chapters later in this book.

Much of the endocrine system is controlled by hormones produced by cells in the hypothalamus. A special system of blood vessels directly connects the hypothalamus with the **anterior pituitary gland.** (See *Figure 3.16.*) The hypothalamic hormones are secreted by specialized neurons called **neurosecretory cells,** located near the base of the pituitary stalk. These hormones stimulate

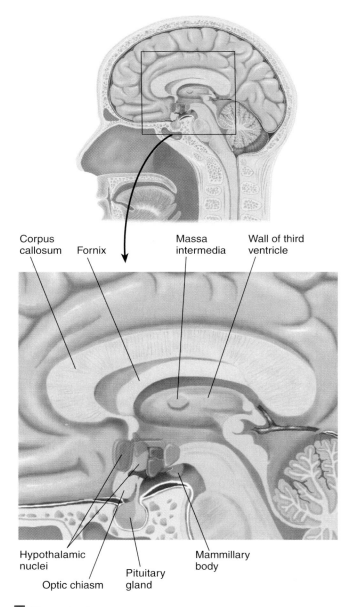

Corpus callosum   Fornix   Massa intermedia   Wall of third ventricle

Hypothalamic nuclei   Mammillary body   Optic chiasm   Pituitary gland

Figure 3.15
A midsagittal view of part of the brain, showing some of the nuclei of the hypothalamus. The nuclei are situated on the far side of the wall of the third ventricle, inside the right hemisphere.

---

medial geniculate nucleus   A group of cell bodies within the medial geniculate body of the thalamus; receives fibers from the auditory system and projects fibers to the primary auditory cortex.

ventrolateral nucleus   A nucleus of the thalamus that receives inputs from the cerebellum and sends axons to the primary motor cortex.

hypothalamus   The group of nuclei of the diencephalon situated beneath the thalamus; involved in regulation of the autonomic nervous system, control of the anterior and posterior pituitary glands, and integration of species-typical behaviors.

optic chiasm *(kye az′ m)*   A cross-shaped connection between the optic nerves, located below the base of the brain, just anterior to the pituitary gland.

anterior pituitary gland   The anterior part of the pituitary gland; an endocrine gland whose secretions are controlled by the hypothalamic hormones.

neurosecretory cell   A neuron that secretes a hormone or hormonelike substance.

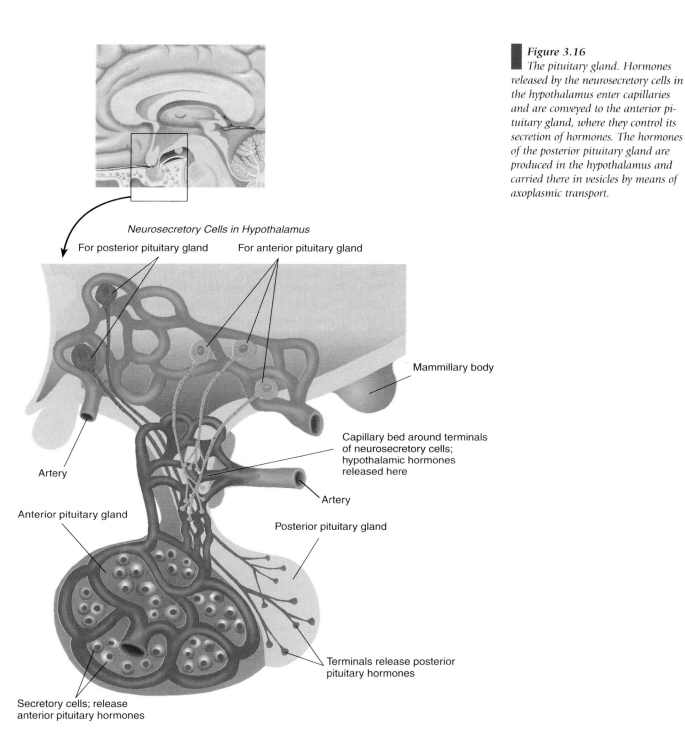

Figure 3.16
The pituitary gland. Hormones released by the neurosecretory cells in the hypothalamus enter capillaries and are conveyed to the anterior pituitary gland, where they control its secretion of hormones. The hormones of the posterior pituitary gland are produced in the hypothalamus and carried there in vesicles by means of axoplasmic transport.

Neurosecretory Cells in Hypothalamus

For posterior pituitary gland   For anterior pituitary gland

Mammillary body

Capillary bed around terminals
of neurosecretory cells;
hypothalamic hormones
released here

Artery

Artery

Anterior pituitary gland

Posterior pituitary gland

Terminals release posterior
pituitary hormones

Secretory cells; release
anterior pituitary hormones

the anterior pituitary gland to secrete its hormones. For example, the *gonadotropin-releasing hormone* causes the anterior pituitary gland to secrete the *gonadotropic hormones*, which play a role in reproductive physiology and behavior.

Most of the hormones secreted by the anterior pituitary gland control other endocrine glands. Because of this function, the anterior pituitary gland has been called the body's "master gland." For example, the gonadotropic hormones stimulate the gonads (ovaries and testes) to release male or female sex hormones. These hormones affect cells throughout the body, including some in the brain. Two other anterior pituitary hormones—prolactin and somatotropic hormone (growth hormone)—do not control other glands but act as the final messenger. The behavioral effects of many of the anterior pituitary hormones are discussed in later chapters.

75

The hypothalamus also produces the hormones of the **posterior pituitary gland** and controls their secretion. These hormones include oxytocin, which stimulates ejection of milk and uterine contractions at the time of childbirth, and vasopressin, which regulates urine output by the kidneys. They are produced by neurons in the hypothalamus whose axons travel down the pituitary stalk and terminate in the posterior pituitary gland. The hormones are carried in vesicles through the axoplasm of these neurons and collect in the terminal buttons in the posterior pituitary gland. When these axons fire, the hormone contained within their terminal buttons is liberated and enters the circulatory system.

● The Mesencephalon

The **midbrain** (also called the **mesencephalon**) surrounds the cerebral aqueduct and consists of two major parts: the tectum and the tegmentum.

Tectum

The **tectum** ("roof") is located in the dorsal portion of the mesencephalon. Its principal structures are the **superior colliculi** and **inferior colliculi,** which appear as four bumps on the surface of the **brain stem.** The brain stem includes the diencephalon, midbrain, and hindbrain, and it is so called because it looks just like that—a stem. Figure 3.17 shows several views of the brain stem: lateral and posterior views of the brain stem inside a semitransparent brain, an enlarged view of the brain stem with part of the cerebellum cut away to reveal the inside of the fourth ventricle, and a cross section through the midbrain. (See *Figure 3.17.*) The inferior colliculi are a part of the auditory system. The superior colliculi are part of the visual system. In mammals they are primarily involved in visual reflexes and reactions to moving stimuli.

Tegmentum

The **tegmentum** ("covering") consists of the portion of the mesencephalon beneath the tectum. It includes the rostral end of the reticular formation, several nuclei controlling eye movements, the periaqueductal gray matter, the red nucleus, the substantia nigra, and the ventral tegmental area. (See *Figure 3.17d.*)

The **reticular formation** is a large structure consisting of many nuclei (over ninety in all). It is also characterized by a diffuse, interconnected network of neurons with complex dendritic and axonal processes. (Indeed, *reticulum* means "little net"; early anatomists were struck by the netlike appearance of the reticular formation.) The reticular formation occupies the core of the brain stem, from the lower border of the medulla to the upper border of the midbrain. (See *Figure 3.17d.*) The reticular formation receives sensory information by means of various pathways and projects axons to the cerebral cortex, thalamus, and spinal cord. It plays a role in sleep and arousal, attention, muscle tonus, movement, and various vital reflexes. Its functions will be described more fully in later chapters.

The **periaqueductal gray matter** is so called because it consists mostly of cell bodies of neurons ("gray matter," as contrasted with the "white matter" of axon bundles) that surround the cerebral aqueduct as it travels from the third to the fourth ventricle. The periaqueductal gray matter contains neural circuits that control sequences of movements that constitute species-typical behaviors, such as fighting and mating. As we will see in Chapter 7, opiates such as morphine decrease an organism's sensitivity to pain by stimulating receptors on neurons located in this region.

The **red nucleus** and **substantia nigra** ("black substance") are important components of the motor system. A bundle of axons that arises from the red nucleus constitutes one of the two major fiber systems that bring motor information from the cerebral cortex and cerebellum to the

posterior pituitary gland   The posterior part of the pituitary gland; an endocrine gland that contains hormone-secreting terminal buttons of axons whose cell bodies lie within the hypothalamus.

midbrain   The mesencephalon; the central of the three major divisions of the brain.

mesencephalon (*mezz en seff a lahn*)   The midbrain; a region of the brain that surrounds the cerebral aqueduct; includes the tectum and the tegmentum.

tectum   The dorsal part of the midbrain; includes the superior and inferior colliculi.

superior colliculi (*ka lik yew lee*)   Protrusions on top of the midbrain; part of the visual system.

inferior colliculi   Protrusions on top of the midbrain; part of the auditory system.

brain stem   The "stem" of the brain, from the medulla to the diencephalon, excluding the cerebellum.

tegmentum   The ventral part of the midbrain; includes the periaqueductal gray matter, reticular formation, red nucleus, and substantia nigra.

reticular formation   A large network of neural tissue located in the central region of the brain stem, from the medulla to the diencephalon.

periaqueductal gray matter   The region of the midbrain surrounding the cerebral aqueduct; contains neural circuits involved in species-typical behaviors.

red nucleus   A large nucleus of the midbrain that receives inputs from the cerebellum and motor cortex and sends axons to motor neurons in the spinal cord.

substantia nigra   A darkly stained region of the tegmentum that contains neurons that communicate with the caudate nucleus and putamen in the basal ganglia.

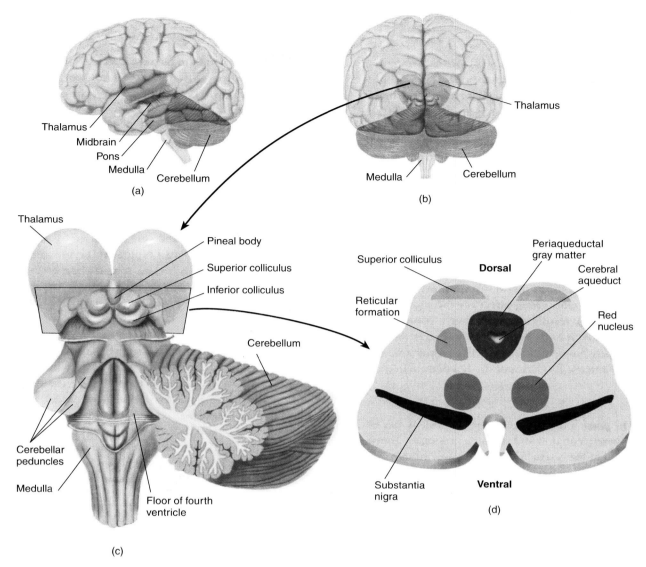

Figure 3.17
The cerebellum and brain stem. (a) Lateral view of a semitransparent brain, showing the cerebellum and brain stem "ghosted in." (b) View from the back of the brain. (c) A dorsal view of the brain stem. The left hemisphere of the cerebellum and part of the right hemisphere have been removed to show the inside of the fourth ventricle and the cerebellar peduncles. (d) A cross section of the midbrain.

spinal cord. The substantia nigra contains neurons whose axons project to the caudate nucleus and putamen, parts of the basal ganglia. As we will see in Chapter 4, degeneration of these neurons causes Parkinson's disease.

● The Hindbrain

The **hindbrain,** which surrounds the fourth ventricle, consists of two major divisions: the metencephalon and the myelencephalon.

Metencephalon

The metencephalon consists of the pons and the cerebellum.

Cerebellum. The **cerebellum** ("little brain"), with its two hemispheres, resembles a miniature version of the cerebrum. It is covered by the **cerebellar cortex** and has a

hindbrain The most caudal of the three major divisions of the brain; includes the metencephalon and myelencephalon.

cerebellum (*sair a **bell** um*) A major part of the brain located dorsal to the pons, containing the two cerebellar hemispheres, covered with the cerebellar cortex; an important component of the motor system.

cerebellar cortex The cortex that covers the surface of the cerebellum.

set of **deep cerebellar nuclei.** These nuclei receive projections from the cerebellar cortex and themselves send projections out of the cerebellum to other parts of the brain. Each hemisphere of the cerebellum is attached to the dorsal surface of the pons by bundles of axons: the superior, middle, and inferior **cerebellar peduncles** ("little feet"). (See *Figure 3.17c.*)

Damage to the cerebellum impairs standing, walking, or performance of coordinated movements. (A virtuoso pianist or other performing musician owes much to his or her cerebellum.) The cerebellum receives visual, auditory, vestibular, and somatosensory information, and it also receives information about individual muscle movements being directed by the brain. The cerebellum integrates this information and modifies the motor outflow, exerting a coordinating and smoothing effect on the movements. Cerebellar damage results in jerky, poorly coordinated, exaggerated movements; extensive cerebellar damage makes it impossible even to stand. Chapter 8 discusses the anatomy and the functions of the cerebellum in more detail.

Pons. The **pons,** a large bulge in the brain stem, lies between the mesencephalon and medulla oblongata, immediately ventral to the cerebellum. *Pons* means "bridge," but it does not really look like one. (Refer to *Figures 3.12* and *3.17a.*) The pons contains, in its core, a portion of the reticular formation, including some nuclei that appear to be important in sleep and arousal. It also contains a large nucleus that relays information from the cerebral cortex to the cerebellum.

Myelencephalon

The myelencephalon contains one major structure, the **medulla oblongata** (literally, "oblong marrow"), usually just called the *medulla.* This structure is the most caudal portion of the brain stem; its lower border is the rostral end of the spinal cord. (Refer to *Figures 3.12* and *3.17a.*) The medulla contains part of the reticular formation, including nuclei that control vital functions such as regulation of the cardiovascular system, respiration, and skeletal muscle tonus.

● The Spinal Cord

The **spinal cord** is a long, conical structure, approximately as thick as our little finger. The principal function of the spinal cord is to distribute motor fibers to the effector organs of the body (glands and muscles) and to collect so-

matosensory information to be passed on to the brain. The spinal cord also has a certain degree of autonomy from the brain; various reflexive control circuits (some of which are described in Chapter 8) are located there.

The spinal cord is protected by the vertebral column, which is composed of twenty-four individual vertebrae of the *cervical* (neck), *thoracic* (chest), and *lumbar* (lower back) regions, and the fused vertebrae making up the *sacral* and *coccygeal* portions of the column (located in the pelvic region). The spinal cord passes through a hole in each of the vertebrae (the *spinal foramens*). Figure 3.18 illustrates the divisions and structures of the spinal cord and vertebral column. (Refer to *Figure 3.18.*) Note that the spinal cord is only about two-thirds as long as the vertebral column; the rest of the space is filled by a mass of **spinal roots** composing the **cauda equina** ("horse's tail"). (Refer to *Figure 3.3a.*)

Early in embryological development the vertebral column and spinal cord are the same length. As development progresses, the vertebral column grows faster than the spinal cord. This differential growth rate causes the spinal roots to be displaced downward; the most caudal roots travel the farthest before they emerge through openings between the vertebrae and thus compose the cauda equina. To produce the **caudal block** sometimes used in pelvic surgery or childbirth, a local anesthetic can be injected into the CSF contained within the sac of dura mater surround-

---

deep cerebellar nuclei   Nuclei located within the cerebellar hemispheres; receive projections from the cerebellar cortex and send projections out of the cerebellum to other parts of the brain.

cerebellar peduncle (*pee* dun kul)   One of three bundles of axons that attach each cerebellar hemisphere to the dorsal pons.

pons   The region of the metencephalon rostral to the medulla, caudal to the midbrain, and ventral to the cerebellum.

medulla oblongata (me *doo* la)   The most caudal portion of the brain; located in the myelencephalon, immediately rostral to the spinal cord.

spinal cord   The cord of nervous tissue that extends caudally from the medulla.

spinal root   A bundle of axons surrounded by connective tissue that occurs in pairs, which fuse and form a spinal nerve.

cauda equina (ee *kwye* na)   A bundle of spinal roots located caudal to the end of the spinal cord.

caudal block   The anesthesia and paralysis of the lower part of the body produced by injection of a local anesthetic into the cerebrospinal fluid surrounding the cauda equina.

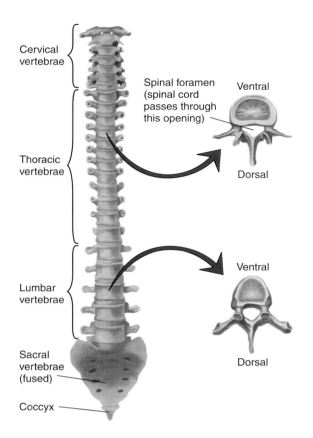

Cervical vertebrae

Spinal foramen (spinal cord passes through this opening)

Ventral

Dorsal

Thoracic vertebrae

Ventral

Lumbar vertebrae

Dorsal

Sacral vertebrae (fused)

Coccyx

Figure 3.18
A ventral view of the human spinal column, with details showing the anatomy of the vertebrae.

ing the cauda equina. The drug blocks conduction in the axons of the cauda equina.

Figure 3.19(a) shows a portion of the spinal cord, with the layers of the meninges that wrap it. Small bundles of fibers emerge from each side of the spinal cord in two straight lines along its dorsolateral and ventrolateral surfaces. Groups of these bundles fuse together and become the thirty-one paired sets of **dorsal roots** and **ventral roots.** The dorsal and ventral roots join together as they pass through the intervertebral foramens and become spinal nerves. (See *Figure 3.19a.*)

Figure 3.19(b) shows a cross section of the spinal cord. Like the brain, the spinal cord consists of white matter and gray matter. Unlike the brain's, its white matter (consisting of ascending and descending bundles of myelinated axons) is on the outside; the gray matter (mostly neural cell bodies and short, unmyelinated axons) is on the inside. In Figure 3.19(b), the ascending tracts are indicated in blue; the descending tracts are indicated in red. (See *Figure 3.19b.*)

Interim Summary

The brain consists of three major divisions, organized around the three chambers of the tube that develops early in embryonic life: the forebrain, the midbrain, and the hindbrain. The development of the CNS is illustrated in Figure 3.8, and Table 3.2 outlines the major divisions and subdivisions of the brain.

The forebrain, which surrounds the lateral and third ventricles, consists of the telencephalon and diencephalon. The telencephalon contains the cerebral cortex, the limbic system, and the basal ganglia. The cerebral cortex is organized into the frontal, parietal, temporal, and occipital lobes. The central sulcus divides the frontal lobe, which deals specifically with movement and the planning of movement, from the other three lobes, which deal primarily with perceiving and learning. The limbic system, which includes the limbic cortex, the hippocampus, and the amygdala, is involved in emotion, motivation, and learning. The basal ganglia participate in the control of movement. The diencephalon consists of the thalamus, which directs information to and from the cerebral cortex, and the hypothalamus, which controls the endocrine system and modulates species-typical behaviors.

The midbrain, which surrounds the cerebral aqueduct, consists of the tectum and tegmentum. The tectum is involved in audition and the control of visual reflexes and reactions to moving stimuli. The tegmentum contains the reticular formation, which is important in sleep, arousal, and movement; the periaqueductal gray matter, which controls various species-typical behaviors; and the red nucleus and the substantia nigra, both parts of the motor system. The hindbrain, which surrounds the fourth ventricle, contains the cerebellum, the pons, and the medulla. The cerebellum plays an important role in integrating and coordinating movements. The pons contains some nuclei that are important in sleep and arousal. The medulla oblongata, too, is involved in sleep and arousal, but it also plays a role in control of movement and in control of vital functions such as heart rate, breathing, and blood pressure.

The outer part of the spinal cord consists of white matter: axons conveying information up or down. The central gray matter contains cell bodies.

dorsal root   The spinal root that contains incoming (afferent) sensory fibers.

ventral root   The spinal root that contains outgoing (efferent) motor fibers.

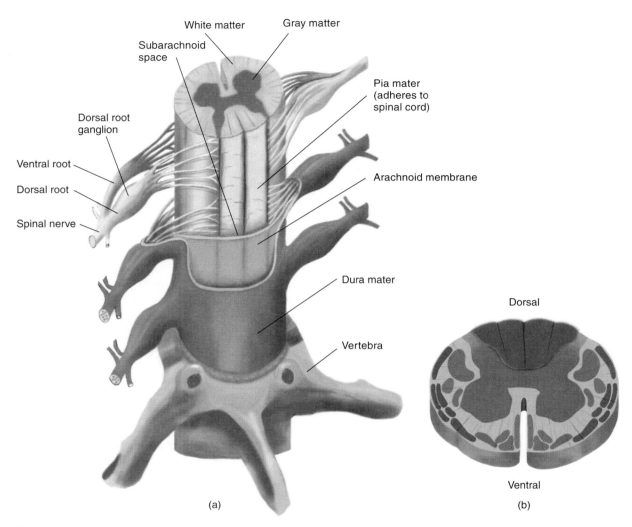

White matter · Gray matter
Subarachnoid space
Pia mater (adheres to spinal cord)
Dorsal root ganglion
Ventral root
Dorsal root
Spinal nerve
Arachnoid membrane
Dura mater
Vertebra
Dorsal
Ventral
(a)
(b)

Figure 3.19
The spinal cord. (a) A portion of the spinal cord, showing the layers of the meninges and the relation of the spinal cord to the vertebral column. (b) A cross section through the spinal cord. Ascending tracts are shown in blue; descending tracts are shown in red.

THE PERIPHERAL NERVOUS SYSTEM

The brain and spinal cord communicate with the rest of the body via the cranial nerves and spinal nerves. These nerves are part of the peripheral nervous system, which conveys sensory information to the central nervous system and conveys messages from the central nervous system to the body's muscles and glands.

● Spinal Nerves

The **spinal nerves** begin at the junction of the dorsal and ventral roots of the spinal cord. The nerves leave the ver-

tebral column and travel to the muscles or sensory receptors they innervate, branching repeatedly as they go. Branches of spinal nerves often follow blood vessels, especially those branches that innervate skeletal muscles. (Refer to *Figure 3.3*.)

Now let us consider the pathways by which sensory information enters the spinal cord and motor information leaves it. The cell bodies of all axons that bring sensory information into the brain and spinal cord are located outside the CNS. (The sole exception is the visual system; the retina of the eye is actually a part of the brain.) These in-

spinal nerve   A peripheral nerve attached to the spinal cord.

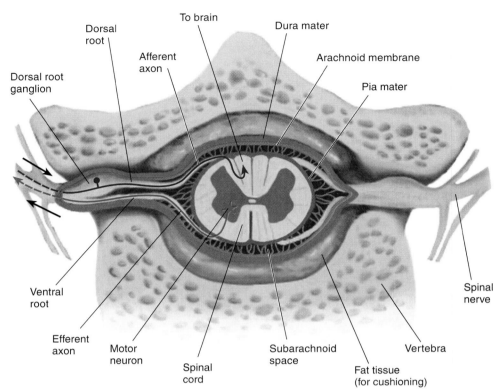

Dorsal root

To brain

Dura mater

Dorsal root ganglion

Afferent axon

Arachnoid membrane

Pia mater

Ventral root

Efferent axon

Motor neuron

Spinal cord

Subarachnoid space

Fat tissue (for cushioning)

Vertebra

Spinal nerve

Figure 3.20
A cross section of the spinal cord, showing the route taken by afferent and efferent axons through the dorsal and ventral roots.

coming axons are referred to as **afferent axons** because they "bear toward" the CNS. The cell bodies that give rise to the axons that bring somatosensory information to the spinal cord reside in the **dorsal root ganglia,** rounded swellings of the dorsal root. (See *Figure 3.20.*) These neurons are of the unipolar type (described in Chapter 2). The axonal stalk divides close to the cell body, sending one limb into the spinal cord and the other limb out to the sensory organ. Note that all of the axons in the dorsal root convey somatosensory information.

Cell bodies that give rise to the ventral root are located within the gray matter of the spinal cord. The axons of these multipolar neurons leave the spinal cord via a ventral root, which joins a dorsal root to make a spinal nerve. The axons that leave the spinal cord through the ventral roots control muscles and glands. They are referred to as **efferent axons** because they "bear away from" the CNS. (See *Figure 3.20.*)

● Cranial Nerves

Twelve pairs of **cranial nerves** leave the ventral surface of the brain. Most of these nerves serve sensory and motor functions of the head and neck region. One of them, the *tenth*, or **vagus nerve,** regulates the functions of organs in

the thoracic and abdominal cavities. It is called the *vagus* ("wandering") nerve because its branches wander throughout the thoracic and abdominal cavities. (The word *vagabond* has the same root.) Figure 3.21 presents a view of the base of the brain and illustrates the cranial nerves and the structures they serve. Note that efferent (motor) fibers are drawn in red and that afferent (sensory) fibers are drawn in blue. (See *Figure 3.21.*)

As I mentioned in the previous section, cell bodies of sensory nerve fibers that enter the brain and spinal cord (except for the visual system) are located outside the central nervous system. Somatosensory information (and the

afferent axon   An axon directed toward the central nervous system, conveying sensory information.

dorsal root ganglion   A nodule on a dorsal root that contains cell bodies of afferent spinal nerve neurons.

efferent axon *(eff ur ent)*   An axon directed away from the central nervous system, conveying motor commands to muscles and glands.

cranial nerve   A peripheral nerve attached directly to the brain.

vagus nerve   The largest of the cranial nerves, conveying efferent fibers of the parasympathetic division of the autonomic nervous system to organs of the thoracic and abdominal cavities.

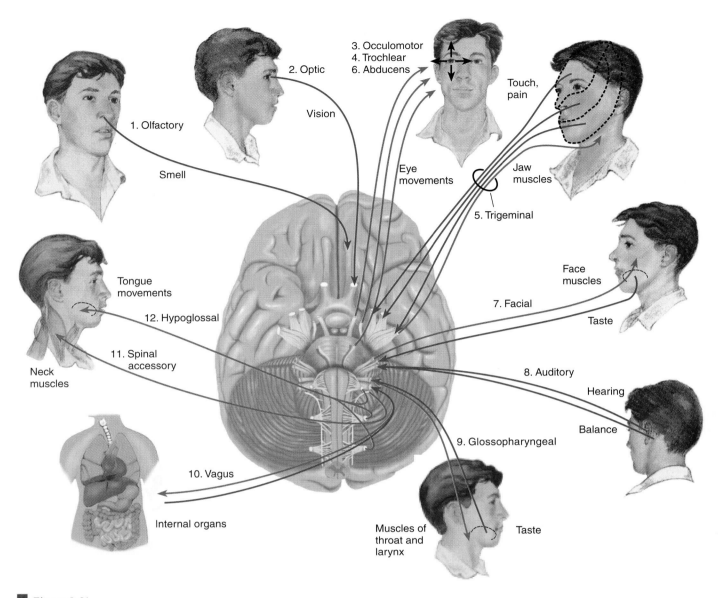

Figure 3.21

The twelve pairs of cranial nerves and the regions and functions they serve. Red lines denote axons that control muscles or glands; blue lines denote sensory axons.

sense of taste) is received, via the cranial nerves, from unipolar neurons. Auditory, vestibular, and visual information is received via fibers of bipolar neurons (described in Chapter 2). Olfactory information is received via the **olfactory bulbs,** which receive information from the olfactory receptors in the nose. The olfactory bulbs are complex structures containing a considerable amount of neural circuitry; actually, they are part of the brain. Sensory mechanisms are described in more detail in Chapters 6 and 7.

● The Autonomic Nervous System

The part of the peripheral nervous system that I have discussed so far—which receives sensory information from the sensory organs and that controls movements of the skeletal muscles—is called the **somatic nervous system.** The other branch of the peripheral nervous system—the **autonomic nervous system (ANS)**—is concerned with reg-

olfactory bulb   The protrusion at the end of the olfactory nerve; receives input from the olfactory receptors.

somatic nervous system   The part of the peripheral nervous system that controls the movement of skeletal muscles or transmits somatosensory information to the central nervous system.

autonomic nervous system (ANS)   The portion of the peripheral nervous system that controls the body's vegetative functions.

ulation of smooth muscle, cardiac muscle, and glands. (*Autonomic* means "self-governing.") Smooth muscle is found in the skin (associated with hair follicles), in blood vessels, in the eyes (controlling pupil size and accommodation of the lens), and in the walls and sphincters of the gut, gallbladder, and urinary bladder. Merely describing the organs innervated by the autonomic nervous system suggests the function of this system: regulation of "vegetative processes" in the body.

The ANS consists of two anatomically separate systems, the *sympathetic division* and the *parasympathetic division*. With few exceptions, organs of the body are innervated by both of these subdivisions, and each has a different effect. For example, the sympathetic division speeds the heart rate, whereas the parasympathetic division slows it.

Sympathetic Division of the ANS

The **sympathetic division** is most involved in activities associated with expenditure of energy from reserves that are stored in the body. For example, when an organism is excited, the sympathetic nervous system increases blood flow to skeletal muscles, stimulates the secretion of epinephrine (resulting in increased heart rate and a rise in blood sugar level), and causes piloerection (erection of fur in mammals that have it and production of "goose bumps" in humans).

The cell bodies of sympathetic motor neurons are located in the gray matter of the thoracic and lumbar regions of the spinal cord (hence the sympathetic nervous system is also known as the *thoracolumbar system*). The fibers of these neurons exit via the ventral roots. After joining the spinal nerves, the fibers branch off and pass into **spinal sympathetic ganglia** (not to be confused with the dorsal root ganglia). Figure 3.22 shows the relation of these ganglia to the spinal cord. Note that the various spinal sympathetic ganglia are connected to the neighboring ganglia above and below, thus forming the **sympathetic ganglion chain.** (See *Figure 3.22*.)

The axons that leave the spinal cord through the ventral root are part of the **preganglionic neurons.** With one exception, all sympathetic preganglionic axons enter the ganglia of the sympathetic chain, but not all of them synapse there. (The exception is the medulla of the adrenal gland, described in the following paragraph.) Some axons leave and travel to one of the other sympathetic ganglia, located among the internal organs. All sympathetic preganglionic axons form synapses with neurons located in one of the ganglia. The neurons with which they form synapses are called **postganglionic neurons.** In turn, the postganglionic neurons send axons to the target organs, such as the intestines, stomach, kidneys, or sweat glands. (See *Figure 3.22*.)

The sympathetic nervous system controls the **adrenal medulla,** a set of cells located in the center of the adrenal gland. The adrenal medulla closely resembles a sympathetic ganglion. It is innervated by preganglionic axons, and its secretory cells are very similar to postganglionic sympathetic neurons. These cells secrete epinephrine and norepinephrine when they are stimulated. These hormones function chiefly as an adjunct to the direct neural effects of sympathetic activity; for example, they increase blood flow to the muscles and cause stored nutrients to be broken down into glucose within skeletal muscle cells, thus increasing the energy available to these cells.

All synapses within the sympathetic ganglia are acetylcholinergic; the terminal buttons on the target organs, belonging to the postganglionic axons, are noradrenergic. (An exception to this rule is provided by the sweat glands, which are innervated by acetylcholinergic terminal buttons.)

Parasympathetic Division of the ANS

The **parasympathetic division** of the autonomic nervous system supports activities that are involved with increases in the body's supply of stored energy. These activities include salivation, gastric and intestinal motility, secretion of digestive juices, and increased blood flow to the gastrointestinal system.

Cell bodies that give rise to preganglionic axons in the parasympathetic nervous system are located in two regions: the nuclei of some of the cranial nerves (especially the

sympathetic division   The portion of the autonomic nervous system that controls functions that accompany arousal and expenditure of energy.

spinal sympathetic ganglia   Sympathetic ganglia either adjacent to the spinal cord in the sympathetic chain or located in the abdominal cavity.

sympathetic ganglion chain   One of a pair of groups of sympathetic ganglia that lie ventrolateral to the vertebral column.

preganglionic neuron   The efferent neuron of the autonomic nervous system whose cell body is located in a cranial nerve nucleus or in the intermediate horn of the spinal gray matter and whose terminal buttons synapse on postganglionic neurons in the autonomic ganglia.

postganglionic neuron   Neurons of the autonomic nervous system that form synapses directly with their target organ.

adrenal medulla   The inner portion of the adrenal gland, located atop the kidney, controlled by sympathetic nerve fibers; secretes epinephrine and norepinephrine.

parasympathetic division   The portion of the autonomic nervous system that controls functions that occur during a relaxed state.

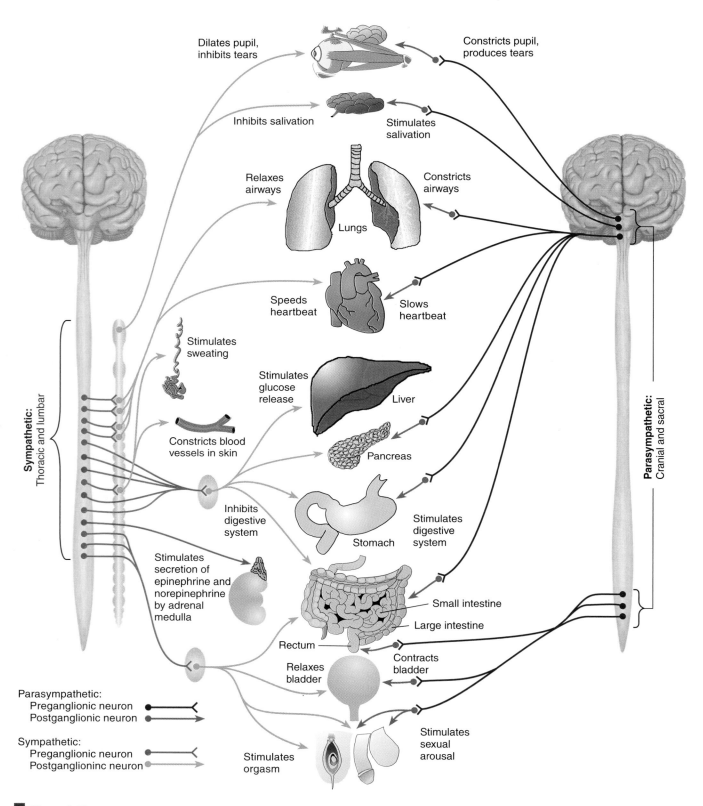

Figure 3.22

The autonomic nervous system and the target organs and functions served by the sympathetic and parasympathetic branches.

Table 3.3
The Major Divisions of the Peripheral Nervous System

Somatic nervous system	Autonomic nervous system (ANS)
Spinal nerves	*Sympathetic branch*
Afferents from sense organs	Spinal nerves (from thoracic and lumbar regions)
Efferents to muscles	Sympathetic ganglia
Cranial nerves	Paravertebral ganglion chain
Afferents from sense organs	Prevertebral ganglia
Efferents to muscles	*Parasympathetic branch*
	Cranial nerves (3rd, 7th, 9th, and 10th)
	Spinal nerves (from sacral region)
	Parasympathetic ganglia (adjacent to organs)

vagus nerve) and the intermediate horn of the gray matter in the sacral region of the spinal cord. Thus, the parasympathetic division of the ANS has often been referred to as the *craniosacral system.* Parasympathetic ganglia are located in the immediate vicinity of the target organs; the postganglionic fibers are therefore relatively short. The terminal buttons of both preganglionic and postganglionic neurons in the parasympathetic nervous system secrete acetylcholine.

Table 3.3 summarizes the major divisions of the peripheral nervous system.

Interim Summary

The spinal nerves and the cranial nerves convey sensory axons into the central nervous system and motor axons out from it. Spinal nerves are formed by the junctions of the dorsal roots, which contain incoming (afferent) axons, and the ventral roots, which contain outgoing (efferent) axons. The autonomic nervous system consists of two divisions: the sympathetic division, which controls activities that occur during excitement or exertion, such as increased heart rate; and the parasympathetic division, which controls activities that occur during relaxation, such as decreased heart rate and increased activity of the digestive system. The pathways of the autonomic nervous system contain preganglionic axons, from the brain or spinal cord to the sympathetic or parasympathetic ganglia, and postganglionic axons, from the ganglia to the target organ. The adrenal medulla, which secretes epinephrine and norepinephrine, is controlled by axons of the sympathetic nervous system.

SUGGESTED READINGS

Diamond, M. C., Scheibel, A. B., and Elson, L. M. *The Human Brain Coloring Book.* New York: Barnes & Noble, 1985.

Gluhbegovic, N., and Williams, T. H. *The Human Brain: A Photographic Guide.* New York: Harper & Row, 1980.

Heimer, L. *The Human Brain and Spinal Cord: Functional Neuroanatomy and Dissection Guide,* 2nd ed. New York: Springer-Verlag, 1995.

Nauta, W. J. H., and Feirtag, M. *Fundamental Neuroanatomy.* New York: W. H. Freeman, 1986.

Netter, F. H. *The CIBA Collection of Medical Illustrations. Vol. 1: Nervous System. Part 1: Anatomy and Physiology.* Summit, NJ: CIBA Pharmaceutical Products Co., 1983.

CHAPTER 4

Psychopharmacology

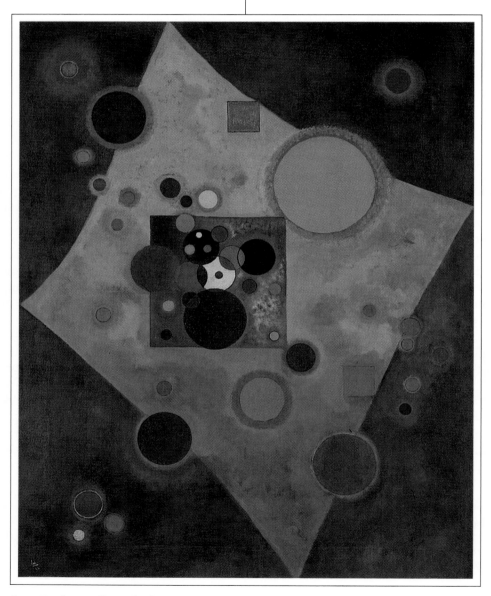

Accent Rose by Wassily Kandinsky.

C hapter 2 introduced you to the cells of the nervous system, and Chapter 3 described its basic structure. Now it is time to build on this information by introducing the field of psychopharmacology. **Psychopharmacology** is the study of the effects of drugs on the nervous system and (of course) on behavior. (*Pharmakon* is the Greek word for "drug.")

But what *is* a drug? Like many words, this one has several different meanings. In one context, it refers to a medication that we would obtain from a druggist—a chemical that has a therapeutic effect on a disease or its symptoms. In another context, the word refers to a chemical that people are likely to abuse, such as heroin or cocaine. The meaning that will be used in this book (and the one generally accepted by pharmacologists) is "an exogenous chemical not necessary for normal cellular functioning that significantly alters the functions of certain cells of the body when taken in relatively low doses." Because the topic of this chapter is *psycho*pharmacology, we will concern ourselves here only with chemicals that alter the functions of cells within the nervous system. The word *exogenous* rules out chemical messengers produced by the body, such as neurotransmitters, neuromodulators, or hormones. (*Exogenous* means "produced from without"—that is, from outside the body.) Chemical messengers produced by the body are not drugs, although synthetic chemicals that mimic their effects are classified as drugs. The definition of a drug also rules out essential nutrients, such as proteins, fats, carbohydrates, minerals, and vitamins that are a necessary constituent of a healthy diet. Finally, it states that drugs are effective in low doses. This qualification is important, because large quantities of al-most any substance—even common ones such as table salt—will alter the functions of cells.

As we will see in this chapter, drugs have *effects* and *sites of action*. **Drug effects** are the changes we can observe in an organism's physiological processes and behavior. For example, the effects of morphine, heroin, and other opiates include decreased sensitivity to pain, slowing of the digestive system, sedation, muscular relaxation, constriction of the pupils, and euphoria. The **sites of action** of drugs are the points at which molecules of drugs interact with molecules located on or in cells of the body, thus affecting some biochemical processes of these cells. For example, the sites of action of the opiates are specialized receptors situated in the membrane of certain neurons. When molecules of opiates attach to and activate these receptors, the drugs alter the activity of these neurons and produce their effects. This chapter considers both the effects of drugs and their sites of action.

Psychopharmacology is an important field of neuroscience. It has been responsible for the development of psychotherapeutic drugs, which are used to treat psychological and behavioral disorders. It has also provided tools that have enabled other investigators to study the func-

psychopharmacology The study of the effects of drugs on the nervous system and on behavior.

drug effects The changes a drug produces in an organism's physiological processes and behavior.

sites of action The locations at which molecules of drugs interact with molecules located on or in cells of the body, thus affecting some biochemical processes of these cells.

tions of cells of the nervous system and the behaviors controlled by particular neural pathways.

This chapter does not contain all this book has to say about the subject of psychopharmacology. Throughout the book you will learn about the use of drugs to investigate the nature of neural circuits involved in the control of perception, memory, and behavior. In addition, Chapter 19 discusses the nature of reinforcement and the physiology of drug abuse, and Chapters 17 and 18 discuss the use of drugs to study and treat mental disorders such as schizophrenia, depression, and the anxiety disorders.

PRINCIPLES OF PSYCHOPHARMACOLOGY

This chapter begins with a description of the basic principles of psychopharmacology: the routes of administration of drugs and their fate in the body. The second section discusses the sites of drug actions. The final section discusses specific neurotransmitters and neuromodulators and the physiological and behavioral effects of specific drugs that interact with them.

● Pharmacokinetics

To be effective, a drug must reach its sites of action. To do so, molecules of the drug must enter the body and then enter the bloodstream so that they can be carried to the organ (or organs) they act on. Once there, they must leave the bloodstream and come in contact with the molecules with which they interact. For almost all of the drugs we are interested in, this means that the molecules of the drug must enter the central nervous system. Some behaviorally active drugs exert their effects on the peripheral nervous system, but these drugs are less important to us than those that affect cells of the CNS.

Molecules of drugs must cross several barriers in order to enter the body and find their way to their sites of action. Some molecules pass through these barriers easily and quickly; others do so very slowly. And once molecules of drugs enter the body they begin to be metabolized—broken down by enzymes—or excreted in the urine (or both). In time, the molecules either disappear or are transformed into inactive fragments. The process by which drugs are absorbed, distributed within the body, metabolized, and excreted is referred to as **pharmacokinetics** ("movements of drugs").

Routes of Administration

First, let's consider the routes by which drugs can be administered. For laboratory animals, the most common

route is injection. The drug is dissolved in a liquid (or, in some cases, suspended in a liquid in the form of fine particles) and injected through a hypodermic needle. The fastest route is **intravenous (IV) injection**—injection into a vein. The drug immediately enters the bloodstream, and it reaches the brain within a few seconds. The disadvantages of IV injections are the increased care and skill they require over other forms of injection and the fact that the entire dose reaches the bloodstream at once. If an organism is especially sensitive to the drug, there may be little time to administer another drug to counteract its effects.

An **intraperitoneal (IP) injection** is rapid, but not as rapid as an IV injection. The drug is injected through the abdominal wall into the *peritoneal cavity*—the space that surrounds the stomach, intestines, liver, and other abdominal organs. IP injections are the most common route for administering drugs to small laboratory animals. An **intramuscular (IM) injection** is made directly into a large muscle, such as found in the upper arm, thigh, or buttocks. The drug is absorbed into the bloodstream through the capillaries that supply the muscle. If very slow absorption is desirable, the drug can be mixed with another drug (such as ephedrine) that constricts blood vessels and retards the flow of blood through the muscle. A drug can also be injected into the space beneath the skin, by means of a **subcutaneous (SC) injection**. A subcutaneous injection is useful only if small amounts of drug need to be administered, because large amounts would be painful. Some fat-soluble drugs can be dissolved in vegetable oil and administered subcutaneously. In this case, molecules of the drug will slowly leave the deposit of oil over a period of several days. If *very* slow and prolonged absorption of a drug is desirable, the drug can be formed into a dry pellet or placed in a sealed silicone rubber capsule and implanted beneath the skin.

Oral administration is the most common form of administering medicinal drugs to humans. Because of the dif-

pharmacokinetics The process by which drugs are absorbed, distributed within the body, metabolized, and excreted.

intravenous (IV) injection Injection of a substance directly into a vein.

intraperitoneal (IP) injection *(in tra pair i toe **nee** ul)* Injection of a substance into the *peritoneal cavity*—the space that surrounds the stomach, intestines, liver, and other abdominal organs.

intramuscular (IM) injection Injection of a substance into a muscle.

subcutaneous (SC) injection Injection of a substance into the space beneath the skin.

oral administration Administration of a substance into the mouth, so that it is swallowed.

ficulty getting laboratory animals to eat something that does not taste good to them, researchers seldom use this route. Some drugs cannot be administered orally because they will be destroyed by stomach acid or digestive enzymes, or because they are not absorbed from the digestive system into the bloodstream. For example, insulin, a peptide hormone, must be injected. **Sublingual administration** of certain drugs can be accomplished by placing them beneath the tongue. The drug is absorbed into the bloodstream by the capillaries that supply the mucous membrane that lines the mouth. (Obviously, this method works only with humans, who will cooperate and leave the capsule beneath their tongue.) Nitroglycerine, a drug that causes blood vessels to dilate, is taken sublingually by people who suffer the pains of angina pectoris, caused by obstructions in the coronary arteries.

Drugs can also be administered at the opposite end of the digestive tract, in the form of suppositories. **Intrarectal administration** is rarely used to give drugs to experimental animals. For obvious reasons, this process would be difficult with a small animal. In addition, when agitated, small animals such as rats tend to defecate, which would mean that the drug would not remain in place long enough to be absorbed. And I'm not sure I would want to try to administer a rectal suppository to a large animal. Rectal suppositories are most commonly used to administer drugs that might upset a person's stomach.

The lungs provide another route for drug administration: **inhalation.** Nicotine, free base cocaine, and marijuana are usually smoked. In addition, drugs used to treat lung disorders are often inhaled in the form of a vapor or fine mist. The route from the lungs to the brain is very short, and drugs administered this way have very rapid effects.

Some drugs can be absorbed directly through the skin, so they can be given by means of **topical administration.** Natural or artificial steroid hormones can be administered this way, as can nicotine (as a treatment to make it easier for a person to stop smoking). The mucous membrane lining the nasal passages also provides a route for topical administration. Commonly abused drugs such as cocaine hydrochloride are often sniffed so that they come in contact with the nasal mucosa. This route delivers the drug to the brain very rapidly. (The technical, rarely used, name for this route is *insufflation.*)

Finally, drugs can be administered directly into the brain. As we saw in Chapter 2, the blood–brain barrier prevents certain chemicals from leaving capillaries and entering the brain. Some drugs cannot cross the blood–brain barrier. If these drugs are to reach the brain, they must be injected directly into the brain or into the cerebrospinal fluid in the brain's ventricular system. To study the effects of a drug in a specific region of the brain (for example, in

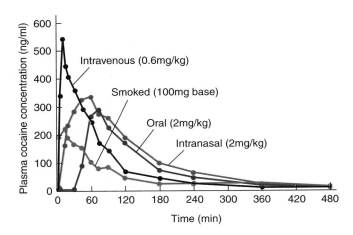

Figure 4.1
The concentration of cocaine in blood plasma after intravenous injection, inhalation, sniffing, and oral administration.
(Adapted from Feldman, Meyer, and Quenzer, 1997; after Jones, 1990.)

a particular nucleus of the hypothalamus), a researcher will inject a very small amount of the drug directly into the brain. This procedure, known as **intracerebral administration,** is described in more detail in Chapter 5. To achieve a widespread distribution of a drug in the brain, a researcher will get past the blood–brain barrier by injecting the drug into a cerebral ventricle. The drug is then absorbed into the brain tissue, where it can exert its effects. This route, **intracerebroventricular (ICV) administration,** is used very rarely in humans—primarily to deliver antibiotics directly to the brain to treat certain types of infections.

Figure 4.1 shows the time course of blood levels of a commonly abused drug, cocaine, after intravenous injection, inhalation, sniffing, and oral administration. The amounts received were not identical, but the graph illustrates the relative rapidity with which the drug reaches the blood. (See *Figure 4.1.*)

sublingual administration *(sub ling wul)* Administration of a substance by placing it beneath the tongue.

intrarectal administration Administration of a substance into the rectum.

inhalation Administration of a vaporous substance into the lungs.

topical administration Administration of a substance directly onto the skin or mucous membrane.

intracerebral administration Administration of a substance directly into the brain.

intracerebroventricular (ICV) administration Administration of a substance into one of the cerebral ventricles.

Distribution of Drugs Within the Body

As we saw, drugs exert their effects only when they reach their sites of action. In the case of drugs that affect behavior, most of these sites are located on or in particular cells in the central nervous system. The previous section described the routes by which drugs can be introduced into the body. With the exception of intracerebral or intracerebroventricular administration, the differences in the routes of drug administration vary only in the rate at which a drug reaches the blood plasma (that is, the liquid part of the blood). But what happens next? All the sites of action of drugs of interest to psychopharmacologists lie outside the blood vessels.

Several factors determine the rate at which a drug present in the bloodstream reaches sites of action within the brain. The first is lipid solubility. The blood–brain barrier is a barrier only for water-soluble molecules. Molecules that are soluble in lipids pass through the cells that line the capillaries in the central nervous system, and they rapidly distribute themselves throughout the brain. For example, diacetylmorphine (more commonly known as heroin) is more lipid soluble than morphine. Thus, an intravenous injection of heroin produces more rapid effects than one of morphine. Even though the molecules of the two drugs are equally effective when they reach their sites of action in the brain, the fact that heroin molecules get there faster means that they produce a more intense "rush" and thus explains why drug addicts prefer heroin to morphine.

Many drugs bind with various tissues of the body or with proteins in the blood—a phenomenon known as **depot binding.** As long as the molecules of the drug are bound to a depot, they cannot reach their sites of action and exert their effects. One source of such binding is **albumin,** a protein found in the blood. Albumin serves to transport free fatty acids, a source of nutrients for most cells of the body, but this protein can also bind with some lipid-soluble drugs. Depot binding can both delay and prolong the effects of a drug. Consider a lipid-soluble drug taken orally. As molecules of the drug are absorbed from the stomach, they begin to bind with albumin in the blood. For a while, very little of the drug reaches the brain. Finally, the albumin molecules can hold no more of the drug, so it begins to enter the brain. Eventually, all the drug is absorbed from the stomach. Then, perhaps over a period of several hours, the albumin molecules will gradually release the molecules of the drug as the plasma concentration of the drug falls. (See *Figure 4.2.*)

Other sources of depot binding include fat tissue, bones, muscles, and the liver. Of course, drugs bind with these depots more slowly than they do with albumin, because they must leave the blood vessels to do so. Thus, these sources

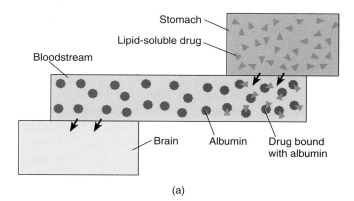

(a)

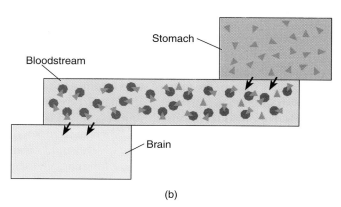

(b)

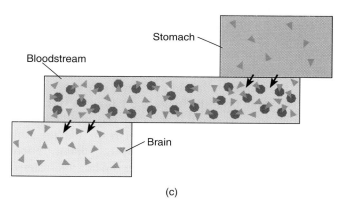

(c)

Figure 4.2
Depot binding with blood albumin protein. (a) The drug begins to be absorbed from the stomach into the bloodstream, where it binds with albumin. (b) The albumin molecules are saturated with the drug and can hold no more. (c) Unbound molecules of the drug begin to enter the brain. Eventually, molecules of the drug will break away from the molecules of albumin and enter the brain.

depot binding   Binding of a drug with various tissues of the body or with proteins in the blood.

albumin *(al **bew** min)*   A protein found in the blood; serves to transport free fatty acids and can bind with some lipid-soluble drugs.

of binding are less likely to interfere with the initial effects of a drug. For example, thiopental, a barbiturate sometimes used to anesthetize the brain, has high lipid solubility. An intravenous injection of this drug reaches the brain within a few seconds after being injected intravenously. The drug also binds very well with muscles and fat tissue, so it soon is taken out of circulation, and the levels of the drug in the brain fall rapidly. Within 30 minutes or so, the drug's anesthetic effect is gone. Eventually, the drug is destroyed by enzymes and excreted by the kidneys.

Inactivation and Excretion

Drugs do not remain in the body indefinitely. Many are deactivated by enzymes and all are eventually excreted—primarily, by the kidneys. The liver plays an especially active role in enzymatic deactivation of drugs, but some deactivating enzymes are also found in the blood. The brain also contains enzymes that destroy some drugs. In some cases, enzymes transform molecules of a drug into other forms that themselves are biologically active. Occasionally, the transformed molecules are *even more* active than the one that was administered. In such cases, the effects of a drug can have a very long duration.

● Drug Effectiveness

Drugs vary widely in their effectiveness. A small dose of a relatively effective drug can equal or exceed the effects of larger amounts of a relatively ineffective drug. The best way to measure the effectiveness of a drug is to plot a **dose-response curve.** To do this, subjects are given various doses of a drug, usually defined as milligrams of drug per kilogram of a subject's body weight, and the effects of the drug are plotted. Because the molecules of most drugs distribute themselves throughout the blood and then throughout the rest of the body, a heavier subject (human or laboratory animal) will require a larger quantity of a drug to achieve the same concentration as a smaller subject. As Figure 4.3 shows, increasingly stronger doses of a drug cause increasingly larger effects, until the point of maximum effect is reached. At this point, increasing the dose of the drug does not produce any more effect. (See *Figure 4.3.*)

Most drugs have more than one effect. Opiates such as morphine and codeine produce analgesia (reduction in sensitivity to pain), but they also depress the activity of neurons in the medulla that control heart rate and respiration. A physician who prescribes an opiate to relieve a patient's pain wants to administer a dose large enough to produce analgesia but not enough to depress heart rate and respiration—effects that could be fatal. Figure 4.4 shows two dose-response curves, one for the analgesic effects of a

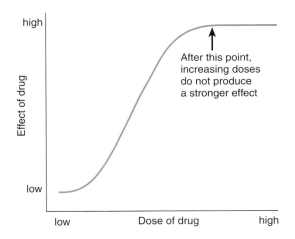

Figure 4.3
A dose-response curve. Increasingly stronger doses of the drug produce increasingly larger effects until the maximum effect is reached. After that point, increments in the dose do not produce any increments in the drug's effect. However, the risk of adverse side effects increases.

painkiller and one for the drug's depressant effects on respiration. The difference between these curves indicates the drug's margin of safety. Obviously, the most desirable drugs have a large margin of safety. (See *Figure 4.4.*)

One measure of a drug's margin of safety is its **therapeutic index.** This measure is obtained by administering varying doses of the drug to a group of laboratory animals such as mice. Two numbers are obtained: the dose that produces the desired effects in 50 percent of the animals and the dose that produces toxic effects in 50 percent of the animals. The therapeutic index is the ratio of these two numbers. For example, if the toxic dose is five times higher than the effective dose, then the therapeutic index is 5.0. The lower the therapeutic index, the more care that must be taken in prescribing the drug. For example, barbiturates have relatively low therapeutic indexes—as low as 2 or 3. In contrast, tranquilizers such as Librium or Valium have therapeutic indexes of well over 100. As a consequence, an accidental overdose of a barbiturate is much more likely to have tragic effects than a similar overdose of Librium or Valium.

---

dose-response curve   A graph of the magnitude of an effect of a drug as a function of the amount of drug administered.

therapeutic index   The ratio between the dose that produces the desired effect in 50 percent of the animals and the dose that produces toxic effects in 50 percent of the animals.

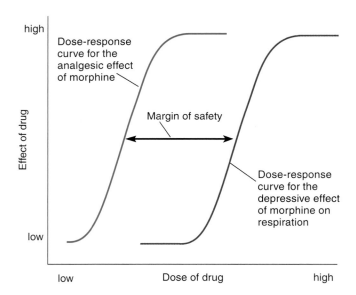

Figure 4.4
Dose-response curves for the analgesic effect of morphine and for the drug's adverse side effects, its depressant effect on respiration. A drug's margin of safety is reflected by the difference between the dose-response curve for its therapeutic effects and its adverse side effects.

Why do drugs vary in their effectiveness? There are two reasons. First, different drugs—even those with the same behavioral effects—may have different sites of action. For example, both morphine and aspirin have analgesic effects, but morphine suppresses the activity of neurons in the spinal cord and brain that are involved in pain perception, whereas aspirin reduces the production of a chemical involved in transmitting information from damaged tissue to pain-sensitive neurons. Because the drugs act very differently, a given dose of morphine (expressed in terms of milligrams of drug per kilogram of body weight) produces much more pain reduction than the same dose of aspirin.

The second reason that drugs vary in their effectiveness has to do with the affinity of the drug with its site of action. As we will see in the next major section of this chapter, most drugs of interest to psychopharmacologists exert their effects by binding with other molecules located in the central nervous system—with presynaptic or postsynaptic receptors, with transporter molecules, or with enzymes involved in the production or deactivation of transmitter substances. Drugs vary widely in their **affinity** for the molecules to which they attach—the readiness with which the two molecules join together. A drug with a high affinity will produce effects at a relatively low concentration, whereas one with a low affinity must be administered in

relatively high doses. Thus, even two drugs with identical sites of action can vary widely in their effectiveness if they have different affinities for their binding sites. In addition, because most drugs have multiple effects, a drug can have high affinities for some of its sites of action and low affinities for others. The most desirable drug has a high affinity for sites of action that produce therapeutic effects and a low affinity for sites of action that produce toxic side effects. One of the goals of research by drug companies is to find chemicals with just this pattern of effects.

● Effects of Repeated Administration

Often, when a drug is administered repeatedly, its effects will not remain constant. In most cases, its effects will diminish—a phenomenon known as **tolerance.** In other cases, a drug becomes more and more effective—a phenomenon known as **sensitization.**

Let's consider tolerance first. Tolerance is seen in many drugs that are commonly abused. For example, a regular user of heroin must take larger and larger amounts of the drug for it to be effective. And once a person has taken an opiate regularly enough to develop tolerance, that individual will suffer **withdrawal symptoms** if he or she suddenly stops taking the drug. Withdrawal symptoms are primarily the opposite of the effects of the drug itself. For example, heroin produces euphoria; withdrawal from it produces *dysphoria*—a feeling of anxious misery. (*Euphoria* and *dysphoria* mean "easy to bear" and "hard to bear," respectively.) Heroin produces constipation; withdrawal from it produces nausea and cramping. Heroin produces relaxation; withdrawal from it produces agitation.

Withdrawal symptoms are caused by the same mechanisms that are responsible for tolerance. Tolerance is the result of the body's attempt to compensate for the effects of the drug. That is, most systems of the body, including those controlled by the brain, are regulated so that they stay at an optimal value. When the effects of a drug alter these systems for a prolonged time, compensatory mechanisms begin to produce the opposite reaction, at least partially

affinity   The readiness with which two molecules join together.

tolerance   A decrease in the effectiveness of a drug that is administered repeatedly.

sensitization   An increase in the effectiveness of a drug that is administered repeatedly.

withdrawal symptom   The appearance of symptoms opposite to those produced by a drug when the drug is administered repeatedly and then suddenly no longer taken.

compensating for the disturbance from the optimal value. These mechanisms account for the fact that more and more of the drug must be taken in order to achieve a given level of effects. Then, when the person stops taking the drug, the compensatory mechanisms make themselves felt, unopposed by the action of the drug.

Research suggests that there are several types of compensatory mechanisms. As we will see, many drugs that affect the brain do so by binding with receptors. The first compensatory mechanism involves a decrease in the effectiveness of such binding. Either the receptors become less sensitive to the drug (that is, their affinity for the drug decreases) or the receptors decrease in number. The second compensatory mechanism involves the process that couples the receptors to ion channels in the membrane or to the production of second messengers. After prolonged stimulation of the receptors, one or more steps in the coupling process become less effective. (Of course, *both* effects can occur.) The details of these compensatory mechanisms are described in Chapter 19, which discusses the causes and effects of drug abuse.

Many drugs have several different sites of action and thus produce several different effects. This means that some of the effects of a drug may show tolerance but others may not. For example, barbiturates cause sedation and also depress neurons that control respiration. The sedative effects show tolerance, but the respiratory depression does not. This means that if larger and larger doses of a barbiturate are taken in order to achieve the same level of sedation, the person begins to run the risk of taking a dangerously large dose of the drug.

Sensitization is, of course, the exact opposite of tolerance: Repeated doses of a drug produce larger and larger effects. Because homeostatic mechanisms tend to correct for deviations away from the optimal values of physiological processes, sensitization is less common than tolerance. And some of the effects of a drug may show sensitization while others show tolerance. For example, repeated injections of cocaine become more and more likely to produce movement disorders and convulsions, whereas the euphoric effects of the drug do not show sensitization—and may even show tolerance.

● Placebo Effects

A **placebo** is an innocuous substance without a specific physiological effect. The word comes from the Latin *placere,* "to please." A physician may sometimes give a placebo to anxious patients to placate them. (You will see that *placate* also has the same root.) But although placebos have no *specific* physiological effect, it is incorrect to say that they have *no* effect. If a person thinks that a placebo has a physiological effect, then administration of the placebo may actually produce that effect. And I do not mean that the patient will *imagine* the effect; it will actually occur.

Consider the following experiment. Levine, Gordon, and Fields (1979) measured people's sensitivity to pain. Next, they gave the subjects an injection of a painkiller—or so they said. Actually, they administered a placebo. When the experimenters again applied some painful stimuli, they found that the subjects were less sensitive to them. Clearly, they had demonstrated a placebo effect. Next, the experimenters administered another injection—some more painkiller, they said. Actually, the injection contained a drug that blocked the brain's opiate receptors. (This drug, naloxone, is described later in this chapter.) The drug abolished the placebo effect; the subjects regained their original sensitivity to pain. Thus, the subjects' belief that they had received a painkiller seems to have been responsible for a real, physiological event: the secretion of an endogenous opiatelike chemical in the brain. (See *Figure 4.5.*)

Clearly, when experimenters want to investigate the behavioral effects of drugs in humans, they must use control groups whose members receive placebos, or they cannot be sure that the behavioral effects they observe were caused by specific effects of the drug. Studies with laboratory animals must also use placebos, even though we need not worry about the animals "beliefs" about the effects of the drugs we give them. Consider what you must do to give a rat an intraperitoneal injection of a drug. You reach into the animal's cage, pick it up, hold it in such a way that its abdomen is exposed and its head is positioned to prevent it from biting you, insert a hypodermic needle through its abdominal wall, press the plunger of the syringe, and replace the animal in its cage, being sure to let go of it quickly so that it cannot turn and bite you. Even if the substance you inject is innocuous, the experience of receiving the injection would activate the animal's autonomic nervous system, cause the secretion of stress hormones, and have other physiological effects. If we want to know what the behavioral effects of a drug are, we must compare the drug-treated animals with other animals who receive a placebo, administered in exactly the same way as the drug. (By the way, a skilled and experienced researcher can handle a rat so gently that it shows very little reaction to a hypodermic injection.)

placebo (*pla* **see** *boh*) An inert substance given to an organism in lieu of a physiologically active drug; used experimentally to control for the effects of mere administration of a drug.

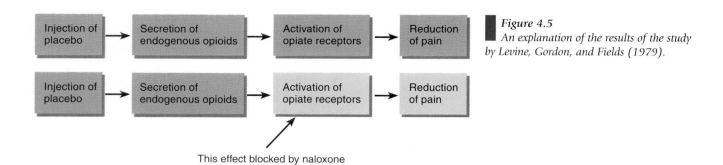

Figure 4.5
An explanation of the results of the study by Levine, Gordon, and Fields (1979).

nterim Summary

Psychopharmacology is the study of the effects of drugs on the nervous system and behavior. Drugs are exogenous chemicals not necessary for normal cellular functioning that significantly alter the functions of certain cells of the body when taken in relatively low doses. Drugs have *effects,* physiological and behavioral, and they have *sites of action*—molecules with which they interact to produce these effects.

Pharmacokinetics is the fate of a drug as it is absorbed into the body, circulates throughout the body, and reaches its sites of action. Drugs may be administered by intravenous, intraperitoneal, intramuscular, and subcutaneous injection; they may be administered orally, sublingually, intrarectally, by inhalation, and topically; and they may be injected intracerebrally or intracerebroventricularly. Lipid-soluble drugs easily pass through the blood–brain barrier, whereas others pass this barrier slowly or not at all.

With the exception of intravenous injection directly into the bloodstream, the time courses of the various routes of drug administration are different. Once molecules of a drug reach the bloodstream, they may bind with albumin protein, and they may bind with storage depots in fat tissue, muscles, or bones. Eventually, drugs disappear from the body. Some are deactivated by enzymes, especially in the liver, and others are simply excreted.

The dose-response curve represents a drug's effectiveness; it relates the amount administered (usually in mg/kg of the subject's body weight) to the resulting effect. Most drugs have more than one site of action and thus more than one effect. The safety of a drug is measured by the difference between doses that produce desirable effects and those that produce adverse side effects. Drugs vary in their effectiveness because of the nature of their sites of action and the affinity between molecules of the drug and these sites of action.

Repeated administration of a drug can cause either tolerance, often resulting in withdrawal symptoms, or sensitization. Tolerance can be caused by decreased affinity of a drug with its receptors, by decreased numbers of receptors, or by decreased coupling of receptors with the biochemical steps it controls. Some of the effects of a drug may show tolerance, while others may not—or may even show sensitization.

Sites of Drug Action

Throughout the history of our species, people have discovered that plants—and a few animals—produce chemicals that act on synapses. (Of course, the people who discovered these chemicals knew nothing about neurons and synapses.) Some of these chemicals have been used for their pleasurable effects; others have been used to treat illness, reduce pain, or poison other animals (or enemies). More recently, scientists have learned to produce completely artificial drugs, some with potencies far greater than the naturally occurring ones. The traditional uses of drugs remain, but in addition, they can be used in research laboratories to investigate the operations of the nervous system. Most drugs that affect behavior do so by affecting synaptic transmission. Drugs that affect synaptic transmission are classified into two general categories. Those that block or inhibit the postsynaptic effects are called **antagonists.** Those that facilitate them are called **agonists.** (The Greek word *agon* means "contest." Thus, an *agonist* is one who takes part in a contest.)

antagonist A drug that opposes or inhibits the effects of a particular neurotransmitter on the postsynaptic cell.
agonist A drug that facilitates the effects of a particular neurotransmitter on the postsynaptic cell.

This section will describe the basic effects of drugs on synaptic activity. Recall from Chapter 2 that the sequence of synaptic activity goes like this: Transmitter substances are synthesized and stored in synaptic vesicles. The synaptic vesicles travel to the presynaptic membrane where they become docked. When an axon fires, voltage-dependent calcium channels in the presynaptic membrane open, permitting the entry of calcium ions. The calcium ions interact with the docking proteins and initiate the release of the transmitter substances into the synaptic cleft. Molecules of the transmitter substance bind with postsynaptic receptors, causing particular ion channels to open, which produces excitatory or inhibitory postsynaptic potentials. The effects of the transmitter substance are kept relatively brief by their reuptake by transporter molecules in the presynaptic membrane or by their destruction by enzymes. In addition, the stimulation of presynaptic autoreceptors regulates the synthesis and release of the transmitter substance. The discussion of the effects of drugs in this section follows the same basic sequence. All of the effects I will describe are summarized in Figure 4.6, with some details shown in additional figures. I should warn you that some of the effects are complex, so the discussion that follows bears careful reading.

● Effects on Production of Transmitter Substances

The first step is the synthesis of the transmitter substance from its precursors. In some cases the rate of synthesis and release of a neurotransmitter is increased when a precursor is administered; in these cases the precursor itself serves as an agonist. (See step 1 in *Figure 4.6*.)

The steps in the synthesis of transmitter substances are controlled by enzymes. Therefore, if a drug inactivates one of these enzymes, it will prevent the transmitter substance from being produced. Such a drug serves as an antagonist. (See step 2 in *Figure 4.6*.)

● Effects on Storage and Release of Transmitter Substances

Transmitter substances are stored in synaptic vesicles, which are transported to the presynaptic membrane, where the chemicals are released. The storage of transmitter substances in vesicles is accomplished by the same kind of transporter molecules that are responsible for reuptake of a transmitter substance into a terminal button. The transporter molecules are situated in the membrane of synaptic vesicles, and their action is to pump molecules of the transmitter substance across the membrane, filling the vesicles. Some of the transporter molecules that fill synaptic vesicles

are capable of being blocked by a drug. Molecules of the drug bind with a particular site on the transporter and inactivate it. Because the synaptic vesicles remain empty, nothing is released when the vesicles eventually rupture against the presynaptic membrane. The drug serves as an antagonist. (See step 3 in *Figure 4.6*.)

Some drugs act as antagonists by preventing the release of transmitter substances from the terminal button. They do so by deactivating the proteins that cause docked synaptic vesicles to fuse with the presynaptic membrane and expel their contents into the synaptic cleft. Other drugs have just the opposite effect: They act as agonists by binding with these proteins and directly triggering the release of the transmitter substance. (See steps 4 and 5 in *Figure 4.6*.)

● Effects on Receptors

The most important—and most complex—site of action of drugs in the nervous system is on receptors, both presynaptic and postsynaptic. Let's consider postsynaptic receptors first. (Here is where the careful reading should begin.) Once a transmitter substance is released, it must stimulate the postsynaptic receptors. Some drugs bind with these receptors, just as the transmitter substance does. Once a drug has bound with the receptor, it can serve as either an agonist or an antagonist.

A drug that mimics the effects of a transmitter substance acts as a **direct agonist.** Molecules of the drug attach to the binding site to which the transmitter substance normally attaches. This binding causes ion channels controlled by the receptor to open, just as they do when the transmitter substance is present. Ions then pass through these channels and produce postsynaptic potentials. (See step 6 in *Figure 4.6*.)

Drugs that bind with postsynaptic receptors can also serve as antagonists. Molecules of such drugs bind with the receptors but *prevent* the ion channels from opening. These drugs are called **receptor blockers,** or **direct antagonists.** (See step 7 in *Figure 4.6*.)

Some postsynaptic receptors have multiple binding sites, to which different ligands can attach. Molecules of the transmitter substance bind with one site, and other substances (such as neuromodulators and various drugs)

---

direct agonist   A drug that binds with and activates a receptor.

receptor blocker   A drug that binds with a receptor but does not activate it; prevents the natural ligand from binding with the receptor.

direct antagonist   A synonym for receptor blocker.

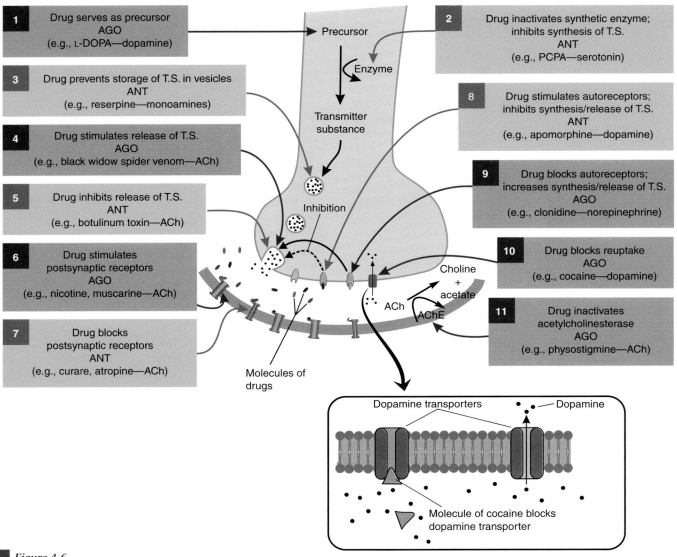

Figure 4.6
A summary of the ways that drugs can affect the synaptic transmission (AGO = agonist; ANT = antagonist; T.S. = transmitter substance). Drugs that act as agonists are marked in blue; drugs that act as antagononists are marked in red.

bind with the others. Binding of a molecule with one of these alternative sites is referred to as **noncompetitive binding,** because the molecule does not compete with molecules of the transmitter substance for the same binding site. If a drug attaches to one of these alternative sites and prevents the ion channel from opening, the drug is said to be an **inverse agonist.** The ultimate *effect* of an inverse agonist is the same as that of a direct antagonist, but its site of action is different. If a drug attaches to one of the alternative sites and *facilitates* the opening of the ion channel, it is said to be an **indirect agonist.** (See *Figure 4.7.*)

As we saw in Chapter 2, the presynaptic membranes of some neurons contain autoreceptors that regulate the amount of transmitter substance that is released. Because stimulation of these receptors causes less transmitter sub-

stance to be released, drugs that selectively activate them but do not activate the postsynaptic receptors act as antagonists. Drugs that *block* presynaptic autoreceptors have the

noncompetitive binding   Binding of a drug to a site on a receptor; does not interfere with the binding site for the principal ligand.

inverse agonist   A drug that attaches to a binding site on a receptor and interferes with the action of the receptor; does not interfere with the binding site for the principal ligand.

indirect agonist   A drug that attaches to a binding site on a receptor and facilitates the action of the receptor; does not interfere with the binding site for the principal ligand.

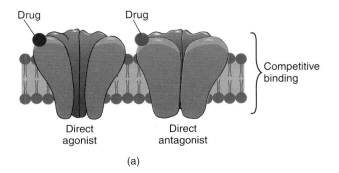

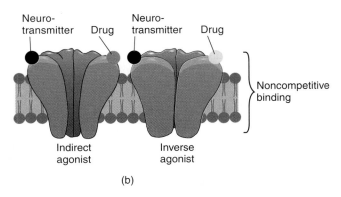

Figure 4.7
Actions of drugs at binding sites on receptors. (a) Competitive binding. Direct agonists and antagonists act on the neurotransmitter binding site. (b) Noncompetitive binding. Inverse agonists and indirect agonists act on an alternative binding site and modify the effects of the neurotransmitter.

opposite effect: They *increase* the release of the transmitter substance, acting as agonists. (Refer to steps 8 and 9 in *Figure 4.6.*)

We also saw in Chapter 2 that some terminal buttons form axoaxonic synapses—synapses of one terminal button with another. Activation of the first terminal button causes presynaptic inhibition or facilitation of the second one. The second terminal button contains **presynaptic heteroreceptors,** which are sensitive to the transmitter substance released by the first one. Presynaptic heteroreceptors that produce presynaptic inhibition do so by inhibiting the opening of voltage-dependent calcium channels located in the presynaptic membrane. As you will recall, the entry of calcium ions into the terminal button is what triggers the release of the neurotransmitter; if calcium ions cannot enter, the neurotransmitter is not released. Conversely, presynaptic heteroreceptors responsible for presynaptic facilitation *facilitate* the opening of voltage-dependent calcium channels. So drugs can block or facilitate presynaptic inhibition or facilitation, depending on whether they block or activate presynaptic heteroreceptors. (See *Figure 4.8.*)

Finally (yes, this is the last site of action I will describe in this subsection), you will recall from Chapter 2 that autoreceptors are located in the membrane of dendrites of

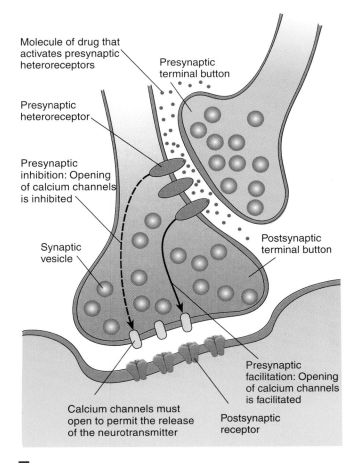

Figure 4.8
Presynaptic heteroreceptors. Presynaptic facilitation is caused by activation of receptors that facilitate the opening of calcium channels near the active zone of the postsynaptic terminal button, which promotes release of the neurotransmitter. Presynaptic inhibition is caused by activation of receptors that inhibit the opening of these calcium channels.

some neurons. When these neurons become active, their dendrites, as well as their terminal buttons, release transmitter substance. The transmitter substance released by the dendrites stimulates autoreceptors located on these same dendrites, which decrease neural firing by producing hyperpolarizations. This mechanism has a regulatory effect, serving to prevent these neurons from becoming too active. Thus, drugs that bind with and *activate* dendritic autoreceptors will serve as *antagonists.* Those that bind with and *block* dendritic autoreceptors will serve as *agonists,* because they will prevent the inhibitory hyperpolarizations. (See *Figure 4.9.*)

presynaptic heteroreceptor A receptor located in the membrane of a terminal button that receives input from another terminal button by means of an axoaxonic synapse; binds with the neurotransmitter released by the presynaptic terminal button.

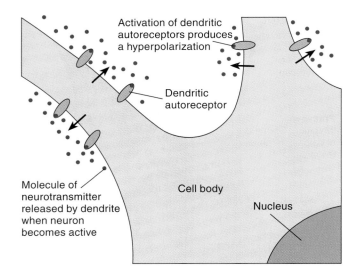

Figure 4.9
Dendritic autoreceptors. The dendrites of certain neurons release some neurotransmitter when the cell is active. The activation of dendritic autoreceptors by the neurotransmitter (or by a drug that binds with these receptors) inhibits the cell's production of the neurotransmitter.

As you will surely realize, the effects of a particular drug that binds with a particular type of receptor can be very complex. The effects depend on where the receptor is located, what its normal effects are, and whether the drug activates the receptor or blocks its actions. To help you review these effects, I have prepared a table that summarizes these effects. (See *Table 4.1*.)

● Effects on Reuptake or Destruction of Transmitter Substance

The next step after stimulation of the postsynaptic receptor is termination of the postsynaptic potential. Two processes accomplish that task: Molecules of the transmitter substance are taken back into the terminal button through the process of reuptake, or they are destroyed by an enzyme. Drugs can interfere with either of these processes. In the first case, molecules of the drug attach to the transporter molecules responsible for reuptake and inactivate them, thus blocking reuptake. In the second case, molecules of the drug bind with the enzyme that normally destroys the transmitter substance and prevents the enzymes from working. The most important example of such an enzyme is acetylcholinesterase, which destroys acetylcholine. Because both types of drugs prolong the presence of the transmitter substance in the synaptic cleft (and hence in a location where they can stimulate postsynaptic receptors), they serve as *agonists*. (Refer to steps 10 and 11 in *Figure 4.6*.)

Interim Summary

The process of synaptic transmission entails the synthesis of the transmitter substance, its storage in synaptic vesicles, its release into the synaptic cleft, its interaction with postsynaptic receptors, and the consequent opening of ion channels in the postsynaptic membrane. The effects of the transmitter substance are then terminated by reuptake into

Table 4.1
Effects of Drugs That Bind with Receptors

Site of action	Effect of activated receptor	Effect of drug on receptor	Effect on synaptic transmission
Postsynaptic receptor	Open postsynaptic ion channel	Stimulate	Agonist
		Block	Antagonist
Presynaptic autoreceptor	Decrease synthesis of transmitter substance	Stimulate	Antagonist
		Block	Agonist
Presynaptic heteroreceptor	Facilitate opening of calcium channels	Stimulate	Agonist
		Block	Antagonist
Presynaptic heteroreceptor	Inhibit opening of calcium channels	Stimulate	Antagonist
		Block	Agonist
Dendritic autoreceptor	Decrease synthesis of transmitter substance	Stimulate	Antagonist
		Block	Agonist

the terminal button, or, in the case of acetylcholine, by enzymatic deactivation.

Each of the steps necessary for synaptic transmission can be interfered with by drugs that serve as *antagonists*, and a few can be stimulated by drugs that serve as *agonists*. Thus, drugs can increase the pool of available precursor, block a biosynthetic enzyme, prevent the storage of transmitter substance in the synaptic vesicles, stimulate or block the release of the transmitter substance, stimulate or block presynaptic or postsynaptic receptors, retard reuptake, or deactivate enzymes that destroy the transmitter substance postsynaptically or presynaptically. A drug that activates postsynaptic receptors serves as an agonist, whereas one that activates presynaptic autoreceptors serves as an antagonist. A drug that blocks postsynaptic receptors serves as an antagonist, whereas one that blocks autoreceptors serves as an agonist. A drug that activates or blocks presynaptic heteroreceptors serves as an agonist or antagonist, depending on whether the heteroreceptors are responsible for presynaptic facilitation or inhibition.

NEUROTRANSMITTERS AND NEUROMODULATORS

Because transmitter substances have two general effects on postsynaptic membranes—depolarization (EPSP) or hyperpolarization (IPSP)—one might expect that there would be two kinds of transmitter substances, excitatory and inhibitory. Instead, there are many different kinds—several dozen, at least. In the brain, most synaptic communication is accomplished by two transmitter substances: one with excitatory effects (glutamate) and one with inhibitory effects (GABA). (Another inhibitory transmitter substance, glycine, is found in the spinal cord and lower brain stem.) Most of the activity of local circuits of neurons involves balances between the excitatory and inhibitory effects of these chemicals, which are responsible for most of the information transmitted from place to place within the brain. In fact, there are probably no neurons in the brain that do not receive excitatory input from glutamate-secreting terminal buttons and inhibitory input from neurons that secrete either GABA or glycine. And with the exception of neurons that detect painful stimuli, all sensory organs transmit information to the brain through axons whose terminals release glutamate. (Pain-detecting neurons secrete a peptide.)

What do all the other transmitter substances do? In general, they have modulating effects rather than information-transmitting effects. That is, the release of transmitter substances other than glutamate and GABA tends to activate or inhibit entire circuits of neurons that are involved in particular brain functions. For example, secretion of acetylcholine activates the cerebral cortex and facilitates learning, but the information that is learned and remembered is transmitted by neurons that secrete glutamate and GABA. Secretion of norepinephrine increases vigilance and enhances readiness to act when a signal is detected. Secretion of serotonin suppresses certain categories of species-typical behaviors and reduces the likelihood that the animal acts impulsively. Secretion of dopamine in some regions of the brain generally activates voluntary movements but does not specify which movements will occur. In other regions, secretion of dopamine reinforces ongoing behaviors and makes them more likely to occur at a later time. Because particular drugs can selectively affect neurons that secrete particular transmitter substances, they can have specific effects on behavior.

This section introduces the most important transmitter substances, discusses some of their behavioral functions, and describes the drugs that interact with them. As we saw in the previous section of this chapter, drugs have many different sites of action. Fortunately for your information-processing capacity (and perhaps your sanity), not all types of neurons are affected by all types of drugs. As you will see, that still leaves a good number of drugs to be mentioned by name. Obviously, some are more important than others. Those whose effects I describe in some detail are more important than those I mention in passing or simply indicate in a figure or a table. If you want to learn more details about these drugs (and many others), you should consult an up-to-date psychopharmacology text. I particularly recommend the one by Feldman, Meyer, and Quenzer (1997).

● Acetylcholine

Acetylcholine is the primary transmitter substance secreted by efferent axons of the central nervous system. All muscular movement is accomplished by the release of acetylcholine, and ACh is also found in the ganglia of the autonomic nervous system and at the target organs of the parasympathetic branch of the ANS. Because ACh is found outside the central nervous system in locations that are easy to study, this transmitter substance was the first to be discovered, and it has received much attention from neuroscientists. Some terminology: These synapses are said to be *acetylcholinergic*. *Ergon* is the Greek word for "work." Thus, *dopaminergic* synapses release dopamine, *serotonergic* synapses release serotonin, and so on. (The suffix *-ergic* is pronounced **ur jik**.)

The axons and terminal buttons of acetylcholinergic neurons are distributed widely throughout the brain. Three

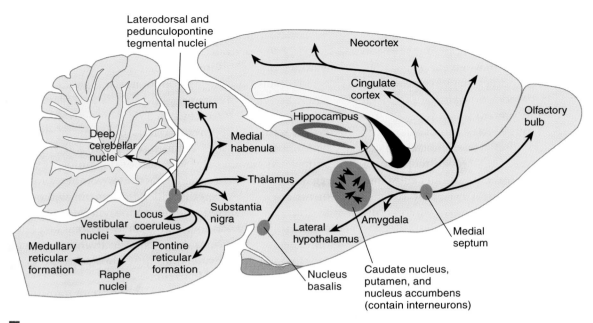

Figure 4.10
A schematic midsagittal section of a rat brain, showing the locations of the most important groups of acetylcholinergic neurons and the distribution of their axons and terminal buttons.
(Adapted from Woolf, 1991.)

systems have received the most attention from neuroscientists: the systems originating in the dorsolateral pons, the basal forebrain, and the medial septum. The effects of ACh release in the brain are generally facilitatory. The acetylcholinergic neurons located in the dorsolateral pons are responsible for eliciting most of the characteristics of REM sleep (the phase of sleep during which dreaming occurs). Those located in the basal forebrain are involved in activating the cerebral cortex and facilitating learning, especially perceptual learning. Those located in the medial septum control the electrical rhythms of the hippocampus and modulate its functions, which include the formation of particular kinds of memories. These functions of acetylcholinergic neurons are described in more detail in Chapters 9, 14, and 15.

Figure 4.10 shows a schematic midsagittal view of a rat brain. On it are indicated the most important sites of acetylcholinergic cell bodies and the regions served by the branches of their axons. The figure illustrates a rat brain because most of the neuroanatomical tracing studies have been performed with rats. Presumably, the location and projections of acetylcholinergic neurons in the human brain resemble those found in the rat brain, but we cannot yet be certain. The methods used for tracing particular systems of neurons in the brain, and the difficulty of doing such studies with the human brain, are described in Chapter 5. (See *Figure 4.10.*)

ACh is composed of two components: *choline*, a substance derived from the breakdown of lipids, and *acetate*, the anion found in vinegar, also called acetic acid. Acetate cannot be attached directly to choline; instead, it is transferred from a molecule of *acetyl-CoA*. CoA (coenzyme A) is a complex molecule, consisting in part of the vitamin pantothenic acid (one of the B vitamins). CoA is produced by the mitochondria, and it takes part in many reactions in the body. **Acetyl-CoA** is simply CoA with an acetate ion attached to it. ACh is produced by the following reaction: In the presence of the enzyme **choline acetyltransferase (ChAT),** the acetate ion is transferred from the acetyl-CoA molecule to the choline molecule, yielding a molecule of ACh and one of ordinary CoA. (See *Figure 4.11.*)

A simple analogy will illustrate the role of coenzymes in chemical reactions. Think of acetate as a hot dog and choline as a bun. The task of the person (enzyme) who operates the hot dog vending stand is to put a hot dog into the bun (make acetylcholine). To do so, the vendor needs a

acetyl-CoA *(a **see** tul)*   A cofactor that supplies acetate for the synthesis of acetylcholine.

choline acetyltransferase (ChAT) *(**koh** leen a see tul **trans** fer ace)*   The enzyme that transfers the acetate ion from acetyl coenzyme A to choline, producing the neurotransmitter acetylcholine.

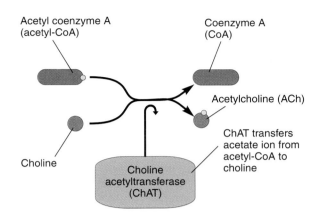

Figure 4.11
The biosynthesis of acetylcholine.

fork (coenzyme) to remove the hot dog from the boiling water. The vendor inserts the fork into the hot dog (attaches acetate to CoA) and transfers the hot dog from fork to bun.

Two drugs, botulinum toxin and the venom of the black widow spider, affect the release of acetylcholine. **Botulinum toxin** is produced by *clostridium botulinum*, a bacterium that can grow in improperly canned food. This drug prevents the release of ACh. The drug is an extremely potent poison; someone once calculated that a teaspoonful of pure botulinum toxin could kill the world's entire human population. In contrast, **black widow spider venom** has the opposite effect: It stimulates the release of ACh. Although the effects of black widow spider venom can also be fatal, the venom is much less toxic than botulinum toxin. In fact, most healthy adults would have to receive several bites, but infants or frail, elderly people would be more susceptible.

You will recall from Chapter 2 that after being released by the terminal button, ACh is deactivated by the enzyme acetylcholinesterase (AChE), which is present in the post-synaptic membrane. The deactivation produces choline and acetate from ACh. Because the amount of choline that is picked up by the soma from the general circulation and then sent to the terminal buttons by means of axoplasmic flow is not sufficient to keep up with the loss of choline by an active synapse, choline must be recycled. After ACh is destroyed by the AChE in the postsynaptic membrane, the choline is returned to the terminal buttons by means of re-uptake. There, it is converted back into ACh. This process has an efficiency of 50 percent; that is, half of the choline is retrieved and recycled. (See *Figure 4.12*.)

Drugs that deactivate or inhibit AChE are used for several purposes. Some are used as insecticides. These drugs readily kill insects but not humans and other mammals, because our blood contains enzymes that destroy them.

(Insects lack the enzyme.) Other AChE inhibitors are used medically. For example, a hereditary disorder called *myasthenia gravis* is caused by an attack of a person's immune system against acetylcholine receptors located on skeletal muscles. The person becomes weaker and weaker as the muscles become less responsive to the neurotransmitter. If given an AChE inhibitor such as **neostigmine,** the person will regain some strength because the acetylcholine that is released has a more prolonged effect on the remaining receptors. (Because neostigmine cannot cross the blood–brain barrier, it does not affect the AChE found in the central nervous system.)

Reuptake of choline can be blocked by a drug called **hemicholinium.** Because this drug prevents the recycling of choline, the terminal button must rely solely on transport of this substance from the cell body. The result is production (and release) of less acetylcholine, which means that hemicholinium serves as an acetylcholine antagonist. (See *Figure 4.12*.)

There are two different types of ACh receptors—one ionotropic and one metabotropic. These receptors were identified when investigators discovered that different drugs activated or inhibited them. The ionotropic ACh receptor is stimulated by nicotine, a drug found in tobacco leaves. (The Latin name of the plant is *Nicotiniana tabacum*.) The metabotropic ACh receptor is stimulated by muscarine, a drug found in the poison mushroom *Amanita muscaria*. Consequently, these two ACh receptors are referred to as **nicotinic receptors** and **muscarinic receptors,** respectively. Because muscle fibers must be able to contract rapidly, they contain the rapid, ionotropic nicotinic receptors. The central nervous system contains both kinds of ACh receptors, but muscarinic receptors predominate.

---

botulinum toxin *(bot you **lin** um)*   An acetylcholine antagonist: prevents release by terminal buttons.

black widow spider venom   A poison produced by the black widow spider that triggers the release of acetylcholine.

neostigmine *(nee o **stig** meen)*   A drug that inhibits the activity of acetylcholinesterase.

hemicholinium *(hem ee koh **lin** um)*   A drug that inhibits the uptake of choline.

nicotinic receptor   An ionotropic acetylcholine receptor that is stimulated by nicotine and blocked by curare.

muscarinic receptor *(muss ka **rin** ic)*   A metabotropic acetylcholine receptor that is stimulated by muscarine and blocked by atropine.

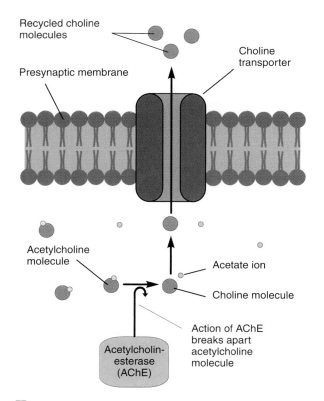

Recycled choline molecules

Presynaptic membrane

Choline transporter

Acetylcholine molecule

Acetate ion

Choline molecule

Action of AChE breaks apart acetylcholine molecule

Acetylcholin-esterase (AChE)

Figure 4.12
The destruction of acetylcholine by acetylcholinesterase and the reuptake of choline. The drug hemicholinium blocks the reuptake of choline.

Because muscarinic receptors are metabotropic in nature, and thus control ion channels through the production of second messengers, their actions are slower and more prolonged than those of nicotinic receptors. In the brain, many nicotinic receptors are found at axoaxonic synapses, where they produce presynaptic facilitation.

Just as two different drugs stimulate the two classes of acetylcholine receptors, two different drugs *block* them. Both drugs were discovered in nature long ago, and both are used by modern medicine. The first, **atropine,** blocks muscarinic receptors. The drug is named after *Atropos,* the Greek fate who cut the thread of life (which a sufficient dose of atropine will certainly do). Atropine is one of several *belladonna alkaloids* extracted from a plant called the "deadly nightshade," and therein lies a tale. Many years ago, women who wanted to increase their attractiveness to men put drops containing belladonna alkaloids into their eyes. In fact, *belladonna* means "pretty lady." Why was the drug used this way? One of the unconscious responses that occurs when we are interested in something is dilation of our pupils. By blocking the effects of acetylcholine on the pupil, belladonna alkaloids such as atropine make the

pupils dilate. This change makes a woman appear more interested in a man when she looks at him, and, of course, this apparent sign of interest makes him regard her as more attractive.

Another drug, **curare,** blocks nicotinic receptors. Because these receptors are the ones found on muscles, curare, like botulinum toxin, causes paralysis. However, the effects of curare are much faster. The drug is extracted from several different species of plants found in South America, where it was discovered long ago by people who used it to coat the tips of arrows and darts. Within minutes of being struck by one of these points, an animal collapses, ceases breathing, and dies. Nowadays, curare (and other drugs with the same site of action) are used to paralyze patients who are to undergo surgery so that their muscles will relax completely and not contract when cut with a scalpel. An anesthetic must also be used, because a person who receives only curare will remain perfectly conscious and sensitive to pain, even though paralyzed. And, of course, a respirator must be used to supply air to the lungs.

The most important drugs that affect acetylcholinergic synapses are summarized in *Table 4.2*.

● The Monoamines

Epinephrine, norepinephrine, dopamine, and serotonin are four chemicals that belong to a family of compounds called **monoamines.** Because the molecular structures of these substances are similar, some drugs affect the activity of all of them, to some degree. The first three—epinephrine, norepinephrine, and dopamine—belong to a subclass of monoamines called **catecholamines.** It is worthwhile learning the terms in Table 4.3, because they will be used many times throughout the rest of this book. (See *Table 4.3*.)

The monoamines are produced by several systems of neurons in the brain. Most of these systems consist of a relatively small number of cell bodies located in the

atropine *(a tro peen)* A drug that blocks muscarinic acetylcholine receptors.

curare *(kew rahr ee)* A drug that blocks nicotinic acetylcholine receptors.

monoamine *(mahn o a meen)* A class of amines that includes indolamines such as serotonin and catecholamines such as dopamine, norepinephrine, and epinephrine.

catecholamine *(cat a kohl a meen)* A class of amines that includes the neurotransmitters dopamine, norepinephrine, and epinephrine.

Table 4.2
Some Drugs That Affect Acetylcholinergic Synapses

Effect of drug	Name of drug	Effect on synaptic transmission
Block release of ACh	Botulinum toxin	Antagonist
Stimulate release of ACh	Black widow spider venom	Agonist
Stimulate nicotinic receptors	Nicotine	Agonist
Block nicotinic receptors	Curare	Antagonist
Stimulate muscarinic receptors	Muscarine	Agonist
Block muscarinic receptors	Atropine	Antagonist
Inhibit acetylcholinesterase	Neostigmine	Agonist
Inhibit reuptake of choline	Hemicholinium	Antagonist

brain stem, whose axons branch repeatedly and give rise to an enormous number of terminal buttons distributed throughout many regions of the brain. Monoaminergic neurons thus serve to modulate the function of widespread regions of the brain, increasing or decreasing the activities of particular brain functions.

Dopamine

The first catecholamine, **dopamine (DA),** produces both excitatory and inhibitory postsynaptic potentials, depending on the postsynaptic receptor. Dopamine is one of the more interesting neurotransmitters because it has been implicated in several important functions, including movement, attention, learning, and the reinforcing effects of drugs that people tend to abuse; thus, it is discussed in Chapters 8, 9, 14, and 19.

The synthesis of the catecholamines is somewhat more complicated than that of ACh, but each step is a simple one. The precursor molecule is modified slightly, step by step, until it achieves its final shape. Each step is controlled by a different enzyme, which causes a small part to be added or taken off. The precursor for the two major cate-cholamine transmitter substances (dopamine and norepinephrine) is *tyrosine,* an essential amino acid that we must obtain from our diet. Tyrosine receives a hydroxyl group (OH—an oxygen atom and a hydrogen atom) and becomes L-DOPA (L-3,4-dihydroxyphenylalanine). The enzyme that adds the hydroxyl group is called *tyrosine hydroxylase.* L-DOPA then loses a carboxyl group (COOH—one carbon atom, two oxygen atoms, and one hydrogen atom) through the activity of the enzyme *DOPA decarboxylase* and becomes dopamine. Finally, the enzyme *dopamine β-hydroxylase* attaches a hydroxyl group to dopamine, which becomes norepinephrine. These reactions are shown in *Figure 4.13*.

The brain contains several systems of dopaminergic neurons. The three most important of these originate in the midbrain: in the substantia nigra and in the ventral tegmental area. (These regions were shown in Figure 3.18.) The cell bodies of neurons of the **nigrostriatal system** are located in the substantia nigra and project their axons to the neostriatum: the caudate nucleus and the putamen. The neostriatum is an important part of the basal ganglia, which is involved in the control of movement. The cell

Table 4.3
Classification of the Monoamine Transmitter Substances

Catecholamines	Indolamines
Dopamine	Serotonin
Norephinephrine	
Epinephrine	

dopamine (DA) *(dope a meen)*   A neurotransmitter; one of the catecholamines.

L-DOPA *(ell dope a)*   The levorotatory form of DOPA; the precursor of the catecholamines; often used to treat Parkinson's disease because of its effect as a dopamine agonist.

nigrostriatal system *(nigh grow stry ay tul)*   A system of neurons originating in the substantia nigra and terminating in the neostriatum (caudate nucleus and putamen).

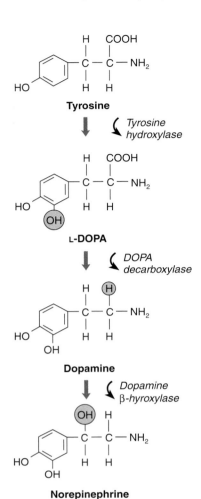

Figure 4.13
Biosynthesis of the catecholamines.

bodies of neurons of the **mesolimbic system** are located in the ventral tegmental area and project their axons to several parts of the limbic system, including the nucleus accumbens, amygdala, and hippocampus. The nucleus accumbens plays an important role in the reinforcing (rewarding) effects of certain categories of stimuli, including those of drugs that people abuse. The cell bodies of neurons of the **mesocortical system** are also located in the ventral tegmental area. Their axons project to the prefrontal cortex. These neurons have an excitatory effect on the frontal cortex and thus affect such functions as formation of short-term memories, planning, and strategy preparation for problem solving. These three systems of dopaminergic neurons are shown in *Figure 4.14*.

Degeneration of dopaminergic neurons that connect the substantia nigra with the caudate nucleus causes **Parkinson's disease,** a movement disorder characterized by

tremors, rigidity of the limbs, poor balance, and difficulty in initiating movements. The cell bodies of these neurons are located in a region of the brain called the *substantia nigra* ("black substance"). This region is normally stained black with melanin, the substance that gives color to skin. This compound is produced by the breakdown of dopamine. (The brain damage that causes Parkinson's disease was discovered by pathologists who observed that the substantia nigra of a deceased person who had had this disorder was pale rather than black.) People with Parkinson's disease are given L-DOPA, the precursor to dopamine. Although dopamine cannot cross the blood–brain barrier, L-DOPA can. Once L-DOPA reaches the brain, it is taken up by dopaminergic neurons and is converted to dopamine. The increased synthesis of dopamine causes more dopamine to be released by the surviving dopaminergic neurons in patients with Parkinson's disease. As a consequence, the patients' symptoms are alleviated.

Another drug, **AMPT** (or α-methyl-*p*-tyrosine), binds with tyrosine hydroxylase, the enzyme that converts tyrosine to L-DOPA. Because this drug interferes with the synthesis of dopamine (and of norepinephrine, as well), it serves as a catecholamine antagonist. The drug is not normally used medically, but it has been used as a research tool in laboratory animals.

The drug **reserpine** prevents the storage of monoamines in synaptic vesicles by blocking the transporters in the membrane that pump monoamines into the vesicles. Because the synaptic vesicles remain empty, no transmitter substance is released when an action potential reaches the terminal button. Reserpine, then, is a monoamine antagonist. The drug, which comes from the root of a shrub, was discovered over three thousand years ago in India, where it was found to be useful in treating snakebite and seemed to

mesolimbic system *(mee zo **lim** bik)* A system of dopaminergic neurons originating in the ventral tegmental area and terminating in the nucleus accumbens, amygdala, and hippocampus.

mesocortical system *(mee zo **kor** ti kul)* A system of dopaminergic neurons originating in the ventral tegmental area and terminating in the prefrontal cortex.

Parkinson's disease A neurological disease characterized by tremors, rigidity of the limbs, poor balance, and difficulty in initiating movements; caused by degeneration of the nigrostriatal system.

AMPT A drug that blocks the activity of tyrosine hydroxylase and thus interferes with the synthesis of the catecholamines.

reserpine *(ree **sur** peen)* A drug that interferes with the storage of monoamines in synaptic vesicles.

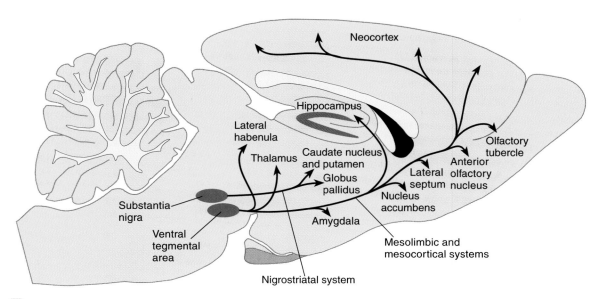

Figure 4.14
A schematic midsagittal section of a rat brain, showing the locations of the most important groups of dopaminergic neurons and the distribution of their axons and terminal buttons.
(Adapted from Fuxe et al., 1985.)

have a calming effect. Pieces of the root are still sold in markets in rural areas of India. In Western medicine, reserpine was previously used to treat high blood pressure, but it has been replaced by drugs with fewer side effects.

At least five types of dopamine receptors have been identified, all metabotropic. Of these, two are the most common: D_1 *dopamine receptors* and D_2 *dopamine receptors*. It appears that D_1 receptors are exclusively postsynaptic, whereas D_2 receptors are found both presynaptically and postsynaptically in the brain. Stimulation of D_1 receptors increases the production of the second messenger cyclic AMP, whereas stimulation of D_2 receptors decreases it, as does stimulation of D_3 and D_4 receptors. Several drugs stimulate or block specific types of dopamine receptors.

Autoreceptors are found in the dendrites, soma, and terminal buttons of dopaminergic neurons. Activation of the autoreceptors in the dendritic and somatic membrane decreases neural firing by producing hyperpolarizations. The presynaptic autoreceptors located in the terminal buttons suppress the activity of the enzyme tyrosine hydroxylase and thus decrease the production of dopamine—and ultimately, its release. Dopamine autoreceptors resemble D_2 receptors, but there seem to be some differences. For example, the drug **apomorphine** is a D_2 agonist, but it seems to have a greater affinity for presynaptic D_2 receptors than postsynaptic D_2 receptors. A low dose of apomorphine acts as an antagonist, because it stimulates the presynaptic receptors and inhibits the production and release of dopa-

mine. Higher doses begin to stimulate postsynaptic D_2 receptors, and the drug begins to act as an agonist. (See *Figure 4.15.*)

Several drugs inhibit the reuptake of dopamine, thus serving as potent dopamine agonists. The best known of these drugs are amphetamine, cocaine, and methylphenidate. The effects of amphetamine are complex. Besides inhibiting dopamine reuptake, this drug causes the release of both norepinephrine and dopamine from the terminal buttons by causing the transporters for these neurotransmitters to run in reverse, propelling DA and NE into the synaptic cleft. Because cocaine also blocks voltage-dependent sodium channels, it is sometimes used as a topical anesthetic, especially in the form of eye drops for eye surgery. **Methylphenidate** (Ritalin) is used to treat children with attention deficit disorder.

The production of the catecholamines is regulated by an enzyme called **monoamine oxidase (MAO).** This en-

apomorphine *(ap o **more** feen)*   A drug that blocks dopamine autoreceptors at low doses; at higher doses blocks postsynaptic receptors as well.

methylphenidate *(meth ul **fen** i date)*   A drug that inhibits the reuptake of dopamine.

monoamine oxidase (MAO) *(**mahn** o a meen)*   A class of enzymes that destroy the monoamines: dopamine, norepinephrine, and serotonin.

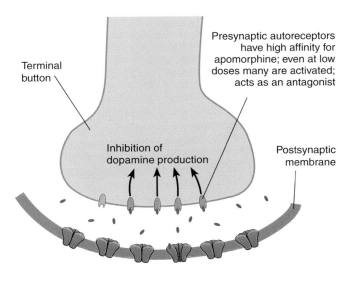

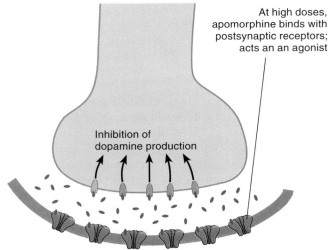

Figure 4.15
The effects of low and high doses of apomorphine. At low doses apomorphine serves as a dopamine agonist; at high doses it serves as an agonist.

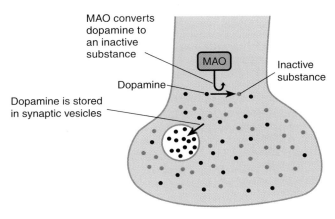

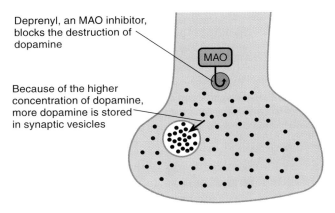

Figure 4.16
The role of monoamine oxidase in dopaminergic terminal buttons and the action of deprenyl.

zyme is found within monoaminergic terminal buttons, where it destroys excessive amounts of transmitter substance. A drug called **deprenyl** destroys the particular form of monoamine oxidase (MAO-B) that is found in dopaminergic terminal buttons. Because deprenyl prevents the destruction of dopamine, more dopamine is released when an action potential reaches the terminal button. Thus, deprenyl serves as a dopamine agonist. (See *Figure 4.16.*)

MAO is also found in the blood, where it deactivates amines that are present in foods such as chocolate and cheese; without such deactivation these amines could cause dangerous increases in blood pressure.

Dopamine has been implicated as a transmitter substance that might be involved in schizophrenia, a serious mental disorder whose symptoms include hallucinations, delusions, and disruption of normal, logical thought processes. Drugs such as **chlorpromazine,** which block D_2 dopamine receptors, alleviate these symptoms. Hence, investigators have speculated that schizophrenia is produced by overactivity of dopaminergic neurons. More recently discovered drugs, such as **clozapine,** may exert their therapeutic effects by blocking D_4 receptors. The physiology of schizophrenia is discussed in Chapter 17.

deprenyl *(depp ra nil)* A drug that blocks the activity of MAO-B; acts as a dopamine agonist.

chlorpromazine *(klor proh ma zeen)* A drug that reduces the symptoms of schizophrenia by blocking dopamine D_2 receptors.

clozapine *(kloz a peen)* A drug that reduces the symptoms of schizophrenia, apparently by blocking dopamine D_4 receptors.

Table 4.4
Some Drugs That Affect Dopaminergic Synapses

Effect of drug	Name of drug	Effect on synaptic transmission
Facilitate synthesis of DA	L-DOPA	Agonist
Inhibit synthesis of DA	AMPT	Antagonist
Inhibit storage of DA in synaptic vesicles	Reserpine	Antagonist
Stimulate D_1 receptors	Dihydrexidine	Agonist
Block D_1 receptors	SCH 23390	Antagonist
Stimulate D_2 receptors	Bromocriptine	Agonist
Block D_2 receptors	Spiroperidol	Antagonist
Stimulate D_3 receptors	7-OH-DPAT	Agonist
Block D_3 receptors	(+)-S 14297	Antagonist
Block D_4 receptors	Clozapine	Antagonist
Block dopamine reuptake	Cocaine	Agonist
Block MAO-B	Deprenyl	Agonist

The symptoms of schizophrenia are occasionally produced by another dopamine agonist, L-DOPA, used to treat the symptoms of Parkinson's disease. Fortunately, these symptoms can usually be eliminated by reducing the drug dosage.

The most important drugs that affect dopaminergic synapses are shown in *Table 4.4.*

Norepinephrine

Because **norepinephrine (NE),** like ACh, is found in neurons in the autonomic nervous system, this neurotransmitter has received much experimental attention. I should note that *Adrenalin* and *epinephrine* are synonymous, as are *noradrenalin* and *norepinephrine*. **Epinephrine** is a hormone produced by the adrenal medulla, the central core of the adrenal glands, located just above the kidneys. Epinephrine also serves as a transmitter substance in the brain, but it is of minor importance compared with norepinephrine. *Ad renal* is Latin for "toward kidney." In Greek, one would say *epi nephron* ("upon the kidney"), hence the term *epinephrine*. The latter term has been adopted by pharmacologists, probably because the word *Adrenalin* was appropriated by a drug company as a proprietary name; therefore, to be consistent with general usage, I will refer to the transmitter substance as *norepinephrine*. The accepted adjectival form is *noradrenergic*; I suppose that *nor-epinephrinergic* never caught on because it takes so long to pronounce.

We have already seen the biosynthetic pathway for norepinephrine in Figure 4.13. The drug AMPT, which prevents the conversion of tyrosine to L-DOPA, blocks the production of norepinephrine as well as dopamine.

Most transmitter substances are synthesized in the cytoplasm of the terminal button and then stored in newly formed synaptic vesicles. However, for norepinephrine the final step of synthesis occurs inside the vesicles themselves. The vesicles are first filled with dopamine. Then, the dopamine is converted to norepinephrine through the action of the enzyme dopamine β-hydroxylase located within the vesicles. The drug **fusaric acid** inhibits the activity of the enzyme dopamine-β-hydroxylase and thus blocks the pro-

norepinephrine (NE) *(nor epp i **neff** rin)*   One of the catecholamines; a neurotransmitter found in the brain and in the sympathetic division of the autonomic nervous system.

epinephrine *(epp i **neff** rin)*   One of the catecholamines; a hormone secreted by the adrenal medulla; serves also as a neurotransmitter in the brain.

fusaric acid *(few **sahr** ik)*   A drug that inhibits the activity of the enzyme dopamine-β-hydroxylase and thus blocks the production of norepinephrine.

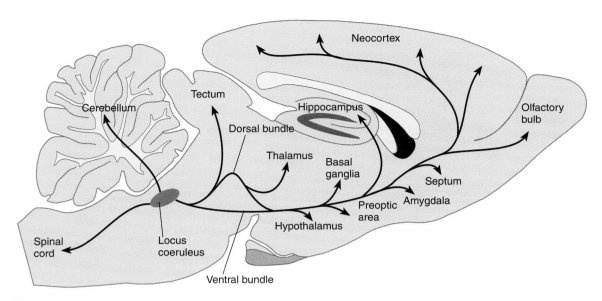

Figure 4.17
A schematic midsagittal section of a rat brain, showing the locations of the most important groups of noradrenergic neurons and the distribution of their axons and terminal buttons.
(Adapted from Cotman and McGaugh, 1980.)

duction of norepinephrine without affecting the production of dopamine.

Excess norepinephrine in the terminal buttons is destroyed by monoamine oxidase, type A. The drug **moclobemide** specifically blocks MAO-A and hence serves as a noradrenergic agonist.

Almost every region of the brain receives input from noradrenergic neurons. The cell bodies of most of these neurons are located in seven regions of the pons and medulla and one region of the thalamus. The cell bodies of the most important noradrenergic system begin in the **locus coeruleus,** a nucleus located in the dorsal pons. The axons of these neurons project to the regions shown in Figure 4.17. As we will see later, the primary effect of activation of these neurons is an increase in vigilance—attentiveness to events in the environment. (See *Figure 4.17.*)

Most neurons that release norepinephrine do not do so through terminal buttons on the ends of axonal branches. Instead, they usually release them through **axonal varicosities,** beadlike swellings of the axonal branches. These varicosities give the axonal branches of catecholaminergic neurons the appearance of beaded chains.

There are several types of noradrenergic receptors, identified by their differing sensitivities to various drugs. Actually, these receptors are usually called *adrenergic* receptors rather than *noradrenergic* receptors, because they are sensitive to epinephrine (Adrenalin) as well as norepinephrine. Neurons in the central nervous system contain β_1- and β_2-*adrenergic receptors* and α_1- and α_2-*adrenergic receptors.* All four kinds of receptors are also found in various organs of the body besides the brain and are responsible for the effects of the catecholamines when they act as hormones outside the central nervous system. A fourth type of adrenergic receptor, the β_3 receptor, is found only outside the central nervous system, primarily in adipose (fat) tissue. In the brain, all autoreceptors appear to be of the α_2 type. All adrenergic receptors are metabotropic, coupled to G proteins that control the production of second messengers.

Adrenergic receptors produce both excitatory and inhibitory effects. In general, the *behavioral* effects of the release of NE are excitatory. In the brain, α_1 receptors produce a slow depolarizing (excitatory) effect on the postsynaptic membrane, while α_2 receptors produce a slow hyperpolarization. Both types of β receptors increase the responsiveness of the postsynaptic neuron to its excitatory inputs. As we will see in Chapter 9, the behavioral conse-

moclobemide *(mak low **bem** ide)*   A drug that blocks the activity of MAO-A; acts as a noradrenergic agonist.

locus coeruleus *(sur **oo** lee us)*   A dark-colored group of noradrenergic cell bodies located in the pons near the rostral end of the floor of the fourth ventricle.

axonal varicosities   Enlarged regions along the length of an axon that contain synaptic vesicles and release a neurotransmitter or neuromodulator.

Table 4.5
Some Drugs That Affect Noradrenergic Synapses

Effect of drug	Name of drug	Effect on synaptic transmission
Inhibit synthesis of NE	Fusaric acid	Antagonist
Inhibit storage of NE in synaptic vesicles	Reserpine	Antagonist
Stimulate α_1 receptors	Phenylephrine	Agonist
Block α_1 receptors	Projosin	Antagonist
Stimulate α_2 receptors	Clonidine	Agonist
Block α_2 receptors	Yohimbine	Antagonist
Stimulate b_1 receptors	Denopamine	Agonist
Block b_1 receptors	Atenolol	Antagonist
Stimulate b_2 receptors	Procaterol	Agonist
Block b_2 receptors	ICI-118,551	Antagonist
Inhibit reuptake of NE	Desipramine	Agonist
Inhibit MAO-A	Moclobemide	Agonist

quence of this effect is to increase an animal's vigilance—its ability to detect the occurrence of important stimuli. Noradrenergic neurons—in particular, α_2 receptors—are also involved in sexual behavior and in the control of appetite, topics that are discussed in Chapters 10 and 13.

The most important drugs that affect noradrenergic synapses are listed in **Table 4.5.**

Serotonin

The third monoamine transmitter substance, **serotonin** (also called **5-HT,** or 5-hydroxytryptamine), has also received much experimental attention. Its behavioral effects are complex. Serotonin plays a role in the regulation of mood; in the control of eating, sleep, and arousal; and in the regulation of pain. Serotonergic neurons are involved somehow in the control of dreaming.

The precursor for serotonin is the amino acid *tryptophan.* The enzyme *tryptophan hydroxylase* adds a hydroxyl group, producing *5-HTP* (5-hydroxytryptophan). The enzyme *5-HTP decarboxylase* removes a carboxyl group from 5-HTP, and the result is 5-HT (serotonin). (See *Figure 4.18.*) The drug **PCPA** (*p*-chlorophenylalanine) blocks the activity of tryptophan hydroxylase and thus serves as a serotonergic antagonist.

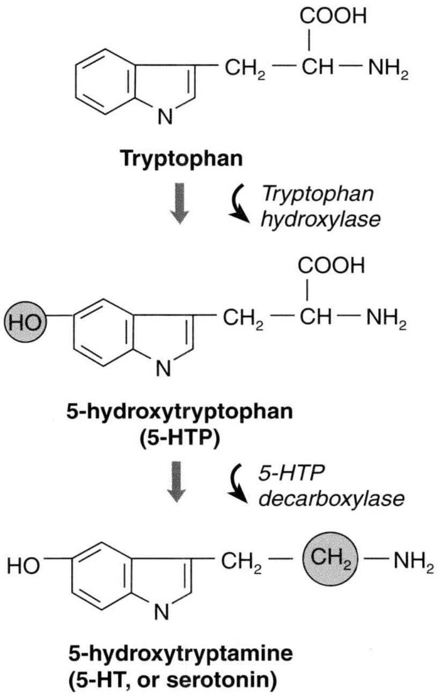

Figure 4.18
Biosynthesis of serotonin (5-hydroxytryptamine, or 5-HT).

serotonin (5-HT) *(sair a **toe** nin)*   An indolamine transmitter substance; also called 5-hydroxytryptamine.

PCPA   A drug that inhibits the activity of tryptophan hydroxylase and thus interferes with the synthesis of 5-HT.

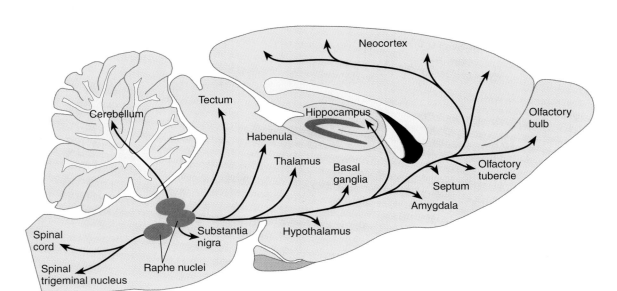

Figure 4.19
*A schematic midsagittal section of a rat brain, showing the locations of the most important groups
of serotonergic neurons and the distribution of their axons and terminal buttons.*
(Adapted from Consolazione and Cuello, 1982.)

The cell bodies of serotonergic neurons are found in nine clusters, most of which are located in the raphe nuclei of the midbrain, pons, and medulla. The two most important clusters are found in the dorsal and medial raphe nuclei, and I will restrict my discussion to these clusters. The word *raphe* means "seam," or "crease," and refers to the fact that most of the raphe nuclei are found at or near the midline of the brain stem. Both the dorsal and median raphe nuclei project axons to the cerebral cortex. In addition, neurons in the dorsal raphe innervate the basal ganglia, and those in the median raphe innervate the dentate gyrus, a part of the hippocampal formation. These and other connections are shown in *Figure 4.19.*

Like norepinephrine, 5-HT is released from varicosities rather than terminal buttons. In fact, there are two types of serotonergic axonal fibers, which appear to have different functions. The **D system** originates in the dorsal raphe nucleus. Its axonal fibers are thin, with spindle-shaped varicosities. These varicosities do not appear to form synapses; that is, the 5-HT that they release diffuses throughout the region, serving as a neuromodulator. The **M system** originates in the median raphe nucleus. Its axonal fibers are thick and rounded, appearing like beads on a chain. These varicosities appear to be located adjacent to postsynaptic membranes, forming conventional synapses. Figure 4.20 is a photomicrograph of both types of fibers, located in the forebrain. Fibers belonging to the D system are indicated with small arrows, and those belonging to the M system are indicated with large open arrows. Almost certainly, these two systems have different behavioral effects. (See *Figure 4.20.*)

Investigators have identified at least nine different types of serotonin receptors: 5-HT_{1A-1B}, 5-HT_{1D-1F}, 5-HT_{2A-2C}, and 5-HT_3. Of these, the 5-HT_{1B} and 5-HT_{1D} receptors serve as presynaptic autoreceptors. In the dorsal and median raphe nuclei, 5-HT_{1A} receptors serve as autoreceptors in the membrane of dendrites and soma. All 5-HT receptors are metabotropic except for the 5-HT_3 receptor, which is ionotropic. The 5-HT_3 receptor controls a chloride channel, which means that it produces inhibitory postsynaptic potentials. These receptors appear to play a role in nausea and vomiting, because 5-HT_3 antagonists have been found to be useful in treating the side effects of chemotherapy and radiotherapy for the treatment of cancer. Pharmacologists have discovered drugs that serve as agonists or antagonists for some, but not all, of the types of 5-HT receptors.

Drugs that inhibit the reuptake of serotonin have found a very important place in the treatment of mental disor-

D system   A system of serotonergic neurons that originates in the dorsal raphe nucleus; its axonal fibers are thin, with spindle-shaped varicosities that do not appear to form synapses with other neurons.

M system   A system of serotonergic neurons that originates in the median raphe nucleus; its axonal fibers are thick and rounded and appear to form conventional synapses with other neurons.

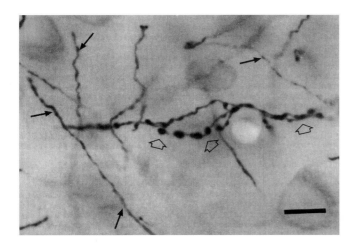

Figure 4.20
A photomicrograph of axonal fibers belonging to the D system and M system of serotonergic neurons.
(From Törk, I. *Annals of the New York Academy of Sciences,* 1990, *600,* 9–35.)

ders. The most popular of these, **fluoxetine** (Prozac), is used to treat depression, some forms of anxiety disorders, and obsessive-compulsive disorder. These disorders—and their treatment—are discussed in Chapters 17 and 18. Another drug, **fenfluramine,** which causes the release of serotonin as well as inhibits its reuptake, is used as an appetite suppressant in the treatment of obesity. Fenfluramine is usually prescribed in combination with phentermine, a drug that acts on catecholamines. This drug has appetite suppressing effects of its own and also counteracts the drowsiness caused by fenfluramine. Chapter 13 discusses the topic of obesity.

Several hallucinogenic drugs appear to produce their effects by interacting with serotonergic transmission. **LSD** (lysergic acid diethylamide) produces distortions of visual perceptions that some people find awesome and fascinating, but that simply frighten other people. This drug, which is effective in extremely small doses, has many sites of action in the brain. For years researchers thought that its behavioral effects were produced by the stimulation of 5-HT autoreceptors located on somatic and dendritic membranes in the raphe nuclei. In this role, LSD acts as a serotonin antagonist. However, more recent studies have concluded that LSD is also a direct agonist for postsynaptic 5-HT$_{2A}$ receptors in the forebrain, and that this action is responsible for the behavioral effects of the drug. Other drugs that act as 5-HT$_{2A}$ agonists also have hallucinogenic effects.

The most important drugs that affect serotonergic synapses are listed in *Table 4.6*.

Amino Acids

So far, all of the transmitter substances I have described are synthesized within neurons: acetylcholine from choline, the catecholamines from the amino acid tyrosine, and serotonin from the amino acid tryptophan. Some neurons secrete simple amino acids as transmitter substances. Because amino acids are used for protein synthesis by all cells of the brain, it is difficult to prove that a particular amino acid is a transmitter substance. However, investigators suspect that at least eight amino acids may serve as transmitter substances in the mammalian central nervous system (CNS). As we saw in the introduction to this section, three of them are especially important because they are the most common transmitter substances in the CNS: glutamate, gamma-aminobutyric acid (GABA), and glycine.

Glutamate

Because **glutamate** (also called *glutamic acid*) and gamma-aminobutyric acid (GABA) are found in very simple organisms, many investigators believe that these neurotransmitters are the first to have evolved. Besides producing postsynaptic potentials by activating postsynaptic receptors, they also have direct excitatory effects (glutamic acid) and inhibitory effects (GABA) on axons; they raise or lower the threshold of excitation, thus affecting the rate at which action potentials occur. These direct effects suggest that these substances had a general modulating role even before the evolutionary development of specific receptor molecules.

Glutamate is the principal excitatory transmitter substance in the brain and spinal cord. It is produced in abundance by the cells' metabolic processes. There is no effective way to prevent its synthesis without disrupting other activities of the cell.

Investigators have discovered four types of glutamate receptors. Three of these receptors are ionotropic and are named after the artificial ligands that stimulate them: the **NMDA receptor,** the **AMPA receptor,** and the **kainate**

---

fluoxetine *(floo ox i teen)*   A drug that inhibits the reuptake of 5-HT.

fenfluramine *(fen fluor i meen)*   A drug that stimulates the release of 5-HT.

LSD   A drug that stimulates 5-HT$_{2A}$ receptors.

glutamate   An amino acid; the most important excitatory transmitter substance in the brain.

NMDA receptor   A specialized ionotropic glutamate receptor that controls a calcium channel that is normally blocked by Mg^{2+} ions; has several other binding sites.

AMPA receptor   An ionotropic glutamate receptor that controls a sodium channel; stimulated by AMPA and blocked by CNQX.

Table 4.6
Some Drugs That Affect Serotonergic Synapses

Effect of drug	Name of drug	Effect on synaptic transmission
Inhibit synthesis of 5-HT	PCPA	Antagonist
Inhibit storage of 5-HT in synaptic vesicles	Reserpine	Antagonist
Stimulate release of 5-HT	Fenfluramine	Agonist
Stimulate 5-HT$_{1A}$ receptors	8-OH-DPAT	Agonist
Block 5-HT$_{1A}$ receptors	SDZ 216-5254	Antagonist
Stimulate 5-HT$_{1B}$ receptors	CP-93,129	Agonist
Stimulate 5-HT$_{1D}$ receptors	Sumatripan	Agonist
Stimulate 5-HT$_{2A}$ receptors	α-methyl-5-HT	Agonist
Block 5-HT$_{2A}$ receptors	Ketanserin	Antagonist
Stimulate 5-HT$_{2B}$ receptors	α-methyl-5-HT	Agonist
Block 5-HT$_{2B}$ receptors	SB 200646A	Antagonist
Stimulate 5-HT$_{2C}$ receptors	α-methyl-5-HT	Agonist
Block 5-HT$_{2C}$ receptors	SB 200646A	Antagonist
Stimulate 5-HT$_3$ receptors	2-methyl-5-HT	Agonist
Block 5-HT$_3$ receptors	Tropisetron	Antagonist
Inhibit reuptake of 5-HT	Fluoxetine	Agonist

receptor. The other glutamate receptor—the **metabotropic receptor**—is (obviously!) metabotropic. Actually, there appear to be at least seven different metabotropic receptors, but little is known about their functions except that some of them serve as presynaptic autoreceptors. The AMPA receptor is the most common glutamate receptor. It controls a sodium channel, so when glutamate attaches to the binding site, it produces EPSPs. The kainate receptor has similar effects.

The NMDA receptor has some special—and very important—characteristics. It contains at least six different binding sites, four located on the exterior of the receptor, and two located deep within the ion channel. When it is open, the ion channel controlled by the NMDA receptor permits both sodium and calcium ions to enter the cell. The influx of both of these ions causes a depolarization, of course, but the entry of calcium (Ca^{2+}) is especially important. Calcium serves as a second messenger, binding with—and activating—various enzymes within the cell. These enzymes have profound effects on the biochemical and structural properties of the cell. As we shall see, one

important result is alteration in the characteristics of the synapse that provide one of the building blocks of a newly formed memory. These effects of NMDA receptors will be discussed in much more detail in Chapter 14.

Figure 4.21 presents a schematic diagram of an NMDA receptor and its binding sites. Obviously, glutamate binds with one of these sites, or we would not call it a glutamate receptor. However, glutamate by itself cannot open the calcium channel. For that to happen, a molecule of glycine must be attached to the glycine binding site, located on the outside of the receptor. (We do not yet understand why glycine—which also serves as an inhibitory neurotransmitter in some parts of the central nervous system—is required for this ion channel to open.) (See *Figure 4.21.*)

---

kainate receptor (*kay in ate*) An ionotropic glutamate receptor that controls a sodium channel; stimulated by kainic acid and blocked by CNQX.

metabotropic receptor (*meh tab a troh pik*) A metabotropic glutamate receptor.

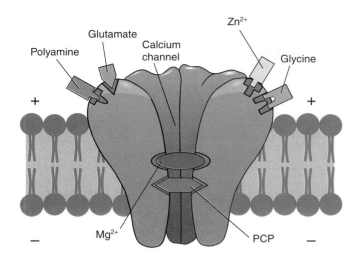

Figure 4.21
A schematic illustration of an NMDA receptor, with its binding sites.

An additional requirement for the opening of the calcium channel is that a magnesium ion *not* be attached to the magnesium binding site, located deep within the channel. Under normal conditions, when the postsynaptic membrane is at the resting potential, a magnesium ion (Mg^{2+}) is attracted to the magnesium binding site and blocks the calcium channel. If a molecule of glutamate attaches to its binding site, the channel widens, but the magnesium ion still blocks it, so no calcium can enter the postsynaptic neuron. However, if the postsynaptic membrane is partially depolarized, the magnesium ion is repelled from its binding site. Thus, the NMDA receptor opens only if glutamate is present *and* the postsynaptic membrane is depolarized. The NMDA receptor, then, is a voltage- and neurotransmitter-dependent ion channel. (See *Figure 4.21.*)

Table 4.7
Behavioral Symptoms of Phencyclidine (PCP)

Altered body image
Feelings of isolation and aloneness
Cognitive disorganization
Drowsiness and apathy
Negativism and hostility
Feelings of euphoria and inebriation
Dreamlike states

Source: Adapted from Feldman, Meyer, and Quenzer, 1997.

What about the other three binding sites? If a zinc ion (Zn^{2+}) binds with the zinc binding site, the activity of the NMDA receptor is decreased. On the other hand, the polyamine site has a facilitatory effect. (Polyamines are chemicals that have been shown to be important for tissue growth and development. The significance of the polyamine binding site is not yet understood.) The PCP site, located deep within the ion channel near the magnesium binding site, binds with a hallucinogenic drug, **PCP** (phencyclidine, also known as "angel dust"). PCP serves as an inverse agonist; when it attaches to its binding site, calcium ions cannot pass through the ion channel. PCP is a synthetic drug, and is not produced by the brain. Thus, it is not the natural ligand of the PCP binding site. What that ligand is and what useful functions it serves are not yet known. The behavioral symptoms of PCP are listed in *Table 4.7*.

Several drugs affect glutamatergic synapses. As you already know, NMDA, AMPA, and kainate serve as direct agonists at the receptors named after them. Agonists and antagonists of glutamate receptors are listed in *Table 4.8*.

GABA

GABA (gamma-aminobutyric acid) is produced from glutamic acid by the action of an enzyme (GAD, or glutamic acid decarboxylase) that removes a carboxyl group. The drug **allylglycine** blocks GAD and thus prevents the synthesis of GABA. GABA is an inhibitory transmitter substance, and it appears to have a widespread distribution throughout the brain and spinal cord. Two GABA receptors have been identified: $GABA_A$ and $GABA_B$. The $GABA_A$ receptor is ionotropic and controls a chloride channel; the $GABA_B$ receptor is metabotropic and controls a potassium channel.

As you know, neurons in the brain are greatly interconnected. Without the activity of inhibitory synapses these interconnections would make the brain unstable. That is, through excitatory synapses, neurons would excite their neighbors, which would then excite *their* neighbors, which would then excite the originally active neurons, and so on, until most of the neurons in the brain would be firing uncontrollably. In fact, this event does sometimes occur, and

PCP Phencyclidine; a drug that binds with the PCP binding site of the NMDA receptor and serves as an inverse agonist.

GABA An amino acid; the most important inhibitory transmitter substance in the brain.

allylglycine A drug that inhibits the activity of GAD and thus blocks the synthesis of GABA.

Table 4.8
Some Drugs That Affect Glutamate Receptors

Effect of drug	Name of drug	Effect on synaptic transmission
Stimulate AMPA receptor	AMPA	Agonist
Block AMPA receptor	CNQX	Antagonist
Stimulate kainate receptor	Kainic acid	Agonist
Block kainate receptor	CNQX	Antagonist
Stimulate NMDA receptor	NMDA	Agonist
Block NMDA receptor	AP5	Antagonist
Stimulate metabotropic receptor	*Trans*-ACPD	Agonist
Block metabotropic receptor	α-methyl-4-carboxyphenylglycine	Antagonist

we refer to it as a *seizure.* (*Epilepsy* is a neurological disorder characterized by the presence of seizures.) Normally, an inhibitory influence is supplied by GABA-secreting neurons, which are present in large numbers in the brain. Some investigators believe that one of the causes of epilepsy is an abnormality in the biochemistry of GABA-secreting neurons or in GABA receptors.

Like NMDA receptors, $GABA_A$ receptors are complex; they contain at least five different binding sites. The primary binding site is, of course, for GABA. The drug **muscimol** (derived from the ACh agonist, muscarine) serves as a direct agonist for this site. Another drug, **bicuculline,** blocks this GABA binding site, serving as a direct antagonist. A second site on the $GABA_A$ receptor binds with a class of tranquilizing drugs called the **benzodiazepines.** These drugs include diazepam (Valium) and chlordiazepoxide (Librium), which are used to reduce anxiety, promote sleep, reduce seizure activity, and produce muscle relaxation. The third site binds with barbiturates. The fourth site binds with various steroids, including some steroids used to produce general anesthesia. The fifth site binds with picrotoxin, a poison found in an East Indian shrub. In addition, alcohol binds with one of these sites—probably the benzodiazepine binding site. (See *Figure 4.22.*)

Barbiturates, drugs that bind to the steroid site, and benzodiazepines all promote the activity of the $GABA_A$ receptor; thus, all these drugs serve as agonists. The benzodiazepines are very effective **anxiolytics,** or "anxiety-dissolving" drugs. They are often used to treat people with anxiety disorders. In addition, some benzodiazepines serve as effective sleep medications, and others are used to treat some types of seizure disorder.

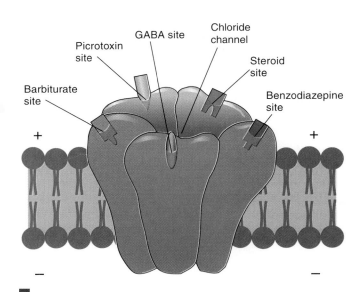

Figure 4.22
A schematic illustration of a $GABA_A$ receptor, with its binding sites.

muscimol (*musk* i *mawl*)   A direct agonist for the GABA binding site on the $GABA_A$ receptor.

bicuculline *(by kew kew leen)*   A direct antagonist for the GABA binding site on the $GABA_A$ receptor.

benzodiazepine *(ben zoe dy azz a peen)*   A category of anxiolytic drugs; an indirect agonist for the $GABA_A$ receptor.

anxiolytic *(angz ee oh lit ik)*   An anxiety-reducing effect.

In low doses barbiturates have a calming effect. In progressively higher doses they produce difficulty in walking and talking, unconsciousness, coma, and death. Although veterinarians sometimes use barbiturates to produce anesthesia for surgery, the therapeutic index—the ratio between a dose that produces anesthesia and one that causes fatal depression of the respiratory centers of the brain—is small. As a consequence, these drugs are rarely used by themselves to produce surgical anesthesia in humans.

Picrotoxin has effects opposite to those of benzodiazepines and barbiturates: It *inhibits* the activity of the GABA$_A$ receptor. In high enough doses, this drug causes convulsions.

Various steroid hormones are normally produced in the body, and some hormones related to progesterone (the principal pregnancy hormone) act on the steroid binding site of the GABA$_A$ receptor, producing a sedative effect. However, the brain does not produce Valium, barbiturates, or picrotoxin. What are the natural ligands for these binding sites? So far, most research has concentrated on the benzodiazepine binding site. These binding sites are more complex than the others. They can be activated by drugs such as the benzodiazepines, which promote the activity of the receptor and thus serve as indirect agonists. They can also be activated by other drugs that have the opposite effect—that inhibit the activity of the receptor, thus serving as inverse agonists. (Indirect and inverse agonists were described earlier; their actions were shown in Figure 4.7.)

There is good evidence that a chemical produced by the brain, **β-CCM,** serves as a natural ligand for the benzodiazepine binding site. β-CCM (known by chemists as methyl-β-carboline-3-carboxylate) acts as an inverse agonist; thus, its behavioral effects are fear, tension, and anxiety, which are just the opposite of those of the benzodiazepines. Perhaps, some investigators believe, β-CCM or other neuromodulators are released in times of danger and motivate the animal to perform behaviors that will permit it to escape or defend itself. Whether the brain also produces chemicals that act as indirect agonists, as the benzodiazepines do, is not yet known.

What about the GABA$_B$ receptor? This metabotropic receptor, coupled to a G protein, serves as both a postsynaptic receptor and a presynaptic autoreceptor. A GABA$_B$ agonist, baclofen, serves as a muscle relaxant. Another drug, CGP 335348, serves as an antagonist. The activation of GABA$_B$ receptors opens potassium channels, producing hyperpolarizing inhibitory postsynaptic potentials.

Glycine

The amino acid **glycine** appears to be the inhibitory neurotransmitter in the spinal cord and lower portions of the brain. Little is known about its biosynthetic pathway; there are several possible routes, but not enough is known to decide how neurons produce glycine. The bacteria that cause tetanus (lockjaw) release a chemical that prevents the release of glycine (and GABA, as well); the removal of the inhibitory effect of these synapses causes muscles to contract continuously.

The glycine receptor is ionotropic, and it controls a chloride channel. Thus, when it is active, it produces inhibitory postsynaptic potentials. The drug **strychnine,** an alkaloid found in the seeds of the *Strychnos nux vomica*, a tree found in India, serves as a glycine agonist. Strychnine is very toxic, and even relatively small doses cause convulsions and death. No drugs have yet been found that serve as specific glycine agonists.

● Peptides

Recent studies have discovered that the neurons of the central nervous system release a large variety of peptides. Peptides consist of two or more amino acids, linked together by peptide bonds. All the peptides that have been studied so far are produced from precursor molecules. These precursors are large polypeptides that are broken into pieces by special enzymes. A neuron manufactures both the polypeptides and the enzymes that it needs to break them apart in the right places. The appropriate sections are retained, and the other ones are destroyed. Because the synthesis of peptides takes place in the soma, vesicles containing these chemicals must be delivered to the terminal buttons by axoplasmic transport.

Peptides are released from all parts of the terminal button, not just from the active zone; thus, only a portion of the molecules are released into the synaptic cleft. The rest presumably act on receptors belonging to other cells in the vicinity. Once released, peptides are deactivated by enzymes. There is no mechanism for reuptake and recycling of peptides.

Several different peptides are released by neurons. Although most peptides appear to serve as neuromodulators, some act as neurotransmitters. One of the most important family of peptides is the **endogenous opioids.**

β-CCM   A direct agonist for the benzodiazepine binding site of the GABA$_A$ receptor.

glycine (*gly* seen)   An amino acid; an important inhibitory transmitter substance in the lower brain stem and spinal cord.

strychnine (*strik* neen)   A direct agonist for the glycine receptor.

endogenous opioid (en *dodge* en us *oh* pee oyd)   A class of peptides secreted by the brain that act as opiates.

(*Endogenous* means "produced from within"; *opioid* means "like opium.") Several years ago it became clear that opiates (drugs such as opium, morphine, and heroin) reduce pain because they have direct effects on the brain. (Please note that the term *opioid* refers to endogenous chemicals, and *opiate* refers to drugs.) Pert, Snowman, and Snyder (1974) discovered that neurons in a localized region of the brain contain specialized receptors that respond to opiates. Then, soon after the discovery of the opioid receptor, other neuroscientists discovered the natural ligands for these receptors (Terenius and Wahlström, 1975; Hughes et al., 1975), which they called **enkephalins** (from the Greek word *enkephalos,* "in the head"). We now know that the enkephalins are only two members of a family of endogenous opiate peptides, all of which are synthesized from one of three large peptides that serve as precursors. In addition, we know that there are at least three different types of opioid receptors: μ (mu), δ (delta), and κ (kappa).

Several different neural systems are activated when opiate receptors are stimulated. One type produces analgesia, another inhibits species-typical defensive responses such as fleeing and hiding, and another stimulates a system of neurons involved in reinforcement ("reward"). The last effect explains why opiates are often abused. The situations that cause neurons to secrete endogenous opioids are discussed in Chapter 7, and the brain mechanisms of opiate addiction are discussed in Chapter 19.

So far, pharmacologists have developed only two types of drugs that affect neural communication by means of opioids: direct agonists and antagonists. Many synthetic opiates, including heroin (dihydromorphine) and Percodan (levorphanol), have been developed and are used clinically as analgesics. Several opiate receptor blockers have also been developed. One of them, **naloxone,** is used clinically to reverse opiate intoxication. This drug has saved the lives of many drug abusers who would otherwise have died of an overdose of heroin. And as we saw earlier in this chapter, naloxone was used to demonstrate that the administration of a placebo can cause analgesia by triggering the release of endogenous opioids.

As we saw in Chapter 2, many terminal buttons contain two different types of synaptic vesicles, each filled with a different substance. These terminal buttons release peptides in conjunction with a "classical" neurotransmitter (one of those I just described). The primary reason for the co-release of peptides is their ability to regulate the sensitivity of presynaptic or postsynaptic receptors to the neurotransmitter. For example, the terminal buttons of the salivary nerve of the cat (which control the secretion of saliva) release both acetylcholine and a peptide called VIP. When the axons fire at a low rate, only ACh is released and only a little saliva is secreted. At a higher rate, both ACh and VIP are secreted and the VIP dramatically increases the sensitivity of the muscarinic receptors in the salivary gland to ACh; thus, much saliva is released.

Several peptide hormones are also found in the brain, where they serve as neurotransmitters or neuromodulators. In some cases, the peripheral and the central peptides perform related functions (Panksepp, 1991). For example, outside the nervous system the hormone angiotensin acts directly on the kidneys and blood vessels to produce effects that help the body cope with the loss of fluid, and inside the nervous system circuits of neurons that use angiotensin as a neurotransmitter perform similar functions, including the activation of neural circuits that produce thirst.

Some of the most important peptides are listed in Table 4.9. Many of these have interesting behavioral effects, which will be discussed in subsequent chapters. (See *Table 4.9.*)

● Lipids

Various substances derived from lipids can serve to transmit messages within or between cells. One of them appears to be the natural ligand for the THC receptor, which is responsible for the physiological effects of the active ingredient in marijuana.

Matsuda et al. (1990) discovered that THC (tetrahydrocannibinal, the active ingredient of marijuana) stimulates specific receptors in specific regions of the brain. (See *Figure 4.23.*) THC produces analgesia and sedation, stimulates appetite, reduces nausea caused by drugs used to treat cancer, relieves asthma attacks, decreases pressure within the eyes in patients with glaucoma, and reduces the symptoms of certain motor disorders. On the other hand, THC interferes with concentration and memory, alters visual and auditory perception, and distorts perceptions of the passage of time. Devane et al. (1992) discovered what appears to be the natural ligand for the THC receptor: a lipid-like substance that they named **anandamide,** from the Sanskrit word *ananda,* or "bliss." Researchers have not yet found how it is released or what physiological functions it performs.

enkephalin *(en **keff** a lin)*   One of the endogenous opioids.

naloxone *(na **lox** own)*   A drug that blocks opioid receptors.

anandamide *(a **nan** da mide)*   A lipid; the endogenous ligand for receptors that bind with THC, the active ingredient of marijuana.

Table 4.9
Some Important Peptides Found in the Central Nervous System

Cholecystokinin (CCK)
Corticotropin releasing factor (CRF)
Neuropeptide Y
Neuropeptide YY
Neurotensin
Oxytocin
Somatostatin
Substance P
Thyroid hormone releasing hormone (TRH)
Vasoactive intestinal peptide (VIP)
Vasopressin
Endogenous opioids
Dynorphin
β-Endorphin
Enkephalin

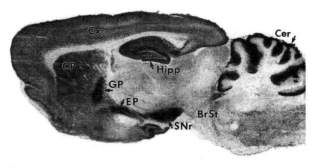

Figure 4.23
An autoradiogram of a sagittal section of a rat brain that has been incubated in a solution containing a radioactive ligand for THC receptors. The receptors are indicated by dark areas. (Autoradiography is described in Chapter 5.) (Br St = brain stem, Cer = cerebellum, CP = caudate nucleus/putamen, Cx = cortex, EP = entopeduncular nucleus, GP = globus pallidus, Hipp = hippocampus, SNr = substantia nigra.)
(Courtesy of Miles Herkenham, National Institute of Mental Health, Bethesda, MD.)

● Nucleosides

A nucleoside is a compound that consists of a sugar molecule bound with a purine or pyrimidine base. One of these compounds, **adenosine** (a combination of ribose and adenine), serves as a neuromodulator in the brain.

Adenosine is known to be released, apparently by glial cells as well as neurons, when cells are short of fuel or oxygen. The release of adenosine activates receptors on nearby blood vessels and causes them to dilate, increasing the flow of blood and helping bring more of the needed substances to the region. Adenosine also acts as a neuromodulator, through its action on at least three different types of adenosine receptors. Adenosine receptors are coupled to G proteins, and their effect is to open potassium channels, producing inhibitory postsynaptic potentials. Because adenosine is present in all cells, investigators have not yet succeeded in distinguishing neurons that release this chemical as a neuromodulator. Thus, circuits of adenosinergic neurons have not yet been identified.

Because adenosine receptors suppress neural activity, adenosine and other adenosine receptor agonists have generally inhibitory effects on behavior. In fact, as we will see in Chapter 9, some investigators believe that adenosine receptors may be involved in the control of sleep. A very common drug, **caffeine,** blocks adenosine receptors and

hence produces excitatory effects. Caffeine is a bitter-tasting alkaloid found in coffee, tea, cocoa beans, and other plants. In much of the world, a majority of the adult population ingests caffeine every day—without apparent harm. (See *Table 4.10.*)

Prolonged use of caffeine leads to a moderate amount of tolerance, and people who suddenly stop taking caffeine complain of withdrawal symptoms, which include headaches, drowsiness, and difficulty in concentrating. If the person continues to abstain, the symptoms disappear within a few days. Caffeine does not produce the compulsive drug-taking behavior often seen in people who abuse amphetamine, cocaine, or the opiates. In addition, laboratory animals do not readily self-administer caffeine, as they do drugs that are commonly abused by humans.

● Soluble Gases

Recently, investigators have discovered that neurons use at least two simple, soluble gases—nitric oxide and carbon monoxide—to communicate with one another. One of these, **nitric oxide (NO),** has received the most attention.

adenosine *(a **den** oh seen)* A nucleoside; a combination of ribose and adenine; serves as a neuromodulator in the brain.

caffeine A drug that blocks adenosine receptors.

nitric oxide (NO) A gas produced by cells in the nervous system; used as a means of communication between cells.

Table 4.10
Typical Caffeine Content of Chocolate and Several Beverages

Item	Caffeine content
Chocolates	
Baking chocolate	35 mg/oz
Milk chocolate	6 mg/oz
Beverages	
Coffee	85 mg/5-oz cup
Decaffeinated coffee	3 mg/5-oz cup
Tea (brewed 3 minutes)	28 mg/5-oz cup
Cocoa or hot chocolate	30 mg/5-oz cup
Cola drink	30-46 mg/12-oz container

Source: Based on data from Somani and Gupta, 1988.

Nitric oxide (not to be confused with nitrous oxide, or laughing gas) is a soluble gas that is produced by the activity of an enzyme found in certain neurons. Researchers have found that NO is used as a messenger in many parts of the body; for example, it is involved in the control of the muscles in the wall of the intestines, it dilates blood vessels in regions of the brain that become metabolically active, and it stimulates the changes in blood vessels that produce penile erections (Culotta and Koshland, 1992). As we will see in Chapter 14, it may also play a role in the establishment of neural changes that are produced by learning. And as we will see in Chapter 8, nitric oxide has also been implicated in the brain degeneration that accompanies Huntington's chorea, a hereditary disorder.

All of the neurotransmitters and neuromodulators discussed so far (with the exception of anandamide and, perhaps, adenosine) are stored in synaptic vesicles and released by terminal buttons. Nitric oxide is produced in several regions of a nerve cell—including dendrites—and is released as soon as it is produced. More accurately, it diffuses out of the cell as soon as it is produced. It does not activate membrane-bound receptors, but enters neighboring cells, where it activates an enzyme responsible for the production of a second messenger, cyclic GMP. Within a few seconds of being produced, nitric oxide is converted into biologically inactive compounds.

Nitric oxide is produced from arginine, an amino acid, by the activation of an enzyme known as **nitric oxide synthase.** This enzyme can be blocked by a drug called L-NAME (nitro-L-arginine methyl ester).

Interim Summary

The nervous system contains a variety of transmitter substances, each of which interacts with a specialized receptor. Those that have received the most study are acetylcholine and the monoamines: dopamine, norepinephrine, and 5-hydroxytryptamine (serotonin). The synthesis of these transmitter substances is controlled by a series of enzymes. Several amino acids also serve as transmitter substances, the most important of which are glutamate (glutamic acid), GABA, and glycine. Glutamate serves as an excitatory transmitter substance; the others serve as inhibitory transmitter substances.

Peptide transmitter substances consist of chains of amino acids. Like proteins, peptides are synthesized at the ribosomes according to sequences coded for by the chromosomes. The best known class of peptides in the nervous system includes the endogenous opioids, whose effects are mimicked by drugs such as opium and heroin. One lipid appears to serve as a chemical messenger: anandamide, the endogenous ligand for the THC (marijuana) receptor. Adenosine, a nucleoside that has inhibitory effects on synaptic transmission, is released by neurons and glial cells in the brain. In addition, two soluble gases—nitric oxide and carbon monoxide—can diffuse out of the cell in which they are produced and trigger the production of a second messenger in adjacent cells.

nitric oxide synthase   The enzyme responsible for the production of nitric oxide.

SUGGESTED READINGS

Cooper, J. R., Bloom, F. E., and Roth, R. H. *The Biochemical Basis of Neuropharmacology,* 7th ed. New York: Oxford University Press, 1996.

Feldman, R. S., Meyer, J. S., and Quenzer, L. F. *Principles of Neuropsychopharmacology.* Sunderland, MA: Sinauer Associates, 1997.

Grilly, D. M. *Drugs and Human Behavior.* Boston: Allyn and Bacon, 1994.

CHAPTER 5

Methods and Strategies of Research

Enigma by Wilfredo Chiesa. Courtesy of the artist.

S tudy of the physiology of behavior involves the efforts of scientists in many disciplines, including physiology, neuroanatomy, biochemistry, psychology, endocrinology, and histology. Pursuing a research project in physiological psychology requires competence in many experimental techniques. Because different procedures often produce contradictory results, investigators must be familiar with the advantages and limitations of the methods they employ. Scientific investigation entails a process of asking questions of nature. The method that is used frames the question. Often we receive a puzzling answer, only to realize later that we were not asking the question we thought we were. As we will see, the best conclusions about the physiology of behavior are made not by any single experiment, but by a program of research that enables us to compare the results of studies that approach the problem with different methods.

An enormous—and bewildering—array of research methods is available to the investigator. If I merely presented a catalog of them, it would not be surprising if you got lost—or simply lost interest. Instead, I will present only the most important and commonly used procedures, organized around a few problems that researchers have studied. This way, it should be easier to see the types of information provided by various research methods and to understand their advantages and disadvantages. It will also permit me to describe the strategies that researchers employ as they follow up the results of one experiment by designing and executing another one.

EXPERIMENTAL ABLATION

One of the most important research methods used to investigate brain functions involves destroying part of the brain and evaluating the animal's subsequent behavior. This method is called **experimental ablation** (from the Latin word *ablatus*, a "carrying away"). In most cases experimental ablation does not involve the removal brain tissue; instead, the researcher destroys some tissue and leaves it in place. Experimental ablation is the oldest method used in neuroscience, and it remains one of the most important ones today.

● Evaluating the Behavioral Effects of Brain Damage

A *lesion* literally refers to a wound or injury, and a researcher who destroys part of the brain usually refers to the damage as a *brain lesion*. Experiments in which part of the brain is damaged and the animal's behavior is subsequently observed are called **lesion studies.** The rationale for lesion studies is that the function of an area of the brain

experimental ablation   The removal or destruction of a portion of the brain of a laboratory animal; presumably, the functions that can no longer be performed are the ones the region previously controlled.
lesion study   A synonym for experimental ablation.

can be inferred from the behaviors that the animal can no longer perform after the area is damaged. For example, if, after part of the brain is destroyed, an animal can no longer perform tasks that require vision, we can conclude that the animal is blind—and that the damaged area plays some role in vision.

We must be very careful in interpreting the effects of brain lesions. For example, how do we ascertain that the lesioned animal is blind? Does it bump into objects, or fail to run through a maze toward a light that signals the location of food, or no longer constrict its pupils to light? An animal could bump into objects because of deficits in motor coordination, it could have lost its appetite for food (and thus its motivation to run through the maze), or it could see quite well but could have lost its visual reflexes. Researchers can often be fooled. Years ago they thought that the albino rat was blind. (It isn't.) Think about it: How would you test whether a rat can see? Remember that rats have vibrissae (whiskers) that can be used to detect a wall before bumping into it or the edge of a table before walking off it. They can also find their way around a room by following odor trails.

Just what can we learn from lesion studies? Our goal is to discover what functions are performed by different regions of the brain and then to understand how these functions are combined to accomplish particular behaviors. The distinction between *brain function* and *behavior* is an important one. Circuits within the brain perform functions, not behaviors. No one brain region or neural circuit is solely responsible for a behavior; each region performs a function (or set of functions) that contributes to performance of the behavior. For example, the act of reading involves functions required for controlling eye movements, focusing the lens of the eye, perceiving and recognizing words and letters, comprehending the meaning of the words, and so on. Some of these functions also participate in other behaviors; for example, controlling eye movement and focusing is required for any task that involves looking, and brain mechanisms used for comprehending the meanings of words also participate in comprehending speech. The task of the researcher is to understand the functions that are required for performing a particular behavior and to determine what circuits of neurons in the brain are responsible for each of these functions.

Let me give an example of how researchers try to deduce the nature of the functions performed by various parts of the brain. Neural circuits located in the cortex covering the parietal lobe perform functions involved in spatial perception and memory. Damage there disrupts people's ability to follow or draw maps, to remember the locations of objects that they have just seen, and so on. In addition, peo-ple with parietal lobe damage often have difficulty performing arithmetic calculations. At first glance, there would not seem to be a relation between this deficit and the spatial functions of the parietal lobe, but in fact they are almost certainly related. To prove this to yourself, try to multiply 55 by 12 without using pencil and paper. Close your eyes and work on the problem for a while. Try to analyze how you did it.

Most people report that they try to imagine the numbers arranged one above the other as they would be if paper and pencil were being used. In other words, they "write" the problem out mentally. Apparently, damage to the parietal lobes makes it difficult for people to put each of the numbers in a particular location in an imaginary "space" and remember what they were.

The interpretation of lesion studies is complicated by the fact that all regions of the brain are interconnected. Suppose that we have a good understanding of the functions required for performance of a particular behavior. We find that damage to brain structure X impairs a particular function. Can we necessarily conclude that the function is performed by circuits of neurons located in structure X? Unfortunately, we cannot. The function we are interested in may actually be performed by neural circuits in another part of the brain.

Let me cite a particular example that illustrates this complication. Damage to one part of the brain (the septum) completely disrupts the maternal behavior of a female rodent. The animal does not build a nest for her offspring, and she does not gather them together all in one place and nurse them. The result is that the pups end up scattered all over the cage, where they eventually starve unless the experimenter rescues them by giving them to a foster mother. What function does the septum perform that is so vital to normal maternal behavior? It happens that a connection between the septum and the hippocampal formation controls the activity of the latter structure—it turns some of the functions of the hippocampus on or off. Among these functions are some that are required for animals to perceive their location in space. When the septum is damaged, these functions are permanently turned off. Thus, the absence of nest-building and pup-gathering is almost certainly caused by disruption of the mother's spatial perception. The septum itself is not directly involved in spatial perception, but through its control of neural circuits located in the hippocampus, its damage disrupts maternal behavior.

● Producing Brain Lesions

How do we produce brain lesions? It is easy to destroy parts of the brain immediately beneath the skull; we anes-

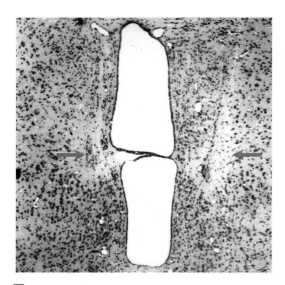

Figure 5.1
Radio frequency lesion. The arrows point to very small lesions produced by passing radio frequency current through the tips of stainless steel electrodes placed in the medial preoptic nucleus of a rat brain. (Frontal section, cell-body stain.)
(From Turkenburg, J. L., Swaab, D. F., Endert, E., Louwerse, A. L., and van de Poll, N. E. *Brain Research Bulletin,* 1988, *21,* 215–224.)

thetize the animal, cut its scalp, remove part of its skull, and cut through the dura mater, bringing the cortex into view. Then we can use a suction device to aspirate the brain tissue. To accomplish this tissue removal, we place a glass pipette on the surface of the brain and suck away brain tissue with a vacuum pump attached to the pipette.

More often, we want to destroy regions that are hidden away in the depths of the brain. Brain lesions of subcortical regions (regions located beneath the cortex) are usually produced by passing electrical current through a stainless steel wire that is coated with an insulating varnish except for the very tip. We guide the wire stereotaxically, so that its end reaches the appropriate location. (Stereotaxic surgery is described in the next subsection.) Then we turn on a lesion-making device, which produces radio frequency (RF) current—alternating current of a very high frequency. The passage of the current through the brain tissue produces heat that kills cells in the region surrounding the tip of the electrode. (See *Figure 5.1.*)

Lesions produced by these means destroy everything in the vicinity of the electrode tip, including neural cell bodies and the axons of neurons that pass through the region. A more selective method of producing brain lesions employs an excitatory amino acid such as *kainic acid,* which

kills neurons by stimulating them to death. (As we saw in Chapter 3, kainic acid stimulates glutamate receptors.) Lesions produced this way are referred to as **excitotoxic lesions.** When an excitatory amino acid is injected through a cannula into a region of the brain, the chemical destroys neural cell bodies in the vicinity but spares axons that belong to different neurons that happen to pass nearby. (See *Figure 5.2.*) This selectivity permits the investigator to determine whether the behavioral effects of destroying a particular brain structure are caused by the death of neurons located there or by the destruction of axons that pass nearby. For example, some researchers discovered that RF lesions of a particular region in the brain stem abolished REM sleep; thus, they believed that this region was involved in the production of this stage of sleep. (REM sleep

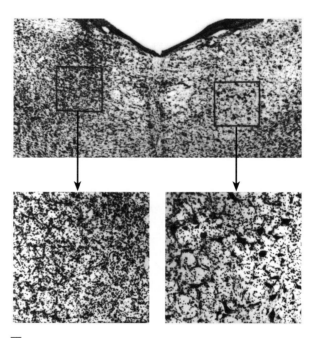

Figure 5.2
Excitotoxic lesion. An excitatory amino acid was injected into one side of the pontine reticular formation of a cat brain. (a) Frontal section. The two photographs in parts (b) and (c) show the brain tissue in more detail (indicated by black squares here). (b) Damaged tissue. Only glial cells can be seen. (c) Normal tissue. Large neurons and small glial cells can be seen.
(From Suzuki, S. S., Siegel, J. M., and Wu, M.-F. *Brain Research,* 1989, *484,* 78–93.)

excitotoxic lesion *(ek sigh tow **tok** sik)* A brain lesion produced by intracerebral injection of an excitatory amino acid, such as kainic acid.

is the stage of sleep during which dreaming occurs.) But later studies showed that when kainic acid was used to destroy the neurons located there, the animals' sleep was *not* affected. Thus, the RF lesions must have altered sleep by destroying the axons that pass through the area.

Even more specific methods of lesion production are available. For example, the drug **6-hydroxydopamine** (6-HD) resembles the catecholamines norepinephrine and dopamine. Because of this resemblance, 6-HD is taken up by transporter molecules in axons and terminal buttons of dopaminergic and noradrenergic neurons. Once inside, the chemical poisons and kills the neurons. Thus, 6-HD can be injected directly into particular regions of the brain to kill specific populations of dopaminergic and noradrenergic neurons.

Note that when we produce subcortical lesions by passing RF current through an electrode or infusing a chemical through a cannula, we always cause additional damage to the brain. When we pass an electrode or a cannula through the brain to get to our target, we inevitably cause a small amount of damage even before turning on the lesion maker or starting the infusion. Thus, we cannot simply compare the behavior of brain-lesioned animals with that of unoperated control animals; the incidental damage to the brain regions above the lesion may actually be responsible for some of the behavioral deficits we see. What we do is operate on a group of animals and produce **sham lesions.** To do so, we anesthetize each animal, put it in the stereotaxic apparatus, cut open the scalp, drill the holes, insert the electrode or cannula, and lower it to the proper depth. In other words, we do everything we would do to produce the lesion except turn on the lesion maker or start the infusion. This group of animals serves as a control group; if the behavior of the animals with brain lesions is different from that of the sham-operated control animals, we can conclude that the lesions caused the behavioral deficits. (As you can see, a sham lesion serves the same purpose as a placebo does in a pharmacology study.)

Most of the time, investigators produce permanent brain lesions, but sometimes it is advantageous to disrupt the activity of a particular region of the brain temporarily. The easiest way to do so is to inject a local anesthetic into the appropriate part of the brain. The anesthetic blocks action potentials in axons entering or leaving that region, thus effectively producing a temporary lesion (usually called a *reversible* brain lesion). Reversible lesions can also be produced by cooling brain tissue enough to suppress neural activity. Figure 5.3 shows a device called a *cryode,* which can be used to produce temporary lesions of a region of the cerebral cortex of the monkey brain. The device consists of a series of stainless steel tubes through which a

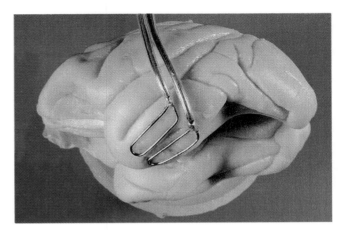

Figure 5.3
A cryode, a device that produces temporary lesions of the cerebral cortex. The device is surgically implanted between the skull and the brain, and the temporary lesion can be produced while the animal is awake and alert. A chilled liquid is circulated through the stainless steel tubes. The cryode shown in the photograph was placed against a region of the visual association cortex of the left hemisphere of a monkey brain.
(Courtesy of James Horel, SUNY Upstate Medical Center.)

chilled liquid can be circulated. It is implanted between the skull and the surface of the brain. (See *Figure 5.3.*)

● Stereotaxic Surgery

So how do we get the tip of an electrode or cannula to a precise location in the depths of an animal's brain? The answer is **stereotaxic surgery.** *Stereotaxis* literally means "solid arrangement"; more specifically, it refers to the ability to locate objects in space. A *stereotaxic apparatus* contains a holder that fixes the animal's head in a standard position and a carrier that moves an electrode or a cannula through measured distances in all three axes of space. However, to perform stereotaxic surgery, one must first study a *stereotaxic atlas.*

6-hydroxydopamine (6-HD) A chemical that is selectively taken up by axons and terminal buttons of noradrenergic or dopaminergic neurons and acts as a poison, damaging or killing them.

sham lesion A "placebo" procedure that duplicates all the steps of producing a brain lesion except for the one that actually causes the brain damage.

stereotaxic surgery *(stair ee oh **tak** sik)* Brain surgery using a stereotaxic apparatus to position an electrode or cannula in a specified position of the brain.

The Stereotaxic Atlas

No two brains of animals of a given species are completely identical, but there is enough similarity among individuals to predict the location of particular brain structures relative to external features of the head. For instance, a subcortical nucleus of a rat might be so many millimeters ventral, anterior, and lateral to a point formed by the junction of several bones of the skull. Figure 5.4 shows two views of a rat skull: a drawing of the dorsal surface and, beneath it, a midsagittal view. (See *Figure 5.4.*) The skull is composed of several bones that grow together and form *sutures* (seams). The heads of newborn babies contain a soft spot at the junction of the coronal and sagittal sutures called the *fontanelle*. Once this gap closes, the junction is called **bregma,** from the Greek word meaning "front of head." We can find bregma on a rat's skull, too, and it serves as a convenient reference point. If the animal's skull is oriented as shown in the illustration, a particular region of the brain is found in a fairly constant position, relative to bregma.

A **stereotaxic atlas** contains photographs or drawings that correspond to frontal sections taken at various distances rostral and caudal to bregma. For example, the page shown in Figure 5.5 is a drawing of a slice of the

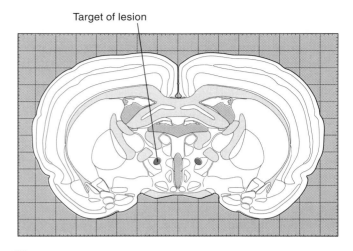

Target of lesion

Figure 5.5
A sample page from a stereotaxic atlas of the rat brain. The target (the fornix) is indicated in red. Labels have been removed for the sake of clarity.
(Adapted from Swanson, L. W. *Brain Maps: Structure of the Rat Brain.* New York: Elsevier, 1992.)

brain that contains a brain structure (shown in red) that we are interested in. If we wanted to place the tip of a wire in this structure (the fornix), we would have to drill a hole through the skull immediately above it. (See *Figure 5.5.*) Each page of the stereotaxic atlas is labeled according to the distance of the section anterior or posterior to bregma. The grid on each page indicates distances of brain structures ventral to the top of the skull and lateral to the midline. To place the tip of a wire in the fornix, we would drill a hole above the target and then lower the electrode through the hole until the tip was at the correct depth, relative to the skull height at bregma. (See *Figures 5.4* and *5.5.*) Thus, by finding a neural structure (which we cannot see in our animal) on one of the pages of a stereotaxic atlas, we can determine the structure's location relative to bregma (which we can see). Note that, because of variations in different strains and ages of animals, the atlas gives only an approximate location. We always have to try out a new set of coordinates, slice and stain the animal's brain, see the actual location of the lesion, correct the numbers, and try again. (Slicing and staining of brains is described later.)

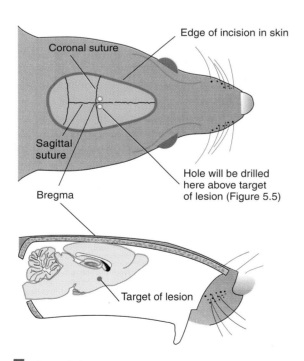

Edge of incision in skin
Coronal suture
Sagittal suture
Bregma
Hole will be drilled here above target of lesion (Figure 5.5)
Target of lesion

Figure 5.4
Relation of the skull sutures to a rat's brain, and the location of a target for an electrode placement. Top: *Dorsal view.* Bottom: *Midsagittal view.*

bregma   The junction of the sagittal and coronal sutures of the skull; often used as a reference point for stereotaxic brain surgery.

stereotaxic atlas   A collection of drawings of sections of the brain of a particular animal with measurements that provide coordinates for stereotaxic surgery.

The Stereotaxic Apparatus

A **stereotaxic apparatus** operates on simple principles. The device includes a head holder, which maintains the animal's skull in the proper orientation, a holder for the electrode, and a calibrated mechanism that moves the electrode holder in measured distances along the three axes: anterior-posterior, dorsal-ventral, and lateral-medial. Figure 5.6 illustrates a stereotaxic apparatus designed for small animals; various head holders can be used to outfit this device for such diverse species as rats, mice, hamsters, pigeons, and turtles. (See *Figure 5.6.*)

Once we obtain the coordinates from a stereotaxic atlas, we anesthetize the animal, place it in the apparatus, and cut the scalp open. We locate bregma, dial in the appropriate numbers on the stereotaxic apparatus, drill a hole through the skull, and lower the device into the brain by the correct amount. Now the tip of the cannula or electrode is where we want it to be, and we are ready to produce the lesion.

Of course, stereotaxic surgery may be used for purposes other than lesion production. Wires placed in the brain may be used to stimulate neurons as well as destroy them, and drugs can be injected that stimulate neurons or block specific receptors. We can attach cannulas or wires permanently by following a procedure that will be described later in this chapter. In all cases, once surgery is complete, the wound is sewed together, and the animal is taken out of the stereotaxic apparatus and allowed to recover from the anesthetic.

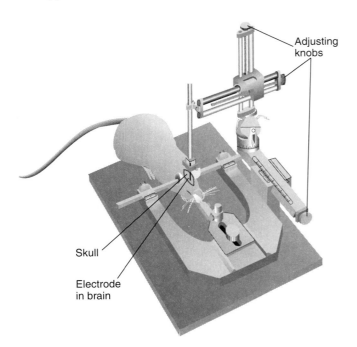

Adjusting
knobs

Skull

Electrode
in brain

Figure 5.6
A stereotaxic apparatus for performing brain surgery on rats.

Stereotaxic apparatuses are made for humans, by the way. Sometimes a neurosurgeon produces subcortical lesions—for example, to reduce severe tremors caused by Parkinson's disease. Usually, the surgeon uses multiple landmarks and verifies the location of the wire (or other device) inserted into the brain by taking MRI scans before producing a brain lesion.

● Histological Methods

After producing a brain lesion and observing its effects on an animal's behavior, we must slice and stain the brain so that we can observe it under the microscope and see the location of the lesion. Brain lesions often miss the mark, so we have to verify the precise location of the brain damage after testing the animal behaviorally. To do so, we must fix, slice, stain, and examine the brain. Together, these procedures are referred to as *histological methods*. (The prefix *histo-* refers to body tissue.)

Fixation and Sectioning

If we hope to study the tissue in the form it had at the time of the organism's death, we must destroy the autolytic enzymes (*autolytic* means "self-dissolving"), which will otherwise turn the tissue into shapeless mush. The tissue must also be preserved to prevent its decomposition by bacteria or molds. To achieve both of these objectives, we place the neural tissue in a **fixative.** The most commonly used fixative is **formalin,** an aqueous solution of formaldehyde, a gas. Formalin halts autolysis, hardens the very soft and fragile brain, and kills any microorganisms that might destroy it.

Before the brain is fixed (that is, put into a fixative solution), it is usually perfused. **Perfusion** of tissue (literally, "a pouring through") entails removal of the blood and its replacement with another fluid. The animal's brain is perfused because better histological results are obtained when there is no blood present in the tissue. The animal whose brain is to be studied is humanely killed with an overdose of a general anesthetic. Blood vessels are opened so that the blood can be drained from them and replaced with a

stereotaxic apparatus   A device that permits a surgeon to position an electrode or cannula into a specific part of the brain.

fixative   A chemical such as formalin; used to prepare and preserve body tissue.

formalin (*for* ma *lin*)   The aqueous solution of formaldehyde gas; the most commonly used tissue fixative.

perfusion (per *few* zhun)   The process by which an animal's blood is replaced by a fluid such as a saline solution or a fixative in preparing the brain for histological examination.

dilute salt solution. The brain is removed from the skull and placed in a jar containing the fixative.

Once the brain has been fixed, we must slice it into thin sections and stain various cellular structures in order to see anatomical details. Slicing is done with a **microtome** (literally, "that which slices small"). Slices prepared for examination under a light microscope are typically 10 to 80 µm in thickness; those prepared for the electron microscope are generally cut at less than 1 µm. (For some reason, slices of brain tissue are usually referred to as *sections*.)

A microtome contains three parts: a knife, a platform on which to mount the tissue, and a mechanism that advances the knife (or the platform) the correct amount after each slice, so that another section can be cut. In most cases, the platform includes an attachment that freezes the brain to make it hard enough to be cut into thin sections. Figure 5.7 shows a microtome. The knife holder slides forward on an oiled rail and takes a section off the top of the tissue mounted on the platform. The platform automatically rises by a predetermined amount as the knife and holder are pushed back, so that the next forward movement of the knife takes off another section. (See *Figure 5.7.*)

After the tissue is cut, we attach the slices to glass microscope slides. We can then stain the tissue by putting the entire slide into various chemical solutions. Finally, we cover the stained sections with a small amount of a transparent liquid known as a *mounting medium* and place a very thin glass coverslip over the sections. The mounting medium keeps the coverslip in position.

Staining

If you looked at an unstained section of brain tissue under a microscope, you would be able to see the outlines of

Figure 5.7
A microtome.

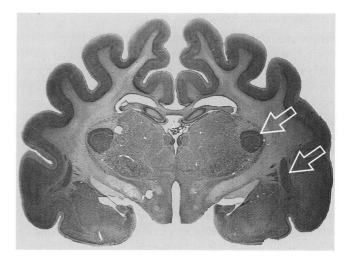

Figure 5.8
A frontal section of a cat brain, stained with cresyl violet, a cell-body stain. The arrowheads point to nuclei, or groups of cell bodies. (Histological material courtesy of Mary Carlson.)

some large cellular masses and the more prominent fiber bundles. However, no fine details would be revealed. For this reason, the study of microscopic neuroanatomy requires special histological stains. Researchers have developed many different stains to identify specific substances within and outside of cells. For verifying the location of a brain lesion, we will use one of the simplest: a cell-body stain.

In the late nineteenth century Franz Nissl, a German neurologist, discovered that a dye known as methylene blue would stain the cell bodies of brain tissue. The material that takes up the dye, known as the *Nissl substance*, consists of RNA, DNA, and associated proteins located in the nucleus and scattered, in the form of granules, in the cytoplasm. Many dyes besides methylene blue can be used to stain cell bodies found in slices of the brain, but the most frequently used is cresyl violet. Incidentally, the dyes were not developed specifically for histological purposes but were originally formulated for use in dyeing cloth.

The discovery of cell-body stains made it possible to identify nuclear masses in the brain. Figure 5.8 shows a frontal section of a cat brain stained with cresyl violet. Note that you can observe fiber bundles by their lighter appearance; they do not take up the stain. (See *Figure 5.8.*) The stain is not selective for *neural* cell bodies; all

microtome (*my* krow tome)   An instrument that produces very thin slices of body tissues.

cells are stained, neurons and glia alike. It is up to the investigator to determine which is which—by size, shape, and location.

Electron Microscopy

The light microscope is limited in its ability to resolve extremely small details. Because of the nature of light itself, magnification of more than approximately 1500 times does not add any detail. To see such small anatomical structures as synaptic vesicles and details of cell organelles, investigators must use an electron microscope. A beam of electrons is passed through the tissue to be examined. A shadow of the tissue is then cast on a sheet of photographic film, which is exposed by the electrons. Electron photomicrographs produced in this way can provide information about structural details on the order of a few ångström units. (See *Figure 5.9.*)

A **scanning electron microscope** provides less magnification than a standard transmission electron microscope, which transmits the electron beam through the tissue. However, it shows objects in three dimensions. The microscope scans the tissue with a moving beam of electrons. The information received from the reflection of the beam is used to produce a remarkably detailed three-dimensional view. (See *Figure 5.10.*)

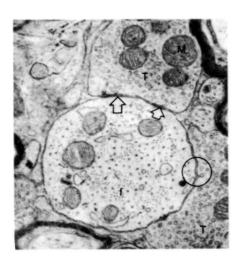

Figure 5.9
An electron photomicrograph of a section through an axodendritic synapse. Two synaptic regions are indicated by arrows, and a circle points out a region of pinocytosis in an adjacent terminal button, presumably representing recycling of vesicular membrane. T = terminal button; f = microfilaments; M = mitochondrion.
(From Rockel, A. J., and Jones, E. G. *Journal of Comparative Neurology,* 1973, *147,* 61–92.)

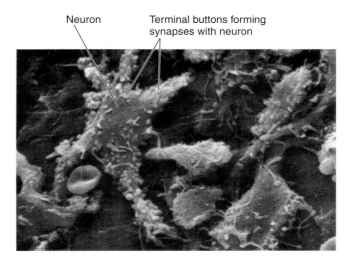

Neuron Terminal buttons forming synapses with neuron

Figure 5.10
A scanning-electron micrograph of neurons and glia.
(From Kessel, R. G., and Kardon, R. H. *Tissues and Organs: A Text-Atlas of Scanning Electron Microscopy.* San Francisco: W. H. Freeman, 1979. By permission.)

● Tracing Neural Connections

Let's suppose that we were interested in discovering the neural mechanisms responsible for reproductive behavior. To start out, we wanted to study the physiology of sexual behavior of female rats. Based on some hints we received by reading reports of experiments by other researchers published in scientific journals, we performed stereotaxic surgery on two groups of female rats. We made a lesion in the ventromedial nucleus of the hypothalamus (VMH) of the rats in the experimental group, and performed sham surgery on the rats in the control group. After a few day's recovery, we placed the animals (individually, of course) with male rats. The females in the control group responded positively to the males' attention; they engaged in courting behavior followed by copulation. However, the females with the VMH lesions rejected the males' attention and refused to copulate with them. We confirmed with histology that the VMH was, indeed, destroyed in the brains of the experimental animals. (One rat did copulate, but we found that we had missed the VMH in that animal, so we discarded the data from that subject.)

The results of our experiment indicate that neurons in the VMH appear to play a role in functions required for

scanning electron microscope A microscope that provides three-dimensional information about the shape of the surface of a small object.

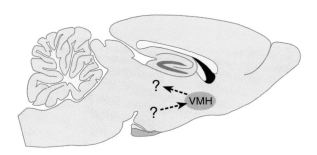

Figure 5.11
Once we know that a particular brain region is involved in a particular function, we may ask what structures provide inputs to the region and what structures receive outputs from it.

copulatory behavior in females. (By the way, it turns out that these lesions do not affect copulatory behavior in males.) So where do we go from here? What is the next step? In fact, there are many questions that we could pursue. One question concerns the system of brain structures that participate in female copulatory behavior. Certainly, the VMH does not stand alone; it receives inputs from other structures and sends outputs to still others. Copulation requires integration of visual, tactile, and olfactory perceptions and organization of patterns of movements in response to those of the partner. In addition, the entire network requires activation by the appropriate sex hormones. What is the precise role of the VMH in this complicated system?

Before we can hope to answer this question, we must know more about the connections of the VMH with the rest of the brain. What structures send their axons to the VMH, and to what structures does the VMH, in turn, send its axons? Once we know what the connections are, we can investigate the role of these structures and the nature of their interactions. (See *Figure 5.11*.)

How do we investigate the connections of the VMH? The question cannot be answered by means of histological procedures that stain all neurons, such as cell-body stains. If we look closely at a brain that has been prepared by these means, we see only a tangled mass of neurons. But in recent years, researchers have developed very precise methods that make specific neurons stand out from all of the others.

Tracing Efferent Axons

Eventually, the VMH must affect behavior. That is, neurons in the VMH must send axons to parts of the brain that contain neurons that are responsible for muscular movements. The pathway is probably not direct; more likely, neurons in the VMH affect neurons in other structures, which influence those in yet other structures, until, eventually, the appropriate motor neurons are stimulated. To discover this system, we want to be able to identify the paths followed by axons leaving the VMH. In other words, we want to trace the *efferent axons* of this structure.

We will use an **anterograde labeling method** to trace these axons. (*Anterograde* means "moving forward.") Anterograde labeling methods employ chemicals that are taken up by dendrites or cell bodies and are then transported through the axons toward the terminal buttons.

Over the years, neuroscientists have developed several different methods for tracing the pathways followed by efferent axons. A recently developed method is replacing earlier ones, so this is what we will use. Cell biologists have discovered that a family of proteins produced by plants bind with specific complex molecules present in cells of the immune system. These proteins, called *lectins*, have also found a use in tracing neural pathways. A particular lectin produced by the kidney bean, **PHA-L** (*phaseolus vulgaris leukoagglutinin*, if you really want to know), is used to identify efferent axons.

To discover the destination of the efferent axons of neurons located within the VMH, we inject a minute quantity of PHA-L into that nucleus. (We use a stereotaxic apparatus to do so, of course.) The molecules of PHA-L are taken up by dendrites and are transported through the soma to the axon, where they travel by means of fast axoplasmic transport to the terminal buttons. Within a few days, the cells are filled in their entirety with molecules of PHA-L: dendrites, soma, axons and all their branches, and terminal buttons. Then, we kill the animal, slice the brain, and mount the sections on microscope slides. A special *immunocytochemical* method is used to make the molecules of PHA-L visible, and the slides are examined under a microscope. (See *Figure 5.12*.)

Immunocytochemical methods take advantage of the immune reaction. The body's immune system has the ability to produce antibodies in response to antigens. *Antigens* are proteins (or peptides), such as those found on the sur-

anterograde labeling method *(ann ter oh grade)* A histological method that labels the axons and terminal buttons of neurons whose cell bodies are located in a particular region.

PHA-L Phaseolus vulgaris leukoagglutinin; a protein derived from lima beans used as an anterograde tracer; taken up by dendrites and cell bodies and carried to the ends of the axons.

immunocytochemical method A histological method that uses radioactive antibodies or antibodies bound with a dye molecule to indicate the presence of particular proteins of peptides.

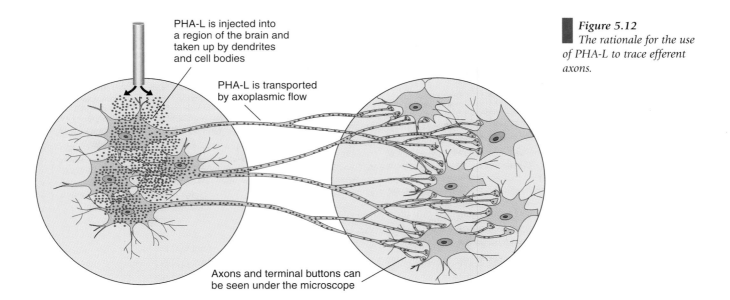

PHA-L is injected into
a region of the brain and
taken up by dendrites
and cell bodies

PHA-L is transported
by axoplasmic flow

Axons and terminal buttons can
be seen under the microscope

Figure 5.12
*The rationale for the use
of PHA-L to trace efferent
axons.*

face of bacteria or viruses. *Antibodies,* which are also proteins, are produced by white blood cells to destroy invading
microorganisms. Antibodies are either secreted by white
blood cells or they are located on their surface, in the way
neurotransmitter receptors are located on the surface of
neurons. When the antigens present on the surface of an
invading microorganism come into contact with the antibodies that recognize them, the antibodies trigger an attack on the invader by the white blood cells.

Cell biologists have developed methods for producing
antibodies to any peptide or protein. The antibody molecules are attached to various types of dye molecules. Some
of these dyes react with other chemicals and stain the tissue
a brown color. Others are fluorescent; they glow when they
are exposed to light of a particular wavelength. To determine where the peptide or protein (the antigen) is located
in the brain, the investigator places fresh slices of brain tissue in a solution that contains the antibody/dye molecules.
The antibodies attach themselves to their antigen. When
the investigator examines the slices with a microscope (under light of a particular wavelength in the case of fluorescent dyes), he or she can see which parts of the brain—even
which individual neurons—contain the antigen.

Figure 5.13 shows how PHA-L can be used to identify
the efferents of a particular region of the brain. Molecules
of this chemical were injected into the VMH. Two days
later, after the PHA-L had been taken up by the neurons
in this region and transported to the ends of their axons,
the animal was killed. Slices of the brain were treated with
an antibody to PHA-L, attached to a dye that stains the tissue a brown color. Figure 5.13(a) shows the site of the in-

jection; as you can see, the lectin fills nearby cell bodies
and dendrites. (See *Figure 5.13a*.) Figure 5.13(b) shows a
photomicrograph of the periaqueductal gray matter
(PAG). As you can see, this region contains some labeled
axons and terminal buttons, which proves that some of
the efferent axons of the VMH terminate in the PAG. (See
Figure 5.13b.)

To continue our study of the role of the VMH in female
sexual behavior, we would find the structures that receive
information from neurons in the VMH (such as the PAG)
and see what happens when each of them is destroyed.
Let's suppose that damage to some of these structures also
impairs female sexual behavior. We will inject these structures with PHA-L and see where *their* axons go. Eventually,
we will discover the relevant pathways from the VMH to
the motor neurons whose activity is necessary for copulatory behavior. (In fact, researchers have done so, and some
of their results are presented in Chapter 10.)

Tracing Afferent Axons

Tracing efferent axons from the VMH will tell us only part
of the story about the neural circuitry involved in female
sexual behavior: the part between the VMH and the motor
neurons. What about the circuits *before* the VMH? Is the
VMH somehow involved in the analysis of sensory information (such as the sight, odor, or touch of the male)? Or
perhaps the activating effect of a female's sex hormones on
her behavior act through the VMH, or through neurons
whose axons form synapses there. To discover the parts of
the brain involved in the "upstream" components of the
neural circuitry, we need to find the inputs of the VMH—

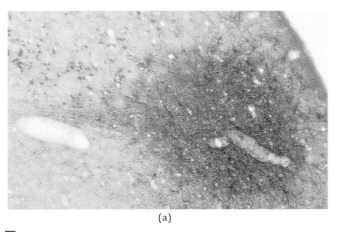

(a)

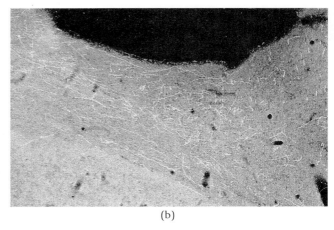

(b)

Figure 5.13
An anterograde labeling method. PHA-L was injected into the ventromedial nucleus of the hypothalamus (VMH), where it was taken up by dendrites and carried through the cells' axons to their terminal buttons. (a) The injection site. (b) Labeled axons and terminal buttons in the periaqueductal gray matter (PAG).
(Courtesy of Kirsten Nielsen Ricciardi and Jeffrey Blaustein, University of Massachusetts.)

its afferent connections. To do so, we will employ a **retrograde labeling method.**

Retrograde means "moving backward." Retrograde labeling methods employ chemicals that are taken up by terminal buttons and carried back through the axons toward the cell bodies. The method for identifying the afferent inputs to a particular region of the brain is similar to the method used for identifying its efferents. First, we will inject a small quantity of a chemical called **fluorogold** into the VMH. The chemical is taken up by terminal buttons and is transported back by means of retrograde axoplasmic transport to the cell bodies. A few days later we kill the animal, slice its brain, and examine the tissue under light of the appropriate wavelength. The molecules of fluorogold fluoresce under this light. We discover that the medial amygdala is one of the regions that provide input to the VMH. (See *Figure 5.14.*)

Together, anterograde and retrograde labeling methods enable us to discover the connections of a particular part of the brain (in this case, the VMH) with other parts of the brain. Thus, these methods help to provide us with a "wiring diagram" of the brain. (See *Figure 5.15.*) Armed with other research methods (including some to be described later in this chapter), we can try to discover the functions of each component of this circuit.

Figure 5.14
A retrograde tracing method. Fluorogold was injected in the VMH, where it was taken up by terminal buttons and transported back through the axons to their cell bodies. The photograph shows these cell bodies, located in the medial amygdala.
(Courtesy of Yvon Delville, University of Massachusetts Medical School.)

retrograde labeling method A histological method that labels cell bodies that give rise to the terminal buttons that form synapses with cells in a particular region.

fluorogold *(flew roh gold)* A dye that serves as a retrograde label; taken up by terminal buttons and carried back to the cell bodies.

● Study of the Living Human Brain

There are many good reasons to investigate the functions of brains of animals other than humans. For one thing, we can compare the results of studies made with different species in order to make some inferences about the evolution of various neural systems. Even if our primary interest is in the functions of the human brain, we certainly cannot ask people to submit to brain surgery for the purposes of research. But diseases and accidents do occasionally damage the human brain, and if we know where the damage occurs, we can study the people's behavior and try to make

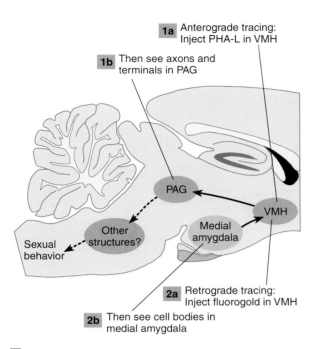

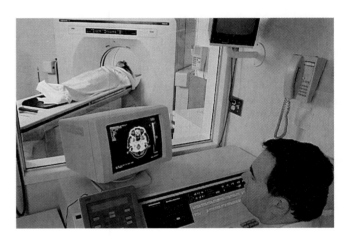

1a Anterograde tracing:
Inject PHA-L in VMH

1b Then see axons and
terminals in PAG

PAG

VMH

Other
structures?

Medial
amygdala

Sexual
behavior

2a Retrograde tracing:
Inject fluorogold in VMH

2b Then see cell bodies in
medial amygdala

Figure 5.15
One of the inputs to the VMH and one of the outputs, as revealed by anterograde and retrograde labeling methods.

the same sorts of inferences we make with deliberately produced brain lesions in laboratory animals. The problem is, where is the lesion?

In past years, a researcher might study the behavior of a person with brain damage and never find out exactly where the lesion was located. The only way to be sure was to obtain the patient's brain when he or she died and examine slices of it under a microscope. But it was often impossible to do so. Sometimes the patient outlived the researcher. Sometimes the patient moved out of town. Sometimes (often, perhaps) the family refused permission for an autopsy. Because of these practical problems, study of the behavioral effects of damage to specific parts of the human brain made rather slow progress.

Recent advances in X-ray techniques and computers have led to the development of several methods for studying the anatomy of the living brain. These advances permit researchers to study the location and extent of brain damage while the patient is still living. The first method to be developed is called **computerized tomography (CT)** (from the Greek for *tomos*, "cut"; *graphein*, "to write"). This procedure, usually referred to as a *CT scan*, works as follows: The patient's head is placed in a large doughnut-shaped ring. The ring contains an X-ray tube and, directly opposite it (on the other side of the patient's head), an X-ray detector. The X-ray beam passes through the patient's head, and

the detector measures the amount of radioactivity that gets through it. The beam scans the head from all angles, and a computer translates the numbers it receives from the detector into pictures of the skull and its contents. (See *Figure 5.16*.)

Figure 5.17 shows a series of these CT scans taken through the head of a patient who sustained a stroke. The stroke damaged a part of the brain involved in bodily awareness and perception of space. The patient lost her awareness of the left side of her body and of items located on her left. You can see the damage as a white spot in the lower left corner of scan 5. (See *Figure 5.17* on page 132.)

An even more detailed picture of what is inside a person's head is provided by a process called **magnetic resonance imaging (MRI).** The MRI scanner resembles a CT scanner, but it does not use X-rays. Instead, it passes an extremely strong magnetic field through the patient's head. When a person's body is placed in a strong magnetic field, the nuclei of some atoms in molecules in the body spin with a particular orientation. If a radio frequency wave is then passed through the body, these nuclei emit radio waves of their own. Different molecules emit energy at dif-

Figure 5.16
A computerized tomography (CT) scanner.
(Larry Mulvehill/Rainbow)

computerized tomography (CT) The use of a device that employs a computer to analyze data obtained by a scanning beam of X rays to produce a two-dimensional picture of a "slice" through the body.

magnetic resonance imaging (MRI) A technique whereby the interior of the body can be accurately imaged; involves the interaction between radio waves and a strong magnetic field.

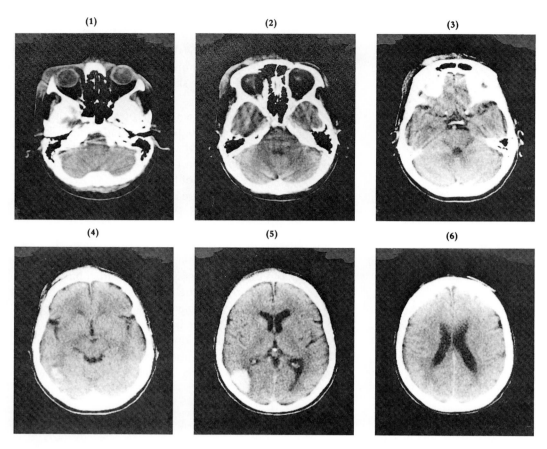

(1) **(2)** **(3)**

(4) **(5)** **(6)**

Figure 5.17
A series of CT scans from a patient with a lesion in the right occipital-parietal area (scan 5). The lesion appears white because it was accompanied by bleeding; blood absorbs more radiation than the surrounding brain tissue. Rostral is up, caudal is down; left and right are reversed. Scan 1 shows a section through the eyes and the base of the brain.
(Courtesy of J. McA. Jones, Good Samaritan Hospital, Portland, Oregon.)

ferent frequencies. The MRI scanner is tuned to detect the radiation from hydrogen molecules. Because these molecules are present in different concentrations in different tissues, the scanner can use the information to prepare pictures of slices of the brain. Unlike CT scans, which are generally limited to the horizontal plane, MRI scans can be taken in the sagittal or frontal planes, as well. (See *Figure 5.18*.)

Interim Summary

The goal of research in physiological psychology is to understand the brain functions required for the performance of a particular behavior and then to learn the location of the neural circuits that perform these functions. The lesion method is the oldest one employed in such research, and

it remains one of the most useful. A subcortical lesion is made under the guidance of a stereotaxic apparatus. The coordinates are obtained from a stereotaxic atlas, and the tip of an electrode or cannula is placed at the target. A lesion is made by passing RF current through the electrode or infusing an excitatory amino acid through the cannula, producing an excitotoxic lesion. The advantage of excitotoxic lesions is that they affect only neural cell bodies; axons passing through the region are not damaged.

The location of a lesion must be determined after the animal's behavior is observed. The animal is killed by humane means, the brain is perfused with a saline solution, and the brain is removed and placed in a fixative such as formalin. A microtome is used to slice the brain, which is usually frozen to make it hard enough to cut into thin sections. These sections are mounted on glass slides, stained with a cell-body stain, and examined under a microscope.

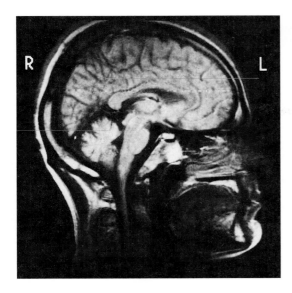

Figure 5.18
A midsagittal MRI scan of a human brain.
(Photo courtesy of Philips Medical Systems.)

The next step in a research program often requires the investigator to discover the afferent and efferent connections of the region of interest with the rest of the brain. Efferent connections (those that carry information from the region in question to other parts of the brain) are revealed with anterograde tracing methods, such as the one that uses PHA-L. Afferent connections (those that bring information to the region in question from other parts of the brain) are revealed with retrograde tracing methods, such as the one that uses fluorogold.

Although brain lesions are not deliberately made in the human brain for the purposes of research, diseases and accidents can cause brain damage, and if we know where the damage is located, we can study people's behavior and make inferences about the location of the neural circuits that perform relevant functions. If the patient dies and the brain is available for examination, ordinary histological methods can be used. Otherwise, the living brain can be examined with CT scanners and MRI scanners.

Table 5.1 summarizes the research methods presented in this section.

Light microscopes enable us to see cells and their larger organelles, but an electron microscope is needed to see small details, such as individual mitochondria and synaptic vesicles. Scanning electron microscopes provide a three-dimensional view of tissue, but at a lower magnification than transmission electron microscopes.

Table 5.1
Research Methods: Part I

Goal of method	Method	Remarks
Destroy or inactivate specific brain region	Radio frequency lesion	Destroys all brain tissue near tip of electrode
	Excitotoxic lesion	Destroys only cell bodies near tip of cannula; spares axons passing through region
	Infusion of local anesthetic	Temporarily inactivates specific brain region; animal can serve as its own control
Place electrode or cannula in specific region within brain	Stereotaxic surgery	Consult stereotaxic atlas for coordinates
Find location of lesion	Perfuse brain; fix brain; slice brain; stain sections	
Identify axons leaving a particular region and the terminal buttons of these axons	Anterograde tracing method, such as PHA-L	
Identify location of neurons whose axons terminate in a particular region	Retrograde tracing method, such as fluorogold	
Find location of lesion in living human brain	Computerized tomography (CT scanner)	Shows "slice" of brain
	Magnetic resonance imaging (MRI scanner)	Shows "slice" of brain; better detail than CT scan

RECORDING AND STIMULATING NEURAL ACTIVITY

The first section of this chapter dealt with the anatomy of the brain and the effects of damage to particular regions. This section considers a different approach: studying the brain by recording or stimulating the activity of particular regions. Brain functions involve activity of circuits of neurons; thus, different perceptions and behavioral responses involve different patterns of activity in the brain. Researchers have devised methods to record these patterns of activity or artificially produce them.

● Recording of Neural Activity

Axons produce action potentials, and terminal buttons elicit postsynaptic potentials in the membrane of the cells with which they form synapses. These electrical events can be recorded (as we saw in Chapter 2), and changes in the electrical activity of a particular region can be used to determine whether that region plays a role in various behaviors. For example, recordings can be made during stimulus presentations, decision making, or motor activities.

Recordings can be made *chronically*, over an extended period of time after the animal recovers from surgery, or *acutely*, for a relatively short period of time during which the animal is kept anesthetized. Acute recordings, made while the animal is anesthetized, are usually restricted to studies of sensory pathways. Acute recordings seldom involve behavioral observations, since the behavioral capacity of an anesthetized animal is limited, to say the least.

Recordings with Microelectrodes

Drugs that affect serotonergic and noradrenergic neurons also affect REM sleep. Suppose that, knowing this fact, we wondered whether the activity of serotonergic and noradrenergic neurons would vary during different stages of sleep. To find out, we would record the activity of these neurons with microelectrodes. **Microelectrodes** have a very fine tip, small enough to record the electrical activity of individual neurons. This technique is usually called **single-unit recording** (a unit refers to an individual neuron).

Microelectrodes can be constructed of fine glass tubes. As we saw in Chapter 2, these electrodes can be used to record action potentials in giant squid axons. Glass tubes have an interesting property. If they are heated until soft, and if the ends are pulled apart, the softened glass will stretch into a very fine filament. However, no matter how thin the filament becomes, it will still have a hole running through it. To construct glass microelectrodes, we heat the middle of a length of capillary tubing (glass with an out-

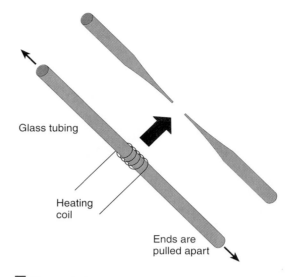

Figure 5.19
Microelectrodes produced by heating the center portion of a length of glass capillary tubing and pulling the ends apart.

side diameter of approximately 1 mm) and then sharply pull the ends apart. The glass tube is drawn out finer and finer, until the tube snaps apart. The result is two microelectrodes, as shown in *Figure 5.19*. (These devices are usually produced with the aid of a special machine, called a *microelectrode puller*.) Glass will not conduct electricity, so we fill the microelectrode with a conducting liquid, such as a solution of potassium chloride.

Because we want to record the activity of single neurons over a long period of time in unanesthetized animals, we want more durable electrodes. Thus, we will make them of fine tungsten wires. We sharpen these wires by etching them in an acid solution. We pass electrical current through a fine wire as we move it in and out of the solution. The tip erodes away, leaving a fine, sharp point. We then insulate the wire with a special varnish. The point is so sharp that it does not retain insulation and thus can record electrical signals.

We implant the electrodes in the brains of animals through stereotaxic surgery. We attach them to miniaturized electrical sockets and bond the sockets to the animals' skull, using plastics originally developed for the dental profession. Then, after recovery from surgery, the animal can be "plugged in" to the recording system. Laboratory animals pay no heed to the electrical sockets on their skulls and behave quite normally. (See *Figure 5.20.*)

microelectrode   A very fine electrode, generally used to record activity of individual neurons.

single-unit recording   Recording of the electrical activity of a single neuron.

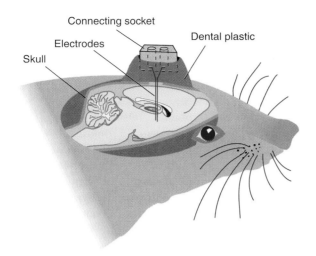

Figure 5.20
A permanently attached set of electrodes, with a connecting socket cemented to the skull.

Researchers often attach rather complex devices to the animals' skulls when they implant microelectrodes. These devices include screw mechanisms that permit the experimenter to move the electrode deeper into the brain, so that they can record from several different neurons during the course of their observations.

The electrical signals detected by microelectrodes are quite small and must be amplified. Amplifiers used for this purpose work just like the amplifiers in a stereo system, converting the weak signals recorded at the brain into stronger ones. These signals can be displayed on an oscilloscope and stored in the memory of a computer for analysis at a later time.

What about our results? As you will learn in Chapter 9, if we record the activity of noradrenergic and serotonergic neurons during various stages of sleep, we will find that the firing rate of these neurons falls almost to zero during REM sleep. This observation suggests that these neurons have an *inhibitory* effect on REM sleep. That is, REM sleep cannot occur until these neurons stop firing.

Recordings with Macroelectrodes

Sometimes, we want to record the activity of a region of the brain as a whole, not the activity of individual neurons located there. To do this we would use macroelectrodes. **Macroelectrodes** do not detect the activity of individual neurons; rather, the records obtained with these devices represent the postsynaptic potentials of many thousands— or millions—of cells in the area of the electrode. These electrodes can consist of unsharpened wires inserted into the brain, screws attached to the skull, or even metal disks attached to the human scalp with a special paste that conducts electricity. Recordings taken from the scalp, especially, represent the activity of an enormous number of neurons, whose electrical signals pass through the meninges, skull, and scalp before reaching the electrodes.

Occasionally, neurosurgeons implant macroelectrodes directly into the human brain. The reason for doing so is to detect the source of abnormal electrical activity that is giving rise to frequent seizures. Once the source is determined, the surgeon can open the skull and remove the source of the seizures—usually scar tissue caused by brain damage that occurred earlier in life. Most often, the electrical activity of a human brain is recorded through electrodes attached to the scalp and displayed on an *ink-writing oscillograph*, commonly called a *polygraph*.

A polygraph contains a mechanism that moves a very long strip of paper past a series of pens. These pens are essentially the pointers of large voltmeters, moving up and down in response to the electrical signal sent to them by the biological amplifiers. Figure 5.21 illustrates a record of electrical activity recorded from macroelectrodes attached to various locations on a person's scalp. (See *Figure 5.21.*)

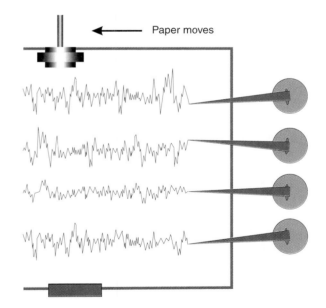

Figure 5.21
A record from an ink-writing oscillograph.

macroelectrode   An electrode used to record the electrical activity of large numbers of neurons in a particular region of the brain; much larger than a microelectrode.

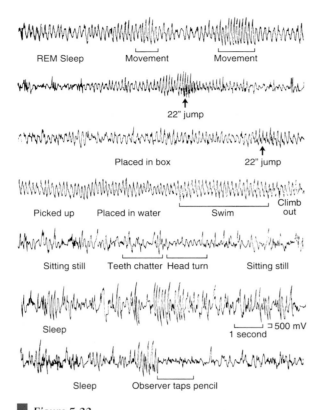

Figure 5.22
EEG activity from the rat hippocampus, recorded during various behaviors.
(From Whishaw, I. Q., and Vanderwolf, C. H. *Behavioral Biology*, 1973, *8*, 461–484.)

Such records are called **electroencephalograms (EEGs),** or "writings of electricity from the head." They can be used to diagnose epilepsy or brain tumors, or to study the stages of sleep and wakefulness, which are associated with characteristic patterns of electrical activity.

Figure 5.22 shows the EEG recorded from the hippocampus of a rat during sleep and during the performance of various behaviors while awake. You will see that the pattern of activity changes drastically during different behaviors. (See *Figure 5.22.*)

● Recording the Brain's Metabolic and Synaptic Activity

Electrical signals are not the only signs of neural activity. If the neural activity of a particular region of the brain increases, the metabolic rate of this region increases, too, largely as a result of increased operation of ion pumps in the membrane of the cells. This increased metabolic rate can be measured. The experimenter injects radioactive **2-deoxyglucose (2-DG)** into the animal. Because this chem-

ical resembles glucose (the principal food for the brain), it is taken into cells. Thus, the most active cells, which use glucose at the highest rate, will take up the highest concentrations of radioactive 2-DG. But unlike normal glucose, 2-DG cannot be metabolized, so it stays in the cell. The experimenter then kills the animal, removes the brain, slices it, and prepares it for *autoradiography*.

Autoradiography can be translated roughly as "writing with one's own radiation." Sections of the brain are mounted on microscope slides. The slides are then taken into a darkroom, where they are coated with a photographic emulsion (the substance found on photographic film). Several weeks later, the slides, with their coatings of emulsion, are developed, just like photographic film. The molecules of radioactive 2-DG show themselves as spots of silver grains in the developed emulsion because the radioactivity exposes the emulsion, just as X rays or light will do.

The most active regions of the brain contain the most radioactivity, showing this radioactivity in the form of dark spots in the developed emulsion. Figure 5.23 shows an autoradiograph of a slice of a rat brain; the dark spots at the

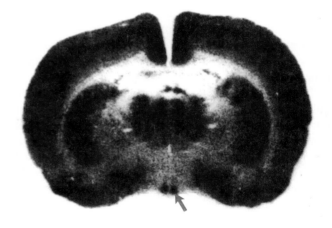

Figure 5.23
A 2-DG autoradiogram of a rat brain (frontal section, dorsal is at top), showing especially high regions of activity in the pair of nuclei in the hypothalamus, at the base of the brain.
(From Schwartz, W. J., and Gainer, H. *Science,* 1977, *197*, 1089–1091.)

electroencephalogram (EEG)   An electrical brain potential recorded by placing electrodes on in the scalp.

2-deoxyglucose (2-DG) *(dee ox ee **gloo** kohss)*   A sugar that enters cells along with glucose but is not metabolized.

autoradiography   A procedure that locates radioactive substances in a slice of tissue; the radiation exposes a photographic emulsion or a piece of film that covers the tissue.

bottom (indicated by the arrow) are nuclei of the hypothalamus with an especially high metabolic rate. Chapter 9 describes these nuclei and their function. (See *Figure 5.23.*)

Another method of identifying active regions of the brain capitalizes on the fact that when neurons are activated (for example, by the terminal buttons that form synapses with them), particular genes in the nucleus are turned on and particular proteins are produced. These proteins then bind with the chromosomes in the nucleus. Exactly what they do is not yet known; the important fact is their presence indicates that the cell has just been activated.

One of the nuclear proteins produced during neural activation is called **Fos.** You will remember that we already did some research on the neural circuitry involved in the sexual behavior of female rats. Suppose we want to use the Fos method in this research project. We place female rats with males and permit the animals to copulate. Then we remove the rats' brains, slice them, and follow a procedure that stains Fos protein. Figure 5.24 shows the results: Neurons in the medial amygdala of a female rat that has just mated show the presence of dark spots, indicating the presence of Fos protein. Thus, these neurons appear to be activated by the physical stimulation of the genitals that occurs during copulatory activity. As you will recall, when we injected a retrograde tracer (fluorogold) into the VMH, we found that this region receives input from the medial amygdala. (See *Figure 5.24.*)

The metabolic activity of specific brain regions can be measured in human brains, too, using a method known as **positron emission tomography,** or PET. First, the patient receives an injection of radioactive 2-DG. (Eventually, the chemical is broken down and leaves the cells. The dose given to humans is harmless.) The person's head is placed in a machine similar to a CT scanner. When the radioactive molecules of 2-DG decay, they emit subatomic particles called positrons, which are detected by the scanner. The computer determines which regions of the brain have taken up the radioactive substance, and it produces a picture of a slice of the brain, showing the activity level of various regions in that slice. (See *Figure 5.25.*)

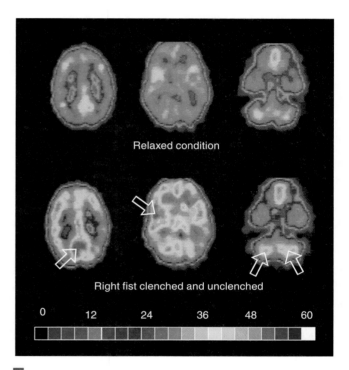

Relaxed condition

Right fist clenched and unclenched

0   12   24   36   48   60

Figure 5.25
PET scans of a human brain (horizontal sections). The top row shows three scans from a person at rest. The bottom row shows three scans from the same person while clenching and unclenching his right fist. The scans show increased uptake of radioactive 2-deoxyglucose in regions of the brain that are devoted to the control of movement, which indicates increased metabolic rate in these areas. Different computer-generated colors indicate different rates of uptake of 2-DG, as shown in the scale below.
(Courtesy of the Brookhaven National Laboratory and the State University of New York, Stony Brook.)

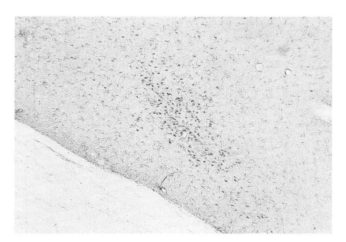

Figure 5.24
Localization of Fos protein. The photomicrograph shows a frontal section of the brain of a female rat, taken through the medial amygdala. The dark spots indicate the presence of Fos protein, localized by means of immunocytochemistry. The synthesis of Fos protein was stimulated by permitting the animal to engage in copulatory behavior.
(Courtesy of Marc Tetel, University of Massachusetts.)

Fos *(fahs)* A protein produced in the nucleus of a neuron in response to synaptic stimulation.

positron emission tomography (PET) The use of a device that reveals the localization of a radioactive tracer in a living brain.

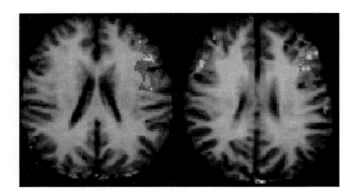

Figure 5.26
A functional MRI scan of a human brain. Localized increases in neural activity of males (left) and females (right) while judging whether pairs of written words rhymed.
(From Shaywitz, B. A., et al., *Nature*, 1995, 373, 607–609. By permission.)

One of the disadvantages of PET scanners is their operating cost. For reasons of safety, the radioactive chemicals that are administered have very short half-lives; that is, they decay and lose their radioactivity very quickly. Because these chemicals decay so quickly, they must be produced on site, in an atomic particle acceleration called a *cyclotron*. Thus, to the cost of the PET scanner must be added the cost of the cyclotron and the salaries of the personnel who operate it.

The most recent development in brain imaging is **functional MRI (fMRI).** Engineers have devised modifications to existing MRI scanners that acquire images very rapidly and permit the measurement of regional metabolism. Functional MRI scans have a higher resolution than PET scans, so they reveal more detailed information about the activity of particular brain regions. (See *Figure 5.26.*)

● Measuring the Brain's Secretions

Sometimes we are interested not in the general metabolic activity of particular regions of the brain, but in the secretion of specific neurotransmitters or neuromodulators in these regions. For example, suppose we know that acetylcholinergic neurons in the brain stem participate in the control of REM sleep. (The experiments that provided this knowledge are described in the next section of this chapter.) One of the characteristics of REM sleep is muscular paralysis, which prevents us from getting out of bed and acting out our dreams. We decide to measure the secretion of acetylcholine in a region of the medulla known to contain neurons that inhibit motor neurons in the spinal cord. To do so, we use a procedure called **microdialysis.**

Dialysis is a process in which substances are separated by means of an artificial membrane that is permeable to some molecules but not others. A microdialysis probe consists of a small metal tube that introduces a solution into a section of dialysis tubing—a piece of artificial membrane shaped in the form of a cylinder, sealed at the bottom. Another small metal tube leads the solution away after it has circulated through the pouch. A drawing of such a probe is shown in *Figure 5.27.*

We use stereotaxic surgery to place a microdialysis probe in a rat's brain so that the tip of the probe is located in the region we are interested in. We pump a small amount of a solution similar to extracellular fluid through one of the small metal tubes into the dialysis tubing. The fluid circulates through the dialysis tubing and passes through the

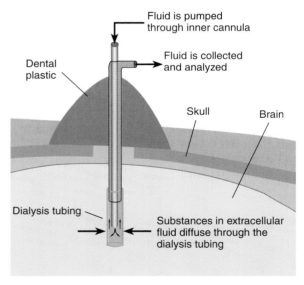

Figure 5.27
Microdialysis. A salt solution is slowly infused into the microdialysis tube, where it picks up molecules that diffuse in from the extracellular fluid. The fluid is then analyzed by high-performance liquid chromatography (HPLC).
(Adapted from Hernandez, L., Stanley, B. G., and Hoebel, B. G. *Life Sciences*, 1986, 39, 2629–2637.)

functional MRI (fMRI)   A modification of the MRI procedure that permits the measurement of regional metabolism in the brain.

microdialysis   A procedure for analyzing chemicals present in the interstitial fluid through a small piece of tubing made of a semipermeable membrane that is implanted in the brain.

second metal tube, from which it is taken for analysis. As the fluid passes through the dialysis tubing, it collects molecules from the extracellular fluid of the brain, which are pushed across the membrane by the force of diffusion.

We analyze the contents of the fluid that has passed through the dialysis tubing by an extremely sensitive analytical method. This method is so sensitive that it can detect transmitter substances (and their breakdown products) that have been released by the terminal buttons and have escaped from the synaptic cleft into the rest of the extracellular fluid. In fact, we find that the amount of acetylcholine present in the extracellular fluid of the nucleus in the medulla *does* increase during REM sleep.

The microdialysis procedure could theoretically be applied to study of the human brain, but ethical and practical reasons prevent us from doing so. Fortunately, there is a noninvasive way to measure neurochemicals in the human brain. Although PET scanners are very expensive machines, they are also very versatile. They can be used to localize *any* radioactive substance that emits positrons.

Several years ago, several young people injected themselves with an illicit drug that was contaminated with a chemical that destroyed their dopaminergic neurons. As a result, they suffered from severe parkinsonism. (This case is described in more detail in Chapter 8.) Recently, neurosurgeons used stereotaxic procedures to transplant fetal dopaminergic neurons into the basal ganglia of some of these patients. Figure 5.28 shows PET scans of the brain of one of them. The patient was given an injection of radioactive L-DOPA one hour before each scan was made. As you learned in Chapter 3, L-DOPA is taken up by the terminals of dopaminergic neurons, where it is converted to dopamine; thus, the radioactivity shown in the scans indicates the presence of dopamine-secreting terminals in the basal ganglia. The scans show the amount of radioactivity before (part a) and after (part b) he received the transplant, which greatly diminished his symptoms. (See *Figure 5.28.*)

● Stimulating Neural Activity

So far, this section has been concerned with research methods that measure the activity of specific regions of the brain. But sometimes we may want to artificially change the activity of these regions to see what effects these changes have on the animal's behavior. For example, female rats will copulate with males only if certain female sex hormones are present. If we remove the rats' ovaries, the loss of these hormones will abolish their sexual behavior. We found in our earlier studies that VMH lesions disrupt this behavior. Perhaps if we *activate* the VMH, we

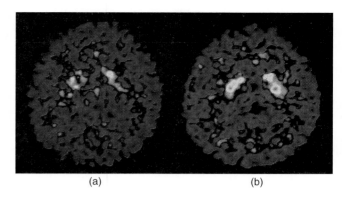

(a)   (b)

Figure 5.28
PET scans showing uptake of radioactive L-DOPA in the basal ganglia of a patient with parkinsonian symptoms induced by a toxic chemical before and after receiving a transplant of fetal dopaminergic neurons. (a) Preoperative scan. (b) Scan taken 13 months postoperatively. The increased uptake of L-DOPA indicates that the fetal transplant was secreting dopamine.
(Adapted from Widner, H., Tetrud, J., Rehncrona, S., Snow, B., Brundin, P., Gustavii, B., Björklund, A., Lindvall, O., and Langston, J. W. *New England Journal of Medicine*, 1992, *327*, 1556–1563. Scans reprinted with permission.)

will make up for the lack of female sex hormones and the rats will copulate again.

How do we activate neurons? We can do so by electrical or chemical stimulation. Electrical stimulation simply involves passing an electrical current through a wire inserted into the brain, as you saw in Figure 5.20. Chemical stimulation is usually accomplished by injecting a small amount of an excitatory amino acid, such as kainic acid or glutamic acid, into the brain. As you learned in Chapter 3, the principal excitatory transmitter substance in the brain is glutamic acid (glutamate), and both of these substances stimulate glutamate receptors, thus activating the neurons on which these receptors are located.

Injections of chemicals into the brain can be done through an apparatus permanently attached to the skull, so that the animal's behavior can be observed several times. We place a metal cannula (a guide cannula) in an animal's brain and cement its top to the skull. At a later date, we place a smaller cannula of measured length inside the guide cannula and then inject a chemical into the brain. Because the animal is free to move about, we can observe the effects of the injection on its behavior. (See *Figure 5.29.*)

The principal disadvantage of chemical stimulation is that it is slightly more complicated than electrical stimulation; chemical stimulation requires cannulas, tubes, special

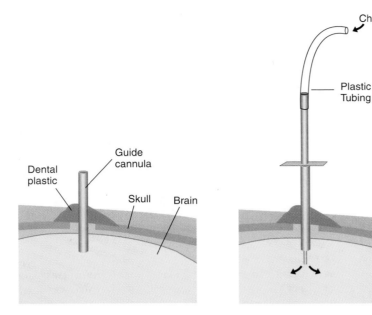

Figure 5.29
An intracranial cannula. A guide cannula is permanently attached to the skull, and at a later time a thinner cannula can be inserted through the guide cannula into the brain. Chemicals can be infused into the brain through this device.

pumps or syringes, and sterile solutions of excitatory amino acids. However, it has a distinct advantage over electrical stimulation: It activates cell bodies but not axons. Because only cell bodies (and their dendrites, of course) contain glutamate receptors, we can be assured that an injection of an excitatory amino acid into a particular region of the brain excites the cells there, but not the axons of other neurons that happen to pass through the region. Thus, the effects of chemical stimulation are more localized than the effects of electrical stimulation.

You may have noticed that I just said that kainic acid, which I described earlier as a neurotoxin, can be used to stimulate neurons. These two uses are not really contradictory. Kainic acid produces excitotoxic lesions by stimulating neurons to death. Whereas large doses of a concentrated solution kill neurons, small doses of a dilute solution simply stimulate them.

What about the results of our experiment? In fact (as we shall see in Chapter 10), VMH stimulation *does* substitute for female sex hormones. Perhaps, then, the female sex hormones exert their effects in this nucleus. We will see how to test this hypothesis in the final section of this chapter.

When drugs are injected into the brain through cannulas, the chemicals diffuse over a region that involves hundreds (or thousands) of neurons. Sometimes, we want to study the effect of chemicals on the activity of a single cell. To do that, we use a technique known as *microiontophoresis.*

When transmitter substances bind with postsynaptic receptors, ion channels open, producing excitatory or inhibitory postsynaptic potentials. These potentials increase or decrease the cell's firing rate. To determine the effects of transmitter substances (or drugs that stimulate or block particular receptors) on the activity of an individual neuron, an investigator uses a **multibarreled micropipette.** This device consists of two or more glass microelectrodes (also called *micropipettes*), bundled together so that their tips are close to one another.

Figure 5.30 illustrates a seven-barreled micropipette glued to a recording microelectrode. Each of the seven micropipettes can be filled with transmitter substances, neuromodulators, hormones, or drugs. The pH (acid-base balance) of the solutions in the micropipettes is adjusted so that the chemicals ionize. Then when an electrical current is passed through one of the micropipettes, some molecules of the substance will be discharged. The injection of extremely small quantities of a chemical this way is called **microiontophoresis** (*iontophoresis* means "ion carrying," from *pherein,* "to bear or carry"). (See *Figure 5.30.*)

The recording microelectrode detects the neural activity of the cell that is being exposed to one of the chemicals placed in the micropipettes—for example, a particular transmitter substance. If the neuron changes its firing rate when some of the hormone is ejected from the micropipette, we can conclude that the neuron contains receptors for that transmitter substance.

● Behavioral Effects of Electrical Brain Stimulation

Stimulation of the brain of a freely moving animal often produces behavioral changes. For example, hypothalamic stimulation can elicit behaviors such as feeding, drinking, grooming, attack, or escape, which suggests that the hypothalamus is involved in their control. Stimulation of the caudate nucleus often halts ongoing behavior, which suggests that this structure is involved in motor inhibition. Brain stimulation can serve as a signal for a learned task or

multibarreled micropipette   A group of micropipettes attached together, used to infuse several different substances by means of iontophoresis while recording from a single neuron.

microiontophoresis   A procedure that uses electricity to eject a chemical from a micropipette in order to determine the effects of the chemical on the electrical activity of a cell.

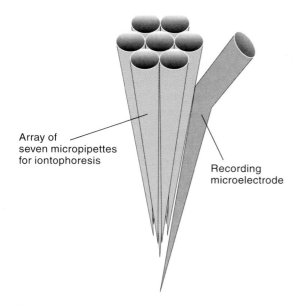

Array of
seven micropipettes
for iontophoresis

Recording
microelectrode

Figure 5.30
Microiontophoresis. Molecules of different chemicals are carried out of the seven micropipettes by an electrical current. The recording microelectrode records the activity of the neuron and determines whether it responds to the chemical.

can even serve as a rewarding or punishing event, as we will see in Chapter 14.

There are problems in interpreting the significance of the effects of brain stimulation, especially when it is produced with electricity. An electrical stimulus (usually a series of pulses) can never duplicate the natural neural processes that go on in the brain. The normal interplay of spatial and temporal patterns of excitation and inhibition is destroyed by the artificial stimulation of an area. Electrical brain stimulation is probably as natural as attaching ropes to the arms of the members of an orchestra and then shaking all the ropes simultaneously to see what they can play. In fact, local stimulation is sometimes used to produce a "temporary lesion," by which the region is put out of commission by the meaningless artificial stimulation. The surprising finding is that stimulation so often *does* produce orderly changes in behavior.

One of the more interesting uses of electrical stimulation of the brain was developed by the late Wilder Penfield (see Penfield and Jasper, 1954) to treat focal-seizure disorders. These problems are produced by localized regions of neural tissue that periodically irritate the surrounding areas, triggering epileptic seizures (wild, sustained firing of cerebral neurons, resulting in some behavioral disruption). If severe cases of focal epilepsy do not respond to medication, surgical excision of the focus may be necessary. The

focus is identified by means of EEG recordings before surgery and is confirmed by EEG recordings during surgery, after the brain is exposed. (As we saw in an earlier section, it can also be identified by special imaging techniques.)

Patients undergoing open-head surgery first have their heads shaved. Then a local anesthetic is administered to the scalp along the line that will be followed by the incision. A general anesthetic is not used, because the method requires that the patient be awake and conscious during surgery. The surgeon cuts the scalp and saws through the skull under the cut so that a piece of skull can then be removed. Next, the surgeon cuts and folds back the dura mater, exposing the brain itself.

When removing an epileptic focus, the surgeon wants to cut away all the abnormal tissue, while sparing neural tissue that performs important functions, such as the comprehension and production of speech. For this reason, Penfield first stimulated parts of the brain to determine which regions he could safely remove, before removing the seizure focus. Penfield touched the tip of a metal electrode to various parts of the brain and observed the effects of stimulation on the patient's behavior. For example, stimulation of the primary motor cortex produced movement, and stimulation of the primary auditory cortex elicited reports of the presence of buzzing noises. Stimulation of portions of the temporal lobe and frontal lobe stopped the patient's ongoing speech and disrupted the ability to understand what the surgeon and his associates were saying.

After the surgeon removes the region of the brain that contains the seizure focus, the dura mater is sewn back together and the piece of skull is replaced.

Besides giving patients relief from their epileptic attacks, the procedure provided Penfield with interesting data. As he stimulated various parts of the brain, he noted the effect and placed a sterile piece of paper, on which a number was written, on the point stimulated. When various points had been stimulated, Penfield photographed the exposed brain with its numbered locations before removing the slips of paper and proceeding with the surgery. After the operation, he could then compare the recorded notes with the photograph of the patient's brain, showing the location of the points of stimulation. (See *Figure 5.31*.)

Interim Summary

When circuits of neurons participate in their normal functions, their electrical activity, metabolic activity, and chemical secretions increase. Thus, by observing these processes as an animal perceives various stimuli or engages in various behaviors, we can make some inferences about the

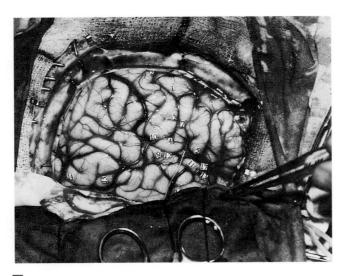

Figure 5.31

The appearance of the cortical surface of a conscious patient whose brain has been stimulated. The points of stimulation are indicated by the numbered tags placed there by the surgeon.

(From Case M. M., in Wilder Penfield, *The Mystery of the Mind: A Critical Study of Consciousness and the Human Brain,* with Discussions by William Feindel, Charles Hendel, and Charles Symonds. Copyright © 1975 by Princeton University Press. Figure 4, p. 24 reprinted by permission of Princeton University Press.)

functions performed by various regions of the brain. Microelectrodes can be used to record the electrical activity of individual neurons. Chronic recordings require that the electrode be attached to an electrical socket, which is fastened to the skull with a plastic adhesive. Macroelectrodes record the activity of large groups of neurons. In rare cases, macroelectrodes are placed in the depths of the human brain, but most often they are placed on the scalp and their activity is recorded on a polygraph.

Metabolic activity can be measured by giving an animal an injection of radioactive 2-DG, which accumulates in metabolically active neurons. The presence of the radioactivity is revealed through autoradiography: Slices of the brain are placed on microscope slides, covered with a photographic emulsion, left to sit a while, and then developed like photographic negatives. When neurons are stimulated, they synthesize the nuclear protein Fos. The presence of Fos, revealed by a special staining method, provides another way to discover active regions of the brain. The metabolic activity of various regions of the living human brain can be revealed by the 2-DG method, but a PET scanner is used to detect the active regions.

The secretions of neurotransmitters and neuromodulators can be measured by implanting the tip of a microdialysis probe in a particular region of the brain. A PET scanner can be used to perform similar observations of the human brain.

Researchers can stimulate various regions of the brain by implanting a macroelectrode and applying mild electrical stimulation. Alternatively, they can implant a guide cannula in the brain; after the animal has recovered from the surgery, they insert a smaller cannula and inject a weak solution of an excitatory amino acid into the brain. The advantage of this procedure is that only neurons whose cell bodies are located nearby will be stimulated; axons passing through the region will not be affected.

Table 5.2 summarizes the research methods presented in this section.

NEUROCHEMICAL METHODS

I have already described some neurochemical methods in the context of damaging or stimulating the brain or measuring neural activity. This section describes several other neurochemical methods that are useful in studying the physiology of behavior.

● Finding Neurons That Produce Particular Neurochemicals

Suppose we learn that a particular drug affects behavior. How would we go about discovering the neural circuits responsible for the drug's effects? To answer this question, let's take a specific example. Physicians discovered several years ago that farm workers exposed to certain types of insecticides (the organophosphates) had particularly intense and bizarre dreams, and even reported having hallucinations while awake. A plausible explanation for these symptoms is that the drug stimulates the neural circuits responsible for dreaming. (After all, dreams are hallucinations that we have while sleeping.) Alternatively, the drug could disrupt inhibitory mechanisms that *prevent* dreaming while we are awake. Other evidence (which will not be described here) indicates that the former hypothesis is true: Organophosphate insecticides directly activate the neural circuits responsible for dreaming. (Other drugs, such as LSD, produce hallucinations by disrupting inhibitory mechanisms.)

The first question to ask relates to how the organophosphate insecticides work. Pharmacologists have the answer: These drugs are acetylcholinesterase inhibitors. As you learned in Chapter 4, acetylcholinesterase inhibitors are potent acetylcholine agonists. By inhibiting AChE, the drugs prevent the rapid destruction of ACh after it is re-

Table 5.2
Research Methods: Part II

Goal of method	Method	Remarks
Record electrical activity of single neurons	Glass or metal microelectrodes	Metal microelectrodes can be implanted chronically to record neural activity as animal moves
Record electrical activity of regions of brain	Metal macroelectrodes	In humans, usually attached to the scalp with a special paste
Record metabolic activity of regions of brain	2-DG autoradiography	Measures local glucose utilization
	Measurement of Fos protein	Identifies neurons that have recently been stimulated
Measure neurotransmitters and neuromodulators released by neurons	2-DG PET scan	Can measure regional metabolic activity of human brain
Measure neurochemicals in the living human brain	Microdialysis	A wide variety of substances can be analyzed
	PET scan	Can localize any radioactive substance in the brain
Simulate neural activity	Electrical stimulation	Stimulates neurons near the tip of the electrode and axons passing through region
	Chemical stimulation with excitatory amino acid	Stimulates only neurons near the tip of the electrode, not axons passing through region

leased by terminal buttons, and thus prolong the postsynaptic potentials at acetylcholinergic synapses.

Now that we understand the action of the insecticides, we know that these drugs act at acetylcholinergic synapses. What neurochemical methods should we use to discover the site of action of the drugs in the brain? There are three possibilities: We could look for neurons that contain acetylcholine, we could look for the enzyme acetylcholinesterase (which must be present in the postsynaptic membranes of cells that receive synaptic input from acetylcholinergic neurons), or we could look for acetylcholine receptors. Let's see how these three methods work.

First, let's consider methods by which we can localize particular neurochemicals, such as neurotransmitters and neuromodulators. (In our case, we are interested in acetylcholine.) There are three basic ways of localizing neurochemicals in the brain: localizing the *chemicals* themselves, localizing the *enzymes* that produce them, and localizing the *messenger RNA* involved in their synthesis.

Peptides (or proteins) can be localized directly by means of immunocytochemical methods, which were described in the first section of this chapter. Slices of brain tissue are exposed to an antibody for the peptide, linked to a dye (usually, a fluorescent dye). The slices are then examined under a microscope using light of a particular wavelength. For example, Figure 5.32 shows the location of axons in the forebrain that contain vasopressin, a peptide neurotransmitter. Two sets of axons are shown. One set, which forms a cluster around the third ventricle at the base of the brain, shows up as a rusty color. The other set, scattered through the lateral septum, look like strands of gold fibers. (As you can see, a properly stained brain section can be beautiful. See *Figure 5.32*.)

But we are interested in acetylcholine, which is not a peptide. Thus, we cannot use immunocytochemical methods to find this neurotransmitter. But we can use these methods to localize the enzyme that produces it. The synthesis of acetylcholine is made possible by the enzyme choline acetyltransferase (ChAT). Thus, neurons that contain this enzyme almost certainly secrete ACh. Figure 5.33 shows acetylcholinergic neurons in the pons that have been identified by means of immunocytochemistry; the brain tissue was exposed to an antibody to ChAT attached to a fluorescent dye. (See *Figure 5.33*.)

Figure 5.32
*Localization of a peptide by means of immunocytochemistry.
The photomicrograph shows a frontal section through the rat fore-
brain. The gold- and rust-colored fibers are axons and terminal
buttons that contain vasopressin, a peptide neurotransmitter.*
(Courtesy of Geert DeVries, University of Massachusetts.)

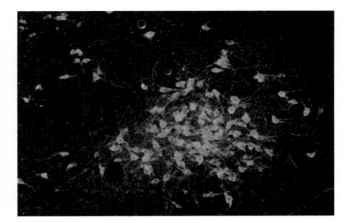

Figure 5.33
*Localization of an enzyme responsible for the synthesis of a neu-
rotransmitter, revealed by immunocytochemistry. The photomicrograph shows a section through the pons. The orange neurons
contain choline acetyltransferase, which implies that they produce
(and thus secrete) acetylcholine.*
(Courtesy of David A. Morilak and Roland Ciaranello, Nancy Pritzker
Laboratory of Developmental and Molecular Neurobiology, Department of Psychiatry and Behavioral Sciences, Stanford University
School of Medicine.)

sticks to molecules of the appropriate messenger RNA.
Then we would use autoradiographic methods (described
in the second section of this chapter) to reveal the location
of the messenger RNA and, by inference, the location of
the protein whose synthesis the RNA initiates.

Figure 5.34 explains the in situ hybridization method
graphically, and Figure 5.35 shows the location of the messenger RNA responsible for the synthesis of a peptide, vasopressin, as revealed by this method. Side lighting of the
microscope slide makes the silver grains in the photographic emulsion show up as white spots. (See *Figures 5.34
and 5.35.*)

● Localizing Particular Receptors

As we saw in Chapter 4, neurotransmitters, neuromodulators, and hormones convey their messages to their target
cells by binding with receptors. The location of these receptors can be determined by two different procedures.

The first procedure uses autoradiography. We expose
slices of brain tissue to a solution containing a radioactive
ligand for a particular receptor. Next, we rinse the slices so
that the only radioactivity remaining in them is that of the

Another indirect way to localize a substance uses a technique known as **in situ hybridization:** All peptides and
proteins (which includes all enzymes, of course) are synthesized according to information contained on the chromosomes. As we saw in Chapter 2, when a particular protein is to be produced, the necessary information is copied
from a chromosome onto a piece of messenger RNA, which
then leaves the nucleus and travels to a ribosome, where
protein synthesis takes place. (This process was illustrated
in Figure 2.5.) The recipe for the protein is coded as a particular sequence of nucleotides that make up the messenger RNA. If this code is known (and in most cases it is),
molecular biologists can synthesize a piece of radioactive
RNA that contains a sequence of nucleotides complementary to the sequence on the messenger RNA. We would expose slices of brain tissue to the radioactive RNA, which

in situ hybridization *(in see* too) The production of
DNA complementary to a particular messenger RNA in
order to detect the presence of the RNA.

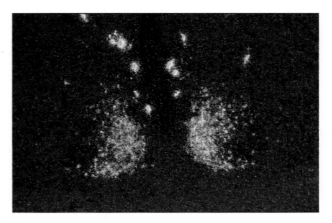

Figure 5.35
In situ hybridization. The tissue was exposed to radioactive RNA that binds with the messenger RNA responsible for the synthesis of vasopressin, a peptide. The location of the radioactive RNA, revealed by means of autoradiography, shows up as white spots. The labeled neurons are located in a pair of nuclei in the hypothalamus.
(Courtesy of Geert DeVries, University of Massachusetts.)

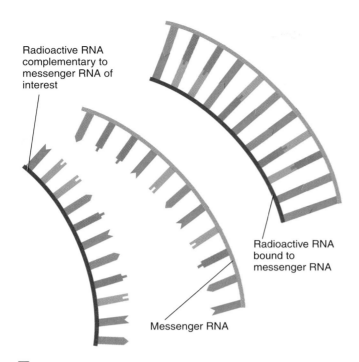

Radioactive RNA complementary to messenger RNA of interest

Radioactive RNA bound to messenger RNA

Messenger RNA

Figure 5.34
An explanation of the use of in situ hybridization to localize messenger RNA that is responsible for the synthesis of a particular protein or peptide.

molecules of the ligand bound to their receptors. Finally, we use autoradiographic methods to localize the radioactive ligand—and thus, the receptors.

The second procedure uses immunocytochemistry. Receptors are proteins; thus we can produce antibodies against them. We expose slices of brain tissue to the appropriate antibody (labeled with a fluorescent dye) and look at the slices with a microscope under light of a particular wavelength.

Let's apply the method for localizing receptors to another line of investigation we considered earlier in this chapter: the role of the ventromedial hypothalamus (VMH) in the sexual behavior of female rats. As we saw, lesions of the VMH abolish this behavior. We also saw that the behavior does not occur if the rat's ovaries are removed but that it can be activated by stimulation of the VMH with electricity or an excitatory amino acid. These results suggest that the sex hormones produced by the ovaries act on neurons in the VMH.

This hypothesis suggests two experiments. First, we could use the procedure shown in Figure 5.29 to place a small amount of the appropriate sex hormone directly into the VMH of female rats whose ovaries we had previously removed. As we shall see in Chapter 10, this procedure

works; the hormone *does* reactivate the animals' sexual behavior. The second experiment would use autoradiography to look for the receptors for the sex hormone. We would expose slices of rat brain to the radioactive hormone, rinse them, and perform autoradiography. If we did so, we would indeed find radioactivity in the VMH. (And if we compared slices from the brains of female and male rats, we would find evidence of more hormone receptors in the female brains.) We could also use immunocytochemistry to localize the hormone receptors, and we would obtain the same results.

A useful property of the various methods of localizing neurochemicals is that they can be combined with anterograde or retrograde tracers. Thus, investigators not only can determine what chemicals a particular neuron contains, but they can also determine what connections these neurons have with other parts of the brain. This method is called **double labeling.** Figure 5.36 shows a group of neurons in the periaqueductal gray matter. The cells that appear brown have been stained with an immunocytochemical method that reveals the presence of receptors for a female sex hormone. The terminal buttons that form synapses with these neurons have been stained with PHA-L, which was injected into the VMH. These results tell us that neurons in the

double labeling Labeling neurons in a particular region by two different means; for example, by using an anterograde tracer and a label for a particular enzyme.

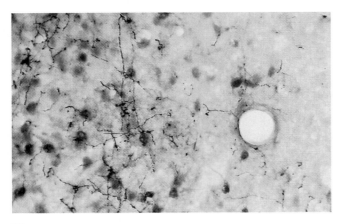

Figure 5.36
Double labeling, using immunocytochemistry and antero-grade tracing. The photomicrograph shows a slice through the periaqueductal gray matter of a guinea pig. The tissue has been treated with an antibody to estradiol receptor protein; a dye label attached to the antibody makes the cells that contain these receptors show up as brown. The purple-colored axons and terminal buttons are labeled with PHA-L, which was injected into the ventromedial nucleus of the hypothalamus.
(Courtesy of Kirsten Nielsen Ricciardi and Jeffrey Blaustein, University of Massachusetts.)

periaqueductal gray matter that are sensitive to estrogens (female sex hormones) also receive input from the ventromedial nucleus of the hypothalamus. (See *Figure 5.36.*)

Interim Summary

Neurochemical methods can be used to determine the location of an enormous variety of substances in the brain. They can identify neurons that secrete a particular neurotransmitter or neuromodulator and those that possess receptors that respond to the presence of these substances. Peptides and proteins can be directly localized, through immunocytochemical methods; the tissue is exposed to an antibody that is linked to a molecule that fluoresces under light of a particular wavelength. Other substances can be detected by immunocytochemical localization of an enzyme required for their synthesis. Peptides and proteins can also be detected by in situ hybridization methods that reveal the presence of the messenger RNA that directs their synthesis.

Receptors for neurochemicals can be localized by two means. The first method uses autoradiography to reveal the distribution of a radioactive ligand to which the tissue has been exposed. The second method uses immunocytochemistry to detect the presence of the receptors themselves, which are proteins. Combined staining methods can localize neurons that possess a particular receptor or a particular peptide and also have connections with particular regions of the brain.

Table 5.3 summarizes the research methods presented in this section.

Table 5.3
Research Methods: Part III

Goal of method	Method	Remarks
Identify neurons producing a particular neurotransmitter or neuromodulator	Immunocytochemical localization of peptide or protein	Requires a specific antibody
	Immunocytochemical localization of enzyme responsible for synthesis of substance	Useful if substance is not a peptide or protein
Identify neurons that contain a particular type of receptor	Autoradiographic localization of radioactive ligand	
	Immunocytochemical localization of receptor	Requires a specific antibody
Identify neurons that produce a particular neurotransmitter, contain a particular type of receptor, and also communicate with other neurons in a specific brain region	Combine any of the methods above with anterograde or retrograde tracing methods	Provides detailed information about the connections of specific types of neurons

SUGGESTED READINGS

Laboratory Manual

Wellman, P. *Laboratory Exercises in Physiological Psychology.* Boston: Allyn and Bacon, 1994.

Stereotaxic Atlases

Paxinos, G., and Watson, C. *The Rat Brain in Stereotaxic Coordinates,* 2nd ed. Sydney: Academic Press, 1986.

Slotnick, B. M., and Leonard, C. M. *A Stereotaxic Atlas of the Albino Mouse Forebrain.* Rockville, MD: Public Health Service, 1975. (U.S. Government Printing Office Stock Number 017–024–00491–0)

Snider, R. S., and Niemer, W. T. *A Stereotaxic Atlas of the Cat Brain.* Chicago: University of Chicago Press, 1961.

Swanson, L. W. *Brain Maps: Structure of the Rat Brain.* Amsterdam: Elsevier, 1992.

Histological Methods

Heimer, L., and Záborsky, L. *Neuroanatomical Tract-Tracing Methods 2: Recent Progress.* New York: Plenum Press, 1989.

Vision

Ocean Park #17 by Richard Diebenkorn.

As we saw in Chapter 3, the brain performs two major functions: It controls the movements of the muscles, producing useful behaviors, and it regulates the body's internal environment. To perform both these tasks, the brain must be informed about what is happening both in the external environment and within the body. Such information is received by the sensory systems. This chapter and the next are devoted to a discussion of the ways in which sensory organs detect changes in the environment and the ways in which the brain interprets neural signals from these organs.

We receive information about the environment from **sensory receptors**—specialized neurons that detect a variety of physical events. (Do not confuse *sensory receptors* with receptors for neurotransmitters, neuromodulators, and hormones. Sensory receptors are specialized neurons, and the other types of receptors are specialized proteins that bind with certain molecules.) Stimuli impinge on the receptors and, through various processes, alter their membrane potentials. This process is known as **sensory transduction** because sensory events are *transduced* ("transferred") into changes in the cells' membrane potential. These electrical changes are called **receptor potentials.** Most receptors lack axons; a portion of their somatic membrane forms synapses with the dendrites of other neurons. Receptor potentials affect the release of transmitter substances and hence modify the pattern of firing in neurons with which these cells form synapses. Ultimately, the information reaches the brain.

People often say that we have five senses: sight, hearing, smell, taste, and touch. Actually, we have more than five, but even experts disagree about how the lines between the various categories should be drawn. Certainly, we should add the vestibular senses; as well as providing us with auditory information, the inner ear supplies information about head orientation and movement. The sense of touch (or, more accurately, *somatosensation*) detects changes in pressure, warmth, cold, vibration, limb position, and events that damage tissue (that is, produce pain). Everyone agrees that we can detect these stimuli; the issue is whether they are detected by separate senses.

This chapter considers vision, the sensory modality that receives the most attention from psychologists, anatomists, and physiologists. One reason for this attention derives from the fascinating complexity of the sensory organs of vision and the relatively large proportion of the brain that is devoted to the analysis of visual information. Another reason, I am sure, is that vision is so important to us as individuals. A natural fascination with such a rich

sensory receptor   A specialized neuron that detects a particular category of physical events.

sensory transduction   The process by which sensory stimuli are transduced into slow, graded receptor potentials.

receptor potential   A slow, graded electrical potential produced by a receptor cell in response to a physical stimulus.

source of information about the world leads to curiosity about how this sensory modality works. Chapter 7 deals with the other sensory modalities: audition, the vestibular senses, the somatosenses, gustation, and olfaction.

THE STIMULUS

As we all know, our eyes detect the presence of light. For humans, light is a narrow band of the spectrum of electromagnetic radiation. Electromagnetic radiation with a wavelength of between 380 and 760 nm (a nanometer, nm, is one-billionth of a meter) is visible to us. (See *Figure 6.1.*) Other animals can detect different ranges of electromagnetic radiation. For example, honeybees can detect differences in ultraviolet radiation reflected by flowers that appear white to us. The range of wavelengths we call *light* is not qualitatively different from the rest of the electromagnetic spectrum; it is simply the part of the continuum that we humans can see.

The perceived color of light is determined by three dimensions: *hue, saturation,* and *brightness.* Light travels at a constant speed of approximately 300,000 kilometers (186,000 miles) per second. Thus, if the frequency of oscillation of the wave varies, the distance between the peaks of the waves will similarly vary, but in inverse fashion. Slower oscillations lead to longer wavelengths, and faster ones to shorter wavelengths. Wavelength determines the first of the three perceptual dimensions of light: **hue.** The visible spectrum displays the range of hues that our eyes can detect.

Light can also vary in intensity, which corresponds to the second perceptual dimension of light: **brightness.** If the intensity of the electromagnetic radiation is increased, the apparent brightness increases, too. The third dimension, **saturation,** refers to the relative purity of the light that is being perceived. If all the radiation is of one wavelength, the perceived color is pure, or fully saturated. Conversely,

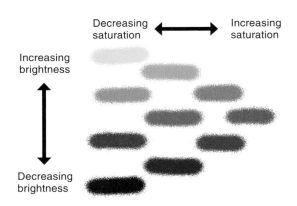

Figure 6.2
Examples of colors with the same dominant wavelength (hue) but different levels of saturations or brightness.

if the radiation contains all wavelengths, it produces no sensation of hue—it appears white. Colors with intermediate amounts of saturation consist of different mixtures of wavelengths. Figure 6.2 shows some color samples, all with the same hue but with different levels of brightness and saturation. (See *Figure 6.2.*)

ANATOMY OF THE VISUAL SYSTEM

For an individual to see, an image must be focused on the retina, the inner lining of the eye. This image causes changes in the electrical activity of millions of neurons in the retina, which results in messages being sent through the optic nerves to the rest of the brain. (I said "the rest" because the retina is actually part of the brain; it and the optic nerve are in the central—not peripheral—nervous system.) This section describes the anatomy of the eyes, the photoreceptors in the retina that detect the presence of light, and the connections between the retina and the brain.

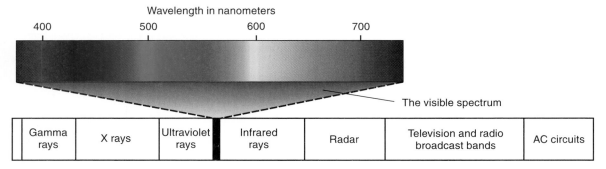

Figure 6.1
The electromagnetic spectrum.

● The Eyes

The eyes are suspended in the *orbits,* bony pockets in the front of the skull. They are held in place and moved by six extraocular muscles attached to the tough, white outer coat of the eye called the *sclera.* (See *Figure 6.3.*) Normally, we cannot look behind our eyeballs and see these muscles, because their attachments to the eyes are hidden by the *conjunctiva.* These mucous membranes line the eyelid and fold back to attach to the eye (thus preventing a contact lens that has slipped off the cornea from "falling behind the eye"). Figure 6.4 illustrates the external and internal anatomy of the eye. (See *Figure 6.4.*)

The eyes make three types of movements: vergence movements, saccadic movements, and pursuit movements. **Vergence movements** are cooperative movements that keep both eyes fixed on the same target—or, more precisely, that keep the image of the target object on corresponding parts of the two retinas. If you hold up a finger in front of your face, look at it, and then bring your finger closer to your face, your eyes will make vergence movements toward your nose. If you then look at an object on the other side of the room, your eyes will rotate outward, and you will see two separate blurry images of your finger.

When you scan the scene in front of you, your gaze does not roam slowly and steadily across its features. Instead, your eyes make jerky **saccadic movements**—you shift your gaze abruptly from one point to another. When you read a line in this book, your eyes stop several times, moving very quickly between each stop. You cannot consciously control the speed of movement between stops; during each *saccade* the eyes move as fast as they can. Only by performing a **pursuit movement**—say, by looking at your finger while you move it around—can you make your eyes move more slowly.

The outer layer of most of the eye, the sclera, is opaque and does not permit entry of light. However, the cornea, the outer layer at the front of the eye, is transparent and admits light. The amount of light that enters is regulated by the size of the pupil, which is an opening in the iris, the pigmented ring of muscles situated behind the cornea. The lens, situated immediately behind the iris, consists of a series of transparent, onionlike layers. Its shape can be altered by contraction of the ciliary muscles. These changes in shape permit the eye to focus images of near or distant objects on the retina—a process called **accommodation.**

After passing through the lens, light traverses the main part of the eye, which contains the *vitreous humor.* Vitreous humor ("glassy liquid") is a clear, gelatinous substance that gives the eye its bulk. After passing through the vitreous humor, light falls on the **retina,** the interior lining of the back of the eye. In the retina are located the receptor cells, the **rods** and **cones** (named for their shapes), collec-

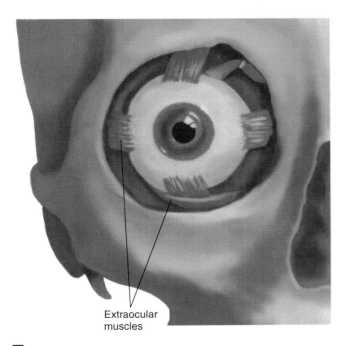

Extraocular
muscles

Figure 6.3
The extraocular muscles, which move the eyes.

hue   One of the perceptual dimensions of color; the dominant wavelength.

brightness   One of the perceptual dimensions of color; intensity.

saturation   One of the perceptual dimensions of color; purity.

vergence movement   The cooperative movement of the eyes, which ensures that the image of an object falls on identical portions of both retinas.

saccadic movement (*suh kad ik*)   The rapid, jerky movement of the eyes used in scanning a visual scene.

pursuit movement   The movement that the eyes make to maintain an image of a moving object on the fovea.

accommodation   Changes in the thickness of the lens of the eye, accomplished by the ciliary muscles, that focus images of near or distant objects on the retina.

retina   The neural tissue and photoreceptive cells located on the inner surface of the posterior portion of the eye.

rod   One of the receptor cells of the retina; sensitive to light of low intensity.

cone   One of the receptor cells of the retina; maximally sensitive to one of three different wavelengths of light and hence encodes color vision.

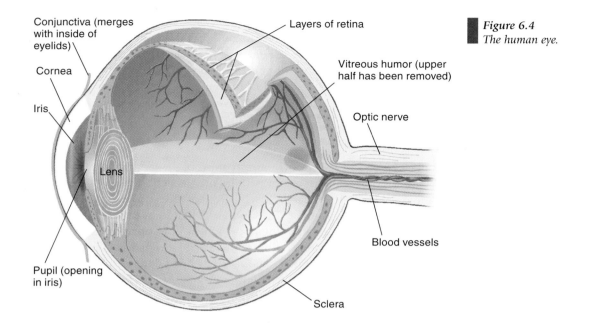

Conjunctiva (merges with inside of eyelids)

Cornea

Iris

Lens

Pupil (opening in iris)

Layers of retina

Vitreous humor (upper half has been removed)

Optic nerve

Blood vessels

Sclera

Figure 6.4
The human eye.

tively known as **photoreceptors.** The human retina contains approximately 120 million rods and 6 million cones. Although they are greatly outnumbered by rods, cones provide us with most of the information about our environment. In particular, they are responsible for our daytime vision. They provide us with information about small features in the environment and thus are the source of vision of the highest sharpness, or *acuity* (from *acus,* "needle"). The **fovea,** or central region of the retina, which mediates our most acute vision, contains only cones. Cones are also responsible for color vision—our ability to discriminate light of different wavelengths. Although rods do not detect different colors and provide vision of poor acuity, they are

more sensitive to light. In a very dimly lighted environment we use our rod vision; therefore, in dim light we are color-blind and lack foveal vision. You may have noticed, while out on a dark night, that looking directly at a dim, distant light (that is, placing the image of the light on the fovea) causes it to disappear.

Another feature of the retina is the **optic disk,** where the axons conveying visual information gather together and leave the eye through the optic nerve. The optic disk produces a *blind spot* because no receptors are located there. We do not normally perceive our blind spots, but their presence can be demonstrated. If you have not found yours, you may want to try the exercise described in *Figure 6.5.*

Optic disk (Blind spot)

Fovea

Figure 6.5
A test for the blind spot. With your left eye closed, look at the + with your right eye and move the page nearer and farther from you. When the page is about 20 cm from your face, the green circle disappears, because its image falls on the blind spot of your right eye.

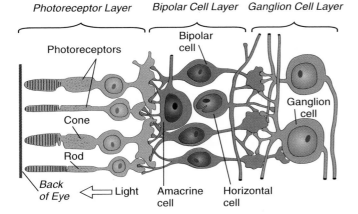

Photoreceptor Layer   Bipolar Cell Layer   Ganglion Cell Layer

Photoreceptors

Bipolar cell

Cone

Ganglion cell

Rod

Back of Eye ⇐ Light   Amacrine cell   Horizontal cell

Figure 6.6
Details of retinal circuitry.
(Adapted from Dowling, J. E., and Boycott, B. B. *Proceedings of the Royal Society of London, B.*, 1966, 166, 80–111.)

Close examination of the retina shows that it consists of several layers of neuron cell bodies, their axons and dendrites, and the photoreceptors. Figure 6.6 illustrates a cross section through the primate retina, which is divided into three main layers: the photoreceptive layer, the bipolar cell layer, and the ganglion cell layer. Note that the photoreceptors are at the *back* of the retina; light must pass through the overlying layers to get to them. Fortunately, these layers are transparent. (See *Figure 6.6.*)

The photoreceptors form synapses with **bipolar cells,** neurons whose two arms connect the shallowest and deepest layers of the retina. In turn, these neurons form synapses with the **ganglion cells,** neurons whose axons travel through the optic nerves (the second cranial nerves) and carry visual information into the brain. In addition, the retina contains **horizontal cells** and **amacrine cells,** both of

which transmit information in a direction parallel to the surface of the retina and thus combine messages from adjacent photoreceptors. (See *Figure 6.6.*)

● Photoreceptors

Figure 6.7 shows a drawing of two rods and a cone. Note that each photoreceptor consists of an outer segment connected by a cilium to the inner segment, which contains the nucleus. (See *Figure 6.7* on page 154.) The outer segment contains several hundred **lamellae,** or thin plates of membrane. (*Lamella* is the diminutive form of *lamina*, "thin layer.")

Let's consider the nature of transduction of visual information. The first step in the chain of events that leads to visual perception involves a special chemical called a photopigment. **Photopigments** are special molecules embedded in the membrane of the lamellae; a single human rod contains approximately 10 million of them. The molecules consist of two parts: an **opsin** (a protein) and **retinal** (a lipid). There are several forms of opsin; for example, the photopigment of human rods, **rhodopsin,** consists of *rod opsin* plus retinal. (*Rhod-* refers to the Greek *rhodon*, "rose," not to *rod*. Before it is bleached by the action of light, rhodopsin has a pinkish hue.) Retinal is synthesized from vitamin A, which explains why carrots, rich in this vitamin, are said to be good for your eyesight.

When a molecule of rhodopsin is exposed to light, it breaks into its two constituents, rod opsin and retinal. When that happens, the rod opsin changes from its rosy color to a pale yellow; hence, we say that the light *bleaches* the photopigment. The splitting of the photopigment causes a change in the membrane potential of the pho-

photoreceptor   One of the receptor cells of the retina; transduces photic energy into electrical potentials.

fovea (foe vee a)   The region of the retina that mediates the most acute vision of birds and higher mammals. Color-sensitive cones constitute the only type of photoreceptor found in the fovea.

optic disk   The location of the exit point from the retina of the fibers of the ganglion cells that form the optic nerve; responsible for the blind spot.

bipolar cell   A bipolar neuron located in the middle layer of the retina, conveying information from the photoreceptors to the ganglion cells.

ganglion cell   A neuron located in the retina that receives visual information from bipolar cells; its axons give rise to the optic nerve.

horizontal cell   A neuron in the retina that interconnects adjacent photoreceptors and the outer processes of the bipolar cells.

amacrine cell (amm a krin)   A neuron in the retina that interconnects adjacent ganglion cells and the inner processes of the bipolar cells.

lamella   A layer of membrane containing photopigments; found in rods and cones of the retina.

photopigment   A protein dye bonded to retinal, a substance derived from vitamin A; responsible for transduction of visual information.

opsin (opp sin)   A class of protein that, together with retinal, constitutes the photopigments.

retinal (rett i nahl)   A chemical synthesized from vitamin A; joins with an opsin to form a photopigment.

rhodopsin (roh dopp sin)   A particular opsin found in rods.

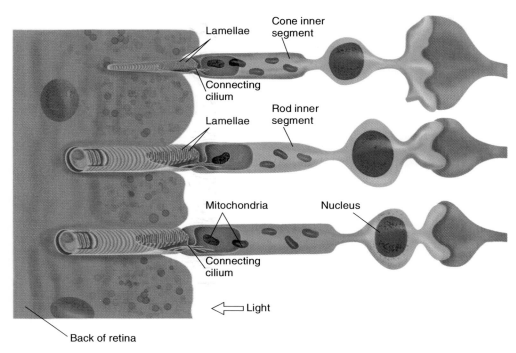

Lamellae

Cone inner segment

Connecting cilium

Lamellae

Rod inner segment

Mitochondria

Nucleus

Connecting cilium

Light

Back of retina

Figure 6.7
Photoreceptors.

toreceptor (the receptor potential), which changes the rate at which the photoreceptor releases its transmitter substance, glutamate.

The membrane of photoreceptors is different from that of other neurons—it contains cation channels that are normally *open* (Baylor, 1996). In the dark, these ion channels, which admit Na^+ and Ca^{+2}, are held open by molecules of cyclic GMP; thus, the resting membrane potential is less polarized than that of other neurons. As a consequence, photoreceptors continuously release glutamate when light is not falling on them. When light strikes a molecule of photopigment and causes it to split, the resulting series of chemical events activates a G protein known as **transducin.** In turn, molecules of transducin activate molecules of the enzyme *phosphodiesterase*, which destroy cyclic GMP, closing the ion channels. Because cations can no longer enter the cell, the membrane then becomes more polarized, and the release of glutamate decreases. (See *Figure 6.8.*)

In the vertebrate retina, photoreceptors provide input to both bipolar cells and horizontal cells. Figure 6.9 shows the neural circuitry from a photoreceptor to a ganglion cell. The circuitry is much simplified and omits the horizontal cells and amacrine cells. The first two types of cells in the circuit—photoreceptors and bipolar cells—do not produce action potentials. Instead, their release of transmitter substance is regulated by the value of their membrane poten-

tial; depolarizations increase the release, and hyperpolarizations decrease it. The circles indicate what would be seen on an oscilloscope screen recording changes in the cells' membrane potentials in response to a spot of light shining on the photoreceptor.

The hyperpolarizing effect of light on the membranes of photoreceptors is shown in the left graph. The hyperpolarization *reduces* the release of transmitter substance by the photoreceptor. Because the transmitter substance normally hyperpolarizes the dendrites of the bipolar cell, a *reduction* in its release causes the membrane of the bipolar cell to *depolarize*. Thus, light hyperpolarizes the photoreceptor and depolarizes the bipolar cell. (See *Figure 6.9.*) The depolarization causes the bipolar cell to release more transmitter substance, which depolarizes the membrane of the ganglion cell, causing it to increase its rate of firing. Thus, light shining on the photoreceptor causes excitation of the ganglion cell.

The circuit shown in Figure 6.9 illustrates a ganglion cell whose firing rate increases in response to light. As we will see, other ganglion cells *decrease* their firing rate in re-

transducin A G protein that is activated when a photon strikes a photopigment; activates phosphodiesterase molecules, which destroy cyclic GMP and close cation channels in the photoreceptor.

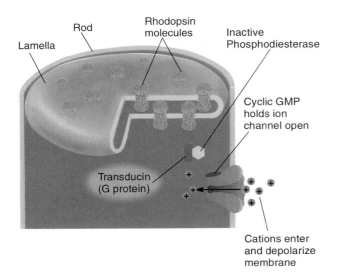

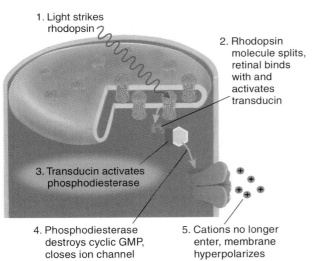

Figure 6.8
Transduction. A hypothetical explanation for the production of receptor potentials in photoreceptors.

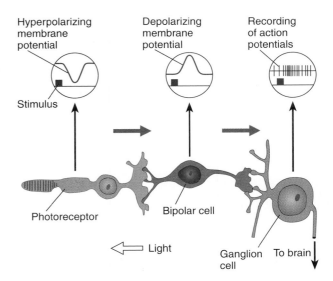

Figure 6.9
Neural circuitry in the retina. Light striking a photoreceptor produces a hyperpolarization, so the photoreceptor releases less transmitter substance. Because the transmitter substance normally hyperpolarizes the membrane of the bipolar cell, the reduction causes a depolarization. This depolarization causes the bipolar cell to release more transmitter substance, which excites the ganglion cell.
(Adapted from Dowling, J. E., in *The Neurosciences: Fourth Study Program,* edited by F. O. Schmitt and F. G. Worden. Cambridge Mass.: MIT Press, 1979.)

sponse to light. These neurons are connected to bipolar cells that form different types of synapses with the photoreceptors. The functions of these two types of circuits are discussed in a later section, Coding of Visual Information in the Retina.

● Connections Between Eye and Brain

The axons of the retinal ganglion cells bring information to the rest of the brain. They ascend through the optic nerves and reach the **dorsal lateral geniculate nucleus** of the thalamus. This nucleus receives its name from its resemblance to a bent knee (*genu* means "knee"). It contains six layers

of neurons, each of which receives input from only one eye. The neurons in the two inner layers contain cell bodies larger than those in the outer four layers. For this reason, the inner two layers are called the **magnocellular layers** and the outer four layers are called the **parvocellular layers** (*parvo-* refers to the small size of the cells). As we will see later, these two sets of layers belong to different systems, which are responsible for the analysis of different types of visual information. They receive input from different types of retinal ganglion cells. (See *Figure 6.10.*)

dorsal lateral geniculate nucleus A group of cell bodies within the lateral geniculate body of the thalamus; receives inputs from the retina and projects to the primary visual cortex.

magnocellular layer One of the inner two layers of cells in the dorsal lateral geniculate nucleus; transmits information necessary for the perception of form, movement, depth, and small differences in brightness.

parvocellular layer One of the four outer layers of cells in the dorsal lateral geniculate nucleus; transmits information necessary for perception of color and fine details.

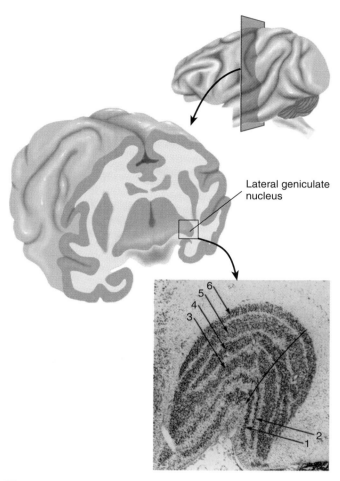

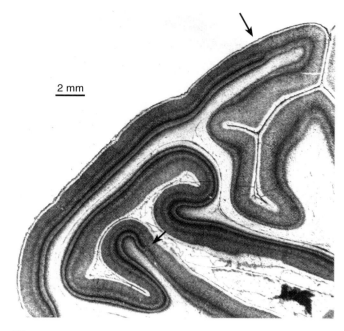

2 mm

Figure 6.11
A photomicrograph of a cross section through the striate cortex of a rhesus macaque monkey. The ends of the striate cortex are shown by arrows.
(From Hubel, D. H., and Wiesel, T. N. *Proceedings of the Royal Society of London, B.*, 1977, 198, 1–59.)

Figure 6.10
A photomicrograph of a section through the right lateral geniculate nucleus of a rhesus monkey (cresyl violet stain). Layers 1, 4, and 6 receive input from the contralateral (left) eye, and layers 2, 3, and 5 receive input from the ipsilateral (right) eye. Layers 1 and 2 are the magnocellular layers; layers 3–6 are the parvocellular layers. The receptive fields of all six layers are in almost perfect registration; cells located along the line of the unlabeled arrow have receptive fields centered on the same point.
(From Hubel, D. H., Wiesel, T. N., and Le Vay, S. *Philosophical Transactions of the Royal Society of London, B.*, 1977, 278, 131–163.)

The neurons in the dorsal lateral geniculate nucleus send their axons via the optic radiations to the primary visual cortex—the region surrounding the **calcarine fissure** (*calcarine* means "spur-shaped"), a horizontal fissure located in the medial and posterior occipital lobe. The primary visual cortex is often called the **striate cortex** because it contains a dark-staining layer *(striation)* of cells. (See *Figure 6.11*.)

Figure 6.12 shows a diagrammatical view of a horizontal section of the human brain. The optic nerves join to-

gether at the base of the brain to form the X-shaped **optic chiasm** (*khiasma* means "cross"). There, axons from ganglion cells serving the inner halves of the retina (the nasal sides) cross through the chiasm and ascend to the dorsal lateral geniculate nucleus of the opposite side of the brain. The axons from the outer halves of the retina (the temporal sides) remain on the same side of the brain. (See *Figure 6.12*.) The lens inverts the image of the world projected on the retina (and similarly reverses left and right). Therefore, because the axons from the nasal halves of the retinas cross to the other side of the brain, each hemisphere receives information from the contralateral half (opposite side) of the visual scene. That is, if a person looks straight ahead, the right hemisphere receives information from the left half of the visual field, and the left hemisphere receives information from the right. (See *Figure 6.12*.)

calcarine fissure (*kal ka rine*) A horizontal fissure on the inner surface of the posterior cerebral cortex; the location of the primary visual cortex.

striate cortex (*stry ate*) The primary visual cortex.

optic chiasm A cross-shaped connection between the optic nerves, located below the base of the brain, just anterior to the pituitary gland.

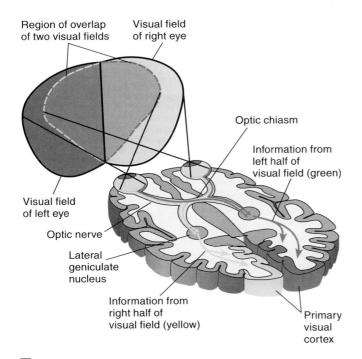

Figure 6.12
The primary visual pathway.

Besides the primary retino-geniculo-cortical pathway, several other pathways are taken by fibers from the retina. For example, one pathway to the hypothalamus synchronizes an animal's activity cycles to the 24-hour rhythms of day and night. (We will study this system in Chapter 9.) Other pathways, especially those that travel to the optic tectum and the pretectal nuclei, coordinate eye movements, control the muscles of the iris (and thus, the size of the pupil) and the ciliary muscles (which control the lens), and help direct our attention to sudden movements in the periphery of our visual field.

Interim Summary

Light consists of electromagnetic radiation, similar to radio waves but of a different frequency and wavelength. Color can vary in three perceptual dimensions: hue, brightness, and saturation, which correspond, respectively, to the physical dimensions of wavelength, intensity, and purity.

The photoreceptors in the retina—the rods and the cones—detect light. Muscles move the eyes so that images of the environment fall on the retina. Accommodation is accomplished by the ciliary muscles, which change the shape of the lens. Photoreceptors communicate through synapses with bipolar cells, which communicate through synapses with ganglion cells. In addition, horizontal cells and amacrine cells combine messages from adjacent photoreceptors.

When light strikes a molecule of photopigment in a photoreceptor, the retinal molecule detaches from the opsin molecule. This detachment activates a G protein called transducin, which activates the enzyme phosphodiesterase, which in turn destroys the molecules of cyclic GMP that are holding cation channels open. The reduction in the influx of Na^+ and Ca^{2+} produces the receptor potential—hyperpolarization of the photoreceptor membrane. As a result, the rate of firing of the ganglion cell changes, signaling the detection of light.

Visual information from the retina reaches the striate cortex surrounding the calcarine fissure after being relayed through the magnocellular and parvocellular layers of the dorsal lateral geniculate nuclei. Several other regions of the brain, including the hypothalamus and the tectum, also receive visual information. These regions help regulate activity during the day–night cycle, coordinate eye and head movements, control attention to visual stimuli, and regulate the size of the pupils.

CODING OF VISUAL INFORMATION IN THE RETINA

This section describes the way in which cells of the retina encode information they receive from the photoreceptors.

● Coding of Light and Dark

One of the most important methods for studying the physiology of the visual system is the use of microelectrodes to record the electrical activity of single neurons. As we saw in the previous section, some ganglion cells become excited when light falls on the photoreceptors with which they communicate. The **receptive field** of a neuron in the visual system is the part of the visual field that neuron "sees"— that is, the part in which light must fall for the neuron to be stimulated. Obviously, the location of the receptive field of a particular neuron depends on the location of the photoreceptors that provide it with visual information. If a neuron receives information from photoreceptors located in the fovea, its receptive field will be at the fixation point—

receptive field   That portion of the visual field in which the presentation of visual stimuli will produce an alteration in the firing rate of a particular neuron.

Figure 6.13

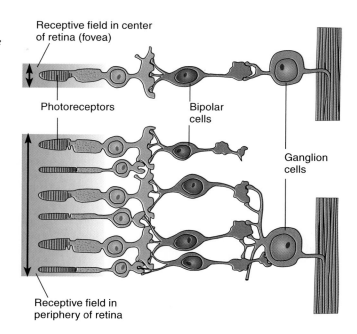

Figure 6.13
Central versus peripheral acuity. Ganglion cells in the fovea receive input from a smaller number of photoreceptors than in the periphery and hence provide more acute visual information.

the point at which the eye is looking. If the neuron receives information from photoreceptors located in the periphery of the retina, its receptive field will be located off to one side.

At the periphery of the retina many individual receptors converge on a single ganglion cell, bringing information from a relatively large area of the retina—and hence a relatively large area of the visual field. However, foveal vision is more direct, with approximately equal numbers of ganglion cells and cones. These receptor-to-axon relationships explain the fact that our foveal (central) vision is very acute, but our peripheral vision is much less precise. (See *Figure 6.13*.)

Over sixty years go, Hartline (1938) discovered that the frog retina contained three types of ganglion cells. ON cells responded with an excitatory burst when the retina was illuminated, OFF cells responded when the light was turned off, and ON/OFF cells responded briefly when the light went on and again when it went off. Kuffler (1952, 1953), recording from ganglion cells in the retina of the cat, discovered that their receptive field consists of a roughly circular center, surrounded by a ring. Stimulation of the center or surrounding fields had contrary effects: ON cells

were excited by light falling in the central field (*center*) and were inhibited by light falling in the surrounding field (*surround*), whereas OFF cells responded in the opposite manner. ON/OFF ganglion cells were briefly excited when light was turned on or off. In the primate retina, these ON/OFF cells project primarily to the superior colliculus (Schiller and Malpeli, 1977); thus, they do not appear to play a direct role in form perception. (See *Figure 6.14*.)

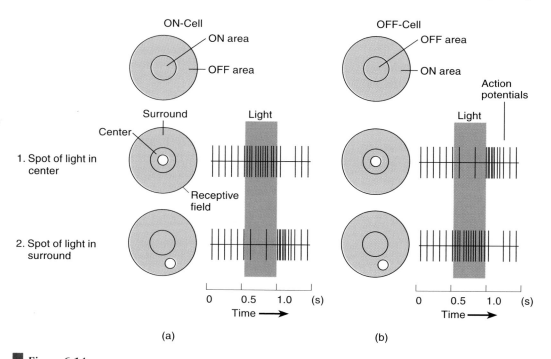

Figure 6.14
Responses of ON and OFF ganglion cells to stimuli presented in the center or the surround of the receptive field.
(Adapted from Kuffler, S. W. *Cold Spring Harbor Symposium for Quantitative Biology*, 1952, *17*, 281–292.)

Figure 6.14 also illustrates a rebound effect that occurs when the light is turned off again. Neurons whose firing is inhibited while the light is on will show a brief burst of excitation when it is turned off. In contrast, neurons whose firing is increased will show a brief period of inhibition when the light is turned off. (See *Figure 6.14.*)

The two major categories of ganglion cells (ON and OFF) and the organization of their receptive fields into contrasting center and surround provide useful information to the rest of the visual system. Let us consider the two types of ganglion cells first. As Schiller (1992) notes, ganglion cells normally fire at a relatively low rate. Then, when the level of illumination in the center of their receptive field increases or decreases (for example, when an object moves or the eye makes a saccade), they signal the change. In particular, ON cells signal increases and OFF cells signal decreases—but both signal them by an increased rate of firing. Such a system is particularly efficient. Theoretically, a single type of ganglion cell could fire at an intermediate rate and signal changes in the level of illumination by increases or decreases in rate of firing. However, in this case the average rate of firing of the one million axons in each optic nerve would have to be much higher.

Several studies have shown that ON cells and OFF cells do, indeed, signal different kinds of information. Schiller, Sandell, and Maunsell (1986) injected monkeys with APB (2-amino-4-phosphonobutyrate), a drug that selectively blocks synaptic transmission in ON bipolar cells. They found that the animals were less able to detect spots that were made brighter than the background but had no difficulty detecting spots slightly darker than the background. In addition, Dolan and Schiller (1989) found that an injection of APB completely blocked vision in very dim light, which is normally mediated by rods. Thus, rod bipolar cells must all be of the ON type. (If you think about it, that arrangement makes sense; in very dim light we are more likely to see brighter objects against a dark background than dark objects against a light background.)

The second characteristic of the receptive fields of ganglion cells—their center-surround organization—enhances

Figure 6.15
Enhancement of contrast. Although each gray square is of uniform darkness, the right edge of each square looks somewhat lighter and the left edge looks somewhat darker. This effect appears to be caused by the opponent center-surround arrangement of the receptive fields of the retinal ganglion cells.

All of the surrounds of the ON cells whose receptive fields fall within the lighter gray are evenly illuminated; this illumination partially inhibits the firing of these cells.

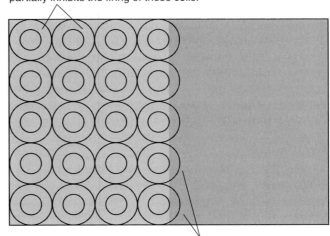

A portion of the inhibitory surrounds of the ON cells near the border receives less illumination; thus, these cells have the highest rate of firing.

Figure 6.16
A schematic explanation of the phenomenon shown in Figure 6.15. Only ON cells are shown; OFF cells are responsible for the darker appearance of the left side of the darker square.

our ability to detect the outlines of objects even when the contrast between the object and the background is low. Figure 6.15 illustrates this phenomenon. This figure shows six gray squares, arranged in order of brightness. The right side of each square looks lighter than the left side, which makes the borders between the squares stand out. But these exaggerated borders do not exist in the illustration; they are added by our visual system because of the center-surround organization of the receptive fields of the retinal ganglion cells. (See *Figure 6.15.*)

Figure 6.16 explains how this phenomenon works. We see the centers and surrounds of the receptive fields of several ganglion cells. (In reality, these receptive fields would be overlapping, but the simplified arrangement is easier to understand. This example also includes only ON cells—again, for simplicity.) The image of the transition between lighter and darker regions falls across some of these receptive fields. The cells whose centers are located in the brighter region but whose surrounds are located at least partially in the darker region will have the highest rate of firing.

● Coding of Color

So far, we have been examining the monochromatic properties of ganglion cells—that is, their responses to light and dark. But, of course, objects in our environment selectively absorb some wavelengths of light and reflect others, which, to our eyes, gives them different colors. Although monochromatic (black-and-white) vision is perfectly adequate for most purposes, color vision gives us, for example, the ability to distinguish ripe fruit from unripe fruit and makes it more difficult for other animals to hide themselves by means of camouflage (Mollon, 1989). The retinas of humans, Old World monkeys, and apes contain three different types of cones, which provides them with the most elaborate form of color vision (Jacobs, 1996).

Color Mixing

Various theories of color vision have been proposed for many years—long before it was possible to disprove or validate them by physiological means. In 1802 Thomas Young, a British physicist and physician, proposed that the eye detected different colors because it contained three types of receptors, each sensitive to a single hue. His theory was referred to as the *trichromatic* (three-color) *theory.* It was suggested by the fact that for a human observer any color can be reproduced by mixing various quantities of three colors judiciously selected from different points along the spectrum.

I must emphasize that *color mixing* is different from *pigment mixing.* If we combine yellow and blue pigments (as when we mix paints), the resulting mixture is green. Color mixing refers to the addition of two or more light sources.

If we shine a beam of red light and a beam of bluish green light together on a white screen, we will see yellow light. If we mix yellow and blue light, we get white light. When white appears on a color television screen or computer monitor, it actually consists of tiny dots of red, blue, and green light. (See *Figure 6.17.*)

Another fact of color perception suggested to a German physiologist, Ewald Hering (1905/1965), that hue might be represented in the visual system as *opponent colors.* Humans have long regarded yellow, blue, red, and green as primary colors. (Black and white are primary, too, but we perceive them as colorless.) All other colors can be described as mixtures of these primary colors. The trichromatic system cannot explain why *yellow* is included in this group. In addition, some colors appear to blend, whereas others do not. For example, one can speak of a bluish green or a yellowish green, and orange appears to have both red and yellow qualities. Purple resembles both red and blue. But try to imagine a reddish green or a bluish yellow. It is impossible; these colors seem to be opposite to each other. Again, these facts are not explained by the trichromatic theory. As we shall see in the following section, the visual system uses both trichromatic and opponent-color systems to encode information related to color.

Photoreceptors: Trichromatic Coding

Physiological investigations of retinal photoreceptors in higher primates have found that Young was right: Three

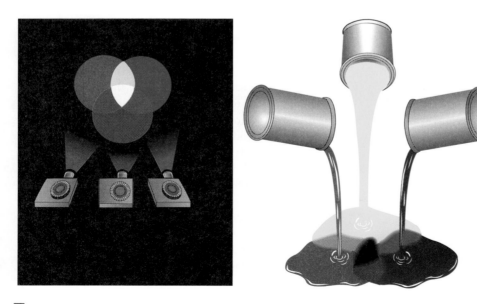

Figure 6.17
Additive color mixing and paint mixing. When blue, red, and green light of the proper intensity are all shone together, the result is white light. When red, blue, and yellow paints are mixed together, the result is a dark gray.

different types of photoreceptors (three different types of cones) are responsible for color vision. Investigators have studied the absorption characteristics of individual photoreceptors, determining the amount of light of different wavelengths that is absorbed by the photopigments. These characteristics are controlled by the particular opsin a photoreceptor contains; different opsins absorb particular wavelengths more readily. Figure 6.18 shows the absorption characteristics of the four types of photoreceptors in the human retina: rods and the three types of cones. (See *Figure 6.18.*)

The peak sensitivities of the three types of cones are approximately 420 nm (blue-violet), 530 nm (green), and 560 nm (yellow-green). The peak sensitivity of the short-wavelength cone is actually 440 nm in the intact eye, because the lens absorbs some short-wavelength light. For convenience, the short-, medium-, and long-wavelength cones are traditionally called "blue," "green," and "red" cones, respectively. The retina contains approximately equal numbers of "red" and "green" cones but a much smaller number of "blue" cones (approximately 8 percent of the total).

Genetic defects in color vision appear to result from anomalies in one or more of the three types of cones (Boynton, 1979; Nathans et al., 1986). The first two kinds of defective color vision described here involve genes on the X chromosome; thus, because males have only one X chromosome, they are much more likely to have this disorder. (Females are likely to have a normal gene on one of

their X chromosomes, which compensates for the defective one.) People with **protanopia** ("first-color defect") confuse red and green. They see the world in shades of yellow and blue; both red and green look yellowish to them. Their visual acuity is normal, which suggests that their retinas do not lack "red" or "green" cones. This fact, and their sensitivity to lights of different wavelengths, suggests that their "red" cones are filled with "green" cone opsin. People with **deuteranopia** ("second-color defect") also confuse red and green and also have normal visual acuity. Their "green" cones appear to be filled with "red" cone opsin.

Tritanopia ("third-color defect") is rare, affecting fewer than 1 in 10,000 people. This disorder involves a faulty gene that is not located on an X chromosome; thus, it is equally prevalent in males and females. People with tritanopia have difficulty with hues of short wavelengths and see the world in greens and reds. To them, a clear blue sky is a bright green, and yellow looks pink. Their retinas appear to lack "blue" cones. Because the retina contains so few of these cones, their absence does not noticeably affect visual acuity.

Retinal Ganglion Cells: Opponent-Process Coding

At the level of the retinal ganglion cell, the three-color code gets translated into an opponent-color system. Daw (1968) and Gouras (1968) found that these neurons respond specifically to pairs of primary colors, with red opposing green and blue opposing yellow. Thus, the retina contains two kinds of color-sensitive ganglion cells: *red-green* and *yellow-blue*. Some color-sensitive ganglion cells respond in a center-surround fashion. For example, a cell might be excited by red and inhibited by green in the center of their receptive field, while showing the opposite response in the surrounding ring. (See *Figure 6.19.*) Other ganglion cells that receive input from cones do not respond differentially to different wavelengths but simply encode relative brightness in the center and surround. These cells serve as "black-and-white" detectors.

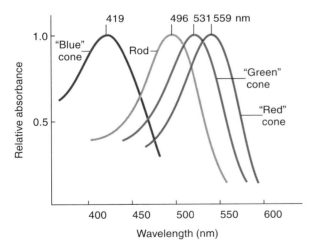

Figure 6.18
Relative absorbance of light of various wavelengths by rods and the three types of cones in the human retina.
(From Dartnall, H. J. A., Bowmaker, J. K., and Mollon, J. D. Human visual pigments: Microspectrophotometric results from the eyes of seven persons. *Proceedings of the Royal Society of London, B.,* 1983, *220,* 115–130.)

protanopia *(pro tan **owe** pee a)*   An inherited form of defective color vision in which red and green hues are confused; "red" cones are filled with "green" cone opsin.

deuteranopia *(dew ter an **owe** pee a)*   An inherited form of defective color vision in which red and green hues are confused; "green" cones are filled with "red" cone opsin.

tritanopia *(try tan **owe** pee a)*   An inherited form of defective color vision in which hues with short wavelengths are confused; "blue" cones are either lacking or faulty.

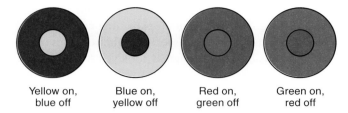

Yellow on, blue off   Blue on, yellow off   Red on, green off   Green on, red off

Figure 6.19
Receptive fields of color-sensitive ganglion cells. When a portion of the receptive field is illuminated with the color shown, the cell's rate of firing increases. When a portion is illuminated with the complementary color, the cell's rate of firing decreases.

The response characteristics of retinal ganglion cells to light of different wavelengths are obviously determined by the particular circuits that connect the three types of cones with the two types of ganglion cells. These circuits involve different types of bipolar cells, amacrine cells, and horizontal cells.

Figure 6.20 helps explain how particular hues are detected by the "red," "green," and "blue" cones and translated into excitation or inhibition of the red-green and yellow-blue ganglion cells. The diagram does not show the actual neural circuitry, which includes the retinal neurons that connect the cones with the ganglion cells. Although some progress is being made (Dacey, 1996; Dacey et al., 1996), the retinal circuitry responsible for color coding in ganglion cells is still largely unknown. The arrows in Figure 6.20 refer merely to the *effects* of the light falling on the retina.

Detection and coding of pure red, green, or blue light is the easiest to understand. For example, red light excites "red" cones, which causes the excitation of red-green ganglion cells. (See *Figure 6.20a.*) Green light excites "green"

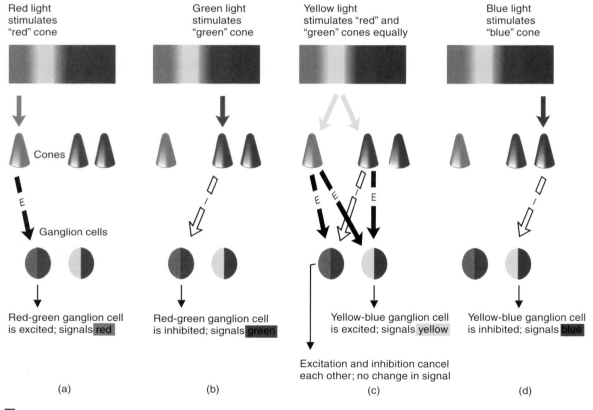

Red light stimulates "red" cone   Green light stimulates "green" cone   Yellow light stimulates "red" and "green" cones equally   Blue light stimulates "blue" cone

Cones

Ganglion cells

Red-green ganglion cell is excited; signals red   Red-green ganglion cell is inhibited; signals green   Yellow-blue ganglion cell is excited; signals yellow   Yellow-blue ganglion cell is inhibited; signals blue

Excitation and inhibition cancel each other; no change in signal

(a)   (b)   (c)   (d)

Figure 6.20
Color coding in the retina. (a) Red light stimulating a "red" cone, which causes excitation of a red-green ganglion cell. (b) Green light stimulating a "green" cone, which causes inhibition of a red-green ganglion cell. (c) Yellow light stimulating "red" and "green" cones equally but not affecting "blue" cones. The stimulation of "red" and "green" cones causes excitation of a yellow-blue ganglion cell. (d) Blue light stimulating a "blue" cone, which causes inhibition of a yellow-blue ganglion cell. The arrows labeled E and I represent neural circuitry within the retina that translates excitation of a cone into excitation or inhibition of a ganglion cell. For clarity, only some of the circuits are shown.

Figure 6.21
A negative afterimage. Stare for approximately 30 seconds at the dot in the center of the left figure; then quickly transfer your gaze to the dot in the center of the right figure. You will see colors that are complementary to the originals.

cones, which causes the *inhibition* of red-green cells. (See *Figure 6.20b.*) But consider the effect of yellow light. Because the wavelength that produces the sensation of yellow is intermediate between red and green, it will stimulate both "red" and "green" cones about equally. Yellow-blue ganglion cells are excited by both "red" and "green" cones, so their rate of firing increases. However, red-green ganglion cells are excited by red and inhibited by green, so their firing rate does not change. The brain detects an increased firing rate from the axons of yellow-blue ganglion cells, which it interprets as yellow. (See *Figure 6.20c.*) Blue light simply inhibits the activity of yellow-blue ganglion cells. (See *Figure 6.20d.*)

The opponent-color system employed by the ganglion cells explains why we cannot perceive a reddish green or a bluish yellow: An axon that signals red or green (or yellow or blue) can either increase or decrease its rate of firing; it cannot do both at the same time. A reddish green would have to be signaled by a ganglion cell firing slowly and rapidly at the same time, which is obviously impossible.

Negative Afterimages

Figure 6.21 demonstrates an interesting property of the visual system: the formation of a **negative afterimage.** Stare at the cross in the center of the image on the left for approximately 30 seconds. Then quickly look at the cross in the center of the white rectangle to the right. You will have a fleeting experience of seeing the red and green colors of a radish—colors that are complementary, or opposite, to the ones on the left. (See *Figure 6.21.*) Complementary items go together to make up a whole. In this context, **com-**

plementary colors are those that make white (or shades of gray) when added together.

The most important cause of negative afterimages is adaptation in the rate of firing of retinal ganglion cells. When ganglion cells are excited or inhibited for a prolonged period of time, they later show a *rebound effect*, firing faster or slower than normal. For example, the green of the radish in Figure 6.21 inhibits some red-green ganglion cells. When this region of the retina is then stimulated with the neutral-colored light reflected off the white rectangle, the red-green ganglion cells—no longer inhibited by the green light—fire faster than normal. Thus, we see a red afterimage of the radish.

Interim Summary

Recordings of the electrical activity of single neurons in the retina indicate that each ganglion cell receives information from photoreceptors—just one in the fovea and more in the periphery. The receptive field of most retinal ganglion cells consists of two concentric circles, with the cells becoming excited when light falls in one region and becoming inhibited when it falls in the other. This arrangement

negative afterimage   The image seen after a portion of the retina is exposed to an intense visual stimulus; consists of colors complementary to those of the physical stimulus.

complementary colors   Colors that make white or gray when mixed together.

enhances the ability of the nervous system to detect contrasts in brightness. ON cells are excited by light in the center and OFF cells are excited by light in the surround. ON cells detect light objects against dark backgrounds; OFF cells detect dark objects against light backgrounds.

Color vision occurs as a result of information provided by three types of cones, each of which is sensitive to light of a certain wavelength: long, medium, or short. The absorption characteristics of the cones are determined by the particular opsin that their photopigment contains. Most forms of defective color vision appear to be caused by alterations in cone opsins. The "red" cones of people with protanopia are filled with "green" cone opsin, and the "green" cones of people with deuteranopia are filled with "red" cone opsin. The retinas of people with tritanopia appear to lack "blue" cones.

Most color-sensitive ganglion cells respond in an opposing center-surround fashion to the pairs of primary colors: red and green, and blue and yellow. The responses of these neurons is determined by the retinal circuitry connecting them with the photoreceptors.

ANALYSIS OF VISUAL INFORMATION: ROLE OF THE STRIATE CORTEX

The retinal ganglion cells encode information about the relative amounts of light falling on the center and surround regions of their receptive field and, in many cases, about the wavelength of that light. The striate cortex performs additional processing of this information, which it then transmits to the visual association cortex.

● Anatomy of the Striate Cortex

The striate cortex consists of six principal layers (and several sublayers), arranged in bands parallel to the surface. These layers contain the nuclei of cell bodies and dendritic trees that show up as bands of light or dark in sections of tissue that have been dyed with a cell-body stain. (See *Figure 6.22.*)

In primates, information from the dorsal lateral geniculate nucleus enters the middle layer (layer IV_c) of the striate cortex. From there, it is relayed upward and downward, to be analyzed by circuits of neurons in different layers.

If we consider the striate cortex as a whole—if we imagine that we remove it and spread it out on a flat surface—we find that it contains a map of the contralateral half of the visual field. (Remember that each side of the brain sees the opposite side of the visual field.) The map is distorted; approximately 25 percent of the striate cortex is devoted to

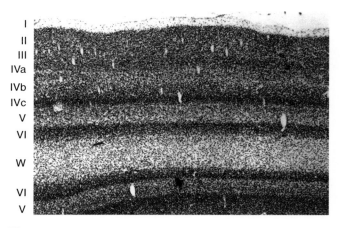

Figure 6.22
A photomicrograph of a small section of striate cortex, showing the six principal layers. The letter W refers to the white matter that underlies the visual cortex; beneath the white matter is layer VI of the striate cortex on the opposite side of the gyrus.
(From Hubel, D. H., and Wiesel, T. N. *Proceedings of the Royal Society of London, B.*, 1977, 198, 1–59. Reprinted with permission.)

the analysis of information from the fovea, which represents a small part of the visual field. (The area of the visual field seen by the fovea is approximately the size of a large grape held at arm's length.)

The pioneering studies of David Hubel and Torsten Wiesel at Harvard University during the 1960s began a revolution in the study of the physiology of visual perception (see Hubel and Wiesel, 1977, 1979). Hubel and Wiesel discovered that neurons in the visual cortex did not simply respond to spots of light; they selectively responded to specific *features* of the visual world. That is, the neural circuitry within the visual cortex combines information from several sources (for example, from axons carrying information received from several different ganglion cells) in such a way as to detect features that are larger than the receptive field of a single ganglion cell. The following subsections describe the visual characteristics that researchers have studied so far: orientation and movement, spatial frequency, texture, retinal disparity, and color.

● Orientation and Movement

Most neurons in the striate cortex are sensitive to *orientation*. That is, if a line is positioned in the cell's receptive field and rotated around its center, the cell will respond only when the line is in a particular position—a particular orientation. (See *Figure 6.23.*) Some neurons respond best to a vertical line, some to a horizontal line, and some to a line oriented somewhere in between.

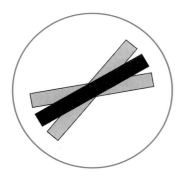

Some orientation-sensitive neurons have receptive fields organized in an opponent fashion. Hubel and Wiesel referred to them as **simple cells.** For example, a line of a particular orientation (say, a dark 45-degree line against a white background) might excite a cell if placed in the center of the receptive field but inhibit it if moved away from the center. (See *Figure 6.24a.*) Another type of neuron, which the researchers referred to as a **complex cell,** also responded best to a line of a particular orientation but did

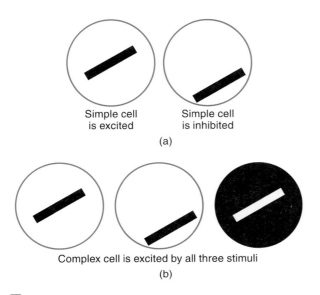

Simple cell
is excited

Simple cell
is inhibited

(a)

Complex cell is excited by all three stimuli

(b)

Figure 6.24
Response characteristics of neurons to orientation in the primary visual cortex. (a) Simple cell. (b) Complex cell.

not show an inhibitory surround; that is, it continued to respond while the line was moved within the receptive field. In fact, many complex cells increased their rate of firing when the line was moved perpendicular to its angle of orientation; thus, they also served as movement detectors. In addition, complex cells responded equally well to white lines against black backgrounds and black lines against white backgrounds. (See *Figure 6.24b.*)

● Spatial Frequency

Although the early studies by Hubel and Wiesel suggested that neurons in the primary visual cortex detected lines and edges, subsequent research found that they actually responded best to sine-wave gratings (De Valois, Albrecht, and Thorell, 1978). Figure 6.25 compares a sine-wave grating with a more familiar square-wave grating. A square-wave grating consists of a simple set of rectangular bars that vary in brightness; the brightness along the length of a line perpendicular to them would vary in a stepwise (square-wave) fashion. (See *Figure 6.25a.*) A **sine-wave grating** looks like a series of fuzzy, unfocused parallel bars. Along any line perpendicular to the long axis of the grating, the brightness varies according to a sine-wave function. (See *Figure 6.25b.*)

A sine-wave grating is designated by its spatial frequency. We are accustomed to the expression of frequencies (for example, of sound waves or radio waves) in terms of time or distance (such as cycles per second or cycles per meter). But because the image of a stimulus on the retina varies in size according to how close it is to the eye, the visual angle is generally used instead of the physical distance between adjacent cycles. Thus, the **spatial frequency** of a sine-wave grating is its variation in brightness measured in cycles per degree of visual angle. (See *Figure 6.26.*)

simple cell   An orientation-sensitive neuron in the striate cortex whose receptive field is organized in an opponent fashion.

complex cell   A neuron in the visual cortex that responds to the presence of a line segment with a particular orientation located within its receptive field, especially when the line moves perpendicularly to its orientation.

sine-wave grating   A series of straight parallel bands varying continuously in brightness according to a sine-wave function, along a line perpendicular to their lengths.

spatial frequency   The relative width of the bands in a sine-wave grating, measured in cycles per degree of visual angle.

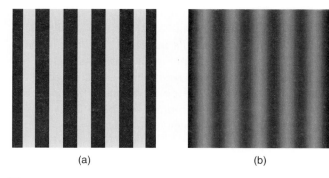

(a)   (b)

Figure 6.25
Parallel gratings. (a) Square-wave grating. (b) Sine-wave grating.

Most neurons in the striate cortex respond best when a sine-wave grating of a particular spatial frequency is placed in the appropriate part of the visual field. Different neurons detect different spatial frequencies. For orientation-sensitive neurons the grating must be aligned at the appropriate angle of orientation. Albrecht (1978) mapped the shapes of receptive fields of simple cells by observing their response while moving a very thin flickering line of the appropriate orientation through their receptive fields. He found that many of them had multiple inhibitory and excitatory regions surrounding the center. The profile of the excitatory and inhibitory regions of the receptive fields of such neurons looked like a modulated sine wave—precisely what would be needed to detect a few cycles of a sine-wave grating. (See **Figure 6.27.**) In most cases a neuron's receptive field is large enough to include between 1.5

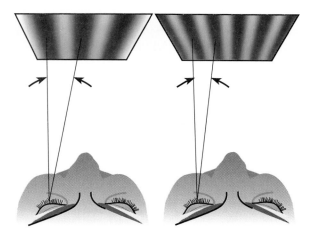

Figure 6.26
The concepts of visual angle and spatial frequency. Angles are drawn between the sine waves, with the apex at the viewer's eye. The visual angle *between adjacent sine waves is smaller when the waves are closer together.*

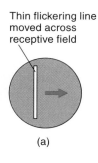

Thin flickering line moved across receptive field

(a)

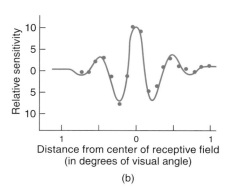

Distance from center of receptive field
(in degrees of visual angle)

(b)

Figure 6.27
The experiment by Albrecht, 1978. (a) The stimulus presented to the animal. (b) The response of a simple cell in the primary visual cortex.
(Adapted from De Valois, R. L., and De Valois, K. K. *Spatial Vision.* New York: Oxford University Press, 1988.)

and 3.5 cycles of the grating (De Valois, Thorell, and Albrecht, 1985).

What is the point of having neural circuits that analyze spatial frequency? A complete answer requires some rather complicated mathematics, so I will give a simplified one here. (If you are interested, you can consult De Valois and De Valois, 1988.) Consider the types of information provided by high and low spatial frequencies. Small objects, details within a large object, and large objects with sharp edges provide a signal rich in high frequencies, whereas large areas of light and dark are represented by low frequencies. An image that is deficient in high-frequency information looks fuzzy and out of focus, like the image seen by a nearsighted person who is not wearing corrective lenses. This image still provides much information about forms and objects in the environment; thus, the most important visual information is that contained in *low spatial frequencies.* When low-frequency information is removed, the shapes of images are very difficult to perceive. (As we will see, the more primitive magnocellular system provides low-frequency information.)

Many experiments have confirmed that the concept of spatial frequency plays a central role in visual perception, and mathematical models have shown that the information present in a scene can be represented very efficiently if it is first encoded in terms of spatial frequency. Thus, the brain probably represents the information in a similar way. Here I will describe just one example to help show the validity of the concept. Look at the two pictures in *Figure 6.28.* You can see that the picture on the right looks much more like the face of Abraham Lincoln than the one on the

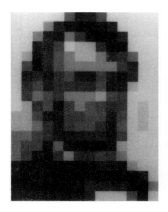

Figure 6.28
Spatial filtering. Both pictures contain the same amount of low-frequency information, but extraneous high-frequency information has been filtered from the picture on the right. If you look at the pictures from across the room, they look identical.
(From Harmon, L. D., and Julesz, B. *Science*, 1973, *180*, 1191–1197. Copyright 1973 by the American Association for the Advancement of Science.)

left. And yet both pictures contain the same information. The creators of the pictures, Harmon and Julesz (1973), used a computer to construct the figure on the left, which consists of a series of squares, each representing the average brightness of a portion of a picture of Lincoln. The one on the right is simply a transformation of the first one in which high frequencies have been removed. Sharp edges contain high spatial frequencies, so the transformation eliminates them. In the case of the picture on the left, these frequencies have nothing to do with the information contained in the original picture; thus, they can be seen as visual "noise." The filtration process (accomplished by a computer) removes this noise—and makes the image much clearer to the human visual system. Presumably, the high frequencies produced by the edges of the squares in the left figure stimulate neurons in the striate cortex that are tuned to high spatial frequencies. When the visual association cortex receives this noisy information, it has difficulty perceiving the underlying form.

If you want to watch the effect of filtering the extraneous high-frequency noise, try the following demonstration. Put the book down and look at the pictures in Figure 6.28 from across the room. The distance "erases" the high frequencies, because they exceed the resolving power of the eye, and the two pictures look identical. Now walk toward the book, focusing on the left figure. As you get closer, the higher frequencies reappear and this face gets harder and harder to recognize. (See *Figure 6.28.*)

● Texture

Recently, von der Heydt, Peterhans, and Dürstler (1992) discovered a new class of neurons in the monkey striate cortex. These neurons respond to "periodic patterns." They do not respond when single lines, bars, or edges are placed in their receptive fields, but they do respond vigorously when a grating (square-wave, sine-wave, or thin-line) of a particular spatial frequency and orientation is presented there. To provide a reliable response, these cells require a minimum of 2–7 alternating dark and light bars. They are not spatial-frequency analyzers like the ones I just described. The proof of this fact is difficult to convey in a few words, because it requires an understanding of the underlying mathematics. Those of you who would like to know more should consult the article.

These neurons showed extreme sensitivity to deviations from their optimal frequency and orientation. Figure 6.29 shows three square-wave gratings. The middle one produced the optimal response in a particular neuron in striate cortex. The one on the left, which has a slightly higher spatial frequency, produced only half as much excitation. The one on the right, which is rotated slightly counterclockwise, also produced only half as much excitation. (See *Figure 6.29.*)

Von der Heydt and his colleagues estimate that approximately 4 million periodic-pattern-selective cells serve the central four degrees of vision in the monkey striate cortex. They suggest that the function provided by these cells is perception of surfaces. Most surfaces (especially those found in nature) have a rough texture, and many of them contain a repeating pattern. For example, tree trunks, grasslands, boulders, leaves of bushes and trees, pebble-strewn ground—even a close-up view of the fur of another animal—contain periodic patterns that potentially could be

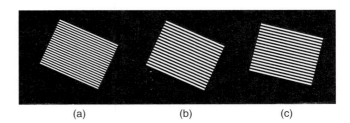

(a)   (b)   (c)

Figure 6.29
Sensitivity of a "texture" cell. The center stimulus (b) produced the highest rate of firing. The firing rate decreased by 50 percent when the spatial frequency of the grating was slightly higher (a) or the grating was rotated slightly (c).
(Adapted from von der Heydt, R., Peterhans, E., and Duersteler, M. R. *Journal of Neuroscience*, 1992, *12*, 1416–1434.)

Figure 6.30
Texture cues. Variations in texture can produce an appearance of distance.
(Nancy Sheehan.)

detected by these cells. These cells could help us discriminate surfaces that differ only in terms of their texture and could help us determine their orientation. As Figure 6.30 shows, texture gradients provide an important cue for perception of distance. (See *Figure 6.30.*)

● Retinal Disparity

We perceive depth by many means, most of which involve cues that can be detected monocularly, by one eye alone. For example, perspective, relative retinal size, loss of detail through the effects of atmospheric haze, and relative apparent movement of retinal images as we move our heads all contribute to depth perception and do not require binocular vision. However, binocular vision provides a vivid perception of depth through the process of stereoscopic vision, or *stereopsis.* If you have used a stereoscope (such as a View Master) or have seen a three-dimensional movie, you know what I mean. Stereopsis is particularly important in the visual guidance of fine movements of the hands and fingers, such as we use when we thread a needle.

Most neurons in the striate cortex are *binocular*—that is, they respond to visual stimulation of either eye. Many of these binocular cells, especially those found in a layer that receives information from the magnocellular system, have response patterns that appear to contribute to the perception of depth (Poggio and Poggio, 1984). In most cases the cells respond most vigorously when each eye sees a stimulus in a slightly *different* location. That is, the neurons respond to **retinal disparity,** a stimulus that produces images on slightly different parts of the retina of each eye. This is exactly the information that is needed for stereopsis; each eye sees a three-dimensional scene slightly differently, and the presence of retinal disparity indicates differences in the distance of objects from the observer.

● Color

In the striate cortex, information from color-sensitive ganglion cells is transmitted, through the parvocellular layers of the dorsal lateral geniculate nucleus, to special cells grouped together in **cytochrome oxidase (CO) blobs.** CO blobs were discovered by Wong-Riley (1978), who found that a stain for cytochrome oxidase, an enzyme present in mitochondria, showed a patchy distribution. Subsequent research with the stain (Horton and Hubel, 1980; Humphrey and Hendrickson, 1980) revealed the presence of a polka-dot pattern of dark columns extending through layers 2 and 3 and (more faintly) layers 5 and 6. The columns are oval in cross section, approximately 150×200 mm in diameter and spaced at 0.5-mm intervals (Fitzpatrick, Itoh, and Diamond, 1983; Livingstone and Hubel, 1987).

Figure 6.31 shows a photomicrograph of a slice through a macaque monkey visual cortex that has been flattened out and stained for the mitochondrial enzyme. You can clearly see the CO blobs within the striate cortex. Because the curvature of the cortex prevents it from being perfectly flattened, some of the tissue is missing in the center of the slice. (See *Figure 6.31.*)

To summarize, neurons in the striate cortex respond to several different features of a visual stimulus, including orientation, movement, spatial frequency, texture, retinal disparity, and color. Now let us turn our attention to the way this information is organized within the striate cortex.

retinal disparity   The fact that points on objects located at different distances from the observer will fall on slightly different locations on the two retinas; provides the basis for stereopsis.

cytochrome oxidase (CO) blob   The central region of a module of the primary visual cortex, revealed by a stain for cytochrome oxidase; contains wavelength-sensitive neurons; part of the parvocellular system.

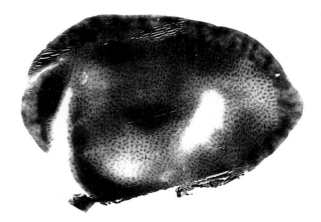

Figure 6.31
A photomicrograph of a slice through the primary visual cortex of a macaque monkey, parallel to the surface. The dark spots are the blobs, colored by a stain for cytochrome oxidase.
(From Hubel, D. H., and Livingstone, M. S. *Journal of Neuroscience*, 1989, 7, 3378–3415.)

Depending on their locations within the module, neurons receive varying percentages of input from each of the eyes.

If we record from neurons anywhere within a single module, we will find that all of their receptive fields overlap. Thus, all the neurons in a module analyze information from the same region of the visual field. Furthermore, if we insert a microelectrode straight down into an interblob region of the striate cortex (that is, in a location outside one of the CO blobs), we will find both simple and complex cells, but all of the orientation-sensitive cells will respond to lines of the same orientation. In addition, they will all share the same **ocular dominance**—that is, the same percentage of input from each of the eyes. If we move our electrode around the module, we will find that these two characteristics—orientation sensitivity and ocular dominance—vary systematically and are arranged at right angles to each other. (See *Figure 6.32.*)

Modular Organization of the Striate Cortex

Most investigators believe that the brain is organized in modules, which probably range in size from a hundred thousand to a few million neurons. Each module receives information from other modules, performs some calculations, and then passes the results to other modules. In recent years investigators have been learning the characteristics of the modules that are found in the visual cortex (De Valois and De Valois, 1988; Livingstone and Hubel, 1988).

The striate cortex is divided into approximately 2500 modules, each approximately 0.5 × 0.7 mm and containing approximately 150,000 neurons. The neurons in each module are devoted to the analysis of various features contained in one very small portion of the visual field. Collectively, these modules receive information from the entire visual field, the individual modules serving like the tiles in a mosaic mural. Input from the parvocellular and magnocellular layers of the dorsal lateral geniculate nucleus is received by different sublayers of the striate cortex: The parvocellular input is received by layer 4Cb, whereas the magnocellular input is received by layer 4Cα.

The modules actually consist of two segments, each surrounding a CO blob. Neurons located within the blobs have a special function: They are sensitive to color and to low spatial frequencies but are relatively insensitive to other visual features. Outside the CO blob, neurons show sensitivity to orientation, movement, spatial frequency, texture, and binocular disparity—but most do not respond to color (Livingstone and Hubel, 1984; Born and Tootell, 1991; Edwards, Purpura, and Kaplan, 1995). Each half of the module receives input from only one eye, but the circuitry within the module combines the information from both eyes, which means that most of the neurons are binocular.

ocular dominance   The extent to which a particular neuron receives more input from one eye than from the other.

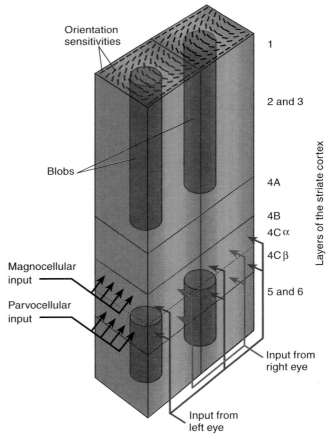

Figure 6.32
One of the modules of the primary visual cortex.

The striate cortex is not rectangular in shape, so its architecture is not like a checkerboard, with the borders of the modules following perfectly straight lines. Blasdel (1992a, 1992b) developed an ingenious technique to visualize just how the modules are arranged. He operated on monkeys, removing part of their skull and placing a glass window over the striate cortex. The window was equipped with a fitting that permitted him to inject a voltage-sensitive dye—a dye that changes its color according to the strength of an electrical field that passes through it.

After the animals recovered from the surgery, Blasdel injected the dye, which spread across the surface of the striate cortex. Then he showed the animals visual stimuli designed to excite neurons that were sensitive to particular features. If a large number of neurons in a particular region were sensitive to that feature, their excitation would change the color of the dye covering that region. Blasdel presented patterns containing lines of different orientations to identify cells that responded to particular orientations, and he presented stimuli monocularly to identify cells that received direct input from either the right or the left eye. During the presentation of the stimuli he used a sensitive video camera to record the pattern of color changes in the dye and analyzed these patterns with a computer.

Figure 6.33 shows some of his results. The colors shown on the figure were produced by the computer and do not represent the actual color of the dye on the surface of the cortex; nor do they represent the sensitivity of cortical neurons to different wavelengths. Instead, the colors represent the orientation sensitivity of the cortical neurons. Neurons in a region colored red are sensitive to horizontal lines; those in a region colored orange are sensitive to a line rotated counterclockwise by 30 degrees; and so on for yellow, green, blue, and violet. You will notice that this sequence of colors corresponds to the sequence of hues in the visual spectrum, as shown in Figure 6.1. Figure 6.33(a) shows how orientation sensitivity (indicated by white lines) is coded by color; as you will see, the red regions contain neurons sensitive to horizontal lines, the green regions contain neurons sensitive to vertical lines, and so on. (See *Figure 6.33a.*)

Figure 6.33(b) shows the relation between orientation sensitivity and *ocular dominance*—that is, the degree to which a cell responds to only one eye. The white lines indicate the location of cells that respond exclusively to one eye; thus, cells that respond equally well to stimuli presented to either eye are located midway between these lines. As you will see, the "rainbows" are lined up along the channels defined by the white lines, which means that changes in orientation sensitivity run at right angles to changes in ocular dominance. The CO blobs, which receive information from only one eye and which contain neurons that are not sensitive to orientation, are located at regular intervals along these white lines. (See *Figure 6.33b.*)

How does spatial frequency fit into this organization? Edwards, Purpura, and Kaplan (1995) found that neurons

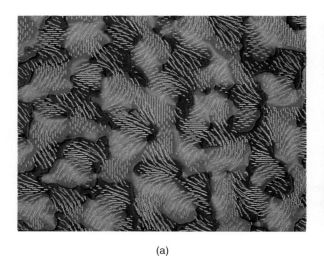

(a)

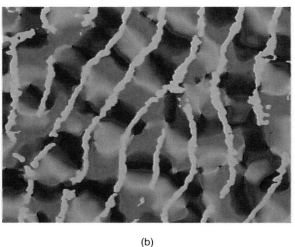

(b)

Figure 6.33
Modular organization of the striate cortex. (a) Distribution of orientation-sensitive cells. The white lines indicate the orientation sensitivity, which is encoded by color. (b) Relation between orientation sensitivity and ocular dominance. The white lines indicate the location of cells that respond exclusively to one eye. Note that the color bands are roughly perpendicular to the white lines.
(From Blasdel, G. G., *Journal of Neuroscience*, 1992b, *12*, 3139–3161. Reprinted by permission.)

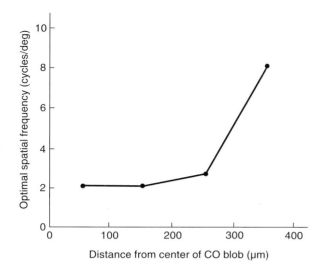

Figure 6.34
Optimal spatial frequency of neurons in striate cortex as a function of the distance of the neuron from the center of the nearest cytochrome oxidase blob.
(Adapted from Edwards, Edwards, D. P., Purpura, K. P., and Kaplan, E. *Vision Research*, 1995, *35*, 1501–1523.)

within the CO blobs responded to low spatial frequencies, but were sensitive to small differences in brightness. Outside the blobs, sensitivity to spatial frequency varied with the distance from the center of the nearest blob. Higher frequencies were associated with greater distances. (See *Figure 6.34*.) However, neurons outside the blobs were less sensitive to contrast; the difference between the bright and dark areas of the sine-wave grating had to be greater for these neurons than for neurons within the blobs.

● Blindsight

Visual perception depends on the integrity of the connections between the retina and the striate cortex. Thus, damage to the eyes, optic nerves, optic tracts, lateral geniculate nucleus, optic radiations, or primary visual cortex itself results in loss of vision in particular portions of the visual field or in complete blindness if the damage is total. However, an interesting phenomenon is seen in people with damage to the optic radiations or primary visual cortex.

It has long been recognized that damage to the optic radiations or primary visual cortex on one side of the brain causes blindness in the contralateral visual field. That is, if the right side of the brain is damaged, the patient will be blind to everything located to the left when he or she looks straight ahead. However, Weiskrantz and his colleagues (Weiskrantz et al., 1974; Weiskrantz, 1987) found that if an

object is placed in the patient's blind field and the patient is asked to reach for it, he or she will be able to do so rather accurately. The patients are surprised to find their hands repeatedly coming in contact with an object in what appears to them as darkness; they say that they see nothing there. The patient is also sensitive to movement and, to a certain extent, to the orientation of objects in the blind field.

This phenomenon, which Weiskrantz called **blindsight,** may depend on the connections that the visual association cortex receives from the superior colliculus and from the dorsal lateral geniculate nucleus (Cowey and Stoerig, 1991). The role of these connections in the intact brain is not known. Most of the inputs to the visual association cortex come directly from the striate cortex, and these connections are obviously necessary for normal visual perception.

Besides telling us something about the functions of the various parts of the visual system, the phenomenon of blindsight also shows that visual information can control behavior without producing a conscious sensation. Although the superior colliculi send visual information to parts of the brain that guide hand movements, they do not appear to send them to parts of the brain responsible for conscious awareness. Perhaps that connection is a more recent evolutionary development. I will have more to say about this topic in Chapters 15 and 16, which discuss memory and communication.

Interim Summary

The striate cortex consists of six layers and several sublayers. Visual information is received from the magnocellular and parvocellular layers of the dorsal lateral geniculate nucleus. The magnocellular system is more primitive, color-blind, and sensitive to movement, depth, and small differences in brightness, and the parvocellular system is more recent, color-sensitive, and able to discriminate finer details.

The striate cortex is organized into modules, each surrounding a pair of CO blobs, which are revealed by a stain for cytochrome oxidase, an enzyme found in mitochondria. Each half of a module receives information from one eye; but because information is shared, most of the neurons respond to input to both eyes. The neurons in the CO blobs are sensitive to color and to low-frequency sine-wave gratings, whereas those between the blobs are sensitive to sine-wave gratings of higher spatial frequencies, orienta-

blindsight The ability of a person to reach for objects located in his or her "blind" field; occurs after damage restricted to the primary visual cortex.

tion, retinal disparity, and movement. Some cells are specifically sensitive to orientation and frequency of gratings and probably are involved in detecting the texture of surfaces.

Damage to the visual system up to the striate cortex produces blindness in all or part of the visual field. However, damage limited to the striate cortex or to the optic radiations leading to them produces a syndrome called blindsight. People with blindsight deny seeing anything in the blind part of their visual field but can nevertheless point to objects located there and discriminate their size and orientation. They are also sensitive to movement. But although their behavior can be affected by objects in their blind field, they have no conscious awareness of the presence of these objects. Their ability to respond to visual stimuli apparently depends on connections from the superior colliculus and the lateral geniculate nucleus to the visual association cortex.

ANALYSIS OF VISUAL INFORMATION: ROLE OF THE VISUAL ASSOCIATION CORTEX

Although the striate cortex is necessary for visual perception, perception of objects and of the totality of the visual scene does not take place there. Each module of the striate cortex sees only what is happening in one tiny part of the visual field. Thus, for us to perceive objects and entire visual scenes, the information from these individual modules must be combined. That combination takes place in the visual association cortex.

● Two Streams of Visual Analysis

Visual information received from the striate cortex is analyzed in the visual association cortex. Based on their own research and on a review of the literature, Ungerleider and Mishkin (1982) concluded that the visual association cortex contains two streams of analysis. Subsequent anatomical studies have confirmed this conclusion (Baizer, Ungerleider, and Desimone, 1991). Both streams begin in the striate cortex, but they begin to diverge in the extrastriate cortex. One stream turns downward, ending in the cortex of the inferior temporal lobe. The other turns upward, ending in the cortex of the posterior parietal lobe. The ventral stream recognizes *what* an object is, and the dorsal stream recognizes *where* the object is located. (See *Figure 6.35*.)

The parvocellular and magnocellular systems provide different kinds of information (Livingstone and Hubel, 1987). The magnocellular system is found in all mammals,

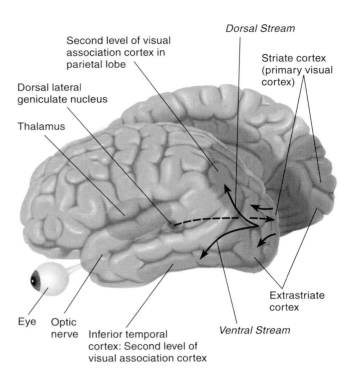

Figure 6.35
The human visual system, from the eye to the two streams of visual association cortex.

whereas the parvocellular system is found only in primates. These two systems receive information from different types of ganglion cells, which are connected to different types of bipolar cells and photoreceptors. Only the cells in the parvocellular system receive information about wavelength from cones; thus, this system analyzes information concerning color. Cells in this system also show high spatial resolution and low temporal resolution; that is, they are able to detect very fine details, but their response is slow and prolonged. In contrast, neurons in the magnocellular system are color-blind, are not able to detect fine details, and respond very briefly to a visual stimulus. And although they appear to be responsible for vision of lower acuity, these neurons are able to detect smaller contrasts between light and dark. They are especially sensitive to movement. (See *Table 6.1.*)

At one time, researchers believed that the dorsal stream received its information from the magnocellular system and the ventral stream received its information from the parvocellular system. But more recent research has shown that both systems contribute information to both streams (Maunsell, 1992). The dorsal stream receives mostly magnocellular input, but the ventral stream receives approximately equal input from both systems.

Table 6.1
Properties of the Magnocellular and Parvocellular Divisions of the Visual System

Property	Magnocellular division	Parvocellular division
Color	No	Yes
Sensitivity to contrast	High	Low
Spatial resolution	Low	High
Temporal resolution	Fast (transient response)	Slow (sustained response)

Source: Adapted from Livingston, M. S., and Hubel, D. H. *Journal of Neuroscience,* 1987, 7, 3416–2468.

Neurons in the striate cortex send axons to the **extrastriate cortex,** the region of the visual association cortex that surrounds the striate cortex (Zeki and Shipp, 1988). The primate extrastriate cortex (sometimes called the prestriate cortex or circumstriate cortex) consists of several regions, each of which contains one or more independent maps of the visual field. Each region is specialized, containing neurons that respond to a particular feature of visual information, such as orientation, movement, spatial frequency, retinal disparity, or color. So far, investigators have identified twenty-five distinct regions and subregions of the visual cortex of the rhesus monkey. These regions are arranged hierarchically, beginning with the striate cortex (Van Essen, Anderson, and Felleman, 1992). Most of the information passes up the hierarchy; each region receives information from regions located beneath it in the hierarchy, analyzes the information, and passes the results on to "higher" regions for further analysis. Some information is also transmitted in the opposite direction, but axons that descend the hierarchy are much less numerous than those that ascend it. Unfortunately, our knowledge of the anatomical details far exceeds our understanding of the functions performed by the subdivisions of the visual cortex.

● **Perception of Color**

As we saw earlier, neurons within the CO blobs in the striate cortex respond to colors. Like the ganglion cells in the retina (and the parvocellular neurons in the dorsal lateral geniculate nucleus), these neurons respond in opponent fashion. This information is analyzed by the regions of the visual association cortex that constitute the ventral stream.

Studies with Laboratory Animals

In the monkey brain, neurons in the CO blobs send information about color to a specific subarea of the extrastriate cortex. Zeki (1980) found that neurons in this subarea

(called V4) also respond selectively to colors, but their response characteristics are much more complex. Unlike the neurons we have encountered so far, these neurons respond to a variety of wavelengths, not just those that correspond to red, green, yellow, and blue.

The appearance of the colors of objects remains much the same whether we observe them under artificial light, under an overcast sky, or at noon on a cloudless day. This phenomenon is known as **color constancy.** Our visual system does not simply respond according to the wavelength of the light reflected by objects in each part of the visual field; instead, it compensates for the source of the light. This compensation appears to be made by simultaneously comparing the color composition of each point in the visual field with the average color of the entire scene. If the scene contains a particularly high level of long-wavelength light (as it would if an object were illuminated by the light of a setting sun), then some long-wavelength light is "subtracted out" of the perception of each point in the scene.

Schein and Desimone (1990) performed a careful study of the response characteristics of neurons in region V4 of the monkey extrastriate cortex. They found that these neurons responded to specific colors. Some also responded to colored bars of specific orientation; thus, area V4 seems to be involved in the analysis of form as well as color. The color-sensitive neurons had a rather unusual secondary receptive field—a large region surrounding the primary field. When stimuli were presented in the secondary receptive field, the neuron did not respond. However, stimuli pre-

extrastriate cortex   A region of visual association cortex; receives fibers from the striate cortex and from the superior colliculi and projects to the inferior temporal cortex.

color constancy   The relatively constant appearance of the colors of objects viewed under varying lighting conditions.

sented there could suppress the neuron's response to a stimulus presented in the primary field. For example, if a cell would fire when a red spot was presented in the primary field, it would fire at a slower rate (or not at all) when an additional red stimulus was presented in the surrounding secondary field. In other words, these cells responded to particular wavelengths of light but subtracted out the amount of that wavelength that was present in the background. As Schein and Desimone point out, this subtraction could serve as the basis for color constancy.

Walsh et al. (1993) confirmed this prediction; damage to area V4 does disrupt color constancy. The investigators found that although monkeys could still discriminate between different colors after area V4 had been damaged, their performance was impaired when the color of the overall illumination was changed. But the fact that the monkeys could still perform a color discrimination task under constant illumination means that some region besides area V4 must be involved in color vision.

A study by Heywood, Gaffan, and Cowey (1995) appears to have found that region—a portion of the temporal cortex just anterior to area V4. The investigators destroyed this region, leaving area V4 intact, and observed severe impairment in color discrimination. Thus, this region may be even more important than V4 for color perception.

Studies with Humans

Lesions of a restricted region of the human extrastriate cortex in the medial occipital lobe can cause loss of color vision without disruption of visual acuity. The patients describe their vision as resembling a black-and-white film. (Damasio et al., 1980; Kennard et al., 1995). The condition is known as **achromatopsia** ("vision without color"). If the brain damage is unilateral, people will lose color vision in only half of the visual field. In addition, they cannot even imagine colors or remember the colors or objects they saw before their brain damage occurred. As we just saw, Heywood, Gaffan, and Cowey (1995) found a region of the rhesus monkey brain whose damage disrupted the ability to make color discriminations. It will be interesting to see whether the regions are analogous in these two species.

Several PET or functional MRI studies confirm the studies of people with brain lesions. For example, Zeki et al. (1991) used a PET scanner to measure regional cerebral blood flow in normal human subjects. At the same time, they showed the subjects a plain gray stimulus or a multicolored pattern made up of rectangles of different sizes. They found that both stimuli increased the metabolic activity of the striate cortex and the region of the extrastriate cortex that surrounds it (region V2). The colored stimulus activated a specific region of the extrastriate cortex: the lingual and fusiform gyri, located in the occipital cortex on the medial surface of the brain.

Of course, perception of colors is useless in itself. The function of our ability to perceive different colors is to help us perceive different objects in our environment. Thus, to perceive and understand what is in front of us, we must have information about color combined with other forms of information. Some people with brain damage lose the ability to perceive shapes but can still perceive colors (Zeki, 1992). They can identify the colors of objects in their visual field, but they cannot say what these objects are.

● Analysis of Form

The analysis of form by the visual cortex begins with neurons in the striate cortex that are sensitive to orientation and spatial frequency. These neurons send information to the extrastriate cortex, which consists of several subregions. These subregions analyze the information and send it along the ventral stream toward the temporal neocortex.

Studies with Laboratory Animals

In primates the recognition of visual patterns and identification of particular objects takes place in the **inferior temporal cortex,** located on the ventral part of the temporal lobe. This region of visual association cortex is located at the end of the ventral stream. It is here that analyses of form and color are put together and perceptions of three-dimensional objects and backgrounds are achieved. The inferior temporal cortex consists of two major regions, areas TE and TEO. Damage to these regions causes severe deficits in visual discrimination (Mishkin, 1966; Gross, 1973; Dean, 1976). (See *Figures 6.36* and *6.37.*)

The receptive fields of neurons in area TEO are quite variable in size, but generally they are larger than those of neurons in area V4 and smaller than those of neurons in area TE (Boussaoud, Desimone, and Ungerleider, 1991). Their primary inputs come from area V4 and their primary outputs go to area TE, which suggests that "the neural coding of visual objects in TEO is based on object features that are more global than those in V4, but not quite as global as those in TE" (Boussaoud et al., 1991, p. 574). Lesions of TEO make it almost impossible for monkeys

---

achromatopsia *(ay krohm a **top** see a)*   Inability to discriminate among different hues; caused by damage to the visual association cortex.

inferior temporal cortex   In primates, the highest level of the ventral stream of the visual association cortex; located on the inferior portion of the temporal lobe.

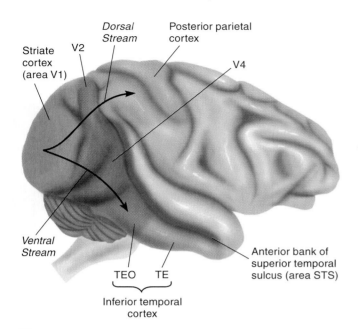

Figure 6.36
Areas of visual cortex in the rhesus monkey brain.
(Adapted from Zeki, S. M. *Journal of Physiology,* 1978, *277,* 227–244.)

to learn a task that requires them to discriminate between two simple two-dimensional patterns differing in form, size, orientation, color, or brightness (Iwai and Mishkin, 1969; Gross, 1973; Dean, 1982; Ungerleider and Mishkin,

1982; Mishkin, Ungerleider, and Macko, 1983). Thus, this region serves as an essential link in the analysis of visual information.

Neurons in area TE have the largest receptive fields of all, often encompassing the entire contralateral half of the visual field. In general, these neurons respond best to three-dimensional objects (or photographs of them). They respond poorly to simple stimuli such as spots, lines, or sine-wave gratings. Most of them continue to respond even when these stimuli are moved to a different location, are changed in size, are placed against a different background, or are partially occluded by another object (Rolls and Baylis, 1986; Kovács, Vogels, and Orban, 1995). Thus, they appear to participate in the recognition of objects rather than the analysis of specific features.

Tanaka and his colleagues (reviewed by Tanaka, 1996) investigated the response characteristics of these neurons. First, they located a single neuron with a microelectrode and then presented a large number of three-dimensional items, such as toy animals, plants, and "junk" objects, until they found one that produced the best response. Then they used a computerized system to present a series of simplified versions of the picture to find the simplest pattern that would still excite the cell. Figure 6.38 illustrates this procedure. The cell responded when the tiger's head was presented, and continued to respond to successively simplified patterns. The cell was activated by a pair of black rectangles superimposed on a white square, but not

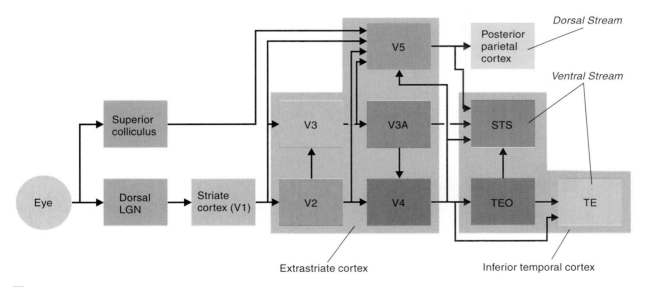

Figure 6.37
Interconnections of areas of visual cortex in the rhesus monkey brain. This diagram is greatly simplified; only the major areas and the most important connections are shown. The colors correspond to those shown in Figure 6.36. Some of the areas are hidden in the depth of sulci and are therefore not visible in Figure 6.36.

by either of the two components of this stimulus (See *Figure 6.38.*)

Obviously, the fact that the cell responded to the tiger's face does not mean that it was a "tiger's face analyzer." As Tanaka observed, no single cell could recognize a complex stimulus found in nature. Instead, particular stimuli would be represented by the activity of a large group of cells, each sensitive to slightly different patterns. It is the *pattern* of activity in circuits of neurons in area TE that represents the perception of particular objects.

Figure 6.39 shows the responses of a cell in area TE that responded to the sight of a water bottle oriented with its spout at ten o'clock. The computer program found that the simplest stimulus that this neuron would respond to was pear-shaped. The neuron would not respond to a circle without the neck, nor would it respond to a pear-shaped object rotated away from ten o'clock. The neuron still responded if the neck was extended or retracted, but did not respond at all if the neck was squared off at the end. (See *Figure 6.39.*)

Like other regions of the visual cortex, the inferior temporal cortex is arranged in columns. Neurons in adjacent regions usually respond to slightly different versions of the same stimuli. For example, several studies (for example, Desimone et al., 1984) have found neurons in the temporal lobe that are specifically excited by the sight of another face—either that of another monkey or that of a human. Some of these neurons respond to full-face views and others respond to profiles. Most of these face-sensitive cells are located in area TE and in the cortex that lines the anterior

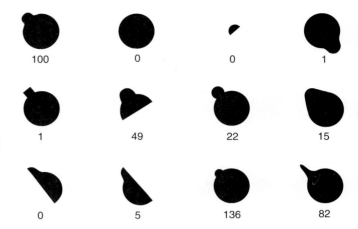

Figure 6.39
Responses of a single neuron in the inferior temporal cortex to variations on the pear-shaped stimulus that best activated the cell. The numbers beneath each shape indicate the relative response rates.
(Adapted from Tanaka, K. *Annual Review of Neuroscience,* 1996, *19,* 109–139.)

bank of the superior temporal sulcus (area STS). (Refer to *Figures 6.36* and *6.37.*)

A study by Wang, Tanaka, and Tanifuji (1996) used an optical recording technique to study the functional organization of the inferior temporal cortex in monkeys. They placed transparent "windows" over the surface of the cortex that permitted them to monitor the surface of the brain. They did not inject a voltage-sensitive dye, as Blasdel did in his study of the striate cortex. Instead, they used a special computer-driven video camera to record changes in the appearance of the cortex caused by changes in the oxidation level of hemoglobin in the cortical capillaries—changes that correlate with neural activity. Figure 6.40 shows the response to different views of a doll's head as it rotated. As you can see from the movement of the dark spot (arrows) from frame to frame, adjacent clusters of neurons were activated by different views of the head. (See *Figure 6.40.*)

Clearly, neurons in the primate inferior temporal cortex respond to very complex shapes, including things the animals have already seen, such as water bottles and faces. The complexity and the specific nature of these features suggest that the development of the circuits responsible for detecting them must involve learning. And, indeed, that seems to be the case. For example, several studies have found neurons in the inferior temporal cortex that respond specifically to objects that the monkeys have already seen many

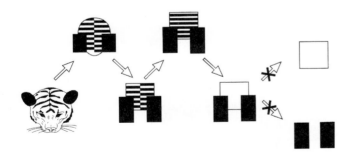

Figure 6.38
An analysis of the response characteristics of a neuron in area TE. The cell responded vigorously to the tiger's face and to the four simplified patterns selected by the computer. It did not respond to the white square or the two black rectangles presented alone.
(From Tanaka, K. *Current Opinion in Neurobiology,* 1992, *2,* 502–505.)

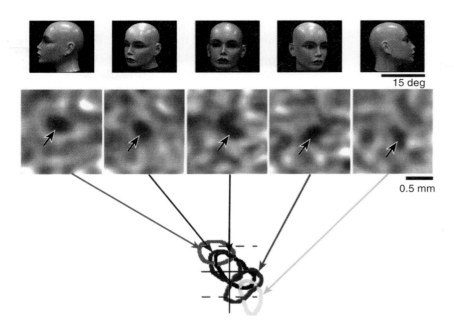

15 deg

0.5 mm

Figure 6.40
Results of the study by Wang, Tanaka, and Tanifuji (1996). Top row: *Views of the doll's head shown to the monkey.* Middle row: *Computer-generated images of the surface of the inferior temporal cortex. The arrows point to dark spots indicating a cluster of activated neurons.* Bottom: *Superimposed drawings of the outline of the clusters of activated neurons.* (Adapted from Wang, G., Tanaka, K., and Tanifuji, M. *Science*, 1996, *272*, 1665–1668.)

times, but not to unfamiliar objects (Kobatake, Tanaka, and Tamori, 1992; Logothetis, Pauls, and Poggio, 1995). Such studies will be discussed in more detail in Chapter 14.

Studies with Humans

Damage to the human visual association cortex can cause a category of deficits known as **visual agnosia.** *Agnosia* ("failure to know") refers to an inability to perceive or identify a stimulus by means of a particular sensory modality, even though its details can be detected by means of that modality and the person retains relatively normal intellectual capacity. *Apperceptive* visual agnosias are failures in high-level perception, whereas *associative* visual agnosias are disconnections between these perceptions and verbal systems. The distinction will be described in more detail later in this section.

People with visual agnosia cannot identify common objects by sight, even though they have relatively normal visual acuity (Warrington and James, 1988). In some cases they can read small print but fail to recognize a common object, such as a wristwatch. However, if they are permitted to hold the object (say, the wristwatch), they can immedi-

ately recognize it by touch and say what it is. Thus, they have not lost their memory for the object or forgotten how to say its name.

Apperceptive Visual Agnosia.   People with **apperceptive visual agnosia** may have normal visual acuity, but they cannot successfully recognize objects visually by their shape. For example, a brain-damaged patient studied by Benson and Greenberg (1969) was initially believed to be blind but was subsequently observed to navigate his wheelchair around the halls of the hospital. Testing revealed that his visual fields were full (there were no blind spots other than ones we all have) and that he could pick up threads placed on a sheet of white paper. He could discriminate among stimuli that differed in size, brightness, or hue but could not distinguish those that differed only in shape.

visual agnosia *(ag **no** zha)*   Deficits in visual perception in the absence of blindness; caused by brain damage.

apperceptive visual agnosia   Failure to perceive objects, even though visual acuity is relatively normal.

A common symptom of apperceptive visual agnosia is **prosopagnosia,** an inability to recognize particular faces (*prosopon* means "face"). That is, the patients can recognize that they are looking at a face, but they cannot say whose face it is—even if it belongs to a relative or close friend. They still remember who these people are, and will usually recognize them when they hear their voice. Prosopagnosia is a subtle deficit that can occur even when a person has no apparent difficulty recognizing common objects visually. Some investigators have speculated that facial recognition is mediated by special circuits in the brain that are devoted to the specific analysis of facial features. Others argue that the distinction between prosopagnosia and visual agnosia for common objects is quantitative, not qualitative; that is, visual agnosia for common objects is simply a more severe deficit, caused by more extensive damage to the relevant parts of the visual association cortex. Alexander and Albert (1983) note that although prosopagnosia can occur without visual-object agnosia, all patients with visual-object agnosia also have prosopagnosia.

Damasio, Damasio, and Van Hoesen (1982) described three patients with prosopagnosia who could recognize common objects but had difficulty discriminating between particular objects of the same class. For example, none of them could recognize their own car, although they could tell a car from other types of motorized vehicles. One of them could find her own car in a parking lot only by reading all the license plates until she found her own. Another patient, a farmer, could no longer recognize his cows (Bornstein, Stroka, and Munitz, 1969). Sergent and Signoret (1990) studied three patients with prosopagnosia who could recognize drawings of objects presented as we normally see them but who could not recognize them when they were presented from unusual viewpoints. For example, they could recognize a drawing of a side view of a coffee cup but could not recognize a drawing of a coffee cup viewed from above. These results suggest that prosopagnosia is simply a relatively mild form of visual agnosia; faces are particularly complex stimuli, and even a mild agnosia will make it difficult for a person to recognize them.

Lesion studies also suggest that the right hemisphere may be more important than the left in the perception of faces. Although most cases of prosopagnosia involve bilateral damage, some cases have resulted from right-hemisphere damage (Sergent and Villemure, 1989; De Renzi et al., 1994; Evans et al., 1995). However, no cases of prosopagnosia that include only left-hemisphere damage have been reported in right-handed people.

Associative Visual Agnosia. A person with apperceptive agnosia who cannot recognize common objects also cannot draw them or copy other people's drawings; thus, we properly speak of a deficit in perception. However, people with an **associative visual agnosia** appear to be able to perceive normally but cannot name what they have seen. In fact, they seem to be *unaware* of these perceptions. For example, a patient studied by Ratcliff and Newcombe (1982) could copy a drawing of an anchor (better than I could have done). Thus, he could perceive the shape of the anchor. However, he could not recognize either the sample or the copy that he had just drawn. When asked on another occasion to draw (not copy) a picture of an anchor, he could not do so. Even though he could copy a real image of an anchor, the word *anchor* failed to produce a mental image of one. (See *Figure 6.41.*) When asked (on yet another occasion) to define *anchor,* he said, "a brake for ships," so we can conclude that he knew what the word meant.

Associative agnosia also extends to prosopagnosia. For example, Sergent and Signoret (1992) reported the case of a patient who could match photos of different views of the same face but could not identify the faces—even when they were pictures of the patient herself. The lesion seems to have affected the ability to identify faces without severely damaging perceptual analysis.

Associative visual agnosia appears to involve difficulty in transferring visual information to verbal mechanisms. That is, the person perceives the object well enough to draw it (or to match it with similar stimuli), but his or her verbal mechanisms do not receive the necessary information to produce the appropriate word. David Margolin and I studied a man who had sustained brain damage from an inflammatory disease that affected his cerebral blood vessels. (The damage was diffuse, so we could not make any conclusions about the anatomy of his disorder.) Suffering from an apparent visual agnosia, he failed to identify most pictures of objects. However, he sometimes made unintentional gestures when he was studying a picture that gave him enough of a clue that he could identify it. For example, on one occasion while puzzling over a picture of a cow, he started making movements with both hands that were unmistakably ones he would make if he were milking a cow. He looked at his hands and said, "Oh, a cow!" (He was a farmer, by the way.)

prosopagnosia (*prah soh pag **no** zha*)   Failure to recognize particular people by the sight of their faces.

associative visual agnosia   Inability to identify objects that are perceived visually, even though the form of the perceived object can be drawn or matched with similar objects.

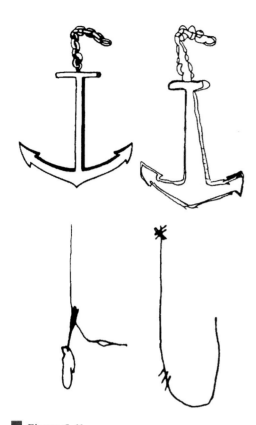

Figure 6.41
Associative visual agnosia. The patient successfully copied an anchor (top) *but failed on two attempts to comply with a request to "draw an anchor"* (bottom).
(From Ratcliff, G., and Newcombe, F., in *Normality and Pathology in Cognitive Functions*, edited by A. W. Ellis. London: Academic Press, 1982.)

We might speculate that his perceptual mechanisms, in the visual association cortex, were relatively normal but that connections between these mechanisms and the speech mechanisms of the left hemisphere were disrupted. However, the connections between the perceptual mechanisms and the motor mechanisms of the frontal lobe were spared, permitting him to make appropriate movements when looking at some pictures. In fact, a particularly observant and conscientious speech therapist helped the patient learn how to read by these means. She taught him the manual alphabet used by deaf people, in which letters are represented by particular hand and finger movements. (This system is commonly called *finger spelling*.) He could then look at individual letters of words he could not read, make the appropriate movements, observe the sequence of letters that he spelled, and decode the word.

Recent studies suggest that associative visual agnosia is best explained as a disruption of connections between the ventral stream of the visual cortex from the brain's verbal mechanisms without damage to the connections between these mechanisms and the dorsal stream. I will say more about these studies in the next subsection.

● Perception of Movement

We need not only to know what things are, but also where they are and where they are going. Without the ability to perceive the direction and velocity of movement of objects, we would have no way to predict where they will be. We would be unable to catch them (or avoid letting them catch us). This section examines the perception of movement; the final section examines the perception of location.

Studies with Laboratory Animals

One of the regions of the extrastriate cortex—area V5, also known as area MT—contains neurons that respond to movement. Damage to this region severely disrupts a monkey's ability to perceive moving stimuli (Siegel and Andersen, 1986). Area V5 receives input directly from the striate cortex and from several regions of the extrastriate cortex. It also receives input from the superior colliculus—directly and from projections relayed through the pulvinar, a nucleus of the thalamus (not shown). (Refer to *Figures 6.36* and *6.37*.)

The input from the superior colliculus contributes in some way to the movement sensitivity of neurons in area V5. Rodman, Gross, and Albright (1989, 1990) found that destruction of the striate cortex or the superior colliculus alone does not eliminate the movement sensitivity of V5 neurons, but destruction of both areas does. The roles played by these two sources of input are not yet known. Clearly, both inputs provide useful information; Seagraves et al. (1987) found that monkeys still could detect movement after lesions of the striate cortex but had difficulty estimating its rate.

Albright, Desimone, and Gross (1984) mapped the characteristics of movement-sensitive neurons in area V5. They found that all V5 neurons responded better to moving stimuli than to stationary ones and that most of them gave the same response regardless of the color or shape of the test stimulus. Most neurons showed directional sensitivity; that is, they responded only to movements in a particular direction. They also found that, like the striate cortex, area V5 is divided into rectangular modules. Traveling along the long axis of a module, they encountered neurons with directional sensitivities that varied systematically, in a clockwise or counterclockwise fashion. The receptive fields of movement-sensitive neurons in area V5 are elongated, with most neurons showing movement sensitivity in a direction at right angles to the long axis. A large antagonistic surround shows sensitivity to movement in the opposite direction (Raiguel et al., 1995).

As we saw in Chapter 5, no single method permits us to be certain that a particular region of the brain is directly involved in a particular function. But if several different methods provide compatible results, we can have more confidence that our conclusions are correct. As you have seen, most experiments investigating the neural basis of visual perception involve recording neural activity (of single units or of regions of the brain) or examining the behavioral effects of destruction of particular brain regions. Salzman et al. (1992) developed an additional approach that permitted them to alter the neural activity of particular neurons to see whether this alteration would affect the animal's perception. If it did, we could be reasonably confident that the activity of these neurons is at least partly responsible for the perception.

Salzman and his colleagues operated on monkeys, attaching a device to their skulls that permitted them to record, without causing discomfort, the activity of single units in area V5 while the animal was awake. Later, they presented the monkeys with a computer-controlled video display that contained an array of randomly located dots. Varying proportions of these dots (from 0 percent to 100 percent) moved in a particular direction. Under the 0 percent (no movement) condition, the dots moved randomly in a display resembling the "snow" seen on the screen of a television tuned between channels. Under the 100 percent condition, the display showed a set of dots all streaming in one direction. The animals' task was to indicate whether they detected coherent movement in the display by directing their gaze toward one of two small lights. Correct responses were rewarded with a small sip of water or fruit juice.

The investigators moved the microelectrode until they found a cluster of neurons that responded to movement in a particular direction. (As we just saw, area V5 is organized in modules, and neurons responsive to movements in a particular direction are clustered together.) Next, they adjusted the display so that it fell on the receptive field of this cluster of neurons and adjusted the proportion of the dots moving in the same direction so that the animals made correct responses on approximately half of the trials. Then, on some of the trials, the researchers applied a weak electrical current through the microelectrode. They found that the stimulation affected the animals' perception; during the stimulation the animals became more likely to perceive movement in the preferred direction of the cluster of neurons.

So far this discussion has been confined to movement of objects in the visual field. But if an animal moves its eyes, its head, or its whole body, the image on the retina will move even if everything within the animal's visual field remains stable. Often, of course, *both* kinds of movements will occur at the same time. The problem for the visual system is to determine which of these images are produced by movements of objects in the environment and which are produced by the animal's own eye, head, and body movements.

To illustrate this problem, think about how the page of this book looks as you read it. If we could make a videotape of one of your retinas, we would see that the image of the page projected there is in constant movement as your eyes make several saccades along a line and then snap back to the beginning of the next line. And yet, the page seems perfectly still to you. On the other hand, if you look at a single point on the page (say, a period at the end of a sentence) and then move the page around while following it with your eyes, you perceive the book as moving, even though the image on your retina remains relatively stable. (Try it.) And then think about the images on your retina while you are driving in busy traffic, constantly moving your eyes around to keep track of your own location and that of other cars moving in different directions at different speeds.

Little is known about how the visual system solves this very complicated problem. One subcortical brain structure has been implicated: the **pulvinar.** This large thalamic nucleus is one of the regions of the brain that has enlarged in size (relative to the rest of the brain) during the evolution of our species. Anatomical evidence and the results of single-unit recording suggest that it plays a role in our ability to compensate for the effects of our own movements on movements of images on the retina (Robinson and Petersen, 1992). The pulvinar receives inputs from the lateral geniculate nucleus and the superior colliculus and has reciprocal connections with all regions of the visual cortex. Some neurons in the pulvinar fire immediately after an eye movement, even when it is made in the dark. Other neurons respond to movements of retinal images, but not to those produced by eye movements (Robinson et al., 1991). Thus, the pulvinar is informed about eye movements and about movements of the visual image.

The pulvinar receives information about eye movements from the superior colliculus, which is interconnected with the brain stem nuclei that control the eye muscles, and it receives information about visual images from the striate cortex. Presumably, the pulvinar puts this infor-

pulvinar *(pull vi nar)* A large thalamic nucleus that projects to the visual association cortex and may play a role in compensating for eye and head movements.

mation together and helps the visual association cortex "subtract out" eye movements from movements of the retinal image. Whether the pulvinar is also involved in compensating for head and body movements is not known.

Studies with Humans

Bilateral damage to parts of the visual association cortex of the human brain can produce an agnosia for movement. For example, Zihl et al. (1991) reported the case of a woman with bilateral lesions of the lateral occipital cortex and middle temporal gyrus and the underlying white matter. The woman had an almost total loss of movement perception. She was unable to cross a street without traffic lights, because she could not judge the speed at which cars were moving. Although she could perceive movements, she found moving objects very unpleasant to look at. For example, while talking with another person, she avoided looking at the person's mouth because she found its movements very disturbing. When the investigators asked her to try to detect movements of a visual target in the laboratory, she said, "First the target is completely at rest. Then it suddenly jumps upwards and downwards" (p. 2244). She was able to see that the target was constantly changing its position, but she was unaware of any sensation of movement.

As we saw in the previous subsection, area V5 is the one region of the monkey brain that is most important for perception of movement. Several PET and functional MRI studies suggest that the region of the human brain that performs this function is located near the junction of the lateral occipital and temporal lobes. For example, Malach et al. (1995) showed people two types of stimuli: pictures of objects, faces, and textures, and moving random patterns of dots. As Figure 6.42 shows, these stimuli activated different regions of extrastriate cortex. The red region was activated by objects, faces, and textures, and the green region (presumably, corresponding to area V5) was activated by movement. (See *Figure 6.42.*)

Perception of movement can even help us perceive three-dimensional forms. Johansson (1973) demonstrated just how much information we can derive from movement. He dressed actors in black and attached small lights to several points on their bodies, such as their wrists, elbows, shoulders, hips, knees, and feet. He made movies of the actors in a darkened room while they were performing various behaviors, such as walking, running, jumping, limping, doing push-ups, and dancing with a partner who was also equipped with lights. Even though observers who watched the films could see only a pattern of moving lights against a dark background, they could readily perceive the pattern as belonging to a moving human and could identify the behavior the actor was performing. Subsequent

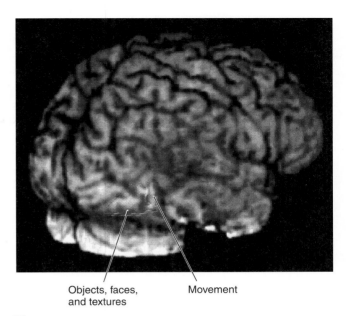

Objects, faces, and textures   Movement

Figure 6.42

Responses to shapes and movement. Averaged PET images of activation in the occipital lobe produced by pictures of objects, faces, and textures (red) and moving random patterns of dots (green).

(From Malach, R., Reppas, J. B., Benson, R. R., Kwong, K. K., Jiang, H., Kennedy, W. A., Ledden, P. J., Brady, T. J., Rosen, B. R., and Tootell, R. B. H. *Proceedings of the National Academy of Sciences, USA,* 1995, 92, 8135–8139.)

studies (Kozlowski and Cutting, 1977; Barclay, Cutting, and Kozlowski, 1978) showed that people could even tell, with reasonable accuracy, the sex of the actor wearing the lights. The cues appeared to be supplied by the relative amounts of movement of the shoulders and hips as the person walked.

Often, people with visual agnosia can still perceive *actions* (such as someone pretending to stir something in a bowl or deal out some playing cards) even though they cannot recognize objects by sight. They may be able to recognize friends by the way they walk, even though they cannot recognize their faces. Presumably, their lesions damage the ventral stream of the visual association cortex but leave intact area V5 and its efferent connections with the rest of the brain.

● Perception of Location

As we just saw, all subareas of the extrastriate cortex send information to the inferior temporal cortex, the region in which object perception appears to take place. In addition, three subareas of the extrastriate cortex—those involved with color, orientation, and movement—send information through area V5 to the parietal cortex. (Refer to *Figures 6.36* and *6.37*.) The parietal lobe is involved in spatial perception, and it is through these connections that it receives its visual input. Damage to the parietal lobes disrupts performance on a variety of tasks that require perceiving and remembering the locations of objects (Ungerleider and Mishkin, 1982).

Haxby et al. (1994) had human subjects perform two different discrimination tasks: one for form (human faces) and the other for spatial location (human faces and random patterns). In both cases, the subjects saw a display showing a face or a pattern, followed by a second display. In the form discrimination task, the subjects had to ignore the location of the faces but decide whether the second display contained the same face as the first. In the spatial location task, they had to ignore the nature of the forms but decide whether the form shown in the second display was in the same *location* as the one shown in the first display. While the subjects were performing the discrimination tasks, the investigators used a PET scanner to record their regional cerebral blood flow. They found that performance of both tasks increased the metabolic activity of much of the extrastriate cortex. However, only the form discrimination task activated the ventral stream and only the location discrimination task activated the dorsal stream. (See *Figure 6.43*.)

A particularly interesting phenomenon called **Balint's syndrome** occurs in people with bilateral damage to the parieto-occipital region—the region bordering the parietal lobe and occipital lobe (Balint, 1909; Damasio, 1985). Balint's syndrome consists of three major symptoms: optic ataxia, ocular apraxia, and simultanagnosia. All three symptoms are related to spatial perception.

Optic ataxia is a deficit in reaching for objects under visual guidance (*ataxia* comes from the Greek word for "disorderly"). A person with Balint's syndrome might be able to perceive and recognize a particular object, but when he or she tries to reach for it, the movement is often misdirected. **Ocular apraxia** (literally "without visual action") is a deficit of visual scanning. If a person with Balint's syndrome looks around a room filled with objects, he or she will see an occasional item and will be able to perceive it normally. However, the patient will not be able to maintain fixation; his or her eyes will begin to wander and another object will come into view for a time. The person is unable to make a systematic scan of the contents of the room and will not be able to perceive the location of the objects he or she sees. If an object moves, or if a light flashes, the person may report seeing something but will not be able to make an eye movement that directs the gaze toward the target.

Simultanagnosia is the most interesting of the three symptoms (Rizzo and Robin, 1990). As I just mentioned, if the gaze of a person with Balint's syndrome happens to fall on an object, he or she will perceive it. But *only one object* will be perceived at a time. For example, if an examiner holds either a comb or a pen in front of a patient's eyes, the patient will recognize the object. But if the examiner holds a pen and a comb together (for example, so that they form the legs of an X), the patient will see either the comb or the pen, but not both. The existence of simultanagnosia means that perception of separate objects takes place at least somewhat independently, even when the outlines of the objects overlap in the visual field.

Goodale and his colleagues (Goodale and Milner, 1992; Goodale et al., 1994) suggested that the primary function of the dorsal stream of the visual cortex is to guide actions rather than simply to perceive spatial locations. As Ungerleider and Mishkin (1982) originally put it, the ventral and dorsal streams tell us "what" and "where." Goodale and his colleagues suggested that the better terms are "what" and

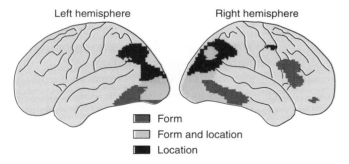

Left hemisphere   Right hemisphere

■ Form
□ Form and location
■ Location

Figure 6.43
Responses to objects and location. Averaged PET images of cortical activation produced by performing an object discrimination (human faces and random patterns) or a spatial location discrimination of the same stimuli.
(Adapted from Haxby, J. V., Horwitz, B., Ungerleider, L. G., Maisog, J. M., Pietrini, P., and Grady, C. L. *Journal of Neuroscience*, 1994, *14*, 6336–6353.)

Balint's syndrome   A syndrome caused by bilateral damage to the parieto-occipital region; includes optic ataxia, ocular apraxia, and simultanagnosia

optic ataxia *(ay tack see a)*   Difficulty in reaching for objects under visual guidance.

ocular apraxia *(ay prak see a)*   Difficulty in visual scanning.

simultanagnosia *(sime ul tane ag no zha)*   Difficulty in perceiving more than one object at a time.

"*how.*" First, they noted that the visual cortex of the parietal lobe is extensively connected to regions of the frontal lobe involved in controlling eye movements, reaching movements of the limbs, and grasping movements of the hands and fingers (Cavada and Goldman-Rakic, 1989; Gentilucci and Rizzolatti, 1990; Broussaud, di Pellegrino, and Wise, 1996). Second, they noted that the optic ataxia and ocular apraxia of Balint's syndrome, which are caused by bilateral damage to the dorsal stream, are deficits in visually guided movements. They cited the case of a person with such lesions who had no difficulty recognizing line drawings (that is, the ventral stream was intact), but who had trouble picking up objects (Jakobson et al., 1991). The patient could easily perceive the difference in the size of wooden blocks set out before her, but she failed to adjust the distance between her thumb and forefinger to the size of the block she was about to pick up. In contrast, a patient with profound visual agnosia could not distinguish between wooden blocks of different sizes, but *could* adjust the distance between her thumb and forefinger when she picked them up. She made this adjustment by means of vision, before she actually touched them (Milner et al., 1991; Goodale et al., 1994).

The suggestion by Goodale and his colleagues seems a reasonable one. Of course, the dorsal stream is involved in perception of the location of objects' space—but then, if its primary role is to direct movements, it *must* be involved in location of these objects, or else how could it direct movements toward them? In addition, it must contain information about the size and shape of objects, or else how could it control the distance between thumb and forefinger?

I mentioned earlier that I would attempt to explain associative visual agnosia as a disruption of the connections between the ventral stream and the brain's verbal mechanisms. As we saw, people with associative agnosia cannot verbally identify visually presented objects or pictures of them, but they can copy them and sometimes they can make hand movements that enable them to guess what the object is. Sirigu, Duhamel, and Poncet (1991) reported the case of a patient with bilateral lesions of the anterior temporal cortex who was able to copy drawings of objects but was unable to name them. However, he was able to say or demonstrate *what to do* with these objects. For example, he said, "You open on one side, stick something on it, close it, and it stays in. I can tell you how it works, but I don't see its exact use" (p. 2555). And what had the investigators shown him? A safety pin. When they showed him a picture of a jackhammer, he acted as if he were holding one, and made shaking movements. What was it for? "Probably to make holes . . . in the wall . . . when you want to hang a picture" (p. 2566).

It is important to realize that the patient recognized *what to do* with objects he saw, not *what they were used for.* He was able to describe or mime behaviors, not functions. Certainly, one would not use a jackhammer to hang a picture on the wall. Consider what he said when shown a pair of pliers: "It is used manually, when you pull apart here [points to handle] it opens up at the other end." So far, so good. But then he went on to say, "Perhaps to hold several pieces of paper together" (p. 2566). When shown an iron, he said "You hold it in one hand, and move it back and forth horizontally." He then mimed the action, as if he were pressing some clothes on an ironing board. "Maybe you can spread glue evenly with it" (p. 2566).

Even though the patient could not identify most objects visually, he accurately answered questions about their physical properties, such as "Which one would feel the heaviest?" "Which one is the softest?" or "Which one would feel the coldest?" The fact that he could answer these questions (and could mime what to do with them) indicates that the circuits responsible for visual form perception (those in the ventral stream) were relatively intact, but that they were no longer connected to the circuits responsible for speech (and for consciousness). His dorsal stream and its connections with speech mechanisms were undamaged, and it was apparently through these connections that he was able to describe how to use the objects. This interpretation is consistent with Goodale and Milner's conclusion that the dorsal stream is primarily occupied with controlling movements, not simply perceiving the location of objects.

Interim Summary

The visual cortex consists of the striate cortex, the extrastriate cortex (also called the prestriate or circumstriate cortex), and the visual association cortex of the inferior temporal lobe and the posterior parietal lobe. There are at least twenty-five different subregions of the visual cortex, arranged in a hierarchical fashion. The extrastriate cortex receives information from the striate cortex and from the superior colliculus. The color-sensitive cells in the CO blobs in the striate cortex send information to area V4 of the extrastriate cortex. Damage to the human extrastriate cortex (presumably, damage to area V4) can cause achromatopsia, a loss of color vision.

The visual cortex is organized into two streams. The ventral stream, which ends with the inferior temporal cortex, is involved with perception of objects. Lesions of this region disrupt visual object perception. Also, single neurons in the inferior temporal cortex respond best to complex stimuli and continue to do so even if the object is moved to a different location, changed in size, placed against a different background, or are partially hidden. The dorsal stream, which ends with the posterior parietal cortex, is involved with perception of location, movement, and control of eye and hand movements. Damage to area V5 or to the posterior parietal cortex disrupts an animal's ability to perceive movement or the spatial location of objects. Microstimulation of clusters of neurons in area V5 can alter a monkey's perception of movement. The pulvinar, a thalamic nucleus that receives information about eye movements from the superior colliculus and information about movement of retinal images from the visual cortex, appears to inform the visual cortex about which movements are caused by eye movements and which are caused by movements in the environment.

PET studies indicate that specific regions of the cortex are involved in perception of form, movement, and color, and these studies will undoubtedly enable us to discover the correspondences between the anatomy of the human visual system and that of laboratory animals. Studies with humans who have sustained damage to the visual association cortex have discovered two basic forms of visual agnosia. Apperceptive visual agnosia involves difficulty in perceiving the shapes of objects, even though the fine details can often be detected. Prosopagnosia, failure to recognize faces, has traditionally been regarded as a separate disorder, but it probably represents a mild form of apperceptive visual agnosia. The second basic form of visual agnosia, associative visual agnosia, is characterized by relatively good object perception (shown by the fact that the patients can copy drawings of objects) but the inability to recognize what is perceived. This disorder is probably caused by damage to axons that connect the visual association cortex with regions of the brain that are important for verbalization and thinking in words. Some patients with this disorder can describe or mime actions appropriate to the objects they see but cannot recognize.

Damage to the human visual association cortex corresponding to area V5 disrupts perception of movement. Sometimes people with visual agnosia caused by damage to the ventral system can still perceive the meanings of actions or recognize friends by the way they walk, which indicates that the dorsal stream of their visual cortex is largely intact. Balint's syndrome, which is caused by bilateral damage to the parieto-occipital region (the dorsal stream), includes the symptoms of optic ataxia, ocular apraxia, and simultanagnosia.

SUGGESTED READINGS

De Valois, R. L., and De Valois, K. K. *Spatial Vision*. New York: Oxford University Press, 1988.

Land, M. F., and Fernald, R. D. The evolution of eyes. *Annual Review of Neuroscience*, 1992, *15*, 1–30.

Merigan, W. H., and Maunsell, J. H. R. How parallel are the primate visual pathways? *Annual Review of Neuroscience*, 1993, *16*, 369–402.

Miyashita, Y. Inferior temporal cortex: Where visual perception meets memory. *Annual Review of Neuroscience*, 1993, *16*, 245–264.

Tanaka, K. Inferotemporal cortex and object vision. *Annual Review of Neuroscience*, 1996, *19*, 100–139.

Valberg, A., and Lee, B. B. *From Pigments to Perception*. New York: Plenum Press, 1991.

Wandell, B. A. *Foundations of Vision*. Sunderland, MA: Sinauer Associates, 1995.

Zeki, S. *A Vision of the Brain*. Oxford: Blackwell Scientific Publications, 1992.

CHAPTER 7

Audition, the Body Senses, and the Chemical Senses

Children Meeting by Elizabeth Murray, 1978.

Oil on canvas, 101 x 127 in. (256.5 x 322.6 cm.) Collection of Whitney Museum of American Art. Purchased with funds from the Louis and Bessie Adler Foundation, Inc., Seymour M. Klein, President.

One chapter was devoted to vision, but the rest of the sensory modalities must share a chapter. This unequal allocation of space reflects the relative importance of vision to our species and the relative amount of research that has been devoted to it. People often say that we have five senses: sight, hearing, smell, taste, and touch. Actually, we have more than five. For example, besides providing us with auditory information, the inner ear supplies information about head orientation and movement. And the sense of touch (more accurately, *somatosensation*) detects changes in pressure, warmth, cold, vibration, limb position, and events that damage tissue (that is, produce pain).

This chapter is divided into five major sections, which discuss audition, the vestibular system, the somatosenses, gustation, and olfaction.

AUDITION

For most people, audition is the second most important sense. The value of verbal communication makes it even more important than vision in some respects; for example,

a blind person can join others in conversation far more easily than a deaf person can. Acoustic stimuli also provide information about things that are hidden from view, and our ears work just as well in the dark. This section describes the nature of the stimulus, the sensory receptors, the brain mechanisms devoted to audition, and some of the details of the physiology of auditory perception.

● The Stimulus

We hear sounds, which are produced by objects that vibrate and set molecules of air into motion. When an object vibrates, its movements cause the air surrounding it alternately to condense and rarefy (pull apart), producing waves that travel away from the object at approximately 700 miles per hour. If the vibration ranges between approximately 30 and 20,000 times per second, these waves will stimulate receptive cells in our ears and will be perceived as sounds. (See *Figure 7.1.*)

In Chapter 6 we saw that light has three perceptual dimensions—hue, brightness, and saturation—that correspond to three physical dimensions. Similarly, sounds vary

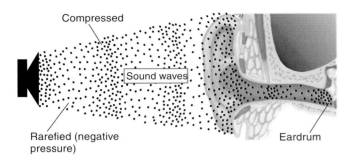

Figure 7.1
Sound waves. Changes in air pressure from sound waves move the eardrum in and out. Air molecules are closer together in regions of higher pressure and farther apart in regions of lower pressure.

in their pitch, loudness, and timbre. The perceived **pitch** of an auditory stimulus is determined by the frequency of vibration, which is measured in **hertz (Hz)**, or cycles per second. (The term honors Heinrich Hertz, a nineteenth-century German physicist.) **Loudness** is a function of intensity—the degree to which the condensations and rarefactions of air differ from each other. More vigorous vibrations of an object produce more intense sound waves and, hence, louder ones. **Timbre** provides information about the nature of the particular sound—for example, the sound of an oboe or a train whistle. Most natural acoustic stimuli are complex, consisting of several different frequencies of vibration. The particular mixture determines the sound's timbre. (See *Figure 7.2.*)

The eye is a *synthetic* organ (literally, "a putting together"). When two different wavelengths of light are mixed, we perceive a single color. For example, when we see a mixture of red and bluish green light, we perceive pure yellow light and cannot detect either of the two constituents. In contrast, the ear is an *analytical* organ (from

analuein, "to undo"). When two different frequencies of sound waves are mixed, we do not perceive an intermediate tone; instead, we hear both original tones. As we will see, the ability of our auditory system to detect the individual component frequencies of a complex tone gives us the capacity to identify the nature of particular sounds, such as those of different musical instruments.

● Anatomy of the Ear

Figure 7.3 shows a section through the ear and auditory canal and illustrates the apparatus of the middle and inner ear. (See *Figure 7.3.*) Sound is funneled via the *pinna* (external ear) through the ear canal to the **tympanic membrane** (eardrum), which vibrates with the sound. We are not very good at moving our ears, but by orienting our heads we can modify the sound that finally reaches the receptors.

The *middle ear* consists of a hollow region behind the tympanic membrane, approximately 2 ml in volume. It contains the bones of the middle ear, called the **ossicles,** which are set into vibration by the tympanic membrane. The **malleus** (hammer) connects with the tympanic membrane and transmits vibrations via the **incus** (anvil) and **stapes** (stirrup) to the **cochlea,** the structure that contains the receptors. The baseplate of the stapes presses against the membrane behind the **oval window,** the opening in the bony process surrounding the cochlea. (See *Figures 7.3* and *7.4* on pages 188 and 189.)

---

pitch   A perceptual dimension of sound; corresponds to the fundamental frequency.

hertz (Hz)   Cycles per second.

Loudness   A perceptual dimension of sound; corresponds to intensity.

timbre (*tim* ber or *tamm* ber)   A perceptual dimension of sound; corresponds to complexity.

tympanic membrane   The eardrum.

ossicle (*ahss* i kul)   One of the three bones of the middle ear.

malleus   The "hammer"; the first of the three ossicles.

incus   The "anvil"; the second of the three ossicles.

stapes (*stay* peez)   The "stirrup"; the last of the three ossicles.

cochlea (*cock* lee uh)   The snail-shaped structure of the inner ear that contains the auditory transducing mechanisms.

oval window   An opening in the bone surrounding the cochlea that reveals a membrane, against which the baseplate of the stapes presses, transmitting sound vibrations into the fluid within the cochlea.

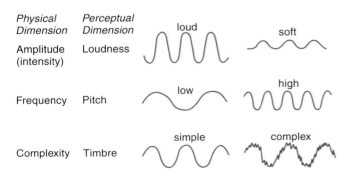

Figure 7.2
The physical and perceptual dimensions of sound waves.

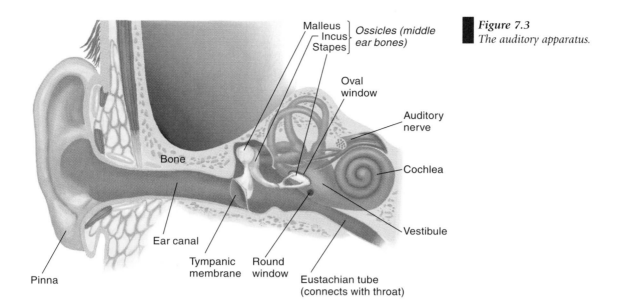

Figure 7.3
The auditory apparatus.

The cochlea is part of the *inner ear.* It is filled with fluid; therefore, sounds transmitted through the air must be transferred into a liquid medium. This process normally is very inefficient—99.9 percent of the energy of airborne sound would be reflected away if the air impinged directly against the oval window of the cochlea. (If you have ever swum underwater, you have probably noted how quiet it is there; most of the sound arising in the air is reflected off the surface of the water.) The chain of ossicles serves as an extremely efficient means of energy transmission. The bones provide a mechanical advantage, with the baseplate of the stapes making smaller but more forceful excursions against the oval window than the tympanic membrane makes against the malleus.

The name *cochlea* comes from the Greek word *kokhlos,* or "land snail." It is indeed snail-shaped, consisting of two and three-quarters turns of a gradually tapering cylinder, 35 mm (1.37 in.) long. The cochlea is divided longitudinally into three sections, the *scala vestibuli* ("vestibular stairway"), the *scala media* ("middle stairway"), and the *scala tympani* ("tympanic stairway"), as shown in *Figure 7.5.* The receptive organ, known as the **organ of Corti,** consists of the *basilar membrane,* the *hair cells,* and the *tectorial membrane.* The auditory receptor cells are called **hair cells,** and they are anchored, via rodlike **Deiters's cells,** to the **basilar membrane.** The cilia of the hair cells pass through the *reticular membrane,* and the ends of some of them attach to the fairly rigid **tectorial membrane,** which projects overhead like a shelf. (See *Figure 7.5.*) Sound waves cause the basilar membrane to move relative to the tectorial membrane, which bends the cilia of the hair cells. This bending produces receptor potentials.

Georg von Békésy—in a lifetime of brilliant studies on the cochleas of various animals, from human cadavers to elephants—found that the vibratory energy exerted on the oval window causes the basilar membrane to bend (von Békésy, 1960). Because of the physical characteristics of the basilar membrane, the portion that bends the most is determined by the frequency of the sound: High-frequency sounds cause the end nearest the oval window to bend.

Figure 7.6 shows this process in a cochlea that has been partially straightened. If the cochlea were a closed system, no vibration would be transmitted through the oval window, because liquids are essentially incompressible. However, there is a membrane-covered opening, the **round win-**

organ of Corti The sensory organ on the basilar membrane that contains the auditory hair cells.

hair cell The receptive cell of the auditory apparatus.

Deiters's cell *(dye* terz) A supporting cell found in the organ of Corti; sustains the auditory hair cells.

basilar membrane *(bazz i ler)* A membrane in the cochlea of the inner ear; contains the organ of Corti.

tectorial membrane *(tek torr ee ul)* A membrane located above the basilar membrane; serves as a shelf against which the cilia of the auditory hair cells move.

round window An opening in the bone surrounding the cochlea of the inner ear that permits vibrations to be transmitted, via the oval window, into the fluid in the cochlea.

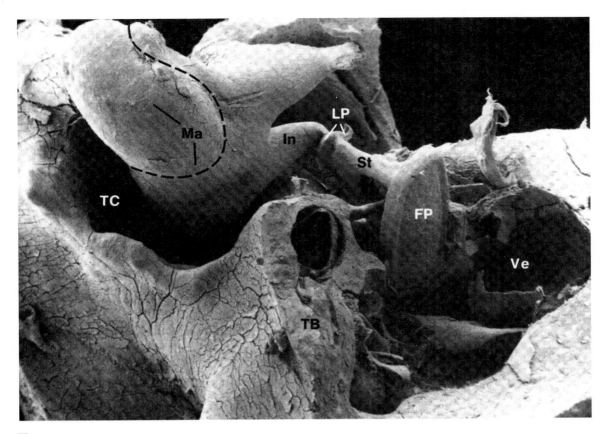

Figure 7.4
A scanning electron micrograph of the stapes and the round window.
(From *Tissues and Organs: A Text-Atlas of Scanning Electron Microscopy.* By Richard G. Kessel and Randy H. Kardon. Copyright © 1979 by W. H. Freeman and Company. Reprinted with permission.)

dow, that allows the fluid inside the cochlea to move back and forth. The baseplate of the stapes vibrates against the membrane behind the oval window and introduces sound waves of high or low frequency into the cochlea. The vibrations cause part of the basilar membrane to flex back and forth. Pressure changes in the fluid underneath the basilar membrane are transmitted to the membrane of the round window, which moves in and out in a manner opposite to the movements of the oval window. That is, when the baseplate of the stapes pushes in, the membrane behind the round window bulges out. As we will see in a later subsection, different frequencies of sound vibrations cause different portions of the basilar membrane to flex. (See *Figure 7.6.*)

Some people suffer from a middle ear disease that causes the bone to grow over the round window. Because their basilar membrane cannot easily flex back and forth, these people have a severe hearing loss. However, their hearing can be restored by a surgical procedure called *fen-*

estration ("window making"), in which a tiny hole is drilled in the bone where the round window should be.

● Auditory Hair Cells and the Transduction of Auditory Information

Two types of auditory receptors, *inner* and *outer* auditory hair cells, lie on the inside and outside of the cochlear coils, respectively. Hair cells contain **cilia** ("eyelashes"), fine hairlike appendages arranged in rows, according to height. The human cochlea contains 3500 inner hair cells and 12,000 outer hair cells. The hair cells form synapses with dendrites of bipolar neurons whose axons bring auditory information to the brain. Figure 7.7 shows the appearance of the inner and outer hair cells and the reticular membrane in a

cilium A hairlike appendage of a cell involved in movement or in transducing sensory information; found on the receptors in the auditory and vestibular system.

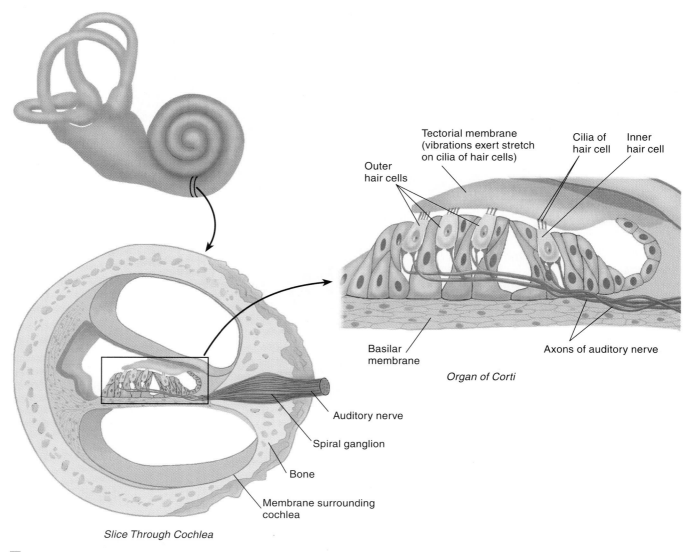

Organ of Corti

Slice Through Cochlea

Figure 7.5
A cross section through the cochlea, showing the organ of Corti.

photograph taken by means of a scanning electron microscope. Note the three rows of outer hair cells on the right and the single row of inner hair cells on the left. (See *Figure 7.7.*)

Sound waves cause both the basilar membrane and the tectorial membrane to flex up and down. These movements bend the cilia of the hair cells in one direction or the other. The tips of the cilia of outer hair cells are attached directly to the tectorial membrane. The cilia of the inner hair cells do not touch the overlying tectorial membrane, but the relative movement of the two membranes causes the fluid within the cochlea to flow past them, making them bend back and forth, too.

Cilia contain actin filaments, which make them stiff and rigid (Flock, 1977). Adjacent cilia are linked to each other by elastic filaments known as **tip links.** Each tip link is attached to the end of one cilium and to the side of an adjacent cilium. The points of attachment, known as **insertional plaques,** look dark under an electron microscope. As we will see, receptor potentials are triggered at the insertional plaques. (See *Figure 7.8* on page 192.)

> **tip link**   Elastic filaments that attach the tip of one cilium to the side of the adjacent cilium.
>
> **insertional plaque**   The point of attachment of a tip link to a cilium.

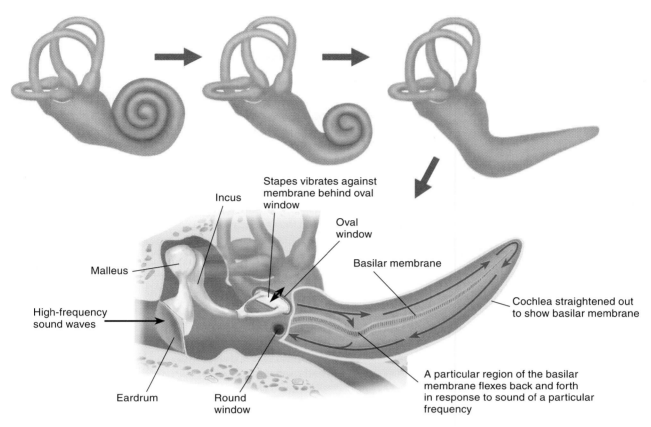

Figure 7.6
Responses to sound waves. When the stapes pushes against the membrane behind the oval window, the membrane behind the round window bulges outward. Different high-frequency and medium-frequency sound vibrations cause flexing of different portions of the basilar membrane. In contrast, low-frequency sound vibrations cause the tip of the basilar membrane to flex in synchrony with the vibrations.

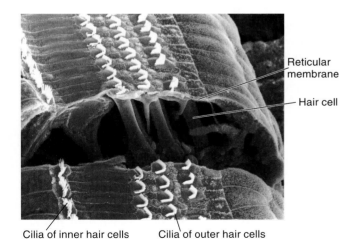

Figure 7.7
A scanning electron photomicrograph of a portion of the organ of Corti, showing the cilia of the inner and outer hair cells.
(Photomicrograph courtesy of I. Hunter-Duvar, The Hospital for Sick Children, Toronto, Ontario.)

Normally, tip links are slightly stretched, which means that they are under a small amount of tension. Thus, movement of the bundle of cilia in the direction of the tallest of them further stretches these linking fibers, whereas movement in the opposite direction relaxes them. The bending of the bundle of cilia causes receptor potentials (Pickles and Corey, 1992; Hudspeth and Gillespie, 1994; Gillespie, 1995; Jaramillo, 1995). The resting potential of an auditory hair cell is approximately -160 mV, and the fluid that surrounds them is rich in potassium. Each insertional plaque contains a single cation channel. When the bundle of hair cells is straight, the probability of an individual ion channel being open is approximately 10 percent. This means that a small amount of K^+ and Ca^{+2} diffuses into the cilium. When the bundle moves toward the tallest one, the increased tension on the tip links opens all the ion channels, the flow of K^+ and Ca^{+2} into the cilium increases, and the membrane depolarizes. As a result, the release of neurotransmitter by the hair cell increases. When the bundle

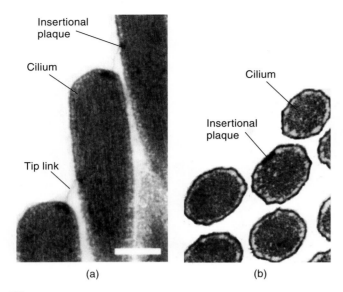

Figure 7.8
Electron micrographs of the transduction apparatus in hair cells. (a) Longitudinal section through three adjacent cilia. Tip links, elastic filaments attached to insertional plaques, link adjacent cilia. (b) A cross section through several cilia, showing an insertional plaque.

moves in the opposite direction, toward the shortest cilium, the relaxation of the tip links allows the opened ion channels to close. The influx of K^+ and Ca^{+2} ceases, the membrane hyperpolarizes, and the release of neurotransmitter decreases. (See *Figure 7.9*.)

The location of the ion channels at the end of each tip link was revealed by use of calcium green, a calcium-sensitive fluorescent dye. Denk et al. (1995) placed tissue containing a group of hair cells in a fluid-filled chamber. They used a special scanning microscope that produced a very fine laser beam of infrared light to detect the presence of calcium in individual cilia. A micropipette located to the side of the bundle of cilia could eject or aspirate a stream of liquid, thus moving the bundle toward or away from the longest cilia. They also attached a recording microelectrode to the hair cell to record receptor potentials. (See *Figure 7.10* on page 194.)

Denk and his colleagues found that deflection of the bundle of cilia toward the tallest one produced a depolarization in the hair cell membrane and was accompanied by the entry of calcium. Larger displacements produced greater depolarizations and resulted in more cilia being filled with calcium. The calcium entered at the tips of the cilia and then spread down toward the body of the hair cells. Previous studies had obtained evidence suggesting that the ion channels were located near the tips of the cilia,

but it had proved impossible to determine whether they were located at both ends of the tip links or only at one end. If ion channels were located at only one end of the tip links, then either the shortest or the longest cilia should not contain ion channels and thus should never be filled with calcium. However, Denk et al. found that cilia in all locations could admit calcium; thus, the ion channels were located at both ends of the tip links. (See *Figure 7.11* on page 194.)

Exactly how does stretching a tip link cause an ion channel to open? Most researchers believe that the tip links are attached directly to the ion channels, and when there is a sufficient amount of tension on them, the pores of the ion channels are pulled open. In fact, Preyer et al. (1995) found that when tip links were dissolved by a special enzyme, displacement of the bundle of cilia no longer produced receptor potentials. Thus, tension on the tip links, and not simple movement of the cilia, is what opens the ion channels.

Figure 7.12 illustrates this process. It also illustrates a hypothetical explanation for the fact that the tension on the tip links is self-adjusting. For the hair cells to be maximally sensitive to movements of the bundle of cilia, the tension on the tip links must be just right. If the tension is too low, the ion channels will not open when the bundle is moved toward the longest cilium. If the tension is too high, the ion channels will always be open. Research in several laboratories (Assad and Corey, 1992; Gillespie, 1995; Jaramillo, 1995) has shown that the ion channel located on the side of a cilium contains a myosin "motor" that is capable of crawling up or down the actin filaments that run the length of the cilia. (The interaction between myosin and actin is what provides the motive force responsible for muscular contraction. This process is described in Chapter 8.) When calcium ions enter an open ion channel, the myosin motor slides down, reducing the tension on the tip link. When the ion channel closes and calcium disappears from the cytoplasm of the cilium, the motor moves up, increasing the tension on the tip link. (See *Figure 7.12* on page 195.)

● The Auditory Pathway

Connections with the Cochlear Nerve

The organ of Corti sends auditory information to the brain by means of the **cochlear nerve,** a branch of the auditory

cochlear nerve The branch of the auditory nerve that transmits auditory information from the cochlea to the brain.

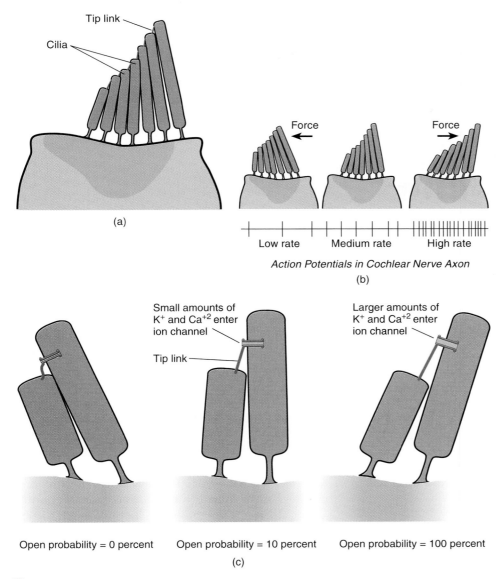

Force

Force

Action Potentials in Cochlear Nerve Axon

Low rate   Medium rate   High rate

(a)

(b)

Small amounts of K⁺ and Ca⁺² enter ion channel

Larger amounts of K⁺ and Ca⁺² enter ion channel

Tip link

Open probability = 0 percent   Open probability = 10 percent   Open probability = 100 percent

(c)

Figure 7.9
*Transduction in hair cells of the inner ear. (a) Appearance of the cilia of an auditory hair cell.
(b) Movement of the bundle of cilia toward the tallest one increases the firing rate of the cochlear
nerve axon attached to the hair cell, while movement away from the tallest one decreases it.
(c) Movement toward the tallest cilium increases tension on the tip links, which opens the ion channels and increases the influx of K⁺ and Ca⁺² ions. Movement toward the shortest cilium removes tension from the tip links, which permits the ion channels to close, stopping the influx of cations.*

nerve (eighth cranial nerve). The neurons that give rise to
the afferent axons that travel through this nerve are of the
bipolar type. Their cell bodies reside in the *cochlear nerve
ganglion.* (This ganglion is also called the *spiral ganglion,*
because it consists of clumps of cell bodies arranged in a
spiral caused by the curling of the cochlea.) These neurons
have axonal processes, capable of sustaining action poten-

tials, that protrude from both ends of the soma. The end of
one process acts like a dendrite, responding with excitatory
postsynaptic potentials when the transmitter substance is
released by the auditory hair cells. The excitatory postsynaptic potentials trigger action potentials in the auditory
nerve axons, which form synapses with neurons in the
medulla. (Refer to *Figure 7.5.*)

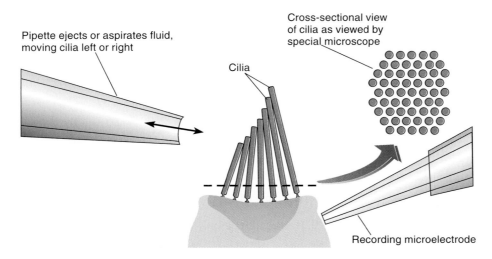

Figure 7.10
The experimental setup used by Denk et al. (1995) to detect the influx of calcium into the cilia of hair cells of the inner ear.
(Adapted from Denk, W., Holt, J. R., Shepherd, G. M. G., and Corey, D. P. *Neuron,* 1995, *15,* 1311–1321.)

Each cochlear nerve contains approximately 50,000 afferent axons. The dendrites of approximately 95 percent of these axons form synapses with the inner hair cells. Most afferent fibers make contact with only one inner hair cell, but each inner hair cell forms synapses with approximately 20 fibers (Dallos, 1992). The axons that receive information from the inner hair cells are thick and myelinated. The other 5 percent of the sensory fibers in the cochlear nerve form synapses with the much more numerous outer hair

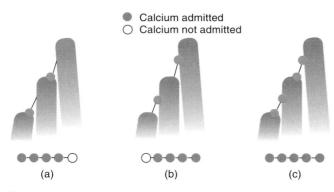

Figure 7.11
Verifying the location of ion channels in hair cells of the inner ear. If ion channels were found only at the insertional plaque located at the tip of the cilia (a) or at the side of the cilia (b), the longest or the shortest cilia should not admit calcium (indicated by the open circles). Because cilia in all locations admitted calcium, there must be an ion channel located at all insertional plaques (c).
(Adapted from Denk, W., Holt, J. R., Shepherd, G. M. G., and Corey, D. P. *Neuron,* 1995, *15,* 1311–1321.)

cells, at a ratio of approximately 1 fiber per 30 outer hair cells. In addition, these axons are thin and unmyelinated. Thus, although the inner hair cells represent only 29 percent of the total number of receptive cells, their connections with auditory nerves suggest that they are of primary importance in the transmission of auditory information to the central nervous system.

Physiological and behavioral studies confirm the inferences made from the synaptic connections of the two types of hair cells: The inner hair cells are necessary for normal hearing. In fact, Deol and Glucksohn-Waelsch (1979) found that a mutant strain of mice whose cochleas contain *only* outer hair cells apparently cannot hear at all. Most investigators currently believe that the outer hair cells are primarily *effector* cells, involved in altering the mechanical characteristics of the basilar membrane and thus influencing the effects of sound vibrations on the inner hair cells. I will discuss this possibility in the section on place coding of pitch.

The cochlear nerve contains efferent axons as well as afferent ones. The source of the efferent axons is the superior olivary complex, a group of nuclei in the medulla; thus, the efferent fibers constitute the **olivocochlear bundle.** The fibers form synapses directly on outer hair cells and on the dendrites that serve the inner hair cells. The transmitter

olivocochlear bundle   A bundle of efferent axons that travel from the olivary complex of the medulla to the auditory hair cells on the cochlea.

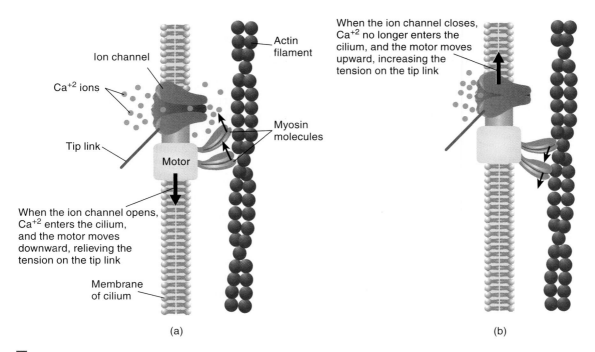

Actin filament

Ion channel

Ca+2 ions

Tip link

Motor

Myosin molecules

When the ion channel opens, Ca+2 enters the cilium, and the motor moves downward, relieving the tension on the tip link

Membrane of cilium

When the ion channel closes, Ca+2 no longer enters the cilium, and the motor moves upward, increasing the tension on the tip link

(a)

(b)

Figure 7.12

Transduction and control of the tension on the tip link. (a) Movement of the bundle of cilia toward the tallest one increases tension on the tip link, which opens the ion channels, permitting K+ and Ca+2 to enter the cilia. When the ion channel is open, the entry of calcium ions causes the myosin motor to move down, reducing the tension on the tip link. (b) When the channel is closed, the disappearance of calcium causes the motor to move up, increasing the tension on the tip link. By these means, tension on the tip links is regulated so that the hair cells are as sensitive as possible to sound vibrations.

(Adapted from Gillespie, P. G. *Current Opinion in Neurobiology*, 1995, *5*, 449–455 and Jaramillo, F. *Neuron*, 1995, *15*, 1227–1230.)

substance at the afferent synapses appears to be an excitatory amino acid such as glutamate or aspartate. The efferent terminal buttons secrete acetylcholine, which appears to have an inhibitory effect on the hair cells.

The Central Auditory System

The anatomy of the auditory system is more complicated than that of the visual system. Rather than give a detailed verbal description of the pathways, I will refer you to *Figure 7.13*. Note that axons enter the **cochlear nucleus** of the medulla and synapse there. Most of the neurons in the cochlear nucleus send axons to the **superior olivary complex,** also located in the medulla. Neurons there project axons through a large bundle of axons called the **lateral lemniscus** to the inferior colliculus, located in the dorsal midbrain. Neurons there project to the medial geniculate nucleus of the thalamus, which sends axons to the auditory cortex of the temporal lobe. As you can see, there are many synapses along the way to complicate the story. Each hemisphere receives information from both ears but primarily

from the contralateral one. And auditory information is relayed to the cerebellum and reticular formation as well.

If we unrolled the basilar membrane into a flat strip and followed afferent axons serving successive points along its length, we would reach successive points in the nuclei of the auditory system and ultimately successive points along the surface of the primary auditory cortex. The *basal* end of the basilar membrane (the end toward the oval window) is represented most medially in the auditory cortex, and the *apical* end is represented most laterally there. Because,

cochlear nucleus One of a group of nuclei in the medulla that receive auditory information from the cochlea.

superior olivary complex A group of nuclei in the medulla; involved with auditory functions, including localization of the source of sounds.

lateral lemniscus A band of fibers running rostrally through the medulla and pons; carries fibers of the auditory system.

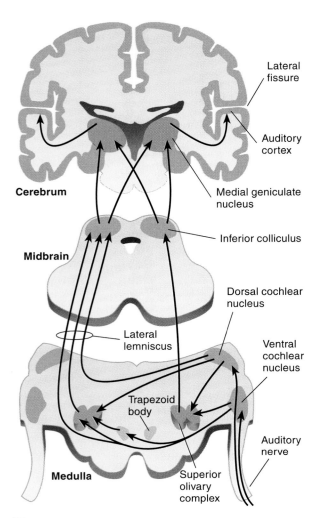

Figure 7.13
The pathway of the auditory system.

Labels on figure: Lateral fissure; Auditory cortex; Medial geniculate nucleus; Inferior colliculus; Dorsal cochlear nucleus; Ventral cochlear nucleus; Auditory nerve; Superior olivary complex; Trapezoid body; Lateral lemniscus; Cerebrum; Midbrain; Medulla

as we will see, different parts of the basilar membrane respond best to different frequencies of sound, this relationship between cortex and basilar membrane is referred to as **tonotopic representation** (*tonos* means "tone" and *topos* means "place").

Neurons in the primary auditory cortex send axons to the auditory association cortex. In Chapter 4, we saw that the primary auditory cortex lies hidden on the inside of the lateral fissure and that the auditory association cortex lies on the superior part of the temporal lobe.

● Detection of Pitch

As we have seen, the perceptual dimension of pitch corresponds to the physical dimension of frequency. The cochlea detects frequency by two means: moderate to high

frequencies by place coding and low frequencies by rate coding. These two types of coding are described next.

Place Coding

The work of von Békésy has shown us that because of the mechanical construction of the cochlea and basilar membrane, acoustic stimuli of different frequencies cause different parts of the basilar membrane to flex back and forth. Figure 7.14 illustrates the amount of deformation along the length of the basilar membrane produced by stimulation with tones of various frequencies. Note that higher frequencies produce more displacement at the basal end of the membrane (the end closest to the stapes). (See *Figure 7.14.*)

These results suggest that at least some frequencies of sound waves are detected by means of a **place code.** In this context a code represents a means by which neurons can represent information. Thus, if neurons at one end of the basilar membrane are excited by higher frequencies and those at the other end by lower frequencies, we can say that the frequency of the sound is *coded* by the particular neurons that are active. In turn, the firing of particular axons in the cochlear nerve tells the brain about the presence of particular frequencies of sound.

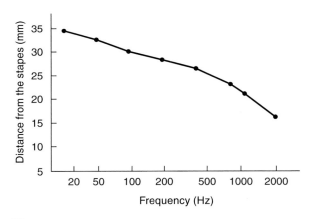

Figure 7.14
Anatomical coding of pitch. Stimuli of different frequencies maximally deform different regions of the basilar membrane.
(From von Békésy, G. *Journal of the Acoustical Society of America*, 1949, *21*, 233–245.)

tonotopic representation *(tonn oh **top** ik)* A topographically organized mapping of different frequencies of sound that are represented in a particular region of the brain.

place code The system by which information about different frequencies is coded by different locations on the basilar membrane.

Evidence for place coding of pitch comes from several sources. High doses of the antibiotic drugs kanamycin and neomycin produce degeneration of the auditory hair cells. Damage to auditory hair cells begins at the basal end of the cochlea and progresses toward the apical end; this pattern can be verified by killing experimental animals after dosing them with the antibiotic for varying amounts of time. Longer exposures to the drug are associated with increased progress of hair cell damage down the basilar membrane. Stebbins et al. (1969) found that the progressive death of hair cells induced by an antibiotic closely parallels a progressive hearing loss: The highest frequencies are the first to go, and the lowest are the last.

Perhaps the best evidence for place coding of pitch (at least, in humans) comes from the effectiveness of cochlear implants. **Cochlear implants** are devices used to restore hearing in people with deafness caused by damage to the hair cells. The external part of a cochlear implant consists of a microphone and a miniaturized electronic signal processor. The internal part contains a very thin, flexible array of electrodes, which the surgeon carefully inserts into the cochlea in such a way that it follows the snaillike curl and ends up resting along the entire length of the basilar membrane. Each electrode in the array stimulates a different part of the basilar membrane. Information from the signal processor is passed to the electrodes by means of flat coils of wire, implanted under the skin.

The primary purpose of a cochlear implant is to restore a person's ability to understand speech. Because most of the important acoustical information in speech is contained in higher frequencies, the multichannel electrode was developed in an attempt to duplicate the place coding of higher frequencies on the basilar membrane (Loeb, 1990). The signal processor in the external device analyzes the sounds detected by the microphone and sends separate signals to the appropriate portions of the basilar membrane. The fact that this device can work so well—some people with cochlear implants can understand speech well enough to use a telephone—indicates the importance of place coding.

The work of von Békésy indicated that although the basilar membrane codes for frequency along its length, the coding was not very specific. His studies, and those of investigators who followed him, indicated that a given frequency causes a large region of the basilar membrane to be deformed. This finding contrasted with the observation that people can detect changes in frequency of only 2 or 3 Hz.

The reason for this discrepancy is now clear. Because of technical limitations, von Békésy had to observe the cochleas of animals that were no longer living, or, at best, cochleas that had been damaged by the procedure necessary to make the measurements. More recently, investigators have used much more sensitive—and less damaging—procedures to observe movements of the basilar membrane in response to different frequencies of sound. It appears that the point of maximum vibration of the basilar membrane to a particular frequency is very precisely localized—but only when the cells in the organ of Corti are alive and healthy (Evans, 1992; Ruggero, 1992).

The fact that the tuning characteristics of the basilar membrane change when the cells in the organ of Corti die suggests that these cells somehow affect the mechanical properties of the basilar membrane. We now know that the outer hair cells are responsible for this selective tuning, but we do not understand yet exactly how they accomplish this feat. As I mentioned earlier, outer hair cells not only are sensory transducers but are also contractile elements, like muscle fibers. When these cells are exposed to an electrical current, or when acetylcholine is placed on them, they contract by up to 10 percent of their length (Brownell et al., 1985; Zenner, Zimmermann, and Schmitt, 1985). Because the tips of their cilia are embedded in the tectorial membrane, contraction would affect the mechanical characteristics of the basilar membrane—and consequently, the response properties of the inner hair cells. Kemp (1978) discovered that when brief sounds are presented to a normal cochlea, it produces a sound itself, which can be detected with a microphone. Presumably, this sound is produced by contraction of the outer hair cells. Most investigators believe that the signals that cause contraction of the outer hair cells come partly from the olivocochlear bundle and partly from local circuits of neurons within the organ of Corti.

Rate Coding

We have seen that the frequency of a sound can be detected by place coding. However, the lowest frequencies do not appear to be accounted for in this manner. Kiang (1965) was unable to find any cells that responded best to frequencies of less than 200 Hz. How, then, can animals distinguish low frequencies? It appears that lower frequencies are detected by neurons that fire in synchrony to the movements of the apical end of the basilar membrane. Thus, lower frequencies are detected by means of **rate coding.**

cochlear implant An electronic device surgically implanted in the inner ear that can enable deaf people to hear.

rate code The system by which information about different frequencies is coded by the rate of firing of neurons in the auditory system.

The most convincing evidence of rate coding of pitch comes from studies of people with cochlear implants. Pijl and Schwartz (1995a, 1995b) found that stimulation of a single electrode with pulses of electricity produced sensations of pitch that were proportional to the frequency of the stimulation. In fact, the subjects could even recognize familiar tunes produced by modulating the pulse frequency. (The subjects had become deaf later in life, after already having learned to recognize the tunes.) As we would expect, the subjects' perceptions were best when the tip of the basilar membrane was stimulated, and only low frequencies could be distinguished by this method.

● Detection of Loudness

The cochlea is an extremely sensitive organ. Wilska (1935) used an ingenious procedure to estimate the smallest vibration needed to produce a perceptible sound. He glued a small wooden rod to a volunteer's tympanic membrane (temporarily, of course) and made the rod vibrate longitudinally by means of an electromagnetic coil that could be energized with alternating current. He could vary the frequency and intensity of the current, which consequently changed the perceived pitch and loudness of the stimulus. He found that subjects could detect a sound even when the eardrum was vibrated over a distance less than the diameter of a hydrogen atom—showing that the auditory system is very sensitive. Thus, in very quiet environments a young, healthy ear is limited in its ability to detect sounds in the air by the masking noise of blood rushing through the cranial blood vessels, rather than by the sensitivity of the auditory system itself. More recent studies using modern instruments (reviewed by Hudspeth, 1983) have essentially confirmed Wilska's measurements. The softest sounds that can be detected appear to move the tip of the hair cells between 1 and 100 picometers (pm; trillionths of a meter). They achieve their maximum response when the tips are moved 100 nm (Corwin and Warchol, 1991).

The axons of the cochlear nerve appear to inform the brain of the loudness of a stimulus by altering their rate of firing. More intense vibrations produce a more intense shearing force on the cilia of the auditory hair cells, presumably causing them to release more transmitter substance, resulting in a higher rate of firing by the cochlear nerve axons. This explanation seems simple for the axons involved in place coding of pitch; in this case pitch is signaled by which neurons fire, and loudness is signaled by their rate of firing. However, the neurons that signal lower frequencies do so by their rate of firing. If they fire more frequently, they signal a higher pitch. Therefore, most investigators believe that the loudness of low-frequency sounds is signaled by the *number* of axons that are active at a given time.

● Detection of Timbre

Although laboratory investigations of the auditory system often employ pure sine waves as stimuli, these waves are seldom encountered outside the laboratory. Instead, we hear sounds with a rich mixture of frequencies—sounds of complex timbre. For example, consider the sound of a clarinet playing a particular note. If we hear it, we can easily say that it is a clarinet and not a flute or a violin. The reason we can do so is that these three instruments produce sounds of different timbre, which our auditory system can distinguish.

Figure 7.15 shows the waveform from a clarinet playing a steady note (*top*). The shape of the waveform repeats itself regularly at the **fundamental frequency,** which corresponds to the perceived pitch of the note. A Fourier analysis of the waveform shows that it actually consists of a series of sine waves that includes the fundamental frequency and many **overtones,** multiples of the fundamental frequency. Different instruments produce overtones with different intensities. (See *Figure 7.15.*) Electronic synthesizers simulate the sounds of real instruments by producing a series of overtones of the proper intensities, mixing them, and passing them through a loudspeaker.

When the basilar membrane is stimulated by the sound of a clarinet, different portions respond to each of the overtones. This response produces a unique anatomically coded pattern of activity in the cochlear nerve, which is subsequently identified by the auditory system of the brain. Just how this analysis is done is not known and probably will not be known for many years. When you consider that we can listen to an orchestra and identify several instruments that are playing simultaneously, you can appreciate the complexity of the analysis performed by the auditory system.

● Feature Detection in the Auditory System

So far, I have discussed coding of pitch, loudness, and timbre only (the last of which is actually a complex frequency analysis). The auditory system also responds to other qual-

fundamental frequency   The lowest, and usually most intense, frequency of a complex sound; most often perceived as the sound's basic pitch.

overtone   The frequency of complex tones that occurs at multiples of the fundamental frequency.

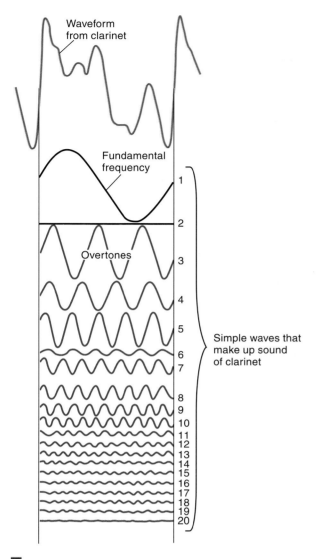

Waveform
from clarinet

Fundamental
frequency

1

2

Overtones

3

4

5

Simple waves that
make up sound
of clarinet

6
7

8
9
10
11
12
13
14
15
16
17
18
19
20

Figure 7.15
The shape of a sound wave from a clarinet (top) *and the individual frequencies into which it can be analyzed.*
(Reprinted from *Stereo Review*, copyright © 1977 by Diamandis Communications Inc.)

ities of acoustic stimuli. For example, our ears are very good at determining whether the source of a sound is to the right or to the left of us. (To discriminate front from back, we merely turn our heads, transforming the discrimination into a left-right decision.) Two separate physiological mechanisms detect the location of sound sources: We use phase differences for low frequencies (less than approximately 3000 Hz) and intensity differences for high frequencies. Stevens and Newman (1936) found that localization is poorest at approximately 3000 Hz, presum-

ably because both mechanisms are rather inefficient at that frequency.

Localization by Means of Arrival Time and Phase Differences

If we are blindfolded, we can still determine with rather good accuracy the location of a stimulus that emits a click. We do so because neurons respond selectively to different *arrival times* of the sound waves at the left and right ears. If the source of the click is to the right or left of the midline, the sound pressure wave will reach one ear sooner and initiate action potentials there first. Only if the stimulus is straight ahead will the ears be stimulated simultaneously. Many neurons in the auditory system respond to sounds presented to either ear. Some of these neurons, especially those in the superior olivary complex of the medulla, respond according to the difference in arrival times of sound waves produced by clicks presented *binaurally* (that is, to both ears). Their response rates reflect differences as small as a fraction of a millisecond.

Of course, we can hear continuous sounds as well as clicks, and we can also perceive the location of their source. We detect the source of continuous low-pitched sounds by means of phase differences. **Phase differences** refer to the simultaneous arrival, at each ear, of different portions (phases) of the oscillating sound wave. For example, if we assume that sound travels at 700 miles per hour through the air, adjacent cycles of a 1000-Hz tone are 12.3 inches apart. Thus, if the source of the sound is located to one side of the head, one eardrum is pulled out while the other is pushed in. The movement of the eardrums will reverse, or be 180° *out of phase.* If the source were located directly in front of the head, the movements would be perfectly in phase (0° out of phase). (See *Figure 7.16.*) Because some auditory neurons respond only when the eardrums (and thus the bending of the basilar membrane) are at least somewhat out of phase, neurons in the superior olivary complex in the brain are able to use the information they provide to detect the source of a continuous sound.

A possible mechanism to explain the ability of the nervous system to detect very short delays in the arrival times of two signals was first proposed by Jeffress (1948). He suggested that neurons received information from two sets of axons coming from the two ears. Each neuron served as a *coincidence detector;* it responded only if it received signals simultaneously from synapses belonging to both sets of ax-

phase difference   The difference in arrival times of sound waves at each of the eardrums.

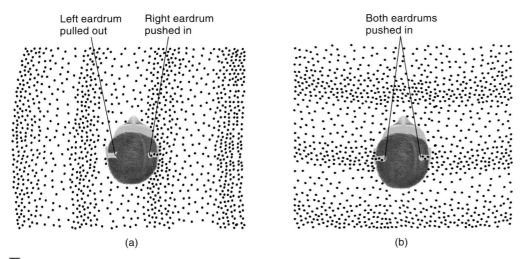

(a)   (b)

Figure 7.16
Localizing the source of medium-frequency and high-frequency sounds through phase differences. (a) Source of a 1000-Hz tone to the right. The pressure waves on each eardrum are out of phase; one eardrum is pushed in while the other is pushed out. (b) Source of a sound directly in front. The vibrations of the eardrums are synchronized (in phase).

ons. If a signal reached the two ears simultaneously, neurons in the middle of the array would fire. If, however, the signal reached one ear before the other, then neurons farther away from the "early" ear would be stimulated. (See *Figure 7.17.*)

In fact, that is exactly how the mechanism works. Carr and Konishi (1989; 1990) obtained anatomical evidence in support of Jeffress's hypothesis from the brain of the barn owl, a nocturnal bird that can detect very accurately the source of a sound (such as that made by an unfortunate

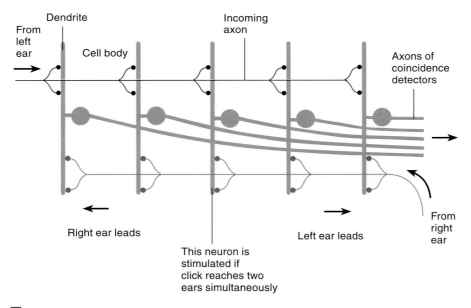

Figure 7.17
A model of a coincidence detector that can determine differences in arrival times at each ear of an auditory stimulus.

mouse). Figure 7.18 shows a drawing of the distribution of the branches of two axons, one from each ear, projecting to the nucleus laminaris, the barn owl analog of the mammalian medial superior olive. As you can see, axons from the ipsilateral and contralateral ears penetrate the nucleus from opposite directions; therefore, dorsally located neurons within the nucleus are stimulated by sounds that first reach the contralateral ear. (Compare *Figures 7.17* and *7.18*.) Carr and Konishi recorded from single units within the nucleus and found that the response characteristics of the neurons located there were perfectly consistent with these anatomical facts.

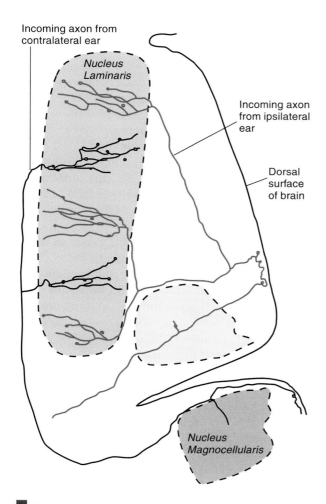

Figure 7.18
Evidence for a coincidence detector in the brain of a barn owl. Compare the branches of the axons with those of Figure 7.17. The drawing was prepared from microscopic examination of sections of stained tissue.

(Adapted from Carr, C. E., and Konishi, M. *Proceedings of the National Academy of Sciences, USA*, 1989, *85*, 8311–8315.)

Localization by Means of Intensity Differences

The auditory system cannot readily detect binaural phase differences of high-frequency stimuli; the differences in phases of such rapid sine waves are just too short to be measured by the neurons. However, high-frequency stimuli that occur to the right or left of the midline stimulate the ears unequally. The head absorbs high frequencies, producing a "sonic shadow," so that the ear closest to the source of the sound receives the most intense stimulation. Some neurons in the auditory system respond differentially to binaural stimuli of different intensity in each ear, which means that they provide information that can be used to detect the source of tones of high frequency.

The neurons that detect binaural differences in loudness are located in the superior olivary complex. But whereas neurons that detect binaural differences in phase or arrival time are located in the *lateral* superior olivary complex, these neurons are located in the *medial* superior olivary complex. Information from both sets of neurons is sent to other levels of the auditory system.

● Behavioral Functions of the Auditory System

Hearing has three primary functions: to detect sounds, to determine the location of their sources, and to recognize the identity of these sources—and thus their meaning and relevance to us (Heffner and Heffner, 1990; Yost, 1991). Let us consider the third function, recognizing the identity of a sound source. Unless you are in a completely silent location, pay attention to what you can hear. Right now, I am sitting in an office and can hear the sound of a fan in a computer, the tapping of the keys as I write this, the footsteps of someone passing outside the door, and the voices of some people talking in the hallway. How can I recognize these sources? The axons in my cochlear nerve contain a constantly changing pattern of activity corresponding to the constantly changing mixtures of frequencies that strike my eardrums. Somehow, the auditory system of my brain recognizes particular patterns that belong to particular sources, and I perceive each of them as independent entities.

The task of the auditory system in identifying sound sources, then, is one of *pattern recognition*. The auditory system must recognize that particular patterns of constantly changing activity belong to different sound sources. And few patterns are simple mixtures of fixed frequencies. For example, when a clarinet plays notes of different pitches, different patterns of activity are produced in our cochlear nerve—and yet we recognize each of the notes as belonging to a clarinet. Needless to say, we are far from understanding how this pattern recognition works.

Although the subcortical components of the auditory system are often referred to as "relay nuclei," it is clear that these nuclei do much more than passively transmit information from the cochlear nerve to the auditory cortex. For example, as we saw earlier in this chapter, the superior olivary complex contains circuits that analyze the location of sound sources according to arrival time (or phase differences) and intensity differences.

Pattern recognition, however, appears to be accomplished by circuits of neurons in the neocortex. We know a little bit about the types of analyses that the auditory cortex accomplishes. Various studies (Whitfield and Evans, 1965; Saitoh, Maruyama, and Kudoh, 1981) have found neurons in the auditory cortex that respond only to the onset or cessation of a sound (or to both), to changes in pitch or intensity (sometimes only to changes in one direction), or to complex stimuli that contain a variety of frequencies. Winter and Funkenstein (1971) found neurons in the auditory cortex of the squirrel monkey that responded specifically to the vocalizations made by members of this species. McKenna, Weinberger, and Diamond (1989) found that when they presented a series of different tones, some neurons in the primary auditory cortex responded to a particular frequency only in a particular context; for example, they would respond if the tone were the last in a series but not if it were the first. Rauschecker, Tian, and Hauser (1995) found that neurons in the auditory association cortex of rhesus monkeys responded much better to sound mixtures than to pure tones. Thus, neurons in the auditory cortex encode rather complex features. Because data are scanty so far, we have no real conception of the coding mechanism that the brain uses for these changes or even of precisely what features are coded.

Bilateral lesions of the auditory cortex in monkeys cause an almost total hearing loss, which eventually shows some recovery (Heffner and Heffner, 1990). The animals' ability to localize sounds is severely disrupted; they can eventually learn to discriminate a sound coming from the left or right from one coming from the center, but they are unable to walk toward the source of the sound. Thus, their sound localizing ability does not translate into useful behavior (Heffner and Heffner, 1990). In addition, lesions of the left auditory cortex disrupt the animals' ability to discriminate the vocalizations made by other members of this species.

As we saw in the previous chapter, lesions of the visual association cortex in humans can produce visual agnosias—the inability to recognize objects even though the visual acuity may be good. Similarly, lesions of the auditory association cortex can produce auditory agnosias, the inability to comprehend the meaning of sounds even though the individuals are not deaf. If the lesion occurs in the left hemisphere, the person will sustain a particular form of language disorder. If it occurs in the right hemisphere, the person will be unable to recognize the nature or location of nonspeech sounds. Because of the importance of audition to language, these topics are discussed in much more detail in Chapter 16.

Interim Summary

The receptive organ for audition is the organ of Corti, located on the basilar membrane. When sound strikes the tympanic membrane, it sets the ossicles into motion, and the baseplate of the stapes pushes against the membrane behind the oval window. Pressure changes thus applied to the fluid within the cochlea cause a portion of the basilar membrane to flex, causing the basilar membrane to move laterally with respect to the tectorial membrane that overhangs it. This movement pulls directly on the cilia of the outer hair cells and causes movements in the fluid within the cochlea, which, in turn, causes the cilia of the inner hair cells to wave back and forth. These mechanical forces open potassium channels in the tips of the hair cells and thus produce receptor potentials.

The hair cells form synapses with the dendrites of the bipolar neurons whose axons give rise to the cochlear branch of the eighth cranial nerve. The central auditory system involves several brain stem nuclei, including the cochlear nuclei, superior olivary complexes, and inferior colliculi. The medial geniculate nucleus relays auditory information to the primary auditory cortex on the medial surface of the temporal lobe.

Pitch is encoded by two means. High-frequency sounds cause the base of the basilar membrane (near the oval window) to flex; low-frequency sounds cause the apex (opposite end) to flex. Because high and low frequencies thus stimulate different groups of auditory hair cells, frequency is encoded anatomically. The lowest frequencies cause the apex of the basilar membrane to flex back and forth in time with the acoustic vibrations. The outer hair cells act as motive elements rather than as sensory transducers, contracting in response to activity of the efferent axons and modifying the mechanical properties of the basilar membrane.

The auditory system is analytical in its operation. That is, it can discriminate between sounds with different timbres by detecting the individual overtones that constitute the sounds and producing unique patterns of neural firing in the auditory system.

Left-right localization is performed by analyzing binaural differences in arrival time, in phase relations, and in intensity. The location of sources of brief sounds (such as clicks) and sounds of frequencies below approximately 3000 Hz is detected by neurons in the lateral superior olivary complex, which respond most vigorously when one ear receives the click first, or when the phase of a sine wave received by one ear leads that received by the other. The location of sources of high-frequency sounds is detected by neurons in the medial superior olivary complex, which respond most vigorously when one organ of Corti is stimulated more intensely than the other.

To recognize the source of sounds, the auditory system must recognize the constantly changing patterns of activity received from the axons in the cochlear nerve. Studies have found neurons in the auditory cortex that respond to complex stimuli, such as ascending or descending pitches, series of tones, combinations of two or more tones, or even species-specific vocalizations. Bilateral lesions of the auditory cortex of monkeys produce severe impairments in hearing, and lesions of the left auditory cortex impair the ability to discriminate the vocalizations of other monkeys.

VESTIBULAR SYSTEM

The vestibular system has two components: the vestibular sacs and the semicircular canals. They represent the second and third components of the *labyrinths* of the inner ear. (We just studied the first component, the cochlea.) The **vestibular sacs** respond to the force of gravity and inform the brain about the head's orientation. The **semicircular canals** respond to angular acceleration—changes in the rotation of the head—but not to steady rotation. They also respond (but rather weakly) to changes in position or to linear acceleration.

The functions of the vestibular system include balance, maintenance of the head in an upright position, and adjustment of eye movement to compensate for head movements. Vestibular stimulation does not produce any readily definable sensation; certain low-frequency stimulation of the vestibular sacs can produce nausea, and stimulation of the semicircular canals can produce dizziness and rhythmic eye movements (*nystagmus*). However, we are not directly aware of the information received from these organs. This section describes the vestibular system: the vestibular apparatus, the receptor cells, and the vestibular pathway in the brain.

● Anatomy of the Vestibular Apparatus

Figure 7.19 shows the labyrinths of the inner ear, which include the cochlea, the semicircular canals, and the two vestibular sacs: the **utricle** ("little pouch") and the **saccule** ("little sack"). (See *Figure 7.19.*) The semicircular canals approximate the three major planes of the head: sagittal, transverse, and horizontal. Receptors in each canal respond maximally to angular acceleration in one plane. Figure 7.20 shows cross sections through one semicircular canal. The semicircular canal consists of a membranous canal floating within a bony one; the membranous canal contains a fluid called *endolymph* and floats within a fluid called *perilymph*. An enlargement called the **ampulla** contains the organ in which the sensory receptors reside. The sensory receptors are hair cells similar to those found in the cochlea. Their cilia are embedded in a gelatinous mass called the **cupula**, which blocks part of the ampulla. (See *Figure 7.20.*)

To explain the effects of angular acceleration on the semicircular canals, I will first describe an "experiment." If we place a glass of water on the exact center of a turntable

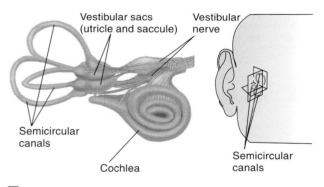

Figure 7.19
The labyrinths of the inner ear.

vestibular sac One of a set of two receptor organs in each inner ear that detect changes in the tilt of the head.

semicircular canal One of the three ringlike structures of the vestibular apparatus that detect changes in head rotation.

utricle (*you* trih kul) One of the vestibular sacs.

saccule (*sak* yule) One of the vestibular sacs.

ampulla (am *pull* uh) An enlargement in a semicircular canal; contains the cupula and the crista.

cupula (*kew* pew luh) A gelatinous mass found in the ampulla of the semicircular canals; moves in response to the flow of the fluid in the canals.

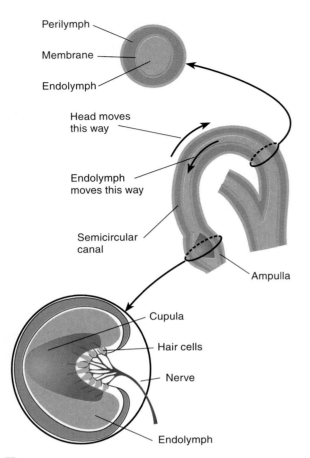

Figure 7.20
Cross sections through one semicircular canal.

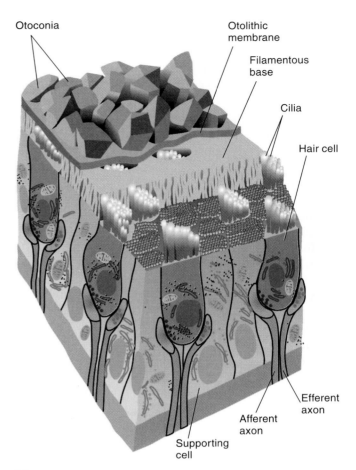

Figure 7.21
The receptive tissue of the utricle and saccule.

and then start the turntable spinning, the water in the glass will, at first, remain stationary (the glass will move with respect to the water it contains). Eventually, however, the water will begin rotating with the container. If we then stop the turntable, the water will continue spinning for a while, because of its inertia.

The semicircular canals operate on the same principle. The endolymph within these canals, like the water in the glass, resists movement when the head begins to rotate. This inertial resistance pushes the endolymph against the cupula, causing it to bend, until the fluid begins to move at the same speed as the head. If the head rotation is then stopped, the endolymph, still circulating through the canal, pushes the cupula the other way. Angular acceleration is thus translated into bending of the cupula, which exerts a shearing force on the cilia of the hair cells. (Of course, unlike the glass of water in my example, we do not normally spin around in circles; the semicircular canals measure very slight and very brief rotations of the head.)

The vestibular sacs (the utricle and saccule) work very differently. These organs are roughly circular, and each contains a patch of receptive tissue. The receptive tissue is located on the "floor" of the utricle and on the "wall" of the saccule when the head is in an upright position. The receptive tissue, like that of the semicircular canals and cochlea, contains hair cells. The cilia of these receptors are embedded in an overlying gelatinous mass, which contains something rather unusual: *otoconia*, which are small crystals of calcium carbonate. (See *Figure 7.21*.) The weight of the crystals causes the gelatinous mass to shift in position as the orientation of the head changes. Thus, movement produces a shearing force on the cilia of the receptive hair cells.

● The Receptor Cells

The hair cells of the semicircular canal and vestibular sacs are similar in appearance. Each hair cell contains several

(a)   (b)

Figure 7.22
*(a) Oblique view of a normal bundle of vestibular hair cells.
(b) Top view of a bundle of hair cells from which the longest has
been detached.*
(From Hudspeth, A. J., and Jacobs, R. *Proceedings of the National Academy of Sciences, USA,* 1979, 76, 1506–1509.)

cilia, graduated in length from short to long. Figure 7.22
shows two views of a hair cell of a bullfrog saccule made by
a scanning electron microscope. (See *Figure 7.22.*)

● The Vestibular Pathway

The vestibular and cochlear nerves constitute the two
branches of the eighth cranial nerve (auditory nerve). The
bipolar cell bodies that give rise to the afferent axons of
the vestibular nerve are located in the **vestibular ganglion,**
which appears as a nodule on the vestibular nerve.

Most of the axons of the vestibular nerve synapse within
the vestibular nuclei in the medulla, but some axons travel
directly to the cerebellum. Neurons of the vestibular nuclei
send their axons to the cerebellum, spinal cord, medulla,
and pons. There also appear to be vestibular projections to
the temporal cortex, but the precise pathways have not
been determined. Most investigators believe that the cortical projections are responsible for feelings of dizziness; the
activity of projections to the lower brain stem can produce
the nausea and vomiting that accompany motion sickness.
Projections to brain stem nuclei controlling neck muscles
are clearly involved in maintaining an upright position of
the head.

Perhaps the most interesting connections are those to
the cranial nerve nuclei (third, fourth, and sixth) that control the eye muscles. As we walk or (especially) run, the
head is jarred quite a bit. The vestibular system exerts direct
control on eye movement, to compensate for the sudden

head movements. This process, called the *vestibulo-ocular
reflex,* maintains a fairly steady retinal image. Test this reflex yourself: Look at a distant object and hit yourself (gently) on the side of the head. Note that your image of the
world jumps a bit, but not too much. People who have suffered vestibular damage, and who lack the vestibulo-ocular
reflex, have difficulty seeing anything while walking or running. Everything becomes a blur of movement.

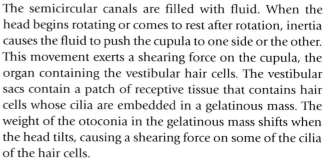

Interim Summary

The semicircular canals are filled with fluid. When the
head begins rotating or comes to rest after rotation, inertia
causes the fluid to push the cupula to one side or the other.
This movement exerts a shearing force on the cupula, the
organ containing the vestibular hair cells. The vestibular
sacs contain a patch of receptive tissue that contains hair
cells whose cilia are embedded in a gelatinous mass. The
weight of the otoconia in the gelatinous mass shifts when
the head tilts, causing a shearing force on some of the cilia
of the hair cells.

Each hair cell contains one long cilium and several
shorter ones. These cells form synapses with dendrites of
bipolar neurons whose axons travel through the vestibular
nerve. The receptors also receive efferent terminal buttons
from neurons located in the cerebellum and medulla, but
the function of these connections is not known. Vestibular
information is received by the vestibular nuclei in the medulla, which relay it on to the cerebellum, spinal cord, medulla, pons, and temporal cortex. These pathways are responsible for control of posture, head movements, eye
movements, and the puzzling phenomenon of motion
sickness.

SOMATOSENSES

The somatosenses provide information about what is happening on the surface of our body and inside it. The **cutaneous senses** (skin senses) include several submodalities
commonly referred to as *touch.* **Kinesthesia** provides information about body position and movement and arises

vestibular ganglion A nodule on the vestibular nerve
that contains the cell bodies of the bipolar neurons that
convey vestibular information to the brain.

cutaneous sense *(kew tane ee us)* One of the somatosenses; includes sensitivity to stimuli that involve
the skin.

kinesthesia Perception of the body's own movements.

from receptors in joints, tendons, and muscles. The muscle receptors are discussed in this section and in Chapter 8. The **organic senses** arise from receptors in and around the internal organs, providing us with unpleasant sensations, such as stomachaches or gallbladder attacks, or pleasurable ones, such as those provided by a warm drink on a cold winter day. Because the cutaneous senses are the most studied of the somatosenses, both perceptually and physiologically, I will devote most of my discussion to them.

● The Stimuli

The cutaneous senses respond to several different types of stimuli: pressure, vibration, heating, cooling, and events that cause tissue damage (and hence, pain). Feelings of pressure are caused by mechanical deformation of the skin. Vibration is produced in the laboratory or clinic by tuning forks or mechanical devices, but it more commonly occurs when we move our fingers across a rough surface. Thus, we use vibration sensitivity to judge an object's roughness. Obviously, sensations of warmth and coolness are produced by objects that change skin temperature from normal. Sensations of pain can be caused by many different types of stimuli, but it appears that most cause at least some tissue damage.

Kinesthesia is provided by stretch receptors in skeletal muscles that report changes in muscle length to the central nervous system and by stretch receptors in tendons that measure the force being exerted by the muscles. Receptors within joints between adjacent bones respond to the magnitude and direction of limb movement. The muscle length detectors (sensory endings on the *intrafusal muscle fibers*) do not give rise to conscious sensations; their information is used to control movement. These receptors will be discussed separately in Chapter 8.

Organic sensitivity is provided by receptors in the linings of muscles, outer layers of the gastrointestinal system and other internal organs, and linings of the abdominal and thoracic cavities. Many of these tissues are sensitive only to stretch and do not report sensations when cut, burned, or crushed. In addition, the stomach and esophagus are responsive to heat and cold and to some chemicals.

● Anatomy of the Skin and Its Receptive Organs

The skin is a complex and vital organ of the body—one that we tend to take for granted. We cannot survive without it; extensive skin burns are fatal. Our cells, which must be bathed by a warm fluid, are protected from the hostile environment by the skin's outer layers. The skin partici-

pates in thermoregulation by producing sweat, thus cooling the body, or by restricting its circulation of blood, thus conserving heat. Its appearance varies widely across the body, from mucous membrane to hairy skin to the smooth, hairless skin of the palms and the soles of the feet.

Skin consists of subcutaneous tissue, dermis, and epidermis and contains various receptors scattered throughout these layers. Figure 7.23 shows cross sections through hairy and **glabrous skin** (hairless skin, such as we have on our fingertips and palms). Hairy skin contains unencapsulated (free) nerve endings and **Ruffini corpuscles,** which respond to low-frequency vibration. Free nerve endings are found just below the surface of the skin, in a basketwork around the base of hair follicles and around the emergence of hair shafts from the skin. (See *Figure 7.23.*)

Glabrous skin contains a more complex mixture of free nerve endings and axons that terminate within specialized end organs (Iggo and Andres, 1982). The increased complexity probably reflects the fact that we use the palms of our hands and the inside surfaces of our fingers to explore the environment actively: We use them to hold and touch objects. In contrast, the rest of our body most often contacts the environment passively; that is, other things come in contact with it.

Pacinian corpuscles are the largest sensory end organs in the body. Their size, approximately 0.5×1.0 mm, makes them visible to the naked eye. They are found in glabrous skin and in the external genitalia, mammary glands, and various internal organs. These receptors consist of up to seventy onionlike layers wrapped around the terminal button of a single myelinated axon. They are sensitive to touch, particularly to high-frequency vibration. **Meissner's corpuscles** are found in *papillae* ("nipples"), small elevations of the dermis that project up into the epidermis. These end organs are innervated by between two and six axons. They respond to low-frequency vibration. **Merkel's disks,** which

---

organic sense A sense modality that arises from receptors located within the inner organs of the body.

glabrous skin (*glab* russ) Skin that does not contain hair; found on the palms and soles of the feet.

Ruffini corpuscle A vibration-sensitive organ located in hairy skin.

Pacinian corpuscle (*pa chin* ee un) A specialized, encapsulated somatosensory nerve ending that detects mechanical stimuli, especially vibrations.

Meissner's corpuscle The touch-sensitive end organs located in the papillae, small elevations of the dermis that project up into the epidermis.

Merkel's disk The touch-sensitive end organs found at the base of the epidermis, adjacent to sweat ducts.

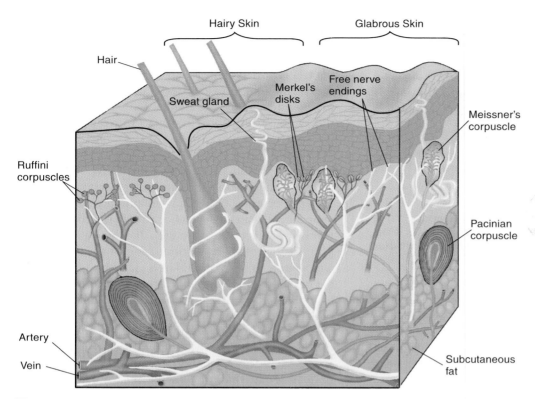

Hairy Skin

Glabrous Skin

Hair

Sweat gland

Merkel's disks

Free nerve endings

Meissner's corpuscle

Ruffini corpuscles

Pacinian corpuscle

Artery

Vein

Subcutaneous fat

Figure 7.23
Sensory receptors. (a) In hairy skin. (b) In glabrous (hairless) skin.

also respond to indentation of the skin, are found at the base of the epidermis, in the same general locations as Meissner's corpuscles, adjacent to sweat ducts. (See *Figure 7.23.*)

● Detection of Cutaneous Stimulation

The three most important qualities of cutaneous stimulation are touch, temperature, and pain. These qualities are described in the sections that follow.

Touch

Sensitivity to pressure and vibration is caused by movement of the skin. The best-studied receptor is the Pacinian corpuscle, which primarily detects vibration. When the corpuscle is bent relative to the axon, the membrane becomes depolarized. If the threshold of excitation is exceeded, an action potential is produced at the first node of Ranvier. Loewenstein and Mendelson (1965) have shown that the layers of the corpuscle alter the mechanical characteristics of the organ, so the axon responds briefly when the intact organ is bent and again when it is released. Thus, this receptor is sensitive to vibration but not to steady pressure.

The bending of the tip of the nerve ending in a Pacinian corpuscle appears to produce a receptor potential by opening ion channels in the membrane. These channels appear to be anchored to protein filaments beneath the membrane and have long carbohydrate chains attached to them. When a mechanical stimulus changes the shape of the nerve ending, tension is exerted on the carbohydrate chains, pulling the channel open. (See *Figure 7.24.*) Most investigators believe that the encapsulated endings serve only to modify the physical stimulus transduced by the axons that enter them.

Adaptation. Investigators have known for a long time that a moderate, constant stimulus applied to the skin fails to produce any sensation after it has been present for a while. For example, we not only ignore the pressure of a wristwatch, but we cannot feel it at all if we keep our arm still (assuming that the band is not painfully tight). Physiological studies have shown that the reason for the lack of sensation is the absence of receptor firing; the receptors adapt to a constant stimulus.

This adaptation is not caused by "fatigue" of physical or chemical processes within the receptor. Instead, adaptation

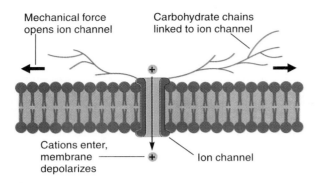

Figure 7.24
A hypothetical explanation of transduction of somatosensory information. Mechanical force on carbohydrate chains linked to ion channels opens the channels, permitting the entry of cations, which depolarizes the membrane potential.

occurs because of the physical construction of the skin and the cutaneous sensory organs. Nafe and Wagoner (1941) recorded the sensations reported by human subjects as a stimulus weight gradually moved downward, deforming the skin. Pressure was reported until the weight finally stopped moving. When the weight was increased, pressure was reported until downward movement stopped again. Pressure sensations were also briefly recorded when the weight was removed, while the surface of the skin regained its normal shape. (You may have noticed that when you first take your hat off, it feels for a few moments as if you were still wearing it.)

Responsiveness to Moving Stimuli. A moderate, constant, nondamaging stimulus is rarely of any importance to an organism, so this adaptation mechanism is useful. Our cutaneous senses are used much more often to analyze shapes and textures of stimulus objects moving with respect to the surface of the skin. Sometimes, the object itself moves; but more often, we do the moving ourselves.

If I placed an object in your palm and asked you to keep your hand still, you would have a great deal of difficulty recognizing the object by touch alone. If I said you could now move your hand, you would manipulate the object, letting its surface slide across your palm and the pads of your fingers. You would be able to describe its three-dimensional shape, hardness, texture, slipperiness, and so on. Obviously, your motor system must cooperate, and you need kinesthetic sensation from your muscles and joints, besides the cutaneous information. If you squeeze the object and feel a lot of well-localized pressure in return, it is hard. If you feel a less intense, more diffuse pressure in return, it is soft. If it produces vibrations as it moves over the ridges on your fingers, it is rough. If very little ef-

fort is needed to move the object while pressing it against your skin, it is slippery. If it does not produce vibrations as it moves across your skin, but moves in a jerky fashion, and if it takes effort to remove your fingers from its surface, it is sticky. Thus, our somatosenses work dynamically with the motor system to provide useful information about the nature of objects that come in contact with our skin.

Temperature

Feelings of warmth and coolness are relative, not absolute (except at the extremes). There is a temperature level that, for a particular region of skin, will produce a sensation of temperature neutrality—neither warmth nor coolness. This neutral point is not an absolute value but depends on the prior history of thermal stimulation of that area. If the temperature of a region of skin is raised by a few degrees, the initial feeling of warmth is replaced by one of neutrality. If the skin temperature is lowered to its initial value, it now feels cool. Thus, increases in temperature lower the sensitivity of warmth receptors and raise the sensitivity of cold receptors. The converse holds for decreases in skin temperature. This adaptation to ambient temperature can be demonstrated easily by placing one hand in a bucket of warm water and the other in a bucket of cool water until some adaptation has taken place. If you then simultaneously immerse both hands in water at room temperature, it will feel warm to one hand and cool to the other.

Thermal receptors are difficult to study, because changes in temperature alter the metabolic activity, and also the rate of axonal firing, of a variety of cells. For example, a receptor that responds to pressure might produce varying amounts of activity in response to the same mechanical stimulus, depending on the temperature. Nevertheless, most investigators agree that changes in temperature are detected by free nerve endings and that warmth and coolness are detected by different populations of receptors (Sinclair, 1981). The transduction of temperature changes into the rate of axonal firing has not yet been explained.

An ingenious experiment by Bazett et al. (1932) showed long ago that receptors for warmth and cold lie at different depths in the skin. The investigators lifted the prepuce (foreskin) of uncircumcised males with dull fishhooks. They applied thermal stimuli on one side of the folded skin and recorded the rate at which the temperature changes were transmitted through the skin by placing small temperature sensors on the opposite side. They then correlated these observations with verbal reports of warmth and coolness. The investigators concluded that cold receptors were close to the skin and that warmth receptors were located deeper in the tissue. (This experiment shows the extremities to which scientists will go to obtain information—pun intended.)

Pain

The story of pain is quite different from that of temperature and pressure; the analysis of this sensation is extremely difficult. It is obvious that our awareness of pain and our emotional reaction to it are controlled by mechanisms within the brain. For example, we can have a tooth removed painlessly while under hypnosis, which has no effect on the stimulation of pain receptors. Stimuli that produce pain also tend to trigger species-typical escape and withdrawal responses. Subjectively, these stimuli *hurt,* and we try hard to avoid them. However, sometimes we are better off ignoring pain and getting on with other tasks. In fact, our brains possess mechanisms that can reduce pain, partly through the action of the endogenous opioids. These mechanisms are described in more detail in a later section of this chapter.

Most investigators identify pain reception with the networks of free nerve endings in the skin. Pain appears to be produced by a variety of procedures. Intense mechanical stimulation activates a class of high-threshold receptors that produce a sensation of pain. However, most painful stimuli cause tissue damage, suggesting that pain is also caused by the release of a chemical by injured cells (Besson et al., 1982). When cells are damaged, they very rapidly synthesize a **prostaglandin,** a category of hormones first discovered in the prostate gland. This chemical sensitizes free nerve endings to another chemical, histamine, which is also released by damaged cells. (The analgesic effect of aspirin occurs by virtue of the fact that it interferes with the synthesis of prostaglandins.)

● The Somatosensory Pathways

Somatosensory axons from the skin, muscles, or internal organs enter the central nervous system via spinal nerves. Those located in the face and head primarily enter through the trigeminal nerve (fifth cranial nerve). The cell bodies of the unipolar neurons are located in the dorsal root ganglia and cranial nerve ganglia. Axons that convey precisely localized information, such as fine touch, ascend through the *dorsal columns* in the white matter of the spinal cord to nuclei in the lower medulla. From there, axons cross the brain and ascend through the *medial lemniscus* to the *ventral posterior nuclei of the thalamus,* the relay nuclei for so-

matosensation. Axons from the thalamus project to the primary somatosensory cortex, which in turn sends axons to the secondary somatosensory cortex. In contrast, axons that convey poorly localized information, such as pain or temperature, form synapses with other neurons as soon as they enter the spinal cord. The axons of these neurons cross to the other side of the spinal cord and ascend through the *spinothalamic tract* to the ventral posterior nuclei of the thalamus. (See *Figure 7.25.*)

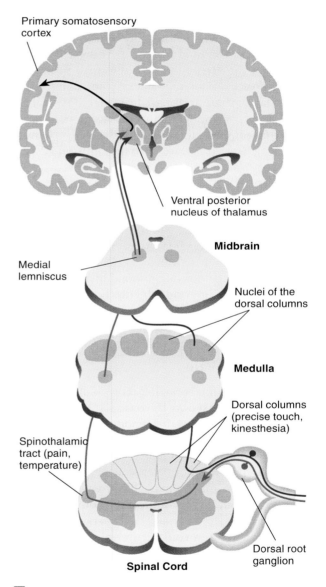

Figure 7.25
The somatosensory pathways from the spinal cord to the somatosensory cortex. Note that precisely localized information (such as fine touch) and imprecisely localized information (such as pain and temperature) are transmitted by different pathways.

prostaglandin   A member of a family of fatty acid derivatives that serve as hormones; first discovered in the prostate gland; involved in many physiological processes, including pain perception.

Recall from Chapter 6 that the primary visual cortex contains columns of cells, each of which responds to particular features, such as orientation, ocular dominance, or spatial frequency. Within these columns are blobs that contain cells that respond to particular colors. The somatosensory cortex also has a columnar arrangement; in fact, cortical columns were discovered there by Mountcastle (1957) before they were found in the visual and auditory cortex. Within a column, neurons respond to a particular type of stimulus (for example, temperature or pressure) applied to a particular part of the body.

Dykes (1983) has reviewed research indicating that the primary and secondary somatosensory cortical areas are divided into at least five (and perhaps as many as ten) different maps of the body surface. Within each map, cells respond to a particular submodality of somatosensory receptors. So far, separate areas have been identified that respond to slowly adapting cutaneous receptors, rapidly adapting cutaneous receptors, receptors that detect changes in muscle length, receptors located in the joints, and Pacinian corpuscles.

As you learned in Chapter 6, the extrastriate cortex consists of several subareas, each of which contains an independent representation of the visual field. For example, one area responds specifically to color and form, and another responds to movement. The somatosensory cortex appears to follow a similar scheme: Each cortical map of the body contains neurons that respond to a specific submodality of stimulation. Undoubtedly, further investigations will provide more accurate functional maps of the cortical subareas of both of these sensory systems.

● Perception of Pain

Pain is a curious phenomenon. It is more than a mere sensation; it can be defined only by some sort of withdrawal reaction or, in humans, by verbal report. Pain can be modified by opiates, by hypnosis, by the administration of pharmacologically inert sugar pills, by emotions, and even by other forms of stimulation, such as acupuncture. Recent research efforts have made remarkable progress in discovering the physiological bases of these phenomena.

We might reasonably ask *why* we experience pain. In most cases pain serves a constructive role. For example, people who have congenital insensitivity to pain suffer an abnormally large number of injuries, such as cuts and burns. One woman did not make the shifts in posture that we normally do when our joints start to ache. As a consequence, she suffered damage to the spine that ultimately resulted in death. Other people have died from ruptured appendixes and ensuing abdominal infections that they

did not feel (Sternbach, 1968). I am sure that a person who is passing a kidney stone would not find much comfort in the fact that pain does more good than ill; but pain is, nevertheless, very important to our existence.

Some environmental events diminish the perception of pain. For example, Beecher (1959) noted that wounded American soldiers back from the battle at Anzio, Italy, during World War II reported that they felt no pain from their wounds—they did not even want medication. It would appear that their perception of pain was diminished by the relief they felt from surviving such an ordeal. There are other instances in which people still report the perception of pain but are not bothered by it. Some tranquilizers have this effect.

A particularly interesting form of pain sensation occurs after a limb has been amputated. After the limb is gone, up to 70 percent of amputees report that they feel as though the missing limb still existed and that it often hurts. This phenomenon is referred to as the **phantom limb** (Melzak, 1992). People with phantom limbs report that the limb feels very real, and they often say that if they try to reach out with it, it feels as though it were responding. Sometimes, they perceive it as sticking out, and they may feel compelled to avoid knocking it against the side of a doorframe or sleeping in a position that would make it come between them and the mattress. People have reported all sorts of sensations in phantom limbs, including pain, pressure, warmth, cold, wetness, itching, sweatiness, and prickliness.

The classic explanation for phantom limbs has been activity of the sensory axons belonging to the amputated limb. Presumably, this activity is interpreted by the nervous system as coming from the missing limb. When nerves are cut and connections cannot be reestablished between the proximal and distal portions, the cut ends of the proximal portions form nodules known as *neuromas*. The treatment for phantom pain has been to cut the nerves above these neuromas, to cut the dorsal roots that bring the afferent information from these nerves into the spinal cord, or to make lesions in somatosensory pathways in the spinal cord, thalamus, or cerebral cortex. Sometimes these procedures work for a while, but often the pain returns.

Melzak suggested that the phantom limb sensation is inherent in the organization of the parietal cortex. As we saw in Chapter 4, the parietal cortex is involved in our awareness of our own bodies. Indeed, people with lesions of the parietal lobe (especially in the right hemisphere) have been known to push their own leg out of bed, believing that it actually belongs to someone else. Melzak reports

phantom limb   Sensations that appear to originate in a limb that has been amputated.

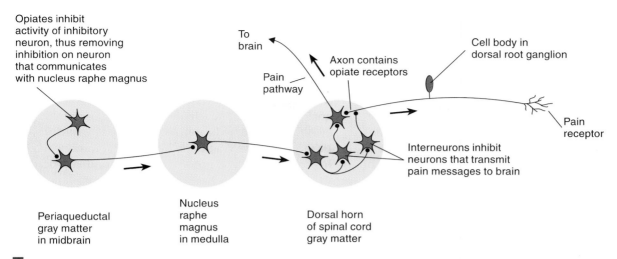

Figure 7.26
The neural circuit that mediates opiate-induced analgesia, as hypothesized by Basbaum and Fields (1978).

In the figure:

- Opiates inhibit activity of inhibitory neuron, thus removing inhibition on neuron that communicates with nucleus raphe magnus
- To brain
- Axon contains opiate receptors
- Pain pathway
- Cell body in dorsal root ganglion
- Pain receptor
- Interneurons inhibit neurons that transmit pain messages to brain
- Periaqueductal gray matter in midbrain
- Nucleus raphe magnus in medulla
- Dorsal horn of spinal cord gray matter

that some people who were born with missing limbs nevertheless experience phantom limb sensations, which would suggest that our brains are genetically programmed to provide sensations for all four limbs.

Modification of Pain Sensitivity: The Endogenous Opioids

For many years investigators have known that perception of pain can be modified by environmental stimuli. Recent work, beginning in the 1970s, has revealed the existence of neural circuits whose activity can produce analgesia. A variety of environmental stimuli can activate these analgesia-producing circuits. Most of these stimuli cause the release of the endogenous opioids, which were described in Chapter 4.

Electrical stimulation of particular locations within the brain can cause analgesia, which can even be profound enough to serve as an anesthetic for surgery in rats (Reynolds, 1969). The most effective locations appear to be within the periaqueductal gray matter and in the rostroventral medulla. For example, Mayer and Liebeskind (1974) reported that electrical stimulation of the periaqueductal gray matter produced analgesia in rats equivalent to that produced by at least 10 milligrams (mg) of morphine per kilogram of body weight, which is a large dose. The technique has even found an application in reducing severe, chronic pain in humans: Fine wires are surgically implanted in parts of the central nervous system and attached to a radio-controlled device that permits the patient to administer electrical stimulation when necessary (Kumar, Wyant, and Nath, 1990).

Analgesic brain stimulation apparently triggers the neural mechanisms that reduce pain, primarily by causing endogenous opioids to be released. Basbaum and Fields (1978, 1984), who summarized their work and that of others, proposed a neural circuit that mediates opiate-induced analgesia. Basically, they proposed the following: Endogenous opioids (released by environmental stimuli or administered as a drug) stimulate opiate receptors on neurons in the periaqueductal gray matter. Because the effect of opiates appears to be inhibitory (Nicoll, Alger, and Nicoll, 1980), Basbaum and Fields proposed that the neurons that contain opiate receptors are themselves inhibitory interneurons. Thus, the administration of opiates activates the neurons on which these interneurons synapse. (See *Figure 7.26.*)

Neurons in the periaqueductal gray matter send axons to the **nucleus raphe magnus,** located in the medulla. The neurons in this nucleus send axons to the dorsal horn of the spinal cord gray matter; destruction of these axons eliminates analgesia induced by an injection of morphine. The inhibitory effects of these neurons apparently involve one or two interneurons in the spinal cord. (See *Figure 7.26.*)

Pain sensitivity can be regulated by direct neural connections, as well as by secretion of the endogenous opioids. The periaqueductal gray matter receives inputs from the frontal cortex, amygdala, and hypothalamus (Beitz, 1982; Mantyh, 1983). These inputs permit learning and emotional reactions to affect an animal's responsiveness to pain even without the secretion of opioids.

Biological Significance of Analgesia

It appears that a considerable amount of neural circuitry is devoted to reducing the intensity of pain. What functions

nucleus raphe magnus A nucleus of the raphe that contains serotonin-secreting neurons that project to the dorsal gray matter of the spinal cord and is involved in analgesia produced by opiates.

do these circuits perform? When an animal encounters a noxious stimulus, it usually stops what it is doing and engages in withdrawal or escape behaviors. Obviously, these responses are quite appropriate. However, they are sometimes counterproductive. For example, if an animal sustains a wound that causes chronic pain, a tendency to engage in withdrawal responses will interfere with its performance of everyday activities, such as obtaining food. Thus, chronic, unavoidable pain would best be diminished.

Another useful function of analgesia is the suppression of pain during important behaviors such as fighting or mating. For example, males fighting for access to females during mating season will fail to pass on their genes if pain elicits withdrawal responses that interfere with fighting. As we will see, these conditions *do* diminish pain.

First, let us consider the effects of unavoidable pain. Several experiments have shown that analgesia can be produced by the application of painful stimuli or even by the presence of nonpainful stimuli that have been paired with painful ones (that is, through classically conditioned analgesia). For example, Maier, Drugan, and Grau (1982) administered inescapable shocks to rats' tails or administered shocks that the animals could learn to escape by making a response. Although both groups of animals received the same amount of shock, only those that received *inescapable* shocks showed analgesia. That is, when their pain sensitivity was tested, it was found to be lower than that of control subjects. The analgesia was abolished by administration of naloxone, which indicates that it was mediated by the release of endogenous opioids. The results make good sense, biologically. If pain is escapable, it serves to motivate the animal to make appropriate responses. If it occurs whatever the animal does, then a reduction in pain sensitivity is in the animal's best interest. Defeat by another animal of the same species or exposure to the sound or smell of a predator all have been reported to produce analgesia (Lester and Fanselow, 1985; Kavaliers, 1988; Hendrie, 1991).

Pain can be reduced by stimulating regions other than those that hurt. For example, people often rub or scratch the area around a wound, in an apparent attempt to diminish the severity of the pain. And as you know, acupuncturists insert needles into various parts of the body to reduce pain. The needle is usually then rotated, thus stimulating axons and nerve endings in the vicinity. Often, the region that is stimulated is far removed from the region that becomes less sensitive to pain.

Several experimental studies have shown that acupuncture does, indeed, produce analgesia (Mann et al., 1973; Gaw, Chang, and Shaw, 1975). Mayer, Price, Rafii, and Barber (1976) reported that the analgesic effects of acupunc-

ture could be blocked by naloxone. However, when pain was reduced by hypnotic suggestion, naloxone had no effect. Thus, acupuncture, but not hypnosis, appears to cause analgesia through the release of endogenous opioids.

Although pain reduction produced by acupuncture may be more effective if a person believes that it will work, belief in its efficacy is not the only reason this procedure works. Many studies have demonstrated that acupuncture reduces the reaction of laboratory animals to pain, where "belief" can certainly not be an issue. Lee and Beitz (1992) reported that acupuncture that was able to reduce an animal's sensitivity to painful stimuli also reduced the production of Fos protein in somatosensory neurons in the dorsal horn of the spinal cord. (You will recall from Chapter 5 that the production of Fos protein in neurons indicates that they have been activated.)

There is evidence that engaging in behaviors that are important to survival also reduces sensitivity to pain. For example, Komisaruk and Larsson (1971) found that gentle probing of a rat's vagina with a glass rod produced analgesia. Such probing also increases the activity of neurons in the periaqueductal gray matter and decreases the responsiveness of neurons in the ventrobasal thalamus to painful stimulation (Komisaruk and Steinman, 1987). The phenomenon also occurs in humans; Whipple and Komisaruk (1988) found that self-administered vaginal stimulation reduces sensitivity to painful stimuli but not to neutral tactile stimuli. Presumably, copulation triggers analgesic mechanisms. The adaptive significance of this phenomenon is clear: Painful stimuli encountered during the course of copulation are less likely to cause the behavior to be interrupted; thus, the chances of pregnancy are increased.

As we saw in Chapter 4, pain can also be reduced, at least in some people, by administering a pharmacologically inert placebo. When some people take a medication that they believe will reduce pain, it triggers the release of endogenous opioids. This effect is eliminated by the opiate receptor-blocker naloxone (Levine, Gordon, and Fields, 1979). Thus, for some people a placebo is not pharmacologically "inert." The placebo effect is probably mediated through connections of the frontal cortex with the periaqueductal gray matter.

Interim Summary

Cutaneous sensory information is provided by specialized receptors in the skin. Pacinian corpuscles provide information about vibration. Ruffini corpuscles, similar to Pacinian corpuscles but considerably smaller, respond to low-frequency vibration, usually referred to as "flutter." Meissner's corpuscles, found in papillae and innervated by several axons, respond to mechanical stimuli. Merkel's disks, also found in papillae, consist of single, flattened dendritic endings next to specialized epithelial cells. These receptors respond to mechanical stimulation. Krause end bulbs, found in the junction between mucous membrane and dry skin (mucocutaneous zones), consist of loops of unmyelinated axons. They probably respond to mechanical stimuli. Painful stimuli are detected primarily by free nerve endings.

Our somatosensory system is most sensitive to changes in mechanical stimuli. Unless the skin is moving, we do not detect nonpainful stimuli, because the receptors adapt to constant mechanical pressure. Temperature receptors also adapt; moderate changes in skin temperature are soon perceived as "neutral," and deviations above or below this temperature are perceived as warmth or coolness.

Precise, well-localized somatosensory information is conveyed by a pathway through the dorsal columns and their nuclei and the medial lemniscus, connecting the dorsal column nuclei with the ventral posterior nuclei of the thalamus. Information about pain and temperature ascends the spinal cord through the spinothalamic system. Organic sensibility reaches the central nervous system by means of axons that travel through nerves of the autonomic nervous systems.

The neurons in the primary somatosensory cortex are topographically arranged, according to the part of the body from which they receive sensory information (somatotopic representation). Columns within the somatosensory cortex respond to a particular type of stimulus from a particular region of the body. Recent studies have shown that different types of somatosensory receptors send their information to separate areas of the somatosensory cortex.

Pain perception is not a simple function of stimulation of pain receptors; it is a complex phenomenon that can be modified by experience and the immediate environment. The phantom limb phenomenon, which often is accompanied by phantom pain, appears to be inherent in the organization of the parietal lobe.

Just as we have mechanisms to perceive pain, we have mechanisms to reduce it—to produce analgesia. Under the appropriate circumstances neurons in the periaqueductal gray matter are stimulated through synaptic connections with the frontal cortex, amygdala, and hypothalamus. In addition, some neurosecretory cells in the brain release enkephalins, a class of endogenous opioids. These neuromodulators activate receptors on neurons in the periaqueductal gray matter and provide additional stimulation of neurons in this region. Connections from the periaque-

ductal gray matter to the nucleus raphe magnus of the medulla activate serotonergic neurons located there. These neurons send axons to the dorsal horn of the spinal cord gray matter, where they inhibit the transmission of pain information to the brain. In humans, chronic pain is sometimes treated by implanting electrodes in the periaqueductal gray matter or the thalamus and permitting the patients to stimulate the brain through these electrodes when the pain becomes severe.

Analgesia occurs when it is important for an animal to continue a behavior that would tend to be inhibited by pain—for example, mating or fighting. In addition, inescapable pain activates brain mechanisms that produce analgesia, but escapable pain does not. This distinction makes sense: If the pain is escapable, its sensation should not be blunted but should serve to motivate the animal's efforts to escape. Because the endogenous opioids are found in several regions of the brain that are apparently not involved in pain perception, these neuromodulators undoubtedly serve functions besides analgesia. The fact that many people have chosen to self-administer opiates extracted from the opium poppy attests to its potency as a reinforcer of behavior.

Analgesia can also be produced by stimulating regions other than those that hurt, which is the basis for acupuncture. This phenomenon can be demonstrated in laboratory animals, which suggests that it has a physiological basis. The administration of a placebo can also produce analgesia. Because this effect is blocked by naloxone, it must involve the release of endogenous opioids.

GUSTATION

The stimuli we have encountered so far produce receptor potentials by imparting physical energy: thermal, photic (involving light), or kinetic. However, the stimuli received by the last two senses to be studied, gustation and olfaction, interact with their receptors chemically. This section discusses the first of them: gustation.

● The Stimuli

Gustation is clearly related to eating; this sense modality helps us determine the nature of things we put in our mouths. For a substance to be tasted, molecules of it must dissolve in the saliva and stimulate the taste receptors on the tongue. Tastes of different substances vary, but much less than we generally realize. There are only four qualities of taste: *bitterness, sourness, sweetness,* and *saltiness.* (As we will see later, researchers have suggested that at least some species can detect two other taste qualities.) Flavor, as opposed to taste, is a composite of olfaction and gustation. Much of the flavor of a steak depends on its odor; to an *anosmic* person (one who lacks the sense of smell) or to a person whose nostrils are stopped up, an onion tastes like an apple, and a steak tastes like salty cardboard.

Most vertebrates possess gustatory systems that respond to all four taste qualities. (An exception is the cat family; lions, tigers, leopards, and house cats do not detect sweetness.) Clearly, sweetness receptors are food detectors. Most sweet-tasting foods, such as fruits and some vegetables, are safe to eat (Ramirez, 1990). Saltiness receptors detect the presence of sodium chloride. In some environments inadequate amounts of this mineral are obtained from the usual source of food, so sodium chloride detectors help the animal detect its presence. Injuries that cause bleeding deplete an organism of its supply of sodium rapidly, so the ability to find it quickly can be critical.

Most species of animals will readily ingest substances that taste sweet or somewhat salty. However, they will tend to avoid substances that taste sour or bitter. Because of bacterial activity, many foods become acidic when they spoil. The acidity tastes sour and causes an avoidance reaction. (Of course, we have learned to make highly preferred mixtures of sweet and sour, such as lemonade.) Bitterness is almost universally avoided and cannot easily be improved by adding some sweetness. Many plants produce poisonous alkaloids, which protect them from being eaten by animals. Alkaloids taste bitter; thus, the bitterness receptor undoubtedly serves to warn animals away from these chemicals.

● Anatomy of the Taste Buds and Gustatory Cells

The tongue, palate, pharynx, and larynx contain approximately 10,000 taste buds. Most of these receptive organs are arranged around *papillae,* small protuberances of the tongue. *Fungiform papillae,* located on the anterior two-thirds of the tongue, contain up to eight taste buds, along with receptors for pressure, touch, and temperature. *Foliate papillae* consist of up to eight parallel folds along each edge of the back of the tongue. Approximately 1300 taste buds are located in these folds. *Circumvallate papillae,* arranged in an inverted V on the posterior third of the tongue, contain approximately 250 taste buds. They are shaped like little plateaus surrounded by moatlike trenches. Taste buds consist of groups of 20–50 receptor cells, arranged somewhat like the segments of an orange. Cilia are located at the end of each cell and project through the opening of the taste

bud (the pore) into the saliva that coats the tongue. Tight junctions between adjacent taste cells prevent substances in the saliva from diffusing freely into the taste bud itself. Figure 7.27 shows the appearance of a circumvallate papilla; a cross section through the surrounding trench contains a taste bud. (See *Figure 7.27.*)

Taste buds that respond to the different taste qualities have different distributions on the tongue. The tip of the tongue is most sensitive to sweetness and saltiness, the sides are most sensitive to sourness, and the back of the tongue, throat, and soft palate are most sensitive to bitterness. This distribution explains why saccharin, an artificial sweetener, tastes both sweet and bitter to some people, producing a sensation of sweetness on the front of the tongue when it is first tasted and then a sensation of bitterness in the back of the mouth when it is swallowed. (See *Figure 7.28.*)

Taste receptors form synapses with dendrites of sensory neurons that convey gustatory information to the brain. The receptors have a life span of only ten days. They quickly wear out, being directly exposed to a rather hostile environment. As they degenerate, they are replaced by newly developed cells; the afferent dendrite is passed on to the new cell (Beidler, 1970).

● Detection of Gustatory Information

Transduction of taste is similar to the chemical transmission that takes place at synapses: The tasted molecule binds with the receptor and produces changes in membrane permeability that cause receptor potentials. Different substances bind with different types of receptors, producing different taste sensations. In this section I will describe what we know about the nature of the molecules with particular tastes and the receptors that detect their presence. I should note that in some cases, researchers have found that more than one type of receptor detects a particular taste and that different types of receptors may be found in different species. Thus, the following description, and the information in Figure 7.29, should be seen as representative rather than definitive.

To taste salty, a substance must ionize. Although the best stimulus for saltiness receptors is sodium chloride (NaCl), a variety of salts containing metallic cations (such as Na^+, K^+, and Li^+) with a halogen or other small anion (such as Cl^-, Br^-, SO_4^{2-}, or NO_3^-) taste salty. The receptor for saltiness seems to be a simple sodium channel. When present in the saliva, sodium enters the taste cell and depolarizes it, triggering action potentials that cause the cell to release transmitter substance (Avenet and Lindemann, 1989; Kinnamon and Cummings, 1992). The best evi-

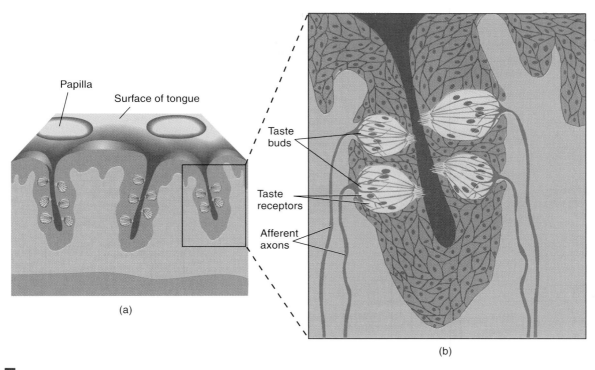

Figure 7.27
The tongue. (a) Papillae on the surface of the tongue. (b) Taste buds.

dence that sodium channels are involved is the fact that amiloride, a drug that is known to block sodium channels, prevents sodium chloride from activating taste cells and blocks sensations of saltiness (Schiffman, Lockhead, and Maes, 1983). (See *Figure 7.29a.*)

Sourness receptors appear to respond to the hydrogen ions present in acidic solutions. However, because the

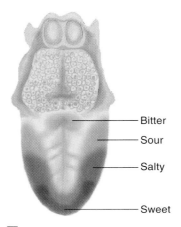

Figure 7.28
Sensitivity of different regions of the tongue to different tastes.

sourness of a particular acid is not simply a function of the concentration of hydrogen ions, the anions must have an effect, as well. The reason for this anion effect is not yet known. Kinnamon, Dionne, and Beam (1988) suggest that sourness is detected by sites on potassium channels in the membrane of taste cell cilia. These channels are normally open, permitting K^+ to flow out of the cell. Hydrogen ions bind with these sites and close the channels. Their closure prevents this outward current and depolarizes the membrane, producing action potentials. (See *Figure 7.29b.*)

Bitter and sweet substances are more difficult to characterize. The typical stimulus for bitterness is a plant alkaloid such as quinine; for sweetness it is a sugar such as glucose or fructose. The fact that some molecules elicit both sensations suggests that bitterness and sweetness receptors may be similar. For example, the Seville orange rind contains a glycoside (complex sugar) that tastes extremely bitter; the addition of a hydrogen ion to the molecule makes it taste intensely sweet (Horowitz and Gentili, 1974). Some amino acids taste sweet. Indeed, the commercial sweetener aspartame consists simply of two amino acids, aspartate and phenylalanine.

The structure of molecules that taste bitter appears to include a hydrophobic residue—that is, a region that is re-

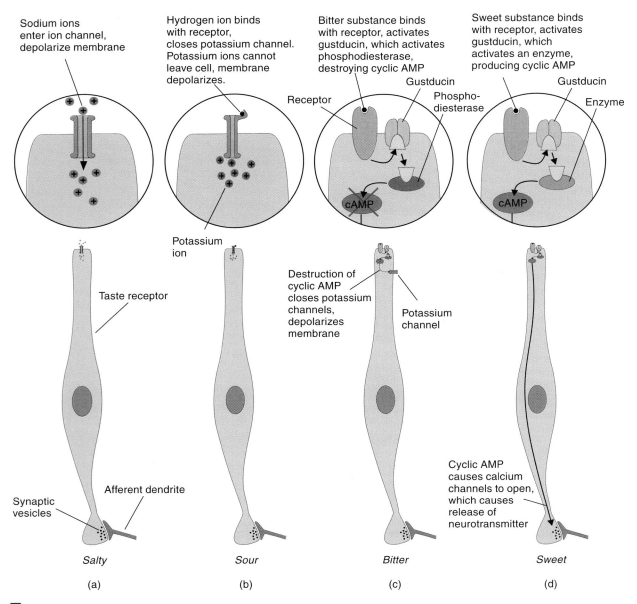

Figure 7.29
Transduction of taste information. (a) Salty taste. (b) Sour taste. (c) Bitter taste. (d) Sweet taste.

pelled by the presence of water. Especially bitter substances also have a region with a positive charge (Kurihara et al., 1994). The bitterness receptors are coupled with a G protein called **gustducin,** which is very similar in structure to *transducin,* the G protein involved in transduction of photic information in the retina (McLaughlin et al., 1993). When a bitter molecule binds with the receptor, gustducin activates phosphodiesterase, an enzyme that destroys cyclic AMP. Thus, detection of a bitter-tasting molecule by the receptor causes a decrease in intracellular cyclic AMP. In taste receptor cells, as in photoreceptors, it appears that potassium channels in the body of the taste receptor cell are normally held open by the action of cyclic AMP, which permits a constant efflux of K^+ cations. Thus, a fall in the level of cyclic AMP causes potassium channels to close, and the membrane depolarizes. (See *Figure 7.29c.*)

gustducin *(gust **doo** sin)*   A G protein that plays a vital role in the transduction of sweetness and bitterness.

Most molecules that taste sweet have a hydrogen ion situated 0.3 nm from a site that will accept a hydrogen ion. Presumably, the sweetness receptor has sites that match these. Sweetness receptors, like bitterness receptors, appear to be coupled to gustducin. Wong, Gannon, and Margolskee (1996) produced a mutation in mice using genetic engineering techniques that permit investigators to "knock out" a particular gene—in this case, the gene responsible for the production of gustducin. As expected, the mice did not respond to bitter substances. But in addition, they failed to respond to sweet substances, as well. (They did respond to sour and salty substances.) The binding of sweet-tasting molecules with their receptors causes an increase in the level of cyclic AMP in the cell. This second messenger causes calcium channels to open, and the subsequent influx of calcium causes the cell to release transmitter substance (Lindemann, 1996). (See *Figure 7.29d.*)

Researchers have proposed two other taste qualities: umami and carbohydrates. **Umami,** a Japanese word that means "good taste," refers to the taste of monosodium glutamate (MSG), a substance often used as a flavor enhancer in Asian cuisine (Kurihara, 1987; Scott and Plata-Salaman, 1991). MSG is present in meats, cheeses, and some vegetables. There is good evidence that the umami receptor exists in several species, but the existence of this taste quality is still not universally accepted in humans. Chaudhari et al. (1996) suggest that a specialized metabotropic glutamate receptor (mGluR4) may be responsible for detecting the taste of glutamate. The investigators found this receptor in taste buds, but not in other parts of the tongue. They also reported that rats did not distinguish the taste of MSG from that of a ligand for this receptor, L-AP4. Some studies suggest that monkeys and rodents can also taste complex carbohydrates (Feigin, Sclafani, and Sunday, 1987; Sunderland and Sclafani, 1988), but further research is needed to be certain.

The Gustatory Pathway

Gustatory information is transmitted through cranial nerves 7, 9, and 10. Information from the anterior part of the tongue travels through the **chorda tympani,** a branch of the seventh cranial nerve (facial nerve). Taste receptors in the posterior part of the tongue send information through the lingual (tongue) branch of the ninth cranial nerve (glossopharyngeal nerve); the tenth cranial nerve (vagus nerve) carries information from receptors of the palate and epiglottis. The chorda tympani gets its name because it passes through the middle ear just beneath the tympanic membrane. Because of its convenient location, it is accessible to a recording or stimulating electrode. Investigators

have even recorded from this nerve during the course of human ear operations.

The first relay station for taste is the **nucleus of the solitary tract,** located in the medulla. In primates the taste-sensitive neurons of this nucleus send their axons to the ventral posteromedial thalamic nucleus, a nucleus that also receives somatosensory information received from the trigeminal nerve (Beckstead, Morse, and Norgren, 1980). Thalamic taste-sensitive neurons send their axons to the primary gustatory cortex, which is located in the frontal insular and opercular cortex (Pritchard et al., 1986). Neurons in this region project to the secondary gustatory cortex, located in the caudolateral orbitofrontal cortex (Rolls, Yaxley, and Sienkiewicz, 1990). Unlike most other sense modalities, taste is ipsilaterally represented in the brain. (See *Figure 7.30.*)

Gustatory information also reaches the amygdala and the hypothalamus and adjacent basal forebrain (Nauta, 1964; Russchen, Amaral, and Price, 1986). Many investigators believe that the hypothalamic pathway plays a role in mediating the reinforcing effects of sweet and salty tastes. In fact, some neurons in the hypothalamus respond to sweet stimuli only when the animal is hungry (Rolls et al., 1986). I will discuss this phenomenon in more detail in Chapter 14.

Neural Coding of Taste

Almost all fibers in the chorda tympani respond to more than one taste quality, and many respond to changes in temperature, as well. However, most show a preference for one of the four qualities (sweet, salty, sour, or bitter). Figure 7.31 shows the average responses of fibers in the rat chorda tympani and glossopharyngeal nerve to sucrose (S), NaCl (N), HCl (H), quinine (Q), and water (W), as recorded by Nowlis and Frank (1977). (See *Figure 7.31.*)

Scott and his colleagues (Scott et al., 1991; Smith-Swintosky, Plata-Salaman, and Scott, 1991) operated on monkeys, attaching devices that permitted them to record the activity of single neurons in the primary gustatory cortex while the animals were awake and alert. They found that

umami *(oo mah mee)* The taste sensation produced by glutamate.

chorda tympani A branch of the facial nerve that passes beneath the eardrum; conveys taste information from the anterior part of the tongue and controls the secretion of some salivary glands.

nucleus of the solitary tract (NST) A nucleus of the medulla that receives information from visceral organs and from the gustatory system.

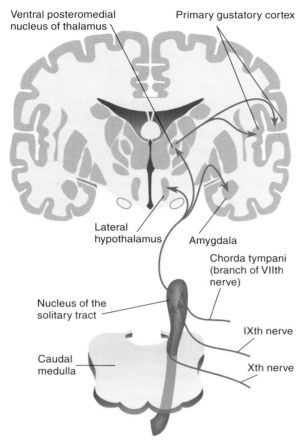

Figure 7.30
Neural pathways of the gustatory system.

slightly over 3 percent of the cells they found responded to taste. Others responded to movement of the mouth or to various somatosensory stimuli. Many cells did not respond to any of the stimuli that the investigators tried.

Although the distribution of the taste-sensitive neurons in the nucleus of the solitary tract and the gustatory thalamus resembles that found on the surface of the tongue (Beckstead, Morse, and Norgren, 1980; Scott et al., 1986), their distribution in the gustatory cortex appears to be unsystematic. However, the investigators did find clusters of neurons with similar response characteristics, which suggests that like other regions of sensory cortex, the gustatory cortex may be organized in columns. They found two major groups of taste-sensitive neurons, sweet and salty. They found cells responsive to sour and bitter also, but the responses were less distinct. They noted that the minimum concentrations of salty, sweet, sour, and bitter substances that produced responses in these neurons were very close to the minimum concentrations of these substances that human subjects can detect. Recording in the secondary gustatory cortex, Rolls and his colleagues (reviewed by Rolls, 1995b) found both narrowly and broadly tuned neurons responding to single taste qualities or to several of them.

Interim Summary

Taste receptors detect only four sensory qualities: bitterness, sourness, sweetness, and saltiness. Bitter foods often contain plant alkaloids, many of which are poisonous.

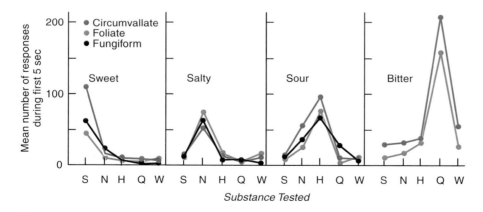

Figure 7.31
Mean number of responses recorded from axons in rat chorda tympani and glossopharyngeal nerve during the first 5 seconds after the application of sugar (S), NaCl (N), HCl (H), quinine (Q), and water (W). The response characteristics of the axons are categorized as sweet, salty, sour, or bitter.
(From Nowlis, G. H., and Frank, M., in *Olfaction and Taste 6,* edited by J. Le Magnen and P. MacLeod. Washington, DC: Information Retrieval, 1977.)

Sour foods have usually undergone bacterial fermentation, which can produce toxins. On the other hand, sweet foods (such as fruits) are usually nutritious and safe to eat, and salty foods contain an essential cation, sodium. The fact that people in affluent cultures today tend to ingest excessive amounts of sweet and salty foods suggests that these taste qualities are naturally reinforcing.

Saltiness receptors appear to be simple sodium channels. Sourness receptors appear to detect the presence of hydrogen ions, which closes potassium channels located on the cilia and depolarizes the membrane of the cell. Both bitter and sweet tastes are detected by receptors bound to gustducin, a G protein. The structure of molecules that taste bitter appears to include a hydrophobic residue, and some also have a region with a positive charge. Bitter molecules activate phosphodiesterase, which destroys cyclic AMP and closes potassium channels, thus depolarizing the membrane of the cell. Most molecules that taste sweet have a hydrogen ion situated 0.3 nm from a site that will accept a hydrogen ion. Sweet molecules *increase* cyclic AMP levels, which opens calcium channels and thus causes the release of the transmitter substance. The taste of glutamate (umami) is—at least, in some species—detected by a particular metabolic glutamate receptor (mGluR4). Some animals may also be able to taste complex carbohydrates.

Gustatory information from the anterior part of the tongue travels through the chorda tympani, a branch of the facial nerve that passes beneath the eardrum on its way to the brain. The posterior part of the tongue sends gustatory information through the glossopharyngeal nerve, and the palate and epiglottis send gustatory information through the vagus nerve. Gustatory information is received by the nucleus of the solitary tract (located in the medulla) and is relayed by the ventral posteromedial thalamus to the primary gustatory cortex in the opercular and insular areas. The caudolateral orbitofrontal cortex contains the secondary gustatory cortex. Gustatory information is also sent to the amygdala, hypothalamus, and basal forebrain.

OLFACTION

Olfaction, the second chemical sense, helps us identify food and avoid food that has spoiled and is unfit to eat. It helps the members of many species to track prey or detect predators and to identify friends, foes, and receptive mates. For humans, olfaction is the most enigmatic of all sensory modalities. Odors have a peculiar ability to evoke memories, often vague ones that seem to have occurred in the distant past—a phenomenon vividly described by Marcel Proust in his book *Remembrance of Things Past*. Although people can discriminate among many thousands of different odors, we lack a good vocabulary to describe them. It is relatively easy to describe sights we have seen or sounds we have heard, but the description of an odor is difficult. At best, we can say it smells like something else. Thus, the olfactory system appears to be specialized for *identifying things*, not for analyzing particular qualities.

The Stimulus

The stimulus for odor consists of volatile substances having a molecular weight in the range of approximately 15 to 300. Almost all odorous compounds are lipid soluble and of organic origin. However, many substances that meet these criteria have no odor at all.

Anatomy of the Olfactory Apparatus

Our 50 million olfactory receptor cells reside within two patches of mucous membrane (the **olfactory epithelium**), each having an area of about 1 square inch. The olfactory epithelium is located at the top of the nasal cavity, as shown in *Figure 7.32*. Less than 10 percent of the air that enters the nostrils reaches the olfactory epithelium; a sniff is needed to sweep air upward into the nasal cavity so that it reaches the olfactory receptors.

The inset in Figure 7.32 illustrates a group of olfactory receptor cells, along with their supporting cells. (See *inset, Figure 7.32*.) Olfactory receptor cells are bipolar neurons whose cell bodies lie within the olfactory mucosa that lines the *cribriform plate*, a bone at the base of the rostral part of the brain. There is a constant turnover of olfactory receptor cells, as there is of gustatory receptor cells; their life cycle is approximately 60 days. The cells send a process toward the surface of the mucosa, which divides into 10 to 20 cilia that penetrate the layer of mucus. Odorous molecules must dissolve in the mucus and stimulate receptor molecules on the olfactory cilia. The axons of olfactory receptor cells enter the skull through small holes in the cribriform ("perforated") plate. The olfactory mucosa also contains free nerve endings of trigeminal nerve axons; these nerve endings presumably mediate sensations of pain that can be produced by sniffing some irritating chemicals, such as ammonia.

The **olfactory bulbs** lie at the base of the brain on the ends of the stalklike olfactory tracts. Each olfactory recep-

olfactory epithelium   The epithelial tissue of the nasal sinus that covers the cribriform plate; contains the cilia of the olfactory receptors.

olfactory bulb   The protrusion at the end of the olfactory tract; receives input from the olfactory receptors.

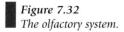

Figure 7.32
The olfactory system.

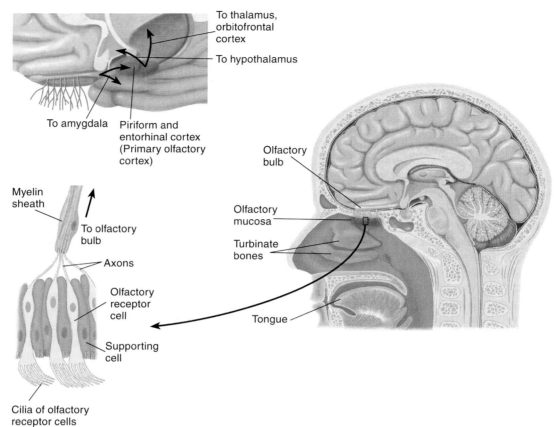

tor cell sends a single axon into the olfactory bulb, where it forms synapses with dendrites of **mitral cells** (named for their resemblance to a bishop's miter). These synapses take place in the complex axonal and dendritic arborizations called **olfactory glomeruli** (from *glomus,* "ball"). There are approximately 10,000 glomeruli, each of which receives input from a bundle of approximately 2000 axons. The axons of the mitral cells travel to the rest of the brain through the olfactory tracts. Some of these axons terminate in the brain; others cross the brain, enter the other olfactory nerve, and terminate in the contralateral olfactory bulb.

Olfactory tract axons project directly to the amygdala and to two regions of the limbic cortex, the pyriform cortex and the entorhinal cortex. (See *Figure 7.32.*) The amygdala sends olfactory information to the hypothalamus, the entorhinal cortex sends it to the hippocampus, and the pyriform cortex sends it to the hypothalamus and to the orbitofrontal cortex, via the dorsomedial nucleus of the thalamus (Buck, 1996; Shipley and Ennis, 1996). As you may recall, the orbitofrontal cortex also receives gustatory information; thus, it may be involved in the

combining of taste and olfaction into flavor. The hypothalamus also receives a considerable amount of olfactory information, which is probably important for the acceptance or rejection of food and for the olfactory control of reproductive processes seen in many species of mammals.

Most mammals have another organ that responds to olfactory stimuli: the *vomeronasal organ.* Because it plays an important role in animals' responses to odors that affect reproductive physiology and behavior, its structure and function are described in Chapter 10.

Efferent fibers from several locations in the brain enter the olfactory bulbs. These include acetylcholinergic, noradrenergic, dopaminergic, and serotonergic inputs (Shipley

mitral cell   A neuron located in the olfactory bulb that receives information from olfactory receptors; axons of mitral cells bring information to the rest of the brain.

olfactory glomerulus *(glow **mare** you luss)*   A bundle of dendrites of mitral cells and the associated terminal buttons of the axons of olfactory receptors.

and Ennis, 1996). As we shall see in Chapter 10, the noradrenergic input appears to be involved in olfactory memories, particularly those involved in reproduction.

Transduction of Olfactory Information

Olfactory cilia contain receptors that are stimulated by odor molecules. Jones and Reed (1989) identified a particular G protein, which they called G_{olf}. This protein is able to activate an enzyme that catalyzes the synthesis of cyclic AMP, which, in turn, can open sodium channels and depolarize the membrane of the olfactory cell (Nakamura and Gold, 1987; Firestein, Zufall, and Shepherd, 1991; Menco et al., 1992).

Buck and Axel (1991) used molecular genetics techniques and discovered a family of genes that code for what is almost certainly the olfactory receptor protein. These proteins contain a sequence common to all receptors linked with G proteins. There appear to be between five hundred and one thousand different receptors in humans and rodents, each sensitive to different odorants (Ressler, Sullivan, and Buck, 1994a).

Detection of Specific Odors

For many years, recognition of specific odors has been an enigma. Humans can recognize up to ten thousand different odorants, and other animals can probably recognize even more of them (Shepherd, 1994). Even if we have one thousand different olfactory receptors, that leaves many odors unaccounted for. And every year, chemists synthesize new chemicals, many with odors unlike those that anyone has previously detected. How can we use a relatively small number of receptors to detect so many different odorants?

Before I answer this question, we should look more closely at the relation between receptors, olfactory neurons, and the glomeruli to which the axons of these neurons project. First, the cilia of each olfactory neuron contain only one type of receptor (Nef et al., 1992; Vassar, Ngai, and Axel, 1993). As we saw, each glomerulus receives information from approximately two thousand different olfactory receptor cells. Using in situ hybridization methods to identify particular receptor proteins in individual cells, Ressler, Sullivan, and Buck (1994) discovered that although a given glomerulus receives information from approxi-

mately two thousand different olfactory receptor cells, each of these cells contains the same type of receptor molecule. Thus, there are as many types of glomeruli as there are types of receptor molecules. Furthermore, the location of particular types of glomeruli (defined by the type of receptor that sends information to them) appears to be the same in each of the olfactory bulbs in a given animal and may even be the same from one animal to another. (See *Figure 7.33.*)

Now let's get back to the question I just posed: How can we use a relatively small number of receptors to detect so many different odorants. The answer is that a particular odorant binds to more than one receptor. Moreover, it binds to some of these receptors better than to others. Thus, because a given glomerulus receives information from only one type of receptor, different odorants produce different *patterns* of activity in different glomeruli. Recognizing a particular odor, then, is a matter of recognizing a particular pattern of activity in the glomeruli. The task of chemical recognition is transformed into a task of spatial recognition.

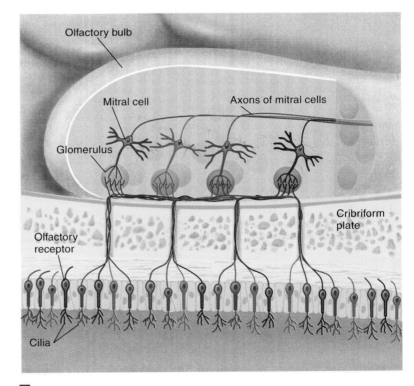

Figure 7.33
Details of the connections of olfactory receptor cells with the glomeruli of the olfactory bulb. Each glomerulus receives information from only one type of receptor cell. Olfactory receptor cells of different colors contain different types of receptor molecules.

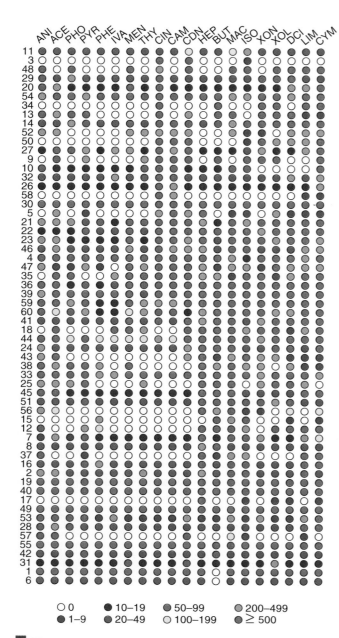

0 0   **●** 10–19   **●** 50–99   **●** 200–499
● 1–9   **●** 20–49   ○ 100–199   **●** ≥ 500

Figure 7.34
Responses of individual olfactory neurons to the presence of different odorants.
(Adapted from Sicard, G., and Holley, A. *Brain Research*, 1984, 292, 282–296.)

Figure 7.34 illustrates this process. The diagram shows the responses of sixty different olfactory neurons to the presence of twenty different odorants (Sicard and Holley, 1984). Each horizontal row of dots indicates the response of a particular neuron to each of the odorants. The color of

each dot indicates the magnitude of the response. As you can see, almost all odorants provoked at least some response in most cells, but different odorants produced different patterns of responses. In recognizing these patterns, the brain recognizes particular odors. (See *Figure 7.34.*)

Just how the brain recognizes these patterns is not yet known. The task is obviously complex. Cain (1988) noted that although most odors are produced by mixtures of many different chemicals, we identify odors as belonging to particular objects. For example, the smells of coffee, fried bacon, and cigarette smoke are each made of up to several hundred different types of molecules. Although each of these odors is a mixture, we recognize them as being unique—we do not detect the individual components. However, if the smells of coffee, fried bacon, and cigarette smoke are mixed together, we still recognize all three odors, even though each one of them is itself a mixture!

Recordings in more central levels of the olfactory system show that neural responses tend to be finely tuned to particular odors. For example, Tanabe et al. (1974) and Tanabe, Iino, and Takagi (1975) found that neurons in the olfactory area of the orbitofrontal cortex of monkeys were rather selective. Of the forty cells from which they recorded, half responded to only one odor, and decreasing numbers responded to two, three, or four different odors. None responded to more than five odors. The nature of the coding system in the olfactory cortex is unknown.

Interim Summary

The olfactory receptors consist of bipolar neurons located in the olfactory epithelium that lines the roof of the nasal sinuses, on the bone that underlies the frontal lobes. The receptors send processes toward the surface of the mucosa, which divide into cilia. The membranes of these cilia contain receptors that detect aromatic molecules dissolved in the air that sweeps past the olfactory mucosa. The axons of the olfactory receptors pass through the perforations of the cribriform plate into the olfactory bulbs, where they form synapses in the glomeruli with the dendrites of the mitral cells. These neurons send axons through the olfactory tracts to the brain, principally to the amygdala, the pyriform cortex, and the entorhinal cortex. The hippocampus, hypothalamus, and orbitofrontal cortex receive olfactory information indirectly.

Aromatic molecules produce membrane potentials by interacting with a newly discovered family of receptor molecules, which may number up to one thousand. These receptors are coupled to a special G protein, G_{olf}. This protein catalyzes the synthesis of cyclic AMP, which opens sodium channels and depolarizes the membrane. Each glomerulus receives information from only one type of olfactory receptor. This means that the task of detecting different odors is a spatial one; the brain recognizes odors by means of the patterns of activity created in the glomeruli.

SUGGESTED READINGS

Audition

Ashmore, J. F. The electrophysiology of hair cells. *Annual Review of Physiology*, 1991, *53*, 465–476.

Corwin, J. T., and Warchol, M. E. Auditory hair cells: Structure, function, development, and regeneration. *Annual Review of Neuroscience*, 1991, *14*, 301–333.

Ehret, G., and Romand, R. *The Central Auditory System*. New York: Oxford University Press, 1997.

Moore, B. C. J. *Hearing: Handbook of Perception and Cognition* (2nd ed.). San Diego: Academic Press, 1995.

Yost, W. A. *Fundamentals of Hearing: An Introduction* (3rd ed.). San Diego: Academic Press, 1994.

Vestibular System

Cohen, B., Tomko, D. L., and Guedry, F. E. *Sensing and Controlling Motion: Vestibular and Sensorimotor Function*. New York: New York Academy of Sciences, 1992.

Somatosenses

Bromm, B., and Desmedt, J. E. *Pain and the Brain: From Nociception to Cognition*. New York: Raven Press, 1995.

García-Añoveros, J., and Corey, D. P. The molecules of mechanosensation. *Annual Review of Neuroscience*, 1997, *20*, 567–594.

Kruger, L. *Pain and Touch: Handbook of Perception and Cognition* (2nd ed.). San Diego: Academic Press, 1996.

Melzak, R. Phantom limbs. *Scientific American*, 1992, *266(4)*, 120–126.

Olfaction and Gustation

Buck, L. B. Information coding in the vertebrate olfactory system. *Annual Review of Neuroscience*, 1996, *19*, 517–544.

Getchell, T. V. *Smell and Taste in Health and Disease*. New York: Raven Press, 1991.

Hildebrand, J. G., and Shepherd, G. M. Mechanisms of olfactory discrimination: Converging evidence for common principles across phyla. *Annual Review of Neuroscience*, 1997, *20*, 595–632.

Laing, D. G., Doty, R. L., and Breipohl, W. *The Human Sense of Smell*. New York: Springer-Verlag, 1991.

Kinnamon, S. C., and Cummings, T. A. Chemosensory transduction mechanisms in taste. *Annual Review of Physiology*, 1992, *54*, 715–731.

CHAPTER 8

Control of Movement

Sweets Crane by William T. Williams.

So far, I have described the nature of neural communication, the basic structure of the nervous system, and the physiology of perception. Now it is time to consider the ultimate function of the nervous system: control of behavior. The brain is the organ that moves the muscles. It does many other things, but all of them are secondary to making our bodies move. This chapter describes the principles of muscular contraction, some reflex circuitry within the spinal cord, and the means by which the brain initiates behaviors. The rest of the book describes the physiology of particular categories of behaviors and the ways in which our behaviors can be modified by experience.

MUSCLES

Mammals have three types of muscles: skeletal muscle, smooth muscle, and cardiac muscle.

● Skeletal Muscle

Skeletal muscles are the ones that move us (our skeletons) around and thus are responsible for our behavior. Most of them are attached to bones at each end and move the bones when they contract. (Exceptions include eye muscles and some abdominal muscles, which are attached to bone at one end only.) Muscles are fastened to bones via *tendons,* strong bands of connective tissue. Several different classes of movement can be accomplished by the skeletal muscles, but I will refer principally to two of them: flexion and extension. Contraction of a flexor muscle produces **flexion,** the drawing in of a limb. **Extension,** which is the opposite movement, is produced by contrac-

tion of extensor muscles. These are the so-called *antigravity muscles*—the ones we use to stand up. When a four-legged animal lifts a paw, the movement is one of flexion. Putting it back down is one of extension. Sometimes, people say they "flex" their muscles. This is an incorrect use of the term. Muscles *contract;* limbs *flex.* Bodybuilders show off their arm muscles by simultaneously contracting the flexor and extensor muscles of that limb.

Anatomy

The detailed structure of a skeletal muscle is shown in *Figure 8.1*. As you can see, it consists of two types of muscle fibers. The **extrafusal muscle fibers** are served by axons of the **alpha motor neurons.** Contraction of these fibers provides the muscle's motive force. The **intrafusal muscle fibers** are specialized sensory organs that are served by two axons, one sensory and one motor. These organs are also called *muscle spindles* because of their shape. In fact, the

---

skeletal muscle   One of the striated muscles attached to bones.

flexion   A movement of a limb that tends to bend its joints; opposite of extension.

extension   A movement of a limb that tends to straighten its joints; the opposite of flexion.

extrafusal muscle fiber   One of the muscle fibers that are responsible for the force exerted by contraction of a skeletal muscle.

alpha motor neuron   A neuron whose axon forms synapses with extrafusal muscle fibers of a skeletal muscle; activation contracts the muscle fibers.

intrafusal muscle fiber   A muscle fiber that functions as a stretch receptor, arranged parallel to the extrafusal muscle fibers, thus detecting changes in muscle length.

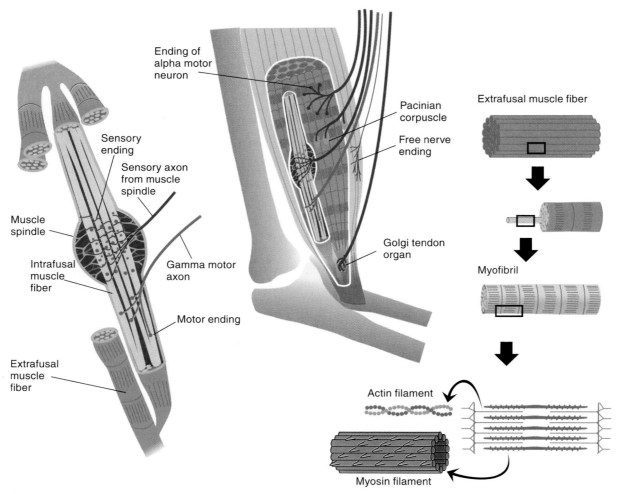

Figure 8.1
Anatomy of skeletal muscle.

Latin word *fusus* means "spindle"; hence *intrafusal* muscle fibers are found within the spindles, and *extrafusal* muscle fibers are found outside them.

The central region (*capsule*) of the intrafusal muscle fiber contains sensory endings that are sensitive to stretch applied to the muscle fiber. Actually, there are two types of intrafusal muscle fibers, but for simplicity's sake only one kind is shown here. The efferent axon of the **gamma motor neuron** causes the intrafusal muscle fiber to contract; however, this contraction contributes an insubstantial amount of force. As we will see, the function of this contraction is to modify the sensitivity of the fiber's afferent ending to stretch.

A single myelinated axon of an alpha motor neuron serves several extrafusal muscle fibers. In primates the number of muscle fibers served by a single axon varies considerably, depending on the precision with which the mus-

cle can be controlled. In muscles that move the fingers or eyes the ratio can be less than one to ten; in muscles that move the leg it can be one to several hundred. An alpha motor neuron, its axon, and associated extrafusal muscle fibers constitute a **motor unit.**

A single muscle fiber consists of a bundle of **myofibrils,** each of which consists of overlapping strands of **actin** and

gamma motor neuron   A neuron whose axons form synapses with intrafusal muscle fibers.

motor unit   A motor neuron and its associated muscle fibers.

myofibril   An element of muscle fibers that consists of overlapping strands of actin and myosin; responsible for muscular contractions.

actin   One of the proteins (with myosin) that provide the physical basis for muscular contraction.

myosin. Note the small protrusions on the myosin filaments; these structures (*myosin cross bridges*) are the motile elements that interact with the actin filaments and produce muscular contractions. (See *Figure 8.1.*) The regions in which the actin and myosin filaments overlap produce dark stripes, or *striations;* hence skeletal muscle is often referred to as **striated muscle.**

The Physical Basis of Muscular Contraction

The synapse between the terminal button of an efferent neuron and the membrane of a muscle fiber is called a **neuromuscular junction.** The terminal buttons of the neurons synapse on **motor endplates,** located in grooves along the surface of the muscle fibers. When an axon fires, acetylcholine is liberated by the terminal buttons and produces a depolarization of the postsynaptic membrane—an **endplate potential.** The endplate potential is much larger than an excitatory postsynaptic potential in synapses between neurons; an endplate potential *always* causes the muscle fiber to fire, propagating the potential along its length. This action potential induces a contraction, or *twitch,* of the muscle fiber.

The depolarization of a muscle fiber opens the gates of voltage-dependent calcium channels, permitting calcium ions to enter the cytoplasm. This event triggers the contraction. Calcium acts as a cofactor that permits the myofibrils to extract energy from the ATP that is present in the cytoplasm. The myosin cross bridges alternately attach to the actin strands, bend in one direction, detach themselves, bend back, reattach to the actin at a point farther down the strand, and so on. Thus, the cross bridges "row" along the actin filaments. Figure 8.2 illustrates this rowing sequence and shows how this sequence results in shortening the muscle fiber. (See *Figure 8.2.*)

A single impulse of a motor neuron produces a single twitch of a muscle fiber. The physical effects of the twitch last considerably longer than will the action potential, because of the elasticity of the muscle and the time required to rid the cell of calcium. (Like sodium, calcium is actively extruded by a pump situated in the membrane.) Figure 8.3 shows how the physical effects of a series of action potentials can overlap, causing a sustained contraction by the muscle fiber. A single motor unit in a leg muscle of a cat can raise a 100-gram weight, which attests to the remarkable strength of the contractile mechanism. (See *Figure 8.3.*)

As you know from your own experience, muscular contraction is not an all-or-nothing phenomenon, as are the twitches of the constituent muscle fibers. Obviously, the strength of a muscular contraction is determined by the average rate of firing of the various motor units. If, at a given

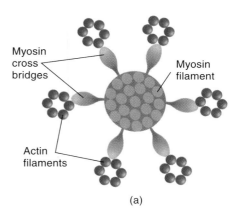

(a)

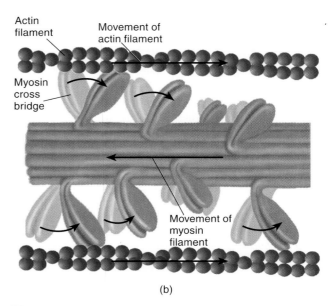

(b)

Figure 8.2
The mechanism by which muscles contract. (a) Cross section through a myosin filament and the surrounding actin filaments. (b) The myosin cross bridges performing "rowing" movements, which cause the actin and myosin filaments to move relative to each other. For the sake of clarity, only two actin filaments are shown.

myosin   One of the proteins (with actin) that provide the physical basis for muscular contraction.

striated muscle   Skeletal muscle; muscle that contains striations.

neuromuscular junction   The synapse between the terminal buttons of an axon and a muscle fiber.

motor endplate   The postsynaptic membrane of a neuromuscular junction.

endplate potential   The postsynaptic potential that occurs in the motor endplate in response to release of acetylcholine by the terminal button.

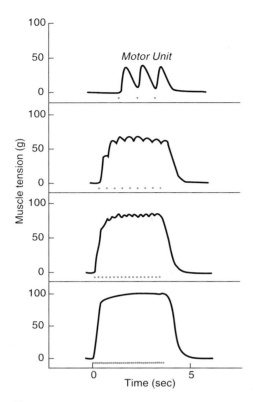

Figure 8.3
Action potentials and contractions. A rapid succession of action potentials can cause a muscle fiber to produce a sustained contraction. Each dot represents an individual action potential.
(Adapted from Devanandan, M. S., Eccles, R. M., and Westerman, R. A. *Journal of Physiology* (London), 1965, *178*, 359–367.)

moment, many units are firing, the contraction will be forceful. If few are firing, the contraction will be weak.

Sensory Feedback from Muscles

As we saw, the intrafusal muscle fibers contain sensory endings that are sensitive to stretch. The intrafusal muscle fibers are arranged in parallel with the extrafusal muscle fibers. Therefore, they are stretched when the muscle lengthens and are relaxed when it shortens. Thus, even though these afferent neurons are *stretch receptors,* they serve as *muscle length detectors.* This distinction is important. Stretch receptors are also located within the tendons, in the **Golgi tendon organ** (GTO). These receptors detect the total amount of stretch exerted by the muscle, through its tendons, on the bones to which the muscle is attached. The stretch receptors of the Golgi tendon organ encode the de-

gree of stretch by the rate of firing. They respond not to a muscle's length but to how hard it is pulling. In contrast, the receptors on intrafusal muscle fibers detect muscle length, not tension.

Figure 8.4 shows the response of afferent axons of the muscle spindles and Golgi tendon organ to various types of movements. Figure 8.4(a) shows the effects of passive lengthening of muscles, the kind of movement that would be seen if your forearm, held in a completely relaxed fashion, were slowly lowered by someone who was supporting it. The rate of firing of one type of muscle spindle afferent neuron (MS_1) increases, while the activity of the afferent of the Golgi tendon organ remains unchanged. (See *Figure 8.4a.*) Figure 8.4(b) shows the results when the arm is dropped quickly; note that this time the second type of muscle spindle afferent neuron (MS_2) fires a rapid burst of impulses. This fiber, then, signals rapid changes in muscle length. (See *Figure 8.4b.*) Figure 8.4(c) shows what would happen if a weight were suddenly dropped into your hand while your forearm was held parallel to the ground. Neurons MS_1 and MS_2 (especially MS_2, which responds to rapid changes in muscle length) briefly fire, because your arm lowers briefly and then comes back to the original position. The Golgi tendon organ, monitoring the strength of contraction, fires in proportion to the stress on the muscle, so it increases its rate of firing as soon as the weight is added. (See *Figure 8.4c.*)

● Smooth Muscle

Our bodies contain two types of **smooth muscle,** both of which are controlled by the autonomic nervous system. *Multiunit smooth muscles* are found in large arteries, around hair follicles (where they produce *piloerection,* or fluffing of fur) and in the eye (controlling lens adjustment and pupillary dilation). This type of smooth muscle is normally inactive, but it will contract in response to neural stimulation or to certain hormones. In contrast, *single-unit smooth muscles* normally contract in a rhythmical fashion. Some of these cells spontaneously produce *pacemaker potentials,*

Golgi tendon organ (GTO)   The receptor organ at the junction of the tendon and muscle that is sensitive to stretch.

smooth muscle   Nonstriated muscle innervated by the autonomic nervous system, found in the walls of blood vessels, in the reproductive tracts, in sphincters, within the eye, in the digestive system, and around hair follicles.

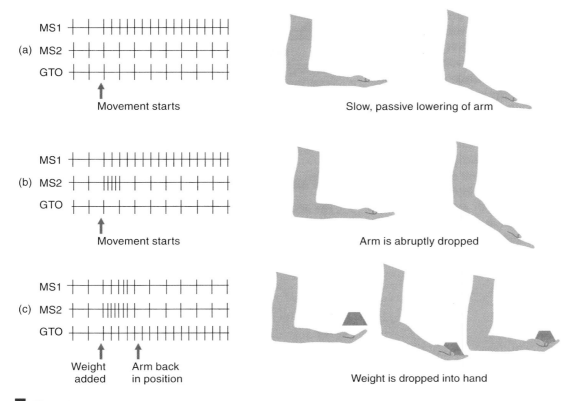

Figure 8.4

Effects of arm movements on the firing of muscle and tendon afferent axons. (a) Slow passive extension of the arm. (b) Rapid extension of the arm. (c) Addition of a weight to an arm held in a horizontal position. MS$_1$ and MS$_2$ are two types of muscle spindles; GTO is an afferent fiber from the Golgi tendon organ.

which we can regard as self-initiated excitatory postsynaptic potentials. These slow potentials elicit action potentials, which are propagated by adjacent smooth muscle fibers, causing a wave of muscular contraction. The efferent nerve supply (and various hormones) can modulate the rhythmical rate, increasing or decreasing it. Single-unit smooth muscles are found chiefly in the gastrointestinal system, uterus, and small blood vessels.

● Cardiac Muscle

As its name implies, **cardiac muscle** is found in the heart. This type of muscle looks somewhat like striated muscle but acts like single-unit smooth muscle. The heart beats regularly, even if it is denervated. Neural activity and certain hormones (especially the catecholamines) serve to modulate the heart rate. A group of cells in the *pacemaker* of the heart are rhythmically active and initiate the contractions of cardiac muscle that constitute the heartbeat.

Interim Summary

Our bodies possess skeletal muscle, smooth muscle, and cardiac muscle. Skeletal muscles contain extrafusal muscle fibers, which provide the force of contraction. The alpha motor neurons form synapses with the extrafusal muscle fibers and control their contraction. Skeletal muscles also contain intrafusal muscle fibers, which detect changes in muscle length. The length of the intrafusal muscle fiber, and hence its sensitivity to increases in muscle length, is controlled by the gamma motor neuron. Besides the intrafusal muscle fibers, the muscles contain stretch receptors in the Golgi tendon organs, located at the ends of the muscles.

cardiac muscle The muscle responsible for the contraction of the heart.

The force of muscular contraction is provided by long protein molecules called actin and myosin, arranged in overlapping parallel arrays. When an action potential, initiated by the synapse at the motor endplate, causes Ca^{2+} to enter the muscle fiber, the myofibrils extract energy from ATP and cause a twitch of the muscle fiber, producing a ratchetlike "rowing" movement of the myosin cross bridges.

Smooth muscle is controlled by the autonomic nervous system through direct neural connections and indirectly through the endocrine system. Multiunit smooth muscles contract only in response to neural or hormonal stimulation. In contrast, single-unit smooth muscles normally contract rhythmically, but their rate is controlled by the autonomic nervous system. Cardiac muscle also contracts spontaneously, and its rate of contraction, too, is influenced by the autonomic nervous system.

REFLEX CONTROL OF MOVEMENT

Although behaviors are controlled by the brain, the spinal cord possesses a certain degree of autonomy. Particular kinds of somatosensory stimuli can elicit rapid responses through neural connections located within the spinal cord. These reflexes constitute the simplest level of motor integration.

● The Monosynaptic Stretch Reflex

The activity of the simplest functional neural pathway in the body is easy to demonstrate. Sit on a surface high enough to allow your legs to dangle freely and have someone lightly tap your patellar tendon, just below the kneecap. This stimulus briefly stretches your quadriceps

Figure 8.5
The monosynaptic stretch reflex. (a) Neural circuit. (b) A useful function.

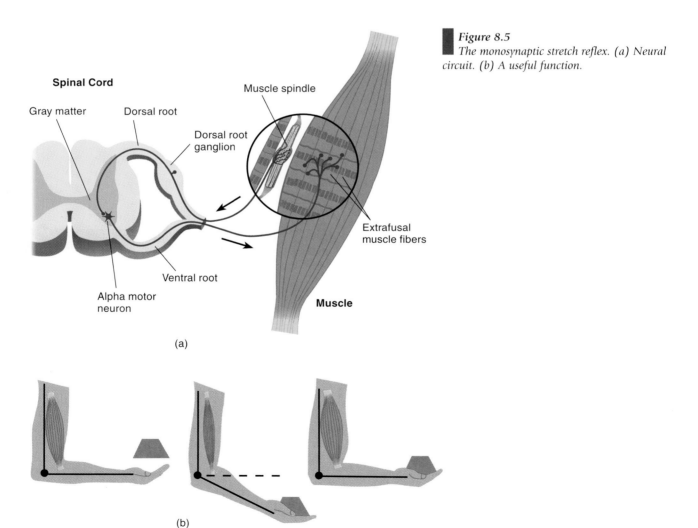

(a)

(b)

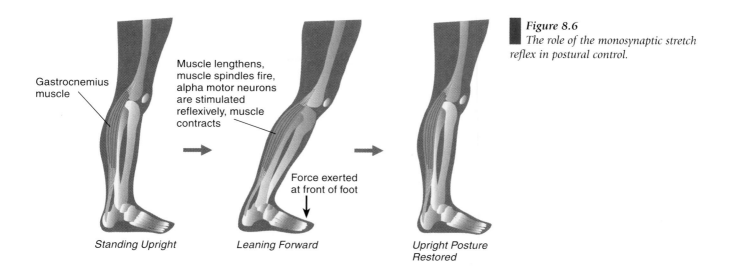

Figure 8.6
■ *The role of the monosynaptic stretch reflex in postural control.*

Gastrocnemius muscle

Muscle lengthens, muscle spindles fire, alpha motor neurons are stimulated reflexively, muscle contracts

Force exerted at front of foot

Standing Upright

Leaning Forward

Upright Posture Restored

muscle, on the top of your thigh. The stretch causes the muscle to contract, which makes your leg kick forward. (I am sure few of you will bother with this demonstration, because you are already familiar with it; physical examinations often include a test of this reflex.) The time interval between the tendon tap and the start of the leg extension is about 50 milliseconds. That interval is too short for the involvement of the brain; it would take considerably longer for sensory information to be relayed to the brain and for motor information to be relayed back. For example, suppose a person is asked to move his or her leg as quickly as possible after being *touched* on the knee. This response would not be reflexive but would involve sensory and motor mechanisms of the brain. In this case the interval between the stimulus and the start of the response would be several times greater than the time required for the patellar reflex.

Obviously, the patellar reflex as such has no utility; no selective advantage is bestowed on animals that kick a limb when a tendon is tapped. However, if a more natural stimulus is applied, the utility of this mechanism becomes apparent. Figure 8.5 shows the effects of placing a weight in a person's hand. This time I have included a piece of the spinal cord, with its roots, to show the neural circuit that composes the **monosynaptic stretch reflex.** First, follow the circuit: Starting at the muscle spindle, afferent impulses are conducted to terminal buttons in the gray matter of the spinal cord. These terminal buttons synapse on an alpha motor neuron that innervates the extrafusal muscle fibers of the same muscle. Only one synapse is encountered along the route from receptor to effector—hence the term *monosynaptic.* (See *Figure 8.5.*)

Now consider a useful function this reflex performs. If the weight the person is holding is increased, the forearm begins to move down. This movement lengthens the muscle and increases the firing rate of the muscle spindle afferent neurons, whose terminal buttons then stimulate the alpha motor neurons, increasing their rate of firing. Consequently, the strength of the muscular contraction increases, and the arm pulls the weight up. (See *Figure 8.5.*)

Another important role played by the monosynaptic stretch reflex is control of posture. In order to stand, we must keep our center of gravity above our feet, or we will fall. As we stand, we tend to oscillate back and forth, and from side to side. Our vestibular sacs and our visual system play an important role in the maintenance of posture. However, these systems are aided by the activity of the monosynaptic stretch reflex. For example, consider what happens when a person begins to lean forward. The large calf muscle (gastrocnemius) is stretched, and this stretching elicits compensatory muscular contraction that pushes the toes down, thus restoring upright posture. (See *Figure 8.6.*)

● The Gamma Motor System

The muscle spindles are very sensitive to changes in muscle length; they will increase their rate of firing when the muscle is lengthened by a very small amount. The interesting thing is that this detection mechanism is adjustable.

monosynaptic stretch reflex   A reflex in which a muscle contracts in response to its being quickly stretched; involves a sensory neuron and a motor neuron, with one synapse between them.

Remember that the ends of the intrafusal muscle fibers can be contracted by activity of the associated efferent axons of the gamma motor neurons; their rate of firing determines the degree of contraction. When the muscle spindles are relaxed, they are relatively insensitive to stretch. However, when the gamma motor neurons are active, they become shorter and hence become much more sensitive to changes in muscle length. This property of adjustable sensitivity simplifies the role of the brain in controlling movement. The more control that can occur in the spinal cord, the fewer messages must be sent to and from the brain.

We already saw that the afferent axons of the muscle spindle help maintain limb position even when the load carried by the limb is altered. Efferent control of the muscle spindles permits these muscle length detectors to assist in changes in limb position, as well. Consider a single muscle spindle. When its efferent axon is completely silent, the spindle is completely relaxed and extended. As the firing rate of the efferent axon increases, the spindle gets shorter and shorter. If, simultaneously, the rest of the entire muscle also gets shorter, there will be no stretch on the central region that contains the sensory endings, and the afferent axon will not respond. However, if the muscle spindle contracts faster than does the muscle as a whole, there will be a considerable amount of afferent activity.

The motor system makes use of this phenomenon in the following way: When commands from the brain are issued to move a limb, both the alpha motor neurons and the gamma motor neurons are activated. The alpha motor neurons start the muscle contracting. If there is little resistance, both the extrafusal and the intrafusal muscle fibers will contract at approximately the same rate, and little activity will be seen from the afferent axons of the muscle spindle. However, if the limb meets with resistance, the intrafusal muscle fibers will shorten more than the extrafusal muscle fibers, and hence sensory axons will begin to fire and cause the monosynaptic stretch reflex to strengthen the contraction. Thus, the brain makes use of the gamma motor system in moving the limbs. By establishing a rate of firing in the *gamma motor system,* the brain controls the length of the muscle spindles and, indirectly, the length of the entire muscle.

● Polysynaptic Reflexes

The monosynaptic stretch reflex is the only spinal reflex we know of that involves only one synapse. All others are *polysynaptic.* Examples include relatively simple ones, like limb withdrawal in response to noxious stimulation, and relatively complex ones, like the ejaculation of semen. Spinal reflexes do not exist in isolation; they are normally

controlled by the brain. For example, Chapter 2 described how inhibition from the brain can prevent a person from dropping a hot casserole dish, even though the painful stimuli received by the fingers serve to cause reflexive extension of the fingers. This section will describe some general principles by which polysynaptic spinal reflexes operate.

Before I begin the discussion, I should mention that the simple circuit diagrams used here (including the one you just looked at in Figure 8.6) are much too simple. Reflex circuits are typically shown as a single chain of neurons, but in reality most reflexes involve thousands of neurons. Each axon usually synapses on many neurons, and each neuron receives synapses from many different axons.

As we previously saw, the afferent axons from the Golgi tendon organ serve as detectors of muscle stretch. There are two populations of afferent axons from the Golgi tendon organ, with different sensitivities to stretch. The more sensitive afferent axons tell the brain how hard the muscle is pulling. The less sensitive ones have an additional function. Their terminal buttons synapse on spinal cord interneurons—neurons that reside entirely within the gray matter of the spinal cord and serve to interconnect other spinal neurons. These interneurons synapse on the alpha motor neurons serving the same muscle. The terminal buttons liberate glycine and hence produce inhibitory postsynaptic potentials on the motor neurons. (See *Figure 8.7.*) The function of this reflex pathway is to decrease the strength of muscular contraction when there is danger of damage to the tendons or bones to which the muscles are attached. Weight lifters can lift heavier weights if their Golgi tendon organs are deactivated with injections of a local anesthetic, but they run the risk of pulling the tendon away from the bone or even breaking the bone.

The discovery of the inhibitory Golgi tendon organ reflex provided the first real evidence of neural inhibition, long before the synaptic mechanisms were understood. A **decerebrate** cat, whose brain stem has been cut through, exhibits a phenomenon known as **decerebrate rigidity.** The animal's back is arched, and its legs are extended stiffly from its body. This rigidity results from excitation originating in the caudal reticular formation, which greatly facilitates all stretch reflexes, especially of extensor muscles, by increasing the activity of the gamma motor system. Ros-

decerebrate Describes an animal whose brain stem has been transected.

decerebrate rigidity Simultaneous contraction of agonistic and antagonistic muscles; caused by decerebration or damage to the reticular formation.

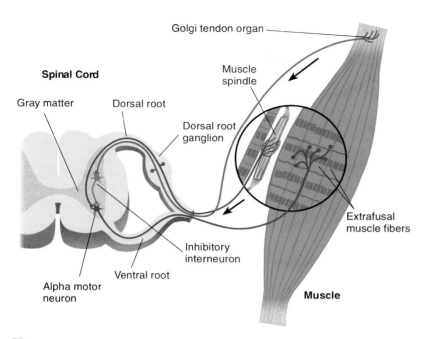

Figure 8.7
Polysynaptic inhibitory reflex. Input from the Golgi tendon organ can cause inhibitory postsynaptic potentials to occur on the alpha motor neuron.

tral to the brain stem transection is an inhibitory region of the reticular formation, which normally counterbalances the excitatory one. The transection removes the inhibitory influence, leaving only the excitatory one. If you attempt to flex the outstretched leg of a decerebrate cat, you will meet with increasing resistance, which suddenly melts away, allowing the limb to flex. It almost feels as though you were closing the blade of a pocketknife—hence the term **clasp-knife reflex.** The sudden release is, of course, mediated by activation of the Golgi tendon organ reflex.

Even the monosynaptic stretch reflex serves as the basis of polysynaptic reflexes. Muscles are arranged in opposing pairs. The **agonist** moves the limb in the direction being studied, and because muscles cannot push back, the **antagonist** muscle must move the limb back in the opposite direction. Consider this finding: When a stretch reflex is elicited in the agonist, it contracts quickly, thus causing the antagonist to lengthen. It would appear, then, that the antagonist is presented with a stimulus that should elicit *its* stretch reflex. And yet the antagonist relaxes instead. Let us see why.

Afferent axons of the muscle spindles, besides sending terminal buttons to the alpha motor neuron and to the brain, also synapse on inhibitory interneurons. The terminal buttons of these interneurons synapse on the alpha motor neurons that innervate the antagonistic muscle. (See

Figure 8.8.) Thus, a stretch reflex excites the agonist and *inhibits the antagonist,* so that the limb can move in the direction controlled by the stimulated muscle.

Interim Summary

Reflexes are simple circuits of sensory neurons, interneurons (usually), and efferent neurons that control simple responses to particular stimuli. In the monosynaptic stretch reflex the terminal buttons of axons that receive sensory information from the intrafusal muscle fibers synapse with alpha motor neurons that innervate the same muscle. Thus, a sudden lengthening of the muscle causes the muscle to contract. By setting the length of the intrafusal muscle fibers, and hence their sensitivity to increases in muscle length, the motor system of the brain can control limb po-

clasp-knife reflex   A reflex that occurs when force is applied to flex or extend the limb of an animal showing decerebrate rigidity; resistance is replaced by sudden relaxation.

agonist   A muscle whose contraction produces or facilitates a particular movement.

antagonist   A muscle whose contraction resists or reverses a particular movement.

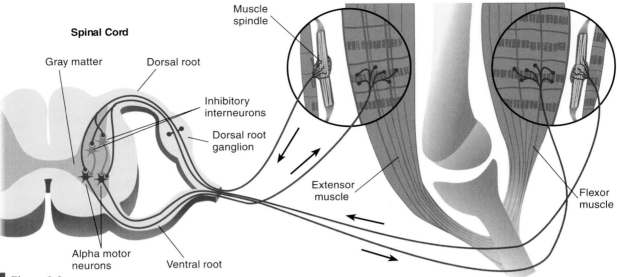

Figure 8.8

Secondary reflexes. Firing of the muscle spindle causes excitation on the alpha motor neuron of the agonist and inhibition on the antagonist.

sition. Changes in a weight being held that cause the limb to move will be quickly compensated for by means of the monosynaptic stretch reflex.

Polysynaptic reflexes contain at least one interneuron between the sensory neuron and the motor neuron. For example, when a strong muscular contraction threatens to damage muscles or limbs, the increased rate of firing of the afferent axons of Golgi tendon organs stimulates inhibitory interneurons, which inhibit the alpha motor neurons of those muscles. And when the afferent axons of intrafusal muscle fibers fire, they excite inhibitory interneurons that slow the rate of firing of the alpha motor neurons that serve the antagonistic muscles, causing the antagonist to relax and the agonist to contract.

CONTROL OF MOVEMENT BY THE BRAIN

Movements can be initiated by several means. For example, rapid stretch of a muscle triggers the monosynaptic stretch reflex, a stumble triggers righting reflexes, and the rapid approach of an object toward the face causes a startle response, a complex reflex consisting of movements of several muscle groups. Other stimuli initiate sequences of movements that we have previously learned. For example, the presence of food causes eating, and the sight of a loved one evokes a hug and a kiss. Because there is no single cause of behavior, we cannot find a single starting point in our search for the neural mechanisms that control movement.

The brain and spinal cord include several different motor systems, each of which can simultaneously control par-

ticular kinds of movements. For example, a person can walk and talk with a friend simultaneously. While doing so, he or she can gesture with the hands to emphasize a point, scratch an itch, brush away a fly, wipe sweat off his or her forehead, and so on. Walking, postural adjustments, talking, movement of the arms, and movements of the fingers all involve different specialized motor systems.

● Organization of Motor Cortex

The primary motor cortex lies on the precentral gyrus, just rostral to the central sulcus. Stimulation studies (including those in awake humans) have shown that the activation of neurons located in particular parts of the primary motor cortex causes movements of particular parts of the body. In other words, the primary motor cortex shows **somatotopic organization** (from *soma,* "body," and *topos,* "place"). Figure 8.9 shows a *motor homunculus* based on the observations of Penfield and Rasmussen (1950). Note that a disproportionate amount of cortical area is devoted to movements of the fingers and muscles used for speech. (See *Figure 8.9.*)

The principal cortical input to the primary motor cortex is the frontal association cortex, located rostral to it. Two regions immediately adjacent to the primary motor cortex—the *supplementary motor area* and the *premotor cortex*—are especially important in the control of movement. Both regions receive sensory information from the parietal and temporal lobes, and both send efferent axons to the pri-

somatotopic organization   A topographically organized mapping of parts of the body that are represented in a particular region of the brain.

234

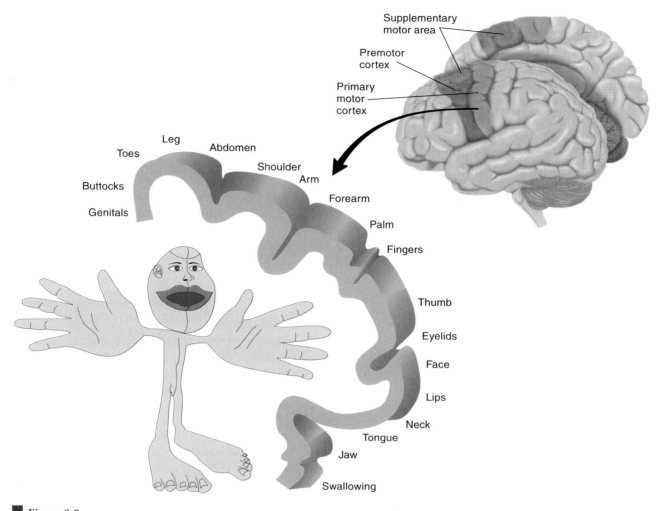

Figure 8.9
Motor cortex and a motor homunculus. Stimulation of various regions of the primary motor cortex causes movement in muscles of various parts of the body.

mary motor cortex. The **supplementary motor area** is located on the medial surface of the brain, just rostral to the primary motor cortex. The **premotor cortex** is located primarily on the lateral surface, also just rostral to the primary motor cortex. (See *Figure 8.9.*)

Lesion studies (some of which I will describe later in this chapter) indicate that the planning of most complex behaviors takes place in the **prefrontal cortex,** the portion of the frontal lobes rostral to the supplementary motor area and premotor cortex. These plans are executed by the primary motor cortex, which directly controls particular movements. Like the supplementary motor area and the premotor cortex, the prefrontal cortex receives information from association areas of the parietal and temporal cortex. As we saw, the occipital and temporal lobes contain the visual association cortex, and the temporal lobe also con-

tains the auditory association cortex. And as we will see later, the association cortex of the parietal lobes is responsible for a person's perception of space. Thus, the frontal cortex receives information about the environment (including memories previously acquired by means of vision, audition, and somatosensation) from the posterior associ-

supplementary motor area   A region of motor association cortex of the dorsal and dorsomedial frontal lobe, rostral to the primary motor cortex.

premotor cortex   A region of motor association cortex of the lateral frontal lobe, rostral to the primary motor cortex.

prefrontal cortex   The neocortex of the frontal lobes rostral to the supplementary motor area and premotor cortex.

ation cortex and uses this information to plan movements. Because the parietal lobes contain spatial information, the pathway from them to the frontal lobes is especially important in controlling both locomotion and arm and hand movements. After all, meaningful locomotion requires us to know where we are, and meaningful movements of our arms and hands require us to know where objects are located in space. (See *Figure 8.10.*)

The primary motor cortex also receives projections from the adjacent primary somatosensory cortex, located just across the central sulcus. The connections between these two areas are quite specific: Neurons in the primary somatosensory cortex that respond to stimuli applied to a particular part of the body send axons to neurons in the primary motor cortex that move muscles in the same part of the body. For example, Asanuma and Rosén (1972) and Rosén and Asanuma (1972) found that somatosensory neurons that respond to a touch on the back of the thumb send axons to motor neurons that cause thumb extension, and somatosensory neurons that respond to a touch on the ball of the thumb send axons to motor neurons that cause thumb flexion. This organization appears to provide rapid feedback to the motor system during manipulation of objects.

Evidence that supports this suggestion was obtained by Evarts (1974), who recorded the activity of single neurons in the precentral gyrus of monkeys. He trained his subjects to move a lever back and forth by means of wrist flexions

and extensions. When the monkeys made the movements in the correct amount of time, they received a squirt of grape juice, a drink they appeared to enjoy. Figure 8.11 shows the experimental preparation as well as the relationship between lever movement and the firing of a cortical neuron. Note that the firing of this neuron is nicely related to the movement, with the rate increasing during flexion. (See *Figure 8.11.*) Evarts trained monkeys to produce a hand movement in response to a flash of a light or to a tactile stimulus delivered through the handle. He found that neurons in the motor cortex began firing 100 msec after a visual stimulus but responded as soon as 25 msec after a tactile stimulus. These results confirm the conclusion that hand and finger movements are controlled by somatosensory feedback received by neurons in the postcentral gyrus.

● Cortical Control of Movement: The Descending Pathways

Neurons in the primary motor cortex control movements by two groups of descending tracts, the **lateral group** and the **ventromedial group,** named for their locations in the white matter of the spinal cord. The lateral group consists of the *corticospinal tract,* the *corticobulbar tract,* and the *rubrospinal tract.* This system is primarily involved in control of independent limb movements, particularly movements of the hands and fingers. *Independent* limb movements mean that the right and left limbs make different movements—or one limb moves while the other remains still. These movements contrast with coordinated limb movements, such as those involved in locomotion. The ventromedial group consists of the *vestibulospinal tract,* the *tectospinal tract,* the *reticulospinal tract,* and the *ventral corticospinal tract.* These tracts control more automatic movements: gross movements of the muscles of the trunk and coordinated trunk and limb movements involved in posture and locomotion.

Let's first consider the lateral group of descending tracts. The **corticospinal tract** consists of axons of cortical neurons that terminate in the gray matter of the spinal cord. The largest concentration of cell bodies responsible for

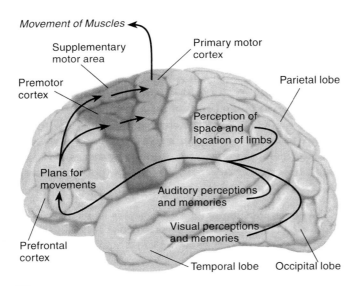

Movement of Muscles
Supplementary motor area
Primary motor cortex
Premotor cortex
Parietal lobe
Perception of space and location of limbs
Plans for movements
Auditory perceptions and memories
Visual perceptions and memories
Prefrontal cortex
Temporal lobe
Occipital lobe

Figure 8.10
Cortical control of movement. The posterior association cortex is involved with perceptions and memories, and the frontal association cortex is involved with plans for movement.

lateral group The corticospinal tract, the corticobulbar tract, and the rubrospinal tract.

ventromedial group The vestibulospinal tract, the tectospinal tract, the reticulospinal tract, and the ventral corticospinal tract.

corticospinal tract The system of axons that originates in the motor cortex and terminates in the ventral gray matter of the spinal cord.

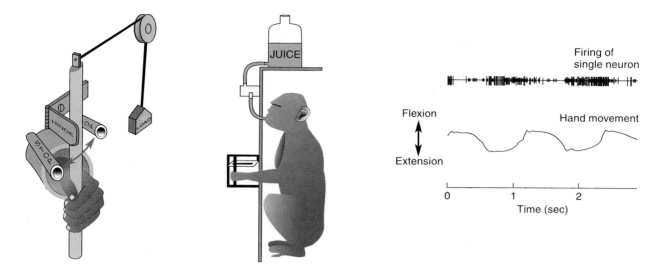

Figure 8.11
The relation between firing of single neurons in the motor cortex and hand movements. The single-unit records are redrawn from the original data and are therefore only approximate representations.
(Redrawn from Evarts, E. V. *Journal of Neurophysiology*, 1968, 31, 14–27.)

these axons is located in the primary motor cortex, but neurons in the parietal and temporal lobes also send axons through the corticospinal pathway. The axons leave the cortex and travel through subcortical white matter to the ventral midbrain, where they enter the cerebral peduncles. They leave the peduncles in the medulla and form the **pyramidal tracts,** so-called because of their shape. At the level of the caudal medulla, most of the fibers decussate (cross over) and descend through the contralateral spinal cord, forming the **lateral corticospinal tract.** The rest of the fibers descend through the ipsilateral spinal cord, forming the **ventral corticospinal tract.** Because of its location and function, the ventral corticospinal tract is actually part of the ventromedial group. (See light and dark blue lines in *Figure 8.12.*)

Most of the axons in the lateral corticospinal tract originate in the regions of the primary motor cortex and supplementary motor area that control the distal parts of the limbs: the arms, hands, and fingers and the lower legs, feet, and toes. They form synapses, directly or via interneurons, with motor neurons in the gray matter of the spinal cord—in the lateral part of the ventral horn. These motor neurons control muscles of the distal limbs, including those that move the arms, hands, and fingers. (See light blue lines in *Figure 8.12.*)

The axons in the ventral corticospinal tract originate in the upper leg and trunk regions of the primary motor cortex. They descend to the appropriate region of the spinal

cord and divide, sending terminal buttons into both sides of the gray matter. They control motor neurons that move the muscles of the upper legs and trunk. (See dark blue lines in *Figure 8.12.*)

Lawrence and Kuypers (1968a) cut both pyramidal tracts in monkeys in order to assess their motor functions. Within six to ten hours after recovery from the anesthesia, the animals were able to sit upright, but their arms hung loosely from their shoulders. Within a day they could stand, hold the cage bars with their hands, and even climb a little. By six weeks the monkeys could walk and climb rapidly. Thus, posture and locomotion were not disturbed. However, the animals' manual dexterity was poor. They could reach for objects and grasp them, but they used their fingers together as though they were wearing mittens; they could not manipulate their fingers independently to pick

pyramidal tract   An alternate term for the corticospinal tract.

lateral corticospinal tract   The system of axons that originates in the motor cortex and terminates in the contralateral ventral gray matter of the spinal cord; controls movements of the distal limbs.

ventral corticospinal tract   The system of axons that originates in the motor cortex and terminates in the ipsilateral ventral gray matter of the spinal cord; controls movements of the upper legs and trunk.

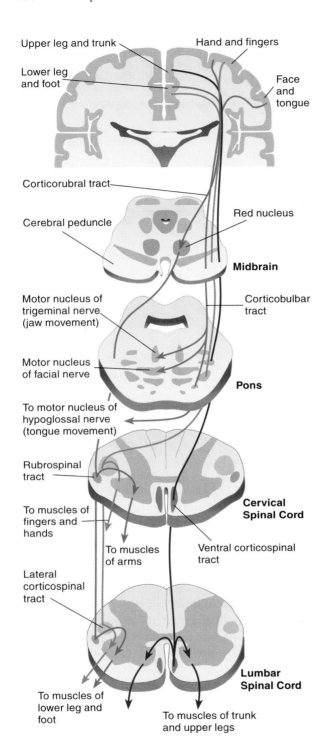

Upper leg and trunk
Lower leg and foot
Hand and fingers
Face and tongue
Corticorubral tract
Cerebral peduncle
Red nucleus
Midbrain
Motor nucleus of trigeminal nerve (jaw movement)
Corticobulbar tract
Motor nucleus of facial nerve
Pons
To motor nucleus of hypoglossal nerve (tongue movement)
Rubrospinal tract
To muscles of fingers and hands
To muscles of arms
Ventral corticospinal tract
Cervical Spinal Cord
Lateral corticospinal tract
To muscles of lower leg and foot
To muscles of trunk and upper legs
Lumbar Spinal Cord

Figure 8.12
The lateral group of descending motor tracts: the lateral corticospinal tract (light blue lines), corticobulbar tract (green lines), and rubrospinal tract (red lines). The ventral corticospinal tract (dark blue lines) is part of the ventromedial group.

The results confirm what we would predict from the anatomical connections: The corticospinal pathway controls hand and finger movements and is indispensable for moving the fingers independently when reaching and manipulating. Postural adjustments of the trunk and use of the limbs for reaching and locomotion are unaffected; therefore, these types of movements are controlled by other systems. Because the monkeys had difficulty releasing their grasp when they picked up objects but had no trouble doing so when climbing the walls of the cage, we can conclude that the same behavior (opening the hand) is controlled by different brain mechanisms in different contexts.

The second of the lateral group of descending pathways, the **corticobulbar tract,** projects to the medulla (sometimes called the *bulb*). This pathway is similar to the corticospinal pathway, except that it terminates in the motor nuclei of the fifth, seventh, ninth, tenth, eleventh, and twelfth cranial nerves (the trigeminal, facial, glossopharyngeal, vagus, spinal accessory, and hypoglossal nerves). These nerves control movements of the face, neck, tongue, and parts of the extraocular eye muscles. (See green lines in *Figure 8.12.*)

The third member of the lateral group is the **rubrospinal tract.** This tract originates in the red nucleus (*nucleus ruber*) of the midbrain. The red nucleus receives its most important inputs from the motor cortex via the **corticorubral tract** and (as we shall see later) from the cerebellum. Axons of the rubrospinal tracts terminate on motor neurons in the spinal cord that control movements of forelimb and hindlimb muscles. (They do not control the muscles that move the fingers.) (See red lines in *Figure 8.12.*)

up small pieces of food. And once they had grasped food with their hand, they had difficulty releasing their grip. They usually had to use their mouth to pry their hand open. In contrast, they had no difficulty releasing their grip when they were climbing the bars of their cage.

corticobulbar pathway A bundle of axons from the motor cortex to the fifth, seventh, ninth, tenth, eleventh, and twelfth cranial nerves; controls movements of the face, neck, tongue, and parts of the extraocular eye muscles.

rubrospinal tract The system of axons that travels from the red nucleus to the spinal cord; controls independent limb movements.

corticorubral tract The system of axons that travels from the motor cortex to the red nucleus.

Lawrence and Kuypers (1968b) destroyed the rubrospinal tract *unilaterally* in some of the animals that had previously received bilateral lesions of the pyramidal tract. The rubrospinal tract lesion severely affected the animals' use of the ipsilateral arm. The arm tended to hang straight from the shoulder, with hand and fingers extended. If they could reach food only with the affected arm, they made a raking movement with the arm as a whole, bending their elbow and wrist as the food approached their mouth. The arm movement was accompanied by movements of the trunk. The monkeys did not hold the food with their hand, even with the mittenlike grasp that is produced by pyramidal tract lesions. The animals managed to hold onto cage bars with their affected hand, but the grip was weaker.

Lawrence and Kuypers concluded that the rubrospinal system controls independent movements of the forearms and hands—that is, movements that are independent of trunk movements. This control overlaps with that of the pyramidal system but does not include independent movements of the fingers.

Now let's consider the second set of pathways originating in the brain stem, the ventromedial group. This group includes the **vestibulospinal tracts,** the **tectospinal tracts,** and the **reticulospinal tracts,** as well as the ventral corticospinal tract (already described). These tracts control motor neurons in the ventromedial part of the spinal cord gray matter. Neurons of all these tracts receive input from the portions of the primary motor cortex that control movements of the trunk and proximal muscles (that is, the muscles located on the parts of the limbs close to the body). In addition, the reticular formation receives a considerable amount of input from the premotor cortex and from several subcortical regions, including the amygdala, hypothalamus, and basal ganglia. The cell bodies of neurons of the vestibulospinal tracts are located in the vestibular nuclei. As you might expect, this system plays a role in the control of posture. The cell bodies of neurons in the tectospinal tracts are located in the superior colliculus and are

involved in coordinating head and trunk movements with eye movements. The cell bodies of neurons of the reticulospinal tracts are located in many nuclei in the brain stem and midbrain reticular formation. These neurons control several automatic functions, such as muscle tonus, respiration, coughing, and sneezing; but they are also involved in behaviors under direct neocortical control, such as walking. (See *Figure 8.13.*)

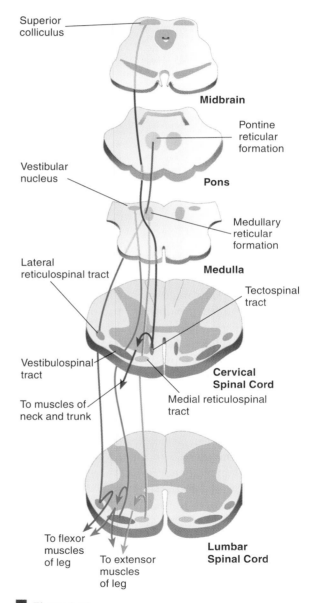

Figure 8.13
The ventromedial group of descending motor tracts: the tectospinal tract (blue lines), lateral reticulospinal tract (purple lines), medial reticulospinal tract (orange lines), and vestibulospinal tract (green lines).

vestibulospinal tract   A bundle of axons that travels from the vestibular nuclei to the gray matter of the spinal cord; controls postural movements in response to information from the vestibular system.

tectospinal tract   A bundle of axons that travels from the tectum to the spinal cord; coordinates head and trunk movements with eye movements.

reticulospinal tract   A bundle of axons that travels from the reticular formation to the gray matter of the spinal cord; controls the muscles responsible for postural movements.

Table 8.1
Major motor pathways

	Origin	Termination	Muscle groups
Corticospinal pathways			
Lateral corticospinal tract	Finger, hand, and arm region of motor cortex	Spinal cord	Fingers, hands, and arms
Ventral corticospinal tract	Trunk and upper leg region of motor cortex	Spinal cord	Trunk and upper legs
Corticobulbar pathway	Face region of motor cortex	Cranial nerve nuclei: 5, 7, 9, 10, 11, and 12	Face and tongue
Ventromedial pathways			
Vestibulospinal tract	Vestibular nuclei	Spinal cord	Trunk and legs
Tectospinal tract	Superior colliculi	Spinal cord	Neck and trunk
Lateral reticulospinal tract	Medullary reticular formation	Spinal cord	Flexor muscles of legs
Medial reticulospinal tract	Pontine reticular formation	Spinal cord	Extensor muscles of legs
Rubrospinal tract	Red nucleus	Spinal cord	Hands (not fingers), lower arms, feet, and lower legs

You will recall that Lawrence and Kuypers (1968a) found no deficits in postural movements after they had destroyed both the right and left pyramidal tracts. Presumably, the animals maintained their control of posture through the ventromedial pathways. Another study confirmed this speculation. Lawrence and Kuypers (1968b) cut the ventromedial fibers of some of the animals that had previously received bilateral pyramidal tract lesions. These animals showed severe impairments in posture. After a long recovery period they could eventually stand with great difficulty but could not take more than a few steps without falling. When they reached for food, their upper arms hung at their sides. Thus, we can conclude that the ventromedial pathways control the muscles of the trunk and proximal limbs, with supplementary control of the trunk muscles coming from the ventral corticospinal tract.

Table 8.1 summarizes the names of these pathways, their locations, and the muscle groups they control. (See *Table 8.1.*)

● Deficits of Verbally Controlled Movements: The Apraxias

Damage to the corpus callosum, frontal lobe, or parietal lobe of the human brain produces a category of deficits called **apraxia.** Literally, the term means "without action," but apraxia differs from paralysis or weakness that occurs when motor structures such as the precentral gyrus, basal ganglia, brain stem, or spinal cord are damaged. Apraxia is the "inability to properly execute a learned skilled movement" (Heilman, Rothi, and Kertesz, 1983, p. 381). Neuropsychological studies of the apraxias have provided information about the way skilled behaviors are organized and initiated.

There are four major types of apraxia, two of which I will discuss in this chapter. *Limb apraxia* refers to problems with movements of the arms, hands, and fingers. *Oral apraxia* refers to problems with movements of the muscles used in speech. *Apraxic agraphia* refers to a particular type of writing deficit. *Constructional apraxia* refers to difficulty in drawing or constructing objects. Because of their relation to language, I will describe oral apraxia and the agraphias in Chapter 16.

Limb Apraxia

Limb apraxia is characterized by movement of the wrong part of the limb, incorrect movement of the correct part, or correct movements but in the incorrect sequence. It is assessed by asking patients to perform movements. The most

apraxia   Difficulty in carrying out purposeful movements, in the absence of paralysis or muscular weakness.

difficult movements involve pantomiming particular acts. For example, the examiner may ask the patient, "Pretend you have a key in your hand and open a door with it." In response, a patient with limb apraxia may wave his wrist back and forth rather than rotate it, or rotate his wrist first and then pretend to insert the key. Or if asked to pretend she is brushing her teeth, a patient may use her finger as though it were a toothbrush, rather than pretend to hold a toothbrush in her hand.

To perform behaviors on verbal command without having a real object to manipulate, a person must comprehend the command and be able to imagine the missing article as well as to make the proper movements; therefore, these requests are the most difficult to carry out. Somewhat easier are tasks that involve imitating behaviors performed by the experimenter. Sometimes, a patient who cannot mime the use of a key can copy the examiner's hand movements. The easiest tasks involve the actual use of objects. For example, the examiner may give the patient a door key and ask him or her to demonstrate its use. If the brain lesion makes it impossible for the patient to understand speech, then the examiner cannot assess the ability to perform behaviors on verbal command. In this case the examiner can only measure the patient's ability to imitate movements or use actual objects. (See Heilman, Rothi, and Kertesz, 1983, for a review.)

Limb apraxia can be caused by three types of lesions. **Callosal apraxia** is apraxia of the left limb that is caused by damage to the anterior corpus callosum. The explanation for the deficit is the following: When a person hears a verbal request to perform a movement, the meaning of the speech is analyzed by circuits in the posterior left hemisphere (discussed in Chapter 16). A neural command to make the movement is conveyed through long transcortical axons to the prefrontal area. There, the command activates neural circuits that contain the memory of the movements that constitute the behavior. This information is transmitted through the corpus callosum to the right prefrontal cortex, and from there to the right precentral gyrus. Neurons in this area control the individual movements. Damage to the anterior corpus callosum prevents communication between the left and right motor cortex. Thus, the right arm can perform the requested movement, but the left arm cannot. (See lesion A in *Figure 8.14.*)

A similar form of limb apraxia is caused by damage to the anterior left hemisphere, sometimes called **sympathetic apraxia.** The damage causes a primary motor impairment of the right arm and hand: full or partial paralysis. As with anterior callosal lesions, the damage also causes apraxia of the left arm. The term *sympathetic* was originally adopted because the clumsiness of the left hand appeared to be a

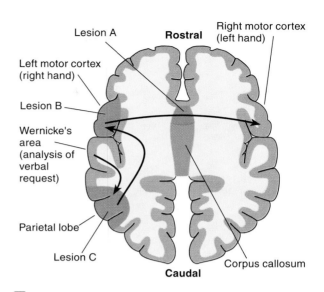

Figure 8.14
Apraxias. Lesion A causes callosal apraxia of the left limb, lesion B causes sympathetic apraxia of the right limb, and lesion C causes left parietal apraxia of both limbs.

"sympathetic" response to the paralysis of the right one. (See lesion B in *Figure 8.14.*)

The third form of limb apraxia is **left parietal apraxia,** caused by lesions of the posterior left hemisphere. These lesions involve both limbs. The posterior parietal lobe contains areas of association cortex that receive information from the surrounding sensory association cortex of the occipital, temporal, and anterior parietal lobes. (See lesion C in *Figure 8.14.*)

From the effects of parietal lobe lesions in humans and monkeys, Mountcastle et al. (1975) suggested that this region contains a sensory representation of the surrounding environment and keeps track of the location of objects in the environment and the location of the organism's body parts in relation to them. Because the right parietal lobe is especially important for perception of three-dimensional space, information about location of objects external to the person is probably supplied from this region. According to

callosal apraxia   An apraxia of the left hand caused by damage to the anterior corpus callosum.

sympathetic apraxia   A movement disorder of the left hand caused by damage to the left frontal lobe; similar to callosal apraxia.

left parietal apraxia   An apraxia caused by damage to the left parietal lobe; characterized by difficulty in producing sequences of movements by verbal request or in imitation of movements made by someone else.

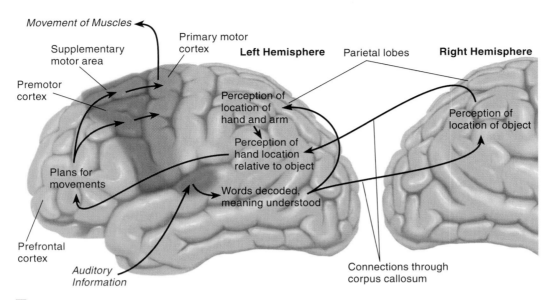

Figure 8.15
The "command apparatus" of the left parietal lobe.

Mountcastle and his colleagues, the left parietal region serves as a "command apparatus for the operation of the limbs, hands, and eyes within immediate extrapersonal space." For example, when a person hears a command to reach for a particular object, the left auditory association cortex decodes the meaning of the request and passes it on to the left parietal association cortex. Using information received from the right parietal association cortex about the spatial location of the object, neural circuits in the left parietal association cortex assess the relative location of the person's hand and the object and send information about the starting and ending coordinates to the left frontal association cortex. There, the sequence of muscular contractions necessary to perform the movement is organized and then executed through the primary motor cortex and its connections with the spinal cord and subcortical motor systems. (See *Figure 8.15*.)

Constructional Apraxia

Constructional apraxia is caused by lesions of the right hemisphere, particularly the right parietal lobe. People with this disorder do not have difficulty making most types of skilled movements with their arms and hands. They have no trouble using objects properly, imitating their use, or pretending to use them. However, they have trouble drawing pictures or assembling objects from elements such as toy building blocks.

The primary deficit in constructional apraxia appears to involve the ability to perceive and imagine geometrical re-

lations. Because of this deficit, a person cannot draw a picture, say, of a cube, because he or she cannot imagine what the lines and angles of a cube look like, not because of difficulty controlling the movements of his or her arm and hand. (See *Figure 8.16*.) Besides being unable to draw accurately, a person with constructional apraxia invariably has trouble with other tasks involving spatial perception, such as following a map.

● The Basal Ganglia

Anatomy and Function

The basal ganglia constitute an important component of the motor system. We know that they are important because their destruction by disease or injury causes severe motor deficits. The motor nuclei of the basal ganglia include the caudate nucleus, putamen, and globus pallidus. The basal ganglia receive most of their input from all regions of the cerebral cortex (but especially the primary motor cortex and primary somatosensory cortex) and the substantia nigra. They have two primary outputs: the primary motor cortex, supplementary motor area, and premotor cortex (via the thalamus), and motor nuclei of the

constructional apraxia Difficulty in drawing pictures or diagrams or in making geometrical constructions of elements such as building blocks or sticks; caused by damage to the right parietal lobe.

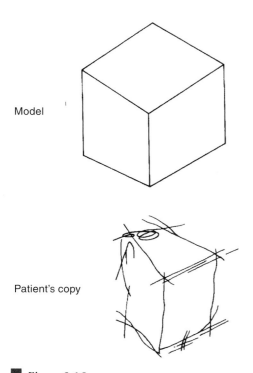

Model

Patient's copy

Figure 8.16
Attempt to copy a cube by a patient with constructional apraxia caused by a lesion of the right parietal lobe.
(From *Fundamentals of Human Neuropsychology,* by B. Kolb and I. Q. Whishaw. W. H. Freeman and Company. Copyright © 1980.)

brain stem that contribute to the ventromedial pathways. Through these connections the basal ganglia influence movements under the control of the primary motor cortex and exert some direct control over the ventromedial system.

Figure 8.17(a) illustrates the components of the basal ganglia: the **caudate nucleus,** the **putamen,** and the **globus pallidus.** It also shows some nuclei associated with the basal ganglia: the **ventral anterior nucleus** and **ventrolateral nucleus** of the thalamus, and the substantia nigra of the ventral midbrain. (See *Figure 8.17a.*)

Figure 8.17(b) shows some of the more important connections of the basal ganglia and helps explain the role that these structures play in the control of movement. First, let's take a quick look at the loop formed between the cortex and the basal ganglia. The primary motor cortex and the primary somatosensory cortex send axons to the putamen, which then connects with the globus pallidus. The globus pallidus sends information back to the motor cortex via the ventral anterior and ventrolateral nuclei of the thalamus, completing the loop. Thus, the basal ganglia can monitor somatosensory information and are informed of movements being planned and executed by the motor cortex. Using this information (and other information they

receive from other parts of the brain), they can then influence the movements controlled by the motor cortex. Throughout this circuit, information is represented somatotopically. That is, projections from neurons in the motor cortex that cause movements in particular parts of the body project to particular parts of the putamen, and this segregation is maintained all the way back to the motor cortex. (See *Figure 8.17b.*)

For the sake of clarity, Figure 8.17(b) leaves out many connections, including inputs to the substantia nigra from the basal ganglia and other structures. One important structure is not shown at all: the caudate nucleus. The caudate nucleus receives input from the association cortex of the frontal, parietal, and temporal lobes and sends information on to the globus pallidus. I prepared a figure that included these connections, but the tangle of arrows and labels was much too complicated. Remember, though, that the basal ganglia do receive information from all association areas of the cerebral cortex as well as from the primary motor and somatosensory cortex.

Another important input to the basal ganglia comes from the substantia nigra of the midbrain. We already saw in Chapter 4 that degeneration of the nigrostriatal bundle, the dopaminergic pathway from the substantia nigra to the caudate nucleus and putamen (the *neostriatum*), causes Parkinson's disease. (I will say more about this disorder later.) Obviously, because the caudate nucleus is not shown in Figure 8.17(b), only the connections with the putamen can be seen. (See *Figure 8.17b.*)

Now let's consider some of the complexities of the cortical-basal ganglia loop. The links in the loop are made by both excitatory (glutamate-secreting) neurons and inhibitory (GABA-secreting) neurons. The putamen receives excitatory input from the cerebral cortex. It sends inhibitory axons to the external and internal divisions of the globus

caudate nucleus   A telencephalic nucleus, one of the input nuclei of basal ganglia; involved with control of voluntary movement.

putamen   A telencephalic nucleus; one of the input nuclei of the basal ganglia; involved with control of voluntary movement.

globus pallidus   A telencephalic nucleus; the primary output nucleus of the basal ganglia; involved with control of voluntary movement.

ventral anterior nucleus (of thalamus)   A thalamic nucleus that receives projections from the basal ganglia and sends projections to the motor cortex.

ventrolateral nucleus (of thalamus)   A thalamic nucleus that receives projections from the basal ganglia and sends projections to the motor cortex.

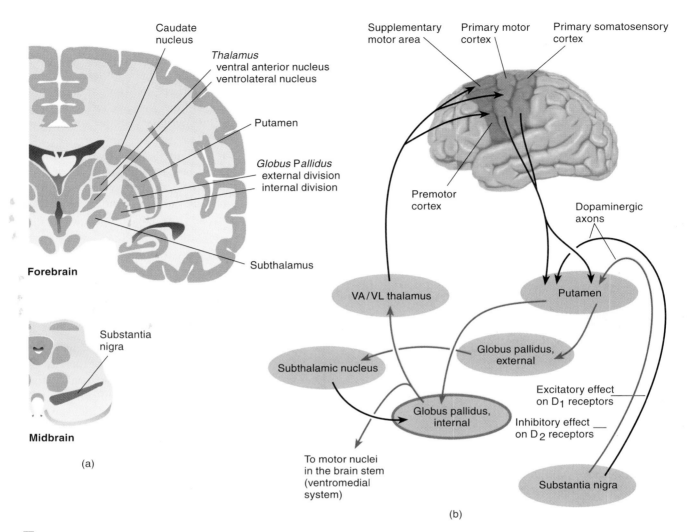

Figure 8.17
*The basal ganglia. (a) The locations of the components of the basal ganglia and associated struc-
tures. (b) The major connections of the basal ganglia and associated structures. Excitatory connections are shown as black lines; inhibitory connections are shown as red lines. The caudate nucleus is
not shown, and many connections, such as the inputs to the substantia nigra, are omitted for clarity.
The internal division of the globus pallidus, the primary output of the basal ganglia and the target of
stereotaxic surgery for Parkinson's disease, is outlined in gray.*

pallidus (the GP_i and the GP_e, respectively). The GP_i sends
inhibitory axons to the ventral anterior and ventrolateral
thalamus (VA/VL thalamus), which send excitatory projections to the motor cortex. The net effect of the loop is excitatory because it contains two inhibitory links. Each
inhibitory link (red arrow) reverses the sign of the input to
that link. Thus, excitatory input to the putamen causes the
putamen to *inhibit* neurons in the GP_i. This inhibition *removes* the inhibitory effect of the connections between the
GP_i on the VA/VL thalamus; in other words, neurons in the

VA/VL thalamus become more excited. This excitation is
passed on to the motor cortex. (See *Figure 8.17b.*)

The GP_e also contributes to the cortical-basal ganglia
loop, but the circuitry is slightly more complex. The external division sends inhibitory input to the subthalamic nucleus, which sends excitatory input to the GP_i. From there
on the circuit is identical to the one we just examined—except that the ultimate effect of this loop on the thalamus
and frontal cortex is inhibitory. And while we're at it, notice also that the globus pallidus sends axons to various

motor nuclei in the brain stem that contribute to the ventromedial system. (See *Figure 8.17b.*)

Parkinson's Disease

Now that you understand the cortical-basal ganglia loop, you can understand the symptoms and treatment of two important neurological disorders: Parkinson's disease and Huntington's chorea. The primary symptoms of Parkinson's disease are muscular rigidity, slowness of movement, a resting tremor, and postural instability. For example, once a person with Parkinson's disease is seated, he or she finds it difficult to arise. Once the person begins walking, he or she has difficulty stopping. Thus, a person with Parkinson's disease cannot easily pace back and forth across a room. Reaching for an object can be accurate, but the movement usually begins only after a considerable delay. Writing is slow and labored, and as it progresses the letters get smaller and smaller. Postural movements are impaired. A normal person who is bumped while standing will quickly move to restore balance—for example, by taking a step in the direction of the impending fall or by reaching out with the arms to grasp onto a piece of furniture. However, a person with Parkinson's disease fails to do so and simply falls. A person with this disorder is even unlikely to put out his or her arms to break the fall.

Parkinson's disease also produces a resting tremor—vibratory movements of the arms and hands that diminish somewhat when the individual makes purposeful movements. The tremor is accompanied by rigidity; the joints appear stiff. However, the tremor and rigidity are not the cause of the slow movements. In fact, some patients with Parkinson's disease show extreme slowness of movements but little or no tremor.

Let's look at Figure 8.17(b) again to see why damage to the nigrostriatal bundle causes slowness of movements and disrupts postural adjustments. The putamen consists of two different zones, both of which receive input from dopaminergic neurons of the substantia nigra. One of these zones contains D_1 dopamine receptors, which produce excitatory effects. Neurons in this zone send their axons to the GP_i. Neurons in the other zone contain D_2 receptors, which produce inhibitory effects. These neurons send their axons to the GP_e. (See *Figure 8.17b.*) The first of these circuits, beginning with the black arrow from the substantia nigra, goes through two inhibitory synapses (red arrows) before it reaches the VA/VL thalamus; thus, this circuit has an excitatory effect on behavior. The second of these circuits begins with an inhibitory input to the putamen, but it goes through *four* inhibitory synapses in the following pathway: substantia nigra → putamen →

GP_e → subthalamic nucleus → GP_i → VA/VL thalamus. Thus, the effect of this pathway, too, is excitatory. And note that the GP_i also sends axons to the ventromedial system. A decrease in this inhibitory output is probably responsible for the muscular rigidity and poor control of posture seen in Parkinson's disease. (See *Figure 8.17b.*)

As we saw in Chapter 4, the standard treatment for Parkinson's disease is L-DOPA, the precursor of dopamine. When an increased amount of L-DOPA is present, the remaining nigrostriatal dopaminergic neurons in a patient with Parkinson's disease will produce and release more dopamine. But this compensation does not work indefinitely; eventually, the number of nigrostriatal dopaminergic neurons declines to such a low level that the symptoms become worse. In addition, high levels of L-DOPA produce side effects by acting on dopaminergic systems other than the nigrostriatal system. Some patients—especially those whose symptoms began when they were relatively young—become bedridden, scarcely able to move.

Neurosurgeons have been developing two stereotaxic procedures designed to alleviate the symptoms of Parkinson's disease that no longer respond to treatment with L-DOPA. The first one, transplantation of fetal tissue, attempts to reestablish the secretion of dopamine in the neostriatum. The tissue is obtained from the substantia nigra of aborted human fetuses and implanted into the caudate nucleus and putamen by means of stereotaxically guided needles. Although the procedure is still experimental, some good results have been obtained. As we saw in Chapter 5, PET scans have shown that fetal cells are able to grow in their new host and secrete dopamine, reducing the patient's symptoms.

Another procedure has a long history, but only recently have technological developments in imaging methods and electrophysiological techniques led to an increase in its popularity. As we saw in Figure 8.17(b), the principal output of the basal ganglia comes from the internal division of the globus pallidus. This output, which is directed toward the motor cortex through the VA/VL thalamus and to components of the ventromedial system in the brain stem, is inhibitory. As we saw, a decrease in the activity of the dopaminergic input to the neostriatum causes an *increase* in the activity of the GP_i. Thus, damage to the GP_i might be expected to relieve the symptoms of Parkinson's disease.

In the 1950s, Leksell and his colleagues performed pallidotomies (surgical destruction of the internal division of the globus pallidus) in patients with severe Parkinson's disease (Svennilson et al., 1960; Laitinen, Bergenheim, and Hariz, 1992). The surgery often reduced the rigidity and enhanced the patient's ability to move. Unfortunately, the surgery occasionally made the patient's symptoms worse and sometimes resulted in partial blindness. (The optic tract is located next to the GP_i.)

With the development of L-DOPA therapy in the late 1960s, pallidotomies were abandoned. However, it eventually became evident that L-DOPA worked for a limited time and that the symptoms of Parkinson's disease would eventually return. For that reason, in the 1990s neurosurgeons again began experimenting with pallidotomies, first with laboratory animals and then with humans (Graybiel, 1996). This time, they used MRI scans to find the location of the GP_i and then inserted an electrode into the target region. They could then pass low-intensity, high-frequency stimulation through the electrode, thus temporarily disabling the region around its tip. If the patient's rigidity disappeared (obviously, the patient is awake during the surgery), then the electrode was in the right place. To make the lesion, the surgeon passes radiofrequency current of sufficient strength to heat and destroy the brain tissue. The results of this procedure have been so promising that several neurological teams have begun promoting its use in the treatment of relatively young patients whose symptoms no longer respond to L-DOPA. PET studies have found that after pallidotomy, the metabolic activity in the premotor and supplementary motor areas, normally depressed in patients with Parkinson's disease, returns to normal levels (Grafton et al., 1995), which indicates that lesions of the GP_i do indeed release the motor cortex from inhibition.

Research suggests that Parkinson's disease may be caused by toxins—present in the environment, caused by faulty metabolism, or produced by unrecognized infectious disorders. Several years ago, a few young people developed symptoms of Parkinson's disease after taking illicit drugs that had been prepared in "underground" laboratories. Unfortunately, the drugs were contaminated with small amounts of a chemical called MPTP, which had the effect of destroying dopaminergic neurons of the substantia nigra (Langston et al., 1983). Further investigation showed that the damage occurs when enzymes present in dopaminergic neurons convert MPTP into an extremely toxic compound called MPP^+. Studies with laboratory animals revealed that injections of a drug that inhibits MAO (the enzyme that breaks down the monoamines, including dopamine) will protect against the damage caused by MPTP (Langston et al., 1984). Presumably, MAO is responsible for converting MPTP into MPP^+. In fact, a more recent clinical trial with deprenyl, a MAO inhibitor, was so encouraging that many patients with Parkinson's disease are now receiving the drug (Tetrud and Langston, 1989). If the drug retards the rate of degeneration of dopaminergic neurons, it will be the most important discovery since L-DOPA for the treatment of this disorder.

Huntington's Chorea

Another basal ganglia disease, **Huntington's chorea,** is caused by degeneration of the caudate nucleus and putamen, especially of GABAergic and acetylcholinergic neurons. (See *Figure 8.18.*) Whereas Parkinson's disease causes a poverty of movements, Huntington's chorea causes uncontrollable ones, especially jerky limb movements. (*Chorea* derives from the Greek *khoros,* meaning "dance.") The movements of Huntington's chorea look like fragments of purposeful movements but occur involuntarily. This disease is progressive and eventually causes death.

The symptoms of Huntington's chorea usually begin in the thirties and forties, but can sometimes begin in the early twenties. The first signs of neural degeneration occur in the putamen, specifically, in the inhibitory neurons that project to the external division of the globus pallidus. The loss of this inhibition increases the activity of the GP_e, which then inhibits the subthalamic nucleus. As a consequence, the activity level of the GP_i decreases and excessive movements occur. (Refer to *Figure 8.17b.*) As the disease progresses, the caudate nucleus and putamen degenerate until almost all of their neurons disappear.

Huntington's chorea is a hereditary disorder, caused by a dominant gene on chromosome 4. In fact, the gene has been located, and its defect has been identified as a repeated sequence of bases that code for the amino acid glutamine (Collaborative Research Group, 1993). This repeated sequence causes the gene product—a protein called *huntingtin*—to contain an elongated stretch of glutamine. Longer stretches of glutamine are associated with patients whose symptoms began at a younger age, which strongly suggests that this abnormal portion of the huntingtin molecule is responsible for the disease.

Subsequent research discovered that other proteins interact with the elongated stretch of glutamine. Burke et al. (1996) found that GADPH, an enzyme that plays a critical role in glucose metabolism, interacts with huntingtin. Possibly, the abnormal huntingtin may somehow interfere with the action of GADPH and cause some cells to starve. Researchers in another laboratory (Li et al., 1995) discovered that huntingtin is associated with another protein found only in the brain, which they called HAP1 (huntingtin-associated protein 1). This team also discovered that HAP1 is found in neurons that contain nitric oxide synthase, the enzyme responsible for the production of nitric

Huntington's chorea A fatal inherited disorder that causes degeneration of the caudate nucleus and putamen; characterized by uncontrollable jerking movements, writhing movements, and dementia.

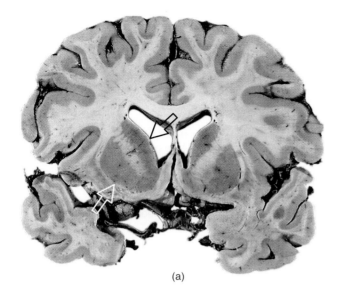

(a)

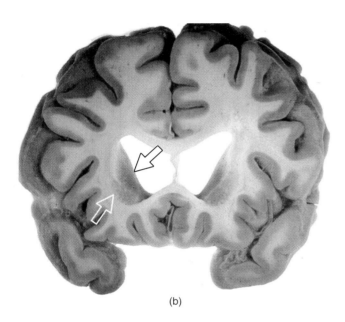

(b)

Figure 8.18
Huntington's chorea. (a) A slice through a normal human brain, showing the normal appearance of the caudate nuclei (arrowheads) and lateral ventricles. (b) A slice through the brain of a person who had Huntington's chorea. The arrowheads indicate the location of the caudate nuclei, which are severely degenerated. As a consequence of the degeneration, the lateral ventricles (open spaces in the middle of the slice) have enlarged.
(Courtesy of Harvard Medical School/Betty G. Martindale and Anthony D'Agostino, Good Samaritan Hospital, Portland, Oregon.)

son, 1995). Its outputs project to every major motor structure of the brain. When it is damaged, people's movements become jerky, erratic, and uncoordinated. The cerebellum consists of two hemispheres that contain several deep nuclei situated beneath the wrinkled and folded cerebellar cortex. Thus, the cerebellum resembles the cerebrum in miniature. The medial part of the cerebellum is phylogenetically older than the lateral part, and it participates in control of the ventromedial system. The **flocculonodular lobe,** located at the caudal end of the cerebellum, receives input from the vestibular system and projects axons to the vestibular nucleus. You will not be surprised to learn that this system is involved in postural reflexes. (See green lines in *Figure 8.19.*) The **vermis** ("worm"), located on the midline, receives auditory and visual information from the tectum and cutaneous and kinesthetic information from the spinal cord. It sends its outputs to the **fastigial nucleus** (one of the set of deep cerebellar nuclei). Neurons in the fastigial nucleus send axons to the vestibular nucleus and to motor nuclei in the reticular formation. Thus, these neurons influence behavior through the vestibulospinal and reticulospinal tracts, two of the three ventromedial pathways. (See blue lines in *Figure 8.19.*)

The rest of the cerebellar cortex receives most of its input from the cerebral cortex, including the primary motor cortex and association cortex. This input is relayed to the cerebellar cortex through the pontine tegmental reticular nucleus. The intermediate zone of the cerebellar cortex projects to the **interposed nuclei,** which in turn project to the

oxide (Li et al., 1996). As they noted, nitric oxide appears to play a role in the generation of excitotoxic lesions; in fact, nitric oxide synthase inhibitors reduce the neurotoxicity of glutamate agonists (Dawson et al., 1993). Thus, this group suggests that the release of nitric oxide may cause the destruction of surrounding neurons. Further research will undoubtedly clarify the role of faulty huntingtin protein in the neuropathology of Huntington's chorea.

● The Cerebellum

The cerebellum is an important part of the motor system. It contains about 50 billion neurons, versus the approximately 22 billion neurons in the cerebral cortex (Robin-

flocculonodular lobe   A region of the cerebellum; involved in control of postural reflexes.

vermis   The portion of the cerebellum located at the midline; receives somatosensory information and helps control the vestibulospinal and reticulospinal tracts through its connections with the fastigial nucleus.

fastigial nucleus   A deep cerebellar nucleus; involved in the control of movement by the reticulospinal and vestibulospinal tracts.

interposed nuclei   A set of deep cerebellar nuclei; involved in the control of the rubrospinal system.

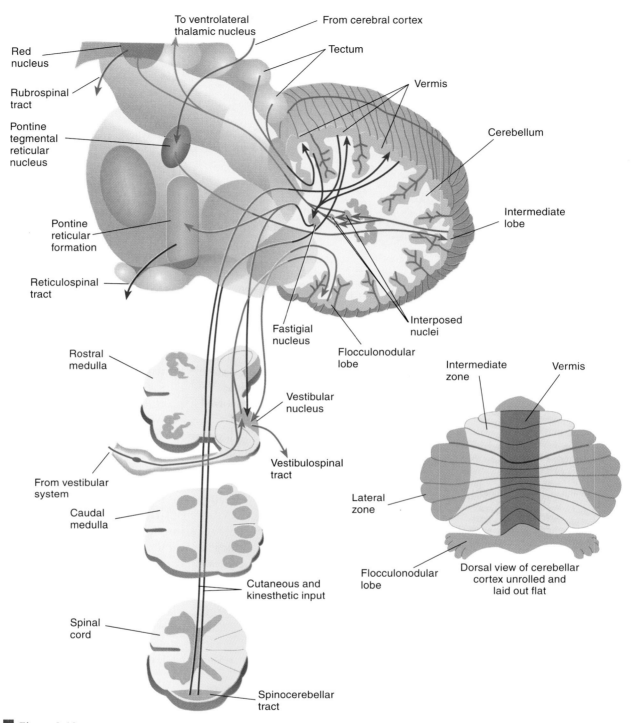

Figure 8.19
Inputs and outputs of three systems of the cerebellum: the flocculonodular lobe (green lines), the vermis (blue lines), and the intermediate zone of the cerebellar cortex (red lines).

red nucleus. Thus, the intermediate zone influences the control of the rubrospinal system over movements of the arms and legs. The interposed nuclei also send outputs to the ventrolateral thalamic nucleus, which projects to the motor cortex. (See red lines, *Figure 8.19.*)

The lateral zone of the cerebellum is involved in the control of independent limb movements, especially rapid, skilled movements. Such movements are initiated by neurons in the frontal association cortex, which control neurons in the primary motor cortex. But although the frontal cortex can plan and initiate movements, it does not contain the neural circuitry needed to calculate the complex, closely timed sequences of muscular contractions that are needed for rapid, skilled movements. That task falls to the lateral zone of the cerebellum.

Both the frontal association cortex and the primary motor cortex send information about intended movements to the lateral zone of the cerebellum via the **pontine nucleus.** The lateral zone also receives information from the somatosensory system, which informs it about the current position and rate of movement of the limbs—information that is necessary for computing the details of a movement. When the cerebellum receives information that the motor cortex has begun to initiate a movement, it computes the contribution that various muscles will have to make to perform that movement. The results of this computation are sent to the **dentate nucleus,** another of the deep cerebellar nuclei. Neurons in the dentate nucleus pass the information on to the ventrolateral thalamus, which projects to the primary motor cortex. The projection from the ventrolateral thalamus to the primary motor cortex enables the cerebellum to modify the ongoing movement that was initiated by the frontal cortex. The lateral zone of the cerebellum also sends efferents to the red nucleus (again, via the dentate nucleus); thus, it helps control independent limb movements through this system as well. (See *Figure 8.20.*)

In humans, lesions of different regions of the cerebellum produce different symptoms. Damage to the flocculonodular lobe or vermis causes disturbances in posture and balance. Damage to the intermediate zone produces deficits in movements controlled by the rubrospinal system; the principal symptom of this damage is limb rigidity. Damage to the lateral zone causes weakness and *decomposition of movement.* For example, a person attempting to bring the hand to the mouth will make separate movements of the joints of the shoulder, elbow, and wrist instead of performing simultaneous smooth movements.

Lesions of the lateral zone of the cerebellar cortex also appear to impair the timing of rapid *ballistic* movements. Ballistic (literally, "throwing") movements occur too fast to be modified by feedback. The sequence of muscular movements must then be programmed in advance, and the individual muscles must be activated at the proper times. You might like to try this common neurological test. Have a

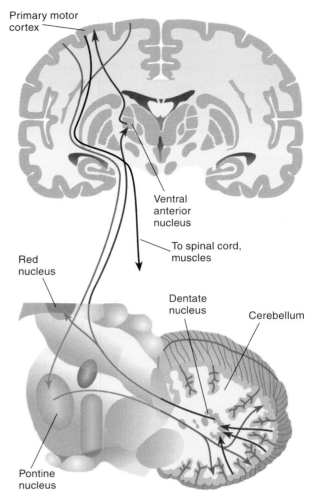

Figure 8.20
Inputs and outputs of the lateral zone of the cerebellar cortex. This zone receives information about impending movements from the frontal lobes and helps smooth and integrate the movements through its connections to the primary motor cortex and red nucleus through the dentate nucleus and ventral thalamus.

friend place his or her finger in front of your face, about three-quarters of an arm's length away. While your friend slowly moves his or her finger around to serve as a moving target, alternately touch your nose and your friend's finger as rapidly as you can. If your cerebellum is normal, you can successfully hit your nose and your friend's finger without too much trouble. People with lateral cerebellar damage have great difficulty; they tend to miss the examiner's hand and poke themselves in the eye. (I have often wondered why neurologists do not adopt a less dangerous test.)

When making rapid, aimed movements, we cannot rely on feedback to stop the movement when we reach the tar-

pontine nucleus   A large nucleus in the pons that serves as an important source of input to the cerebellum.

dentate nucleus   A deep cerebellar nucleus; involved in the control of rapid, skilled movements by the corticospinal and rubrospinal systems.

get. By the time we perceive that our finger has reached the proper place, it is too late to stop the movement, and we will overshoot the target if we try to stop it then. Instead of relying on feedback, the movement appears to be timed. We estimate the distance between our hand and the target, and our cerebellum calculates the amount of time that the muscles will have to be turned on. After the proper amount of time the cerebellum briefly turns on antagonistic muscles to stop the movement. In fact, Kornhuber (1974) suggested that one of the primary functions of the cerebellum is timing the duration of rapid movements. Obviously, learning must play a role in controlling such movements.

The cerebellum also appears to integrate successive *sequences* of movements that must be performed one after the other. For example, Holmes (1939) reported that one of his patients said, "The movements of my left arm are done subconsciously, but I have to think out each movement of the right [affected] arm. I come to a dead stop in turning and have to think before I start again." Thach (1978) obtained experimental evidence that corroborates this role. He found that many neurons in the dentate nuclei (which receive inputs from the lateral zone of the cerebellar cortex) showed response patterns that predicted the *next* movement in a sequence rather than the one that was currently taking place. Presumably, the cerebellum was planning these movements.

●The Reticular Formation

The reticular formation consists of a large number of nuclei located in the core of the medulla, pons, and midbrain. The reticular formation controls the activity of the gamma motor system and hence regulates muscle tonus. In addition, the pons and medulla contain several nuclei with specific motor functions. For example, different locations in the medulla control automatic or semiautomatic responses such as respiration, sneezing, coughing, and vomiting. As we saw, the ventromedial pathways originate in the superior colliculi, vestibular nuclei, and reticular formation. Thus, the reticular formation plays a role in the control of posture.

The reticular formation also plays a role in locomotion. Stimulation of the **mesencephalic locomotor region,** located ventral to the inferior colliculus, causes a cat to make pacing movements (Shik and Orlovsky, 1976). The mesencephalic locomotor region does not send fibers directly to the spinal cord but apparently controls the activity of reticulospinal tract neurons.

Other motor functions of the reticular formation are also being discovered. Siegel and McGinty (1977) recorded from thirty-five single neurons in the reticular formation of unanesthetized, freely moving cats. Thirty-two of these neurons responded during *specific* movements of the head, tongue, facial muscles, ears, forepaw, or shoulder. The specific nature of the relations suggests that the neurons play some role in controlling the movements. For example, one neuron responded when the tongue moved out and to the left. The function of these neurons and the range of movements they control are not yet known.

Interim Summary

The motor systems of the brain are complex. (Having read this section, you do not need me to tell you that.) A good way to review the systems is through an example. While following my description, you might want to look at Table 8.1 and Figures 8.12 and 8.13 again. Suppose you see, out of the corner of your eye, that something is moving. You quickly turn your head and eyes toward the source of the movement and discover that a vase of flowers on a table someone has just bumped is ready to fall. You quickly reach forward, grab it, and restore it to a stable upright position. (For simplicity's sake, I will assume that you are right-handed.)

The rapid movement of your head and eyes is controlled by mechanisms that involve the superior colliculi and nearby nuclei. The head movement and corresponding movement of the trunk are mediated by the tectospinal tract. You perceive the tipping vase because of the activity of neurons in your visual association cortex. Your visual association cortex also contributes information about depth to your right parietal lobe, whose association cortex determines the exact spatial location of the vase. Your left parietal lobe uses the spatial information, together with its own record of the location of your hand, to compute the path your hand must travel to intercept the vase. The information is relayed to your left frontal lobe, where the motor association cortex starts the movement. Because the movement will have to be a ballistic one, the cerebellum controls its timing, based on information it receives from the association cortex of the frontal and parietal lobes. Your hand stops just as it touches the vase, and connections between the somatosensory cortex and the primary motor cortex initiate a reflex that closes your hand around the vase.

mesencephalic locomotor region   A region of the reticular formation of the midbrain whose stimulation causes alternating movements of the limbs normally seen during locomotion.

The movement of your hand is controlled through a cooperation between the corticospinal, rubrospinal, and ventromedial pathways. Even before your hand moves, the ventral corticospinal tract and the ventromedial pathways (vestibulospinal and reticulospinal system, largely under the influence of the basal ganglia) begin adjusting your posture so that you will not fall forward when you suddenly reach in front of you. Depending on how far forward you will have to reach, the reticulospinal tract may even cause one leg to step forward in order to take your weight. The rubrospinal tract controls the muscles of your upper arm, and the lateral corticospinal tract controls your finger and hand movements. Perhaps you say, triumphantly, "I got it!" The corticobulbar pathway, under the control of speech mechanisms in the left hemisphere, causes the muscles of your vocal apparatus to say these words.

A person with apraxia will have difficulty making controlled movements of the limb in response to a verbal request. Most cases of apraxia are produced by lesions of the left parietal lobe, which sends information about the requested movement to the left frontal association cortex. This region directly controls movement of the right limb by activating neurons in the left primary motor cortex and indirectly controls movement of the left limb by sending information to the right frontal association cortex. Damage to the left frontal association cortex or its connections with the right hemisphere also produce apraxia.

SUGGESTED READINGS

Kandel, E. R., Schwartz, J. H., and Jessell, T. M. *Principles of Neural Science,* 3rd ed. Norwalk, CT: Appleton & Lange, 1992.

Kolb, B., and Whishaw, I.Q. *Fundamentals of Human Neuropsychology,* 4th ed. New York: W. H. Freeman, 1996.

Nicholls, J. G., Martin, A. R., Wallace, B. G., and Kuffler, S. W. *From Neuron to Brain,* 3rd ed. Sunderland, MA: Sinauer Associates, 1992.

Schneider, J. S., and Lidsky, T. I. *Basal Ganglia and Behavior: Sensory Aspects and Motor Functioning.* Bern: Hans Huber, 1987.

CHAPTER 9

Sleep and Biological Rhythms

Hagoromo by Kenzo Okada.

Why do we sleep? Why do we spend at least one-third of our lives doing something that provides most of us with only a few fleeting memories? I will attempt to answer this question in several ways. In the first two parts of this chapter I will describe what is known about the phenomenon of sleep: How much do we sleep? What do we do while asleep? What happens if we do not get enough sleep? Does sleep perform a restorative function? In the third part of the chapter I will describe the search for the chemicals and the neural circuits that control sleep and wakefulness. In the fourth section I will explore whether sleeping medications are effective and what we know about sleepwalking and other sleep-related disorders. In the final part of the chapter I will discuss the brain's biological clock—the mechanism that controls daily rhythms of sleep and activity.

A PHYSIOLOGICAL AND BEHAVIORAL DESCRIPTION

Sleep is a behavior. That statement may seem peculiar, because we usually think of behaviors as activities that involve movements, such as walking or talking. Except for the rapid eye movements that accompany a particular stage, sleep is not distinguished by movement. What characterizes sleep is that the insistent urge of sleepiness forces us to seek out a quiet, comfortable place, lie down, and re-

main there for several hours. Because we remember very little about what happens while we sleep, we tend to think of sleep more as a state of consciousness than as a behavior. The change in consciousness is undeniable, but it should not prevent us from noticing the behavioral changes.

Stages of Sleep

The best research on human sleep is conducted in a sleep laboratory. A sleep laboratory, usually located at a university or medical center, consists of one or several small bedrooms adjacent to an observation room, where the experimenter spends the night (trying to stay awake). The experimenter prepares the sleeper for electrophysiological measurements by attaching electrodes to the scalp to monitor the electroencephalogram (EEG) and to the chin to monitor muscle activity, recorded as the **electromyogram (EMG)**. Electrodes attached around the eyes monitor eye movements, recorded as the **electro-oculogram (EOG).** In addition, other electrodes and transducing devices can be

electromyogram (EMG) *(my oh gram)* An electrical potential recorded from an electrode placed on or in a muscle.
electro-oculogram (EOG) *(ah kew loh gram)* An electrical potential from the eyes, recorded by means of electrodes placed on the skin around them; detects eye movements.

used to monitor autonomic measures such as heart rate, respiration, and skin conductance. Wires from the electrodes are bundled together in a "ponytail," which is then plugged into a junction box at the head of the bed. (See *Figure 9.1.*)

During wakefulness the EEG of a normal person shows two basic patterns of activity: *alpha activity* and *beta activity.* **Alpha activity** consists of regular, medium-frequency waves of 8–12 Hz. The brain produces this activity when a person is resting quietly, not particularly aroused or excited and not engaged in strenuous mental activity (such as problem solving). Although alpha waves sometimes occur when a person's eyes are open, they are much more prevalent when the eyes are closed. The other type of waking EEG pattern, **beta activity,** consists of irregular, mostly low-amplitude waves of 13–30 Hz. This activity occurs when a person is alert and attentive to events in the environment or is thinking actively. (See *Figure 9.2.*)

What is the significance of these two types of waveforms? As we saw in Chapter 5, the EEG is a recording of the summed postsynaptic activity of cerebral neurons (mostly, neurons in the cerebral cortex). Therefore, a low-frequency, high-voltage EEG (alpha activity, as opposed to beta activity) reflects neural **synchrony.** These waves are

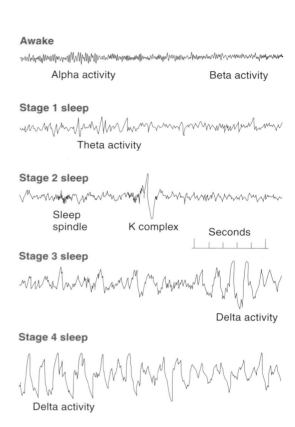

Awake

Alpha activity   Beta activity

Stage 1 sleep

Theta activity

Stage 2 sleep

Sleep
spindle   K complex   Seconds

Stage 3 sleep

Delta activity

Stage 4 sleep

Delta activity

REM sleep

Theta activity   Beta activity

Figure 9.2
An EEG recording of the stages of sleep.
(From Horne, J.A. *Why We Sleep: The Functions of Sleep in Humans and Other Mammals.* Oxford, England: Oxford University Press, 1988.)

produced by a regular, synchronized pattern of activity in a large number of neurons. The activity of the individual neurons is analogous to a large number of people chanting the same words together (speaking *synchronously*). Similarly, beta activity is referred to as **desynchrony;** it is like a

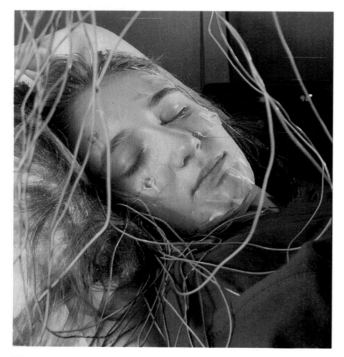

Figure 9.1
A subject prepared for a night's sleep in a sleep laboratory.
Philippe Platilly/Science Photo Library/Photo Researchers Inc.

alpha activity   Smooth electrical activity of 8–12 Hz recorded from the brain; generally associated with a state of relaxation.

beta activity   Irregular electrical activity of 13–30 Hz recorded from the brain; generally associated with a state of arousal.

synchrony   High-voltage, low-frequency EEG activity, characteristic of slow-wave sleep or coma, during which neurons fire together in a regular fashion.

desynchrony   Irregular electrical activity recorded from the brain, generally associated with periods of arousal.

large number of people broken into many small groups, each carrying on an individual conversation.

The analogy helps explain why desynchrony is generally assumed to represent activation, whereas synchrony reflects a resting or depressed state. A group of people who are all chanting the same message will process very little information; only one message is being produced. On the other hand, a desynchronized group will process and transmit many different messages. The alert, waking state of the brain is more like the desynchronized group of people, with much information processing going on. During synchrony the neurons of the resting brain (especially the cortex) quietly murmur the same message in unison.

Let us look at a typical night's sleep of a female college student on her third night in the laboratory. (Of course, we would obtain similar results from a male, with one exception, which is noted later.) The experimenter attaches the electrodes, turns the lights off, and closes the door. Our subject becomes drowsy and soon enters stage 1 sleep, marked by the presence of some **theta activity** (3.5–7.5 Hz). This stage is actually a transition between sleep and wakefulness; if we watch our volunteer's eyelids, we will see that from time to time they slowly open and close and that her eyes roll upward and downward. (See *Figure 9.2.*) About 10 minutes later she enters stage 2 sleep. The EEG during this stage is generally irregular but contains periods of theta activity, *sleep spindles,* and *K complexes*. Sleep spindles are short bursts of waves of 12–14 Hz that occur between two and five times a minute during stages 1–4 of sleep. Some investigators believe that sleep spindles represent the activity of a mechanism that decreases the brain's sensitivity to sensory input—disconnects the brain from the outside world, so to speak—and thus permits the person to enter deeper stages of sleep (Bowersox, Kaitin, and Dement, 1985; Steriade, 1992). The sleep of older people contains fewer sleep spindles and is generally accompanied by more awakenings during the night. K complexes are sudden, sharp waveforms, which, unlike sleep spindles, are usually found only during stage 2 sleep. They spontaneously occur at the rate of approximately one per minute but often can be triggered by noises—especially unexpected noises (Niiyama et al., 1995; 1996). Some investigators believe that they, too, represent mechanisms involved in keeping the person asleep (Wauquier, Aloe, and Declerck, 1995). (See *Figure 9.2.*)

The subject is sleeping soundly now; but if awakened, she might report that she has not been asleep. This phenomenon often is reported by nurses who awaken loudly snoring patients early in the night (probably to give them a sleeping pill) and find that the patients insist they were lying there awake all the time. About 15 minutes later the subject enters stage 3 sleep, signaled by the occurrence of high-amplitude **delta activity** (less than 3.5 Hz). (See *Figure 9.2.*) The distinction between stage 3 and stage 4 is not clear-cut; stage 3 contains 20–50 percent delta activity, and stage 4 contains more than 50 percent. (See *Figure 9.2.*)

About 90 minutes after the beginning of sleep (and about 45 minutes after the onset of stage 4 sleep), we notice an abrupt change in a number of physiological measures recorded from our subject. The EEG suddenly becomes mostly desynchronized, with a sprinkling of theta waves, very similar to the record obtained during stage 1 sleep. (See *Figure 9.2.*) We also note that her eyes are rapidly darting back and forth beneath her closed eyelids. We can see this activity in the EOG, recorded from electrodes attached to the skin around her eyes, or we can observe the eye movements directly—the cornea produces a bulge in the closed eyelids that can be seen to move about. We also see that the EMG becomes silent; there is a profound loss of muscle tonus. In fact, physiological studies have shown that, aside from occasional twitching, a person actually becomes paralyzed during REM sleep.

This peculiar stage of sleep is quite distinct from the quiet sleep we saw earlier. It is usually referred to as **REM sleep** (for the **r**apid **e**ye **m**ovements that characterize it). It has also been called *paradoxical sleep,* because of the presence of beta activity, which is usually seen during wakefulness or stage 1 sleep. The term *paradoxical* merely reflects people's surprise at observing an unexpected phenomenon, but the years since its first discovery (reported by Aserinsky and Kleitman in 1955) have blunted the surprise value.

At this point, I should introduce some terminology. Stages 1–4 are usually referred to as **non-REM sleep.** Stages 3 and 4 are referred to as **slow-wave sleep,** because of the presence of delta activity. As we will see, research has focused on the role of REM sleep and of slow-wave sleep; most investigators believe that the other stages of non-REM

theta activity   EEG activity of 5–8 Hz that occurs intermittently during early stages of slow-wave sleep and REM sleep.

delta activity   Regular, synchronous electrical activity of approximately 1–4 Hz recorded from the brain; occurs during the deepest stages of slow-wave sleep.

REM sleep   A period of desynchronized EEG activity during sleep, at which time dreaming, rapid eye movements, and muscular paralysis occur; also called *paradoxical sleep.*

non-REM sleep   All stages of sleep except REM sleep.

slow-wave sleep   Non-REM sleep, characterized by synchronized EEG activity during its deeper stages.

sleep, stages 1 and 2, are less important than the others. (As we shall see, when people are sleep deprived, they make up most of their slow-wave sleep and REM sleep, but not their stage 1 and stage 2 sleep.) By some criteria, stage 4 is the deepest stage of sleep; only loud noises will cause a person to awaken, and when awakened, the person acts groggy and confused. During REM sleep a person may not react to noises, but he or she is easily aroused by meaningful stimuli, such as the sound of his or her name. Also, when awakened from REM sleep, a person appears alert and attentive.

If we arouse our volunteer during REM sleep and ask her what was going on, she will almost certainly report that she had been dreaming. The dreams of REM sleep tend to be narrative in form; there is a storylike progression of events. If we wake her during slow-wave sleep and ask, "Were you dreaming?" she will most likely say, "No." However, if we question her more carefully, she might report the presence of a thought, an image, or some emotion. I will return to this issue later.

During the rest of the night our subject's sleep alternates between periods of REM and non-REM sleep. Each cycle is approximately 90 minutes long, containing a 20- to 30-minute bout of REM sleep. Thus, an 8-hour sleep will contain four or five periods of REM sleep. Figure 9.3 shows a graph of a typical night's sleep. The x-axis indicates the EEG activity that is being recorded; thus REM sleep and stage 1 sleep are placed on the same line because similar patterns of EEG activity occur at these times. Note that most slow-wave sleep (stages 3 and 4) occurs during the first half of night. Subsequent bouts of non-REM sleep contain more and more stage 2 sleep, and bouts of REM sleep (indicated by the horizontal bars) become more prolonged. (See *Figure 9.3*.)

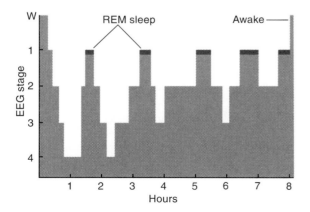

Figure 9.3
A typical pattern of the stages of sleep during a single night. The dark blue shading indicates REM sleep.

The fact that REM sleep occurs at regular 90-minute intervals suggests that a brain mechanism alternately causes REM and slow-wave sleep. Normally, a period of slow-wave sleep must precede REM sleep. In addition, there seems to be a refractory period after each occurrence of REM sleep, during which time REM sleep cannot take place again. In fact, the cyclical nature of REM sleep appears to be controlled by a "clock" in the brain that also controls an activity cycle that continues through waking. The first suggestion that a 90-minute activity cycle occurs throughout the day came from the observation that infants who are fed on demand show regular feeding patterns (Kleitman, 1961). Later studies found 90-minute cycles of rest and activity, including such activities as eating, drinking, smoking, heart rate, oxygen consumption, stomach motility, urine production, and performance on various tasks that make demands upon a person's ability to pay attention. Kleitman termed this phenomenon the **basic rest–activity cycle (BRAC).** (See Kleitman, 1982, for a review.) As we will see later in this chapter, an internal "clock," probably located in the medulla, causes regular changes in activity and alertness during the day and controls periods of slow-wave and REM sleep at night.

As we saw, during REM sleep we become paralyzed; most of our spinal and cranial motor neurons are strongly inhibited. (Obviously, the ones that control respiration and eye movements are spared.) At the same time, the brain is very active. Cerebral blood flow and oxygen consumption are accelerated. In addition, a male's penis will become at least partially erect, and a female's vaginal secretions will increase. However, Fisher, Gross, and Zuch (1965) found that in males, genital changes do not signify that the person is experiencing a dream with sexual content. (Of course, people can have dreams with frank sexual content. In males some dreams culminate in ejaculation—the so-called nocturnal emissions, or "wet dreams." Females, too, sometimes experience orgasm during sleep.)

The fact that penile erections occur during REM sleep, independent of sexual arousal, has been used clinically to assess the causes of impotence (Karacan, Salis, and Williams, 1978; Singer and Weiner, 1996). A subject sleeps in the laboratory with a device attached to his penis that measures its circumference. If penile enlargement occurs during REM sleep, then his failure to obtain an erection during attempts at intercourse is not caused by physiological problems such as nerve damage or a circulatory disorder.

basic rest–activity cycle (BRAC) A 90-min cycle (in humans) of waxing and waning alertness, controlled by a biological clock in the caudal brain stem; controls cycles of REM sleep and slow-wave sleep.

Table 9.1
Principal characteristics of REM and slow-wave sleep

REM Sleep	Slow-Wave Sleep
EEG desynchrony	EEG synchrony
Lack of muscle tonus	Moderate muscle tonus
Rapid eye movements	Slow or absent eye movements
Penile erection or vaginal secretion	Lack of genital activity
PGO waves	Lack of PGO waves
Narrative-type dreams	Static dreams

(A neurologist told me that there is a less expensive way to gather the same data. The patient obtains a strip of postage stamps, moistens them, and applies them around his penis before going to bed. In the morning he checks to see whether the perforations are broken.)

The important differences between REM and slow-wave sleep are listed in *Table 9.1.*

● Mental Activity During Sleep

Although sleep is a period during which we do not respond very much to the environment, it is incorrect to refer to sleep as a state of unconsciousness. Consciousness during sleep certainly differs from waking consciousness, but we *are* conscious then. In the morning we usually forget what we experienced while asleep, so in retrospect we conclude that we were unconscious. However, when experimenters wake sleeping subjects, the reports that the subjects give make it clear that they were conscious.

Some people insist that they never dream. They are wrong; everyone dreams. What does happen, however, is that most dreams are subsequently forgotten. Unless a person awakens during or immediately after a dream, the dream will not be remembered. Many people who thought they had not had a dream for years have been startled by the vivid narrations they were able to supply when roused during REM sleep in the laboratory. Even the most vivid experiences can be completely erased from consciousness. I am sure that many of you have had the experience of waking during a particularly interesting dream. You decide to tell your friends about it, and you start to review what you will say. As you do so, the memory just slips away. You can't remember the slightest detail of the dream, which was so vivid and real just a few seconds ago. You may feel that if you could remember just one detail about it, everything would come back. Understanding this phenomenon would probably tell us much about the more general issue of learning and forgetting.

Madsen et al. (1991) found that the rate of cerebral blood flow in the human brain during REM sleep was high in the visual association cortex but low in the inferior frontal cortex. As we shall see in Chapter 14, the inferior frontal cortex is involved in making plans and keeping track of the organization of events in time. As Madsen and his colleagues noted, dreams are characterized by good visual images (undoubtedly involving the visual association cortex), but they are poorly organized with respect to time; for example, past, present, and future are often interchanged (Hobson, 1988). And as Melges (1982) put it, "the dreamer often has no feeling of striving for long-term goals but rather is carried along by the flow of time by circumstances that crop up in an unpredictable way." This quote could just as well be describing the daily life of a person whose inferior frontal cortex has been damaged.

Several investigators have suggested that the eye movements made during REM sleep are related to the visual imagery that occurs while we dream. Roffwarg et al. (1962) recorded the eye movements of subjects during REM sleep and then awakened them and asked them to describe what had been happening in their dreams. They found that the eye movements were similar to what would have been expected if the subjects had actually been watching these events. Miyauchi, Takino, and Azakami (1990) recorded the EEG of sleeping subjects and found that a particular wave accompanied eye movements during REM sleep. This wave was also seen when waking subjects scanned a scene—but it was *not* seen when they simply made eye movements in a dark room. Thus, the EEG wave is not produced by eye movements themselves, but may actually indicate that the subjects had been scanning a visual image during a dream.

Evidence indicates that the particular brain mechanisms that become active during a dream are those that would become active if the events in the dream were actually occurring. For example, cortical and subcortical motor mechanisms become active during a dream that contains movement—as if the person were actually moving (McCarley and Hobson, 1979). In addition, if a dream involves talking and listening, regions of the dreamer's brain that are involved in speaking and listening become especially active (Hong et al., 1996). (Brain mechanisms of verbal communication are discussed in Chapter 15.)

Although narrative, storylike dreaming occurs during REM sleep, mental activity can also accompany slow-wave sleep. Some of the most terrifying nightmares occur during

Figure 9.4
The Nightmare, *1781, by Henry Fuseli, Swiss, 1741–1825.*
(Gift of Mr. and Mrs. Bert L. Smokler and Mr. and Mrs. Lawrence A.
Fleischman, Acc. No. 55.5. Courtesy of The Detroit Institute of Arts.)

slow-wave sleep, especially stage 4 sleep (Fisher et al., 1970). If people are awakened from slow-wave sleep, they are unlikely to report a storylike dream. Instead, they often report a situation, such as being crushed or suffocated, or simply a feeling of fear or dread. This common sensation is reflected in the terms that some languages use for describing what we call a *nightmare.* For example, in French the word is *cauchemar,* or "pressing devil." Figure 9.4 shows a victim of a nightmare (undoubtedly in the throes of stage 4 slow-wave sleep) being squashed by an *incubus* (from the Latin *incubare,* "to lie upon"). (See **Figure 9.4.**)

Interim Summary

Sleep is generally regarded as a state, but it is, nevertheless, a behavior. As we will see later in this chapter, we do not sleep because our brains "run down"; instead, active brain mechanisms cause us to engage in the behavior of sleep. The stages of non-REM sleep, stages 1 through 4, are defined by EEG activity. Slow-wave sleep (stages 3 and 4) comprises the two deepest stages. Alertness consists of desynchronized beta activity (13–30 Hz); relaxation and drowsiness consist of alpha activity (8–12 Hz); stage 1 sleep consists of alternating periods of alpha activity, irregular fast activity, and theta activity (3.5–7.5 Hz); the EEG of stage 2 sleep lacks alpha activity but contains sleep spindles (short periods of 12–14 Hz activity) and occasional K complexes; stage 3 sleep consists of 20–50 percent

delta activity (less than 3.5 Hz); and stage 4 sleep consists of more than 50 percent delta activity. About 90 minutes after the beginning of sleep, people enter REM sleep. Cycles of REM and slow-wave sleep alternate in periods of approximately 90 minutes.

REM sleep consists of rapid eye movements, a desynchronized EEG, sensitivity to external stimulation, muscular paralysis, genital activity, and dreaming. Mental activity can accompany slow-wave sleep, too, but it is usually static in nature rather than narrative, like dreams during REM sleep.

WHY DO WE SLEEP?

We all know how insistent the urge to sleep can be and how uncomfortable we feel when we have to resist it and stay awake. With the exception of the effects of severe pain and the need to breathe, sleepiness is probably the most insistent drive. People can commit suicide by refusing to eat or drink, but even the most stoical person cannot indefinitely defy the urge to sleep. Sleep will come, sooner or later, no matter how hard a person tries to stay awake. However, despite the insistent nature of sleepiness, researchers have not yet found a simple answer to the question posed in the title of this section. The two major hypotheses that have been proposed are discussed next.

Sleep as an Adaptive Response

Sleep is a universal phenomenon among vertebrates. As far as we know, all mammals and birds sleep (Durie, 1981). Reptiles also sleep, and fish and amphibians enter periods of quiescence that probably can be called sleep. However, only warm-blooded vertebrates (mammals and birds) exhibit unequivocal REM sleep, with EEG signs of desynchrony along with rapid eye movements. (Obviously, birds such as flamingos, which sleep while perched on one leg, do not lose tone in the muscles they use to remain standing.) This special form of sleep will be discussed separately, in a later section.

Some investigators believe that the best way to understand sleep is to see it as a useful behavior that we have inherited from our ancestors. For example, Webb (1975, 1982) suggested that sleep might not have special restorative properties but might simply be a behavior that keeps an animal out of harm's way when there is nothing important to do. We can imagine that our primitive ancestors benefited from irresistible periods of sleep that kept them from stumbling around in the dark, when predators were harder to see, when food was difficult to find, and when injuries were more likely to occur.

Many animals obtain food during only part of the day–night cycle. These animals profit from a period of inactivity, during which less energy is expended. In fact, animals that have safe hiding places (such as rabbits) sleep a lot, unless they are very small and need to eat much of the time (such as shrews). Large predators such as lions can sleep safely wherever and whenever they choose, and indeed, they sleep many hours of the day. In contrast, large animals that are preyed upon and have no place to hide (such as cattle) sleep very little. Presumably, they must remain awake to be alert for predators.

An argument *against* the suggestion that sleep serves merely as an adaptive response is the fact that sleep is found in some species of mammals that would seem to be better off without it. For example, the Indus dolphin *(Platanista indi)* lives in the muddy waters of the Indus estuary in Pakistan (Pilleri, 1979). Over the years it has become blind, presumably because vision is not useful in the animal's environment. (It has an excellent sonar system, which it uses to navigate and find prey.) However, despite the dangers caused by sleeping, sleep has not disappeared. The Indus dolphin never stops swimming; doing so would result in injury, because of the dangerous currents and the vast quantities of debris carried by the river during the monsoon season. Pilleri captured two dolphins and studied their habits. He found that they slept a total of 7 hours a day, in brief naps of 4–60 seconds each. If sleep were simply an adaptive response, why was it not eliminated (as vision was) through the process of natural selection?

Some other species of marine mammals have developed an extraordinary pattern of sleep: The cerebral hemispheres take turns sleeping, presumably because that strategy always permits at least one hemisphere to be alert. The bottlenose dolphin *(Tursiops truncatus)* and the porpoise *(Phocoena phocoena)* both sleep this way (Mukhametov, 1984). Figure 9.5 shows the EEG recordings from the two hemispheres; note that slow-wave sleep occurs independently in the left and right hemispheres. (See *Figure 9.5*.)

Undoubtedly, sleep *does* serve as a useful behavior. The fact that sleeping time varies with environmental factors suggests that the amount of sleep an organism engages in is somewhat flexible. But its presence in all species of mammals and birds suggests that at least a certain amount of sleep is necessary.

● Sleep as a Restorative Process

Most investigators believe that sleep accomplishes some sort of restoration from the effects of wear and tear that oc-

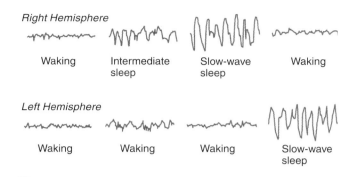

Figure 9.5
Sleep in a dolphin. The two hemispheres sleep independently, presumably so that the animal remains behaviorally alert. (Adapted from Mukhametov, L.M., in *Sleep Mechanisms,* edited by A.A. Borbély and J.L. Valatx. Munich: Springer-Verlag, 1984.)

cur during wakefulness. However, until recently, evidence for this hypothesis was very thin, indeed. In fact, sleep does not seem to be related to physical exercise; thus, its most important role is probably not rest and recuperation of the body. However, it *does* appear to be needed to keep the brain functioning normally. (For convenience, I will talk about the "body" and the "brain" in the following section, even though we both know that the brain is a part of the body.)

Effects of Sleep Deprivation

When we are forced to miss a night's sleep, we become very sleepy. The fact that sleepiness is so motivating suggests that sleep is a necessity of life. If so, it should be possible to deprive people or laboratory animals of sleep and see what functions are disrupted. We should then be able to infer the role that sleep plays. However, the results of sleep deprivation studies have not revealed as much as investigators had originally hoped.

Studies with Humans. Deprivation studies have not obtained persuasive evidence that sleep is needed to keep the body functioning normally. Horne (1978) reviewed over fifty experiments in which humans had been deprived of sleep. He reported that most of them found that sleep deprivation did not interfere with people's ability to perform physical exercise. In addition, the studies found no evidence of a physiological stress response to sleep deprivation. If people encounter stressful situations that cause illness or damage to various organ systems, changes can be seen in such physiological measures as blood levels of cortisol and epinephrine. (The physiology of stress is described in more detail in Chapter 18.) Generally, these changes did not occur.

Sleep deprivation does appear to disrupt cognitive functions, and it has profound effects on people's mood (Pilcher and Huffcutt, 1996). Several studies have found that after staying awake for a few days, people begin to report perceptual distortions or even hallucinations. For example, Morris, Williams, and Lubin (1960) reported that sleep-deprived subjects made statements such as, "The floor seems wavy," "That black mark looked like it was changing into different rock formations," or "I thought steam was rising from the floor, so I tested my eyes to check whether it was real." The effects on a subject without a history of mental illness are never particularly severe—the subjects realize that the perceptual distortions and hallucinations are not real—but they do suggest that sleep deprivation adversely affects some brain functions.

What happens to sleep-deprived subjects after they are permitted to sleep again? Most of them sleep longer the next night or two, but they never regain all of the sleep they lost. In one remarkable case a seventeen-year-old boy stayed awake for 264 hours so that he could obtain a place in the *Guinness Book of World Records* (Gulevich, Dement, and Johnson, 1966). After his ordeal the boy slept for a little less than 15 hours and awoke feeling fine. He slept slightly more than 10 hours the second night and just under 9 hours the third. Almost 67 hours were never made up. However, percentages of recovery were not equal for all stages of sleep. Only 7 percent of stages 1 and 2 were made up, but 68 percent of stage 4 slow-wave sleep and 53 percent of REM sleep were made up. Other studies (for example, Kales et al., 1970) have found similar results, which suggests that stage 4 sleep and REM sleep are more important than the other stages.

As I mentioned earlier, REM sleep will be discussed later. But what do we know about the possible functions of slow-wave sleep? What happens then that is so important? Both cerebral metabolic rate and cerebral blood flow decline during slow-wave sleep, falling to about 75 percent of the waking level during stage 4 sleep (Sakai et al., 1979; Buchsbaum et al., 1989; Maquet, 1995). In particular, the regions that have the highest levels of activity during waking show the highest levels of delta waves—and the lowest levels of activity—during slow-wave sleep. Thus, the presence of delta activity in a particular region of the brain appears to indicate that that region is resting. As we know from behavioral observation, people are unreactive to all but intense stimuli during slow-wave sleep and, if awakened, act groggy and confused—as if their cerebral cortex has been shut down and has not yet resumed its functioning. These observations suggest that during stage 4 sleep the brain is, indeed, resting.

A study by Bonnet and Arand (1996) provides further evidence for the restorative value of slow-wave sleep. They kept volunteers awake until 2:00 A.M., gave them either 400 mg of caffeine or a placebo, and then allowed them to sleep for approximately 3.5 h. Measurements indicated that although all subjects slept for the same amount of time, those who received caffeine obtained less of stage 4 slow-wave sleep—and these subjects performed more poorly on cognitive tests the next day. Presumably, the brains of the subjects who took the caffeine were less rested the next day because the drug had interfered with stage 4 sleep.

An inherited neurological disorder called **fatal familial insomnia** results in damage to portions of the thalamus (Sforza et al., 1995; Gallassi et al., 1996). The symptoms of this disease include deficits in attention and memory, followed by a dreamlike, confused state; loss of control of the autonomic nervous system and the endocrine system; and insomnia. The first signs of sleep disturbances are reductions in sleep spindles and K complexes. As the disease progresses, slow-wave sleep completely disappears and only brief episodes of REM sleep (without the accompanying paralysis) remain. As the name indicates, the disease is fatal. Whether the insomnia, caused by the brain damage, contributes to the other symptoms and to the patient's death is not known. In any case, as we shall see in the next section, when laboratory animals are kept awake indefinitely, they, too, will die.

Studies with Laboratory Animals. Until recently, sleep deprivation studies with animals have provided us with little insight into the role of sleep. Because animals cannot be "persuaded" to stay awake, it is especially difficult to separate the effects of sleep deprivation from those caused by the method used to keep the animals awake. We can ask a human volunteer to try to stay awake and can expect some cooperation. He or she will say, "I'm getting sleepy—help me to stay awake." However, animals are interested only in getting to sleep and must constantly be stimulated—and hence, stressed. Rechtschaffen and his colleagues (Rechtschaffen et al., 1983, 1989; Rechtschaffen and Bergmann, 1995) devised a procedure to control for the effects of forced exercise that are necessary to keep an animal from sleeping. They constructed a circular platform on which two rats lived, each restrained in a plastic cage. When the platform was rotated by an electrical motor, the rats were

fatal familial insomnia   A fatal inherited disorder characterized by progressive insomnia.

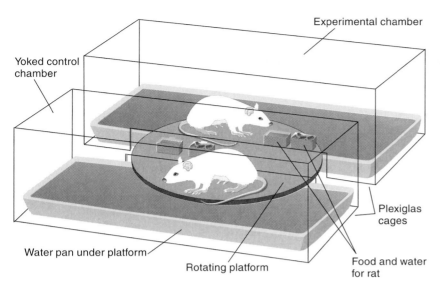

Yoked control chamber

Experimental chamber

Water pan under platform

Rotating platform

Plexiglas cages

Food and water for rat

Figure 9.6
The apparatus used to deprive rats of sleep. Whenever one of the pair of rats in the experimental chambers fell asleep, the turntable was rotated until the animal was awake for 6 seconds. (Redrawn from Rechtschaffen, A., Gilliland, M.A., Bergmann, B.M., and Winter, J.B. *Science*, 1983, 221, 182–184.)

forced to walk to avoid falling into a pool of water. (See *Figure 9.6.*)

The investigators employed a *yoked-control* procedure to deprive one rat of sleep but force both members of the pair to exercise an equal amount of time. (The term is used for any experiment in which two animals receive the same treatment at the same time, like two oxen fastened together with a yoke.) A computer recorded the EEGs and EMGs of both rats and detected both slow-wave and REM sleep. One rat served as the experimental (sleep-deprived) animal, and the other served as the yoked control. As soon as the EEG recording indicated that the experimental animal was falling asleep, the computer turned on the motor that rotated the disk, forcing both animals to exercise. Because the platform rotated whenever the experimental animal started to sleep, the procedure reduced the experimental animal's total sleep time by 87 percent. However, the sleep time of the yoked-control rat was reduced by only 31 percent.

Sleep deprivation had serious effects. The control animals remained in perfect health. However, the experimental animals looked sick and stopped grooming their fur. They became weak and uncoordinated and lost their ability to regulate their body temperature. (As we will see later, neurons involved in sleep also appear to be involved in thermoregulation.) Although they began eating much more food than normal, their metabolic rates became so high that they continued to lose weight. Eventually, the rats died. The cause of death is still not certain. The rats' brains appeared to be normal, and there were no obvious signs of inflammation or damage to other internal organs. The animals' levels of stress hormones were not unusually high,

so the deaths could not be attributed to simple stress. If they were given a high-calorie diet to compensate for their increased metabolic rate, the rats lived longer, but eventually they succumbed (Everson and Wehr, 1993). Everson (1995) suggested that the sleep deprivation may disrupt the immune system and, as a consequence, the animals develop toxic infections of the blood.

As we saw, the effects of sleep deprivation are less drastic in humans than in rats. Perhaps human sleep deprivation studies have just not continued long enough to cause serious harm. The human body is much larger than that of a rat, and changes in metabolic rate would take much longer to affect body weight—and prolonged sleep deprivation of human subjects would clearly be unethical.

Effects of Exercise on Sleep

Sleep deprivation studies with humans suggest that the brain may need slow-wave sleep in order to recover from the day's activities but that the rest of the body does not. Another way to determine whether sleep is needed for restoration of physiological functioning is to look at the effects of daytime activity on nighttime sleep. If the function of sleep is to repair the effects of activity during waking hours, then we should expect that sleep and exercise are related. That is, we should sleep more after a day of vigorous exercise than after a day spent quietly at an office desk.

However, the relation between sleep and exercise is not very compelling. For example, Ryback and Lewis (1971) found no changes in slow-wave or REM sleep of healthy subjects who spent six weeks resting in bed. If sleep repairs wear and tear, we would expect these people to sleep less.

Adey, Bors, and Porter (1968) studied the sleep of *completely* immobile quadriplegics and paraplegics and found only a small decrease in slow-wave sleep as compared with uninjured people.

Horne (1981, 1988) reported that some studies have found that exercise increases slow-wave sleep but others have not. He noted that an important factor seems to be the climate in which the exercise occurs. If the temperature and the humidity are high, the exercise is likely to increase slow-wave sleep. Horne suggested that the important variable might be whether the exercise succeeded in heating the body.

To test this hypothesis, Horne and Moore (1985) had subjects exercise on a treadmill. Some subjects were cooled by electric fans, and their skin was periodically sprayed with water. Their body temperature rose only 1° C. That night, the slow-wave sleep of the "hot exercised" subjects rose by 25 percent, whereas that of the "cool exercised" subjects was unchanged. Horne (1988) now believes that the increased body temperature itself is not the significant factor but that an increase in brain temperature is. Perhaps, he said, an increase in brain temperature raises its metabolic rate and hence its demand for more slow-wave sleep. A preliminary study suggests that this hypothesis may have some merit. Horne and Harley (1989) warmed subjects' heads and faces with a hair dryer, which raised their brain temperature by an estimated 1° C. Four of the six subjects showed an increase in slow-wave sleep the next night. Clearly, further research is needed.

Effects of Mental Activity on Sleep

If the primary function of slow-wave sleep is to permit the brain to rest and recover from its daily activity, then we might expect that a person would spend more time in slow-wave sleep after a day of intense cerebral activity. Indeed, as we just saw, that is precisely the way that Horne interpreted the effects of increased body temperature. First of all, tasks that demand alertness and mental activity *do* increase glucose metabolism in the brain, as measured by a PET scanner (Roland, 1984). The most significant increases are seen in the frontal lobes, where delta activity is most intense during slow-wave sleep. In an experiment that supports this interpretation, Kattler, Kijk, and Borbély (1994) stimulated a person's hand with a vibrator, which activated the contralateral somatosensory cortex. The next night, a recording of the subject's EEG showed more delta activity in that region of the brain. Presumably, the increased activity of the cortical neurons called for more rest during the following night's sleep.

In an ingenious study Horne and Minard (1985) found a way to increase mental activity without affecting physical activity and without causing stress. The investigators told subjects to show up for an experiment in which they were supposed to take some tests designed to measure reading skills. When the subjects turned up, however, they were told that the plans had been changed. They were invited for a day out, at the expense of the experimenters. (Not surprisingly, the subjects willingly accepted.) They spent the day visiting an art exhibition, a shopping center, a museum, an amusement park, a zoo, and an interesting mansion. After a scenic drive through the countryside they watched a movie in a local theater. They were driven from place to place and certainly did not become overheated by exercise. After the movie they returned to the sleep laboratory. They said they were tired, and they readily fell asleep. Their sleep duration was normal, and they awoke feeling refreshed. However, their slow-wave sleep—particularly stage 4 sleep—was increased.

● Sleep and Thermoregulation

As we have seen, prolonged sleep deprivation disrupts an animal's ability to regulate its body temperature. Berger and Phillips (1995) suggested that sleep and thermoregulation are closely linked processes. They hypothesized that sleep emerged as a response to the evolution of endothermy. Endothermic animals (*endo-*, "within"; *thermë*, "heat") warm their bodies with the heat produced by their metabolism—the so-called *homoiothermic*, or "warm-blooded" animals. *Poikilothermic* ("cold-blooded") animals do not really have cold blood, but they maintain their body temperature by absorbing heat from the environment. Thus, if the weather gets cold and they cannot find a sunny spot, their body temperature falls. The brains of endothermic animals have a sort of thermostat that detects when their body temperature gets too high or too low, and they have mechanisms to raise or lower their temperature (shivering, sweating or panting, and so on).

Endothermy is very costly, especially for small animals. Heat is primarily lost through the skin, and the smaller an animal is, the more skin it has, relative to its body mass. As a result, it must eat often to maintain a high rate of metabolism. Berger and Phillips suggested that sleep not only keeps an animal quiet so that it is not needlessly exercising, but it also provides an opportunity for the animal to lower its thermostat, thus reducing the number of calories it must expend to maintain its body temperature.

Many studies have shown that sleep and thermoregulation are closely related. As we saw, physical exercise that causes a person's body temperature to rise increases the amount of slow-wave sleep the next night—and so do warm baths (Horne and Reid, 1985). In addition, Morairty et al. (1993) found that rats exhibited more slow-wave sleep after they had spent some time in a warm, temperature-controlled chamber. In addition, as we shall see later in this chapter, the anterior hypothalamus and the adjacent preoptic area contain neural circuits involved in both sleep and thermoregulation.

How can we explain the relation between thermoregulation and sleep? Horne (1992) argued that the hypothesis that the primary function of sleep is to lower the body temperature and save energy does not seem plausible for animals as large as ourselves. Although a small rodent may save a considerable amount of energy by lowering its body temperature while it sleeps, a human who sleeps for 8 hours will expend only a little less energy than someone who sits quietly for the same amount of time: the calories contained in a small slice of bread. So far, the hypothesis that sleep permits the brain to rest and recover from a day's activity seems to have received the most support. Of course, a reduction in *brain* temperature may play an important role in that rest and recovery.

● The Functions of REM Sleep

Clearly, REM sleep is a time of intense physiological activity. The eyes dart about rapidly, the heart rate shows sudden accelerations and decelerations, breathing becomes irregular, and the brain becomes more active. It would be unreasonable to expect that REM sleep has the same functions as slow-wave sleep. An early report on the effects of REM sleep deprivation (Dement, 1960) observed that as the deprivation progressed, subjects had to be awakened from REM sleep more frequently; the "pressure" to enter REM sleep built up. Furthermore, after several days of REM sleep deprivation, subjects would show a **rebound phenomenon** when permitted to sleep normally; they spent a much greater-than-normal percentage of the recovery night in REM sleep. This rebound suggests that there is a need for a certain amount of REM sleep—that REM sleep is controlled by a regulatory mechanism. If selective deprivation causes a deficiency in REM sleep, the deficiency is made up later, when uninterrupted sleep is permitted.

How have investigators explained the occurrence of REM sleep? The similarities between REM sleep and waking have led some to suggest that REM sleep permits an animal to become more sensitive to its environment and avoid being surprised by predators (Snyder, 1966). (You will recall that during REM sleep humans are more sensitive to meaningful stimuli, such as the sound of their name.) Of course, given that an animal spends only a portion of its total sleep time in REM sleep, a predator would

have to come by at just the right time for its potential prey to hear it coming.

Other investigators have suggested that REM sleep has a special role in learning. Some investigators suggest that memories of events of the previous day—especially those dealing with emotionally related information—are consolidated and integrated with existing memories (Greenberg and Pearlman, 1974); others have suggested that this time is utilized to accomplish the opposite function—to flush useless information from memory, to prevent the storage of useless clutter (Crick and Mitchison, 1983, 1995). Another investigator (Jouvet, 1980) has suggested that REM sleep helps integrate learned and instinctive behaviors—it provides a time to modify the neural circuits controlling species-typical behaviors according to the experience gained in the past day. The fact that the sleep of infants consists mainly of REM sleep has suggested to others that this stage is associated with brain development (Roffwarg, Muzio, and Dement, 1966). The association could go either way; brain development could cause REM sleep (perhaps to tidy up after spurts of neural growth), or REM sleep could be setting the stage for brain growth to occur.

As you can see, many hypotheses have been advanced to explain the rather puzzling phenomenon of REM sleep. In the previous two paragraphs I mentioned four categories: *vigilance, learning* (either consolidation or flushing), *species-typical reprogramming*, and *brain development*. It is probably safe to say that when there are so many hypothetical explanations for a phenomenon, we do not know very much about its causes. So far, none of the hypotheses have been either unambiguously supported or proved wrong. REM sleep deprivation, imposed after a session of training, does impair learning—especially of complicated tasks—but the effect is not very large (McGrath and Cohen, 1978; Smith, 1985). Similarly, a training session does increase REM sleep—especially early in the sleep period. Thus, the learning hypothesis receives a certain amount of support. The vigilance and reprogramming hypotheses have not been developed enough to make specific predictions that can be tested experimentally.

The developmental hypothesis is supported by the fact that infant animals born with well-developed brains (such as guinea pigs) spend proportionally less time in REM sleep than infant animals born with less-developed brains (such as rats, cats, or humans). Researchers have long been struck by the fact that the highest proportion of REM sleep

rebound phenomenon   The increased frequency or intensity of a phenomenon after it has been temporarily suppressed; for example, the increase in REM sleep seen after a period of REM sleep deprivation.

is seen during the most active phase of brain development. Perhaps, then, REM sleep plays a role in this process. Studies of human fetuses and infants born prematurely indicate that REM sleep begins to appear 30 weeks after conception and peaks at around 40 weeks (Roffwarg, Muzio, and Dement, 1966; Petre-Quadens and De Lee, 1974; Inoue et al., 1986). Approximately 70 percent of a newborn infant's sleep is REM sleep. By six months of age, this proportion has declined to approximately 30 percent. By eight years of age, it has fallen to approximately 22 percent, and by late adulthood, it is less than 15 percent.

Mirmiran (1995) described a series of studies he and his colleagues performed with infant rats. They injected the rats with drugs that suppressed REM sleep during the second and third weeks of life and found that the animals showed behavioral abnormalities as adults. In addition, their cerebral cortexes and brain stems were smaller than those of control subjects. Marks et al. (1995) found that brain lesions that disrupted one of the phenomena of REM sleep (PGO waves, described later) also disrupted development of the animals' visual systems. Of course, we cannot be sure that the effects of the drugs or the brain lesions on brain development were caused by the REM sleep deprivation; the treatments may have had additional effects.

If the function of REM sleep is to promote brain development, why do adults have REM sleep? One possibility is that REM sleep facilitates the massive changes in the brain that occur during development but also the more modest changes responsible for learning that occur later in life. Studies with laboratory animals suggest that REM sleep performs functions that facilitate learning. Investigators have carried out two types of experiments. In the first, they train animals in a learning task and then deprive them of REM sleep for a period of time. If REM sleep facilitates learning—perhaps by promoting changes in the brain that store the information just acquired—then animals deprived of the opportunity to engage in REM sleep after the training session should not learn as well as control subjects. In the second type of experiment, investigators train animals in a learning task and then monitor their sleep for several hours. An increase in REM sleep suggests that learning increases the need for this stage of sleep.

Experiments of both types have obtained positive results. For example, when animals are deprived of REM sleep after participating in a training session, they learn the task more slowly; thus, REM sleep deprivation retards memory formation. Most investigators believe that a learning experience starts a process that results in structural and biochemical changes in the brain. Perhaps some part of this process requires REM sleep to operate most effectively. In fact, if animals are deprived of sleep at the appropriate time after a training session (for a rat, this usually occurs around 8 hours later), their performance will be poorer than that of animals permitted to obtain REM sleep (Smith, 1996).

In an example of the second type of experiment, Bloch, Hennevin, and Leconte (1977) gave rats daily training trials in a complex maze. They found that the experience enhanced subsequent REM sleep. Moreover, daily performance was related to subsequent REM sleep. The lower curve in Figure 9.7 shows REM sleep as a percentage of total sleep. The upper curve illustrates the animals' performance in the maze. You can see that the largest increase in running speed (possibly representing the largest increase in learning) was accompanied by the largest amount of REM sleep. Also note that once the task was well learned (after day 6), REM sleep declined to baseline levels. (See *Figure 9.7*.)

In contrast to the studies with laboratory animals, studies with human subjects show that REM sleep deprivation has only a small effect on a person's ability to learn or to remember what was previously learned. But several studies have found that learning can affect the amount of REM sleep a person obtains. For example, several studies found that retarded children engaged in less REM sleep than normal children and that intellectually gifted children engaged in more (Dujardin, Guerrien, and Leconte, 1990). In addition, Smith and Lapp (1991) found that REM sleep

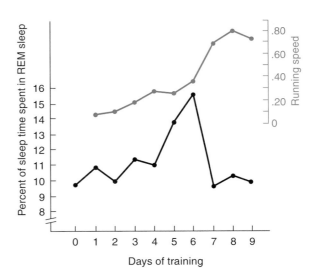

Figure 9.7
Percentage of sleep time spent in REM sleep (lower curve) *as a function of maze-learning performance* (upper curve). (From Bloch, V., Hennevin, E., and Leconte, P., in *Neurobiology of Sleep and Memory*, edited by R.R. Drucker-Colín and J.L. McGaugh. New York: Academic Press, 1978.)

of college students increased during exam time, when they presumably were spending more time learning new information.

As we saw, REM sleep seems to be regulated. If a person (or a laboratory animal) is deprived of REM sleep, he or she will show a rebound effect later when permitted to sleep undisturbed. In other words, going without REM sleep causes a REM deficit to accumulate, just as staying awake causes a general sleep deficit to accumulate. But what contributes to the REM deficit? It is possible that REM sleep and slow-wave sleep both help the brain rest and recuperate from the wear and tear caused by wakefulness. On the other hand, it is possible that only slow-wave sleep provides rest and recuperation but has some deleterious side effects—and that REM sleep provides an antidote for these side effects. In other words, it is possible that slow-wave sleep repairs the effects of waking and that REM sleep repairs the effects of slow-wave sleep. Benington and Heller (1994) suggested that, indeed, REM sleep serves slow-wave sleep, not waking. They noted that in healthy individuals, REM sleep does not occur until after a period of slow-wave sleep. In addition, the amount of REM sleep during a given night is related to the total time the person sleeps, not how long the person was awake the previous day. (See *Figure 9.8.*)

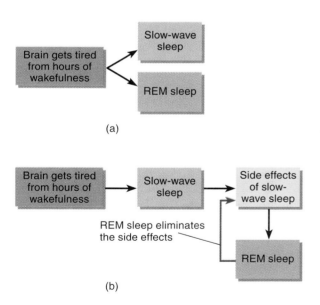

Figure 9.8
Two possible explanations for the relation between waking, slow-wave sleep, and REM sleep. (a) The wear and tear on the brain produced by wakefulness produces a need for both slow-wave sleep and REM sleep. (b) Wakefulness produces a need for slow-wave sleep, which, as it repairs this need, produces side effects that can be repaired only by REM sleep.

A particularly interesting case of brain damage suggests that whatever the functions of REM sleep may be, they do not appear to be necessary for survival. Lavie et al. (1984) reported that a 33-year-old man whose head was injured by shrapnel at age 20 engaged in almost no REM sleep. In the sleep laboratory the man slept an average of 4.5 hours. On three of eight nights he engaged in no REM sleep; the average on the other five nights was approximately 6 minutes. The pieces of metal damaged the pons, left temporal lobe, and left thalamus. As we shall see later in this chapter, the pons seems to be the part of the brain that controls REM sleep. The almost complete lack of REM sleep did not appear to cause serious side effects. After receiving his injury, the man completed high school, attended law school, and began practicing law. (I have a feeling that I could work in a lawyer joke here, but I think I'll refrain.)

Interim Summary

The two principal explanations for sleep are that sleep serves as an adaptive response or that it provides a period of restoration. The fact that a species' degree of safety and rate of metabolism are related to the amount of sleep it engages in supports the adaptive hypothesis, but the fact that all vertebrates sleep, including some that would seem to be better off without it, does not.

In humans, the effects of several days of sleep deprivation include difficulty performing tasks that require prolonged concentration, emotional changes, and perceptual distortions and (sometimes) mild hallucinations. These effects suggest that sleep deprivation impairs cerebral functioning. Deep slow-wave sleep appears to be the most important stage, and perhaps its function is to permit the brain (but not necessarily the rest of the body) to recuperate. Animals that are sleep-deprived eventually die. Their symptoms include increased body temperature and metabolic rate, voracious eating, weight loss, but no obvious signs of a stress response. Fatal familial insomnia is an inherited disease that results in degeneration of parts of the thalamus, deficits in attention and memory, a dreamlike state, loss of control of the autonomic nervous system and the endocrine system, insomnia, and death.

Exercise can increase the amount of slow-wave sleep a person receives, but only if the brain temperature rises; the effect can be abolished by cooling the person's head and face. Perhaps, then, the most important function of slow-wave sleep is to lower the brain's metabolism and permit it to rest. In support of this hypothesis, research has shown that increased mental activity can cause an increase in slow-wave sleep the next night. Some investigators have suggested that by causing a slight decrease in body temperature, sleep saves energy. However, this factor does not appear to be important in animals as large as ourselves.

The functions of REM sleep are even less understood than those of slow-wave sleep. REM sleep may promote vigilance, learning, species-typical reprogramming, or brain development. So far, the evidence is inconclusive, although several studies have shown a moderate relation between REM sleep and learning. It appears that REM sleep is a response to slow-wave sleep. Whatever functions it performs, it's absence, unlike that of slow-wave sleep, is not fatal.

PHYSIOLOGICAL MECHANISMS OF SLEEP AND WAKING

So far, I have discussed the nature of sleep, its functions, problems associated with it, and the control of biological rhythms. Now it is time to examine what researchers have discovered about the physiological mechanisms that are responsible for the behavior of sleep, and for its counterpart, alert wakefulness. But before doing so, I must emphasize that sleep does not occur simply because neurons get tired and begin to fire more slowly. Like other behaviors, sleep occurs when certain neural circuits become *active*.

● Chemical Control of Sleep

As we have seen, sleep is *regulated;* that is, if an organism is deprived of slow-wave sleep or REM sleep, the organism will make up at least part of the missed sleep when permitted to do so. In addition, the amount of slow-wave sleep that a person obtains during a daytime nap is deducted from the amount of slow-wave sleep he or she obtains the next night (Karacan et al., 1970). These facts suggest that some physiological mechanism monitors the amount of sleep that an organism receives. What might this mechanism be?

The most obvious explanation would be that the body produces either *sleep-promoting substances* during wakefulness or *wakefulness-promoting* substances during sleep. For example, a sleep-promoting substance might accumulate in the blood during wakefulness and be destroyed during sleep. The longer someone is awake, the longer he or she has to sleep in order to deactivate this substance. Obviously, because slow-wave sleep and REM sleep are mostly independent of each other, there would have to be two substances, one for each stage of sleep. As we saw earlier, Benington and Heller (1994) suggested that although slow-wave sleep may provide an opportunity for the brain

to rest, it creates its own need for REM sleep. Of course, the opposite could be true; sleep could be regulated by a *wakefulness-promoting* substance. This substance would be used up during wakefulness and be manufactured only during sleep. A *decline* in the blood level of this substance would cause sleepiness. (See *Figure 9.9.*)

Where might these substances be located? They do not appear to be found in the general circulation of the body. As we saw earlier, the cerebral hemispheres of the bottlenose dolphin sleep at different times (Mukhametov, 1984). If sleep were controlled by *blood-borne* chemicals, the hemispheres should sleep at the same time. This observation suggests that if sleep is controlled by chemicals, these chemicals are produced within the brain and act there. In a fifty-two-page article that cites over four hundred papers, Borbély and Tobler (1989) reported that the search for sleep-promoting substances within the brain had not yet yielded unambiguous results. And studies performed since that time have not yielded unambiguous results, either. Several different categories of chemicals affect sleep and wakefulness, but we cannot yet conclude that they are responsible for the insistent urge to sleep that inevitably comes after a long period of wakefulness.

An important category of drugs, the benzodiazepines, promotes sleep. In fact, they are widely used to treat insomnia. As we saw in Chapter 4, these drugs act on the benzodiazepine binding site located at the $GABA_A$ receptor. The existence of a special receptor suggests the existence of at least one endogenous ligand for this receptor, and this ligand could be involved in the control of sleep. However, no one has yet discovered a benzodiazepinelike substance whose concentration in the brain varies as a function of sleepiness.

A second category of drugs affects both sleep and body temperature. For example, anti-inflammatory drugs such as aspirin and ibuprofen reduce body temperature and interfere with sleep (Murphy et al., 1994), and a class of chemicals known as cytokines increases body temperature and produces drowsiness (Knefati et al., 1995; Krueger and Majde, 1995). As we saw earlier in this chapter, sleep and thermoregulation are closely related functions. It is possible that the anti-inflammatory drugs and the cytokines affect sleep indirectly, through their effects on body temperature.

Several peptides that appear to affect sleep have been extracted from the brain (Seifritz et al., 1995; De Lecea et al., 1996), but their role as endogenous sleep modulators is still unproved. As we saw earlier in this chapter, evidence seems to support the hypothesis that slow-wave sleep serves as a period of rest and recuperation for the brain. Presumably, increased mental activity makes the brain become "tired," and the brain displays more delta activity the fol-

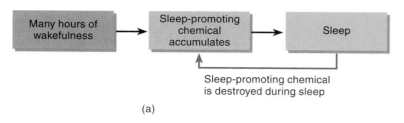

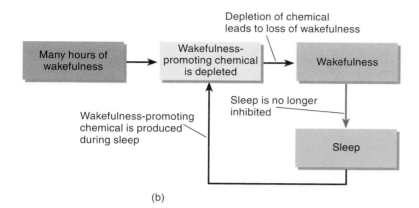

(a)

(b)

Figure 9.9
Hypothetical roles of chemicals in sleep. (a) A sleep-promoting chemical accumulates during wakefulness and is destroyed during sleep. (b) A wakefulness-promoting chemical is depleted during waking and is produced during sleep.

lowing night. But what, exactly, does it mean for the brain to become "tired"? The answer is that we do not yet know for certain, but Benington, Kodali, and Heller (1995) have suggested the following hypothesis: The primary nutrient of the brain is glucose, carried to it by the blood. The blood supply usually delivers an adequate amount of glucose, but if some regions of the brain become especially active, the cells located there consume the glucose faster than it can be supplied. In such cases, extra nutrients are supplied by astrocytes (Swanson, 1992; Swanson et al., 1992.). As we saw in Chapter 2, astrocytes maintain a small stock of nutrients in the form of glycogen, an insoluble carbohydrate that is also stocked by the liver and the muscles. The metabolism of glycogen causes an increase in the levels of adenosine, a neuromodulator that has inhibitory effects. Benington and his colleagues suggested that this accumulation of adenosine produces increased amounts of delta activity during the next night's sleep. The cells in that region rest, and the astrocytes renew their stock of glycogen. If wakefulness is prolonged, even more adenosine accumulates, producing the cognitive and emotional effects seen during sleep deprivation. In support of this hypothesis, the investigators found that when they administered a drug that stimulates adenosine receptors, they saw increases in delta activity during the animals' slow-wave sleep.

● Neural Control of Arousal

As we have seen, sleep is not a unitary condition but consists of several different stages with very different characteristics. Wakefulness, too, is nonuniform; sometimes we are alert and attentive, and sometimes we fail to notice much about what is happening around us. Of course, sleepiness has an effect on wakefulness; if we are fighting to stay awake, the struggle might impair our ability to concentrate on other things. But everyday observations suggest that even when we are not sleepy, our alertness can vary. For example, when we observe something very interesting (or frightening, or simply surprising), we feel ourselves become more activated and aware of our surroundings.

Experimental evidence suggests that the brain stem contains circuits of neurons that can increase an animal's level of alertness and activation—what is commonly referred to as *arousal*. In 1949 Moruzzi and Magoun found that electrical stimulation of the brain stem reticular formation produced arousal. The reticular formation, which occupies the central core of the brain stem, receives collateral axons from ascending sensory pathways. Presumably, sensory input, the event that normally produces arousal, activates the reticular formation by means of these collateral axons. The activated reticular formation then arouses the cerebral cortex by means of two pathways (Jones, 1990). The dorsal pathway projects to the medial and intralaminar nuclei of the thalamus, which in turn projects to the cerebral cortex; and the ventral pathway projects to the lateral hypothalamus, basal ganglia, and basal forebrain region. One part of the basal forebrain region projects extensively to the cerebral cortex, and another part projects to the hippocampus. (See *Figure 9.10*.)

At least three different systems of neurons play a role in some aspect of arousal and wakefulness: noradrenergic, acetylcholinergic, and serotonergic (Marrocco, Witte, and

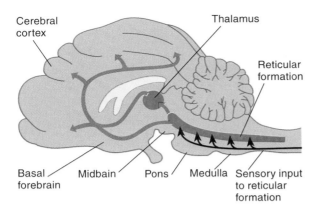

Figure 9.10
A midsagittal view of a cat brain, showing the reticular formation and its hypothesized role in arousal.

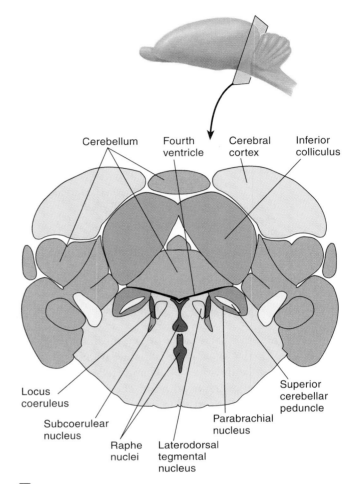

Figure 9.11
A section through the pons of a rat, showing the location of the locus coeruleus, which contains the cell bodies of most of the brain's noradrenergic neurons. Also shown are some structures that play a role in REM sleep, which is discussed later.
(Adapted from Paxinos, G., and Watson, C. *The Rat Brain in Stereotaxic Coordinates.* Sydney: Academic Press, 1982. Redrawn with permission.)

Davidson, 1994). Investigators have long known that catecholamine agonists such as amphetamine produce arousal and sleeplessness. These effects appear to be primarily mediated by the noradrenergic system of the **locus coeruleus,** located in the dorsal pons. Neurons of the locus coeruleus send axons that branch widely, releasing norepinephrine (from axonal varicosities) throughout the neocortex, hippocampus, thalamus, cerebellar cortex, pons, and medulla; thus, they potentially affect widespread and important regions of the brain. (See *Figure 9.11.*)

Aston-Jones and Bloom (1981a) recorded from noradrenergic neurons of the locus coeruleus (LC) across the sleep-waking cycle in unrestrained rats. As Figure 9.12 shows, these neurons exhibited a close relation to behavioral arousal. Note the decline in firing rate before and during sleep and the abrupt increase when the animal wakes. The rate of firing of neurons in the locus coeruleus falls almost to zero during REM sleep and increases dramatically when the animal wakes. As we shall see later in this chapter, these facts suggest that these neurons (along with serotonergic neurons) play a role in controlling REM sleep. (See *Figure 9.12.*)

Aston-Jones and Bloom (1981a, 1981b) found that although sudden environmental stimuli presented during sleep or quiet wakefulness increased the activity of noradrenergic LC neurons, the firing rate of these neurons was very low while the animals were performing activities that are normally accompanied by a high level of arousal, such as grooming or drinking sweetened water. In particular, the neurons became active when the experimenters presented stimuli that disrupted the animals' ongoing behavior. Stimuli that did not produce a behavioral change had little or no effect. The researchers suggested that these neurons showed the highest level of activity when the animals were *vigilant*—paying attention to stimuli in their environment.

In a subsequent study, Aston-Jones et al. (1994) recorded the electrical activity of noradrenergic LC neurons in monkeys. The monkeys watched stimuli on a video display. When one stimulus was presented (the S⁺), the monkeys would receive a sip of fruit juice if they moved a lever.

locus coeruleus *(sa **roo** lee us)* A dark-colored group of noradrenergic cell bodies located in the pons near the rostral end of the floor of the fourth ventricle; involved in arousal and vigilance.

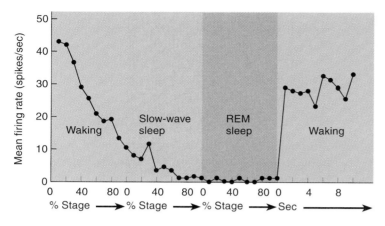

Figure 9.12
Activity of noradrenergic neurons in the locus coeruleus of freely moving cats during various stages of sleep and waking. (From Aston-Jones, G., and Bloom, F.E. *The Journal of Neuroscience*, 1981, *1*, 876–886. Copyright 1981, The Society for Neuroscience.)

When another stimulus was presented (the S⁻), responses were not reinforced. The investigators found that the noradrenergic neurons did not respond when the monkey made the lever response, when they sipped the fruit juice, or when the S⁻ was presented. However, the neurons showed a large burst of activity when the S⁺ was presented, about 200 ms prior to a response. (See *Figure 9.13.*) In addition, the monkeys performed best when the rate of firing of the LC neurons was high. After working for a long time at the task, the neurons' rate of firing fell—and so did the monkeys' performance. These results support the conclusion that the activation of LC neurons (and their release of norepinephrine) increases vigilance.

The second neurotransmitter involved in arousal is acetylcholine. Two groups of acetylcholinergic neurons, one in the pons and one located in the basal forebrain, produce activation and cortical desynchrony when they are stimulated (Jones, 1990; Steriade, 1996). Researchers have long known that acetylcholinergic antagonists decrease EEG signs of cortical arousal and that acetylcholinergic agonists increase them (Vanderwolf, 1992). Day, Damsma, and Fibiger (1991) used microdialysis probes to measure the release of acetylcholine in the striatum, hippocampus, and frontal cortex—three regions whose activity is closely related to an animal's alertness and behavioral arousal. They found that the levels of ACh in these regions were closely related to the animals' level of activity. In addition, Rasmusson, Clow, and Szerb (1994) electrically stimulated a region of the pontine reticular formation and found that the stimulation activated the cerebral cortex and increased the release of acetylcholine there by 350 percent (as measured by microdialysis probes). A group of acetylcholinergic neurons located in the basal forebrain forms an essential part of the pathway responsible for this effect. If these neurons were deactivated by an infusion of drugs

that interfere with axonal conduction or synaptic transmission, the activating effects of the pontine stimulation were abolished.

A third neurotransmitter, serotonin (5-HT) also appears to play a role in activating behavior. Almost all of the

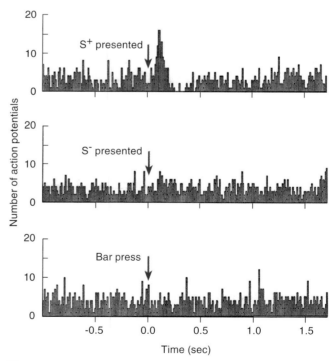

Figure 9.13
Firing rate of a noradrenergic neuron in a monkey's locus coeruleus while performing a vigilance task. Note that the neuron became more active immediately after the target was presented. (From Aston-Jones, G., Rajkowski, J., Kubiak, P., and Alexinsky, T. *Journal of Neuroscience*, 1994, *14*, 4467–4480.)

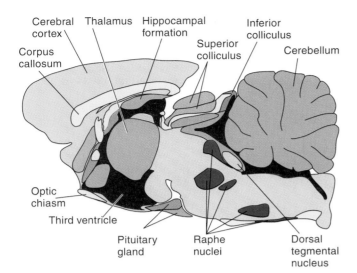

Figure 9.14
The raphe nuclei, the location of the cell bodies of most of the brain's serotonergic neurons.
(Adapted from Paxinos, G., and Watson, C. *The Rat Brain in Stereo-taxic Coordinates.* Sydney: Academic Press, 1982. Redrawn with permission.)

brain's serotonergic neurons are found in the **raphe nuclei,** which are located in the medullary and pontine regions of the reticular formation. (See *Figure 9.14.*) The axons of these neurons project to many parts of the brain, including the thalamus, hypothalamus, basal ganglia, hippocampus, and neocortex. Stimulation of the raphe nuclei causes locomotion and cortical arousal (as measured by the EEG), whereas PCPA, a drug that prevents the synthesis of serotonin, reduces cortical arousal (Peck and Vanderwolf, 1991). Unlike noradrenergic neurons, which increase their rate of firing during stressful situations, serotonergic neurons do *not* respond to external stimuli that produce pain or induce a stress response (Jacobs, Wilkinson, and Fornal, 1990).

Jacobs and Fornal (1993) suggested that one specific contribution of serotonergic neurons to activation is facilitation of continuous, automatic movements, such as pacing, chewing, and grooming. On the other hand, when animals engage in orienting responses to novel stimuli, the activity of serotonergic neurons decreases. Perhaps serotonergic neurons are involved in facilitating ongoing activities and suppressing impulsive responding that might disrupt them (Marrocco, Witte, and Davidson, 1994).

Figure 9.15 shows the activity of serotonergic neurons, recorded by Trulson and Jacobs (1979). As you can see, these neurons, like the noradrenergic neurons studied by

Aston-Jones and Bloom (1981a), were most active during waking. Their firing rate declined during slow-wave sleep and became virtually zero during REM sleep. However, once the period of REM sleep ended, the neurons temporarily became very active again. (See *Figure 9.15.*)

● Neural Control of Slow-Wave Sleep

Although sleep is a behavior that involves most of the brain, one region seems to be particularly important: the **basal forebrain region,** located just rostral to the hypothalamus. Nauta (1946) found that destruction of this area produced total insomnia in rats. The animals subsequently fell into a coma and died; the average survival time was only three days. McGinty and Sterman (1968) found that cats reacted somewhat differently; the animals did not become sleepless until several days after the lesion was made. Two of the cats, whose sleep was totally suppressed, died within ten days. Infusions of kainic acid into the basal forebrain region, which destroys cell bodies without damaging axons passing through the region, also suppresses sleep (Szymusiak and McGinty, 1986b).

The effects of these lesion experiments are corroborated by the effects of electrical stimulation of the basal forebrain region. Sterman and Clemente (1962a, 1962b) found that electrical stimulation of this region produced signs of drowsiness in the behavior and the EEG of unanesthetized, freely moving cats. The average latency period between the stimulation and the changes in the EEG was 30 seconds, but sometimes the effect was immediate. The animals often subsequently fell asleep.

A considerable amount of evidence suggests that forebrain mechanisms involved in sleep are closely linked to those involved in thermoregulation—an animal's ability to regulate its body temperature. Part of the basal forebrain, the preoptic area and the adjacent anterior hypothalamus—often referred to as the **POAH**—contains neurons involved in thermoregulation. Some of these neurons are directly sensitive to changes in brain temperature, and

raphe nuclei *(ruh fay)*   A group of nuclei located in the reticular formation of the medulla, pons, and midbrain, situated along the midline; contain serotonergic neurons.

basal forebrain region   The region at the base of the forebrain rostral to the hypothalamus; involved in thermoregulation and control of sleep.

POAH   The region of the preoptic area and the adjacent anterior hypothalamus, involved in thermoregulation and induction of slow-wave sleep.

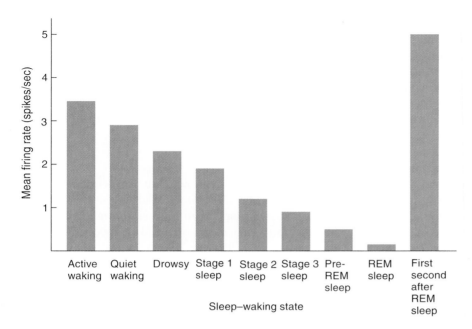

Figure 9.15
Activity of serotonergic (5-HT-secreting) neurons in the dorsal raphe nuclei of freely moving cats during various stages of sleep and waking.
(Adapted from Trulson, M.E., and Jacobs, B.L. *Brain Research*, 1979, *163*, 135–150. Redrawn with permission.)

some receive information from thermosensors located in the skin. Warming of the POAH, like electrical stimulation, induces slow-wave sleep (McGinty, Szymusiak, and Thomson, 1994). Thus, a more "natural" stimulation mimics the effects of electrical stimulation. In addition, many neurons in the POAH increase their rate of firing when the animal falls asleep, and most of them also do so in response to increases in body temperature (Scammell, Price, and Sagar, 1993; Alam, McGinty, and Szymusiak, 1995a, 1995b). The excessive sleepiness that accompanies a fever may be produced by this mechanism. And perhaps the connections between the thermosensors in the skin and the POAH account for the drowsiness and lassitude we feel on a hot day. (See *Figure 9.16*.)

As we saw earlier in this chapter, the most likely function of slow-wave sleep is to permit the brain to rest. As Horne and his colleagues showed, when people's brains are warmed during the day, they engage in more sleep the following night. And sleep appears to reduce brain temperature. You will recall that the cerebral hemispheres of dolphins take turns sleeping. Kolvalzon and Mukhametov (1982) found that the temperature of the sleeping hemisphere was always lower than that of the awake one. Furthermore, the injection of prostaglandins into the preoptic area raises body temperature and increases slow-wave sleep (Hayaishi, 1988), whereas drugs that inhibit the synthesis of prostaglandins (such as aspirin or ibuprofen) lower body temperature and reduce slow-wave sleep (Naito et al., 1988; Murphy et al., 1994).

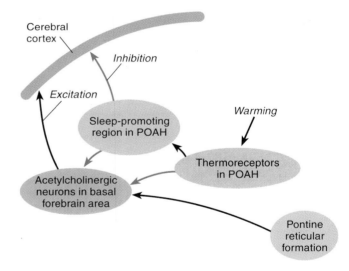

Figure 9.16
A schematic diagram of the role of the POAH in the sleep-promoting effects of warming and the wakefulness-promoting effects of the pontine reticular formation. The role of the thalamus is omitted for simplicity.

● Neural Control of REM Sleep

As we saw earlier in this chapter, REM sleep consists of desynchronized EEG activity, muscular paralysis, rapid eye movements, and (in humans, at least) increased genital activity. The rate of cerebral metabolism is as high as it is during waking (Maquet et al., 1990) and, were it not for the state of paralysis, the level of *physical* activity would also be high. In laboratory animals, REM sleep also includes *PGO waves*. **PGO waves** (for **p**ons, **g**eniculate, and **o**ccipital) are the first manifestation of REM sleep. They consist of brief, phasic bursts of electrical activity that originate in the pons and are propagated to the lateral geniculate nuclei and then to the primary visual (occipital) cortex. They can be seen only when electrodes are placed directly into the brain, so they have not been recorded in humans. It seems likely, however, that they occur in our species, too. Figure 9.17 shows the typical onset of REM sleep, recorded in a cat. The first sign of an impending bout of REM sleep is the presence of PGO waves—in this case, recorded from electrodes implanted in the lateral geniculate nucleus. Next, the EEG becomes desynchronized, and then muscular activity ceases and rapid eye movements commence. (See *Figure 9.17.*)

As we shall see, REM sleep is controlled by mechanisms located within the pons. The executive mechanism (that is, the one whose activity turns on the various components of REM sleep) consists of a group of neurons that secrete acetylcholine. During waking and slow-wave sleep, REM sleep is inhibited by the serotonergic neurons of the raphe nuclei and the noradrenergic neurons of the locus coeruleus.

The Executive Mechanism

Researchers have long known that acetylcholinergic agonists facilitate REM sleep. Stoyva and Metcalf (1968) found that people who have been exposed to organophosphate insecticides, which act as acetylcholine agonists, spend an increased time in REM sleep. In a controlled experiment with human subjects, Sitaram, Moore, and Gillin (1978) found that an ACh agonist (arecoline) shortened the interval between periods of REM sleep and that a cholinergic antagonist (scopolamine) lengthened it.

Jasper and Tessier (1969) analyzed the levels of acetylcholine that had been released by terminal buttons in the cat cerebral cortex. They found that the levels of ACh were highest during waking and REM sleep and were lowest during slow-wave sleep. Using 2-DG autoradiography in cats, Lydic et al. (1991) found that the rate of glucose metabolism was elevated in those regions of the brain that contain ACh-secreting neurons or that receive input from the axons of these neurons. As we saw earlier in this chapter, acetylcholinergic neurons play an important role in cerebral activation during alert wakefulness. The findings I just cited suggest that these neurons are also responsible for the cerebral activation seen during REM sleep.

The brain contains several groups of acetylcholinergic neurons. The ones that play the most central role in triggering the onset of REM sleep are found in the dorsolateral pons, primarily in the *pedunculopontine tegmental nucleus* (PPT) and *laterodorsal tegmental nucleus* (LDT) (Jones and Beaudet, 1987). Most investigators now refer to this region as the **peribrachial area,** because it is located in the region of the brachium conjunctivum. Figure 9.18 contains two drawings through the brain stem of a cat, prepared by

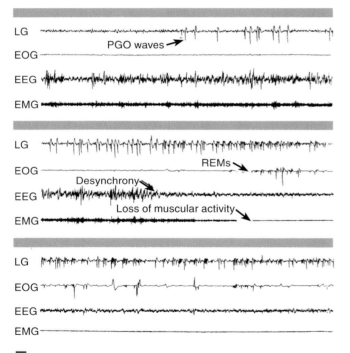

Figure 9.17
Onset of REM sleep in a cat. The arrows indicate the onset of PGO waves, EEG desynchrony, loss of muscular activity, and rapid eye movements. LG = lateral geniculate nucleus; EOG = electrooculogram (eye movements).
(Adapted from Steriade, M., Paré, D., Bouhassira, D., Deschênes, M., and Oakson, G. *Journal of Neuroscience,* 1989, 9, 2215–2229. Reprinted with permission.)

PGO wave Bursts of phasic electrical activity originating in the pons, followed by activity in the lateral geniculate nucleus and visual cortex; a characteristic of REM sleep.

peribrachial area *(pair ee **bray** kee ul)* The region around the brachium conjunctivum, located in the dorsolateral pons; contains acetylcholinergic neurons involved in the initiation of REM sleep.

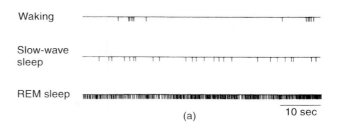

(a)

10 sec

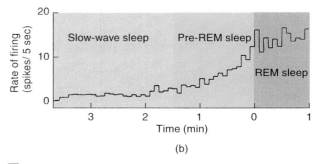

(b)

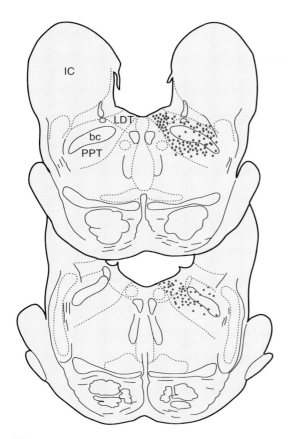

Figure 9.18
Acetylcholinergic neurons (colored circles) in the peribrachial area of the cat, as revealed by a stain for choline acetyltransferase. LDT = lateral tegmental nucleus; PPT = pedunculopontine tegmental nucleus; bc = brachium conjunctivum, IC = inferior colliculus.
(Adapted from Jones, B.E., and Beaudet, A. *Journal of Comparative Neurology,* 1987, *261,* 15–32. Reprinted with permission.)

Figure 9.19
Firing pattern of an acetylcholinergic REM-ON cell in the peribrachial area of the pons. (a) Action potentials during 60-min intervals during waking, slow-wave sleep, and REM sleep. (b) Rate of firing just before and after the transition from slow-wave sleep to REM sleep. The increase in activity begins approximately 80 sec before the onset of REM sleep.
(Adapted from El Mansari, M., Sakai, K., and Jouvet, M. *Experimental Brain Research,* 1989, 76, 519–529.)

Jones and Beaudet (1987). The locations of acetylcholinergic cell bodies (identified by a stain for choline acetyltransferase) are shown by colored circles. As you can see, these neurons surround the brachium conjunctivum (bc). (See *Figure 9.18.*)

Several studies (for example, El Mansari, Sakai, and Jouvet, 1989; Steriade et al., 1990; Kayama, Ohta, and Jodo, 1992) have shown that the activity of single neurons in the peribrachial area is related to the sleep cycle. Most of these neurons fire at a high rate during REM sleep or during both REM sleep and active wakefulness. Figure 9.19 shows the activity of a so-called *REM-ON* cell, which fires at a high rate only during REM sleep. As you can see, this neuron increased its activity approximately 80 sec before the onset of REM sleep. The increase in the activity of these acetylcholinergic cells may be the event that initiates a bout of REM sleep. (See *Figure 9.19.*)

Webster and Jones (1988) made lesions of the peribrachial area by infusing kainic acid into this region. They found that REM sleep was drastically reduced. The amount of REM sleep that remained was directly related to the number of cholinergic neurons that were spared. Figure 9.20(a) contains a photomicrograph through the pons of a normal cat, and part (b) that of a cat with a kainic acid lesion. Acetylcholinergic neurons show up as black granules. As you can see, very few of them remain in the cat with the lesion. (See *Figure 9.20.*)

Where do the acetylcholinergic neurons of the peribrachial area exert their effects? The axons of these neurons project to the medial pontine reticular formation; to several regions of the forebrain, including the thalamus, basal ganglia, preoptic area, hippocampus, hypothalamus, and cingulate cortex; and to several brain stem regions involved with the control of eye movements (Cornwall, Cooper, and Phillipson, 1990; Bolton, Cornwall, and Phillipson, 1993).

Let us examine the role of these connections. If a small amount of **carbachol,** a drug that stimulates acetylcholine

carbachol *(car ba call)* A drug that stimulates acetylcholine receptors.

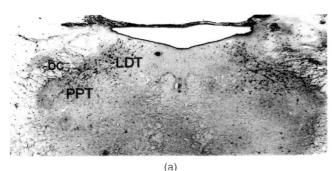

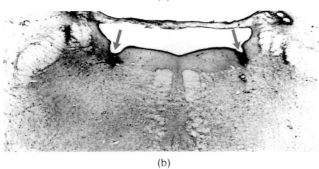

(a)

(b)

Figure 9.20
*Destruction of acetylcholine-secreting neurons in the pons.
(a) A section through the pons of an intact brain. (b) A section
through the pons after infusions of kainic acid. Acetylcholine-
secreting neurons show up as black spots in (a). LDT = lateral
tegmental nucleus; PPT = pedunculopontine tegmental nucleus;
bc = brachium conjunctivum.*
(From Jones, B.E., and Webster, H.H. *Brain Research,* 1988, 451,
13–32. Reprinted with permission.)

receptors, is infused into the region of the pons ventral to
the locus coeruleus, the animal will display some or all of
the components of REM sleep (Katayama et al., 1986;
Callaway et al., 1987). Some investigators refer to the general region of these infusions as the *mesopontine* (or *medial
pontine*) *reticular formation,* others call it the *nucleus reticularis pontis oralis (RPO),* and yet others call it the *giganto-
cellular tegmental field (FTG)* (Siegel, 1989). Unfortunately,
although the regions referred to by these names overlap,
the terms are not completely synonymous, which makes
for confusion when reading the research literature. I will
refer to the region as the **medial pontine reticular formation,** or **MPRF.** Carbachol is effective when infused into
the MPRF because it stimulates postsynaptic acetylcholine
receptors of neurons that receive projections from the
ACh cells of the peribrachial area (Quattrochi et al.,
1989). For this reason, this region is often referred to as
the *cholinoceptive* region of the MPRF (because it is *receptive* to ACh).

The critical cholinoceptive region of the MPRF—the region where infusions of carbachol produce all of the components of REM sleep—is still disputed. Reinoso-Suárez et
al. (1994) found that extremely small infusions of carbachol would produce REM sleep only in the ventral portion
of the MPRF in cats, while Shiromani et al. (1995) found
that somewhat larger infusions into the central and dorsal
MPRF were effective. As you might expect, lesions of the
MPRF, like those of the peribrachial area, reduce or abolish REM sleep (Siegel, 1989). (See *Figure 9.21.*)

If the acetylcholinergic neurons in the peribrachial area
of the pons are responsible for the onset of REM sleep, how
do they control each of its components, cortical arousal,
PGO waves, rapid eye movements, and muscular paralysis? As we saw, the acetylcholinergic neurons of the pons
comprise an integral part of the reticular activating system.
They send axons directly to regions of the thalamus that are

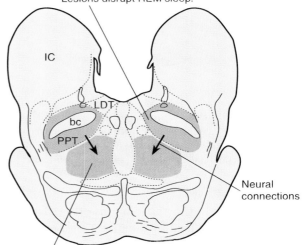

Peribrachial area contains
ACh-secreting neurons.
Lesions disrupt REM sleep.

IC

LDT

bc

PPT

Neural
connections

Medial pontine reticular formation (MPRF)
contains cholinoceptive cells. Infusions of
carbachol stimulate components of REM
sleep. Lesions disrupt REM sleep.

Figure 9.21
*A cross section through the pons of a cat, showing the locations
of the peribrachial area and the medial pontine reticular formation
(MPRF), regions involved in the control of REM sleep.*

medial pontine reticular formation (MPRF)   A region
that contains neurons involved in the initiation of REM
sleep; activated by acetylcholinergic neurons of the
peribrachial area.

involved in the control of cortical arousal. In addition, these neurons send axons to glutamergic neurons in the mesopontine reticular formation, which, in turn, send axons to the acetylcholinergic neurons of the basal forebrain. Activation of the forebrain neurons produces arousal and cortical desynchrony. PGO waves appear to be controlled by direct connections between the peribrachial area and the lateral geniculate nucleus (Sakai and Jouvet, 1980; Steriade et al., 1990). The control of rapid eye movements appears to be achieved by projections from the peribrachial area to the tectum (Webster and Jones, 1988).

The last of the REM-related phenomenon, muscular paralysis, is particularly interesting. As we will see, some patients with lesions in the brain stem fail to become paralyzed during REM sleep and thus act out their dreams. (This phenomenon is called *REM without atonia.*) The same thing happens—that is, assuming that cats dream—when a lesion is placed just caudal to the peribrachial area of the pons. Jouvet (1972) described this phenomenon:

> To a naive observer, the cat, which is standing, looks awake since it may attack unknown enemies, play with an absent mouse, or display flight behavior. There are orienting movements of the head or eyes toward imaginary stimuli, although the animal does not respond to visual or auditory stimuli. These extraordinary episodes . . . are a good argument that "dreaming" occurs during [REM sleep] in the cat. (Jouvet, 1972, pp. 236–237)

Jouvet's lesions destroyed a set of neurons responsible for the muscular paralysis that occurs during REM sleep. These neurons, which are activated by nonacetylcholinergic neurons, are located just ventral to the locus coeruleus—in the subcoerulear region. Their axons travel caudally to the **magnocellular nucleus,** located in the medial medulla (Sakai, 1980). Neurons in the magnocellular nucleus send axons to the spinal cord, where they form inhibitory synapses with motor neurons (Morales, Boxer, and Chase, 1987).

There is good evidence that this pathway is responsible for the atonia that accompanies REM sleep. Shouse and Siegel (1992) found that lesions of the subcoerulear region had no effect on REM sleep itself but abolished the atonia that accompanies it. Kanamori, Sakai, and Jouvet (1980) recorded from single neurons in the magnocellular nucleus in unrestrained cats and found that they became active during REM sleep. Sakai (1980) found that electrical stimulation of this nucleus caused paralysis in awake cats, and Schenkel and Siegel (1989) found that lesions of the magnocellular nucleus produced REM without atonia. Fort et al. (1990) found that the magnocellular nucleus contains glycine-secreting neurons, and this inhibitory transmitter substance is undoubtedly responsible for the inhibition of the motor neurons located in the spinal cord.

The fact that our brains contain an elaborate mechanism whose sole function is to keep us paralyzed while we dream—that is, to prevent us from acting out our dreams—suggests that the motor components of dreams are as important as the sensory components. Perhaps the practice our motor system gets during REM sleep helps us improve our performance of behaviors we have learned that day. The inhibition of the motor neurons in the spinal cord prevents the movements being practiced from actually occurring, with the exception of a few harmless twitches of the hands and feet.

As you will certainly appreciate, the neural circuitry controlling REM sleep is rather complicated. Figure 9.22 summarizes the evidence I have just reviewed. The first event preceding a bout of REM sleep appears to be activation of acetylcholinergic neurons in the peribrachial area of the dorsolateral pons. These neurons directly activate brain stem mechanisms responsible for rapid eye movements and trigger PGO waves through their connections with the lateral geniculate nucleus of the thalamus. They also activate neurons in the subcoerulear area that, through their connections with the nucleus magnocellularis of the medulla, produce atonia. Finally, these neurons activate neurons in the MPRF that, in turn, activate acetylcholinergic neurons of the basal forebrain responsible for the cortical activation that accompanies REM sleep. (See *Figure 9.22.*)

Why, you might ask, does an infusion of an ACh agonist such as carbachol into the MPRF induce REM sleep? After all, neurons in the MPRF seem to be directly involved in producing just one component of REM sleep—cortical activation. The other components of REM sleep are produced directly by neurons in the peribrachial area or the subcoerulear region. The answer seems to lie in the fact that neurons in the MPRF send axons to the peribrachial area (Reinoso-Suárez et al., 1994). Presumably, the activation of neurons in the MPRF with carbachol causes the neurons in the peribrachial region to be activated as well, triggering the rest of the components of REM sleep. (See *Figure 9.22.*)

As we saw earlier, when an animal (including a member of our own species) is deprived of REM sleep, it shows a rebound effect when the period of deprivation ends. Mallick,

magnocellular nucleus A nucleus in the medulla; involved in the atonia (muscular paralysis) that accompanies REM sleep.

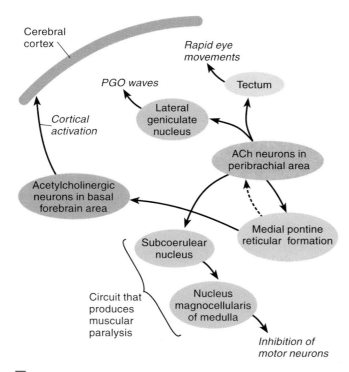

Figure 9.22

A summary of the neural circuitry thought to be responsible for REM sleep. The dashed arrow represents a connection from the MPRF to the peribrachial area that appears to be responsible for some of the phenomena of REM sleep produced by infusion of carbachol into the MPRF.

Siegel, and Fahringer (1989) placed recording electrodes next to "REM-on" neurons in the peribrachial area of the pons—that is, near those neurons that become active during REM sleep. They found that short-term REM sleep deprivation increased the activity of these neurons, even while the cats were awake. They suggested that this activity might represent the "REM pressure" that is responsible for the rebound effect. Of course, the experiment does not reveal *why* REM sleep deprivation makes these neurons become more active. When we find the answer to that question, we will learn more about the functions of REM sleep.

One of the factors (but certainly not the only one) that stimulates REM sleep is temperature. As we saw, brain temperature falls during slow-wave sleep; in fact, this fall in temperature (reflecting a decrease in metabolic activity of the brain) may even be one of the major functions of this phase of sleep. The fall in temperature appears to stimulate neurons responsible for REM sleep (Jouvet, 1975). The increased brain activity that occurs during REM sleep causes a rise in brain temperature, which then falls again during the subsequent period of slow-wave sleep.

Serotonin and Norepinephrine

As you will learn in a discussion of sleep disorders later in this chapter, serotonergic and noradrenergic agonists have inhibitory effects on REM sleep. In addition, the rate of activity in the serotonergic neurons of the raphe nuclei and the noradrenergic neurons of the locus coeruleus are at their very lowest levels during sleep. The patterns of firing of noradrenergic neurons of the locus coeruleus and the serotonergic neurons of the raphe nuclei were presented in Figures 9.12 and 9.15.

Evidence suggests that the activity of neurons in the locus coeruleus and the dorsal raphe nucleus normally inhibits REM sleep and that a reduction in the rate of firing of these neurons is the event that triggers a bout of REM sleep. For example, Figure 9.23 shows the very close linkage between the activity of a single unit in the dorsal raphe nucleus and the occurrence of PGO waves, the first manifestation of REM sleep (Lydic, McCarley, and Hobson, 1983). Note that the PGO waves occur only when the serotonergic neuron is silent. (See *Figure 9.23.*)

Anatomical and pharmacological studies provide further evidence. Acetylcholinergic neurons in the peribrachial area receive both serotonergic and noradrenergic inputs (Honda and Semba, 1994; Leonard et al., 1995). In addition, the cholinoceptive region of the MPRF also receives both serotonergic and noradrenergic inputs (Semba, 1993). Portas et al. (1996) infused a drug into the dorsal raphe nucleus that inhibits the release of serotonin. As a result, the animals exhibited a three-fold increase in REM sleep. Bier and McCarley (1994) found that infusions of a noradrenergic antagonist into the MPRF also causes an increase in REM sleep.

Several unanswered questions await further research. What makes the neurons of the locus coeruleus and the dorsal raphe nuclei become silent? Is there an excitatory input to the peribrachial area as well as the inhibitory ones whose activity *increases* at the beginning of REM sleep?

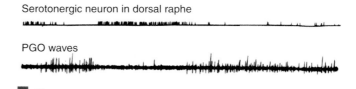

Serotonergic neuron in dorsal raphe

PGO waves

Figure 9.23

Activity of a single unit in the dorsal raphe nucleus. Note that the activity is inversely related to the occurrence of PGO waves, the first sign of REM sleep.

(Adapted from Lydic, R., McCarley, R.W., and Hobson, J.A. *Brain Research*, 1983, *274*, 365–370. Redrawn with permission.)

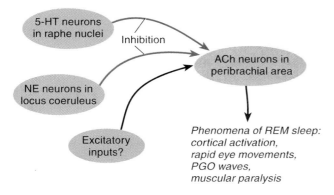

Figure 9.24
Interactions between serotonergic, noradrenergic, and acetyl-cholinergic neurons in the control of REM sleep.

Where is the pacemaker that controls the regular cycles of REM and slow-wave sleep, and how is this pacemaker connected to the REM sleep mechanisms in the pons? And finally, are rises and falls in brain temperature partly responsible for these cycles? (See *Figure 9.24*.)

Interim Summary

The fact that the amount of sleep is regulated suggests that sleep-promoting substances (produced during wakefulness) or wakefulness-promoting substances (produced during sleep) may exist. The sleeping pattern of the dolphin brain suggests that such substances do not accumulate in the blood. They may accumulate in the brain, but so far, attempts to find them have not been successful. One hypothesis suggests that adenosine, released when neurons are obliged to utilize the supply of glycogen stored in astrocytes, serves as the link between increased brain metabolism and the necessity of sleep.

Three systems of neurons appear to be important for alert, active wakefulness: the noradrenergic system of the locus coeruleus, involved in vigilance; the acetylcholinergic system of the peribrachial area of the pons and the basal forebrain, involved in cortical activation; and the serotonergic system of the raphe nuclei, involved in activation of automatic behaviors such as locomotion and grooming.

Slow-wave sleep occurs when neurons in the basal forebrain become active. These neurons are also sensitive to changes in temperature, leading some investigators to suggest that an important function of slow-wave sleep is to lower brain temperature (and permit the brain to rest). REM sleep occurs when the activity of acetylcholinergic

neurons in the peribrachial area increases. These neurons initiate PGO waves and cortical arousal through their connections with the thalamus, and they activate neurons in the MPRF whose axons travel to the acetylcholinergic neurons of the basal forebrain. The peribrachial neurons also produce rapid eye movements. Atonia (muscular paralysis that prevents our acting out our dreams) is produced by a group of acetylcholinergic neurons located in the subcoerulear nucleus that activate other neurons located in the magnocellular nucleus of the medulla, which in turn produce inhibition of motor neurons in the spinal cord. REM sleep, too, is related to temperature; it occurs only after the brain temperature has been lowered by a period of slow-wave sleep.

The noradrenergic neurons of the locus coeruleus and the serotonergic neurons of the raphe nuclei have inhibitory effects on pontine neurons responsible for REM sleep. Bouts of REM sleep begin only after the activity of the noradrenergic and serotonergic neurons ceases; whether this event is the only one to trigger REM sleep or whether direct excitation of acetylcholinergic neurons also occurs is not yet known.

DISORDERS OF SLEEP

Insomnia

Insomnia is a problem said to affect at least 20 percent of the population at some time (Raybin and Detre, 1969). At the outset I must emphasize that there is no single definition of insomnia that can apply to all people. The amount of sleep that individuals require is quite variable. A short sleeper may feel fine with 5 hours; a long sleeper may still feel unrefreshed after 10 hours of sleep. Insomnia must be defined in relation to a person's particular sleep needs. Some short sleepers have sought medical assistance because they thought that they were supposed to get more sleep, even though they felt fine. These people should be reassured that whatever amount of sleep seems to be enough *is* enough. Meddis, Pearson, and Langford (1973) reported the case of a 70-year-old woman who slept approximately 1 hour each day (documented by sessions in a sleep laboratory). She felt fine and was of the opinion that most people "wasted much time" in bed.

Ironically, one of the most important causes of insomnia seems to be sleeping medication. Insomnia is not a disease that can be corrected with a medicine, in the way that diabetes can be treated with insulin. Insomnia is a symptom. If it is caused by pain or discomfort, the physical ailment that leads to the sleeplessness should be treated. If it is secondary to personal problems or psychological disorders, these problems should be dealt with directly. Patients who receive a sleeping medication develop a tolerance to the drug and suffer rebound symptoms if it is withdrawn (Weitzman, 1981). That is, the drug loses its effectiveness, so the patient requests larger doses from the physician. If the patient attempts to sleep without the accustomed medication or even takes a smaller dose one night, he or she is likely to experience a withdrawal effect: a severe disturbance of sleep. The patient becomes convinced that the insomnia is even worse than before and turns to more medication for relief. This common syndrome is called **drug dependency insomnia.** Kales et al. (1979) found that withdrawal of some sleeping medications produced a rebound insomnia after the drugs were used for as few as three nights.

Most patients who receive a prescription for a sleeping medication are given one on the basis of their own description of their symptoms. That is, they tell their physician that they sleep very little at night, and the drug is prescribed on the basis of this testimony. Very few patients are observed during a night's sleep in a sleep laboratory; thus, insomnia is one of the few medical problems that physicians treat without having direct clinical evidence for its existence. But studies on the sleep of people who complain of insomnia show that most of them grossly underestimate the amount of time they actually sleep. The U.S. Institute of Medicine (1979) found that most insomniacs, even without sleeping medication, fall asleep in less than 30 minutes and sleep for at least 6 hours. *With* sleeping medication they obtained less than a 15-minute reduction in falling asleep, and their sleep length was increased by only about 30 minutes. Given the unfortunate side effects, sleeping medication does not seem to be worthwhile, except perhaps on a short-term basis.

For many years, the goal of sleeping medication was to help people fall asleep, and when drug companies evaluated potential medications they concentrated on that property. However, if we think about the ultimate goal of sleeping medication, it is to make the person feel more refreshed the next day. If a medication puts people to sleep right away but produces a hangover of grogginess and difficulty concentrating the next day, it is worse than useless. In fact, many drugs traditionally used to treat insomnia had just this effect. More recently, researchers have recognized that the true evaluation of a sleeping medication must be made the following day (Word Health Organization, 1991; American Psychiatric Association, 1994), and "hangover-free" drugs are finally being developed (Hajak et al., 1995).

A particular form of insomnia is caused by the inability to sleep and breathe at the same time. Patients with this disorder, called **sleep apnea,** fall asleep and then cease to breathe. (Nearly all people, especially people who snore, have occasional episodes of sleep apnea, but not to the extent that it interferes with sleep.) During a period of sleep apnea the level of carbon dioxide in the blood stimulates chemoreceptors (neurons that detect the presence of certain chemicals), and the person wakes up, gasping for air. The oxygen level of the blood returns to normal, the person falls asleep, and the whole cycle begins again. Fortunately, many cases of sleep apnea are caused by an obstruction of the airway that can be corrected surgically or relieved by a device that attaches to the sleeper's face and provides pressurized air that keeps the airway open (Sher, 1990; Westbrook, 1990).

● Problems Associated with REM Sleep

Narcolepsy (*narke* means "numbness," and *lepsis* means "seizure") is a neurological disorder characterized by sleep (or some of its components) at inappropriate times. The symptoms can be described in terms of what we know about the phenomena of sleep. The primary symptom of narcolepsy is the **sleep attack.** The narcoleptic sleep attack is an overwhelming urge to sleep that can happen at any time but occurs most often under monotonous, boring conditions. Sleep (which appears to be entirely normal) generally lasts for 2 to 5 minutes. The person usually wakes up feeling refreshed.

Another symptom of narcolepsy—in fact, the most striking one—is **cataplexy** (from *kata*, "down," and *plexis*, "stroke"). During a cataplectic attack a person will suddenly wilt and fall like a sack of flour. The person will lie there, *fully conscious*, for a few seconds to several minutes. What apparently happens is that one of the phenomena of REM sleep—muscular paralysis—occurs at an inappropriate time. As we saw, this loss of tonus is caused by massive inhibition of motor neurons in the spinal cord. When this

---

drug dependency insomnia   An insomnia caused by the side effects of ever-increasing doses of sleeping medications.

sleep apnea (*app nee a*)   Cessation of breathing while sleeping.

narcolepsy (*nahr ko lep see*)   A sleep disorder characterized by periods of irresistible sleep, attacks of cataplexy, sleep paralysis, and hypnagogic hallucinations.

sleep attack   A symptom of narcolepsy; an irresistible urge to sleep during the day, after which the person awakes feeling refreshed.

cataplexy (*kat a plex ee*)   A symptom of narcolepsy; complete paralysis that occurs during waking.

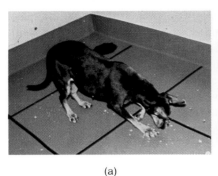  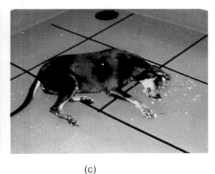

(a)   (b)   (c)

Figure 9.25
A dog undergoing a cataplectic attack triggered by its excitement at finding some food on the floor. (a) Sniffing the food. (b) Muscles beginning to relax. (c) Dog is temporarily paralyzed, as it would be during REM sleep.
(Photos courtesy of the Sleep Disorders Foundation, Stanford University.)

happens during waking, the victim of a cataplectic attack falls as suddenly as if a switch had been thrown.

Cataplexy is quite different from a narcoleptic sleep attack; cataplexy is usually precipitated by strong emotion or by sudden physical effort, especially if the patient is caught unawares. Laughter, anger, or an effort to catch a suddenly thrown object can trigger a cataplectic attack. In fact, as Guilleminault, Wilson, and Dement (1974) noted, even people who do not have cataplexy sometimes lose muscle strength after a bout of intense laughter. (Perhaps that is why we say a person can become "weak from laughter.") Common situations that bring on cataplexy are attempting to discipline one's children or making love (an awkward time to become paralyzed!).

REM sleep paralysis sometimes intrudes into waking, but at a time that does not present any physical danger—just before or just after normal sleep, when a person is already lying down. This symptom of narcolepsy is referred to as **sleep paralysis,** an inability to move just before the onset of sleep or upon waking in the morning. A person can be snapped out of sleep paralysis by being touched or by hearing someone call his or her name. Sometimes, the mental components of REM sleep intrude into sleep paralysis; that is, the person dreams while lying awake, paralyzed. These episodes, called **hypnagogic hallucinations,** are often alarming or even terrifying. (The term *hypnagogic* comes from the Greek words *hupnos,* "sleep," and *agogos,* "leading.")

Almost certainly, narcolepsy is produced by a brain abnormality that causes the neural mechanisms responsible for various aspects of REM sleep to become active at inappropriate times. Indeed, Rechtschaffen et al. (1963) found that narcoleptic patients generally skip the slow-wave sleep that normally begins a night's sleep; instead, they go di-

rectly into REM sleep from waking. This finding suggests that in the brains of narcoleptics, the neural mechanisms that produce REM sleep are poorly controlled.

Narcolepsy is primarily a genetic disorder, caused by one of two different mutations (Aldrich, 1992). Occasionally, the disorder can also be caused by brain damage (D'Cruz et al., 1994). Researchers have even successfully bred dogs that are afflicted with narcolepsy. (See **Figure 9.25.**) Slices of the dogs' brains do not show any obvious abnormalities in brain structure, but Nishino et al. (1994, 1995) found that acetylcholinergic neurons involved in control of REM sleep in these animals were more excitable than those in normal brains. Another study (Nitz et al., 1995) found that the brains of narcoleptic dogs contained a larger number of these neurons.

The symptoms of narcolepsy can be successfully treated with drugs. As we saw, both noradrenergic and serotonergic neurons exert inhibitory control over the acetylcholinergic neurons in the peribrachial area. Sleep attacks are diminished by stimulants such as amphetamine, a catecholamine agonist. The REM sleep phenomena (cataplexy, sleep paralysis, and hypnagogic hallucinations) can be alleviated by antidepressant drugs, which facilitate both serotonergic and noradrenergic activity (Mitler, 1994; Hublin, 1996). Often, the drugs are given together.

Several years ago, Schenck et al. (1986) reported the existence of an interesting disorder. The formal name is *REM*

sleep paralysis   A symptom of narcolepsy; paralysis occurring just before a person falls asleep.

hypnagogic hallucination (*hip na gah jik*)   A symptom of narcolepsy; vivid dreams that occur just before a person falls asleep; accompanied by sleep paralysis.

sleep behavior disorder, but a better name is **REM without atonia.** (*Atonia* refers to the lack of muscular activity seen during paralysis.) As you now know, REM sleep is accompanied by paralysis. Despite the fact that the motor cortex and subcortical motor systems are extremely active (McCarley and Hobson, 1979), people are unable to move at this time. The fact that they are dreaming suggests the possibility that but for the paralysis, they would act out their dreams. Indeed, they would. The behavior of people who exhibit REM without atonia corresponds with the contents of their dreams. Consider the following case:

> I was a halfback playing football, and after the quarterback received the ball from the center he lateraled it sideways to me and I'm supposed to go around end and cut back over tackle and—this is very vivid—as I cut back over tackle there is this big 280-pound tackle waiting, so I, according to football rules, was to give him my shoulder and bounce him out of the way . . . when I came to I was standing in front of our dresser and I had [gotten up out of bed and run and] knocked lamps, mirrors and everything off the dresser, hit my head against the wall and my knee against the dresser. (Schenck et al., 1986, p. 294)

Like narcolepsy, REM without atonia appears to be an inherited disorder (Schenck et al., 1996). In addition, it can be caused by brain damage—apparently, to the pathway between the subcoerulear region to the magnocellular nucleus (Culebras and Moore, 1989). The symptoms of REM without atonia are the opposite of those of cataplexy; that is, rather than exhibit paralysis outside REM sleep, patients with REM without atonia *fail* to exhibit paralysis *during* REM sleep. As you might expect, the drugs used to treat the symptoms of cataplexy will aggravate the symptoms of REM without atonia (Schenck and Mahowald, 1992). REM without atonia is usually treated by clonazepam, a benzodiazepine (Schenck, Hurwitz, and Mahowald, 1993).

● Problems Associated with Slow-Wave Sleep

Some maladaptive behaviors occur during slow-wave sleep, especially during its deepest phase, stage 4. These behaviors include bedwetting (*nocturnal enuresis*), sleepwalking (*somnambulism*), and night terrors (*pavor nocturnus*). All three events occur most frequently in children. Often bedwetting can be cured by training methods, such as having a special electronic circuit ring a bell when the first few drops of urine are detected in the bed sheet (a few drops usually precede the ensuing flood). Night terrors consist of anguished screams, trembling, a rapid pulse, and usually no memory for what caused the terror. Night terrors and somnambulism usually cure themselves as the child gets

older. Neither of these phenomena is related to REM sleep; a sleepwalking person is *not* acting out a dream. Most authorities firmly advise that the best treatment for these two disorders is no treatment at all. There is no evidence that they are associated (at least in childhood) with mental disorders or personality variables.

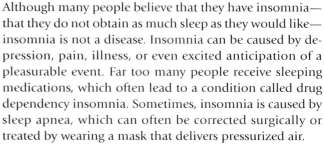

Interim Summary

Although many people believe that they have insomnia—that they do not obtain as much sleep as they would like—insomnia is not a disease. Insomnia can be caused by depression, pain, illness, or even excited anticipation of a pleasurable event. Far too many people receive sleeping medications, which often lead to a condition called drug dependency insomnia. Sometimes, insomnia is caused by sleep apnea, which can often be corrected surgically or treated by wearing a mask that delivers pressurized air.

Narcolepsy is characterized by four symptoms. *Sleep attacks* consist of overwhelming urges to sleep for a few minutes. *Cataplexy* is sudden paralysis, during which the person remains conscious. *Sleep paralysis* is similar to cataplexy, but it occurs just before sleep or on waking. *Hypnagogic hallucinations* are dreams that occur during periods of sleep paralysis, just before a night's sleep. Sleep attacks are treated with stimulants such as amphetamine, and the other symptoms are treated with serotonin agonists. Studies with narcoleptic dogs suggest that the disorder may involve biochemical abnormalities in the brain. Another disorder associated with REM sleep, REM without atonia, is a genetic disorder that can also be produced by damage to brain stem mechanisms that produce paralysis during REM sleep.

During slow-wave sleep, especially during stage 4, some people are afflicted by bedwetting (nocturnal enuresis), sleepwalking (somnambulism), or night terrors (pavor nocturnus). These problems are most common in children, who usually outgrow them. Only if they occur in adults do they suggest the existence of a physical or psychological disorder.

BIOLOGICAL CLOCKS

Much of our behavior follows regular rhythms. For example, we saw that the stages of sleep are organized around a 90-minute cycle of REM and slow-wave sleep. The same

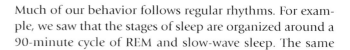

REM without atonia *(ay **tone** ee a)* A neurological disorder in which the person does not become paralyzed during REM sleep and thus acts out dreams.

rhythm continues during the day as the basic rest–activity cycle (BRAC). And, of course, our daily pattern of sleep and waking follows a 24-hour cycle. Finally, many animals display seasonal breeding rhythms in which reproductive behaviors and hormone levels show yearly fluctuations. In recent years investigators have learned much about the neural mechanisms responsible for these rhythms.

● Circadian Rhythms and Zeitgebers

Daily rhythms in behavior and physiological processes are found throughout the plant and animal world. These cycles are generally called **circadian rhythms.** (*Circa* means "about," and *dies* means "day"; therefore, a circadian rhythm is one that varies on a cycle of approximately 24 hours.) Some of these rhythms are passive responses to changes in illumination. However, other rhythms are controlled by mechanisms within the organism—by "internal clocks." For example, Figure 9.26 shows the activity of a rat during various conditions of illumination. Each horizontal line represents 24 hours. Vertical tick marks represent the animal's activity in a running wheel. The upper portion of the figure shows the activity of the rat during a normal day-night cycle, with alternating 12-hour periods of light and dark. Notice that the animal is active during the night, which is normal for a rat. (See *Figure 9.26.*)

Next, the dark-light cycle was shifted by 6 hours; the animal's activity cycle quickly followed the change. (See *Figure 9.26.*) Finally, dim lights were left on continuously. The cyclical pattern in the rat's activity remained. Because there were no cycles of light and dark in the rat's environment, the source of rhythmicity must be located within the animal; that is, the animal must possess an internal, biological clock. You can see that the rat's clock was not set precisely to 24 hours; when the illumination was held constant, the clock ran a bit slow. The animal began its bout of activity almost one hour later each day. (See *Figure 9.26.*)

The phenomenon illustrated in Figure 9.26 is typical of the circadian rhythms shown by many species. A free-running clock, with a cycle a little longer than 24 hours, controls some biological functions—in this case, motor activity. Regular daily variation in the level of illumination (that is, sunlight and darkness) normally keeps the clock adjusted to 24 hours. Light serves as a **zeitgeber** (German for "time giver"); it synchronizes the endogenous rhythm. Studies with many species of animals have shown that if they are maintained in constant darkness (or constant dim light), a brief period of bright light will reset their internal clock, advancing or retarding it, depending upon when the light flash occurs (Aschoff, 1979). For example, if an animal is exposed to bright light soon after dusk, the biolog-

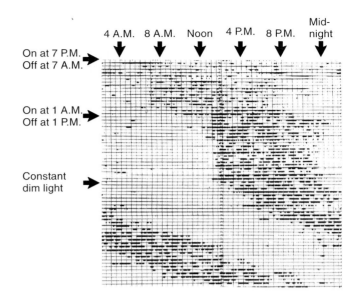

Figure 9.26

Wheel-running activity of a rat. Note that the animal's activity occurs at "night" (that is, during the 12 hours the light is off) and that the active period is reset when the light period is changed. When the animal is maintained in constant dim illumination, it displays a free-running activity cycle of approximately 25 hours. (From Groblewski, T.A., Nuñez, A., and Gold, R.M. Paper presented at the meeting of the Eastern Psychological Association, April 1980.)

ical clock is set back to an earlier time—as if dusk had not yet arrived. On the other hand, if the light occurs late at night, the biological clock is set ahead to a later time—as if dawn had already come.

Like other animals, humans exhibit circadian rhythms. Our normal period of inactivity begins several hours after the start of the dark portion of the day–night cycle and persists for a variable amount of time into the light portion. Without the benefits of modern civilization we would probably go to sleep earlier and get up earlier than we do; we use artificial lights to delay our bedtime and window shades to extend our time for sleep. Under constant illumination our biological clocks will run free, gaining or losing time like a watch that runs too slow or too fast. Different people have different cycle lengths, but most people in that situation will begin to live a "day" that is ap-

circadian rhythm (*sur* **kay** *dee un* or *sur ka* **dee** *un*)   A daily rhythmical change in behavior or physiological process.

zeitgeber (*tsite gay ber*)   A stimulus (usually the light of dawn) that resets the biological clock responsible for circadian rhythms.

proximately 25 hours long. This works out quite well, because the morning light, acting as a zeitgeber, simply resets the clock.

● The Suprachiasmatic Nucleus

Role of the SCN

Researchers working independently in two laboratories (Moore and Eichler, 1972; Stephan and Zucker, 1972) discovered that the primary biological clock of the rat is located in the **suprachiasmatic nucleus (SCN)** of the hypothalamus; they found that lesions disrupted circadian rhythms of wheel running, drinking, and hormonal secretion. The SCN also provides the primary control over the timing of sleep cycles. Rats are nocturnal animals; they sleep during the day and forage and feed at night. Lesions of the SCN abolish this pattern; sleep occurs in bouts randomly dispersed throughout both day and night (Ibuka and Kawamura, 1975; Stephan and Nuñez, 1977). However, rats with SCN lesions still obtain the same amount of sleep that normal animals do. The lesions disrupt the circadian pattern but do not affect the total amount of sleep.

Figure 9.27 shows the suprachiasmatic nuclei in a cross section through the hypothalamus of a mouse; they appear as two clusters of dark-staining neurons at the base of the brain, just above the optic chiasm. (See *Figure 9.27.*) The suprachiasmatic nuclei of the rat consist of approximately ten thousand small neurons, tightly packed into a volume of between 0.1 and 0.3 mm^3 (Meijer and Rietveld, 1989).

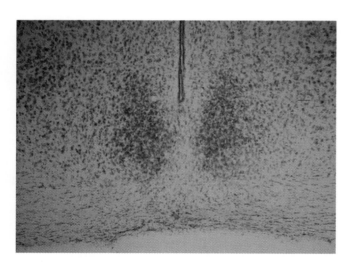

Figure 9.27
A cross section through a rat brain, showing the location and appearance of the suprachiasmatic nuclei. Cresyl violet stain.
(Courtesy of Geert DeVries, University of Massachusetts.)

The dendrites of these neurons form synapses with one another—a phenomenon that is found only in this part of the hypothalamus and that probably relates to the special function of these nuclei. A group of neurons is found clustered around the capillaries that serve the SCN. These neurons contain a large amount of rough endoplasmic reticulum, which suggests that they may be neurosecretory cells (Card, Riley, and Moore, 1980; Moore, Card, and Riley, 1980). Thus, some of the control that the SCN exerts over other parts of the brain may be accomplished by the secretion of neuromodulators.

Because light is the primary zeitgeber for most mammals' activity cycles, we would expect that the SCN receives fibers from the visual system. Indeed, anatomical studies have revealed a direct projection of fibers from the retina to the SCN: the *retinohypothalamic pathway* (Hendrickson, Wagoner, and Cowan, 1972; Aronson et al., 1993). If you look carefully at Figure 9.27, you can see small dark spots within the optic chiasm, just ventral and medial to the base of the SCN; these are cell bodies of oligodendroglia that serve axons that enter the SCN and provide information from the retina. (See *Figure 9.27.*)

Investigators do not yet know the nature of the photoreceptors in the retina that provide photic information to the SCN. Studies with the *rd/rd* mouse suggest that the photosensitive cells may be some form of cone. These mice have a genetic disorder that causes degeneration of retinal photoreceptors: total degeneration of rods and near-total degeneration of cones. Notwithstanding this loss of photoreceptors, the circadian rhythms of *rd/rd* mice—who are blind—are still as sensitive to light as those of normal mice (Foster et al., 1991; Jiminez et al., 1996). It is possible that the information is provided by some as-yet undiscovered photoreceptor.

Pulses of light that reset an animal's circadian rhythm also trigger the production of Fos protein in the SCN, which indicates that the light initiates a period of neural activity in this nucleus (Rusak et al., 1990, 1992). (The significance of the Fos protein as an indicator of neural activation was discussed in Chapter 5.) The synaptic connections between the retina and the SCN appear to be glutamatergic; drugs that block glutamate receptors prevent a period of bright light from stimulating Fos production and resetting circadian rhythms (Abe, Rusak, and Robertson, 1991; Vindlacheruvu et al., 1992). (See *Figure 9.28.*)

suprachiasmatic nucleus (SCN) *(soo pra ky az **mat** ik)*
A nucleus situated atop the optic chiasm. It contains a biological clock responsible for organizing many of the body's circadian rhythms.

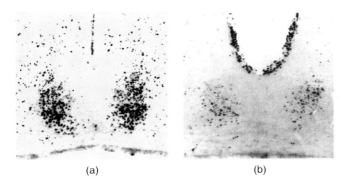

(a)   (b)

Figure 9.28
A cross section through the suprachiasmatic nuclei of two hamster brains stained for the Fos protein. The animals received an injection into the third ventricle 10 minutes before being presented with a pulse of light. (a) Control animal, who received an injection of a placebo. (b) Experimental animal, who received an injection of a drug that blocks glutamate receptors.
(From Vindlacheruvu, R.R., Ebling, F.J.P., Maywood, E.S., and Hastings, M.H. *European Journal of Neuroscience*, 1992, 4, 673–679. Reprinted with permission.)

Besides receiving visual information directly from the retina via the retinohypothalamic pathway, the SCN also receives such information indirectly, from the **intergeniculate leaflet (IGL),** a part of the lateral geniculate nucleus (Aronson et al., 1993; Moore and Card, 1994). (You will recall from Chapter 6 that the *dorsal* lateral geniculate nucleus sends visual information to the striate cortex.) The IGL receives photic information from the retina; in fact, the axons of the retinohypothalamic pathway divide near the optic chiasm and send one collateral to the SCN and another to the IGL. The terminal buttons of the neurons that connect the IGL to the SCN co-release GABA and a substance called **neuropeptide Y**. The connection between the IGL and the SCN (the *geniculohypothalamic pathway*) appears to play a role in resetting circadian rhythms; electrical stimulation of the IGL leaflet or microinfusion of neuropeptide Y directly into the SCN shifts the timing of circadian rhythms (Albers and Ferris, 1984; Rusak, Meijer, and Harrington, 1989). Damage to the geniculohypothalamic pathways reduces, but does not abolish, the effects of changes in the light-dark cycle on an animal's circadian rhythms (Harrington and Rusak, 1986). Thus, both the direct pathway from the retina to the SCN and the indirect pathway through the thalamus mediate the effects of light as a zeitgeber.

Evidence suggests that the IGL plays a special role in mediating the effects of zeitgebers other than light. Although light is the most potent stimulus for resetting circadian rhythms, other environmental stimuli, such as loud noises or sudden changes in temperature, can do so, too. In addition, an animal's own activity can affect its circadian rhythm. For example, if a hamster is suddenly given access to a running wheel, its burst of activity in the wheel will advance or retard the animal's circadian rhythm, according to the time of day during which the access occurs (Reebs and Mrosovski, 1989; Wickland and Turek, 1991). Wickland and Turek (1994) found that this effect was abolished by lesions of the IGL. Thus, it appears that the geniculohypothalamic tract connecting the IGL with the SCN is the sole pathway for at least one zeitgeber. More recently, Amir and Stewart (1996) found that zeitgebers could be classically conditioned. They found that after a neutral stimulus had been paired with bright lights, this stimulus could itself serve as a zeitgeber, provoking the production of Fos in the SCN and resetting circadian activity rhythms. It would be interesting to see whether damage to the IGL would disrupt this effect, too.

How does the SCN control drinking, eating, sleep cycles, and hormone secretion? Neurons of the SCN project caudally to the midbrain and to other hypothalamic nuclei, dorsally to other diencephalic regions, and rostrally to other hypothalamic nuclei and to the septum. If all of these connections are severed by large semicircular knife cuts around most of the SCN, circadian rhythms are disrupted (Meijer and Rietveld, 1989). However, we cannot conclude that the effects result from damage to efferent axons of the SCN. For one thing, knife cuts do not simply sever axons; they also cut blood vessels and interrupt patterns of blood flow. In addition, transplantation studies suggest that the control that the SCN exerts over some functions may be mediated by the secretion of chemical signals.

Lehman et al. (1987) destroyed the SCN and then transplanted in their place a new set of suprachiasmatic nuclei obtained from donor animals. The grafts succeeded in reestablishing circadian rhythms, even though very few efferent connections were observed between the graft and the recipient's brain. More recent studies have shown that the transplant need not even be placed in the normal location of the SCN. Aguilar-Roblero et al. (1994) found that SCN tissue restored circadian rhythms in a recipient animal if it was transplanted into the lateral ventricle, dorsal

intergeniculate leaflet (IGL)   A part of the lateral geniculate nucleus that receives information from the retina and projects to the SCN.

neuropeptide Y   A peptide released by the terminals of the neurons that project from the IGL to the SCN.

third ventricle, or caudal third ventricle adjacent to the cerebral aqueduct. The fact that the placement of the transplant was not critical suggests that the circadian rhythms may be controlled by chemicals secreted by the SCN tissue and carried to the critical regions of the brain through the cerebrospinal fluid. But the most convincing evidence comes from a transplantation study by Silver et al. (1996). Silver and her colleagues first destroyed the SCN in a group of hamsters, abolishing their circadian rhythms. Then, a few weeks later, they removed SCN tissue from donor animals and placed it in semipermeable capsules, which they then implanted in the animals' third ventricles. Nutrients and other chemicals could pass through the walls of the capsules, keeping the SCN tissue alive, but the neurons inside the capsules were not able to establish synaptic connections with the surrounding tissue. Nevertheless, the transplants re-established circadian rhythms in the recipient animals.

The Nature of the Clock

All clocks must have a time base. Mechanical clocks use flywheels or pendulums; electronic clocks use quartz crystals. The SCN, too, must contain a physiological mechanism that parses time into units. After years of research, investigators are finally beginning to discover the nature of the biological clock in the SCN.

First, let us examine some evidence that the SCN does, in fact, contain a clock. So far, we have seen that zeitgebers act through their connections with the SCN. We have also seen that circadian rhythms require that the animal have an intact SCN or a transplant placed in or near the lateral or third ventricles. However, I have not yet described evidence that proves that a clock is located there—the clock could be located elsewhere but fail to run unless it is exposed to chemicals secreted by the SCN.

Several studies have demonstrated daily activity rhythms in the SCN, which indicates that the circadian clock is located there. A study by Schwartz and Gainer (1977) nicely demonstrated day–night fluctuations in the activity of the SCN. These investigators injected rats with radioactive 2-deoxyglucose (2-DG). As you will recall from Chapter 5, this chemical is structurally similar to ordinary glucose; thus, it is taken up by cells that are metabolically active. However, it cannot be utilized, nor can it leave the cell. Therefore, metabolically active cells will accumulate radioactivity.

Schwartz and Gainer injected some rats with radioactive 2-DG during the day and injected others at night. The animals were then killed, and autoradiographs of cross sections through the brain were prepared. Figure 9.29 shows photographs of two of these cross sections. Note the evi-

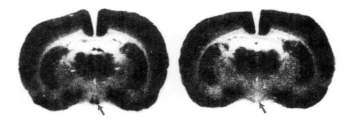

Figure 9.29

Autoradiographs of cross sections through the brains of rats that had been injected with carbon 14-labeled 2-deoxyglucose during the day (left) *and the night* (right). *The dark region at the base of the brain* (arrows) *indicates increased metabolic activity of the suprachiasmatic nuclei.*
(From Schwartz, W.J., and Gainer, H. *Science,* 1977, *197,* 1089–1091. Reprinted with permission.)

dence of radioactivity (and hence a high metabolic rate) in the SCN of the brain that was injected during the day (*left*). (See **Figure 9.29.**)

Schwartz and his colleagues (Schwartz et al., 1983) found a similar pattern of activity in the SCN of squirrel monkeys, which are diurnal animals (active during the day). These results suggest that it is not differences in the SCN that determine whether an animal is nocturnal or diurnal but differences elsewhere in the brain. The SCN keeps track of day and night, but it is up to mechanisms located elsewhere to determine when the animal is to be awake or asleep.

The "ticking" of the biological clock within the SCN could involve interactions of circuits of neurons, or it could be intrinsic to individual neurons themselves. Evidence suggests the latter—that each neuron contains a clock. Moore and Bernstein (1989) studied the prenatal and postnatal development of the SCN in the rat. Previous reports (Reppert and Schwartz, 1984) had shown that circadian rhythms in glucose metabolism are found in these nuclei prenatally, as early as the nineteenth day after conception. However, Moore and Bernstein found that at this time, the SCN contains fewer than one synapse per neuron, which seems to indicate that the neurons are "ticking" independently. One synapse per neuron is just not enough to synchronize the activity of a group of neurons. In addition, Schwartz, Gross, and Morton (1987) found that continuous infusion of TTX (tetrodotoxin), a drug that prevents action potentials by blocking voltage-dependent sodium channels, abolishes circadian rhythms. However, the drug does not appear to stop the "ticking" of the individual cells; when the infusions are stopped, the animals' circadian rhythms continued as if the clock had been running the whole time.

Several studies have succeeded in keeping individual SCN neurons alive in a culture medium. For example, Welsh et al. (1995) removed tissue from the rat SCN and dissolved the connections between the cells with papain, an enzyme sometimes used as a meat tenderizer. The cells were placed on top of an array of microelectrodes so that their electrical activity could be measured. Although these neurons did re-establish synaptic connections, they displayed individual, independent, circadian rhythms in activity. Figure 9.30 shows the activity cycles of four neurons. As you can see, all showed circadian rhythms, but their periods of peak activity occurred at different times of day. (See *Figure 9.30*.)

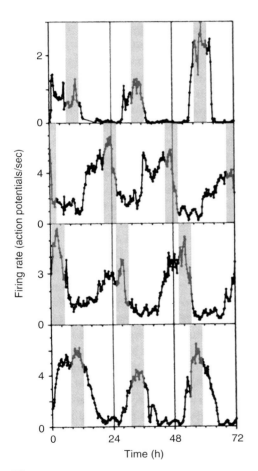

Figure 9.30
Firing rate of individual SCN neurons in a tissue culture. Color bars have been added to emphasize the daily peaks. Note that although each neuron has a period of approximately one day, their activity cycles are not synchronized.
(From Welsh, D.K., Logothetis, D.E., Meister, M., and Reppert, S.M. *Neuron*, 1995, *14*, 697–706.)

As we have just seen, both in vivo and in vitro evidence suggests that "ticking" occurs in individual neurons. But the activity cycles of neurons in the SCN of an intact animal are all synchronized—their peaks of activity occur at the same time each day. What synchronizes these cycles? The most obvious answer would seem to be the synaptic connections between them. However, studies have shown this explanation to be incorrect. For example, Bouskila and Dudek (1993) prepared slices of the rat hypothalamus that included the SCN and kept them alive in a culture medium. They found that the activity cycles of the neurons were all synchronized. The investigators then placed the slices in a culture medium that contained no calcium. As we saw in Chapter 2, the release of transmitter substance requires the entry of calcium into the terminal button; thus, the lack of extracellular calcium blocks synaptic transmission. Despite the absence of synaptic activity, the activity cycles of the SCN neurons in the slice remained synchronized. The most likely explanation is that the neurons (or perhaps the glial cells that surround them) release chemicals that synchronize their activity.

What causes intracellular ticking? Researchers have uncovered some of the details of one mechanism so far—that of the circadian clock of *Drosophila melanogaster*, the common fruit fly (Hunterensor, Ousley, and Sehgal, 1996; Lee et al., 1996; Myers et al., 1996; Zeng et al., 1996). For many years, investigators have believed that circadian rhythms were produced by the production of a protein that, when it reached a certain level in the cell, inhibited its own production. As a result, the levels of the protein would begin to decline, which would remove the inhibition, starting the production cycle again. It appears that, at least in the fruit fly, two proteins are involved, and one of them is involved in mediating the effects of a zeitgeber.

The clock seems to work like this: At sunrise, two genes, *per* and *tim*, become active. Copies of the information they encode are transcribed onto molecules of messenger RNA, which leave the nucleus, join with ribosomes, and trigger the production of the proteins PER and TIM. However, the TIM protein is immediately destroyed by the presence of light. (How this occurs is not yet known.) Then, at dusk, the concentration of TIM rises. Molecules of PER and TIM link together and travel to the nucleus, where they suppress the activity of the *per* and *tim* genes. With no more messenger RNA being produced, the levels of PER and TIM begin to decline. Then, at dawn, light destroys TIM. As a result, the *per* and *tim* genes become active again, which brings us to the beginning of the cycle.

As we saw earlier, exposure of pulses of light at different times of day has different effects on an animal's circadian rhythms. The same is true of fruit flies. If a fruit fly is ex-

After dusk, PER and TIM join, and PER-TIM enters the nucleus, suppressing *per* and *tim*. No more messenger RNA is made.

A few hours before dawn, levels of PER-TIM are low. After dawn, light destroys PER-TIM, so the genes *per* and *tim* become active again.

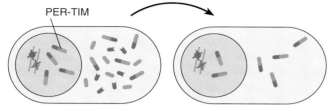

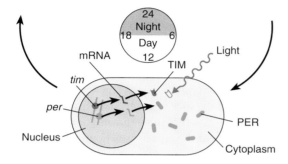

The *per* and *tim* genes are active; messenger RNA leaves the nucleus and causes the production of PER and TIM. However, light destroys TIM.

Figure 9.31
A schematic explanation of the hypothesized role of PER and TIM in control of circadian rhythms in the fruit fly.

posed to light an hour or two after dusk, the destruction of TIM disrupts the suppression of the *per* and *tim* genes that has just begun. This means that PER and TIM proteins continue to be produced, so the shut-down of gene activity is delayed. However, if a fruit fly is exposed to light an hour or two before dawn, gene production is already shut down. The destruction of TIM removes the inhibition, and *per* and *tim* become active right away, starting the cycle earlier than usual. (See *Figure 9.31*.)

What about the mammalian clock? Is this mechanism peculiar to insects, or do cells in the SCN work this way, too? Although it is too early to say, it does appear that a PER-like protein is produced in the rat SCN (Rosewell, Siwicki, and Wise, 1994). We will have to await the results of further research.

● Control of Seasonal Rhythms: The Pineal Gland and Melatonin

Although the SCN has an intrinsic rhythm of approximately 24 hours, it plays a role in much longer rhythms. (We could

say that it is involved in a biological calendar as well as a biological clock.) Male hamsters show annual rhythms of testosterone secretion, which appear to be based on the amount of light that occurs each day. Their breeding season begins as the day length increases and ends when it decreases. Lesions of the SCN abolish these annual breeding cycles; the animals' testes then secrete testosterone all year (Rusak and Morin, 1976). Possibly, the lesions disrupt these annual cycles because they destroy the 24-hour clock against which the daily light period is measured to determine the season. That is, if the light period is considerably shorter than 12 hours, the season is winter; if it is considerably longer than 12 hours, the season is summer.

The control of seasonal rhythms involves another part of the brain: the **pineal gland** (Bartness et al., 1993; Moore, 1995). This structure sits on top of the midbrain, just in front of the cerebellum. (See *Figure 9.32*.) The pineal gland secretes a hormone called **melatonin,** so named because it has the ability in certain animals (primarily fish, reptiles, and amphibians) to turn the skin temporarily dark. (The dark color is produced by a chemical known as *melanin*.) In mammals, melatonin controls seasonal rhythms. Neurons in the SCN make synaptic connections with neurons in the *paraventricular nucleus of the hypothalamus* (the PVN). The axons of these neurons travel all the way to the spinal cord, where they form synapses with preganglionic neurons of the sympathetic nervous system. The postganglionic neurons innervate the pineal gland and control the secretion of melatonin.

In response to input from the SCN, the pineal gland secretes melatonin during the night. This melatonin acts back on various structures in the brain (including the SCN, whose cells contain melatonin receptors) and controls hormones, physiological processes, and behaviors that show seasonal variations. During long nights a large amount of melatonin is secreted, and the animals go into the winter phase of their cycle. Lesions of the SCN, the paraventricular nucleus (PVN), or the pineal gland disrupt seasonal rhythms that are controlled by day length—and so do knife cuts that interrupt the neural connection between the SCN and the PVN, which indicates that this is one function of the SCN that is mediated through its neural connections with another structure. Furthermore, although transplants

pineal gland *(py **nee** ul)* A gland attached to the dorsal tectum; produces melatonin and plays a role in circadian and seasonal rhythms.

melatonin *(mell a **tone** in)* A hormone secreted during the night by the pineal body; plays a role in circadian and seasonal rhythms.

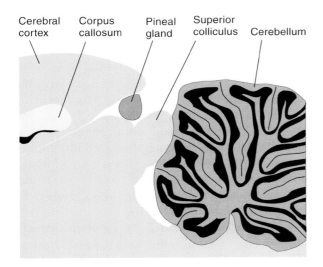

Cerebral cortex   Corpus callosum   Pineal gland   Superior colliculus   Cerebellum

Figure 9.32
The pineal gland, located on the dorsal surface of the midbrain.
(Adapted from Paxinos, G., and Watson, C. *The Rat Brain in Stereotaxic Coordinates.* Sydney: Academic Press, 1982. Redrawn with permission.)

of fetal suprachiasmatic nuclei will restore circadian rhythms, they will not restore seasonal rhythms, because the transplanted tissue does not establish neural connections with the PVN (Ralph and Lehman, 1991).

● Changes in Circadian Rhythms: Shift Work and Jet-Lag

When people abruptly change their daily rhythms of activity, their internal circadian rhythms, controlled by the SCN, become desynchronized with those in the internal environment. For example, if a person who normally works on the day shift begins working on a night shift or if someone travels east or west across several time zones, his or her SCN will signal the rest of the brain that it is time to sleep during the work shift (or the middle of the day, in the case of jet travel). This disparity between internal rhythms and the external environment results in sleep disturbances and mood changes and interferes with people's ability to function during waking hours.

Jet lag is a temporary phenomenon; after several days, people who have crossed several time zones find it easier to fall asleep at the appropriate time, and their daytime alertness improves. Shift work can present a more enduring problem when people are required to change shifts frequently. Obviously, the solution to jet lag and to the problems caused by shift work is to get the internal clock

synchronized with the external environment as quickly as possible. The most obvious way to start is to try to provide strong zeitgebers at the appropriate time. If a person is exposed to bright light before the low-point in the daily rhythm of body temperature (which occurs an hour or two before the person usually awakens), the person's circadian rhythm is delayed. If the exposure to bright light occurs after the low-point, the circadian rhythm is advanced (Dijk et al., 1995). In fact, several studies have shown that exposure to bright lights at the appropriate time help ease the transition (Boulos et al., 1995). Houpt, Boulos, and Moore-Ede (1996) have even developed a computer program that helps determine the optimal pattern of light exposure to minimize the effects of jet travel between various parts of the world. Similarly, people adapt to shift work more rapidly if artificial light is kept at a brighter level and if their bedroom is kept as dark as possible (Eastman et al., 1995).

As we saw in the previous subsection, the role of melatonin in seasonal rhythms is well established. Studies in recent years suggest that melatonin may also be involved in circadian rhythms, as well. As we saw, melatonin is secreted during the night, which, for diurnal mammals such as ourselves, is the period during which we sleep. But although our species lacks strong seasonal rhythms, the daily rhythm of melatonin secretion persists. Thus, melatonin must have some functions besides regulation of seasonal rhythms.

Recent studies have found that melatonin, acting on receptors in the SCN, can affect the sensitivity of SCN neurons to zeitgebers and can itself alter circadian rhythms (Gillette and McArthur, 1995; Starkey et al., 1995). Researchers do not yet understand exactly what role melatonin plays in the control of circadian rhythms, but they have already discovered practical applications. Melatonin secretion normally reaches its highest levels early in the night, at around bedtime. Investigators have found that the administration of melatonin at the appropriate time (in most cases, just before going to bed) significantly reduces the adverse effects of both jet-lag and shifts in work schedules (Arendt et al., 1995; Deacon and Arendt, 1996). Bedtime melatonin has even helped synchronize circadian rhythms and improved the sleep of blind people for whom light cannot serve as a zeitgeber (Skene, Deacon, and Arendt, 1996).

Interim Summary

Our daily lives are characterized by cycles in physical activity, sleep, body temperature, secretion of hormones, and many other physiological changes. Circadian rhythms—those with a period of approximately one day—are controlled by biological clocks in the brain. The principal biological clock appears to be located in the suprachiasmatic nuclei of the hypothalamus; lesions of these nuclei disrupt most circadian rhythms, and the activity of neurons located there correlates with the day–night cycle. Light serves as a zeitgeber for most circadian rhythms. That is, the biological clocks tend to run a bit slow, with a period of approximately 25 hours. The sight of sunlight in the morning is conveyed from the retina to the SCN—directly and via the IGL of the lateral geniculate nucleus. The effect of the light is to reset the clock to the start of a new cycle.

Individual neurons, rather than circuits of neurons, are responsible for the "ticks." Studies with tissue cultures suggest that synchronization of the firing patterns of individual neurons is accomplished by means of chemical communication between cells, perhaps involving astro-

cytes. In the fruit fly, two genes, *tim* and *per*, are responsible for circadian rhythms. These genes' proteins (TIM and PER) bind, travel to the nucleus, and inhibit further protein synthesis until they disintegrate and the cycle begins again. Light causes TIM to be destroyed, so it can serve as a zeitgeber, advancing or retarding the cycle according to the time during which it occurs.

The SCN and the pineal gland control annual rhythms. During the night, the SCN signals the pineal gland to secrete melatonin. Prolonged melatonin secretion, which occurs during winter, causes the animals to enter the winter phase of their annual cycle. Melatonin also appears to be involved in synchronizing circadian rhythms: The hormone can help people adjust to the effects of shift work or jet-lag and even synchronize the daily rhythms of blind people for whom light cannot serve as a zeitgeber.

Suggested Readings

Cohen, D.B. *Sleep and Dreaming: Origins, Nature and Functions.* Oxford: Pergamon Press, 1979.

Hastings, J.W., Rusak, B., and Boulos, Z. Circadian rhythms: The physiology of biological timing. In *Neural and Integrative Animal Physiology,* edited by C.L. Prosser. New York: Wiley-Liss, 1991.

Horne, J. *Why We Sleep: The Functions of Sleep in Humans and Other Mammals.* Oxford: Oxford University Press, 1988.

Kryger, M.H., Roth, T., and Dement, W.C. *Principles and Practices of Sleep Disorders in Medicine.* New York: W.B. Saunders, 1989.

Mancia, M., and Marini, G. *The Diencephalon and Sleep.* New York: Raven Press, 1990.

Webb, W. *Sleep: The Gentle Tyrant,* 2nd ed. Bolton, MA: Anker, 1992.

CHAPTER 10

Reproductive Behavior

Composition by Lee Krasner.

Reproductive behaviors constitute the most important category of social behaviors, because without them, most species would not survive. These behaviors—which include courting, mating, parental behavior, and most forms of aggressive behaviors—are the most striking categories of **sexually dimorphic behaviors,** that is, behaviors that differ in males and females (*di + morphous,* "two forms"). As you will see, hormones present both before and after birth play a very special role in the development and control of sexually dimorphic behaviors.

This chapter describes male and female sexual development and then discusses the neural and hormonal control of two sexually dimorphic behaviors most important to reproduction: sexual behavior and maternal behavior.

SEXUAL DEVELOPMENT

A person's chromosomal sex is determined at the time of fertilization. However, this event is merely the first in a series of steps that culminate in the development of a male or female. This section considers the major features of sexual development.

● Production of Gametes and Fertilization

All cells of the human body (other than sperms or ova) contain twenty-three pairs of chromosomes. The genetic information that programs the development of a human is contained in the DNA that constitutes these chromosomes. We pride ourselves on our ability to miniaturize computer circuits on silicon chips, but that accomplishment looks primitive when we consider that the blueprint for a human being is too small to be seen by the naked eye.

The production of **gametes** (ova and sperms; *gamein* means "to marry") entails a special form of cell division. This process produces cells that contain one member of each of the twenty-three pairs of chromosomes. The development of a human begins at the time of fertilization, when a single sperm and ovum join, sharing their twenty-three single chromosomes to reconstitute the twenty-three pairs.

A person's genetic sex is determined at the time of fertilization by the father's sperm. Twenty-two of the twenty-three pairs of chromosomes determine the organism's physical development independent of its sex. The last pair consists of two **sex chromosomes,** which determine whether the offspring will be a boy or a girl.

There are two types of sex chromosomes: X chromosomes and Y chromosomes. Females have two X chromo-

---

sexually dimorphic behavior A behavior that has different forms or that occurs with different probabilities or under different circumstances in males and females.

gamete *(gamm eet)* A mature reproductive cell; a sperm or ovum.

sex chromosome The X and Y chromosomes, which determine an organism's gender. Normally, XX individuals are female, and XY individuals are male.

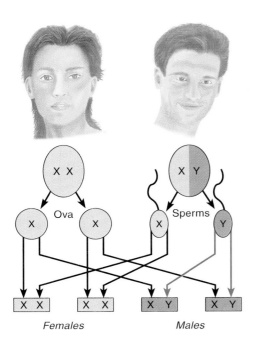

Figure 10.1
Determination of gender. The gender of the off-spring depends on whether the sperm cell that fertilizes the ovum carries an X or a Y chromosome.

somes (XX); thus, all the ova that a woman produces will contain an X chromosome. Males have an X and a Y chromosome (XY). When a man's sex chromosomes divide, half the sperms contain an X chromosome and the other half contain a Y chromosome. A Y-bearing sperm produces an XY-fertilized ovum and therefore a male. An X-bearing sperm produces an XX-fertilized ovum and therefore a female. (See *Figure 10.1.*)

● Development of the Sex Organs

Men and women differ in many ways: Their bodies are different, parts of their brains are different, and their reproductive behaviors are different. Are all these differences encoded on the tiny Y chromosome, the sole piece of genetic material that distinguishes males from females? The answer is no. The X chromosome and the twenty-two non-sex chromosomes found in the cells of both males and females contain all the information needed to develop the bodies of either sex. Exposure to sex hormones, both before and after birth, is responsible for our sexual dimorphism. What the Y chromosome does control is the development of the glands that produce the male sex hormones.

Gonads

There are three general categories of sex organs: the gonads, the internal sex organs, and the external genitalia. The **gonads**—testes or ovaries—are the first to develop. Gonads (from the Greek *gonos,* "procreation") have a dual function: They produce ova or sperms, and they secrete hormones. Through the fourth week of prenatal development, male and female fetuses are identical. Both sexes have a pair of identical undifferentiated gonads, which have the potential of developing into either testes or ovaries. The factor that controls their development appears to be a single gene on the Y chromosome called *SRY*. This gene produces an enzyme called *testis-determining factor,* which causes the undifferentiated gonads to become testes. If the gene is not present, they become ovaries (Smith, 1994). In fact, if this gene is inserted into one of the X chromosomes of a female (XX) embryonic mouse, the animal will develop as a male (Koopman et al., 1991).

Once the gonads have developed, a series of events is set into action that determines the individual's gender. These events are directed by hormones, which affect sexual development in two ways. During prenatal development these hormones have **organizational effects,** which influence the development of a person's sex organs and brain. These effects are permanent; once a particular path is followed in the course of development, there is no going back. The second role of sex hormones is their **activational effect.** These effects occur later in life, after the sex organs have developed. For example, hormones activate the production of sperms, make erection and ejaculation possible, and induce ovulation. Because the bodies of adult males and females have been organized differently, sex hormones will have different activational effects in the two sexes.

Internal Sex Organs

Early in embryonic development, the internal sex organs are *bisexual;* that is, all embryos contain the precursors for both female and male sex organs. However, during the third month of gestation only one of these precursors develops; the other withers away. The precursor of the internal female sex organs, which develops into the *fimbriae* and *Fallopian tubes,* the *uterus,* and the *inner two-thirds of the*

gonad *(rhymes with **moan** ad)*   An ovary or testis.
organizational effect (of hormone)   The effect of a hormone on tissue differentiation and development.
activational effect (of hormone)   The effect of a hormone that occurs in the fully developed organism; may depend on the organism's prior exposure to the organizational effects of hormones.

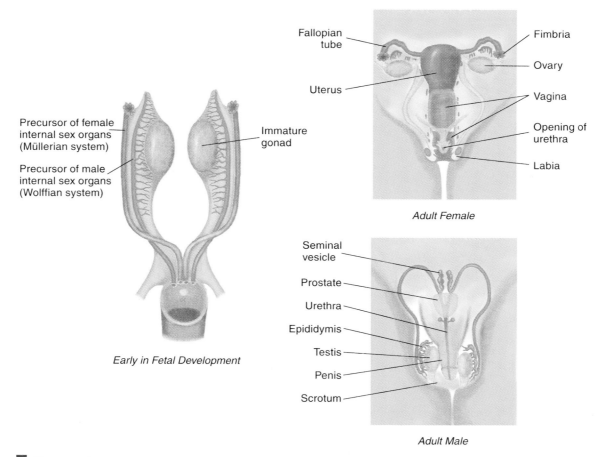

Fallopian tube

Uterus

Fimbria

Ovary

Vagina

Opening of urethra

Labia

Adult Female

Precursor of female internal sex organs (Müllerian system)

Precursor of male internal sex organs (Wolffian system)

Immature gonad

Early in Fetal Development

Seminal vesicle

Prostate

Urethra

Epididymis

Testis

Penis

Scrotum

Adult Male

Figure 10.2
Development of the internal sex organs.

vagina, is called the **Müllerian system.** The precursor of the internal male sex organs, which develops into the *epididymis, vas deferens, seminal vesicles,* and *prostate,* is called the **Wolffian system.** (These systems were named after their discoverers, Müller and Wolff. See *Figure 10.2.*)

The gender of the internal sex organs of a fetus is determined by the presence or absence of hormones secreted by the testes. If these hormones are present, the Wolffian system develops. If they are not, the Müllerian system develops. The Müllerian (female) system needs no hormonal stimulus from the gonads to develop; it just normally does so. In contrast, the cells of the Wolffian (male) system do not develop unless they are stimulated to do so by a hormone. Thus, testes secrete two types of hormones. The first, a peptide hormone called **anti-Müllerian hormone,** does exactly what its name says: It prevents the Müllerian (female) system from developing. It therefore has a **defeminizing effect.** The second, a set of steroid hormones called **androgens,** stimulates the development of the Wolffian system. (This class of hormone is also aptly named: *andros* means "man," and *gennan* means "to produce.") Androgens have a **masculinizing effect.**

Two different androgens are responsible for masculinization. The first, **testosterone,** is secreted by the testes—and gets its name from these glands. An enzyme called *5α*

Müllerian system   The embryonic precursors of the female internal sex organs.

Wolffian system   The embryonic precursors of the male internal sex organs.

anti-Müllerian hormone   A peptide secreted by the fetal testes that inhibits the development of the Müllerian system, which would otherwise become the female internal sex organs.

defeminizing effect   An effect of a hormone present early in development that reduces or prevents the later development of anatomical or behavioral characteristics typical of females.

androgen (*an dro jen*)   A male sex steroid hormone. Testosterone is the principal mammalian androgen.

masculinizing effect   An effect of a hormone present early in development that promotes the later development of anatomical or behavioral characteristics typical of males.

reductase converts some of the testosterone into another androgen, known as **dihydrotestosterone.**

As you will recall from Chapter 2, hormones exert their effects on target cells by stimulating the appropriate hormone receptor. Thus, the precursor of the male internal sex organs—the Wolffian system—contains androgen receptors that are coupled to cellular mechanisms that promote growth and division. When molecules of androgens bind with these receptors, the epididymis, vas deferens, and prostate develop and grow. In contrast, the cells of the Müllerian system contain receptors for anti-Müllerian hormone that *prevent* growth and division. Thus, anti-Müllerian hormone prevents the development of the female internal sex organs.

The fact that the internal sex organs of the human embryo are bisexual and could potentially develop as either male or female is dramatically illustrated by two genetic disorders: *androgen insensitivity syndrome* and *persistent Müllerian duct syndrome.* Some people are insensitive to androgens; they have **androgen insensitivity syndrome,** one of the more aptly named disorders (Money and Ehrhardt, 1972; MacLean, Warne, and Zajac, 1995). The cause of androgen insensitivity syndrome is a genetic mutation that prevents the formation of functioning androgen receptors. (The gene for the androgen receptor is located on the X chromosome.) The primitive gonads of a genetic male fetus with androgen insensitivity syndrome become testes and secrete both anti-Müllerian hormone and androgens. The lack of androgen receptors prevents the androgens from having a masculinizing effect; thus, the epididymis, vas deferens, seminal vesicles, and prostate fail to develop. However, the anti-Müllerian hormone still has its defeminizing effect, preventing the female internal sex organs from developing. The uterus, fimbriae, and Fallopian tubes fail to develop, and the vagina is shallow. Their external genitalia are female, and at puberty they develop a woman's body. Of course, lacking a uterus and ovaries, these people cannot have children. (See *Figure 10.3.*)

The second genetic disorder, **persistent Müllerian duct syndrome,** is caused by defective receptors for Müllerian inhibiting hormone (Behringer, 1995; Imbeaud et al., 1995). When this syndrome occurs in genetic males, androgens have their masculinizing effect but defeminization does not occur. Thus, the person is born with *both* sets of internal sex organs, male and female. The presence of the additional female sex organs usually interferes with normal functioning of the male sex organs.

So far, I have been discussing only male sex hormones. What about prenatal sexual development in females? A genetic anomaly indicates that female sex organs are not needed for development of the Müllerian system. This fact

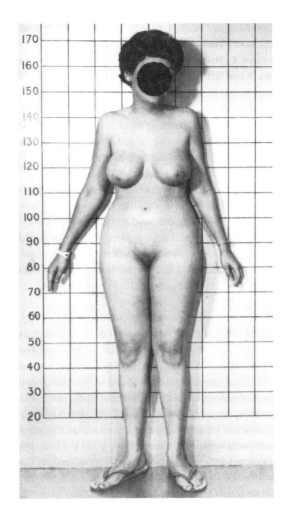

Figure 10.3
An XY female displaying androgen insensitivity syndrome.
(From Money, J., and Ehrhardt, A.A. *Man & Woman, Boy & Girl.* Copyright 1973 by The Johns Hopkins University Press, Baltimore, Maryland. By permission.)

testosterone *(tess **tahss** ter own)* The principal androgen found in males.

dihydrotestosterone *(dy hy dro tess **tahss** ter own)* An androgen, produced from testosterone through the action of the enzyme 5α reductase.

androgen insensitivity syndrome A condition caused by a congenital lack of functioning androgen receptors; in a person with XY sex chromosomes, causes the development of a female with testes but no internal sex organs.

persistent Müllerian duct syndrome A condition caused by a congenital lack of functioning anti-Müllerian hormone receptors; in a male, causes development of both male and female internal sex organs.

has led to the dictum "Nature's impulse is to create a female." People with **Turner's syndrome** have only one sex chromosome: an X chromosome. (Thus, instead of having XX cells, they have X0 cells—0 indicating a missing sex chromosome.) In most cases, the existing X chromosome comes from the mother, which means that the cause of the disorder lies with a defective sperm (Knebelmann et al., 1991). Because a Y chromosome is not present, testes do not develop. In addition, because two X chromosomes are needed to produce ovaries, these glands are not produced, either. But even though people with Turner's syndrome have no gonads at all, they develop into females, with normal female internal sex organs and external genitalia—which proves that fetuses do not need ovaries or the hormones they produce to develop as females. Of course, they cannot bear children, because without ovaries they cannot produce ova.

External Genitalia

The external genitalia are the visible sex organs, including the penis and scrotum in males and the labia, clitoris, and outer part of the vagina in females. (See *Figure 10.4.*) As we just saw, the external genitalia do not need to be stimulated by female sex hormones to become female; they just naturally develop that way. However, masculine development requires the presence of androgens—in particular, the presence of dihydrotestosterone (Josso et al., 1991). Thus, the gender of a person's external genitalia is determined by the presence or absence of testes—or, more precisely, by the presence or absence of the androgens they secrete. This fact explains why people with Turner's syndrome have female external genitalia even though they lack ovaries.

Figure 10.5 summarizes the factors that control the development of the gonads, internal sex organs, and genitalia. (See *Figure 10.5.*)

● Sexual Maturation

The *primary* sex characteristics include the gonads, internal sex organs, and external genitalia. These organs are present at birth. The *secondary* sex characteristics, such as enlarged breasts and widened hips or a beard and deep voice, do not appear until puberty. Without seeing genitals, we must guess the sex of a prepubescent child from his or her haircut and clothing; the bodies of young boys and girls are rather similar. However, at puberty the gonads are stimulated to produce their hormones, and these hormones cause the person to mature sexually. The onset of puberty occurs when cells in the hypothalamus secrete **gonadotropin-releasing hormones** (GnRH), which stimulate the production and release of two **gonadotropic hormones** by

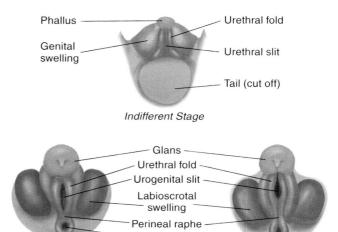

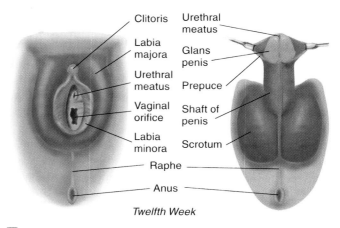

Figure 10.4
Development of the external genitalia.
(Adapted from Spaulding, M.H., in *Contributions to Embryology*, Vol. 13. Washington, D.C.: Carnegie Institute of Washington, 1921.)

the anterior pituitary gland. The gonadotropic ("gonad-turning") hormones stimulate the gonads to produce *their* hormones, which are ultimately responsible for sexual maturation. (See *Figure 10.6.*)

Turner's syndrome The presence of only one sex chromosome (an X chromosome); characterized by lack of ovaries but otherwise normal female sex organs and genitalia.

gonadotropin-releasing hormone (*go nad oh **trow** pin*) A hypothalamic hormone that stimulates the anterior pituitary gland to secrete gonadotropic hormone.

gonadotropic hormone A hormone of the anterior pituitary gland that has a stimulating effect on cells of the gonads.

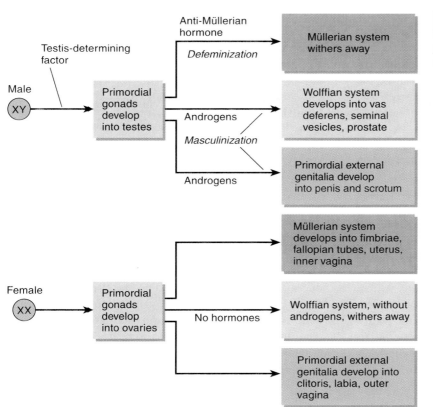

Figure 10.5
Hormonal control of masculinization and de-feminization of the internal sex organs and external genitalia.

The two gonadotropic hormones are **follicle-stimulating hormone (FSH)** and **luteinizing hormone (LH),** named for the effects they produce in the female (production of a *follicle* and its subsequent *luteinization,* to be described in the next section of this chapter). However, the same hormones are produced in the male, where they stimulate the testes to produce sperms and to secrete testosterone. If male and female pituitary glands are exchanged in rats, the ovaries and testes respond perfectly to the hormones secreted by the new glands (Harris and Jacobsohn, 1951–1952).

In response to the gonadotropic hormones (usually called *gonadotropins*), the gonads secrete steroid sex hormones. The ovaries produce **estradiol,** one of a class of hormones known as **estrogens.** As we saw, the testes produce testosterone, an androgen. Both types of glands also pro-

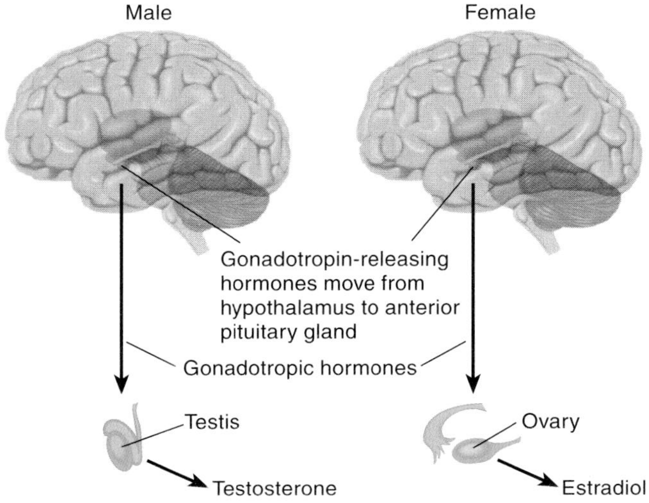

Figure 10.6
Sexual maturation. Puberty is initiated when the hypothalamus secretes gonadotropin-releasing hormones.

follicle-stimulating hormone (FSH)   The hormone of the anterior pituitary gland that causes development of an ovarian follicle and the maturation of its oocyte into an ovum.

luteinizing hormone (LH) *(lew tee a nize ing)*   A hormone of the anterior pituitary gland that causes ovulation and development of the ovarian follicle into a corpus luteum.

estradiol *(ess tra **dye** ahl)*   The principal estrogen of many mammals, including humans.

estrogen *(ess trow jen)*   A class of sex hormones that cause maturation of the female genitalia, growth of breast tissue, and development of other physical features characteristic of females.

duce a small amount of the hormones of the other sex. The gonadal steroids affect many parts of the body. Both estradiol and testosterone initiate closure of the growing portions of the bones and thus halt skeletal growth. Estradiol also causes breast development, growth of the lining of the uterus, changes in the deposition of body fat, and maturation of the female genitalia. Testosterone stimulates growth of facial, axillary (underarm), and pubic hair; lowers the voice; alters the hairline on the head (often causing baldness later in life); stimulates muscular development; and causes genital growth. This description leaves out two of the female secondary characteristics: axillary and pubic hair. These characteristics are produced not by estradiol but rather by androgens secreted by the cortex of the adrenal glands. Even a male who is castrated before puberty (whose testes are removed) will grow axillary and pubic hair, stimulated by his own adrenal androgens. A list of the principal sex hormones and examples of their effects are presented in Table 10.1. Note that some of these effects are discussed later in this chapter. (See *Table 10.1.*)

The bipotentiality of some of the secondary sex characteristics remains throughout life. If a man is treated with an estrogen (for example, to control an androgen-dependent tumor), he will grow breasts, and his facial hair will become finer and softer. However, his voice will remain low, because the enlargement of the larynx is permanent. Conversely, a woman who receives high levels of an androgen (usually, from a tumor that secretes androgens) will grow a beard, and her voice will become lower.

Interim Summary

Gender is determined by the sex chromosomes: XX produces a female, and XY produces a male. Males are produced by the action of the SRY gene on the Y chromosome, which contains the code for the production of the testis-determining protein, which in turn, causes the primitive gonads to become testes. The testes secrete two kinds of hormones that cause a male to develop. Testosterone (an

Table 10.1
Classification of Sex Hormones

Class	Principal hormones in humans (where produced)	Examples of effects
Androgens	Testosterone (testes)	Development of Wolffian system; production of sperms, growth of facial, pubic, and axillary hair; muscular development; enlargement of larynx; inhibition of bone growth; sex drive in men (and women?)
	Dihydrotestosterone (produced from testosterone by action of 5α reductase)	Maturation of male external genitalia
	Androstenedione (adrenal glands)	In women, growth of pubic and axillary hair; less important than testosterone in men
Estrogens	Estradiol (ovaries)	Maturation of female genitalia; growth of breasts; alterations in fat deposits; growth of uterine lining; inhibition of bone growth; sex drive in women (?)
Gestagens	Progesterone (ovaries)	Maintenance of uterine lining
Hypothalamic hormones	Gonadotrophin-releasing hormone (hypothalamus)	Secretion of gonadotropins
Gonadotropins	Follicle-stimulating hormone (anterior pituitary)	Development of ovarian follicle
	Luteinizing hormone (anterior pituitary)	Ovulation; development of corpus luteum
Other hormones	Prolactin (posterior pituitary)	Milk production; male refractory period (?)
	Oxytocin (posterior pituitary)	Milk ejection; orgasm; male refractory period (?); social bonding (?)

androgen) stimulates the development of the Wolffian system (masculinization), and anti-Müllerian hormone suppresses the development of the Müllerian system (defeminization). Androgen insensitivity syndrome results from a hereditary defect in androgen receptors, and persistent Müllerian duct syndrome results from a hereditary defect in anti-Müllerian hormone receptors.

By default, the body is female ("Nature's impulse . . . "); only by the actions of testicular hormones does it become male. Masculinization and defeminization are referred to as *organizational* effects of hormones; *activational* effects occur after development is complete. A person with Turner's syndrome (X0) fails to develop gonads but nevertheless develops female internal sex organs and external genitalia. The external genitalia develop from common precursors. In the absence of gonadal hormones, the precursors develop the female form; in the presence of androgens (primarily dihydrotestosterone, which derives from testosterone through the action of 5α reductase), they develop the male form (masculinization).

Sexual maturity occurs when the hypothalamus begins secreting gonadotropin-releasing hormone, which stimulates the secretion of follicle-stimulating hormone and luteinizing hormone by the anterior pituitary gland. These hormones stimulate the gonads to secrete their hormones, thus causing the genitals to mature and the body to develop the secondary sex characteristics (activational effects).

HORMONAL CONTROL OF SEXUAL BEHAVIOR

We have seen that hormones are responsible for sexual dimorphism in the structure of the body and its organs. Hormones have organizational and activational effects on the internal sex organs, genitals, and secondary sex characteristics. Naturally, all of these effects influence a person's behavior. Simply having the physique and genitals of a man

menstrual cycle (*men* strew al) The female reproductive cycle of most primates, including humans; characterized by growth of the lining of the uterus, ovulation, development of a corpus luteum, and (if pregnancy does not occur), menstruation.

estrous cycle The female reproductive cycle of mammals other than primates.

ovarian follicle A cluster of epithelial cells surrounding an oocyte, which develops into an ovum.

corpus luteum (*lew* tee um) A cluster of cells that develops from the ovarian follicle after ovulation; secretes estradiol and progesterone.

or a woman exerts a powerful effect. But hormones do more than give us masculine or feminine bodies; they also affect behavior by interacting directly with the nervous system. Androgens present during prenatal development affect the development of the nervous system. In addition, both male and female sex hormones have activational effects on the adult nervous system that influence both physiological processes and behavior. This section considers some of these hormonal effects.

● Hormonal Control of Female Reproductive Cycles

The reproductive cycle of female primates is called a **menstrual cycle** (from *mensis,* meaning "month"). Females of other species of mammals also have reproductive cycles, called **estrous cycles.** *Estrus* means "gadfly"; when a female rat is in estrus, her hormonal condition goads her to act differently than she does at other times. (For that matter, it goads male rats to act differently, too.) The primary feature that distinguishes menstrual cycles from estrous cycles is the monthly growth and loss of the lining of the uterus. The other features are approximately the same—except that the estrous cycle of rats takes four days. Also, the sexual behavior of female mammals with estrous cycles is linked with ovulation, whereas most female primates can mate at any time during their menstrual cycle.

Menstrual cycles and estrous cycles consist of a sequence of events that are controlled by hormonal secretions of the pituitary gland and ovaries. These glands interact, the secretions of one affecting those of the other. A cycle begins with the secretion of gonadotropins by the anterior pituitary gland. These hormones (especially FSH) stimulate the growth of **ovarian follicles,** small spheres of epithelial cells surrounding each ovum. Women normally produce one ovarian follicle each month; if two are produced and fertilized, dizygotic (fraternal) twins will develop. As ovarian follicles mature, they secrete estradiol, which causes the growth of the lining of the uterus in preparation for implantation of the ovum, should it be fertilized by a sperm. Feedback from the increasing level of estradiol eventually triggers the release of a surge of LH by the anterior pituitary gland. (See *Figure 10.7.*)

The LH surge causes *ovulation:* The ovarian follicle ruptures, releasing the ovum. Under the continued influence of LH the ruptured ovarian follicle becomes a **corpus luteum** ("yellow body"), which produces estradiol and **progesterone.** (See *Figure 10.7.*) The latter hormone promotes pregnancy *(gestation).* It maintains the lining of the uterus, and it inhibits the ovaries from producing another follicle. Meanwhile, the ovum enters one of the Fallopian tubes

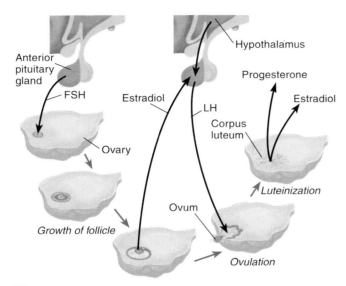

Figure 10.7
Neuroendocrine control of the menstrual cycle.

and begins its progress toward the uterus. If it meets sperm cells during its travel down the Fallopian tube and becomes fertilized, it begins to divide, and several days later it attaches itself to the uterine wall.

If the ovum is not fertilized, or if it is fertilized too late to develop sufficiently by the time it gets to the uterus, the corpus luteum will stop producing estradiol and progesterone, and then the lining of the walls of the uterus will slough off. At this point menstruation will commence.

● Hormonal Control of Sexual Behavior of Laboratory Animals

The interactions between sex hormones and the human brain are difficult to study. We must turn to two sources of information: experiments with animals and various developmental disorders in humans, which serve as nature's own "experiments." Let us first consider the evidence gathered from research with laboratory animals.

Males

Male sexual behavior is quite varied, although the essential features of *intromission* (entry of the penis into the female's vagina), *pelvic thrusting* (rhythmic movement of the hindquarters, causing genital friction), and *ejaculation* (discharge of semen) are characteristic of all male mammals. Humans, of course, have invented all kinds of copulatory and noncopulatory sexual behavior. For example, the pelvic movements leading to ejaculation may be performed

by the woman, and sex play can lead to orgasm without intromission.

The sexual behavior of rats has been studied more than that of any other laboratory animal. When a male rat encounters a receptive female, he will spend some time nuzzling her and sniffing and licking her genitals, mount her, and engage in pelvic thrusting. He will mount her several times, achieving intromission on most of the mountings. After eight to fifteen intromissions approximately 1 minute apart (each lasting only about one-quarter of a second), the male will ejaculate.

After ejaculating, the male refrains from sexual activity for a period of time (minutes, in the rat). Most mammals will return to copulate again and again, showing a longer pause, called a **refractory period,** after each ejaculation. (The term comes from the Latin *refringere,* "to break off.") An interesting phenomenon occurs in some mammals. If a male, after finally becoming "exhausted" by repeated copulation with the same female, is presented with a new female, he begins to respond quickly—often as fast as he did in his initial contact with the first female. Successive introductions of new females can keep up his performance for prolonged periods of time. This phenomenon is undoubtedly important in species in which a single male inseminates all the females in his harem. Species with approximately equal numbers of reproductively active males and females are less likely to act this way.

The phenomenon I have just described, also seen in roosters, is usually called the **Coolidge effect.** The following story is reputed to be true, but I cannot vouch for that fact. (If it is not true, it ought to be.) The late former U.S. president Calvin Coolidge and his wife were touring a farm, when Mrs. Coolidge asked the farmer whether the continuous and vigorous sexual activity among the flock of hens was the work of just one rooster. The reply was yes. "You might point that out to Mr. Coolidge," she said. The president then asked the farmer whether a different hen was involved each time. The answer, again, was yes. "You might point that out to Mrs. Coolidge," he said.

---

progesterone *(pro **jess** ter own)* A steroid hormone produced by the ovary that maintains the endometrial lining of the uterus during the later part of the menstrual cycle and during pregnancy; along with estradiol, it promotes receptivity in female mammals with estrous cycles.

refractory period *(ree **frak** to ree)* A period of time after a particular action (for example, an ejaculation by a male) during which that action cannot occur again.

Coolidge effect The restorative effect of introducing a new female sex partner to a male that has apparently become "exhausted" by sexual activity.

Sexual behavior of male rodents depends on testosterone, a fact that has long been recognized (Bermant and Davidson, 1974). If a male rat is castrated (that is, if his testes are removed), his sexual activity eventually ceases. However, the behavior can be reinstated by injections of testosterone. I will describe the neural basis of this activational effect later in this chapter.

As we saw earlier, testosterone can be converted, through the action of the enzyme 5α reductase, to dihydrotestosterone, which is responsible for some of the masculinization that occurs during prenatal development. Testosterone can be converted into yet another hormone: estradiol. The process, called **aromatization,** is accomplished by an enzyme called an *aromatase*. (In chemistry an *aromatic compound* is one that contains a particular six-carbon ring.) Many cells of the brain contain aromatase; when molecules of testosterone enter them, they are converted into estradiol. The molecules of estradiol travel to the nucleus, bind with estrogen receptors, and trigger their physiological effects. (See *Figure 10.8.*)

At least some of the activational effects of testosterone on male sexual behavior are produced by the action of aromatized testosterone (that is, estradiol) on estrogen receptors. Zumpe, Bonsall, and Michael (1993) found that a drug that blocks aromatase (the enzyme that converts testosterone to estrogen) decreased the sexual behavior of adult male monkeys by 40 percent.

Other hormones play a role in male sexual behavior. **Oxytocin** is a hormone produced by the posterior pituitary gland that contracts the milk ducts—and thus causes milk ejection in lactating females. It is also produced in males, where it obviously plays no role in lactation. Oxytocin is released at the time of orgasm in both males and females and appears to contribute to the contractions of the smooth muscle in the male ejaculatory system and of the vagina and uterus (Carter, 1992; Carmichael et al., 1994). The effects of this hormonal release can easily be seen in lactating women, who often eject some milk at the time of orgasm. As we shall see later in this chapter, oxytocin also serves as a neurotransmitter or neuromodulator in the brain, where it may have facilitatory effects on sexual behavior.

The refractory period that occurs after an ejaculation may be produced by another hormone, perhaps in conjunction with oxytocin. **Prolactin,** a hormone secreted by the anterior pituitary gland, stimulates milk production by the mammary glands. Like oxytocin, prolactin is released

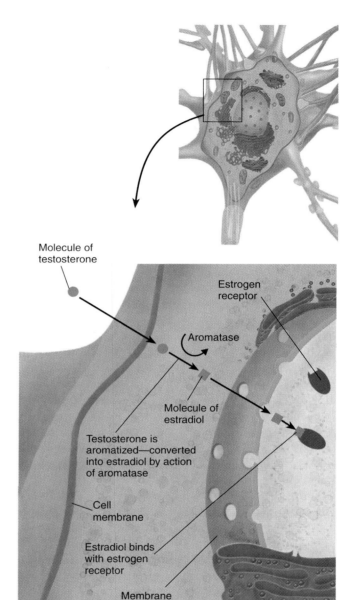

Figure 10.8
Aromatization. In some cells the effects of testosterone are carried out by an estrogen. Testosterone is aromatized into estradiol, which activates estrogen receptors in the nucleus.

aromatization *(air oh mat i zay shun)* A chemical reaction catalyzed by an aromatase; the process by which testosterone is transformed into estradiol.

oxytocin *(ox ee tow sin)* A hormone secreted by the posterior pituitary gland; causes contraction of the smooth muscle of the milk ducts, the uterus, and the male ejaculatory system; also serves as a neurotransmitter in the brain.

prolactin A hormone of the anterior pituitary gland, necessary for production of milk; has an inhibitory effect on male sexual behavior.

by male rats after ejaculation (Oaknin et al., 1989). In addition, prolactin has an inhibitory effect on male sexual behavior; in fact, one of the symptoms of *hyperprolactinemia* (oversecretion of prolactin) is loss of sexual desire (Foster et al., 1990). Doherty, Baum, and Todd (1986) transplanted a pituitary gland into males rats, which causes their blood level of prolactin to increase dramatically. The investigators found that the hormone severely depressed mounting behavior and intromissions. Mas et al. (1995) observed similar effects when they injected small amounts of prolactin directly into male rats' brains, into a region known to be involved in male sex behavior (the *MPA*, discussed later in this chapter).

Females

The mammalian female has been described as the passive participant in copulation. It is true that in some species the female's role during the act of copulation is merely to assume a posture that exposes her genitals to the male. This behavior is called the **lordosis** response (from the Greek *lordos*, meaning "bent backward"). The female will also move her tail away (if she has one) and stand rigidly enough to support the weight of the male. However, the behavior of a female rodent in *initiating* copulation is often very active. Certainly, if a male attempts to copulate with a nonestrous rodent, the female will either actively flee or rebuff him. But when the female is in a receptive state, she will often approach the male, nuzzle him, sniff his genitals, and show behaviors characteristic of her species. For example, a female rat will exhibit quick, short, hopping movements and rapid ear wiggling, which most male rats find irresistible (McClintock and Adler, 1978).

Sexual behavior of female rodents depends on the gonadal hormones present during estrus: estradiol and progesterone. In rats, estradiol increases about 40 hours before the female becomes receptive; just before receptivity occurs, the corpus luteum begins secreting large quantities of progesterone (Feder, 1981). Ovariectomized rats (rats whose ovaries have been removed) are not sexually receptive. Although sexual receptivity can be produced in ovariectomized rodents by administering large doses of estradiol alone, the most effective treatment duplicates the normal sequence of hormones: a small amount of estradiol, followed by progesterone. Progesterone alone is ineffective; thus, the estradiol "primes" its effectiveness. Priming with estradiol takes about 16–24 hours, after which an injection of progesterone produces receptive behaviors within an hour (Takahashi, 1990). The neural mechanisms that are responsible for these effects will be described later in this chapter.

The sequence of estradiol followed by progesterone has three effects on female rats: It increases their receptivity, their proceptivity, and their attractiveness. *Receptivity* refers to their ability and willingness to copulate—to accept the advances of a male by holding still and displaying lordosis when he attempts to mount her. *Proceptivity* refers to a female's eagerness to copulate, as shown by the fact that she seeks out a male and engages in behaviors that tend to arouse his sexual interest. *Attractiveness* refers to physiological and behavioral changes that affect the male. The male rat (along with many other male mammals) is most responsive to females who are in estrus ("in heat"). Males will ignore a female whose ovaries have been removed, but injections of estradiol and progesterone will restore her attractiveness (and also change her behavior toward the male). The stimuli that arouse a male rat's sexual interest include her odor and her behavior. In some species, visible changes, such as the swollen sex skin in the genital region of a female monkey, also affect sex appeal.

● Organizational Effects of Androgens on Behavior: Masculinization and Defeminization

The dictum "Nature's impulse is to create a female" applies to sexual behavior as well as to sex organs. That is, if a rodent's brain is *not* exposed to androgens during a critical period of development, the animal will engage in female sexual behavior as an adult (if then given estradiol and progesterone). Fortunately for experimenters, this critical time comes shortly after birth for rats and for several other species of rodents that are born in a rather immature condition. Thus, if a male rat is castrated immediately after birth, permitted to grow to adulthood, and then given injections of estradiol and progesterone, it will respond to the presence of another male by arching its back and presenting its hindquarters. In other words, it will act as if it were a female (Blaustein and Olster, 1989).

In contrast, if a rodent brain is exposed to androgens during development, two phenomena occur: behavioral defeminization and behavioral masculinization. *Behavioral defeminization* refers to the organizational effect of androgens that prevents the animal from displaying female sexual behavior in adulthood. As we shall see later, this effect is accomplished by suppressing the development of neural circuits controlling female sexual behavior. For example, if

lordosis A spinal sexual reflex seen in many four-legged female mammals; arching of the back in response to approach of a male or to touching the flanks, which elevates the hindquarters.

a female rodent is ovariectomized and given an injection of testosterone immediately after birth, she will *not* respond to a male rat when, as an adult, she is given injections of estradiol and progesterone. *Behavioral masculinization* refers to the organizational effect of androgens that enables animals to engage in male sexual behavior in adulthood. This effect is accomplished by stimulating the development of neural circuits controlling male sexual behavior. For example, if the female rodent in my previous example is given testosterone in adulthood, rather than estradiol and progesterone, she will mount and attempt to copulate with a receptive female. (See Breedlove, 1992, and Carter, 1992, for references to specific studies.) (See *Figure 10.9.*)

The two organizational effects of androgens on the brain—behavioral masculinization and behavioral defeminization—are, of course, stimulated by testosterone, but they appear to involve estrogen receptors. As you will recall, aromatase, an enzyme present in some cells, converts testosterone into estradiol, which then stimulates estrogen receptors located in the nucleus. (Refer to *Figure 10.8.*) If male rats are treated early in life with drugs that block aromatization, they become less likely to show male sexual behavior and more likely to show female sexual behavior and prefer the company of males rather than females (Brand et al., 1991; Houtsmuller et al., 1994; Bakker, Van Ophemert, and Slob, 1996). These results indicate that behavioral defeminization is largely (but not completely) accomplished by the indirect effects of aromatized testosterone on estrogen receptors.

You might wonder why *all* fetuses—male and female—do not become masculinized and defeminized through exposure to estrogens. First, the ovaries of females do not secrete significant amounts of estradiol until puberty, so their brains are not exposed to their own ovarian hormones during brain development. Second, although all fetuses are exposed to their mother's estradiol, their blood contains a substance called *α-fetoprotein*, which binds with estradiol and inactivates it (Breedlove, 1992). This means that the only estradiol that has organizational effects in the developing brain is that produced *inside* the cell by the action of aromatase on molecules of testosterone—and only male brains are exposed to significant levels of testosterone during brain development.

Research by Moore and her colleagues (reviewed by Moore, 1986) indicates that some of the masculinizing and defeminizing effects of androgens are even more indirect. As we will see in a later section in this chapter, female rats spend a considerable amount of time licking the genital region of their offspring. This behavior is very useful, because it stimulates urination and permits the mother to ingest the water and minerals that are released so they can be recycled in her milk.

Moore and her colleagues discovered that mothers spent much more time licking their male offspring and wondered whether this licking could have any effects on the sexual behavior of these offspring later in life. Indeed, it did. First, the experimenters found that androgens caused the secretion of an odorous chemical in the male pups' urine, which was attractive to the mothers. Next, they found that if they destroyed the mothers' ability to smell the odor, the mothers failed to give the males special attention—and that these males showed decreases in their sexual behavior in adulthood. But if the experimenters stroked the genitals of the male pups with a small brush each day, the animals showed a greater level sexual behavior when they grew up. Thus, at least some of the organizational effects of androgens are accomplished through an intermediary—the infant's mother.

● Effects of Pheromones

Hormones transmit messages from one part of the body (the secreting gland) to another (the target tissue). Another class of chemicals, called **pheromones,** carries messages

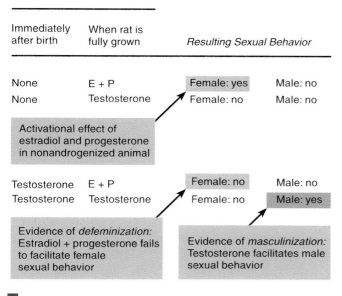

Figure 10.9
Organizational effects of testosterone. Around the time of birth, testosterone masculinizes and defeminizes rodents' sexual behavior.

pheromone (*fair* oh moan)   A chemical released by one animal that affects the behavior or physiology of another animal; usually smelled or tasted.

from one animal to another. Some of these chemicals, like hormones, affect reproductive behavior. Karlson and Luscher (1959) coined the term, from the Greek *pherein*, "to carry," and *horman*, "to excite." Pheromones are released by one animal and directly affect the physiology or behavior of another. In mammalian species, most pheromones are detected by means of olfaction.

Pheromones can affect reproductive physiology or behavior. First, let us consider the effects on reproductive physiology. When groups of female mice are housed together, their estrous cycles slow down and eventually stop. This phenomenon is known as the **Lee–Boot effect** (van der Lee and Boot, 1955). If groups of females are exposed to the odor of a male (or of his urine), they begin cycling again, and their cycles tend to be synchronized. This phenomenon is known as the **Whitten effect** (Whitten, 1959). The **Vandenbergh effect** (Vandenbergh, Whitsett, and Lombardi, 1975) is the acceleration of the onset of puberty in a female rodent caused by the odor of a male. Both the Whitten effect and the Vandenbergh effect are caused by a pheromone present only in the urine of intact adult males; the urine of a juvenile or castrated male has no effect. Thus, the production of the pheromone requires the presence of testosterone.

The **Bruce effect** (Bruce, 1960a, 1960b) is a particularly interesting phenomenon: When a recently impregnated female mouse encounters a normal male mouse other than the one with which she mated, the pregnancy is very likely to fail. This effect, too, is caused by a substance secreted in the urine of intact males—but not of males that have been castrated. Thus, a male mouse that encounters a pregnant female is able to prevent the birth of infants carrying another male's genes and subsequently impregnate the female himself. And this phenomenon is advantageous even from the female's point of view. The fact that the new male has managed to take over the old male's territory indicates that he is probably healthier and more vigorous—and therefore his genes will contribute to the formation of offspring more likely to survive.

As you learned in Chapter 7, detection of odors is accomplished by the olfactory bulbs, which constitute the primary olfactory system. However, the four effects that pheromones have on reproductive cycles appear to be mediated by another organ—the **vomeronasal organ**—which consists of a small group of sensory receptors arranged around a pouch connected by a duct to the nasal passage. The vomeronasal organ, which is present in all orders of mammals except for cetaceans (whales and dolphins), projects to the **accessory olfactory bulb**, located immediately behind the olfactory bulb (Wysocki, 1979). (See *Figure 10.10*.) The vomeronasal organ probably does not detect

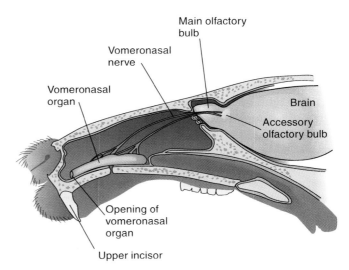

Figure 10.10
The rodent accessory olfactory system.
(Adapted from Wysocki, C.J. *Neuroscience & Biobehavioral Reviews,* 1979, 3, 301–341.)

airborne molecules, as the olfactory bulbs do, but instead is sensitive to nonvolatile compounds found in urine or other substances. In fact, stimulation of a nerve that serves the nasal region of the hamster causes fluid to be pumped into the vomeronasal organ, which exposes the receptors to any substances that may be present (Meredith and O'Connell, 1979). This pump is activated whenever the animal encounters a novel stimulus (Meredith, 1994).

Lee–Boot effect   The increased incidence of false pregnancies seen in female animals that are housed together; caused by a pheromone in the animals' urine; first observed in mice.

Whitten effect   The synchronization of the menstrual or estrous cycles of a group of females, which occurs only in the presence of a pheromone in a male's urine.

Vandenbergh effect   The earlier onset of puberty seen in female animals that are housed with males; caused by a pheromone in the male's urine; first observed in mice.

Bruce effect   Termination of pregnancy caused by the odor of a pheromone in the urine of a male other than the one that impregnated the female; first identified in mice.

vomeronasal organ *(voah mer oh **nay** zul)*   A sensory organ that detects the presence of certain chemicals, especially when a liquid is actively sniffed; mediates the effects of some pheromones.

accessory olfactory bulb   A neural structure located in the main olfactory bulb that receives information from the vomeronasal organ.

Removal of the accessory olfactory bulb disrupts the Lee–Boot effect, the Whitten effect, the Vandenbergh effect, and the Bruce effect; thus, this organ is essential for these phenomena (Halpern, 1987). The accessory olfactory bulb sends axons to the **medial nucleus of the amygdala,** which in turn projects to the preoptic area and anterior hypothalamus and to the ventromedial nucleus of the hypothalamus. (As you learned in Chapter 7, so does the main olfactory bulb.) Thus, the neural circuit responsible for the effects of these pheromones appears to involve these regions. As we shall see, the preoptic area, the medial amygdala, and the ventromedial nucleus of the hypothalamus all play important roles in reproductive behavior. (See *Figure 10.11.*)

The Bruce effect involves learning; the female obviously learns to recognize the odor of the male with which she mates, because his odor will not cause her to abort if she encounters it later. This learning appears to require the activity of a set of noradrenergic axons that enter the olfactory bulbs and form synapses with neurons in both the main and accessory olfactory bulbs. Keverne and de la Riva

(1982) found that after these axons had been destroyed with infusions of 6-hydroxydopamine (6-HD), a female mouse would not learn to recognize the odor of the male that mated with her; even *his* odor would cause her to abort.

It is possible that the stimuli associated with copulation trigger the noradrenergic mechanism and "imprint" the odor of the male on the female, ensuring that she will not abort if she later encounters his odor. Indeed, Rosser and Keverne (1985) found that vaginal stimulation increases the activity in the noradrenergic axons that serve the olfactory bulbs. As other studies have shown (Gray, Freeman, and Skinner, 1986; Leon, 1987), the release of norepinephrine in the olfactory bulbs is necessary for olfactory learning.

Besides having effects on reproductive physiology, some pheromones directly affect behavior. For example, pheromones present in the vaginal secretions of female hamsters stimulate sexual behavior in males. Males are attracted to the secretions of females, and they sniff and lick the female's genitals before copulating. In fact, there may be two categories of pheromones, one detected by the vomeronasal organ and another detected by the olfactory epithelium; mating behavior of male hamsters is disrupted only if *both* systems are interrupted (Powers and Winans, 1975; Winans and Powers, 1977). As we saw, both the primary and accessory olfactory systems send fibers to the medial nucleus of the amygdala. Lehman and Winans (1982) found that lesions of the medial amygdala abolished the sexual behavior of male hamsters. Thus, the amygdala is part of the system that mediates the effects of pheromones on the sexual behavior of male hamsters.

Singer and his colleagues (Singer et al., 1986; Singer, 1991) succeeded in isolating and analyzing the molecular structure of a sex-attractant pheromone in the vaginal discharge of female hamsters, a protein that they named *aphrodisin.* They tested the effectiveness of this pheromone by swabbing it on the hindquarters of an anesthetized male hamster; test males who sniffed the substance subsequently attempted to mount the animal.

Some evidence suggests that males may also produce sex-attractant pheromones that affect the behavior of females. If given a choice, receptive female rats prefer to be close to normal males rather than to males that have been castrated; this preference disappears after the vomeronasal

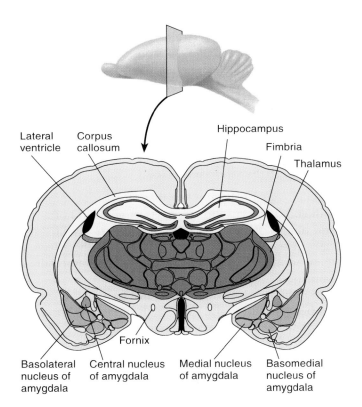

Lateral ventricle

Corpus callosum

Hippocampus

Fimbria

Thalamus

Fornix

Basolateral nucleus of amygdala

Central nucleus of amygdala

Medial nucleus of amygdala

Basomedial nucleus of amygdala

▌ *Figure 10.11*
A cross section through the rat brain showing the location of the amygdala.
(Adapted from Swanson, L.W. *Brain Maps: Structure of the Rat Brain.* New York: Elsevier, 1992.)

medial nucleus of the amygdala *(a **mig** da la)* A nucleus that receives olfactory information from the olfactory bulb and accessory olfactory bulb; involved in the effects of odors and pheromones on reproductive behavior.

organ is destroyed (Romero et al., 1990). In addition, females who mate briefly with a series of males become more and more receptive. Rajendren, Dudley, and Moss (1990) found that this increased receptivity, too, is abolished by destruction of the vomeronasal organ.

It appears that at least some pheromone-related phenomena occur in humans. McClintock (1971) studied the menstrual cycles of women attending an all-female college. She found that women who spent a large amount of time together tended to have synchronized cycles—their menstrual periods began within a day or two of one another. In addition, women who regularly spent some time in the presence of men tended to have shorter cycles than those who rarely spent time with (smelled?) men.

Russell, Switz, and Thompson (1977) obtained direct evidence that olfactory stimuli can synchronize women's menstrual cycles. The investigators collected daily samples of a woman's underarm sweat. They dissolved the samples in alcohol and swabbed them on the upper lips of a group of women three times each week, in the order in which they were originally taken. The cycles of the women who received the extract (but not those of control subjects whose lips were swabbed with pure alcohol) began to synchronize with the cycle of the odor donor.

Some investigators have studied the possibility that odors produced by vaginal secretions may affect a woman's sexual attractiveness. Doty et al. (1975) found, however, that both males and females rated these odors as unpleasant—although secretions obtained around the time of ovulation were rated as less unpleasant. Thus, a woman's menstrual cycle appears to affect the odor of her vaginal secretions, but there is no direct evidence that these changes increase her sexual attractiveness.

Cowley and Brookshank (1991) obtained some interesting evidence that suggests that pheromones may affect the social behavior of humans. They asked male and female college students to wear necklaces overnight and to keep a record of their social interactions the following day. Some of the necklaces contained *androstenol,* a substance found in human underarm sweat—especially that of males. Other necklaces contained an inert control substance. The investigators found that the androstenol had no effect on the social interactions of male subjects, but that female subjects engaged in more social exchanges with men. Thus, exposure to a substance normally produced by men has at least a small effect on women's tendency to engage in social interactions with men.

Although there is currently only scanty evidence that pheromones play a role in sexual attraction in higher primates, the familiar odor of a sex partner may have a positive effect on sexual arousal. We are not generally conscious of the fact, but we can identify other people on the basis of olfactory cues. For example, a study by Russell (1976) found that people were able to distinguish by odor between T-shirts that they had worn and those previously worn by other people. They could also tell whether the unknown owner of a T-shirt was male or female. Thus, it is likely that men and women can *learn* to be attracted by their partners' characteristic odors, just as they can learn to be attracted by the sound of their voice. In an instance like this, the odors are serving simply as sensory cues, not as pheromones.

In the past, most investigators believed that the human nose did not contain a vomeronasal organ, and thus they assumed that all effects of pheromones on humans involved the main olfactory system. However, recent studies suggests that we do have such an organ, and that this organ contains chemosensitive neurons. Two plastic surgeons, Garcia-Velasco and Mondragon (1991), on examining the olfactory mucosae of 1000 patients during surgical reconstructions of their noses, found vomeronasal organs in virtually every case. Monti-Bloch et al. (1994) stimulated the vomeronasal organ and the olfactory epithelium with various chemicals suggested by previous research to act as pheromones and recorded the organ's electrical activity. The investigators found that some chemicals produced electrical responses in men, while others produced responses in women. The chemicals did not affect the activity of the olfactory system. Whether these chemicals serve as pheromones in humans—and if they do, what functions they serve—is still not known.

● Human Sexual Behavior

Human sexual behavior, like that of other mammals, is influenced by activational effects of gonadal hormones and, almost certainly, organizational effects as well. But as we will see in the following subsections, the effects of these hormones are different in our species—especially in women.

If hormones have organizational effects on human sexual behavior, they must exert these effects by altering the development of the brain. Although there is good evidence that prenatal exposure to androgens affects development of the human brain, we cannot yet be certain that this exposure has long-lasting behavioral effects. The evidence pertaining to these issues is discussed later, in a section on sexual orientation.

Activational Effects of Sex Hormones in Women

As we saw, the sexual behavior of most female mammals other than higher primates is controlled by the ovarian hormones estradiol and progesterone. (In some species, such as cats and rabbits, only estradiol is necessary.) As Wallen (1990) pointed out, the ovarian hormones control not only the *willingness* (or even eagerness) of an estrous female to mate but also her *ability* to mate. That is, a male rat cannot copulate with a female rat that is not in estrus. Even if he would overpower her and mount her, her lordosis response would not occur, and he would be unable to achieve intromission. (The neural control of the lordosis response and the effects of ovarian hormones on it are described later in this chapter.)

In higher primates (including our own species), the ability to mate is not controlled by ovarian hormones. There are no physical barriers to sexual intercourse during any part of the menstrual cycle. If a woman or other female primate consents to sexual activity at any time (or is forced to submit by a male), intercourse can certainly take place.

This difference between females with estrous cycles and menstrual cycles has obscured the effects of ovarian hormones on the sexual behavior of female primates. Most studies have reported that fluctuations in the level of the ovarian hormones have only a minor effect on women's sexual interest (Adams, Gold, and Burt, 1978; Morris et al., 1987). However, as Wallen (1990) pointed out, these studies have almost all involved married women who live with their husbands. In stable, monogamous relationships in which the partners are together on a daily basis, sexual activity can be instigated by either of them. Normally, a husband does not force his wife to have intercourse with him, but even if she is not interested in engaging in sexual activity at that moment, she may find that she wants to do so because of her affection for him. In fact, a study of lesbian couples (whose menstrual cycles are likely to be synchronized) found a significant increase in sexual interest and activity during the middle portions of the women's cycles (Matteo and Rissman, 1984).

Several studies have found that the sexual behavior of female monkeys is only poorly related to their menstrual cycles. However, most of these studies were carried out with small numbers of monkeys living in small cages. Thus, intercourse was as likely to be instigated by a male as by the female. Wallen et al. (1986) observed female monkeys that were housed in large groups in large cages, in a situation in which a female could seek out a sex partner if she wanted one but could avoid sexual contact if she preferred. Figure 10.12 contrasts the results of these two types of studies; note that the sexual activity of females housed in large-group situations closely corresponded with their cycles of ovarian hormones. (See *Figure 10.12.*)

These results pose an interesting question. If all of a woman's sexual encounters were initiated by her, without

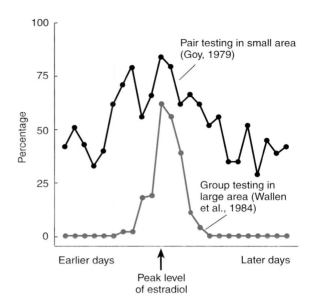

Figure 10.12
Percentage of tests in which ejaculations occurred in the course of a female monkey's menstrual cycle.
(Adapted from Wallen, K. *Neuroscience and Biobehavioral Reviews*, 1990, *14*, 233–241; after Goy, 1979 and Wallen et al., 1984.)

regard to her partner's desires, would we find as strong an effect of ovarian hormones as Wallen and his colleagues found in monkeys? As Alexander et al. (1990) showed, women taking oral contraceptives (which prevent the normal cycles in secretion of ovarian hormones) were less likely to show fluctuations in sexual interest during the menstrual cycle. In any event, the more recent results with monkeys indicate that the possibility remains that ovarian hormones *do* have a significant effect on a woman's sexual desire.

Where higher primates and animals with estrous cycles differ is in their reaction to androgens. In mammals other than primates, androgens stimulate only male sexual behavior. Persky et al. (1978) studied the sexual activity and blood levels of various hormones in married couples over a period of three menstrual cycles. They found that the frequency of intercourse over the entire cycle was at least moderately correlated with the wife's peak testosterone level, which occurs around the time of ovulation. In addition, the wives reported more sexual gratification when their testosterone levels were high. A follow-up study by Morris et al. (1987) found similar results. And in a study of women using oral contraceptives, Alexander and Sherwin (1993) found that plasma testosterone levels were correlated with the women's "sexual desire, sexual thoughts, and anticipation of sexual activity."

In a carefully controlled study, Sherwin, Gelfand, and Brender (1985) investigated the effects of testosterone on sexual interest in women who had undergone hysterectomies and ovariectomies. They found the hormone increased the intensity of the women's sexual desire and the frequency of sexual fantasies. As Sherwin (1994) concluded in a review of the relevant literature, "it would now seem that testosterone is the hormone most crucially implicated in the maintenance of . . . sexual desire, in women just as it is in men." (p. 423)

Another hormone, oxytocin, may play a role in a woman's sexual response. As we saw earlier in this chapter, oxytocin appears to stimulate contractions of the uterus and vagina that accompany orgasm, and some investigators have suggested that the pleasant "afterglow" that follows sexual intercourse may involve the action of oxytocin. Whether this hormone actually plays a role in pair-bonding in humans has yet to be established. I find it difficult to imagine how this question could be addressed through scientific study.

Activational Effects of Sex Hormones in Men

Although women and mammals with estrous cycles differ in their behavioral responsiveness to sex hormones, men resemble other mammals in their behavioral responsiveness to testosterone. With normal levels they can be potent and fertile; without testosterone, sperm production ceases and, sooner or later, so does sexual potency. Some investigators have said that the sexual activity of humans is "emancipated" from the effects of hormones. In one sense this is true. Many men who have been castrated (for medical reasons) do report a continuing interest in sexual activity with their wives. Even if sexual activity no longer takes the form of intercourse, other types of sexual contact can occur.

The decline of sexual activity after castration is quite variable. As reported by Money and Ehrhardt (1972), some men lose potency immediately, whereas others show a slow, gradual decline over several years. Perhaps at least some of the variability is a function of prior experience; practice not only may "make perfect" but may also forestall a decline in function. Although there is no direct evidence with respect to this possibility in humans, Rosenblatt and Aronson (1958a, 1958b) found that male cats that had engaged in high levels of sexual activity remained potent for a longer time after they were castrated. Also, there are other sources of androgens besides the testes that may supply at least small amounts of male sex hormones: the adrenal glands, the prostate gland, and even fat tissue (Carter, 1992).

Testosterone not only affects sexual activity but also is affected by it—or even by thinking about it. A scientist stationed on a remote island (Anonymous, 1970) removed his beard with an electrical shaver each day and weighed the clippings. Just before he left for visits to the mainland (and to the company of a female companion), his beard began growing faster. Because rate of beard growth is related to androgen levels, the effect indicates that his anticipation of sexual activity stimulated testosterone production. Confirming these results, Hellhammer, Hubert, and Schurmeyer (1985) found that watching an erotic film increased men's testosterone level.

As we saw earlier in this chapter, oxytocin and prolactin may play a role in male sexual behavior. Both hormones are secreted during orgasm, and both may be at least partly responsible for the refractory period. In addition, oxytocin may even contribute to the "afterglow" that is usually experienced by both partners after making love.

● Sexual Orientation

What controls a person's sexual orientation—the gender of the preferred sex partner? Some people (especially males) who are essentially heterosexual engage in homosexual episodes sometime during their lives. Although many animals occasionally engage in sexual activity with a member of the same sex, *exclusive* homosexuality appears to occur only in humans (Ehrhardt and Meyer-Bahlburg, 1981). Animals of other species, if they are not exclusively heterosexual, are likely to be bisexual, engaging in sexual activity with members of both sexes. In contrast, the number of men and women who describe themselves as exclusively homosexual exceeds the number who describe themselves as bisexual.

Some investigators believe that homosexuality is a result of childhood experiences, especially interactions between the child and parents. A large-scale study of several hundred male and female homosexuals reported by Bell, Weinberg, and Hammersmith (1981) attempted to assess the effects of these factors. The researchers found no evidence that homosexuals had been raised by domineering mothers or submissive fathers, as some clinicians had suggested. The best predictor of adult homosexuality was a self-report of homosexual feelings, which usually preceded homosexual activity by three years. The investigators concluded that their data did not support social explanations for homosexuality but were consistent with the possibility that homosexuality is at least partly biologically determined.

If homosexuality does have a physiological cause, it certainly is not variations in the levels of sex hormones during adulthood. Many studies have examined the levels of sex steroids in male homosexuals (Meyer-Bahlburg, 1984), and the vast majority of them found these levels to be similar to those of heterosexuals. A few studies suggest that about 30 percent of female homosexuals have elevated levels of testosterone (but still lower than those found in men). Whether these differences are related to a biological cause of lesbianism or whether differences in lifestyles may increase the secretion of testosterone is not yet known.

A more likely biological cause of homosexuality is a subtle difference in brain structure caused by differences in the amount of prenatal exposure to androgens. Perhaps, then, the brains of male homosexuals are neither masculinized nor defeminized, those of female homosexuals are masculinized and defeminized, and those of bisexuals are masculinized but not defeminized. Of course, these are *speculations* that so far cannot be supported by human data; they are not *conclusions.* They should be regarded as suggestions to guide future research.

Prenatal Androgenization of Genetic Females

Evidence suggests that prenatal androgens can affect human social behavior and sexual orientation, as well as anatomy. In a disorder known as **congenital adrenal hyperplasia (CAH),** the adrenal glands secrete abnormal amounts of androgens. (*Hyperplasia* means "excessive formation.") The secretion of androgens begins prenatally; thus, the syndrome causes prenatal masculinization. Boys born with CAH develop normally; the extra androgen does not seem to have significant effects. However, a girl with CAH will be born with an enlarged clitoris, and her labia may be partly fused together. (As Figure 10.4 shows, the scrotum and labia develop from the same tissue in the fetus.) If the masculinization of the genitals is pronounced, surgery will be performed to correct them. In any event, once the syndrome is identified, the person will be given a synthetic hormone that suppresses the abnormal secretion of androgens.

Money, Schwartz, and Lewis (1984) studied thirty young women with a history of CAH. They had all been born with enlarged clitorises and partly fused labia, which led to the diagnosis. (A few mild cases were not diagnosed for several years.) Once the diagnosis was made, they were treated with drugs that suppress the secretion of adrenal androgens and, if necessary, genital surgery was performed. Money and his colleagues asked the young women to describe their sexual orientation. Thirty-seven percent of the women described themselves as bisexual or homosexual, 40 percent said they were exclusively heterosexual, and 23 percent refused to talk about their sex lives. If the non-committal women are excluded from the sample, the percentage of homosexuality or bisexuality rises to 48 percent.

The Kinsey report on sexuality in women (Kinsey et al., 1943) reported that approximately 10 percent of American women had had some sexual contact with another woman by the age of 20; in the sample of women exposed prenatally to androgens the percentage was at least four times as high. The results therefore suggest that the exposure of a female fetus to an abnormally high level of androgens does affect sexual orientation. A plausible explanation is that the effect takes place in the brain, but we must remember that the androgens also affect the genitals; possibly, the changes in the genitals played a role in shaping the development of the girls' sexual orientation. If the differences seen in sexual orientation *were* caused by effects of the prenatal androgens on brain development, then we could reasonably conclude that androgens have this effect in males, too. That is, these results support the hypothesis that male sexual orientation is at least partly determined by masculinizing (and defeminizing) effects of androgens on the human brain.

Because controlled experiments cannot be performed on humans, some investigators have turned to our close relatives to see whether exposure to prenatal androgens has enduring behavioral effects. Goy, Bercovitch, and McBrair (1988) administered injections of testosterone to pregnant monkeys. The testosterone entered the blood supply of the fetuses and masculinized them. Female infants that had been exposed to androgens during early fetal development were born with masculinized genitals; the genitals of those that had been exposed to androgens later were normal. *Both* groups showed differences in their sociosexual interactions with peers, displaying a higher proportion of male-like behavior than normal females did. For example, even as young adults, the group with normal genitals continued to mount their peers significantly more than normal females did. The results suggest that genital changes cannot account for all the behavioral effects of prenatal exposure to androgens in primates. Whether *human* primates share these characteristics is, of course, another question.

Failure of Androgenization of Genetic Males

As we saw, genetic males with androgen insensitivity syndrome develop as females, with female external genitalia—but also with testes and without uterus or Fallopian tubes. If an individual with this syndrome is raised as a girl, all is well. Normally, the testes are removed because they often become cancerous; but if they are not, the body will mature into that of a woman at the time of puberty through the effects of the small amounts of estradiol produced by

congenital adrenal hyperplasia (CAH) (*hy per **play** zha*) A condition characterized by hypersecretion of androgens by the adrenal cortex; in females, causes masculinization of the external genitalia.

the testes. (If the testes are removed, the person will be given estradiol to accomplish the same result.) At adulthood the individual will function sexually as a woman, although surgical lengthening of the vagina may be necessary. Women with this syndrome report average sex drives, including normal frequency of orgasm in intercourse. Most marry and lead normal sex lives.

Studies of the social behavior of people with androgen insensitivity syndrome indicate that they tend to be very "feminine" (Money and Ehrhardt, 1972). There is no indication of sexual orientation toward women. Thus, the lack of androgen receptors appears to prevent both the masculinizing and defeminizing effects of androgens on a person's sexual interest. But you will recall that, at least in laboratory animals, prenatal masculinization and defeminization of sexual behavior are accomplished largely by stimulation of intracellular estrogen receptors by testosterone that has been aromatized to estradiol. The lack of masculinization or defeminization seen in genetic males with androgen insensitivity syndrome suggests that in humans, these effects are carried out by the action of testosterone on androgen receptors, not by aromatized testosterone. Of course, it is also possible that rearing a child as a girl could play an important role in that person's sexual orientation.

Sexual Orientation and the Brain

The human brain is a sexually dimorphic organ. This fact has long been suspected, even before confirmation was received from anatomical studies and studies of regional cerebral metabolism using PET and functional MRI. For example, neurologists discovered that the two hemispheres of a woman's brain appear to share functions more than those of a man's brain do. If a man sustains a stroke that damages the left side of the brain, he is more likely to show impairments in language than a woman with similar damage. Presumably, the woman's right hemisphere shares language functions with the left, so that damage to one hemisphere is less devastating than it is in men. Also, men's brains are, on average, somewhat larger—apparently because men's bodies are generally larger than those of women's. In addition, the sizes of some specific regions of the telencephalon and diencephalon are different in males and females, and the shape of the corpus callosum may also be sexually dimorphic. (See Breedlove, 1994 and Swaab, Gooren, and Horman, 1995, for specific references.)

Most investigators believe that the sexual dimorphism of the human brain is a result of differential exposure to androgens prenatally and during early postnatal life. Of course, additional changes could occur at the time of puberty, when another surge in androgens occurs. The differences could even be a result of differences in the social environments of males and females. We cannot manipulate the hormone levels of humans before and after birth as we can with laboratory animals, so it may be a long time before enough evidence is gathered to permit us to make definite conclusions.

Several studies have examined the brains of deceased heterosexual and homosexual men and heterosexual women. So far, these studies have found differences in the size of three different subregions of the brain: the suprachiasmatic nucleus, a sexually dimorphic nucleus of the hypothalamus, and the anterior commissure (Swaab and Hofman, 1990; LeVay, 1991; Allen and Gorski, 1992). You are already familiar with the suprachiasmatic nucleus from Chapter 9; the anterior commissure is a fiber bundle that interconnects parts of the left and right temporal lobes. The suprachiasmatic nucleus was found to be larger in homosexual men and smaller in heterosexual men and women; a sexually dimorphic nucleus of the hypothalamus (the *third interstitial nucleus of the anterior hypothalamus*, or *INAH-3*) was found to be larger in heterosexual men and smaller in homosexual men and heterosexual women; and the anterior commissure was found to be larger in homosexual men and heterosexual women and smaller in heterosexual men. Obviously, the differences did not follow a simple pattern.

Although this section has been considering sexual orientation—the sex of a person to whom an individual is sexually and romantically attracted—another sexual characteristic is related to structural differences in the brain. Zhou et al. (1995) found that the size of a particular region of the forebrain, the central subdivision of the *bed nucleus of the stria terminalis (BNST)*, is larger in males than in females. They also found that in male transsexuals, this nucleus is as small as it is in females. The size of this nucleus was as large in male homosexuals as in male heterosexuals. Thus, its size was related to sexual *identity*, not to sexual *orientation*. (See *Figure 10.13.*) Male transsexuals are men who regard themselves as females trapped in male bodies. Some go so far as to seek medical assistance to obtain female sex hormones and sex-change operations. (Most male homosexuals have male sexual identities; although they are romantically and sexually oriented toward other men, they do not regard themselves as women nor do they wish to be.) Whether the BNST actually plays a role in a person's sexual identity will have to be determined by further research.

We cannot necessarily conclude that any of the brain regions I just mentioned are directly involved in people's sexual orientation (or sexual identity), but the results do

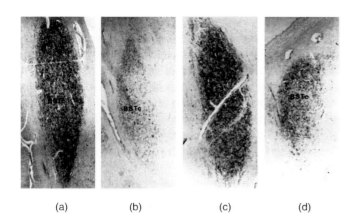

(a)   (b)   (c)   (d)

Figure 10.13
Photomicrographs of slices of the human brain containing the central subdivision of the bed nucleus of the stria terminalis (BNST). (a) From a heterosexual man. (b) From a heterosexual woman. (c) From a homosexual man. (d) From a male-to-female transsexual. (BSTc = central subdivision of the bed nucleus of the stria terminalis.)
(From Zhou, J.-N., Hofman, M.A., Gooren, L.J.G., and Swaab, D.F. *Nature*, 1995, *378*, 68–70. Reprinted with permission.)

suggest the following: The brains of heterosexual women, heterosexual men, and homosexual men may have been exposed to different patterns of hormones prenatally. The *real* differences—if indeed sexual orientation is determined by prenatal exposure to androgens—may lie elsewhere in the brain, but at least we have an indication that differences do exist. There remains also the possibility that a person's lifestyle may affect the structure of parts of his or her brain; thus, the differences mentioned in this section could be the *result* of people's sexual orientation rather than the cause. In any event, more research must be done on this subject.

Possible Causes of Differences in Brain Development

If sexual orientation is, indeed, affected by differences in exposure of the developing brain to androgens, what factors might cause this exposure to vary? Presumably, something must decrease the prenatal androgen levels to which male homosexuals are exposed and increase the levels to which female homosexuals are exposed. As we saw, congenital adrenal hyperplasia exposes the developing fetus to increased levels of androgens, but most homosexual women do not have CAH. So far, no other plausible sources of high levels of prenatal androgens have been proposed.

Studies performed with laboratory animals suggest an event that could potentially interfere with prenatal andro-

genization of males: maternal stress. Ward (1972) subjected pregnant rats to periods of stress by confining them and exposing them to a bright light, which suppresses androgen production in male fetuses. The male rats born to the stressed mothers were less likely than control subjects to display male sexual behavior and were more likely to display female sexual behavior when they were given injections of estradiol and progesterone. Another study (Ward and Stehm, 1991) found that the play behavior of juvenile male rats whose mothers were stressed while pregnant resembled that of females more than that of males—that is, the animals showed less rough-and-tumble play. Thus, the behavioral effects caused by prenatal stress are not restricted to changes in sexual behavior.

Other studies with laboratory animals have shown that besides having behavioral effects, prenatal stress reduces the size of a sexually dimorphic nucleus of the preoptic area, which normally is larger in males than in females, and which plays an important role in male sex behavior (Anderson et al., 1986). Although we cannot assume that prenatal stress in humans and laboratory animals has similar effects on the brain and behavior, the results of these studies are consistent with the hypothesis that male homosexuality may be related to events that reduce exposure to prenatal androgens.

Heredity and Sexual Orientation

Another factor that may play a role in sexual orientation is heredity. Twin studies take advantage of the fact that identical twins have identical genes, whereas the genetic similarity between fraternal twins is, on the average, 50 percent. Bailey and Pillard (1991) studied pairs of male twins in which at least one member identified himself as homosexual. If both twins are homosexual, they are said to be *concordant* for this trait. If only one is homosexual, the twins are said to be *discordant*. Thus, if homosexuality has a genetic basis, the percentage of monozygotic twins concordant for homosexuality should be higher than that for dizygotic twins. And this is exactly what Bailey and Pillard found: The concordance rate was 52 percent for identical twins and only 22 percent for fraternal twins.

Genetic factors also appear to affect female homosexuality. Bailey et al. (1993) found that the concordance of female monozygotic twins for homosexuality was 48 percent, while that of dizygotic twins was 16 percent. Another study, by Pattatucci and Hamer (1995), found an increased incidence of homosexuality and bisexuality in sisters, daughters, nieces, and female cousins (through a paternal uncle) of homosexual women.

To summarize, evidence suggests that two biological factors—prenatal hormonal exposure and heredity—may affect a person's sexual orientation. These research findings certainly contradict the suggestion that a person's sexual orientation is a moral issue. It appears that homosexuals are no more responsible for their sexual orientation than heterosexuals are. Ernulf, Innala, and Whitam (1989) found that people who believed that homosexuals were "born that way" expressed more positive attitudes toward them than people who believed that they "chose to be" or "learned to be" that way. Thus, we can hope that research on the origins of homosexuality will reduce prejudice based on a person's sexual orientation. The question, "Why does someone become homosexual?" will probably be answered when we find out why someone becomes *heterosexual*.

Interim Summary

Sexual behaviors are controlled by the organizational and activational effects of hormones. The female reproductive cycle (menstrual cycle or estrous cycle) begins with the maturation of one or more ovarian follicles, which occurs in response to the secretion of FSH by the anterior pituitary gland. As the ovarian follicle matures, it secretes estradiol, which causes the lining of the uterus to develop. When estradiol reaches a critical level, it causes the pituitary gland to secrete a surge of LH, triggering ovulation. The empty ovarian follicle becomes a corpus luteum, under the continued influence of LH, and secretes estradiol and progesterone. If pregnancy does not occur, the corpus luteum dies and stops producing hormones, and menstruation begins.

The sexual behavior of males of all mammalian species appears to depend on the presence of androgens. Oxytocin has a facilitatory effect on erection and ejaculation, whereas prolactin has a generally inhibitory effect. Both hormones may be involved in the male refractory period, and oxytocin in particular may be involved in social bonding. The proceptivity, receptivity, and attractiveness of female mammals other than primates depend primarily on estradiol and progesterone. In particular, estradiol has a priming effect on the subsequent appearance of progesterone. Oxytocin also may facilitate social bonding in females.

In most mammals, female sexual behavior is the norm, just as the female body and female sex organs are the norm. That is, unless prenatal androgens masculinize and defeminize the animal's brain, its sexual behavior will be feminine. Behavioral masculinization refers to the androgen-stimulated development of neural circuits that respond to testosterone in adulthood, producing male sexual behavior. Behavioral defeminization refers to the inhibitory effects of androgens on the development of neural circuits that respond to estradiol and progesterone in adulthood, producing female sexual behavior. Behavioral defeminization is caused by intracellular estradiol, derived from testosterone through the action of aromatase.

Some organizational effects of androgens are indirect. Androgens cause the secretion of a chemical into the urine of male rat pups that makes it more attractive to their mothers, which spend more time licking their anogenital region. This tactile stimulation contributes to their behavioral masculinization.

Pheromones can affect sexual physiology and behavior. Odorants present in the urine of female mice affect their estrous cycles, lengthening and eventually stopping them (Lee–Boot effect). Odorants present in the urine of male mice abolish these effects and cause the females' cycles to become synchronized (Whitten effect). (Phenomena similar to the Lee–Boot effect and the Whitten effect also occur in women.) Odorants can also accelerate the onset of puberty in females (Vandenbergh effect). In addition, the odor of the urine from a male other than the one that impregnated a female mouse will cause her to abort (Bruce effect). The Bruce effect involves learning the odor of the male that impregnates the female, and the activity of a noradrenergic input to the olfactory bulb (triggered by vaginal stimulation) is involved in this learning.

In the hamster, the attractiveness of an estrous female to the male derives in part from chemicals present in her vaginal secretions, detected by the olfactory epithelium and vomeronasal organ. Connections between the olfactory system and the amygdala appear to be important in stimulating male sexual behavior. One sex-attractant chemical, a protein named aphrodisin, has been isolated from the urine of female hamsters.

Males produce pheromones that affect female behavior. Female rats prefer to be near intact adult males rather than those whose testes have been removed, and contact with several males increases their level of sexual arousal; both phenomena disappear after removal of the vomeronasal system. The search for sex attractant pheromones in humans has so far been fruitless, although we may well recognize our sex partners by their odors. One study does suggest that exposure to androstenol, a substance present in male underarm sweat, may increase a woman's tendency to engage in social interchanges with men.

The behavioral effects of prenatal exposure to androgens in humans, if any, are not well understood. Studies of prenatally androgenized girls suggest that organizational effects may well influence the development of sexual orientation; androgenization appears to increase the incidence of homosexuality. If androgens cannot act (as they cannot in cases of androgen insensitivity syndrome), then the person's anatomy and behavior are feminine. Testosterone has an activational effect on the sexual behavior of men, just as it does on the behavior of other male mammals. Women do not require estradiol or progesterone in order to experience sexual interest or to engage in sexual behavior. These hormones may affect the quality and intensity of their sex drive, and studies comparing the sexual behavior of female monkeys housed in small groups with those housed in large groups in large cages suggest that the sexual proceptivity may be related to ovarian hormones, even in higher primates. However, the strongest hormonal effect on women's sex drives appears to come from androgens.

Sexual orientation (that is, heterosexuality or homosexuality) may be influenced by prenatal exposure to androgens. So far, researchers have obtained evidence that suggests that the sizes of three brain regions are related to a man's sexual orientation, and studies with rats have shown that events that cause stress during pregnancy can interfere with defeminization of the sexual behavior of the male offspring. The size of another part of the brain has been found to be related to sexual identity in males. In addition, twin studies suggest that heredity may play a role in sexual orientation in both men and women.

NEURAL CONTROL OF SEXUAL BEHAVIOR

The control of sexual behavior—at least in laboratory animals—involves different brain mechanisms in males and females. This section describes these mechanisms.

● Males

Spinal Mechanisms

Some sexual responses are controlled by neural circuits contained within the spinal cord. For example, genital stimulation can elicit sexual movements and postures in female cats and rats even after their spinal cord is transected below the brain (Beach, 1967; Hart, 1969). In male dogs with spinal cord transections genital stimulation can produce erection and ejaculation (Hart, 1967). Thus, the brain is not required for these reflexes.

In humans, too, erection and ejaculation are controlled by spinal reflexes. Men with spinal damage have become fathers when their wives have been artificially inseminated with semen obtained by mechanical stimulation (Hart, 1978). Because the spinal damage prevents sensory information from reaching the brain, these men do not experience an orgasm; thus, they are unaware of the erection and ejaculation unless they see it happening. However, they do occasionally experience a "phantom erection" along with an orgasm (Money, 1960; Comarr, 1970). Nothing happens to their genitals or internal sex organs, but the spontaneous activity of various brain mechanisms gives rise to feelings of arousal and orgasm.

Breedlove and Arnold (1980, 1983) discovered striking sex differences in the size of a nucleus in the ventral horn of the lumbar region of the spinal cord of rats. This structure, called the **spinal nucleus of the bulbocavernosus (SNB),** contains motor neurons whose axons innervate the bulbocavernosus muscle, which is attached to the base of the penis and is involved in sexual activity. Although the muscle is not present in female rats, it is present in both sexes in humans. (It is usually called the *sphincter vaginae* in women.) The size of this nucleus—which is larger in males than in females—is controlled by the level of androgens present in a newborn rat (Arnold and Jordan, 1988).

As we saw earlier in this chapter, Moore and her colleagues have found that in rats some of the masculinizing and defeminizing effects of androgens on behavior are indirect. That is, androgens make the urine of infant male pups more attractive to the mothers, which spend more time licking their anogenital region, which affects their behavior in adulthood. Moore, Dou, and Juraska (1992) found that this licking also affects the development of the structure of the nervous system. They found that when they destroyed the mothers' sense of smell so that they spent less time licking their male offspring, the animals showed 11 percent fewer neurons in the SNB. Thus, although androgens have direct effects on the survival of these motor neurons, tactile stimuli delivered by the mother reinforce these effects.

Brain Mechanisms

The **medial preoptic area (MPA),** located just rostral to the hypothalamus, is the forebrain region most critical for male sexual behavior. (As we will see later in this chapter and in Chapter 11, it is also critical for other sexually dimorphic behavior, including maternal behavior and territorial aggression.) Electrical stimulation of this region elicits male copulatory behavior (Malsbury, 1971), and sexual activity increases the firing rate of single neurons in the MPA (Shimura, Yamamoto, and Shimokochi, 1994; Mas,

---

spinal nucleus of the bulbocavernosus (SNB) *(bul bo kav er no sis)* A nucleus located in the lower spinal cord; in some species of rodents, present only in males.

medial preoptic area (MPA) An area of cell bodies just rostral to the hypothalamus; plays an essential role in male sexual behavior.

1995). In addition, the act of copulation increases the metabolic activity of the MPA and induces the production of Fos protein (Oaknin et al., 1989; Robertson et al., 1991; Wood and Newman, 1993). (The significance of the Fos protein as an indicator of neural activation was discussed in Chapter 5.) Finally, destruction of the MPA permanently abolishes male sexual behavior (Heimer and Larsson, 1966/1967).

Of course, the MPA does not stand alone. It receives chemosensory input from the vomeronasal organ through connections with the medial amygdala and the bed nucleus of the stria terminalis (BNST). (You will recall that in humans, the BNST is sexually dimorphic, and that it is smaller in transsexual males.) The MPA also receives somatosensory information from the genitals through connections with the midbrain reticular formation and the medial amygdala. (See *Figure 10.14.*)

The organizational effects of androgens are responsible for sexual dimorphisms in brain structure. Gorski et al. (1978) discovered a nucleus within the MPA of the rat that is three to seven times larger in males than in females. This area is called (appropriately enough) the **sexually dimorphic nucleus (SDN)** of the preoptic area. The size of this nucleus is controlled by the amount of androgens present during fetal development. According to Rhees, Shryne, and Gorski (1990a, 1990b), the critical period for masculinization of the SDN appears to start on the 18th day of gestation and end once the animals are five days old. (Normally, rats are born on the 22nd day of gestation. See *Figure 10.15.*)

In the section on sexual orientation I mentioned that Anderson et al. (1986) found that prenatal stress reduced the size of the SDN in male rats. These investigators also found that volume of the SDN in an individual male rat was directly related to the animal's level of sexual activity. De Jonge et al. (1989) confirmed the importance of these results, observing that lesions of the SDN decrease masculine sexual behavior. In addition, Humm, Lambert, and Kinsley (1995) found that when prenatally stressed male rats were exposed to sexually receptive females, little Fos protein was seen in the MPA.

Androgens exert their activational effects on neurons in the medial preoptic area. If a male rodent is castrated in adulthood, its sexual behavior will cease. However, the behavior can be reinstated by implanting a small amount of testosterone directly into the medial preoptic area (Davidson, 1980; Nyby, Matochik, and Barfield, 1992). This region has been shown to contain a high concentration of androgen receptors in the male rat brain—more than five times as many as are found in females (Roselli, Handa, and Resko, 1989).

The precise role of the medial preoptic area in male sexual behavior is still being debated. According to some researchers, damage to this structure seems to disrupt copulatory ability rather than sexual motivation. For example, Slimp, Hart, and Goy (1975) found that male monkeys whose medial preoptic areas had been damaged would no longer copulate with a female, but they would often masturbate while watching a female in an adjacent cage. However, Shimura, Yamamoto, and Shimokochi (1994) found that some neurons in the MPA became active while a male rat was pursuing a receptive female. The activity started a few seconds before the animal actually started moving, which suggests that these neurons play a role in motivation rather than performance of copulatory behaviors.

Neurons in the medial preoptic area send axons to the lateral tegmental field of the midbrain (just dorsal and me-

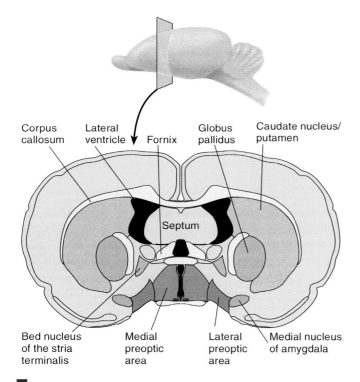

Corpus callosum   Lateral ventricle   Fornix   Globus pallidus   Caudate nucleus/ putamen

Septum

Bed nucleus of the stria terminalis   Medial preoptic area   Lateral preoptic area   Medial nucleus of amygdala

Figure 10.14
A cross section through the rat brain showing the location of the medial preoptic area (MPA), the medial amygdala, and the bed nucleus of the stria terminalis (BNST).
(Adapted from Swanson, L.W. *Brain Maps: Structure of the Rat Brain.* New York: Elsevier, 1992.)

sexually dimorphic nucleus   A nucleus in the preoptic area that is much larger in males than in females; first observed in rats; plays a role in male sexual behavior.

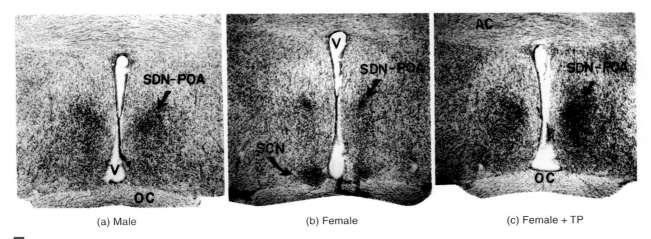

(a) Male   (b) Female   (c) Female + TP

Figure 10.15
Photomicrographs of sections through the preoptic area of the rat brain. (a) Normal male. (b) Normal female. (c) Androgenized female. SDN-POA = sexually dimorphic nucleus of the preoptic area; OC = optic chiasm; V = third ventricle; SCN = suprachiasmatic nucleus; AC = anterior commissure.
(From Gorski, R.A., in *Neuroendocrine Perspectives*, Vol. 2, edited by E.E. Müller and R.M. MacLeod. Amsterdam: Elsevier-North Holland, 1983.)

dial to the substantia nigra), and destruction of these axons disrupts male sexual behavior (Brackett and Edwards, 1984). In addition, Shimura and Shimokochi (1990) recorded from single neurons in the lateral tegmental field and found that the activity of virtually all neurons increased during various aspects of copulatory behavior. For example, some increased their firing rate only when the male achieved intromission. These results suggest that the medial preoptic area exerts its effect on male sexual behavior by activating motor mechanisms in the midbrain.

Other parts of the brain play a role in sexual behavior, too. As we saw, the medial amygdala receives information from the olfactory bulbs and the vomeronasal organ, and damage to this region disrupts many of the effects produced by pheromones. The medial amygdala is sexually dimorphic: One region within this structure (which contains an especially high concentration of androgen receptors) is 85 percent larger in male rats than in female rats (Hines, Allen, and Gorski, 1992). In addition, destruction of the medial amygdala disrupts the sexual behavior of male rats. De Jonge et al. (1992) found that the rats with these lesions took longer to mount receptive females and to ejaculate. Wood and Newman (1993) observed that mating increased the production of Fos protein in the medial amygdala, as well as the BNST and MPA. They also found that many of the activated neurons in these regions contained androgen receptors.

In humans, temporal lobe dysfunctions are often correlated with decreased sex drives. (The temporal lobes contain the amygdala, but the hippocampus and the temporal neocortex may also be involved.) For example, seizures that originate from localized, irritative lesions of the tem-

poral lobes are often associated with lack of interest in sexual activity (Blumer and Walker, 1975; Morrell, 1991). Morrell et al. (1994) found that men with temporal lobe epilepsy were much less likely than other men to have penile erections while watching an erotic film. Usually, if the seizures are successfully treated by medication or by surgical removal of the affected tissue, the person attains normal sexual interest.

Several neurotransmitters appear to affect male sexual behavior. As we saw earlier, oxytocin, a hormone secreted by the posterior pituitary gland, may play a role in ejaculation and its aftereffects. Oxytocin is also a transmitter substance in the brain (Arletti, Benelli, and Bertolini, 1992). Several studies (see Argiolas and Gessa, 1991) have shown that injections of oxytocin into the brains of male rats increase the likelihood of penile erections. Arletti, Benelli, and Bertolini (1992) found that intracerebral injections of this peptide had no effect on mounting behavior, but caused the rats to ejaculate sooner; thus, the role of this hormone in sexual behavior may be limited to its effects on erection and ejaculation.

Another peptide hormone secreted by the posterior pituitary gland, **vasopressin**, serves as a transmitter substance in the brain. (As we shall see in Chapter 12, vasopressin is involved in control of kidney function.) Vasopressin-secreting neurons are found in the medial amygdala and BNST and are found in higher numbers in males (Wang

vasopressin *(vay zo **press** in)* A hormone secreted by the posterior pituitary gland that controls the secretion of urine by the kidneys; also serves as a neurotransmitter in the brain.

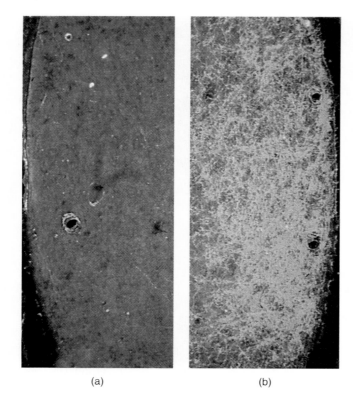

(a)　　　　　　　　(b)

Figure 10.16
Photomicrographs of frontal sections through half of the septum of two rats, arranged side by side for comparison. The bright yellow fibers are vasopressin-containing axons, stained by means of im-munocytochemistry. (a) The brain of a male castrated three months previously. The loss of testosterone has caused the vasopressin-con-taining axons to disappear. (b) The brain of a normal male.
(Courtesy of Geert DeVries, University of Massachusetts.)

rats. As we saw, when a male is castrated, its sexual performance declines. De Vries and his colleagues (see De Vries, 1990) found that this decline was reflected in a decrease in brain vasopressin. (See *Figure 10.16.*) If the animals were given drugs that stimulate vasopressin receptors in the brain, their sexual behavior declined more slowly. And when testosterone was administered to rats that had been castrated several weeks earlier, sexual activity and brain vasopressin returned at the same time.

Several studies have shown that the activity of dopaminergic synapses in the MPA is essential for male sexual behavior. In a microdialysis study, Hull et al. (1995) found that sexual activity increased the release of dopamine in the MPA. Microinjection of a dopamine antagonist in this region disrupts copulation and pursuit of females, whereas microinjection of a dopamine agonist facilitates erections and increases the rate of intromissions (Hull et al., 1986; Warner et al., 1991.)

Figure 10.17 summarizes the evidence I have presented in this section. (See *Figure 10.17.*)

and DeVries, 1995). Vasopressin appears to play an important role in male sexual behavior. Argiolas et al. (1988) found that administration of a vasopressin antagonist directly into the brain disrupted the sexual behavior of male

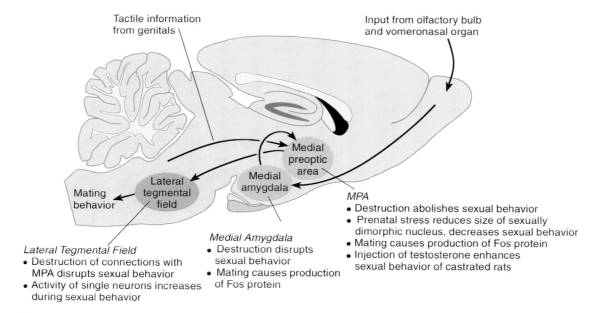

Figure 10.17
A possible explanation of the interacting excitatory effects of pheromones, genital stimulation, and testosterone on male sexual behavior.

314

● Females

Just as the MPA plays an essential role in male sex behavior, another region in the ventral forebrain plays a similar role in female sexual behavior: the **ventromedial nucleus of the hypothalamus (VMH).** A female rat with bilateral lesions of the ventromedial nuclei will not display lordosis, even if she is treated with estradiol and progesterone. Conversely, electrical stimulation of the ventromedial nucleus facilitates female sexual behavior (Pfaff and Sakuma, 1979). (See *Figure 10.18.*)

As we saw in the previous section, the medial amygdala of males receives chemosensory information from the vomeronasal system and somatosensory information from the genitals, and it sends efferent axons to the medial preoptic area. These connections are found in females as well. In addition, neurons in the medial amygdala also send efferent axons to the VMH. In fact, copulation or mechanical stimulation of the genitals or flanks increases the production of Fos protein in both the medial amygdala and the VMH (Pfaus et al, 1993; Tetel, Getzinger, and Blaustein, 1993).

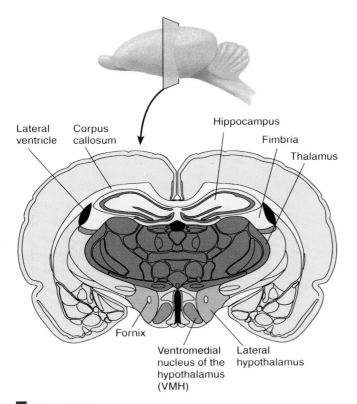

Lateral ventricle

Corpus callosum

Hippocampus

Fimbria

Thalamus

Fornix

Ventromedial nucleus of the hypothalamus (VMH)

Lateral hypothalamus

▌ *Figure 10.18*
▌ *A cross section through the rat brain showing the location of the ventromedial nucleus of the hypothalamus.*
(Adapted from Swanson, L.W. *Brain Maps: Structure of the Rat Brain.* New York: Elsevier, 1992.)

As we saw earlier, sexual behavior of female rats is activated by a priming dose of estradiol, followed by progesterone. The estrogen sets the stage, so to speak, and the progesterone stimulates the sexual behavior. Injections of these hormones directly into the VMH will stimulate sexual behavior even in females whose ovaries have been removed (Rubin and Barfield, 1980; Pleim and Barfield, 1988). And if a chemical that blocks the production of progesterone receptors is injected into the VMH, the animal's sexual behavior is disrupted (Ogawa et al., 1994). Thus, estradiol and progesterone exert their effects on female sexual behavior by activating neurons in this nucleus.

Rose (1990) recorded from single neurons in the ventromedial hypothalamus of freely moving female hamsters and found that injections of progesterone (following estradiol pretreatment) increased the activity level of these neurons, particularly when the animals were displaying lordosis. In a double-labeling study, Tetel, Celentano, and Blaustein (1994) found that neurons in both the VMH and the medial amygdala that showed increased Fos production when the animal's genitals were stimulated also contained estrogen receptors. Thus, the stimulating effects of estradiol and genital stimulation converge on the same neurons.

The mechanism by which estrogen primes a female's sensitivity to progesterone appears to be simple: Estradiol increases the production of progesterone receptors, which greatly increases the effectiveness of progesterone. Blaustein and Feder (1979) administered estradiol to ovariectomized guinea pigs and found a 150 percent increase in the number of progesterone receptors in the hypothalamus. Presumably, the estradiol activates genetic mechanisms in the nucleus that are responsible for the production of progesterone receptors.

Figure 10.19 shows two slices through the hypothalamus of ovariectomized guinea pigs, stained for progesterone receptors. One of the animals had previously received a priming dose of estradiol; the other had not. As this figure shows, the estradiol dramatically increased the number of cells containing progesterone receptors. (See *Figure 10.19.*)

The neurons of the ventromedial nucleus send axons to the **periaqueductal gray matter (PAG)** of the midbrain,

ventromedial nucleus of the hypothalamus (VMH) A large nucleus of the hypothalamus located near the walls of the third ventricle; plays an essential role in female sexual behavior.

periaqueductal gray matter (PAG) The region of the midbrain that surrounds the cerebral aqueduct; plays an essential role in various species-typical behaviors, including female sexual behavior.

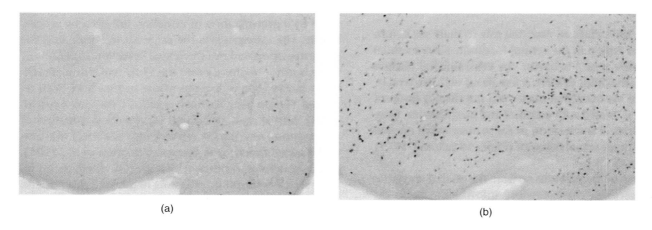

(a)   (b)

Figure 10.19
Photomicrographs of sections through the hypothalamus of ovariectomized guinea pigs, stained for progesterone receptors. (a) No priming. (b) After receiving a priming dose of estradiol.
(Courtesy of Joanne Turcotte and Jeffrey Blaustein, University of Massachusetts.)

which surrounds the cerebral aqueduct. This region, too, has been implicated in female sexual behavior; Sakuma and Pfaff (1979a, 1979b) found that electrical stimulation of the PAG facilitates lordosis in female rats and that lesions there disrupt it. In addition, Hennessey et al. (1990) found that lesions that disconnect the VMH from the PAG abolish female sexual behavior. Finally, Sakuma and Pfaff (1980a, 1980b) found that estradiol treatment or electrical stimulation of the ventromedial nuclei increased the firing rate of neurons in the PAG. (The PAG contains both estrogen and progesterone receptors.)

The neurons of the periaqueductal gray matter send axons to the reticular formation of the medulla, and cells there send axons to the spinal cord. It seems likely that this pathway is the final link between the hormone-sensitive neurons in the ventromedial nucleus of the hypothalamus and the muscles that are responsible for the lordosis response.

As we saw earlier, oxytocin serves both as a hormone and a neurotransmitter or neuromodulator. Schumacher et al. (1990) found that injections of progesterone in female rats previously primed with estradiol increased the number of oxytocin receptors in the ventromedial hypothalamus. Also, injections of oxytocin directly into the VMH facilitated lordosis—but only after the animal had been treated with estradiol and progesterone (Schumacher et al., 1989). Finally, intracerebral injections of an oxytocin antagonist into the VMH decreased sexual behavior of female rats (McCarthy et al., 1994).

Several other neurotransmitters appear to play a role in female sexual behavior, but the one that has received the most attention is norepinephrine. Crowley, Rodriguez-Sierra, and Komisaruk (1977) found that stimulation of the vagina and cervix increased the activity of noradrenergic neurons. (As we saw in the section on pheromones, this effect enables a female mouse to remember the odor of the male that inseminated her.) Damage either to the noradrenergic axons that project to the spinal cord or to those that project to the forebrain decreases lordosis (Hansen, Stanfield, and Everitt, 1980; Hansen and Ross, 1983). Injection of norepinephrine or an NE agonist directly into the hypothalamus facilitates estrous behavior, whereas injection of a NE antagonist inhibits it (Crowley, Nock, and Feder, 1978; Fernandez-Guasti, Larsson, and Beyer, 1985).

Figure 10.20 shows the effects of estradiol, then progesterone, and then the introduction of an active male on the secretion of norepinephrine in the VMH of freely moving female rats, as measured by microdialysis (Vathy and Etgen, 1989). As you can see, the presence of a male provokes a very large release of norepinephrine, but only in rats that have been primed with estradiol and progesterone. The effect seems to be specific to sexual activity, because the release of norepinephrine in another part of the hypothalamus, which does not appear to be involved in female sexual behavior, was *not* increased. (See *Figure 10.20.*)

Interim Summary

Sexual reflexes such as sexual posturing, erection, and ejaculation are organized in the spinal cord. The spinal cord contains at least one sexually dimorphic region, the spinal

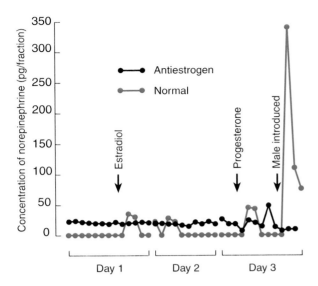

Figure 10.20

Norepinephrine concentration in the ventromedial hypothalamus of female rats, measured by microdialysis. One rat was given a priming dose of estradiol, then progesterone, and then a male was introduced. The other rat received an antiestrogenic drug along with the estradiol, which blocked its behavioral effects and prevented the release of norepinephrine. (Adapted from Vathy, I.U., and Etgen, A.M. *Journal of Neuroendocrinology*, 1989, 1, 383–388.)

nucleus of the bulbocavernosus (SNB), whose size is controlled by prenatal androgens. In rats, at least part of the masculinization of this nucleus is a result of tactile stimulation delivered by the animal's mother.

In laboratory animals, different brain mechanisms control male and female sexual behavior. The medial preoptic area is the forebrain region most critical for male sexual behavior. Stimulating this area produces copulatory behavior; destroying it permanently abolishes the behavior. The sexually dimorphic nucleus, located in the medial preoptic area, develops only if an animal is exposed to androgens early in life. This nucleus is found in humans, as well. The size of the SDN (part of the MPA) is reduced by prenatal stress and correlates with an animal's level of sexual behavior; its destruction impairs such behavior.

Neurons in the MPA contain testosterone receptors. Copulatory activity causes an increase in the activity of neurons in this region. Implantation of testosterone directly into the MPA reinstates copulatory behavior that was previously abolished by castration in adulthood. Neurons in the MPA send their axons to various regions, including the lateral tegmental field, where lesions also disrupt male sexual behavior.

The temporal lobes also appear to play a role in sexual interest; damage to the medial amygdala (which receives input from both the main and accessory olfactory systems) disrupts male sexual behavior. In humans, sexual dysfunctions are associated with seizure activity originating in the temporal lobes.

The level of vasopressin, a hormone secreted by the posterior pituitary gland that also serves as a neurotransmitter, is correlated with male sexual activity. Axons with terminal buttons secreting this neurotransmitter disappear after castration and reappear after the animal is given testosterone. In addition, the injection of vasopressin agonists into the brain decreases male sexual behavior, while vasopressin agonists facilitate it. The activity of dopamine in the MPA is also related to male sexual activity.

The most important forebrain region for female sexual behavior is the ventromedial nucleus of the hypothalamus (VMH). Its destruction abolishes copulatory behavior, and its stimulation facilitates this behavior. Both estradiol and progesterone exert their facilitating effects on female sexual behavior in this region, and studies have confirmed the existence of progesterone and estrogen receptors there. The priming effect of estradiol is caused by an increase in progesterone receptors in the VMH. The steroid-sensitive neurons of the VMH send axons to the periaqueductal gray matter (PAG) of the midbrain; presumably, neurons in the midbrain, through their connections with the medullary reticular formation, control the particular responses that constitute female sexual behavior.

Two neurotransmitters, oxytocin and norepinephrine, appear to facilitate female sexual behavior. Both substances appear to act in the VMH.

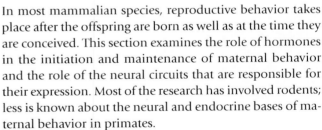

PARENTAL BEHAVIOR

In most mammalian species, reproductive behavior takes place after the offspring are born as well as at the time they are conceived. This section examines the role of hormones in the initiation and maintenance of maternal behavior and the role of the neural circuits that are responsible for their expression. Most of the research has involved rodents; less is known about the neural and endocrine bases of maternal behavior in primates.

Although most research on the physiology of parental behavior has focused on maternal behavior, some researchers are now studying paternal behavior shown by the males of some species of rodents. It goes without saying that the human paternal behavior is very important for the offspring of our species, but the physiological basis of this behavior has not yet been studied.

● Maternal Behavior of Rodents

The final test of the fitness of an animal's genes is the number of offspring that survive to a reproductive age. Just as the process of natural selection favors reproductively competent animals, it favors those that care adequately for their young (if their young in fact require care). Rat and mouse pups certainly do; they cannot survive without a mother to attend to their needs.

At birth, rats and mice resemble fetuses. The infants are blind (their eyes are still shut), and they can only helplessly wriggle. They are poikilothermous ("cold-blooded"); their brain is not yet developed enough to regulate body temperature. They even lack the ability to release their own urine and feces spontaneously and must be helped to do so by their mother. As we will see shortly, this phenomenon actually serves a useful function.

During gestation, female rats and mice build nests. The form this structure takes depends on the material available for its construction. In the laboratory the animals are usually given strips of paper or lengths of rope or twine. A good *brood nest,* as it is called, is shown in Figure 10.21. This nest is made of hemp rope; a piece of the rope is shown below the nest. The mouse laboriously shredded the rope and then wove an enclosed nest, with a small hole for access to the interior. (See *Figure 10.21.*)

Figure 10.21
A mouse's brood nest. Beside it is a length of the kind of rope the mouse used to construct it.

At the time of **parturition** (delivery of offspring) the female begins to groom and lick the area around the vagina. As a pup begins to emerge, she assists the uterine contractions by pulling the pup out with her teeth. She then eats the placenta and umbilical cord and cleans off the fetal membranes—a quite delicate operation. (A newborn pup looks like it is sealed in very thin plastic wrap.) After all the pups are born and cleaned up, the mother will probably nurse them. Milk is usually present in the mammary glands very near the time of birth.

Periodically, the mother licks the pups' anogenital region, stimulating reflexive urination and defecation. Friedman and Bruno (1976) have shown the utility of this mechanism. They noted that a lactating female rat produces approximately 48 grams (g) of milk on the tenth day of lactation. This milk contains approximately 35 milliliters (ml) of water. The experimenters injected some of the pups with tritiated (radioactive) water and later found radioactivity in the mother and in the littermates. They calculated that a lactating rat normally consumes 21 ml of water in the urine of her young, thus recycling approximately two-thirds of the water she gives to the pups in the form of milk. The water, traded back and forth between mother and young, serves as a vehicle for the nutrients—fats, protein, and sugar—contained in milk. Because each day the milk production of a lactating rat is approximately 14 percent of her body weight (for a human weighing 120 lb, that would be around 2 gal), the recycling is extremely useful, especially when the availability of water is a problem.

Besides cleaning, nursing, and purging her offspring, a female rodent will retrieve pups if they leave or are removed from the nest. The mother will even construct another nest in a new location and move her litter there, should the conditions at the old site become unfavorable (for example, when an inconsiderate experimenter puts a heat lamp over it). The way a female rodent picks up her pup is quite consistent: She gingerly grasps the animal by the back, managing not to injure it with her very sharp teeth. (I can personally attest to the ease with which these teeth can penetrate skin.) She then carries the pup with a characteristic prancing walk, her head held high. (See *Figure 10.22.*) The pup is brought back to the nest and is left there. The female then leaves the nest again to search for another pup. She continues to retrieve pups until she finds no more; she does not count her pups and stop retrieving when they are all back. A mouse or rat will usually accept all the pups she is offered, if they are young enough. I once observed two lactating female mice with nests in corners of

parturition *(par tew **ri** shun)* The act of giving birth.

Figure 10.22
A female mouse carrying one of her pups.

the same cage, diagonally opposite each other. I disturbed their nests, which triggered a long bout of retrieving, during which each mother stole youngsters from the other's nest. The mothers kept up their exchange for a long time, passing each other in the middle of the cage.

Maternal behavior begins to wane as the pups become more active and begin to look more like adults. At around sixteen to eighteen days of age they are able to get about easily by themselves, and they begin to obtain their own food. The mother ceases to retrieve them when they leave the nest and will eventually run away from them if they attempt to nurse.

● Stimuli That Elicit and Maintain Maternal Behavior

As we saw earlier in this chapter, most sexually dimorphic behaviors are controlled by the organizational and activational effects of sex hormones. Maternal behavior is somewhat different in this respect. First, there is no evidence that organizational effects of hormones play a role; as we will see, under the proper conditions even males will take care of infants. (Obviously, they cannot provide them with milk.) Second, although maternal behavior is affected by hormones, it is not *controlled* by them.

Most virgin female rats will begin to retrieve and care for young pups after having infants placed with them for several days (Wiesner and Sheard, 1933). And once the rats are sensitized, they will thereafter take care of pups as soon as they encounter them; sensitization lasts for a lifetime.

Olfaction plays an important role in sensitization—at least, in species such as the rat. A virgin female rat does not normally approach a rat pup; in fact, when she encounters one, she retreats from the pup as if she were repelled by the pup's odor. Fleming and Rosenblatt (1974) confirmed that the avoidance is, indeed, based on smell. They rinsed the olfactory mucosa of virgin female rats with zinc sulfate, which temporarily eliminates olfactory sensitivity. The treatment abolished the animals' natural aversion to the pups, and soon they started taking care of them. Thus, sensitization involves overcoming a natural aversion to the odor of pups.

Fleming et al. (1979) found that cutting the vomeronasal nerve, which disrupts the accessory olfactory system, also facilitates the responsiveness of virgin females to pups. Thus, both the primary and the accessory olfactory systems play a role in olfactory control of maternal behavior. You will recall that both the primary and accessory olfactory systems project to the medial amygdala. Fleming, Vaccarino, and Luebke (1980) found that lesions of the medial amygdala also facilitated responsiveness, as did lesions of the **stria terminalis,** a fiber bundle that connects the medial amygdala with various forebrain regions, including the medial preoptic area. As we will see, the medial preoptic area is essential for maternal behavior. (Refer to *Figure 10.11.*) Note that lesions of the amygdala or stria terminalis do not abolish the sense of smell; they only abolish the animals' aversion to the smell of pups.

Although olfaction seems to play the most important role in sensitizing maternal behavior of virgin female rats, the act of parturition has more important effects in natural situations. As we saw, female rodents normally begin taking care of their pups as soon as they are born. Some of this effect is caused by prenatal hormones, but the passage of the pups through the birth canal also stimulates maternal behavior: Artificially distending the birth canal in nonpregnant females stimulates maternal behavior, whereas deafferenting the birth canal retards the appearance of maternal behavior (Graber and Kristal, 1977; Yeo and Keverne, 1986).

stria terminalis *(stree a ter mi nal is)*   A long fiber bundle that connects portions of the amygdala with the hypothalamus.

The most important sense modalities in the *initiation* of maternal behavior in rodents appears to be olfaction and somatosensation. However, other sense modalities are involved in its control. For example, mouse, rat, and hamster pups emit at least two different kinds of ultrasonic calls (Noirot, 1972; Hofer and Shair, 1993; Ihnat, White, and Barfield, 1995). These sounds cannot be heard by humans; they have to be translated into lower frequencies by a special device (a "bat detector") in order to be perceived by the experimenter. Of course, the mother can hear these calls. When a pup gets cold (as it would if it were removed from the nest), it emits a characteristic call that brings the mother out of her nest. The sound is so effective that female mice have been observed to chew the cover off a loudspeaker that is transmitting a recording of this call. Once out of the nest, the female uses olfactory cues as well as auditory ones to find the pups; she can find a buried, anesthetized baby mouse that is unable to make any noise. The second call is made in response to rough handling. When a mother hears this sound, she stops what she is doing. Typically, it is she that is administering the rough handling, and the distress call makes her stop. This mechanism undoubtedly plays an important role in training mother mice to handle pups properly.

Stern (1989a, 1989b) reviewed experimental findings that indicate that tactile stimuli also play an important role in the maintenance and control of maternal behavior. She noted that most maternal behaviors include the use of the mouth: nuzzling, licking, and carrying pups; building and repairing nests; attacking and biting intruders. Many of these behaviors are initiated by somatosensory information received by the region around the mouth as the mother sniffs the pups and nuzzles them with her mouth. For example, when the region around the mouth (the *perioral region*) is desensitized by cutting nerves or injecting a local anesthetic, female rats are less likely to lick their pups, retrieve them, build or repair a nest, or attack an intruder. Tactile feedback from the pups against the mother's ventral surface is important, too. When the regions around pups' mouths are anesthetized so that they cannot root against their mother, she will not show the crouching posture that is necessary for nursing. She will, however, retrieve them and lick them.

● Hormonal Control of Maternal Behavior

As we have just seen, hormones are not essential for the activation of maternal behavior; mere exposure to pups will accomplish that. (Of course, hormones are necessary for milk production.) However, many aspects of maternal behavior are facilitated by hormones. Nest-building behavior is facilitated by progesterone, the principal hormone of pregnancy. Lisk, Pretlow, and Friedman (1969) found that nonpregnant female mice built brood nests after a pellet of progesterone was implanted under the skin. The pellet slowly dissolved, maintaining a continuously high level of progesterone. The enhanced nest building was suppressed by the administration of estradiol. After parturition, mothers continue to maintain their nests, and they construct new nests if necessary, even though their blood level of progesterone is very low then. Voci and Carlson (1973) found that hypothalamic implants of prolactin as well as progesterone facilitated nest building in mice. Presumably, nest building can be facilitated by either hormone: progesterone during pregnancy and prolactin after parturition. (Prolactin, produced by the anterior pituitary gland, is responsible for milk production.)

Although pregnant female rats will not immediately care for foster pups that are given to them during pregnancy, they will do so as soon as their pups are born. A female rodent's responsiveness to her offspring appears to be triggered by the hormones present during pregnancy. Figure 10.23 shows the levels of the three hormones that have been implicated in maternal behavior: estradiol, progesterone, and prolactin. Note that just before parturition the level of estradiol begins rising, then the level of progesterone falls dramatically, followed by a sharp increase in prolactin. (See *Figure 10.23*.) If ovariectomized virgin female rats are given estradiol and progesterone in a pattern that duplicates this sequence, the time it takes to sensitize their maternal behavior is drastically reduced (Moltz, Lubin, Leon, and Numan, 1970; Bridges, 1984). Prolactin is not necessary.

Fleming et al. (1989) found that the administration of progesterone and estradiol produced effects similar to those of sensitization. First, the hormone-treated rats became less timid in a strange environment that contained novel odors. Second, the animals spent more time near a jar containing some bedding material removed from a nest containing a lactating female and her pups. These effects may be the ones that occur during sensitization: The animal is no longer repelled by (frightened by?) the strange odor of pups and, indeed, comes to prefer the smell. In addition, Fleming and Sarker (1990) found that sensitization produces stronger long-term effects if the animal is first primed with estradiol and progesterone.

Another hormone present during lactation—prolactin—may also have stimulating effects on maternal behavior; and its effects, like those of estradiol, may be exerted in the medial preoptic area. Bridges et al. (1990) infused minute quantities of prolactin into the lateral ventricles or directly into the MPA of virgin female rats. They found that

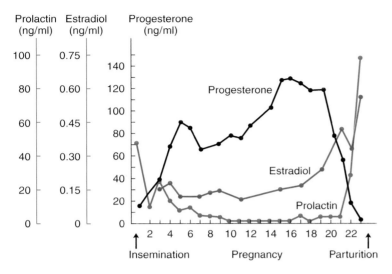

Figure 10.23
Blood levels of progesterone, estradiol, and prolactin in pregnant rats.
(From Rosenblatt, J.S., Siegel, H.I., and Mayer, A.D. *Advances in the Study of Behavior*, 1979, 10, 225–310.)

the animals quickly began taking care of pups. The effect occurred only if the animals were first given a series of injections of progesterone and estradiol; thus, the maternal behavior of normal females may depend on an interaction between several hormones.

● Neural Control of Maternal Behavior

The medial preoptic area, the region of the forebrain that plays the most critical role in male sexual behavior, appears to play a similar role in maternal behavior. Numan (1974) found that lesions of the MPA disrupted both nest building and pup care. The mothers simply ignored their offspring. However, female sexual behavior was unaffected by these lesions.

As we saw in the previous section, distension of the birth canal, normally caused by passage of a pup, provides an important stimulating effect on maternal behavior. Del Cerro et al. (1995) found that the act of parturition increased the metabolic activity of the MPA, measured by 2-DG autoradiography. They also found that virgin females whose maternal behavior had been sensitized by exposure to pups showed a similar increase. Thus, stimuli associated with pup care activate the MPA.

As you learned earlier, in the discussion of the neural basis of male sexual behavior, the MPA sends axons to the midbrain. Numan and his colleagues found that the pathway critical for maternal behavior runs from the MPA to the **ventral tegmental area (VTA)** of the midbrain. Numan and Smith (1984) found that lesions that interrupted this pathway disrupted maternal behavior. A later study (Numan and Numan, 1991) found that lesions of the ventral tegmental area made by injecting an excitatory amino acid (which kills cell bodies but spares axons that are passing

through the region) did not disrupt maternal behavior. However, knife cuts caudal to the VTA did; thus, the critical axons pass through the VTA and form synapses with neurons farther back in the brain stem. Where they do so is not yet known.

The medial preoptic area appears to be the place where estradiol affects maternal behavior. The MPA contains estrogen receptors (Pfaff and Keiner, 1973). Giordano et al. (1989) found that the concentration of estrogen receptors in the MPA increases during pregnancy and appears to reflect the priming effect produced by the sequence of hormones that occurs during pregnancy. In addition, direct implants of estradiol in the MPA facilitate maternal behavior (Numan, Rosenblatt, and Komisaruk, 1977) and injections of an antiestrogen into the MPA block it (Adieh, Mayer, and Rosenblatt, 1987).

As we just saw, zinc sulfate treatment (which abolishes olfactory sensitivity), lesions of the medial amygdala, or lesions of the stria terminalis (which connects the medial amygdala with the medial preoptic area) all facilitate maternal behavior in virgin female rats by eliminating the inhibitory effects caused by the odor of pups. Perhaps the stimulating effect of estradiol on the medial preoptic area works in a similar fashion, removing the inhibitory influence of the amygdala. (See *Figure 10.24*.)

● Neural Control of Paternal Behavior

Newborn infants of most species of mammals are cared for by their mother, and it is, of course, their mother that feeds

ventral tegmental area A nucleus in the ventral midbrain; plays an essential role in maternal behavior.

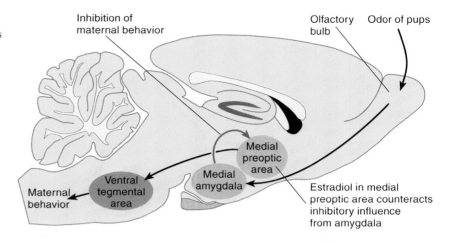

Figure 10.24
A possible explanation of the facilitating effects of estradiol on maternal behavior.

them. However, males of a few species of rodents share the task of infant care with the mothers, and the brains of these nurturing fathers show some interesting differences compared with those of nonpaternal fathers of other species.

Several laboratories have been investigating parental behavior in some closely related species of voles (small rodents often mistaken for mice). Prairie voles *(Microtus ochrogaster)* and pine voles *(Microtus pinetorum)* are monogamous; males and females form pair bonds after mating, and the fathers help care for the pups. Montane voles *(Microtus montanus)* and meadow voles *(Microtus pennsylvanicus)* are promiscuous; after mating, the male leaves, and the mother cares for the pups by herself. The size of the MPA, which plays an essential role in maternal behavior, shows less sexual dimorphism in monogamous prairie voles than in promiscuous montane voles (Shapiro et al., 1991).

Kirkpatrick, Kim, and Insel (1994) found that when male prairie voles were exposed to a pup, Fos production increased in the MPA (and also several other regions of the forebrain), which suggests that this brain region may be involved in paternal behavior as well as maternal behavior. The only study I could find that reported the effects of MPA lesions on paternal behavior was performed with a non-mammalian species—ring doves. Slawski and Buntin (1995) found that preoptic lesions did, indeed, disrupt paternal behavior that had been induced by prolactin. Whether similar effects would be obtained in male mammals is not yet known.

As we saw earlier, vasopressin appears to be involved in male sexual behavior. It also appears to play a role in parental behavior. Research by De Vries and his colleagues (Bamshad, Novak and De Vries, 1993, 1994; Wang et al., 1994) indicates that both mating and the birth of pups increase vasopressin production in the brains of male prairie

voles, but not in meadow voles, which do not show maternal behavior. In addition, Wang, Ferris, and De Vries (1994) found that injections of vasopressin into the lateral septum (a major projection region for vasopressin-secreting axons) stimulated paternal behavior of sexually naive male prairie voles. Injections of a vasopressin antagonist blocked such behavior. (See *Figure 10.25.*)

Interim Summary

Many species must care for their offspring. Among most rodents, this duty falls to the mother, who must build a nest, deliver her own pups, clean them, keep them warm,

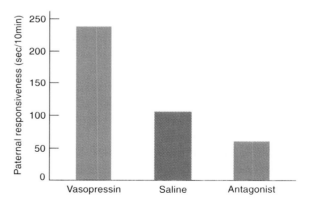

Figure 10.25
Effects of injections of vasopressin, saline (control injection), and a vasopressin antagonist injected into the lateral septum on paternal behavior in monogamous prairie voles.
(Adapted from Wang, Z., Ferris, C.F., and De Vries, G.J. *Proceedings of the National Academy of Sciences (USA)*, 1994, *91*, 400–404.)

nurse them, and retrieve them if they are moved out of the nest. They must even induce their pups' urination and defecation, and their ingestion of the urine recycles water, which is often a scarce commodity.

Exposure to young pups stimulates maternal behavior within a few days. Apparently, the odor of pups elicits handling and licking, whereas the sound of their distress calls elicits nest building. Unsensitized virgin female rats appear to be repelled by the odor of pups, but temporary deactivation of the olfactory system with zinc sulfate abolishes this aversion and causes the animals to begin caring for pups more quickly. The inhibitory effect of the odor of pups may be mediated by the accessory olfactory system; cutting the vomeronasal nerve facilitates maternal behavior. Both components of the olfactory system project to the medial amygdala. Lesions of the medial amygdala or the stria terminalis also facilitate maternal responsiveness. Therefore, the inhibitory effects of olfaction on maternal behavior may be mediated by the pathway from the olfactory system to the medial amygdala to the medial preoptic area, via the stria terminalis.

Nest building appears to be facilitated by progesterone during pregnancy and by prolactin during the lactation period. Injections of progesterone and estradiol that duplicate the sequence that occurs during pregnancy facilitate of maternal behavior, as does injection of prolactin directly into the brain.

The medial preoptic area is the most important forebrain structure for maternal behavior, and the ventral tegmental area of the midbrain is the most important brain stem structure. Neurons in the medial preoptic area send axons caudally through the ventral tegmental area toward more caudal regions of the brain stem. If these connections are interrupted bilaterally, rats cease providing maternal care.

Paternal behavior is relatively rare in mammalian species, but research indicates that sexual dimorphism of the MPA is less pronounced in monogamous species of voles in which both the male and the female care for the offspring. In addition, vasopressin secretion stimulates paternal behavior in male voles of monogamous, but not promiscuous, species.

SUGGESTED READINGS

Becker, J.B., Breedlove, S.M., and Crews, D. *Behavioral Endocrinology.* Cambridge, MA: MIT Press, 1992.

Bornstein, M.H. *Handbook of Parenting. Vol. 2: Biology and Ecology of Parenting.* Mahwah, NJ: Lawrence Erlbaum Associates, 1995.

Gerall, A.A., Moltz, H., and Ward, I.I. *Handbook of Behavioral Neurobiology. Vol. 11: Sexual Differentiation.* New York: Plenum Press, 1992.

Knobil, E., and Neill, J. *The Physiology of Reproduction.* New York: Raven Press, 1988.

Krasnegor, N.A., and Bridges, R.S. *Mammalian Parenting: Biochemical, Neurobiological, and Behavioral Determinants.* New York: Oxford University Press, 1990.

Rosen, R.C., and Beck, J.G. *Patterns of Sexual Arousal.* New York: Guilford Press, 1988.

CHAPTER 11

Emotion

Red Admiral by William T. Williams. Courtesy SBC Communications Inc.

The word *emotion* can mean several things. Most of the time, it refers to positive or negative feelings that are produced by particular situations. For example, being treated unfairly makes us angry, seeing someone suffer makes us sad, and being close to a loved one makes us feel happy. Emotions consist of patterns of physiological responses and species-typical behaviors. In humans these responses are accompanied by feelings. In fact, most of us use the word *emotion* to refer to the feelings, not to the behaviors. But it is behavior, and not private experience, that has consequences for survival and reproduction. Thus, the useful purposes served by emotional behaviors are what guided the evolution of our brain. The feelings that accompany these behaviors came rather late in the game.

This chapter is divided into four major sections. The first considers the patterns of behavioral and physiological responses that constitute emotions. It describes the nature of these response patterns, their neural control, and the perception of situations that give rise to emotions; and it includes a discussion of prefrontal lobotomy and other types of psychosurgery. The second section describes the communication of emotions—their expression and recognition. The third section examines the nature of the feelings that accompany emotions. Finally, the fourth section considers the neural and hormonal control of aggressive and defensive behaviors.

EMOTIONS AS RESPONSE PATTERNS

An emotional response consists of three types of components: behavioral, autonomic, and hormonal. The *behav-*

ioral component consists of muscular movements appropriate to the situation that elicits them. For example, a dog defending its territory against an intruder first adopts an aggressive posture, growls, and shows its teeth. If the intruder does not leave, the defender runs toward it and attacks. *Autonomic* responses facilitate the behaviors and provide quick mobilization of energy for vigorous movement. In this example the activity of the sympathetic branch increases while that of the parasympathetic branch decreases. As a consequence, the dog's heart rate increases, and changes in the size of blood vessels shunt the circulation of blood away from the digestive organs toward the muscles. *Hormonal* responses reinforce the autonomic responses. The hormones secreted by the adrenal medulla—epinephrine and norepinephrine—further increase blood flow to the muscles and cause nutrients stored in the muscles to be converted into glucose. In addition, the adrenal cortex secretes steroid hormones, which also help make glucose available to the muscles.

This section discusses research on the control of overt emotional behaviors and the autonomic and hormonal responses that accompany them. Special behaviors that serve to communicate emotional states to other animals, such as the threat gestures that precede an actual attack and the smiles and frowns used by humans, will be discussed in the second section of the chapter. As you will see, negative emotions receive much more attention than positive ones. Most of the research on the physiology of emotions has been confined to fear and anxiety—emotions associated with situations in which we must defend ourselves or our loved ones. The physiology of behaviors associated with positive emotions—such as those associated with lovemaking, caring for one's offspring, enjoying a good meal or a cool drink of water (or an alcoholic beverage)—is described in other chapters but not in the specific context of emotions. And Chapter 18 discusses the long-term consequences of situations that evoke negative emotions—stress.

● Neural Control of Emotional Response Patterns: Role of the Amygdala

As we will see, stimulation of various parts of the brain can induce an animal to attack another one or can cause it to make vigorous attempts to escape. In other words, the stimulation can produce the behaviors associated with anger or fear. The overt behaviors, the autonomic responses, and the hormonal secretions associated with these emotional reactions are controlled by separate neural systems. The *integration* of these responses appears to be controlled by the amygdala.

Research with Laboratory Animals

The amygdala plays a special role in physiological and behavioral reactions to objects and situations that have special biological significance, such as those that warn of pain or other unpleasant consequences or signify the presence of food, water, salt, potential mates or rivals, or infants in need of care. Researchers in several different laboratories have shown that single neurons in various nuclei of the amygdala become active when emotionally relevant stimuli are presented. For example, these neurons are excited by such stimuli as the sight of a device that has been used to squirt either a bad-tasting or a sweet solution into the animal's mouth, the sound of another animal's vocalization, the sound of the opening of the laboratory door, the smell of smoke, or the sight of another animal's face (O'Keefe and Bouma, 1969; Jacobs and McGinty, 1972; Rolls, 1982; Leonard et al., 1985). As we have already seen in Chapter 10, the amygdala is involved in the effects of pheromones on reproductive physiology and behavior (including maternal behavior). This section describes research on the role of the amygdala in organizing emotional responses produced by aversive stimuli.

The amygdala (or more precisely, the *amygdaloid complex*) is located within the temporal lobes. It consists of several groups of nuclei, each with different inputs and outputs—and with different functions (Canteras, Simerly, and Swanson, 1995; Pitkaenen et al., 1995; Savander et al., 1995). The major parts of the amygdala are the *medial nucleus,* the *lateral/basolateral nuclei,* the *central nucleus,* and the *basal nucleus.* The **medial nucleus** consists of several subnuclei that receive sensory input (including informa-

tion about the presence of odors and pheromones) and relay the information to the medial basal forebrain and to the hypothalamus. Reproductive functions of the medial nucleus were discussed in Chapter 10. Another role of the medial nucleus—participation in control of sodium intake—is discussed in Chapter 12. The **lateral/basolateral nuclei** receives sensory information from the primary sensory cortex, association cortex, thalamus, and hippocampal formation. These nuclei project to the ventral striatum (a region involved in the effects of reinforcing stimuli on learning) and to the dorsomedial nucleus of the thalamus, whose projection region is the prefrontal cortex. They also provide sensory input to the **central nucleus,** which is the part of the amygdala that will most concern us in this chapter. The central nucleus projects to regions of the hypothalamus, midbrain, pons, and medulla that are responsible for the expression of the various components of emotional responses. The **basal nucleus** consists of several subnuclei that, like the central nucleus, receive sensory input from the lateral and basolateral nuclei and relay information to other amygdaloid nuclei and to the periaqueductal gray matter of the midbrain. (See *Figure 11.1.*)

The central nucleus of the amygdala is the single most important part of the brain for the expression of emotional responses provoked by aversive stimuli. When threatening stimuli are presented, both the neural activity of the central nucleus and the production of Fos protein increase (Pascoe and Kapp, 1985; Campeau et al., 1991). Damage to the central nucleus (or to the lateral/basolateral nuclei, which provide it with sensory information) reduces or abolishes a wide range of emotional behaviors and physiological responses. After the central nucleus has been destroyed, animals no longer show signs of fear when confronted with stimuli that have been paired with aversive

medial nucleus   A group of subnuclei of the amygdala that receives sensory input, including information about the presence of odors and pheromones, and relays it to the medial basal forebrain and hypothalamus.

lateral/basolateral nuclei   Nuclei of the amygdala that receive sensory information from the neocortex, thalamus, and hippocampus and send projections to the ventral striatum, dorsomedial nucleus of the thalamus, and the central nucleus.

central nucleus   The region of the amygdala that receives information from the basolateral division and sends projections to a wide variety of regions in the brain; involved in emotional responses.

basal nucleus   A group of subnuclei of the amygdala that receives sensory input from the lateral and basolateral nuclei and relays information to other amygdaloid nuclei and to the periaqueductal gray matter.

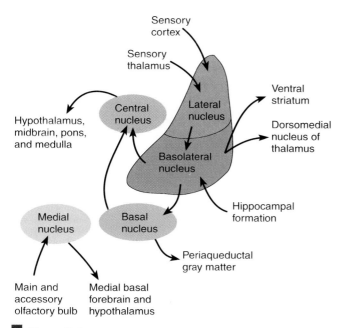

Figure 11.1
A much-simplified diagram of the major divisions and connections of the amygdala.

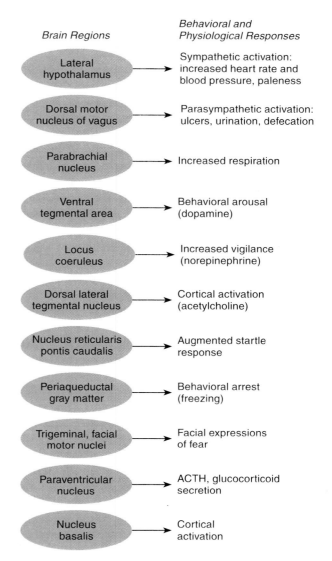

Figure 11.2
Some important brain regions that receive input from the central nucleus of the amygdala and the emotional responses controlled by these regions.
(Adapted from Davis, M., *Trends in Pharmacological Sciences*, 1992, 13, 35–41.)

events. They also act more tamely when handled by humans, their blood levels of stress hormones are lower, and they are less likely to develop ulcers or other forms of stress-induced illnesses (Coover, Murison, and Jellestad, 1992; Davis, 1992b; LeDoux, 1992). In contrast, when the central amygdala is stimulated by means of electricity or by an injection of an excitatory amino acid, the animal shows physiological and behavioral signs of fear and agitation (Davis, 1992b), and long-term stimulation of the central nucleus produces stress-induced illnesses such as gastric ulcers (Henke, 1982). These observations suggest that the autonomic and endocrine responses controlled by the central nucleus are among those responsible for the harmful effects of long-term stress, which are discussed in Chapter 18.

As we saw earlier, neurons in the central nucleus of the amygdala send axons to regions of the brain that are responsible for the expression of the various components of emotional responses. Rather than describe each of these regions and the responses they control, I will refer you to Figure 11.2, which summarizes them. (See *Figure 11.2*.)

The central amygdala is particularly important for aversive emotional learning. A few stimuli automatically produce fear reactions—for example, loud unexpected noises, the approach of large animals, heights, or (for some species) specific sounds or odors. Even more important, however, is the fact that we can *learn* that a particular situation is dangerous or threatening. Once the learning has taken place, we will become frightened when we encounter

that situation—our heart rate and blood pressure will increase, our muscles will become more tense, our adrenal glands will secrete epinephrine, and we will proceed cautiously, alert and ready to respond.

Let's examine a specific (if somewhat contrived) example. A **conditioned emotional response** is produced by a

conditioned emotional response A classically conditioned response that occurs when a neutral stimulus is followed by an aversive stimulus; usually includes autonomic, behavioral, and endocrine components such as changes in heart rate, freezing, and secretion of stress-related hormones.

neutral stimulus that has been paired with an emotion-producing stimulus. For example, suppose you are helping a friend prepare a meal. You pick up an electric mixer to mix some batter for a cake. Before you can turn the mixer on, the device makes a sputtering noise and then gives you a painful electrical shock. Your first response would be a defensive reflex: You would let go of the mixer, which would end the shock. This response is *specific*; it is aimed at terminating the painful stimulus. In addition, the painful stimulus would elicit *nonspecific* responses controlled by your autonomic nervous system: Your eyes would dilate, your heart rate and blood pressure would increase, you would breathe faster, and so on. The painful stimulus would also trigger the secretion of some stress-related hormones, another nonspecific response.

Suppose that a while later you visit your friend again and once more agree to make a cake. Your friend tells you that the electric mixer is perfectly safe—it has been fixed. Just seeing the mixer and thinking of holding it again makes you a little nervous, but you accept your friend's assurance and pick it up. Just then, it makes the same sputtering noise that it did when it shocked you. What would your response be? Almost certainly, you would drop the mixer again, even if it did not give you a shock. And your pupils would dilate, your heart rate and blood pressure would increase, and your endocrine glands would secrete some stress-related hormones. In other words, the sputtering sound would trigger a conditioned emotional response.

The word *conditioned* refers to the process of *classical conditioning*, which is described in more detail in Chapter 14. Briefly, classical conditioning occurs when a neutral stimulus is regularly followed by a stimulus that automatically evokes a response. For example, if a dog regularly hears a bell ring just before it receives some food that makes it salivate, it will begin salivating as soon as it hears the sound of the bell. (You probably already know that this phenomenon was discovered by Ivan Pavlov.)

If an organism learns to make a specific response that avoids contact with the aversive stimulus (or at least minimizes its painful effect), most of the nonspecific "emotional" responses will eventually disappear. That is, if the organism learns a successful **coping response**—a response that terminates, avoids, or minimizes an aversive stimulus—the emotional responses will no longer occur. For example, suppose you suspect that your friend's electric mixer is still defective but you are determined to make the cake anyway. You get your gloves from the pocket of your overcoat and put them on. Now you can safely handle the mixer; the gloves provide electrical insulation for your hands. This time the sputtering noise does not bother you because you are protected from electrical shocks. The noise

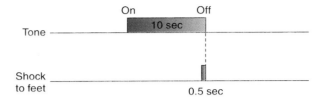

Figure 11.3
The procedure used to produce conditioned emotional responses.

does not activate your autonomic nervous system (at least, not very much), nor does it cause your glands to secrete stress-related hormones.

Several laboratories have investigated the role of the central nucleus of the amygdala in the development of classically conditioned emotional responses. For example, LeDoux and his colleagues have studied these responses in rats by pairing an auditory stimulus with a brief electrical shock delivered to the feet (reviewed by LeDoux, 1995). In their studies they presented an 800-Hz tone for 10 sec, and then they delivered a brief (0.5-sec) shock to the floor on which the animals were standing. (See *Figure 11.3*.) By itself, the shock produces an *unconditional* emotional response: The animal jumps into the air, its heart rate and blood pressure increase, its breathing becomes more rapid, and its adrenal glands secrete catecholamines and steroid stress hormones. The experimenters presented several pairings of the two stimuli, which established classical conditioning.

The investigators tested conditioned emotional responses the next day by presenting the 800-Hz tone several times and measuring the animals' blood pressure and heart rate and observing their behavior. (This time, they did not present the shock.) Upon hearing the tone, the rats showed the same type of physiological responses as when they were shocked the previous day. In addition, they showed behavioral arrest—a species-typical defensive response called *freezing*. That is, the animals acted as if they were expecting to receive a shock.

LeDoux and his colleagues have shown that the central nucleus is necessary for the development of a conditioned emotional response (LeDoux, 1987). If this nucleus is destroyed, conditioning does not take place. In addition, LeDoux et al. (1988) destroyed two regions that receive projections from the central nucleus: the lateral hypothal-

coping response A response through which an organism can avoid, escape from, or minimize an aversive stimulus; reduces the stressful effects of an aversive stimulus.

amus and the caudal periaqueductal gray matter. They found that lesions of the lateral hypothalamus interfered with the change in blood pressure, whereas lesions of the periaqueductal gray matter interfered with the freezing response. Thus, two different mechanisms, both under the control of the central nucleus of the amygdala, are responsible for the autonomic and behavioral components of conditioned emotional responses. (As you saw in Figure 11.3, activation of the central nucleus produces many other responses, but not all of them have been studied in this situation.)

Although most of the experiments investigating the role of the central nucleus of the amygdala in conditioned emotional responses have used auditory stimuli, results from studies using stimuli of other sensory modalities are consistent with the ones I have reviewed. For example, lesions of the central nucleus disrupt conditioned responses evoked by visual or olfactory stimuli that have been paired with a foot shock, and they make an animal act less timid in a strange environment (Hitchcock and Davis, 1986; Sananes and Campbell, 1989; Grijalva et al., 1990). (By the way, timidity in a strange environment is a useful trait; animals that enter an unfamiliar place boldly and heedlessly may find something awaiting them that will end their opportunity to contribute to the gene pool.)

Another behavioral measure of fear has received considerable attention: the augmented startle response. When an animal hears a sudden, loud noise, its muscles suddenly contract. An especially strong response may even cause a four-footed animal such as a rat to jump into the air. The magnitude of the startle response is strongly modulated by fear. For example, if a rat is placed in a chamber in which it previously received electrical shocks, a sudden noise makes it jump much more than it otherwise would. In fact, an animal's "jumpiness" is an excellent indication of its level of fear.

Davis and his colleagues (see Davis, 1992a, 1992b; Davis, Rainnie, and Cassell, 1994) have investigated the neural circuits responsible for this phenomenon. They measured the startle response by placing a rat in a cage equipped with pressure transducers that provided an electrical signal any time the floor of the cage was jostled. Thus, when an animal made a sudden movement, the pressure transducers would send a signal that could be analyzed electronically. The investigators produced a conditioned fear to light by turning on a light and then shocking the animal. The next day, they placed the rat in the apparatus and measured the magnitude of its startle response to a sudden sound—in the dark and then with the light on. Clearly, the light provoked fear; the animals were more "jumpy" when it was on than when it was off. (See *Figure 11.4.*)

Training: light and shock paired

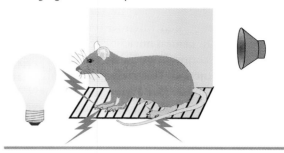

Testing: noise-alone trial

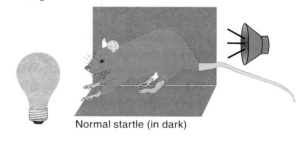

Normal startle (in dark)

Testing: light + noise trial

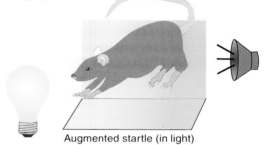

Augmented startle (in light)

Figure 11.4
The method used by Davis and his colleagues to investigate the augmented startle response.
(Adapted from Davis, M., *Trends in Pharmacological Sciences*, 1992, *13*, 35–41.)

The first step in the investigation was to trace the pathway from the ear to the muscles. The researchers found that the first relay is in the auditory system, in the *ventral cochlear nucleus*. The next relay is in the *ventral nucleus of the lateral lemniscus*, and the next in the *nucleus reticularis pontis caudalis*, which projects directly to motor neurons in the spinal cord that are directly responsible for the muscular contractions. Davis and his colleagues found that the augmentation of the startle response was accomplished by a connection between the central nucleus of the amygdala and the nucleus reticularis pontis caudalis—usually referred to as the *rpc*. The central nucleus receives both visual information (light) and somatosensory information (foot shock). The pairing of these two stimuli causes changes to take place in this nucleus—changes that are responsible for classical conditioning. Then when the visual stimulus is presented by itself, the central nucleus becomes active and, through its efferent connections, raises the level of excitation of neurons in the rpc. This increased excitation augments the startle response. (See *Figure 11.5*.)

Research on the details of the physical changes responsible for classical conditioning—including the role of the central nucleus of the amygdala—has provided some interesting information about the physiology of learning and memory. This research will be discussed in more detail in Chapter 14.

Some of the effects of anxiolytic (anxiety-reducing) drugs appear to be produced through the central nucleus. The amygdala contains a high concentration of benzodiazepine receptors—especially the basolateral nucleus, which projects to the central nucleus—and the central nucleus itself contains a high concentration of opiate receptors. The infusion of either opiates or benzodiazepine tranquilizers into the amygdala decreases both the learning and the expression of conditioned emotional responses (Kapp et al., 1982; Davis, 1992a). In addition, Sanders and Shekhar (1995) found that an injection of a benzodiazepine antagonist into the basolateral nucleus blocked the anxiolytic effects of an intraperitoneal injection of chlordiazepoxide

(*Librium*). Thus, tranquilizers appear to exert their anxiolytic effect in the basolateral amygdala. It is possible that some other regions are also involved in this effect; Yadin et al. (1991) found that even after the amygdala is destroyed, benzodiazepines still have some anxiolytic effect. And as we will see in Chapter 19, opiates have effects on many different parts of the brain.

As we will see in Chapter 18, some evidence suggests that increased activity of the neural mechanisms described in this section are associated with a fairly common category of psychological disorders—the *anxiety disorders*. Some investigators have suggested that anxiety disorders are caused by hyperactivity of the central nucleus of the amygdala, perhaps as a result of increased secretion of endogenous anxiety-producing ligands for the $GABA_A$ receptor, of which the benzodiazepine receptor is a part. Whether the primary cause of the increased anxiety lies within these circuits or elsewhere in the brain (or in people's environments and past histories) has yet to be determined.

Another neuropeptide, *cholecystokinin* (CCK), has anxiety-producing effects in the brain. As we shall see in Chapter 13, CCK is a hormone that controls several functions of the digestive system, and may also have an inhibitory effect on eating. Like many other peptide hormones, CCK is also secreted in the brain, where it has behavioral effects. Several studies (see Frankland et al., 1997, for a review) have

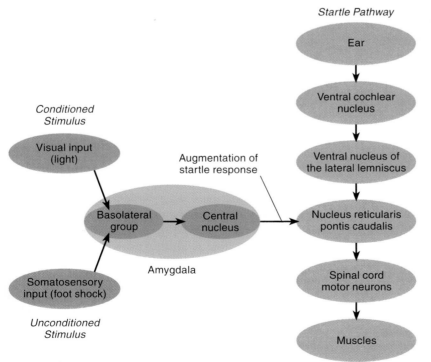

Figure 11.5
The neural circuits responsible for an auditory startle response and for its augmentation by conditioned aversive stimuli.
(Adapted from Davis, M., *Trends in Pharmacological Sciences*, 1992, 13, 35–41.)

found that injections of agonists for the CCK_B receptor produce both behavioral and autonomic changes associated with fear and anxiety, whereas CCK_B antagonists reduce them. At least some of these effects appear to be mediated by the amygdala. First, the amygdala contains many CCK-secreting neurons (Ingram et al., 1989; Schiffmann and Vanderhaeghen, 1991). Second, events that increase fear also increase the levels of endogenous CCK in the amygdala. For example, Pavlasevic et al. (1993) found that presenting rats with a cloth scented with the odor of a predator increased the levels of CCK in the amygdala, and Pratt and Brett (1995) found that administration of an inverse agonist for the benzodiazepine receptor, which produces anxiety, also increased CCK levels in the amygdala. Finally, Frankland et al. (1997) found that injection of a CCK_B agonist directly into the amygdala produced signs of anxiety (an augmented startle response) and that injections of a CCK_B antagonist had the opposite effect.

We will also see in Chapter 13 that the amygdala is involved in behaviors associated with another negative emotion—disgust. When an animal (including a member of our own species) becomes nauseated as a result of eating tainted food (or receiving an injection of a nausea-inducing drug), the animal develops an aversion to the flavor of the last thing it ate or drank prior to the nausea. This form of learning is abolished by lesions of the basolateral amygdala.

Research with Humans

A considerable amount of evidence indicates that the amygdala is involved in emotional responses in humans. One of the earliest studies observed the reactions of people who were being evaluated for surgical removal of parts of the brain to treat severe seizure disorders. These studies found that stimulation of parts of the brain (for example, the hypothalamus) produced autonomic responses often associated with fear and anxiety, but that only when the amygdala was stimulated did people also report that they actually felt afraid (White, 1940; Halgren et al., 1978; Gloor et al., 1982).

Lesions of the amygdala decrease people's emotional responses. Two studies (LaBar et al., 1995; Bechara et al., 1995) found that people with lesions of the amygdala showed impaired acquisition of a conditioned emotional response, just as rats do. Angrilli et al. (1996) found that the startle response of a man with a localized lesion of the right amygdala was not augmented by an unpleasant emotion. Normally, a person's startle response, elicited by a sudden noise, is larger when the person looks at unpleasant photos than when he or she looks at neutral ones. Presumably, the augmentation is produced by the negative

emotion elicited by the unpleasant scene. Angrilli and his colleagues did not observe this effect in their patient—the man showed the same startle response regardless of the nature of the photographs.

Damage to the amygdala interferes with the effects of emotions on memory. Normally, when people encounter events that produce a strong emotional response, they are more likely to remember these events. Cahill et al. (1995) studied a patient with bilateral degeneration of the amygdala. The investigators narrated a story about a young boy walking with his mother on his way to visit his father at work. To accompany the story, they showed a series of slides. During one part of the story, the boy was injured in a traffic accident, and gruesome slides illustrated his injuries. When this slide show is presented to normal subjects, they remember more details from the emotion-laden part of the story. However, a patient with amygdala damage showed no such increase in memory.

Several imaging studies have shown that the human amygdala participates in emotional responses. For example, Cahill et al. (1996) had people watch both neutral and emotionally arousing films (such as scenes of violent crimes). Later, the experimenters placed the subjects in a PET scanner and asked them to recall the films. The activity of the right amygdala increased while the subjects recalled the emotionally arousing films but not when they recalled the neutral ones. Schneider et al. (1996) had people attempt to solve anagrams (rearrangements of scrambled words into sentences). Some of the anagrams could be solved relatively easily, but others were actually impossible to solve. When well-motivated people work on such tasks, they tend to become tense and unhappy and usually report feelings of frustration. A PET scanner showed that the blood flow in the amygdala increased while the subjects were working on the unsolvable anagrams but not when working on the solvable ones.

As we saw in the previous subsection, CCK, a neuropeptide, has been implicated in fear and anxiety, and its site of action appears to be the amygdala. Benkelfat et al. (1995) found that injections of CCK, which increase people's anxiety, also increase blood flow in the amygdala, as measured by functional MRI.

● Social Judgments and Emotions: Role of the Orbitofrontal Cortex

We humans are capable of reacting emotionally to very complex situations, especially those involving other people. Perceiving the meaning of social situations is obviously more complex than perceiving individual stimuli. The analysis of social situations involves much more than

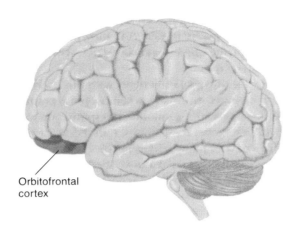

Figure 11.6
The orbitofrontal cortex.

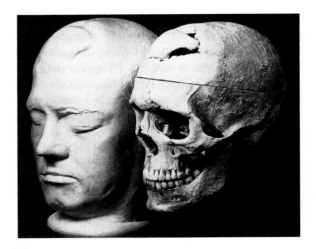

Figure 11.7
A bust and skull of Phineas Gage. The steel rod entered his left cheek and exited through his left forehead.
(From Warren Museum, Harvard Medical School. Reprinted with permission.)

sensory analysis; it involves experiences and memories, inferences and judgments. In fact, the skills involved include some of the most complex ones we possess. These skills are not localized in any one part of the cerebral cortex, although research does suggest that the right hemisphere is more important than the left. But one region of the brain—the orbitofrontal cortex—plays a special role.

The **orbitofrontal cortex** is located at the base of the frontal lobes. It covers the part of the brain just above the *orbits*—the bones that form the eye sockets—hence the term *orbitofrontal.* (See *Figure 11.6.*) The orbitofrontal cortex receives direct inputs from the dorsomedial thalamus, temporal cortex, ventral tegmental area, olfactory system, and amygdala. Its outputs go to several brain regions, including the cingulate cortex, hippocampal formation, temporal cortex, lateral hypothalamus, and amygdala. Finally, it communicates with other regions of the frontal cortex. Thus, its inputs provide it with information about what is happening in the environment and what plans are being made by the rest of the frontal lobes, and its outputs permit it to affect a variety of behaviors and physiological responses, including emotional responses organized by the amygdala.

The fact that the orbitofrontal cortex plays an important role in emotional behavior is shown by the effects of damage to this region. The first—and most famous—case comes from the mid-1800s. Phineas Gage, a dynamite worker, was using a steel rod to ram a charge of dynamite into a hole drilled in solid rock. Suddenly, the charge exploded and sent the rod into his cheek, through his brain, and out the top of his head. (See *Figure 11.7.*) He survived, but he was a different man. Before his injury he was serious, industrious, and energetic. Afterward, he became child-

ish, irresponsible, and thoughtless of others. He was unable to make or carry out plans, and his actions appeared to be capricious and whimsical. His accident largely destroyed the orbitofrontal cortex (Damasio et al., 1994).

Over the succeeding years physicians reported several cases similar to that of Phineas Gage. In general, damage to the orbitofrontal cortex reduced people's inhibitions and self-concern; they became indifferent to the consequences of their actions. In addition, although they remained sensitive to noxious stimuli, the pain no longer bothered them—it no longer produced an emotional reaction. Then in 1935 the report of an experiment with a chimpanzee triggered events whose repercussions are still felt today.

Jacobsen, Wolf, and Jackson (1935) tested some chimpanzees on a behavioral task that requires the animal to remain quiet and remember the location of food that the experimenter has placed behind a screen. One animal, Becky, displayed a violent emotional reaction whenever she made an error while performing this task. "[When] the experimenter lowered . . . the opaque door to exclude the animal's view of the cups, she immediately flew into a temper tantrum, rolled on the floor, defecated, and urinated. After a few such reactions during the training period, the animal would make no further responses. . . . " After the chimpanzee's frontal lobes were removed, it became a model of good comportment. It "offered its usual friendly

orbitofrontal cortex   The region of the prefrontal cortex at the base of the anterior frontal lobes.

greeting, and eagerly ran from its living quarters to the transfer cage, and in turn went properly to the experimental cage. . . .If the animal made a mistake, it showed no evidence of emotional disturbance but quietly awaited the loading of the cups for the next trial" (Jacobsen, Wolf, and Jackson, 1935, pp. 9–10).

These findings were reported at a scientific meeting in 1935, which was attended by Egas Moniz, a Portuguese neuropsychiatrist. He heard the report by Jacobsen and his colleagues and also one by Brickner (1936), which indicated that radical removal of the frontal lobes in a human patient (performed because of a tumor) did not appear to produce intellectual impairment—thus, people could presumably get along without their frontal lobes. These two reports suggested to Moniz that "if frontal-lobe removal . . . eliminates frustrational behavior, why would it not be feasible to relieve anxiety states in man by surgical means?" (Fulton, 1949, pp. 63–64). In fact, Moniz persuaded a neurosurgeon to do so, and approximately one hundred operations were eventually performed under his supervision. (In 1949 Moniz received the Nobel Prize for the development of this procedure.)

Three paragraphs ago, I wrote that the repercussions of the 1935 meeting are still felt today. Since that time tens of thousands of people have received prefrontal lobotomies, primarily to reduce symptoms of emotional distress, and many of these people are still alive. At first, the procedure was welcomed by the medical community because it provided their patients with relief from emotional anguish. Only after many years were careful studies performed on the side effects of the procedure. These studies showed that although patients did perform well on standard tests of intellectual ability, they showed serious changes in personality, becoming irresponsible and childish. They also lost the ability to carry out plans and most were unemployable. And although pathological emotional reactions were eliminated, so were normal ones. Because of these findings, and because of the discovery of drugs and therapeutic methods that relieve the patients' symptoms without producing such drastic side effects, neurosurgeons eventually abandoned the prefrontal lobotomy procedure (Valenstein, 1986).

I should point out that the prefrontal lobotomies performed under Moniz's supervision, and by the neurosurgeons who followed, were not as drastic as the surgery performed by Jacobsen and his colleagues on Becky, the chimpanzee. In fact, no brain tissue was removed. Instead, the surgeons introduced various kinds of cutting devices into the frontal lobes and severed white matter (bundles of axons). One rather gruesome procedure did not even require an operating room; it could be performed in a physi-

cian's office. A *transorbital leucotome*, shaped like an ice pick, was introduced into the brain by passing it beneath the upper eyelid until the point reached the orbital bone above the eye. The instrument was hit with a mallet, driving it through the bone into the brain. The end was then swept back and forth so that it cut through the white matter. The patient often left the office within an hour. (See *Figure 11.8.*)

Many physicians objected to the "ice pick" procedure because it was done blind (that is, the surgeon could not see just where the blade of the leucotome was located) and because it produced more damage than was necessary. Also, the fact that it was so easy and left no external signs other than a pair of black eyes may have tempted its practitioners to perform it too casually. In fact, at least twenty-five hundred patients received this form of surgery (Valenstein, 1986).

What we know today about the effects of prefrontal lobotomy—whether done transorbitally or by more conventional means—tells us that such radical surgery should never have been performed. For too long the harmful side effects were ignored. (As we will see later in Chapter 18, neurosurgeons eventually developed a much restricted version of this surgery, which reduces the symptoms without producing the harmful side effects.) But the fact remains that the surgery *did* reduce people's emotional suffering, or it would never have become so popular. Primarily, the surgery reduced anxiety, obsessions, and compulsions.

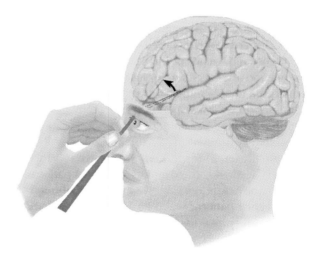

Figure 11.8
"Ice pick" prefrontal lobotomy. The sharp metal rod is inserted under the eyelid and just above the eye, so that it pierces the skull and enters the base of the frontal lobe.
(Adapted from Freeman, W., *Proceedings of the Royal Society of Medicine*, 1949, 42(suppl.), 8–12.)

People's groundless fears disappeared, and they no longer felt compelled to perform rituals to ward off some (imaginary) disastrous events. Before the surgery the world was a threatening place, and their emotional responses and behavior caused them anguish and made shambles of their lives. After surgery their cares disappeared.

All types of prefrontal lobotomies disrupted the functions of the frontal lobes (primarily the orbitofrontal cortex) by severing connections between this area and the rest of the brain. Some procedures approached the frontal lobes from the base of the brain, primarily cutting their connections with the diencephalon and temporal lobes. Other procedures approached the frontal lobes from above and disconnected the orbitofrontal cortex from the cingulate gyrus. In either case the patients' emotional distress was usually reduced.

What, exactly, does the orbitofrontal cortex do? One possibility is that it is involved in assessing the personal consequences of what is presently happening. However, this analysis does not appear to be correct. People whose orbitofrontal cortex has been damaged by disease or accident are still able to accurately assess the significance of particular situations, but only in a *theoretical* sense. For example, Eslinger and Damasio (1985) found that a patient with bilateral damage of the orbitofrontal cortex (produced by a benign tumor, which was successfully removed) displayed excellent social judgment. When he was given hypothetical situations that required him to make decisions about what the people involved should do—situations involving moral, ethical, or practical dilemmas—he always gave sensible answers and justified them with carefully reasoned logic. However, his own life was a different matter. He frittered away his life's savings on investments that his family and friends pointed out were bound to fail. He lost one job after another because of his irresponsibility. He became unable to distinguish between trivial decisions and important ones, spending hours trying to decide where to have dinner but failing to use good judgment in situations that concerned his occupation and family life. (His wife finally left him and sued for divorce.) As the authors noted, "He had learned and used normal patterns of social behavior before his brain lesion, and although he could recall such patterns when he was questioned about their applicability, *real-life situations failed to evoke them*" (p. 1737). Thus, it appears that the orbitofrontal cortex is not directly involved in making judgments and conclusions about events (these occur elsewhere in the brain) but in translating these judgments into appropriate feelings and behaviors.

As I mentioned earlier, in performing prefrontal lobotomies, neurosurgeons have made two different approaches toward the frontal lobes. The ventral connections with the diencephalon and temporal lobes presumably bring environmental information to the orbitofrontal cortex, tell it about emotionally relevant activity of the amygdala, and permit it to influence the amygdala, in turn. The dorsal connections with the cingulate gyrus presumably provide a way for the orbitofrontal cortex to influence both behavior and the autonomic nervous system.

The cingulate gyrus deserves some discussion. The cortex that covers this gyrus is an important part of the limbic system. It appears to provide an interface between the decision-making processes of the frontal cortex, the emotional functions of the amygdala, and the brain mechanisms controlling movement. It communicates (in both directions) with the rest of the limbic system, as well as with other regions of the frontal cortex. Electrical stimulation of the cingulate gyrus in humans can produce feelings of either positive or negative emotions (Talairach et al., 1973). Damage to this region leads to **akinetic mutism,** a syndrome accurately described by its name—the patient stops talking and moving (Amyes and Nielsen, 1955). If the damage is severe, the patient dies. Thus, the cingulate gyrus plays an excitatory role in emotions and in motivated behavior in general.

Interim Summary

The word *emotion* refers to behaviors, physiological responses, and feelings. This section has discussed emotional response patterns, which consist of behaviors that deal with particular situations and physiological responses (both autonomic and hormonal) that support the behaviors. The amygdala organizes behavioral, autonomic, and hormonal responses to a variety of situations, including those that produce fear, anger, or disgust. In addition, it is involved in the effects of odors and pheromones on sexual and maternal behavior. It receives inputs from the olfactory system, the association cortex of the temporal lobe, the frontal cortex, and the rest of the limbic system. Its outputs go to the frontal cortex, hypothalamus, hippocampal formation, and brain stem nuclei that control autonomic functions and some species-typical behaviors. Damage to specific brain regions that receive these outputs will abolish particular components of emotional response patterns. Electrical recordings of single neurons in the amygdala in-

akinetic mutism   A motor disorder characterized by a relative lack of movement and lack of speech; caused by damage to the cingulate gyrus.

dicate that some of them respond when the animal perceives particular stimuli with emotional significance. Stimulation of the amygdala leads to emotional responses, and its destruction disrupts them. Receptors in the amygdala are largely responsible for the anxiolytic effects of the benzodiazepine tranquilizers and the opiates, whereas CCK, a neuropeptide, exerts its anxiety-producing effects there. Studies of people with amygdala lesions and PET and functional MRI studies with humans indicate that the amygdala is involved in emotional reactions in our species, too.

The orbitofrontal cortex plays an important role in emotional reactions. People with orbitofrontal lesions are able to explain the implications of complex social situations but are unable to respond appropriately when these situations concern *them*. Thus, this region does not appear to be necessary for making judgments about the personal significance of social situations, but it does appear to be necessary for translating these judgments into actions and emotional responses. The orbitofrontal cortex receives information from other regions of the frontal lobes, from the temporal pole, and from the amygdala and other parts of the limbic system via the mediodorsal nucleus of the thalamus. It produces emotional reactions through its connections with the amygdala and the cingulate gyrus.

The cingulate gyrus is involved in the activation of behavior—what we might refer to as motivation. Damage to the cingulate gyrus produces akinetic mutism and, if the damage is severe, causes death. Electrical stimulation produces feelings of both positive and negative emotions. Its outputs include the rest of the limbic system and most of the frontal cortex.

Between the late 1930s and the late 1950s many people received prefrontal lobotomies, which involved cutting the white matter in the ventromedial frontal lobes. Although the operations affected many parts of the frontal lobes, the most important region was probably the orbitofrontal cortex. The surgery did often relieve emotional anguish and the suffering caused by pain, but it also made people become largely indifferent to the social consequences of their own behavior and to the feelings of others, and it interfered with their ability to make and execute plans. Prefrontal lobotomies are no longer performed.

EXPRESSION AND RECOGNITION OF EMOTIONS

The previous section described emotions as organized responses (behavioral, autonomic, and hormonal) that prepare an animal to deal with existing situations in the environment, such as events that pose a threat to the or-

ganism. For our earliest premammalian ancestors, that is undoubtedly all there was to emotions. But over time other responses, with new functions, evolved. Many species of animals (including our own) communicate their emotions to others by means of postural changes, facial expressions, and nonverbal sounds (such as sighs, moans, and growls). These expressions serve useful social functions; they tell other individuals how we feel and—more to the point—what we are likely to do. For example, they warn a rival that we are angry or tell friends that we are sad and would like some comfort and reassurance. In many species they indicate that a danger may be present or that something interesting seems to be happening. This section examines such expression and communication of emotions.

● Facial Expression of Emotions: Innate Responses

Charles Darwin (1872/1965) suggested that human expressions of emotion have evolved from similar expressions in other animals. He said that emotional expressions are innate, unlearned responses consisting of a complex set of movements, principally of the facial muscles. Thus, a man's sneer and a wolf's snarl are biologically determined response patterns, both controlled by innate brain mechanisms, just as coughing and sneezing are. (Of course, men can sneer and wolves can snarl for quite different reasons.) Some of these movements resemble the behaviors themselves and may have evolved from them. For example, a snarl shows one's teeth and can be seen as an anticipation of biting.

Darwin obtained evidence for his conclusion that emotional expressions were innate by observing his own children and by corresponding with people living in various isolated cultures around the world. He reasoned that if people all over the world, no matter how isolated, show the same facial expressions of emotion, then these expressions must be inherited instead of learned. The logical argument goes like this: When groups of people are isolated for many years, they develop different languages. Thus, we can say that the words people use are arbitrary; there is no biological basis for using particular words to represent particular concepts. However, if facial expressions are inherited, then they should take approximately the same form in people from all cultures, despite their isolation from one another. And Darwin did, indeed, find that people in different cultures used the same patterns of movement of facial muscles to express a particular emotional state.

Research by Ekman and his colleagues (Ekman and Friesen, 1971; Ekman, 1980) tends to confirm Darwin's hypothesis that facial expression of emotion uses an innate, species-typical repertoire of movements of facial muscles (Darwin, 1872/1965). For example, Ekman and Friesen (1971) studied the ability of members of an isolated tribe in New Guinea to recognize facial expressions of emotion produced by westerners. They had no trouble doing so and themselves produced facial expressions that westerners readily recognized. Figure 11.9 shows four photographs taken from videotapes of a man from this tribe reacting to stories designed to evoke facial expressions of sadness, disgust, happiness, and anger. I am sure that you will have no trouble recognizing which is which. (See *Figure 11.9.*)

Because the same facial expressions were used by people who had not previously been exposed to each other, Ekman and Friesen concluded that the expressions were unlearned behavior patterns. In contrast, different cultures use different words to express particular concepts; production of these words does not involve innate responses but must be learned.

Other researchers have compared the facial expressions of blind and normally sighted children. They reasoned that

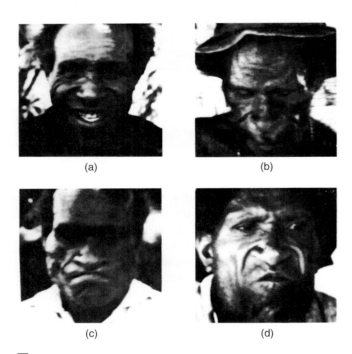

(a)

(b)

(c)

(d)

Figure 11.9
A member of an isolated New Guinea tribe, studied by Ekman and Friesen, making faces when told stories. (a) "Your friend has come and you are happy." (b) "Your child had died." (c) "You are angry and about to fight." (d) "You see a dead pig that has been lying there a long time."
(From Ekman, P., *The Face of Man: Expressions of Universal Emotions in a New Guinea Village*. New York: Garland STPM Press, 1980. Reprinted with permission.)

if the facial expressions of both groups are similar, then the expressions are natural for our species and do not require learning by imitation. (Studies of blind adults would not be conclusive, because adults would have heard enough descriptions of facial expressions to be able to pose them.) In fact, the facial expressions of young blind and sighted children are very similar (Woodworth and Schlosberg, 1954; Izard, 1971). Thus both the cross-cultural studies and the investigations with blind children confirm the naturalness of these expressions.

Although facial expressions of emotion seems to be innate, we all realize that our expressions of emotions can be perceived by other people. Consequently, we sometimes try to hide our true feelings, attempting to appear impassive or even to display an emotion different from what we feel. At other times, we may exaggerate our emotional response to make sure that others see how we feel. For example, if a friend tells us about a devastating experience, we make sure that our facial expression conveys sadness and sympathy. Although the patterns of muscular movements that accompany particular feelings are biologically determined, these movements can, to a certain extent, be modulated.

Cultures, as well as situations, influence our expressions of emotions. According to Ekman and Friesen (1975), the expression of emotions often follows culturally determined **display rules**—rules that prescribe under what situations we should or should not display signs of particular emotions. For example, in Western society it is impolite for a winner to show too much pleasure and for a loser to show too much disappointment. The expression of these emotions is supposed to be modulated downward. Also, in many societies it is unmanly to cry or show fear and unfeminine to show anger. Ekman and his colleagues (Ekman, Friesen, and Ellsworth, 1972; Friesen, 1972) attempted to assess a different kind of culturally determined display rule. They showed a distressing film to Japanese and American college students, singly and in the presence of a visitor, who was described to the subjects as a scientist. Because the Japanese culture discourages public display of emotion, the researchers expected that the Japanese students would show fewer facial expressions of emotion when in public than when alone.

The researchers recorded the facial expressions of their subjects with hidden cameras while the subjects viewed a film showing a gruesome and bloody coming-of-age rite in a primitive tribe. The results were as predicted. When the

display rule A culturally determined rule that modifies the expression of emotion in a particular situation.

subjects were alone, American and Japanese subjects showed the same facial expressions. When they were with another person, the Japanese students were less likely to express negative emotions and more likely to mask these expressions with polite smiles. Thus, people from both societies used the same facial expressions of emotion but were subject to different social display rules.

Investigators have not yet determined whether other means of communicating emotions, such as tone of voice or changes in body posture, are learned or are at least partly innate. However, as we will see, some progress has been made in studying the neuroanatomical basis of expressing and recognizing emotions.

● Neural Basis of the Communication of Emotions: Recognition

Effective communication is a two-way process. That is, the ability to display one's emotional state by changes in expression is useful only if other people are able to recognize them. In fact, Kraut and Johnston (1979) unobtrusively observed people in circumstances that would be likely to make them happy. They found that happy situations (such as making a strike while bowling, seeing the home team score, or experiencing a beautiful day) produced only small signs of happiness when the people were alone. However, when the people were interacting socially with other people, they were much more likely to smile. For example, bowlers who made a strike usually did not smile when the ball hit the pins, but when they turned around to face their companions, they often smiled. Jones et al. (1991) found that even ten-month-old children showed this tendency.

We recognize other people's feelings by means of vision and audition—seeing their facial expressions and hearing their tone of voice and choice of words. Many studies have found that the right hemisphere plays a more important role than the left hemisphere in comprehension of emotion. For example, many investigators have found a left-ear and a left-visual field advantage in recognition of emotionally related stimuli. The rationale for these studies is that each hemisphere directly receives information from the contralateral part of the environment. For example, when a person looks directly ahead, visual stimuli to the left of the fixation point (seen with *both* eyes) are transmitted to the right hemisphere, and stimuli to the right are transmitted to the left hemisphere. Of course, the hemispheres exchange information by means of the corpus callosum, but it appears that this transcommissural information is not as precise and detailed as information that is directly received. Similarly, although each hemisphere receives auditory information from both ears, the contralat-

eral projections are richer than the ipsilateral ones. Thus, when stimuli are presented to the left visual field or left ear, the right hemisphere receives more specific information than the left hemisphere does.

In studies of hemispherical differences in visual recognition, stimuli are usually presented to the left or right visual field so rapidly that the subject does not have time to move his or her eyes. Many studies (reviewed by Bryden and Ley, 1983) have shown that the left hemisphere is better than the right at recognizing words or letter strings, but that the right hemisphere is better at detecting differences in facial expressions of emotion. Similarly, subjects can more easily understand the verbal content of a message presented to the left hemisphere but can more accurately detect the emotional tone of the voice presented to the right hemisphere. These results suggest that when a message is heard, the right hemisphere assesses the emotional expression of the voice while the left hemisphere assesses the meaning of the words.

Blonder, Bowers, and Heilman (1991) found that patients with right hemisphere lesions had no difficulty making emotional judgments about particular situations but were severely impaired in judging the emotions conveyed by facial expressions or hand gestures. For example, they had no difficulty deciding what emotion would be evoked by the situations described in sentences like *After you drink the water, you see the sign* (fear) or *Your house seems empty without her* (sadness). However, these patients had difficulty recognizing the emotions depicted by sentences like *He scowled, Tears fell from her eyes,* or *He shook his fist.* In addition, Bowers et al. (1991) found that patients with right hemisphere damage had difficulty producing or describing mental images of facial expressions of emotions. Subjects were asked to imagine the face of someone who was very happy (or very sad, angry, or afraid). Then they were asked questions about the facial expression—for example, *Do the eyes look twinkly? Is the brow raised? Are the corners of the lips raised up?* People with right hemisphere damage had trouble answering these questions but could easily answer questions about nonemotional images, such as *What's higher off the ground, a horse's knee or the top of its tail?* or *What number from one to ten does a peanut look like?* or *What's bigger, a thimble or a pencil eraser?*

Several PET studies have confirmed these results. For example, George et al. (1996) measured subjects' regional cerebral blood flow with a PET scanner while they listened to some sentences and identified their emotional content. In one condition, the subjects listened to the meaning of the words and said whether they described a situation in which someone would be happy, sad, angry, or neutral. In another condition, they judged the emotional state from

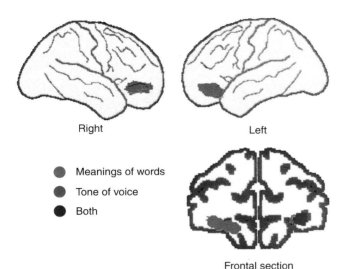

Right   Left

● Meanings of words
● Tone of voice
● Both

Frontal section

Figure 11.10
PET scans indicating brain regions activated by listening to emotions expressed by tone of voice or meanings of words.
(From George, M.S., Parekh, P.I., Rosinsky, N., Ketter, T.A., Kimbrell, T.A., Heilman, K.M., Herscovitch, P., and Post, R.M., *Archives of Neurology*, 1996, 53, 665–670.)

the tone of the voice. In a control condition, they simply repeated the second word they heard from each sentence. The investigators found that comprehension of emotion from word meaning increased the activity of both frontal lobes, the left more than the right. Comprehension of emotion from tone of voice increased the activity of only the right prefrontal cortex. (See *Figure 11.10.*)

Observations of people with brain damage are consistent with the studies with normal subjects. Heilman, Scholes, and Watson (1975) had patients with unilateral lesions of the temporal-parietal region listen to sentences with neutral content (such as *The boy went to the store*) said in a happy, sad, angry, or indifferent tone of voice. Patients with right hemisphere damage judged the emotion being expressed less accurately. Heilman, Watson, and Bowers (1983) recorded a particularly interesting case of a man with a disorder called *pure word deafness* (described in Chapter 16). The man could not comprehend the meaning of speech but had no difficulty identifying the emotion being expressed by its intonation. This case, like the study by George et al., indicates that comprehension of words and recognition of tone of voice are independent functions.

As we saw in Chapter 6, damage to the visual association cortex can cause *prosopagnosia*—inability to recognize particular faces. Just as recognition of the meaning of words and the emotion expressed by tone of voice are ac-

complished by different brain functions, so are recognition of particular faces and facial expressions of emotions. Some patients can recognize faces but not the emotions they express, and others can recognize the emotions but not the faces (Bowers and Heilman, 1981; Humphreys, Donnelly, and Riddoch, 1993). In addition, most patients who cannot recognize facial expressions can easily recognize emotions from tone of voice.

Perrett and his colleagues (see Perrett et al., 1992) have discovered an interesting brain function that may be related to recognition of emotional expression. They found that neurons in the monkey's superior temporal sulcus are involved in recognition of the direction of another monkey's gaze—or even that of a human. They found that some neurons in this region responded when the monkey looked at photographs of a monkey's face or a human face, but only when the gaze of the face in the photograph was oriented in a particular direction. For example, Figure 11.11 shows the activity level of a neuron that responded when a human face was looking up. (See *Figure 11.11.*)

Why is gaze important in recognition of emotions? First, it is important to know whether an emotional expression is directed toward you or toward someone else. For example, an angry expression directed toward you means something very different from a similar expression directed toward someone else. And if someone else shows signs of fear, the expression can serve as a useful warning to us, but only if we can figure out what he or she is looking at. The neocortex that lines the superior temporal sulcus seems to provide such information. Lesions there disrupt monkeys' ability to discriminate the direction of another animal's gaze, but they do not impair their ability to recognize other animals' faces (Campbell et al., 1990; Heywood and Cowey, 1992). As we saw in Chapter 6, the parietal lobe—the endpoint of the dorsal stream of visual analysis—is concerned with perceiving the location of objects in space. Presumably, the connections that exist between the superior temporal sulcus and the parietal cortex enable the orientation of another animal's gaze to direct one's attention to a particular location in space (Harries and Perrett, 1991).

As we saw in the previous section, the amygdala plays a special role in emotional responses. It may play a role in emotional recognition, as well. For example, several studies have found that lesions of the amygdala (the result of degenerative diseases or surgery for severe seizure disorders) impair people's ability to recognize facial expressions of emotion—especially expressions of fear (Adolphs et al., 1994, 1995; Young et al., 1995; Calder et al., 1996). These lesions sometimes impair perception of gaze direction, too. Scott et al. (1997) report the case of a woman with bi-

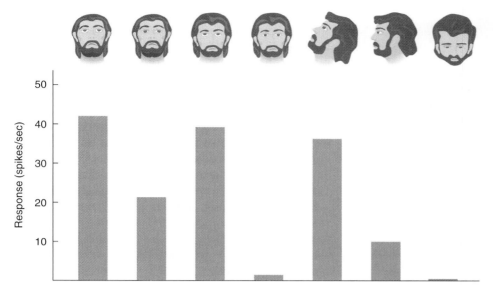

Figure 11.11
Responses of a single neuron in the cortex lining the superior temporal sulcus of a monkey's brain. The cell fired most vigorously when the monkey was presented a photograph of a face looking up.
(From Perrett, D.I., Harries, M.H., Mistlin, A.J., Hietanen, J.K., Benson, P.J., Bevan, R., Thomas, S., Oram, M.W., Ortega, J., and Brierley, K., *International Journal of Comparative Psychology*, 1990, 4, 25–55.)

lateral amygdala lesions who had normal hearing but had difficulty recognizing emotions—particularly fear and anger—expressed in a person's tone of voice. Finally, Morris et al. (1996) found a large increase in the activity of the amygdala (measured by PET) when people viewed photographs of faces expressing fear but only a small increase when they looked at photographs of happy faces.

● Neural Basis of the Communication of Emotions: Expression

Facial expressions of emotion are automatic and involuntary (although, as we saw, they can be modified by display rules). It is not easy to produce a realistic facial expression of emotion when we do not really feel that way. In fact, Ekman and Davidson have confirmed an early observation by a nineteenth-century neurologist, Guillaume-Benjamin Duchenne de Boulogne, that genuinely happy smiles, as opposed to false smiles or smiles people make when they greet someone else, involve contraction of a muscle near the eyes, the lateral part of the orbicularis oculi—now sometimes referred to as Duchenne's muscle (Ekman, 1992; Ekman and Davidson, 1993). As Duchenne put it, "The first [zygomatic major muscle] obeys the will but the second [orbicularis oculi] is only put in play by the sweet emotions of the soul; the . . . fake joy, the deceitful laugh, cannot provoke the contraction of this latter muscle" (Duchenne, 1862/1990, p. 72). The difficulty actors have in voluntarily producing a convincing facial expression of emotion is one of the reasons that led Konstantin Stanislavsky to develop his system of *method acting*, in which ac-

tors attempt to imagine themselves in a situation that would lead to the desired emotion. Once the emotion is evoked, the facial expressions follow naturally.

This observation is confirmed by two neurological disorders with complementary symptoms (Hopf et al., 1992). The first, **volitional facial paresis,** is caused by damage to the face region of the primary motor cortex or to the fibers connecting this region with the motor nucleus of the facial nerve, which controls the muscles responsible for movement of the facial muscles. (*Paresis,* from the Greek "to let go," refers to a partial paralysis.) The interesting thing about volitional facial paresis is that the patient cannot voluntarily move the facial muscles, but will express a genuine emotion with those muscles. For example, Figure 11.12a shows a woman trying to pull her lips apart and show her teeth. Because of the lesion in the face region of her right primary motor cortex, she could not move the left side of her face. However, when she laughed (Figure 11.12b), both sides of her face moved normally. (See *Figure 11.12a* and *11.12b.*) In contrast, **emotional facial paresis** is caused by damage to the insular region of the pre-

volitional facial paresis   Difficulty in moving the facial muscles voluntarily; caused by damage to the face region of the primary motor cortex or its subcortical connections.

emotional facial paresis   Lack of movement of facial muscles in response to emotions in people who have no difficulty moving these muscles voluntarily; caused by damage to the insular prefrontal cortex, subcortical white matter of the frontal lobe, or parts of the thalamus.

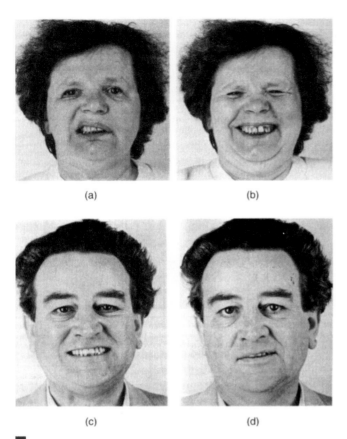

Figure 11.12
Emotional and volitional paresis. (a) A woman with volitional facial paresis caused by a right hemisphere lesion trying to pull her lips apart and show her teeth. Only the right side of her face responds. (b) The same woman showing a genuine smile. (c) A man with emotional facial paresis caused by a left-hemisphere lesion showing his teeth. (d) The same man smiling. Only the left side of his face responds.
(From Hopf, H.C., Mueller-Forell, W., and Hopf, N.J., *Neurology*, 1992, 42, 1918–1923.)

frontal cortex, to the white matter of the frontal lobe, or to parts of the thalamus. People with this disorder can move their face muscles voluntarily, but do not express emotions on the affected side of the face. Figure 11.12c shows a man pulling his lips apart to show his teeth, which he had no trouble doing. Figure 11.12d shows him smiling; as you can see, only the left side of his mouth is raised. He had a stroke that damaged the white matter of the left frontal lobe. (See *Figure 11.12c* and *11.12d*.) These two syndromes clearly indicate that different brain mechanisms are responsible for voluntary movements of the facial muscles and automatic, involuntary expression of emotions involving the same muscles.

As we saw in the previous subsection, the right hemisphere plays a more significant role in recognizing emotions in the voice or facial expressions of other people—especially negative emotions. The same hemispheric specialization appears to be true for expressing emotions. When people show emotions with their facial muscles, the left side of the face usually makes a more intense expression. For example, Sackheim and Gur (1978) cut photographs of people who were posing emotions into right and left halves, prepared mirror images of each of them, and pasted them together, producing so-called *chimerical faces* (from the mythical Chimera, a fire-breathing monster, part goat, part lion, and part serpent). They found that the left halves were more expressive than the right ones. (See *Figure 11.13.*) Because motor control is contralateral, the results suggest that the right hemisphere is more expressive than the left.

Moscovitch and Olds (1982) made more natural observations of people in restaurants and parks and found that the left side of their faces appeared to make stronger expressions of emotions. They confirmed these results in the laboratory by analyzing videotapes of people telling sad or humorous stories.

Using the chimerical faces technique, Hauser (1993) found that rhesus monkeys, like humans, express emotions more strongly in the left sides of their faces. Analysis of videotapes further showed that emotional expressions also begin sooner in the left side of the face. These findings suggest that hemispherical specialization for emotional expression appeared before the emergence of our own species. Figure 11.14 shows six videotape frames of a monkey's fear grimace expressed during the course of an interaction with a more dominant monkey. (See *Figure 11.14.*)

Left hemisphere lesions do not usually impair vocal expressions of emotion. For example, people with Wernicke's aphasia (described in Chapter 16) usually modulate their voice according to mood, even though the words they say make no sense. In contrast, right hemisphere lesions, do impair expression of emotion, both facially and by tone of voice.

Interesting information about hemispherical specialization in the expression of emotion has been obtained during the Wada test. The **Wada test** (named after its developer) is performed before a person receives surgery for removal of a seizure focus. (The reason for the procedure is described in more detail in Chapter 15.) Ross, Homan,

Wada test   A test often performed before brain surgery; verifies the functions of one hemisphere by testing patients while the other hemisphere is anesthetized.

 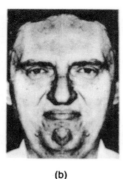 

(a)   (b)   (c)

Figure 11.13
An example of a stimulus used by Sackheim and Gur
(1978). (a) Original photo. (b) Composite of the right
side of the man's face. (c) Composite of the left side of the
man's face.
(Reprinted with permission from *Neuropsychologia*, 16, H.A.
Sackheim and R.C. Gur, Lateral asymmetry in intensity of
emotional expression. Copyright 1978, Pergamon Press.)

and Buck (1994) asked people about to be evaluated for
seizure surgery about experiences they had had that caused
an intense emotion. The subjects narrated their experiences
and described their feelings at the time. Then, while the
right hemisphere was anesthetized with a fast-acting barbiturate injected into the right carotid artery, the subjects
were asked about these experiences again. This time, most
of the subjects described less intense emotions. For example, one subject described an accident in which he had
wrecked his car. Before the injection, he said, "I was scared,
scared to death. I could have run off the road and killed
myself or someone else . . . I was really scared." During the
right hemisphere anesthesia he said that after the accident
he felt "silly . . . silly." Another patient described an accident with a truck as the scariest situation he had ever experienced. While his right hemisphere was anesthetized,
he said he was "sort of scared" but denied that the accident
was the scariest event in his life. Another patient said he

was very angry when he learned that his wife was having an
affair and threw a phone across the room. During the anesthesia he said that he had become "a little angry" and
"kind'a tossed the phone." Ross and his colleagues suggest
that the right hemisphere plays a role in what they call *primary* emotions, most of which are negative. The left hemisphere, they believe, is involved in modulating emotional
displays controlled by the right hemisphere and organizing
social displays of positive emotions, such as the quick
smile we flash when we meet someone we know. These social displays are different from the expressions of genuine
emotions—for example, the social smile does not involve
the contraction of Duchenne's muscle. Unfortunately, it is
not possible to query people about their emotional responses while the left hemisphere is anesthetized, because
the anesthesia of the speech mechanisms in the left hemisphere prevents them from speaking or understanding the
speech of other people.

Interim Summary

We (and members of other species) communicate our
emotions primarily through facial gestures. Darwin believed that such expressions of emotion were innate—that
these muscular movements were inherited behavioral patterns. Ekman and his colleagues performed cross-cultural
studies with members of an isolated tribe in New Guinea.
Their results supported Darwin's hypothesis. But although
expressions of genuine emotions are automatic and innate,
research has shown that people can follow culturally determined display rules and exert a certain amount of control over their emotional expressions.

Recognition of other people's emotional expressions involves the right hemisphere more than the left. Studies
with normal people have shown that people can judge facial expressions or tone of voice better when the informa-

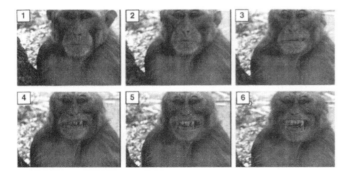

Figure 11.14
Successive frames from a videotape of a rhesus monkey showing
a fear grimace in response to an interaction with a more dominant
monkey.
(From Hauser, M.D., *Science*, 1993, 261, 475–477.)

tion is presented to the right hemisphere than when it is presented to the left hemisphere. PET scans made while people judge the emotions of voices activate the right hemisphere more than the left. The right hemisphere plays a special role in recognition of negative emotions; a conditioned emotional response can most easily be established with an angry face presented to the right hemisphere. Studies of people with left or right hemisphere brain damage corroborate these findings. In addition, they show that recognition of particular faces involves neural circuits different from those needed to recognize facial expressions of emotions. Finally, the amygdala plays a role in recognition in emotions; lesions of the amygdala disrupt this ability, and PET scans show increased activity of the amygdala while engaging in this task.

Facial expression of emotions (and other stereotypical behaviors such as laughing and crying) are almost impossible to simulate. For example, only a genuine smile of pleasure causes the contraction of the lateral part of the orbicularis oculi (Duchenne's muscle). Genuine expressions of emotion are controlled by special neural circuits. The best evidence for this assertion comes from the complementary syndromes of emotional and volitional facial paresis. People with emotional facial paresis can move their facial muscles voluntarily but not in response to an emotion, whereas people with volitional facial paresis show the opposite symptoms. In addition, the left halves of people's faces—and the faces of monkeys—tend to be more expressive than the right halves. While the right hemisphere is anesthetized during the Wada test, the emotional feelings that accompany people's recollection of memories generally become less intense.

FEELINGS OF EMOTIONS

So far, we have examined two aspects of emotions: the organization of patterns of responses that deal with the situation that provokes the emotion, and the communication of emotional states with other members of the species. The final aspect of emotion to be examined in this chapter is the subjective component—feelings of emotion.

● The James–Lange Theory

William James (1842–1910), an American psychologist, and Carl Lange (1834–1900), a Danish physiologist, independently suggested similar explanations for emotion, which most people refer to collectively as the **James–Lange theory** (James, 1884; Lange, 1887). Basically, the theory states that emotion-producing situations elicit an appro-

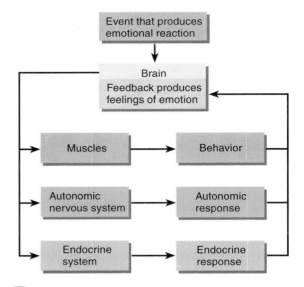

Figure 11.15
A diagrammatic representation of the James–Lange theory of emotion. An event in the environment triggers behavioral, autonomic, and endocrine responses. Feedback from these responses produces feelings of emotions.

priate set of physiological responses, such as trembling, sweating, and increased heart rate. The situations also elicit behaviors, such as clenching of the fists or fighting. The brain receives sensory feedback from the muscles and from the organs that produce these responses, and it is this feedback that constitutes our feeling of emotion.

James says that our own emotional feelings are based on what we find ourselves doing and on the sensory feedback we receive from the activity of our muscles and internal organs. Thus, when we find ourselves trembling and feel queasy, we experience fear. Where feelings of emotions are concerned, we are self-observers. Thus, the two aspects of emotions reported in the first two sections of this chapter (patterns of emotional responses and expressions of emotions) give rise to the third—feelings. (See *Figure 11.15*.)

James's description of the process of emotion might strike you as being at odds with your own experience. Many people think that they experience emotions directly, internally. They consider the outward manifestations of

James–Lange theory A theory of emotion that suggests that behaviors and physiological responses are directly elicited by situations and that feelings of emotions are produced by feedback from these behaviors and responses.

emotions to be secondary events. But have you ever found yourself in an unpleasant confrontation with someone else and discovered that you were trembling, even though you did not think that you were so bothered by the encounter? Or did you ever find yourself blushing in response to some public remark that was made about you? Or did you ever find tears coming to your eyes while watching a film that you did not think was affecting you? What would you conclude about your emotional states in situations like these? Would you ignore the evidence from your own physiological reactions?

A well-known physiologist, Walter Cannon, criticized James's theory. He said that the internal organs were relatively insensitive and that they could not respond very quickly, so feedback from them could not account for our feelings of emotions. In addition, he observed that cutting the nerves that provide feedback from the internal organs to the brain did not alter emotional behavior (Cannon, 1927). However, subsequent research indicated that Cannon's criticisms are not relevant. For example, although the viscera are not sensitive to some kinds of stimuli, such as cutting and burning, they provide much better feedback than Cannon suspected. Moreover, many changes in the viscera can occur rapidly enough so that they could be the causes of feelings of emotion.

Cannon cited the fact that cutting the sensory nerves between the internal organs and the central nervous system does not abolish emotional behavior in laboratory animals. However, this observation misses the point. It does not prove that feelings of emotion survive this surgical disruption—only that emotional *behaviors* do. We do not know how the animals feel; we know only that they will snarl and attempt to bite if threatened. In any case, James did not attribute all feelings of emotion to the internal organs; he also said that feedback from muscles was important. The threat might make the animal snarl and bite, and the feedback from the facial and neck muscles might constitute a "feeling" of anger, even if feedback from the internal organs was cut off. But we have no way to ask the animal how it felt.

James's theory is difficult to verify experimentally, because it attempts to explain *feelings* of emotion, not the causes of emotional responses—and feelings are private events. Some anecdotal evidence supports the theory. For example, Sweet (1966) reported the case of a man in whom some sympathetic nerves were severed on one side of the body to treat a cardiovascular disorder. The man—a music lover—reported that the shivering sensation he felt while listening to music now occurred only on the unoperated side of his body. He still enjoyed listening to music, but the surgery altered his emotional reaction.

In one of the few tests of James's theory, Hohman (1966) collected data from people with spinal cord damage. He asked these people about the intensity of their emotional feelings. If feedback is important, one would expect that emotional feelings would be less intense if the injury were high (that is, close to the brain) than if it were low, because a high spinal cord injury would make the person become insensitive to a larger part of the body. In fact, this result is precisely what Hohman found: The higher the injury, the less intense the feeling was. As one of Hohman's subjects said:

> I sit around and build things up in my mind, and I worry a lot, but it's not much but the power of thought. I was at home alone in bed one day and dropped a cigarette where I couldn't reach it. I finally managed to scrounge around and put it out. I could have burned up right there, but the funny thing is, I didn't get all shook up about it. I just didn't feel afraid at all, like you would suppose. (Hohman, 1966, pp. 150–151)

Another subject showed that angry behavior (an emotional response) does not appear to depend on *feelings* of emotion. Instead, the behavior is evoked by the situation (and by the person's evaluation of it) even if the spinal cord damage has reduced the intensity of the person's emotional feelings.

> Now, I don't get a feeling of physical animation, it's sort of cold anger. Sometimes I act angry when I see some injustice. I yell and cuss and raise hell, because if you don't do it sometimes, I've learned people will take advantage of you, but it doesn't have the heat to it that it used to. It's a mental kind of anger. (Hohman, 1966, pp. 150–151)

● Feedback from Simulated Emotions

James stressed the importance of two aspects of emotional responses, emotional behaviors and autonomic responses. As we saw earlier in this chapter, a particular set of muscles—those of the face—helps us communicate our emotional state to other people. Several experiments suggest that feedback from the contraction of facial muscles can affect people's moods and even alter the activity of the autonomic nervous system.

Ekman and his colleagues (Ekman, Levenson, and Friesen, 1983; Levenson, Ekman, and Friesen, 1990) asked subjects to move particular facial muscles to simulate the emotional expressions of fear, anger, surprise, disgust, sadness, and happiness. They did not tell the subjects what emotion they were trying to make them produce but only what movements they should make. For example, to simulate fear, they told the subjects to "Raise your brows. While

Figure 11.16
Photographs of happy, sad, and surprised faces posed by an adult, and the responses made by the infant.
(From Field, T., in *Development of Nonverbal Behavior in Children,* edited by R.S. Feldman. New York: Springer-Verlag, 1982. Reprinted with permission.)

fear increased heart rate but decreased skin temperature, and happiness decreased heart rate without affecting skin temperature.

Why should a particular pattern of movements of the facial muscles cause changes in mood or in the activity of the autonomic nervous system? Perhaps the connection is a result of experience; in other words, perhaps the occurrence of particular facial movements along with changes in the autonomic nervous system leads to classical conditioning, so that feedback from the facial movements becomes capable of eliciting the autonomic response—and a change in perceived emotion. Or perhaps the connection is innate. As we saw earlier, the adaptive value of emotional expressions is that they communicate feelings and intentions to others. One of the ways we communicate feelings may be through imitation.

When people see someone expressing an emotion, they tend to imitate the expression. This tendency to imitate appears to be innate. Field et al. (1982) had adults make facial expressions in front of infants. The infants' own facial expressions were videotaped and were subsequently rated by people who did not know what expressions were being displayed by the adults. Field and her colleagues found that even newborn babies (with an average age of 36 hours) tended to imitate the expressions they saw. Clearly, the effect occurs too early in life to be a result of learning. Figure 11.16 shows three photographs of the adult expressions and the expressions they elicited in a baby. Can you look at them yourself without changing your own expression, at least a little? (See *Figure 11.16.*)

Perhaps imitation provides one of the channels by which organisms communicate their emotions. For example, if we see someone looking sad, we tend to assume a sad expression ourselves. The feedback from our own expression helps put us in the other person's place and makes us more likely to respond with solace or assistance. And perhaps one of the reasons we derive pleasure from making others smile is that their smile makes *us* smile and feel happy.

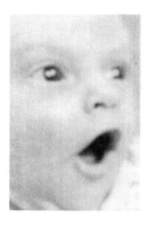

holding them raised pull your brows together. Now raise your upper eyelids and tighten the lower eyelids. Now stretch your lips horizontally." (These movements produce a facial expression of fear.) While the subjects made the expressions, the investigators monitored several physiological responses controlled by the autonomic nervous system.

The simulated expressions *did* alter the activity of the autonomic nervous system. In fact, different facial expressions produced somewhat different patterns of activity. For example, anger increased heart rate and skin temperature,

Interim Summary

From the earliest times people recognized that emotions were accompanied by feelings that seemed to come from inside the body, which probably provided the impetus for developing physiological theories of emotion. James and

Lange suggested that emotions were primarily responses to situations. Feedback from the physiological and behavioral reactions to emotion-producing situations gave rise to the feelings of emotion; thus, feelings are the *results*, not the *causes*, of emotional reactions. Hohman's study of people with spinal cord damage supported the James–Lange theory; people who could no longer feel the reactions from most of their body reported that they no longer experienced intense emotional states.

Ekman and his colleagues have shown that even simulating an emotional expression causes changes in the activity of the autonomic nervous system. Perhaps feedback from these changes explains why an emotion can be "contagious": We see someone smile with pleasure, we ourselves imitate the smile, and the internal feedback makes us feel at least somewhat happier.

AGGRESSIVE BEHAVIOR

Almost all species of animals engage in aggressive behaviors, which involve threatening gestures or actual attack directed toward another animal. Aggressive behaviors are species-typical; that is, the patterns of movements (for example, posturing, biting, striking, and hissing) are organized by neural circuits whose development is largely programmed by an animal's genes. Many aggressive behaviors are related to reproduction. For example, aggressive behaviors that gain access to mates, defend territory needed to attract mates or to provide a site for building a nest, or defend offspring against intruders can all be regarded as reproductive behaviors. Other aggressive behaviors are related to self-defense, such as that of an animal threatened by a predator.

Aggressive behavior can consist of actual attacks, or they may simply involve **threat behaviors,** which consist of postures or gestures that warn the adversary to leave or it will become the target of an attack. The threatened animal might show **submissive behaviors,** which indicate that it accepts defeat and will not challenge the other animal. In the natural environment most animals display far more threats than actual attacks. Threat behaviors are useful in reinforcing social hierarchies in organized groups of animals or in warning intruders away from an animal's territory. They have the advantage of not involving actual fighting, which can harm one or both of the combatants.

Predation is the attack of a member of one species on that of another, usually because the latter serves as food for the former. While engaged in attacking a member of the same species or defending oneself against the attack, an animal appears to be extremely aroused and excited, and the

activity of the sympathetic branch of its autonomic nervous system is high. In contrast, the attack of a predator is much more "cold-blooded"; it is generally efficient and not accompanied by a high level of sympathetic activation.

Neural Control of Aggressive Behavior

The neural control of aggressive behavior is hierarchical. That is, the particular muscular movements an animal makes in attacking or defending itself are programmed by neural circuits in the brain stem. Whether an animal attacks depends on many factors, including the nature of the eliciting stimuli in the environment and the animal's previous experience. The activity of the brain stem circuits appears to be controlled by the hypothalamus and the amygdala, which also influence many other species-typical behaviors. And, of course, the activity of the limbic system is controlled by perceptual systems that detect the status of the environment, including the presence of other animals.

Both **defensive behavior** and predation can be elicited by stimulating the periaqueductal gray matter (PAG) of a cat's midbrain. It may seem surprising that a cat should need any special treatment to induce it to attack a rat, but most laboratory cats do *not* spontaneously attack rats. During a defensive display, a cat turns sideways, arches its back, and its fur stands on end, making the animal look larger. It also retracts its ears, unsheathes its claws, and growls and hisses. A predatory attack is directed against a small animal such as a rat. Predation is not accompanied by a strong display of rage. A cat stalks a rat and suddenly pounces on it, directing powerful bites to the head and neck region. The cat does not growl or scream, and it stops attacking once the rat ceases to move. Although a cat looks excited when it pounces on a rat and bites it, it does not show signs of "rage." The attack appears cold-blooded and ruthless.

Although predation obtains food, the brain mechanisms that organize predatory behavior are not identical to those that organize eating; these two sets of mechanisms

threat behavior A species-typical behavior that warns another animal that it may be attacked if it does not flee or show a submissive behavior.

submissive behavior A stereotypical behavior shown by an animal in response to threat behavior by another animal; serves to prevent an attack.

predation Attack of one animal directed at an individual of another species, on which the attacking animal normally preys.

defensive behavior A species-typical behavior by which an animal defends itself against the threat of another animal.

can be excited independently. Roberts and Kiess (1964) implanted stimulating electrodes in the brains of cats in a location that produced predatory attack. (These cats were not natural rat killers.) The experimenters taught the cats to run through a maze in order to obtain a rat to attack. The animals would do so only while the brain stimulation was turned on; when it was off, they would not seek out the rat. When the brain stimulation was turned on, a hungry cat would even leave a dish of food to run through the maze and attack the rat, which it would *not* subsequently eat. Therefore, predatory attack is not synonymous with feeding. It provides a means for carnivores to obtain food, but the neural mechanisms for attack and eating are different.

As we all know, a cat will often stalk and kill rodents and birds even when it is not hungry; it seems to enjoy this activity independent of its food-getting utility. In contrast, animals that are fighting do not act as if they are enjoying themselves. Panksepp (1971) observed a significant difference in rats' preference for receiving electrical brain stimulation that elicits predatory attack or defensive attack. If he turned on the stimulation that produced defensive attack but permitted the rats to press a lever to turn it off, they quickly learned to do so. Thus, brain stimulation that elicits defensive attack appears to be aversive. In contrast, rats quickly learned to press a lever that turned *on* stimulation that elicited predatory attack. Thus, stimulation of the brain regions involved in the elicitation of attack is reinforcing.

A series of studies by Shaikh, Siegel, and their colleagues (Shaikh and Siegel, 1989; Shaikh, Steinberg, and Siegel, 1993; Shaikh, Schubert, and Siegel, 1994; Siegel, Schubert, and Shaikh, 1995; Han, Shaikh, and Siegel, 1996a, 1996b) investigated the neural circuitry involved in defensive behavior and predation in cats. The investigators placed electrodes in various regions of the brain and observed the effects of electrical stimulation of these regions on the animals' behavior. In some cases, the electrode was actually a stainless-steel cannula, coated with an insulating material except for the tip. These devices (called *cannula electrodes*) could be used to infuse chemicals into the brain as well as to stimulate it. The investigators found that defensive behavior and predation can be elicited by stimulation of different parts of the PAG and that the hypothalamus and the amygdala influence these behaviors through excitatory and inhibitory connections with the PAG.

Rather than describe the details of all the experiments, I will describe just one of them, which illustrates the procedure the investigators used. Schubert, Shaikh, and Siegel (1996) placed a cannula electrode in the dorsal PAG and a standard wire electrode in the medial hypothalamus. Other studies had already shown that stimulation of the dorsal PAG elicits defensive rage in cats, and that simulta-

neous stimulation of the medial hypothalamus enhances this behavior. Schubert and her colleagues confirmed these findings and then showed that infusion of AP-7 into the dorsal PAG blocked the effects of medial hypothalamic stimulation. (AP-7 blocks NMDA receptors, a category of ionotropic glutamate receptors.) They also injected the retrograde tracer fluorogold into the dorsal PAG and found labeled neurons in the medial hypothalamus, which confirms a direct connection between these two brain regions. In addition, they incubated slices of the PAG in a solution containing radioactive NMDA and confirmed the presence of a dense concentration of NMDA receptors in this area by means of autoradiography. Finally, a double-labeling procedure showed that neurons in the medial hypothalamus that send axons to the dorsal PAG are glutamatergic. (If you want to review the use of retrograde tracers, autoradiography, and double labeling procedures, you can find a discussion of these methods in Chapter 5.)

Using similar methods, Shaikh and his colleagues found that the three principal regions of the amygdala and two regions of the hypothalamus affect defensive rage and predation, both of which appear to be organized by the PAG. (They assessed predation by presenting the cats with an anesthetized rat, so no pain was inflicted.) A possible connection between the lateral hypothalamus and the ventral PAG has not yet been verified. Rather than list the connections and their effects, I will direct you to *Figure 11.17*.

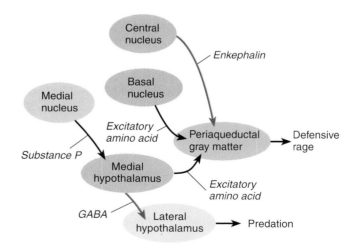

Figure 11.17
Results of the studies by Shaikh, Siegel, and their colleagues. The diagram shows interconnections of parts of the amygdala, hypothalamus, and periaqueductal gray matter and their effects on defensive rage and predation in cats. Black arrows indicate excitation; red arrows indicate inhibition.

Of course, brain regions other than the amygdala, hypothalamus, and periaqueductal gray matter are involved in aggressive behavior. In general, increased activity of serotonergic synapses inhibits aggression. For this reason, some clinicians have used serotonergic drugs to treat violent behavior in humans. Destruction of serotonergic axons in the forebrain facilitates aggressive attack, presumably by removing an inhibitory effect (Vergnes et al., 1988). A group of researchers has studied the relation between serotonergic activity and aggressiveness in a free-ranging colony of rhesus monkeys (Mehlman et al., 1995; Higley et al. 1996a, 1996b). They assessed serotonergic activity by capturing the monkeys and removing a sample of cerebrospinal fluid and analyzing it for 5-HIAA, a metabolite of serotonin (5-HT). When 5-HT is released, most of the neurotransmitter is taken back into the terminal buttons by means of reuptake, but some escapes and is broken down to 5-HIAA, which finds its way into the cerebrospinal fluid. Thus, high levels of 5-HIAA in the CSF indicates an elevated level of serotonergic activity. The investigators found that young male monkeys with the lowest levels of 5-HIAA showed a pattern of risk-taking behavior, including high levels of aggression directed toward animals older and much larger than themselves. They were much more likely to take dangerous unprovoked long leaps from tree to tree at a height of more than 7 m (27.6 ft). They were also more likely to pick fights that they could not possibly win. Of 49 preadolescent male monkeys that the investigators followed for four years, 46 percent of those with the lowest 5-HIAA levels died, while all of the monkeys with the highest levels survived. (See *Figure 11.18.*) Most of the monkeys were killed by other monkeys. In fact, the first monkey to be killed had the lowest level of 5-HIAA and was seen attacking two mature males the night before his death.

It is clear that serotonin does not simply inhibit aggression; rather, it exerts a controlling influence on risky behavior, which includes aggression. A study by Raleigh et al. (1991) removed the dominant male from each of several groups of vervet monkeys and treated the top two remaining males with serotonergic drugs: One received an agonist, and the other received an antagonist. The monkeys who received the serotonin agonist became dominant, while the status of those who received the antagonist declined. You might think that removing some inhibitory control over aggressiveness would increase a monkey's dominance. However, dominance and aggression are not synonymous. Certainly, a dominant animal will use aggression if it is overtly challenged by a rival. However, becoming the dominant animal in a group of monkeys requires good social skills. As Mehlman et al. (1995) noted in their naturalistic study, the monkeys with low levels of

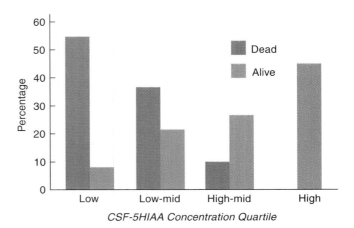

Figure 11.18
Percentage of young male monkeys alive or dead as a function of 5-HIAA level in the CSF, measured four years previously.
(Adapted from Higley, J.D., Mehlman, P.T., Higley, S.B., Fernald, B., Vickers, J., Lindell, S.G., Taub, D.M., Suomi, S.J., and Linnoila, M., *Archives of General Psychiatry*, 1996, *53*, 537–543.)

serotonergic activity showed the lowest levels of social competency.

Two studies with targeted mutations in mice confirm the conclusion that serotonin has an inhibitory role in aggression. Saudou et al. (1994) found that mice lacking 5-HT$_{1B}$ receptors attacked an intruder more quickly and intensely than normal mice, but otherwise, their behavior appeared normal. Chen et al. (1994) tested mice with a targeted mutation of an enzyme (α-CaMKII) that resulted in reduced release of serotonin by neurons of the dorsal raphe nucleus. The animals exhibited decreased fear and increased defensive aggression.

Several studies have found that serotonergic neurons play an inhibitory role in human aggression. (See Coccaro, 1996, for a review.) For example, Brown et al. (1979, 1982) found that a history of aggressiveness and psychological test scores indicating antisocial tendencies was related to low levels of CSF 5-HIAA in a group of naval recruits. Coccaro et al. (1994) studied a group of men with personality disorders (including a history of impulsive aggression). They found that the men with the lowest serotonergic activity were more likely to have close relatives with a history of similar behavior problems. The study did not collect evidence needed to determine whether the association was genetic or environmental (or both).

Another study (Brunner et al., 1993) found a potential genetic link between serotonin and violent, antisocial behavior, but the results are somewhat puzzling. The authors studied a Dutch family that contained many men who displayed antisocial behavior, including impulsive aggression, attempted rape, arson, and exhibitionism. They discovered that the antisocial syndrome was caused by a mutation of the gene for monoamine oxidase type A (MAO-A), which is located on the X chromosome. (Because males have only one X chromosome and females have two, an X-linked disorder is much more frequent in males.) MAO-A is the enzyme responsible for the destruction of serotonin. But although these results are interesting, they are somewhat puzzling. Just why a deficiency in this enzyme should produce a syndrome of antisocial behavior is not at all clear—after all, MAO-A destroys serotonin, and one might expect that a lack of this enzyme would *increase* the release of serotonin. In fact, Cases et al. (1995) found that mice with a targeted mutation for the MAO-A receptor gene were hyperaggressive and that their brains contained an extremely high level of serotonin. However, there were other abnormalities in the brain, and it is possible that down-regulation of postsynaptic 5-HT receptors prevented serotonin from having its usual effects. In any case, we need more research to resolve these speculations.

● Hormonal Control of Aggressive Behavior

As we saw, many instances of aggressive behavior are in some way related to reproduction. For example, males of some species establish territories that attract females during the breeding season. To do so, they must defend them against the intrusion of other males. Even in species in which breeding does not depend on the establishment of a territory, males may compete for access to females, which also involves aggressive behavior. Females, too, often compete with other females for space in which to build nests or dens in which to rear their offspring, and they will defend their offspring against the intrusion of other animals. As you learned in Chapter 10, most reproductive behaviors are controlled by the organizational and activational effects of hormones; thus, we should not be surprised that many forms of aggressive behavior are, like mating, affected by hormones.

Aggression in Males

Adult males of many species fight for territory or access to females. In laboratory rodents androgen secretion occurs prenatally, decreases, and then increases again at the time of puberty. Intermale aggressiveness also begins around the time of puberty, which suggests that the behavior is controlled by neural circuits that are stimulated by androgens. Indeed, many years ago Beeman (1947) found that castration reduced aggressiveness and that injections of testosterone reinstated it.

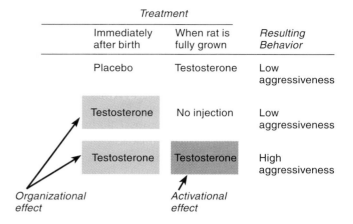

Figure 11.19
Organizational and activational effects of testosterone on social aggression.

In Chapter 10 we saw that early androgenization has an *organizational effect*. The secretion of androgens early in development modifies the developing brain, making neural circuits that control male sexual behavior become more responsive to testosterone. Similarly, early androgenization has an organizational effect that stimulates the development of testosterone-sensitive neural circuits that facilitate intermale aggression. (See *Figure 11.19*.)

The organizational effect of androgens on intermale aggression (aggressive displays or actual fights between two males of the same species) is important, but it is not an all-or-none phenomenon. Prolonged administration of testosterone will eventually induce intermale aggression even in rodents that were castrated immediately after birth. Data reviewed by vom Saal (1983) show that exposure to androgens early in life decreases the amount of exposure that is necessary to activate aggressive behavior later in life. Thus, early androgenization *sensitizes* the neural circuits—the earlier the androgenization, the more effective the sensitization.

As we saw in Chapter 10, when a pregnant female is subjected to stress, her male offspring show less male sexual behavior, presumably because the stress interferes with the prenatal secretion of androgens. Kinsley and Svare (1986) found that prenatal stress also reduces intermale aggression. They subjected pregnant female mice to stress by restraining them several times in a plastic tube that was placed under bright lights. The male offspring were tested as adults for intermale aggression by placing them in a cage with an unfamiliar male. The prenatally stressed animals were much less likely than the control animals to attack the intruder. Thus, a treatment that interferes with prena-

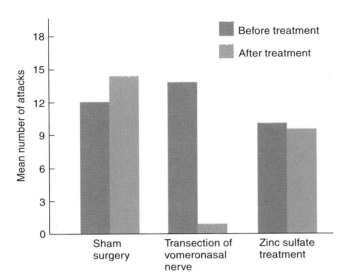

Figure 11.20
Effects of transection of the vomeronasal nerve and anosmia produced by zinc sulfate treatment on intermale aggression in mice.
(Adapted from Bean, N.J., *Physiology and Behavior,* 1982, 29, 433–437.)

tal masculinization of sexual behavior also interferes with the masculinization of aggressive behavior.

We also saw in Chapter 10 that androgens stimulate male sexual behavior by interacting with androgen receptors in neurons located in the medial preoptic area (MPA). This region also appears to be important in mediating the effects of androgens on intermale aggression. Bean and Conner (1978) found that implanting testosterone in the MPA reinstated intermale aggression in castrated male rats. Presumably, the testosterone directly activated the behavior by stimulating the androgen-sensitive neurons located there. The medial preoptic area, then, appears to be involved in several behaviors related to reproduction: male sexual behavior, maternal behavior, and intermale aggression.

Males readily attack other males but usually do not attack females. Their ability to discriminate the sex of the intruder appears to be based on the presence of particular pheromones. Bean (1982) found that intermale aggression was abolished in mice by cutting the vomeronasal nerve, which deprives the brain of input from the vomeronasal organ. Rinsing the olfactory epithelium with zinc sulfate (which temporarily deactivates the primary olfactory system) had no effect. (See *Figure 11.20.*) Thus, intermale aggression of mice (and probably of other species of rodents) depends on a pheromonal stimulus, not on odors detected by the primary olfactory system. It seems reasonable to pre-

dict that the medial amygdala plays a role in modulating this effect, as it does in all other phenomena controlled by pheromones. Pheromones (or perhaps odors) also appear to be responsible for the inhibition of a male's attack on a female. If the urine of female mice is painted on a male mouse, it will not be attacked if it is introduced into another male's cage (Dixon and Mackintosh, 1971; Dixon, 1973).

Aggression in Females

Two adult female rodents that meet in a neutral territory are less likely than males to fight. But aggression between females, like aggression between males, appears to be facilitated by testosterone. Van de Poll et al. (1988) ovariectomized female rats and then give them daily injections of testosterone, estradiol, or a placebo for fourteen days. The animals were then placed in a test cage and an unfamiliar female was introduced. As Figure 11.21 shows, testosterone increased aggressiveness, whereas estradiol had no effect. (See *Figure 11.21.*)

Androgens have an organizational effect on the aggressiveness of females, and a certain amount of prenatal androgenization appears to occur naturally. Most rodent fetuses share their mother's uterus with brothers and sisters, arranged in a row like peas in a pod. A female mouse may have zero, one, or two brothers adjacent to her. Researchers refer to these females as 0M, 1M, or 2M, respectively. (See *Figure 11.22.*) Being next to a male fetus has an effect on a female's blood levels of androgens prenatally. Vom Saal and Bronson (1980) found that females located

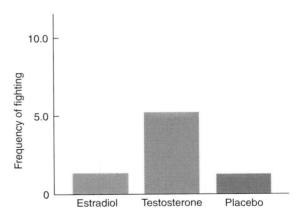

Figure 11.21
Effects of estradiol and testosterone on interfemale aggression in rats.
(Adapted from van de Poll, N.E., Taminiau, M.S., Endert, E., and Louwerse, A.L., *International Journal of Neuroscience,* 1988, 41, 271–286.)

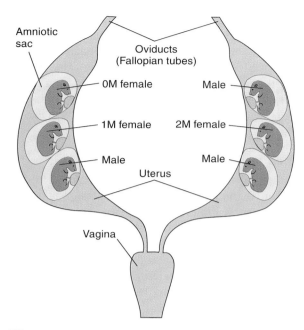

Figure 11.22
0M, 1M, and 2M female mouse fetuses.
(Adapted from vom Saal, F.S., in *Hormones and Aggressive Behavior*, edited by B.B. Svare. New York: Plenum Press, 1983.)

between two males had significantly higher levels of testosterone in their blood than females located between two females (or between a female and the end of the uterus). When they are tested as adults, 2M females are more likely to exhibit interfemale aggressiveness.

Females of some primate species (for example, rhesus monkeys and baboons) are more likely to engage in fights around the time of ovulation (Carpenter, 1942; Saayman, 1971). This phenomenon is probably caused by their increased sexual interest and consequent proximity to males. As Carpenter noted, "She actively approaches males and must overcome their usual resistance to close association, hence she becomes an object of attacks by them" (p. 136). Another period of fighting occurs just before menstruation (Sassenrath, Powell, and Hendrickx, 1973; Mallow, 1979). During this time females tend to attack other females.

Researchers have studied the possibility that irritability and aggressiveness may increase in women just before the time of menstruation, as it does in some other primate species. Floody (1983) reviewed the literature on the so-called *premenstrual syndrome* (PMS). Almost all studies that observed actual aggressiveness, primarily of women in institutions, found decreases around the time of ovulation and increases just before menstruation. Clearly, the changes in irritability are not universal; some women experience little or no mood shift before menstruation. And

even if changes in mood occur, most women do not actually become aggressive. Although women with a history of criminal behavior (such as those in prison) may indeed exhibit premenstrual aggressiveness, emotionally stable women may fail to show even a small increase in aggressiveness (Persky, 1974). Depending on their history and temperament, different people respond differently to similar physiological changes.

Maternal Aggression

Most parents who actively raise their offspring will vigorously defend them against intruders. In laboratory rodents the responsible parent is the female, so the most commonly studied form of parental defense is maternal aggression. Female mice very effectively defend their young, driving away intruding adults of either sex. Counterattacks by the intruder are rare (Svare, Betteridge, Katz, and Samuels, 1981). Whereas strange males who encounter each other engage in mutual investigation for a minute or two before fighting begins, the attack of a lactating female on an intruder is immediate (Svare, 1983).

Maternal aggressiveness actually begins during pregnancy. Like maternal nest building, it appears to be stimulated by progesterone. The onset of aggressiveness in pregnant mice occurs when progesterone levels begin to rise significantly (Mann, Konen, and Svare, 1984). Immediately after birth, for a period of approximately 48 hours, female mice become completely docile; they do not attack intruders (Ghiraldi and Svare, 1989). As Svare (1989) noted, it is at this time that female mice typically mate again; thus, the fact that they do not attack a male is biologically significant. This phenomenon is probably caused by the high level of estradiol that is present at that time. Ghiraldi and Svare found that removing a female mouse's ovaries just before parturition shortened the period of docility by 24 hours, and administering estradiol restored it.

The tendency for a lactating female mouse to attack a stranger is induced by stimuli provided by her offspring. If the newborn mice are removed, the mother fails to become aggressive. Two activating stimuli appear to be important: suckling and odors. First, let us consider the tactile stimulation produced by suckling. Normally, maternal aggressiveness begins after the mother has suckled her young for 48 hours. If the mother's nipples are surgically removed, she does not become aggressive, even if pups are present (Svare and Gandelman, 1976; Gandelman and Simon, 1980). These effects do not depend on the presence of ovarian or pituitary hormones (Svare et al., 1982.)

Prenatal exposure to androgens appears to have an organizational effect on maternal aggression. As we saw in the previous section, female mice who were located between two males in the uterus (2M females) are more likely to attack other females and are more responsive to the activating effects of androgens in adulthood. Vom Saal and Bronson (1980a) also found that 2M females are more maternally aggressive than 0M females. Kinsley, Konen, Miele, Ghiraldi, and Svare (1986) found that they were also more likely to exhibit aggressiveness during pregnancy.

Infanticide

Although the evolutionary process has selected parents who nurture and defend their young, adults—both male and female—sometimes kill infants, including their own. Although this behavior may appear to be aberrant and maladaptive, under some circumstances it has survival value for the species.

Hrdy (1977), in a report of infanticide among langurs (a primate species), suggested that the killing of infants by a male who was not the father "is a reproductive strategy whereby the usurping male increases his own reproductive success at the expense of the former leader (presumably the father of the infant killed)" (p. 48). Because lactation suppresses a female's fertility, she is unlikely to become pregnant by the new male. However, when the male kills her offspring, she soon becomes fertile and thus capable of becoming pregnant by him. (The male tends *not* to kill his own offspring.)

You will recall a related phenomenon that I mentioned in Chapter 10: the Bruce effect (Bruce, 1960a, 1960b). When a newly pregnant mouse encounters the odor of a strange male, she tends to abort spontaneously. Thus, the male unintentionally kills her yet-unborn offspring, making it possible for him to impregnate her and propagate his own genes.

Vom Saal (1985) discovered that the tendency of male mice to kill infants is regulated by copulation. He found that after male mice successfully copulated and ejaculated, the likelihood of infanticide increased within a few days, but then decreased nineteen days later, around the time that the pups would be born. In fact, the males not only did not kill pups, but they actually cared for them, just as their mothers do. This docility and solicitude lasted until about fifty days after the time of copulation, which is about the time that the pups would be weaned. Thus, the act of ejaculation initiates a series of events that increases the likelihood that a would-be father mouse kills the infants of other males but not his own.

The timing of these behavioral changes is remarkable. What internal mechanism keeps track of the nineteen-day gestation period of the female? Perrigo, Bryant, and vom Saal (1990) found that however this mechanism works, it does so by counting days, not hours. They permitted male mice to copulate and then divided them into two groups, which they put in rooms with light/dark cycles of different lengths: 22 or 27 hours. They found that the reduction in the likelihood of infanticide occurred after approximately eighteen "days," whether the days were short or long. It will be interesting to discover the mechanism that permits the mouse brain to count to eighteen.

Female rodents sometimes kill their own pups. Obviously, infanticide by males and females must occur for different reasons. Indeed, female infanticide appears to achieve at least two advantages: It decreases crowding, and it helps attain an optimal litter size. The first hypothetical advantage was supported by Calhoun (1962), who reported that severe crowding greatly increased the incidence of female infanticide in rats. Presumably, this behavior helped prevent the crowding from increasing still further. Gandelman and Simon (1978) obtained data that supported the second hypothetical advantage. They adjusted the size of litters of newborn mice to either twelve or sixteen pups by adding foster pups or removing them. In both groups the mean number of surviving offspring was nine. The mothers with sixteen pups tended to kill more than those with twelve pups. The smallest pups were most likely to be killed. Because these pups were probably the least fit, the behavior tends to select for an optimally sized litter that consists of the healthiest pups. (Mice have ten nipples, which suggests that the optimal size is ten or fewer.)

Effects of Androgens on Human Aggressive Behavior

Boys are generally more aggressive than girls. Clearly, Western society tolerates assertiveness and aggressive behavior from boys more than from girls. Without doubt, the way we treat boys and girls and the models we expose them to play important roles in sex differences in aggressiveness in our species. The question is not whether socialization has an effect (certainly, it does) but whether biological influences, such as exposure to androgens, have an effect, too.

Prenatal androgenization increases aggressive behavior in all species that have been studied, including primates. Therefore, if androgens did not affect aggressive behavior in humans, our species would be exceptional. After puberty, androgens also begin to have activational effects. Boys' testosterone levels begin to increase during the early teens, at which time aggressive behavior and intermale fighting also increase (Mazur, 1983). Of course, boys' social status changes during puberty, and their testosterone affects their muscles as well as their brains; so we cannot be sure that the effect is hormonally produced or, if it is, that it is mediated by the brain.

Scientifically rigorous evidence that androgens increase aggression in humans is difficult to obtain. Obviously, we cannot randomly castrate some men to see whether their aggressiveness declines. In the past, authorities have attempted to suppress sex-related aggression by castrating convicted male sex offenders. Investigators have reported that both heterosexual and homosexual aggressive attacks disappear, along with the offender's sex drive (Hawke, 1951; Sturup, 1961; Laschet, 1973). However, the studies typically lack appropriate control groups and usually do not measure aggressive behavior directly.

Some cases of aggressiveness, especially sexual assault, have been treated with synthetic steroids that inhibit the production of androgens by the testes. Clearly, treatment with drugs is preferable to castration, because the effects are not irreversible. However, the efficacy of treatment with antiandrogens has yet to be established conclusively. According to Walker and Meyer (1981), these drugs decrease sex-related aggression but have no effect on other forms of aggression. In fact, Zumpe et al. (1991) found that one of these drugs decreased sexual activity and aggression toward females when administered to male monkeys but that it actually *increased* intermale aggression.

Another way to determine whether androgens affect aggressiveness in humans is to examine the testosterone levels of people who exhibit varying levels of aggressive behavior. However, even though this approach poses fewer ethical problems, it presents methodological ones. First, let me review some evidence. In a review of the literature, Archer (1994) found that most studies found a positive relation between men's testosterone levels and their level of aggressiveness. For example, Dabbs and Morris (1990) studied 4462 US military veterans. The men with the highest testosterone levels had records of more antisocial activities, including assaults of other adults and histories of more trouble with parents, teachers, and classmates during adolescence. The largest effects were seen in men of lower socioeconomic status. Dabbs et al. (1987) measured the testosterone levels of male prison inmates and found a significant correlation with several measures of violence, including the nature of the crime for which they were convicted, infractions of prison rules, and ratings of "toughness" by their peers. These relations are also seen in female prison inmates; Dabbs et al. (1988) found that women prisoners who showed unprovoked violence and had several prior convictions also showed higher levels of testosterone. (As we saw earlier, testosterone increases interfemale aggression in laboratory animals as well.)

But we must remember that *correlation* does not necessarily indicate *causation*. A person's environment can affect his or her testosterone level. For example, losing a tennis match or a wrestling competition causes a fall in blood levels of testosterone (Mazur and Lamb, 1980; Elias, 1981). Even winning or losing a simple game of chance carried out in a psychology laboratory can affect participants' testosterone levels: Winners feel better afterward and have a higher level of testosterone (McCaul, Gladue, and Joppa, 1992). In a very elaborate study Jeffcoate et al. (1986) found that the blood levels of a group of five men confined on a boat for fourteen days changed as they established a dominance-ranking among themselves: The higher the rank a person eventually achieved, the higher his testosterone level. Thus, we cannot be sure in any correlational study that high testosterone levels *cause* people to become dominant or aggressive; perhaps their success in establishing a position of dominance increases their testosterone levels relative to those of the people they dominate.

A few studies have looked at the behavioral effects of administering androgens. Because of ethical concerns, people cannot be given androgen supplements for any length of time merely to see whether they become more aggressive—excessive amounts of androgens have deleterious effects on a person's health. Thus, the only evidence we have of the effects of long-term administration comes from case studies in which people with abnormally low levels of testosterone (the *hypogonadal syndrome*) are given an androgen to replace what would normally be present. In general, such people feel happier and their sexual activity increases, but they do not usually show more aggressiveness (Skakkebaek et al., 1981; O'Carroll, Shapiro, and Bancroft, 1985). One double-blind study (Su et al., 1993) did administer testosterone for several days to a group of normal volunteers, men aged 18 to 42 years. Those receiving the highest doses reported more euphoria and sexual arousal but also more irritability and feelings of hostility. However, the effects were small, and the investigators did not observe behaviors, only self-reports of feelings.

As everyone knows, some athletes take anabolic steroids to increase their muscle mass and strength and, supposedly, to increase their competitiveness. Anabolic steroids include natural androgens and synthetic hormones with androgenic effects. Thus, we might expect that these hormones would increase aggressiveness. Indeed, several studies have found exactly that. For example, Yates, Perry, and Murray (1992) found male weight lifters who were taking anabolic steroids to be more aggressive and hostile than those who were not. But as the authors note, we cannot be certain that the steroid is responsible for the increased aggressiveness; it could simply be that the men who were already more competitive and aggressive were the ones who chose to take the steroids.

An interesting set of experiments with another species of primates may have some relevance to human aggression. As you undoubtedly know, alcohol intake is often associated with aggression in humans. Alcohol increases intermale aggression in dominant male squirrel monkeys, but only during the mating season, when their blood level of testosterone is two to three times higher than during the nonmating season (Winslow and Miczek, 1985, 1988). Alcohol does *not* increase the aggressive behavior of subordinate monkeys at any time of the year. These studies suggest that the effects of alcohol interact with both social status and with testosterone. (See *Figure 11.23.*) This suggestion was confirmed by Winslow, Ellingoe, and Miczek (1988), who tested monkeys during the nonmating season. They found that alcohol increased the aggressive behavior of dominant monkeys if they were also given injections of testosterone. However, these treatments were ineffective in subordinate monkeys, who had presumably learned not to be aggressive. The next step will be to find the neural mechanisms that are responsible for these interactions.

Interim Summary

Aggressive behaviors are species-typical and serve useful functions most of the time. In addition, animals may exhibit threat or submissive behaviors, which may avoid an actual fight.

The periaqueductal gray matter appears to be involved in defensive behavior and predation. These mechanisms are modulated by the hypothalamus and amygdala. Activation of the central nucleus inhibits defensive aggression, while stimulation of the basolateral or medial amygdala stimulates it. Stimulation of the medial hypothalamus also facilitates defensive aggression but, through inhibitory connections with the lateral hypothalamus, inhibits predation.

Because many aggressive behaviors are related to reproduction, they are influenced by hormones, especially sex steroid hormones. Androgens primarily affect offensive attack; they are not necessary for defensive behaviors, which are shown by females as well as males. In males, androgens have organizational and activational effects on offensive attack, just as they have on male sexual behavior. The effects of androgens on intermale aggression appear to be mediated by the medial preoptic area.

Female rodents will fight when they meet in neutral territory, but less often than males. Female rodents who have been slightly androgenized (2M females) are more likely to attack other females. Female primates are most likely to fight around the time of ovulation, perhaps because their

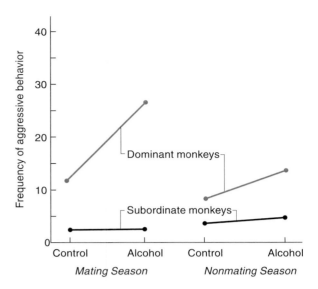

Figure 11.23
Effect of alcohol intake on frequency of aggressive behavior of dominant and subordinate male squirrel monkeys during the mating season and the nonmating season.
(Based on data from Winslow, J.T., and Miczek, J.A., *Psychopharmacologia*, 1988, 95, 92–98.)

increased sexual interest brings them closer to males. Although some women report irritability just before menstruation, the phenomenon is not universal.

Maternal aggression is a very swift and effective behavior. It begins during pregnancy, apparently triggered by the secretion of progesterone. After parturition maternal aggression is stimulated by the tactile feedback from suckling. The odor of pups is also necessary. Prenatal androgens have an organizational effect on maternal aggression; 2M females are more likely than 0M females to display maternal aggression.

Infanticide by male mice is regulated by copulation; after ejaculating, the males become more likely to kill infants, but around the time that their pups would be born, this tendency is suppressed. In males, infanticide is promoted by androgens; its occurrence is decreased by castration. Female infanticide appears to promote optimal litter size and tends to weed out less healthy offspring.

Androgens apparently promote aggressive behavior in humans, but this topic is more difficult to study in our species than in laboratory animals. Differences in testosterone levels have been observed in criminals with a history of violence, but we cannot be sure whether higher androgen levels promote violence or whether successful aggression increases androgen levels. Studies with monkeys suggest that testosterone and alcohol have synergistic effects, particularly in dominant animals. (*Synergy*, from a Greek word meaning "working together," refers to combinations of factors that are more effective than the sum of their individual actions.) Perhaps these effects are related to our observations that some men with a history of violent behavior become more aggressive when they drink.

SUGGESTED READINGS

Aggleton, J. (ed.). *The Amygdala: Neurobiological Aspects of Emotion, Memory, and Mental Dysfunction.* New York: Wiley-Liss, 1992.

Damasio, A.R. *Decartes' Error: Emotion, Reason, and the Human Brain.* New York: G.P. Putnam, 1994.

LeDoux, J.E. *The Emotional Brain: The Mysterious Underpinnings of the Emotional Life.* New York: Simon and Schuster, 1996.

McNaughton, Neil. *Biology and Emotion.* Cambridge, England: Cambridge University Press, 1989.

Stein, N.L., Leventhal, B., and Trabasso, T. (eds.). *Psychological and Biological Approaches to Emotion.* Hillsdale, NJ: Lawrence Erlbaum Associates, 1990.

CHAPTER 12

Ingestive Behavior: Drinking

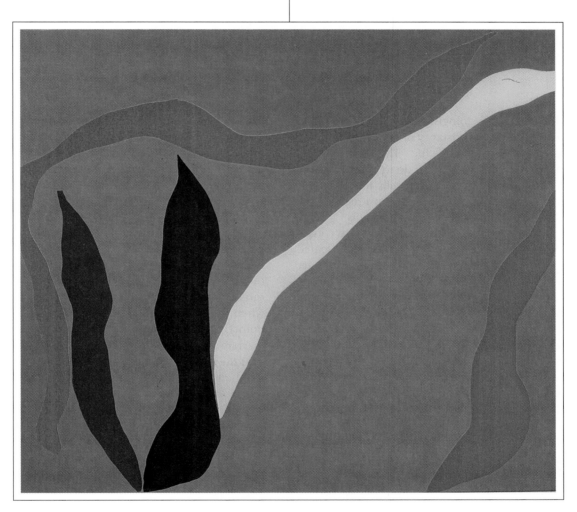

Curling Red by Raymond Parker.

As the French physiologist Claude Bernard (1813–1878) said, "The constancy of the internal milieu is a necessary condition for a free life." This famous quote succinctly says what organisms must do to be able to exist in environments hostile to the living cells that compose them (that is, to live a "free life"): They must regulate the nature of the internal fluid that bathes their cells.

The physiological characteristics of the cells that constitute our bodies evolved long ago, when these cells floated freely in the ocean. In essence, what the evolutionary process has accomplished is the ability to make our own seawater for bathing our cells, to add to this seawater the oxygen and nutrients that our cells need, and to remove from it waste products that would otherwise poison our cells. To perform these functions, we have digestive, respiratory, circulatory, and excretory systems. We also have the behaviors necessary for finding and ingesting food, water, and certain minerals.

Regulation of the fluid that bathes our cells is part of a process called **homeostasis** ("similar standing"). This chapter discusses the means by which we mammals achieve homeostatic control of the vital characteristics of our extracellular fluid through our **ingestive behavior:** intake of food, water, and minerals such as sodium. First, we will examine the general nature of regulatory mechanisms; then we will consider our drinking and eating behavior.

THE NATURE OF PHYSIOLOGICAL REGULATORY MECHANISMS

A physiological regulatory mechanism is one that maintains the constancy of some internal characteristic of the organism in the face of external variability—for example,

keeping body temperature constant despite changes in the ambient temperature. A regulatory mechanism contains four essential features: the **system variable** (the characteristic to be regulated), a **set point** (the optimal value of the system variable), a **detector** that monitors the value of the system variable, and a **correctional mechanism** that restores the system variable to the set point.

An example of a regulatory system is a room whose temperature is regulated by a thermostatically controlled heater. The system variable is the air temperature of the room, and the detector for this variable is a thermostat. This device can be adjusted so that contacts of a switch will be closed when the temperature falls below a preset value (the set point). Closure of the contacts turns on the correctional mechanism—the coils of the heater. (See *Figure 12.1.*)

If the room cools below the set point of the thermostat, the thermostat turns the heater on, and the heater warms the room. The rise in room temperature causes the thermostat to turn the heater off. Because the activity of the correctional mechanism (heat production) feeds back to

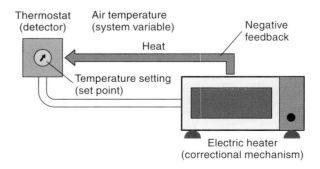

Figure 12.1
An example of a regulatory system.

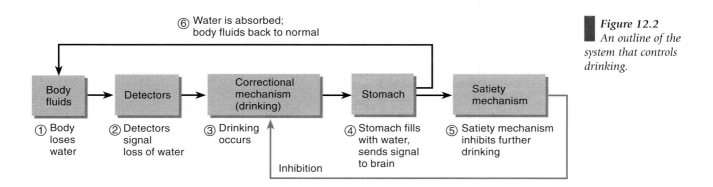

Figure 12.2
An outline of the system that controls drinking.

the thermostat and causes it to turn the heater off, this process is called **negative feedback.** Negative feedback is an essential characteristic of all regulatory systems.

This chapter and Chapter 13 consider regulatory systems that involve ingestive behaviors: drinking and eating. These behaviors are correctional mechanisms that replenish the body's depleted stores of water or nutrients. Because of the delay between ingestion and replenishment of the depleted stores, ingestive behaviors are controlled by **satiety mechanisms** as well as by detectors that monitor the system variables. Satiety mechanisms are required because of the physiology of our digestive system. For example, suppose you spend some time in a hot, dry environment and lose body water. The loss of water causes internal detectors to initiate the correctional mechanism—drinking. You quickly drink a glass or two of water and then stop. What stops your ingestive behavior? The water is still in your digestive system, not yet in the fluid surrounding your cells, where it is needed. Therefore, although drinking was initiated by detectors that measure your body's need for water, *it was stopped by other means.* There must be a satiety mechanism that says, in effect, "Stop—this water, when absorbed by the digestive system into the blood, will eventually replenish the body's need." Satiety mechanisms monitor the activity of the correctional mechanism (in this case, drinking), not the system variables themselves. When a sufficient amount of drinking occurs, the satiety mechanisms stop further drinking *in anticipation* of the replenishment that will occur later. (See *Figure 12.2.*)

SOME FACTS ABOUT FLUID BALANCE

Before you can understand the physiological control of drinking, you must know something about the fluid compartments of the body and their relations with one another. And to understand these facts, you must also know something about the functions of the kidney.

● The Fluid Compartments of the Body

The body contains four major fluid compartments: one compartment of intracellular fluid and three compartments of extracellular fluid. Approximately two-thirds of the body's water is contained in the **intracellular fluid**—the fluid portion of the cytoplasm of cells. The rest is **extracellular fluid,** which includes the **intravascular fluid** (the blood plasma), the cerebrospinal fluid, and

homeostasis *(home ee oh **stay** sis)*   The process by which the body's substances and characteristics (such as temperature and glucose level) are maintained at their optimal level.

ingestive behavior *(in **jess** tiv)*   Eating or drinking.

system variable   A variable that is controlled by a regulatory mechanism; for example, temperature in a heating system.

set point   The optimal value of the system variable in a regulatory mechanism.

detector   In a regulatory process, a mechanism that signals when the system variable deviates from its set point.

correctional mechanism   In a regulatory process, the mechanism that is capable of changing the value of the system variable.

negative feedback   A process whereby the effect produced by an action serves to diminish or terminate that action; a characteristic of regulatory systems.

satiety mechanism   A brain mechanism that causes cessation of hunger or thirst, produced by adequate and available supplies of nutrients or water.

intracellular fluid   The fluid contained within cells.

extracellular fluid   All body fluids outside cells: interstitial fluid, blood plasma, and cerebrospinal fluid.

intravascular fluid   The fluid found within the blood vessels.

the **interstitial fluid.** *Interstitial* means "standing between"; indeed, the interstitial fluid stands between our cells—it is the "seawater" that bathes them. For the purposes of this chapter I will ignore the cerebrospinal fluid and concentrate on the other three compartments. (See *Figure 12.3.*)

The fluid compartments are separated by semipermeable barriers, which permit the passage of some substances but not others. The walls of the capillaries separate the intravascular fluid (blood plasma) from the interstitial fluid, and the cell membranes separate the interstitial fluid from the intracellular fluid. The volume of the intracellular fluid is controlled by the concentration of solutes in the interstitial fluid. (*Solutes* are the solid substances dissolved in a solution.) Normally, the interstitial fluid is **isotonic** (from the Greek *isos*, "same," and *tonos*, "tension") with the intracellular fluid. That is, the concentration of solutes in the cells and in the interstitial fluid that bathes them is balanced, so that water does not tend to move into or out of the cells. If the interstitial fluid loses water (becomes more concentrated, or **hypertonic**), water will then diffuse out of the cells. On the other hand, if the interstitial fluid gains water (becomes more dilute, or **hypotonic**), water will diffuse into the cells. (See *Figure 12.4.*) Either condition endangers cells; a loss of water deprives them of the ability to perform many chemical reactions, and a gain of water can cause their membrane to rupture. Thus, the concentration of the interstitial fluid must be regulated closely.

The volume of the blood plasma must be closely regulated because of the mechanics of the operation of the

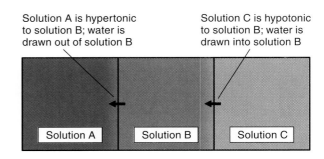

Solution A is hypertonic to solution B; water is drawn out of solution B

Solution C is hypotonic to solution B; water is drawn into solution B

Solution A   Solution B   Solution C

Figure 12.4
Effects of differences in solute concentration on the movement of water molecules.

heart. If the blood volume becomes too high, blood pressure can reach dangerously high levels. If the blood volume becomes too low, the heart can no longer pump the blood effectively; and if the volume is not restored, heart failure will result. This condition is called **hypovolemia,** literally "low volume of the blood" (*-emia* comes from the Greek *haima*, "blood"). The vascular system of the body can make some adjustments for loss of blood volume by contracting the muscles present in the walls of the smaller veins and arteries, thereby presenting a smaller space for the blood to fill, but this correctional mechanism has definite limits.

The volume of the interstitial fluid need not be regulated closely. The most important reason is that when the volumes of the intracellular and intravascular fluid compartments are kept within normal limits, the volume of the interstitial fluid will automatically stay within its normal limits. Only in certain pathological conditions—such as capillary damage, heart failure, or a very low level of protein in the blood—will the volume of the interstitial fluid become abnormally high. (There is no way for it to become abnormally low without the other fluid compart-

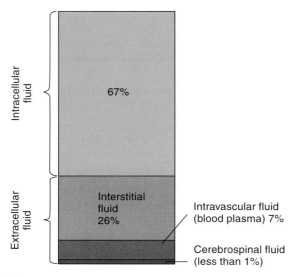

67%

Interstitial fluid 26%

Intravascular fluid (blood plasma) 7%

Cerebrospinal fluid (less than 1%)

Intracellular fluid

Extracellular fluid

Figure 12.3
The relative size of the body's fluid compartments.

interstitial fluid   The fluid that bathes the cells, filling the space between the cells of the body (the "interstices").

isotonic   Equal in osmotic pressure to the contents of a cell. A cell placed in an isotonic solution neither gains nor loses water.

hypertonic   The characteristic of a solution that contains enough solute that it will draw water out of a cell placed in it, through the process of osmosis.

hypotonic   The characteristic of a solution that contains so little solute that a cell placed in it will absorb water, through the process of osmosis.

hypovolemia *(hy poh voh lee mee a)*   Reduction in the volume of the intravascular fluid.

ments becoming abnormal.) However, although the *volume* of the interstitial fluid is normally not a matter of concern, its *tonicity* (solute concentration) must be closely regulated, because this variable is what determines whether water diffuses into cells or out of them.

As we will see, the intracellular fluid and the blood volume are monitored by two different sets of receptors. A single set of receptors would not work, because it is possible for one of these fluid compartments to be changed without affecting the other. For example, a loss of blood (obviously) reduces the volume of the intravascular fluid, but it has no effect on the volume of the intracellular fluid. On the other hand, a salty meal will increase the solute concentration of the interstitial fluid and draw water out of the cells. These cells will remain dehydrated even after the kidney has gotten rid of the excess sodium (and a quantity of water to flush it away) and has restored the blood volume back to normal. Thus, the body needs two sets of receptors: one for measuring blood volume and another for measuring cell volume.

Just as there are two sets of receptors, there are two sets of correctional mechanisms. One set involves the ingestion and excretion of water, and the other involves the ingestion and excretion of sodium. Obviously, the excretions of water and sodium are accomplished by the kidney, and the ingestion of these substances is accomplished by the behavior of eating salt (or foods containing salt) and drinking water.

Most of the time, we drink more water than our body needs, and the excess is excreted by the kidneys. Similarly, we ingest more sodium than we need, and the kidneys get rid of this surplus, too. Thus, if we want to understand the means of regulating our water and sodium balance, we must understand what the kidneys do and how they are controlled.

● The Kidneys

A human kidney consists of approximately a million functional units called **nephrons.** Each nephron extracts fluid from the blood and carries it, through collecting ducts, to the **ureter.** The ureter, in turn, connects the kidney to the urinary bladder, where urine is stored until it can be released at a convenient time. (This behavior, which physiologists politely refer to as *micturition,* from the Latin word for "urinate," has absolutely nothing to do with regulation. Once the urine is in the bladder, it is out of the body as far as the three fluid compartments are concerned.) (See *Figure 12.5.*)

The kidneys control the amount of water and sodium that the body excretes, which controls both the volume

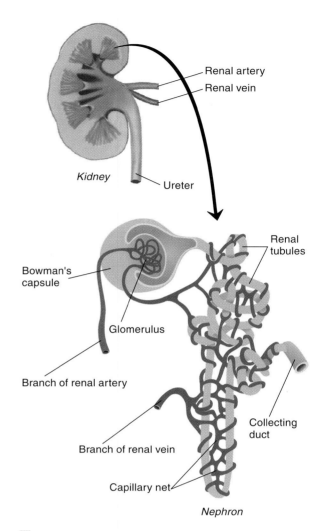

Figure 12.5
Anatomy of the kidney and an individual nephron.

and the concentration (tonicity) of the extracellular fluid. If we drink a large amount of water and must get rid of the excess, our kidneys pass a large quantity of urine to the bladder. Similarly, if we eat salty food and must get rid of the excess sodium, our kidneys extract the sodium from our blood and pass it on to the bladder. However, if the organism has lost water through evaporation, the kidneys

nephron   A functional unit of the kidney; extracts fluid from the blood and carries the fluid, through collecting ducts, to the ureter.

ureter (*your* eh ter)   One of two tubes that carries urine from the kidneys to the bladder.

conserve water, producing the minimum quantity of urine. In addition, if the body becomes deficient in sodium, the kidneys will begin to excrete a very small amount of this mineral in the urine.

The amounts of sodium and water that the kidneys excrete are controlled by two hormones: aldosterone and vasopressin. Sodium excretion is controlled by **aldosterone,** a steroid hormone secreted by the adrenal cortex. High levels of aldosterone cause the kidneys to retain sodium in the body—to pass very little sodium on to the bladder. Thus, if the body contains too much sodium, the level of aldosterone secretion falls and sodium is excreted in the urine. If too little salt is present, a high aldosterone level causes it to be conserved. (See *Figure 12.6.*)

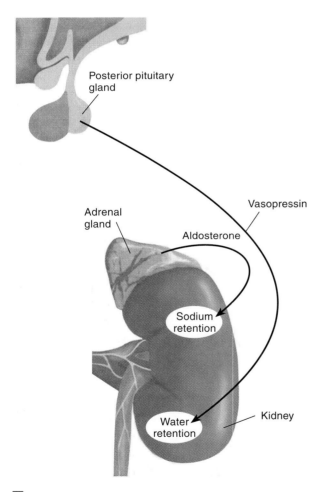

Figure 12.6
Hormonal control of the kidney. Aldosterone, secreted by the cortex of the adrenal gland, causes sodium retention by the kidney. Vasopressin, secreted by the posterior pituitary gland, causes water retention.

The excretion of water by the kidneys is controlled by a hormone called **vasopressin.** The name of this hormone does not describe its primary function with respect to control of fluid homeostasis, which is to instruct the kidneys how much water to retain. High levels of vasopressin will cause the kidneys to retain as much water as possible, only excreting as much as is needed to rid the body of the waste products of metabolism. The term *vasopressin* refers to its ability under certain circumstances to cause blood vessels to contract (*vas* means "vessel" in Latin). A more descriptive term is *antidiuretic hormone.* (*Diuresis* comes from the Greek *dia,* "through," and *ouron,* "urine"; thus, *anti*diuretic hormone reduces the production of urine.) Nevertheless, vasopressin is the name that most physiologists use.

Vasopressin is a peptide hormone secreted by the posterior pituitary gland. It is produced in the cell bodies of neurons located in two nuclei of the hypothalamus: the **supraoptic nucleus** and the **paraventricular nucleus.** The hormone is stored in vesicles and travels through axons to the posterior pituitary gland, where it collects in the terminal buttons. When the neurons in the supraoptic and paraventricular nuclei become active, their terminal buttons release vasopressin, which enters the blood supply. Thus, the production, storage, and release of vasopressin is exactly like that of any peptide transmitter substance, except that it affects receptors in another part of the body, not in a membrane across a synaptic cleft.

If we drink more water than our body needs, the posterior pituitary gland reduces its secretion of vasopressin, and the kidneys excrete the excess water. If we become dehydrated, the posterior pituitary gland increases vasopressin secretion, and the kidneys excrete a minimum amount of water. (See *Figure 12.6.*)

The importance of vasopressin in the retention of water is demonstrated by the disease produced by the lack of this

aldosterone (*al **dahs** ter own*)   A hormone of the adrenal cortex that causes the retention of sodium by the kidneys.

vasopressin (*vay zo **press** in*)   A hormone secreted by the posterior pituitary gland that causes the kidneys to excrete a more concentrated urine, thus retaining water in the body.

supraoptic nucleus (*sue pra **op** tik*)   A hypothalamic nucleus that contains cell bodies of neurons that produce vasopressin and transport it through their axons to the posterior pituitary gland.

paraventricular nucleus   A hypothalamic nucleus that contains cell bodies of neurons that produce vasopressin and oxytocin and transport them through their axons to the posterior pituitary gland.

hormone: **diabetes insipidus**. The term literally means "a tasteless passing through," because the urine of a person with diabetes insipidus is so dilute that it has little taste. People with untreated diabetes insipidus will excrete approximately 25 liters (over 6.5 gallons) of water each day, which means that they will have to stay close to a bathroom and a source of water. The treatment is, of course, vasopressin—administered in the form of a nasal spray, which is absorbed into the bloodstream.

So far, I have been talking only about system variables and correctional mechanisms. What about detectors? It turns out that the detectors that control the secretion of aldosterone and vasopressin (and thus control the excretion of sodium and water by the kidneys) are among those that control the intake of water and salt. Thus, I will discuss them in the next section.

Interim Summary

A regulatory system contains four features: a system variable (the variable that is regulated), a set point (the optimal value of the system variable), a detector to measure the system variable, and a correctional mechanism to change it. Physiological regulatory systems, such as control of body fluids and nutrients, require a satiety mechanism to anticipate the effects of the correctional mechanism, because the changes brought about by eating and drinking occur only after a considerable period of time.

The body contains three major fluid compartments: the intracellular fluid, the interstitial fluid, and the intravascular fluid. Sodium and water can pass easily between the intravascular fluid and the interstitial fluid, but sodium cannot penetrate the cell membrane. The solute concentration of the interstitial fluid must be closely regulated. If it becomes hypertonic, cells lose water; if it becomes hypotonic, they gain water. The volume of the intravascular fluid (blood plasma) must also be kept within bounds.

The kidneys regulate the excretion of water and sodium; in the process of excreting water, waste products are carried away by the urine. Aldosterone, a steroid hormone released by the adrenal cortex, causes sodium retention. Vasopressin, a peptide hormone produced by the supraoptic and paraventricular nuclei and released by the posterior pituitary gland, causes water retention.

DRINKING AND SALT APPETITE

As we just saw, for our bodies to function properly, the volume of two fluid compartments—intracellular and intra-

vascular—must be regulated. Most of the time we ingest more water and sodium than we need, and the kidneys excrete the excess. However, if the level of water or sodium falls too low, a correctional mechanism—drinking of water or ingestion of sodium—is activated. Everyone is familiar with the sensation of thirst, which occurs when we need to ingest water. However, a salt appetite is much rarer, because it is difficult for people *not* to get enough sodium in their diet, even if they do not put extra salt on their food. Nevertheless, the mechanisms to increase sodium intake exist, even though they are seldom called on in members of our species.

Because loss of water from either the intracellular or intravascular fluid compartments stimulates drinking, researchers have adopted the terms *osmometric thirst* and *volumetric thirst* to describe them (Fitzsimons, 1972; Epstein, 1973). The term *volumetric* is clear—it refers to the metering (measuring) of the volume of the blood plasma. The term *osmometric* requires more explanation, which I will provide in the next section. The term *thirst* means different things in different circumstances. Its original definition referred to a sensation that people say they have when they are dehydrated. Here I use it in a descriptive sense. Because we do not know how laboratory animals feel, *thirst* simply means a tendency to seek water and to ingest it.

● Osmometric Thirst

Osmometric thirst occurs when the tonicity (solute concentration) of the interstitial fluid increases. This increase draws water out of the cells, so they shrink in volume. The term *osmometric* refers to the fact that the detectors are actually responding to (metering) differences in the concentration of their own intracellular fluid and that of the interstitial fluid that surrounds them. *Osmosis* is the movement of water through a semipermeable membrane, from a region of low solute concentration to one of high solute concentration.

Verney (1947) first hypothesized that the brain contained neurons that respond to changes in the solute concentration of the interstitial fluid. He called these neurons

diabetes insipidus *(in **sipp** i duss)* The loss of excessive amounts of water through the kidneys; caused by lack of secretion of vasopressin.

osmometric thirst Thirst produced by an increase in the osmotic pressure of the interstitial fluid relative to the intracellular fluid, thus producing cellular dehydration.

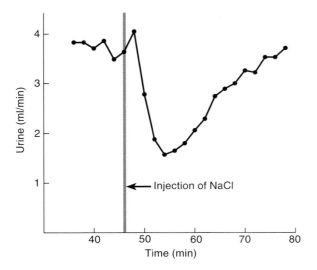

Figure 12.7
Effects of an injection of hypertonic saline solution into a dog's carotid artery. The solution removed water from cells in the brain and caused the posterior pituitary gland to secrete vasopressin. The hormone caused water to be retained by the kidneys, reducing the flow of urine.
(From Verney, E.G. *Proceedings of the Royal Society of London, B.*, 1947, *135*, 25–106.)

osmoreceptors. He found that an infusion of hypertonic sodium chloride into a dog's carotid artery would stimulate the secretion of vasopressin and thus cause the kidneys to decrease their excretion of water. Figure 12.7 shows how the injection caused an almost immediate decrease in the production of urine. (See *Figure 12.7.*)

Verney hypothesized that osmoreceptors were neurons whose firing rate was affected by their level of hydration. That is, if the interstitial fluid surrounding them became more concentrated, they would lose water through osmosis. The shrinkage would cause them to alter their firing rate, which would send signals to the neurons that control the rate of vasopressin secretion. (See *Figure 12.8.*) As we

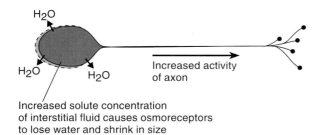

Increased solute concentration
of interstitial fluid causes osmoreceptors
to lose water and shrink in size

Figure 12.8
A hypothetical explanation of the workings of an osmoreceptor.

will see, more recent studies have confirmed that osmoreceptors do exist and that they can initiate drinking as well as vasopressin secretion.

Before I discuss the evidence concerning the existence and location of osmoreceptors, I want to say more about the conditions that cause osmometric thirst. Our bodies lose water continuously, primarily through evaporation. Each breath exposes the moist inner surfaces of the respiratory system to the air; thus, each breath causes the loss of a small amount of water. In addition, our skin is not completely waterproof; some water finds its way through the layers of the skin and evaporates from the surface. The moisture lost through evaporation is, of course, pure distilled water. (Sweating loses water, too; but because it loses salt along with the water, it produces a sodium need as well.) When we lose water through evaporation, we lose it from all fluid compartments, intracellular, interstitial, and intravascular. Thus, normal dehydration produces both *osmometric* and *volumetric* thirst.

Figure 12.9 illustrates how the loss of water through evaporation depletes both the intracellular and intravascular fluid compartments. For the sake of simplicity, only a few cells are shown, and the volume of the interstitial fluid is greatly exaggerated. Water is lost directly from the interstitial fluid, which becomes slightly more concentrated than either the intracellular or the intravascular fluid. Thus, water is drawn from both the cells and the blood plasma. When enough water is lost from the cells, the secretion of vasopressin will be stimulated, and urine production will diminish. And eventually, the loss of water from the cells and the blood plasma will be great enough that both osmometric and volumetric thirst will be produced. (See *Figure 12.9.*)

If evaporation were the only way that the distribution of water in the three fluid compartments could be disturbed, then we would not need two kinds of detectors to stimulate thirst; a set of osmoreceptors would be sufficient. However, it is possible to incur a loss of intracellular fluid without losing intravascular fluid. (And as we shall see in the next section, the opposite condition is possible, too.)

The most common way to incur a loss of just intracellular fluid is to eat a salty meal. The salt is absorbed from the digestive system into the blood plasma; hence the blood plasma becomes hypertonic. This condition draws water from the interstitial fluid, which makes this compartment become hypertonic, too, and thus causes water to

osmoreceptor A neuron that detects changes in the solute concentration of the interstitial fluid that surrounds it.

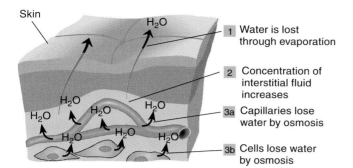

1 Water is lost through evaporation

2 Concentration of interstitial fluid increases

3a Capillaries lose water by osmosis

3b Cells lose water by osmosis

Figure 12.9
The loss of water through evaporation.

diffuse out of the cells. As the blood plasma increases in volume, the kidneys begin excreting large amounts of both sodium and water. Eventually, the excess sodium is excreted, along with the water that was taken from the interstitial and intracellular fluid. The net result is a loss of water from the cells. *At no time did the volume of the blood plasma fall;* in fact, it was temporarily higher than normal, which is what triggered the excretion of sodium and water by the kidneys.

As we saw earlier, Verney hypothesized that the loss of water by the cells of the body is the stimulus that produces osmometric thirst. Fitzsimons (1972) obtained evidence that supports Verney's hypothesis by demonstrating that the stimulus for osmometric thirst is not simply a change in the solute concentration of the interstitial fluid but the *effect* that these changes have on the water content of the cells. Fitzsimons removed the kidneys of a group of rats to prevent the kidneys from eliminating water or any of the substances he administered to the animals. Next, he injected the animals with hypertonic solutions of substances that can enter cells (such as glucose and urea) or substances that cannot (such as sodium chloride, sodium sulfate, and sucrose—table sugar). All of the substances that he injected would increase the solute concentration of the interstitial fluid. However, only the substances that *cannot* enter cells would draw water from them. For example, an increased concentration of urea in the interstitial fluid has no effect on cells, because the urea freely diffuses into them, and a concentration gradient is not set up.

In fact, the only animals that drank excessively were those that received substances that could not enter the cells and hence drew water from them; thus, cell dehydration is the stimulus for osmometric thirst. In addition, Fitzsimons found that an injection of urea produced a small amount of drinking. The reason for this effect is that urea passes slowly through the blood–brain barrier. Therefore, an in-jection of urea produces a slight, and temporary, increase in the solute concentration of the blood plasma relative to that of the brain, which causes water to diffuse from the brain into the intravascular fluid. Thus, urea produces a temporary dehydration of the brain. The fact that *brain* dehydration produces drinking suggests that the osmoreceptors that produce thirst are located there. (I will return to this finding later.)

Fitzsimons was not the first to obtain evidence that osmoreceptors that produce thirst were located in the brain. Andersson (1953) found that injections of hypertonic saline solution into the rostrolateral hypothalamus produced drinking but not vasopressin release, whereas injections into caudal hypothalamic regions stimulated vasopressin secretion but not thirst. Thus, different sets of receptors appear to mediate drinking and vasopressin release in response to hypertonicity.

The location of the osmoreceptors that control drinking is not yet settled. An extensive mapping study by Peck and Blass (1975) suggested that the osmoreceptors that stimulate thirst in rats are located in the medial portion of the lateral preoptic area. They found that injections of hypertonic sucrose in this region produced drinking. In addition, Blass and Epstein (1971) found that when a rat was made thirsty by giving it a subcutaneous injection of hypertonic saline, drinking could be inhibited by injecting water into the preoptic area. Presumably, the water turned off the signal for thirst at the detectors. (This manipulation was similar to what would happen if we heated the thermostat in a cold room; we would "fool" the thermostat and cause it to turn off the furnace.)

A more recent study failed to confirm these findings. Andrews et al. (1992) used special minipumps to continuously infuse small quantities of hypertonic and hypotonic solutions bilaterally into the preoptic area. They found that the infusions had variable effects on the rats' drinking: Sometimes infusions of hypertonic saline would *reduce* the animals' drinking and infusions of water would *increase* it. Also, several studies (for example, Coburn and Stricker, 1978; Saad et al., 1996) have found that rats still show osmometric thirst after the lateral preoptic area has been destroyed.

So where are the osmoreceptors? Most researchers now believe that they are located more medially, in the region that borders the anteroventral tip of the third ventricle (the *AV3V*). Buggy et al. (1979) found that injections of hypertonic saline directly into the AV3V produced drinking, whereas injections into the lateral preoptic area did not. In some species (such as the dog) the osmoreceptors may be located in a specialized *circumventricular organ* located just rostral to the AV3V. The brain contains several circumventricular organs—specialized regions with rich blood supplies located along the ventricular system. You are already familiar with two of these: the area postrema and the pineal gland (discussed in Chapters 2 and 9). You will learn about two more in this chapter: the OVLT and the SFO.

The **OVLT** (if you really want to know, that stands for the **organum vasculosum of the lamina terminalis**), like the other circumventricular organs, is located on the *blood* side of the blood–brain barrier. That means that substances dissolved in the blood pass easily into the interstitial fluid within this organ. (The importance of this fact will become apparent soon.) Thrasher and Keil (1987) found that after the OVLT was destroyed, dogs no longer drank when given injections of hypertonic saline—nor did they show increases in vasopressin secretion. However, studies by Johnson and his colleagues (see Johnson and Edwards, 1990) found that in rats, lesions of the OVLT alone did not abolish osmometric drinking; the lesions had to include additional brain tissue around the AV3V. Thus, although some of the osmoreceptors in the rat brain may be located in the OVLT, others are located in the medial preoptic area.

As we saw earlier, when rats are given an injection of urea, they show a small amount of osmometric thirst, presumably because the urea temporarily dehydrates the brain. But urea does not dehydrate any of the tissue *outside* the blood–brain barrier, which includes the OVLT. Thus, Johnson and Edwards must be right—some of the osmoreceptors must be located *inside* the blood–brain barrier.

● Volumetric Thirst

Volumetric thirst occurs when the volume of the blood plasma—the intravascular volume—decreases. As we saw earlier, when we lose water through evaporation, we lose it from all three fluid compartments, intracellular, interstitial, and intravascular. Thus, evaporation produces both volumetric thirst and osmometric thirst. If evaporation were the only way that our body lost fluids, we would not need to have drinking mechanisms controlled by detectors that monitor blood volume. However, it is possible to incur a loss in intravascular volume without affecting the interstitial compartment.

Loss of blood is the most obvious cause of pure volumetric thirst. From the earliest recorded history, reports of battles note that the wounded survivors called out for water. (More prosaically, vomiting or diarrhea rids the body of isotonic fluid and hence lowers the volume of the intravascular fluid.) Thus, volumetric thirst provides a second line of defense against a loss of water should the osmometric system be damaged, and it provides the means

for the loss of isotonic fluid to instigate drinking. In addition, because hypovolemia involves a loss of sodium as well as water (that is, the sodium that was contained in the isotonic fluid that was lost), hypovolemia leads to a salt appetite.

The easiest way to produce hypovolemia in experimental animals such as rats would be to remove some of their blood. A less drastic procedure is to inject a **colloid** into the animal's abdominal cavity or under the loose skin of the back (Fitzsimons, 1961). Colloids are gluelike substances (from the Greek *kolla*, "glue") made of large molecules that cannot cross cell membranes. Thus, they stay in the abdominal cavity or in the space under the skin. Because the solution of molecules is hypertonic, it draws extracellular fluid out of tissue. The fluid that leaves the blood plasma is isotonic; as water molecules move down the concentration gradient produced by the colloid, they draw sodium chloride with them. Initially, the water comes from the interstitial fluid, but as the volume of this fluid space decreases the pressure of the blood causes fluid from the blood plasma to begin to fill the vacant space. Fluid does *not* leave the cells, because the solute concentration of the interstitial fluid remains stable. Within an hour the posterior pituitary gland begins to release vasopressin, and urine volume drops. At about the same time the animal begins to drink, and it continues to do so until most of the volume of fluid stolen from the extracellular fluid has been replaced.

Let us look at a specific experiment that produced volumetric thirst. Fitzsimons (1961) injected a colloid called *polyethylene glycol* into the abdominal cavity of rats and later drained the fluid that accumulated, ridding the body of the colloid along with the water and sodium chloride it had drawn from the extracellular fluid. The loss of fluid caused a considerable thirst; the animals drank water copiously. The next day, he presented the rats with both water and a hypertonic 1.8 percent saline solution, which rats normally refuse to drink. This time, the rats avidly consumed the saline solution. Why did they do so? Because the procedure had removed both water and salt, they needed both substances to restore their fluid compart-

---

OVLT (organum vasculosum of the lamina terminalis)
A circumventricular organ located anterior to the anteroventral portion of the third ventricle; served by fenestrated capillaries and thus lacks a blood–brain barrier.

volumetric thirst   Thirst produced by hypovolemia.

colloid (*kalh* oyd)   A soluble, gluelike substance made of large molecules that cannot penetrate cell membranes.

ments to normal. Thus, the loss of salt induced a strong **salt appetite.**

What detectors are responsible for initiating volumetric thirst and a salt appetite? In fact, there are at least two sets of receptors: one in the kidneys, and one in the heart and large blood vessels.

The Renin-Angiotensin System

The kidneys contain cells that are able to detect decreases in flow of blood to the kidneys. The primary cause of a reduced flow of blood is a loss of blood volume; thus, these cells detect the presence of hypovolemia. When the flow of blood to the kidneys decreases, these cells secrete an enzyme called **renin.** Renin enters the blood, where it catalyzes the conversion of a protein called **angiotensinogen** into a hormone called **angiotensin.** (In fact, there are two forms of angiotensin. Angiotensinogen becomes angiotensin I, which is quickly converted by an enzyme to angiotensin II. The active form is angiotensin II, which I shall abbreviate as *AII.*)

Angiotensin II has several physiological effects: It stimulates the adrenal cortex to secrete aldosterone, it stimulates the posterior pituitary gland to secrete vasopressin, and it increases blood pressure by causing the muscles in the small arteries to contract. (Recall that the presence of aldosterone inhibits the kidneys from excreting sodium, and the presence of vasopressin inhibits them from excreting water.) In addition, AII has two behavioral effects: It initiates drinking, and (through its stimulation of aldosterone secretion, and perhaps directly, as well), it produces a salt appetite. Therefore, a reduction in the flow of blood to the kidneys causes water and sodium to be retained by the body, helps compensate for their loss by reducing the size of the blood vessels, and encourages the animal to find and ingest both water and salt. (See *Figure 12.10.*)

Baroreceptors

The second set of receptors for volumetric thirst lies within the heart. Physiologists had long known that the atria of the heart (the parts that receive blood from the veins) contain sensory neurons that detect stretch. The atria are filled passively with blood being returned from the body by the veins. The more blood that is present, the fuller the atria become just before each contraction of the heart. Thus, when the volume of the blood plasma falls, the stretch receptors within the atria will detect the change. These receptors occupy the best possible location to detect the presence of hypovolemia.

Fitzsimons and Moore-Gillon (1980) showed that information from the atrial baroreceptors can stimulate thirst. They operated on dogs, placing a small balloon in

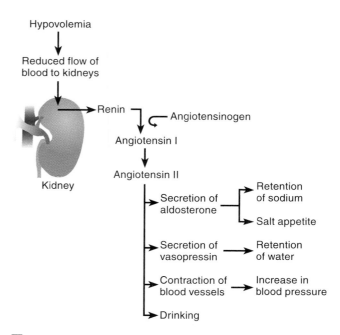

Figure 12.10
Detection of hypovolemia by the kidney and the renin-angiotensin system.

the inferior vena cava, the vein that brings blood from most of the body (excluding the head and arms) to the heart. When the balloon was inflated, it reduced the flow of blood to the heart and thus lowered the amount of blood that entered the right atrium. Within 30 minutes the dogs began to drink. The effect occurred even when the investigators administered **saralasin,** a drug that blocks angiotensin receptors; thus, it was not produced by secretion of renin by the kidneys. In another experiment Moore-Gillon and Fitzsimons (1982) implanted a small balloon in the junction between one of the large veins from the lungs and the left atrium of the heart. (They removed the part of the lung served by the vein so that inflating the balloon had no effect on the flow of blood into the heart.) In-

---

salt appetite   A craving for sodium chloride.

renin (*ree* nin)   A hormone secreted by the kidneys that causes the conversion of angiotensinogen in the blood into angiotensin.

angiotensinogen (*ann gee oh ten **sin** oh jen*)   A protein in the blood that can be converted by renin to angiotensin.

angiotensin (*ann gee oh **ten** sin*)   A peptide hormone that constricts blood vessels, causes the secretion of aldosterone, and produces thirst and a salt appetite.

saralasin (*sair a **lay** sin*)   A drug that blocks angiotensin receptors.

flation of the balloon directly stimulated stretch receptors in the left atrium—and reduced the amount of water that the animals drank. Finally, Quillen, Keil, and Reid (1990) found that when the nerves connecting the atrial baroreceptors with the brain were cut, the animals drank much less water when the blood flow to their heart was temporarily reduced.

● Food-Related Drinking

Although research on the physiology of drinking has generally focused on drinking caused by need (that is, by hypovolemia or by cellular dehydration), most drinking occurs *in anticipation* of actual need, during meals (de Castro, 1988; Kraly, 1990). For two reasons, eating produces a need for water. First, eating causes water to be diverted from the rest of the body into the stomach and small intestine, where it is needed for the digestive process (Lepkovsky et al., 1957). Second, once food is absorbed (especially salty food or food rich in amino acids), it increases the solute concentration of the blood plasma and thus induces an osmometric thirst. But animals do not wait until they need the water; they drink it with their meal. Fitzsimons and Le Magnen (1969) found that when rats were switched from a high-carbohydrate diet to a high-protein diet, they increased their water intake. At first, they drank most of the water *after* the meal, when the osmotic demands were being felt. However, within a few days the animals began drinking more water with the meals. They apparently learned the association of the new diet with subsequent thirst and drank in anticipation of that thirst.

According to research by Kraly and his colleagues, food-related drinking appears to involve angiotensin. The movement of water into the digestive system during and after a meal causes hypovolemia (Nose et al., 1986). As we just saw, hypovolemia stimulates the kidneys to secrete renin, which results in increased blood levels of angiotensin II. Rowland (1995) found that when rats ate a normal-size meal, the level of renin in their blood doubled. The angiotensin production triggered by this secretion of renin appears to be at least partly responsible for food-related drinking; Kraly and Corneilson (1990) found that when they administered a drug that blocks the production of AII, rats drank less water with their meals.

Food-related drinking also involves histamine, a compound that serves as a transmitter substance in the nervous system. If, prior to eating a meal, a rat is given drugs that block histamine receptors, the animal will drink much less water with that meal (Kraly and Specht, 1984). Kraly and Corneilson (1990) suggest that histamine may play a role in the secretion of angiotensin that accompanies a meal.

They note that subcutaneous injections of histamine cause rats to drink (Kraly and June, 1982) and that the secretion of renin is controlled by histamine receptors on cells in the kidney (Radke et al., 1986). They found that a drug that blocks the synthesis of angiotensin II abolishes the stimulating effect of histamine on drinking. Kraly, Kim, and Tribuzio (1995) found that the drinking caused by eating a small meal could be eliminated by cutting the nerves to the kidney. Presumably, the presence of food in the stomach activates brain mechanisms that trigger the release of histamine in the kidneys. The kidneys secrete renin, which catalyzes the synthesis of angiotensin, which activates drinking mechanisms in the brain.

● Salt Appetite

You will recall from Chapter 7 that the tongue contains four types of taste receptors, which provide the sensations of sweetness, bitterness, sourness, and saltiness. As we have seen, the reason our tongue has receptors that specifically detect the presence of sodium chloride is that this mineral plays a vital role in maintaining our fluid balance. A fall in the body's level of sodium makes it impossible to maintain the intravascular fluid at its proper level.

The primary stimulus for a salt appetite is the presence of aldosterone, whose secretion is under the control of angiotensin. When an animal becomes hypovolemic, the blood flow to the kidneys decreases, renin is secreted, angiotensin is produced, and the adrenal glands begin secreting aldosterone. The aldosterone acts directly on the brain, as we will see in the next section.

Besides aldosterone, there are two other possible signals for salt appetite: angiotensin and the atrial baroreceptors. So far, researchers have not been able to prove unequivocally that AII stimulates a salt appetite directly, by binding with angiotensin receptors in one of the circumventricular organs, just as it stimulates drinking. The primary reason for this uncertainty is that angiotensin has several different effects, including increased blood pressure, which inhibit salt intake unless the animal is already sodium deficient (Sakai, Chow, and Epstein, 1990; Thunhorst and Fitts, 1994; Weisinger et al., 1996).

What about the third possible signal of hypovolemia, detected by the atrial baroreceptors? Thornton, Sanchez, and Nicolaïdis (1994) found that penthonium, a drug that lowers blood pressure, induced a salt appetite in rats. This salt appetite was not blocked by an injection of **losartan,** a

losartan (*low **sar** tan*) A drug that blocks angiotensin receptors.

drug that blocks angiotensin receptors, directly into the third ventricle. Thus, the salt appetite persisted even when the contribution of angiotensin was eliminated. Presumably, this appetite was stimulated by the atrial baroreceptors.

Interim Summary

Osmometric thirst occurs when the interstitial fluid becomes hypertonic, drawing water out of cells. This event, which can be caused by evaporation of water from the body or by ingestion of a salty meal, is detected by osmoreceptors in the region of the anteroventral third ventricle (the AV3V). The receptors are located both in OVLT, a circumventricular organ, and in adjacent regions of the brain. Activation of the osmoreceptors increases vasopressin secretion and stimulates drinking.

Volumetric thirst occurs along with osmometric thirst when the body loses fluid through evaporation. Pure volumetric thirst is caused by the loss of blood, vomiting, and diarrhea, or through experimental manipulations such as the injection of a colloid. One stimulus for volumetric thirst is provided by a fall in blood flow to the kidneys, which triggers the secretion of renin. Renin converts plasma angiotensinogen to angiotensin I, which becomes AII. AII then stimulates the secretion of aldosterone (which conserves salt, needed to maintain the plasma volume), increases blood pressure, and causes drinking and a salt appetite. Volumetric drinking can also be stimulated by a set of baroreceptors in the atria of the heart that sends messages to the brain.

Much drinking occurs with meals, in anticipation of the need for water produced by the digestive process and by the addition of solutes to the body's fluid compartments. The hypovolemia that accompanies a meal induces drinking through the release of AII, which may be triggered by the release of histamine by the terminals of axons that innervate the kidneys.

Hypovolemia induces a salt appetite, because animals must ingest sodium as well as water in order to regain their normal plasma volume. The primary stimulus for a salt appetite is reduction of blood flow to the kidneys, which results in the secretion of renin. The resulting angiotensin II triggers the cortex of the adrenal glands to secrete aldosterone, a steroid hormone that acts on the brain and stimulates the ingestion of salt. Angiotensin may also directly stimulate a salt appetite by binding with receptors in the circumventricular organs, but the evidence is not yet conclusive. Some evidence also suggests that the atrial baroreceptors may also produce a salt appetite.

BRAIN MECHANISMS OF THIRST AND SALT APPETITE

As we saw, the osmoreceptors responsible for thirst appear to be located in the region that borders the anteroventral tip of the third ventricle (the AV3V). The regions that play an important role in volumetric drinking and salt appetite also appear to be located in the forebrain. However, the picture of the neural circuitry that has been obtained so far is still fuzzy; at best, we can say that some structures have been implicated in the physiological and behavioral control of fluid balance, but the exact roles these structures play is still uncertain.

● Neural Control of Thirst

The Circumventricular System

As we saw earlier in this chapter, the brain region around the anteroventral third ventricle (including the OVLT) contains the osmoreceptors that stimulate thirst and vasopressin secretion. The entire region around the anterior third ventricle—dorsal as well as ventral—seems to be the part of the brain where osmometric and volumetric signals are integrated and drinking, salt appetite, and vasopressin secretion are controlled.

As you have already learned, the osmoreceptors that initiate drinking and vasopressin secretion are located in the OVLT and (in some species, at least) in the brain tissue around the AV3V. This region also appears to receive information from the baroreceptors located in the atria of the heart. Sensory information received from the internal organs (and from the taste buds, as well) is received by a nucleus in the medulla: the **nucleus of the solitary tract.** The nucleus of the solitary tract sends efferent axons to many parts of the brain, including the region around the AV3V (see Johnson and Edwards, 1990).

Thornton, de Beaurepaire, and Nicolaïdis (1984) recorded the activity of single neurons in the region just in front of the AV3V. They found that the neurons were sensitive to changes in blood pressure that occurred spontaneously or were induced by temporary removal of small amounts of blood from a vein. Possibly, these neurons receive information via the nucleus of the solitary tract from stretch receptors located in the atria of the heart, and they

nucleus of the solitary tract   A nucleus of the medulla that receives information from visceral organs and from the gustatory system.

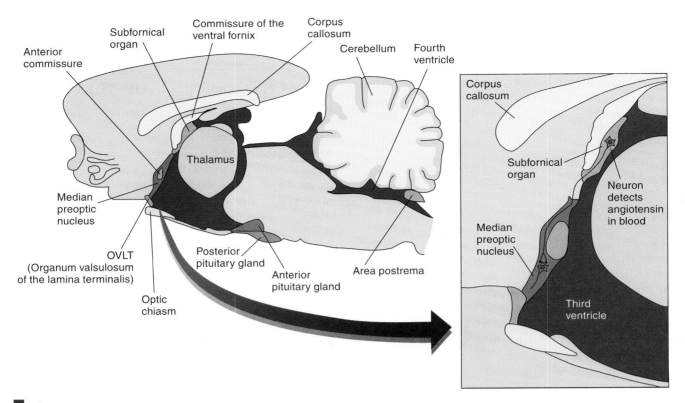

Figure 12.11
A sagittal section of the rat brain, showing the location of the circumventricular organs. Inset: A hypothetical circuit connecting the subfornical organ with the median preoptic nucleus.

may be part of a neural circuit responsible for volumetric thirst.

The region of the AV3V seems to play a critical role in fluid regulation in humans, as well. For example, McIver et al. (1991) reported that brain damage that includes this region can cause both diabetes insipidus and *adipsia*—lack of drinking. The patients report no sensation of thirst, even after they are given an injection of hypertonic saline. To survive, they must deliberately drink water at regular intervals each day, even though they feel no need to do so.

Another thirst signal, angiotensin, is a peptide composed of eight amino acids. As far as we know, all peptides that directly affect behavior do so by interacting with specific receptors in neural membranes. Therefore, researchers hypothesized that the brain contains neurons that initiate thirst when they detect the presence of angiotensin. Because angiotensin does not cross the blood–brain barrier, a likely site of action would be one of the circumventricular organs, which lack this barrier. Angiotensin could leave the capillaries in one of these organs, enter the interstitial fluid, and stimulate angiotensin receptors.

Although all of the circumventricular organs contain angiotensin receptors, one of them, the **subfornical organ (SFO)**, appears to be the site at which blood angiotensin acts to produce thirst. This structure gets its name from its location, just below the commissure of the ventral fornix. (See *Figure 12.11*.)

Evidence clearly indicates that the subfornical organ is the site of action of angiotensin. Simpson, Epstein, and Camardo (1978) found that very low doses of angiotensin injected directly into the SFO caused drinking and that destruction of the SFO or injection of saralasin, which blocks angiotensin receptors, abolished the drinking response to injections of angiotensin into the blood. Phillips and Felix (1976) found that microiontophoretic injections of angiotensin into the SFO increased the firing rate of single neurons located there. Kadekaro et al. (1989) found that an intravenous injection of AII caused the metabolic activity of the SFO to increase. This increase occurred even when the axons connecting the SFO with the rest of the brain had been cut, which indicates that the hormone acted directly on the SFO. Finally, Smith, Beninger, and Ferguson (1995) found that electrical stimulation of the subfornical organ induced drinking.

subfornical organ (SFO)   A small organ located in the confluence of the lateral ventricles, attached to the underside of the fornix; contains neurons that detect the presence of angiotensin in the blood and excite neural circuits that initiate drinking.

The subfornical organ, whose primary role is to detect the presence of a hormone in the blood, has few neural inputs but sends axons to several parts of the brain. As Miselis, Weiss, and Shapiro (1987) noted, the outputs of the SFO fall into three categories: endocrine, autonomic, and behavioral. As we saw earlier, angiotensin has five major effects: It stimulates aldosterone secretion, it stimulates vasopressin secretion, it increases blood pressure, it causes drinking, and it causes a sodium appetite.

The first of these effects, aldosterone secretion, occurs directly in the cortex of the adrenal gland. The other effects involve the brain. The *endocrine outputs* of the SFO include axons that project to the neurons in the supraoptic and paraventricular nuclei that are responsible for production and secretion of the posterior pituitary hormones, vasopressin and oxytocin. (The reason for the connection with the vasopressin neurons is obvious, but the function of the connection with the oxytocin neurons is still not understood.) The *autonomic outputs* include axons that project to the cells of the paraventricular nucleus and other parts of the hypothalamus, which in turn send axons to brain stem nuclei that control the sympathetic and parasympathetic nervous system. This system is responsible for the effects of angiotensin on blood pressure. The most important *behavioral outputs,* which control drinking, are probably those to a region of the basal forebrain just in front of the ventral portion of the anterior third ventricle.

Let us consider the behavioral outputs of the SFO—the efferent connections that are responsible for its effects on drinking. Lind, Thunhorst, and Johnson (1984) found that lesions of the ventral stalk of the SFO, which destroy its efferent connections, abolished the drinking response that is produced by injecting AII into a vein. Thus, the thirst produced by the renin-angiotensin system is mediated by efferent axons of the SFO that pass through the ventral stalk. However, these lesions had only a small effect on the drinking response that is produced by injecting AII into the third ventricle. These results indicate that angiotensin receptors located elsewhere in the brain are capable of stimulating drinking.

Many of these receptors are located in the **median preoptic nucleus** (not to be confused with the *medial* preoptic nucleus), which is shaped like half a doughnut, wrapped around the front of the anterior commissure, a fiber bundle that connects the amygdala and anterior temporal lobe. (See inset, *Figure 12.11.*) The median preoptic nucleus is

on the *brain* side of the blood–brain barrier; thus, its angiotensin receptors are never exposed to angiotensin present in the blood. Only when angiotensin is injected directly into the third ventricle can it reach them.

If angiotensin cannot get from the blood to the median preoptic nucleus, what is the point of having angiotensin receptors there? Lind and Johnson (1982) proposed the following answer: When neurons in the SFO are stimulated by the presence of angiotensin in the blood, a message is sent down their axons to the neurons in the median preoptic nucleus. The terminal buttons of these axons release angiotensin *as a transmitter substance.* Thus, the angiotensin receptors in the median preoptic nucleus are not there to detect the presence of a hormone; instead, they are postsynaptic receptors for a peptide transmitter substance that just happens to be a hormone, too.

There is considerable evidence to support Lind and Johnson's hypothesis. For example, after the median preoptic nucleus has been destroyed, injections of AII into the blood or the third ventricle have no effect on drinking (Johnson and Cunningham, 1987). In addition, Tanaka and Nomura (1993) found that an injection of saralasin directly into the median preoptic nucleus blocks drinking caused by the injection of AII directly into the SFO. (See inset, *Figure 12.11.*)

Thrasher and his colleagues (see Thrasher, 1989) suggest that the region in front of the third ventricle acts as an integrating system for most or all of the stimuli for osmometric and volumetric thirst. As we have already seen, the OVLT contains osmoreceptors and the SFO contains receptors that detect angiotensin present in the blood. Both circumventricular organs communicate with the median preoptic nucleus. In addition, the median preoptic nucleus receives information from the atrial baroreceptors via the nucleus of the solitary tract, located in the medulla. This nucleus integrates the information and through its efferent connections with other parts of the brain, controls both drinking and the secretion of vasopressin. (The roles of the lateral hypothalamus and the zona incerta are described later.) (See *Figure 12.12.*)

As we have already seen, lesions of the SFO disrupt angiotensin-induced drinking and lesions of the OVLT (and the surrounding region of the AV3V) disrupt osmometric drinking. Neurotoxic lesions of the median preoptic nucleus (which spare axons passing through the region) almost totally abolish drinking in response to injections of angiotensin or hypertonic saline (Cunningham et al., 1992). (See *Figure 12.13.*) However, the lesions did not completely abolish drinking; thus, we cannot conclude that *all* signals for drinking are routed through the median preoptic nucleus. In fact, it is unlikely that the evolution-

median preoptic nucleus   A small nucleus situated around the decussation of the anterior commissure; plays a role in thirst stimulated by angiotensin.

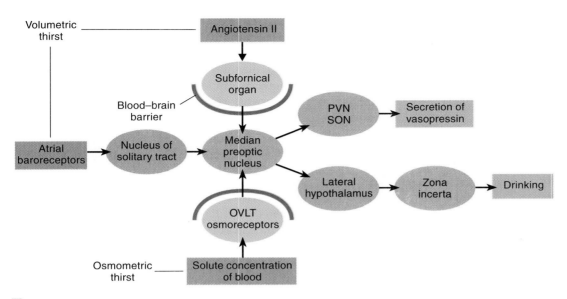

Figure 12.12
*Neural circuitry concerned with the control of drinking. Not all connections are shown, and some
connections may be indirect. PVN = paraventricular nucleus; SON = supraoptic nucleus.*
(Adapted from Thrasher, T.N. *Acta Physiologica Scandanivica*, 1989, *136*, 141–150.)

ary process would have entrusted such an important function to a single brain structure. Undoubtedly, there is some
redundancy in the control of water intake.

The Lateral Hypothalamus and Zona Incerta

The control of osmometric and volumetric drinking, initiated by the median preoptic area, involves other brain
structures. Many years ago, investigators discovered that lesions of the lateral hypothalamus abolished drinking behavior. (As we will see in Chapter 13, the lesions also
abolished eating and other behaviors.) Eventually, through
careful nursing, the animals began drinking again, but
only during meals (Teitelbaum and Epstein, 1962). In
other words, lesions of the hypothalamus disrupt osmometric and volumetric thirst, but do not disrupt meal-
associated drinking.

Another structure involved in osmometric drinking is
the **zona incerta.** This region is an oblong extension of the
midbrain reticular formation; its posterior end is in the
midbrain, between the substantia nigra and the ventral
tegmental area, and its anterior end is in the diencephalon,
just lateral and dorsal to the paraventricular nuclei of the
hypothalamus. It receives input from several forebrain regions, including the lateral hypothalamus.

Huang and Mogenson (1972) found that electrical
stimulation of the rostral zona incerta elicited drinking in
rats, indicating that this region is connected to motor

mechanisms responsible for drinking behavior. Walsh and
Grossman (1978) found that lesions of the zona incerta
caused a profound deficit in osmometric drinking; injections of hypertonic sodium chloride did not induce drinking. In addition, neither did rats with these lesions drink
when they were given an injection of angiotensin, but they
did drink if they were given an injection of polyethylene
glycol. Thus, damage to the zona incerta also disrupts the
hormonal stimulus for volumetric thirst but not the neural
one that originates in the atrial baroreceptors.

Mok and Mogenson (1986) recorded from single neurons in the zona incerta. They found that injections of hypertonic saline, hypertonic sucrose, or distilled water into
the basal forebrain anterior to the third ventricle changed
the firing rate of these neurons. In addition, Czech and
Stein (1992) found that injections of angiotensin into a
cerebral ventricle increased the metabolic activity of several regions, including the lateral hypothalamus and the
zona incerta. Then, when the animal began drinking, the
metabolic activity of these regions returned to normal
levels.

The zona incerta sends axons to many brain structures
involved in movement, including the basal ganglia, the

zona incerta *(in **sir** ta)*   An oblong extension of the
midbrain reticular formation, extending from the midbrain to the medial diencephalon.

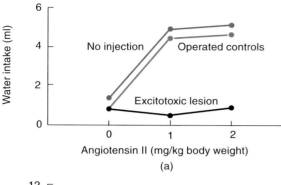

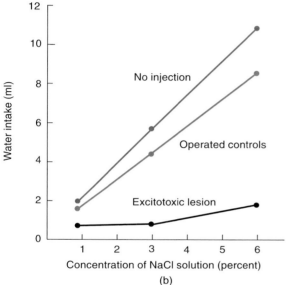

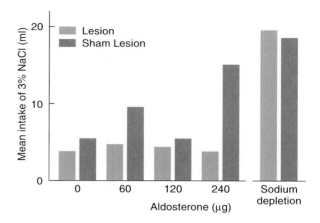

Figure 12.14
Effects of lesions of the medial amygdala on salt intake of rats produced by aldosterone or sodium depletion.
(Adapted from Schulkin, J., Marini, J., and Epstein, A.N. *Behavioral Neuroscience*, 1989, *103*, 178–185.)

Figure 12.13
The effects of lesions of the median preoptic nucleus on drinking produced by (a) injections of angiotensin II and (b) a hypertonic saline solution.
(Adapted from Cunningham, T.J., Beltz, T., Johnson, R.F., and Johnson, A.K. *Brain Research*, 1992, *580*, 325–330.)

brain stem reticular formation, the red nucleus, the periaqueductal gray matter, and the ventral horn of the spinal cord (Ricardo, 1981). Thus, the zona incerta appears to be in an excellent position to influence drinking behavior.

● Neural Control of Salt Appetite

We already saw that a sodium deficiency causes hypovolemia, which stimulates the secretion of renin. The increased blood level of angiotensin that results stimulates the adrenal glands to secrete aldosterone, which produces a salt appetite. In addition, angiotensin may produce a salt appetite directly, by acting on angiotensin receptors in the brain.

First let's consider the role of aldosterone. This hormone appears to exert its behavioral effects by stimulating receptors in the medial nucleus of the amygdala. First, the medial nucleus contains aldosterone receptors (Coirini et al., 1985). In addition, Schulkin, Marini, and Epstein (1989) found that lesions of the medial region of the amygdala specifically abolished the effects of aldosterone on salt intake. However, when the investigators induced a sodium deficiency (by feeding the animals a sodium-free diet and giving them an injection of **furosemide,** a drug that causes the kidneys to excrete sodium), the rats ingested a normal amount of a sodium chloride solution. Thus, aldosterone cannot be the sole stimulus for salt appetite. (See *Figure 12.14.*)

As we saw earlier, some evidence suggests that AII stimulates a salt appetite directly. If so, where does it act? The obvious candidates are the SFO and the OVLT. In fact, damage to either of these two structures decreases sodium intake in rats (Weisinger et al., 1990; Fitts, Tjepkes, and Bright, 1990). Thus, angiotensin receptors in *both* of the anterior circumventricular organs may be involved in salt appetite.

As we saw in the previous subsection, the zona incerta plays a critical role in osmometric drinking and drinking stimulated by angiotensin. It also appears to play a role in the development of salt appetite. Grossman and Grossman (1978) found that when a hypertonic sodium chloride so-

furosemide *(few **row** se myde)* A diuretic; a drug that increases the production of urine.

lution is presented to sodium-depleted rats with lesions of the zona incerta, the animals will consume much less salt than a normal animal will. Conversely, electrical stimulation of parts of the zona incerta will induce salt intake (Gentil, Mogenson, and Stevenson, 1971). Thus, the stimulation of aldosterone receptors in the medial amygdala must be communicated to the neurons in the zona incerta.

Interim Summary

Volumetric thirst stimulated by AII involves one of the anterior circumventricular organs: the subfornical organ. Volumetric thirst stimulated by the atrial stretch receptor system reaches the AV3V region via a relay in the nucleus of the solitary tract. Neurons in the SFO, the AV3V region, and the OVLT (which, you will remember, contains osmoreceptors) all send axons to the median preoptic nucleus.

Neurons in the median preoptic nucleus stimulate the secretion of vasopressin through their connections with the supraoptic and paraventricular nuclei. They stimulate drinking through their connections with the lateral hypothalamus and the zona incerta. The zona incerta sends axons to many parts of the brain involved in motor control.

The medial amygdala appears to be involved in salt appetite. Aldosterone exerts its effect on receptors located there. Angiotensin may also stimulate a salt appetite directly, by acting on receptors in the SFO and the OVLT. The zona incerta is involved in sodium appetite as well as in drinking; lesions there decrease salt intake, whereas stimulation increases it.

MECHANISMS OF SATIETY

As I explained in the first part of this chapter, an anticipatory mechanism, which we call satiety, is needed to stop drinking even before the system variables (cellular dehydration or hypovolemia) have been restored. In this section I will consider satiety produced by drinking and satiety caused by ingestion of sodium chloride.

● Drinking

Normally, when a thirsty animal is given the opportunity to drink, it will rapidly drink enough water to restore its loss and then stop. In most cases satiety occurs before substantial amounts of water are absorbed from the digestive system. For example, a dog consumes the water it needs within 2 to 3 minutes (Adolph, 1939). However, replenishment of the water previously lost from the blood plasma does not begin for 10 to 12 minutes and is not completed until 40 to 45 minutes (Ramsay, Rolls, and Wood, 1977). Perhaps receptors in the mouth and throat are responsible for satiety.

Receptors in the mouth and throat *do* influence the amount of water an organism drinks, but their effects are secondary to those of receptors located farther along the digestive system. Receptors in the digestive system send a signal to the brain that water has been received and is therefore making progress along the way to absorption. Miller, Sampliner, and Woodrow (1957) allowed thirsty rats to drink 14 ml of water or administered it directly into the stomach through a tube that had been placed there previously. At various times after the preload the rats were permitted to drink. As Figure 12.15 shows, rats that received the 14-ml preload by mouth drank less than those that received it directly into the stomach. In other words, water placed directly into the stomach is less satiating than water that gets there after being tasted and swallowed. Thus, receptors in the mouth and throat play a role in satiety. (See *Figure 12.15.*)

It is clear, however, that satiety produced by receptors in the mouth and throat does not last long. Many studies,

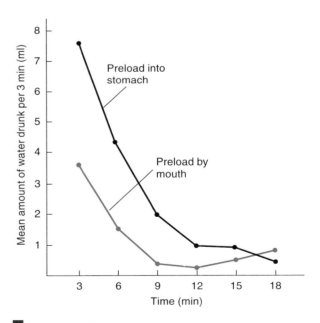

Figure 12.15
Effects of receiving 14 ml of water by mouth or through a tube inserted into the stomach on subsequent drinking of thirsty rats.
(From Miller, N.E., Sampliner, R.I., and Woodrow, P. *Journal of Comparative and Physiological Psychology,* 1957, *50,* 1–5. Copyright 1957 by the American Psychological Association. Reprinted with permission of the author.)

dating from Bernard (1856), have shown that when water that an animal drinks is not allowed to reach the stomach, an animal may pause for a while the first time it drinks but will soon resume drinking and will continue to do so until it is exhausted. These experiments used a surgical procedure called an **esophageal fistula.** (A *fistula* is an abnormal or artificial opening between one hollow organ and another or between a hollow organ and the outside of the body.) An esophageal fistula causes water that is swallowed to fall to the ground. (After the animal's behavior has been tested, the experimenter puts water directly into its stomach.)

Hall (1973) and Hall and Blass (1977) obtained evidence that receptors in the stomach are less important for satiety than those of the duodenum or liver. They prepared a noose out of fine fishing line, passed it around the **pylorus,** the junction of the small intestine with the stomach, and threaded the line through a plastic tube. They brought the end of the tube through the rat's skin and fastened it to the top of the rat's head. The experimenters could tighten and loosen the noose without disturbing the rats. (See *Figure 12.16.*) When the experimenters tightened the noose, the pylorus closed, and contents of the stomach could not enter the intestine. When water could not leave the stomach, thirsty rats drank *more* water than when the noose was open. These results suggest that signals from the small intestine or liver are important in satiety; the noose prevented water from reaching them, thus preventing these signals from being sent.

Before I say more about these potential signals, I should describe two important parts of the body: the small intestine and the liver. The first part of the small intestine,

which receives food and water from the stomach, is called the **duodenum.** The original Greek name for this part of the gut was *dodekadaktulon,* or "twelve fingers long." In fact, the duodenum is twelve finger *widths* long. The walls of the duodenum contain receptors, some of which may communicate with the brain through the nerves that serve the intestine. The liver is the first organ to receive substances from the digestive system. It receives them through the *hepatic portal system,* a special vascular system. (The adjective *hepatic* refers to the liver.) Water and nutrients enter the blood supply through capillaries located in the small intestine. These capillaries collect into larger and larger veins and finally into the **hepatic portal vein,** which travels to the liver and branches into capillaries again. (See *Figure 12.17.*)

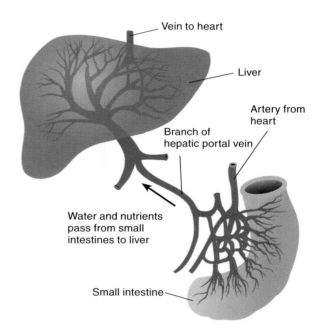

Figure 12.17
The hepatic portal blood supply. The liver receives water, minerals, and nutrients from the digestive system through this system.

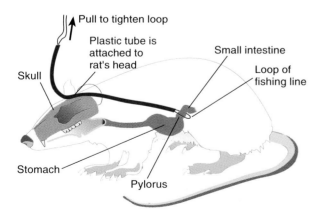

Figure 12.16
The procedure used by Hall and Blass (1977) to prevent water from leaving the stomach.

esophageal fistula *(ee soff a jee ul fiss tew la)*   A diversion of the esophagus so that when an animal eats or drinks, the substance does not reach the stomach.

pylorus *(pie lorr us)*   The ring of smooth muscle at the junction of the stomach and duodenum that controls the release of the stomach contents.

duodenum *(doo oh dee num)*   The portion of the small intestine immediately adjacent to the stomach.

hepatic portal vein   The vein that receives blood from the digestive system and passes it to the liver.

At present, I know of no evidence that indicates that receptors in the duodenum are involved in satiety, although they well may be. However, there is good evidence that the liver plays such a role. Kozlowski and Drzewiecki (1973) obtained evidence supporting this hypothesis. They infused small quantities of water into the hepatic portal vein, which conveys blood from the intestine to the liver. Thus, this vein carries substances absorbed from the intestines—including water. The infusions inhibited osmometric drinking initiated by injections of hypertonic saline. (Control infusions of the same amount of water in the jugular vein had no effect.) More recently, Kobashi and Adachi (1992) found that infusions of water into the hepatic portal vein suppressed drinking in rats that had been made thirsty by 24 hours of water deprivation. Infusions of isotonic or hypertonic saline did not increase drinking; thus, the osmoreceptors in the liver are responsible for satiation of thirst, but not for the induction of thirst. This effect did not occur when the branch of the vagus nerve that connects the liver to the brain was severed (Kobashi and Adachi, 1993). Presumably, the satiety signals are carried to the brain by means of this nerve.

● Salt Appetite

Satiety associated with salt intake has received less attention than satiety associated with drinking, but some general conclusions can be made. First, although an animal identifies the presence of sodium in the diet by tasting it, receptors in the mouth do not appear to play a role in satiety; a sodium-deficient rat will continue to drink a concentrated salt solution if a gastric fistula allows it to escape from the stomach (Mook, 1969). In addition, stomach or duodenal receptors do not appear to be important; an injection of a salt solution directly into the stomach of a sodium-deficient rat does not have an immediate effect on salt appetite, although it will inhibit sodium intake after a delay of several hours (Wolf, Schulkin, and Simson, 1984).

Tordoff, Schulkin, and Friedman (1987) obtained evidence that suggests that sodium receptors in the liver contribute to the satiation of a sodium appetite. The investigators placed catheters into rats' hepatic portal vein and jugular vein. Thus, they were able to make injections into the veins while the rats were moving around freely. They induced a sodium deficiency in order to provoke a sodium appetite. They found that an injection of a hypertonic sodium chloride solution into the hepatic portal vein, which directly enters the liver, reduced the amount of salt solution that an animal would drink. Thus, the experiment provides evidence that the liver detects the presence of

sodium in the blood it receives from the digestive system and sends a satiety signal to the brain.

Another satiety signal for salt appetite comes from a hormone secreted in what might seem to be an unlikely place: the atria of the heart. As we saw earlier, the atria of the heart provide a perfect location to detect a fall in blood volume. Similarly, they provide a perfect location to detect a *rise* in blood volume.

De Bold and his colleagues discovered that a hormone, **atrial natriuretic peptide (ANP),** is secreted by the atria of the heart (De Bold et al., 1981; De Bold, 1985). The term *natriuretic* (not the easiest word to pronounce) comes from the fact that the hormone promotes the excretion of sodium (in Latin, *natrium*) by the kidneys. ANP appears to be an emergency backup system that helps prevent disastrously high volumes of blood plasma. The hormone is secreted when the atria are stretched more than usual by the presence of too much fluid in the blood plasma. Because plasma volume is largely controlled by the sodium concentration, eliminating sodium is obviously a useful response. But ANP does more than produce sodium excretion; it also increases the excretion of water, inhibits the secretion of renin, vasopressin, and aldosterone, and inhibits both drinking and sodium appetite. (See Tarjan, Denton, and Weisinger, 1988, for a review.) ANP receptors are found in the adrenal medulla, the pituitary gland, and the brain; presumably, these sites are responsible for the effects of the hormone on the endocrine system and on behavior (Quirion, 1989).

Some of the inhibitory effect of ANP on drinking appears to be exerted in the subfornical organ, which contains ANP receptors (Quirion et al., 1984). Nermo-Lindquist et al. (1990) found that injection of ANP blocked the excitatory effect of angiotensin on the metabolic activity of the SFO. The injection also decreased the rats' drinking. Ehrlich and Fitts (1990) found that injection of ANP directly into the SFO also blocked angiotensin-induced drinking.

Interim Summary

Although receptors in the mouth and throat play a role in anticipatory satiety produced by drinking, the most important detectors appear to be in the duodenum or liver;

atrial natriuretic peptide (ANP) *(nay tree ur **ett** ik)*   A peptide secreted by the atria of the heart when blood volume is higher than normal; increases water and sodium excretion, inhibits renin, vasopressin, and aldosterone secretion, and inhibits sodium appetite.

when the pylorus is held shut, an animal drinks more than when it is open. Water infused into the hepatic portal vein will inhibit osmometric drinking, and water-deprived rats will drink more water if the hepatic branch of the vagus nerve is cut. Thus, osmoreceptors in the liver appear to play a role in satiety for drinking.

Although receptors on the tongue detect the presence of salt for a sodium-depleted animal, their stimulation does not produce satiety; that occurs only when the salt solution is permitted to accumulate in the stomach. Here, too, osmoreceptors in the liver play a role; an infusion of hyper-tonic sodium chloride into the hepatic portal vein reduces the intake of a sodium chloride solution by a sodium-depleted rat.

The atria of the heart secrete a peptide hormone, atrial natriuretic peptide, that is secreted in response to significant increases in blood volume. ANP stimulates sodium excretion by the kidneys and inhibits the secretion of renin, vasopressin, and aldosterone, and inhibits sodium appetite and drinking. At least some of the inhibitory effects of ANP are exerted in the SFO.

SUGGESTED READINGS

De Caro, G., Epstein, A.N., and Massi, M. *The Physiology of Thirst and Sodium Appetite.* New York: Plenum, 1986.

Gross, P. *Circumventricular Organs and Body Fluids. Vol. III.* Boca Raton, FL: CRC Press, 1987.

Johnson, A.K., and Edwards, G.L. The neuroendocrinology of thirst: Afferent signaling and mechanisms of central integration. *Current Topics in Neuroendocrinology,* 1990, *10,* 149–190.

Stricker, E.M. *Handbook of Behavioral Neurobiology. Vol. 10. Neurobiology of Food and Fluid Intake.* New York: Plenum Press, 1990.

CHAPTER 13

Ingestive Behavior: Eating

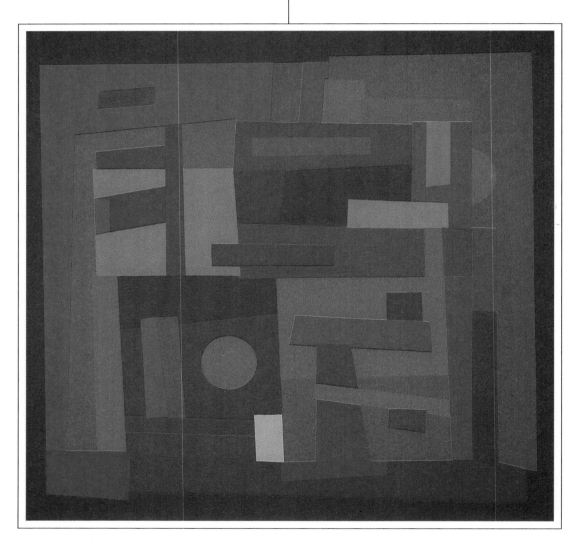

Number 30, 1938, by Ad Reindardt.

Clearly, eating is one of the most important things we do—and it can also be one of the most pleasurable. Much of what an animal learns to do is motivated by the constant struggle to obtain food; thus, the need to ingest undoubtedly shaped the evolutionary development of our own species. After having read Chapter 12, in which you saw that the signals that cause thirst are well understood, you may be surprised to learn that researchers are only now discovering what the system variables for hunger are. Control of ingestive behavior is even more complicated than the control of drinking and sodium intake. We can achieve water balance by the intake of two ingredients: water and sodium chloride. When we eat, we must obtain adequate amounts of carbohydrates, fats, amino acids, vitamins, and minerals other than sodium. Thus, our food-ingestive behaviors are more complex, as are the physiological mechanisms that control them.

This chapter describes research on the control of eating: metabolism, regulation of body weight, the environmental and physiological factors that begin and stop a meal, and the neural mechanisms that monitor the nutritional state of our bodies and control our ingestive behavior. It also describes the most serious eating disorders, obesity and anorexia nervosa. Despite all the effort that has gone into understanding the physiology of ingestive behavior, these disorders are still difficult to treat. Our best hope of finding effective treatments is to achieve a better understanding of the physiology of metabolism and ingestive behavior.

SOME FACTS ABOUT METABOLISM

As you saw in Chapter 12, you must know something about the fluid compartments of the body and the functions of the kidney in order to understand the physiology of drinking. Thus, you will not be surprised that this chapter begins with a discussion of metabolism. Your first inclination may be to skip over this section; but if you do so, you will find that you will not understand experiments that are described later. For example, the system variables that cause an animal to seek food and eat it are obviously related to the animal's metabolism. This section will discuss only as much about this subject as you will need to understand these experiments.

● Absorption, Fasting, and the Two Nutrient Reservoirs

When we eat, we incorporate into our own bodies molecules that were once part of other living organisms, plant and animal. We ingest these molecules for two reasons: to construct and maintain our own organs and to obtain energy for muscular movements and for keeping our bodies warm. In other words, we need both building blocks and fuel. Although food used for building blocks is essential, I will discuss only the food used for fuel, because most of the molecules we eat get "burned" to provide energy for movement and heating.

To stay alive, our cells must be supplied with fuel and oxygen. Obviously, fuel comes from the digestive tract, and its presence there is a result of eating. But the digestive tract is sometimes empty; in fact, most of us wake up in the morning in that condition. So there has to be a reservoir that stores nutrients to keep the cells of the body nourished when the gut is empty. Indeed, there are two reservoirs—one short-term and the other long-term. The short-term reservoir stores carbohydrates, and the long-term reservoir stores fats.

The short-term reservoir is located in the cells of the liver and the muscles, and it is filled with a complex, insoluble carbohydrate called **glycogen.** I will consider only the most important of these locations—the liver. Cells in the liver convert glucose (a simple, soluble carbohydrate) into glycogen and store the glycogen. They are stimulated to do so by the presence of **insulin,** a peptide hormone produced by the pancreas. Thus, when glucose and insulin are present in the blood, some of the glucose is used as a fuel and some of it is stored as glycogen. Later, when all of the food has been absorbed from the digestive tract, the level of glucose in the blood begins to fall.

The fall in glucose is detected by cells in the brain, which cause an increase in the activity of sympathetic axons that innervate the pancreas. This activity inhibits the secretion of insulin and causes another set of cells of the pancreas to begin secreting a different peptide hormone, **glucagon.** The effect of glucagon is opposite that of insulin: It stimulates the conversion of glycogen into glucose. (Unfortunately, the terms *glucose, glycogen,* and *glucagon* are similar enough that it is easy to confuse them. Even worse, you will soon encounter another one, *glycerol.*) (See *Figure 13.1.*) Thus, the liver soaks up excess glucose and stores it as glycogen when plenty of glucose is available, and it releases glucose from its reservoir when the digestive tract becomes empty and the level of glucose in the blood begins to fall.

The carbohydrate reservoir in the liver is primarily reserved for the central nervous system. When you wake in the morning, your brain is being fed by your liver, which is in the process of converting glycogen to glucose and releasing it into the blood. The glucose reaches the CNS,

where it is absorbed and metabolized by the neurons and the glia. This process can continue for a few hours, until all of the carbohydrate reservoir in the liver is used up. (The average liver holds approximately 300 calories of carbohydrate.) Usually, we eat some food before this reservoir gets depleted, which permits us to refill it. But if we do not eat, the CNS has to start living on the products of the long-term reservoir.

Our long-term reservoir consists of adipose tissue (fat tissue). This reservoir is filled with fats, or, more precisely, with **triglycerides.** Triglycerides are complex molecules that contain **glycerol** (a soluble carbohydrate, also called *glycerine*) combined with three **fatty acids** (stearic acid, oleic acid, and palmitic acid). Adipose tissue is found beneath the skin and in various locations in the abdominal cavity. It consists of cells capable of absorbing nutrients from the blood, converting them to triglycerides, and storing them. These cells can expand enormously in size; in fact, the primary physical difference between an obese person and a person of normal weight is the size of their fat cells, which is determined by the amount of triglycerides that these cells contain.

The long-term fat reservoir is obviously what keeps us alive when we are fasting. As we begin to use the contents of our short-term carbohydrate reservoir, fat cells start converting triglycerides into fuels that the cells can use and releasing these fuels into the bloodstream. As we just saw, when we wake in the morning with an empty digestive tract, our brain (in fact, all of the central nervous system) is living on glucose released by the liver. But what about the other cells of the body? They are living on fatty acids,

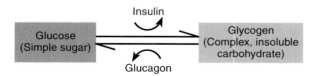

Figure 13.1
Effects of insulin and glucagon on glucose and glycogen.

glycogen (*gly* ko jen)   A polysaccharide often referred to as *animal starch;* stored in liver and muscle; constitutes the short-term store of nutrients.

insulin   A pancreatic hormone that facilitates entry of glucose and amino acids into the cell, conversion of glucose into glycogen, and transport of fats into adipose tissue.

glucagon (*gloo* ka gahn)   A pancreatic hormone that promotes the conversion of liver glycogen into glucose.

triglyceride (*try* **gliss** er ide)   The form of fat storage in adipose cells; consists of a molecule of glycerol joined with three fatty acids.

glycerol (*gliss* er all)   A substance (also called glycerine) derived from the breakdown of triglycerides, along with fatty acids; can be converted by the liver into glucose.

fatty acid   A substance derived from the breakdown of triglycerides, along with glycerol; can be metabolized by most cells of the body except for the brain.

sparing the glucose for the brain. As you will recall from Chapter 3, the sympathetic nervous system is primarily involved in the breakdown and utilization of stored nutrients. When the digestive system is empty, there is an increase in the activity of the sympathetic axons that innervate adipose tissue, the pancreas, and the adrenal medulla. All three effects (direct neural stimulation, secretion of glucagon, and secretion of catecholamines) cause triglycerides in the long-term fat reservoir to be broken down into glycerol and fatty acids. The fatty acids can be directly metabolized by cells in all of the body *except the brain*, which needs glucose. That leaves glycerol. The liver takes up glycerol and converts it to glucose. That glucose, too, is available to the brain.

You may be asking *why* the cells of the rest of the body treat the brain so kindly, letting it consume almost all the glucose that the liver releases from its carbohydrate reservoir and constructs from glycerol. The answer is simple: Insulin has several other functions besides causing glucose to be converted to glycogen. One of these functions is the control of the entry of glucose into cells. Glucose easily dissolves in water, but it will not dissolve in fats. Cell membranes are made of lipids (fatlike substances); thus, glucose cannot directly pass through them. To be taken into a cell, glucose must be transported there by *glucose transporters*—protein molecules that are situated in the membrane and are similar to those responsible for the reuptake of transmitter substances. Glucose transporters contain insulin receptors, which control their activity; only when insulin binds with these receptors can glucose be transported into the cell. But the cells of the nervous system are an exception to this rule. Their glucose transporters do not contain insulin receptors; thus, these cells can absorb glucose *even when insulin is not present*.

Figure 13.2 reviews what I have said so far about the metabolism that takes place while the digestive tract is empty, which physiologists refer to as the **fasting phase** of metabolism. A fall in the blood glucose level causes the pancreas to stop secreting insulin and to start secreting glucagon. The absence of insulin means that most of the cells of the body can no longer use glucose; thus, all the glucose present in the blood is reserved for the central nervous system. The presence of glucagon instructs the liver to start drawing on the short-term carbohydrate reservoir—to start converting its glycogen into glucose. The presence of glucagon, along with increased activity of the sympathetic nervous system, also instructs fat cells to start drawing on the long-term fat reservoir—to start breaking down triglycerides into fatty acids and glycerol. Most of the body lives on the fatty acids, and the glycerol, which is converted into glucose by the liver, gets used by the brain. If fasting is prolonged, pro-

teins (especially protein found in muscle) will be broken down to amino acids, which can be metabolized by all of the body except for the central nervous system. (See *Figure 13.2.*)

The phase of metabolism that occurs when food is present in the digestive tract is called the **absorptive phase.** Now that you understand the fasting phase, this one is simple. Suppose that we eat a balanced meal of carbohydrates, proteins, and fats. The carbohydrates are broken down into glucose and the proteins are broken down into amino acids. The fats basically remain as fats. Let us consider each of these three nutrients.

1. As we start absorbing the nutrients, the level of glucose in the blood rises. This rise is detected by cells in the brain, which causes the activity of the sympathetic nervous system to decrease and the activity of the parasympathetic nervous system to increase. This change tells the pancreas to stop secreting glucagon and to begin secreting insulin. The insulin permits all the cells of the body to use glucose as a fuel. Extra glucose is converted into glycogen, which fills the short-term carbohydrate reservoir. If some glucose is left over, fat cells absorb it and convert it to triglycerides.
2. A small proportion of the amino acids received from the digestive tract are used as building blocks to construct proteins and peptides; the rest are converted to fats and stored in adipose tissue.
3. Fats are not used at this time; they are simply stored in adipose tissue. (See *Figure 13.2.*)

● Is Total Body Fat Regulated?

No one questions the fact that body fluids are regulated, but some people have suggested that body weight (or, more accurately, total body fat) might not be. The reason for this suggestion is easy to see: Many people are obese, and some of those who are not say that they have to make a real effort to remain thin. If total body fat is truly regulated, then we might expect that people should get hungry only when they need to eat and should stop eating when

fasting phase   The phase of metabolism during which nutrients are not available from the digestive system; glucose, amino acids, and fatty acids are derived from glycogen, protein, and adipose tissue during this phase.

absorptive phase   The phase of metabolism during which nutrients are absorbed from the digestive system; glucose and amino acids constitute the principal source of energy for cells during this phase, and excess nutrients are stored in adipose tissue in the form of triglycerides.

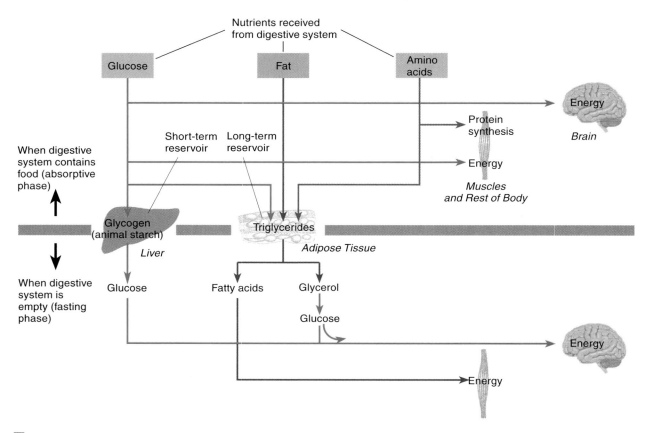

Figure 13.2
Metabolic pathways during the fasting phase and absorptive phase of metabolism.

they have eaten enough. But obviously, we sometimes eat when we are not really hungry, and we continue to eat even when we have had enough.

There are several reasons to explain the apparent failure of the body to regulate weight. First, as we shall see, some of the eating habits imposed on us by our society interfere with regulatory mechanisms that evolved in different types of environments. Second, regulation is not as bad as it may seem. The fact that many people show visible fat in their abdomens or in their hips and thighs does not mean that their body weights are not regulated; it may mean only that the amount of fat that is normal for them is higher than what we find aesthetically pleasing nowadays. Consider the purpose of fat—to provide a reservoir that can be drawn on in time of need. In the past (and in the present, in some parts of the world), the supply of food was (is) unreliable. When certain plants were in season, when the fish were running in the river, or when migratory animals were passing through the region, there was plenty to eat. At other times people ate very little and made up the difference by living off their fat. If they had *not* stored some fat

during the good seasons, they would have died during times when food was harder to find.

As we will see in the section on eating disorders near the end of this chapter, heredity plays an important role in determining a person's body size and shape. Primarily because of genetic differences, some people are just naturally fatter than others. In other words, people's "set points" can vary. The reasons for these differences and their implications for control of total body fat will be discussed later.

Perhaps the best evidence that there are some controls over total body fat comes from studies that indicate that changes in diet cause compensatory changes in behavior or in metabolism. For example, if animals are given a diet with fewer calories, they soon eat more of it; whereas if they are given a richer diet, they begin to eat less. People respond this way too; Foltin et al. (1990) found that when they varied the number of calories in people's lunches (by changing either the carbohydrate or the fat content), the subjects altered the amount of food they ate the rest of the day, keeping the intake of calories relatively constant. In addition, if animals are force-fed through a tube placed in their stomach so that they become fat, they will subsequently reduce their food intake until their weight returns to normal levels (Hoebel and Teitelbaum, 1966; Steffens, 1975).

Interim Summary

Metabolism consists of two phases. During the absorptive phase we receive glucose, amino acids, and fats from the intestines. The blood level of insulin is high, which permits all cells to metabolize glucose. In addition, the liver and the muscles convert glucose to glycogen, which replenishes the short-term reservoir. Excess carbohydrates and amino acids are converted to fats, and fats are placed into the long-term reservoir in the adipose tissue.

During the fasting phase the activity of the parasympathetic nervous system falls and the activity of the sympathetic nervous system increases. In response, the level of insulin falls, and the level of glucagon and the adrenal catecholamines rises. These events cause liver glycogen to be converted to glucose and triglycerides to be broken down into glycerol and fatty acids. In the absence of insulin only the central nervous system can use the glucose available in the blood; the rest of the body lives on fatty acids. Glycerol is converted to glucose by the liver, and the glucose is metabolized by the brain.

Body weight (or, more likely, quantity of adipose tissue) is regulated, although the amount of fat people's bodies contain can vary widely. Both people and laboratory animals will eat less of a rich diet and more of a diet low in calories and they will change their food intake if their metabolic requirements change.

WHAT STARTS A MEAL?

The heading to this section is a very simple question, but the answer is complex. The short answer, I suppose, is that we still are not sure, but that will not stop me from writing more. In fact, many factors start a meal, including the presence of appetizing food, the company of people who are eating, or the words "It's time to eat!" More fundamentally, there must be some sort of signal that tells the brain that the supply of nutrients has gotten low and that it is time to begin looking for, and ingesting, some food. This section considers all of these factors.

Before I begin, I will point out that the physiological signals that cause a meal to begin are different from the ones that cause it to end. As I said in the discussion of regulatory systems at the beginning of Chapter 12, there is a considerable delay between the act of eating (the correctional mechanism) and a change in the system variable. We may start eating because the supply of nutrients has fallen below a certain level, but we certainly do not stop eating because the level of those nutrients has been restored to normal. In fact, we stop eating long before that happens, because digestion takes several hours. Thus, the signals for hunger and satiety are sure to be different.

● Social and Environmental Factors

Most people, if they were asked why they eat, would say that they do so because they get hungry. By that, they probably mean that something happens inside their body that provides a sensation that makes them want to eat. In other words, we tend to think of eating as something provoked by physiological factors. But often we eat because of habit or because of some stimuli present in our environment. These stimuli include a clock indicating that it is time to eat, the sight of a plate of food, the smell of food cooking in the kitchen, or the presence of other people sitting around the table. Many studies have shown that eating can be classically conditioned in both humans and laboratory animals. For example, Weingarten (1983) presented hungry rats with a buzzer and a light (CS^+) followed by food six times a day for eleven days. Another stimulus, a tone (CS^-), was turned on intermittently between meals. During test days following the training, he periodically turned on the CS^+ and the CS^- and observed the animals' eating behavior. The rats began eating within 5 seconds after the CS^+ was presented, even when they were satiated, but did not react to the CS^-. (See *Figure 13.3.*) Birch et al. (1989) observed a similar phenomenon in nursery school children. Thus, it seems reasonable to suppose that stimuli naturally associated with eating can provoke a meal.

One of the most important variables affecting appetite is the meal schedule. We tend to take our meals at fixed times: soon after waking, at midday, and in the evening. This custom makes it difficult for us to adjust the timing of our meals, as other animals can do. What we do instead is adjust the *size* of our meals. If we have eaten recently or if the previous meal was large, we tend to eat a smaller meal (Jiang and Hunt, 1983; de Castro et al., 1986). Other animals tend to be less schedule-bound. For example, when a rat is free to eat whenever it wants, the size of the meal is primarily determined by external factors, such as the taste and texture of the food. However, the *time* of the next meal is related to the size of the one just eaten; that is, if a rat eats a large meal, it waits longer until the next one (Le Magnen and Tallon, 1963, 1966). The difference between our pattern and that of animals such as rats seems to be caused by

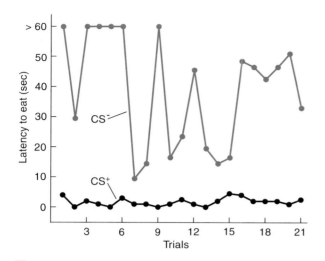

Figure 13.3
Classical conditioning of eating; latency to eat after the presentation of the stimulus previously associated with the presence (CS⁺) or absence (CS⁻) of food.
(Adapted from Weingarten, H.P. *Science*, 1983, *220*, 431–432.)

our habit of eating at fixed times. If people live in isolation, away from cues that indicate the time of day, their meal patterns resemble those of rats: The bigger the meal, the longer the wait until the next one (Bernstein, 1981).

The presence of other people is yet another factor that strongly affects our eating behavior. De Castro and de Castro (1989) asked people to keep diaries that listed all the food they ate during a seven-day period and the number of other people who were present while they were eating. The investigators found that the amount of food eaten was directly related to the number of other people who were present—the more people present, the more the subjects ate. In addition, the correlation that is normally seen between the time since the previous meal and the size of the present meal was observed only when the subjects ate alone; when other people were present, the correlation was abolished. Thus, social factors can overcome the effects of metabolic factors.

● Dietary Selection: Responding to the Consequences

Animals need to obtain a variety of different nutrients: carbohydrates, fats, essential amino acids, minerals, and various chemicals that the body cannot make, which we call vitamins. Some animals can get along well eating only one type of food. For example, the physiology of a koala is perfectly suited to a diet of eucalyptus leaves, and that of a giant panda to bamboo shoots. Predators can count on their

prey to get a balanced diet and, by eating them, obtain all the nutrients, vitamins, and minerals they need. But animals that eat only one type of food will be limited by the distribution of their food; you will not find koalas where there are not eucalyptus trees, nor giant pandas where there are not bamboo forests. Similarly, predators are dependent on their prey; if an epidemic decimates the population of rabbits in a particular region, the number of wolves is also affected.

It is probably not a coincidence that two of the most successful species on earth, humans and rats, are omnivores. (Please excuse the comparison.) Omnivores ("all-devouring creatures") are liberated from dependency on a particular type of food. As always, however, with freedom comes responsibility. The metabolism of omnivores is such that no single food will provide all essential nutrients. Thus, it is advantageous to eat many different kinds of foods. As we shall see, we tend to do that, naturally. But in some situations, when the foods available at a particular time and place lack an essential nutrient, such as a vitamin or mineral, the animal must make special efforts to find a food that supplies what is needed. In addition, omnivores are exposed to foods that may contain toxic substances. All plants produce chemicals designed by the evolutionary process to poison animals (primarily insects) that might eat them. Most of these poisons are harmless to mammals, but some are not. In addition, food that has been infected with various types of bacteria or molds can become toxic. Thus, omnivores must learn to avoid foods that might cause harm.

Let us consider the tendency to obtain a varied diet. Most of us find a meal that consists of moderate quantities of several different foods to be more interesting than a huge platter of only one food. If we eat a single food, we soon become tired of it, a phenomenon that has been labeled **sensory-specific satiety**. Le Magnen (1956) demonstrated this phenomenon elegantly. He fed rats a diet to which he could add a flavoring. He let the rats eat one flavor for 30 minutes. By that time they had pretty much stopped eating. He replaced the dish with a second flavor, and the rats began eating again. He presented a total of four different flavors (of the same basic food, remember) and found that the rats would eat a meal that was two to three times larger than a 2-hour meal consisting of a single course. Rolls et al. (1981) observed the same phenomenon in humans; they found that people would eat a larger meal

sensory-specific satiety Satiety for a specific food that has been ingested recently in the absence of general satiety for all foods.

when they were offered four types of sandwich fillings or four different flavors of yogurt. Obviously, the phenomenon of sensory-specific satiety encourages the consumption of a varied diet.

Of course, it is not enough simply to get a varied diet. Foods differ in their ability to provide needed calories and specific nutrients. Omnivores are able to learn about the consequences of eating different kinds of food. For example, Sclafani and Nissenbaum (1988) showed that rats can learn which flavors provide them with calories. The investigators gave rats flavored water to drink. On some days the water was cherry-flavored; on other days it was grape-flavored. The rats drank the flavored water from a special drinking tube that permitted the experimenters to detect each lick that the animals took. As the animals drank the flavored water, an automatic pump delivered either water or a nutritive starch solution into their stomachs, through tubes that had been previously placed there. For each rat a particular flavor was paired with the injection of the starch solution. After four days of training the rats were permitted to chose between the two flavors. They overwhelmingly chose the flavor that had been paired with the starch infusions; thus, rats are able to learn which flavor is associated with the delivery of a nutritive substance to their stomach. (See *Figure 13.4*.)

As we saw in Chapter 7, most mammals come provided with specialized receptors that detect substances that are possibly poisonous. Our tongue contains receptors that detect alkaloids and acids (the bitterness and sourness detectors), many of which are poisonous. Thus, we tend to reject bitter or sour tastes. (As we shall see, this tendency is controlled by mechanisms in the brain stem; thus, it is undoubtedly a very primitive reaction.) But taste tells us about the nature of food only when it is in the mouth, so taste provides us with a limited range of information. Much more information is provided by the olfactory system. There are many odors that almost everyone finds disgusting, such as the smell of rotten meat (you'll be able to think of some others), and such odors quickly reduce a person's appetite. Some odor aversions are undoubtedly learned socially; we see that our parents find an odor disgusting, and we learn to do so, too. But others are learned by direct experience of the consequences of ingestion.

If an animal encounters a particular food, eats it, becomes sick, and survives, the animal will avoid eating that food afterward. That is, the animal will have formed a **conditioned flavor aversion.** The aversion can be formed simply on the basis of taste; but more often, olfaction is also involved, because flavor is a composite of taste and olfaction. The phenomenon was first experimentally demonstrated by Garcia and Koelling (1966). The investigators let rats taste some saccharin and then injected them with lithium chloride, which produces nausea. (Rats cannot vomit, but their behavior indicates that lithium chloride makes them feel ill.) Afterward, the rats refused to drink saccharin. Other studies have shown that conditioned aversions can readily be formed to the complex flavors of particular foods, which are the composites of odors and tastes.

If a rat encounters a new and potentially interesting food, it takes only a small nibble of the food. If the food contained something toxic and if it survives its subsequent illness, it will never eat that food again. But if it does *not* get ill, it will take a larger meal the next time; it acts as if it has learned that the food is safe. Humans, too, can form conditioned flavor aversions. These aversions can sometimes occur by chance. A friend of mine often took trips on airplanes with her parents when she was a child. Unfortunately, she usually got airsick. Just before takeoff, her mother would give her some spearmint-flavored chewing gum to help relieve the pressure on her eardrums that would occur when the plane ascended. Yes, she developed a conditioned flavor aversion to spearmint gum. In fact, the odor of the gum still makes her feel nauseated. A more

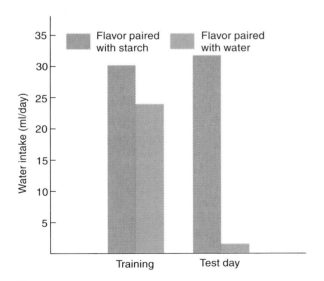

Figure 13.4
Preference for a flavor paired with an infusion of starch into the stomach.
(Based on data from Sclafani, A., and Nissenbaum, J.W. *American Journal of Physiology*, 1988, *255*, R672–R675.)

conditioned flavor aversion   The avoidance of a relatively unfamiliar flavor that previously caused (or was followed by) illness.

serious problem is encountered by patients undergoing chemotherapy for cancer. The drugs they are given often cause nausea, and the patients can form an aversion to the foods they eat during the course of therapy (Bernstein, 1978).

Rozin and Kalat (1971) described an interesting phenomenon: Conditioned flavor aversions can motivate an animal to find a nutrient that it needs. As we saw in Chapter 12, if a rat is fed a food that is deficient in sodium, it will develop a sodium appetite and will seek foods that contain sodium, which it is able to taste. This tendency need not be learned; it is innate. However, rats (and humans) cannot innately recognize the flavor of vital ingredients of the diet, such as vitamins or minerals other than sodium. If a rat is fed a food that is deficient in a particular vitamin, such as thiamine, it will become ill. Its illness will cause the formation of a conditioned aversion to that food. If it is offered another, it will eat it; and if it gets well after eating that food (because it contains the ingredient lacking in its diet), it will learn to prefer that food over the old one.

Thus, we omnivores are endowed with some innate tendencies and with the ability to learn from our experience with particular foods. These tendencies and abilities permit us to obtain the nutrients we need from an enormous variety of foodstuffs, while avoiding foods that could be dangerous to us.

● Physiological Hunger Signals

Most of the time, we begin a meal because it is time to eat. The amount of food we eat during that meal depends on several factors, including the amount and variety of food available to us, how good the food tastes to us, and (as we just saw) the presence of other people. But the amount of food we eat also depends on metabolic factors. If we skip several meals, we get hungrier and hungrier, presumably because of physiological signals indicating that we have been withdrawing nutrients from our long-term reservoir. And all other things being equal, the hungrier we are, the more we will eat. In addition, as we saw in the previous section, if clocks and dinner bells are not present, we eat soon after a small meal but wait longer after a large one. These facts suggest that the amount of food we eat is inversely related to the amount of nutrients left over from previous meals.

What happens to the level of nutrients in our body as time passes after a meal? As you learned earlier in this chapter, during the absorptive phase of metabolism we live on food that is being absorbed from the digestive tract. After that, we start drawing on our nutrient reservoirs: The brain lives on glucose and the rest of the body lives on fatty acids. Although the metabolic needs of the cells of the body are being met, we are taking fuel out of our long-term reservoir—making withdrawals rather than deposits. Clearly, this is the time to start thinking about our next meal.

As we will see, evidence suggests that the brain responds to two types of hunger signals, short term and long term. Receptors in the liver and the brain detect the short-term hunger signals, which are determined by the availability of nutrients in the blood. Long-term signals are provided by adipose tissue, which contains the long-term nutrient reservoir. If this reservoir is full (that is, if the fat cells contain plenty of triglycerides), they secrete a peptide hormone that has an inhibitory effect on the brain mechanisms that control eating. When the level of this hormone is high, the brain becomes less sensitive to short-term hunger signals, and as a consequence, the animal eats less. But if a long period of fasting starts depleting the long-term nutrient reservoir, fat cells decrease their secretion of this hormone, and the brain mechanisms that control eating become more sensitive to short-term hunger signals. In other words, we get hungrier and eat more.

Short-Term Hunger Signals: Glucoprivation and Lipoprivation

A fall in blood glucose level (a condition known as *hypoglycemia*) is a potent stimulus for hunger. Hypoglycemia can be produced experimentally by giving an animal a large injection of insulin, which causes liver cells and fat cells to take up glucose and store it away. We can also deprive cells of glucose by injecting an animal with 2-deoxyglucose (2-DG). You are already familiar with this chemical, because I have described several experiments that used radioactive 2-DG in conjunction with PET scanners or autoradiography to study the metabolic rate of different parts of the brain. When (nonradioactive) 2-DG is given in large doses, it interferes with glucose metabolism by competing with glucose for access to the mechanism that transports glucose through the cell membrane and for access to the enzymes that metabolize glucose. (A similar chemical, *5-TG*, has the same effect.) Both hypoglycemia and 2-DG cause **glucoprivation;** that is, they deprive cells of glucose. And glucoprivation, whatever its cause, stimulates eating.

glucoprivation A dramatic fall in the level of glucose available to cells; can be caused by a fall in the blood level of glucose or by drugs that inhibit glucose metabolism.

Hunger can also be produced by causing **lipoprivation**—depriving cells of lipids. More precisely, they are deprived of the ability to metabolize fatty acids through injection of one of two drugs, **methyl palmoxirate (MP)** or **mercaptoacetate (MA).**

Glucose and fatty acids are only two of the three major nutrients. However, less is known about the importance of amino acids in the body's metabolism. One of the problems in studying the role of amino acids in hunger is that they are essential for protein synthesis. Thus, a diet low in amino acids interferes with many biological processes. Similarly, a diet that is very high in amino acids produces toxic waste products. Thus, experimental manipulations in the amino acid content of diets cause effects unrelated to energy metabolism. For that reason (and the fact that there is no simple way to produce *aminoprivation*), experimenters have concentrated on carbohydrates and lipids.

Severe glucoprivation or severe lipoprivation causes hunger. However, Friedman, Tordoff, and Ramirez (1986) found that *moderate* glucoprivation or *moderate* lipoprivation alone has only a small effect on eating; but when they are combined, an animal eats much more. They administered moderate doses of 2-DG or MP separately or together; only when they were given together did the animals eat large quantities of food. (See *Figure 13.5.*) Presumably, when the metabolism of only one fuel was reduced, the rats simply relied more heavily on the other type of fuel. The investigators also found that if rats were fed a diet high in fats but low in carbohydrates, treatment with MP alone

caused food intake to increase. With no carbohydrates for the animals to fall back on, a treatment that interferes with fatty acid metabolism is enough to stimulate eating.

What is the nature of the detectors that monitor the level of metabolic fuels, and where are they located? The evidence gathered so far indicates that there are two sets of detectors—one set located in the brain, and the other set located in the liver. The detectors in the brain monitor the nutrients available on their side of the blood–brain barrier, and the detectors in the liver monitor the nutrients available to the rest of the body. Because the brain can use only glucose, its detectors are sensitive to glucoprivation, and because the rest of the body can use both glucose and fatty acids, the detectors in the liver are sensitive to both glucoprivation and lipoprivation.

Let's first review the evidence for the detectors in the liver. A study by Novin, VanderWeele, and Rezek (1973) suggested that receptors in the liver can stimulate glucoprivic hunger; when these neurons are deprived of nutrients, they cause eating. The investigators infused 2-DG into the hepatic portal vein. (As we saw in Chapter 12, this vein brings blood from the intestines to the liver; thus, an injection of a drug into this vein delivers it directly to the liver.) Because the animals had been eating a high-carbohydrate, low-fat diet, the 2-DG effectively starved the cells of the liver. The investigators found that the intraportal infusions of 2-DG caused immediate eating. When they cut the vagus nerve, which connects the liver with the brain, the infusions no longer stimulated eating. Thus, the brain receives the hunger signal through this connection.

What about liproprivic hunger? Ritter and Taylor (1989) administered intraperitoneal (IP) injections of capsaicin to rats. **Capsaicin,** a neurotoxin found in red peppers, destroys fine-diameter, unmyelinated sensory axons of the vagus nerve. The capsaicin blocked lipoprivic hunger but did not affect glucoprivic hunger. After this treatment the rats increased their food intake when they were given intravenous injections of 2-DG but not when they were given MA. These results indicate that the signal for lipoprivation originates in the internal organs. (Because the in-

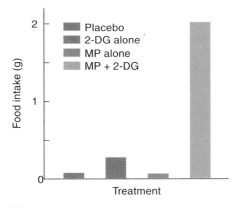

Figure 13.5
Effects of lipoprivation (MP treatment) and glucoprivation (2-DG treatment) on food intake of rats. Intake is stimulated much more when both fatty acid and carbohydrate metabolism are impaired.
(Adapted from Friedman, M.I., Tordoff, M.G., and Ramirez, I. *Brain Research Bulletin,* 1986, *17,* 855–859.)

lipoprivation   A dramatic fall in the level of fatty acids available to cells; usually caused by drugs that inhibit fatty-acid metabolism.

methyl palmoxirate (MP)   A drug that inhibits fatty-acid metabolism and produces lipoprivic hunger.

mercaptoacetate (MA)   A drug that inhibits fatty-acid metabolism and produces lipoprivic hunger.

capsaicin *(kap **say** sin)*   An ingredient in hot peppers that can destroy small, unmyelinated sensory axons that innervate the internal organs.

jections of 2-DG were not made directly into the portal vein, they reached all of the body—including the brain. As we shall see, detectors in the brain were responsible for the glucoprivic hunger seen after the capsaicin treatment.) (See *Figure 13.6.*)

Ritter and Taylor (1990) found that cutting the vagus nerve as it entered the abdominal cavity also abolished lipoprivic hunger (but, again, not glucoprivic hunger). Thus, the receptors that detect low availability of fatty acids seem to be located in the abdominal cavity and send their information to the brain through small-diameter, unmyelinated axons in the vagus nerve.

Several studies have shown that detectors in the liver are also responsible for lipoprivic hunger. One possibility would be that this lipoprivic signal is produced by neurons sensitive to blood lipid levels. However, this is not the case. The detectors appear to be specialized neurons that are sensitive to their own internal rate of metabolism, not to the presence of particular nutrients in the blood. If plenty of fuel is available to them—either in the form of carbohydrates or lipids—the neurons remain quiet. Only if the level of *both* kinds of nutrients falls will they send a hunger signal through the vagus nerve to the brain.

Tordoff, Rawson, and Friedman (1991) injected **2,5-AM** (2,5-anhydro-D-mannitol), a drug that interferes with the production of ATP from glucose, into the hepatic portal vein. The injection caused the animals to eat. An intraportal injection of radioactive 2,5-AM produced no radioactivity in the brain, so the effects of the drug could not have occurred there. In addition, when the investigators cut the branch of the vagus nerve that connects the liver with the brain, the effect of the drug was abolished. Rawson, Ulrich,

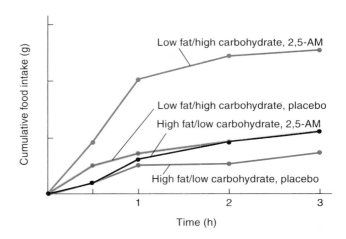

Figure 13.7
Cumulative food intake of rats fed a high-fat/low-carbohydrate or a low-fat/high-carbohydrate diet and given injections of 2,5-AM or a placebo.
(Adapted from Rawson, N.E., Ulrich, P.M., and Friedman, M.I. *American Journal of Physiology: Regulatory, Integrative and Comparative Physiology*, 1996, *271*, R144–R148.)

and Friedman (1996) found that 2,5-AM stimulated eating only in rats that had been living on a low-fat/high-carbohydrate diet. Rats that had been living on a high-fat/low-carbohydrate diet did *not* increase their food intake, because their liver cells were primarily using lipids. (See *Figure 13.7.*)

The studies I have cited indicate that neurons in the liver responsible for hunger signals change their firing rate when their own metabolic rate falls because of inadequate amounts of nutrients. This change in firing rate informs the brain of the need to look for something to eat. It is possible, of course, that two different sets of neurons detect levels of glucose and lipids in the blood, but evidence suggests that this is not the case. For example, people with untreated diabetes are chronically hungry, even though their blood level of glucose is very high. If the nutrient detectors measured the amount of glucose in the blood, these people should not be hungry. But because these people lack insulin, the glucose in their blood cannot enter cells and be metabolized. Thus, their cells starve in the midst of plenty. Clearly, the monitoring of available fuels must take place *inside* the cells that serve as nutrient detectors.

Although different metabolic pathways exist for glucose and fatty acids, the end product of these pathways is the

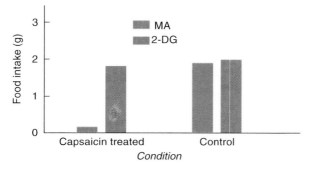

Figure 13.6
Effects of capsaicin-induced damage to unmyelinated peripheral axons on lipoprivic hunger (MA treatment) and glucoprivic hunger (2-DG treatment). Only lipoprivic hunger is affected.
(Based on data from Ritter, S., and Taylor, J.S. *American Journal of Physiology*, 1989, *256*, R1232–R1239.)

2,5-AM A drug that inhibits carbohydrate metabolism in the liver by making phosphate unavailable, thus blocking the production of ATP.

same: the production of ATP. A cell's activities are powered by molecules of ATP, which yield energy when they are broken down; thus, the ATP within a cell constitutes the cell's private stock of energy. Rawson and her colleagues (Rawson et al., 1994; Rawson, Ulrich, and Friedman, 1994) found that eating can be stimulated by two drugs, 2,5-AM (which we encountered two paragraphs ago) and **L-ethionine.** These two drugs block the production of ATP in the liver, but they do so by very different means: 2,5-AM makes phosphate unavailable, and L-ethionine makes adenosine unavailable. (ATP, or adenosine triphosphate, is made of adenosine and phosphate.) These results are consistent with the *ischymetric hypothesis* of hunger (from the Greek word *ischis,* "power") proposed by Nicolaïdis (1974, 1987). Nicolaïdis suggested that some neurons serve as witnesses that testify to the rest of the nervous system about the level of nutrients available to them. The firing rate of their axons is very sensitive to the cells' metabolic rate. If the level of fuels falls (or if drugs interfere with their rate of energy production), their metabolic rate falls too, and the change in the firing rate of their axons tells other neurons that it is time to start thinking about the next meal.

Now let's look at some of the evidence that indicates that the brain has its own nutrient detectors. Because the brain can use only glucose, it would make sense that these detectors respond to glucoprivation—and, indeed, they do. Ritter, Slusser, and Stone (1981) injected some silicone grease into the cerebral aqueduct, which blocked communication between the third and fourth ventricles. Next, they injected 5-TG into either the third ventricle or the fourth ventricle. (5-TG, like 2-DG, produces glucoprivation.) Injections into the fourth ventricle stimulated eating, but injections into the third ventricle (located in the middle of the diencephalon) had no effect. Presumably, the 5-TG diffused out of the fourth ventricle into the surrounding brain tissue and inhibited glucose metabolism in neurons in the hindbrain.

The location of the hindbrain nutrient receptors is not yet known, but one possible location is the area postrema or the adjacent nucleus of the solitary tract, located in the medulla. Bird, Cardone, and Contreras (1983) found that after the area postrema had been destroyed, an injection of 5-TG into the ventricular system no longer stimulated food intake. Also, Yettefti, Orsini, and Perrin (1997) found that the firing rate of some neurons in the nucleus of the solitary tract changed when the investigators infused glucose into that region by means of iontophoresis or injected glucose intravenously.

To summarize: The brain contains detectors that monitor the availability of glucose (its only fuel) inside the blood–brain barrier, and the liver contains detectors that monitor the availability of nutrients (glucose and fatty acids) outside the blood–brain barrier.

Before closing this section I should note that no single set of receptors is solely responsible for the information the brain uses to control eating. For example, Tordoff, Hopfenbeck, and Novin (1982) found that cutting the hepatic branch of the vagus nerve, which prevents hunger signals originating in the liver from reaching the brain, had little effect on an animal's day-to-day eating. In addition, lesions of the area postrema and the nucleus of the solitary tract, which abolish both glucoprivic and lipoprivic signals, do not lead to long-term disturbances in the control of feeding (Ritter et al., 1992). Apparently, the control of metabolism and ingestive behavior is just too important to entrust to one mechanism.

Interim Summary

Many stimuli, environmental and physiological, can initiate a meal. Stimuli associated with eating—such as clocks pointing to lunchtime or dinnertime, the smell or sight of food, or (especially) the taste of food—increase appetite. The size of a meal taken by a rat (or a person living in isolation) determines the interval until the next one. In contrast, most people eat at fixed times but vary their intake according to how much (or when) they ate the previous meal. The presence of other people tends to increase our meal and removes the controlling effect of the previous meal.

Omnivores are naturally attracted to sweet tastes and avoid sour or bitter ones. The phenomenon of sensory-specific satiety encourages omnivores to eat a varied diet. In addition, they can learn to avoid (form an aversion to) the flavors of foods that make them ill. If they eat a diet that lacks an essential ingredient, their illness produces an aversion to their present diet and motivates them to seek another. If that diet cures them, they learn to prefer it.

Studies with inhibitors of the metabolism of glucose (2-DG or 5-TG) and fatty acids (MP or MA) indicate that low levels of both of these nutrients are involved in hunger; that is, animals will eat in response to both glucoprivation and lipoprivation. Studies with capsaicin and drugs that block metabolism in the liver (2,5-AM or L-ethionine) indicate that the signal for lipoprivic eating is detected by receptors in the liver and transmitted through unmyelinated sensory axons of the vagus nerve. Actually, the detectors in

L-ethionine   A drug that inhibits carbohydrate metabolism in the liver by making adenosine unavailable, thus blocking the production of ATP.

the liver appear to monitor the amount of ATP present in the cells, and if this level falls for any reason, a hunger signal is sent to the brain. Glucoprivic eating can also be stimulated by interfering with glucose metabolism in the region surrounding the fourth ventricle by injecting 5-TG into the fourth ventricle; thus, the brain stem contains its own glucose-sensitive detectors. Although the evidence is not yet conclusive, these detectors may lie in the area postrema/nucleus of the solitary tract, which also receives information from the detectors in the liver.

WHAT STOPS A MEAL?

As we saw, the signals that stop a meal are different from those that start it. However, these two types of signals interact. If a meal is started when there is not much physiological need for nutrients (that is, when the nutrient reservoirs are well stocked), the meal will be a small one. If, however, a meal is started after a long fast, when the nutrient reservoirs are somewhat depleted, the meal will be a large one. In other words, if the hunger signal is moderate, a moderate satiety signal will stop the meal. If the hunger signal is strong, only a strong satiety signal will stop it.

There are two primary sources of satiety signals—the signals that stop a meal. Short-term satiety signals come from the immediate consequence of eating a particular meal. To search for these signals, we follow the pathway traveled by ingested food: the eyes, nose, and mouth; the stomach; the duodenum; and the liver. Each of these locations can potentially provide a signal to the brain that indicates that food has been ingested and is progressing on the way toward absorption. Long-term satiety signals arise in the adipose tissue, which contains the long-term nutrient reservoir. These signals do not control the beginning and end of a particular meal, but they do, in the long run, control the intake of calories by modulating the sensitivity of brain mechanisms involved in hunger.

● Head Factors

The term *head factors* refers to several sets of receptors located in the head: the eyes, the nose, the tongue, and the throat. Information about the appearance, odor, taste, texture, and temperature of food has some automatic effects on food intake, but most of the effects involve learning. The mere act of eating does not produce long-lasting satiety; an animal with a gastric fistula (a tube placed in the stomach that drains food out of the stomach before it can be digested) will eat indefinitely.

Undoubtedly, the most important role of head factors in satiety is the fact that taste and odor of food can serve as stimuli that permit animals to learn about the caloric contents of different foods. Thus, animals can learn to adjust their intake according to the caloric value of what they are eating. For example, Mather, Nicolaïdis, and Booth (1978) found that rats learned to eat less of a food with a particular flavor when the eating of that food was accompanied by intravenous infusions of glucose, which supplied extra calories.

● Gastric Factors

Although most people associate feelings of hunger with "hunger pangs" in the stomach and feelings of satiety with an impression of gastric fullness, the stomach is not necessary for feelings of hunger. Humans whose stomachs have been removed because of cancer or the presence of large ulcers still periodically get hungry (Ingelfinger, 1944). Of necessity, these people eat frequent, small meals; in fact, a large meal causes nausea and discomfort, apparently because the duodenum quickly fills up. (As you will recall from Chapter 12, the duodenum is the part of the small intestine that attaches to the stomach.) However, although the stomach may not be especially important in producing hunger, it does appear to play an important role in satiety.

The stomach apparently contains receptors that can detect the presence of nutrients. Davis and Campbell (1973) allowed rats to eat their fill, and shortly thereafter, they removed food from the rats' stomachs through an implanted tube. When the rats were permitted to eat again, they ate almost exactly the same amount of food that had been taken out. This finding suggests that animals are able to monitor the amount of food in their stomachs.

Deutsch and Gonzalez (1980) confirmed and extended these findings. They operated on rats and attached an inflatable cuff around the pylorus—something that looked like a miniature blood pressure cuff. The cuff could be inflated by remote control, which would cause it to compress the pylorus, preventing the stomach from emptying. (As we saw in Chapter 12, Hall and Blass used a similar device, in which a noose of fishing line could be tightened to prevent water from leaving the stomach. The pylorus is located at the junction of the stomach and the duodenum, and contains a sphincter that regulates the flow of nutrients out of the stomach.) With their device Deutsch and Gonzalez could confine food to the stomach, eliminating the possible influence of receptors in the intestine or liver. After observations were made, the cuff could be deflated so that the stomach would empty normally.

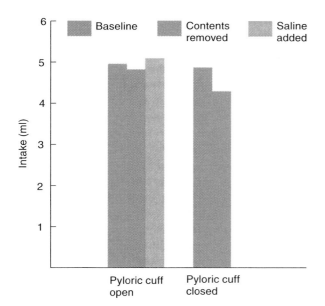

Figure 13.8

Evidence for a gastric satiety signal. Rats compensate for the removal of food from the stomach and ignore the addition of a saline solution. To permit direct comparisons, the amount drunk does not reflect the amount removed from the stomach.

(Based on data from Deutsch, J.A., and Gonzalez, M.F. *Behavioral and Neural Biology*, 1980, *31*, 113–116.)

Each day, the investigators inflated the pyloric cuff and gave the rats a 30-minute opportunity to drink a commercial high-calorie liquid diet. Because the rats had not eaten for 15 hours, they readily consumed the liquid diet. After the meal the investigators removed 5 ml of the stomach's contents through an implanted tube. On some days they replaced the contents with a saline solution, and on others they let the rats eat without intervention. The rats adjusted their food intake perfectly, compensating for the calories that were removed but ignoring the added nonnutritive saline solution. (See *Figure 13.8.*) The results indicate that animals can monitor the total amount of nutrients received by the stomach. They do not do so simply by measuring the volume of the food there, because they are not fooled by the infusion of a saline solution. And the detec-

sham feeding   Feeding behavior of an animal with an open gastric or esophageal fistula that prevents food from remaining in the stomach.

cholecystokinin (CCK) *(coal i sis toe **ky** nin)*   A hormone secreted by the duodenum that regulates gastric motility and causes the gallbladder (cholecyst) to contract; appears to provide a satiety signal transmitted to the brain through the vagus nerve.

tion takes place in the stomach, not the intestine, because the pyloric cuff keeps all the food in the stomach. Of course, this study only proves that the stomach contains nutrient receptors—it does not prove that there are not detectors in the intestines, as well.

● Intestinal Factors

Indeed, the intestines do contain nutrient detectors. Studies have shown that afferent axons arising from the duodenum are sensitive to the presence of glucose, amino acids, and fatty acids (Ritter et al., 1992). These axons may transmit a satiety signal to the brain. In fact, studies have replicated the findings of Deutsch and Gonzalez but have shown that the animals eat the same amount of food whether the pyloric cuff is open or closed (Rauhofer, Smith, and Gibbs, 1993; Seeley, Kaplan, and Grill, 1995).

Greenberg, Smith, and Gibbs (1990) showed that the entry of food into the duodenum suppresses food intake. They attached gastric fistulas to a group of rats so that when the animals drank a liquid diet, it would drain out of their stomachs. Under these conditions animals will eat for a long time, because food does not accumulate in the digestive system. (This behavior is referred to as **sham feeding** because it is an imitation of the real thing.) The researchers infused *Intralipid*, a commercial mixture of lipids and fatty acids, into the rats' duodenums. The infusion inhibited the sham feeding, which indicates the presence of a duodenal satiety signal. When the researchers added a local anesthetic to the liquid diet, the infusion was much less effective in reducing sham feeding. Thus, the signal seems to arise from nutrient detectors located inside the duodenum—the local anesthetic prevented these detectors from sending a signal to the brain, and the animals continued to eat. In support of this conclusion Greenberg et al. (1991) found that the satiating effect of an injection of radioactively labeled *Intralipid* into the duodenum occurred before radioactivity was seen in the blood of the hepatic portal vein. Thus, the satiating effect occurred before digestion had taken place.

After food reaches the stomach, it is mixed with hydrochloric acid and pepsin, an enzyme that breaks proteins into their constituent amino acids. As digestion proceeds, food is gradually introduced into the duodenum. There, the food is mixed with bile and pancreatic enzymes, which continue the digestive process. The duodenum controls the rate of stomach emptying by secreting a peptide hormone called **cholecystokinin (CCK).** This hormone receives its name from the fact that it causes the gallbladder (cholecyst) to contract, injecting bile into the duodenum. (Bile breaks fats down into small particles so that they can be absorbed from the intestines.) CCK is secreted in response to the presence of fats, which are detected by receptors in the walls of the duodenum. In addition to stimulating contraction of the gallbladder, CCK causes the pylorus to constrict and inhibits gastric contractions, thus keeping the stomach from giving it more food.

Obviously, the blood level of CCK must be related to the amount of nutrients (particularly fats) that the duodenum receives from the stomach. Thus, this hormone could potentially provide a satiety signal to the brain, telling it that the duodenum was receiving food from the stomach. In fact, many studies have indeed found that injections of CCK suppress eating (Gibbs, Young, and Smith, 1973; Smith, Gibbs, and Kulkosky, 1982). Because CCK cannot cross the blood–brain barrier, its site of actions must be either outside the central nervous system or in one of the circumventricular organs (like that of angiotensin).

In fact, CCK seems to act peripherally. Smith, Gibbs, and Kulkosky (1982) reported that the inhibitory effect of CCK on food intake was abolished by cutting the gastric branch of the vagus nerve, which disconnects the stomach from the brain. Evidence suggests that the pylorus, a region rich in CCK receptors, may be an important site of action. Moran et al. (1989) removed rats' pyloruses, attaching the stomach directly to the cut end of the duodenum. After the surgery the suppressive effect of CCK on the animals' eating was significantly decreased. However, by 2 to 3 months after the surgery the junction between the stomach and the duodenum had grown new CCK receptors, and the hormone again suppressed food intake. (See *Figure 13.9.*)

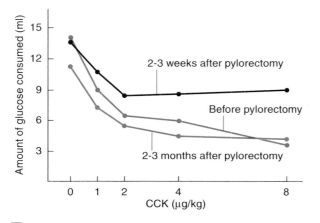

Figure 13.9
Effects of cholecystokinin (CCK) on the amount of glucose consumed by rats before and after removal of the pyloric region. (Based on data from Moran, Shnayder, Hostetler, and McHugh, 1989.)

The suppressive effect of CCK on eating is well established. However, several investigators have questioned whether the suppression is caused by *aversion* or by *satiety*. That is, CCK might simply make the animals feel nauseated, so they stop eating. Deutsch and Hardy (1977) found that when an injection of CCK was paired with a particular flavor, rats formed a conditioned aversion to that flavor. In addition, Moore and Deutsch (1985) found that an injection of an *antiemetic* drug (one that suppresses nausea and vomiting) diminished the inhibitory effect of CCK on eating. Also, Bowers et al. (1992) found that rats that received low doses of CCK after drinking sweetened condensed milk from a drinking spout in their home cage would later not only avoid drinking the milk but also bury the drinking spout with the bedding material—a response that rats make when they encounter something that appears to be dangerous. Finally, Stricker and his colleagues (McCann, Verbalis, and Stricker, 1989; Stricker and Verbalis, 1991) found that several chemicals known to produce nausea, including lithium chloride, copper sulfate, and apomorphine, cause a release of oxytocin by the posterior pituitary gland; thus, they consider oxytocin release an indicator of malaise. They found that injections of CCK, too, cause a release of oxytocin. Satiety produced by eating a normal meal does *not* cause the release of oxytocin.

● Liver Factors

As we saw earlier, detectors in the liver send a hunger signal to the brain when the level of nutrients available to them falls. These detectors appear to play a role in satiety, as well. Satiety produced by head factors and gastric factors is anticipatory; that is, these factors predict that the food in the digestive system will, when absorbed, eventually restore the system variables that cause hunger. Food in the mouth or stomach does not restore the body's store of nutrients. Not until nutrients are absorbed from the intestines are the internal system variables that cause hunger returned to normal. The last stage of satiety appears to occur in the liver, which is the first organ to learn that food is finally being received from the intestines.

Over twenty years ago, Russek (1971) noted that although intravenous (IV) injections of glucose had little effect on food intake, intraperitoneal injections (injections into the abdominal cavity) suppressed eating. Russek realized that most of the glucose injected into the abdominal cavity is taken up by the liver and stored as glycogen. The fact that the glucose injected intraperitoneally probably got no farther than the liver but nevertheless inhibited eating suggested to him that the liver might contain detectors that were sensitive to glucose. Perhaps these detectors send signals to the brain that activate mechanisms that control eating.

To test this hypothesis, Russek attached two chronic cannulas in a dog, one in the hepatic portal vein and another in the jugular vein, located in the neck. Injection in the jugular vein introduces a substance into the general circulation. By the time the substance reaches the liver, it is already diluted by the blood. In contrast, injection in the hepatic portal vein introduces a substance directly into the liver. Russek found that an injection of glucose into the hepatic portal vein produced long-lasting satiety, whereas a similar injection into the jugular vein had no effect on food intake. Since then, many other studies (for example, Novin et al., 1983) have confirmed these results.

Tordoff and Friedman (1988) demonstrated that this effect seems to be localized in the liver. They infused small amounts of two nutrients, glucose and fructose, into the hepatic portal vein. The amounts they used were similar to those that are produced when a meal is being digested. Both nutrients reduced the amount of food that the rats ate. Almost certainly, the signal was detected by the liver. First, neither the glucose nor the fructose increased the animals' blood levels of glucose, free fatty acids, glycerol, or other nutrients; thus, the infusions did not provide a signal that could be detected directly by nutrient receptors in the brain. Second, fructose cannot cross the blood–brain barrier and is metabolized very poorly by cells in the rest of the body—but it can readily be metabolized by the liver. Therefore, the results strongly suggest that when the liver receives nutrients from the intestines, it sends a signal to the brain that produces satiety. (More accurately, the signal *continues* the satiety that was already started by signals arising from the stomach and duodenum.)

Of course, we cannot necessarily conclude that a treatment produces *satiety* just because it inhibits eating. (As we saw, the researchers disagree about whether the suppression of food intake produced by CCK should be called satiety.) However, the effects of infusions of nutrients into the hepatic portal vein do not appear to be aversive. Tordoff and Friedman (1986) infused either a saline solution or a solution of glucose into the hepatic portal blood supply of rats while the animals were eating. The two solutions were randomly paired with two nonnutritive flavors added to their food: chicken or chocolate. As expected, the glucose suppressed eating. But later, when the rats were permitted to choose between the two flavors of food, they preferred the one associated with the glucose infusion. Thus, not only is the infusion not aversive, but it is also actually reinforcing. As we saw earlier, Sclafani and Nissenbaum (1988) found that an infusion of starch into the stomach produced a preference for a flavor associated with

the infusion; thus, the brain interprets the signals from the stomach and the liver not simply as satiety signals but as signals that a beneficial event has occurred.

● Long-Term Satiety: Signals from Adipose Tissue

So far, I have discussed satiety factors arising from a meal. But as we saw in the first section of this chapter, total body fat appears to be regulated over a long-term basis. If an animal is force-fed so that it becomes fatter than normal, it will reduce its food intake once it is permitted to choose how much to eat (Wilson et al., 1990). (See *Figure 13.10.*) Similar studies have shown that an animal will adjust its food intake appropriately if it is given a high-calorie or low-calorie diet. And if an animal is put on a diet that reduces its body weight, gastric satiety factors become much less effective (Cabanac and Lafrance, 1991). Thus, signals arising from the long-term nutrient reservoir may either suppress hunger signals or augment satiety signals.

Koopmans (1985) demonstrated the interaction between long-term and short-term signals in the control of food intake. He operated on pairs of rats, surgically producing "Siamese twins." He attached them side by side and connected their intestines in such a way that much of the food that one rat ate was actually absorbed by the other rat. The animals exchanged very little blood, so their nutrient reservoirs did not mix. (See *Figure 13.11.*) (The rats were

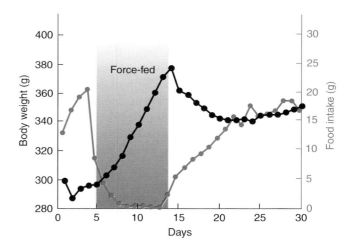

Figure 13.10

Food intake and body weight of rats that received an excess of their normal food intake through force feeding. Their food intake fell during the period of force feeding and recovered only when their body weight returned to normal.

(Adapted from Wilson, B.E., Meyer, G.E., Cleveland, J.C., and Weigle, D.S. *American Journal of Physiology,* 1990, 259, R1148–R1155.)

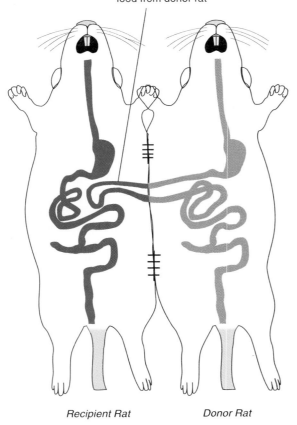

Loop of recipient rat's small intestine receives food from donor rat

Recipient Rat   Donor Rat

Figure 13.11
A surgical preparation used by Koopmans (1985) to cause most of the nutrients eaten by one rat to be absorbed in the body of its partner.

genetically identical members of an inbred strain, so there was no problem with tissue rejection.) The rat that received the extra nutrients from its partner began eating much less, and the donor began eating much more. Although satiety signals arising from the stomachs and duodenums of both rats were unaffected by the surgery, signals arising from the depletion of the animals' long-term nutrient reservoirs were obviously able to override these signals.

What exactly is the system variable that permits the body weight of most organisms to remain relatively stable? It seems highly unlikely that body *weight* itself is regulated—this variable would have to be measured by detectors in the soles of our feet or (for those of us who are sedentary) in the skin of our buttocks. What is more likely is that some variable related to body fat is regulated. As we saw earlier, the basic difference between obese and non-obese people is the amount of fat stored in their adipose tissue. Perhaps fat tissue provides a signal to the brain that indicates how much of it there is. If so, the signal is almost certainly some sort of chemical, because cutting the nerves

that serve the fat tissue in an animal's body does not affect its total body fat.

For years, researchers have been trying to identify a signal from fat tissue that could tell the brain how well stocked the long-term reservoir was. Finally, they succeeded. The discovery came after years of study with a strain of genetically obese mice. The **ob mouse** (as this strain is called) has a low metabolism, overeats, and gets exceedingly fat. It also develops diabetes in adulthood, just as many obese people do. Researchers in several laboratories have discovered the cause of the obesity (Campfield et al., 1995; Halaas et al., 1995; Pelleymounter et al., 1995). A particular gene, called OB, normally produces a protein that has been given the name **leptin** (from the Greek word *leptos*, "thin"). Leptin is normally secreted by fat cells that contain a large amount of triglycerides. Because of a genetic mutation, the fat cells of ob mice are unable to produce leptin.

Leptin has profound effects on metabolism and eating, acting as an antiobesity hormone. If ob mice are given daily injections of leptin, their metabolic rate increases, their body temperature rises, they become more active, and they eat less. As a result, their weight returns to normal. Figure 13.12 shows a picture of an untreated ob mouse and

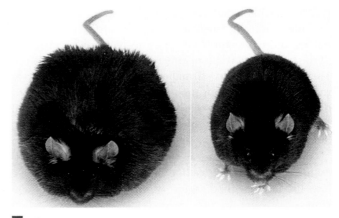

Figure 13.12
The effects of leptin on obesity in mice of the ob (obese) strain. The ob mouse on the left is untreated; the one on the right received daily injections of leptin.
(Photo courtesy of Dr. J. Sholtis, The Rockefeller University. Copyright © 1995 Amgen, Inc.)

ob mouse   A strain of mice whose obesity and low metabolic rate is caused by a mutation that prevents the production of leptin.

leptin   A hormone secreted by adipose tissue; decreased food intake and increased metabolic rate, primarily by inhibiting NPY-secreting neurons in the arcuate nucleus.

an ob mouse that has received injections of leptin. (See *Figure 13.12.*)

The discovery of leptin has stimulated much interest among researchers interested in finding ways to treat human obesity. Because it is a natural hormone, it might provide a way to help people lose weight without the use of drugs with potentially harmful effects. The next section describes the brain mechanisms responsible for its effects on metabolism and behavior, and the final section explores the possibilities of its use in treating obesity.

Interim Summary

Because of the long delay between swallowing food and digesting it, the regulation of food intake requires a satiety mechanism; without it, we would overeat and damage our stomachs. The feedback produced by tasting, smelling, and swallowing food provides the first satiety signal, but unless this signal is followed by feedback from the stomach indicating that food has arrived there, the animal will eat again. The stomach contains nutrient detectors that tell the brain how much food has been received. If some food is removed from the stomach, the animal eats enough to replace it, even if the experimenter tries to fool the animal by injecting an equal volume of a saline solution.

Signals originating in the intestines may also produce satiety. Several investigators have suggested that cholecystokinin, released by the duodenum when it receives fat-rich food from the stomach, provides a satiety signal. The inhibitory effect of CCK on eating appears to be mediated by receptors in the pylorus and transmitted to the brain via the vagus nerve. However, studies have shown that CCK has an aversive effect. The duodenum also appears to contain nutrient detectors that send a satiety signal to the brain without the intermediate of a hormone; infusion of a mixture of lipids and fatty acids suppresses sham feeding.

Another satiety signal comes from the liver, which detects nutrients being received from the intestines. Infusion of glucose or fructose (which do not cross the blood–brain barrier) directly into the hepatic portal vein suppresses food intake of hungry animals. The signal from the liver does not appear to be aversive; it can even be used to reinforce the consumption of a particular flavor.

Signals arising from nutrient reservoirs affect food intake on a long-term basis. Force-feeding facilitates satiety, and starvation inhibits it. A study with surgically produced "Siamese twins" showed that long-term food intake is in-

fluenced by the quantity of nutrients actually received from the digestive system. Studies of the ob mouse led to the discovery of leptin, a peptide hormone secreted by well nourished adipose tissue that increases an animal's metabolic rate and decreases food intake.

BRAIN MECHANISMS

Although hunger and satiety signals originate in the digestive system and in the body's nutrient reservoirs, the target of these signals is the brain. This section looks at some of the research on brain mechanisms of food intake and metabolism.

Brain Stem

Ingestive behaviors are phylogenetically ancient; obviously, all our ancestors ate and drank or died. Thus, we should expect that the basic ingestive behaviors of chewing and swallowing are programmed by phylogenetically ancient brain circuits. Indeed, studies have shown that these behaviors can be performed by decerebrate rats, whose brains were transected between the diencephalon and the midbrain (Norgren and Grill, 1982; Grill and Kaplan, 1990). Decerebration disconnects the motor neurons of the brain stem and spinal cord from the neural circuits of the cerebral hemispheres (such as the cerebral cortex and basal ganglia) that normally control them. The only behaviors that decerebrate animals can display are those that are directly controlled by neural circuits located within the brain stem. A decerebrate rat cannot approach and eat food; the experimenters must place food, in liquid form, into their mouths. Decerebrate rats can distinguish between different tastes; they drink and swallow sweet or slightly salty liquids and spit out bitter ones. They even respond to hunger and satiety signals. They drink more sucrose after having been deprived of food for 24 hours, and they drink less of it if some sucrose is first injected directly into their stomachs.

The area postrema and the nucleus of the solitary tract (henceforth referred to as the AP/NST) receive taste information from the tongue and a variety of sensory information from the internal organs—including hunger signals from detectors in the liver. In addition, we saw that this region appears to contain a set of detectors sensitive to the brain's own fuel, glucose. All this information is transmitted to regions of the forebrain more directly involved in control of eating and metabolism.

Several kinds of evidence indicate the importance of the AP/NST to hunger. Ritter, Dinh, and Friedman (1994) found that injections of 2,5-AM (which disrupt liver metabolism and produce hunger) stimulated Fos production in the AP/NST. (The presence of Fos protein is a sign of neural activation.) They found that both eating and Fos production were abolished by cutting the branch of the vagus nerve that connects the liver to the brain. In addition, Ritter and Taylor (1990) found that lesions of the NST and the area postrema (AP/NST) abolished both glucoprivic and lipoprivic feeding. (See *Figure 13.13.*)

As we will see, the most important interactions between hunger and satiety signals take place in the forebrain. However, there is some evidence that such interactions take place even in the brain stem. Giza, Scott, and VanderWeele (1992) recorded the activity of taste-sensitive neurons in the NST that responded to the application of glucose placed on the tongue. They found that intravenous injections of glucose or glucagon, which produce satiety, decreased the response of these neurons to the sweet taste. This interaction may be at least partly responsible for the effects of hunger and satiety signals on the ingestive behavior of decerebrate rats described in the first paragraph of this subsection.

Information from the tongue and internal organs received by the AP/NST is relayed to the **lateral parabrachial nucleus** of the pons. Lesions of the lateral parabrachial nucleus eliminate the effects of hunger signals detected by the liver; they disrupt both lipoprivic feeding and feeding elicited by 2,5-AM (Calingasan and Ritter, 1993; Grill et al., 1995). These lesions do *not* disrupt feeding produced

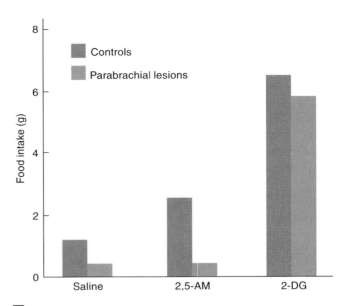

Figure 13.14
Effects of parabrachial lesions on glucoprivic hunger signaled by detectors in the liver (2,5-AM treatment) or in the brain stem (2-DG treatment).
(Adapted from Grill, H.J., Friedman, M.I., Norgren, R., Scalera, G., and Seeley, R. *American Journal of Physiology*, 1995, *268*, R676–R682.)

by 2-DG, which indicates that information from the brain's own glucose-sensitive detectors reaches the forebrain by a different pathway. The route these neurons take is not yet known. (See *Figure 13.14.*)

● Hypothalamus

Discoveries made in the 1940s and 1950s focused the attention of researchers interested in ingestive behavior on two regions of the hypothalamus: the lateral area and the ventromedial nucleus. For many years investigators believed that these two regions controlled hunger and satiety, respectively; one was the accelerator, and the other was the brake. The basic findings were these: After the lateral hypothalamus was destroyed, animals stopped eating or drinking (Anand and Brobeck, 1951; Teitelbaum and Stellar, 1954). Electrical stimulation of the same region would produce eating, drinking, or both behaviors. Conversely, lesions of the ventromedial hypothalamus produced overeating that led to gross obesity, whereas electrical stim-

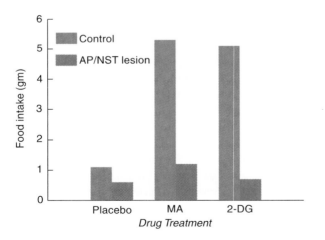

Figure 13.13
Effects of lesions of the nucleus of the solitary tract and adjacent area postrema on glucoprivic hunger (MA treatment) and lipoprivic hunger (2-DG treatment).
(Based on data from Ritter, S., and Taylor, J.S. *American Journal of Physiology*, 1990, *258*, R1395–R1401.)

lateral parabrachial nucleus   A nucleus in the pons that receives gustatory information and information from the liver and digestive system and relays it to the forebrain.

ulation suppressed eating (Hetherington and Ranson, 1942). The story was too simple, of course. Although both the lateral and the ventromedial hypothalamus participate in the control of food intake, both regions appear to play both excitatory and inhibitory roles.

Role in Hunger

For approximately two decades after the discovery that lesions of the lateral hypothalamus abolished eating behavior, most investigators subscribed to the hypothesis that this region was a "feeding center." (See *Figure 13.15.*) During the 1970s researchers finally began to pay attention to the fact that rats with these lesions have other types of behavioral impairments. In fact, they hardly move at all and pay little attention to stimuli around them. Stricker and Zigmond (1976) reviewed the existing evidence and concluded that the behavioral effects of lateral hypothalamic

lesions, including the suppression of eating, were produced by damage to dopaminergic axons of the nigrostriatal bundle that passes through this region, which is known to play a role in the control of movement.

Subsequent research has shown that the lateral hypothalamus does after all play a role in eating. Neurotoxic lesions of the lateral hypothalamus made with ibotenic acid, which kills cells while sparing axons passing through the region, produce a long-lasting decrease in food intake and body weight (Stricker, Swerdloff, and Zigmond, 1978; Dunnett, Lane, and Winn, 1985). The lesions do not affect dopamine levels in the forebrain. In addition, stimulation of the lateral hypothalamus with direct injections of excitatory amino acids produces eating (Stanley et al., 1993a), and injections of a glutamate antagonist in this region decrease food intake (Stanley et al., 1996). (See *Figure 13.16.*)

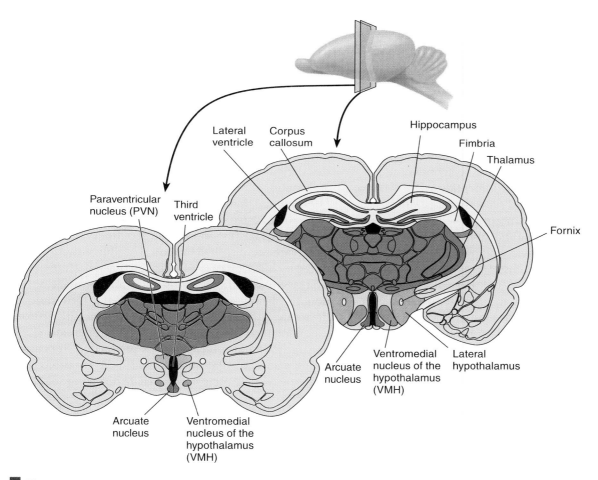

Figure 13.15
Cross sections through the rat brain, showing the location of regions of the hypothalamus that play a role in the control of eating and metabolism.
(Adapted from Swanson, L.W. *Brain Maps: Structure of the Rat Brain.* New York: Elsevier, 1992.)

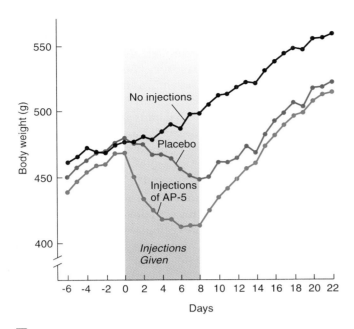

Figure 13.16
Body weight of rats that received twice-daily injections of a glutamate antagonist into the lateral hypothalamus.
(Adapted from Stanley, B.G., Willett, V.L., Donias, H.W., Dee, M.G., and Duva, M.A. *American Journal of Physiology: Regulatory, Integrative and Comparative Physiology*, 1996, 270, R443–R449.)

Another piece of evidence indicating that the lateral hypothalamus plays a role in ingestive behavior is the fact that a neurotransmitter called **neuropeptide Y (NPY)** is an extremely potent stimulator of food intake (Clark et al., 1984). Infusion of this substance into the hypothalamus produces ravenous, almost frantic eating. Rats who receive an infusion of this peptide will work very hard, pressing a lever many times for each morsel of food; they will eat food made bitter with quinine; and they will continue to drink milk even when doing so means that they receive an electric shock to their tongue (Flood and Morley, 1991; Jewett et al., 1992). The potency of this peptide suggests that it plays an important role in the control of food intake.

Neuropeptide Y appears to have at least two sites of action in the hypothalamus. When infused into the midlateral hypothalamus, just medial to the fornix, it produces eating (Stanley et al., 1993b). When infused into the paraventricular nucleus, located in the medial hypothalamus around the dorsal part of the third ventricle, it produces metabolic effects, including insulin and glucocorticoid secretion, decreased breakdown of triglycerides, and a decrease in body temperature (Wahlestedt et al., 1987; Abe, Saito, and Shimazu, 1989; Currie and Coscina, 1996). (Refer to *Figure 13.15.*)

Neuropeptide Y is found in neurons that project from regions of the brain stem to the hypothalamus, often colocalized with both epinephrine and norepinephrine (Sawchenko et al.,1985). Just how neuropeptide Y interacts with these catecholamines is not known, but drugs that block adrenergic α_2 receptors decrease eating produced by hypothalamic infusions of NPY (Clark et al., 1988). Levels of neuropeptide Y are affected by hunger and satiety signals; Sahu, Kalra, and Kalra (1988) found that hypothalamic levels of NPY are increased by food deprivation and lowered by eating. In addition, Myers et al. (1995) found that hypothalamic injections of a drug that blocks neuropeptide Y receptors suppress eating caused by food deprivation or by hypothalamic injections of NPY. This last finding, in particular, provides strong evidence that normal food intake is at least partially stimulated by neuropeptide Y.

The neurons that secrete NPY are found in the **arcuate nucleus,** located in the hypothalamus at the base of the third ventricle. The arcuate nucleus also contains neurosecretory cells whose hormones control the secretions of the anterior pituitary gland. (Refer to *Figure 13.15.*) The NPY-containing neurons send a dense projection of axons to the paraventricular nucleus—the region where infusions of NPY affect metabolic functions (Bai et al., 1985). They also send a lighter projection elsewhere in the hypothalamus. Presumably, the latter set of projections are responsible for the direct effects of NPY on eating. Several studies indicate that these neurons do, indeed, play a direct role in hunger and control of metabolism. For example, Akabayashi et al. (1994) found that infusion of a chemical that prevents the synthesis of NPY directly into the arcuate nucleus suppresses both feeding and insulin secretion.

Minami et al. (1995) found that glucoprivation produced by injection of 2-DG into the cerebral ventricles activates NPY-secreting neurons in the arcuate nucleus. In a double-labeling study, they showed glucoprivation induced the production of Fos protein in arcuate neurons that contained messenger RNA for neuropeptide Y. The glucoprivation also increased Fos production in neurons in the paraventricular nucleus, which receive projections from the NPY neurons in the arcuate nucleus. (See *Figure*

neuropeptide Y (NPY) A peptide neurotransmitter whose release stimulates feeding, insulin and glucocorticoid secretion, decreased breakdown of triglycerides, and a decrease in body temperature.

arcuate nucleus A nucleus in the base of the hypothalamus that controls secretions of the anterior pituitary gland; contains NPY-secreting neurons involved in feeding and control of metabolism.

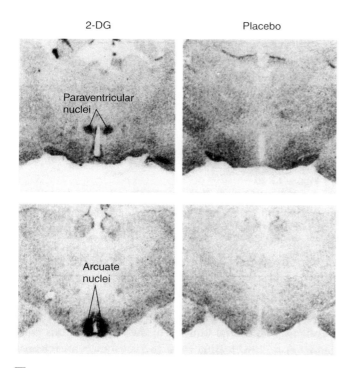

2-DG   Placebo

Paraventricular
nuclei

Arcuate
nuclei

Figure 13.17
The effects of glucoprivic hunger induced by intracerebroven-tricular injection of 2-DG in expression of c-Fos messenger RNA. The treatment activated neurons in the arcuate nucleus and the paraventricular nucleus of the hypothalamus.

(From Minami, S., Kamegai, J., Sugihara, H., Suzuki, N., Higuchi, H., and Wakabayashi, I. *Molecular Brain Research*, 1995, *33*, 305–310. Reprinted by permission.)

level in females of many species, they stop ovulating, which prevents them from becoming pregnant. Pregnancy is a costly enterprise, because the female must feed her fetuses as well as herself, and such an enterprise should not be undertaken in times of famine. Studies suggest that increased activity of NPY-secreting neurons in the arcuate nucleus inhibit the secretion of gonadotropic hormones by the anterior pituitary gland, which results in temporary sterility. The fact the neuropeptide Y suppresses reproduction, decreases metabolism, and stimulates hunger indicates that this peptide, like angiotensin, is responsible for several effects with a common purpose.

Neuropeptide Y is not the only hypothalamic neurotransmitter involved in hunger. Rats, being nocturnal animals, generally sleep and fast during the day; then, when night comes, they take their first big meal. This meal tends to be high in carbohydrates, which are the most easily digested and metabolized nutrients; later meals are higher in fats and protein (Leibowitz, Weiss, and Shor-Posner, 1988). This carbohydrate appetite appears to be stimulated by the release of norepinephrine in the hypothalamus—particularly, in the paraventricular nucleus.

Leibowitz et al. (1985) found that microinfusion of NE into the PVN stimulates eating, especially of carbohydrates. (See **Figure 13.18**.) In fact, if a noradrenergic agonist is continuously infused into the PVN, the animal will overeat and get fat; and if AMPT (a drug that blocks the synthesis of NE) is infused, the animal will undereat and lose weight (Yee et al., 1987). Lesions of the PVN or destruction of the

13.17.) These neurons appear to respond only to signals received from neurons that detect glucoprivation on the brain side of the blood–brain barrier. Akabayashi et al. (1993) found that an intraperitoneal injection of MA, which stimulates a lipoprivic signal in the liver, did not increase levels of NPY in the arcuate nucleus.

As we saw in Chapter 12, another peptide, angiotensin, produces a variety of effects, including contraction of blood vessels, secretion of aldosterone, sodium appetite, and thirst. All these effects serve a common purpose: to increase blood volume and maintain normal blood pressure during a period of hypovolemia. Neuropeptide Y may also have multiple effects. Besides stimulating eating, neuropeptide Y appears to reduce energy expenditure (Egawa, Yoshimatsu, and Bray, 1991). It also suppresses ovulation by suppressing gonadotropin release, and it inhibits sexual behavior (Clark, Kalra, and Kalra, 1985). As Wade and his colleagues have shown (Wade, Schneider, and Li, 1996), when the level of available nutrients falls below a certain

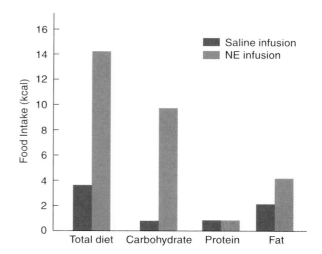

Figure 13.18
Effects of infusion of norepinephrine into the paraventricular nucleus on intake of carbohydrate, protein, and fat.
(Adapted from Leibowitz, S.F., Weiss, G.F., Yee, F., and Tretter, J.B. *Brain Research Bulletin*, 1985, *14*, 561–567.)

noradrenergic axons that enter it disrupts an animal's ability to regulate its carbohydrate intake (Shor-Posner et al., 1986). It is not clear whether the effects of NE stimulate eating directly or whether they do so indirectly, by increasing the secretion of insulin by the pancreas. (If an animal is already in the fasting phase of metabolism, as a rat would normally be at the end of its period of sleep and inactivity, secretion of insulin lowers the blood sugar level and stimulates eating.) Sawchenko, Gold, and Leibowitz (1981) found that after they cut the branch of the vagus nerve that serves the pancreas, animals showed a smaller intake of food when they put NE in the PVN, which suggests that the eating may at least in part be stimulated by the secretion of insulin.

The level of NE release is correlated with an animal's eating habits. Stanley et al. (1989) placed a microdialysis probe in the paraventricular nucleus of rats and recorded the level of extracellular NE across the sleep–waking cycle. The investigators found that the level of NE showed a sharp rise just after the onset of the dark phase of the light cycle, at about the time when the animals ate their first meal. (See *Figure 13.19.*)

So far, little is known about the control of NE secretion in the PVN. Perhaps the activity of the noradrenergic neurons is regulated by signals from nutrient detectors in the brain stem and liver, by taste signals from the tongue and by information from the suprachiasmatic nucleus, that the active period of the light–dark cycle has begun.

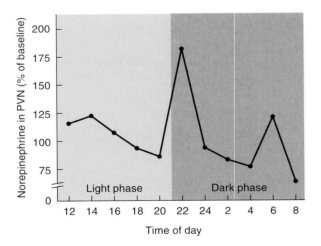

Figure 13.19
Extracellular norepinephrine levels in the paraventricular nucleus during the light and dark phases of the day–night cycle, as measured by microdialysis.
(Adapted from Stanley, B.G., Schwartz, D.H., Hernandez, L., Hoebel, B.G., and Leibowitz, S.F. *Life Sciences*, 1989, 45, 275–282.)

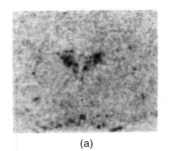 

(a) (b)

0.5 mm

Figure 13.20
Autoradiogram of cells that express mRNA for galanin in the paraventricular nucleus of a rat that preferred a low-fat diet (a) and a rat that preferred a high-fat diet (b).
(From Akabayashi, A., Koenig, J.I., Watanabe, Y., Alexander, J.T., and Leibowitz, S.F. *Proceedings of the National Academy of Sciences*, 1994, 91, 10375–10379. Reprinted by permission.)

Another peptide, **galanin,** is colocalized with norepinephrine in terminal buttons in the hypothalamus (Melander et al., 1987). Thus, these two substances are released together. Infusion of galanin into the PVN produces eating. In particular, when rats that receive such an infusion are permitted to choose among carbohydrates, fats, and proteins, they choose to eat fats (Tempel, Leibowitz, and Leibowitz, 1988). Infusion of galanin also alters the secretion of insulin and corticosterone, which indicates that it has metabolic as well as behavioral effects (Tempel and Leibowitz, 1990), and rats that show a natural preference for a high-fat diet have higher levels of galanin in the PVN (Akabayashi et al., 1994). (See *Figure 13.20.*) A neuroanatomical study by Horvath et al. (1996) found that NPY-secreting terminals appear to form synapses with galanin-secreting neurons. Otherwise, little is known about the control of galanin secretion.

Role in Satiety

One of the most striking effects of a localized brain lesion is the overeating and obesity that is produced by a lesion of the ventromedial hypothalamus (VMH). The simplest explanation for a brain lesion causing an increase in eating is that it damages satiety mechanisms, and this explanation was accepted for many years. However, the *VMH syndrome* (the set of behaviors that accompany these lesions) turns out to be much more complex than a loss of inhibitory control of eating. Animals with VMH lesions are "finicky"; they will not overeat if some quinine is added to

galanin *(gal a nin)* A peptide neurotransmitter whose release stimulates ingestion of fats.

their diet (Ferguson and Keesey, 1975). If given a choice of different diets, animals with VMH lesions will primarily overeat carbohydrates (Sclafani and Aravich, 1983). And in addition to affecting behavior, VMH lesions disrupt the control of the autonomic nervous system. In particular, they cause an increase in parasympathetic activity of the vagus nerve, which stimulates the secretion of insulin and inhibits the secretion of glucagon and adrenal catecholamines (Weingarten, Chang, and McDonald, 1985). Thus, the liver and adipose tissue of an animal with a VMH lesion are unable to release their nutrients during the fasting phase of metabolism; although the nutrient reservoirs are full, their contents are inaccessible. Consequently, the animal *has* to eat to keep up the supply of nutrients in its blood.

The VMH syndrome is complex anatomically as well as behaviorally. In fact, VMH lesions destroy not only the ventromedial hypothalamus but also axons that connect the paraventricular nucleus of the hypothalamus (PVN) with structures in the brain stem. Kirchgessner and Sclafani (1988) found that the destination of the axons from cells in the VMH and the PVN seems to be the nucleus of the solitary tract and the dorsal motor nucleus of the vagus. As we just saw, the nucleus of the solitary tract receives nutrient-related information from the tongue, stomach, duodenum, and liver; thus, changes in its activity could affect an animal's intake of food. The dorsal motor nucleus of the vagus nerve controls the activity of the parasympathetic axons that stimulate insulin secretion; thus, the increased insulin secretion produced by VMH lesions may be caused by disruption of this pathway.

As we saw in the previous subsection, the release of NE and NPY increases food intake. The release of another transmitter substance, 5-HT, has the opposite effect: It *inhibits* the eating of carbohydrates. The inhibitory effects of 5-HT are not precisely localized; Leibowitz, Weiss, and Suh (1990) found that injections of 5-HT into the PVN, VMH, and suprachiasmatic nucleus (SCN) all suppressed carbohydrate intake. This effect occurred only if the neurotransmitter was injected early in the dark part of the day–night cycle, when rats normally eat a high-carbohydrate meal. Perhaps, the authors suggested, the 5-HT interferes with a signal that originates in the SCN, which (as you learned in Chapter 9) serves as the circadian pacemaker.

Drugs that destroy serotonergic neurons, inhibit the synthesis of 5-HT, or block 5-HT receptors have an effect opposite that of 5-HT: They *increase* food intake, especially carbohydrates (Breisch, Zemlan, and Hoebel, 1976; Saller and Stricker, 1976; Stallone and Nicolaïdis, 1989). Dryden et al. (1995) found that an IP injection of methysergide, a 5-HT antagonist, increased the secretion of NPY in the hy-

pothalamus and (as you might expect) increased food intake. This finding suggests that 5-HT somehow inhibits the activity of NPY neurons.

As we will see later, a 5-HT agonist, **fenfluramine (FEN),** is often used to suppress appetite in obese people who are trying to lose weight. The appetite-suppressing effects of FEN do not take place in the PVN; Fletcher et al. (1993) found that IP injections of the drug still decreased food intake after the PVN had been destroyed. And although 5-HT receptors are found outside the brain, injections of fenfluramine still activate neurons in the AP/NST and parabrachial nucleus (as measured by the production of Fos protein) even after the vagus nerve has been cut (Li and Rowland, 1995). Thus, 5-HT receptors in the brain but outside the PVN alter the activity of neurons that play a role in eating. At least one site of action of FEN could be in the brain stem; Li, Spector, and Rowland (1994) found that the appetite-suppressing effect of the drug was reduced after destruction of the lateral parabrachial nucleus.

As we saw, leptin, a hormone secreted by well-fed adipose tissue, has an inhibitory effect on eating. The interaction of this long-term satiety signal with neural circuits involved in hunger are now being discovered. Leptin appears to produce its effects by binding with receptors in the brain. Schwartz et al. (1996) found that infusions of leptin into the cerebral ventricles, which inhibit eating, also inhibit the production of neuropeptide Y in the arcuate nucleus. As you will recall, the arcuate nucleus contains the largest concentration of NPY-secreting neurons, and the axons of these neurons project to the PVN and to other regions of the hypothalamus involved in hunger and the control of metabolism. Two double-labeling studies (Hakansson et al., 1996; Mercer et al., 1996) found that neuropeptide Y–secreting neurons in the PVN contain leptin receptors. (See *Figure 13.21.*)

Glaum et al. (1996) obtained direct evidence that activation of leptin receptors on NPY-secreting neurons in the arcuate nucleus has an inhibitory effect. They used micropipettes to record postsynaptic potentials from these neurons while infusing small amounts of chemicals by means of iontophoresis. They found that infusion of glutamate produced excitatory postsynaptic potentials and that infusion of leptin decreased the magnitude of these potentials. These findings suggest that glutamatergic input to the arcuate nucleus excites NPY-secreting cells, resulting in hunger and metabolic changes associated with the fasting phase of metabolism, and that leptin inhibits these effects. (See *Figure 13.22.*)

fenfluramine (FEN)   A drug that causes the release of serotonin and inhibits eating.

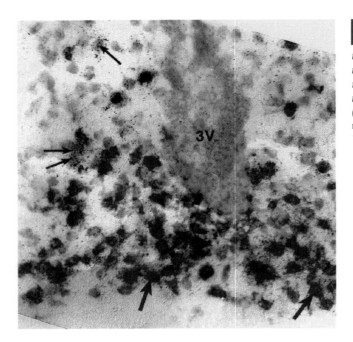

Figure 13.21
Double-labeling of cells in the arcuate nucleus of the hypothalamus that express mRNA for leptin receptors (black grains) and neuropeptide Y (dark purple color). Large arrows point to neurons that contain mRNA for both leptin receptors and neuropeptide; small arrows point to neurons that contain mRNA for only leptin receptors.
(From Mercer, J.G., Hoggard, N., Williams, L.M., Lawrence, C.B., Hannah, L.T., Morgan, P.J., and Trayhurn, P. *Journal of Neuroendocrinology*, 1996, 8, 733–735. Reprinted by permission.)

leptin must have other effects beside inhibition of NPY release. They also suggest that NPY is not the only appetite-promoting neurotransmitter.

Interim Summary

The brain stem contains neural circuits that are able to control acceptance or rejection of sweet or bitter foods and can even be modulated by satiation or physiological hunger signals, such as a decrease in glucose metabolism or the presence of food in the digestive system. The nucleus of the solitary tract and area postrema (AP/NST) receive signals from the tongue, stomach, small intestine, and liver and send the information on to the lateral parabrachial nucleus of the pons, which passes the information on to many regions of the forebrain. These signals interact and help control food intake. Lesions of the AP/NST disrupt both glucoprivic and lipoprivic eating, whereas lesions of the lateral parabrachial nucleus disrupt only liproprivic eating.

Stimulation of the lateral hypothalamus with electricity or excitatory amino acids produces eating, while lesions or infusion of glutamate antagonists decreases eating. The release of neuropeptide Y in the lateral hypothalamus induces ravenous eating. When NPY is infused in the paraventricular nucleus, it decreases metabolic rate. The cell bodies of most NPY-secreting neurons are located in the arcuate nucleus, the region that controls the secretion of the anterior pituitary gland. Glucoprivation caused by injection of 2-DG into the cerebral ventricles increases the activity of NPY-secreting neurons. Neuropeptide Y also suppresses sexual behavior and stops ovulation—responses that occur when food is scarce. Secretion of another peptide, galanin, increases the intake of fats.

The first meal of the active portion of the dark–light cycle tends to be high in carbohydrates. It is preceded by a large increase in norepinephrine in the PVN. In addition, when NE is infused into the PVN, the animal eats—especially carbohydrates. The response may be a result of changes in the activity of the autonomic nervous system as well as direct stimulation of circuits that control eating.

Lesions of the ventromedial hypothalamus produce overeating and obesity, and electrical or chemical stimula-

Erickson, Hollopeter, and Palmiter (1996) prepared a targeted mutation of the gene responsible for production of NPY in ob mice. Thus, the mice had two mutations: a natural one that prevented them from producing leptin, and a genetically engineered one, preventing them from producing NPY. If the only effect of leptin were to inhibit the release of NPY, we would expect these mice to be thin. But Erickson et al. found that their body weight was about midway between that of a normal mouse and an ob mouse without the targeted mutation. These findings indicate that

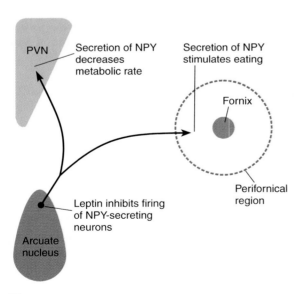

Figure 13.22
A schematic diagram of the interactions between leptin and NPY-secreting neurons.

tion of this area inhibits eating. However, this region is not a simple "satiety center." The lesions make an animal finicky and increase the secretion of insulin (thus forcing the animal to eat more). Some (perhaps most) of the VMH syndrome is caused by damage to fibers that innervate the nucleus of the solitary tract and the dorsal motor nucleus of the vagus. This damage increases fat storage as well as eating.

Another transmitter substance, 5-HT, has an inhibitory effect on eating in the PVN. Although investigators suggest that 5-HT is involved in satiety, it appears to be secreted even before a meal is consumed. The most common appetite suppressant, fenfluramine, is a 5-HT agonist.

Leptin, the long-term satiety hormone secreted by well-stocked adipose tissue, desensitizes the brain to hunger signals. It binds with receptors in the arcuate nucleus of the hypothalamus, where it inhibits NPY-secreting neurons, increasing metabolic rate and suppressing eating.

EATING DISORDERS

Unfortunately, some people are susceptible to the development of eating disorders. Some people grow obese, even though our society regards this condition as unattractive and even though obese people tend to have more health problems—and to die sooner—than people of normal weight. Other people (especially young women) can become obsessed with losing weight, eating little and increasing their activity level until their body weight becomes extremely low—sometimes fatally so. Others manage to keep from losing or gaining weight, but often lose control of intake, eating enormous amounts of food and then taking strong laxatives or forcing themselves to vomit. Has what we have learned about the physiology of appetite helped us understand these conditions?

● Obesity

Obesity is a widespread problem that can have serious medical consequences. In the United States, approximately 34 million people are overweight, 12.5 million of them severely so (Kuczmarski, 1992). The known health hazards include hypertension, diabetes, and cardiovascular disease (Pi-Sunyer, 1991). The economic costs from obesity-related diseases in the United States alone have been estimated at over $39 billion per year (Colditz, 1992).

Possible Causes

There are undoubtedly many causes of obesity, including learning and innate or acquired differences in metabolism.

The behavior of eating, like most other behaviors, is subject to modification through learning. Unfortunately, many aspects of modern, industrialized societies tend to weaken physiological controls over eating. For example, as children we learn to eat what is put on our plates; indeed, many children are praised for eating all they have been given and punished for failing to do so. As Birch et al. (1987) showed, the effect of this kind of training can be to make children less sensitive to the nutrient content of their diet. As we get older, our metabolic requirements decrease; and if we continue to eat as we did when we were younger, we tend to accumulate fat. The inhibitory signals associated with food consumption are certainly not absolute; they can be overridden by habit or by the simple pleasure of ingesting good-tasting food. In fact, the arrangement of meals into courses followed by a dessert inhibits the development of sensory-specific satiety and encourages increased food intake.

Obesity is extremely difficult to treat; the enormous financial success of diet books, fat farms, and weight reduction programs attests to the trouble people have losing weight. More precisely, many programs help people lose weight initially, but then the weight is quickly regained. Kramer et al. (1989) reported that four to five years after participating in a fifteen-week behavioral weight loss program, fewer than 3 percent of the participants managed to maintain the weight loss they had achieved during the program. Some experts have suggested that given the extremely low long-term success rate, perhaps we should stop treating people for obesity until our treatments are more successful. As Wooley and Garner (1994) said:

> We should stop offering ineffective treatments aimed at weight loss. Researchers who think they have invented a better mousetrap should test it in controlled research before setting out their bait for the entire population. Only by admitting that our treatments do not work—and showing that we mean it by refraining from offering them—can we begin to undo a century of recruiting fat people for failure. (p. 656)

Many psychological variables have been suggested as causes of obesity, including field dependence, lack of impulse control, poor ability to delay gratification, and maladaptive eating styles (primarily eating too fast). However, in a review of the literature Rodin, Schank, and Striegel-Moore (1989) found that none of these suggestions has received empirical support. Rodin and her colleagues also found that unhappiness and depression seem to be the *effects* of obesity, not its causes, and that dieting behavior seems to make the problem worse.

One reason that many people have so much difficulty losing weight is that metabolic factors appear to play an important role in obesity. In fact, a good case can be made that obesity is most often not an *eating disorder* (despite the title of this section), but a *metabolic disorder*. Rodin and her colleagues found that most studies comparing the amounts of food eaten by obese people and people of normal weight failed to show a significant difference. But unfortunately, we cannot take all these studies at face value. Lichtman et al. (1992) studied a group of obese people who had a history of *diet resistance*—difficulty in losing weight even on a reduced-calorie diet. The investigators made direct measurements of these people's actual intake and physical activity during a fourteen-day stay in a controlled environment and compared these measurements with self-reports. They found that the subjects underreported their actual intake by an average of 47 percent and overreported their physical activity by 51 percent. The subjects were surprised and distressed to learn afterward that their reported figures were so far off the mark; apparently, they were not intentionally trying to deceive the investigators.

Almost all excess body weight is carried in the form of fat. Normally, we carry a certain amount of fat in our long-term nutrient reservoir, making deposits and withdrawals each day during the absorptive and fasting phases of metabolism but keeping the total amount stable. Obesity occurs when deposits exceed withdrawals. We expend energy in two basic ways: through exercise (muscular activity) and through the production of heat. Actually, *most* of our energy expenditure is in the form of heat production; according to Calles-Escandon and Horton (1992), 70–85 percent of a person's energy expenditure is made through the resting metabolism and the energy needed to digest and assimilate food. Physical activity accounts for a small proportion of energy expenditure.

Just as cars differ in their fuel efficiency, so do people. Rose and Williams (1961) studied pairs of people who were matched for weight, height, age, and activity. Some of these matched pairs differed by a factor of two in the number of calories they ate each day. People with an efficient metabolism have calories left over to deposit in the long-term nutrient reservoir; thus, they have difficulty keeping this reservoir from growing. In contrast, people with an inefficient metabolism can eat large meals without getting fat. Thus, whereas a fuel-efficient automobile is desirable, a fuel-efficient body runs the risk of becoming obese.

Nonobese people respond to overeating very differently from obese people. For example, Sims and Horton (1968) enlisted the participation of some prison inmates in an experiment to determine the effects of overeating on body weight. The subjects, men of normal weight, were fed varied and tasty meals several times a day and were asked to eat all they could. Some participants ate up to 8000 calories a day, an enormous quantity for relatively sedentary people. Their weight gain was rather modest, and at the end of the experiment, when the subjects were permitted to select their own diet, they quickly returned to their normal weights.

Differences in body weight (perhaps reflecting differences in metabolism) appear to have a hereditary basis. Twin studies suggest that between 40 and 85 percent of the variability in body fat is due to genetic differences (Price and Gottesman, 1991; De Castro, 1993; Allison et al., 1996). Bouchard (1989, 1991) concluded that heredity probably plays a role in people's resting metabolic rate, in the amount of heat produced by the body after a meal, in the energy expended during exercise, and in the likelihood that ingested calories will be stored as fat. And the family environment in which people are raised apparently has no significant effect on their body weight as adults; Stunkard et al. (1986) found that the body weight of a sample of people who had been adopted as infants was highly correlated with their *biological* parents but not with their *adoptive* parents. Sørrensen et al. (1989) came to similar conclusions in a study comparing adopted people with their full and half siblings, with whom they had not been raised.

Why are there genetic differences in metabolic efficiency? James and Trayhurn (1981) suggested that under some environmental conditions metabolic efficiency is advantageous. That is, in places where food is only intermittently available in sufficient quantities, being able to stay alive on small amounts of food and to store up extra nutrients in the form of fat when food becomes available for a while is a highly adaptive trait. When the famine comes, it is the people with efficient metabolisms and adequate supplies of fat—and their genes—who survive. Therefore, people's metabolic rates may reflect the nature of the environment experienced by their ancestors

James and Trayhurn's hypothesis has received support from epidemiological studies. The tiny island of Nauru, containing only eight square miles of territory, contains a stock of seabird guano, which is now mined for its rich source of phosphate by companies that sell fertilizer. The average per capita income of Nauru suddenly went from very low to one of the highest in the world (Gibbs, 1996). With this wealth came a much less active lifestyle and the ability to buy expensive, imported foods. In the course of a generation the Nauru islanders became some of the most obese people on earth. Ravussin et al. (1994) studied two groups of Pima Indians, who live in the southwestern United States and northwestern Mexico. Members of both groups appear to have the same genetic background; they share the same language and share common historical traditions. The two groups separated 700–1000 years ago and now live under very different environmental conditions. The Pima Indians in the southwestern United States eat a high-fat American diet and weigh an average of 90 kg (198 lb), men and women combined. In contrast, the lifestyle of the Mexican Pimas is probably similar to that of their ancestors. They spend long hours working at subsistence farming and eat a low-fat diet—and weigh an average of 64 kg (141 lb). The cholesterol level of the American Pimas is much higher than that of the Mexican Pimas, and their rate of diabetes is more than five times higher. These findings show that genes that promote an efficient metabolism are of benefit to people who must work hard for their calories, but that these same genes turn into a liability when people live in an environment where the physical demands are low and high-calorie food is cheap and plentiful.

As we saw earlier, study of the ob mouse led to the discovery of leptin, the hormone secreted by well-nourished adipose tissue. The explanation of obesity in the ob mouse was simple: The animals could not produce leptin. Following this discovery, researchers have been trying to determine whether understanding the role of leptin can help us understand at least some of the causes of obesity in humans.

So far, no studies have found evidence that obesity in humans is caused by a deficiency in secretion of leptin. Schwartz et al. (1996) found that plasma levels of leptin were related to total body fat in lean and obese people. It is possible, of course, that a small number of obese people owe their condition to a mutation of the gene responsible for leptin production, just like the mutation that produces the ob mouse. A study by Ravussin et al. (1997) found some evidence for differences in leptin levels of Pima Indians who became obese compared with those who did not. However, most investigators believe that if leptin plays a role in human obesity, the likely mechanism is reduced *sensitivity* to the hormone, and not decreased secretion. Leptin is a peptide, and peptides normally cannot cross the blood–brain barrier. However, an active mechanism transports molecules of leptin across this barrier so that it can exert its behavioral and metabolic effects (Banks et al., 1996; Golden, Maccagnan, and Pardridge, 1997). Caro et al. (1996) suggested that differences in the effectiveness of this transport system may be one cause of obesity. If not much leptin gets across the blood–brain barrier, the leptin signal in the brain will be weaker than it should be. Caro and his colleagues found that although the level of leptin in the blood was 318 percent higher in obese people, it was only 30 percent higher in the cerebrospinal fluid (which is presumably related to the concentration of the hormone in the brain). Another possible cause of leptin insensitivity is a mutation of the gene responsible for production of the leptin receptor. In fact, three strains of obese rodents—the *db mouse*, the *corpulent rat*, and the *Zucker rat*—all have mutations of the leptin receptor gene (Gura, 1997). So far there is no evidence that obese humans have mutations of this gene.

Another mutation found in mice suggests yet another possible cause of hereditary obesity. The **agouti mouse** has a genetic defect that causes bright yellow fur and obesity that shows up later in life, as it often does in humans. (The obesity that is, not the fur.) The mutation does not interfere with the production of a protein—it causes a protein normally produced only in hair follicles to be produced all over the body. The agouti protein is an antagonist of the **melanocortin-4 receptor (MC4-R)**; it binds with and blocks the receptor (Lu et al., 1994). The natural ligand for the MC4 receptor is melanocortin, a hormone that causes the production of melanin, a black pigment found in skin and hair. Until recently, researchers had no reason to suspect that MC4 receptors were found in the brain or that they had anything to do with eating or metabolism. But Mountjoy et al. (1994) found that these receptors can be found in locations throughout the brain, including the arcuate nucleus. Stimulation of these receptors with their natural ligand has an inhibitory effect on eating; Fan et al. (1997) found that injection of MC4-receptor agonists into the cerebral ventricles inhibited eating, while MC4-receptor blockers increased it. In addition, Huszar et al. (1997) found that a targeted mutation of the gene responsible for production of the MC4 receptor caused obesity. The links between MC4 receptors and neural mechanisms that control eating and metabolism are not yet known, but several laboratories are actively pursuing this topic. There is no evidence that the agouti mutation is responsible for obesity in humans, but understanding the function of the MC4 receptor may provide some clues about the factors that regulate body weight.

A review by Roberts and Greenberg (1996) mentions several genetic models that might help researchers understand the causes of obesity. Besides the genetic defects I

agouti mouse   A strain of mice whose yellow fur and obesity are caused by a mutation that causes the production of a peptide that blocks MC4 receptors in the brain.

melanocortin-4 receptor (MC4-R)   A receptor normally stimulated by the hormone melanocortin; responsible for the production of melanin; also plays a role in control of appetite.

have already mentioned, the authors note that the results of recent research suggest four candidate "obesity genes"— genes responsible for the production of chemicals involved in metabolic changes that may make it difficult for some people to remain thin. The functions of *apolipoproteins* are not understood, but they may be involved in the transport of lipids. Another substance, *uncoupling protein*, is involved in heat production. (The production of heat is responsible for most of our energy expenditure.) *Lipoprotein lipase* is an enzyme involved in the uptake of triglycerides into adipose tissue and muscles, and *sodium-potassium ATPase* is an enzyme involved in the oxidation of fat. In addition, some evidence suggests that mutations of the gene responsible for the production of adrenergic β_3 receptors (found on fat cells) may make it more difficult for adipose tissue to release lipids when it is stimulated to do so by activity of the sympathetic nervous system (Clément et al., 1995).

Treatment of Obesity

Whatever the cause of obesity, the metabolic fact of life is this: If calories in exceed calories out, then body fat will increase. Because it is difficult to increase the "calories out" side of the equation enough to bring an obese person's weight back to normal, most treatments for obesity attempt to reduce the "calories in." The extraordinary difficulty that obese people have in reducing caloric intake for a sustained period of time (that is, for the rest of their lives) has led to the development of some extraordinary means. In this section I shall describe mechanical, surgical, and pharmacological methods that have been devised to make obese people eat less.

Eating requires that we open our mouths. This obvious fact led to the development of jaw wiring, a procedure in which wires are attached to a person's teeth to keep the jaw from opening. The patient is not left to starve; he or she is given a liquid diet to sip through a straw. Of course, there is no guarantee that a person will ingest fewer calories each day simply because he or she is deprived of the opportunity to chew. In fact, Munro et al. (1987) reported that some of their patients managed to *gain* weight on a liquid diet. However, many patients do manage to lose weight. Unfortunately, almost all of them regain it once the wires are removed, and many become even more obese than when they started out.

To reduce the recidivism rate, some therapists have fastened a nylon cord around the waist of their patients after they had lost weight through a jaw-wiring procedure. The ends of the cord were fused together so that the cord could not be removed without cutting it. Unfortunately, about half of the patients did just that.

Surgeons have also become involved in trying to help obese people lose weight. The procedures they have developed either reduce the amount of food that can be eaten during a meal or interfere with absorption of calories from the intestines. Surgery has been aimed at the stomach, the small intestine, or both.

The most common surgical procedure for reducing food intake has been to make the person's stomach smaller. Early procedures actually removed some of the stomach, but more recent methods have stapled part of it shut or have put bands around it so that it can expand only a limited amount—a procedure known as *gastroplasty* (literally, "a reshaping of the stomach"). Ideally, gastroplasty should result in a feeling of satiety after the ingestion of a small amount of food. But in fact, the surgery usually produces *nimiety,* or an aversive feeling of overfullness (from the Latin *nimius,* "excessive"). The meal stops not because the patients feel satisfied but because they feel so uncomfortable they cannot go on.

Surgeons have developed several procedures that reduce the absorption of food from the intestines. All of these procedures rearrange the intestines so that food takes a shorter path to the large intestine, leaving less time for nutrients to be absorbed. The unabsorbed nutrients are evacuated from the body, of course, so it should come as no surprise that diarrhea and flatulence (excessive intestinal gas) are commonly associated with these procedures. Many types of intestinal bypass operations do not simply interfere with absorption—they also reduce food intake by producing nimiety. After some surgical procedures, relatively undigested food is dumped into regions of the intestines that normally receive only well-digested food, and the result is a feeling of discomfort.

Besides producing diarrhea and flatulence, intestinal bypass surgery can produce undesirable side effects such as bacterial overgrowth and production of toxins in a bypassed segment of intestine; deficiencies of iron, vitamin B_{12}, vitamin B_1, or protein; and abnormalities in calcium metabolism. A severe vitamin B_1 (thiamine) deficiency can damage the nervous system; as you will learn in Chapter 15, the result can be a permanent memory loss. Of course, if a patient's condition is carefully monitored by a physician after receiving the surgery, these complications can be avoided or corrected; but not all patients cooperate with their physicians for postsurgical care.

To avoid the necessity of surgery, some therapists have tried putting balloons in people's stomachs and then inflating them to reduce the amount of food they will hold. The results have not been entirely successful; as Kral (1989) noted, "After a brief period of extraordinary financial success for the gastroenterologists placing the balloons, the 'Gastric Bubble' has been taken off the market in the United States, largely because of proven lack of efficacy and the realization that chronic balloon placement is not tolerated by the gastric mucosa" (p. 254).

A less drastic form of therapy for obesity—drug treatment—shows some promise. As we saw earlier in this chapter, serotonergic agonists suppress eating. A review by Bray (1992) concluded that serotonin agonists can be of benefit in weight loss programs. The use of fenfluramine, a drug that directly stimulates the release of 5-HT, has recently been approved by the Federal Drug Administration of the United States. (The drug has been in use for several years in other countries.) Figure 13.23 shows the effects of this drug on the body weight of a group of 176 patients. As you can see, the patients showed a stable weight loss during the twelve months they took the drug but then largely regained their weight after they discontinued it. (See *Figure 13.23.*) More recent studies (for example, O'Connor et al., 1995) have obtained similar results; patients regain their weight after the drug is discontinued, even if they remain in weight loss programs.

As Bray noted, regulatory agencies are reluctant to endorse the long-term use of drugs to treat obesity, which is most assuredly a chronic problem. Certainly, drugs such as fenfluramine do not *cure* obesity; but then many drugs in common use do not cure the conditions they are used for.

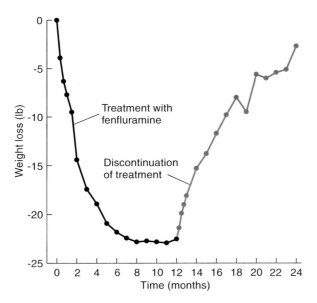

Figure 13.23
Mean weight change during twelve months of treatment with fenfluramine.
(Adapted from Bray, 1992; after Hudson, K.D. *Journal of the Royal College of General Practitioners*, 1977, *27*, 497–501.)

For example, glaucoma is treated by pilocaprine; if the drug is discontinued, the glaucoma will recur. In contrast, according to Bray, physicians have been disciplined by regulatory boards for prescribing appetite-suppressing drugs for more than a few weeks. He suggested that this double standard is based on the common belief that obesity results from a failure of will—that people could lose weight if they would only push themselves away from the table sooner.

The variety of methods—surgical, mechanical, behavioral, and pharmacological—that therapists and surgeons have developed to treat obesity attests to the tenacity of the problem. The basic difficulty, beyond that caused by having an efficient metabolism, is that eating is pleasurable and satiety signals are easy to ignore or override. Despite the fact that relatively little success has been seen until now, I am personally optimistic about what the future may hold. I think that if we learn more about the physiology of hunger signals, satiety signals, and the reinforcement provided by eating, we will be able to develop safe and effective drugs that attenuate the signals that encourage us to eat and strengthen those that encourage us to stop eating. Of course, we will also have to overcome our prejudices against the long-term use of these drugs.

Do the discoveries of the antiobesity effects of leptin and of activation of the MC4 receptor hold any promise for the treatment of obesity? Is there any possibility that researchers will find drugs that will stimulate leptin or MC4 receptors—or perhaps block neuropeptide Y receptors—thus decreasing people's appetite and increasing the rate at which they metabolize fats? Unfortunately there is no immediate prospect of such medications. As we saw, the level of leptin is high in most obese people, so increasing it would probably not be of benefit. If the reason for their leptin insensitivity is an inefficient transport mechanism of leptin molecules through the blood–brain barrier, then perhaps pharmacologists will be able to discover a leptin receptor agonist that will pass through this barrier, bypassing the transport system. In a review of recent research on obesity, Gibbs (1996) presented a list of potential antiobesity medications that are currently being developed by drug companies. Researchers are targeting both behavioral and metabolic variables controlled by the brain, the digestive system, fat tissues, and muscles. (See *Table 13.1.*)

● Anorexia Nervosa/Bulimia Nervosa

Most people, if they have an eating problem, tend to overeat. However, some people, especially young adolescent women, have the opposite problem: They eat too little, even to the point of starvation. This disorder is called

Table 13.1
Antiobesity Drugs Under Development or Recently Approved

Tissue	Drug name	Action	Status
Brain	Dexfenfluramine	Stimulates release of 5-HT	Approved
	Sibutramine	5-HT and NE agonist	Submitted for approval
	NPY inhibitors	Block NPY receptors or production of NPY	Clinical tests of safety
	Bromocriptine	DA agonist; may reduce blood sugar level and fat production by liver	Clinical tests of efficacy
Brain and digestive system	CCK$_A$ promoters	Upregulate CCK$_A$ receptors	Laboratory research
	Butabindide	Blocks enzyme that deactivates CCK	Laboratory research
Digestive system	Orlistat	Inhibits pancreatic enzyme that participates in fat digestion	Approval imminent
	Insulinotropin	Synthetic hormone that may increase insulin levels and slow gastric emptying	Clinical tests of efficacy
Adipose tissue	Bta-243	β_3 agonist that stimulates breakdown of triglycerides	Laboratory research
Muscles	Troglitazone	Synthetic hormone that promotes fatty-acid metabolism in muscle cells.	Approved in Japan; clinical tests of efficacy in U.S.

Source: Adapted from W. W. Gibbs, Gaining on fat. *Scientific American,* 1996, 88–94.

anorexia nervosa. Another eating disorder, **bulimia nervosa,** is characterized by a loss of control of food intake. (The term *bulimia* comes from the Greek *bous,* "ox," and *limos,* "hunger.") People with bulimia nervosa periodically gorge themselves with food, especially dessert or snack food, and especially in the afternoon or evening. These binges are usually followed by self-induced vomiting or the use of laxatives, along with feelings of depression and guilt (Mawson, 1974; Halmi, 1978). With this combination of binging and purging, the net nutrient intake (and consequently, the body weight) of bulimics can vary; Weltzin et al. (1991) reported that 44 percent of bulimics undereat, 37 percent eat a normal amount, and 44 percent overeat. Episodes of bulimia are seen in some patients with anorexia nervosa.

The literal meaning of the word *anorexia* suggests a loss of appetite, but people with this disorder are usually interested in—even preoccupied with—food. They may enjoy preparing meals for others to consume, collect recipes, and even hoard food that they do not eat. Broberg and Bernstein (1989) presented anorexic and lean (but nonanorexic) young women with a warm, appetizing cinnamon roll. They cut the roll and said that they could eat it if they wanted. For the next 10 minutes the experimenters withdrew blood samples and analyzed the insulin content. They found that both groups of subjects showed an increase in insulin level; surprisingly, the increase was even higher in the anorexic subjects. Thus, we cannot conclude that anorexics are simply unresponsive to food. (See *Figure 13.24.*) Incidentally, as you might expect, the normal subjects ate the roll, but the anorexics did not, saying that they were not hungry.

Although anorexics may not be oblivious to the effects of food, they express an intense fear of becoming obese, which continues even if they become dangerously thin. Many exercise by cycling, running, or almost constant walking and pacing. Studies with animals suggest that the increased activity may be a result of the fasting. When rats are deprived of food, they will spend more and more time

anorexia nervosa   A disorder that most frequently afflicts young women; exaggerated concern with overweight that leads to excessive dieting and often compulsive exercising; can lead to starvation.

bulimia nervosa   Bouts of excessive hunger and eating, often followed by forced vomiting or purging with laxatives; sometimes seen in people with anorexia nervosa.

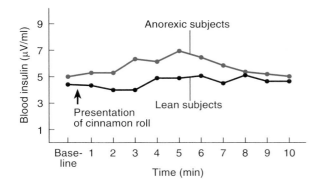

Figure 13.24
Effects of the sight and smell of a warm cinnamon roll on insulin secretion in anorexic women and thin, nonanorexic women. (Adapted from Broberg, D.J., and Bernstein, I.L. *Physiology and Behavior,* 1989, 45, 871–874.)

running in a wheel if one is available, even though doing so means that the animals will lose weight faster (Routtenberg, 1968). Some investigators believe that the exercise stimulates the breakdown of lipids into fatty acids and glycerol and thus actually reduces feelings of hunger. Wilckens, Schweiger, and Pirke (1992) found that deprivation-induced wheel running can be inhibited by drugs that stimulate 5-HT_{1C} receptors.

The fact that anorexia nervosa is seen primarily in young women has prompted both biological and social explanations. Most psychologists favor the latter, concluding that the emphasis our society places on slimness—especially in women—is responsible for this disorder. However, the success of therapy is not especially encouraging; Ratnasuriya et al. (1991) reported that twenty years later, only 29 percent of a group of patients treated for anorexia nervosa showed a good recovery. Almost 15 percent of the patients had died of suicide or complications of the disease. Many anorexics suffer from osteoporosis, and bone fractures are common. When the weight loss becomes severe enough, they cease menstruating. Some disturbing reports (Artmann et al., 1985; Herholz, 1996; Kingston et al., 1996) indicate that CT scans revealed enlarged ventricles and widened sulci, which indicates shrinkage of brain tissue. The widened sulci, but not the enlarged ventricles, apparently return to normal after recovery.

There is good evidence, primarily from twin studies, that hereditary factors play an important role in the development of anorexia (Russell and Treasure, 1989; Walters and Kendler, 1995). The existence of hereditary factors suggests that abnormalities in physiological mechanisms may be involved. As you might suspect, many investigators have

suggested that anorexia and bulimia may be caused by biochemical or structural abnormalities in the brain mechanisms that control metabolism or eating. In a review of the literature Fava et al. (1989) reported that studies have found evidence for changes in NE, 5-HT, and opioids in people with anorexia nervosa, and changes in NE and 5-HT in people with bulimia nervosa. Many studies have reported changes in endocrine levels of anorexic patients, but these changes are probably effects of the disorder, not causes. In most cases, when a patient recovers, the endocrine system returns to normal.

Some investigators have suggested that neuropeptide Y may play a role in anorexia (Kaye et al., 1990; Kaye, 1996). Kaye and his colleagues found elevated levels of NPY in the cerebrospinal fluid of severely underweight anorexics. However, once the patients regained their normal weights, the levels of the peptide returned to normal. The investigators suggested that the increased level of NPY is a response to the loss of weight and at least partly accounts for the obsession with food that is typical in anorexia. In addition, the high level of NPY is probably responsible for the absence of menstruation in these patients. (You will recall that neuropeptide Y suppresses ovulation in laboratory animals.)

We cannot rule out the possibility that some biochemical disturbance in brain functions related to metabolism or food intake underlie anorexia nervosa. Measurement of neurotransmitters, neuromodulators, and their metabolites in the cerebrospinal fluid is a crude and indirect indication of the release and activity of these substances in the brain. Unfortunately, we do not have a good animal model of anorexia to study in the laboratory.

Researchers have tried to treat anorexia nervosa with many drugs that increase appetite in nonanorexics or in laboratory animals—for example, antipsychotic medications, drugs that stimulate adrenergic α_2 receptors, L-DOPA, and THC (the active ingredient in marijuana). Unfortunately, none of these drugs have shown themselves to be helpful (Mitchell, 1989). One study (Halmi et al., 1986) found that cyproheptadine, an antihistaminergic drug that also has an antiserotonergic effect, may speed the recovery of anorexics. The drug only aided patients who did not exhibit bulimia; the drug actually interfered with the recovery of those who did exhibit bulimia. These results have not yet been confirmed by other investigators. And in any event, the fact that anorexics are usually obsessed with food (and show high levels of neuropeptide Y in their CSF) suggests that the disorder is not caused by the absence of hunger. Researchers have had better luck with bulimia nervosa; several studies suggest that serotonin agonists such as fenfluramine (also used to treat obesity) and fluoxetine (an antidepressant drug best known as Prozac) may aid in the treatment of this disorder (Kennedy and Goldbloom, 1991; Advokat and Kutlesic, 1995).

Anorexia nervosa is a serious condition; understanding its causes is more than an academic matter. We can hope that research on the biological and social control of feeding and metabolism will help us understand this puzzling and dangerous disorder.

Interim Summary

Two sets of eating disorders, obesity and anorexia/bulimia nervosa, present serious health problems. Although environmental effects, such as learning to eat everything on the plate and arranging food in appetizing courses, may contribute to overeating, the most important cause appears to be an efficient metabolism, which permits fat to accumulate easily. Metabolic rates are controlled by hereditary and environmental factors. Adoption studies find no evidence that a person's early family environment has a significant effect on his or her body weight in adulthood. But other environmental factors do play an important role in the development of obesity. A high percentage of Pima Indians who live in the United States and consume a high-fat diet become obese and, as a consequence, develop diabetes. In contrast, Mexican Pima Indians, who work hard at subsistence farming and eat a low-fat diet, remain thin and have a low incidence of obesity.

So far, there is little evidence that obesity in humans is related to a deficient secretion of leptin, as it is in ob mice; in general, obese people have very high levels of leptin in their blood. Nor is there good evidence that obese people have faulty leptin receptors, as do db mice and Zucker rats.

One possible reason for insensitivity to leptin in obese people might be inefficient transport of leptin through the blood–brain barrier.

The agouti mouse has a genetic defect that produces yellow fur and obesity. The mutation responsible for this syndrome causes the production of the agouti protein all over the body, which blocks the brain's melanocortin-4 receptors. Other possible "obesity genes" are those responsible for production of proteins involved in control of metabolism.

Researchers have tried many mechanical, surgical, and pharmacological treatments for obesity, but no panacea has yet been found. The best hope probably comes from drugs; specific serotonin agonists suppress eating and decrease body weight, but so far the medical community has been reluctant to use such drugs on a long-term basis. At present, many pharmaceutical companies are trying to apply the results of the discoveries described in this chapter to the development of antiobesity drugs.

Anorexia nervosa is a serious—even life-threatening—disorder. Although anorexic patients avoid eating, they often remain preoccupied with food, and their insulin level rises when they are presented with an appetizing stimulus. Bulimia nervosa (sometimes associated with anorexia) consists of periodic binging and purging.

Researchers are beginning to study possible abnormalities in the regulation of transmitter substances and neuropeptides that seem to play a role in normal control of feeding to see whether medical treatments for anorexia and bulimia can be discovered. So far, no useful drugs have been found to treat anorexia nervosa; but fenfluramine—a serotonin agonist also used to treat obesity—and fluoxetine—a serotonin agonist used to treat depression—may help suppress episodes of bulimia.

SUGGESTED READINGS

Bouchard, C., and Bray, G.A. *Regulation of Body Weight: Biological and Behavioral Mechanisms.* New York: John Wiley & Sons, 1996.

Brownell, K.D., and Fairburn, C.G. *Eating Disorders and Obesity: A Comprehensive Handbook.* New York: Guilford Press, 1995.

Capaldi, E.D. *Why We Eat What We Eat: The Psychology of Eating.* Washington, DC: American Psychological Association, 1996.

Friedman, M.I., Tordoff, M.G., and Kare, M.R. *Chemical Senses. Vol. 4: Appetite and Nutrition.* New York: Dekker, 1991.

Legg, C.R., and Booth, D.A. *Appetite: Neural and Behavioural Bases.* Oxford: Oxford University Press, 1994.

Le Magnen, J. *Neurobiology of Feeding and Nutrition.* San Diego: Academic Press, 1992.

Ritter, S., Ritter, R.C., and Barnes, C.D. *Neuroanatomy and Physiology of Abdominal Vagal Afferents.* Boca Raton, FL: CRC Press, 1992.

Stricker, E.M. *Handbook of Behavioral Neurobiology. Vol. 10. Neurobiology of Food and Fluid Intake.* New York: Plenum Press, 1990.

CHAPTER 14

Learning and Memory: Basic Mechanisms

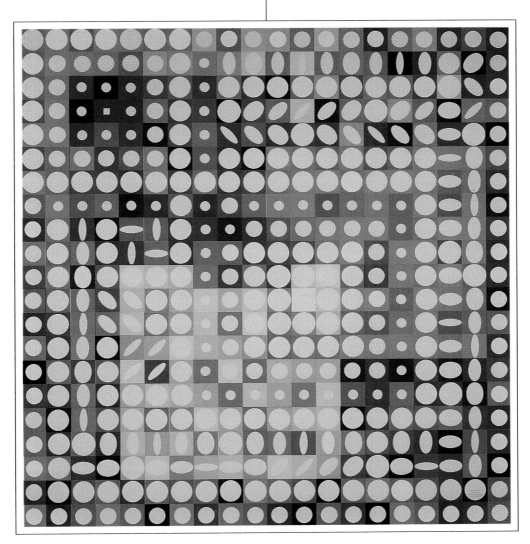

Orion by Victor Vasarely.

E xperiences change us; encounters with our environment alter our behavior by modifying our nervous system. As many investigators have said, an understanding of the physiology of memory is the ultimate challenge to neuroscience research. The brain is complex, and so is learning and remembering. Although the individual changes that occur within the cells of the brain may be relatively simple, the brain consists of many billions of neurons. Therefore, isolating and identifying the particular changes that are responsible for a particular memory is exceedingly difficult. Similarly, although the elements of a particular learning task may be simple, its implications for an organism may be complex. The behavior that the investigator observes and measures may be only one of many that change as a result of an experience. However, despite the difficulties, the long years of work finally seem to be paying off. New approaches and new methods have evolved from old ones, and real progress has been made in understanding the anatomy and physiology of learning and remembering.

THE NATURE OF LEARNING

Learning refers to the process by which experiences change our nervous system and hence our behavior. We refer to these changes as *memories*. Although it is convenient to describe memories as if they were notes placed in filing cabinets, this is certainly not the way experiences are reflected within the brain. Experiences are not "stored"; rather, they change the way we perceive, perform, think, and plan. They do so by physically changing the structure of the nervous system, altering neural circuits that participate in perceiving, performing, thinking, and planning.

The primary function of the ability to learn is to develop behaviors that are adapted to an ever-changing environment. The ability to learn permits us to find food when we are hungry, warmth when we are cold, companions when we are lonely. It also permits us to avoid objects or situations that might harm us. However, the fact that the ultimate function of learning is a useful change in behavior does not mean that learning takes place only in the parts of the brain that control movement. Learning can take at least four basic forms: perceptual learning, stimulus-response learning, motor learning, and relational learning. This chapter discusses the first three forms, and Chapter 15 discusses relational learning.

Perceptual learning is the ability to learn to recognize stimuli that have been perceived before. The primary function of this type of learning is the ability to identify and categorize objects (including other members of our own species) and situations. Unless we have learned to recognize something, we cannot learn how we should behave with respect to it—we will not profit from our experiences with it, and profiting from experience is what learning is all about.

Each of our sensory systems is capable of perceptual learning. We can learn to recognize objects by their visual appearance, the sounds they make, how they feel, or how they smell. We can recognize people by the shape of their

perceptual learning Learning to recognize a particular stimulus.

faces, the movements they make when they walk, or the sound of their voices. When we hear people talk, we can recognize the words they are saying and, perhaps, their emotional state. As we shall see, perceptual learning appears to be accomplished primarily by changes in the sensory association cortex. That is, learning to recognize complex visual stimuli involves changes in the visual association cortex, learning to recognize complex auditory stimuli involves changes in the auditory association cortex, and so on. (Very simple stimuli, such as changes in brightness, do not require the neocortex; learning that involves these stimuli can be accomplished by subcortical components of the sensory systems.)

Stimulus-response learning is the ability to learn to perform a particular behavior when a particular stimulus is present. Thus, it involves the establishment of connections between circuits involved in perception and those involved in movement. The behavior could be an automatic response such as a defensive reflex, or it could be a complicated sequence of movements that was learned previously. Stimulus-response learning includes two major categories of learning that psychologists have studied extensively: *classical conditioning* and *instrumental conditioning*.

Classical conditioning is a form of learning in which an unimportant stimulus acquires the properties of an important one. It involves an *association between two stimuli*. A stimulus that previously had little effect on behavior becomes able to evoke a reflexive, species-typical behavior. For example, a defensive eyeblink response can be conditioned to a tone. If we direct a brief puff of air toward a rabbit's eye, the eye will automatically blink. The response is called an **unconditional response (UR)** because it occurs unconditionally, without any special training. The stimulus that produces it (the puff of air) is called an **unconditional stimulus (US)**. Now we begin the training. We present a series of brief 1000-Hz tones, each followed 500 ms later by a puff of air. After several trials, the rabbit's eye begins to close even before the puff of air occurs. Classical conditioning has occurred; the **conditional stimulus (CS—the 1000-Hz tone)** now elicits the **conditional response (CR—the eye blink)**. (See *Figure 14.1*.)

When classical conditioning takes place, what kinds of changes occur in the brain? Figure 14.1 shows a simplified neural circuit that could account for this type of learning. For the sake of simplicity, we will assume that the US (the puff of air) is detected by a single neuron in the somatosensory system, and the CS (the 1000-Hz tone) is detected by a single neuron in the auditory system. We will also assume that the response—the eyeblink—is controlled by a single neuron in the motor system. (See *Figure 14.1*.)

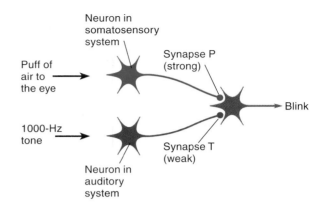

Figure 14.1
A simple neural model of classical conditioning. When the 1000-Hz tone is presented just before the puff of air to the eye, synapse T is strengthened.

Now let us see how the circuits work. If we present a 1000-Hz tone, we find that the animal makes no reaction, because the synapse connecting the tone-sensitive neuron with the neuron in the motor system is weak. However, if we present a puff of air to the eye, the eye blinks. This reaction occurs because nature has provided the animal with a strong synapse between the somatosensory neuron and the motor neuron that causes a blink (synapse P, for "puff"). To establish classical conditioning, we first present the 1000-Hz tone and then almost immediately follow it with a puff of air. After we repeat these pairs of stimuli several times, we find that we can dispense with the air puff; the 1000-Hz tone produces the blink all by itself.

Over forty years ago, Donald Hebb proposed a rule that might explain how neurons are changed by experience in a way that would cause changes in behavior (Hebb, 1949). The **Hebb rule** says that if a synapse repeatedly becomes ac-

stimulus-response learning   Learning to make a particular response automatically in the presence of a particular stimulus; includes classical and instrumental conditioning.

classical conditioning   A learning procedure; when a stimulus that initially produces no particular response is followed several times by an **unconditional stimulus** that produces a defensive or appetitive response (the **unconditional response**), the first stimulus (now called a **conditional stimulus**) itself evokes the response (now called a **conditional response**).

Hebb rule   The hypothesis proposed by Donald Hebb that the cellular basis of learning involves strengthening of a synapse that is repeatedly active when the postsynaptic neuron fires.

tive at about the same time that the postsynaptic neuron fires, changes will take place in the structure or chemistry of the synapse that will strengthen it. How would the Hebb rule apply to our circuit? If the 1000-Hz tone is presented first, then weak synapse T (for "tone") becomes active. If the puff is presented immediately afterward, then strong synapse P becomes active and makes the motor neuron fire. The act of firing then strengthens any synapse with the motor neuron *that has just been active*. Of course, this means synapse T. After several pairings of the two stimuli, and after several increments of strengthening, synapse T becomes strong enough to cause the motor neuron to fire by itself. Learning has occurred. (See *Figure 14.1.*)

Obviously, the rabbit's auditory system contains more than one neuron, and so does its motor system. Neurons in the auditory system have connections with all kinds of neurons in the motor system—with neurons that control ear wiggling, nose twitching, running, sniffing, chewing, and other things rabbits can do. But before learning takes place, all of these connections are weak; hearing a 1000-Hz tone produces so little activation of the neurons in the motor system that the animal does not make an overt response. (Of course, the noise may startle the animal, but this response usually disappears after the tone is presented a few times.) Of all the thousands of synapses in the motor system that become activated by the 1000-Hz tone, only those located on neurons that have just fired will become strengthened. If the US has just been presented and the animal has just blinked, most of the recently activated cells will be those controlling eyeblinks—and only synapses on these cells will be strengthened.

When Hebb formulated his rule, he was unable to determine whether it was true or false. Now, finally, enough progress has been made in laboratory techniques that the strength of individual synapses can be determined, and investigators are studying the physiological bases of learning. We will see the results of some of these approaches in the next section of this chapter.

The second major class of stimulus-response learning is **instrumental conditioning** (also called *operant conditioning*). Whereas classical conditioning involves automatic, species-typical responses, instrumental conditioning involves behaviors that have been learned. And whereas classical conditioning involves an association between two stimuli, instrumental conditioning involves an *association between a response and a stimulus*. Instrumental conditioning is a more flexible form of learning. It permits an organism to adjust its behavior according to the consequences of that behavior. That is, when a behavior is followed by favorable consequences, the behavior tends to occur more frequently; when it is followed by unfavorable

consequences, it tends to occur less frequently. Collectively, "favorable consequences" are referred to as **reinforcing stimuli,** and "unfavorable consequences" are referred to as **punishing stimuli.** For example, a response that enables a hungry organism to find food will be reinforced, and a response that causes pain will be punished. (Psychologists often refer to these terms as *reinforcers* and *punishers.*)

Let's consider the process of reinforcement. Briefly stated, reinforcement causes changes in an animal's nervous system that increase the likelihood that a particular stimulus will elicit a particular response. For example, when a hungry rat is first put in an operant chamber (a "Skinner box"), it is not very likely to press the lever mounted on a wall. However, if it does press the lever, and if it receives a piece of food immediately afterward, the likelihood of making another response increases. Put another way, reinforcement causes the sight of the lever to serve as the stimulus that elicits the lever-pressing response. It is not accurate to say simply that a particular behavior becomes more frequent. If no lever is present, a rat that has learned to press one will not wave its paw around in the air. The *sight of a lever* is needed to produce the response. Thus, the process of reinforcement strengthens a connection between neural circuits involved in perception (the sight of the lever) and those involved in movement (the act of lever pressing). As we will see later in this chapter, the brain contains reinforcement mechanisms that control this process. (See *Figure 14.2.*)

The third major category of learning, **motor learning**, is actually a component of stimulus-response learning. For simplicity's sake, we can think of perceptual learning as the establishment of changes within the sensory systems of the brain, stimulus-response learning as the establishment of connections between sensory systems and motor systems, and motor learning as the establishment of changes within motor systems. But, in fact, motor learning cannot occur without sensory guidance from the environment. For example, most skilled movements involve interactions with

instrumental conditioning   A learning procedure whereby the effects of a particular behavior in a particular situation increase (reinforce) or decrease (punish) the probability of the behavior; also called *operant conditioning.*

reinforcing stimulus   An appetitive stimulus that follows a particular behavior and thus makes the behavior become more frequent.

punishing stimulus   An aversive stimulus that follows a particular behavior and thus makes the behavior become less frequent.

motor learning   Learning to make a new response.

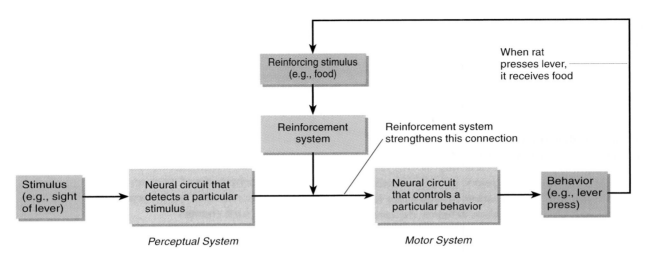

Figure 14.2
A simple neural model of instrumental conditioning.

objects: bicycles, pinball machines, knitting needles, and so on. Even skilled movements we make by ourselves, such as solitary dance steps, involve feedback from the joints, muscles, vestibular apparatus, eyes, and contact between the feet and the floor. Motor learning differs from other forms of learning primarily in the degree to which new forms of behavior are learned; the more novel the behavior, the more the neural circuits in the motor systems of the brain must be modified. (See *Figure 14.3.*)

A particular learning situation can involve varying amounts of all three types of learning that I have described so far: perceptual, stimulus-response, and motor. For example, if we teach an animal to make a new response whenever we present a stimulus it has never seen before, it must learn to recognize the stimulus (perceptual learning) and make the response (motor learning), and a connection must be established between these two new memories (stimulus-response learning). If we teach it to make a response it has already learned whenever we present a new stimulus, only perceptual learning and stimulus-response learning will take place.

The three forms of learning I have described so far consist primarily of changes in one sensory system, between one sensory system and the motor system, or in the motor system. But obviously, learning is usually more complex than that. The fourth form of learning involves learning the *relations* among individual stimuli. For example, a somewhat more complex form of perceptual learning involves connections between different areas of the association cortex. When we hear the sound of a cat meowing in the dark, we can imagine what a cat looks like and what it would feel like if we stroked its fur. Thus, the neural circuits in the auditory association cortex that recognize the meow are somehow connected to the appropriate circuits in the visual association cortex and the somatosensory association cortex. These interconnections, too, are accomplished as a result of learning.

Perception of spatial location—*spatial learning*—also involves learning about the relations among many stimuli. For example, consider what we must learn in order to become familiar with the contents of a room. First, we must learn to recognize each of the objects. But then, in addi-

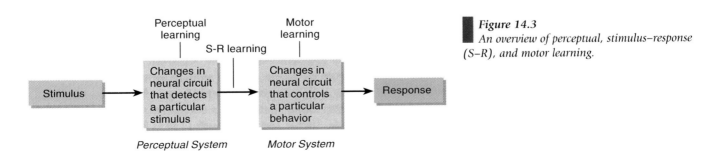

Figure 14.3
An overview of perceptual, stimulus–response (S–R), and motor learning.

tion, we must learn the relative locations of the objects with respect to each other. As a result, when we find ourselves located in a particular place in the room, our perceptions of these objects and their locations relative to us tell us exactly where we are.

Other types of relational learning are even more complex. *Episodic learning*—remembering sequences of events (episodes) that we witness—requires us to keep track not only of individual stimuli but also of the order in which they occur. *Observational learning*—learning by watching and imitating other people—requires us to remember what someone else does, the situation in which the behavior is performed, and the relation between the other person's movements and our own. As we will see in Chapter 15, a special system that involves the hippocampus and associated structures appears to perform coordinating functions that are necessary for many types of learning that go beyond single regions of the cerebral cortex.

Interim Summary

Learning produces changes in the way we perceive, act, think, and feel. It does so by producing changes in the nervous system in the circuits responsible for perception, in those responsible for the control of movement, and in connections between the two.

Perceptual learning consists primarily of changes in perceptual systems that make it possible for us to recognize stimuli so that we can respond to them appropriately. Stimulus-response learning consists of connections between perceptual and motor systems. The most important forms are classical and instrumental conditioning. Classical conditioning occurs when a neutral stimulus is followed by an unconditional stimulus (US) that naturally elicits an unconditional response (UR). After this pairing, the neutral stimulus becomes a conditional stimulus (CS); it now elicits the conditional response (CR) by itself.

Instrumental conditioning occurs when a response is followed by a reinforcing stimulus, such as a drink of water for a thirsty animal. The reinforcing stimulus increases the likelihood that the other stimuli present when the response was made will evoke the response. Both forms of stimulus-response learning may occur as a result of strengthened synaptic connections, as described by the Hebb rule.

Motor learning, although it may primarily involve changes within neural circuits that control movement, is guided by sensory stimuli; thus, it is actually a form of stimulus-response learning. Relational learning, the most complex form of learning, is described in Chapter 15. It includes the ability to recognize objects through more than

one sensory modality, to recognize the relative location of objects in the environment, and to remember the sequence in which events occurred during particular episodes.

LEARNING AND SYNAPTIC PLASTICITY

On theoretical considerations alone, it would appear that learning must involve synaptic plasticity—changes in the structure or biochemistry of synapses that alter their effects on postsynaptic neurons. But is there evidence that learning does cause such changes?

Effects of Learning on Neural Structure and Functions

Is there evidence that learning causes changes in neural structure and function? The answer is clearly yes. More than thirty years ago, Rosenzweig and his colleagues began a research program in which they placed animals in an environment in which they would learn many things, then compared their brains with those of animals that learned very little (see Weiler, Hawrylak, and Greenough, 1995; and Rosenzweig and Bennett, 1996, for reviews). That way the researchers might be able to see the kinds of changes that learning produces, even though they would not be able to determine which changes were caused by which experiences. The experimenters divided litters of rats and placed the animals into two kinds of environments: enriched and impoverished. The enriched environment contained such things as running wheels, ladders, slides, and "toys" that the animals could explore and manipulate. The experimenters changed these objects every day to maximize the animals' experiences and thus ensure that they would learn as much as possible. The impoverished environments were plain cages in a dimly illuminated, quiet room.

Rosenzweig and his colleagues found many differences in the brains of animals raised in the two environments. The brains of rats raised in the enriched environment had a thicker cortex, a better capillary supply, more glial cells, more protein content, and more acetylcholinesterase (and, by inference, more acetylcholine-secreting terminal buttons). As we will see later in this chapter, acetylcholine appears to play a role in learning; thus, this last finding may be especially noteworthy. Subsequent studies found that even the brains of older animals were this way by exposure to a complex environment (Riege, 1971). Researchers have also found changes on a microanatomical level; for example, Turner and Greenough (1985) found increases in the size of postsynaptic densities in the brains of rats that had spent time in a complex environment. Because measurement of postsynaptic densities constitutes an index of the size of the active zone of a synapse, these findings suggest that the synapses had been strengthened by the animals' experiences.

Greenough, Juraska, and Volkmar (1979) succeeded in finding specific learning-induced changes in the brains of adult animals. They gave rats extensive training in a series of mazes, which contrasted with the relative lack of visual stimulation received by the control animals. The investigators found larger dendritic fields in the animals' visual cortex. Of course, the changes could have been caused by factors not specific to learning, such as increased exercise or changes in hormone levels. However, Chang and Greenough (1982) showed that the changes were caused by visual stimulation received during training. They divided the rats' cerebral hemispheres by cutting the corpus callosum and placed an opaque contact lens on one eye. This treatment permitted visual information from the maze training to reach only one hemisphere. Changes in dendritic fields were seen only on the side of the brain that received the increased visual stimulation.

● Induction of Long-Term Potentiation

As we just saw, learning causes changes in neural structure and function. But what, exactly, triggers these changes? As we saw in the first section of this chapter, the Hebb rule states that if a synapse is active at about the same time that the postsynaptic neuron is active, that synapse will be strengthened. Research on a phenomenon originally discovered in the hippocampal formation has discovered at least one way that the Hebb rule may operate.

Electrical stimulation of circuits within the hippocampal formation can lead to long-term synaptic changes that seem to be among those responsible for learning. Lømo (1966) discovered that intense electrical stimulation of axons leading from the entorhinal cortex to the dentate gyrus caused a long-term increase in the magnitude of excitatory postsynaptic potentials in the postsynaptic cells; this increase has come to be called **long-term potentiation.** (The word *potentiate* means "to strengthen, to make more potent.")

First, let us review some anatomy. The **hippocampal formation** is a specialized region of the limbic cortex located in the temporal lobe. (Its location in a human brain is shown in Figure 3.13.) Because the hippocampal formation is folded in one dimension and then curved in another, it has a complex, three-dimensional shape. Thus, it is difficult to show what it looks like with a diagram on a two-dimensional sheet of paper. Fortunately, the structure of the hippocampal formation is orderly; a slice taken anywhere contains the same set of circuits.

The hippocampal formation includes the entorhinal cortex, the subicular complex, the hippocampus itself, and the dentate gyrus. Figure 14.4(a) shows a photomicrograph of a horizontal section through the hippocampal formation of a rat brain and part (b) shows its intrinsic connections. The major neocortical inputs and outputs of the hippocampal formation are channeled through the **entorhinal cortex.** Neurons in the entorhinal cortex relay incoming information to the **granule cells** of the **dentate gyrus.** These neurons then send axons into **field CA3** of the hippocampus itself. The hippocampus is also called "Ammon's horn," or, in Latin, *cornu ammonis.* That fact may seem like a piece of trivia, but it explains why its two major divisions are called CA1 and CA3. (CA2 and CA4 exist, too, but we will not need to talk about them.) The terminals of the fibers from the dentate gyrus form synapses with dendritic spines of the **pyramidal cells** of field CA3. The cell bodies of pyramidal cells are shaped just as their name suggests. An axon grows downward, out of the base of the pyramid, while a long, thick dendritic trunk grows out of the top. This dendrite and its branches are studded with approximately 30,000 dendritic spines. As we will see, these spines are the site of the structural and biochemical changes that are responsible for long-term potentiation.

The axons of CA3 pyramidal cells branch in two directions. One branch terminates in the adjacent **field CA1,** where it forms synapses with the dendritic spines of other

long-term potentiation   A long-term increase in the excitability of a neuron to a particular synaptic input caused by repeated high-frequency activity of that input.

hippocampal formation   A forebrain structure of the temporal lobe, constituting an important part of the limbic system; includes the hippocampus proper (Ammon's horn), dentate gyrus, and subiculum.

entorhinal cortex   A region of the limbic cortex that provides the major source of input to the hippocampal formation.

granule cell   A small, granular cell; those found in the dentate gyrus send axons to field CA3 of the hippocampus.

dentate gyrus   Part of the hippocampal formation; receives inputs from the entorhinal cortex and projects to field CA3 of the hippocampus.

field CA3   Part of the hippocampus; receives inputs from the dentate gyrus and projects to field CA1.

pyramidal cell   A category of large neurons with a pyramid shape; found in the cerebral cortex and Ammon's horn of the hippocampal formation.

field CA1   Part of the hippocampus; receives inputs from field CA3 and projects out of the hippocampal formation via the subiculum.

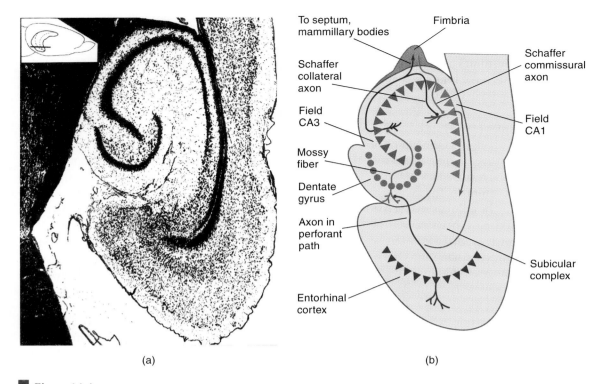

(a)   (b)

Figure 14.4
Connections of the components of the hippocampal formation.
(Photograph from Swanson, L.W., Köhler, C., and Björklund, A., in *Handbook of Chemical Neuroanatomy. Vol. 5.: Integrated Systems of the CNS, Part I.* Amsterdam: Elsevier Science Publishers, 1987.)

pyramidal cells. The other branch travels through the fornix to structures in the basal forebrain, including the septum and the mammillary bodies. Another system of axons connects CA1 pyramidal cells with their counterparts on the opposite side of the brain. CA1 pyramidal cells provide the primary output of the hippocampus: They send axons to neurons in the subicular complex, whose axons then project out of the hippocampal formation to the entorhinal cortex and also through the fimbria to the basal forebrain. (See *Figure 14.4.*)

Figure 14.5 shows a typical procedure for producing long-term potentiation. A stimulating electrode is placed among the axons that project to the dentate gyrus, and a recording electrode is placed in the dentate gyrus, near the granule cells. (See *Figure 14.5.*) First, a single pulse of electrical stimulation is delivered to the perforant path, and then the resulting population EPSP is recorded in the dentate gyrus. The **population EPSP** is an extracellular measurement of the excitatory postsynaptic potentials (EPSP) produced by the synapses of the perforant path axons with the dentate granule cells. The size of the first population EPSP indicates the strength of the synaptic connections before long-term potentiation has taken place. Long-term potentiation can be induced by stimulating the axons in the perforant path with a burst of approximately one hundred pulses of electrical stimulation, delivered within a few seconds. Evidence for

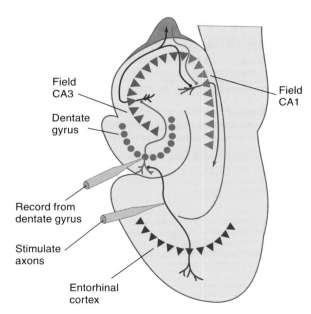

Figure 14.5
The procedure for producing long-term potentiation.

population EPSP   An evoked potential that represents the EPSPs of a population of neurons.

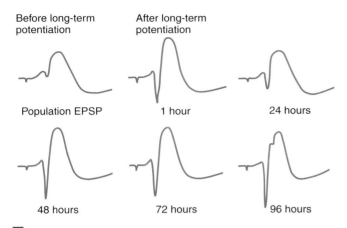

Before long-term potentiation | After long-term potentiation

Population EPSP | 1 hour | 24 hours

48 hours | 72 hours | 96 hours

Figure 14.6
Population EPSPs recorded from the dentate gyrus before and after electrical stimulation that led to long-term potentiation.
(From Berger, T.W. *Science*, 1984, *224*, 627–630. Copyright 1984 by the American Association for the Advancement of Science.)

long-term potentiation is obtained by periodically delivering single pulses to the perforant path and recording the response in the dentate gyrus. If the response is greater than it was before the burst of pulses was delivered, long-term potentiation has occurred. (See *Figure 14.6.*)

Long-term potentiation can be produced in other regions of the hippocampal formation and, as we shall see, in other places in the brain. It can last for several months (Bliss and Lømo, 1973). It can be produced in isolated

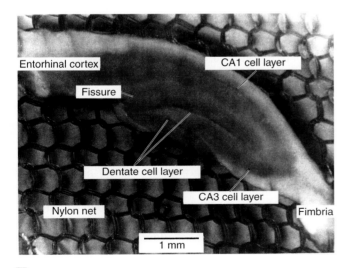

Entorhinal cortex
Fissure
CA1 cell layer
Dentate cell layer
CA3 cell layer
Nylon net
Fimbria
1 mm

Figure 14.7
A photograph of a hippocampal slice in a tissue chamber.
(From Teyler, T.J. *Brain Research Bulletin*, 1980, *5*, 391–403. Reprinted with permission.)

slices of the hippocampal formation as well as in the brains of living animals, which allows researchers to stimulate and record from individual neurons and to analyze biochemical changes. The brain is removed from the skull, the hippocampal complex is dissected, and slices are placed in a temperature-controlled chamber filled with liquid that resembles interstitial fluid. Figure 14.7 shows a 400-micrometer slice of the hippocampal formation being maintained in a tissue chamber. Under optimal conditions a slice remains alive for up to 40 hours. (See *Figure 14.7.*)

Many experiments have demonstrated that long-term potentiation in hippocampal slices can follow the Hebb rule. That is, when weak and strong synapses to a single neuron are stimulated at approximately the same time, the weak synapse becomes strengthened. This phenomenon is called **associative long-term potentiation,** because it is produced by the association (in time) between the activity of the two sets of synapses. Kelso and Brown (1986) stimulated two different weak inputs (W1 and W2) and one strong input (S) to pyramidal cells in the CA1 field. (See *Figure 14.8.*) In some cases they paired W1 with S; in oth-

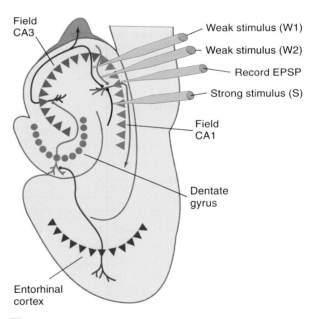

Field CA3
Weak stimulus (W1)
Weak stimulus (W2)
Record EPSP
Strong stimulus (S)
Field CA1
Dentate gyrus
Entorhinal cortex

Figure 14.8
The procedure used by Kelso and Brown (1986) to demonstrate associative long-term potentiation.

associative long-term potentiation A long-term potentiation in which concurrent stimulation of weak and strong synapses to a given neuron strengthens the weak ones.

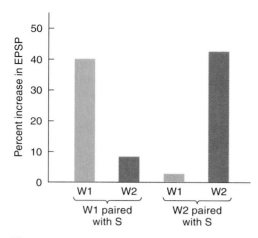

Figure 14.9
Differential associative long-term potentiation.
(Data from Kelso, S.R., and Brown, T.H. *Science*, 1986, *232*, 85–87.)

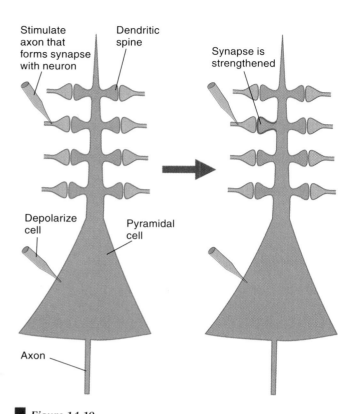

Figure 14.10
Long-term potentiation. Synaptic strengthening occurs when synapses are active while the postsynaptic membrane of the cell is depolarized.

ers they paired W2 with S. They found that only the synapses stimulated at the same time as the strong input were strengthened. (See **Figure 14.9.**) These results are particularly important because they indicate that the pairing did not simply make the CA1 pyramidal cells become more sensitive to *all* its inputs. Thus, the strengthening occurs in *specific synapses.*

● Role of NMDA Receptors

Long-term potentiation requires some sort of additive effect. That is, a series of pulses delivered at a high rate all in one burst will produce long-term potentiation, but the same number of pulses given at a slow rate will not. (In fact, as we shall see, low-frequency stimulation can lead to the opposite phenomenon: long-term *depression*.) The reason for this phenomenon is now clear. Several experiments have shown that synaptic strengthening occurs when molecules of the neurotransmitter bind with postsynaptic receptors located in a dendritic spine that is already depolarized. Kelso, Ganong, and Brown (1986) found that if they artificially depolarized CA1 neurons and then stimulated the axons that formed synapses with them, the synapses became stronger. However, if the stimulation of the synapses and the depolarization of the neuron occurred at different times, no effect was seen; thus, the two events had to occur together. (See **Figure 14.10.**)

Experiments such as the ones I just described indicate that long-term potentiation requires two events: activation of synapses and depolarization of the postsynaptic neuron. The explanation for this phenomenon, at least in some parts of the brain, lies in the characteristics of a very special receptor. As we saw in Chapter 4, the most important excitatory neurotransmitter in the brain is glutamic acid (usually referred to as *glutamate*). We also saw that the postsynaptic effects of glutamate are mediated by several different types of receptors. One of them, the NMDA receptor (short for *N*-methyl-D-aspartate), plays a critical role in long-term potentiation.

The **NMDA receptor** has some unusual properties. It is found in the hippocampal formation, especially in field CA1. The NMDA receptor controls a calcium ion channel. However, this channel is normally blocked by a magnesium ion (Mg^{2+}), which prevents calcium ions from entering the cell, even when the receptor is stimulated by glutamate. But if the postsynaptic membrane is depolarized, the Mg^{2+} is ejected from the ion channel, and the channel is free to admit Ca^{2+} ions. Thus, calcium ions en-

NMDA receptor A specialized ionotropic glutamate receptor that controls a calcium channel that is normally blocked by Mg^{2+} ions; involved in long-term potentiation.

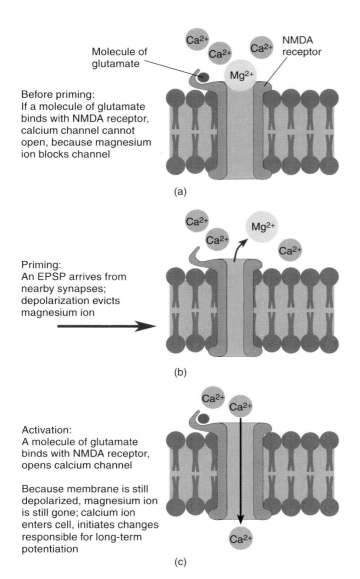

Molecule of glutamate

Ca²⁺   Ca²⁺   Ca²⁺   NMDA receptor

Mg²⁺

Before priming:
If a molecule of glutamate binds with NMDA receptor, calcium channel cannot open, because magnesium ion blocks channel

(a)

Ca²⁺   Mg²⁺

Ca²⁺   Ca²⁺

Priming:
An EPSP arrives from nearby synapses; depolarization evicts magnesium ion

(b)

Ca²⁺   Ca²⁺

Activation:
A molecule of glutamate binds with NMDA receptor, opens calcium channel

Because membrane is still depolarized, magnesium ion is still gone; calcium ion enters cell, initiates changes responsible for long-term potentiation

Ca²⁺

(c)

Figure 14.11
The NMDA receptor. (a) Before priming. (b) Priming. Depolarization from nearby non-NMDA glutamate receptors evicts the magnesium ion. (c) Activation. When glutamate attaches to the binding site, the ion channel opens, allowing calcium ions to enter the dendritic spine.

ter the cells through the channels controlled by NMDA receptors only when glutamate is present *and* when the postsynaptic membrane is already depolarized. That means that the ion channel controlled by the NMDA receptor is a neurotransmitter- *and* voltage-dependent channel. (See *Figure 14.11*.)

The strongest evidence implicating NMDA receptors in long-term potentiation comes from research with drugs that block NMDA receptors, such as **AP5** (2-amino-5-phosphonopentanoate). AP5 prevents the establishment of long-term potentiation in field CA1 and the dentate gyrus. However, it has no effect on long-term potentiation that has already been established (Brown et al., 1989). Thus, although the activation of NMDA receptors is necessary for long-term potentiation, transmission in the potentiated synapses involves *non*-NMDA receptors—primarily, **AMPA receptors.**

Cell biologists have discovered that the calcium ion is used by many cells as a second messenger. The entry of calcium ions through the ion channels controlled by NMDA receptors is an essential step in long-term potentiation. Lynch et al. (1984) demonstrated this fact by injecting EGTA directly into hippocampal pyramidal cells. This chemical binds with calcium and makes it insoluble, destroying its biological activity. The EGTA blocked the establishment of long-term potentiation in the injected cells; their excitability was not increased by high-frequency stimulation of axons that formed synapses with them. However, neighboring cells, which were not injected with EGTA, showed long-term potentiation.

Malenka et al. (1988) demonstrated that not only is calcium *necessary* for long-term potentiation, but it is *sufficient*. They injected a chemical called nitr-5 into CA1 pyramidal cells and then exposed them to ultraviolet light. Nitr-5 is a special calcium chelator. When it is exposed to ultraviolet light, it releases its hold on calcium ions; thus, when Malenka and his colleagues exposed the cells to ultraviolet light, their intracellular concentration of free calcium ions suddenly increased. This increase produced a large enhancement of synaptic transmission between these cells and their inputs. (See *Figure 14.12*.)

In Chapter 2 you learned that only axons are capable of producing action potentials. Actually, they can also occur in dendrites of some types of pyramidal cells, including those in field CA1 of the hippocampal formation. The threshold of excitation for **dendritic spikes** (as these action potentials are called) is rather high. So far as we know, they occur only when an action potential is triggered in the axon of the pyramidal cell. The backwash of depolarization across the cell body triggers a dendritic spike, which is propagated up the trunk of the dendrite. This means that

AP5 2-amino-5-phosphonopentanoate; a drug that blocks NMDA receptors.

AMPA receptor An ionotropic glutamate receptor that controls a sodium channel; when open, produces EPSPs.

dendritic spike An action potential that occurs in the dendrite of some types of pyramidal cells.

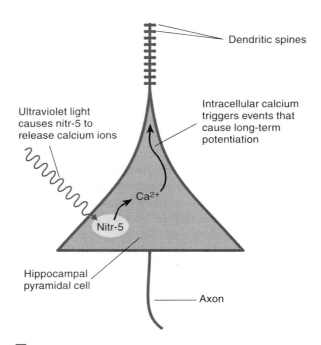

Figure 14.12
An explanation of the experiment by Malenka et al. (1988), which demonstrated that increased intracellular calcium in CA1 pyramidal cells produced long-term potentiation.

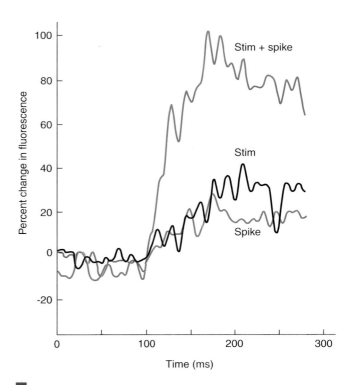

Figure 14.13
The procedure and results of the experiment by Yuste and Denk (1995). (a) The experimental procedure. (b) Changes in calcium concentration in single dendritic spines, measured as percentage change in fluorescence. Stim = *stimulate axon alone*, Spike = *trigger action potential alone*, Stim + spike = *stimulate axon and trigger action potential simultaneously.*
(Graph adapted from Yuste, R., and Denk, W. *Nature*, 1995, *375*, 682–684.)

whenever a pyramidal cell fires, all of its dendritic spines become depolarized for a brief time.

The development of a special technique, two-photon fluorescence microscopy, now enables researchers to visualize individual spines on dendrites of pyramidal cells in hippocampal slices. Yuste and Denk (1995) injected individual CA1 pyramidal cells in hippocampal slices with calcium-green-1, a fluorescent dye that permitted them to observe the influx of calcium. They found that the activity of individual synapses triggered the entry of a small amount of calcium into the dendritic spine. The influx of calcium occurred within a few milliseconds and did not spread to adjacent spines. When an action potential was triggered in the axon of the pyramidal cell, a wave of depolarization washed back through the dendrite, which caused a small amount of calcium to enter the dendrite and all of its spines. When these two events—activation of individual synapses and depolarization of the entire dendrite—occurred at the same time, a large amount of calcium entered the active spines. The amount of calcium that entered was much greater than the sum of the two small amounts. (See *Figure 14.13.*)

A study by Magee and Johnston (1997) proved that the simultaneous occurrence of synaptic activation and a den-

dritic spike strengthens the active synapse. The investigators measured both calcium influx into individual dendrites of CA1 pyramidal cells and the excitatory postsynaptic potentials produced by activation of terminals that formed synapses with these dendrites. Like Yuste and Denk (1995), they found that when synapses became active at the same time a dendritic spike had been triggered, calcium "hotspots" occurred near the activated synapses. Moreover, the size of the excitatory postsynaptic potential produced by these activated synapses became larger. In other words, these synapses became strengthened. To confirm that the dendritic spikes were necessary for the synaptic potentiation to take place, the investigators infused a small amount of TTX (tetrodotoxin) onto the base of the dendrite just before triggering an action potential. (The TTX prevented the formation of dendritic spikes by blocking voltage-dependent ion channels.) Under these conditions, potentiation did not occur. (See *Figure 14.14.*)

Figure 14.14

Figure 14.14
Long-term potentiation caused by pairing of synaptic activation with dendritic spikes triggered by stimulation of the pyramidal cells. The effect was abolished by the infusion of TTX, which blocks the formation of dendritic spikes.
(Adapted from Magee, J.C., and Johnston, D. *Science*, 1997, *275*, 209–213.)

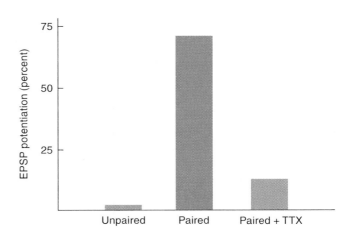

I think that considering what you already know about associative long-term potentiation, you can anticipate the role that NMDA receptors play in this phenomenon. If weak synapses are active by themselves, nothing happens, because the membrane of the dendritic spine does not depolarize sufficiently for the calcium channels controlled by the NMDA receptors to open. (Remember that in order for these channels to open, the postsynaptic membrane must depolarize and displace the Mg^{2+} ions that normally block them.) However, if the activity of strong synapses located elsewhere on the postsynaptic cell have caused the cell to fire, then a dendritic spike will depolarize the postsynaptic membrane enough for calcium to enter the ion channels controlled by the NMDA receptors. Thus, the special properties of NMDA receptors account not only for the exis-

tence of long-term potentiation but also for its associative nature. (See *Figure 14.15.*)

● Mechanisms of Synaptic Plasticity

What is responsible for the increases in synaptic strength that occur during long-term potentiation? These increases

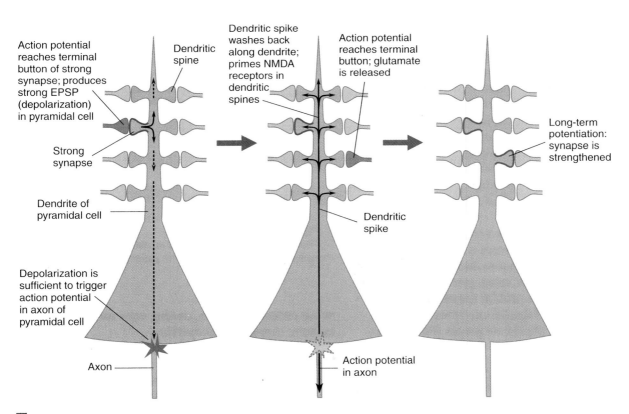

Figure 14.15
Associative long-term potentiation. If the activity of strong synapses is sufficient to trigger an action potential in the neuron, the dendritic spike will depolarize the membrane of dendritic spines, priming NMDA receptors so that any weak synapses active at that time will become strengthened.

could be caused by several different means. They could be produced presynaptically, through increased release of transmitter substance; or they could be produced postsynaptically, through an increased number of receptors, an increased ability of the receptors to activate changes in the permeability of the postsynaptic membrane, or increased communication between the region of the postsynaptic membrane and the rest of the neuron. They could also be produced by an increased number of synapses, which would involve both presynaptic and postsynaptic changes. (See *Figure 14.16.*) As we shall see, *each* of these possibilities has at least some supporting evidence.

Several studies have found that NMDA-mediated long-term potentiation increases the number of postsynaptic AMPA receptors—that is, *non*NMDA glutamate receptors. For example, Tocco et al. (1992) established long-term potentiation in the dentate gyrus in intact animals by stimulating the perforant path. One hour later, they removed and sliced the brains, incubated alternate slices with radioactive ligands for NMDA and AMPA receptors, and looked at the density and distribution of these receptors by means of autoradiography. They found evidence for increased sensitivity (or numbers) of AMPA receptors—but not NMDA receptors. Liao, Hessler, and Malinow (1995) recorded postsynaptic potentials produced by the activity of single synapses on dendritic spines of CA1 pyramidal cells. By either depolarizing the postsynaptic membrane or holding it at the resting potential, they could control whether NMDA receptors were blocked by Mg²⁺. Initially, they found evidence that the spines of many of the synapses contained only NMDA receptors. But after inducing long-term potentiation in the inputs to the cells, they found evidence that the spines now contained AMPA receptors as well. Thus, one of the effects of long-term potentiation appears to be insertion of new AMPA receptors in the postsynaptic membrane.

Researchers agree that long-term potentiation produced by the activation of NMDA receptors is initiated postsynaptically, by the entry of calcium ions. Most also agree that the entry of calcium activates some special calcium-dependent enzymes known as **protein kinases.** Protein kinases are inactive until a calcium ion binds with them; when activated, they add phosphate groups (PO_4) to par-

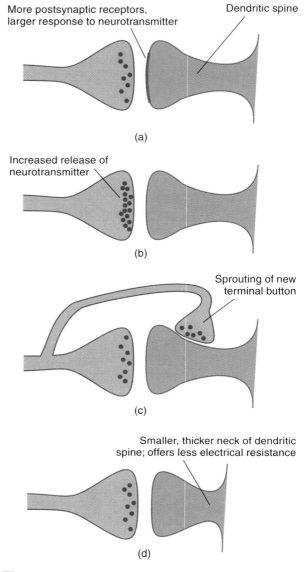

Figure 14.16
Hypothetical changes that could account for the synaptic strengthening produced by long-term potentiation.

---

protein kinase   An enzyme that attaches a phosphate (PO_4) to a protein and thereby causes it to change its shape.

CaM-KII   Type II calcium-calmodulin kinase, an enzyme that must be activated by calcium; may play a role in the establishment of long-term potentiation.

---

ticular protein molecules, causing some part of the protein to move, changing its properties.

One of these enzymes, type II calcium-calmodulin kinase (best known as **CaM-KII**), is present in especially high concentrations in the postsynaptic thickening of neurons in the hippocampal formation. Silva et al. (1992) obtained evidence that this enzyme plays an important role in synaptic plasticity. The investigators produced a targeted mutation of the gene responsible for the production of CaM-KII in mice. The mice had no obvious neuroanatomical de-

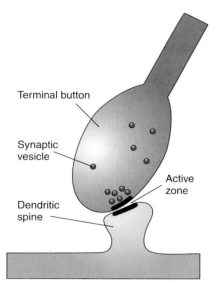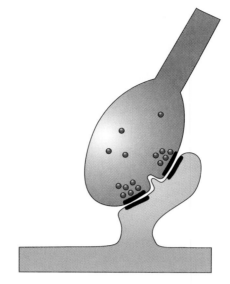

Before long-term potentiation   After long-term potentiation

Terminal button

Synaptic
vesicle

Dendritic
spine

Active
zone

Figure 14.17
Hypothetical changes in the structure of synapses on dendritic spines produced by long-term potentiation.
(Adapted from Hosokawa, T., Rusakov, D.A., Bliss, T.V.P., and Fine, A. *Journal of Neuroscience*, 1995, *15*, 5560–5573.)

fects, and the responses of NMDA receptors were normal. However, the investigators were unable to produce long-term potentiation in field CA1 of hippocampal slices taken from these animals. A targeted mutation of the *fyn* gene, which is responsible for the production of **tyrosine kinase,** another protein kinase, also interferes with the production of long-term potentiation in CA1 pyramidal neurons (Grant et al., 1992).

As we have seen, evidence indicates that long-term potentiation involves an increase in postsynaptic AMPA receptors, which makes the postsynaptic membrane of the dendritic spine more sensitive to the release of glutamate by the presynaptic terminal button. Several studies have also found evidence for structural changes, as well. One of the most compelling studies was performed by Hosokawa et al. (1995), who used a confocal microscope to observe individual dendritic spines of CA1 pyramidal cells before and after long-term potentiation. A confocal microscope uses special optics to examine an extremely thin "slice" of tissue located beneath the surface of a specimen, screening out all elements that are out of focus. What they saw indicated that a subpopulation of small spines grew in length and changed their orientation toward the shaft of the dendrite away from the perpendicular. Figure 14.17 shows a drawing of hypothetical changes in a dendritic spine that are consistent with the observed changes. (See *Figure 14.17*.)

As you can see in Figure 14.17, as the dendritic spine and terminal button elongate, two active zones appear. Several studies (for example, Geinisman, de Toledo-Mor-

rell, and Morrell, 1991; Geinisman et al., 1996) have found that long-term potentiation increased the number of such features, which they referred to as "perforated synapses." Using a special stain that labeled calcium in dendritic spines, Buchs and Muller (1996) found that after long-term potentiation, most of the labeled spines formed perforated synapses with the presynaptic terminals. Thus, perforated synapses appear to be one of the characteristic features of strengthened synapses.

Edwards (1995) suggested that the development of perforated synapses is a means by which the number of postsynaptic AMPA receptors increases. First, the dendritic spine develops a fingerlike projection that projects into the terminal button, dividing the active zone into two parts. Each active zone then grows. In the terminal button, more machinery necessary for the release of the neurotransmitter is inserted into the presynaptic membrane. (See *Figure 14.18*.) In the dendritic spine, more AMPA receptors are inserted into the postsynaptic membrane. Edwards noted that previous studies showed that horizontal cells in the retina of some species project similar "fingers" into the photoreceptors with which they form synapses. After 30 minutes in the dark these fingers disappear, only to reappear when the retina is again exposed to light. The regrowth of these "fingers" depends on the entry of calcium into the cell (Wagner, 1980; Schmitz and Drenckhahn, 1991).

tyrosine kinase A type of protein kinase that may play a role in the establishment of long-term potentiation.

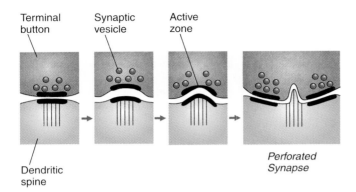

Figure 14.18

A hypothetical description of the synaptic changes in a synapse on a dendritic spine caused by long-term potentiation. The dendritic spine develops a fingerlike projection that projects into the terminal button, dividing the active zone into two parts. Each active zone grows and, in the terminal button, more machinery necessary for the release of the neurotransmitter is inserted into the presynaptic membrane.

(Based on Edwards, F.A. *Trends in Neuroscience*, 1995, 18, 250–255.)

For several years after its discovery, researchers believed that long-term potentiation involved a single process. Since then it has become clear that *long-lasting*, long-term potentiation requires protein synthesis. Frey et al. (1988) found that anisomycin, a drug that blocks protein synthesis, could block the establishment of long-lasting, long-term potentiation in field CA1. If the drug was administered before, during, or immediately after delivering a prolonged burst of stimulation, long-term potentiation occurred, but it disappeared a few hours later. If, however, the drug was administered one hour after stimulating the synapses, the long-term potentiation persisted. Apparently, the protein synthesis necessary for establishing the later phase of long-lasting, long-term potentiation is accomplished within an hour of stimulation.

Where does the protein synthesis take place? As we saw, long-term potentiation involves individual synapses. Only those synapses that are activated when the postsynaptic membrane is depolarized are strengthened. But protein synthesis normally takes place in the cell body. If the long-lasting phase of long-term potentiation requires protein synthesis, then it would seem that the proteins synthesized in the cell body would have to be delivered only to the appropriate dendritic spines. But how could this targeted delivery process be accomplished?

The answer seems to be that the protein synthesis takes place where the proteins are needed—in the dendrites themselves. Tiedge and Brosius (1996) have shown that

dendrites contain all they need to synthesize proteins: ribosomes, transfer RNAs, and various enzymes that participate in the process. An analysis of the messenger RNAs present in dendrites indicates that they code for the production of components of the cytoskeleton, protein kinases, and receptors. Clearly, these products could be involved in establishing the structural changes needed for long-lasting, long-term potentiation.

What about the possibility of presynaptic changes? How could a process that occurs postsynaptically, in the dendritic spines, cause presynaptic changes? A possible answer comes from the discovery that a simple molecule, nitric oxide, can communicate messages from one cell to another. As we saw in Chapter 4, nitric oxide is a soluble gas produced by the activity of an enzyme known as **nitric oxide synthase.** Researchers have found that nitric oxide (NO) is used as a messenger in many parts of the body; for example, it is involved in the control of the muscles in the wall of the intestines, it dilates blood vessels in regions of the brain that become metabolically active, and it stimulates the changes in blood vessels that produce penile erections (Culotta and Koshland, 1992). Once produced, NO lasts only a short time before it is destroyed. Thus, if it were produced in dendritic spines in the hippocampal formation, it could diffuse only as far as the nearby terminal buttons, where it might produce changes related to the induction of long-term potentiation.

Several experiments suggest that NO may, indeed, be a retrograde messenger involved in long-term potentiation. (*Retrograde* means "moving backward"; in this context it refers to messages sent from the dendritic spine back to the terminal button.) East and Garthwaite (1991) found that when hippocampal slices were exposed to NMDA, levels of cyclic GMP increased. This increase did not occur when the investigators administered a drug that prevents the synthesis of nitric oxide, so the activation of NMDA must have resulted in the production of NO. Soon after these studies appeared, four laboratories reported that drugs that block nitric oxide synthase prevented the establishment of long-term potentiation in hippocampal slices (O'Dell et al., 1991; Schuman and Madison, 1991; Bon et al., 1992; Haley, Wilcox, and Chapman, 1992). Endoh, Maiese, and Wagner (1994) found that a calcium-activated NO synthase is found in several regions of the brain, including the dentate gyrus and fields CA1 and CA3 of the hippocampus. Zhang and Wong-Riley (1996) found that most cells that contain NO synthase also contain NMDA receptors.

nitric oxide synthase An enzyme responsible for the production of nitric oxide.

Figure 14.19 summarizes the biochemistry discussed in this subsection. I suspect that you may feel overwhelmed by all the new terms I have introduced here, and I hope that the figure will help clarify things. The evidence we have seen so far indicates that the entry of calcium ions through channels controlled by NMDA receptors activates calcium-dependent protein kinases, including CaM-KII and tyrosine kinase. These enzymes may activate biochemical processes that produce postsynaptic changes that cause the insertion of AMPA receptors into the postsynaptic membrane and change the physical structure of the synapse. (See *Figure 14.19.*) In addition, the entry of calcium activates a calcium-dependent NO synthase, and the newly produced NO then presumably diffuses out of the dendritic spine, back to the terminal button. There, it activates soluble guanylyl cyclase, an enzyme found in the cytoplasm that triggers the synthesis of cyclic GMP. The cyclic GMP then catalyzes unknown chemical reactions that increase the release of glutamate. (See *Figure 14.19.*)

● Long-Term Depression

I mentioned earlier that low-frequency stimulation of the synaptic inputs to a cell can *decrease* rather than increase their strength. This phenomenon, known as **long-term depression,** also plays a role in learning. After all, although the number of synapses in the brain is very large, it is still finite, and animals can continue to learn throughout their lives. Thus, it seems unlikely that once a synapse is strengthened it must remain that way forever. Dudek and Bear (1992) stimulated Schaffer collateral inputs to CA1 neurons in hippocampal slices with 900 pulses of electrical current, delivered at rates ranging from 1 to 50 Hz. They found that frequencies above 10 Hz caused long-term potentiation, whereas those below 10 Hz caused long-term depression. Both of these effects were blocked by application of AP5, the NMDA receptor blocker; thus, both effects require the activation of NMDA receptors. (See *Figure 14.20.*)

Stanton and Sejnowski (1989) demonstrated *associative* long-term depression in field CA1. They found that when

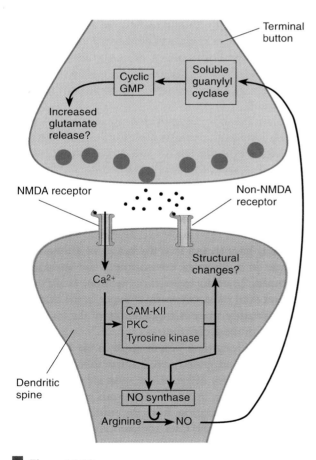

Figure 14.19
A summary of the chemical reactions triggered by the entry of an adequate amount of calcium into the dendritic spine.

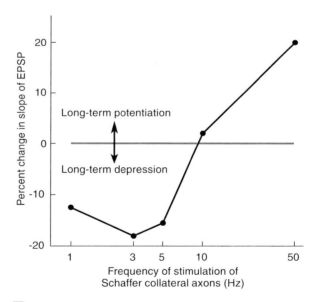

Figure 14.20
Changes in the sensitivity of synapses of Schaffer collateral axons with CA1 pyramidal cells after electrical stimulation at various frequencies.
(Adapted from Dudek, S.M., and Bear, M.F. *Proceedings of the National Academy of Sciences,* 1992, 89, 4363–4367.)

long-term depression A long-term decrease in the excitability of a neuron to a particular synaptic input caused by stimulation of the terminal button while the postsynaptic membrane is hyperpolarized or only slightly depolarized.

a weak input was paired with a strong input, long-term potentiation was produced. However, when the two inputs were stimulated at different times, long-term *depression* was produced. Other studies have shown that long-term depression is produced when synaptic inputs are activated at the same time that the postsynaptic membrane is either weakly depolarized or hyperpolarized (Debanne, Gähwiler, and Thompson, 1994; Thiels et al., 1996). Thus, at least at some synapses the Hebb rule appears to work in both directions: Inputs correlated with strong inputs (or with activation of the postsynaptic neuron) are strengthened, whereas inputs *not* correlated with strong inputs (or correlated with *nonactivation* of the postsynaptic neuron) are weakened. This mechanism could conceivably allow for the reversal of previously established synaptic changes when the contingencies in the environment change.

● Other Forms of Long-Term Potentiation

Long-term potentiation was discovered in the hippocampal formation and has been studied more in this region than in others, but it also occurs elsewhere in the brain. So far, it has been demonstrated in the prefrontal cortex, piriform cortex, entorhinal cortex, motor cortex, visual cortex, thalamus, and amygdala (Gerren and Weinberger, 1983; Clugnet and LeDoux, 1990; Aroniadou and Teyler, 1991; Baranyi, Szente, and Woody, 1991; Lynch et al., 1991). It has even been demonstrated in slices of human neocortex, removed during surgery to treat seizure disorders (Chen et al., 1996). NMDA receptors are probably involved in the potentiation that takes place in the piriform and entorhinal cortex and in the amygdala, but research on the role of these receptors in the other regions has not yet been reported. At least one form of long-term potentiation that takes place in the visual cortex does not involve NMDA receptors (Aroniadou and Teyler, 1991).

In the hippocampal formation NMDA receptors are present in highest concentrations in field CA1 and in the dentate gyrus. However, very few NMDA receptors are found in the region of field CA3 that receives mossy fiber input from the dentate gyrus (Monaghan and Cotman, 1985). High-frequency stimulation of the mossy fibers produces long-term potentiation that gradually decays over a period of several hours (Lynch et al., 1991). AP5, the drug that blocks NMDA receptors and prevents the establishment of long-term potentiation in CA1 neurons, has no effect on long-term potentiation in field CA3. The mechanism responsible for this phenomenon is not yet known.

In recent years the phenomenon of long-term potentiation has received a considerable amount of attention from scientists interested in the cellular basis of learning, and

their interest appears to be justified. The fact that long-term potentiation can be produced in several regions besides the hippocampal formation suggests that the mechanisms that underlie this phenomenon may be widespread in the brain. The discovery of the functions of the NMDA receptor provides solid evidence for at least one mechanism that produces the type of synapse that Hebb predicted a half-century ago. However, other mechanisms of synaptic plasticity also exist, and little is known about them. The progress of the last few years in research on the cellular basis of learning suggests that someday we really may come to understand it.

● Role of Long-Term Potentiation in Learning

If the synaptic changes that constitute learning are accomplished by long-term potentiation, then we should suspect that disruption of long-term potentiation should also disrupt learning; and it does. The injection of AP5 into the hippocampal formation, which disrupts NMDA-mediated long-term potentiation, interferes with learning. In addition, certain learning experiences produce synaptic changes in the hippocampal formation. Because the role of the hippocampus in learning is complex, research on this topic is discussed in Chapter 15, which deals with relational learning.

Several studies have investigated the relationship between long-term potentiation elsewhere in the brain and the acquisition of a classically conditioned emotional response; these studies are discussed later in this chapter.

Interim Summary

Many studies have shown that the brains of animals that spend time in a complex environment are themselves more complex. Learning experiences facilitate brain development and even cause structural changes in the brains of adults. Presumably, these changes represent the memories that result from these experiences.

The study of long-term potentiation in the hippocampal formation has suggested a mechanism that might be responsible for at least some of the synaptic changes that occur during learning. A circuit of neurons passes through the hippocampal formation, from the entorhinal cortex to the dentate gyrus, to field CA3, to field CA1, to the subiculum. High-frequency stimulation of the axons in this circuit strengthens synapses; it leads to an increase in the size of the EPSPs in the dendritic spines of the postsynaptic neurons. Associative long-term potentiation can also occur, in which weak synapses are strengthened by the action of strong ones. In fact, the only requirement for long-term potentiation is that the postsynaptic membrane be depolarized at the same time that the synapses are active.

In field CA1 and in the dentate gyrus, NMDA receptors play a special role in long-term potentiation. These receptors, sensitive to glutamate, control calcium channels but can open them only if the membrane is already depolarized. Thus, the combination of membrane depolarization (for example, from a dendritic spike produced by the activity of strong synapses) and activation of a NMDA receptor causes the entry of calcium ions. The increase in calcium activates several calcium-dependent enzymes. Inhibition of these enzymes disrupts long-term potentiation; presumably, they cause the insertion of AMPA receptors into the membrane of the dendritic spine, increasing its sensitivity to glutamate released by the terminal button. This change is accompanied by structural alterations in the shape of the dendritic spine, including the appearance of synapse perforated by "fingers" inserted into the terminal button. The enzymes may also produce presynaptic changes, through the activation of NO synthase, an enzyme responsible for the production of nitric oxide. This soluble gas may diffuse into nearby terminal buttons where it triggers the synthesis of cyclic GMP. This messenger may facilitate the release of glutamate. Long-lasting, long-term potentiation requires protein synthesis, which appears to take place in the dendrite adjacent to the dendritic spines.

Long-term depression occurs when a synapse is activated at the time that the postsynaptic membrane is hyperpolarized or only slightly depolarized. If long-term potentiation and long-term depression occurred only in the hippocampal formation, their discovery would still be an interesting finding, but the fact that they also occur in several other regions of the brain suggests that they may play an important role in many forms of learning.

PERCEPTUAL LEARNING

Learning enables us to adapt to our environment and to respond to changes in it. In particular, it provides us with the ability to perform an appropriate behavior in an appropriate situation. Situations can be as simple as the sound of a buzzer or as complex as the social interactions of a group of people. The first part of learning involves learning to perceive.

Perceptual learning involves learning *about* things, not *what to do* when they are present. (Learning what to do is discussed in the subsequent sections of this chapter.) Per-

ceptual learning can involve learning to recognize entirely new stimuli, or it can involve learning to recognize changes or variations in familiar stimuli. For example, if a friend gets a new hairstyle or replaces glasses with contact lenses, our visual memory of that person changes. We also learn that particular stimuli are found in particular locations or contexts or in the presence of other stimuli. We can even learn and remember particular *episodes:* sequences of events taking place at a particular time and place. The more complex forms of perceptual learning will be discussed in Chapter 15, which is devoted to relational learning.

Simple perceptual learning—learning to recognize particular stimuli or categories of stimuli—appears to take place in appropriate regions of sensory association cortex. That is, learning to recognize particular sounds takes place in the auditory association cortex; learning to recognize particular objects by sight takes place in the visual association cortex; and so on. *Very* simple perceptual learning—for example, of simple sounds—can even be accomplished subcortically, presumably by mechanisms we inherited from our remote ancestors, who lived before the evolution of the cerebral cortex. This section describes research on visual and auditory learning that illustrates some of the progress that has been made in understanding this topic.

● Learning to Recognize Visual Stimuli

In mammals with large and complex brains objects are recognized visually by circuits of neurons in the visual association cortex. As we saw in Chapter 6, the primary visual cortex receives information from the lateral geniculate nucleus of the thalamus. Within the primary visual cortex individual modules of neurons analyze information from restricted regions of the visual scene that pertain to movement, orientation, color, binocular disparity, and spatial frequency. Information about each of these attributes is collected in subregions of the extrastriate cortex, which surrounds the primary visual cortex (striate cortex). For example, specific regions are devoted to the analysis of form, color, and movement. After analyzing particular attributes of the visual scene, the subregions of the extrastriate cortex send the results of their analysis to the next level of the visual association cortex. As we saw in Chapter 6, the second level of the visual association cortex is divided into two "streams." The *ventral stream,* which is involved with object recognition, begins in the extrastriate cortex and continues ventrally into the inferior temporal cortex. The *dorsal stream,* which is involved with perception of the location of objects, also begins in the extrastriate cortex of the occipital lobe, but it continues dorsally into the posterior parietal cortex. As some investigators have said, the ventral stream

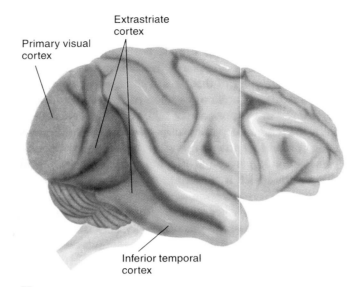

Figure 14.21
The major divisions of the visual cortex of the rhesus monkey. The arrows indicate the primary direction of the flow of information in the dorsal and ventral streams.

is involved with the *what* of visual perception; the dorsal stream is involved with the *where*. (See *Figure 14.21*.)

Let's first consider the ventral stream. Many studies have shown that lesions that damage the inferior temporal cortex disrupt the ability to discriminate between different visual stimuli. Mishkin (1966) showed that if visual information were prevented from reaching the inferior temporal cortex, monkeys lost the ability to distinguish between different visual patterns. First, he removed the striate cortex on one side of the brain and tested the animals' ability to discriminate between visual patterns. They performed well. Next, he removed the contralateral inferior temporal cortex; again, no deficit. Finally, he cut the corpus callosum, which isolated the remaining inferior temporal cortex from the remaining primary visual cortex. This time, the animals could no longer perform the visual discrimination task. Therefore, we can conclude that the inferior temporal cortex is necessary for visual pattern discrimination and that it must receive information from the primary visual cortex. (See *Figure 14.22*.)

Presumably, learning to recognize a particular visual stimulus is accomplished by changes in synaptic connections in the inferior temporal cortex that establish new neural circuits—changes such as the ones described in the previous section of this chapter. At a later time, when the animal sees the same stimulus again and the same pattern of activity is transmitted to the inferior temporal cortex, these circuits become active again. This activity constitutes

the recognition of the stimulus—the "readout" of the visual memory, so to speak.

As we saw in Chapter 6, some neurons in the inferior temporal cortex show remarkable specificity in their response characteristics, which suggests that they are part of circuits that detect the presence of specific stimuli. For example, neurons located near the superior temporal sulcus become active when the animal is shown pictures of faces. Baylis, Rolls, and Leonard (1985) found that most of these neurons are sensitive to *particular* faces. Rolls and Baylis (1986) found that the responses of some of these neurons remain constant even if the picture is blurred or changed in color, size, or distance. Thus, these neurons belong to circuits of neurons that recognize the *identities* of particular faces, not simply a specific view.

Rolls et al. (1989) found that as monkeys became familiar with particular faces, the response characteristics of

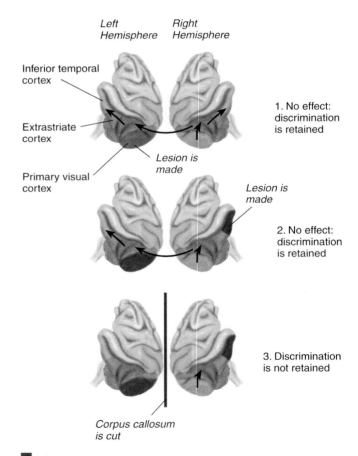

Figure 14.22
The procedure used by Mishkin (1966). Not all of the control groups used in the experiment are shown here.
(Adapted from Mishkin, M., in *Frontiers in Physiological Psychology*, edited by R.W. Russell. New York: Academic Press, 1966.)

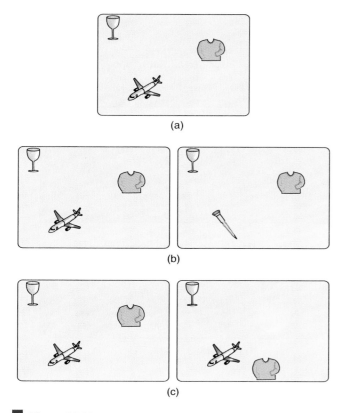

Figure 14.23
Examples of the types of stimuli used in the PET-scanning study by Moscovitch et al., 1995. (a) One of the stimuli to be memorized. (b) The object-memory retrieval task. One of the objects in the right-hand figure is incorrect. (c) The spatial-memory retrieval task. One of the objects in the right-hand figure is located in the wrong place.
(Adapted from Moscovitch, M., Kapur, S., Koehler, S., and Houle, S. *Proceedings of the National Academy of Sciences*, 1995, 92, 3721–3725.)

some face-sensitive neurons in the inferior temporal cortex changed. They presented monkeys with pictures of human and monkey faces on the screen of a video monitor. They found that many cells showed changes in their response characteristic when new faces were shown to the monkey. For example, in one experiment they showed the same set of five faces, one at a time, for several trials. Most neurons showed rather stable responses. Then the experimenters introduced a new face into the series. After one or two presentations the response pattern to the familiar faces changed. This finding suggests that learning caused a "rewiring" of the neural circuits to which these neurons belonged.

Perceptual learning can take place very rapidly, and the number of items that can be remembered is enormous. In fact, Standing (1973) showed people 10,000 color slides and found that they could recognize most of them weeks

later. Other primates are capable of remembering items they have seen for just a few seconds, and the experience changes the responses of neurons in their visual association cortex (Rolls, 1995a).

Two recent studies using PET scanners (Moscovitch et al., 1995; Owen et al., 1996) have found that the recall of perceptual memories of the identities and locations of objects in the human brain involve activity in the ventral and dorsal streams, respectively. Let's consider just one of these studies. Moscovitch and his colleagues measured the activity of the human brain during the recall of the identity and location of visual stimuli—in other words, the retrieval of perceptual memories of objects and their locations. First, they had people study and memorize 28 different visual displays such as the ones illustrated in Figure 14.23. Each display contained a set of three objects placed in specific locations on the screen. Later, the subjects were shown a pair of displays, one that they had seen before and one that they had never seen, and were asked to indicate which was which. The displays differed in one of two ways. During the *object-memory retrieval task*, one of the objects from the familiar display was replaced with a new object. During the *spatial-memory retrieval task*, all three objects were the same, but one of them was shown in a new location. The PET scanner recorded the subjects' regional cerebral blood flow while they were performing these tasks. (See *Figure 14.23.*)

The results of the experiment are shown in Figure 14.24. As you can see, both tasks produced activity in the visual association cortex of the occipital, temporal, and parietal lobes, as well as a region of the frontal cortex. (See *Figure 14.24a.*) The two scans at the bottom show the differences between the upper two scans. As you can see, the object-memory retrieval task activated the ventral stream in the inferior temporal cortex, while the spatial-memory retrieval task activated the dorsal stream in the posterior parietal cortex. (See *Figure 14.24b.*)

● Visual Short-Term Memory

So far, all the studies I have mentioned involved simple recognition of visual stimuli, either particular objects or their locations. What neural circuits are involved not only in recognizing stimuli but in remembering them for a period of time? As we will see, **short-term memory**—memory of information that has just been presented, involves the prefrontal cortex as well as the sensory association cortex.

short-term memory   Memory for a stimulus that has just been perceived.

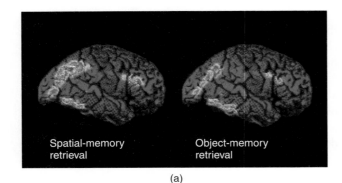

(a)

Spatial-memory retrieval

Object-memory retrieval

Posterior parietal cortex

Inferior temporal cortex

Spatial retrieval minus object retrieval

Object retrieval minus spatial retrieval

(b)

Figure 14.24
The results of PET scans from the task shown in Figure 14.23. (From Moscovitch, M., Kapur, S., Koehler, S., and Houle, S. *Proceedings of the National Academy of Sciences,* 1995, 92, 3721–3725.)

Most studies of short-term memory employ a **delayed matching-to-sample task,** which requires an animal to remember a particular stimulus for a period of time. For example, Fuster and Jervey (1981) trained monkeys on such a task. They turned on a colored light (yellow, green, red, or blue) behind a translucent disk (the *sample stimulus*), turned it off, and, after a delay interval, turned on yellow, green, red, and blue lights behind four other disks (the *test stimuli*). (See *Figure 14.25.*) If the monkey pressed the disk whose color matched the one it had just seen, it received a piece of food.

While the monkeys were performing this task, the experimenters recorded the activity of single neurons in the inferior temporal cortex. Some neurons responded selectively to color: to yellow, red, green, or blue. Presumably, they became active because the *circuits* of neurons of which they were a part became active. It is these circuits, not individual neurons, that recognize particular stimuli. In addition, many of these neurons remained active during the delay interval. For example, Figure 14.26 shows data from a neuron that responded to red light, but not to green light, during a 16-second delay interval. The horizontal lines

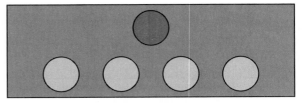

Sample stimulus

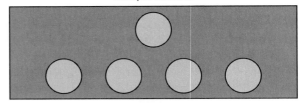

Delay interval

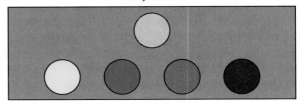

Matching stimuli

Figure 14.25
The delayed matching-to-sample procedure used by Fuster and Jervey (1981).

above each graph represent individual trials; vertical tick marks represent action potentials. The graphs beneath the horizontal lines are sums of the individual trials, showing the total responses during successive intervals. As you can see, when the sample stimulus consisted of a red light, the neuron became active—and remained active even after the sample stimulus went off. (See *Figure 14.26.*) Under normal conditions a stimulus causes a neuron to respond briefly. Thus, the sustained response during the delay interval suggests that the neuron was part of a circuit involved in a particular visual short-term memory: remembering that a red light was presented. Similar experiments have shown that neurons in the posterior parietal lobe—in the dorsal stream—retain information about the location of a visual stimulus that has just been perceived (Constantinidis and Steinmetz, 1996).

Visual short-term memory appears to *require* the activity of neurons in the inferior temporal cortex throughout the delay interval. Kovner and Stamm (1972) implanted electrodes in the inferior temporal cortex of monkeys and

delayed matching-to-sample task   A task that requires the subject to indicate which of several stimuli has just been perceived.

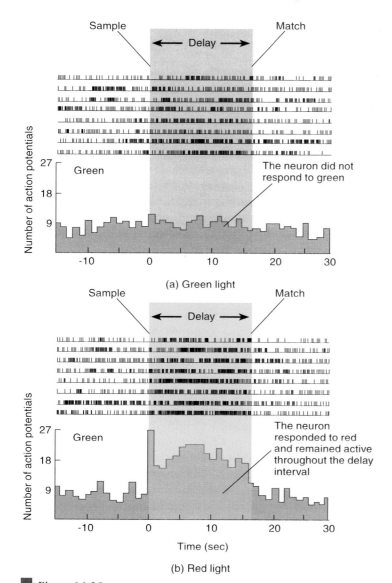

Sample   Match

← Delay →

Number of action potentials

27

18

9

-10   0   10   20   30

Green

The neuron did not respond to green

(a) Green light

Sample   Match

← Delay →

Number of action potentials

27

18

9

-10   0   10   20   30

Green

The neuron responded to red and remained active throughout the delay interval

Time (sec)

(b) Red light

Figure 14.26

Responses of a single unit during the presentation of the sample stimulus, the delay interval, and the presentation of matching stimuli in the experiment outlined in Figure 14.25.

(From Fuster, J.M., in *Conditioning: Representation of Involved Neural Functions,* edited by C.D. Woody. New York: Plenum Press, 1982. Reprinted with permission.)

trained them on a visual delayed matching-to-sample task. Once the monkeys had learned the task, they electrically stimulated the cortex through the electrodes from time to time while the animals were performing. When they administered the stimulation during the delay interval, just before they showed the monkeys the test stimuli, the animals performed poorly on that trial. It was as if the stimulation had disrupted the normal activity in the cortex and erased the memory of the stimulus the monkeys had just seen.

A similar experiment suggests that short-term memory of the location of objects requires neural activity of the

posterior parietal lobe. Oyachi and Ohtsuka (1995) temporarily disrupted the activity of the human posterior parietal cortex by means of **transcranial magnetic stimulation.** When alternating current is passed through an electromagnetic coil placed against the skull, the magnetic field temporarily disrupts the activity of the neural circuits in the brain located beneath the coil. The investigators found that disruption of the right posterior parietal cortex disrupted performance of a delayed matching-to-sample task that required people to move their eyes toward the location of a stimulus that had been presented two seconds earlier.

Although the neural circuits responsible for visual memories appear to reside in the visual association cortex, short-term memory involves other brain regions, as well—especially the prefrontal cortex. Both major regions of the visual association cortex—the ventral stream of the inferior temporal cortex and the dorsal stream of the posterior parietal cortex—have direct connections with the dorsolateral prefrontal cortex. Each of these regions of visual association cortex is individually connected with a particular region of the prefrontal cortex (Wilson, Scalaidhe, and Goldman-Rakic, 1993). In fact, the dorsolateral prefrontal cortex is involved in short-term memory for all sense modalities. Damage to this region or temporary deactivation by cooling the cortex disrupts performance on a variety of delayed matching-to-sample tasks using visual, tactile, or auditory stimuli (Passingham, 1975; Bauer and Fuster, 1976; Shindy, Posley, and Fuster, 1994; Bodner, Kroger, and Fuster, 1996).

As we saw, researchers have found that neurons in the visual association cortex appear to encode short-term memory for visual stimuli. Several studies have found that neurons in the dorsolateral prefrontal cortex do so as well. For example, Miller, Erickson, and Desimone (1996) found many neurons in this region that responded selectively to particular visual stimuli and maintained their activity during the delay period of a delayed matching-to-sample task. In addition, many neurons responded differently to a test stimulus depending on whether it matched the sample stimulus. But why should there be neural activity encoding sensory information in the frontal lobes? Most researchers believe that the reciprocal connections

transcranial magnetic stimulation Stimulation of the cortex by the magnetic field produced by alternating current passing through a coil placed against the skull; disrupts normal activity of the affected brain region.

between the dorsolateral prefrontal cortex and various regions of sensory association cortex in the parietal and temporal lobes form feedback loops. Sensory information activates circuits of neurons in the sensory association cortex that are responsible for perceptual memories. These circuits transmit information to the dorsolateral prefrontal cortex, and activity in the connections between the two regions maintains the information as long as it is required.

Quintana and Fuster (1992) found that under some conditions, neurons in the dorsolateral prefrontal cortex also encode information about the response that the animal is about to make. In the delayed matching-to-sample tasks I have described so far, the animals did not know what response they should make until the test stimuli were presented. Thus, the only way they could make the correct response would be to remember the sample stimulus. Quintana and Fuster's task was somewhat different. They trained monkeys on a delayed responding task in which the color of a signal light indicated which of two responses should be made. A yellow signal meant that the monkey should press the right-hand button after a delay period, and a blue signal meant that it should press the left-hand button. Thus, as soon as the monkeys saw the stimulus they knew what response should be made. The investigators found that some neurons in the dorsolateral prefrontal cortex encoded information about the color of the signal light during the delay interval and that others encoded information about the nature of the response that was to be made.

The study by Quintana and Fuster suggests that some tasks permit the subject to remember a *response*, not simply the stimulus that was presented. For example, if someone shows you a written word, you can remember what the word looks like, what it sounds like, or what movements you would make to pronounce it. We might predict, then, that seeing a word would first activate neurons in the visual association cortex, but after that neurons in the auditory association cortex or motor association cortex would become active. As we shall see in a discussion of verbal abilities in Chapter 16, this appears to be exactly what happens.

● Auditory Learning: Role of Acetylcholine

Although visual learning has received more attention than other forms of perceptual learning, it is clear that learning to recognize stimuli presented to the other sense modalities involves changes in neural circuits located in other areas of sensory association cortex. I will discuss one other example of perceptual learning: recognition of an auditory stimulus that evokes a conditioned emotional response.

This example provides the opportunity to describe the effects of arousal on synaptic plasticity within the neocortex.

By itself, perceptual learning is useless. The function of perceptual learning is to permit us to recognize particular people, objects, and events and respond appropriately. In other words, perceptual learning is useful only in conjunction with other forms of learning, which guide our behavior. Although we can learn to recognize stimuli even when nothing important happens, the occurrence of an important stimulus—one that motivates us to approach or escape from it—facilitates perceptual learning. In other words, we are more likely to remember stimuli associated with events that affect us emotionally.

As we saw in Chapter 4, several systems of neurons project their axons to widespread regions of the brain. The most important of these release acetylcholine, dopamine, norepinephrine, and serotonin. As we saw in Chapters 9 and 11, the release of norepinephrine appears to increase an animal's vigilance, and the release of serotonin appears to inhibit species-typical reactions such as aggressive behaviors. As we shall see later in this chapter, the release of dopamine appears to reinforce ongoing behavior, thus facilitating instrumental conditioning. That leaves acetylcholine. We saw in Chapter 9 that the release of acetylcholine activates the cerebral cortex. As we shall now see, this activation appears to facilitate perceptual learning.

Investigators have long known that the administration of drugs that disrupt acetylcholinergic transmission in the brain impairs learning (Deutsch, 1983). In addition, one of the first signs of Alzheimer's disease, a disease that results in widespread neural degeneration in the brain, is loss of memory. At first, the person may have difficulty remembering appointments and sometimes fails to think of words or people's names. As time passes, he or she shows increasing confusion and increasing difficulty with tasks such as balancing a checkbook. If the person ventures outside alone, he or she is likely to get lost. Eventually, as the degeneration continues, the person becomes bedridden and completely helpless and finally succumbs.

Acetylcholinergic neurons are among the first neurons to degenerate in Alzheimer's disease; thus, loss of these neurons may be, at least in part, responsible for the memory impairments. The cell bodies of ACh-secreting neurons reside in subcortical areas. The cell bodies of neurons that project to the neocortex are found in the nucleus basalis, located in the basal forebrain near the preoptic area, and those that project to the hippocampus are found in the medial septum. Both of these nuclei degenerate in the brains of patients with Alzheimer's disease (Nakano and Hirano, 1982; Whitehouse et al., 1982).

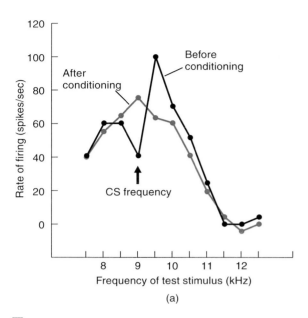

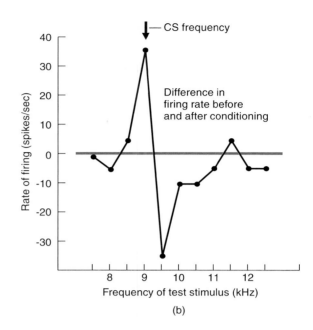

(a)

(b)

Figure 14.27
Rate of firing of a single neuron in the primary auditory cortex to tones of various frequencies.
(a) Responses before (black) and after (color) classical conditioning. The CS was a tone of 9 kHz
(arrow). (b) Changes in responses caused by conditioning.
(Adapted from Bakin, J.S., and Weinberger, N.M. *Brain Research,* 1990, 536, 271–286.)

A series of experiments by Weinberger and his colleagues showed that an auditory learning task modifies the response characteristics of neurons in various parts of the auditory system (Bakin and Weinberger, 1990; Edeline and Weinberger, 1991a; 1991b; 1992). The researchers established a classically conditioned emotional response in guinea pigs by pairing a tone of a particular frequency with a brief foot shock. As we saw in Chapter 11, after these stimuli are paired, the tone becomes a CS; it elicits a range of behavioral, autonomic, and hormonal responses, such as freezing, increased blood pressure, secretion of adrenal stress hormones, and so on. Before the training the researchers implanted microelectrodes in various parts of the auditory system. They presented the animals with a series of tones of different frequencies and recorded the rate of neural firing to each frequency. Most neurons in the auditory system are frequency-sensitive; that is, they are activated more by some frequencies than by others.

After determining the cells' responses to tones of different frequencies, the experimenters presented the animals with the tone–shock pairs and again recorded the cells' responses. They found that the training changed the pattern of many of the neurons' responses. Figure 14.27(a) shows the record obtained from one such cell, located in the pri-

mary auditory cortex. The pretraining response is shown in black, and the posttraining response (obtained 1 hour after training) is shown in color. As you can see, before the training the cell responded best to a 9.5-kHz tone. After the training the cell responded best to the 9-kHz training tone and reduced its response to the 9.5-kHz tone. Figure 14.27(b) shows the difference between the two curves. (See *Figure 14.27.*)

In the next section of this chapter I will review the evidence concerning the location of the synaptic changes responsible for acquisition of a classically conditioned emotional response. For now, we will concern ourselves with the auditory learning that takes place in this situation. As we just saw, the training changes the response characteristics of neurons in the primary auditory cortex. These changes are long-lasting; they are still seen up to 8 weeks later. Auditory information is provided by the ventral division of the medial geniculate nucleus of the thalamus. When an animal receives a footshock, the painful stimulus activates the central nucleus of the amygdala, which, as we saw in Chapter 11, is responsible for a constellation for emotional responses. (The pathway by which information about aversive stimuli reaches the central nucleus is described later in this chapter.)

Besides organizing an emotional response, the central nucleus activates the **nucleus basalis,** the nucleus that contains acetylcholinergic neurons that innervate the cerebral cortex. The acetylcholinergic input to the auditory cortex tells the cells to pay particular attention to the input they are currently receiving from the ventral division of the medial geniculate nucleus and to become more sensitive to that input. The results are changes in the response characteristics of the auditory cortex neurons. (See *Figure 14.28.*)

Weinberger and his colleagues have shown that the release of acetylcholine in the primary auditory cortex is the event that induces synaptic changes in the auditory cortex. As a result of these changes, neurons become more sensitive to the auditory information they are currently receiving—that is, to the CS. Bakin and Weinberger (1996) found that when they simultaneously presented a tone of a particular frequency and electrically stimulated the nucleus basalis, causing the release of acetylcholine in the neocortex, neurons in the auditory cortex became more sensitive to that frequency. This effect was blocked by atropine, a drug that blocks acetylcholine receptors. Cruikshank and Weinberger (1996) found that this effect resembled long-term potentiation. When they simultaneously presented a tone and directly depolarized a neuron in the auditory cortex with a microelectrode, the neuron became more sensitive to tones of that frequency.

The results of these experiments indicate that perceptual learning is an important component of classical conditioning; animals are more likely to learn to recognize stimuli that are important to them. As we shall see in the next major section of this chapter, recent research is beginning to discover the neural circuits responsible for several forms of classical conditioning.

Interim Summary

Perceptual learning occurs as a result of changes in synaptic connections within the sensory association cortex. Damage to a monkey's inferior temporal cortex—the highest level of visual association cortex—disrupts visual discriminations. Electrical recording studies have shown that some neurons respond preferentially to particular complex stimuli, including faces. When new stimuli are presented, the response patterns of some neurons in the inferior temporal cortex change, which suggests that "rewiring" may be taking place. PET studies with humans have shown that retrieval of visual memories of objects activates the inferior temporal cortex and that retrieval of memories of locations activates the posterior parietal cortex.

Visual short-term memory involves the activation of neurons in the visual association cortex. Electrical-recording studies have shown that some neurons in the inferior temporal cortex encode the information presented during the sample period of a delayed matching-to-sample task and continue to fire during the delay interval. Electrical stimulation of the inferior temporal cortex during the delay interval of this task disrupts performance, as if the memory of the stimulus had been erased. Erasure of visual short-term memories can also be produced in human subjects by transcranial magnetic stimulation. The dorsolateral prefrontal cortex is also involved in short-term memory. Lesions or temporary deactivation of this brain region disrupts performance on delayed matching-to-sample tasks using a variety of different sense modalities. Neurons in this region encode information pertaining to the stimulus that must be remembered or, in some tasks, to the response to be made.

A series of studies using auditory stimuli suggest that when a tone is paired with an aversive stimulus, changes can be seen in the responses of neurons in the auditory cortex when that stimulus is presented again. The change appears to be triggered by the activation of the central nucleus of the amygdala which plays an important role in emotional responses. The central nucleus activates the nu-

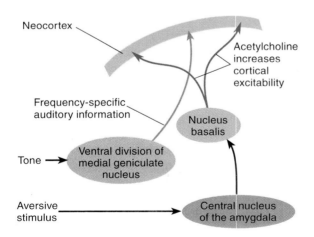

Figure 14.28
Weinberger's hypothetical explanation for the changes in frequency responses of neurons in the primary auditory cortex that occur after a tone is paired with an aversive stimulus.

nucleus basalis A nucleus of the basal forebrain that contains most of the acetylcholine-secreting neurons that send axons to the neocortex; degenerates in patients with Alzheimer's disease.

cleus basalis, which results in the release of acetylcholine in the cortex. The changes in the response characteristics of the cortical neurons are triggered by the depolarizing effects of this neurotransmitter.

CLASSICAL CONDITIONING

Neuroscientists have studied the anatomy and physiology of classical conditioning using many models, such as the gill withdrawal reflex in *Aplysia* (a marine invertebrate) or the eyeblink reflex in the rabbit (Carew, 1989; Lavond, Kim, and Thompson, 1993). I have chosen to describe a simple mammalian model of classical conditioning—the conditioned emotional response—to illustrate the results of such investigations.

The central nucleus of the amygdala plays an important role in organizing a pattern of emotional responses that are provoked by aversive stimuli, both learned and unlearned. As we saw in Chapter 11, when this nucleus is activated, its efferent connections with other regions of the brain trigger several behavioral, autonomic, and endocrine responses that are elicited by aversive stimuli. Most stimuli that cause an aversive emotional response are not intrinsically aversive; we have to *learn* to fear them. The central nucleus of the amygdala is part of an important system involved in a particular form of stimulus–response (S–R) learning: the classically conditioned emotional responses.

As we saw earlier in this chapter, one of the things that the central nucleus of the amygdala does when it is activated is stimulate the release of acetylcholine in the cerebral cortex. This release facilitates perceptual learning: It activates cortical neurons and facilitates the establishment of neural circuits sensitive to the CS. Presumably, the rewiring of these circuits is accomplished by means of long-term potentiation.

What about classical conditioning itself? A conditioned emotional response to a very simple auditory stimulus can occur in the absence of the auditory cortex (LeDoux et al., 1984); thus, I will confine my discussion to the subcortical components of this process. Information about the CS (the tone) reaches a part of the thalamus known as the **MGm** (the medial division of the medial geniculate nucleus). Information about the US (the foot shock) reaches both the MGm and the basolateral amygdala. Thus, there is convergence of information about the CS and the US in two regions: the MGm and the basolateral amygdala. Synaptic changes responsible for learning could take place in either (or both) of these locations.

A hypothetical neural circuit is shown in Figure 14.29. When a rat encounters a painful stimulus, strong synapses

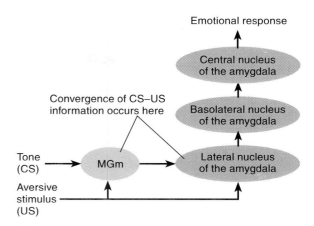

Figure 14.29
The probable location of the changes in synaptic strength produced by the classically conditioned emotional response that results from pairing a tone with a foot shock.

in the MGm and the basolateral amygdala are activated; as a result, neurons in the central nucleus begin firing, evoking an unlearned (unconditioned) emotional response. If a tone is paired with the painful stimulus, the weak synapses in the MGm and the basolateral amygdala are strengthened, through the action of the Hebb rule. (See *Figure 14.29*.)

This hypothesis has a considerable amount of support. Lesions of the MGm, basolateral amygdala, or central nucleus disrupt conditioned emotional responses that involve a simple auditory stimulus as a CS and a shock to the feet as a US (Iwata et al., 1986; LeDoux et al., 1986, 1990; Sananes and Davis, 1992). Thus, the synaptic changes responsible for this learning appear to take place within this circuit.

There is evidence for synaptic changes in both the MGm and the basolateral amygdala. A single-unit-recording study by Weinberger and his colleagues (reported by Weinberger, 1982) showed that neurons in the MGm increased their responsiveness to the auditory CS after this stimulus was paired with an aversive US.

Quirk, Repa, and LeDoux (1995) found similar changes in the lateral amygdala. They recorded the activity of neurons in the lateral amygdala in freely moving rats before, during, and after pairing of a tone with footshock. Within a few trials, neurons became more responsive to the tone, and many neurons that had not previously responded to

MGm The medial division of the medial geniculate nucleus; transmits auditory and somatosensory information to the lateral nucleus of the amygdala.

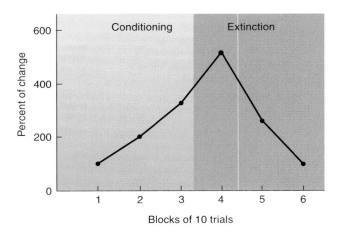

Figure 14.30
Change in rate of firing of neurons in the lateral amygdala in response to the tone, relative to baseline levels.
(Adapted from Quirk, G.J., Repa, J.C., and LeDoux, J.E. *Neuron*, 1995, *15*, 1029–1039.)

the tone began doing so. (See *Figure 14.30.*) The greatest augmentation was seen in short-latency responses, which are received directly from the thalamus; thus, the synaptic changes must have been occurring in the circuit shown in Figure 14.30, not elsewhere in the brain. Quirk and his colleagues suggest that although changes take place in both the thalamus and the amygdala, the amygdala appears to be a more important site of learning. They note that in the lateral nucleus of the amygdala, 88 percent of the neurons that respond to a tone also respond to footshock, whereas in the MGm, the figure is only 38 percent. (As we saw in the beginning of this chapter, classical conditioning requires that information from the CS and the US converge on the same neuron.)

Seeing that it is likely that the synaptic changes responsible for classically conditioned emotional responses take place in two particular locations, we can ask whether these changes may be produced by a phenomenon we already know something about: long-term potentiation. Indeed, studies have shown that long-term potentiation can take place in the synaptic connections in both the MGm and the basolateral amygdala. Gerren and Weinberger (1983) found that high-frequency stimulation of the axons that bring auditory information into the MGm produced long-term potentiation in this nucleus, and Clugnet and Le-Doux (1990) found that stimulation of the medial geniculate nucleus produced long-term potentiation in the lateral amygdala. Even more significantly, Rogan and LeDoux (1995) found that when long-term potentiation was produced in the lateral nucleus of the amygdala, neurons there became more responsive to auditory stimuli.

As we saw, long-term potentiation in at least some parts of the brain is accomplished through the activation of NMDA receptors. Several experiments suggest that these receptors also participate in the synaptic plasticity that occurs in the amygdala. When AP5 (a drug that blocks NMDA receptors) is injected directly into the basolateral amygdala, rats no longer learned a conditioned emotional response. However, if the AP5 is injected *after* a classically conditioned emotional response has been established, the drug had no effect (Campeau, Miserendino, and Davis, 1992; Fanselow and Kim, 1994). Thus, it seems that AP5 can disrupt the establishment of learning by blocking synaptic plasticity in the basolateral amygdala, but the drug does not affect synaptic changes that have already taken place.

Some experimental evidence suggests that synaptic plasticity controlled by the activation of NMDA receptors may play a role in *extinction* of a classically conditioned emotional response. Classical conditioning is not always forever. If, after classical conditioning has been established by pairing a CS and a US, the CS is presented repeatedly by itself, the conditioned response will eventually disappear—a process known as **extinction.** Falls, Miserendino, and Davis (1992) found that thirty presentations of the CS alone were sufficient to extinguish a classically conditioned emotional response. However, if they injected AP5 into the amygdala just before these thirty extinction trials, the response did *not* extinguish. Thus, NMDA-mediated synaptic plasticity seems to be necessary for both learning and extinction. From what we learned earlier in this chapter, it would appear that these changes involve the phenomenon of long-term *depression.*

Interim Summary

You have already encountered the conditioned emotional response in Chapter 11 and in the previous section of this chapter, where I discussed perceptual learning. When an auditory stimulus (CS) is paired with a foot shock (US), the two types of information converge in the medial division of the medial geniculate nucleus (MGm) and again in the lateral amygdala. The lateral amygdala is connected, via the basolateral nucleus, with the central nucleus, which is responsible for the various components of the emotional

extinction With respect to classical conditioning, the reduction or elimination of a conditional response by repeatedly presenting the conditional stimulus without the unconditional stimulus.

response. Lesions anywhere in this circuit disrupt the response.

Recordings of single neurons in both the MGm and the lateral nucleus of the amygdala indicate that classical conditioning changes the response of neurons to the CS. The mechanism of synaptic plasticity in this system appears to be NMDA-mediated long-term potentiation. High-frequency electrical stimulation of the inputs to both the MGm and the lateral amygdala produces long-term potentiation, and long-term potentiation in the lateral nucleus increases the responses of neurons there to auditory stimuli. The establishment of long-term potentiation in the basolateral amygdala increases the sensitivity of neurons there to auditory stimuli. In addition, the infusion of AP5 into the lateral amygdala prevents classical conditioning from taking place but has no effect on conditioning that was established earlier. It also prevents the *extinction* of a conditioned emotional response.

INSTRUMENTAL CONDITIONING AND MOTOR LEARNING

Instrumental (operant) conditioning is the means by which we (and other animals) profit from experience. If, in a particular situation, we make a response that has favorable outcomes, we will tend to make the response again. Sometimes the response is one we already know how to perform, which means that all that needs to occur is a strengthening of connections between neural circuits that detect the relevant stimuli and those that control the relevant response. However, if the response is one we have not made before, our performance is likely to be slow and awkward. As we continue to practice the response, our behavior becomes faster, smoother, and more automatic. In other words, motor learning takes place, as well. This section first describes the neural pathways involved in instrumental conditioning and its close relative, motor learning, and then discusses the neural basis of reinforcement.

● Basal Ganglia

As we saw earlier in this chapter, instrumental conditioning entails the strengthening of connections between neural circuits that detect a particular stimulus and neural circuits that produce a particular response. Clearly, the circuits responsible for instrumental conditioning begin in various regions of the sensory association cortex, where perception takes place, and end in the motor association cortex of the frontal lobe, which controls movements. But what pathways are responsible for these connections, and

where do the synaptic changes responsible for the learning take place?

There are two major pathways between the sensory association cortex and the motor association cortex: direct transcortical connections and connections via the basal ganglia and thalamus. (A third pathway, involving the cerebellum and thalamus, also exists, but the role of this pathway in instrumental conditioning has until very recently received little attention from neuroscientists.) Both of these pathways appear to be involved in instrumental conditioning, but they play different roles.

The direct connections between the sensory association cortex and the motor association cortex are, as we saw earlier, involved in short-term memory. In conjunction with the hippocampal formation, they are also involved in the acquisition of episodic memories—complex perceptual memories of sequences of events that we witness or are described to us. (The acquisition of these types of memories is discussed in Chapter 15.) The transcortical connections are also involved in the acquisition of complex behaviors that involve deliberation or instruction. For example, a person learning to drive a car with a manual transmission might say: "Let's see, push in the clutch, move the shift lever to the left and then away from me—there, it's in gear—now let the clutch come up—oh! It died—I should have given it more gas. Let's see, clutch down, turn the key. . . ." A memorized set of rules (or an instructor sitting next to us) provides a script for us to follow. Of course, this process does not have to be audible or even involve actual movements of the speech muscles; a person can think in words with neural activity that does not result in overt behavior. (Animals that cannot communicate by means of language can acquire complex responses by observing and imitating the behavior of other animals.)

At first, performing a behavior through observation or by following a set of rules is slow and awkward. And because so much of the brain's resources are involved with recalling the rules and applying them to our behavior, we cannot respond to other stimuli in the environment—we must ignore events that might distract us. But then, with practice, the behavior becomes much more fluid. Eventually, we perform it without thinking and can easily do other things at the same time, such as carry on a conversation with passengers as we drive our car.

Evidence suggests that as learned behaviors become automatic and routine, they are "transferred" to the basal ganglia. The process seems to work like this. As we deliberately perform a complex behavior, the basal ganglia receive information about the stimuli that are present and the responses we are making. At first, the basal ganglia are passive "observers" of the situation, but as the behaviors are re-

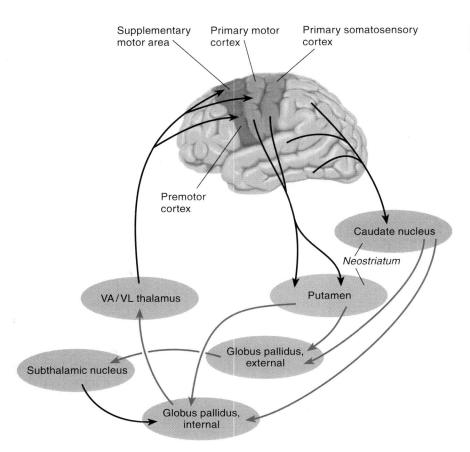

Figure 14.31
A schematic diagram of the basal ganglia and their connections.

peated again and again, they begin to learn what to do. Eventually, they take over most of the details of the process, leaving the transcortical circuits free to do something else. We need no longer think about what we are doing.

Before I discuss some evidence that supports the assertion that the basal ganglia are involved in instrumental conditioning, let me review the anatomy of the basal ganglia, first described in Chapter 8. The neostriatum—the caudate nucleus and the putamen—receive sensory information from all regions of the cerebral cortex. They also receive information from the frontal lobes about movements that are planned or are actually in progress. (So as you can see, the basal ganglia have all the information they need to monitor the progress of someone learning to drive a car.) The outputs of the caudate nucleus and the putamen are sent to another part of the basal ganglia: the globus pallidus. The outputs of this structure are sent to the frontal cortex—to the premotor and supplementary motor cortex, where plans for movements are made, and to the primary motor cortex, where they are executed. (See *Figure 14.31*.)

Now let's review some evidence that supports the assertion that the basal ganglia are involved in learning. Stud-

ies with laboratory animals have found that lesions of the basal ganglia disrupt instrumental conditioning but do not affect other forms of learning. Divac, Rosvold, and Szcwarcbart (1967) found that lesions of the caudate nucleus in monkeys disrupted acquisition of a simple instrumental conditioning task—a visual discrimination task. Gaffan and his colleagues (Gaffan and Harrison, 1987; Gaffan and Eacott, 1995) found that cutting all the connections between the visual association cortex and the frontal cortex *except* for the connections via the basal ganglia had no effect on a visual discrimination task. By a process of elimination, they said, acquisition of this task must involve the connections through the basal ganglia.

McDonald and White (1993) obtained similar results with rats. They tested three groups of animals, with lesions of three different parts of the brain, on three different learning tasks. One task involved episodic learning (remembering what places the rat had visited that day), another involved learning that a particular stimulus was associated with reinforcement, and the other involved an instrumental task: a simple brightness discrimination. Damage to the hippocampal formation disrupted only the episodic learn-

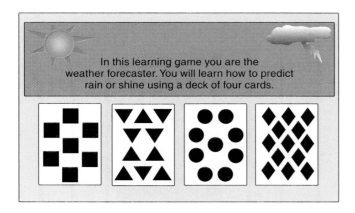

Figure 14.32
The probability learning task used by Knowlton, Mangels, and Squire.
(Adapted from Knowlton, B.J., Mangels, J.A., and Squire, L.R. *Science,* 1996, *273,* 1399–1402.)

ing, damage to the amygdala disrupted only the ability to learn the association of a stimulus with reinforcement, and damage to the caudate nucleus and putamen disrupted the ability to learn the instrumental task. Clearly, different neural pathways are involved in different types of learning.

Studies with humans also indicate that the basal ganglia play an important role in automatic, nondeliberate learning. Investigators have studied people with Parkinson's disease, a neurological disorder that affects the basal ganglia. As we saw in Chapters 4 and 8, Parkinson's disease is caused by degeneration of the dopaminergic neurons of the nigrostriatal system. The cell bodies of these neurons are located in the substantia nigra of the midbrain, and their axons terminate in the neostriatum: the caudate nucleus and the putamen. When the degeneration causes the release of dopamine in the neostriatum to fall to a sufficiently low level, the basal ganglia cease to function normally.

In the past, the symptoms of Parkinson's disease have been described as "motor deficits." However, some of them can be seen as failures of automated memories. For example, although people with Parkinson's disease have sufficient muscular strength, they have difficulty performing many everyday tasks, such as getting out of a chair. Also, if someone bumps into them while they are standing, they are likely to fall—and they will not put their hands out in front of them to catch themselves. These symptoms can, of course, be viewed as motor deficits. But we can also regard them as failure to remember how to do something. We do not think of rising from a chair as a learned behavior, but it surely must be. It involves leaning forward to bring our center of gravity over our feet before beginning to contract

the extensor muscles of our legs. Unless the disease is well advanced, people with Parkinson's disease can eventually stand up from a chair, but it takes them some time, as if they to have to think about how to do it. Similarly, we do not think of putting our hands out in front of us to break a fall as a learned response, but perhaps it is.

Several experiments have shown that people with Parkinson's disease have deficits that can definitely be attributed to difficulty in learning automatic responses. For example, Owen et al. (1992) found that patients with Parkinson's disease were impaired on learning a visual discrimination task. The patients performed normally on a test of visual recognition, which indicates that their impairment was not caused by a perceptual deficit.

Knowlton, Mangels, and Squire (1996) found that patients with Parkinson's disease did poorly on a probability learning task. The task required them to predict the weather. On each trial the subjects were shown one to three cards, each of which contained a particular pattern. Each pattern predicted either sunshine or rain, with a probability ranging from 25 percent to 75 percent. (See *Figure 14.32.*) Normal subjects gradually get better and better at this task, but most of them remain unaware of what they have learned—they are unable to state explicitly the rules they use to predict the weather. Knowlton and her colleagues found that the patients with Parkinson's disease failed to learn this task. Clearly, the results cannot be attributed to a motor deficit. (See *Figure 14.33.*)

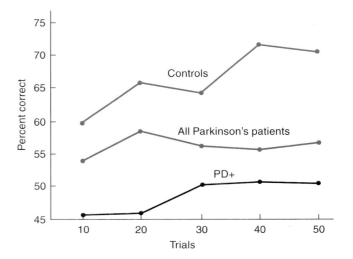

Figure 14.33
Results of subjects on the task illustrated in Figure 14.32. The curve labeled PD+ refers to those patients with Parkinson's disease who exhibited the worst motor symptoms.
(Adapted from Knowlton, B.J., Mangels, J.A., and Squire, L.R. *Science,* 1996, *273,* 1399–1402.)

● Premotor Cortex

The evidence I have reviewed indicates that the basal ganglia are involved in learning. And as we saw in the previous section of this chapter, the dorsolateral prefrontal cortex, along with the sensory association cortex, is involved in remembering stimuli that have just been perceived and, in some cases, the response that is about to be made. As we saw in Chapter 8, most of the output from the basal ganglia is directed, via the thalamus, to the premotor cortex and the adjacent supplementary motor area. (See *Figure 14.34.*) Because these cortical regions are involved in the planning and execution of movements, we might expect that they are also involved in learning—especially motor learning.

A considerable amount of research indicates that they are. Damage to the supplementary motor area does not appear to seriously disrupt simple discrimination tasks, in which a stimulus serves as a signal for the subject to make a response. However, it does disrupt self-initiated responses or sequences of responses in which the performance of one response serves as the signal that the next response must be made. Thaler et al. (1995) attempted to train normal monkeys and monkeys with lesions of the supplementary motor area on a simple instrumental task. All the monkeys had to do was extend their arm through an opening in the cage and raise it. Each time a monkey raised its arm, a machine dispensed a peanut into a hopper placed within easy reach. (See *Figure 14.35.*) The animals with lesions of the supplementary motor cortex were

Figure 14.35
The operant task from the study by Thaler et al., 1995. The monkey received a piece of food each time it raised its arm. (Adapted from Thaler, D., Chen, Y.-C., Nixon, P.D., Stern, C.E., and Passingham, R.E. *Experimental Brain Research*, 1995, *102*, 445–460.)

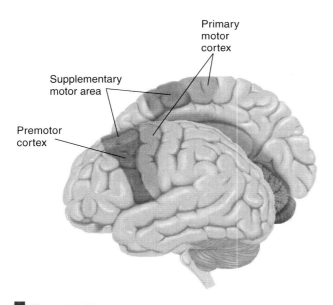

Figure 14.34
The premotor cortex: Lateral premotor cortex and supplementary motor area.

unable to learn this task. However, they had no difficulty learning to raise their arm in response to an auditory stimulus—a 700-Hz tone. Thus, their problem was not an inability to make the required movement, nor was it an inability to learn an instrumentally conditioned response. What they could not do was learn to make a *self-initiated* movement. In a second study by the same laboratory, Chen et al. (1995) found that lesions of the supplementary motor area severely impaired monkeys' ability to perform a perform a simple sequence of two responses. The task required them to push a lever in and then turn it to the left, receiving a peanut after each response. (See *Figure 14.36.*)

A single-unit recording study came to similar conclusions. Mushiake, Inase, and Tanji (1991) trained monkeys to perform a memorized series of responses, pressing each of three buttons in a specific sequence. While the monkeys were performing this task, more than half of the neurons in the supplementary motor area became activated. However, when the sequence was cued by visual stimuli—the monkeys simply had to press the button that was illuminated—these neurons showed little activity.

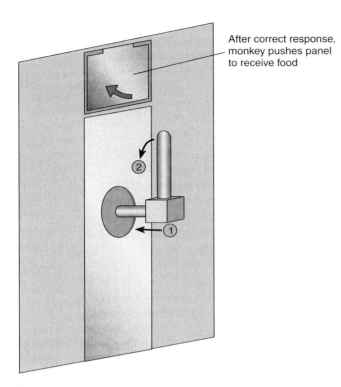

After correct response, monkey pushes panel to receive food

Figure 14.36
The handle used in the experiment by Chen et al., 1995. The monkey was required to push the handle in and then turn it to the left, receiving a piece of food in the door above the lever after each component of the sequence.
(Adapted from Chen, Y.-C., Thaler, D., Nixon, P.D., Stern, C.E., and Passingham, R.E. *Experimental Brain Research*, 1995, *102*, 461–473.)

A PET study with human subjects obtained similar results. Hikosaka et al. (1996) had people learn a sequence of button presses while their heads were placed in the scanner. During learning the anterior supplementary motor area became activated, and then during performance of the learned sequence the posterior supplementary motor area—the part immediately adjacent to the primary motor cortex—became activated. As anatomical studies have shown, the anterior and posterior supplementary motor areas have different inputs and outputs. The anterior region appears to be "upstream" from the posterior region. Only the posterior region has direct connections with the primary motor cortex (Luppino et al., 1993).

● Reinforcement

As we saw, learning provides a means for us to profit from experience—to make responses that provide favorable outcomes. When good things happen (that is, when reinforcing stimuli occur), reinforcement mechanisms in the brain become active, and the establishment of synaptic changes is facilitated. The discovery of the existence of such reinforcement mechanisms occurred by accident.

Discovery of Reinforcing Brain Stimulation

In 1954 James Olds was trying to determine whether electrical stimulation of the reticular formation might increase arousal and thus facilitate learning. He was assisted in this project by Peter Milner, who was a graduate student at the time. Olds had heard a talk by Neal Miller that described the aversive effects of electrical stimulation of the brain. He therefore decided to make sure that stimulation of the reticular formation was not aversive—if it were, the effects of this stimulation on the speed of learning would be difficult to assess. Fortunately for the investigators, one of the electrodes missed its target; the tip wound up some millimeters away, probably in the hypothalamus. (Unfortunately, the brain of the animal was lost, so histological verification could not be obtained.) If all of the electrodes had reached their intended target, Olds and Milner would not have discovered what they did.

Here is Olds's description of what happened when he tested this animal to see whether the brain stimulation was aversive:

> I applied a brief train of 60-cycle sine-wave electrical current whenever the animal entered one corner of the enclosure. The animal did not stay away from the corner, but rather came back quickly after a brief sortie which followed the first stimulation and came back even more quickly after a briefer sortie which followed the second stimulation. By the time the third electrical stimulus had been applied the animal seemed indubitably to be "coming back for more." (Olds, 1973, p. 81)

Olds and Milner were intrigued and excited by this result. They implanted electrodes in the brains of a group of rats and allowed the animals to administer their own stimulation by pressing a lever-operated switch in an operant chamber. (See *Figure 14.37*.) The animals readily pressed the lever; in their initial study Olds and Milner (1954) reported response rates of over seven hundred per hour. (The self-administration of electrical brain stimulation is usually referred to as **self-stimulation**.) In subsequent studies rates of many thousands of responses per hour have been obtained. Clearly, electrical stimulation of the brain can be a very potent reinforcer.

self-stimulation Making a response that causes the electrical stimulation of a particular region of the brain through an implanted electrode.

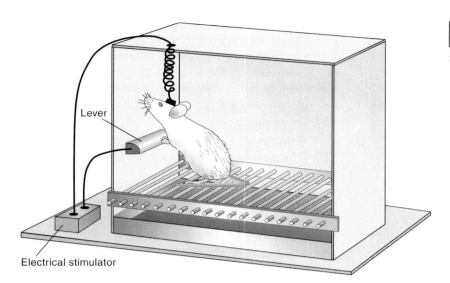

Lever

Electrical stimulator

Figure 14.37
An operant chamber with a lever, used in studies of the effects of reinforcing brain stimulation.

Neural Circuits Involved in Reinforcement

An animal's behavior can be reinforced by electrical stimulation of many parts of the brain, including the olfactory bulb, prefrontal cortex, nucleus accumbens, caudate nucleus, putamen, various thalamic nuclei, reticular formation, amygdala, ventral tegmental area, substantia nigra, and locus coeruleus (Olds and Fobes, 1981). Undoubtedly, this means that there is more than one reinforcement mechanism. The best and most reliable location is the **medial forebrain bundle (MFB)**, a bundle of axons that travel in a rostral-caudal axis from the midbrain to the rostral basal forebrain. The MFB passes through the lateral hypothalamus, and it is in this region that most investigators place the tips of their electrodes. The MFB contains long ascending and descending axons that interconnect forebrain and midbrain structures and short axons that connect adjacent regions. It also contains ascending dopaminergic, noradrenergic, and serotonergic axons on their way from the brain stem to their projection areas in the forebrain. As we will see, the activity of dopaminergic neurons plays a particularly important role in this phenomenon.

There are several systems of neurons whose terminal buttons secrete dopamine. The major pathways begin in two regions of the midbrain: the substantia nigra and the ventral tegmental area (Lindvall, 1979; Fallon, 1988). Although the cell bodies of these neurons are gathered together in compact clusters, their axons divide extensively; each axon can give rise to several hundred thousand terminal buttons. Thus, the activity of a small number of cell bodies can affect an enormous number of neurons in widespread areas of the brain.

The **mesolimbic system** begins in the ventral tegmental area (located in the midbrain—mesencephalon—just adjacent to the substantia nigra) and projects through the medial forebrain bundle to the amygdala, the lateral septum, the bed nucleus of the stria terminalis, the hippocampus, and the nucleus accumbens. Much of the research on the physiology of reinforcement has focused on the last of these structures. The **nucleus accumbens** is located in the basal forebrain rostral to the preoptic area and immediately adjacent to the septum. (In fact, the full name of this region is the *nucleus accumbens septi*, or "nucleus leaning against the septum.") (See *Figure 14.38.*)

Another system of dopaminergic axons, the **mesocortical system,** also plays a role in reinforcement. This system

medial forebrain bundle (MFB) A fiber bundle that runs in a rostral-caudal direction through the basal forebrain and lateral hypothalamus; electrical stimulation of these axons is reinforcing.

mesolimbic system A system of dopaminergic neurons whose cell bodies are located in the ventral tegmental area and whose terminal buttons are located in the nucleus accumbens, amygdala, lateral septum, hippocampus, and bed nucleus of the stria terminalis.

nucleus accumbens A nucleus of the basal forebrain near the septum; receives dopamine-secreting terminal buttons from neurons of the ventral tegmental area and is thought to be involved in reinforcement and attention.

mesocortical system A system of dopaminergic neurons whose cell bodies are located in the ventral tegmental area and whose terminal buttons are located in the cerebral cortex and hippocampus.

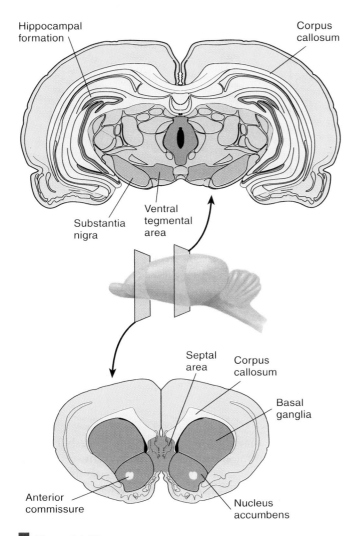

Figure 14.38
Sections through a rat brain showing the location of the ventral tegmental area and the nucleus accumbens.
(Adapted from Swanson, L.W. *Brain Maps: Structure of the Rat Brain.* New York: Elsevier, 1992.)

also begins in the ventral tegmental area. In rats, the neurons project to the prefrontal neocortex, limbic cortex (entorhinal, suprarhinal, and anterior cingulate cortex), and hippocampus. In primates, the mesocortical projections are much more widespread; in addition to the regions just listed, all of the frontal lobes and all regions of association cortex in the parietal and temporal lobes receive dopaminergic innervation (Berger, Gaspar, and Verney, 1991).

The nigrostriatal system, which provides dopaminergic innervation of the neostriatum, may also be involved in reinforcement. In fact, the evidence that people with Parkinson's disease have difficulty learning certain types of tasks suggests strongly that it does.

A large body of experimental evidence indicates that the mesolimbic pathway—particularly the branch that terminates in the nucleus accumbens—is at least partly responsible for the reinforcing effects of electrical stimulation of the medial forebrain bundle. It also plays an important role in the reinforcing effects of amphetamine and cocaine and other addictive drugs. (This role is discussed in much more detail in Chapter 19.) Treatments that stimulate dopamine receptors in the nucleus accumbens will reinforce behaviors; thus, animals will press a lever that causes electrical stimulation of the ventral tegmental area, medial forebrain bundle, or nucleus accumbens itself (Routtenberg and Malsbury, 1969; Crow, 1972; Olds and Fobes, 1981). They will also press a lever that delivers direct injections of very small amounts of dopamine or amphetamine directly into the nucleus accumbens (Hoebel et al., 1983; Guerin et al., 1984).

If the activation of dopamine receptors in the nucleus accumbens is one of the events responsible for reinforcement, then we would expect that the injection of drugs that block these receptors would interfere with reinforcement. And it does. Stellar, Kelley, and Corbett (1983) trained rats to travel through a runway in order to receive electrical stimulation of the medial forebrain bundle. They found that when they injected a dopamine receptor blocker into the nucleus accumbens, they had to turn up the current level of the stimulator in order to get the animals to run. That is, the drug reduced the reinforcing value of the electrical brain stimulation. (See *Figure 14.39.*)

Chapter 5 described a research technique called *microdialysis*, which enables an investigator to analyze the contents of the interstitial fluid within a specific region of the brain. Researchers using this method have shown that reinforcing electrical stimulation of the medial forebrain bundle or the ventral tegmental area, or the administration of cocaine or amphetamine causes the release of dopamine in the nucleus accumbens (Moghaddam and Bunney, 1989; Nakahara et al., 1989; Phillips et al., 1992). (See *Figure 14.40.*) Microdialysis studies have also found that the presence of natural reinforcers, such as water, food, or a sex partner, stimulate the release of dopamine in the nucleus accumbens. Thus, the effects of reinforcing brain stimulation seem to be similar in many ways to those of natural reinforcers.

I should note that microdialysis studies have found that aversive stimuli, as well as reinforcing stimuli, can cause the release of dopamine in various parts of the brain—including the nucleus accumbens (Salamone, 1992). Thus, it is clear that reinforcement is not the sole function of dopaminergic neurons; these neurons appear to be involved in stress, as well. Also, because the stimulation of so

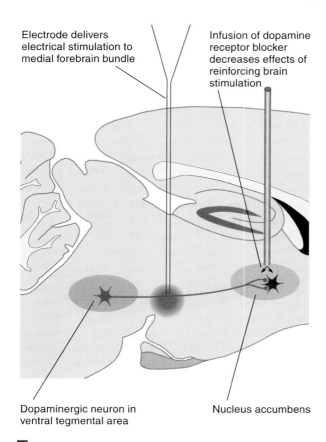

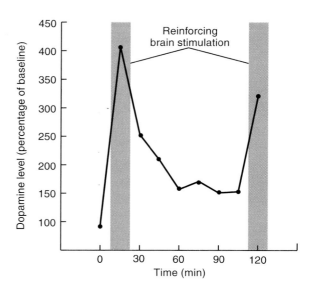

Figure 14.40
Release of dopamine in the nucleus accumbens, measured by microdialysis, produced when a rat pressed a lever that delivered electrical stimulation to the ventral tegmental area. (Adapted from Phillips, A.G., Coury, A., Fiorino, D., LePiane, F.G., Brown, E., and Fibiger, H.C. *Annals of the New York Academy of Sciences,* 1992, *654,* 199–206.)

Figure 14.39
The experiment by Stellar, Kelley, and Corbett (1983). Blocking dopamine receptors in the nucleus accumbens reduces the reinforcing effects of electrical stimulation of the medial forebrain bundle.

many regions of the brain is reinforcing, the mesolimbic system is only one of several reinforcement systems. The mesolimbic system is by far the one that has received the most attention, so little is known about other possible mechanisms.

Functions of the Reinforcement System

What does reinforcing brain stimulation tell us about the brain mechanisms involved in instrumental conditioning? Almost all investigators believe that electrical stimulation of some parts of the brain is reinforcing because it activates the same systems that are activated by natural reinforcers, such as food, water, or sexual contact. A reinforcement system must perform two functions: detect the presence of a reinforcing stimulus, and strengthen the connections between the neurons that detect the discriminative stimulus (such as the sight of a lever) and the neurons that produce the instrumental response (a lever press).

Assuming that this proposed mechanism is correct, there are three major questions: (1) What activates the dopaminergic neurons in the midbrain, causing their terminal buttons to release dopamine? (2) What role does the release of dopamine play in strengthening synaptic connections? (3) Where do these synaptic changes take place? Research that suggests some preliminary answers to these three questions is discussed in the rest of this section.

Detecting reinforcing stimuli. Reinforcement occurs when neural circuits detect a reinforcing stimulus and cause the activation of dopaminergic neurons in the ventral tegmental area. Detection of a reinforcing stimulus is not a simple matter; a stimulus that serves as a reinforcer on one occasion may fail to do so on another. For example, the presence of food will reinforce the behavior of a hungry organism but not one that has just eaten. Thus, the reinforcement system is not automatically activated when particular stimuli are present; its activation also depends on the state of the organism.

In general, if a stimulus causes the animal to engage in an appetitive behavior (that is, if it approaches the stimulus rather than runs away from it), the reinforcement mechanism is activated, and the link between the discriminative stimulus and the instrumental response is strengthened. The ventral tegmental area seems to be an important focal point in the process of reinforcement. Ljungberg, Apicella, and Schultz (1992) operated on monkeys and implanted microelectrodes so that they could record the electrical activity of dopaminergic neurons in the ventral tegmental area when the animals were awake and alert. They put the animals in a chair facing a panel that contained a small door with a sliding panel. During pretraining they opened the door from time to time. The first few times the door opened, the animals looked at it (the door made a noise as it slid open), and the activity of many of the dopaminergic neurons briefly increased. After a few times, the animals stopped looking at the door, and the neurons stopped responding.

Then the experimenters began placing a small piece of apple behind the door from time to time. As you might expect, the animals began looking at the door again—and the dopaminergic neurons began firing again, too. Now that the sound and sight of the door opening was paired with an occasional piece of apple (which the monkeys reached for and ate), this stimulus became capable of triggering the release of dopamine. Thus, a stimulus that previously had no effect on the activity of dopaminergic neurons began to excite them once it was paired with an appetitive stimulus.

This experiment indicates that dopaminergic neurons in the ventral tegmental area are activated not only by primary reinforcing stimuli such as food but also by conditioned reinforcers. When a neutral stimulus is paired several times with a reinforcing stimulus, it acquires the ability to serve as a reinforcing stimulus itself—it becomes a **conditioned reinforcer.** The process of classical conditioning is responsible for this phenomenon: The response an animal makes to the primary reinforcer becomes attached to the conditioned reinforcer. Similarly, when a neutral stimulus is paired with an aversive stimulus, it becomes a **conditioned punisher.** Our behavior can be reinforced by an enormous variety of conditioned reinforcers, including money, good grades, and words of praise. It can also be punished by conditioned punishers such as fines, bad grades, and signs of disapproval.

What neural circuits are responsible for detecting the presence of a reinforcing stimulus (primary or conditioned) and then activating dopaminergic neurons in this

conditioned reinforcer   A previously neutral stimulus that has been paired with an appetitive stimulus, which then itself becomes capable, of reinforcing a response.

conditioned punisher   A previously neutral stimulus that has been followed by an aversive stimulus, which then itself becomes capable of punishing a response.

region? The ventral tegmental area receives inputs from many regions of the brain. Although we still know very little about how reinforcing stimuli are detected, the three inputs that probably play the most important role in reinforcement are the amygdala, the lateral hypothalamus, and the prefrontal cortex.

As we saw in Chapter 11 and again in this chapter, the amygdala is involved in classically conditioned emotional responses. Several studies suggest that it is also involved in conditioned reinforcement. For example, destruction of the amygdala or its disconnection from the visual system has no effect on monkeys' ability to recognize particular visual stimuli by sight, but it does disrupt their ability to remember which of them has been paired with food (Spiegler and Mishkin, 1981; Gaffan, Gaffan, and Harrison, 1988). In addition, Cador, Robbins, and Everitt (1989) and Everitt, Cador, and Robbins (1989) found that neurotoxic lesions of the basolateral amygdala reduced the reinforcing value of stimuli that had been paired with natural reinforcers: water (in thirsty rats) and sexual contact. The experimenters paired the reinforcing stimuli with a flashing light and found that later, the animals would press a lever that turned on the flashing light. Thus, the flashing light had become a conditioned reinforcer. The lesions of the amygdala severely depressed the animals' rate of responding for the flashing light, without otherwise affecting their motor performance.

The inputs to the ventral tegmental area from the lateral hypothalamus may also play a role in the detection of reinforcing stimuli. Burton, Rolls, and Mora (1976) studied the response characteristics of single neurons in the lateral hypothalamus and substantia innominata (a nearby region in the basal forebrain). They found that some neurons located there respond to either the sight or taste of food, but they do so *only if the animal is hungry.* Rolls et al. (1986) found that the firing rate of these neurons was related to an animal's willingness to eat a particular type of food. For example, one neuron showed a high rate of firing when the monkey was shown a peanut, a banana, an orange, or a syringe that was used to squirt a glucose solution into its mouth. The animal was then given repeated drinks of the glucose solution. At first it drank the solution enthusiastically, but after a while acceptance turned to rejection. At the same time the neuron responded less and less when the monkey was shown the syringe. However, the neuron still responded to the sight of a peanut, an orange, or a banana. The monkey was then allowed to eat all the bananas it wanted. The neuron stopped responding to the sight of the banana, but it still responded to the sight of the peanut. It pretty much stopped responding to the sight of an orange, too, but perhaps after drinking 440 milliliters of a glucose

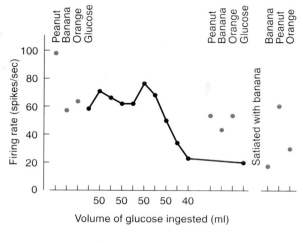

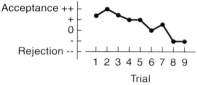

Figure 14.41
Sensory-specific satiety. The graph plots the firing rate of a single neuron in a monkey's lateral hypothalamus when the animal is shown various foods. The smaller graph at the right indicates ratings of the monkey's acceptance or rejection of the glucose solution, presented nine times.
(Adapted from Rolls, E.T., Murzi, E., Yaxley, S., Thorpe, S.J., and Simpson, S.J. *Brain Research*, 1986, *368*, 79–86.)

solution and eating all the bananas one wants, an orange provides less of a flavor contrast than a peanut does. Thus, the connections between the lateral hypothalamus and the ventral tegmental area may convey information about the presence of reinforcing stimuli. (See *Figure 14.41.*)

The prefrontal cortex also provides an important input to the ventral tegmental area. The terminal buttons of the axons connecting these two areas secrete glutamate, an excitatory transmitter substance, and the activity of these synapses makes dopaminergic neurons in the ventral tegmental area fire in a bursting pattern, which greatly increases the amount of dopamine they secrete in the nucleus accumbens (Gariano and Groves, 1988). The prefrontal cortex is generally involved in devising strategies, making plans, evaluating progress made toward goals, judging the appropriateness of one's own behavior, and so on (Mesulam, 1986). Perhaps the prefrontal cortex turns on the reinforcement mechanism when it determines that the ongoing behavior is bringing the organism nearer to its goals—that the present strategy is working.

Even private behaviors such as thinking and planning may be subject to reinforcement. For example, recall the last time you were thinking about a problem and suddenly had an idea that might help you solve it. Did you suddenly feel excited and happy? It would be interesting if we could record the activity of the axons leading from your frontal cortex to your ventral tegmental area at times like that.

Strengthening Neural Connections: Dopamine and Neural Plasticity

Like classical conditioning, instrumental conditioning involves strengthening of synapses located on neurons that have just been active. For example, let us consider a hungry rat learning to press a lever and obtain food. As we saw, the neural circuit responsible for this response consists of strengthened connections between neurons in the visual system that detect the presence of the lever and those that control the muscular movements required to press the lever. The reinforcing stimulus (the food) turns on the reinforcement mechanism, which strengthens the synapses between terminal buttons that have just been active and motor neurons that have just fired.

There is an important difference between classical conditioning and instrumental conditioning: Instrumental conditioning requires a reinforcement system. As we saw in a previous section, NMDA receptors appear to be responsible for some of the interactions between the strong and weak synapses activated by the CS and the US. But classical conditioning involves only two elements, a CS and a

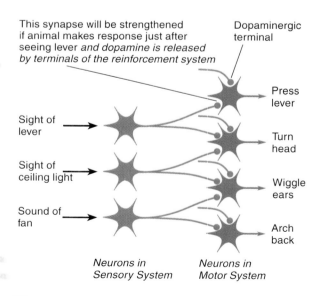

Figure 14.42
A hypothetical explanation for the reinforcing effects of dopamine on associative long-term potentiation.

US, whereas instrumental conditioning involves three elements: a discriminative stimulus, a response, and a reinforcing stimulus. How are the neural manifestations of these three elements combined?

As in classical conditioning, one element (the discriminative stimulus) activates a weak synapse. The second element—the particular circumstance that happened to induce the animal to press the lever—activates a strong synapse, making the neuron fire. The third element comes into play only if the response is followed by a reinforcing stimulus. If it is, the reinforcement mechanism triggers the secretion of a neurotransmitter or neuromodulator throughout the region in which the synaptic changes take place. This chemical is the third element; only if it is present can weak synapses be strengthened. Dopamine appears to serve such a role, but other neurotransmitters may do so as well. (See *Figure 14.42.*)

Stein and Belluzzi (1989) obtained evidence that dopamine can facilitate synaptic strengthening. They prepared slices of the hippocampus, and they recorded from single pyramidal neurons in field CA1, which are known to contain dopamine receptors. They attempted to reinforce bursts of neural activity by infusing dopamine or dopamine agonists onto the neuron through a micropipette. Whenever the neuron spontaneously produced a burst of action po-

tentials lasting at least 0.5 second, they applied the dopamine. Figure 14.43 shows the results of administering dopamine, cocaine, or saline. *Baseline* refers to periods during which they simply recorded the number of bursts of action potentials. During *reinforcement* periods they followed each burst with the infusion. During *noncontingent* periods they administered infusions that were not paired with the bursts. As you can see, both dopamine and cocaine increased the rate of the bursts but only when they were applied contingently. (See *Figure 14.43.*)

These findings indicate that if dopamine is administered at the time that cells are already firing in bursts, their firing rate will increase. Although Stein and Belluzzi did not record the activity of the inputs to the pyramidal neurons, it seems likely that the bursts occur when excitatory synaptic inputs to these neurons become active. Perhaps the dopamine acts by increasing the strength of the "successful" synapses—those that are firing at the same time that the pyramidal cell is bursting. The effect of this strengthening would be to increase the rate of firing of the pyramidal cell.

The Location of Synaptic Changes

Clearly, reinforcement strengthens synaptic connections somewhere in the brain—but where? As we saw, reinforc-

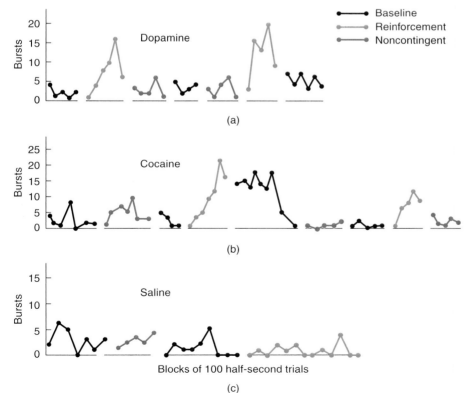

(a)

(b)

(c)

Blocks of 100 half-second trials

Figure 14.43
Instrumental conditioning of single neurons in the CA1 field of the hippocampal formation. (a) Dopamine infusion. (b) Cocaine infusion. (c) Saline infusion. (Adapted from Stein, L., and Belluzzi, J.D., in *Brain Reward Systems and Abuse,* edited by J. Engel and L. Oreland. New York: Raven Press, 1987.)

ing brain stimulation increases the secretion of dopamine in the nucleus accumbens, which suggests that at least some of the synaptic changes may take place there.

Nucleus accumbens. Microdialysis studies show that natural reinforcers, as well as electrical stimulation of the medial forebrain bundle, triggers the release of dopamine in the nucleus accumbens: drinking, induced by dehydration or by an injection of angiotensin; salt intake, induced by sodium depletion; or eating, induced by food deprivation (Blander et al., 1988; Chang et al., 1988; Hernandez and Hoebel, 1988).

Sexual behavior, too, causes the release of dopamine in the nucleus accumbens (Pfaus et al., 1990; Damsma et al., 1992). Figure 14.44 shows the effects of sexual contact on the level of dopamine in the nucleus accumbens of a male rat. When the rat was placed in the test chamber (where he had copulated before), the dopamine level increased. Next, a female rat was introduced behind a wire screen; the dopamine level increased further. Finally, the screen was removed and the rats were permitted to copulate; the dopamine level increased still further. After copulation, the female was removed and the dopamine level declined. (See *Figure 14.44.*)

As I mentioned earlier in this chapter, when a stimulus is paired with a reinforcing or punishing stimulus, it ac-

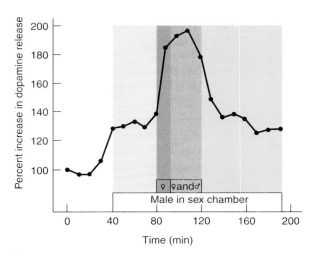

Figure 14.44
Levels of extracellular dopamine in the nucleus accumbens of a male rat before, during, and after engaging in sexual behavior, measured by microdialysis. [♀] = female, [♂] = male.
(Adapted with permission from Pfaus, J.G., Damsma, G., Nomikos, G.G., Wenkstern, D.G., Blaha, C.D., Phillips, A.G., and Fibiger, H.C. *Brain Research*, 1990, *530*, 345–348.)

quires the reinforcing (or punishing) properties of the second stimulus. As we saw in Chapter 13, a conditioned flavor aversion can be established by pairing a particular flavor with treatments that produce illness, such as an injection of lithium chloride. Mark et al. (1989) found that although the taste of saccharin normally caused an increase in dopamine release in the nucleus accumbens of naive animals, it caused a *decrease* in dopamine release if the flavor had previously been paired with an injection of lithium chloride. Thus, the same stimulus can have very different effects on the activity of dopaminergic neurons, depending on the animal's prior experience with this stimulus.

Several studies have shown that disruption of dopaminergic transmission in the nucleus accumbens also impairs the expression of behaviors that are reinforced by natural stimuli. Salamone et al. (1991) trained rats to press a lever in order to obtain some highly preferred food. When the animals were placed in the operant chamber, they pressed the lever to obtain this food, ignoring some less preferred food that was freely available. When the investigators injected a dopamine receptor blocker in the nucleus accumbens, the rats stopped pressing the lever. But the drug did not affect the animals' hunger; they began eating the less preferred food that they could obtain without making the instrumental response.

In a follow-up study performed by the same laboratory, Cousins et al. (1996) trained rats in a T maze. If the rats entered one arm of the maze, they received four pieces of food, but they first had to climb over a tall barrier to get to them. If they entered the other arm, they received only two pieces of food, but there was no barrier. All rats chose to climb the barrier and eat the larger amount of food. Then the experimenters injected 6-HD into the nucleus accumbens of some of the rats, destroying the dopaminergic input to this structure. These rats stopped climbing the barrier, and chose to eat the smaller amount of food instead. It was not that the dopamine depletion prevented the animals from climbing the barrier; in fact, if the only food to be found was located behind a barrier, these animals would climb it. These two studies suggest that the release of dopamine in the nucleus accumbens activates responses reinforced by appetitive stimuli. In the absence of dopamine release, animals can still perform responses that they have learned to make but they are less motivated to do so.

Motor systems. If one of the effects of reinforcement is the release of dopamine in the nucleus accumbens, how does this event affect behavior? Neurons in the nucleus accumbens send axons to several regions of the brain involved in movement, including the globus pallidus and the mesencephalic locomotor region of the pedunculopontine nucleus. In turn, axons in the globus pallidus project (via the thalamus) to the prefrontal cortex, premotor cortex, and supplementary motor area. Thus, the direct or indirect outputs of the nucleus accumbens include important motor systems of the brain (Scheel-Krüger and Willner, 1991).

As we saw, lesions of the basal ganglia in both humans and laboratory animals do disrupt behaviors learned through instrumental conditioning—especially those that involve well-practiced, automatic responses. The basal ganglia receive dopaminergic innervation from the substantia nigra. This innervation certainly plays an important role in motor performance; Parkinson's disease is caused by its degeneration. Whether this innervation also plays a role in synaptic plasticity in the basal ganglia is not yet known.

As I mentioned earlier, the prefrontal cortex may activate the reinforcement system when it detects that the animal's behavior is resulting in progress toward a goal. But the prefrontal and premotor cortex are *targets* of dopaminergic neurons as well as a source of their control. As we saw, these regions play a role in learning. The dopaminergic system of the frontal cortex certainly seems to be involved in reinforcement. For example, Stein and Belluzzi (1989) found that rats will press a lever that produces an injection of a dopamine agonist into this region. Duvauchelle and Ettenberg (1991) found that if a rat's prefrontal cortex is electrically stimulated while the animal is in a particular location, it will learn to prefer that location to others where the stimulation did not take place. This effect appears to involve the release of dopamine, because it is blocked by injections of a drug that blocks dopamine receptors. And in a microdialysis study Hernandez and Hoebel (1990) found that when rats were performing a food-reinforced lever-pressing task, the levels of dopamine in the prefrontal cortex increased.

Interim Summary

Instrumental conditioning entails the strengthening of connections between neural circuits that detect stimuli and neural circuits that produce responses. One of the locations of these changes appears to be the basal ganglia—especially the changes responsible for learning of automated and routine behaviors. The basal ganglia receive sensory information and information about plans for movement from the neocortex. Damage to the basal ganglia disrupt instrumental conditioning in laboratory animals, and Parkinson's disease disrupts automatic motor responses

(as opposed to deliberate ones) and even impairs learning of some tasks that do not involve learning particular movements. Damage to the premotor cortex also impairs learning, especially of self-initiated responses—those not made in response to external stimuli. Electrical recording studies and PET studies have shown that learning sequences of movements increases the activity of the premotor cortex.

Olds and Milner discovered that rats would perform a response that caused electrical current to be delivered through an electrode placed in their brain; thus, the stimulation was reinforcing. Subsequent studies found that stimulation of many locations had reinforcing effects but that the medial forebrain bundle produced the strongest and most reliable ones.

Although several neurotransmitters may play a role in reinforcement, one is particularly important: dopamine. The cell bodies of the most important system of dopaminergic neurons are located in the ventral tegmental area, and their axons project to the nucleus accumbens, prefrontal cortex, and amygdala.

Infusions of dopamine antagonists directly into the nucleus accumbens will reinforce an animal's behavior. Both laboratory animals and humans will self-administer dopamine agonists such as amphetamine or cocaine; laboratory animals will press a lever to have amphetamine injected directly into the nucleus accumbens. Microdialysis studies have also shown that natural and artificial reinforcers stimulate the release of dopamine in the nucleus accumbens. The system of neurons that detect reinforcing stimuli and activate the dopaminergic neurons in the mesolimbic and mesocortical systems probably involves the amygdala and lateral hypothalamus; these neurons fire in response to food-related stimuli capable of reinforcing an animal's behavior. Damage to the amygdala disrupts conditioned reinforcement. The frontal cortex may play a role in reinforcement that occurs when our own behavior brings us nearer to a goal.

Dopamine (and, almost certainly, other neurotransmitters such as acetylcholine and norepinephrine) induces synaptic plasticity by facilitating associative long-term potentiation. Direct evidence for this phenomenon was seen in a study with hippocampal slices. An increase in the spontaneous response rate of CA1 neurons can be increased by contingent infusions of dopamine; thus, single neurons can be instrumentally conditioned.

The location of synaptic changes responsible for instrumental conditioning may be the nucleus accumbens, basal ganglia, and frontal cortex. Microdialysis studies suggest that the release of dopamine in the prefrontal cortex may also be important. The release of dopamine in the prefrontal cortex is reinforcing.

SUGGESTED READINGS

Graf, P., and Masson, M.E.J. *Implicit Memory: New Directions in Cognition, Development, and Neuropsychology.* Hillsdale, NJ: Erlbaum Associates, 1993.

Ono, T. *Brain Mechanisms of Perception and Memory: From Neuron to Behavior.* New York: Oxford University Press, 1992.

Squire, L.R., and Butters, N. *Neuropsychology of Memory.* New York: Guilford Press, 1992.

Squire, L.R., Weinberger, N.M., Lynch, G., and McGaugh, J.L. *Memory: Organization and Locus of Change.* New York: Oxford University Press, 1991.

Thompson, R.F. Mammalian brain substrates of aversive classical conditioning. *Annual Review of Psychology,* 1993, *43,* 317–342.

CHAPTER 15

Relational Learning and Amnesia

The Snail, 1953, by Henri Matisse.

Chapter 14 discussed relatively simple forms of learning, which can be understood as changes in circuits of neurons that detect the presence of particular stimuli or as strengthened connections between neurons that analyze sensory information and those that produce responses. But most forms of learning are more complex; most memories of real objects and events are related to other memories. Seeing a photograph of an old friend may remind you of the sound of the person's name and of the movements you have to make to pronounce it. You may also be reminded of things you have done with your friend: places you have visited, conversations you have had, experiences you have shared. Each of these memories can contain a series of events, complete with sights and sounds, that you will be able to recall in the proper sequence. Obviously, the neural circuits in the inferior temporal cortex that recognize your friend's face are connected to circuits in many other parts of the brain, and these circuits are connected to many others. This chapter discusses research on relational learning, which includes the establishment and retrieval of memories of events and episodes.

HUMAN ANTEROGRADE AMNESIA

One of the most dramatic and intriguing phenomena caused by brain damage is *anterograde amnesia*, which, at first glance, appears to be the inability to learn new information. However, when we examine the phenomenon more carefully, we find that the basic abilities of perceptual learning, stimulus-response learning, and motor learning are intact but that complex relational learning, of the type I just described, is gone. This section discusses the nature of anterograde amnesia in humans and its anatomical ba-

sis. The section that follows discusses related research with laboratory animals.

The term **anterograde amnesia** refers to difficulty in learning new information. A person with pure anterograde amnesia can remember events that occurred in the past, during the time before the brain damage occurred, but cannot retain information he or she encounters *after* the damage. In contrast, **retrograde amnesia** refers to the inability to remember events that happened *before* the brain damage occurred. (See *Figure 15.1*.) As we will see, pure anterograde amnesia is rare; usually, there is also a retrograde amnesia for events that occurred for a period of time before the brain damage occurred.

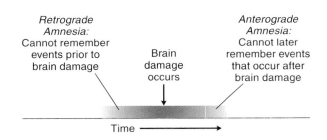

Figure 15.1
A schematic definition of retrograde amnesia and anterograde amnesia.

anterograde amnesia   Amnesia for events that occur after some disturbance to the brain, such as head injury or certain degenerative brain diseases.

retrograde amnesia   Amnesia for events that preceded some disturbance to the brain, such as a head injury or electroconvulsive shock.

In 1889, Sergei Korsakoff, a Russian physician, first described a severe memory impairment caused by brain damage, and the disorder was given his name. The most profound symptom of **Korsakoff's syndrome** is a severe anterograde amnesia: The patients appear to be unable to form new memories, although they can still remember old ones. They can converse normally and can remember events that happened long before their brain damage occurred, but they cannot remember events that happened afterward.

Korsakoff's syndrome is usually (but not always) a result of chronic alcoholism. The disorder actually results from a thiamine (vitamin B$_1$) deficiency caused by the alcoholism (Adams, 1969; Haas, 1988). Because alcoholics receive a substantial number of calories from the alcohol they ingest, they usually eat a poor diet, so their vitamin intake is consequently low. Furthermore, alcohol interferes with intestinal absorption of thiamine. The ensuing deficiency produces brain damage. Thiamine is essential for a step in metabolism: the carboxylation of pyruvate, an intermediate product in the breakdown of carbohydrates, fats, and amino acids. Korsakoff's syndrome sometimes occurs in people who have been severely malnourished and have then received intravenous infusions of glucose; the sudden availability of glucose to the cells of the brain without adequate thiamine with which to metabolize it damages the cells, probably because they accumulate pyruvate. Hence, standard medical practice is to administer thiamine along with intravenous glucose to severely malnourished patients. I will discuss the location of the brain damage that causes Korsakoff's syndrome later in this section.

Another symptom of Korsakoff's syndrome is **confabulation.** When people with this disorder are asked about events that occurred recently, they often describe a fictitious event rather than simply saying, "I don't remember." (Notice that *confabulate* has the same root as *fable.*) Confabulations can contain mixtures of things that really occurred, or they can be completely imaginary. People who confabulate are not deliberately trying to deceive; they appear to believe that what they are saying really occurred. I will describe some research on confabulation later in this chapter.

Anterograde amnesia can also be caused by damage to the temporal lobes. Scoville and Milner (1957) reported that bilateral removal of the medial temporal lobe produced a memory impairment in humans that was apparently identical to that seen in Korsakoff's syndrome. Thirty operations had been performed on psychotic patients in an attempt to alleviate their mental disorder, but it was not until this operation was performed on patient H.M. that the anterograde amnesia was discovered. The psychotic patients' behavior was already so disturbed that their amnesia was not detected. However, patient H.M. was reasonably intelligent and was not psychotic; therefore, his postoperative deficit was discovered immediately. He had received the surgery in an attempt to treat his very severe epilepsy, which could not be controlled even by high doses of anticonvulsant medication.

The surgery successfully treated H.M.'s seizure disorder, but it became apparent that the operation had produced a serious memory impairment. Subsequently, Scoville and Milner (1957) examined eight of the psychotic patients who were coherent enough to cooperate with them. Careful testing revealed that some of these patients also had anterograde amnesia; the deficit appeared to occur only when the hippocampus was removed. They concluded that the hippocampus was the critical structure destroyed by the surgery. Later in this chapter, I will say more about the anatomical basis of anterograde amnesia caused by medial temporal lobe damage.

Once it was discovered that bilateral medial temporal lobectomy causes anterograde amnesia, neurosurgeons stopped performing them and are now careful to operate on only one temporal lobe. (Unilateral temporal lobectomy may cause minor memory problems, but nothing like what occurs after bilateral operations.) In a few cases, surgeons were surprised to find that unilateral removal of the medial temporal lobe produced anterograde amnesia. When the patients eventually died and their brains were examined, the investigators discovered that the hippocampus on the other side of the brain had been damaged, too—probably very early in life (Penfield and Milner, 1958; Warrington and Duchen, 1992). Thus, the operation on the undamaged medial temporal lobe left the patients without a functioning hippocampal formation. To prevent such cases physicians now administer a *Wada test* (Wada and Rasmussen, 1960). Before a patient receives a unilateral temporal lobectomy, a short-acting anesthetic is injected into the carotid artery that serves the hemisphere that is to be operated on. If the patient is able to learn and remember items that are presented while that hemisphere is anesthetized, we can conclude that the other hemisphere contains a functioning hippocampal formation and the one in the anesthetized hemisphere can safely be removed. The Wada test has detected unexpected damage to the hip-

Korsakoff's syndrome   Permanent anterograde amnesia caused by brain damage resulting from chronic alcoholism or malnutrition.

confabulation   The reporting of memories of events that did not take place without the intention to deceive; seen in people with Korsakoff's syndrome.

pocampal system and has thus prevented new cases of anterograde amnesia.

● Basic Description

In order for you to understand more fully the nature of anterograde amnesia, I will discuss the case of patient H.M. in more detail (Milner, Corkin, and Teuber, 1968; Milner, 1970; Corkin et al., 1981). Patient H.M. has been extensively studied because his amnesia is relatively pure. His intellectual ability and his immediate verbal memory appear to be normal. He can repeat seven numbers forward and five numbers backward, and he can carry on conversations, rephrase sentences, and perform mental arithmetic. He has a retrograde amnesia for events that occurred during several years preceding the operation, but he can recall older memories very well. He showed no personality change after the operation, and he appears to be generally polite and good-natured.

However, since the operation, H.M. has been unable to learn anything new. He cannot identify by name people he has met since the operation (performed in 1953, when he was twenty-seven years old), nor can he find his way back home if he leaves his house. (His family moved to a new house after his operation, and he never learned how to get around in the new neighborhood. He now lives in a nursing home, where he can be cared for.) He is aware of his disorder and often says something like this:

> Every day is alone in itself, whatever enjoyment I've had, and whatever sorrow I've had. Right now, I'm wondering. Have I done or said anything amiss? You see, at this moment everything looks clear to me, but what happened just before? That's what worries me. It's like waking from a dream; I just don't remember. (Milner, 1970, p. 37)

H.M. is capable of remembering a small amount of verbal information as long as he is not distracted; constant rehearsal can keep information in his immediate memory for a long time. However, rehearsal does not appear to have any long-term effects; if he is distracted for a moment, he will completely forget whatever he had been rehearsing. He works very well at repetitive tasks. Indeed, because he so quickly forgets what previously happened, he does not easily become bored. He can endlessly reread the same magazine or laugh at the same jokes, finding them fresh and new each time. His time is typically spent solving crossword puzzles and watching television.

From these findings, Milner and her colleagues made the following conclusions:

1. *The hippocampus is not the location of long-term memories; nor is it necessary for the retrieval of long-term memories.* If

it were, H.M. would not have been able to remember events from early in his life, he would not know how to talk, he would not know how to dress himself, and so on.

2. *The hippocampus is not the location of immediate (short-term) memories.* If it were, H.M. would not be able to carry on a conversation, because he would not remember what the other person said long enough to think of a reply.

3. *The hippocampus is involved in converting immediate (short-term) memories into long-term memories.* This conclusion is based on a particular hypothesis of memory function: that our immediate memory of an event is retained by neural activity and that long-term memories consist of relatively permanent biochemical or structural changes in neurons. The conclusion seems a reasonable explanation for the fact that when presented with new information, H.M. seems to understand it and remember it as long as he thinks about it but that a permanent record of the information is just never made.

As we will see, these three conclusions are too simple. Subsequent research on patients with anterograde amnesia indicates that the facts are more complicated—and more interesting—than they first appeared to be. But to appreciate the significance of the findings of more recent research, we must understand these three conclusions and remember the facts that led to them.

Many psychologists believe that learning consists of at least two stages: short-term memory and long-term memory. They conceive of short-term memory as a means of storing a limited amount of information temporarily and long-term memory as a means of storing an unlimited amount (or at least an enormously large amount) of information permanently. **Short-term memory** is an immediate memory for stimuli that have just been perceived. We can remember a new item of information (such as a telephone number) for as long as we want to by engaging in a particular behavior: rehearsal. However, once we stop rehearsing the information, we may or may not be able to remember it later; that is, the information may or may not get stored in **long-term memory.**

Short-term memory can hold only a limited amount of information. To demonstrate this fact, read the following

short-term memory Immediate memory for events, which may or may not be consolidated into long-term memory.

long-term memory Relatively stable memory of events that occurred in the more distant past, as opposed to short-term memory.

numbers to yourself just once, and then close your eyes and recite them back.

1 4 9 2 3 0 7

You probably had no trouble remembering them. Now, try the following set of numbers, and go through them *only once* before you close your eyes.

7 2 5 2 3 9 1 6 5 8 4

Very few people can repeat eleven numbers; in fact, you may not have even bothered to try, once you saw how many numbers there were. Therefore, short-term memory has definite limits. But of course, if you wanted to, you could recite the numbers again and again until you had memorized them; that is, you could rehearse the information in short-term memory until it was eventually stored in long-term memory. Long-term memory has no known limits; and as its name suggests, it is relatively durable. Presumably, it is a result of changes in synaptic strength, such as the ones responsible for long-term potentiation. If we stop thinking about something we have just perceived (that is, something contained in short-term memory), we may or may not remember the information later. However, information in long-term memory need not be continuously rehearsed; once we have learned something, we can stop thinking about it until we need the information at a future time.

The most simple model of the memory process says that sensory information enters short-term memory, rehearsal keeps it there, and eventually, the information makes its way into long-term memory, where it is permanently stored. The conversion of short-term memories into long-term memories has been called **consolidation,** because the memories are "made solid," so to speak. (See *Figure 15.2.*)

Now you can understand the original conclusions of Milner and her colleagues: If H.M.'s short-term memory is intact and if he can remember events from before his operation, then the problem must be that consolidation does not take place. Therefore, the role of the hippocampal formation in memory is consolidation—converting short-term memories to long-term memories.

● Spared Learning Abilities

H.M.'s memory deficit is striking and dramatic. However, when he and other patients with anterograde amnesia are studied more carefully, it becomes apparent that the amnesia does not represent a total failure in learning ability. When the patients are appropriately trained and tested, we find that they are capable of three of the four major types of learning described in Chapter 14: perceptual learning, sensory-response learning, and motor learning.

First, let us consider perceptual learning. Figure 15.3 shows two sample items from a test of the ability to recognize broken drawings; note how the drawings are successively more complete. (See *Figure 15.3.*) Subjects are first shown the least complete set (set I) of each of twenty different drawings. If they do not recognize a figure (and most people do not recognize set I), they are shown more complete sets until they identify it. One hour later, the subjects

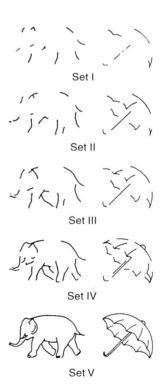

Set I

Set II

Set III

Set IV

Set V

Figure 15.3
Examples of broken drawings.
(Reprinted with permission of author and publisher from Gollin, E.S. Developmental studies of visual recognition of incomplete objects. *Perceptual and Motor Skills, 1960, 11, 289–298.*)

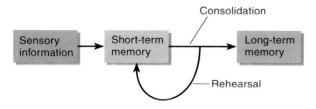

Figure 15.2
A simple model of the learning process.

consolidation The process by which short-term memories are converted into long-term memories.

are tested again for retention, starting with set I. H.M. was given this test and, when retested an hour later, showed considerable improvement (Milner, 1970). When he was retested four months later, he *still* showed this improvement. His performance was not as good as that of normal control subjects, but he showed unmistakable evidence of long-term retention.

The incomplete drawing task is known as a *priming task*. **Priming** refers to the fact that when people perceive a particular stimulus, it becomes easier for them to perceive it again. As we will see, researchers have used several different types of priming tasks to investigate the nature of anterograde amnesia. Priming need not involve familiar objects, as the broken-drawings study did. For example, Gabrieli et al. (1990) presented H.M. and nonamnesic control subjects with a series of patterns of five dots connected by straight lines. (These patterns were referred to as the *targets*.) They asked the subjects to copy the lines on sheets of paper that contained identical dot patterns. (See *Figure 15.4*.) Later, they gave the subjects fresh sheets of papers with the dot patterns and asked them to connect the dots with whatever pattern of straight lines they chose. And all the subjects—H.M. as well as the nonamnesic controls—showed a priming effect, drawing significantly more target patterns than would be expected by chance.

Johnson, Kim, and Risse (1985) found that patients with anterograde amnesia could learn to recognize faces

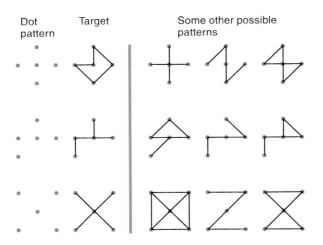

Figure 15.4
Stimuli used in the priming experiment by Gabrieli et al. (1990). The subjects copied the straight lines of the targets onto the dot patterns, which were printed on sheets of paper. Examples of some other possible patterns of lines are shown in the right-hand column.
(Adapted from Gabrieli, J.D.E., Milberg, W., Keane, M.M., and Corkin, S. *Neuropsychologia*, 1990, 28, 417–427.)

and melodies. They played unfamiliar melodies from Korean songs to amnesic patients and found that when they were tested later, the patients preferred these melodies to ones they had not heard before. The experimenters also presented photographs of two men along with stories of their lives: One man was dishonest, mean, and vicious, and the other was nice enough to invite home to dinner. Twenty days later, the amnesic patients said they liked the picture of the "nice" man better than that of the "nasty" one.

Investigators have also succeeded in demonstrating stimulus-response learning by H.M. and other amnesic subjects. For example, Woodruff-Pak (1993) found that H.M. and another patient with anterograde amnesia could acquire a classically conditioned eyeblink response. H.M. even showed retention of the task two years later: He acquired the response again in one-tenth the number of trials that were needed previously. Sidman, Stoddard, and Mohr (1968) successfully trained patient H.M. on an instrumental conditioning task—a visual discrimination task in which pennies were given for correct responses.

Finally, Milner (1965) demonstrated motor learning. She and her colleagues presented H.M. with a mirror-drawing task. This procedure requires the subject to trace the outline of a figure (in this case, a star) with a pencil while looking at the figure in a mirror. (See *Figure 15.5*.) The task may seem simple, but it is actually rather difficult and requires some practice to perform well. With practice, H.M. became proficient at mirror drawing; his errors were reduced considerably during the first session, and his improvement was retained on subsequent days of testing. He also learned a pursuit rotor task, which required him to try to keep a pointer placed above a spot of light moving in a circular path. Thus, several different forms of long-term memory can certainly be established in patients with anterograde amnesia.

● Declarative and Nondeclarative Memories

If amnesic patients can learn tasks like these, you might ask, why do we call them *amnesic?* The answer is this: Although the patients can learn to perform these tasks, they do not remember anything about having learned them. They do not remember the experimenters, the room in which the training took place, the apparatus that was used, or any events that occurred during the training. Although H.M. learned to recognize the broken drawings, he denied

priming A phenomenon in which exposure to a particular stimulus automatically facilitates perception of that stimulus or related stimuli.

Figure 15.5
The mirror-drawing task.

the amygdala play very different roles in the development of emotional and episodic memories. The investigators studied three patients with different brain lesions. Patient S.M. had bilateral amygdala damage, patient W.C. had bilateral hippocampal damage, and patient R.H. had bilateral damage to both structures. The patients were shown a random series of red, green, yellow, and blue lights. Each time the blue light was presented, the experimenters sounded a boat horn that made a very loud—and very unpleasant—noise. The noise elicited an emotional reaction in all subjects—a change in the electrical resistance of the skin that is caused by increased activity of the sympathetic nervous system. Patient S.M., who had only hippocampal damage, showed a conditioned emotional response: a change in skin resistance when the blue light was presented. As we would predict, patients S.M. and R.H., whose amygdalas were damaged, did not show such a response. Thus, amygdala lesions disrupt the establishment of conditioned emotional responses, but hippocampal lesions do not. The opposite pattern was seen when the patients were asked about what had happened. Patient R.H., with only amygdala damage, said that the boat horn was sounded every time the blue light was presented. Patients S.M. and W.C., who had hippocampal damage, could not remember anything about what had occurred during the experimental procedure. Clearly, episodic memories and conditioned emotional memories involve different neural circuits, and knowing that a stimulus is associated with the occurrence of a noxious event is not the same as having a conditioned fear response to that stimulus.

The distinction between what people with anterograde amnesia can and cannot learn is obviously important, because it reflects the basic organization of the learning process. Clearly, there are at least two major categories of memories. Psychologists have given them several different names. For example, some investigators (Eichenbaum, Otto, and Cohen, 1992; Squire, 1992) suggest that patients with anterograde amnesia are unable to form **declarative memories,** which have been defined as those that are "explicitly available to conscious recollection as facts, events, or specific stimuli" (Squire, Shimamura, and Amaral, 1989, p. 218). The term *declarative* obviously comes from *declare,* which means "to proclaim; to announce." The term reflects the fact that patients with anterograde amnesia cannot talk about experiences that they have had since the time of their brain damage. And note that the definition refers specifically to *stimuli*. Thus, according to Squire and his col-

that he had ever seen them before. Although he drew many of the patterns of lines he had seen in the pattern-priming task (the one with the dots), he did not remember having seen them before. Although the amnesic patients in the study by Johnson, Kim, and Risse learned to like some melodies better, they did not recognize that they had heard them before; nor did they remember having seen the pictures of the two young men. Although H.M. successfully acquired a classically conditioned eyeblink response, he did not remember the experimenter, the apparatus, or the headband he wore that held the device that delivered a puff of air to his eye. Similarly, in the experiment by Sidman, Stoddard, and Mohr, although H.M. learned to make the correct response (press a panel with a picture of a circle on it), he was unable to recall having done so. In fact, once H.M. had learned the task, the experimenters interrupted him, had him count his pennies (to distract him for a little while), and then asked him to say what he was supposed to do. He seemed puzzled by the question; he had absolutely no idea. But when they turned on the stimuli again, he immediately made the correct response.

It should be clear by now that the words *learning* and *memory* refer to a variety of different processes. For example, as we saw in Chapters 11 and 14, the amygdala is involved in emotional learning—in particular, in the establishment of conditioned emotional responses. A study by Bechara et al. (1995) showed that the hippocampus and

declarative memory   Memory that can be verbally expressed, such as memory for events in a person's past.

leagues, declarative memory is a form of *perceptual memory*—specifically, memory of events that we can think and talk about.

The other category of memories, often called **nondeclarative memories,** includes instances of perceptual, stimulus-response, and motor learning that we are not necessarily conscious of. (Some psychologists refer to these two categories as *explicit* and *implicit* memories, respectively.) Nondeclarative memories appear to operate automatically. They do not require deliberate attempts on the part of the learner to memorize something. They do not seem to include facts; instead, they control behaviors. If someone asks us a question about a fact that we have learned or something that we have experienced, the question evokes images in the declarative (or explicit) memory system that we can then describe in words. For example, suppose that someone asks you how many windows your house has. If you have never answered that question before, you will probably do so by taking a mental tour of your house, going from room to room and counting the windows you see there. The question evokes the image (that is, gets you to call up a memory), which you then examine.

In contrast, nondeclarative (implicit) memories are not something we answer questions about. Suppose we learn to ride a bicycle. We do so quite consciously and develop declarative memories about our attempts: who helped us learn, where we rode, how we felt, how many times we fell, and so on. But we also form nondeclarative stimulus-response and motor memories; *we learn to ride.* We learn to make automatic adjustments with our hands and bodies that keep our center of gravity above the wheels. Most of us cannot describe the rules that govern our behavior. For example, what do you think you must do if you start falling to the right while riding a bicycle? Many cyclists would say that they compensate by leaning to the left. But they are wrong; what they really do is turn the handlebars to the right. Leaning to the left would actually make them fall faster, because it would force the bicycle even farther to the right. The point is that although they have learned to make the appropriate movements (which involve stimulus-response and motor learning), they cannot necessarily describe in words what these movements are.

Graf, Squire, and Mandler (1984) demonstrated a priming effect for verbal stimuli in subjects with anterograde amnesia. They showed lists of six-letter words to amnesic and nonamnesic subjects and asked them to study each one carefully and rate how much they liked them. The purpose of the rating was to make sure that the subjects spent some time thinking about each word. The investigators then administered two types of memory tests. In the *ex-*

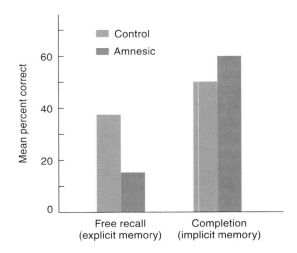

Figure 15.6
Explicit and implicit memory of amnesic patients and control subjects. The performance of amnesic patients was impaired when they were instructed to try to recall the words they had previously seen but not when they were asked to say the first word that came into their minds. (Based on data from Graf, Squire, and Mandler, 1984.)

plicit memory (declarative memory) condition they asked the subjects to recall the words they had seen. In the *implicit memory* (nondeclarative memory) condition they presented cards containing the first three letters of the words. For example, if one of the words had been DEFINE, they would have been shown a card on which DEF was printed. Several different six-letter words besides *define* begin with the letters DEF, such as *deface, defame, defeat, defect, defend, defied,* and *deform,* so there are several possible responses. The investigators asked the subjects simply to say the first word that started with those letters that came into their minds. As Figure 15.6 shows, the amnesic subjects explicitly remembered fewer than half as many words as the control subjects, but both groups performed equally well on the implicit memory task. (See *Figure 15.6.*)

A particularly interesting experiment by Squire et al. (1992) showed that the priming task that I just described does not involve the hippocampus but that a test of declarative memory does. Normal subjects were given lists of words to study. Then they were placed in a PET scanner that recorded regional brain activation. They were shown

nondeclarative memory Memory whose formation does not depend on the hippocampal formation; a collective term for perceptual, stimulus-response, and motor memory.

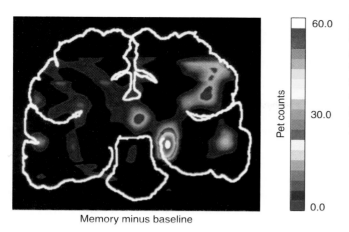

Memory minus baseline

Figure 15.7

PET scan of regional cerebral blood flow. The image represents the difference between blood flow during the baseline condition and during performance of the memory task, averaged across fourteen normal subjects. The peak activity (white center ringed by red, yellow, green, and blue) is located in the region of the hippocampal formation and parahippocampal gyrus.

(From Squire, L.R., Ojemann, J.G., Miezin, F.M., Petersen, S.E., Videen, T.O., and Raichle, M.E. *Proceedings of the National Academy of Sciences,* 1992, 89, 1837–1841. Reprinted with permission.)

the first three letters of the words and were asked either to say the first word that came to mind (*priming task*) or to use the letter sequences as cues and try to remember the words they saw on the list (*declarative memory task*). Note that the stimuli were the same in both cases; only the instructions were different.

When the subjects performed the declarative memory task, increased activity was seen in the right hippocampus and right prefrontal cortex. When they performed the priming task, changes were seen in a region of the visual association cortex, but no changes were seen in the hippocampus. (See *Figure 15.7.*)

Table 15.1 lists the declarative and nondeclarative memory tasks that I have described so far. (See *Table 15.1.*)

● Anterograde Amnesia: Failure of Relational Learning

As we have seen, anterograde amnesia appears to be a loss of the ability to establish new declarative memories; the ability to establish new nondeclarative memories (perceptual, stimulus-response, or motor learning) is intact. What, exactly, are declarative memories? Are they *verbal* memories? Is it simply that people with anterograde amnesia cannot learn new verbal information?

Clearly, verbal learning *is* disrupted in anterograde amnesia. Gabrieli, Cohen, and Corkin (1988) found that patient H.M. does not seem to have learned any words that have been introduced into the English language since his

Table 15.1
Examples of Declarative and Nondeclarative Memory Tasks

Declarative Memory Tasks	
Remembering past experiences	
Learning new words	
Recalling words (DEF____)	

Nondeclarative Memory Tasks	Type of learning
Broken drawings	perceptual
Connecting dots	perceptual (and motor?)
Recognizing faces	perceptual (and stimulus-response?)
Recognizing melodies	perceptual
Classical conditioning (eyeblink)	stimulus-response
Instrumental conditioning (choose circle)	stimulus-response
Mirror drawing	motor
Pursuit rotor	motor
Conditioned emotional response (blue light + boat horn)	stimulus-response
Word completion (DEF____)	stimulus-response

surgery. For example, he defined *biodegradable* as "two grades," *flower child* as "a young person who grows flowers," and *soul food* as "forgiveness." As the authors noted, for H.M., modern-day English is partly a foreign language. But declarative memories are not necessarily *verbal* memories; they are retelling of things or events we have previously experienced.

But anterograde amnesia includes more than a verbal memory deficit. Let us consider the most complex forms of declarative memories: memories of particular episodes. Episodic memories consist of collections of perceptions of events organized in time and identified by a particular context. For example, consider my memory of this morning's breakfast. I put on my robe and slippers, walked downstairs, made coffee, drank some orange juice, made waffle batter, baked a waffle, and ate it at the table next to the window. If I wanted to (and if I thought you were interested), I could give you many more details. The point is that the memory contains many events, organized in time. But would we say that my memory is a *verbal* memory? Clearly not; what I remember about my experience this morning is perceptions of a series of *events*, not a series of *words*. I remember not words but perceptions: the sight of the snow falling outside, the feel of the cold floor replaced by the comfortable warmth of my slippers, the smell of the coffee beans as I opened the container, the rasping sound made by the coffee grinder, and so on.

What started my reminiscence about this morning's breakfast? In this case it was prompted by my thinking about how to explain a particular concept to you. But suppose that you had asked me to tell you about this morning's breakfast. Your words would bring to mind memories of what happened, and I would then describe these memories to you. That sounds simple enough, but in fact, what happens must be extraordinarily complex. The phrase *this morning's breakfast* makes me think of a particular episode. My memory contains many details about many breakfasts, and if I wanted to, I could describe a good number of them. The distinguishing feature among them is the context: today's breakfast, yesterday's breakfast, the first breakfast in a hotel room in Paris, and so on. How do I keep them straight and tell you about the right one?

Obviously, memories must be organized. When you ask me about this morning's breakfast, your words bring to mind a *set* of perceptual memories—memories of events that occurred at a particular time and place. What does the hippocampal formation have to do with that ability? The most likely explanation is that during the original experience, it somehow ties together a series of perceptions in such a way that their memories, too, are linked. The hippocampal formation enables us to learn the *relation* be-

tween the stimuli that were present at the time—the *context* in which the episode occurred—and the events themselves. As we saw, people with anterograde amnesia can form perceptual memories. As the priming studies have shown, once they see something, they are more likely to recognize it later. But their perceptual memories are isolated; the memories of individual objects and events are not tied together or to the context in which they occurred. Thus, seeing a particular person does not remind them of other times they have seen that person or of the things they have done together. Anterograde amnesia appears to be a loss of the ability to learn about the relations among stimuli, including the time and place in which they occurred and the order of their occurrence.

Why have I introduced the term *relational learning?* Why not simply use the term *declarative?* If we consider only humans, there would probably be no reason to introduce a new term. But as we will see later in this chapter, nonverbal animals can have anterograde amnesia, too. And obviously, the term *declarative* cannot apply to animals that cannot talk. Therefore, we must look beyond a verbal-nonverbal distinction to understand what functions have been disrupted. And that is exactly what we will do when we consider research with laboratory animals later in this chapter. I will develop the idea of relational learning more fully there, in the section devoted to theoretical explanations of hippocampal functioning.

● Anatomy of Anterograde Amnesia

The phenomenon of anterograde amnesia—and its implications for the nature of relational learning—has led investigators to study this phenomenon in laboratory animals. But before I review this research (which has provided some very interesting results), we should examine the brain damage that produces anterograde amnesia. One fact is clear: Damage to the hippocampus, or to regions that supply its inputs and receive its outputs, causes anterograde amnesia. As you will recall, Scoville and Milner (1957) studied patients who had received temporal lobectomies and concluded that anterograde amnesia occurred only when the hippocampus was bilaterally damaged. After many years of controversy, researchers have finally concluded that they were right.

Connections of the Hippocampal Formation with the Rest of the Brain

I will spare you the controversy and present the most conclusive evidence that is available from anatomical studies with both humans and laboratory animals. But first let us examine some relevant anatomy.

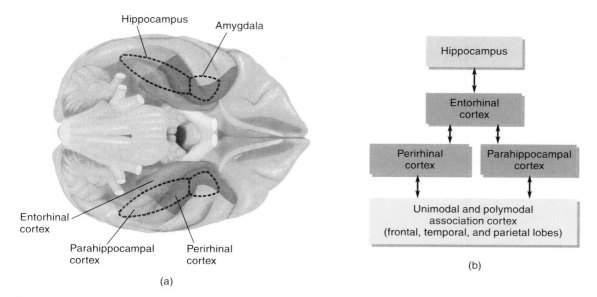

Figure 15.8
Cortical connections of the hippocampal formation. (a) A view of the base of a monkey's brain.
(b) Connections with the cerebral cortex.
(Adapted from Squire, L.R. *Psychological Review,* 1992, 99, 195–231.)

As we saw in Chapter 14, the hippocampal formation consists of the dentate gyrus, the CA fields of the hippocampus itself, and the subiculum (and its subregions). The most important input to the hippocampal formation is the entorhinal cortex; neurons there have axons that terminate in the dentate gyrus, CA3, and CA1. The entorhinal cortex receives its inputs from the amygdala, various regions of the limbic cortex, and all association regions of the neocortex, either directly or via two adjacent regions of limbic cortex: the **perirhinal cortex** and the **parahippocampal cortex.** (See *Figure 15.8.*)

The outputs of the hippocampal system come primarily from field CA1 and the subiculum. Most of these outputs are relayed back through the entorhinal, perirhinal, and parahippocampal cortex to the same regions of association cortex that provide inputs.

The hippocampal formation also receives input from subcortical regions via the fornix. As far as we know, these inputs select and modulate the functions of the hippocampal formation but do not supply it with specific information. (An analogy may make this distinction clearer: An antenna supplies a radio with information that is being broadcast, whereas the on-off switch, the volume control, and the station selector control the radio's functions.) The hippocampal formation receives dopaminergic input from the ventral tegmental area, noradrenergic input from the locus coeruleus, serotonergic input from the raphe nuclei,

and acetylcholinergic input from the medial septum. The release of these neurotransmitters modulates hippocampal functions. The hippocampal formation also sends a set of efferent fibers through the fornix to nuclei contained in the mammillary bodies, located at the caudal end of the hypothalamus. These fibers *do* seem to contain information that has been processed by the hippocampal formation. The mammillary bodies send axons to the anterior thalamus, which in turn sends axons to the cingulate cortex. (See *Figure 15.9.*)

Evidence That Hippocampal Damage Causes Anterograde Amnesia

The clearest evidence that damage to the hippocampal formation produces anterograde amnesia came from a case studied by Zola-Morgan, Squire, and Amaral (1986). Patient R.B., a 52-year-old man with a history of heart trouble, sustained a cardiac arrest. Although his heart was suc-

perirhinal cortex   A region of limbic cortex adjacent to the hippocampal formation that, along with the parahippocampal cortex, relays information between the entorhinal cortex and other regions of the brain.

parahippocampal cortex   A region of limbic cortex adjacent to the hippocampal formation that, along with the perirhinal cortex, relays information between the entorhinal cortex and other regions of the brain.

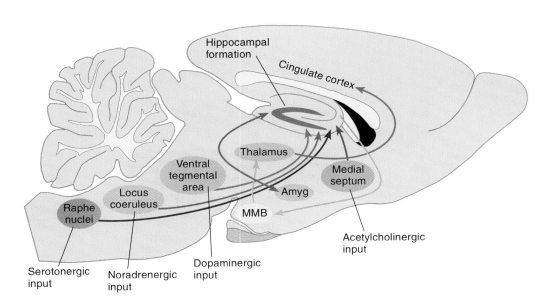

Figure 15.9
A midsagittal view of a rat brain showing the major subcortical connections of the hippocampal formation.

cessfully restarted, the period of anoxia caused by the temporary halt in blood flow resulted in brain damage. The primary symptom of this brain damage was a permanent anterograde amnesia, which Zola-Morgan and his colleagues carefully documented. Five years after the onset of the amnesia, R.B. died of heart failure. His family gave permission for histological examination of his brain.

The investigators discovered that field CA1 of the hippocampal formation was gone; its neurons had completely degenerated. Subsequent studies reported other patients with anterograde amnesia caused by CA1 damage (Victor and Agamonolis, 1990; Kartsounis, Rudge, and Stevens, 1995; Rempel-Clower et al., 1996). (See *Figure 15.10.*) In addition, several studies have found that a period of anoxia causes damage to field CA1 in monkeys and in rats and that the damage causes anterograde amnesia in these species, too (Auer, Jensen, and Whishaw, 1989; Zola-Morgan et al., 1992).

Why is field CA1 of the hippocampus so sensitive to anoxia? The answer appears to lie in the fact that this region is especially rich in NMDA receptors. For some reason, metabolic disturbances of various kinds, including seizures, anoxia, or hypoglycemia, cause glutamatergic terminal buttons to release glutamate at abnormally high levels. The effect of this glutamate release is to stimulate NMDA receptors, which permit the entry of calcium. Within a few minutes, excessive amounts of intracellular calcium begins to destroy the neurons. If animals are pretreated with drugs that block NMDA receptors, a period of anoxia is much less likely to produce brain damage. (See Rothman and Olney, 1987, for a review.) CA1 neurons

contain many NMDA receptors, and so long-term potentiation can quickly become established there. This flexibility undoubtedly contributes to our ability to learn as quickly as we do. But it also renders these neurons particularly susceptible to damage by metabolic disturbances.

Although the evidence I have discussed in this section indicates that hippocampal damage can cause anterograde amnesia, it does not rule out the possibility that other structures are also involved. In fact, the amnesia produced by damage limited to CA1 is not as severe as that caused by medial temporal lobectomy, which destroys other parts of the hippocampal formation, the amygdala, and the surrounding cortex. As we saw earlier, damage to the amygdala causes a deficit in emotional learning but does not produce anterograde amnesia. However, damage to the limbic cortex that funnels information into and out of the hippocampal formation does contribute to anterograde amnesia. Studies with monkeys have shown that damage to the perirhinal and parahippocampal cortex surrounding the entorhinal cortex produces anterograde amnesia or contributes to the severity of amnesia produced by hippocampal damage (Zola-Morgan et al., 1989b, 1993). These results are not surprising; when the major inputs and outputs of the hippocampus are damaged, it obviously cannot function normally.

Evidence for Involvement of Other Brain Structures

We can conclude that bilateral lesions of the medial temporal lobes cause anterograde amnesia because they damage the hippocampal formation and the region of cortex that surrounds it, but what about Korsakoff's syndrome?

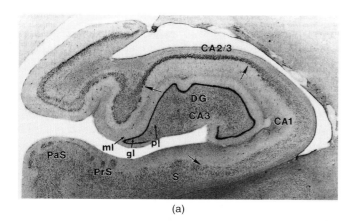

(a)

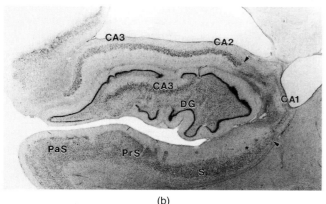

(b)

Figure 15.10
Damage to field CA1 caused by anoxia. (a) Section through a normal hippocampus. (b) Section through the hippocampus of patient G.D. The pyramidal cells of field CA1 (between the two arrowheads) have degenerated. (DG = dentate gyrus, gl, ml, pl = layers of the dentate gyrus, PaS = parasubiculum, PrS = presubiculum, S = subiculum, F = fornix).
(From Rempel-Clower, N.L., Zola, S.M., Squire, L.R., and Amaral, D.G. *Journal of Neuroscience,* 1996, *16,* 5233–5255. Reprinted with permission.)

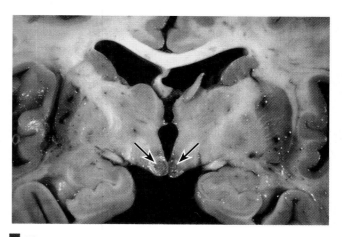

Figure 15.11
Degeneration of the mammillary bodies in a patient with Korsakoff's syndrome.
(Courtesy of A. D'Agostino, Good Samaritan Hospital, Portland, Oregon.)

You will recall that I promised earlier to discuss the anatomy of this disorder. Postmortem examination of the brains of patients with Korsakoff's syndrome almost always reveal severe degeneration of the mammillary bodies (Kopelman, 1995). As we saw, most of the efferent axons of the fornix, which originates in the subiculum, terminate in the mammillary bodies. Thus, it would appear that this pathway plays a role in relational learning. (See *Figure 15.11.*)

Patients with Korsakoff's syndrome almost always have damage to several regions of the brain, so it is not possible to make definitive conclusions about the anatomy of anterograde amnesia by studying these people. However,

study of the symptoms of people with brain damage produced by other means does support the conclusion that damage to any part of the neural circuit that includes the hippocampus, fornix, mammillary bodies, and anterior thalamus causes amnesia. Several studies (for example, Calabrese et al., 1995; D'Esposito et al., 1995; McMackin et al., 1995) have reported that damage to the fornix caused by head injury or surgery to remove tumors or cysts causes anterograde amnesia. In fact, McMackin et al. (1995) found that the amount of damage to the fornix was correlated to the severity of the patients' symptoms. Malamut et al. (1992) found that a patient with a bilateral thalamic lesion that severed the mammillothalamic tract (the fiber bundle that connects the mammillary bodies with the anterior thalamus) had anterograde amnesia. Most investigators believe that the amnesia in cases such as these is caused by interrupting the outflow of information from the hippocampal formation to the diencephalon through the fornix. However, the fornix also carries axons *into* the hippocampus, so it is possible that damage to these fibers is responsible for the memory deficits.

You will recall that one of the symptoms of Korsakoff's syndrome is confabulation—the reporting of memories of events that did not really occur. Direct damage to the fornix, mammillary bodies, or thalamus does not cause confabulation, so damage elsewhere must be responsible for this phenomenon. A study by Benson et al. (1996) suggests that confabulation may be a result of disruption of the normal functions of the prefrontal cortex. The investigators reported the case of a man who developed Korsakoff's syndrome, complete with confabulation. Neuropsychological testing found symptoms that indicate frontal lobe dysfunction, and a PET scan revealed hypoactivity of the medial and orbital prefrontal cortex. Four months later, the confabulation was gone, the neuropsychological tests did not show frontal lobe symptoms, and another PET scan revealed that the activity of the prefrontal cortex was back to normal.

Another study supports the suggestion that the frontal lobes may be involved in distinguishing between real and imaginary memories. Schacter et al. (1996) reported that a man with damage to the right frontal lobe showed an unusually high rate of false alarms in a test of memory for written and spoken words, sounds, and pictures. The experimenters presented sets of items and later tested the patient by presenting him with items he had seen or heard, along with some that had never been presented before. The patient correctly recognized items he had seen or heard but also claimed to recognize many of the new items. (In this context, a *false alarm* is the incorrect identification of a novel item as one that has been perceived before.) The patient made false alarms only when an item bore some similarity to the items that were previously presented. For example, if he studied items that fell into particular categories, he made many false alarms to novel items that also belonged to these categories but very seldom made false alarms to items that belong to categories he had *not* studied. Schacter and his colleagues suggested that the frontal lobes may help us to distinguish items with general familiarity from specific items we have encountered before.

● The Role of Hippocampal Damage in Retrograde Amnesia

As we saw, anterograde amnesia is usually accompanied by retrograde amnesia—the inability to remember events that occurred for a period of time before the brain damage occurred. I said, *"usually* accompanied by retrograde amnesia" because in some rare instances, patients will display only anterograde amnesia. Rempel-Clower et al. (1996) studied three patients with anterograde amnesia caused by hippocampal degeneration. They found that if the damage was limited to field CA1, the patient did not show retrograde amnesia. If the damage extended to other regions of the hippocampus (but still did not involve any structures outside the hippocampus), the patient showed a retrograde amnesia of up to 15 years. What about damage to structures outside the hippocampus? Korsakoff's syndrome is invariably accompanied by retrograde amnesia, but as we saw, it is also invariably accompanied by degeneration of many parts of the brain. Several studies have reported

that lesions restricted to the fornix or mammillary bodies can produce anterograde amnesia without retrograde amnesia (Calabrese et al., 1995; Kapur et al., 1996).

Retrograde amnesia is something of a puzzle. Patients with retrograde amnesia are unable to remember events for several years before the time of their brain damage but can remember events from the remote past. This finding means that we need our hippocampus to retrieve relatively young declarative memories but do not need it to retrieve old ones. What happens over the course of several years that makes declarative memories accessible without the use of the hippocampus? Is it simply a matter of practice? Does the act of remembering something again and again, over a period of years, somehow reinforce that memory so that it can be more easily retrieved later? We do not yet know the answer to these questions.

Interim Summary

Brain damage can produce anterograde amnesia, which consists of the inability to remember events that happen after the damage occurs, even though short-term memory (such as that needed to carry on a conversation) is largely intact. The patients also have a retrograde amnesia of several years' duration but can remember information from the distant past. Anterograde amnesia can be caused by the thiamine deficiency that sometimes accompanies chronic alcoholism (Korsakoff's syndrome), or it can be produced by bilateral removal of the medial temporal lobes. Most patients with Korsakoff's syndrome show confabulation, which may be caused by disruption of the frontal lobes.

The first explanation for anterograde amnesia was that the ability of the brain to consolidate short-term memories into long-term memories was damaged. However, ordinary perceptual, stimulus-response, and motor learning do not appear to be impaired; people can learn to recognize new stimuli, they are capable of instrumental and classical conditioning, and they can acquire motor memories. But they are not capable of *declarative learning*—of describing events that happen to them. The amnesia has also been called a deficit in explicit memory. An even more descriptive term—one that applies to laboratory animals as well as to humans—is *relational learning*. People with anterograde amnesia are also unable to learn the meanings of words they did not know before the brain damage took place.

Although other structures may be involved, researchers are now confident that the primary cause of anterograde amnesia is damage to the hippocampal formation or to its inputs and outputs. Temporary anoxia damages field CA1 (because of the high concentration of NMDA receptors there) and produces anterograde amnesia. The entorhinal cortex receives information from all regions of the association cortex, directly and through its connections with the perirhinal and parahippocampal cortex that surrounds it. The outputs of the hippocampal formation are relayed through these same regions. Subcortical inputs and outputs to the hippocampal formation pass through the fornix.

Korsakoff's syndrome is apparently caused by damage to the mammillary bodies, which receive input from the hippocampal formation via the fornix and relay it to the anterior thalamus. Traumatic or surgical damage to the fornix, mammillary bodies, or the connection between the mammillary bodies and the anterior thalamus also produce anterograde amnesia.

An unresolved puzzle is why damage to the hippocampal formation does not disrupt recall of memories that occurred early in a person's life but do disrupt recall of more recent memories. The period of retrograde amnesia of a person with severe anterograde amnesia can be as long as fifteen years.

RELATIONAL LEARNING IN LABORATORY ANIMALS

The discovery that hippocampal lesions produced anterograde amnesia in humans stimulated interest in the exact role that this structure plays in the learning process. To pursue this interest, many investigators turned to studies with laboratory animals. After the discovery that lesions of the hippocampus caused anterograde amnesia, experimenters began making lesions of the hippocampal formation in animals and testing their learning ability. They quickly found that the animals remained capable of learning most tasks. At the time they were surprised, and some even thought that the hippocampal formation had different functions in humans than it had in other animals. We now realize that most of the learning tasks that the animals were given tested simple sensory-response learning, and as we saw in the previous section, even humans with anterograde amnesia can do well on such tasks. People's anterograde amnesia becomes apparent only when we talk with them—which is something we cannot do with other animals. However, researchers have developed other tasks that require relational learning, and on such tasks, laboratory animals with hippocampal lesions show memory deficits, just as humans do.

● Working Memory: Remembering Places Visited

Olton and Samuelson (1976) devised a task that requires rats to remember where they have just been. The investigators placed the rats on a circular platform located at the junction of eight arms, which radiated away from the center like the spokes of a wheel. (See *Figure 15.12*.) The entire maze was elevated high enough above the ground so that the rats would not jump to the floor. Before placing the rats on the platform in the center, the experimenters put a piece of food at the end of each of the arms. The rats (who were hungry, of course) were permitted to explore the maze and eat the food. The animals soon learned to retrieve the food efficiently, entering each arm once. After twenty trials, most animals did not enter an arm from which they had already obtained food during that session. A later study (Olton, Collison, and Werz, 1977) showed that rats could perform well even when they were prevented from following a fixed sequence of visits to the arms; thus, they had to remember where they had been, not simply follow the same pattern of responses each time. Control procedures in several studies ruled out the possibility that the rats simply smelled their own odor in arms they had previously visited.

The radial-arm-maze task uses a behavioral capacity that is well developed in rats. Rats are scavengers and often find food in different locations each day. Thus, they must be able to find their way around the environment efficiently, not getting lost and not revisiting too soon a place where they previously found food. Of course, they must also

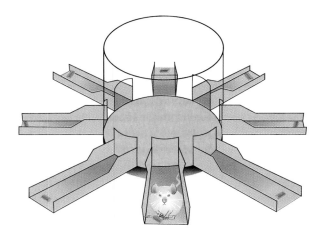

Figure 15.12
An eight-arm radial maze.

learn which places in the environment are likely to contain food and visit them occasionally. Although these two abilities might appear to require the same brain functions, they do not. Let us consider the ability to avoid revisiting a place where food was just found. Olton and his colleagues (reviewed by Olton, 1983) found that lesions of the hippocampus, fornix, or entorhinal cortex severely disrupted the ability of rats to visit the arms of a radial maze efficiently. In fact, their postoperative performance reached chance levels; they acted as if they had no memory of which arms they had previously entered. They eventually obtained all the food, but only after entering many of the arms repeatedly.

The problem was not that the rats could not distinguish among the eight arms of the maze; indeed, they could. Rats with hippocampal lesions can learn that particular locations sometimes contain food or never do. This type of learning is a form of stimulus-response learning; thus, it is analogous to nondeclarative (implicit) learning. Olton and Papas (1979) demonstrated the distinction between explicit and implicit learning in a single experiment. They trained rats in a seventeen-arm radial maze. Before each session, eight of the arms were baited with food; the other nine *never* were. Although rats with lesions of the fornix visited the baited arms randomly, failing to avoid visiting the ones in which they had just eaten, they learned to stay away from the nine arms that never contained food. They apparently could not remember where they had just been, but they could learn which locations regularly contained food. (See *Figure 15.13*.)

On the basis of such results, Olton (1983) has suggested that lesions of the hippocampus or its connections impair working memory but leave reference memory relatively intact. **Working memory** consists of information about things that have just happened, information that is useful in the immediate future but may change from day to day. Thus, it is "erasable" memory that is replaced on a regular basis. **Reference memory** is permanent, long-term memory, produced by consistent conditions.

Although these results can be explained by the concepts of working memory and reference memory, they can also be explained in terms of relational memory. Each set of trials can be seen as a separate episode, during which the animal enters the arms in a particular order. The study with the seventeen-arm maze proves that rats with hippocampal lesions have no trouble learning the association between a particular arm and the presence or absence of food. But the task in the eight-arm maze is more complicated than that: The animal must remember where it has been *that day*. Somehow, the memory of today's explorations must be kept separate from the memory of yesterday's explorations, and

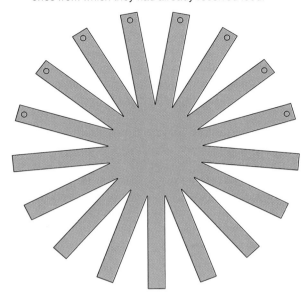

Eight arms always contained food; rats with hippocampal lesions entered them aimlessly, visiting ones from which they had already received food.

Nine arms never contained food; rats with hippocampal lesions learned not to enter them.

Figure 15.13
An explanation of the experiment by Olton and Papas (1979).

those of the day before, and so on. If we think of each day's trials as separate episodes, we can see the similarity to the ability of humans to remember today's breakfast without confusing it with yesterday's or that of the day before. Of course, the rats are not telling us about what they remember, but their performance suggests that without a functioning hippocampal system they cannot keep the episodes straight. In this case, all episodes take place in the same location, so the nature of the contextual stimulus is *time*.

● Spatial Perception and Learning

Hippocampal lesions disrupt the ability to keep track of and remember spatial locations. As we saw, H.M. never

working memory Memory of what has just been perceived and what is currently being thought about; consists of new information and related information that has recently been "retrieved" from long-term memory.

reference memory A form of long-term memory of stable conditions and contingencies in the environment; includes perceptual memory and stimulus-response memory.

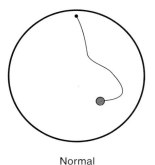
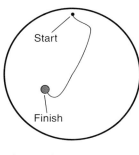
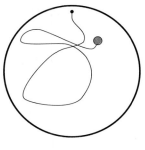

Normal

Neocortical control lesion

Hippocampal lesion

Figure 15.14
Effects of hippocampal lesions and neocortical control lesions on performance in the circular "milk maze." The small circle marks the location of the submerged platform.
(Reprinted by permission from Morris, R.G.M., Garrud, P., Rawlins, J.N.P., and O'Keefe, J. *Nature*, 1982, 297, 681–683. Copyright © 1982, Macmillan Journals Limited.)

learned to find his way home when his parents moved after his surgery. Laboratory animals show similar problems in navigation. Morris et al. (1982) developed a task that has been adopted by other researchers as a standard test of rodents' spatial abilities. The task requires rats to find a particular location in space solely by means of visual cues external to the apparatus. The "maze" consists of a circular pool, 1.3 meters in diameter, filled with a mixture of water and powdered milk. The milk mixture hides the location of a small platform, situated just beneath the surface of the liquid. The experimenters put the rats into the milky water and let them swim until they encountered the hidden platform and climbed onto it. They released the rats from a new position on each trial. After a few trials, normal rats learned to swim directly to the hidden platform from wherever they were released. However, rats with hippocampal lesions swam in what appeared to be an aimless fashion until they encountered the platform. Figure 15.14 shows the performance of three rats: a normal rat, one with a neocortical lesion (to control for the fact that removal of the hippocampus entails damage to the overlying neocortex), and one with a hippocampal lesion. The results speak for themselves. (See *Figure 15.14.*)

The Morris milk maze requires relational learning; to navigate around the maze, the animals get their bearings from the relative locations of stimuli located outside the maze. But the maze can be used for nonrelational, stimulus-response learning, too. If the platform is elevated just above the surface of the water so that the rats can see it, even those with hippocampal lesions quickly learn to swim directly toward it. Similarly, if the animals are always released at the same place, they learn to head in a particular direction—say, toward a particular landmark they can

see above the wall of the maze (Eichenbaum, Stewart, and Morris, 1990). I will say more later about why spatial learning is an example of relational learning.

Many different types of studies have confirmed the importance of the hippocampus in spatial learning. For example, Bingman and Mench (1990) found that hippocampal lesions disrupted navigation in homing pigeons. The lesions did not seem to disrupt the birds' ability to get their initial bearing toward the home roost. Instead, the lesions disrupted their ability to keep track of where they were when they got near the end of their flight—at a time during which the birds begin to use familiar landmarks to determine where they are. In addition, Rehkämper, Haase, and Frahm (1988) found that homing pigeons have larger hippocampal formations than breeds of pigeons that do not have such good navigational ability. In a review of the literature, Sherry, Jacobs, and Gaulin (1992) reported that the hippocampal formation of species of birds and rodents that normally store seeds in hidden caches and later retrieve them (and that have excellent memories for spatial locations) is larger than that of animals without this ability. Smulders, Sasson, and DeVoogd (1995) even found that the size of the hippocampal formation of the black-capped chickadee increased during late fall, a time when the birds spend a lot of time hoarding food.

● Place Cells in the Hippocampal Formation

One of the most intriguing discoveries about the hippocampal formation was made by O'Keefe and Dostrovsky (1971), who recorded the activity of individual pyramidal cells in the hippocampus as an animal moved around the

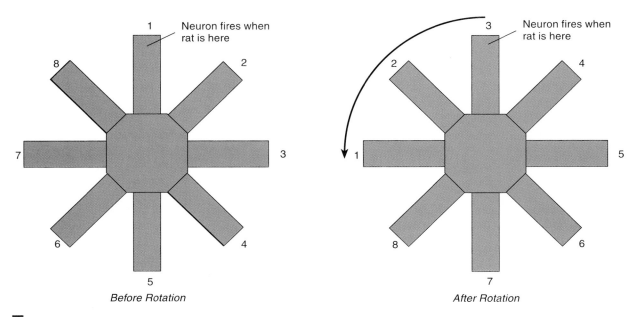

Figure 15.15
Response of place cells to environmental cues. If the maze is rotated 90 degrees, place cells maintain their locations relative to objects located outside the maze.

environment. The experimenters found that some neurons fired at a high rate only when the rat was in a particular location. Different neurons had different *spatial receptive fields;* that is, they responded when the animals were in different locations. For obvious reasons these neurons were named **place cells.** When, for example, a rat is exploring a radial-arm maze, place cells in its hippocampus respond to places defined in relation to objects in the environment outside the maze (for example, lighting fixtures, cabinets, and racks of cages). If a particular place cell is active when the rat is at the end of the arm that points north, it will continue to fire in the end of the northern arm, even after the maze is rotated so that a different arm points north. (See *Figure 15.15.*)

When a rat is placed in a symmetrical chamber, where there are few cues to distinguish one part of the apparatus from another, the animal must keep track of its location from objects it sees (or hears) in the environment outside the maze. Changes in these items affect the firing of the rats' place cells as well as their navigational ability. When experimenters move the stimuli as a group, maintaining their relative positions, the animals simply reorient their responses accordingly. However, when the experimenters interchange the stimuli so that they are arranged in a new order, the animals' performance (and the firing of their place cells) is disrupted. (Imagine how disoriented you might be if you entered a familiar room and found that the windows, doors, and furniture were in new positions.)

Hippocampal place cells are obviously guided by visual stimuli, because their receptive fields change when objects outside an environment are moved. They also receive internally generated stimuli. Hill and Best (1981) deafened and blindfolded rats and found that the spatial receptive fields of most of their place cells remained constant—even when the experimenters rotated the maze. At first the experimenters were surprised and puzzled by the results, but then it occurred to them that the animals might have been keeping track of where they were by feedback from proprioceptive cues. The rats might have been keeping track of their starting point, left and right turns, and so on, which kept resetting their "mental map." To test this hypothesis, Hill and Best wrapped their deafened and blindfolded rats in a towel, spun them around, and then placed them in the maze. (If you have ever played blindman's buff or pin-the-tail-on-the-donkey, you will understand how disorienting this treatment is.) The experimenters' hypothesis was correct; after the rats had been spun, the receptive fields of their place cells were disrupted.

Other investigators have confirmed these results, using somewhat different procedures. McNaughton, Leonard,

place cells   A neuron of the hippocampus that becomes active when the animal is in a particular location in the environment.

and Chen (1989) let rats become familiar with an eight-arm radial maze and then found single neurons in the hippocampus that had spatial receptive fields. Next, they introduced the rats into the maze in complete darkness, *using different starting points on each trial*. Because the animals could no longer see the cues outside the maze—and because they could not know their starting point—they could not tell which way the arms of the maze were oriented with respect to the room. Indeed, the receptive fields of the place cells were disrupted. Then the experimenters turned on the lights briefly, showing the rats the environmental cues that surrounded the maze. The receptive fields reoriented themselves and continued to respond appropriately even when the lights were turned off again.

How does a rat keep track of its location in the dark, when it cannot see any landmarks outside the chamber? McNaughton et al. (1989) obtained evidence that the parietal cortex provides the information that the hippocampal formation needs. They recorded from single neurons in the parietal cortex and found that their responses encoded various types of spatial information provided by movements that the rat made. For example, some responded when the rat turned left or right, some when it moved toward the center or toward the outside of the maze, and so on. Presumably, the hippocampus makes use of this information to keep track of its location in the maze when the external cues are not visible. It appears also to receive information from the vestibular system. Wiener et al. (1995) had rats explore a square chamber in the dark. The thirsty animals could receive drinks of water by alternating between the southeast corner and the center of the chamber. Periodically, the experimenters rotated the chamber by 90, 180, or 270 degrees. The animals compensated for the rotation, going to the corner that was now located toward the southeast. A similar compensation was also seen in the firing patterns of many of their hippocampal place cells.

The hippocampus appears to receive its spatial information through the entorhinal cortex. Quirk et al. (1992) found that neurons in the entorhinal cortex have spatial receptive fields, although these fields are not nearly as clear-cut as those of hippocampal pyramidal cells. These results corroborated those of Rose (1983), who had found that single granule cells in the dentate gyrus also had spatial receptive fields. (As you know, neurons in the dentate gyrus receive input from those in the entorhinal cortex.) Damage to the entorhinal cortex impairs animals' ability to navigate in spatial tasks; it also disrupts the spatial receptive fields of place cells in the hippocampus (Miller and Best, 1980).

The fact that neurons in the hippocampal formation have spatial receptive fields does not mean that each neuron encodes a particular location. Instead, this information is undoubtedly represented by particular *patterns* of activity in circuits of neurons within the hippocampal formation. Muller and Kubie (1987) examined the spatial receptive fields of hippocampal place cells in different environments. They found that if environments differed only in size, the receptive fields would be found in the same relative locations. However, if the environments differed in shape, the locations of the receptive fields would be located in places that the investigators were not able to predict. Receptive fields also adapted themselves to changes in the environment. For example, if the experimenters placed a barrier in the middle of a neuron's receptive field, the shape of the field would change; but if the barrier was outside the field, no change would occur.

Most investigators believe that when animals encounter new environments, they learn their layout and establish "maps" in their hippocampus. (Presumably, these maps are formed through the process of synaptic strengthening that is responsible for long-term potentiation.) An animal's location within each environment (the animal's place on the map) is encoded by the pattern of firing of these neurons. Obviously, a useful map must remain stable over time. Indeed, Thompson and Best (1990) obtained evidence that the hippocampal maps *are* stable; they found that the receptive fields of hippocampal neurons remained unchanged for as long as they were able to record from them—up to 153 days in one case.

Although the most striking characteristic of pyramidal cells in the hippocampal formation is their encoding of spatial location, these neurons also respond to nonspatial cues. For example, Young, Fox, and Eichenbaum (1994) constructed a radial maze out of four arms, which were painted with different patterns and were lined with materials having very different textures, such as sandpaper, corrugated rubber, and plastic mesh. The locations of the arms were varied randomly so that the rats had to remember which arms they had visited, not where the arms were located. The experimenters found that some hippocampal cells fired when the rat was in particular locations (that is, in the north, south, east, or west arm), some fired when the rat was in a particular arm, but most responded to *both* cues, firing only when the rat was in a particular arm that had been placed in a particular location. For example, the cell represented in Figure 15.16 fired when the rat was in arm C, but only when that arm was located to the north. (See *Figure 15.16.*)

The hippocampal formations of monkeys, like those of rodents, also contain neurons that respond to location, but most of them encode information about what part of the environment the animal is *looking at* rather than where the

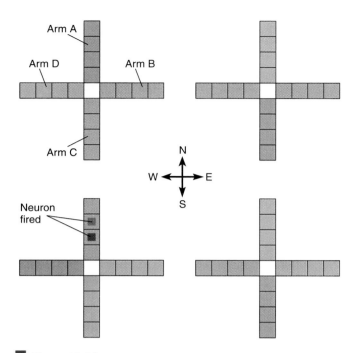

Arm A

Arm D   Arm B

Arm C

N
W ◄──►► E
S

Neuron
fired

Figure 15.16
Response pattern of a hippocampal neuron that fired only in arm C of the four-arm radial maze, but only when that arm was pointing north.
(Adapted from Young, B.J., Fox, G.D., and Eichenbaum, H. *Journal of Neuroscience*, 1994, 14, 6553–6563.)

animal is located. Rolls (1996) refers to these neurons as *spatial view cells* and suggests that their presence in the hippocampus of the monkey reflects the fact that vision is such an important sense modality for primates. The hippocampus of the monkey also contains place cells that respond the way they do in the hippocampus of the rat, but these cells are relatively less numerous (O'Mara et al., 1994).

● Role of Long-Term Potentiation in Hippocampal Functioning

In Chapter 14 we saw how synaptic connections could be quickly modified in the hippocampal formation, leading to long-term potentiation or long-term depression. How are these changes in synaptic strength related to the role the hippocampus plays in learning?

As you just learned, place cells in the hippocampal formation become active when the animal is present in particular locations. The sensory information reaches the dentate gyrus from the entorhinal cortex. Does this increased activity cause changes in the excitability of neurons in the hippocampal formation? The answer is clearly yes.

Green and Greenough (1986) raised rats in a complex environment, which, as we saw in Chapter 14, increases the number of neurons in the brain and their synaptic connections. The experimenters removed hippocampal slices from these animals and found that the synaptic connections between the entorhinal cortex and dentate gyrus appeared to be stronger. More recently, Kemperman, Kuhn, and Gage (1997) found that weanling mice who were put in a complex environment for 40 days had a larger dentate gyrus, which included 15 percent more granule cells than control animals. In addition, these animals learned the Morris milk maze more rapidly. Mitsuno et al. (1994) found that as rats learned a radial-arm maze, the strength of the population EPSP in field CA3 increased. Thus, when animals learn tasks that involve the hippocampal formation, the experience appears to induce the same types of changes that are produced by long-term potentiation.

Learning experiences that involve the hippocampal formation also induce biochemical changes that have been implicated in long-term potentiation. As we saw in Chapter 14, the enzymes PKC and CaM-KII play important roles in synaptic plasticity. When animals participate in spatial learning tasks, the levels of these enzymes in the hippocampal formation increases (Van der Zee et al., 1992; Tan and Liang, 1996).

If the kinds of neural changes seen in long-term potentiation are really those that take place during learning, then treatments that interfere with long-term potentiation should also interfere with learning. And they do. In Chapter 14 we saw that researchers produced targeted mutations in mice to "knock out" the genes responsible for the production of PKC and CaM-KII. These mutations suppressed long-term potentiation. They also produced impairments in the animals' ability to learn the Morris milk maze (Grant et al., 1992; Silva et al., 1992).

More recently, researchers have developed targeted mutations of the gene responsible for the production of NMDA receptors, which, as we saw in Chapter 14, are responsible for long-term potentiation in several parts of the hippocampal formation. Two studies from the same laboratory (McHugh et al., 1996; Tsien, Huerta, and Tonegawa, 1996) used a newly developed method to produce a targeted mutation of the NMDA receptor gene that affected only the CA1 pyramidal cells. NMDA receptors in these neurons failed to develop; in all other parts of the brain these receptors were normal. Figure 15.17 shows photomicrographs of slices through the hippocampus of a normal mouse and a "knock out" mouse, showing in situ hybridization of the messenger RNA for the NMDA receptor. As you can see, this chemical is missing in the CA1 field of the mouse with the targeted mutation. (See *Figure 15.17*.)

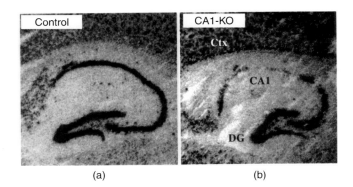

Control   CA1-KO

Ctx

CA1

DG

(a)   (b)

Figure 15.17

Effects of a targeted mutation ("knock out") of the NMDA receptor gene expressed only in field CA1 of the hippocampus. Photomicrographs of sections through the hippocampus showing in situ hybridization of messenger RNA responsible for the production of NMDA receptors. (a) Normal mouse. (b) Mouse with the targeted mutation (CA1 "knock out"). Ctx = neocortex, CA1 = hippocampal field CA1, DG = dentate gyrus.

(From Tsien, J.Z., Huerta, P.T., and Tonegawa, S. *Cell*, 1996, 87, 1327–1338. Reprinted by permission.)

As you might expect, the experimenters found that the lack of NMDA receptors prevented the establishment of long-term potentiation in field CA1 in the mice with the targeted mutation. In addition, although the pyramidal cells of CA1 did show spatial receptive fields, these fields were larger and less focused than those shown by cells in normal animals. Finally, the "knock out" mice learned a Morris milk maze much more slowly than mice whose CA1 neurons contained NMDA receptors.

● Modulation of Hippocampal Functions by Monoaminergic and Acetylcholinergic Inputs

I mentioned earlier that the hippocampal formation receives input from acetylcholinergic, noradrenergic, dopaminergic, and serotonergic neurons. These neurons, which innervate widespread regions of the brain, do not appear to convey specific information that becomes part of memories. Instead, they appear to control the information-processing functions of the hippocampal formation, which affects what is learned.

Serotonin appears to have a suppressive effect on the establishment of long-term potentiation in the hippocampal formation, apparently by inhibiting the release of glutamate (Stäubli and Otaky, 1994; Matsuyama, Nei, and Tanaka, 1996; Reznic and Stäubli, 1997). Conversely, norepinephrine has a facilitatory effect, particularly on syn-

apses of terminals of entorhinal neurons with granule cells of the dentate gyrus (Dahl and Sarvey, 1989; Klukowski and Harley, 1994; Bramham, Bacher-Svendsen, and Sarvey, 1997). In fact, long-term potentiation at these synapses does not require activation of NMDA receptors but does require activation of noradrenergic β receptors.

Dopamine also has excitatory effects on long-term potentiation and, apparently, memory-related functions of the hippocampal formation. As we saw in Chapter 14, bursting of individual CA1 pyramidal cells can be reinforced by infusions of dopamine or cocaine (Stein and Belluzzi, 1989). Presumably, this effect is caused by synaptic plasticity induced by simultaneous depolarization of CA1 neurons and activation of dopamine receptors on these neurons. Gasbarri et al. (1996) infused 6-HD, a chemical toxic to dopaminergic neurons, into the hippocampal formation. The infusions, which destroyed dopaminergic axons in field CA1 and the subiculum, disrupted the animals' performance on the Morris milk maze.

One of the most important modulatory inputs to the hippocampus comes from the medial septum, whose acetylcholinergic axons enter the hippocampal formation via the fornix. Activity of these neurons is responsible for hippocampal **theta rhythms**—medium-amplitude, medium-frequency (5–8 hertz) waves (Stewart and Fox, 1990). These waves influence the establishment of long-term potentiation in the hippocampus. Pavlides et al. (1988) found that when bursts of electrical stimulation coincided with the peaks of the theta waves, long-term potentiation was more easily established. Subsequent studies showed that depolarizing stimulation that coincided with the peaks of the theta waves produced long-term potentiation, while stimulation that coincided with the troughs produced long-term *depression* (Huerta and Lisman, 1996). In other words, theta activity consists of waxing and waning excitability of the hippocampal formation that alternately facilitate or inhibit synaptic strengthening. (See *Figure 15.18.*)

If hippocampal theta activity is disrupted, animals show deficits in learning tasks that are affected by hippocampal lesions. For example, Givens and Olton (1990) found that injections of scopolamine, a drug that blocks muscarinic acetylcholine receptors, suppressed hippocampal theta rhythms and impaired learning of a spatial alternation task that required rats to remember in which arm of a T-maze they had most recently entered. Givens (1995) found that low doses of alcohol, which in-

theta rhythm EEG activity of 5–8 Hz; an important indication of the physiological state of the hippocampus.

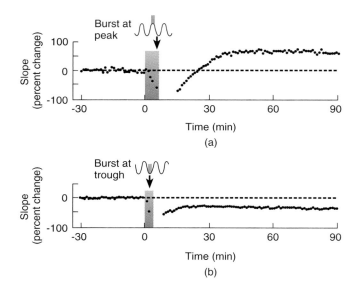

Figure 15.18

Long-term potentiation or long-term depression produced by stimulation of CA1 neurons at (a) the peak or (b) the trough of hippocampal theta waves.

(Adapted from Huerta, P.T., and Lisman, J.E. *Hippocampus,* 1996, *6,* 58–61.)

terfere with spatial working memory, also disrupted hippocampal theta rhythms. Presumably, at least some of alcohol's memory deficits are produced by its effects on hippocampal theta rhythms.

Several studies have shown that transplantation of acetylcholine-secreting cells from the medial septum into the hippocampus can partially reverse the effects of damage to its cholinergic input. For example, such transplants can restore theta activity and spatial receptive fields that are lost by cutting the fornix in rats (Buzsáki, Gage, and Czopf, 1987; Shapiro et al., 1989). These transplants can also reduce deficits in performance in the Morris milk maze caused by fornix lesions (Nilsson et al., 1987). Similar results were obtained in monkeys (Ridley et al., 1991). In all cases, histological examination of the tissue after the experiment was over showed that the transplants took and that they began secreting acetylcholine.

One of the effects of aging is a loss of acetylcholinergic neurons. Studies have shown that manipulations that increase the release of acetylcholine in the hippocampal formation can reduce the deficit in relational memory that occurs in older animals. For example, Gage et al. (1984) found that transplanting fetal medial septal tissue into the hippocampus of aged rats significantly improved their performance on the Morris milk maze. Olton et al. (1991) found that the performance of old rats (but not young

ones) on a test of relational learning was improved by an injection of an acetylcholinergic agonist into the medial septum. The drug stimulated the neurons there to release more acetylcholine in the hippocampal formation.

Vanderwolf and his colleagues (Vanderwolf, 1969; Vanderwolf et al., 1975) observed that hippocampal theta activity is closely related to the type of behavior the animal is performing. In rats, *theta behaviors* are associated with exploration or investigation; they include such behaviors as walking, running, rearing up on the hind legs, sniffing, and manipulating objects with the forepaws. They also occur during REM sleep (when the animal is dreaming?). *Nontheta behaviors* are not involved with exploration; they include alert immobility ("freezing"), drinking, and various self-directed behaviors.

Many investigators believe that the presence of theta rhythms is correlated with the acquisition of sensory information by the hippocampal formation. When a rat investigates odors in the environment, its rate of sniffing is synchronized with the waves of its hippocampal theta rhythm (Wiener, Paul, and Eichenbaum, 1989). And as we saw, when pulses of electrical stimulation are delivered to the perforant pathway in synchrony with the peaks of the theta waves, long-term potentiation can be established more easily. Buzsáki (1989, 1996) suggests that during theta rhythms, information is sampled by the dentate gyrus and CA3 field. Then after the bout of exploration is over, the cessation of the theta rhythms permits the information to be transferred to the CA1 field. During slow-wave sleep, information is transferred in bursts from the hippocampal formation to the neocortex, where the long-term memories are stored. Hippocampal theta waves are somewhat reminiscent of the cycles of a computer; whether they actually function this way will have to be resolved by future research.

● Theoretical Explanations of Hippocampal Functioning

As we saw earlier, people with anterograde amnesia can learn to recognize new stimuli, can learn new responses, and can learn to make a particular response when a particular stimulus is presented. What they cannot do is to talk about what they have learned. Anterograde amnesia appears to be a loss of the ability to learn about complex relations between many stimuli, including the order of their occurrence in time. How does research with laboratory animals help us understand this process?

Many investigators have come to the conclusion that the deficit in spatial learning produced by hippocampal lesions is caused by a failure to learn complex relations among stimuli—patterns of stimuli rather than the individual stimuli themselves. For example, according to Wiener, Paul, and Eichenbaum (1989), "An emerging consensus has indicated that the hippocampus is critical to learning and memory over a large range of information modalities that share a common demand for representing relationships among multiple independent percepts, but not for acquiring independent stimulus-reinforcement associations" (p. 2761). Sutherland and Rudy (Sutherland and Rudy, 1989; Rudy and Sutherland, 1995) present a "configural association theory," which suggests that the hippocampal system "combines the representations of elementary stimulus events to construct unique representations and allows for the formation of associations between these configural representations and other elementary representations" (Sutherland and Rudy, 1989, p. 129).

I think it is likely that the original function of the hippocampus was to help the animal learn to navigate in the environment. Later, the process of evolution gave the hippocampus the ability to detect other types of contexts, also. Let's first consider the spatial functions. Suppose you are standing in an environment similar to the circular milk maze I described earlier: a large field covered with grass and surrounded by distinctive objects such as trees and buildings. You are familiar with the environment, having walked across it and played games on it many times. If someone blindfolds you and then picks you up and drops you somewhere on the field, you will recognize your location as soon as you remove the blindfold. Your location is defined by the *configuration* of objects you see—the *relation* they have with respect to each other. You will get a different view of these objects from each position on the field. Of course, if there are distinctive objects present on the field itself (trees, garbage cans, drinking fountains), the task will be even easier, because you can judge your position relative to nearby objects as well as distant ones.

Spatial location obviously involves contextual stimuli. Another contextual stimulus is *time*. Several experiments have shown that the hippocampal formation is involved in an animal's ability to distinguish between situations that differ only in terms of time. Raffaele and Olton (1988) trained rats in a nonspatial alternation task that required animals to remember what happened in the context of time. They constructed a Y-shaped maze with movable arms. The arms were distinctively different, so the rats had no trouble distinguishing them. The rats received a piece of food in one of the arms on the first trial and then, on the next trial, received food only if they entered the other arm. The locations of the arms were varied randomly from trial

to trial, so the animals had to remember the particular arm they had just visited, not its location. In this task, the animals had to remember what happened in the context of time. They had already entered each of the arms on many occasions, so their choice had to be based on their memory of the arm they had visited most recently. Normal rats readily learned this task, but rats with lesions of the fornix, which disrupts normal functioning of the hippocampus, could not do so.

How can we put all the information about the hippocampal complex together? As you will recall, the hippocampal complex receives information from all regions of the sensory association cortex and from the motor association cortex of the frontal lobe. It also receives information from the amygdala concerning odors and dangerous stimuli. Thus, the hippocampal complex knows what is going on in the environment, where the animal is located, and what responses it has just made. It also knows about the animal's emotional state: whether the animal is hungry, sexually aroused, frightened, and so on. Thus, when something happens, the hippocampal system has all the information necessary to put that event into the proper context.

Several experiments indicate that damage to the hippocampal formation does, indeed, disrupt an animal's ability to distinguish particular contexts. For example, Phillips and LeDoux (1992) placed normal rats, rats with amygdala lesions, rats with hippocampal lesions, and rats with control lesions of the neocortex in a distinctive chamber and then established a conditioned emotional response (freezing) by presenting a tone paired with a foot shock several times. The following day, the experimenters placed the animals in the same chamber, watched them for a while, and then presented the tone (without the shock) several times. The control animals showed signs of conditioned fear as soon as they entered the chamber; they froze, indicating that they recognized the environment as one in which they had received shocks. As expected, the amygdala lesions disrupted all signs of conditioned fear—both to the context and to the tones. The hippocampal lesions had no effect on fear that was conditioned to the tone, but the animals showed very few signs of fear to the context. They did not seem to acquire a memory of the episode. (See *Figure 15.19.*)

As we saw in Chapter 14, synaptic changes in the amygdala appear to be responsible for conditioned emotional responses. If contextual stimuli are detected by the hippocampal formation, then classical conditioning of emotional responses to contextual stimuli must involve the transfer of information from the hippocampus to the amygdala. The hippocampal formation is connected directly to

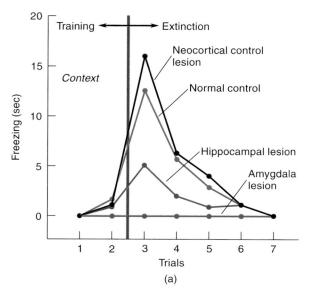

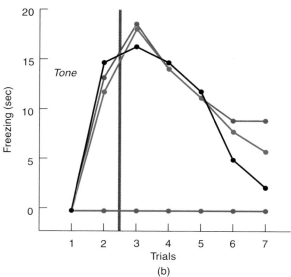

Figure 15.19

Effects of context: Conditioned emotional responses (freezing) during five days of extinction produced by (a) the context (the experimental chamber) and by (b) the CS (a tone).

(Adapted from Phillips, R.G., and LeDoux, J.E. *Behavioral Neuroscience*, 1992, 106, 274–285.)

the basolateral amygdala by means of the **ventral angular bundle,** which conveys information from parts of field CA1, the entorhinal cortex, and the subiculum. Maren and Fanselow (1995) found that stimulation of the ventral angular bundle produced long-term potentiation in the basolateral amygdala. This synaptic plasticity could be prevented by prior infusion of AP5, a drug that blocks NMDA

receptors. Furthermore, lesions of the parts of the hippocampal formation that contribute to the ventral angular bundle disrupted the acquisition of a conditioned emotional response to a contextual stimulus.

What does context have to do with declarative memory deficits in humans? Let's go back to a study involving a human with hippocampal damage and consider why the person can learn a nondeclarative task but cannot recall anything about the experience later. Consider a normal person learning to press a panel with a picture of a circle on it, as patient H.M. did in the experiment by Sidman, Stoddard, and Mohr (1968). While the person is seated in front of the apparatus, his or her hippocampal formation receives information about the context in which the learning is taking place: the room, the other people present, the person's mood, and so on. These pieces of information are collected and are somehow attached to the patterns of activity in the association cortex in several different regions of the brain. Later, when the person is asked about the task, the question reactivates the pattern of activity in the hippocampus, which causes the retrieval of the memory of the episode, pieces of which are stored all over the brain. Patient H.M., lacking a functioning hippocampal system, is unable to accomplish this act.

How might the hippocampus recognize a particular context? Rolls (1989, 1996) presents a hypothetical model of the role of the hippocampal formation in learning and memory that may prove to be useful. Like other researchers who study the physiology of learning and memory, he believes that perceptual learning takes place in the neocortex. The neocortex then sends information about events and episodes to the hippocampal formation, where it is further analyzed. The information reaches the entorhinal cortex and is then relayed to the dentate gyrus, fields CA3 and CA1, and finally to the subiculum, which conveys the results of the hippocampal information processing back to the neocortex, both directly and indirectly, through the entorhinal cortex. (Rolls's theory does not yet specifically address the role of the hippocampal efferents that travel through the fornix to structures in the basal forebrain.) Field CA3 contains a large number of **recurrent collaterals**—branches of axons leaving the region that turn back and form synapses with other neurons in field CA3. Rolls suggests that this field contains a network of neurons that

ventral angular bundle The bundle of axons that conveys information from the hippocampal formation to the basolateral amygdala.

recurrent collateral A branch of an axon leaving a particular region of the brain that turns back and forms synapses with neurons near the one that gives rise to it.

functions as an *autoassociator.* An autoassociative network quickly and efficiently learns to recognize particular pattern of inputs and produces a unique output for each pattern. Then if a similar pattern is presented later—or if parts of the pattern are presented—the network produces the appropriate output, which it sends on to field CA1.

Neural networks such as the one that Rolls proposes are capable of *pattern completion:* When they are presented with a fuzzy version of the original pattern or simply a fragment of it, they supply the complete pattern in their output. Let's go back to an example I described earlier—this morning's breakfast. When I got up, put on my slippers and robe, and went downstairs to have breakfast, my hippocampus received information from multiple sites in the neocortex about where I was, what time it was, how I was feeling, and so on. That is, it registered the context of that situation. As I went about preparing my breakfast, the memories of what was happening were being recorded in the form of synaptic changes in various regions of my sensory association cortex. The hippocampus communicated with these regions, somehow tying together these memories as they were being formed.

When you asked me about what I had for breakfast this morning, the words were recognized and understood by language mechanisms in my left temporal and parietal lobes (more about that in Chapter 16). Information about this recognition was sufficient for my hippocampal formation to recognize the context—to *complete the pattern.* The pattern was broadcast through outputs of the hippocampal formation to the locations in my neocortex that contain the individual components of the memory of the episode, and I told you about my breakfast.

This analysis is certainly speculative, but I think it is consistent with the experimental data I have presented in this chapter. Of course, it is vague about many parts of the process. For example, just how does asking someone a question activate the pattern of activity in the hippocampus? And how, exactly, are memories "tied together"? How are pieces of information collected and attached to sets of neural circuits? Obviously, we need to think about these questions, design clever experiments to obtain useful information, think about the questions in light of the new information, and design more clever experiments.

Interim Summary

Studies with laboratory animals indicate that damage to the hippocampal formation disrupts the ability to learn spatial relations and to distinguish events that have just occurred from those that have occurred at another time. For example, rats with hippocampal damage cannot remember which arms of a radial maze they have just visited, but they can learn to visit only those arms that contain food. Also, they cannot learn the Morris milk maze unless they can see the platform or they are always released from the same place in the maze. The basic deficit appears to be an inability to distinguish among different contexts, which includes locations in space and in time.

The hippocampal formation contains neurons that respond when the animal is in a particular location, which implies that the hippocampus contains neural networks that keep track of the relations among stimuli in the environment that define the animal's location. These networks also receive information concerning the animal's own locomotion, even when the animal moves about in the darkness. Much of this information is received from the parietal cortex, via the entorhinal cortex. Neurons in the hippocampal formation also respond to particular visual and tactual cues, such as those on the floors and walls of particular arms of a maze. Place cells in primates tend to respond according to the particular location the animal is looking at.

Long-term potentiation appears to be related to learning. When rats are raised in complex environments, the synaptic connections between the entorhinal cortex and the dentate gyrus are strengthened, and the animals are able to learn the Morris milk maze more rapidly. In addition, spatial learning tasks increase the levels of two enzymes involved in long-term potentiation—PKC and CaM-KII—in the hippocampal formation. Targeted mutations against these enzymes disrupt both long-term potentiation and the animals' ability to learn the Morris milk maze. Finally, a unique targeted mutation against the NMDA receptor gene in field CA1 disrupts long-term potentiation and the ability to learn the Morris milk maze.

Hippocampal theta activity, controlled by acetylcholinergic neurons in the medial septum, appears to be a time during which the hippocampus receives and stores sensory input. In addition, the establishment of long-term potentiation is modulated by the presence of theta waves: Bursts of hippocampal stimulation delivered during the peaks of the waves produce long-term potentiation, and stimulation delivered during the troughs produces long-term depression. Drugs that block muscarinic acetylcholine receptors disrupt hippocampal theta rhythms and impair spatial working memory. The memory deficits produced by fornix lesions, which appear to be caused by loss of acetylcholinergic neurons that send axons to the hippocampal formation, can be ameliorated by hippocampal transplants of fetal brain tissue that is rich in ACh-secreting neurons. The performance of aged rats can also be improved by these transplants.

The original role of the hippocampal formation may well have been to provide animals with the ability to orient in space, keeping track of the multiple stimuli that define spatial location; but it is clear that its role has expanded to learning relations among nonspatial stimuli and situations, as well. For example, lesions of the fornix disrupt animals' ability to remember which of two stimuli they had most recently perceived. More generally, the hippocampus is important in distinguishing one context from another. Although rats with hippocampal lesions can acquire a conditioned emotional response to a simple stimulus such as a tone, they do not learn to fear the chamber in which they received the shock. This contextual information appears to be transmitted from the hippocampus to the basolateral amygdala via the ventral angular bundle. Presumably, people with anterograde amnesia can no longer learn about episodes in their lives because their inability to distinguish one context from another prevents the elements that make up an episode from being tied together.

SUGGESTED READINGS

Cohen, N.J., and Eichenbaum, H. *Memory, Amnesia, and the Hippocampal System.* Cambridge, MA: MIT Press, 1993.

Graf, P., and Masson, M.E.J. *Implicit Memory: New Directions in Cognition, Development, and Neuropsychology.* Hillsdale, NJ: Erlbaum Associates, 1993.

McGaugh, J.L., Weinberger, N.M., and Lynch, G. *Brain and Memory: Modulation and Mediation of Neuroplasticity.* New York: Oxford University Press, 1995.

Ono, T., McNaughton, B.L., Molotchnikoff, S., Rolls, E.T., and Nishijo, H. *Perception, Memory and Emotion: Frontier in Neuroscience.* Amsterdam: Elsevier, 1996.

Schacter, D.L. *Searching for Memory: The Brain, the Mind, and the Past.* New York: Basic Books, 1996.

Squire, L.R., and Butters, N. *Neuropsychology of Memory.* New York: Guilford Press, 1992.

CHAPTER 16

Human Communication

Sail Baby by Elizabeth Murray.

Collection of the Walker Art Center, Minneapolis MN,
Walker Special Purchase Fund, 1984.

Verbal behaviors constitute one of the most important classes of human social behavior. Our cultural evolution has been possible because we can talk and listen, write and read. Language enables our discoveries to be cumulative; knowledge gained by one generation can be passed on to the next.

The basic function of verbal communication is seen in its effects on other people. When we talk to someone, we almost always expect our speech to induce the person to engage in some sort of behavior. Sometimes, the behavior is of obvious advantage to us, as when we ask for an object or for help in performing a task. At other times we are simply asking for a social exchange: some attention and perhaps some conversation. Even "idle" conversation is not idle, because it causes another person to look at us and say something in return.

This chapter discusses the neural basis of verbal behavior: talking, understanding speech, reading, and writing.

SPEECH PRODUCTION AND COMPREHENSION: BRAIN MECHANISMS

Our knowledge of the physiology of language has been obtained primarily by observing the effects of brain lesions on people's verbal behavior. Although investigators have studied people who have undergone brain surgery or who have sustained head injuries, brain tumors, or infections, most of the observations have been made on people who have suffered strokes, or **cerebrovascular accidents.** The most common type of cerebrovascular accident is caused by obstruction of a blood vessel. The interruption in blood flow deprives a region of the brain of its blood supply, which causes cells in that region to die.

Another source of information about the brain mechanisms of verbal communication has been studies of pa-

tients with seizure disorders that are severe enough to require brain surgery. As we saw in Chapter 5, seizure surgery usually entails removal of a seizure focus—a region of the brain that includes scar tissue or other abnormalities that irritates neurons in the vicinity and periodically triggers a seizure. Sometimes, before the surgery is performed, a set of electrodes will be temporarily implanted in the patient's brain. Electrical recordings can be made through these electrodes to try to find the location of the seizure focus, and the patient's reactions can be studied while electrical stimulation is delivered through the electrodes. Then, if the patient is operated on, the surgeon can stimulate various regions of the brain and observe the effects of the stimulation on the patient's verbal behavior. (As we saw in Chapter 5, such surgery is performed under local anesthesia so that the patient can remain conscious.) Finally, if part of the brain is removed, the patient's behavior before the surgery can be compared with his or her behavior after removal of the brain tissue.

Although one might think that patients like these would be ideal subjects for studies of the brain mechanisms of language, we must remember that their brains contain abnormalities. If they did not, they would not be candidates for surgery. Many of these abnormalities occurred early in life—for example, as a consequence of obstetric difficulties. We know that when damage occurs in the immature brain, the course of development is altered. Thus, the brain of an adult with a long-standing seizure disorder is likely to be different from that of a person without such a disorder. In fact, Devinsky et al. (1993) used cortical stimulation to map the location of speech areas of the temporal lobe of seizure patients and found a more widespread or

cerebrovascular accident A "stroke"; brain damage caused by occlusion or rupture of a blood vessel in the brain.

atypical distribution of these areas in patients with a history of early onset of seizures. Thus, we must be careful in drawing conclusions about the location of brain regions that are involved in specific functions from patients undergoing seizure surgery.

The most important category of speech disorders is **aphasia,** a primary disturbance in the comprehension or production of speech, caused by brain damage. Not all speech disturbances are aphasias; a patient must have difficulty comprehending, repeating, or producing meaningful speech, and this difficulty must not be caused by simple sensory or motor deficits or by lack of motivation. For example, inability to speak caused by deafness or paralysis of the speech muscles is not considered to be aphasia. In addition, the deficit must be relatively isolated; that is, the patient must appear to be aware of what is happening in his or her environment and to comprehend that others are attempting to communicate.

● Lateralization

Verbal behavior is a *lateralized* function; most language disturbances occur after damage to the left side of the brain. The best way to determine which side of the brain is dominant for speech is to perform a *Wada test,* named after its inventor. (As we saw in Chapter 15, this test is also used to assess memory functions.) A patient who is about to undergo surgery that might encroach on a speech area receives a short-acting anesthetic in one carotid artery and then, when the effects have worn off, in the other. This procedure anesthetizes first one cerebral hemisphere and then the other; thus, in a few minutes the involvement of each hemisphere in speech functions can be assessed. In over 95 percent of right-handed people the left hemisphere is dominant for speech. That is, when the left hemisphere is anesthetized, the person loses the ability to speak. However, when the right hemisphere is anesthetized, the person can still talk and carry on a conversation. The figure is somewhat lower in left-handed people: approximately 70 percent. Therefore, unless I say otherwise, you can assume that the brain damage described in this chapter is located in the left (speech-dominant) hemisphere.

Why is one hemisphere specialized for speech? The perceptual functions of the left hemisphere are more specialized for the analysis of sequences of stimuli, occurring one after the other. The perceptual functions of the right hemisphere are more specialized for the analysis of space and geometrical shapes and forms, the elements of which are all present at the same time. Speech is certainly sequential; it consists of sequences of words, which are composed of sequences of sounds. Therefore, it makes sense for the left

hemisphere to have become specialized at perceiving speech. In addition, as we saw in Chapter 8, the left hemisphere is involved in the control of sequences of voluntary movements. Perhaps this fact accounts for the localization of neural circuits involved in speech production, as well as speech perception, in the left hemisphere.

The brain is asymmetrical in structure as well as in function. For example, the size of speech areas in the frontal and temporal lobes is larger in the speech-dominant hemisphere, and there is even some evidence for differences in the size of some populations of neurons in these regions (Galaburda, Rosen, and Sherman, 1991; Hayes and Lewis, 1993; Foundas et al., 1996).

Although the circuits that are *primarily* involved in speech comprehension and production are located in the left hemisphere, it would be a mistake to conclude that the right hemisphere plays no role in speech. Speech is not simply a matter of talking—it is also having something to say. Similarly, listening is not simply hearing and recognizing words—it is understanding the meaning of what has been said. When we hear and understand words, and when we talk about or think about our own perceptions or memories, we are using neural circuits besides those directly involved in speech. Thus, these circuits, too, play a role in verbal behavior. For example, damage to the right hemisphere makes it difficult for a person to read maps, perceive spatial relations, and recognize complex geometrical forms. People with such damage also have trouble talking about things like maps and complex geometrical forms or understanding what other people have to say about them. The right hemisphere also appears to be involved in organizing a narrative—selecting and assembling the elements of what we want to say (Gardner et al., 1983). As we saw in Chapter 11, the right hemisphere is involved in the expression and recognition of emotion in the tone of voice. And as we shall see in this chapter, it is also involved in control of *prosody*—the normal rhythm and stress found in speech. Therefore, both hemispheres of the brain have a contribution to make to our language abilities.

● Speech Production

Being able to talk—that is, to produce meaningful speech—requires several abilities. First, the person must have something to talk about. Let us consider what this means. We can talk about something that is currently happening

aphasia   Difficulty in producing or comprehending speech not produced by deafness or a simple motor deficit; caused by brain damage.

or something that happened in the past. In the first case we are talking about our perceptions: things we are seeing, hearing, feeling, smelling, and so on. In the second case we are talking about our memories of what happened in the past. Both perceptions of current events and memories of events that occurred in the past involve brain mechanisms in the posterior part of the cerebral hemispheres (the occipital, temporal, and parietal lobes). Thus, this region is largely responsible for our having something to say.

Of course, we can also talk about something that *did not* happen. That is, we can use our imagination to make up a story (or to tell a lie). We know very little about the neural mechanisms that are responsible for imagination, but it seems likely that they involve the mechanisms that are responsible for perceptions and memories; after all, when we make up a story, we must base it on knowledge that we originally acquired through perception and have retained in our memory.

Given that a person has something to say, actually doing so requires some additional brain functions. As we shall see in this section, the conversion of perceptions, memories, and thoughts into speech makes use of neural mechanisms located in the frontal lobes.

Damage to a region of the inferior left frontal lobe (Broca's area) disrupts the ability to speak: It causes **Broca's aphasia.** This disorder is characterized by slow, laborious, and nonfluent speech. When trying to talk with patients who have Broca's aphasia, most people find it hard to resist supplying the words the patients are obviously groping for. But although they often mispronounce words, the ones they manage to come out with are usually meaningful. The posterior part of the cerebral hemispheres has something to say, but the damage to the frontal lobe makes it difficult for the patients to express these thoughts.

People with Broca's aphasia find it easier to say some types of words than others. They have great difficulty saying the little words with grammatical meaning, such as *a, the, some, in,* or *about.* These words are called **function words,** because they have important grammatical functions. The words that they do manage to say are almost entirely **content words**—words that convey meaning, including nouns, verbs, adjectives, and adverbs, such as *apple, house, throw,* or *heavy.* Here is a sample of speech from a man with Broca's aphasia, who is telling the examiner why he has come to the hospital. As you will see, his words are meaningful, but what he says is certainly not grammatical. The dots indicate long pauses.

> Ah . . . Monday . . . ah Dad and Paul [patient's name] . . . and Dad . . . hospital. Two . . . ah doctors . . . , and ah . . . thirty minutes . . . and yes . . . ah . . . hospital. And, er Wednesday . . . nine o'clock. And er Thursday,

ten o' clock . . . doctors. Two doctors . . . and ah . . . teeth. Yeah, . . . , fine. (Goodglass, 1976, p. 278)

People with Broca's aphasia can comprehend speech much better than they can produce it. In fact, some observers have said that their comprehension is unimpaired, but as we will see, this is not quite true. Broca (1861) suggested that this form of aphasia is produced by a lesion of the frontal association cortex, just anterior to the face region of the primary motor cortex. Subsequent research proved him to be essentially correct, and we now call the region **Broca's area.** (See *Figure 16.1.*)

Lesions that produce Broca's aphasia are certainly centered in the vicinity of Broca's area. However, damage that is restricted to the cortex of Broca's area does not appear to produce Broca's aphasia; the damage must extend to surrounding regions of the frontal lobe and to the underlying subcortical white matter (H. Damasio, 1989; Naeser et al.,

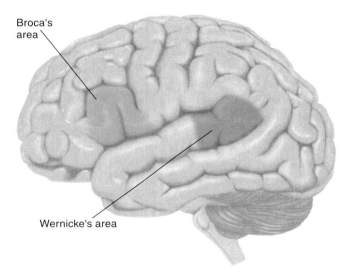

Broca's area

Wernicke's area

Figure 16.1
The location of the primary speech areas of the brain. (Wernicke's area will be described later.)

Broca's aphasia   A form of aphasia characterized by agrammatism, anomia, and extreme difficulty in speech articulation.

function word   A preposition, article, or other word that conveys little of the meaning of a sentence but is important in specifying its grammatical structure.

content word   A noun, verb, adjective, or adverb that conveys meaning.

Broca's area   A region of frontal cortex, located just rostral to the base of the left primary motor cortex, that is necessary for normal speech production.

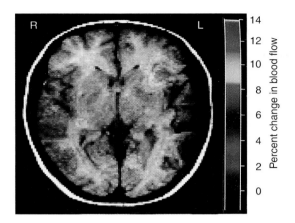

14
12
10
8
6
4
2
0

Percent change in blood flow

Figure 16.2
An averaged plot of PET scans of regional cerebral blood flow, superimposed on an MRI scan, taken while the subjects were reading words aloud. Note that the region of activation includes subcortical regions as well as the cerebral cortex of Broca's area. Also note that left and right are reversed.
(From Leblanc, R., Meyer, E., Bub, D., Zatorre, R.J., and Evans, A.C. *Neurosurgery,* 1992, *31,* 369–373. Reprinted with permission.)

1989). In addition, there is evidence that lesions of the basal ganglia—especially the head of the caudate nucleus—can also produce a Broca-like aphasia (Damasio, Eslinger, and Adams, 1984). Figure 16.2 shows the averaged plot of PET scans of regional blood flow from a group of subjects who were reading words aloud (Leblanc et al., 1992). As you can see, the task activated subcortical regions under Broca's area (including the head of the caudate nucleus) as well as the neocortex. (See *Figure 16.2.*)

Recent studies using PET scanners have shown that a *functional* lesion can often be much more extensive than the area of primary tissue damage. For example, Metter (1991) notes that small lesions in the basal ganglia and in the adjacent subcortical white matter can cause decreased metabolism of a fairly large region of the frontal cortex— even when autopsy shows no loss of neurons in the cortex. In addition, lesions in the frontal lobe can often cause decreased metabolism in the temporal and parietal lobes, presumably because the lesions disrupt connections between these areas. Thus the full extent of a lesion will often be underestimated by examining CT or MRI scans alone.

What do the neural circuits in and around Broca's area do? Wernicke (1874) suggested that Broca's area contains motor memories—in particular, *memories of the sequences of muscular movements that are needed to articulate words.* Talk-

ing involves rapid movements of the tongue, lips, and jaw, and these movements must be coordinated with each other and with those of the vocal cords; thus talking requires some very sophisticated motor control mechanisms. Obviously, circuits of neurons somewhere in our brain will, when properly activated, cause these sequences of movements to be executed. Because damage to the inferior caudal left frontal lobe (including Broca's area) disrupts the ability to articulate words, this region is the most likely candidate for the location of these "programs." The fact that this region is directly connected to the part of the primary motor cortex that controls the muscles used for speech certainly supports this conclusion.

But the speech functions of the left frontal lobe include more than programming the movements used to speak. Broca's aphasia is much more than a deficit in pronouncing words. In general, three major speech deficits are produced by lesions in and around Broca's area: *agrammatism, anomia,* and *articulation difficulties.* Although most patients with Broca's aphasia will have all of these deficits to some degree, their severity can vary considerably from person to person—presumably, because their brain lesions differ.

Agrammatism refers to a patient's difficulty in using grammatical constructions. This disorder can appear all by itself, without any difficulty in pronouncing words (Nadeau, 1988). As we saw, people with Broca's aphasia rarely use function words. In addition, they rarely use grammatical markers such as *-ed* or auxiliaries such as *have* (as in *I have gone*). For some reason, they *do* often use *-ing,* perhaps because this ending converts a verb into a noun. A study by Saffran, Schwartz, and Marin (1980) illustrates this difficulty. The following quotations are from agrammatic patients attempting to describe pictures:

Picture of a boy being hit in the head by a baseball

The boy is catch . . . the boy is hitch . . . the boy is hit the ball. (Saffran, Schwartz, and Marin, 1980, p. 229)

Picture of a girl giving flowers to her teacher

Girl . . . wants to . . . flowers . . . flowers and wants to. . . . The woman . . . wants to. . . . The girl wants to . . . the flowers and the woman. (Saffran, Schwartz, and Marin, 1980, p. 234)

So far, I have described Broca's aphasia as a disorder in speech *production.* In an ordinary conversation, Broca's aphasics seem to understand everything that is said to

agrammatism One of the usual symptoms of Broca's aphasia; a difficulty in comprehending or properly employing grammatical devices, such as verb endings and word order.

them. They appear to be irritated and annoyed by their inability to express their thoughts well, and they often make gestures to supplement their scanty speech. The striking disparity between their speech and their comprehension often leads people to assume that their comprehension is normal. But it is not. Schwartz, Saffran, and Marin (1980) showed Broca's aphasics pairs of pictures in which agents and objects of the action were reversed: for example, a horse kicking a cow and a cow kicking a horse, a truck pulling a car and a car pulling a truck, and a dancer applauding a clown and a clown applauding a dancer. As they showed each pair of pictures, they read the subject a sentence, for example, *The horse kicks the cow.* The subjects' task was to point to the appropriate picture, indicating whether they understood the grammatical construction of the sentence. (See *Figure 16.3.*) They performed very poorly.

The correct picture in the study by Schwartz and her colleagues was specified by a particular aspect of grammar: word order. The agrammatism that accompanies Broca's aphasia appears to disrupt patients' ability to use grammatical information, including word order, to decode the meaning of a sentence. Thus, their deficit in comprehension parallels their deficit in production. If they heard a sentence such as *The man swats the mosquito,* they would understand that it concerns a man and a mosquito and the action of swatting. They would have no trouble figuring out who is doing what to whom. But a sentence such as *The*

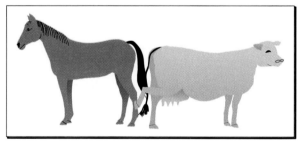

Figure 16.3
An example of the stimuli used in the experiment by Schwartz, Saffran, and Marin (1980).

horse kicks the cow does not provide any extra cues; if the grammar is not understood, neither is the meaning of the sentence.

The second major speech deficit seen in Broca's aphasia is **anomia** ("without name"). Anomia refers to a word-finding difficulty; and because all aphasics omit words or use inappropriate ones, anomia is actually a primary symptom of *all* forms of aphasia. However, because the speech of Broca's aphasics lacks fluency, their anomia is especially apparent; their facial expression and frequent use of sounds like "uh" make it obvious that they are groping for the correct words.

The third major characteristic of Broca's aphasia is *difficulty with articulation.* Patients mispronounce words, often altering the sequence of sounds. For example, *lipstick* might be pronounced "likstip." People with Broca's aphasia recognize that their pronunciation is erroneous, and they usually try to correct it.

These three deficits are seen in various combinations in different patients, depending on the exact location of the lesion and, to a certain extent, on their stage of recovery. We can think of these deficits as constituting a hierarchy. On the lowest, most elementary level is control of the sequence of movements of the muscles of speech; damage to this ability leads to articulation difficulties. The next higher level is selection of the particular "programs" for individual words; damage to this ability leads to anomia. Finally, the highest level is selection of grammatical structure, including word order, use of function words, and word endings; damage to this ability leads to agrammatism.

We might expect that the direct control of articulation would involve the face area of the primary motor cortex and portions of the basal ganglia, while the selection of words, word order, and grammatical markers would involve Broca's area and adjacent regions of the frontal association cortex. Some recent studies indicate that different categories of symptoms of Broca's aphasia do, indeed, involve different brain regions. Dronkers (1996) appears to have found a critical location for control of speech articulation: the left precentral gyrus of the insula. The insular cortex is located on the lateral wall of the cerebral hemisphere behind the anterior temporal lobe. Normally, this region is hidden and can be seen only when the temporal lobe is dissected away. (See *Figure 16.4.*) Dronkers discovered the apparent role of this region by plotting the lesions of patients with and without apraxia of speech who had

anomia Difficulty in finding (remembering) the appropriate word to describe an object, action, or attribute; one of the symptoms of aphasia.

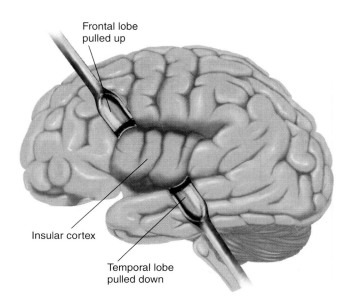

Figure 16.4
The insular cortex, normally hidden behind the rostral temporal lobe.

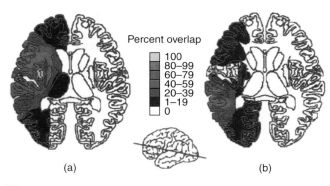

Figure 16.5
Evidence for involvement of the insular cortex in speech articulation. Percentage overlap in the lesions of twenty-five patients (a) with apraxia of speech and (b) without apraxia of speech. The only region common to all lesions that produced apraxia of speech was the precentral gyrus of the insular cortex.
(From Dronkers, N.F. *Nature*, 1996, *384*, 159–161.)

strokes that damaged the same general area of the brain. (**Apraxia of speech** is an impairment in the ability to program movements of the tongue, lips, and throat that are required to produce the proper sequence of speech sounds.) Figure 16.5(a) shows the overlap of the lesions of twenty-five patients with apraxia of speech. As you can see, a region of 100 percent overlap, shown in yellow, falls on the left precentral gyrus of the insula. (See *Figure 16.5a.*) In contrast, *none* of the lesions of nineteen patients who did not show apraxia of speech included damage to this region. (See *Figure 16.5b.*)

The agrammatism and anomia of Broca's aphasia are normally caused by subcortical damage or damage to the neocortex of the inferior frontal lobe. These findings are supported by a PET study by Stromswold et al. (1996). Subjects listened to syntactically complex sentences and had to decide whether they made sense. For example, "The dog that the cat scratched chased the mouse" makes sense, while "The mouse that the cat scratched chased the dog" does not. Listening to such sentences and judging their plausibility certainly exercises neural circuits involved in comprehension of grammar—and the investigators found that doing so increased the activity of Broca's area, especially the part closest to the lateral fissure.

Experiments have shown that people with Broca's aphasia have difficulty carrying out a sequence of commands such as "Pick up the red circle and touch the green square

with it" (Boller and Dennis, 1979). This finding, along with the other symptoms I have described in this section, suggests that an important function of the left frontal lobe is sequencing—of movements of the muscles of speech (producing words) and of words (comprehending and producing grammatical speech).

One study has found that agrammatism can be caused by damage to the cerebellum. Traditionally, the cerebellum has been regarded as a computer involved in coordinating movements, especially those involving precise timing. Neurologists have long recognized the fact that damage to the cerebellum can disrupt motor control of speech, which is not surprising when we consider the role the cerebellum plays in all forms of rapid, skilled movements. The speech of patients who have cerebellar damage is slow and monotonous, syllables tend to be separated by brief pauses, and enunciation is imprecise (Adams and Victor, 1981). However, the advent of PET and functional MRI scanning has found that even when movement is controlled for, engaging in various types of verbal activity activates the cerebellum (Fiez, 1996). The cerebellum may even be involved in grammatical aspects of speech. Silveri, Leggio, and Molinari (1994) studied a patient with cerebellar damage with agrammatic speech, characterized by uninflected verb forms. The following quotation (a word-by-

apraxia of speech Impairment in the ability to program movements of the tongue, lips, and throat required to produce the proper sequence of speech sounds.

word translation from the original Italian) illustrates the agrammatic nature of this patient's speech:

> I was watching television. One moment after, immediately after, to feel one half not to go. To have an attack, to be unable to speak. Upstairs there was my wife sleeping because it was midnight. I suddenly to stand up suddenly to fall down. Not to do anything because there was the carpet. Not to speak then to vomit all night long. I to vomit. My son came, soon an injection he gives and the drips. I to wait that here at the Polyclinic is admitted that free the bed. To wait that here to be the bed free to give the bed free.

● Speech Comprehension

Comprehension of speech obviously begins in the auditory system, which detects and analyzes sounds. But *recognizing* words is one thing; *comprehending* them—understanding their meaning—is another. Recognizing a spoken word is a complex perceptual task that relies on memories of sequences of sounds. This task appears to be accomplished by neural circuits in the middle and posterior portion of the superior temporal gyrus of the left hemisphere—a region that has come to be known as **Wernicke's area.** (Refer to *Figure 16.1.*)

Wernicke's Aphasia: Description

The primary characteristics of **Wernicke's aphasia** are poor speech comprehension and production of meaningless speech. Unlike Broca's aphasia, Wernicke's aphasia is fluent and unlabored; the person does not strain to articulate words and does not appear to be searching for them. The patient maintains a melodic line, with the voice rising and falling normally. When you listen to the speech of a person with Wernicke's aphasia, it appears to be grammatical. That is, the person uses function words such as *the* and *but* and employs complex verb tenses and subordinate clauses. However, the person uses few content words, and the words that he or she strings together just do not make sense. In the extreme, speech deteriorates into a meaningless jumble, illustrated by the following quotation:

Examiner: What kind of work did you do before you came into the hospital?

Patient: Never, now mista oyge I wanna tell you this happened when happened when he rent. His—his kell come down here and is—he got ren something. It happened. In thesse ropiers were with him for hi—is friend—like was. And it just happened so I don't know, he did not bring around anything. And he did not pay it. And he roden all o these arranjen from the pedis on

from iss pescid. In these floors now and so. He hadn't had em round here. (Kertesz, 1981, p. 73)

Because of the speech deficit of people with Wernicke's aphasia, when we try to assess their ability to comprehend speech, we must ask them to use nonverbal responses. That is, we cannot assume that they do not understand what other people say to them just because they do not give the proper answer. A commonly used test of comprehension assesses their ability to understand questions by pointing to objects on a table in front of them. For example, they are asked to "Point to the one with ink." If they point to an object other than the pen, they have not understood the request. When tested this way, people with severe Wernicke's aphasia do indeed show poor comprehension.

A remarkable fact about people with Wernicke's aphasia is that they often seem unaware of their deficit. That is, they do not appear to recognize that their speech is faulty, nor do they recognize that they cannot understand the speech of others. They do not look puzzled when someone tells them something, even though they obviously cannot understand what they hear. Perhaps their comprehension deficit prevents them from realizing that what they say and hear makes no sense. They still follow social conventions, taking turns in conversation with the examiner, even though they do not understand what the examiner says—and what they say in return makes little sense. They remain sensitive to the other person's facial expression and tone of voice and begin talking when he or she asks a question and pauses for an answer. One patient with Wernicke's aphasia made the following responses when asked to name ten common objects.

toothbrush → "stoktery"		*quarter* → "minkt"
cigarette → "cigarette"		*pen* → "spentee"
pen → "tankt"		*matches* → "senktr"
knife → "nike"		*key* → "seek"
fork → "fahk"		*comb* → "sahk"

He acted sure of himself and gave no indication that he recognized that most of his responses were meaningless. The responses he made were not simply new words that he had invented; he was asked several times to name the ob-

Wernicke's area A region of auditory association cortex on the left temporal lobe of humans, which is important in the comprehension of words and the production of meaningful speech.

Wernicke's aphasia A form of aphasia characterized by poor speech comprehension and fluent but meaningless speech.

jects and gave different responses each time (except for *cigarette*, which he always named correctly).

Wernicke's Aphasia: Analysis

Because the superior temporal gyrus is a region of auditory association cortex, and because a comprehension deficit is so prominent in Wernicke's aphasia, this disorder has been characterized as a *receptive* aphasia. Wernicke suggested that the region that now bears his name is the location of *memories of the sequences of sounds that constitute words*. This hypothesis is reasonable; it suggests that the auditory association cortex of the superior temporal gyrus recognizes the sounds of words, just as the visual association cortex of the inferior temporal gyrus recognizes the sight of objects.

But why should damage to an area that is responsible for the ability to recognize spoken words disrupt people's ability to speak? In fact, it does not; Wernicke's aphasia, like Broca's aphasia, actually appears to consist of several deficits. The abilities that are disrupted include *recognition of spoken words, comprehension of the meaning of words,* and the *ability to convert thoughts into words*. Let us consider each of these abilities in turn.

Recognition: Pure Word Deafness.   As I said in the introduction to this section, *recognizing* a word is not the same as *comprehending* it. If you hear a foreign word several times, you will learn to recognize it; but unless someone tells you what it means, you will not comprehend it. Recognition is a perceptual task; comprehension involves retrieval of additional information from memory.

Damage to the left temporal lobe can produce a disorder of auditory word recognition, uncontaminated by other problems. This syndrome is called **pure word deafness.** Although people with pure word deafness are not deaf, they cannot understand speech. As one patient put it, "I can hear you talking, I just can't understand what you're saying." Another said, "It's as if there were a bypass somewhere, and my ears were not connected to my voice" (Saffran, Marin, and Yeni-Komshian, 1976, p. 211). These patients can recognize nonspeech sounds such as the barking of a dog, the sound of a doorbell, and the chirping of a bird. Often, they can recognize the emotion expressed by the intonation of speech even though they cannot understand what is being said. More significantly, their own speech is excellent. They can often understand what other people are saying by reading their lips. They can also read and write, and sometimes, they ask people to communicate with them in writing. Clearly, pure word deafness is not an inability to comprehend the meaning of words; if it were, people with this disorder would not be able to read people's lips or read words written on paper.

Functional imaging studies confirm that perception of speech sounds activates neurons in the auditory association cortex of the superior temporal gyrus. Binder et al. (1994) found that the sounds of real words (such as *barn* and *box*) and pseudowords containing speech sounds (such as *narb* and *skob*) activated this region better than noise did. The stimuli activated the left and right hemispheres equally.

What is involved in the analysis of speech sounds? Just what tasks does the auditory system have to accomplish? And what are the differences in the functions of the auditory association cortex of the left and right hemispheres? Most researchers believe that the left hemisphere is primarily involved in judging the timing of the components of rapidly changing complex sounds, whereas the right hemisphere is primarily involved in judging more slowly changing components, including melody. Evidence suggests that the most crucial aspect of speech sounds is timing, not pitch. We can recognize words whether they are conveyed by the low pitch of a man or the high pitch of a woman or child. In fact, Shannon et al. (1995) found that people had no difficulty understanding speech from which the experimenters had removed almost all the tonal information, leaving only some noise modulated by the rapid stops and starts that characterize human speech sounds. On the other hand, emphasis or the emotional state of the speaker is conveyed by the pitch and melody of speech and by much slower changes in rhythm. In other words, the sounds that convey the identity of words are very brief, whereas those that convey prosody (emphasis and emotion) are of longer duration. Perhaps the auditory system of the left hemisphere is simply specialized for the recognition of acoustical events of short duration.

In a review of the literature, Phillips and Farmer (1990) suggest precisely this hypothesis. They note that careful studies of patients with pure word deafness have shown that the patients can distinguish between different vowels but not between different consonants—especially between different stop consonants, such as /t/, /d/, /k/, or /p/. (Linguists represent speech sounds by putting letters or special phonetic symbols between pairs of slashes.) Patients with pure word deafness *can* generally recognize consonants with a long duration, such as /s/, /z/, or /f/. (Say these consonants to yourself and you will see how different they sound from the first four examples.)

---

pure word deafness   The ability to hear, to speak, and (usually) to read and write without being able to comprehend the meaning of speech; caused by damage to Wernicke's area or disruption of auditory input to this region.

Phillips and Farmer note that the important acoustical events in speech sounds fall within a time range of a few milliseconds to a few tens of milliseconds. Speech sounds are made by rapidly moving lips, tongue, and soft palate, which produce acoustical events that can be distinguished only by a fine-grained analysis. In contrast, most environmental sounds do not contain such a fine temporal structure. The authors also note that "pure" word deafness is not absolutely pure. That is, when people with this disorder are tested carefully with recordings of a variety of environmental sounds, they have difficulty recognizing at least some of them. Although *most* environmental sounds do not contain a fine temporal structure, some do—and patients have difficulty recognizing them. For example, one patient with pure word deafness could no longer understand messages in Morse code but could still *send* messages that way.

Apparently, two types of brain injury can cause pure word deafness: disruption of auditory input to Wernicke's area or damage to Wernicke's area itself. Disruption of auditory input can be produced by bilateral damage to the primary auditory cortex, or it can be caused by damage to the white matter in the left temporal lobes that cuts axons bringing auditory information from the primary auditory cortex to Wernicke's area (Digiovanni et al., 1992; Takahashi et al., 1992). Either type of damage—disruption of auditory input or damage to Wernicke's area—disturbs the analysis of the sounds of words and hence prevents people from recognizing other people's speech. (See *Figure 16.6.*)

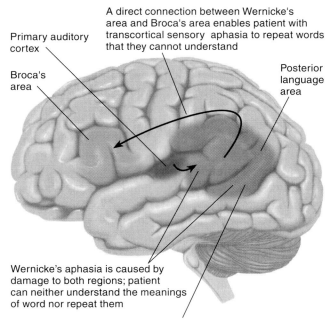

Figure 16.7
The location and interconnections of the posterior language area and an explanation of its role in transcortical sensory aphasia and Wernicke's aphasia.

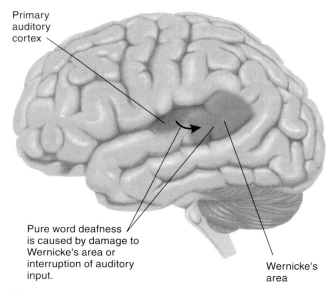

Figure 16.6
The brain damage that causes pure word deafness.

Comprehension: Transcortical Sensory Aphasia. The other symptoms of Wernicke's aphasia—failure to comprehend the meaning of words and inability to express thoughts in meaningful speech—appear to be produced by damage that extends beyond Wernicke's area into the region that surrounds the posterior part of the lateral fissure, near the junction of the temporal, occipital, and parietal lobes. For want of a better term, I will refer to this region as the *posterior language area.* (See *Figure 16.7.*) The posterior language area appears to serve as a place for interchanging information between the auditory representation of words and the meanings of these words, stored as memories in the rest of the sensory association cortex.

Damage to the posterior language area alone, which isolates Wernicke's area from the rest of the posterior language area, produces a disorder known as **transcortical sensory aphasia.** (See *Figure 16.7.*) The difference between transcortical sensory aphasia and Wernicke's aphasia is that patients with this disorder *can repeat what other people say to them;* therefore, they can recognize words. However, *they cannot comprehend the meaning of what they hear and repeat; nor can they produce meaningful speech of their own.* How can these people repeat what they hear? Because the posterior language area is damaged, repetition does not involve this part of the brain. Obviously, there must be a direct connection between Wernicke's area and Broca's area that bypasses the posterior language area. (See *Figure 16.7.*)

The fact that recognition and comprehension of speech require separate brain functions is illustrated dramatically by a case reported by Geschwind, Quadfasel, and Segarra (1968). The patient sustained extensive brain damage from carbon monoxide produced by a faulty water heater. (The damage included considerably more brain tissue than occurs in most cases of transcortical sensory aphasia, but it illustrates the distinction between the recognition and comprehension of speech.) The patient spent several years in the hospital before she died, without ever saying anything meaningful on her own. She did not follow verbal commands or otherwise give signs of understanding them. However, she often repeated what was said to her. The repetition was not parrotlike; she did not imitate accents different from her own, and if someone made a grammatical error while saying something to her, she sometimes repeated correctly, without the error. She could also recite poems if someone started them. For example, when an examiner said "Roses are red, violets are blue," she continued with "Sugar is sweet and so are you." She could sing and would do so when someone started singing a song she knew. She even learned new songs from the radio while in the hospital. Remember, though, that she gave *no signs of understanding anything she heard or said.* This disorder, along with pure word deafness, clearly confirms the conclusion that *recognizing* spoken words and *comprehending* them involve different brain mechanisms.

In conclusion, transcortical sensory aphasia can be seen as Wernicke's aphasia without a repetition deficit. To put it another way, the symptoms of Wernicke's aphasia consist of those of pure word deafness plus those of transcortical sensory aphasia. (See *Figure 16.7.*)

What Is Meaning?   As we have seen, Wernicke's area is involved in the analysis of speech sounds and thus in the recognition of words. Damage to the posterior language area does not disrupt people's ability to recognize words, but it does disrupt their ability to understand them or to produce meaningful speech of their own. But what, exactly, do we mean by the word *meaning*? And what types of brain mechanisms are involved?

Words refer to objects, actions, or relations in the world. Thus, the meaning of a word is defined by particular memories associated with it. For example, knowing the meaning of the word *tree* means being able to imagine the physical characteristics of trees: what they look like, what

the wind sounds like blowing through their leaves, what the bark feels like, and so on. It also means knowing facts about trees: about their roots, buds, flowers, nuts, wood, and the chlorophyll in their leaves. These memories are stored not in the primary speech areas but in other parts of the brain, especially regions of the association cortex. Different categories of memories may be stored in particular regions of the brain, but they are somehow tied together, so that hearing the word *tree* activates all of them. (As we saw in Chapter 15, the hippocampal formation is involved in this process of tying related memories together.)

In thinking about the brain's verbal mechanisms involved in recognizing words and comprehending their meaning, I find that the concept of a dictionary serves as a useful analogy. Dictionaries contain entries (the words) and definitions (the meanings of the words). In the brain we have at least two types of entries: auditory and visual. That is, we can look up a word according to how it sounds or how it looks (in writing). Let us just consider just one type of entry: the sound of a word. (I will discuss reading and writing later in this chapter.) We hear a familiar word and understand its meaning. How do we do so?

First, we must recognize the sequence of sounds that constitute the word—we find the auditory entry for the word in our "dictionary." As we saw, this entry appears in Wernicke's area. Next, the memories that constitute the meaning of the word must be activated. Presumably, Wernicke's area is connected—through the posterior language area—with the neural circuits that contain these memories. (See *Figure 16.8.*)

The process works in reverse when we describe our thoughts or perceptions in words. Suppose we want to tell someone about a tree that we just planted in our yard. Thoughts about the tree (for example, a visual image of it) occur in our association cortex—the visual association cortex, in this example. Information about the activity of these circuits is sent first to the posterior language area and then to Broca's area, which causes the words to be set into a grammatical sentence and pronounced. (See *Figure 16.8.*)

What evidence do we have that meanings of words are represented by neural circuits in various regions of the association cortex? The best evidence comes from the fact that damage to particular regions of the sensory association cortex can damage particular kinds of information

transcortical sensory aphasia   A speech disorder in which a person has difficulty comprehending speech and producing meaningful spontaneous speech but can repeat speech; caused by damage to the region of the brain posterior to Wernicke's area.

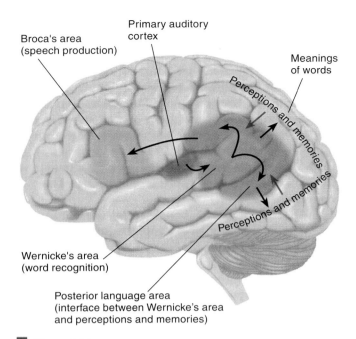

Broca's area
(speech production)

Primary auditory
cortex

Meanings
of words

Perceptions and memories

Perceptions and memories

Wernicke's area
(word recognition)

Posterior language area
(interface between Wernicke's area
and perceptions and memories)

Figure 16.8
The "dictionary" in the brain. Wernicke's area contains the auditory entries of words; the meanings are contained as memories in the sensory association areas. Black arrows represent comprehension of words—the activation of memories that correspond to a word's meaning. Red arrows represent translation of thoughts or perceptions into words.

and thus abolish particular kinds of meanings. For example, I met a patient who had recently had a stroke that damaged a part of her right parietal lobe that played a role in spatial perception. She was alert and intelligent and showed no signs of aphasia. However, she was confused about directions and other spatial relations. When asked to, she could point to the ceiling and the floor, but she could not say which was *over* the other. Her perception of other people appeared to be entirely normal, but she could not say whether a person's head was at the *top* or *bottom* of the body.

I wrote a set of multiple-choice questions to test her ability to use words denoting spatial relations. The results of the test indicated that she did not know the meaning of words such as *up*, *down*, and *under* when they referred to spatial relations, but she could use these words normally when they referred to nonspatial relations. For example, here are some of her incorrect responses when the words referred to spatial relations:

A tree's branches are *under* its roots.
The sky is *down*.
The ceiling is *under* the floor.

She made only ten correct responses on the sixteen-item test. In contrast, she got all eight items correct when the words referred to nonspatial relations like the following:

After exchanging pleasantries, they got *down* to business.
He got sick and threw *up*.

Damage to part of the association cortex of the *left* parietal lobe can produce an inability to name the body parts. The disorder is called **autotopagnosia,** or "poor knowledge of one's own topography." (A better name would have been *autotopanomia,* "poor naming of one's own topography.") People who can otherwise converse normally cannot reliably point to their elbow, knee, or cheek when asked to do so and cannot name body parts when the examiner points to them. However, they have no difficulty understanding the meaning of other words.

Other investigators have reported verbal deficits that include disruption of particular categories of meaning. McCarthy and Warrington (1988) reported the case of a man with left temporal lobe damage (patient T.B.) who was unable to explain the meaning of words that denoted living things. For example, when he was asked to define the word *rhinoceros*, he said, "Animal, can't give you any functions." However, when he was shown a *picture* of a rhinoceros, he said, "Enormous, weighs over one ton, lives in Africa." Similarly, when asked what a *dolphin* was, he said, "a fish or a bird"; but he responded to a *picture* of a dolphin by saying, "Dolphin lives in water . . . they are trained to jump up and come out . . . In America during the war years they started to get this particular animal to go through to look into ships." Clearly, patient T.B. has not lost his knowledge of specific animals but only the ability to name them. Presumably, the damage to his brain disconnected circuits involved in the recognition of words from those involved in his memories of animals. When T.B. was asked to define the meanings of words that denoted inanimate objects (such as *lighthouse* or *wheelbarrow*), he had no trouble at all.

Functional imaging studies of people without brain damage confirm these findings. Several experiments have found that perception of words and concepts from different categories activate different parts of the brain. For example, Spitzer et al. (1995) had people name pictures of items that belonged to four different categories: animals, furniture, fruit, and tools. Functional MRI scans revealed some category-specific sites of activation in the frontal and temporal lobes.

More widespread damage to the temporal and parietal lobes can cause a general loss in comprehension—and not

autotopagnosia Inability to name body parts or to identify body parts that another person names.

simply naming—presumably because of damage to regions of the brain that contain specific memories. For example, Damasio and Tranel (1990) studied a patient who had sustained severe damage to the temporal lobes. Besides becoming amnesic (his hippocampal formation was destroyed bilaterally), he had lost a considerable amount of specific information. For example, he recognized that a raccoon was an animal but had no idea of where it lived, what it ate, or what its name was. Hodges et al. (1992) reported several similar cases, caused by progressive degeneration of the temporal lobes. One patient was asked, "Have you been to America?" She replied, "What's America?" When she was asked, "What is your favorite food?" she said, "Food, food, I wish I knew what that was" (p. 1786). Another patient was frightened when he found a snail in his garden and thought that a goat was a strange creature. Hodges and his colleagues suggest the term *semantic aphasia* to refer to this syndrome.

So far, most of the studies I have described have dealt with comprehension of simple concepts: spatial direction and orientation, body parts, animals, and other concrete objects. But speech also conveys abstract concepts, some of them quite subtle. What parts of the brain are responsible for comprehending the meaning behind proverbs such as "People who live in glass houses shouldn't throw stones" or the moral of stories such as the one about the race between the tortoise and the hare?

Studies of brain-damaged patients suggest that comprehension of the more subtle, figurative aspects of speech involves the right hemisphere in particular (Brownell et al., 1983, 1990). Functional imaging studies confirm these observations. Bottini et al. (1994) had people listen to sentences and judge their plausibility. Some sentences were straightforward and factual. For example, "The old man has a branch as a walking stick" is plausible, whereas "The lady has a bucket as a walking stick" is not. Other sentences presented metaphors, the comprehension of which goes beyond the literal meaning of the words. For example, "The old man had a head full of dead leaves" is plausible, whereas "The old man had a head full of barn doors" is not. The investigators found that judging the metaphors activated parts of the right hemisphere, while judging factual sentences did not. Nichelli et al. (1995) found that judging the moral of Aesop's fables (as opposed to judging more superficial aspects of the stories) also activated additional regions of the right hemisphere.

Repetition: Conduction Aphasia.   As we saw earlier in this section, the fact that people with transcortical sensory aphasia can repeat what they hear suggests that there is a direct connection between Wernicke's area and Broca's

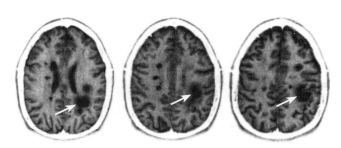

Figure 16.9
MRI scans showing subcortical damage responsible for a case of conduction aphasia. This lesion damaged the arcuate fasciculus, a fiber bundle connecting Wernicke's area and Broca's area.
(From Arnett, P.A., Rao, S.M., Hussain, M., Swanson, S.J., and Hammeke, T.A. *Neurology,* 1996, *47,* 576–578.)

area—and there is, the **arcuate fasciculus** ("arch-shaped bundle"). This bundle of axons appears to convey information about the *sounds* of words but not their *meanings.* The best evidence for this conclusion comes from a syndrome known as conduction aphasia, which is produced by damage to the inferior parietal lobe that extends into the subcortical white matter and damages the arcuate fasciculus (Damasio and Damasio, 1980). (See *Figure 16.9.*)

Conduction aphasia is characterized by meaningful, fluent speech; relatively good comprehension; but very poor repetition. For example, the spontaneous speech of patient L.B. (observed by Margolin and Walker, 1981) was excellent; he made very few errors and had no difficulty naming objects. But let us see how patient L.B. performed when he was asked to repeat words.

Examiner: bicycle
Patient: bicycle
Examiner: hippopotamus
Patient: hippopotamus
Examiner: blaynge
Patient: I didn't get it.
Examiner: Okay, some of these won't be real words, they'll just be sounds. Blaynge.
Patient: I'm not . . .
Examiner: blanch

arcuate fasciculus   A bundle of axons that connects Wernicke's area with Broca's area; damage causes conduction aphasia.

conduction aphasia   An aphasia characterized by inability to repeat words that are heard but normal speech and the ability to comprehend the speech of others.

Patient: blanch
Examiner: north
Patient: north
Examiner: rilld
Patient: Nope, I can't say.

You will notice that the patient can repeat individual words (all nouns, in this case) but utterly fails to repeat nonwords. People with conduction aphasia can repeat speech sounds that they hear *only if these sounds have meaning.*

Sometimes, when a person with conduction aphasia is asked to repeat a word, he or she says a word with the same meaning—or at least, one that is related. For example, if the examiner says *house,* the patient may say *home.* If the examiner says *chair,* the patient may say *sit.* One patient made the following response when asked to repeat an entire sentence:

Examiner: The auto's leaking gas tank soiled the roadway.
Patient: The car's tank leaked and made a mess on the
street.

The symptoms that are seen in transcortical sensory aphasia and conduction aphasia lead to the conclusion that there are pathways connecting the speech mechanisms of the temporal lobe with those of the frontal lobe. The direct pathway through the arcuate fasciculus simply conveys speech sounds to the frontal lobes. We use this pathway to repeat unfamiliar words—for example, when we are learning a foreign language or a new word in our own language or when we are trying to repeat a nonword such as *blaynge.* The second pathway is indirect and is based on the *meaning* of words, not the sounds they make. When patients with conduction aphasia hear a word or a sentence, the meaning of what they hear evokes some sort of image related to that meaning. (The patient in the second example presumably imagined the sight of an automobile leaking fuel onto the pavement.) They are then able to describe that image, just as they would put their own thoughts into words. Of course, the words they choose may not be the same as the ones used by the person who spoke to them. (See *Figure 16.10.*)

The symptoms of conduction aphasia indicate that the connection between Wernicke's area and Broca's area appears to play an important role in short-term memory of words and speech sounds that have just been heard. Presumably, rehearsal of such information can be accomplished by "talking to ourselves" inside our head without actually having to say anything aloud. Imagining ourselves saying the word activates the region of Broca's area, while imagining that we are hearing it activates the auditory association area of the temporal lobe. These two regions,

Damage to the arcuate fasciculus disrupts repetition of speech sounds; causes conduction aphasia

Broca's area (speech production)

Meanings of words

Perceptions and memories

Perceptions and memories

This connection enables patients with conduction aphasia to express their thoughts in words

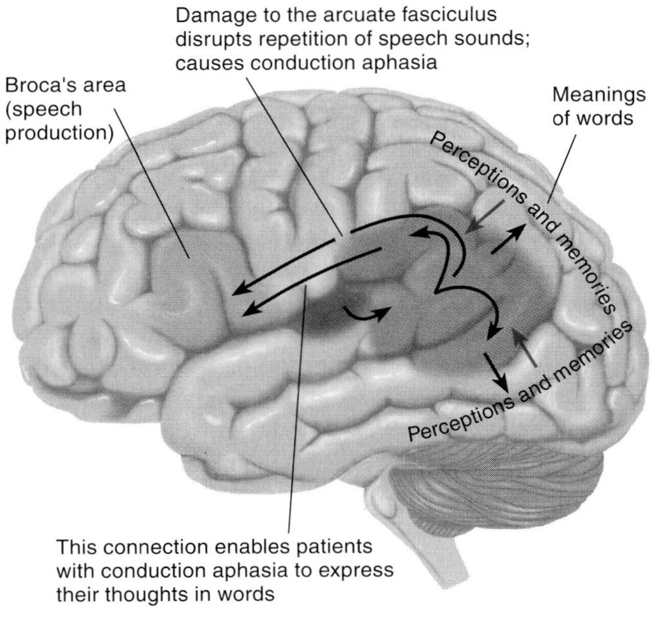

Figure 16.10
A hypothetical explanation of conduction aphasia. A lesion that damages the arcuate fasciculus disrupts transmission of auditory information, but not information related to meaning, to the frontal lobe.

connected by means of the arcuate fasciculus (which contains axons traveling in *both* directions) circulate information back and forth, keeping the short-term memory alive. Baddeley (1992) refers to this circuit as the *phonological loop.*

Functional imaging studies support this hypothesis. For example, Paulesu, Frith, and Frackowiak (1993) observed activation of Broca's area and a region within the posterior language area while subjects were remembering sets of six consonants. (See *Figure 16.11.*) Fiez et al. (1996) obtained similar results in a task that required subjects to remember pronounceable pseudowords. They found that the subjects who performed best at this task showed the greatest activation of Broca's area, while subjects who did poorly showed greater activation of the occipital lobe. The subjects read the pseudowords on a screen before the PET scan and then remembered them during the 40 seconds that the machine was performing a scan. Perhaps, reasoned Fiez and her colleagues, the subjects who did poorly were trying to remember what the pseudowords looked like rather than how they sounded, a less effective strategy in such a task.

Memory of Words: Anomic Aphasia

As I already noted, anomia, in one form or other, is a hallmark of aphasia. However, one category of aphasia con-

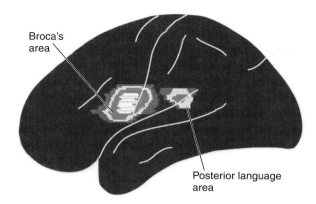

Figure 16.11
The phonological loop. A PET scan showing activation of Broca's area and the auditory association cortex during rehearsal of six consonants.
(Adapted from Baddeley, A.D. *Current Biology*, 1993, *3*, 563–565; after data from Paulesu, E., Frith, C.D., and Frackowiak, R.S.J. *Nature*, 1993, *362*, 342–344.)

Figure 16.12
The drawing of the kitchen story, part of the Boston Diagnostic Aphasia Test.
(From Goodglass, H., and Kaplan, E. *The Assessment of Aphasia and Related Disorders*, 2nd ed. Philadelphia: Lea & Febiger, 1983. Reprinted with permission.)

sists of almost pure anomia, the other symptoms being inconsequential. Speech of patients with anomic aphasia is fluent and grammatical, and their comprehension is excellent, but they have difficulty finding the appropriate words. They often employ **circumlocutions** (literally, "speaking in a roundabout way") to get around missing words. Anomic aphasia is different from Wernicke's aphasia. People with anomic aphasia can understand what other people say, and what they say makes perfect sense, even if they often choose roundabout ways to say it.

The following quotation is from a patient that some colleagues and I studied (Margolin, Marcel, and Carlson, 1985). We asked her to describe the picture shown in *Figure 16.12*. Her pauses, which are marked with three dots, indicate word-finding difficulties. In some cases, when she could not find a word, she supplied a definition instead (a form of circumlocution) or went off on a new track. I have added the words in brackets that I think she intended to use.

Examiner: Tell us about that picture.
Patient: It's a woman who has two children, a son and a daughter, and her son is to get into the . . . cupboard in the kitchen to get out [*take*] some . . . cookies out of the [*cookie jar*] . . . that she possibly had made, and consequently he's slipping [*falling*] . . . the wrong direction [*backward*] . . . on the . . . what he's standing on [*stool*], heading to the . . . the cupboard [*floor*] and if he falls backwards he could have some problems [*get hurt*], because that [*the stool*] is off balance.

Anomia has been described as a partial amnesia for words. It can be produced by lesions in either the anterior or posterior regions of the brain, but only posterior lesions produce a *fluent* anomia. The most likely location of lesions that produce anomia without the other symptoms of aphasia, such as comprehension deficits, agrammatism, or difficulties in articulation, is the left temporal or parietal lobe, usually sparing Wernicke's area. In the case of the woman described above, the damage included the middle and inferior temporal gyri, which includes an important region of the visual association cortex. (See *Figure 16.13*.)

When my colleagues and I were studying the anomic patient, I was struck by the fact that she seemed to have more difficulty finding nouns than other types of words. I informally tested her ability to name actions by asking her what people shown in a series of pictures were doing. She made almost no errors finding verbs. For example, although she could not say what a boy was holding in his hand, she had no trouble saying that he was *throwing* it. Similarly, she knew that a girl was *climbing* something but could not tell me the name of what she was climbing (a fence). In addition, she had no trouble finding nonvisual adjectives; for example, she could say that lemons tasted *sour*, that ice was *cold*, and that a cat's fur felt *soft*.

circumlocution   A strategy by which people with anomia find alternative ways to say something when they are unable to think of the most appropriate word.

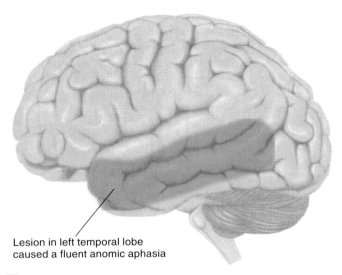

Lesion in left temporal lobe
caused a fluent anomic aphasia

Figure 16.13
The location of the brain damage of patient R.F.

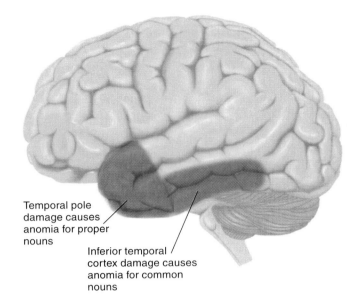

Temporal pole
damage causes
anomia for proper
nouns

Inferior temporal
cortex damage causes
anomia for common
nouns

Figure 16.14
The location of brain damage that causes anomia for proper or common nouns, according to Damasio et al. (1992).

For several years I thought that our patient was unique. But more recently, similar patterns of deficits have been reported in the literature. For example, Manning and Campbell (1992) described a patient who had difficulty naming objects but not actions. Some patients have even more specific deficits; Semenza and Zettin (1989) described a patient who had great difficulty with proper nouns (names of people and places). Damasio et al. (1991) studied several patients with similar deficits and concluded that anomia for proper nouns is caused by damage to the temporal pole, whereas anomia for common nouns is caused by damage to the inferior temporal cortex. Damage to both regions causes anomia for both types of nouns. They suggest that the important distinction between the two types of words is that proper nouns are specific to particular individuals (people or places) whereas common nouns apply to *categories*. Presumably, the cortex of the temporal pole is specifically involved with recognition of individuals. (See *Figure 16.14.*)

What about the ability to name actions? As we saw, the anomic patient my colleagues and I studied had no trouble with verbs. Neither did the anomic patients studied by Semenza and Zettin (1989), Manning and Campbell (1992), or Damasio et al. (1992). Several studies have found that anomia for verbs (more correctly called *averbia*) is caused by damage to the frontal cortex, in and around Broca's area (Damasio and Tranel, 1993; Daniele et al., 1994). If you think about it, that makes sense. The frontal lobes are devoted to planning, organizing, and executing actions, so it should not surprise us that they are involved in the task of remembering the names of actions.

Several functional imaging studies have confirmed the importance of Broca's area and the region surrounding it in production of verbs (Petersen et al., 1988; Wise et al., 1991; McCarthy et al., 1993; Fiez et al., 1996). In these studies, subjects either read or heard nouns and then had to say (or think to themselves) verbs describing actions appropriate to these nouns. For example, on reading or hearing the noun *hammer*, they might think of the verb *pound*. Figure 16.15 shows a PET scan from people who generated verbs in response to written nouns. The activity produced by simply reading nouns aloud has been subtracted out, leaving only the activity associated with the verb generation process. Presumably, the activity in the temporal lobe represents neural processes involved with comprehension of the nouns, while the activity in the frontal lobe represents the neural processes directly involved with thinking of appropriate actions and the associated verbs. (See *Figure 16.15.*)

The picture I have drawn so far suggests that comprehension of speech includes a flow of information from Wernicke's area to the posterior language area to the sensory association cortex. Production of spontaneous speech involves the flow of information concerning perceptions and memories from the posterior language area to Broca's area. This model is certainly an oversimplification, but it is

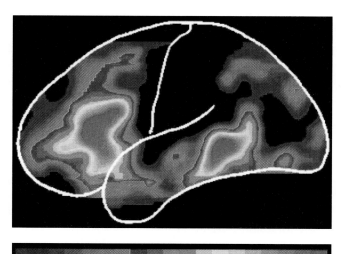

Low   High
Activity Level

Figure 16.15
A PET scan showing the regions of activation while people thought of verbs that depicted actions appropriate to nouns supplied by the experimenters.
(From Fiez, J.A., Raichle, M.E., Balota, D.A., Tallal, P., and Petersen, S.E. *Cerebral Cortex*, 1996, 6, 1–10.)

a useful starting point in conceptualizing basic mental processes. For example, thinking in words probably involves two-way communication between the speech areas and surrounding association cortex (and subcortical regions such as the hippocampus, of course).

Aphasia in Deaf People

So far, I have restricted my discussion to brain mechanisms of spoken and written language. But communication among members of the Deaf community involves another medium—sign language. Sign language is expressed manually, by movements of the hands. Sign language is *not* English; nor is it French, Spanish, or Chinese. The most common sign language in North America is ASL—American Sign Language. ASL is a full-fledged language, having signs for nouns, verbs, adjectives, adverbs, and all the other parts of speech contained in oral languages. People can converse rapidly and efficiently by means of sign language, can tell jokes, and can even make puns based on the similarity between signs. They can also use their language ability to think in words.

The grammar of ASL is based on its visual, spatial nature. For example, if a person makes the sign for *John* in one place and later makes the sign for *Mary* in another place, she can place her hand in the *John* location and move it toward the *Mary* location while making the sign for *love*. As you undoubtedly figured out for yourself, she is saying, "John loves Mary." Signers can also modify the meaning of signs through facial expressions or the speed and vigor with which they make a sign. Thus, many of the prepositions, adjectives, and adverbs found in spoken languages do not require specific words in ASL. The fact that signed languages are based on three-dimensional hand and arm movements accompanied by facial expressions means that their grammars are very different from those of spoken languages. Therefore, a word-for-word translation from a spoken language to a signed language (or vice versa) is impossible.

The fact that the grammar of ASL is spatial suggests that aphasic disorders in deaf people who use sign language might be caused by lesions of the right hemisphere, which is primarily involved in spatial perception and memory. However, all the cases of deaf people with aphasia for signs reported in the literature so far have involved lesions of the left hemisphere (Hickok, Bellugi, and Klima, 1996). Therefore, sign language, like auditory and written language, appears to rely primarily on the left hemisphere for comprehension and expression.

Lipreading

When deaf people communicate with hearing people who do not know sign language, they must do so in writing or by reading the hearing people's lips. What most people do not realize is that even hearing people sometimes use visual information about movements of a speaker's mouth to assist their comprehension of speech. Many studies have shown that in noisy environments, speech comprehension is much improved when the listener can watch the speaker's lips. People are not usually aware of this phenomenon, although they become acutely aware of a desynchronization between lip movements and speech sounds, such as that produced by a movie with a faulty sound track. Two recent studies have investigated the neural basis of lipreading. Campbell, De Gelder, and De Haan (1996) found that although the right hemisphere is more important in judging the identity of faces, the left hemisphere is more important in judging the positions that the lips take when a person is producing different vowel sounds. (For example, the lips describe a circle when we say /oo/, but the corners of the lips are drawn apart when we say /ee/.)

Calvert et al. (1997) obtained functional MRI scans from people who were watching a silent videotape of speakers slowly saying a list of numbers. The subjects had

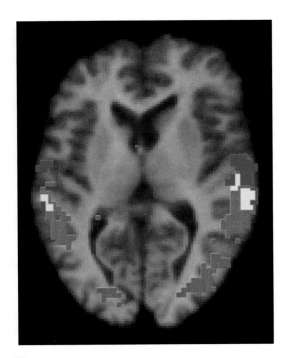

Figure 16.16
A PET scan showing regions of activation that accompanied auditory speech perception (blue), silent lipreading (magenta) and their overlap (yellow).
(From Calvert, G.A., Bullmore, E.T., Brammer, M.J., Campbell, R., Williams, S.C.R., McGuire, P.K., Woodruff, P.W.R., Iversen, S.D., and David, A.S. *Science,* 1997, *276,* 593–596.)

to repeat silently to themselves the numbers they saw being mouthed. The regions of the brain activated by performance of this lipreading task included parts of the visual association cortex (including area V5, which is devoted to the analysis of movement), the angular gyrus of the parietal lobe, and the primary auditory cortex and auditory association cortex of the temporal lobe—especially in the left hemisphere. (See *Figure 16.16.*) A similar pattern of activation was seen when subjects watched videotapes of people saying pronounceable pseudowords but not when they watched people making movements of their jaws and lower face with the lips closed.

● Prosody: Rhythm, Tone, and Emphasis in Speech

When we speak, we do not merely utter words. Our speech has a regular rhythm and cadence; we give some words stress (that is, we pronounce them louder), and we vary the pitch of our voice to indicate phrasing and to distinguish between assertions and questions. In addition, we can impart information about our emotional state through the rhythm, emphasis, and tone of our speech. These rhythmic, emphatic, and melodic aspects of speech are referred to as **prosody.** The importance of these aspects of speech is illustrated by our use of punctuation symbols to indicate some elements of prosody when we write. For example, a comma indicates a short pause; a period indicates a longer one with an accompanying fall in the pitch of the voice; a question mark indicates a pause and a rise in the pitch of the voice; an exclamation mark indicates that the words are articulated with special emphasis; and so on.

The prosody of people with fluent aphasias, caused by posterior lesions, sounds normal. Their speech is rhythmical, pausing after phrases and sentences, and has a melodic line. Even when the speech of a person with severe Wernicke's aphasia makes no sense, the prosody sounds normal. As Goodglass and Kaplan (1972) note, a person with Wernicke's aphasia may "sound like a normal speaker at a distance, because of his fluency and normal melodic contour of his speech." (Up close, of course, we hear the speech clearly enough to realize that it is meaningless.) In contrast, just as the lesions that produce Broca's aphasia destroy grammar, they also severely disrupt prosody. In patients with Broca's aphasia, articulation is so labored and words are uttered so slowly that there is little opportunity for the patient to demonstrate any rhythmic elements; and because of the relative lack of function words, there is little variation in stress or pitch of voice.

Evidence from studies of normal people and patients with brain lesions suggests that prosody is a special function of the right hemisphere. This function is undoubtedly related to the more general role of this hemisphere in musical skills and the expression and recognition of emotions: Production of prosody is rather like singing, and prosody often serves as a vehicle for conveying emotion.

Weintraub, Mesulam, and Kramer (1981) tested the ability of patients with right-hemisphere damage to recognize and express prosodic elements of speech. In one experiment they showed their subjects two pictures, named one of them, and asked the subjects to point to the appropriate one. For example, they showed them a picture of a greenhouse and a house that was painted green. In speech we distinguish between *greenhouse* and *green house* by stress: *GREEN house* means the former, and *GREEN*

prosody The use of changes in intonation and emphasis to convey meaning in speech besides that specified by the particular words; an important means of communication of emotion.

HOUSE (syllables equally stressed) means the latter. In a second experiment, Weintraub and her colleagues tested the subjects' ability simply to detect differences in prosody. They presented pairs of sentences and asked the subjects whether they were the same or different. The pairs of sentences either were identical or differed in terms of intonation (for example, *Margo plays the piano?* and *Margo plays the piano*) or location of stress (for example, *STEVE drives the car* and *Steve drives the CAR*). The patients with right-hemisphere lesions (but not control subjects) performed poorly on both of these tasks. Thus, they showed a deficit in prosodic comprehension.

To test production, the investigators presented two written sentences and asked a question about them. For example, they presented the following pair:

The man walked to the grocery store.
The woman rode to the shoe store.

The subjects were instructed to answer questions by reading one of the sentences. Try this one yourself. Read the question below and then read aloud the sentence (above) that answers it.

Who walked to the grocery store, the man or the woman?

The question asserts that someone walked to the grocery store but asks who that person was. When answering a question like this, people normally stress the requested item of information—in this case they say, "The *man* walked to the grocery store." However, Weintraub and her colleagues found that although patients with right-hemisphere brain damage chose the correct sentence, they either failed to stress a word or stressed the wrong one. Thus, the right hemisphere plays a role in production as well as perception of prosody.

Interim Summary

Two regions of the brain are especially important in understanding and producing speech. Broca's area, in the frontal lobe just rostral to the region of the primary motor cortex that controls the muscles of speech, is involved with speech production. This region contains memories of the sequences of muscular movements that produce words, each of which is connected with its auditory counterpart in the posterior part of the brain. Broca's aphasia—which is caused by damage to Broca's area, adjacent regions of the frontal cortex, and underlying white matter—consists of varying degrees of agrammatism, anomia, and articulation difficulties.

Wernicke's area, in the posterior superior temporal lobe, is involved with speech perception. The region just adjacent to Wernicke's area, which I have called the posterior language area, is necessary for speech comprehension and the translation of thoughts into words. Presumably, Wernicke's area contains memories of the sounds of words, each of which is connected through the posterior language area with memories about the properties of the things the words denote. Damage restricted to Wernicke's area causes pure word deafness—loss of the ability to understand speech but intact speech production, reading, and writing. Wernicke's aphasia, caused by damage to Wernicke's area and the posterior language area, consists of poor speech comprehension, poor repetition, and production of fluent, meaningless speech. Transcortical sensory aphasia, caused by damage to the posterior speech area, consists of poor speech comprehension and production, but the patients can repeat what they hear. Thus, the symptoms of Wernicke's area consist of those of transcortical sensory aphasia plus those of pure word deafness. The fact that people with transcortical sensory aphasia can repeat words they cannot understand suggests that there is a direct connection between Wernicke's area and Broca's area. Indeed, there is—the arcuate fasciculus. Damage to this bundle of axons produces conduction aphasia: disruption of the ability to repeat exactly what was heard without disruption of the ability to comprehend speech.

The meanings of words are our memories of objects, actions, and other concepts associated with them. These meanings are memories and are stored in the association cortex, not in the speech areas themselves. Pure anomia, caused by damage to the temporal or parietal lobes, consists of difficulty in word finding—particularly in naming objects. Some patients have a specific difficulty with proper nouns, while others have difficulty with common nouns; most patients have little difficulty with verbs. Damage to Broca's area and surrounding regions disrupts the ability to name actions—to think of appropriate verbs. Brain damage can also disrupt the "definitions" as well as the "entries" in the mental dictionary; damage to specific regions of the association cortex effectively erases some categories of the *meanings* of words.

Prosody includes changes in intonation, rhythm, and stress that add meaning, especially emotional meaning, to the sentences that we speak. The neural mechanisms that control the prosodic elements of speech appear to be in the right hemisphere.

Because so many terms and symptoms were described in this section, I have provided a table that summarizes them. (See *Table 16.1.*)

Table 16.1
Aphasic Syndromes Produced by Brain Damage

Disorder	Areas of lesion	Spontaneous speech	Comprehension	Repetition	Naming
Wernicke's aphasia	Posterior portion of superior temporal gyrus (Wernicke's area) and posterior language area	Fluent	Poor	Poor	Poor
Pure word deafness	Wernicke's area or its connection with primary auditory cortex	Fluent	Poor	Poor	Good
Broca's aphasia	Frontal cortex rostral to base of primary motor cortex (Braca's area)	Nonfluent	Good	Poor[a]	Good
Conduction aphasia	White matter beneath parietal lobe superior to lateral fissure (arcuate fasciculus)	Fluent	Good	Poor	Good
Anomic aphasia	Various parts of parietal and temporal lobes	Fluent	Good	Good	Poor
Transcortical sensory aphasia	Posterior language area	Fluent	Poor	Good	Poor

[a]May be better than spontaneous speech.

DISORDERS OF READING AND WRITING

Reading and writing are closely related to listening and talking; thus, oral and written language abilities have many brain mechanisms in common. This section discusses the neural basis of reading and writing disorders. As you will see, the study of these disorders has provided us with some useful and interesting information.

● Relation to Aphasia

The reading and writing skills of people with aphasia almost always resemble their speaking and comprehending abilities. For example, patients with Wernicke's aphasia have as much difficulty reading and writing as they do speaking and understanding speech. Patients with Broca's aphasia comprehend what they read about as well as they can understand speech, but their reading aloud is poor, of course. If their speech is agrammatical, so is their writing; and to the extent that they fail to comprehend grammar when listening to speech, they fail to do so when reading. Patients with conduction aphasia generally have some difficulty reading; and when they read aloud, they often make semantic paraphasias (saying synonyms for some of the words they read), just as they do when attempting to repeat

what they hear. Depending on the location of the lesion, some patients with transcortical sensory aphasia may read aloud accurately but fail to comprehend what they read.

There are a few exceptions to this general rule. For example, Semenza, Cipolotti, and Denes (1992) studied a patient with a severe fluent aphasia. Although she could not understand the speech of others, she could read. She clearly understood what she was reading, because she could follow written instructions. And although her spontaneous speech was meaningless and she could not say the names of objects, she could write their names, and she could read aloud. Clearly, her comprehension and production of oral language was very different from that of written language. Although cases like this one are rare, they do indicate that our verbal abilities make use of a large number of individual neural modules. Reading and writing undoubtedly share many modules with oral comprehension and production, but some modules are devoted to particular methods of communication.

● Pure Alexia

Dejerine (1892) described a remarkable syndrome, which we now call **pure alexia,** or sometimes *pure word blindness*

pure alexia   Loss of the ability to read without loss of the ability to write; produced by brain damage.

or *alexia without agraphia*. His patient had a lesion in the visual cortex of the left occipital lobe and the posterior end of the corpus callosum. The patient could still write, although he had lost the ability to read. In fact, if he was shown some of his own writing, he could not read it.

Several years ago, some colleagues and I studied a man with pure alexia who discovered his ability to write in an interesting way. A few months after he sustained a head injury that caused his brain damage, he and his wife were watching a service person repair their washing machine. The patient wanted to say something privately to his wife, so he picked up a pad of paper and jotted a note. As he was handing it to her, they suddenly realized with amazement that although he could not read, he was able to write. His wife brought the note to their neurologist, who asked the patient to read it. Although he remembered the gist of the message, he could not read the words. (See *Figure 16.17*.)

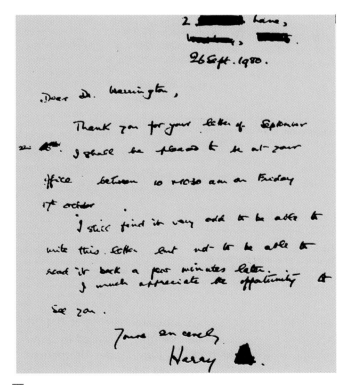

Figure 16.17
A letter written to Dr. Elizabeth Warrington by a patient with pure alexia. The letter reads as follows: "Dear Dr. Warrington, Thank you for your letter of September 16th. I shall be pleased to be at your office between 10–10:30 am on Friday 17th october. I still find it very odd to be able to write this letter but not to be able to read it back a few minutes later. I much appreciate the opportunity to see you. Yours sincerely, Harry X.
(From McCarthy, R.A., and Warrington, E.K. *Cognitive Neuropsychology: A Clinical Introduction*. San Diego: Academic Press, 1990. Reprinted with permission.)

Although patients with pure alexia cannot read, they can recognize words that are spelled aloud to them; therefore, they have not lost their memories of the spellings of words. Pure alexia is obviously a perceptual disorder; it is similar to pure word deafness, except that the patient has difficulty with visual input, not auditory input. The disorder is caused by lesions that prevent visual information from reaching the extrastriate cortex of the left hemisphere (Damasio and Damasio, 1983, 1986). Figure 16.18 explains why Dejerine's original patient could not read. The first diagram shows the pathway that visual information would take if a person had damage *only to the left primary visual cortex*. In this case the person's right visual field would be blind; he or she would see nothing to the right of the fixation point. But people with this disorder can read. Their only problem is that they must look to the right of each word so that they can see all of it, which means that they read somewhat more slowly than someone with full vision.

Let us trace the flow of visual information for a person with this brain damage. Information from the left side of the visual field is transmitted to the right striate cortex (primary visual cortex) and then to the lingual and fusiform gyri—a region of extrastriate cortex involved in the recognition of written text. From there, the information crosses the posterior corpus callosum and is transmitted to the left extrastriate cortex and then to speech mechanisms located in the left frontal lobe. Thus, the person can read the words aloud. (See *Figure 16.18a.*)

The second diagram shows Dejerine's patient. Notice how the additional lesion of the corpus callosum prevents visual information concerning written text from reaching the posterior left hemisphere. Without this information, the patient cannot read. (See *Figure 16.18b.*)

If this model presented in Figure 16.18 is correct, we would predict that a lesion restricted to the posterior corpus callosum should cause a left *hemialexia*—an inability to read words presented entirely in the left visual field. In fact, Binder et al. (1992) studied a patient who had precisely that lesion and precisely that deficit. Their patient, a thirty-year-old woman, was operated on to remove a vascular malformation in her brain. While removing the malformation, the surgeons were obliged to damage the posterior end of the corpus callosum. When Binder and his colleagues tested the woman later, they found that she often made errors in reading that involved the left side of words—the part that would fall into her "word blind" visual field. For example, she read *car* as *ear* and *seat* as *heat*. In addition, she could not read simple three-letter words presented to her left visual field. (See *Figure 16.18c.*)

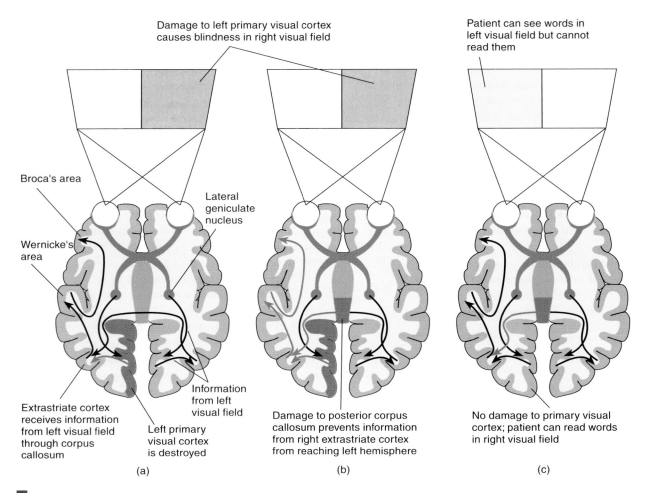

Figure 16.18
Pure alexia. Red arrows indicate the flow of information that has been interrupted by brain damage. (a) The route followed by information as a person with damage to the left primary visual cortex reads aloud. (b) Additional damage to the posterior corpus callosum interrupts the flow of information and produces pure alexia. (c) Damage to the posterior corpus callosum alone produces left hemialexia: an inability to read words presented in the left visual field.

I must note that the diagrams shown in Figure 16.18 are as simple and schematic as possible. They illustrate only the pathway involved in seeing a word and pronouncing it, and they ignore neural structures that would be involved in understanding its meaning. As we will see later in this chapter, evidence from patients with brain lesions indicates that seeing and pronouncing words can take place independently of understanding them. Thus, although the diagrams are simplified, they are not unreasonable, given what we know about the neural components of the reading process.

You will recall that writing is not the only form of visible language; deaf people can communicate by means of sign language just as well as hearing people can commu-

nicate by means of spoken language. Hickok et al. (1995) reported on a case of "sign blindness" caused by damage similar to that which causes pure alexia. The patient, a right-handed deaf woman, sustained a stroke that damaged her left occipital lobe and the posterior corpus callosum. The lesion did not impair her ability to sign in coherent sentences, so she did not have a Wernicke-like aphasia. However, she could no longer understand other people's sign language, and she lost her ability to read. She had some ability to comprehend single signs (corresponding to single words), but she could not comprehend signed sentences.

You will recall from Chapter 6 that visual agnosia is a perceptual deficit in which people with bilateral damage to the visual association cortex cannot recognize objects by sight. Patients with pure alexia do *not* have visual agnosia; they can recognize objects and supply their names. Similarly, people with visual agnosia can still read. Thus, the perceptual analysis of objects and words requires different mechanisms. I find this fact both interesting and puzzling. Certainly, the ability to read cannot have shaped the evolution of the human brain, because the invention of writing is only a few thousand years old, and until very recently, the vast majority of the world's population was illiterate. Thus, reading and object recognition use brain mechanisms that undoubtedly existed even before the invention of writing. What is the nature of these mechanisms? What features of the world around us require analysis similar to the analysis we use to recognize objects versus words?

Although these questions have not yet been answered, a region of the extrastriate cortex that is essential for visual analysis of written text has been identified. Petersen et al. (1990) used a PET scanner to measure regional cerebral blood flow while presenting subjects with four types of visual stimuli: unfamiliar letterlike forms, strings of consonants, pronounceable nonwords, and real words. They found that one region of the extrastriate cortex was activated only by pronounceable nonwords or real words. Their finding suggests that this region, which includes the fusiform and lingual gyri, plays a role in recognition of familiar combinations of letters. (See *Figure 16.19.*)

● Toward an Understanding of Reading

Most investigators believe that reading involves at least two different processes: direct recognition of the word as a whole and sounding it out letter by letter. When we see a familiar word, we normally recognize it by its shape and pronounce it—a process known as **whole-word reading.** (With very long words we might instead perceive segments of several letters each.) The second method, which we use for unfamiliar words, requires recognition of individual letters and knowledge of the sounds they make. This process is known as **phonetic reading.**

Evidence for our ability to sound out words is easy to obtain. In fact, you can prove to yourself that phonetic reading exists by trying to read the following words:

glab trisk chint

Well, as you could see, they are not really words, but I doubt that you had trouble pronouncing them. Obviously, you did not *recognize* them, because you probably never saw them before. Therefore, you had to use what you know about the sounds that are represented by particular letters

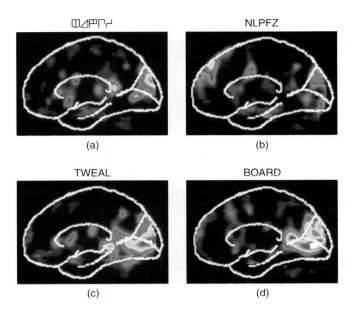

Figure 16.19
PET scans of the medial surface of the brains of subjects who read (a) letterlike forms, (b) strings of consonants, (c) pronounceable nonwords, or (d) real words.
(From Petersen, S.E., Fox, P.T., Snyder, A.Z., and Raichle, M.E. *Science,* 1990, *249,* 1041–1044. Reprinted with permission.)

(or groups of letters, such as *ch*) to figure out how to pronounce the words.

The best evidence that proves that people can read words without sounding them out, using the whole-word method, comes from studies of patients with acquired dyslexias. *Dyslexia* means "faulty reading." *Acquired* dyslexias are those caused by damage to the brains of people who already know how to read. In contrast, *developmental* dyslexias refer to reading difficulties that become apparent when children are learning to read. Developmental dyslexias, which may involve anomalies in brain circuitry, are discussed in a later section.

Figure 16.20 illustrates some elements of the reading processes. The diagram is an oversimplification of a very complex process, but it helps to organize some of the facts that investigators have obtained. It considers only reading and pronouncing single words, not understanding the meaning of text. When we see a familiar word, we nor-

whole-word reading   Reading by recognizing a word as a whole; "sight reading."

phonetic reading   Reading by decoding the phonetic significance of letter strings; "sound reading."

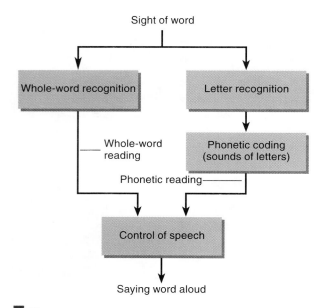

Figure 16.20
A simplified model of the reading process, showing whole-word and phonetic reading. Whole-word reading is used for most familiar words; phonetic reading is used for unfamiliar words and for nonwords such as glab, trisk, *or* chint.

mally recognize it as a whole and pronounce it. If we see an unfamiliar word or a pronounceable nonword, we must try to read it phonetically. (See *Figure 16.20.*)

Although investigators have reported several types of acquired dyslexias, I will mention five of them here. **Surface dyslexia** is a deficit in whole-word reading (Marshall and Newcombe, 1973; McCarthy and Warrington, 1990). The term *surface* reflects the fact that people with this disorder make errors related to the visual appearance of the words and to pronunciation rules, not to the meaning of the words, which is metaphorically "deeper" than the appearance. Because patients with surface dyslexia have difficulty recognizing words as a whole, they are obliged to sound them out. Thus, they can easily read words with regular spelling, such as *hand, table,* or *chin.* However, they have difficulty reading words with irregular spelling, such as *sew, pint,* and *yacht.* In fact, they may read these words as *sue, pinnt,* and *yatchet.* They have no difficulty reading pronounceable nonwords, such as *glab, trisk,* and *chint.* Because people with surface dyslexia cannot recognize whole words by their appearance, they must, in effect, listen to their own pronunciation to understand what they are reading. If they read the word *pint* and pronounce it *pinnt,* they will say that it is not an English word (which it is not, pronounced that way). If the word is one member of a homo-

phone, it will be impossible to understand it unless it is read in the context of a sentence. For example, if you hear the single word "pair," without additional information, you cannot know whether the speaker is referring to *pair, pear,* or *pare.* Thus, a patient with surface dyslexia who reads the word *pair* might say " . . . it could be two of a kind, apples and . . . or what you do with your fingernails" (Gurd and Marshall, 1993, p. 594). (See *Figure 16.21.*)

Patients with **phonological dyslexia** have the opposite problem; they can read by the whole-word method but cannot sound words out. Thus, they can read words that they are already familiar with but have great difficulty figuring out how to read unfamiliar words or pronounceable nonwords (Beauvois and Dérouesné, 1979; Dérouesné and Beauvois, 1979). (In this context, *phonology*—loosely translated as "laws of sound"—refers to the relation between letters and the sounds they represent.) People with phonological dyslexia may be excellent readers if they had already acquired a good reading vocabulary before their brain damage occurred.

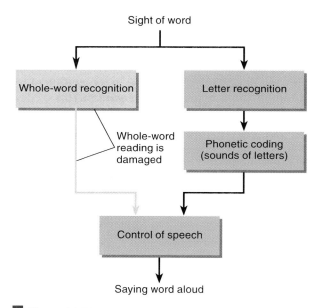

Figure 16.21
A hypothetical explanation of surface dyslexia. Whole-word reading is damaged; only phonetic reading remains.

surface dyslexia A reading disorder in which a person can read words phonetically but has difficulty reading irregularly spelled words by the whole-word method.

phonological dyslexia A reading disorder in which a person can read familiar words but has difficulty reading unfamiliar words or pronounceable nonwords.

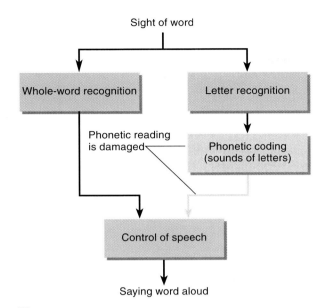

Sight of word

Whole-word recognition

Letter recognition

Phonetic reading is damaged

Phonetic coding (sounds of letters)

Control of speech

Saying word aloud

Figure 16.22
A hypothetical explanation of phonological dyslexia. Phonetic reading is damaged; only whole-word reading remains.

Phonological dyslexia provides further evidence that whole-word reading and phonological reading involve different brain mechanisms. Phonological reading, which is the only way we can read nonwords or words we have not yet learned, entails some sort of letter-to-sound decoding. Obviously, phonological reading of English requires more than decoding of the sounds produced by single letters, because, for example, some sounds are transcribed as two-letter sequences (such as *th* or *sh*) and the addition of the letter *e* to the end of a word lengthens an internal vowel (*can* becomes *cane*). (See *Figure 16.22.*)

The Japanese language provides a particularly interesting distinction between phonetic and whole-word reading. The Japanese language makes use of two kinds of written symbols. *Kanji* symbols are pictographs, adopted from the Chinese language (although they are pronounced as Japanese words). Thus, they represent concepts by means of visual symbols but do not provide a guide to their pronunciation. Reading words expressed in kanji symbols is analogous, then, to whole-word reading. *Kana* symbols are phonetic representations of syllables; thus, they encode acoustical information. These symbols are primarily used to represent foreign words or Japanese words that the average reader would be unlikely to recognize if they were represented by their kanji symbols. Reading words expressed in kana symbols is obviously phonetic.

Studies of Japanese people with localized brain damage have shown that the reading of kana and kanji symbols in-

volves different brain mechanisms (Iwata, 1984; Sakurai et al., 1994). In general, dyslexia for kanji symbols is caused by damage to the left posterior inferior temporal lobe; the damage that causes dyslexia for kana symbols is less certain. Difficulty reading kanji symbols is analogous to surface dyslexia, whereas difficulty reading kana symbols is analogous to phonological dyslexia.

What would happen if individuals sustained brain damage that did not make them blind but destroyed their ability to read words either by the whole-word or phonetic methods? Would they be *completely* unable to read? The answer is no—not quite. They would have a disorder known as **word-form dyslexia** or **spelling dyslexia** (Warrington and Shallice, 1980). Although patients with word-form dyslexia cannot either recognize words as a whole or sound them out phonetically, they can still recognize individual letters and can read the words if they are permitted to name the letters, one at a time. Thus, they read very slowly, taking more time with longer words. As you might expect, patients with word-form dyslexia can identify words that someone else spells aloud, just as they can recognize their own oral spelling. Sometimes, the deficit is so severe that patients have difficulty identifying individual letters, in which case they make mistakes in spelling that prevent them from reading test words. For example, a patient studied by Patterson and Kay (1980) was shown the word *men* and said, "h, e, n, hen." (See *Figure 16.23.*)

As we saw earlier in this chapter, recognizing a spoken word is different from understanding it. For example, patients with transcortical sensory aphasia can repeat what is said to them even though they show no signs of understanding what they hear or say. The same is true for reading. **Direct dyslexia** resembles transcortical sensory aphasia, except that the words in question are written, not spoken (Schwartz, Marin, and Saffran, 1979; Lytton and Brust, 1989). Patients with direct dyslexia are able to read aloud *even though they cannot understand the words they are saying.* After sustaining a stroke that damaged his left frontal and temporal lobes, Lytton and Brust's patient lost the ability to communicate verbally; his speech was meaningless, and he was unable to comprehend what other people said to him. However, he could read words with which he was already familiar. He could *not* read pronounceable

word-form dyslexia A disorder in which a person can read a word only after spelling out the individual letters.
spelling dyslexia An alternative name for word-form dyslexia.
direct dyslexia A language disorder caused by brain damage in which the person can read words aloud without understanding them.

Sight of word

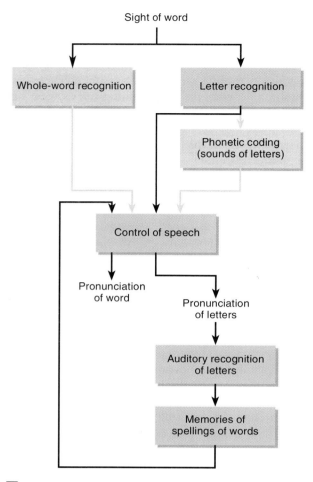

Figure 16.23
A hypothetical explanation of spelling dyslexia. The patient pronounces the letters, recognizes the words, and then says them.

tree
flag
pole
flare

Figure 16.24
An item from a task given to patient R.F. Although she could not read, she could choose the word that went with the picture.

nonwords; therefore, he had lost the ability to read phonetically. His comprehension deficit seemed complete; when the investigators presented him with a word and several pictures, one of which corresponded to the word, he read the word correctly but had no idea what picture went with it.

Several investigators have reported a deficit opposite to that of direct dyslexia. People with this unnamed disorder (we could call it *comprehension without reading*) show some comprehension of words that they cannot read (Margolin, Marcel, and Carlson, 1985). Our patient, R.F., sustained a head injury in an automobile accident that destroyed much of her left temporal lobe and part of the anterior occipital lobe. She had a classic case of anomic aphasia—in fact, I quoted her in the section on that topic earlier in this chapter. Although her speech was fluent and she could re-

peat whatever we said to her, she could not name most common objects, nor could she read most words. Nevertheless, she could match pictures of *objects she could not name* with *words she could not read*. For example, when we showed her the picture and words that appear in Figure 16.24, she immediately pointed to the correct word, *flag*, even though she could not name the object or read any of the words. (See *Figure 16.24.*)

Patient R.F. was utterly unable to read words phonetically. However, the fact that she could match words with pictures indicates that she could still *perceive* them by the whole-word method. This fact was made especially apparent one day when she was trying (without success) to read some words that I had typed. Suddenly, she said, "Hey! You spelled this one wrong." I looked at the word and realized that she was right; I had. But even though she saw that the word was misspelled, she still could not say what it was, even when she tried very hard to sound it out. That evening I made up a list of eighty pairs of words, one spelled correctly and the other incorrectly. The next day she was able to go through the list quickly and easily, correctly identifying 95 percent of the misspelled words. She was able to *read* only five of them.

Toward an Understanding of Writing

Writing depends on knowledge of the words that are to be used, along with the proper grammatical structure of the sentences they are to form. Thus, if a patient is unable to express himself or herself by speech, we should not be surprised to see a writing disturbance as well.

One type of writing disorder involves difficulties in motor control—in directing the movements of a pen or pencil to form letters and words. Investigators have reported surprisingly specific types of writing disorders that fall under this category. For example, some patients can write numbers but not letters, some can write uppercase letters but not lowercase letters, some can write consonants but not vowels, some can write cursively but not print uppercase letters, and others can write letters normally but have difficulty placing them in an orderly fashion on the page (Cubelli, 1991; Alexander et al., 1992; Margolin and Goodman-Schulman, 1992; Silveri, 1996).

The second type of writing disorder involves problems in the ability to spell words, as opposed to problems with making accurate movements of the fingers. I will devote the rest of this section to this type of disorder. Like reading, writing (or more specifically, spelling) involves more than one method. The first is related to audition. When children acquire language skills, they first learn the sounds of words, then learn to say them, then learn to read, and then learn to write. Undoubtedly, reading and writing depend heavily on the skills that are learned earlier. For example, to write most words, we must be able to "sound them out in our heads," that is, to hear them and to articulate them subvocally. If you want to demonstrate this to yourself, try to write a long word such as *antidisestablishmentarianism* from memory and see whether you can do it without saying the word to yourself. If you recite a poem or sing a song to yourself under your breath at the same time, you will see that the writing comes to a halt.

A second way of writing involves transcribing an image of what a particular word looks like—copying a visual mental image. Have you ever looked off into the distance to picture a word so that you can remember how to spell it? Some people are not very good at phonological spelling and have to write some words down to see whether they look correct. This method obviously involves *visual* memories, not acoustical ones.

A third way of writing involves memorization of letter sequences. We learn these sequences the way we learn poems or the lyrics to a song. For example, many Americans learned to spell *Mississippi* with a singsong chant that goes like this: **M**-i-s-s-**i**-s-s-**i**-p-p-**i**, emphasizing the boldfaced letters. (Similarly, most speakers of English say the alpha-

bet with the rhythm of a nursery song that is commonly used to teach it.) This method involves memorizing sequences of letter names, not translating sounds into the corresponding letters. As you will recognize, it is exactly this method that permits people with word-form dyslexia to recognize words as they spell out their letters, one by one.

Finally, the fourth way of writing involves motor memories. We undoubtedly memorize motor sequences for very familiar words, such as our own names. Most of us need not sound out our names to ourselves when we write our signature, nor need we say the sequence of letters to ourselves, nor need we imagine what our signature looks like.

Neurological evidence supports at least the first three of these speculations. Brain damage can impair the first of these methods: phonetic writing. This deficit is called **phonological dysgraphia** (Shallice, 1981). (*Dysgraphia* refers to a writing deficit just as *dyslexia* refers to a reading deficit.) People with this disorder are unable to sound out words and write them phonetically. Thus, they cannot write unfamiliar words or pronounceable nonwords, such as the ones I presented in the section on reading. They can, however, visually imagine familiar words and then write them. **Orthographic dysgraphia** is just the opposite—a disorder of visually based writing. People with orthographic dysgraphia can *only* sound words out; thus, they can spell regular words such as *care* or *tree,* and they can write pronounceable nonsense words. However, they have difficulty spelling irregular words such as *half* or *busy* (Beauvois and Dérouesné, 1981); they may write *haff* or *bizzy.* According to Benson and Geschwind (1985), phonological dysgraphia (impaired phonological writing) is caused by damage to the superior temporal lobe, whereas orthographic dysgraphia (impaired visual, whole-word writing) is usually caused by damage to the inferior parietal lobe.

The third method of spelling depends on a person's having memorized sequences of letters that spell particular words. Cipolotti and Warrington (1996) reported the case of a patient who lacked this ability. The patient sustained a left-hemisphere stroke that severely disrupted his ability to spell words orally and impaired his ability to recognize words that the examiners would spell aloud. Presumably, his ability to spell written words depended on the first two methods of writing—auditory and visual. The ex-

phonological dysgraphia   A writing disorder in which the person cannot sound out words and write them phonetically.

orthographic dysgraphia   A writing disorder in which the person can spell regularly spelled words but not irregularly spelled ones.

aminers noted that when they spelled out words to him, he would make writing movements with his hand on top of his knee. When they asked him to clasp his hands together so that he could not make these writing movements, his ability to recognize four-letter words being spelled aloud dropped from 66 percent to 14 percent. It appears that he was using feedback from hand movements to recognize the words he was "writing" on his knee.

Japanese patients show writing deficits similar to those of patients whose languages use the Roman alphabet; some patients have difficulty writing kana symbols, and others have difficulty with kanji symbols (Iwata, 1984; Yokota et al., 1990). Kawamura, Hirayama, and Yamamoto (1989) reported a particularly interesting case of a man with damage to the middle part of the corpus callosum who could write kana symbols with both hands and could write kanji symbols with the right hand but not the left. He could *copy* kanji symbols with his left hand; he just could not write them down when the investigators dictated them to him. (See *Figure 16.25.*) Another patient, reported by Tei, Soma, and Maruyama (1994), had the opposite symptoms: very bad kana writing with the nondominant hand but better kanji writing.

These results have interesting implications. Writing appears to be organized in the speech-dominant hemisphere (normally, the left hemisphere). That is, the information needed to specify the shape of the symbols is provided by circuits in this hemisphere. When a person uses his or her left hand to write these symbols, the information must be sent across the corpus callosum to the motor cortex of the right hemisphere, which controls the left hand. Apparently, information about the two forms of Japanese symbols is transmitted through different parts of the corpus callosum; the brain damage of the patient studied by Kawamura and

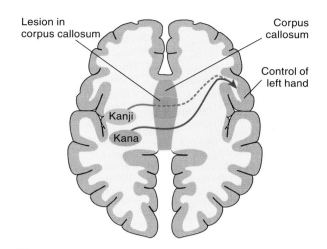

Figure 16.26
The role of the corpus callosum in Japanese writing. Information about kana and kanji characters apparently crosses different parts of the corpus callosum.

his colleagues disrupted one of these pathways but not the other. (See *Figure 16.26.*)

As we saw in the section on reading, some patients (those with direct dyslexia) can read aloud without being able to understand what they are reading. Similarly, some patients can write words that are dictated to them even though they cannot understand these words (Roeltgen, Rothi, and Heilman, 1986; Lesser, 1989). Of course, they cannot communicate by means of writing, because they cannot translate their thoughts into words. (In fact, because most of these patients have sustained extensive brain damage, their thought processes themselves are severely disturbed.) Some of these patients can even spell pronounceable nonwords, which indicates that their ability to spell phonetically is intact. Roeltgen et al. (1986) referred to this disorder as *semantic agraphia,* but perhaps the term *direct dysgraphia* would be more appropriate, because of the parallel with direct dyslexia.

● Developmental Dyslexias

Some children have great difficulty learning to read and never become fluent readers, even though they are otherwise intelligent. Specific language learning disorders, called **developmental dyslexias,** tend to occur in families, a finding that suggests a genetic (and hence bio-

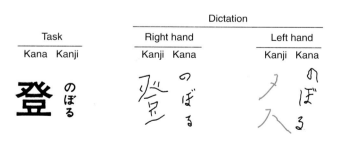

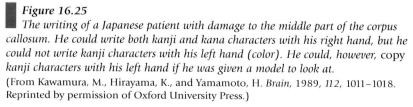

Figure 16.25
The writing of a Japanese patient with damage to the middle part of the corpus callosum. He could write both kanji and kana characters with his right hand, but he could not write kanji characters with his left hand (color). He could, however, copy kanji characters with his left hand if he was given a model to look at.
(From Kawamura, M., Hirayama, K., and Yamamoto, H. *Brain,* 1989, *112,* 1011–1018. Reprinted by permission of Oxford University Press.)

logical) component (Pennington et al., 1991; Wolff and Melngailis, 1994). Linkage studies suggest that the chromosomes 6 and 15 may contain genes responsible for different components of this disorder (Grigorenko et al., 1997). A study of fifty-six dyslexic boys in Sydney, Australia, found that two-thirds of them showed impairments in both phonological and word-form reading. Among the other third, 64 percent had difficulty only with phonological reading, and 46 percent had difficulty only with word-form reading (Castles and Coltheart, 1993). (You will recall that phonological difficulty is the primary symptom of phonological dyslexia, while word-form difficulty is the primary symptom of surface dyslexia.)

Several studies (Galaburda et al., 1985; Galaburda, 1988; Humphreys, Kaufmann, and Galaburda, 1990) found evidence that brain abnormalities may be responsible for at least some cases of developmental dyslexia. The investigators obtained the brains of deceased people with histories of developmental dyslexia. In all cases they found abnormalities in the **planum temporale,** a part of Wernicke's area. Figure 16.27 shows a section through the left planum temporale of a normal person (a) and of a dyslexic accident victim (b). Notice the regular columnar arrangement of cells in the normal brain but not in the brain of the dyslexic accident victim. (See *Figure 16.27.*) The investigators attributed these microscopic abnormalities to problems in prenatal development of the brain. In addition, the right and left planum temporale were approximately the same size. In the brains of people without developmental dyslexia the left planum temporale is normally much larger than the right.

Some subsequent studies have supported these findings; others have not. In a review of the literature, Filipek (1995) concluded that imaging studies have failed to find a "marker" for developmental dyslexia—that is, a reliable abnormality that is universally found in a particular location in the brains of dyslexics. Over the years, investigators have reported finding differences in the size or shape of the corpus callosum or various parts of the region around the posterior part of the lateral fissure, but follow-up studies have been equivocal.

One finding has been receiving a considerable amount of attention in recent years. Galaburda and Livingstone (1993) found evidence for a deficit in the magnocellular layers of the lateral geniculate nucleus. As we saw in Chapter 6, the visual system has two major components, named after two types of layers in the lateral geniculate nucleus, which relays information from the retina to the visual cortex. The *magnocellular system* is more ancient. It consists of two layers of neurons with large cell bodies that transmit information about movement, depth, and small differ-

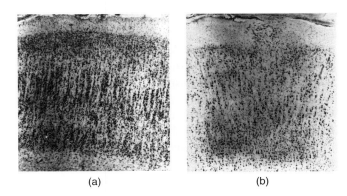
(a)   (b)

Figure 16.27
Photomicrographs of the left planum temporale (a portion of Wernicke's area). (a) A control subject. (b) A person with developmental dyslexia. Nissl stain.
(Photographs courtesy of A. Galaburda.)

ences in contrast. The *parvocellular system*, which evolved more recently, consists of four layers of neurons that transmit information about color and fine details. Galaburda and Livingstone studied the brains of deceased patients with developmental dyslexia and discovered that the magnocellular layers of these people were disorganized. The cell bodies in these layers were 27 percent smaller, and they were more variable in their size and shape. The parvocellular layers were normal.

Why should abnormalities in the magnocellular system impair people's ability to read? Stein and Walsh (1997) note that the primary target of the magnocellular system is the posterior parietal lobe, the endpoint of the dorsal stream of the visual system. As we saw in Chapter 6, this system is concerned with the "where" of vision, while the ventral stream, which terminates in the inferior temporal lobe, is concerned with the "what" of vision. But why should the "where" system be so important to reading? Stein and Walsh point out that dyslexics often have trouble with spatial perception and of movements in space. They often transpose letters (for example, reading *saw* as *was*), they are often clumsy and have difficulties with balance, their handwriting tends to be very poor, they learn to walk later than most other children and have trouble learning to ride a bike, they are slower to learn to tell time or learn the days of the week and months of the year, they have diffi-

developmental dyslexia A reading difficulty in a person of normal intelligence and perceptual ability; of genetic origin or caused by prenatal or perinatal factors.

planum temporale A region of the superior temporal lobe; normally larger in the left hemisphere.

culty reading maps and distinguishing between left and right, and they tend not to establish strong handedness. Such problems are often associated with damage or developmental abnormalities in the posterior parietal lobe. Perhaps, Stein and Walsh suggest, abnormal input to the parietal lobe caused by an abnormal magnocellular system impairs the development of this region and causes a variety of symptoms, including dyslexia.

In support of their hypothesis, Stein and Walsh note that many dyslexics complain that when they try to read, letters move around, merge, and become blurry. Their gaze is often unsteady, and their ability to read is sometimes improved by providing them with text with larger type (Cornelissen et al., 1991). They also note that monkeys with lesions of the posterior parietal lobes have no trouble discriminating between different shapes but have trouble distinguishing between reversals of the same shape, such as < versus > or **b** versus **d** (Walsh and Butler, 1996).

Eden et al. (1996) performed a functional MRI study that provides further support for Stein and Walsh's hypothesis. They found that although no differences were seen in the activity of the primary visual cortex to stationary visual stimuli, there were differences in activation of visual area V5 by moving stimuli. Area V5 receives input from the magnocellular system and is involved in the perception of motion. As Figure 16.28 shows, looking at a pattern of black dots moving against a gray background activated area V5 in control subjects (white arrows), but such activation was not seen in the brains of subjects with developmental dyslexia. (See *Figure 16.28.*)

Geschwind and Behan (1984) noted that investigators have long recognized that a disproportionate number of people with developmental dyslexias are also left-handed. Furthermore, clinical observations suggested a relation between left-handedness and various immune disorders. Therefore, Geschwind and Behan studied a group of left-handed and right-handed people to see whether the relations were statistically significant. They found that they were: The left-handed subjects were ten times more likely to have specific learning disorders (10 percent versus 1 percent) and two and one-half times more likely to have immune disorders (8 percent versus 3 percent). The immune disorders included various thyroid and bowel diseases, diabetes, and rheumatoid arthritis. Of course, although the relation was statistically significant, it was not perfect. After all, most left-handed people are healthy and are good readers.

Geschwind and Behan suggest that left-handedness, developmental dyslexia, and immune disorders are causally related. They note that although the superior temporal gyrus develops one to two weeks earlier on the right, the

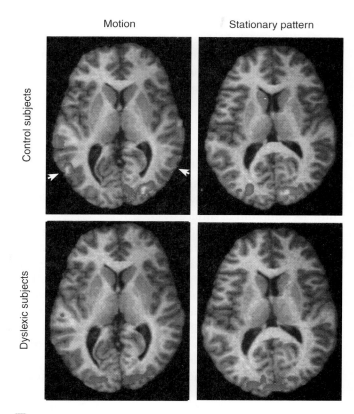

Figure 16.28

Functional MRI scans from dyslexics and control subjects looking at a stationary pattern (a plus sign against a gray background) or at a moving pattern (an array of black dots moving against a gray background). Note that viewing the moving pattern activated area V5 of the visual association cortex in control subjects (white arrows) but not in dyslexics.

(From Eden, G.F., VanMeter, J.W., Rumsey, J.M., Maisog, J.M., Woods, R.P., and Zeffiro, T.A. *Nature*, 1996, *382*, 66–69.)

left superior temporal gyrus ultimately becomes larger (Chi, Dooling, and Gilles, 1977). In fact, slowing the rate of development may be the mechanism that causes the left language area to become larger than the corresponding region of the right hemisphere; by growing more slowly, it ultimately achieves a larger size. Perhaps dyslexia occurs when the development of the left hemisphere is suppressed so much that it fails to develop normally.

Humphreys, Kaufmann, and Galaburda (1990) propose a specific mechanism to explain the microscopic brain abnormalities. They suggest that pregnant women who belong to families with a genetic predisposition to developmental dyslexia may produce antibodies against the cells that make up capillaries and small arteries in the cerebral cortex. These antibodies attack these cells during a critical stage of prenatal development and cause the abnormalities. These hypotheses are interesting, but much research is still to be done to test them experimentally.

Interim Summary

Brain damage can produce reading and writing disorders. With few exceptions, aphasias are accompanied by writing deficits that parallel the speech production deficits and by reading deficits that parallel the speech comprehension deficits. Pure alexia is caused by lesions that produce blindness in the right visual field and that destroy fibers of the posterior corpus callosum. Damage that is restricted to the posterior corpus callosum produces alexia only in the left visual field.

Research in the past few decades has discovered that acquired reading disorders (dyslexias) can fall into one of several categories, and the study of these disorders has provided neuropsychologists and cognitive psychologists with thought-provoking information that has helped them understand how normal people read. Surface dyslexia is a loss of whole-word reading ability. Phonological dyslexia is loss of the ability to read phonetically. Word-form (spelling) dyslexia is caused by a deficit in both phonetic and whole-word reading; patients can still recognize individual letters and can read slowly by pronouncing each letter. Direct dyslexia is analogous to transcortical sensory aphasia; the patients can read words aloud but cannot understand what they are reading. Some dyslexia patients can at least partially comprehend written words without being able to pronounce them; they can match corresponding words and pictures and recognize misspelled words they cannot read.

Brain damage can disrupt writing ability by impairing people's ability to form letters—or even specific types of letters, such as uppercase or lowercase letters, or vowels. Other deficits involve the ability to spell words. We normally use at least four different strategies to spell words: phonetic (sounding the word out), visual (remembering how it looks on paper), sequential (recalling memorized sequences of letters), and motor (recalling memorized hand movements in writing very familiar words). Two types of dysgraphia—phonological and orthographic—represent difficulties implementing phonetic and visual strategies, respectively. The existence of these two disorders indicates that several different brain mechanisms are involved in the process of writing. In addition, some patients have a deficit parallel to direct dyslexia; they can write words they cannot understand. Developmental dyslexia may involve abnormal development of parts of the brain that play a role in language, perhaps because of a hereditary condition that affects the immune system. Recent evidence suggests that abnormal development of the magnocellular system of the lateral geniculate nucleus, seen in people with developmental dyslexia, may impair normal development of the posterior parietal lobe. A better understanding of the components of reading and writing may help us develop effective teaching methods that will permit people with dyslexia to take advantage of the abilities that they do have.

Table 16.2 summarizes the disorders described in this section.

Table 16.2
Reading and Writing Disorders Produced by Brain Damage

Reading Disorders	Whole-word reading	Phonetic reading	Remarks
Pure alexia	Poor	Poor	Can write
Surface dyslexia	Poor	Good	
Phonological dyslexia	Good	Poor	
Spelling dyslexia	Poor	Poor	Can read words letter-by-letter
Direct dyslexia	Good	Good	Cannot comprehend words
Comprehension without reading	Poor	Poor	Show some comprehension of words
Writing Disorders	Whole-word writing	Phonetic writing	
Phonological dysgraphia	Good	Poor	
Orthographic dysgraphia	Poor	Good	

SUGGESTED READINGS

Kolb, B., and Whishaw, I.Q. *Fundamentals of Human Neuropsychology,* 4th ed. New York: W.H. Freeman, 1996.

Margolin, D.I. *Cognitive Neuropsychology in Clinical Practice.* New York: Oxford University Press, 1992.

McCarthy, R.A., and Warrington, E.K. *Cognitive Neuropsychology: A Clinical Introduction.* San Diego: Academic Press, 1990.

Parkin, A.J. *Explorations in Cognitive Neuropsychology.* Oxford: Blackwell Publishers, 1996.

Posner, M.I., and Raichle, M.E. *Images of Mind.* New York: Scientific American Library, 1994.

CHAPTER 17

Schizophrenia and the Affective Disorders

Ready to Wear, 1955, by Stuart Davis. VAGA, New York.

Most of the discussion in this book has concentrated on the physiology of normal, adaptive behavior. The last three chapters summarize research on the nature and physiology of syndromes characterized by maladaptive behavior: mental disorders and drug abuse. The symptoms of mental disorders include deficient or inappropriate social behaviors; illogical, incoherent, or obsessional thoughts; inappropriate emotional responses, including depression, mania, or anxiety; and delusions and hallucinations. Research in recent years indicates that many of these symptoms are caused by abnormalities in the brain, both structural and biochemical.

This chapter discusses two serious mental disorders: schizophrenia and the major affective disorders. Chapter 18 discusses anxiety disorders, autism, and disorders caused by stress. Chapter 19 discusses drug abuse.

SCHIZOPHRENIA

● Description

Schizophrenia afflicts approximately 1 percent of the world's population. Descriptions of symptoms in ancient writings indicate that the disorder has been around for thousands of years (Jeste et al., 1985). The major symptoms of schizophrenia are universal, and clinicians have developed criteria for reliably diagnosing the disorder in people of a wide variety of cultures (Flaum and Andreasen, 1990). *Schizophrenia* is probably the most misused psychological term in existence. The word literally means "split mind," but it does *not* imply a split or multiple personality. People often say that they "feel schizophrenic" about an issue when they really mean that they have mixed feelings about it. A person who sometimes wants to build a cabin in Alaska and live off the land and at other times wants to take over the family insurance business may be

undecided, but he or she is not schizophrenic. The man who invented the term, Eugen Bleuler (1911/1950), intended it to refer to a break with reality caused by disorganization of the various functions of the mind, so that thoughts and feelings no longer worked together normally.

Schizophrenia is characterized by two categories of symptoms, positive and negative (Crow, 1980; Andreasen, 1995). **Positive symptoms** make themselves known by their presence. They include thought disorders, hallucinations, and delusions. A **thought disorder**—disorganized, irrational thinking—is probably the most important symptom of schizophrenia. Schizophrenics have great difficulty arranging their thoughts logically and sorting out plausible conclusions from absurd ones. In conversation they jump from one topic to another as new associations come up. Sometimes, they utter meaningless words or choose words for rhyme rather than for meaning. **Delusions** are beliefs that are obviously contrary to fact. Delusions of *persecution* are false beliefs that others are plotting and conspiring against oneself. Delusions of *grandeur* are false beliefs in one's power and importance, such as a conviction that one has godlike powers or has special knowledge that no one else possesses. Delusions of *control* are related to delusions of persecution; the person believes (for example) that he or she is being controlled by others through such means as radar or tiny radio receivers implanted in his or her brain.

schizophrenia   A serious mental disorder characterized by disordered thoughts, delusions, hallucinations, and often bizarre behaviors.

positive symptom   A symptom of schizophrenia evident by its presence: delusions, hallucinations, or thought disorders.

thought disorder   Disorganized, irrational thinking.

delusion   A belief that is clearly in contradiction to reality.

Table 17.1
Positive and Negative Symptoms of Schizophrenia

Schizophrenic Symptom
Positive
Hallucinations
Thought disorders
Delusions
Persecution
Grandeur
Control
Negative
Flattened emotional response
Poverty of speech
Lack of initiative and persistence
Anhedonia (inability to experience pleasure)
Social withdrawal

The third positive symptom of schizophrenia is **halluci-nations,** perceptions of stimuli that are not actually present. The most common schizophrenic hallucinations are auditory, but they can also involve any of the other senses. The typical schizophrenic hallucination consists of voices talking to the person. Sometimes, they order the person to do something; sometimes, they scold the person for his or her unworthiness; sometimes, they just utter meaningless phrases. Olfactory hallucinations are also fairly common; often they contribute to the delusion that others are trying to kill the person with poison gas. (See *Table 17.1.*)

In contrast to the positive symptoms, the **negative symp-toms** of schizophrenia are known by the absence of normal behaviors: flattened emotional response, poverty of speech, lack of initiative and persistence, inability to experience pleasure, and social withdrawal. Negative symptoms are not specific to schizophrenia; they are seen in many neurological disorders that involve brain damage, especially to the frontal lobes. As we will see later in this chapter, evidence suggests that these two sets of symptoms result from different physiological disorders: Positive symptoms appear to involve excessive activity in some neural circuits that include dopamine as a neurotransmitter, and negative symptoms appear to be caused by brain damage. Some researchers believe that these two sets of symptoms involve a common set of underlying causes. (See *Table 17.1.*)

● Heritability

One of the strongest pieces of evidence that schizophrenia is a biological disorder is that it appears to be heritable.

Two approaches have established a link between schizophrenia and genes: adoption studies and twin studies.

Kety et al. (1968) performed one of the earliest and best-known adoption studies. Kety and his colleagues identified a group of schizophrenic people who had been adopted when they were children. They found that the incidence of schizophrenia in the adopted families of the patients was exactly what would be expected in the general population. Thus, it did not appear that the patients became schizophrenic because they were raised in a family of schizophrenics. However, the investigators did find an unusually high incidence of schizophrenia in the patients' *biological* relatives (parents and siblings), even though the patients were not raised by and with them—and probably, in most cases, did not even know them. The results clearly favor the conclusion that a tendency to develop schizophrenia is heritable. A follow-up study of a larger population confirmed these results (Kety et al., 1994).

Twin studies have produced similar results. These studies take advantage of the fact that monozygotic twins have identical genotypes, whereas the genetic similarity between dizygotic twins is, on the average, 50 percent. Investigators study records to identify pairs of twins in which at least one member has received a diagnosis of schizophrenia or perhaps of a related but milder condition, such as schizotypal personality disorder. If both twins have been diagnosed as having schizophrenia, then they are said to be *concordant.* If only one has received this diagnosis, the twins are said to be *discordant.* Thus, if a disorder has a genetic basis, the percentage of monozygotic twins who are concordant for the diagnosis will be higher than that for dizygotic twins. As many studies have shown, this is exactly what occurs (Gottesman and Shields, 1982; Tsuang, Gilbertson, and Faraone, 1991). According to these studies, the concordance rate for monozygotic twins is at least four times higher than the concordance rate for dizygotic twins, a finding that provides strong evidence that schizophrenia is a heritable trait.

If schizophrenia were a simple trait produced by a single gene, we would expect to see this disorder in at least 50 percent of the children of two schizophrenic parents if the gene were dominant. If it were recessive, *all* children of two schizophrenic parents should become schizophrenic. However, the actual incidence is less than 50 percent,

hallucination Perception of a nonexistent object or event.

negative symptom A symptom of schizophrenia characterized by the absence of behaviors that are normally present: social withdrawal, lack of affect, and reduced motivation.

which means either that several genes are involved or that having a "schizophrenia gene" imparts a *susceptibility* to develop schizophrenia, the disease itself being triggered by other factors.

If the susceptibility hypothesis is true, then we would expect that some people carry a "schizophrenia gene" but do not express it; that is, their environment is such that schizophrenia is never triggered. One such person would be the nonschizophrenic member of a pair of monozygotic twins who are discordant for schizophrenia. The logical way to test this hypothesis is to examine the children of both members of discordant pairs. Gottesman and Bertelsen (1989) found that the percentage of schizophrenic children was identical for both members of such pairs: 16.8% for the schizophrenic parents and 17.4% for the nonschizophrenic parents. For the dizygotic twins the percentages were 17.4% and 2.1%, respectively. These results provide strong evidence for the heritability of schizophrenia and also support the conclusion that carrying a "schizophrenia gene" does not mean that a person will necessarily become schizophrenic. (See *Figure 17.1.*)

Studies have suggested several possible locations for a "schizophrenia gene." Bassett et al. (1988) found a schizophrenic man with a schizophrenic maternal uncle, both of whom had an abnormality of the long arm of chromosome 5; they had three copies of this arm rather than two. The abnormality suggested that this region might be a worthwhile place to look for a defective gene. Sherrington et al. (1988) used DNA markers to study five families in Iceland and two in England that had some schizophrenic members, and they found evidence that implicated this location. Other studies (Kennedy et al., 1988; St. Clair et al., 1989) failed to confirm the results, but Silverman et al. (1996) found evidence for a defective gene in the *short* arm of chromosome 5. Finally, several researchers have found evidence that implicates chromosome 6 (Dawson and Murray, 1996). Undoubtedly, more than one gene is involved in susceptibility to schizophrenia.

As we shall see in the next section, the positive symptoms of schizophrenia are diminished by drugs that block dopamine receptors. This fact has led some investigators to suggest that the hypothetical "schizophrenia gene" may actually be involved in the production of these receptors; for example, it could produce abnormally sensitive postsynaptic receptors or abnormally insensitive presynaptic receptors. So far, researchers have cloned five different dopamine receptors and have determined the location of the genes that produce them. But as Coon et al. (1993) report, studies of nine different multigenerational families have found no evidence that schizophrenia is linked to any of these genes. If susceptibility to schizophrenia is caused by a small number of genes, geneticists will undoubtedly succeed in finding them some day. Once they are found, other researchers will try to determine what role these genes play, which should provide useful information about the causes of schizophrenia.

● Pharmacology of Schizophrenia: The Dopamine Hypothesis

Pharmacological evidence suggests that the positive symptoms of schizophrenia are caused by a biochemical disorder. The explanation that has accrued the most evidence is the *dopamine hypothesis*, which suggests that schizophrenia is caused by overactivity of dopaminergic neurons, probably those of the mesolimbic pathway, which projects from the ventral tegmental area to the nucleus accumbens and amygdala.

Effects of Dopamine Agonists and Antagonists

The treatments for most physiological disorders are developed after we understand their causes. For example, once it was discovered that diabetes was caused by the lack of a hormone produced by the pancreas, researchers were able to extract a substance from pancreatic tissue (insulin) that would alleviate the symptoms of this disease. However, in some cases, treatments are discovered before the causes of the disease. For example, natives of tropical regions discovered that tea made from the bark of the cinchona tree would prevent death from malaria many years before sci-

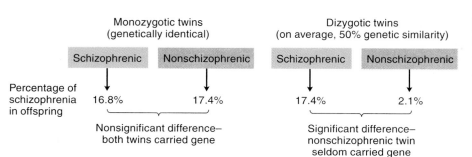

Figure 17.1
An explanation for evidence that people can have an unexpressed "schizophrenia gene."

entists discovered that this disease is caused by microscopic parasites that are transmitted in the saliva of certain species of mosquito. (The bark of the cinchona tree contains quinine, which is now used to treat malaria.)

In the case of schizophrenia a treatment was discovered before its causes were understood. (In fact, its causes are *still* not completely understood.) The discovery was accidental (Snyder, 1974). Antihistamine drugs were discovered in the early 1940s and were found to be useful in the treatment of allergic reactions. Because one of the effects of histamine release is a lowering of blood pressure, a French surgeon named Henri Laborit began to study the effects of antihistamine drugs on the sometimes fatal low blood pressure that can be produced by surgical shock. He found that one of the drugs, promethazine, had an interesting effect: It reduced anxiety in his presurgical patients without causing mental confusion.

Laborit's findings spurred drug companies to examine other antihistamine drugs for sedative effects. Paul Charpentier, a chemist with a French drug company, developed **chlorpromazine,** which appeared to be promising from tests with animals. Laborit tried the drug in humans and found that it had profound calming effects but did not seem to decrease the patient's alertness. This drug produced "not any loss in consciousness, nor any change in the patient's mentality but a slight tendency to sleep and above all 'disinterest' for all that goes on around him" (Laborit, 1950, quoted by Snyder, 1974). Chlorpromazine was tried on patients with a variety of mental disorders: mania, depression, anxiety, neuroses, and schizophrenia (Delay and Deniker, 1952a, 1952b). The drug was not very effective in treating neuroses or affective disorders, but it had dramatic effects on schizophrenia.

The discovery of the antipsychotic effects of chlorpromazine profoundly altered the way in which physicians treated schizophrenic patients and made prolonged hospital stays unnecessary for many of them (the patients, that is). The efficacy of antipsychotic drugs has been established in many double-blind studies (Baldessarini, 1977). They actually eliminate, or at least diminish, the patients' positive symptoms; they do not simply mask them by tranquilizing the patients. Unfortunately, these drugs have little or no effect on negative symptoms.

Since the discovery of chlorpromazine, many other drugs have been discovered that relieve the positive symptoms of schizophrenia. These drugs were found to have one property in common: They block dopamine receptors (Creese, Burt, and Snyder, 1976). Other drugs that interfere with dopaminergic transmission, such as reserpine (which prevents the storage of monoamines in synaptic vesicles) or α-methyl *p*-tyrosine (which blocks the synthesis of dopamine), either facilitate the antipsychotic action of drugs such as chlorpromazine or themselves exert antipsychotic effects (Tamminga et al., 1988). Thus, the positive symptoms of schizophrenia are reduced by a variety of drugs with one common effect: antagonism of dopaminergic transmission.

Another category of drugs has the opposite effect, namely, the *production* of the positive symptoms of schizophrenia. The drugs that can produce these symptoms have one known pharmacological effect in common: They act as dopamine agonists. These drugs include amphetamine, cocaine, and methylphenidate (which block the reuptake of dopamine) and L-DOPA (which stimulates the synthesis of dopamine). The symptoms that these drugs produce can be alleviated with antipsychotic drugs, which further strengthens the argument that these drugs exert their therapeutic effects by blocking dopamine receptors.

An example of the psychosis-inducing effect of amphetamine was demonstrated by Griffith, Cavanaugh, Held, and Oates (1972). The investigators recruited a group of people who had a history of amphetamine use and gave them large doses (10 milligrams) of dextroamphetamine every hour for up to five days. (Experimentally, it would have been better to study nonusers. Ethically, it was better not to introduce this drug to people who did not normally use it.) None of the subjects had prior histories of psychotic behavior. All seven volunteers became psychotic within two to five days. They became suspicious and began to believe that the experimenters were trying to poison them. One developed a delusion that an electric dynamo was controlling his thoughts. Most had auditory hallucinations. Similar symptoms—the classic positive symptoms of schizophrenia—are seen today in many people who abuse cocaine.

Dopamine, Reinforcement, and Positive Symptoms of Schizophrenia

Before looking at further evidence concerning the dopamine hypothesis, let's consider why overactivity at dopaminergic synapses might cause the symptoms of schizophrenia. As we saw, schizophrenia is characterized by both positive and negative symptoms. Because antipsychotic drugs reduce only the positive symptoms, the dopamine hypothesis cannot account for the negative symptoms. (Possible relationships between the positive and negative symptoms of schizophrenia are discussed later in this chapter.)

As we saw in Chapters 4 and 14, the most important systems of dopaminergic neurons begin in two midbrain

chlorpromazine   A dopamine receptor blocker; a most commonly prescribed antischizophrenic drug.

nuclei, the substantia nigra and the ventral tegmental area. Most researchers believe that the mesolimbic pathway, which begins in the ventral tegmental area and ends in the nucleus accumbens and amygdala, is more likely to be involved in the symptoms of schizophrenia. The nigrostriatal pathway, whose axons project from the substantia nigra to the neostriatum (the caudate nucleus and putamen), plays an important role in movement and motor learning. (As you will recall, degeneration of the nigrostriatal pathway results in Parkinson's disease, the symptoms of which involve certain learning deficits as well as motor disorders.) Overactivity of the neurons of the nigrostriatal pathway produces involuntary movements but not the symptoms of schizophrenia.

Why might overactivity of dopaminergic synapses in the nucleus accumbens and amygdala produce the symptoms of schizophrenia? As we saw in Chapter 14, the activity of dopaminergic synapses in the nucleus accumbens appears to be a vital link in the process of reinforcement. Drugs that act as agonists at these synapses (such as cocaine and amphetamine) strongly reinforce behavior; if taken in large doses, they also produce the positive symptoms of schizophrenia. Perhaps the two effects of the drugs are related. If reinforcement mechanisms were activated at inappropriate times, then inappropriate behaviors—including delusional thoughts—might be reinforced. At one time or other, all of us have had some irrational thoughts, which we normally brush aside and forget. But if neural mechanisms of reinforcement became active while these thoughts were occurring, we would tend to take them more seriously. In time, full-fledged delusions might develop.

As Snyder (1974) notes, schizophrenics often report feelings of elation and euphoria at the beginning of a schizophrenic episode, when their symptoms flare up. Presumably, this euphoria is caused by hyperactivity of dopaminergic neurons involved in reinforcement. But the positive symptoms of schizophrenia also include disordered thinking and unpleasant, often terrifying delusions. The disordered thinking may be caused by disorganized attentional processes; the indiscriminate activity of the dopaminergic synapses in the nucleus accumbens makes it difficult for the patients to follow an orderly, rational thought sequence. Fibiger (1991) suggests that paranoid delusions may be caused by increased activity of the dopaminergic input to the amygdala. As we saw in Chapter 11, the central nucleus of the amygdala is involved with conditioned emotional responses elicited by aversive stimuli. The central nucleus receives a strong projection from the mesolimbic dopaminergic system, so Fibiger's suggestion is certainly plausible.

The Search for Abnormalities in Dopamine Transmission in the Brains of Schizophrenic Patients

Before I discuss the search for abnormalities in dopamine transmission in the brains of schizophrenic patients, let's consider the possibilities. (These possibilities are based on what you learned about the pharmacology of neurons in Chapter 4.) First, too much dopamine might be released. This increased release could be caused by more activity of dopaminergic neurons, which itself could be a result of increased excitatory input to these neurons, decreased inhibitory input, or some change in the physiological properties of these neurons that makes them more sensitive to excitatory input. Another reason for increased dopamine release could be decreased numbers of dopamine autoreceptors, whose normal function is to prevent excessive release of the neurotransmitter. A second possibility could be that neurons that receive dopaminergic input are excessively sensitive to that input. For example, these postsynaptic neurons could contain more dopamine receptors, or some biochemical differences in the neurons could produce a greater response when the receptors are stimulated by the neurotransmitter. A third possibility could be that a slow reuptake mechanism in dopaminergic terminals keeps molecules of dopamine in the synaptic cleft for an unusually long time, resulting in prolonged activation of the postsynaptic dopamine receptors. A possible cause of slow reuptake could be some deficit in the number or efficiency of dopamine transporter molecules. (See *Table 17.2*.)

Let's consider these possibilities. First, there is little evidence to suggest that the production and release of dopamine in the brains of schizophrenic patients is abnormally high (Wyatt, Kirch, and DeLisi, 1988; Pickar et

Table 17.2
Possible Causes of Increased Dopaminergic Transmission in the Brains of Schizophrenic Patients

Increased dopamine release
More excitatory input to dopaminergic neurons
Less inhibitory input to dopaminergic neurons
Fewer or defective autoreceptors on dopaminergic neurons
Increased postsynaptic response to dopamine release
More postsynaptic dopamine receptors
More response in postsynaptic neuron to activation of dopamine receptors
Prolonged activation of postsynaptic receptors
Decreased reuptake of dopamine by dopaminergic terminal button

al., 1990). In fact, some studies have found *decreased* levels of the principal breakdown product of dopamine (homovanillic acid) in the cerebrospinal fluid. However, as we shall see later in this chapter, the ventricles of patients with schizophrenia tend to be larger than those of nonschizophrenics; thus, the substance could simply be diluted in a larger pool of CSF (Reynolds, 1989).

One recent study found some indirect evidence that dopaminergic neurons release more dopamine. Laruelle et al. (1996) used a device similar to a PET scanner to estimate the release of dopamine caused by an intravenous injection of amphetamine. As we saw in Chapter 4, amphetamine stimulates the release of dopamine, apparently by causing the dopamine transporters that are present in the terminal buttons to run backward, pumping dopamine out rather than retrieving it after it has been released. Of course, this effect inhibits the reuptake of dopamine as well. Laruelle and his colleagues found that the amphetamine caused the release of more dopamine in the striatum of schizophrenic patients. They also found that subjects with greater amounts of dopamine release showed greater increases in positive symptoms. Because of the limited resolution of the scanner, the investigators could not determine whether the increased dopamine release took place in the neostriatum (which is probably not involved in schizophrenia) or in the nucleus accumbens (which probably is). (See *Figure 17.2.*)

The second possibility—that the brains of schizophrenic patients contain a greater number of dopamine receptors—has received much more attention. Because the earliest antipsychotic drugs appeared to work by blocking D_2 receptors, the earliest studies looked for increases in the numbers of these receptors in the brains of schizophrenics.

How can the researchers measure the numbers of particular receptors in the human brain? There are two methods, one used on brain tissue from deceased persons and another that can be used with living persons. Postmortem measurements of dopamine receptors are performed by removing the regions of the brain that contain dopaminergic terminals, homogenizing the tissue, extracting the cell membranes, and incubating them with a radioactive ligand of dopamine receptors. The degree of radioactivity of the tissue reveals the relative number of dopamine receptors. Measurement of levels of receptors in the living brain uses a PET scanner. The person is given an injection of a radioactive ligand for the receptor in question, and the location of the receptors to which the ligand is bound is determined with the scanner.

Many studies have found that the brains of deceased schizophrenic patients contain an excess of D_2 dopamine receptors. Jaskiw and Kleinman (1988) reviewed twelve

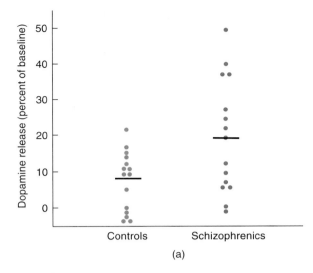

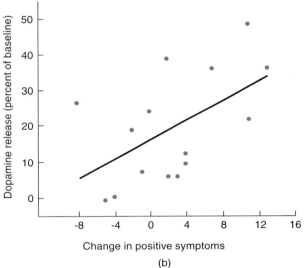

Figure 17.2
Results of the study by Laruelle et al. (1996). (a) Relative amount of dopamine released in response to amphetamine. (b) Relation between dopamine release and changes in positive symptoms of schizophrenic patients.
(Adapted from Laruelle, M., Abi-Dargham, A., Van Dyck, C.H., Gil, R., D'Souza, C.D., Erdos, J., McCance, E., Rosenblatt, W., Fingado, C., Zoghbi, S.S., Baldwin, R.M., Seibyl, J.P., Krystal, J.H., Charney, D.S., and Innis, R.B. *Proceedings of the National Academy of Sciences, USA,* 1996, *93,* 9235–9240.)

such studies published between 1978 and 1987 and found that ten of them observed an increase in the number of these in the neostriatum (caudate nucleus and putamen). Measurements of levels of D_2 receptors in the brains of living schizophrenic patients have yielded mixed results. Wong et al. (1986) found evidence for an increased number of receptors, but Farde et al. (1990) and Martinot et al. (1990), using even more specific ligands for D_2 receptors, found no differences between the level of these receptors in schizophrenic and normal brains.

What conclusion can we make? Most investigators believe that the evidence for increases in D_2 receptors is not very convincing. First, most of the patients had received antipsychotic drugs for a long time, and several studies have shown that, at least in laboratory animals, the administration of an antipsychotic medication for several days increases the number of D_2 receptors in the neostriatum (Burt, Creese, and Snyder, 1977). One exception is the PET study by Farde et al. (1990), which did *not* find an increase in D_2 receptors.

The failure to obtain solid, unambiguous evidence that dopaminergic synapses are hyperactive in schizophrenic patients does not mean that the dopamine hypothesis should be abandoned. First, the early studies were probably looking in the wrong part of the brain. The neostriatum is large relative to the nucleus accumbens and amygdala, and it contains a very high concentration of dopamine receptors. Thus, it seemed like a logical place to look. But as we saw, the nucleus accumbens and the amygdala, not the neostriatum, are involved in functions that might be related to the positive symptoms of schizophrenia. Second, the early studies were probably concerned with the wrong type of receptors.

The older antipsychotic drugs certainly act as D_2-receptor antagonists, and they do have a strong effect in the neostriatum. This action undoubtedly accounts for the motor side effects that these drugs produce. (I will say more about this matter later.) But the affinity for D_2 receptors does not necessarily account for the ability of these drugs to relieve the symptoms of schizophrenia. **Clozapine,** a more recently developed drug, is a very effective antipsychotic medication, and its site of action is primarily on the nucleus accumbens, not the neostriatum (Kinon and Lieberman, 1966). In addition, it has little effect on D_2 receptors (Pickar, 1995). Instead, clozapine serves as a potent blocker of the recently discovered D_4 dopamine receptor; in fact, it has ten times more affinity for D_4 receptors than for D_2 receptors (Van Tol et al., 1991). Consequently, researchers are beginning to turn their attention to these receptors. They are also beginning to examine the possible role of another recently discovered dopamine receptor—the D_3 receptor—which is found in especially high concentrations in the human nucleus accumbens (Murray et al., 1994).

Two recent studies have found evidence for increased amounts of D_3 and D_4 dopamine receptors in the brains of deceased schizophrenics. Murray et al. (1995) found a twofold increase in the concentration of D_4 receptors in

the nucleus accumbens of schizophrenic patients. They found no evidence of messenger RNA for D_4 receptors in the nucleus accumbens, which indicates that these receptors were not being produced by cells located there. This finding means that D_4 receptors could not be serving as postsynaptic receptors in the nucleus accumbens; if cells in the nucleus accumbens contained D_4 receptors in their dendrites, then their cell bodies would have to contain the messenger RNA needed to manufacture them. Murray and his colleagues concluded that the D_4 receptors in the nucleus accumbens were probably presynaptic autoreceptors found on the terminal buttons of dopaminergic axons, manufactured in the cell bodies located in the ventral tegmental area. Gurevich et al. (1997) found a twofold increase in D_3 receptors in both the neostriatum and nucleus accumbens of schizophrenic patients. The patients had been drug free for at least one month before their deaths, so the increased concentration of D_3 receptors is unlikely to have been caused by medication. In fact, patients who had been receiving antipsychotic drugs just before their deaths showed a *decreased* concentration of D_3 receptors in the nucleus accumbens. (See *Figure 17.3.*)

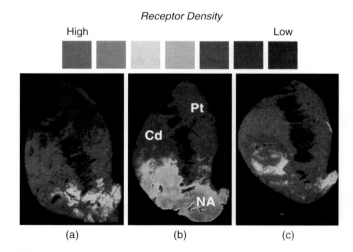

Receptor Density

High   Low

(a)   (b)   (c)

Figure 17.3
Pseudocolor images of concentrations of D_3-receptor binding in the human striatum. (a) Control subject. (b) Unmedicated schizophrenic patient. (c) Schizophrenic patient receiving antipsychotic medication. Cd = caudate nucleus, Pt = putamen, NA = nucleus accumbens.
(From Gurevich, E.V., Bordelon, Y., Shapiro, R.M., Arnold, S.E., Gur, R.E., and Joyce, J.N. *Archives of General Psychiatry,* 1997, *54,* 225–232.)

clozapine   An "atypical" antipsychotic drug; blocks D_4 receptors in the nucleus accumbens.

Although the recent discovery of the D_3 and D_4 dopamine receptors is stimulating research activity, it is still possible that nothing is wrong with dopaminergic neurons or dopamine receptors in the brains of patients with schizophrenia. Instead, the abnormality could lie elsewhere. As I mentioned earlier, overactivity of neurons that excite dopaminergic neurons or underactivity of neurons that inhibit them would both result in dopaminergic activation. I will discuss some specific hypotheses later in this chapter.

Consequences of Long-Term Drug Treatment of Schizophrenia

The discovery of drugs that reduce or eliminate the symptoms of schizophrenia has had a revolutionary effect on the treatment of this disorder. Prior to this discovery, many schizophrenics spent much of their lives in psychiatric hospitals. Now many of these people receive antipsychotic medication on an outpatient basis and are able to live normal lives. But not everyone is helped; the symptoms of up to one-third of all schizophrenic patients are not substantially reduced by antipsychotic drugs. Another problem with antipsychotic drugs is that they sometimes produce serious side effects. Until recently, all the drugs commonly used to treat schizophrenia caused at least some symptoms resembling those of Parkinson's disease: slowness in movement, lack of facial expression, and general weakness. For most patients these symptoms are temporary, but for some they are so severe that the patients cannot tolerate a dose of the drug strong enough to alleviate their schizophrenic symptoms.

Antipsychotic drugs also appear to be responsible for another motor problem: **tardive dyskinesia.** *Tardus* means "slow" and *dyskinesia* means "faulty movement"; thus, tardive dyskinesia is a late-developing movement disorder. This syndrome includes peculiar facial tics and gestures, including tongue protrusion, cheek puffing, and pursing of the lips. In some cases, speech is affected. Sometimes, writhing movements of the hands and trunk are also seen. Tardive dyskinesia is seen in approximately 10 percent of the patients who receive antipsychotic drugs.

The symptoms of tardive dyskinesia are the opposite of those of Parkinson's disease. (Indeed, dyskinesia commonly occurs when patients with Parkinson's disease re-

ceive too much L-DOPA.) In schizophrenic patients, tardive dyskinesia is made *worse* by discontinuing the antipsychotic drug and is improved by increasing the dose. The symptoms are also intensified by dopamine agonists such as L-DOPA or amphetamine (Baldessarini and Tarsy, 1980). Therefore, the disorder appears to be produced by an *overstimulation* of dopamine receptors of the neostriatum. If it is, why should it be caused by antipsychotic drugs, which are dopamine antagonists?

The answer appears to be provided by a phenomenon called **supersensitivity.** If the afferent axons to a neuron are cut or the release of neurotransmitter is prevented with a drug, the postsynaptic membrane often develops an increased sensitivity to the neurotransmitter. This phenomenon is usually caused by an increase in the number of postsynaptic receptors. Thus, supersensitivity is a compensatory mechanism in response to decreased synaptic activity (Baldessarini and Tarsy, 1980). In the case of tardive dyskinesia, blocking dopamine receptors in the neostriatum causes a compensatory supersensitivity to dopamine. This supersensitivity results in dyskinesia when the drug is withdrawn. In cases in which the antipsychotic medication continues for a long time, the supersensitivity becomes so great that it *overcompensates* for the effects of the drug, causing the tardive dyskinesia to occur even while the drug is still being administered.

As we saw, clozapine, an "atypical" antipsychotic drug, has relatively little effect on neurons in the neostriatum. Clozapine has only 10 percent as much affinity for the dopamine D_2 receptor as traditional antipsychotic drugs (hence the term *atypical*), but it is at least as effective in reducing schizophrenic symptoms (Davis et al., 1991). In fact, it often helps patients whose symptoms are not reduced by the more traditional medications (Meltzer, 1992). Because the drug is much less likely to produce parkinsonian side effects, it can be given to patients who cannot tolerate other antipsychotic drugs. Most investigators therefore believe that long-term use of the drug will not cause tardive dyskinesia. Unfortunately, the use of clozapine has been associated with a potentially fatal blood disease, which means that the blood of patients receiving this drug must be tested periodically. Some more recently developed drugs, currently undergoing clinical trials, appear to be just as effective as clozapine but free of other risks.

● Schizophrenia as a Neurological Disorder

So far, I have been discussing the physiology of the positive symptoms of schizophrenia—principally, hallucinations, delusions, and thought disorders. These symptoms are plausibly related to one of the known functions of dopa-

tardive dyskinesia A movement disorder that can after prolonged treatment with antipsychotic medication, characterized by involuntary movements of the face and neck.

supersensitivity The increased sensitivity of neurotransmitter receptors; caused by damage to the afferent axons or long-term blockage of neurotransmitter release.

minergic neurons: reinforcement. But the negative symptoms of schizophrenia—flattened emotional response, poverty of speech, lack of initiative and persistence, inability to experience pleasure, and social withdrawal—are very different. Whereas the positive symptoms are unique to schizophrenia (and to amphetamine or cocaine psychosis), the negative symptoms are similar to those produced by brain damage caused by several different means. Many pieces of evidence suggest that the negative symptoms of schizophrenia are indeed a result of brain damage.

Evidence for Brain Damage in Schizophrenia

Although schizophrenia has traditionally been labeled as a psychiatric disorder, most patients with schizophrenia exhibit neurological symptoms that suggest the presence of brain damage. These symptoms include catatonia; facial dyskinesias; unusually high or low rates of blinking; staring and avoidance of eye contact; absent blink reflex in response to a tap on the forehead; episodes of deviation of the eyes (especially to the right), accompanied by speech arrest; paroxysmal bursts of jerky eye movements; very poor visual pursuit of a smoothly moving object; inability to move the eyes without moving the head; poor pupillary light reactions; and continuous elevation of the brows, causing characteristic horizontal creasing of the forehead (Stevens, 1982). Although these symptoms can be caused by a variety of neuropathological conditions and hence are not unique to schizophrenia, their presence suggests that schizophrenia may be associated with brain damage of some kind.

Many studies have found evidence of brain damage in CT and MRI scans of schizophrenic patients. In one of the earliest studies, Weinberger and Wyatt (1982) obtained CT scans of eighty chronic schizophrenics and sixty-six normal controls of the same mean age (twenty-nine years). Without knowledge of the patients' diagnoses they measured the area of the lateral ventricles in the scan that cut through them at their largest extent, and they expressed this area relative to the area of brain tissue in the same scan. The relative ventricle size of the schizophrenic patients was more than twice as great as that of normal control subjects. (See *Figure 17.4*.) The most likely cause of the enlarged ventricles is loss of brain tissue; thus, the CT scans provide evidence that chronic schizophrenia is associated with brain damage.

Subsequent studies have found evidence for degeneration (or developmental abnormalities) in several parts of the brain. Abnormalities are commonly seen in the medial temporal lobes (Breier et al., 1992; Degreef et al., 1992; Bogerts et al., 1993), in the frontal lobes (Klausner et al., 1992; Raine et al., 1992; Turetsky et al., 1995), and in the medial diencephalon (Bornstein et al., 1992; D'Amato et

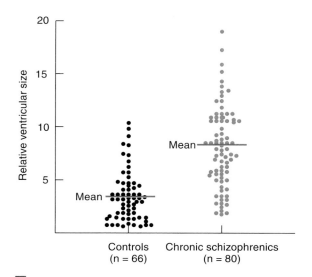

Figure 17.4
Relative ventricular size in chronic schizophrenics and controls. (From Weinberger, D.R., and Wyatt, R.J., in *Schizophrenia as a Brain Disease*, edited by F.A. Henn and H.A. Nasrallah. New York: Oxford University Press, 1982. Reprinted with permission.)

al., 1992; Andreasen et al., 1994). In several of these studies, the severity of the brain abnormalities was correlated with the severity of the patients' negative symptoms.

Possible Causes of the Brain Damage

As we saw earlier, schizophrenia is a heritable disease, but its heritability is less than perfect. Why do fewer than half the children of parents with chronic schizophrenia become schizophrenic? Perhaps what is inherited is a defect that renders people susceptible to some environmental factors that adversely affect brain development or cause brain damage later in life. According to this hypothesis, having a "schizophrenia gene" makes a person more likely to develop schizophrenia if exposed to these factors. In other words, schizophrenia is caused by an interaction between genetic and environmental factors. But as we shall see, the absence of a "schizophrenia gene" does not guarantee that a person will not develop schizophrenia; some cases of schizophrenia occur even in families with no history of schizophrenia or related mental illnesses. Let's look at the evidence concerning environmental factors that increase the risk of schizophrenia.

Epidemiological Studies. **Epidemiology** is the study of the distribution and causes of diseases in populations.

epidemiology The study of the distribution and causes of diseases in populations.

Thus, epidemiological studies examine the relative frequency of diseases in groups of people in different environments and try to correlate the disease frequencies with factors that are present in these environments. Evidence from these studies indicates that the incidence of schizophrenia is related to several environmental factors: season of birth, viral epidemics, population density, latitude, maternal malnutrition, and maternal stress. Let's examine each of these factors in turn.

Many studies have shown that people born during the late winter and early spring are more likely to develop schizophrenia—a phenomenon known as the **seasonality effect.** For example, Kendell and Adams (1991) studied the month of birth of over 13,000 schizophrenic patients born in Scotland between 1914 and 1960. They found that disproportionately more patients were born in February, March, April, and May. (See *Figure 17.5.*) These results have been confirmed by studies in several parts of the world, including Japan (Takei et al., 1995) and Taiwan (Tam and Sewell, 1995). In the southern hemisphere, a disproportionate number of schizophrenic births also take place during late winter and early spring—during the months of August through December (McGrath, Welham, and Pemberton, 1995).

What factors might be responsible for the seasonality effect? One possibility is that pregnant women may be more likely to contract a viral illness during a critical phase of their infants' development. The brain development of

their fetuses may be adversely affected either by a toxin produced by the virus or by the mother's antibodies against the virus. As Pallast et al. (1994) note, the winter flu season coincides with the second trimester of pregnancy of babies born in late winter and early spring. (As we shall see later, evidence suggests that critical aspects of brain development occur during the second trimester.) In fact, Kendell and Adams (1991) found that the relative number of schizophrenic births in late winter and early spring was especially high if the temperature was lower than normal during the previous autumn—a condition that keeps people indoors and favors the transmission of viral illnesses.

In a review of the relevant literature, Franzek and Beckmann (1996) noted that several studies have found that the seasonality effect occurs primarily in cities but is rarely found in the countryside. Because viruses are more readily transmitted in regions with high population densities, this finding is consistent with the hypothesis that at least one of the causes of the seasonality effect is exposure of pregnant women to viral illnesses during the second trimester.

If the viral hypothesis is true, then an increased incidence of schizophrenia should be seen in babies born a few months after an influenza epidemic, whatever the season. Several studies have observed just that. For example, a study of the offspring of women who were pregnant during an epidemic of type A2 influenza in Finland during 1957 showed an elevated incidence of schizophrenia (Mednick, Machon, and Huttunen, 1990). The increased incidence was seen only in the children of women who were in the second trimester of their pregnancy when the epidemic occurred. Another study (Sham et al., 1992) confirmed these findings in a study of infants born to mothers who were pregnant during several influenza epidemics in England and Wales between 1939 and 1960. As Figure 17.6 shows, the peak number of schizophrenic births occurred five months after the start of the epidemic, which means that the greatest susceptibility appears to occur during the second trimester of pregnancy. (See *Figure 17.6.*)

Several studies have reported that people born farther from the equator are more likely to develop schizophrenia. This phenomenon has been termed the **latitude effect.** For example, people born in northern Sweden or the northern United States are more likely to develop schizophrenia than those born in the southern parts of these

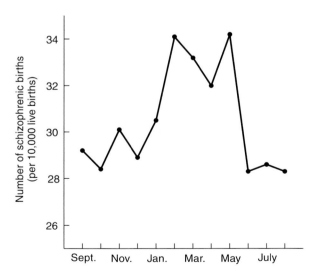

Figure 17.5
The seasonality effect. The graph shows the number of schizophrenic births per 10,000 live births.
(Based on data from Kendell, R.E., and Adams, W. *British Journal of Psychiatry,* 1991, *158,* 758–763.)

seasonality effect   The increased incidence of schizophrenia in people born during late winter and early spring.

latitude effect   The increased incidence of schizophrenia in people born far from the equator.

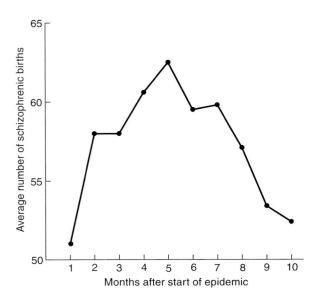

Figure 17.6
Average number of schizophrenic births in each of the ten months following an influenza epidemic in England and Wales between 1939 and 1960.
(Adapted from Sham, P.C., O'Callaghan, E., Takei, N., Murray, G.K., Hare, E.H., and Murray, R.M. *British Journal of Psychiatry*, 1992, *160*, 461–466. Reprinted with permission.)

countries (Dalen, 1968; Torrey, Torrey, and Peterson, 1979). A similar phenomenon is seen in multiple sclerosis, an autoimmune disease that attacks the white matter of the central nervous system (Stevens, 1988). One possible explanation for the latitude effect is that the climate is colder in higher latitudes, and the decreased winter temperature might simply magnify the seasonality effect.

Another prenatal effect was discovered by Susser and Lin (1992), who studied the offspring of women who were pregnant during the *Hunger Winter*—a severe food shortage that occurred in the Netherlands when Germany blockaded the country during World War II. The investigators found that the daughters (but not the sons) of these women were more likely to become schizophrenic. In a more extensive follow-up study, Susser and his colleagues found a twofold increase in the incidence of schizophrenia in both sons and daughters of women who were pregnant during the famine (Susser et al., 1996). Davis and Bracha (1996) suggest that the specific cause of the famine-related schizophrenia may have been a thiamine deficiency—or, more precisely, a sudden buildup of toxins in the brains of the developing fetuses when their mothers suddenly began eating a normal diet when the blockade ended in May 1945. As we saw in Chapter 15, sudden refeeding after a

thiamine deficiency can cause brain damage in an adult, so it is certainly plausible that it could interfere with the brain development of a fetus. As Davis and Bracha note, the end of the fast occurred during the second trimester of the babies born during the time that an increased incidence of schizophrenia was seen.

The final prenatal effect I will mention may be independent of the ones I have described so far, or it may also involve viral infections. Huttunen and Niskanen (1978) reported a higher incidence of schizophrenia in the children born to women who learned that their husbands had been killed in combat during World War II. The stress of this news may have had direct effects on development of the women's fetuses, or it may have suppressed their immune systems, increasing the likelihood of their contracting a viral illness. As we will see in Chapter 18, stress has an inhibitory effect on the immune system.

As we have seen, a wide variety of factors that adversely influence prenatal development can increase the likelihood of schizophrenia. The precise effects of these factors, and the nature of their interaction with genetic factors, continues to be the subject of much research effort.

Evidence for Abnormal Brain Development. So far, the evidence that I have cited concerning developmental factors in schizophrenia is epidemiological, having come from studies of populations, not individuals. Is there any direct evidence that abnormal prenatal development is associated with schizophrenia? The answer is yes; studies have reported both behavioral and anatomical evidence for developmental abnormalities. Walker and her colleagues (Walker, Savoie, and Davis, 1994; Walker, Lewine, and Neumann, 1996) obtained home movies from families with a schizophrenic child. They had independent observers examine the behavior of the children. In comparison with their normal siblings, the children who subsequently became schizophrenic displayed more negative affect in their facial expressions and were more likely to show abnormal movements. (The ratings were done blind; the observers did not know which children subsequently became schizophrenic.) These results are consistent with the hypothesis that the prenatal brain development of the children who became schizophrenic was not entirely normal.

The second trimester of pregnancy is a critical time for brain development—especially of the cerebral cortex. During this time, neurons migrate from the location near the border of the tube that becomes the ventricular system and find their final resting places. One group of cortical neurons contains an enzyme known as *NADPH-d* (nicotinamide-adenine dinucleotide phosphate-diaphorase, if you really want to know). In a follow-up to some earlier studies, Akbarian et al. (1996) studied the brains of twenty deceased schizophrenics and found that the distribution of three different populations of neurons in the white matter underlying the prefrontal cortex was abnormal. According to the authors, the most likely cause of this abnormal distribution was disturbance in the normal migration of these neurons.

As I mentioned earlier, some monozygotic twins are discordant for schizophrenia; that is, one of them develops schizophrenia and the other does not. Suddath et al. (1990) obtained evidence that differences in the structure of the brain may account for the discordance. The investigators examined MRI scans of monozygotic twins who were discordant for schizophrenia and found that in almost every case the twin with schizophrenia had larger lateral and third ventricles. In addition, the anterior hippocampus was smaller in the schizophrenic twins, and the total volume of the gray matter in the left temporal lobe was reduced. Figure 17.7 shows a set of MRI scans from a pair of twins; as you can see, the lateral ventricles are larger in the brain of the twin with schizophrenia. (See *Figure 17.7.*)

In the past, most researchers assumed that discordance for schizophrenia in monozygotic twins must be caused by differential exposure to some environmental factors after birth. Monozygotic twins not are not only genetically identical, they also share the same intrauterine environment. Thus, because all prenatal factors should be identical, any differences must be a result of factors in the postnatal environment. However, some investigators have pointed out that the prenatal environment of monozygotic

twins is *not* identical. In fact, there are two types of monozygotic twins: monochorionic and dichorionic. The formation of monozygotic twins occurs when the blastocyst (the developing organism) splits in two—when it clones itself. If twinning occurs before day 4, the two organisms develop independently, each forming its own placenta. (That is, the twins are *dichorionic*. The *chorion* is the outer layer of the blastocyst, which gives rise to the placenta.) If twinning occurs after day 4, the two organisms become *monochorionic*, sharing a single placenta. (See *Figure 17.8.*)

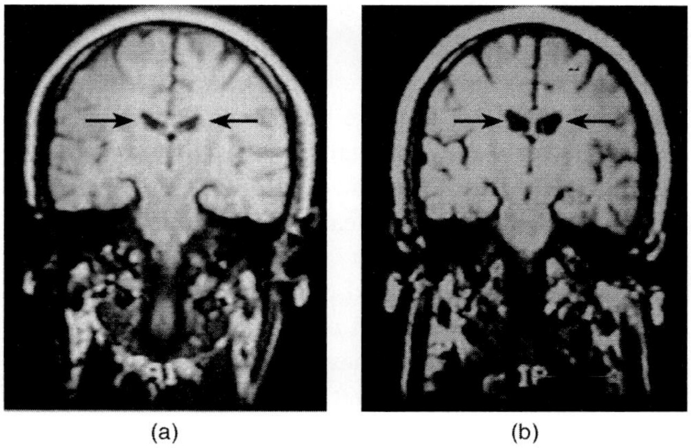

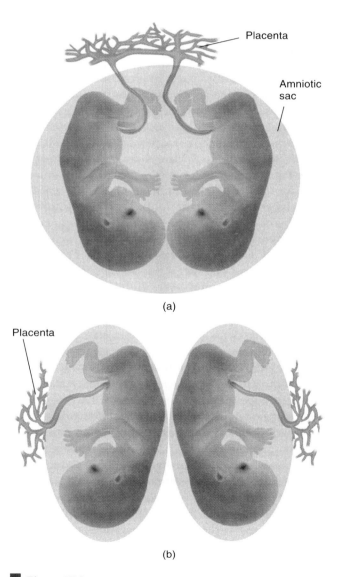

(a)

(b)

Figure 17.8
Monozygotic twins. (a) Monochorionic twins, sharing a single placenta. (b) Dichorionic twins, each with its own placenta.

Figure 17.7
MRI scans of the brains of twins discordant for schizophrenia. The arrows point to the lateral ventricles. (a) Normal twin. (b) Twin with schizophrenia.
(Courtesy of D.R. Weinberger, National Institute of Mental Health, Saint Elizabeth's Hospital, Washington, DC.)

The placenta plays an extremely important role in prenatal development. It transports nutrients to the developing organism from the mother's circulation and transports waste products to her, which she metabolizes in her liver or excretes in her urine. It also constitutes the barrier through which toxins or infectious agents must pass if they are to affect fetal development. The prenatal environments of monochorionic twins, who share a single placenta, are obviously more similar than those of dichorionic twins. Thus, we might expect that the concordance rates for schizophrenia of *monochorionic* monozygotic twins should be higher than those of *dichorionic* monozygotic twins. And, as Davis, Phelps, and Bracha (1995) reported, they are. Davis and his colleagues examined sets of monozygotic twins who were concordant and discordant for schizophrenia. They used several indices to estimate whether a given pair was monochorionic or dichorionic. (For example, twins with mirror images of physical features such as fingerprints, handedness, birthmarks, or hair swirls are more likely to be monochorionic.) The investigators estimated that the concordance rate for schizophrenia was 10.7 percent in the dichorionic twins and 60 percent in the monochorionic twins. These results provide strong evidence for an interaction between heredity and environment during prenatal development.

Bracha et al. (1992) also looked at the fingerprints of monozygotic twins who were concordant or discordant for schizophrenia, but for a different reason. As we saw, the migration of neurons into the cerebral cortex takes place during the second trimester of prenatal development. During this period, cells in the skin of the fingertips also migrate, forming the ridges that give us our fingerprints. (The central nervous system and the skin both originate from cells in the ectoderm, the outer embryonic layer.) Bracha and his colleagues reasoned that if something were interfering with the brain development of one of the twins, it might show itself in the development of that individual's fingerprints, too. And they found exactly that. The fingerprints of the twins who were concordant for schizophrenia were nearly identical, whereas the fingerprints of many of the discordant twins showed distinctive differences. A follow-up study looking at lines in twins' palms (which form at about the same time) confirmed these results (Davis and Bracha, 1996).

The evidence I have cited so far indicates that at least one cause—and perhaps the most important cause—of schizophrenia is disturbance of normal prenatal brain development. Presumably, genetic factors make some fetuses more sensitive to events that can disturb development. There is good evidence that obstetric complications can also cause schizophrenia. In fact, several studies have found that if a schizophrenic person does not have relatives with a schizophrenic disorder, that person is more likely to have had a history of complications at or around the time of childbirth—and the person is more likely to develop the schizophrenic symptoms at an earlier age (Schwarzkopf et al., 1989; O'Callaghan, 1990; O'Callaghan et al., 1992). Sometimes, brain damage received during adulthood can produce the symptoms of schizophrenia. Buckley et al. (1993) found three such cases and reported that MRI scans revealed damage in the left temporal lobe. Thus, brain damage that is *not related to heredity* may also be a cause of schizophrenia.

Although studies have found that people who develop schizophrenia show some abnormalities even during childhood, the symptoms of schizophrenia itself rarely occur before late adolescence or early adulthood. (It also rarely occurs later in life.) Even if most cases of schizophrenia involve abnormalities in prenatal brain development, something else must happen later in life to cause the onset of schizophrenic symptoms. Researchers have proposed various hypotheses to account for this phenomenon. For example, Squires (1997) notes that the total number of synapses in the brain reaches a peak at five years of age and then declines until the age of fifteen to twenty years. Perhaps, he suggests, a prenatal viral infection kills some neurons in the developing brain and it is not until more synapses are lost during the period of "synaptic pruning" that the loss of these neurons manifests itself. Other investigators have suggested that the emergence of the schizophrenic symptoms could be caused by a process instigated by the surge in hormones that occurs around the time of puberty (Torrey, 1991).

Relation Between Brain Damage and Positive and Negative Symptoms

The evidence I just reviewed indicates that schizophrenia is associated with brain damage, which may occur prenatally, during childbirth, or postnatally. Even if the brain damage associated with schizophrenia can be caused by several different means, we would at least expect some similarity in the location of the damage.

As we have seen, CT and MRI scans have found that schizophrenia is associated with damage to the frontal lobes, medial temporal lobes, and diencephalon. Weinberger (1988) suggested that the negative symptoms of schizophrenia are caused primarily by damage to the frontal lobes—in particular, the dorsolateral prefrontal cortex. One of the most reliable tests of the functions of the dorsolateral prefrontal cortex is the Wisconsin Card Sort Test (WCST). In this test, subjects are presented with a deck of cards that contain patterns that differ in number, shape, and color. The cards contain between one and four objects having one of four shapes and one of four differ-

Figure 17.9
Examples of the type of cards used in the Wisconsin Card Sort Test (WCST).

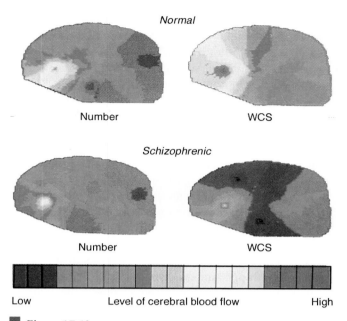

Figure 17.10
Maps of regional cerebral blood flow. The upper two scans are averages from a group of normal subjects, and the lower two scans are averages from a group of schizophrenic subjects. During the scan the subjects were attempting to solve two different problems ("Number" and "WCS"). The schizophrenic subjects fail to show an increased rate of blood flow in the dorsolateral prefrontal cortex during the "WCS" task.
(From Weinberger, D.R., Berman, K.F., and Zec, R.F. *Archives of General Psychiatry*, 1986, 43, 113–124. Reprinted by permission.)

ent colors. (See *Figure 17.9.*) The subjects are instructed to pick up the cards, one at a time, and place each of them in one of four piles, according to the card's number, shape, or color. The experimenter does not tell the subjects what the criterion is; he or she simply says "right" or "wrong" after each response. Once the subjects learn to respond appropriately (which usually does not take very long), the experimenter changes the criterion without warning. For example, if the first criterion was number, the second one might be color. People with damage to the dorsolateral prefrontal cortex learn the first task as rapidly as normal subjects do, but they have great difficulty switching their strategy when the criterion changes; they persist with the outmoded strategy. Thus, one of the functions of the dorsolateral prefrontal cortex is related to behavioral flexibility.

Weinberger, Berman, and Zec (1986) tested schizophrenic patients and normal control subjects on a computerized version of the WCST, in which patterns were presented on a color video screen and subjects had to respond by pressing one of four switches. While the subjects were performing the task, the investigators measured their regional cerebral blood flow.

The investigators found that the schizophrenic patients performed poorly on the task, just as subjects with lesions of the dorsolateral prefrontal cortex do. In addition, whereas the lateral prefrontal cortex of the normal subjects showed an increased blood flow during the card-sorting task, the cortex of the schizophrenic subjects did not. The results are shown in Figure 17.10. The two scans on the left were made while the subjects were performing a simple number-matching task that is not impaired by lesions of the dorsolateral prefrontal cortex; as you can see, the blood flow is similar for both groups. The two scans on the right were made during the sorting task; in this case, only the normal subjects showed signs of increased activation of the lateral prefrontal cortex. (See *Figure 17.10.*)

These results have been confirmed by other investigators. In a review of the literature, Taylor (1996) found that most functional imaging studies of the prefrontal cortex of schizophrenic patients found evidence for decreased activity—particularly when they were being challenged by tasks such as the WCST.

What might cause the "hypofrontality" that so many studies have observed? Weinberger and his colleagues suggest that the primary cause may be subcortical lesions or abnormalities that reduce the dopaminergic input to the prefrontal cortex. Dopamine does indeed play an important role in the normal functioning of the prefrontal cortex; studies with monkeys indicate that destruction of the dopaminergic input to the prefrontal cortex lowers its metabolic rate and leads to cognitive dysfunctions (Brozowski et al., 1979; Schwartzman et al., 1987). In addition, Daniel et al. (1991) found that when they administered amphetamine to schizophrenic patients, the blood flow in their dorsolateral prefrontal cortex increased—and their performance on the WCST improved.

Weinberger et al. (1992) studied a group of monozygotic twins who were discordant for schizophrenia. Each schizophrenic subject, then, had a genetically identical control with which comparisons could be made. The investigators took MRI scans and PET scans of the subjects' brains to measure structural brain abnormalities and differences in regional cerebral blood flow. They found that, relative to their nonschizophrenic siblings, the schizophrenic subjects had smaller hippocampal formations and showed lower metabolic activity in the dorsolateral prefrontal cortex while performing the WCST. In addition, the decreased volume of the hippocampal formation was strongly correlated with the hypofrontality. Studies in laboratory animals have shown that the hippocampal formation sends efferent axons to the ventral tegmental area, the source of the dopaminergic input to the prefrontal cortex. Perhaps the abnormality in the hippocampal formation results in decreased activity of the dopaminergic projection to the prefrontal cortex, which accounts for the hypofrontality. Confirming these results, Arnold et al. (1995) found smaller neurons in several regions of the hippocampal formation of deceased schizophrenic patients. The regions in which the smaller neurons were found included the parts of the hippocampal formation that communicate directly with the rest of the brain (the subiculum, field CA1, and the entorhinal cortex).

What relation does hypoactivity of the prefrontal cortex have to the positive symptoms of schizophrenia, which appear to be produced by *hyperactivity* of dopaminergic synapses in the nucleus accumbens? Weinberger, Berman, and Zec (1986) suggest that the hypoactivity of the prefrontal cortex causes an excitation of the mesolimbic dopamine system. Considerable evidence indicates that neurons in the prefrontal cortex regulate the basal release of dopamine in the ventral tegmental area. *Basal* release refers to the continuous, low-level release of dopamine that occurs when the organism is resting quietly. (I say *organism* rather than *person* because the evidence has been obtained from studies with laboratory animals.) Excitatory glutamatergic neurons of the prefrontal cortex send axons to the ventral tegmental area, where they form synapses with dopaminergic neurons that project to the nucleus accumbens (Sesack and Pickel, 1992). Karreman and Moghaddam (1996) placed a microdialysis probe in the nucleus accumbens to record the release of dopamine there. When they injected an inhibitory drug into the prefrontal cortex, the basal level of dopamine release in the nucleus accumbens fell. In contrast, when they injected an excitatory drug, the level of dopamine release increased.

Grace (1991) suggests the following hypothesis: Hypofrontality results in a low rate of activity of the glutamatergic axons in the prefrontal cortex that regulate the release of dopamine in the nucleus accumbens. The low activity of the glutamatergic terminals results in a low tonic release of dopamine, which causes a compensatory increase in the sensitivity of postsynaptic dopamine recep-

tors. Then when the dopaminergic neurons in the mesolimbic pathway are activated by environmental events, the neurons in the nucleus accumbens overreact—and lead to the occurrence of the positive symptoms of schizophrenia. (See *Figure 17.11.*)

In the interest of clarity and brevity, I have been selective in my review of research on schizophrenia. This puzzling and serious disorder has stimulated many ingenious hypotheses and much research. Some hypotheses have been proved wrong; others have not yet been adequately tested. Possibly, future research will find that all of these

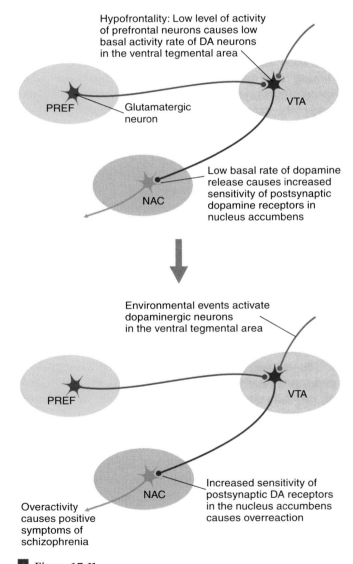

Figure 17.11

A hypothetical explanation for the relation between hypofrontality and the positive symptoms of schizophrenia. PREF = prefrontal cortex, VTA = ventral tegmental area, NAC = nucleus accumbens.

hypotheses (including the ones I have discussed) are incorrect, or one that I have not mentioned is correct. However, I am impressed with recent research, and I believe that we have real hope of finding the causes of schizophrenia in the near future. With the discovery of the causes we can hope for the discovery of methods of prevention.

Interim Summary

Researchers have made considerable progress in the past few years in their study of the physiology of mental disorders, but many puzzles still remain. Schizophrenia consists of positive and negative symptoms, the former involving the presence of an unusual behavior and the latter involving the absence of a normal behavior. Because schizophrenia is at least somewhat heritable, it appears to have a biological basis. But evidence indicates that not all cases are caused by heredity, and some people who appear to carry a "schizophrenia gene" do not become schizophrenic. Some evidence suggests that the location of this gene (if, indeed, a single gene exists) may be on chromosome 5 or 6.

The dopamine hypothesis—inspired by the findings that dopamine antagonists alleviate the positive symptoms of schizophrenia and that dopamine agonists increase or even produce them—is still dominant. This hypothesis states that the positive symptoms of schizophrenia are caused by hyperactivity of dopaminergic synapses. The involvement of dopamine in reinforcement could plausibly explain the positive effects of schizophrenia; inappropriately reinforced thoughts could persist and become delusions. Paranoid thoughts may be caused by dopaminergic activation of the central nucleus of the amygdala, a region involved in negative emotional responses. There is no evidence that an abnormally large amount of dopamine is released under resting conditions, but a PET study indicates that the administration of amphetamine causes a larger release of dopamine in the brains of schizophrenics. Some studies indicate that the brains of schizophrenic patients contain increased numbers of D_2 dopamine receptors in the neostriatum. However, some investigators have suggested that the increase is caused by the administration of antipsychotic drugs. It is still possible that an abnormality exists in the dopaminergic systems that project to the nucleus accumbens. Studies suggest that the nucleus accumbens in the brains of schizophrenic patients may contain increased numbers of D_3 or D_4 dopamine receptors.

That some patients are not helped by antipsychotic drugs poses an unsolved problem for the dopamine hypothesis. In addition, these drugs cause parkinsonian side effects (usually temporary) and, in some cases, tardive dyskinesia. An atypical antipsychotic drug, clozapine, binds with dopamine D_4 receptors and decreases dopaminergic activity in the nucleus accumbens and not in the neostriatum. Thus, this drug does not produce parkinsonian side effects and, one hopes, will not produce tardive dyskinesia. In addition, the drug reduces the symptoms of some patients who are not helped by traditional antipsychotic medication.

CT and MRI scans indicate that brain damage—especially in the frontal lobes, medial temporal lobes, and diencephalon—is associated with the negative symptoms of schizophrenia. Studies of the epidemiology of schizophrenia indicate that season of birth, viral epidemics during pregnancy, population density, latitude of birth, prenatal malnutrition, and prenatal stress all contribute to the occurrence of schizophrenia. In addition, home movies of very young children who became schizophrenic indicate the early presence of abnormalities in movements and facial expressions. All these factors provide evidence for problems with prenatal development. A study of NADPH-d, an enzyme found in some neurons, provides direct evidence of developmental abnormalities in the brains of schizophrenics. Further evidence is provided by the presence of an increased size of the third and lateral ventricles and a decreased size of the hippocampus in the schizophrenic member of monozygotic twins discordant for schizophrenia. The increased concordance rate of monochorionic monozygotic twins provides further evidence that hereditary and prenatal environmental factors may interact. Finally, comparisons of the fingerprints and palm prints of twins who are concordant and discordant for schizophrenia provide evidence for factors that disturb prenatal development during the second trimester.

Some evidence suggests that the hypofrontality that is responsible for at least some of the negative symptoms of schizophrenia may be caused by decreased dopaminergic activity in the prefrontal cortex. Abnormalities in the hippocampal formation may be responsible for this decreased dopaminergic activity. And the hypofrontality may cause increased dopaminergic activity in the nucleus accumbens, thus producing positive symptoms. The mechanism for this increase may be decreased tonic release of dopamine, which causes a compensatory increase in reactivity to dopamine when it is phasically released.

MAJOR AFFECTIVE DISORDERS

Affect, as a noun, refers to feelings or emotions. Just as the primary symptom of schizophrenia is disordered thoughts, the **major affective disorders** (also called *mood disorders*) are characterized by disordered feelings.

● Description

Feelings and emotions are essential parts of human existence; they represent our evaluation of the events in our lives. In a very real sense, feelings and emotions are what human life is all about. The emotional state of most of us reflects what is happening to us: Our feelings are tied to events in the real world, and they are usually the result of reasonable assessments of the importance these events have for our lives. But for some people, affect becomes divorced from reality. These people have feelings of extreme elation (*mania*) or despair (*depression*) that are not justified by events in their lives. For example, depression that accompanies the loss of a loved one is normal, but depression that becomes a way of life—and will not respond to the sympathetic effort of friends and relatives or even to psychotherapy—is pathological.

There are two principal types of major affective disorders. The first type is characterized by alternating periods of mania and depression—a condition called **bipolar disorder.** This disorder afflicts men and women in approximately equal numbers. Episodes of mania can last a few days or several months, but they usually take a few weeks to run their course. The episodes of depression that follow generally last three times as long as the mania. The second type is **unipolar depression,** or depression without mania. This depression may be continuous and unremitting or, more typically, may come in episodes. Unipolar depression strikes women two to three times more often than men. Mania without periods of depression sometimes occurs, but it is rare.

Severely depressed people usually feel extremely unworthy and have strong feelings of guilt. The affective disorders are dangerous; a person who suffers from a major affective disorder runs a considerable risk of death by suicide. According to Chen and Dilsaver (1996), 15.9 percent of people with unipolar depression and 29.2 percent of people with bipolar disorder attempt to commit suicide. Depressed people have very little energy, and they move and talk slowly, sometimes becoming almost torpid. At other times they may pace around restlessly and aimlessly. They may cry a lot. They are unable to experience pleasure; they lose their appetite for food and sex. Their sleep is disturbed; they usually have difficulty falling asleep and awaken early and find it difficult to get to sleep again. Even their body functions become depressed; they often become constipated, and secretion of saliva decreases.

Episodes of mania are characterized by a sense of euphoria that does not seem to be justified by circumstances. The diagnosis of mania is partly a matter of degree—one would not call exuberance and a zest for life pathological. People with mania usually exhibit nonstop speech and motor activity. They flit from topic to topic and often have delusions, but they lack the severe disorganization that is seen in schizophrenia. They are usually full of their own importance and often become angry or defensive if they are contradicted. Frequently, they go for long periods without sleep, working furiously on projects that are often unrealistic. (Sometimes, their work is fruitful; George Frideric Handel wrote *The Messiah*, one of the masterpieces of choral music, during one of his periods of mania.)

● Heritability

The tendency to develop an affective disorder appears to be heritable. (See Moldin, Reich, and Rice, 1991, for a review.) For example, Rosenthal (1971) found that close relatives of people who suffer from affective psychoses are ten times more likely to develop these disorders than people without afflicted relatives. Gershon et al. (1976) found that if one member of a set of monozygotic twins was afflicted with an affective disorder, the likelihood that the other twin was similarly afflicted was 69 percent. In contrast, the concordance rate for dizygotic twins was only 13 percent. Furthermore, the concordance rate for monozygotic twins appears to be the same whether the twins were raised together or apart (Price, 1968). The heritability of the affective disorders implies that they have a physiological basis.

Evidence suggests that a single dominant gene is responsible for susceptibility to developing bipolar disorder (Spence et al., 1995). For years, several groups of researchers have been trying to find the location of this gene. Early studies suggested that it might be located on chromosome 11, but follow-up studies found that it was not (Egeland et al., 1987; Kelsoe et al., 1989). More recent studies suggest that the "bipolar gene" might be located on chromosome 5, near the gene responsible for the dopamine transporter (Kelsoe et al., 1996) or on chromosome 18 (Detera-Wadleigh et al., 1995; Stine et al., 1995).

---

major affective disorder   A serious mood disorder; includes unipolar depression and bipolar disorder.

bipolar disorder   A serious mood disorder characterized by cyclical periods of mania and depression.

unipolar depression   A serious mood disorder that consists of unremitting depression or periods of depression that do not alternate with periods of mania.

● Physiological Treatments

There are four effective biological treatments for depression: monoamine oxidase (MAO) inhibitors, drugs that inhibit the reuptake of norepinephrine and serotonin, electroconvulsive therapy (ECT), and sleep deprivation. (Sleep deprivation is discussed in a later section.) Bipolar disorder can be effectively treated by lithium salts. The fact that these disorders respond to medical treatment provides additional evidence that they have a physiological basis. Furthermore, the fact that lithium is very effective in treating bipolar affective disorders but not unipolar depression suggests that there is a fundamental difference between these two illnesses.

Before the 1950s there was no effective drug treatment for depression. In the late 1940s, clinicians noticed that some drugs used for treating tuberculosis seemed to elevate the patient's mood. Researchers subsequently found that a derivative of these drugs, iproniazid, reduced symptoms of psychotic depression (Crane, 1957). Iproniazid inhibits the activity of MAO, which destroys excess monoamine transmitter substances within terminal buttons. Thus, the drug increases the release of dopamine, norepinephrine, and serotonin. Other MAO inhibitors were soon discovered. Unfortunately, MAO inhibitors can have harmful side effects. The most common problem is the *cheese effect*. Many foods (for example, cheese, yogurt, wine, yeast breads, chocolate, and various fruits and nuts) contain *pressor amines*—substances similar to catecholamines. Normally, these amines are deactivated by MAO, which is present in the blood and in other tissues of the body. But a person who is being treated with an MAO inhibitor may suffer a serious sympathetic reaction after eating food containing pressor amines. The pressor amines simulate the effects of increased activity of the sympathetic nervous system, increasing blood pressure and heart rate. The reaction can raise blood pressure enough to produce intracranial bleeding or cardiovascular collapse.

Fortunately, another class of antidepressant drugs was soon discovered that did not produce a cheese effect: the **tricyclic antidepressants.** These drugs were found to inhibit the reuptake of 5-HT and norepinephrine by terminal buttons. By retarding reuptake, the drugs keep the neurotransmitter in contact with the postsynaptic receptors, thus prolonging the postsynaptic potentials. Thus, both the MAO inhibitors and the tricyclic antidepressant drugs are monoaminergic agonists.

Since the discovery of the tricyclic antidepressants, other drugs have been discovered that have similar effects. The most important of these are the **specific serotonin reuptake inhibitors (SSRI),** whose action is described by their name. One of them, fluoxetine (Prozac) is widely prescribed for its antidepressant properties and for its ability to reduce the symptoms of obsessive-compulsive disorder and social phobia (described in Chapter 18).

The third biological treatment for depression has an interesting history. Earlier in this century, a physician named von Meduna noted that psychotic patients who were also subject to epileptic seizures showed improvement immediately after each attack. He reasoned that the violent storm of neural activity in the brain that constitutes an epileptic seizure somehow improved the patients' mental condition. He developed a way to produce seizures by administering a drug, but the procedure was dangerous to the patient. In 1937, Ugo Cerletti, an Italian psychiatrist, developed a less dangerous method for producing seizures. He had previously learned that the local slaughterhouse applied a jolt of electricity to animals' heads to stun them before killing them. The electricity appeared to produce a seizure that resembled an epileptic attack. He decided to attempt to use electricity to induce a seizure more safely.

Cerletti tried the procedure on dogs and found that an electrical shock to the skull did produce a seizure and that the animals recovered with no apparent ill effects. He then used the procedure on humans and found it to be safer than the chemical treatment that was previously used. As a result, **electroconvulsive therapy (ECT)** became a common treatment for mental illness. Before a person receives ECT, he or she is anesthetized and is given a drug similar to curare, which paralyzes the muscles, preventing injuries that might be produced by a convulsion. (Of course, the patient is attached to a respirator until the effects of this drug wear off.) Electrodes are placed on the patient's scalp (most often, to the nonspeech-dominant hemisphere, to avoid damaging verbal memories), and a jolt of electricity triggers a seizure. Usually, a patient receives three treatments per week until maximum improvement is seen, which usually involves six to twelve treatments. The effectiveness of ECT has been established by placebo studies, in which some patients are anesthetized but not given shocks (Weiner and Krystal, 1994). Although ECT was originally

---

tricyclic antidepressant   A class of drugs used to treat depression; inhibits the reuptake of norepinephrine and serotonin; named for the molecular structure.

specific serotonin reuptake inhibitor (SSRI)   A drug that inhibits the reuptake of serotonin without affecting the reuptake of other neurotransmitters.

electroconvulsive therapy (ECT)   A brief electrical shock, applied to the head, that results in an electrical seizure; used therapeutically to alleviate severe depression.

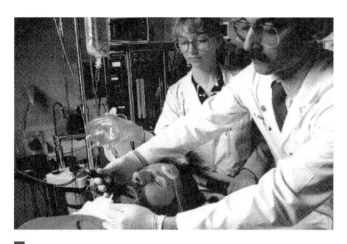

Figure 17.12
A patient being prepared for electroconvulsive therapy.
(Will & Deni McIntyre/Photo Researchers, Inc.)

used for a variety of disorders, including schizophrenia, we now know that its usefulness is limited to treatment of mania and depression. (See *Figure 17.12.*)

A depressed patient does not respond immediately to treatment with antidepressant drugs; improvement in symptoms is not usually seen before two to three weeks of drug treatment. In contrast, the effects of ECT are more rapid. A few seizures induced by ECT can often snap a person out of a deep depression within a few days. Although prolonged and excessive use of ECT causes brain damage, resulting in long-lasting impairments in memory (Squire, 1974), the judicious use of ECT during the interim period before antidepressant drugs become effective has undoubtedly saved the lives of some suicidal patients (Baldessarini, 1977). In addition, some severely depressed people are not helped by drug therapy; for them, occasional ECT is the only effective treatment.

The therapeutic effect of **lithium,** the drug used to treat bipolar affective disorders, is very rapid. This drug, which is administered in the form of lithium carbonate, is most effective in treating the manic phase of a bipolar affective disorder; once the mania is eliminated, depression usually does not follow (Gerbino, Oleshansky, and Gershon, 1978). Many clinicians and investigators have referred to lithium as psychiatry's wonder drug: It does not suppress normal feelings of emotions, but it leaves patients able to feel and express joy and sadness in response to events in their lives. Similarly, it does not impair intellectual processes; many patients have received the drug continuously for years without any apparent ill effects (Fieve, 1979). Between 70 and 80 percent of patients with bipolar

disorder show a positive response to lithium within a week or two (Price and Heninger, 1994).

Lithium does have adverse side effects. The therapeutic index (the difference between an effective dose and an overdose) is low. Side effects include hand tremors, weight gain, excessive urine production, and thirst. Toxic doses produce nausea, diarrhea, motor incoordination, confusion, and coma. Because of the low therapeutic index, patients' blood levels of lithium must be tested regularly to be certain that they do not receive an overdose. Unfortunately, some patients are not able to tolerate the side effects of lithium.

One of the most serious difficulties in treating bipolar disorder is compliance with the prescribed treatment. After taking lithium for a while, some patients find that they miss the intense pleasure they felt during their manic periods. Some of them apparently tell themselves that now that they are "cured," they can stop taking their medication—and when they do, their cycling begins again. Then the pain of the depression usually motivates them to start taking the drug again. Several studies suggest that strong efforts should be made to convince patients with bipolar disorder not to discontinue their medication, because occasionally the drug is no longer effective after a relapse (Suppes et al., 1991; Post et al., 1992).

Investigators have not yet discovered the pharmacological effects of lithium that are responsible for its ability to eliminate mania. Some suggest that the drug stabilizes the population of certain classes of neurotransmitter receptors in the brain (especially serotonin receptors), thus preventing wide shifts in neural sensitivity. This effect may involve interference with the production of a class of second messengers, the **phosphoinositide system** (Atack, Broughton, and Pollack, 1995; Jope et al., 1996).

Because some patients cannot tolerate the side effects of lithium, and because of the potential danger of overdose, researchers have been searching for alternative medications for bipolar disorder. One medication that has shown considerable promise is **carbamazepine** (Tegretol), a drug used to treat seizures that originate in the medial temporal lobes. Although carbamazepine is effective in treating the depressed phase of bipolar disorder, its effects on mania are more impressive (Post et al., 1984). (See *Figure 17.13.*)

lithium   An element; lithium carbonate is used to treat bipolar disorder.

phosphoinositide system   A biochemical pathway that is responsible for the production of several second messengers.

carbamazepine   A drug (trade name: Tegretol) that is used to treat seizures originating from a focus, generally in the medial temporal lobe.

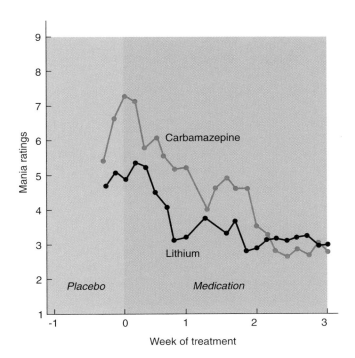

Figure 17.13
The effects of lithium carbonate and carbamazepine on symptoms of mania in patients with bipolar disorder.
(Adapted from Feldman, R.S., Meyer, J.S., and Quenzer, L.F. *Principles of Neuropsychopharmacology.* Sunderland, MA: Sinauer Associates, 1997. After Post et al., 1984.)

In addition, it appears to help some bipolar patients who do not respond to treatment with lithium (Post, Weiss, and Chuang, 1992).

● Role of Monoamines

The fact that depression can be treated effectively with MAO inhibitors and drugs that inhibit the reuptake of norepinephrine suggested the **monoamine hypothesis:** Depression is caused by insufficient activity of monoaminergic neurons. Because the symptoms of depression do not respond to potent dopamine agonists such as amphetamine or cocaine, most investigators have focused their research efforts on the other two monoamines: norepinephrine and serotonin.

The Monoamine Hypothesis

As we saw, the dopamine hypothesis of schizophrenia receives support from the fact that dopamine agonists can produce the symptoms of schizophrenia. Similarly, the monoamine hypothesis of depression receives support from the fact that depression can be caused by monoamine

antagonists. Many hundreds of years ago, an alkaloid extract from *Rauwolfia serpentina,* a shrub of Southeast Asia, was found to be useful for treating snake bite, circulatory disorders, and insanity. Modern research has confirmed that the alkaloid, now called reserpine, has both an antipsychotic effect and a hypotensive effect (that is, it lowers blood pressure). The effect on blood pressure precludes its use in treating schizophrenia, but the drug is still occasionally used to treat patients with high blood pressure.

Reserpine has a serious side effect: It can cause depression. In fact, in the early years of its use as a hypotensive agent, up to 15 percent of the people who received it became depressed (Sachar and Baron, 1979). Reserpine interferes with the storage of monoamines in synaptic vesicles, reducing the amount of neurotransmitter released by the terminal buttons. Thus, the drug serves as a potent norepinephrine, dopamine, and serotonin antagonist. The pharmacological and behavioral effects of reserpine complement the pharmacological and behavioral effects of the drugs used to treat depression—MAO inhibitors and drugs that block the reuptake of norepinephrine and serotonin. That is, a monoamine antagonist produces depression, whereas monoamine agonists alleviate it.

Several studies have found that suicidal depression is related to decreased CSF levels of **5-HIAA** (5-hydroxyindoleacetic acid), a metabolite of serotonin that is produced when serotonin is destroyed by MAO. A decreased level of 5-HIAA implies that less 5-HT (serotonin) is being produced and released in the brain. Träskmann et al. (1981) found that CSF levels of 5-HIAA in people who had attempted suicide were significantly lower than those in controls. In a follow-up study of depressed and potentially suicidal patients, 20 percent of those with levels of 5-HIAA below the median subsequently killed themselves, whereas none of those with levels above the median committed suicide. More recent studies have confirmed these results (Roy, De Jong, and Linnoila, 1989).

Sedvall et al. (1980) analyzed the CSF of healthy, nondepressed volunteers. The families of subjects with unusually low levels of 5-HIAA were more likely to include people with depression. The results suggest that serotonin metabolism or release is genetically controlled and is linked to depression. Thus, these findings clearly support the monoamine hypothesis.

monoamine hypothesis   A hypothesis that states that depression is caused by a low level of activity of one or more monoaminergic synapses.

5-HIAA   A breakdown product of the neurotransmitter serotonin (5-HT).

As we saw in Chapter 11, the activity of serotonergic neurons appears to inhibit aggression. Some investigators have suggested that this role is consistent with the findings of Sedvall et al. Suicide can be seen as a form of aggression—self-directed aggression (Siever et al., 1991); thus, the decreased CSF levels of 5-HIAA may simply indicate a lower level of impulse control. Of course, the fact that serotonin is involved in aggression does not rule out the possibility that low levels of serotonin are for depressed mood as well.

Delgado et al. (1990) used a different approach to study the role of serotonin in depression—the **tryptophan depletion procedure.** They studied depressed patients who were receiving antidepressant medication and were currently feeling well. For one day, they had the patients follow a low-tryptophan diet (for example, salad, corn, cream cheese, and a gelatin dessert). Then the next day, the patients drank an amino acid "cocktail" that contained no tryptophan. The uptake of amino acids through the blood–brain barrier is accomplished by amino acid transporters. Because the patients' blood level of tryptophan was very low and that of the other amino acids was high, very little tryptophan found its way into the brain, and the level of tryptophan in the brain fell drastically. As you will recall, tryptophan is the precursor of 5-HT, or serotonin. Thus, the treatment lowered the level of serotonin in the brain.

Delgado and his colleagues found that the tryptophan depletion caused most of the patients to relapse back into depression. Then when they began eating a normal diet again, they recovered. These results strongly suggest that the therapeutic effect of at least some antidepressant drugs depends on the availability of serotonin in the brain.

Subsequent studies have confirmed these results. These studies also indicate that tryptophan depletion has little or no effect on the mood of healthy subjects, but it does lower the mood of people with a family history of affective disorders (Benkelfat et al., 1994). Also, tryptophan depletion (which affects brain serotonin levels) causes relapses in patients who are successfully being treated with serotonin reuptake inhibitors but not in those who are being treated with norepinephrine reuptake inhibitors. In contrast, administration of AMPT, a drug that inhibits the synthesis of dopamine and norepinephrine, causes relapses only in patients who are being successfully treated with norepinephrine reuptake inhibitors (Heninger, Delgado, and Charney, 1996). (See *Figure 17.14*.)

Bremner et al. (1997) used a PET scanner to try to determine the brain regions involved in the relapse of depression caused by tryptophan depletion. To do so, they measured patients' regional cerebral metabolic rate before and after the patients drank a placebo or the amino acid

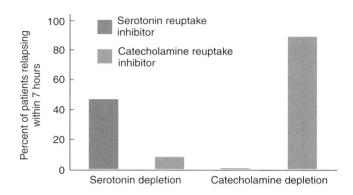

Figure 17.14
Effects of tryptophan depletion and catecholamine depletion on the symptoms of depressed patients receiving a serotonin reuptake inhibitor or a norepinephrine reuptake inhibitor.
(Adapted from Heninger, G.R., Delgado, P.L., and Charney, D.S. *Pharmacopsychiatry,* 1996, 29, 2–11.)

"cocktail." They found that patients whose depression returned showed a decrease in brain metabolism in the dorsolateral prefrontal cortex, orbitofrontal cortex, and thalamus. Patients who did not relapse did not show these changes. These results are consistent with the general finding (discussed in Chapter 11) that the prefrontal cortex is involved in emotions.

Long-Term Changes in Receptor Sensitivity

Although researchers have known for a long time that depression does not respond immediately to antidepressant medication, most studies of their pharmacological effects in laboratory animals have investigated the acute, immediate effects of these drugs. But perhaps the *acute* effects of the drugs are not the ones that relieve the symptoms of depression. Instead, the relevant effects may take two to three weeks to develop, because the delay in symptom reduction takes this long.

Sulser and Sanders-Bush (1989) reviewed research that suggested that the long-term effect of biological treatments for depression causes a **subsensitivity** of postsynaptic noradrenergic β receptors. The subsensitivity, which is just the opposite of supersensitivity, appears to be caused by a de-

tryptophan depletion procedure   A procedure involving a low-tryptophan diet and a tryptophan-free amino acid "cocktail" that lowers brain tryptophan and consequently decreases the synthesis of 5-HT.

subsensitivity   Decreased sensitivity of neurotransmitter receptors; a compensatory response to their prolonged stimulation.

creased number of β receptors. To be effective, these treatments must be applied chronically, over many days; subsensitivity is not produced by short-term treatment; thus, subsensitivity of β receptors seemed to be a reasonable mechanism to explain the long-term therapeutic effects of a variety of treatments with different short-term effects. However, more recent research indicates that some very effective antidepressant drugs do not affect the sensitivity of β receptors (Dechant and Clissold, 1991).

Artigas et al. (1996) propose an alternative hypothesis for the delayed effect of antidepressant drugs. As we saw in the previous subsection, considerable evidence indicates that serotonin plays a role in depression. Artigas and his colleagues suggest that drugs that increase the extracellular concentration of 5-HT in the brain temporarily inhibit the activity of serotonergic neurons in the raphe nuclei. During this period of inhibition the release of serotonin in the brain regions innervated by these neurons is suppressed. Not until the period of inhibition ends does the drugs' action as a serotonin agonist affect these regions.

Let's see how this process works. Studies with laboratory animals has shown that short-term administration of specific serotonin reuptake inhibitors or MAO inhibitors reduce the firing of serotonergic neurons of the dorsal raphe (Aghajanian, Graham, and Sheard, 1970). This effect is mediated by presynaptic 5-HT$_{1A}$ receptors located on the dendritic membranes of these neurons (Blier, De Montigny, and Chaput, 1987). As we saw in Chapter 4, drugs that bind with dendritic autoreceptors decrease the rate of neural firing and thus act as antagonists. By inhibiting the rate of serotonin reuptake, antidepressant drugs cause the concentration of serotonin in the raphe nuclei to increase (Invernizzi, Belli, and Samanin, 1992), thus stimulating these receptors. (As we also saw in Chapter 4, the dendrites of serotonergic neurons, as well as their axons, release the neurotransmitter.)

The inhibitory effect of antidepressant drugs on the firing rate of serotonergic neurons is short-lived. After two to three weeks the dendritic 5-HT$_{1A}$ receptors become desensitized, and the activity of the neurons returns to normal. At this time the antidepressant effects of the drug start taking effect. The serotonin that is released in the projection regions of these neurons (primarily the frontal cortex, hippocampus, and basal ganglia) remains in the synaptic cleft for a longer time because of the inhibitory effect of the drug on reuptake. (See *Figure 17.15.*)

If the therapeutic effect of antidepressant drugs is, indeed, retarded by temporary activation of 5-HT$_{1A}$ dendritic autoreceptors, then a drug that blocks these receptors should permit the antidepressant drugs to act sooner. In fact, some preliminary trials suggest that this is the case.

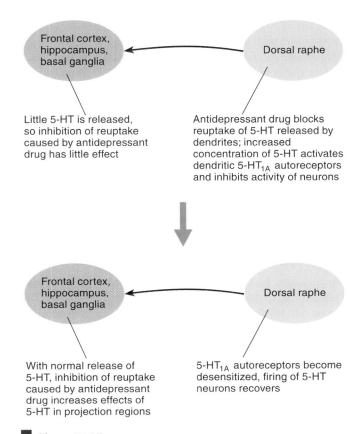

Figure 17.15
An explanation of the hypothesis that the delayed therapeutic effect of serotonergic reuptake inhibitors is caused by activation of dendritic 5-HT$_{1A}$ receptors in the dorsal raphe.

Two studies found that administration of pindol, a drug that blocks 5-HT$_{1A}$ receptors in the dorsal raphe, resulted in improvement of depressive symptoms in approximately one week, as opposed to the more typical two to three weeks (Artigas, Péres, and Alvarez, 1993; Blier and Bergeron, 1995).

As we saw in the previous subsection, some antidepressant drugs inhibit the reuptake of norepinephrine rather than serotonin. Whether these two types of drugs act independently on different systems or whether they have some common effects has yet to be discovered.

As you learned in Chapter 14, reinforcement involves the release of dopamine in the nucleus accumbens. Because inability to experience pleasure is one of the most important symptoms of depression, we might expect to find some involvement of dopaminergic neurons in this disorder. However, dopaminergic agonists such as cocaine and amphetamine do not relieve depression; they simply make depressed patients become agitated. In addition, Reynecke et al. (1989) found that chronic treatment with an antidepressant drug had no effect on the sensitivity of D_1 or D_2 dopamine receptors in the nucleus accumbens; nor did it affect the release of dopamine by electrical stimulation. Therefore, although we do not yet have enough evidence to rule out a role for dopamine in depression, only serotonin and norepinephrine have been shown to play a role.

● Evidence for Brain Abnormalities

As we saw earlier in this chapter, many studies have found structural and biochemical abnormalities in the brains of schizophrenic patients. Some studies have reported abnormalities in patients with affective disorders, but the evidence is still inconclusive. A recent review by Soares and Mann (1997) noted that investigators have reported abnormalities in the prefrontal cortex, basal ganglia, hippocampus, thalamus, cerebellum, and temporal lobe. The most reliable findings were abnormalities in the prefrontal cortex, basal ganglia, and cerebellum of patients with unipolar depression and abnormalities of the cerebellum (and perhaps the temporal lobe) in those with bipolar disorder. Elkis et al. (1996) found evidence for a decreased amount of tissue in the prefrontal cortex of young patients with unipolar depression, which suggests the presence of a developmental abnormality or a degenerative process that occurs early in life.

Several imaging studies using PET or functional MRI have found evidence for increased regional metabolic activity in depressed patients. For example, Drevets et al. (1992) found an increase in the prefrontal cortex and the amygdala, and Wu et al. (1992) found an increase in the anterior cingulate cortex. Nobler et al. (1994) scanned patients before and after ECT treatment and found a reduction in the metabolic activity of the prefrontal cortex. In fact, the amount of reduction was correlated with a positive response to the treatment. (See *Figure 17.16.*)

As we saw earlier in this chapter, evidence indicates that schizophrenia can be produced by brain damage resulting from obstetric complications. Kinney et al. (1993) found that patients with bipolar disorder were more likely than their normal siblings to have a record of obstetric complications. The complications were mostly minor, so the authors suggest that they probably served as a contributing factor to the development of the disorder rather than the sole cause.

● Role of Circadian Rhythms

One of the most prominent symptoms of depression is disordered sleep. The sleep of people with depression tends to be shallow; slow-wave delta sleep (stages 3 and 4) is re-

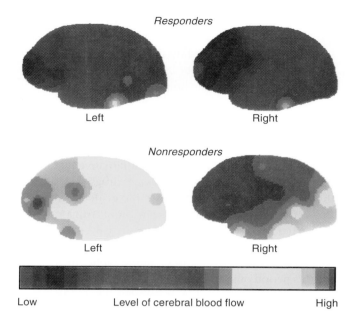

Figure 17.16
Mean changes in cerebral blood flow after bilateral ECT. The largest reductions were seen in the prefrontal cortex of subjects whose symptoms improved after ECT (responders).
(From Nobler, M.S., Sackeim, H.A., Prohovnik, I., Moeller, J.R., Mukherjee, S., Schnur, D.B., Prudic, J., and Devanand, D.P. *Archives of General Psychiatry*, 1994, *51*, 884–897.)

duced, and stage 1 is increased. Sleep is fragmented; people tend to waken frequently, especially toward the morning. In addition, REM sleep occurs earlier, the first half of the night contains a higher proportion of REM periods, and REM sleep contains an increased number of rapid eye movements (Kupfer, 1976; Vogel et al., 1980). (See *Figure 17.17.*)

REM Sleep Deprivation

One of the most effective antidepressant treatments is sleep deprivation, either total or selective. Selective deprivation of REM sleep, accomplished by monitoring people's EEG and awakening them whenever they show signs of REM sleep, alleviates depression (Vogel et al., 1975; Vogel et al., 1990). The therapeutic effect, like that of the antidepressant medications, occurs slowly, over the course of several weeks. Some patients show long-term improvement even after the deprivation is discontinued; thus, it is a practical as well as an effective treatment. In addition, regardless of their specific pharmacological effects, other treatments for depression suppress REM sleep, delaying its onset and decreasing its duration. These facts suggest that REM sleep and mood might somehow be causally related.

Scherschlicht et al. (1982) examined the effects of twenty antidepressant drugs on the sleep cycles of cats and

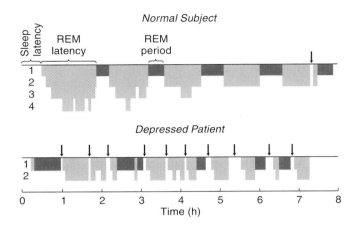

Figure 17.17
Patterns of the stages of sleep of a normal subject and of a patient with endogenous depression. Note the reduced sleep latency, reduced REM latency, reduction in slow-wave sleep (stages 3 and 4), and general fragmentation of sleep (arrows) in the depressed patient.
(From Gillin, J.C., and Borbély, A.A. *Trends in Neurosciences,* 1985, *8,* 537–542. Reprinted with permission.)

found that all of them profoundly reduced REM sleep and most of them increased slow-wave sleep. In an extensive review of the literature, Vogel et al. (1990) found that all drugs that suppressed REM sleep (and produced a rebound effect when their administration was discontinued) acted as antidepressants. As a consequence, an increased amount of delta sleep occurs during the first pre-REM period. Kupfer et al. (1994) found that the effects of antidepressant drugs on sleep persisted throughout long-term treatment. (They observed patients for as long as three years.) These results suggest that the primary effect of antidepressant medication may be to suppress REM sleep, and the changes in mood may be a result of this suppression. However, some drugs that relieve the symptoms of depression (such as iprindole and trimipramine) do not suppress REM sleep. Thus, suppression of REM sleep cannot be the *only* way that antidepressant drugs work.

Studies of families with a history of major depression also suggest a link between this disorder and abnormalities in REM sleep. For example, Giles, Roffwarg, and Rush (1987) found that first-degree relatives of people with depression are likely to show a short REM sleep latency, even if they have not yet had an episode of depression. Giles et al. (1988) found that the members of these families who had the lowest REM latency had the highest risk of subsequently becoming depressed. Abnormalities in REM sleep are seen early in life; Coble et al. (1988) found that newborn infants of mothers with a history of major depression showed patterns of REM sleep that were different from those of the infants of mothers without such a history.

Vogel et al. (1990) have developed what they believe to be an animal model of depression, which may be useful in studying the physiological basis of this disorder. They gave young rats injections of clomipramine (an antidepressant drug that blocks the reuptake of 5-HT) twice a day from age eight days to twenty-one days. This early treatment appears to have affected the development of the brain; perhaps, the authors suggest, it permanently decreased the sensitivity of postsynaptic serotonin receptors. Later, when the rats reached maturity, they showed many of the symptoms of depression: decreased sexual behavior, increased irritability, and decreased pleasure-seeking behavior (specifically, decreased willingness to work for reinforcing brain stimulation or for a taste of sucrose). The animals' sleep was also altered; the latency to the first bout of REM sleep was shorter, and the proportion of REM sleep was higher. The animals even responded to antidepressant treatment; imipramine and REM sleep deprivation both increased sexual behavior. A follow-up study (Yavari, Vogel, and Neill, 1993) found that early clomipramine treatment decreased the rate of firing of serotonergic neurons in the dorsal raphe nucleus in the adult rat, which is consistent with the hypothesis that depression is caused by decreased serotonergic activity.

Total Sleep Deprivation

Total sleep deprivation also has an antidepressant effect. Unlike specific deprivation of REM sleep, which takes several weeks to reduce depression, total sleep deprivation produces immediate effects (Wu and Bunney, 1990). Figure 17.18 shows the mood rating of a patient who stayed awake one night; as you can see, the depression was lifted by the sleep deprivation but returned the next day, after a normal night's sleep. (See *Figure 17.18.*)

Wu and Bunney suggest that during sleep a substance is produced that has a *depressogenic* effect. That is, the substance produces depression in a susceptible person. Presumably, this substance is produced in the brain and acts as a neuromodulator. During waking, this substance is gradually metabolized and hence inactivated. Some of the evidence for this hypothesis is presented in Figure 17.19. The data are taken from eight different studies (cited by Wu and Bunney, 1990) and show self-ratings of depression of people who did and did not respond to sleep deprivation. (Total sleep deprivation improves the mood of patients with major depression approximately two-thirds of the time.) (See *Figure 17.19.*)

Why do only some people profit from sleep deprivation? This question has not yet been answered, but several

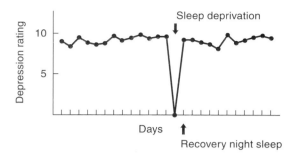

Figure 17.18
Changes in the depression rating of a depressed patient produced by a single night's total sleep deprivation.
(From Wu, J.C., and Bunney, W.E. *American Journal of Psychiatry*, Vol. 147, pp. 14–21, 1990. Copyright 1990, the American Psychiatric Association. Reprinted by permission.)

studies have shown that it is possible to predict who will profit and who will not (Reinink et al., 1990; Riemann, Wiegand, and Berger, 1991; Haug, 1992). In general, depressed patients whose mood remains stable throughout the day will probably not benefit from sleep deprivation, whereas those whose mood fluctuates probably will. The patients who are most likely to respond are those who feel depressed in the morning but then gradually feel better as the day progresses. In these people, sleep deprivation appears to prevent the depressogenic effects of sleep from taking place and simply permits the trend to continue. If you examine Figure 17.19, you can see that the responders were already feeling better by the end of the day. This improvement continued through the sleepless night and during the following day. The next night they were permitted to sleep normally, and their depression was back the following morning. As Wu and Bunney note, these data are consistent with the hypothesis that sleep produces a substance with a depressogenic effect. (See *Figure 17.19*.)

An alternative interpretation of the results we just saw is that waking might produce a substance with *antidepressant* effects, which is destroyed during sleep. However, Wu and Bunney point out that several studies have found that for some subjects a short nap reinstates the depression that had been reduced by sleep deprivation. In some cases a nap as short as 90 seconds (timed by EEG monitoring) can eliminate the beneficial effects of sleep deprivation. They conclude that the simplest hypothesis is that a nap produces a sudden secretion of a substance that causes depression. It seems less likely that a nap could be responsible for the sudden *destruction* of a substance with an antidepressant effect.

The antidepressant effects of REM sleep deprivation and that of total sleep deprivation appear to be different; one is slow and long-lasting, whereas the other is fast and short-lived. In addition, total sleep deprivation can even trigger an episode of mania in patients with bipolar disorder (Wehr, 1992). (Even nondepressed people often report feeling "high" after spending a night without sleep.) The fact that a person's mood can so quickly be altered suggests that it would be worthwhile to look for physiological changes before and after sleep deprivation to try to identify those that may play a role in the control of mood.

Although total sleep deprivation is not a practical method for treating depression (it is impossible to keep people awake indefinitely), several studies suggest that *partial* sleep deprivation can hasten the beneficial effects of antidepressant drugs (Szuba, Baxter, and Fairbanks, 1991; Leibenluft and Wehr, 1992). According to Szuba et al., the best method is to awaken patients at 2:00 A.M. and keep them awake until 9:00 P.M. Some investigators have found that *intermittent* total sleep deprivation (say, twice a week for four weeks) can have beneficial results (Papadimitriou et al., 1993).

Riemann et al. (1996) found that advancing the time of day that depressed patients sleep can prolong the beneficial effects of total sleep deprivation. Patients who slept between 5:00 P.M. and midnight after total sleep deprivation were less likely to relapse than those who slept between 11:00 P.M. and 6:00 A.M. The early sleepers also showed a more normal distribution of REM sleep.

Role of Zeitgebers

Yet another phenomenon relates depression to sleep and waking—or, more specifically, to the mechanisms respon-

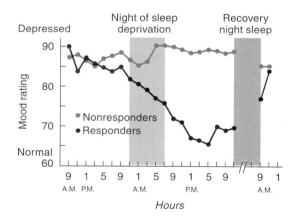

Figure 17.19
Mean mood rating of responding and nonresponding patients deprived of one night's sleep as a function of the time of day.
(From Wu, J.C., and Bunney, W.E. *American Journal of Psychiatry*, Vol. 147, pp. 14–21, 1990. Copyright 1990, the American Psychiatric Association. Reprinted by permission.)

sible for circadian rhythms. Some people become depressed during the winter season, when days are short and nights are long (Rosenthal et al., 1984). The symptoms of this form of depression, called **seasonal affective disorder,** are somewhat different from those of major depression; both forms include lethargy and sleep disturbances, but seasonal depression includes a craving for carbohydrates and an accompanying weight gain. (As you will recall, people with major depression tend to lose their appetite.) A much smaller percentage of the population becomes depressed during the summer (Wehr, Sack, and Rosenthal, 1987). People with **summer depression** are more likely to sleep less, lose their appetite, and lose weight (Wehr et al., 1991).

Seasonal affective disorder, like unipolar depression and bipolar disorder, appears to have a genetic basis. In a study of 6,439 adult twins, Madden et al. (1996) found that seasonal affective disorder ran in families, and they estimated that at least 29 percent of the variance in seasonal mood disorders could be attributed to genetic factors.

Seasonal affective disorder can be treated by **phototherapy:** exposing people to bright light for several hours a day (Rosenthal et al., 1985; Stinson and Thompson, 1990). As you will recall, circadian rhythms of sleep and wakefulness are controlled by the activity of the suprachiasmatic nucleus of the hypothalamus. Light serves as a *zeitgeber;* that is, it synchronizes the activity of the biological clock to the day–night cycle. One possibility is that people with seasonal affective disorder require a stronger-than-normal zeitgeber to reset their biological clock. However, two studies found that light therapy had an antidepressant effect no matter what time of day it occurred (Wirz-Justice et al., 1993; Meesters et al., 1995). If the light were simply serving as a zeitgeber, we would expect different effects depending on the time of day the phototherapy occurred.

Phototherapy has even been found to help patients with unipolar depression. Neumeister et al. (1996) found that patients with unipolar depression who responded to total sleep deprivation were less likely to relapse later if they received phototherapy in the early morning and late afternoon. Patients who sat in front of a dim light (the placebo treatment) quickly relapsed.

Many people are sensitive to seasonal changes in the hours of sunlight and darkness. Ninety-two percent of the respondents to a survey by Kasper et al. (1989a) said that they noticed seasonal changes in their mood, 27 percent reported that these changes caused problems, and 4 percent reported problems severe enough to qualify as a seasonal affective disorder. Kasper et al. (1989b) recruited people with "winter blahs" through newspaper advertisements. They excluded people with evidence of a true sea-

sonal affective disorder and exposed the others to bright light each day. They found that the exposure to bright light improved the mood of the subjects with the "blahs," whereas the mood of normal subjects was not changed. The study suggests that we should consider increasing the level of illumination in the home or workplace. The only negative aspect of the change would seem to be a higher electric bill.

According to a study by Wirz-Justice et al. (1996), even a high electric bill can be avoided. They found that a one-hour walk outside each morning reduced the symptoms of seasonal affective disorder. The investigators note that even on an overcast winter day, the early morning sky provides considerably more illumination than normal indoor artificial lighting, so a walk outside increases a person's exposure to light. (The exercise probably doesn't hurt, either.)

Interim Summary

The major affective disorders include bipolar affective disorder, with its cyclical episodes of mania and depression, and unipolar depression. Heritability studies suggest that genetic anomalies are at least partly responsible for these disorders. Depression can be successfully treated by MAO inhibitors, drugs that block the reuptake of norepinephrine and serotonin, electroconvulsive therapy, and sleep deprivation. Bipolar disorder can be successfully treated by lithium salts. Lithium appears to stabilize neural transmission, especially in serotonin-secreting neurons. It may do so by interfering with the phosphoinositide system, which is responsible for the production of several categories of second messengers.

The therapeutic effect of noradrenergic and serotonergic agonists and the depressant effect of reserpine, a monoaminergic antagonist, suggested the monoamine hypothesis of depression. Several other lines of evidence support this hypothesis. Low levels of 5-HIAA (a serotonin metabolite) in the cerebrospinal fluid correlate with attempts at suicide. It is possible that these results are related to the effects of serotonin on (self-directed) aggression. Depletion of tryptophan (the precursor of 5-HT) in the brain reverses

seasonal affective disorder   A mood disorder characterized by depression, lethargy, sleep disturbances, and craving for carbohydrates during the winter season when days are short.

summer depression   A mood disorder characterized by depression, sleep disturbances, and loss of appetite.

phototherapy   Treatment of seasonal affective disorder by daily exposure to bright light.

the therapeutic effects of antidepressant medication, which lends further support to the conclusion that 5-HT plays a role in mood. Functional imaging studies suggest that depression involves a decrease in the dorsolateral prefrontal cortex, orbitofrontal cortex, and thalamus.

Early studies on the physiological effects of antidepressant drugs focused on their acute effects. However, because the effects of antidepressant treatment are delayed, more recent investigations have studied the chronic effects, some of which are quite different. The delayed therapeutic effect appears to be caused by the activation of dendritic $5\text{-}HT_{1A}$ autoreceptors on neurons in the dorsal raphe. Eventual desensitization of these receptors permits the drug to exert its antidepressant effects.

Several studies have looked for abnormalities in the brains of depressed patients. In general, patients with uni-polar depression show abnormalities in the prefrontal cortex, basal ganglia, and cerebellum, while patients with bipolar disorder show abnormalities in the cerebellum and (perhaps) temporal lobe.

Sleep disturbances are characteristic of affective disorders. In fact, total sleep deprivation rapidly (but temporarily) reduces depression in many people, and selective deprivation of REM sleep does so slowly (but more lastingly). In addition, almost all effective antidepressant treatments suppress REM sleep. Finally, a specific form of depression, seasonal affective disorder, can be treated by exposure to bright light, the zeitgeber that resets the biological clock. Clearly, the mood disorders are somehow linked to biological rhythms.

SUGGESTED READINGS

Depue, R.A., and Iacono, W.G. Neurobehavioral aspects of affective disorders. *Annual Review of Psychology,* 1989, *40,* 457–492.

Goodwin, D.W., and Guze, S.B. *Psychiatric Diagnosis,* 5th ed. New York: Oxford University Press, 1989.

Mednick, S.A. *Fetal Neural Development and Adult Schizophrenia.* New York: Cambridge University Press, 1991.

Miller, R. Schizophrenia as a progressive disorder: Relations to EEG, CT, neuropathological and other evidence. *Progress in Neurobiology,* 1989, *33,* 17–44.

Strange, P.G. *Brain Biochemistry and Brain Disorders.* Oxford: Oxford University Press, 1992.

CHAPTER 18

Anxiety Disorders, Autistic Disorder, and Stress Disorders

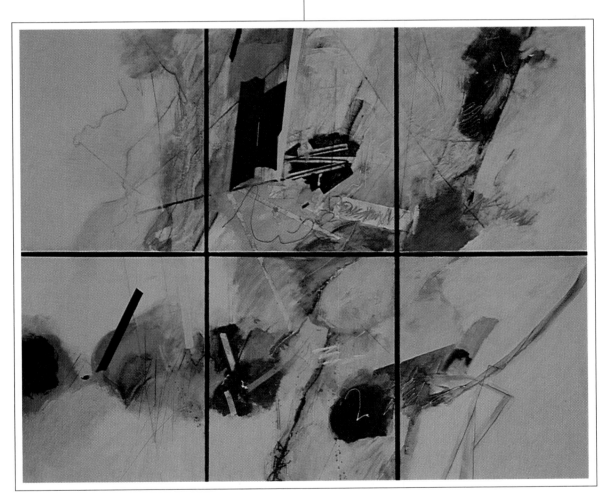

Over the Rail by William T. Kendall. Courtesy of the artist.

Not too many years ago, the first two topics discussed in this chapter, the anxiety disorders and autism, would not be covered in a book concerned with the physiology of behavior. (The importance of physiology to the third topic, stress, has long been recognized.) The anxiety disorders and autism were believed to be learned, primarily from parents who did a bad job raising their children. Although there was always at least some support for the suggestion that serious psychoses such as schizophrenia had a biological basis, other mental disorders were almost universally believed to be psychogenic in origin—that is, produced by "psychological" factors.

The tide has turned (or the pendulum has swung back, if you prefer that metaphor). Certainly, a person's family environment, social class, economic status, and similar factors affect the likelihood that he or she will develop a mental disorder and may help or hinder recovery. But physiological factors, including inherited ones and those that adversely affect development or damage the brain, play an important role, too. The first two sections of this chapter are devoted to research on these physiological factors. The final section of this chapter considers the physiology of stress—the harmful aspects of negative emotional reactions.

ANXIETY DISORDERS

As we saw in Chapter 17, the affective disorders are characterized by unrealistic extremes of emotion: depression or elation (mania). The **anxiety disorders** are characterized by unrealistic, unfounded fear and anxiety. This section describes two of the anxiety disorders that appear to have biological causes: panic disorder and obsessive-compulsive disorder.

● Panic Disorder

Description

People with **panic disorder** suffer from episodic attacks of acute anxiety—periods of acute and unremitting terror that grip them for variable lengths of time, from a few seconds to a few hours. The estimated incidence of panic disorder is between 1 and 2 percent of the population (Robbins et al., 1984). The disorder usually has its onset in young adulthood; it rarely begins after age thirty-five (Woodruff, Guze, and Clayton, 1972).

The basic symptoms of panic attack appear to be universal. For example, these symptoms are similar in residents of the United States, Puerto Rico, Germany, Lebanon, Korea, and New Zealand (Weissman et al., 1995). Panic attacks include many physical symptoms, such as shortness of breath, clammy sweat, irregularities in heartbeat, dizziness, faintness, and feelings of unreality. The victim of a panic attack often feels that he or she is going to die. Anxiety is a normal reaction to many stresses of life, and none of us is completely free from it. In fact, anxiety is undoubtedly useful in causing us to be more alert and to take important things seriously. However, the anxiety that we all feel from time to time is obviously different from the intense fear and terror experienced by a person gripped by a panic attack.

anxiety disorder   A psychological disorder characterized by tension, overactivity of the autonomic nervous system, expectation of an impending disaster, and continuous vigilance for danger.

panic disorder   A disorder characterized by episodic periods of symptoms such as shortness of breath, irregularities in heartbeat, and other autonomic symptoms, accompanied by intense fear.

Between panic attacks many people with panic disorder suffer from **anticipatory anxiety**—the fear that another panic attack will strike them. This anticipatory anxiety often leads to the development of a serious phobic disorder: **agoraphobia** (*agora* means "open space"). According to the American Psychiatric Association's official *Diagnostic and Statistical Manual IV*, agoraphobia associated with panic attacks is a fear of "being in places or situations from which escape might be difficult (or embarrassing) or in which help might not be available in the event of . . . a Panic Attack." Agoraphobia can be severely disabling; some people with this disorder have stayed inside their houses or apartments for years, afraid to venture outside. Although the incidence of panic disorder without agoraphobia is equal in men and women, women are twice as likely to develop panic disorder with agoraphobia (Bradwejn and Koszycki, 1994).

Possible Causes

Because the physical symptoms of panic attacks are so overwhelming, many patients reject the suggestion that they have a mental disorder, insisting that their problem is medical. In fact, a considerable amount of evidence suggests that panic disorder may have biological origins. First, the disorder appears to be hereditary; there is a higher concordance rate for the disorder between monozygotic twins than between dizygotic twins (Slater and Shields, 1969), and almost 30 percent of the first-degree relatives of a person with panic disorder also have panic disorder (Crowe et al., 1983). The pattern of panic disorder within a family tree suggests that the disorder is caused by a single, dominant gene (Crowe et al., 1987).

Panic attacks can be triggered in people with a history of panic disorder by a variety of conditions that activate the autonomic nervous system. These include injections of lactic acid (a by-product of muscular activity) or yohimbine (an α_2 adrenoreceptor antagonist), ingesting caffeine, and breathing air containing an elevated amount of carbon dioxide (Stein and Uhde, 1994). Lactic acid and breathing carbon dioxide both increase heart rate and rate of respiration, just as exercise do; yohimbine and caffeine have direct pharmacological effects on the nervous system.

Some investigators have suggested that people with panic attacks simply have more reactive autonomic nervous systems. That is, a stressful event produces a stronger reaction in the ANS, resulting in an emotional response that the patient interprets as a medical crisis. However, Roth et al. (1992) found no evidence for increased autonomic reactivity. The investigators had normal subjects and subjects with panic disorder breathe air containing 5 percent carbon dioxide. Forty-six percent of the subjects with panic disorder reported having a panic attack; none of

the normal subjects did. However, physiological measures of autonomic arousal showed no differences in reactivity between the two groups. These measures did show, though, that even before breathing the carbon dioxide, the subjects with panic disorder had a higher level of arousal; thus, they appeared to be chronically fearful.

Susceptibility to lactate-induced panic attacks appears to be at least partly heritable. Balon et al. (1989) infused forty-five normal subjects with sodium lactate and found that ten of them had panic attacks. The investigators obtained the family history of their subjects, using an interviewer who did not know which subjects had had panic attacks. They found that over 24 percent of the relatives of the subjects with the panic attacks themselves had a history of anxiety disorders, compared with less than 8 percent in the nonresponders.

Anxiety disorders are usually treated by a combination of behavior therapy and a benzodiazepine. As we saw in Chapter 4, benzodiazepines have strong anxiolytic ("anxiety-dissolving") effects. The brain possesses benzodiazepine receptors, which are part of the GABA$_A$ receptor complex. When a benzodiazepine agonist binds with its receptor, it increases the sensitivity of the GABA binding site and produces an anxiolytic effect. On the other hand, when a benzodiazepine antagonist occupies the receptor site, it *reduces* the sensitivity of the GABA binding site and *increases* anxiety. Anxiety disorders, then, might be caused by a diminished number of benzodiazepine receptors or by the secretion of a neuromodulator that blocks the benzodiazepine binding site at the GABA$_A$ receptor.

As we saw in Chapter 17, rats that receive an antidepressant medication (clomipramine) early in life later develop the symptoms of depression, which can be reduced by an antidepressant drug or by REM sleep deprivation. Similarly, fearfulness can be produced in cats by prenatal administration of a benzodiazepine tranquilizer. Marczynski and Urbancic (1988) gave pregnant cats injections of diazepam (Valium) and assessed the fearfulness of the offspring of these cats when they were one year old. They found that the animals showed restlessness and anxiety in novel situations. This fearfulness could be reduced with an injection of diazepam. Afterward, they measured the level of benzodiazepine receptors in the animals' brains and found a decrease in the hypothalamus, frontal cortex, anterior parietal cortex, and midline thalamus. Thus, fearfulness appears

anticipatory anxiety   A fear of having a panic attack; may lead to the development of agoraphobia.

agoraphobia   A fear of being away from home or other protected places.

to be associated with a decreased number of benzodiazepine receptors and, presumably, lower sensitivity to the endogenous benzodiazepine agonist, whatever that may be.

Two other substances have been implicated in panic disorder: cholecystokinin and serotonin. As we saw in Chapter 13, cholecystokinin (CCK) may play a role in satiety. This peptide is produced by cells in the duodenum and also by neurons in the brain, where it is co-released with neurotransmitters such as dopamine. In a review of the literature, Bradwejn and Koszycki (1994)) conclude that there is good evidence that CCK may be involved in anxiety. In a double-blind study, Bradwejn, Koszycki, and Meterissian (1990) found that an injection of CCK-4 (a form of CCK that crosses the blood–brain barrier) triggered panic attacks in subjects with panic disorder but not in normal controls. A study with rats found that injection of CCK directly into the amygdala causes an anxiety reaction that can be blocked by injection of a benzodiazepine (Csonka et al., 1988). However, a double-blind study by Adams et al. (1995) found that a CCK-receptor antagonist had no effects on panic attacks. Because these contradictory results have yet to be explained, the role of CCK in panic disorder is still uncertain.

As we saw in Chapter 17, serotonin appears to play a role in depression. Some evidence suggests that serotonin may play a role in anxiety disorders, too. Even though the symptoms of panic disorder and obsessive-compulsive disorder (described in the next section) are very different, drugs that serve as serotonin agonists (such as fluoxetine) have been successfully used to treat both disorders (Coplan, Gorman, and Klein, 1992). You will recall from Chapter 17 that short-term tryptophan depletion, caused by a low-tryptophan diet followed by the drinking of an amino acid "cocktail" that is deficient in tryptophan, rapidly increases the symptoms of depression in people with a history of unipolar depression. (The tryptophan depletion interferes with the synthesis of 5-HT.) Goddard et al (1994) found that tryptophan depletion had no effects in people with a history of panic disorder. These results have yet to be reconciled with the fact that serotonin agonists such as fluoxetine reduce the symptoms of panic disorder.

● Obsessive-Compulsive Disorder

Description

As the name implies, people with an **obsessive-compulsive disorder** suffer from **obsessions**—thoughts that will not leave them—and **compulsions**—behaviors that they cannot keep from performing. Obsessions are seen in a variety of mental disorders, including schizophrenia. However, unlike schizophrenics, people with obsessive-compulsive

disorder recognize that their thoughts and behaviors are senseless and desperately wish that they would go away. Compulsions often become more and more demanding until they interfere with people's careers and daily lives.

The incidence of obsessive-compulsive disorder is 1–2 percent. Females are slightly more likely than males to have this diagnosis. Like panic disorder, obsessive-compulsive disorder most commonly begins in young adulthood (Robbins et al., 1984). Cross-cultural studies find that the symptoms of this disorder are similar in various racial and ethnic groups (Akhtar et al., 1975; Khanna and Channabasavanna, 1987; Hinjo et al., 1989). People with this disorder are unlikely to marry, perhaps because of the common obsessional fear of dirt and contamination or because of the shame associated with the rituals they are compelled to perform, which causes them to avoid social contacts (Turner, Beidel, and Nathan, 1985).

Most compulsions fall into one of four categories: *counting, checking, cleaning,* and *avoidance*. For example, people might repeatedly check burners on the stove to see that they are off and windows and locks to be sure that they are locked. Davison and Neale (1974) reported the case of a woman who washed her hands more than five hundred times a day because she feared being contaminated by germs. The hand washing persisted even when her hands became covered with painful sores. Other people meticulously clean their apartment or endlessly wash, dry, and fold their clothes. Some become afraid to leave home because they fear contamination, and they refuse to touch other members of their family. If they do accidentally become "contaminated," they usually have lengthy purification rituals. (See *Table 18.1.*)

Some investigators believe that the compulsive behaviors seen in obsessive-compulsive disorder are forms of species-typical behaviors—for example, grooming, cleaning, and attention toward sources of potential danger—that are released from normal control mechanisms by a brain dysfunction (Wise and Rapoport, 1988). Fiske and Haslam (1997) suggest that the behaviors seen in obsessive-compulsive disorder are simply pathological examples of a natural behavioral tendency to develop and practice social rituals. For example, people perform cultural rituals to mark transitions or changes in social status, to diagnose or treat illnesses, to restore relationships with deities, or to

obsessive-compulsive disorder   A mental disorder characterized by obsessions and compulsions.

obsession   An unwanted thought or idea with which a person is preoccupied.

compulsion   The feeling that one is obliged to perform a behavior, even if one prefers not to do so.

Table 18.1
Reported Obsessions and Compulsions of Child and Adolescent Patients

Major Presenting Symptoms	Percent Reporting Symptom at Initial Interview
Obsession	
Concern or disgust with bodily wastes or secretions (urine, stool, saliva), dirt, germs, environmental toxins, etc.	43
Fear something terrible might happen (fire, death/illness of loved one, self, or others)	24
Concern or need for symmetry, order, or exactness	17
Scrupulosity (excessive praying or religious concerns out of keeping with patient's background)	13
Lucky/unlucky numbers	18
Forbidden or perverse sexual thoughts, images, or impulses	14
Intrusive nonsense sounds, words, or music	11
Compulsion	
Excessive or ritualized hand washing, showering, bathing, toothbrushing, or grooming	85
Repeating rituals (going in/out of door, up/down from chair, etc.)	51
Checking doors, locks, stove, appliances, car brakes, etc.	46
Cleaning and other rituals to remove contact with contaminants	23
Touching	20
Ordering/arranging	17
Measures to prevent harm to self or others (e.g., hanging clothes a certain way)	16
Counting	18
Hoarding/collecting	11
Miscellaneous rituals (e.g., licking, spitting, special dress pattern)	26

Source: From Rapoport, J.L. *Journal of the American Medical Association*, 1988, *260*, 2888–2890.

ensure the success of hunting or planting. These rituals define the status of individuals and their relationships with other members of the society, and they provide comfort in knowing that the structure of the society approves the transition or change in status or is doing all it can to avert misfortune. Consider the following scenario (from Fiske and Haslam, 1997):

> Imagine that you are traveling in an unfamiliar country. Going out for a walk, you observe a man dressed in red, standing on a red mat in a red-pained gateway. . . . He utters the same prayer six times. He brings out six basins of water and meticulously arranges them in a symmetrical configuration in front of the gateway. Then he washes his hands six times in each of the six basins, using precisely the same motions each time. As he does this, he repeats the same phrase, occasionally tapping his right finger on his earlobe. Through your interpreter, you ask him what he is doing. He replies that there are dangerous polluting substances in the ground, . . . [and that] he must purify himself or something terrible will happen. He seems eager to tell you about his concerns. (p. 211)

Why is the man acting this way? Is he a priest following a sacred ritual or does he have obsessive-compulsive disorder? Without knowing more about the spiritual rituals followed by the man's culture we cannot say. Fiske and Haslam compared the features of obsessive-compulsive disorder and other psychological disorders in descriptions of rituals, work, or other activities in fifty-two cultures. They found that the features of obsessive-compulsive disorder (for example, observing lucky or unlucky numbers or colors with special significance, repeating activities, ordering or arranging things in specific configurations, or paying special attention to thresholds or entrances) were found in rituals in these cultures. The features of other psychological disorders were much less common. On the whole, the evidence suggests that the symptoms of obsessive-compulsive disorder represent an exaggeration of natural human tendencies.

Possible Causes

Evidence is beginning to accumulate suggesting that obsessive-compulsive disorder may have a genetic origin. Family studies have found that this disorder is associated with neurological disorders that appears during childhood (Pauls and Leckman, 1986; Pauls et al., 1986). This disorder, **Tourette's syndrome,** is characterized by muscular and vocal tics: facial grimaces, squatting, pacing, twirling, barking, sniffing, coughing, grunting, or repeating specific words (especially vulgarities). Leonard et al. (1992a, 1992b) found that many patients with obsessive-compulsive disorder had tics and that many patients with Tourette's syndrome showed obsessions and compulsions. Both groups of investigators believe that the two disorders are produced by the same underlying causes, which may be the result of a single, dominant gene. It is not clear why some people with the faulty gene develop Tourette's syndrome early in childhood and others develop obsessive-compulsive disorder later in life.

As with schizophrenia, not all cases of obsessive-compulsive disorder have a genetic origin; the disorder sometimes occurs after brain damage caused by various means, such as birth trauma, encephalitis, and head trauma (Berthier et al., 1966; Hollander et al., 1990). In particular, the symptoms appear to be associated with damage to or dysfunction of the basal ganglia, cingulate gyrus, and prefrontal cortex (Giedd et al., 1995; Robinson et al., 1995).

Several investigators have found that obsessive-compulsive disorder sometimes accompanies Huntington's chorea and Sydenham's chorea, both of which involve degeneration of the basal ganglia (Swedo et al., 1989a; Cummings and Cunningham, 1992). **Sydenham's chorea** usually occurs in childhood or adolescence, after a group A β-hemolytic streptococcal infection (a "strep throat"). Like rheumatic fever (which usually involves the heart valves), Sydenham's chorea is an autoimmune disease, in which the patient's immune system attacks and damages certain tissues of the body—in this case, parts of the brain. Presumably, the obsessive and compulsive symptoms of Sydenham's chorea are caused by this damage. Husby et al. (1976) found evidence that the immune system of patients with Sydenham's chorea contained antibodies against proteins found in the subthalamic nucleus and parts of the basal ganglia.

Several studies using PET scans have found evidence of increased activity in the frontal lobes and cingulate gyrus (Baxter et al., 1989; Swedo et al., 1989b; Rubin et al., 1992; Lucey et al., 1997). Some studies have found evidence of decreased activity in the basal ganglia (consistent with the lesion studies I cited earlier), while others have reported an *increase*. Several studies have use functional imaging to measure regional brain activity of patients with obsessive-compulsive disorder before and after successful treatment with drugs or behavior therapy (Swedo et al., 1992; Rubin et al., 1995; Schwartz et al., 1996). In general, the im-

provements in a patient's symptoms was correlated with a reduction in the activity of the prefrontal cortex. These results provide especially strong evidence that the prefrontal cortex plays an important role in this disorder. And the fact that behavior therapy and drug therapy produced similar results is especially remarkable: It indicates that very different procedures may be bringing about physiological changes that alleviate a serious mental disorder.

Breiter et al. (1996) performed a particularly intriguing study with a group of patients with obsessive-compulsive disorder. They used functional MRI to measure their subjects' regional cerebral metabolism before and after having them hold some "contaminated" items. These items included tissue soaked in toilet water, plastic bags from contaminated waste barrels, and tissues into which someone had blown his nose. They also gave them some innocuous stimuli, including tissue soaked in clean water and new plastic bags. In fact, *all* the items the experimenters actually put in the subjects' hands were clean, but the switch was made out of the subjects' sight, so they believed that they were handling some items that were contaminated. Apparently, the act was convincing, because the subjects were quite disturbed by the "contaminated" objects. When the subjects were holding the "contaminated" items, the anterior cingulate cortex, the basal ganglia, the amygdala, and several regions of the prefrontal cortex showed increased activity. (You may be wondering how the experimenters induced the subjects to hold the "contaminated" items. I did, too, but the authors did not explain their methods of persuasion.)

As we saw in Chapter 11, the prefrontal cortex (particularly the orbitofrontal cortex) and the cingulate cortex are involved in emotional reactions, so it is not surprising to learn that they might be implicated in obsessive-compulsive disorder. In fact, some patients with severe obsessive-compulsive disorder have been successfully treated with surgical destruction of specific fiber bundles in the subcortical frontal lobe, including the cingulum bundle (which connects the prefrontal and cingulate cortex with the limbic cortex of the temporal lobe) and a region that contains fibers that connect the basal ganglia with the prefrontal cortex (Ballantine et al., 1987; Mindus, Rasmussen, and

Tourette's syndrome   A neurological disorder characterized by tics and involuntary vocalizations and sometimes by compulsive uttering of obscenities and repetition of the utterances of others.

Sydenham's chorea   An autoimmune disease that attacks parts of the brain, including the basal ganglia, and produces involuntary movements and often the symptoms of obsessive-compulsive disorder.

Lindquist, 1994) These operations, which are performed only when a patient has serious obsessive and compulsive symptoms that do not respond to behavior therapy or drugs, have a reasonably good success rate. Baer et al. (1995) studied patients whose cingulum bundles were destroyed through MRI-guided stereotaxic surgery destruction and found that 27 percent showed definite improvement, 27 percent showed probable improvement, and 46 percent showed no improvement. Sachdev and Hay (1995) found that patients who received neurosurgery for obsessive-compulsive disorder using modern methods were very unlikely to show negative personality changes. Of course, neurosurgery cannot be undone, so such procedures must be considered only as a last resort.

In one extraordinary case a patient performed his own psychosurgery. Solyom, Turnbull, and Wilensky (1987) reported the case of a young man with a serious obsessive-compulsive disorder whose ritual hand washing and other behaviors made it impossible for him to continue his schooling or lead a normal life. Finding that his life was no longer worthwhile, he decided to end it. He placed the muzzle of a .22-caliber rifle in his mouth and pulled the trigger. The bullet entered the base of the brain and damaged the frontal lobes. He survived, and he was amazed to find that his compulsions were gone. Fortunately, the damage did not disrupt his ability to make or execute plans; he went back to school and completed his education and now has a job. His IQ was unchanged. Ordinary surgery would have been less hazardous and messy, but it could hardly have been more successful.

By far, the most effective treatment of obsessive-compulsive disorder is drug therapy. To date, three effective drugs have been found: clomipramine, fluoxetine, and fluvoxamine. Although these drugs are also effective antidepressants, their antidepressant action does not seem to be related to their ability to relieve the symptoms of obsessive-compulsive disorder. For example, Leonard et al. (1989) compared the effects of clomipramine and desipramine (an antidepressant drug that does not affect the reuptake of serotonin) on the symptoms of children and adolescents with severe obsessive-compulsive disorder. For three weeks, all patients received a placebo. Then for five weeks, half of them received clomipramine (CMI) and the other half received desipramine (DMI), on a double-blind basis. At the end of that time the drugs were switched. As Figure 18.1 shows, CMI was a much more effective drug; in fact, when the patients were switched from CMI to DMI, their symptoms got worse. (See *Figure 18.1.*)

All of the effective antiobsessional drugs are specific blockers of 5-HT reuptake; thus, they are specific serotonergic agonists. When patients are given a serotonin *antago-*

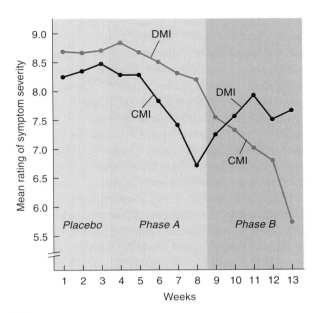

Figure 18.1
Mean rating of symptom severity of patients with obsessive-compulsive disorder treated with desipramine (DMI) or clomipramine (CMI).
(From Leonard, H.L., Swedo, S.E., Rapoport, J.L., Koby, E.V., Lenane, M.C., Cheslow, D.L., and Hamburger, S.D. *Archives of General Psychiatry*, 1989, *46*, 1088–1092. Copyright 1989, American Medical Association.)

nist, their symptoms get worse (Hollander et al., 1992). However, Barr et al. (1994) found that tryptophan depletion does not increase the symptoms of obsessive-compulsive disorder, even though the treatment reduced the level of plasma tryptophan by 84 percent. In general, serotonin has an inhibitory effect on species-typical behaviors, which has tempted several investigators to speculate that these drugs alleviate the symptoms of obsessive-compulsive disorder by reducing the strength of the washing, cleaning, and danger avoidance behaviors that may underlie this disorder.

The importance of serotonergic activity in inhibiting compulsive behaviors is underscored by three interesting compulsions: trichotillomania, onychophagia, and acral lick dermatitis. *Trichotillomania* is compulsive hair pulling. People with this disorder (almost always females) often spend hours each night pulling hairs out one by one, sometimes eating them (Rapoport, 1991). *Onychophagia* is compulsive nail biting, which in its extreme can cause severe damage to the ends of the fingers. (For those who are sufficiently agile, toenail biting is not uncommon.) Double-blind studies have shown that both of these disorders can successfully be treated by clomipramine, the drug of choice for obsessive-compulsive disorder (Leonard et al., 1992).

Acral lick dermatitis is a disease of dogs, not humans. Some dogs will continuously lick at a part of their body, especially their wrist or ankle (called the *carpus* and the *hock*). The licking removes the hair and often erodes away the skin as well. The disorder seems to be genetic; it is seen almost exclusively in large breeds such as Great Danes, Labrador retrievers, and German shepherds, and it runs in families. A double-blind study found that clomipramine reduces this compulsive behavior (Rapoport, Ryland, and Kriete, 1992). At first, when I read the term "double-blind" in the report by Rapoport and her colleagues, I was amused to think that the investigators were careful not to let the dogs learn whether they were receiving clomipramine or a placebo. Then I realized that, of course, it was the dogs' owners who had to be kept in the dark.

Interim Summary

The anxiety disorders severely disrupt some people's lives. People with panic disorder periodically have panic attacks, during which they experience intense symptoms of autonomic activity and often feel as if they were going to die. Frequently, panic attacks lead to the development of agoraphobia, an avoidance of being away from a safe place, such as home. Panic disorder is at least partly heritable, which suggests that it has biological causes.

Panic attacks can be triggered in many susceptible people by conditions that activate the autonomic nervous system, such as an caffeine, yohimbine, injection of lactate, or inhalation of air containing an elevated amount of carbon dioxide. Panic attacks can be alleviated by the administration of a benzodiazepine, a finding that suggests that the disorder may involve decreased numbers of benzodiazepine receptors or an inadequate secretion of an endogenous benzodiazepine agonist. Cats that are given a benzodiazepine prenatally will become especially fearful when they reach adulthood, and the treatment decreases the number of benzodiazepine receptors in parts of their brain. Cholecystokinin (CCK) increases the likelihood of panic attacks, and serotonin reuptake inhibitors decrease it.

Obsessive-compulsive disorder is characterized by obsessions—unwanted thoughts—and compulsions—uncontrollable behaviors, especially those involving cleanliness and attention to danger. Some investigators believe that these behaviors represent overactivity of species-typical behavioral tendencies.

Obsessive-compulsive disorder has a heritable basis and is related to Tourette's syndrome, a neurological disorder characterized by tics and strange verbalizations. It can also be caused by brain damage at birth, encephalitis, and head injuries, especially when the basal ganglia are involved. PET scans indicate that people with obsessive-compulsive disorder tend to show increased glucose metabolism in the frontal lobes and cingulate gyrus, structures that are probably involved in emotional reactions. The destruction of the cingulum bundle, which links them with the anterior temporal lobe, reduces the symptoms, as do drugs such as clomipramine, which specifically block the reuptake of serotonin. Some investigators believe that clomipramine and related drugs alleviate the symptoms of obsessive-compulsive disorder by increasing the activity of serotonergic pathways that play an inhibitory role on species-typical behaviors. Three other compulsions, hair pulling, nail biting, and (in dogs) acral lick syndrome, are also suppressed by clomipramine.

AUTISTIC DISORDER

● Description

When a child is born, the parents normally expect to love and cherish it and to be loved and cherished in return. Unfortunately, approximately 4 in every 10,000 infants are born with a disorder that impairs their ability to return their parents' affection. The symptoms of **autistic disorder** include a failure to develop normal social relations with other people, impaired development of communicative ability, and lack of imaginative ability. The syndrome was named and characterized by Kanner (1943), who chose the term (*auto*, "self," *-ism*, "condition") to refer to the child's apparent self-absorption. The disorder afflicts boys three times more often than girls.

Infants with autistic disorder do not seem to care if they are held, or they may arch their backs when picked up, as if they do not want to be held. They do not look or smile at their caregivers. If they are ill, hurt, or tired, they will not look to someone else for comfort. As they get older, they do not enter into social relationships with other children and avoid eye contact with them. Their language development is abnormal or even nonexistent. They often echo what is said to them, and they may refer to themselves as others do—in the second or third person. For example,

> **autistic disorder** A chronic disorder whose symptoms include failure to develop normal social relations with other people, impaired development of communicative ability, lack of imaginative ability, and repetitive, stereotyped movements.

they may say, "You want some milk?" to mean "I want some milk." They may learn words and phrases by rote, but they fail to use them productively and creatively. Those who do acquire reasonably good language skills talk about their own preoccupations, without regard for other people's interests. They usually interpret other people's speech literally. For example, when an autistic person is asked, "Can you pass the salt?" he may simply say "Yes"—and not because he is trying to be funny or sarcastic.

Autistic people generally show abnormal interests and behaviors. For example, they may show stereotyped movements, such as flapping their hand back and forth or rocking back and forth. They may become obsessed with investigating objects, sniffing them, feeling their texture, or moving them back and forth. They may become attached to a particular object and insist on carrying it around with them. They may become preoccupied in lining up objects or in forming patterns with them, oblivious to everything else that is going on about them. They often insist on following precise routines and may become violently upset when they are hindered from doing so. They show no make-believe play and are uninterested in stories that involve fantasy. Although most autistic people are mentally retarded, not all are; and unlike most retarded people, they may be physically adept and graceful. Some have isolated skills, such as the ability to multiply two four-digit numbers very quickly, without apparent effort.

As you can see, autistic disorder includes affective, cognitive, and behavioral abnormalities. Frith, Morton, and Leslie (1991) suggest that the impaired socialization, communicative ability, and imagination that characterize autism stem from abnormalities in the brain that prevent the person from forming a "theory of mind." That is, the person is unable "to predict and explain the behavior of other humans in terms of their mental states" (p. 434). He or she just cannot see things from another person's point of view. As one autistic man complained, "Other people seem to have a special sense by which they can read other people's thoughts" (Rutter, 1983).

Frith and her colleagues cite an experiment of Baron-Cohen, Leslie, and Frith (1985), who administered the following test: Children were presented with a puppet show in which Sally put a marble in a basket and then left the room. The other puppet, Anne, took the marble out of the basket and put it in a box. When Sally returned, she wanted to play with the marble. Where will she look for it? (See *Figure 18.2.*) A normal four-year-old child will say, "In the basket," because he or she realizes that Sally does not know that Anne has moved it into the box. So will a retarded child with a mental age of five or six years. However, sixteen of twenty autistic children with a mean mental age of

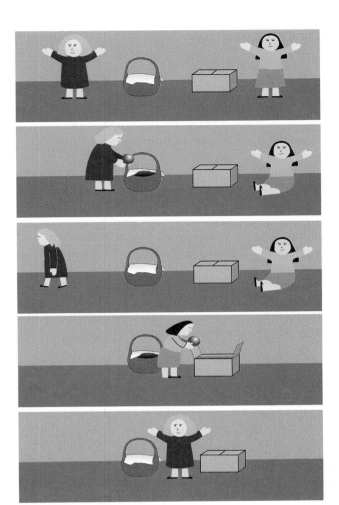

Figure 18.2
A test of the ability of children to understand what another person might be thinking. Sally has a marble and puts it in a basket and leaves the room. Anne takes it out of the basket and puts it into the box. Sally returns and wants to play with her marble. Where will she look for it? Autistic children were more likely to say "in the box."
(Adapted from Frith, U., Morton, J., and Leslie, A.M. *Trends in Neuroscience*, 1991, 14, 433–438.)

nine years said that Sally would look in the box. Apparently, they were unable to understand that people can hold beliefs different from their own.

Of course, this explanation does not account for all the symptoms of autism. For example, it does not explain why autistic children engage in stereotyped behaviors and seem to have a need for sameness in their environment. But it does suggest that a careful analysis of the syndrome may yield some hints about the underlying brain functions that are disrupted.

● Possible Causes

When Kanner first described autism, he suggested that it was of biological origin; but not long afterward, influential clinicians argued that autism was learned. More precisely, it was taught—by cold, insensitive, distant, demanding, introverted parents. Bettelheim (1967) believed that autism was similar to the apathetic, withdrawn, and hopeless behavior seen in some of the survivors of the German concentration camps of World War II. You can imagine the guilt felt by parents who were told by a mental health professional that they were to blame for their child's pitiful condition. Some professionals saw the existence of autism as evidence for child abuse and advocated that autistic children be removed from their families and placed with foster parents.

Nowadays, researchers and mental health professionals almost universally believe that autism is caused by biological factors and that parents should be given help and sympathy, not blame. Careful studies have shown that the parents of autistic children are just as warm, sociable, and responsive as other parents (Cox et al., 1975). In addition, parents with one autistic child often raise one or more normal children. If the parents were at fault, we should expect *all* of their offspring to be autistic.

Heritability

Like all the mental disorders I have described so far, at least some forms of autism appear to be heritable. As we shall see, there appear to be *several* hereditary causes, as well as some nonhereditary ones. Between 2 and 3 percent of the siblings of people with autism are themselves autistic (Folstein and Piven, 1991; Bailey, 1993). That figure may seem low, but it is between 50 and 100 times the expected frequency of autism in the general population (4 cases per 10,000 people). As Jones and Szatmari (1988) note, many parents stop having children after an autistic child is born for fear of having another one with the same disorder; if they did not, the percentage of autistic siblings would be even larger.

The best evidence for genetic factors in autism comes from twin studies. These studies indicate that the concordance rate for monozygotic twins is as high as 96 percent, while the rate for dizygotic twins appears to be no higher than that for normal siblings (Folstein and Piven, 1991; Bailey et al., 1995). This difference is extremely large and indicates that autism is highly heritable. It also implies that autism is caused by a combination of several genes. Folstein and Piven also report that in the relatively few cases of monozygotic twins who are discordant for autism, the affected member was likely to have had a history of ob-

stetric complications. This finding suggests that like schizophrenia and obsessive-compulsive disorder, autism can be caused by both hereditary and nonhereditary factors.

Investigators have suggested that autism is associated with some specific genetic disorders, such as phenylketonuria, Tourette's syndrome, and fragile X syndrome. **Phenylketonuria** (PKU) is caused by an inherited lack of an enzyme that converts phenylalanine (an amino acid) into tyrosine (another amino acid). Excessive amounts of phenylalanine in the blood interfere with the myelinization of neurons in the central nervous system, much of which takes place after birth. When PKU is diagnosed soon after birth, it can be treated by putting the infant on a low-phenylalanine diet. The diet keeps the blood level of phenylalanine low, and myelinization of the central nervous system takes place normally. However, if PKU is not diagnosed and an infant born with this disorder receives foods containing phenylalanine, the amino acid accumulates and the brain fails to develop normally. The result is a severe mental retardation—and, in some cases, autism (Lowe et al., 1980; Folstein and Rutter, 1988).

As we saw earlier in this chapter, obsessive-compulsive disorder and Tourette's syndrome appear to be linked genetically. The same may be true for autism. As several investigators have noted, children with autism show obsessive interest in particular inanimate objects and engage in compulsive, stereotyped behaviors and rituals; thus, there is some similarity between the symptoms of these three disorders. Comings and Comings (1991) note that autistic patients and patients with Tourette's syndrome have the following symptoms in common: "attention deficits, babbling, echolalia, palilalia, echopraxia, facial grimacing, hand flicking, hyperactivity, inappropriate anger, obsessive-compulsive behaviors, onset in childhood, panic at minor environmental change, perseveration, poor control of speech volume, sniffing and smelling of objects, [and] stereotyped movements" (p. 180). (*Palilalia* is incessant repetition of words and phrases, and *echopraxia* is imitation of motions made by other people.) Comings and Comings also note that previous studies reported forty-one cases of autistic patients who subsequently developed Tourette's syndrome and described sixteen more such patients. Sverd (1991) reported ten additional patients with symptoms of both autism and Tourette's syndrome whose families contained relatives with Tourette's syndrome and related disorders. Two of these cases are listed in *Table 18.2.*

phenylketonuria   A hereditary disorder caused by the absence of an enzyme that converts the amino acid phenylalanine to tyrosine; causes brain damage unless a special diet is implemented soon after birth.

Table 18.2
Symptoms and Family Histories of Two Patients with Autistic Disorder and Tourette's Syndrome

Patient	Autistic symptoms	Tourette's symptoms	Family history
Case 6 Anna 4 years old	Poor eye contact. Disregarded people and ran into them as if they did not exist. Sometimes too attached to mother. Inconsistent response to verbal stimuli. Preferred solitary play. Echolalic, pronominal reversal. Unable to initiate and engage in conversation. Lined up toys. Flicks light switch on and off. Hand flapping. Covers ears when upset. Acute episode of agitation and aggressivity.	Onset age 3—eye blinking, facial tics, repetitive face touching and pushing hair from face, growling noises.	Father—eye blinking. Uncle—head tics. Grandfather—mouth stretches, eye twitches, delusional episode. Great aunt—facial grimaces. Delusions she is a world-class musician. Great uncle—claimed he controlled weather with a machine. Maternal uncle—socially awkward as adult, socially isolated as schoolboy. Uncle—fidgety, tapped fingers. Grandfather—socially awkward.
Case 7 Ronald 8 years old	Ignored people. Ran over children as if they did not exist. Poor eye contact. "Doesn't know how to address children and get into their circle." Brings up irrelevant topics "out of blue." No imaginative play. Used single words until age 3. Echolalic. Lined up toys. Markedly restricted interests and activities. Hyperactive.	Onset age 6—eye blinking, head jerks, shoulder shrugs, hand clapping, finger snapping, throat clearing, clucking noises.	Father—head jerks, shoulder shrugs, eye blinking. Doesn't work. Paternal uncle—throat clearing, head jerks, doesn't work. Paternal grandfather—strange, impulsive, fidgety.

Source: Adapted from Sverd, J. *American Journal of Medical Genetics*, 1991, *39*, 173–179.

Another disorder, **fragile X syndrome,** is currently the leading hereditary cause of mental retardation. (As we will see in Chapter 19, alcoholism is the leading nonhereditary cause.) This syndrome, caused (as you might expect) by a faulty gene on the X chromosome, results in mental retardation and, sometimes, the symptoms of autism (Reiss and Freund, 1992). However, it seems likely that autistic symptoms are not specific to the fragile X syndrome but are simply an occasional consequence of mental retardation. Fisch (1992) analyzed previously published data and found that 5.4 percent of 1006 autistic males tested positive for the fragile X, compared with 5.5 percent of 5601 mentally retarded males. Not surprisingly, these percentages were not statistically different. In a subsequent study, Hallmayer et al. (1996) concluded that the X chromosome contained none of the genes that played a major role in the development of autism.

Brain Pathology

The fact that autism is highly heritable is presumptive evidence that the disorder is a result of structural or biochemical abnormalities in the brain. In addition, a variety of nongenetic pathological conditions can produce the symptoms of autism. For example, women who have contracted an infectious disease such as rubella (German measles) during pregnancy sometimes give birth to an autistic child (Chess, Fernandez, and Korn, 1971). Fernell, Gillberg, and Von Wendt (1991) found that 23 percent of children with infantile hydrocephalus showed autistic symptoms and that the severity of the hydrocephalus was correlated with the severity of the symptoms. Of course, hydrocephalus causes widespread brain damage, so this finding does not help us decide what part of the brain might be involved in autism.

Studies by Miller and Strömland (1993) and Strömland et al. (1994) suggests that events that interfere with prenatal development early in pregnancy can increase the likelihood of autism. Thalidomide, a drug that was given to pregnant women in some countries during the 1960s to treat the symptoms of morning sickness, was later found to cause serious birth defects. Miller, Strömland, and their colleagues studied eighty-six people whose mothers had taken thalidomide during pregnancy and found that five of them were autistic. (This rate is 145 times higher than the

fragile X syndrome   A genetic disorder caused by a faulty gene on the X chromosome; the leading genetic cause of mental retardation.

rate of autism in the population as a whole.) All of the autistic people had been exposed to thalidomide between prenatal days 20 and 24. As Rodier et al. (1996) note, the only part of the central nervous system that forms at this time is the brain stem.

Ritvo et al. (1990) found the presence of twelve rare diseases in 26 of 233 autistic individuals studied in an epidemiological survey. The authors estimate the probability of finding twelve such rare and diverse diseases in 11 percent of a random sample of the population at 16 in 100 million. Thus, we can safely conclude that the occurrence of these diseases is *not* due to chance and that the diseases are probably related to the development of the disorder. Besides providing further evidence that autism is caused by biological factors, this finding suggests that autism is not a single-disease entity but that its symptoms can be produced by several means.

Researchers have found evidence for both structural and biochemical abnormalities in the brains of autistics, but so far we cannot point to any single abnormality as the cause of the disorder. MRI scans and histological examination of the brains of deceased autistic patients have found evidence for abnormalities in the medial temporal lobe, the brain stem, and the cerebellum (DeLong, 1992; Happé and Frith, 1996). In a review of the literature, Courchesne (1991) concluded that the vermis of the cerebellum is less developed in cases of autism. In support of this conclusion, Holroyd, Reiss, and Bryan (1991) reported that *Joubert syndrome*, a genetic disorder that results in lack of development of the cerebellar vermis, produced symptoms of autism. Figure 18.3 shows midsagittal MRI scans of a normal subject and two patients with Joubert syndrome. As you can see, the vermis is absent or severely underdeveloped in the Joubert patients. (See *Figure 18.3.*) Although some studies failed to find cerebellar abnormalities in autistic patients, more recent ones support Courchesne's conclusion (Hashimoto et al., 1995; Haas et al., 1996). *Why* cerebellar abnormalities might produce the symptoms of autism is not at all clear. There is no evidence that damage to the cerebellum later in life—or damage to any other part of the brain, for that matter—causes pure autism (Happé and Frith, 1996). Thus, autism seems to be a result of some combination of brain abnormalities that occurs only during development.

Interim Summary

Autistic disorder occurs in 3–5 out of 10,000 infants. It is characterized by poor or absent social relations, communicative abilities, and imaginative abilities and the presence of repetitive, purposeless movements. Although autis-

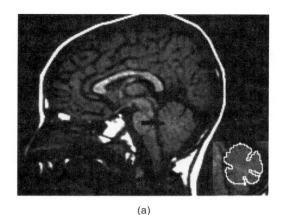

(a)

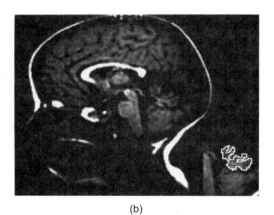

(b)

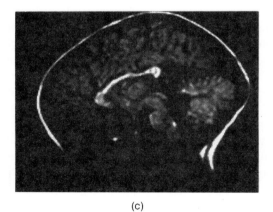

(c)

Figure 18.3
Midsagittal MRI scans. The cerebellar vermis is shown in the lower right corner of each panel, outlined in white. (a) From a normal child. (b) and (c) From two children with Joubert syndrome, who also showed symptoms of autism. The vermis is completely lacking in (c).
(From Holroyd, S., Reiss, A.L., and Bryan, R.N. *Biological Psychiatry,* 1991, *29,* 287–294. Reprinted with permission.)

tics are usually, but not always, retarded, they may have a particular, isolated, talent. Some investigators believe that the most important cognitive deficit is the inability to imagine what others know or think about something and how they feel.

In the past, clinicians blamed parents for autism, but now it is generally accepted as a disorder with biological roots. Twin studies have shown that autism is highly heritable but that several genes are responsible for its development. It is often associated with Tourette's syndrome (as obsessive-compulsive disorder is) and can be caused by untreated phenylketonuria. Some investigators have suggested a link with fragile X syndrome, the leading genetic cause of mental retardation, but more recent research suggests that the two disorders are independent. Autism can also be caused by events that interfere with prenatal development, such as drugs or maternal infection with rubella; with hydrocephalus; and with a wide variety of rare diseases. MRI studies suggest that autism is associated with abnormalities in the medial temporal lobe, the brain stem, and the cerebellum.

STRESS DISORDERS

Aversive stimuli can harm people's health. Many of these harmful effects are produced not by the stimuli themselves but by our reactions to them. Walter Cannon, the physiologist who criticized the James–Lange theory described in Chapter 11, introduced the term **stress** to refer to the physiological reaction caused by the perception of aversive or threatening situations.

The word *stress* was borrowed from engineering, in which it refers to the action of physical forces of mechanical structures. The word can be a noun or a verb; and the noun can refer to situations or the individual's response to them. Because of this potential confusion, I will refer to "stressful" stimuli and situations as **stressors** and to the individual's reaction as a **stress response.** The word *stress* will refer to the general process (as in the title to this section).

The physiological responses that accompany the negative emotions prepare us to threaten rivals or fight them, or to run away from dangerous situations. Walter Cannon in-

stress A general, imprecise term that can refer either to a stress response or to a stressor (stressful situation).

stressor A stimulus (or situation) that produces a stress response.

stress response A physiological reaction caused by the perception of aversive or threatening situations.

fight-or-flight response A species-typical response preparatory to fighting or fleeing; thought to be responsible for some of the deleterious effects of stressful situations on health.

troduced the phrase **fight-or-flight response** to refer to the physiological reactions that prepare us for the strenuous efforts required by fighting or running away. Normally, once we have bluffed or fought with an adversary or run away from a dangerous situation, the threat is over and our physiological condition can return to normal. The fact that the physiological responses may have adverse long-term effects on our health is unimportant as long as the responses are brief. But sometimes, the threatening situations are continuous rather than episodic, producing a more or less continuous stress response.

● Physiology of the Stress Response

As we saw in Chapter 11, emotions consist of behavioral, autonomic, and endocrine responses. The latter two components, the autonomic and endocrine responses, are the ones that can have adverse effects on health. (Well, I guess the behavioral components can, too, if a person rashly gets into a fight with someone much bigger and stronger.) Because threatening situations generally call for vigorous activity, the autonomic and endocrine responses that accompany them are catabolic; that is, they help to mobilize the body's energy resources. The sympathetic branch of the autonomic nervous system is active, and the adrenal glands secrete epinephrine, norepinephrine, and steroid stress hormones. Because the effects of sympathetic activity are similar to those of the adrenal hormones, I will limit my discussion to the hormonal responses.

Epinephrine affects glucose metabolism, causing the nutrients stored in muscles to become available to provide energy for strenuous exercise. Along with norepinephrine, the hormone also increases blood flow to the muscles by increasing the output of the heart. In doing so, it also increases blood pressure, which, over the long term, contributes to cardiovascular disease.

Besides serving as a stress hormone, norepinephrine is (as you know) secreted in the brain as a neurotransmitter. Some of the behavioral and physiological responses produced by aversive stimuli appear to be mediated by noradrenergic neurons. For example, microdialysis studies have found that stressful situations increase the release of norepinephrine in the hypothalamus, frontal cortex, and lateral basal forebrain (Yokoo et al. 1990; Cenci et al. 1992). Montero, Fuentes, and Fernandez-Tome (1990) found that destruction of the noradrenergic axons that ascend from the brain stem to the forebrain prevented the rise in blood pressure that is normally produced by social isolation stress. Presumably, the release of norepinephrine in the brain is produced by a pathway from the central nucleus of the amygdala to the norepinephrine-secreting regions of the brain stem (Wallace, Magnuson, and Gray, 1992).

The other stress-related hormone is *cortisol,* a steroid secreted by the adrenal cortex. Cortisol is called a **glucocorticoid** because it has profound effects on glucose metabolism. (Aldosterone, the other steroid secreted by the adrenal cortex, is called a *mineralocorticoid* because of its effects on sodium metabolism, which were described in Chapter 12.) In addition, glucocorticoids help break down protein and convert it to glucose, help make fats available for energy, increase blood flow, and stimulate behavioral responsiveness, presumably by affecting the brain. They decrease the sensitivity of the gonads to luteinizing hormone (LH), which suppresses the secretion of the sex steroid hormones. In fact, Singer and Zumoff (1992) found that the blood level of testosterone in male hospital residents was severely depressed, presumably because of the stressful work schedule they are obliged to follow. Glucocorticoids have other physiological effects, too, some of which are only poorly understood. Almost every cell in the body contains glucocorticoid receptors, which means that few of them are unaffected by these hormones.

The secretion of glucocorticoids is controlled by neurons in the paraventricular nucleus of the hypothalamus (PVN), whose axons terminate in the median eminence, where the hypothalamic capillaries of the portal blood supply to the anterior pituitary gland are located. (The pituitary portal blood supply was described in Chapter 3.) The neurons of the PVN secrete a peptide called **corticotropin-releasing factor (CRF),** which stimulates the anterior pituitary gland to secrete **adrenocorticotropic hormone (ACTH).** ACTH enters the general circulation and stimulates the adrenal cortex to secrete glucocorticoids. (See *Figure 18.4.*)

CRF is also secreted within the brain, where it serves as a neuromodulator/neurotransmitter, especially in regions of the limbic system involved in emotional responses, such as the periaqueductal gray matter, the locus coeruleus, and the central nucleus of the amygdala. The behavioral effects produced by an injection of CRF into the brain are similar to those produced by aversive situations; thus, some elements of the stress response appear to be produced by the release of CRF by neurons in the brain. For example, intracerebroventricular injection of CRF decreases the amount of time a rat spends in the center of a large open chamber (Britton et al., 1982), it enhances the acquisition of a classically conditioned fear response (Cole and Koob, 1988), and it increases the startle response elicited by a sudden loud noise (Swerdlow et al., 1986). On the other hand, intracerebroventricular injection of a CRF antagonist *reduces* the anxiety caused by a variety of stressful situations (Kalin, Sherman, and Takahaski, 1988; Heinrichs, et al., 1994; Skutella et al., 1994).

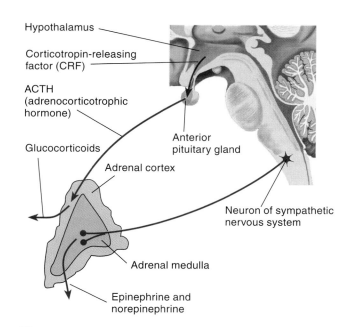

Figure 18.4
Control of the secretion of glucocorticoids by the adrenal cortex and of catecholamines by the adrenal medulla.

The secretion of glucocorticoids does more than help an animal react to a stressful situation: It helps the animal survive. If a rat's adrenal glands are removed, it becomes much more susceptible to the effects of stress. In fact, a stressful situation that a normal rat would take in its stride may kill one whose adrenal glands have been removed. And physicians know that if an adrenalectomized human is subjected to stressors, he or she must be given additional amounts of glucocorticoid (Tyrell and Baxter, 1981).

● Health Effects of Long-Term Stress

Many studies of humans who have been subjected to stressful situations have found evidence of ill health. For example, survivors of concentration camps, who were ob-

glucocorticoid   One of a group of hormones of the adrenal cortex that are important in protein and carbohydrate metabolism, secreted especially in times of stress.

corticotropin-releasing factor (CRF)   A hypothalamic hormone that stimulates the anterior pituitary gland to secrete ACTH (adrenocorticotrophic hormone).

adrenocorticotropic hormone (ACTH)   A hormone released by the anterior pituitary gland in response to CRF; stimulates the adrenal cortex to produce glucocorticoids.

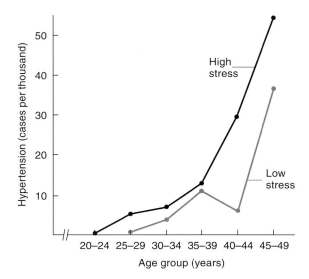

Figure 18.5
Incidence of hypertension in various age groups of air traffic controllers at high-stress and low-stress airports.
(Based on data from Cobb and Rose, 1973.)

viously subjected to long-term stress, have generally poorer health later in life than other people of the same age (Cohen, 1953). Drivers of subway trains that injure or kill people are more likely to suffer from illnesses several months later (Theorell et al., 1992). Air traffic controllers—especially those who work at busy airports where the danger of collisions is greatest—show a greater incidence of high blood pressure, which gets worse as they grow older (Cobb and Rose, 1973). (See **Figure 18.5.**) They also are more likely to suffer from ulcers or diabetes.

A pioneer in the study of stress, Hans Selye, suggested that most of the harmful effects of stress were produced by the prolonged secretion of glucocorticoids (Selye, 1976). Although the short-term effects of glucocorticoids are essential, the long-term effects are damaging. These effects include increased blood pressure, damage to muscle tissue, steroid diabetes, infertility, inhibition of growth, inhibition of the inflammatory responses, and suppression of the immune system. High blood pressure can lead to heart attacks and stroke. Inhibition of growth in children who are subjected to prolonged stress prevents them from attaining their full height. Inhibition of the inflammatory response makes it more difficult for the body to heal itself after an injury, and suppression of the immune system makes an individual vulnerable to infections and (perhaps) cancer.

The adverse effects of stress on healing were demonstrated in a study by Kiecold-Glaser et al. (1995), who performed punch biopsy wounds in the subjects' forearms, a

harmless procedure used often in medical research. The subjects were people who were providing long-term care for relatives with Alzheimer's disease—a situation known to cause stress—and control subjects of the same approximate age and family income. The investigators found that healing of the wounds took significantly longer in the caregivers (48.7 days versus 39.3 days). (See **Figure 18.6.**)

Sapolsky and his colleagues have investigated one rather serious long-term effect of stress: brain damage. As you learned in Chapter 15, the hippocampal formation plays a crucial role in learning and memory, and evidence suggests that one of the causes of memory loss that occurs with aging is degeneration of this brain structure. Research with animals has shown that long-term exposure to glucocorticoids destroys neurons located in field CA1 of the hippocampal formation. The hormone appears to destroy the neurons by making them more susceptible to potentially harmful events, such as decreased blood flow, which often occurs as a result of the aging process. The primary effect of the hormone is to lower the ability of the neurons in the hippocampus to utilize glucose, so when the blood flow decreases, their metabolism falls and they begin to die (Sapolsky, 1986; Sapolsky, Krey, and McEwen, 1986). Perhaps, then, the stressors to which people are subjected throughout their lives increases the likelihood of memory

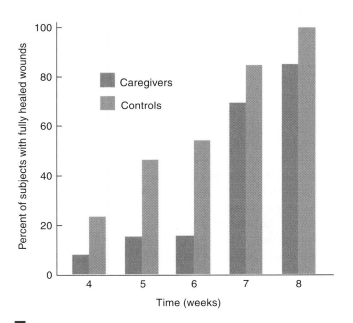

Figure 18.6
Percentage of caregivers and control subjects whose wounds had healed as a function of time after the biopsy was performed.
(Adapted from Kiecolt-Glaser, J.K., Marucha, P.T., Malarkey, W.B., Mercado, A.M., and Glaser, R. *Lancet*, 1995, *346*, 1194–1196.)

problems as they grow older. In fact, Lupien et al. (1996) found that elderly people with elevated blood levels of glucocorticoids learned a maze more slowly than did those with normal levels.

Uno et al. (1989) found that if stress is intense enough, it can even cause brain damage in young primates. The investigators studied a colony of vervet monkeys housed in a primate center in Kenya. They found that some monkeys died, apparently from stress. Vervet monkeys have a hierarchical society, and monkeys near the bottom of the hierarchy are picked on by the others; thus, they are almost continuously subjected to stress. (Ours is not the only species with social structures that cause a stress reaction in some of its members.) The deceased monkeys had gastric ulcers and enlarged adrenal glands, which are signs of chronic stress. And as Figure 18.7 shows, neurons in the CA1 field of their hippocampal formation were completely destroyed. (See *Figure 18.7.*) Severe stress appears to cause brain damage in humans as well; Jensen, Genefke, and Hyldebrandt (1982) found evidence of brain degeneration in CT scans of people who had been subjected to torture.

As we saw in Chapter 10, prenatal stress tends to inhibit androgenization of the fetuses. That is, when a pregnant female is exposed to stressors, the behavior and brain structure of her male offspring appear less masculinized and defeminized than control animals. Prenatal stress also appears to produce long-term effects on animals' stress reactions; Takahashi, Turner, and Kalin (1992) found that rats whose mothers had been stressed reacted more strongly when they were presented with stressful stimuli during adulthood.

The effects of prenatal stress, like the effects of stress in adulthood, appear to be mediated by the secretion of glucocorticoids. Barbazanges et al. (1996) subjected pregnant female rats to stress and later observed the effects of stress on their offspring in adulthood. They found that the prenatally stressed rats showed a prolonged secretion of glucocorticoids when they were subjected to restraint stress (placement in a small chamber. However, if the mothers' adrenal glands had been removed so that glucocorticoids could not be secreted during the stressful situation, their offspring reacted normally in adulthood. (The experimenters gave the adrenalectomized mothers controlled amounts of glucocorticoids to maintain them in good health.) (See *Figure 18.8.*)

● Posttraumatic Stress Disorder

The aftermath of tragic and traumatic events such as those that accompany wars and natural disasters often includes psychological symptoms that persist long after the stressful

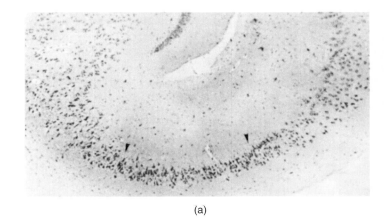

(a)

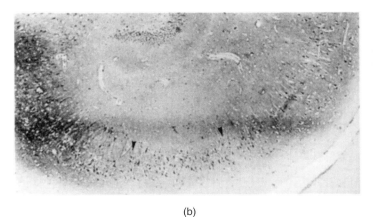

(b)

Figure 18.7
Photomicrographs showing brain damage caused by stress.
(a) Section through the hippocampus of a normal monkey.
(b) Section through the hippocampus of a monkey of low social status subjected to stress. Compare the regions between the arrowheads, normally filled with large pyramidal cells.
(From Uno, H., Tarara, R., Else, J.G., Suleman, M.A., and Sapolsky, R.M. *Journal of Neuroscience,* 1989, 9, 1706–1711. Reprinted by permission of the *Journal of Neuroscience.*)

events are over. According to the DSM IV, **posttraumatic stress disorder** is caused by a situation in which a person "experienced, witnessed, or was confronted with an event or events that involved actual or threatened death or serious injury, or a threat to the physical integrity of self or others" that provoked a response that "involved intense fear, helplessness, or horror." The symptoms produced by such

posttraumatic stress disorder A psychological disorder caused by exposure to a situation of extreme danger and stress; symptoms include recurrent dreams or recollections; can interfere with social activities and a feeling of hopelessness.

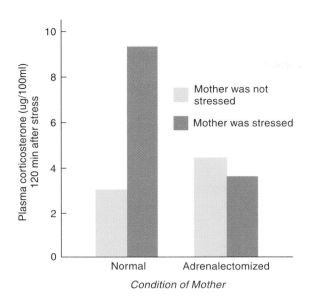

Figure 18.8
Effects of prenatal stress and glucocorticoid level on the stress response of adult rats. Adrenalectomy of the mother before she was subjected to stress prevented the development of an elevated stress response in the offspring during adulthood.
(Adapted from Barbazanges, A., Piazza, P.V., Le Moal, M., and Maccari, S. *Journal of Neuroscience*, 1996, 16, 3943–3949.)

exposure include recurrent dreams or recollections of the event, feelings that the traumatic event is recurring ("flashback" episodes), and intense psychological distress. These dreams, recollections, or flashback episodes lead the person to avoid thinking about the traumatic event, which often results in diminished interest in social activities, feelings of detachment from others, suppressed emotional feelings, and a sense that the future is bleak and empty. Particular psychological symptoms include difficulty falling or staying asleep, irritability, outbursts of anger, difficulty in concentrating, and heightened reactions to sudden noises or movements.

Posttraumatic stress disorder can strike people at any age. Children may show particular symptoms that are not usually seen in adulthood, such as loss of recently acquired language skills or toilet training, and somatic complaints such as stomachaches and headaches. Usually, the symptoms begin immediately after the traumatic event, but they are sometimes delayed for several months or years.

Some studies suggest that preexisting personality factors may play a role in the development of posttraumatic stress disorder. For example, Mikulincer and Solomon (1988) studied Israeli soldiers who suffered a combat stress reaction during the 1982 war in Lebanon and found that those who tended to brood about their feelings were more likely to go on to develop posttraumatic stress disorder. The National Vietnam Veterans Readjustment Study carried out by the U.S. government found that four factors increased the likelihood that a soldier subjected to combat stress would develop posttraumatic stress disorder: being raised in a household with financial difficulty, having a history of drug abuse or dependency, having a history of affective disorders, and having a history of childhood behavior problems (Kulka et al., 1990). Because heredity plays an important role in shaping people's personality traits, we might expect that genetic factors might play some role in determining a person's susceptibility to developing posttraumatic stress disorder. In fact, twin studies indicate that they do (True et al., 1993).

As we will see in Chapter 19, evidence suggests that the presence of a particular allele of the gene responsible for the production of the dopamine D_2 receptor may be associated with susceptibility to developing alcoholism. Comings, Muhleman, and Gysin (1996) found that the presence of this allele (the A1 allele) may also be associated with susceptibility to developing posttraumatic stress disorder. The investigators studied a group of Vietnam veterans who had been exposed to severe combat stress and found that 61.5 percent of those with posttraumatic stress disorder possessed the A1 allele, whereas only 5.3 percent of those without the disorder possessed this allele.

As we saw earlier, prolonged exposure to glucocorticoids can cause brain damage, particularly in the hippocampus. At least two MRI studies have found evidence of hippocampal damage in veterans with combat-related posttraumatic stress disorder (Bremner et al., 1995; Gurvits et al., 1996). In the study by Gurvits et al., the volume of the hippocampal formation was reduced by over 20 percent, and the loss was proportional to the amount of combat exposure the veteran had experienced.

A PET study by Shin et al. (1997) investigated the effects of combat-related imagery on regional cerebral metabolism. The experimenters showed combat veterans with and without posttraumatic stress disorder pictures that showed innocuous items or combat-related items, such as bodybags (the plastic bags in which soldiers killed in battle were placed). Then while the subjects' heads were placed in the PET scanner, the experimenters read aloud sentences concerning the pictures the subjects had seen and asked them to imagine them. Imagining the combat-related pictures increased the activity in the anterior cingulate gyrus and right amygdala of the subjects with posttraumatic stress disorder, relative to control subjects. As we saw in Chapters 11 and earlier sections of this chapter, both of these brain regions are involved in reactions to situations that provoke anxiety and other negative emotional reactions.

Stress and Cardiovascular Disease

One of the most important causes of death is cardiovascular diseases—diseases of the heart and the blood vessels. Cardiovascular diseases can cause heart attacks and strokes; heart attacks occur when the blood vessels that serve the heart become blocked, while strokes involve the blood vessels in the brain. The two most important risk factors in cardiovascular disease are high blood pressure and a high level of cholesterol in the blood.

The degree to which people react to potential stressors may affect the likelihood that they will suffer from cardiovascular disease. For example, Wood et al. (1984) examined the blood pressure of people who had been subjected to a *cold pressor test* in 1934, when they were children. The cold pressor test reveals how people's blood pressure reacts to the stress caused by their hand being placed in a container of ice water for 1 minute. Wood and his colleagues found that 70 percent of the subjects who hyperreacted to cold pressor test when they were children had high blood pressure, compared with 19 percent of those who showed little reaction to the test.

A study with monkeys showed that individual differences in emotional reactivity are a risk factor for cardiovascular disease. Manuck et al. (1983, 1986) fed a high-cholesterol diet to a group of monkeys, which increases the likelihood of their developing coronary artery disease. They measured the animals' emotional reactivity by threatening to capture the animals. (Monkeys avoid contact with humans, and they perceive being captured as a stressful situation.) The animals who showed the strongest negative reactions eventually developed the highest rates of coronary artery disease. Presumably, these animals reacted more strongly to all types of stressors, and their reactions had detrimental effects on their health.

Apparently, at least some of the differences in emotional reactivity displayed by individual animals are caused by genetic differences in brain chemistry and function. Eilam et al. (1991) transplanted some tissue from the hypothalamus of genetically hypertensive rats into normal rats and found that the blood pressure of the recipient rats increased by an average of 31 percent. (Transplants of hypothalamic tissue from normotensive rats did not increase recipients' blood pressure.) (See *Figure 18.9.*)

The Coping Response

As we have seen, many of the harmful effects of long-term stress are caused by our own reactions primarily the secre-

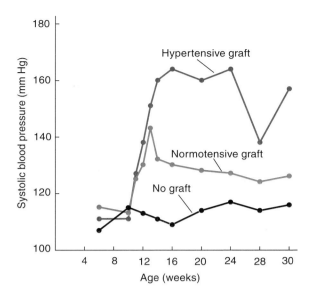

Figure 18.9
Systolic blood pressure in normal rats, rats with grafts of hypothalamic tissue from normal rats, and rats with grafts from genetically hypertensive rats.
(Adapted from Eilam, R., Malach, R., Bergmann, F., and Segal, M. *Journal of Neuroscience,* 1991, *11,* 401–411.)

tion of stress hormones. Some events that cause stress responses, such as prolonged exertion or extreme cold, cause damage directly. These stressors will affect everyone; their severity will depend on each person's physical capacity. The effects of other stressors, such as situations that cause fear or anxiety, depend on people's perceptions and emotional reactivity. That is, because of individual differences in temperament or experience with a particular situation, some people may find a situation stressful and others may not. In these cases it is the perception that counts.

One of the most important variables that determines whether an aversive stimulus will cause a stress reaction is the degree to which the situation can be controlled. As we saw in Chapter 11, when an animal can learn a *coping response* that avoids contact with an aversive stimulus or decreases its severity, its emotional response will disappear. Weiss (1968) found that rats who learned to minimize (but not completely avoid) shocks by making a response whenever they heard a warning tone developed fewer stomach ulcers than did rats who had no control over the shocks. The effect was not caused by the pain itself, because both groups of animals received exactly the same number of shocks. Thus, being able to exert some control over an aversive situation reduces an animal's stress response. Humans react similarly. Situations that permit some control are less likely to produce signs of stress than those in which other people (or machines) control the situation (Gatchel, Baum, and Krantz, 1989). Perhaps this phenomenon explains why some people like to have a magic charm or other "security blanket" with them in stressful situations. Perhaps even the *illusion* of control can be reassuring.

We do not yet understand the neural mechanisms responsible for coping responses, but a study by Drugan et al. (1994) suggests that one of their effects may be the secretion of endogenous benzodiazepines. The experimenters trained rats in a task similar to the one by Weiss (1968) that I just described. That is, all rats received shocks from time to time, but only the rats in the "coping" group could turn the shock off by making a response. As we just saw, the ability to make a coping response reduces stress. Drugan and his colleagues found that the level of endogenous benzodiazepines in the brain was higher in the animals in the "coping" group, compared with animals who rested in their home cages or those who had no control over the shock. As we saw in Chapter 4, endogenous benzodiazepines are neuromodulators produced in the brain that serve as ligands for binding sites on the GABA$_A$ receptor. They have the same anxiolytic effects as the benzodiazepine drugs such as Valium. (See *Figure 18.10.*)

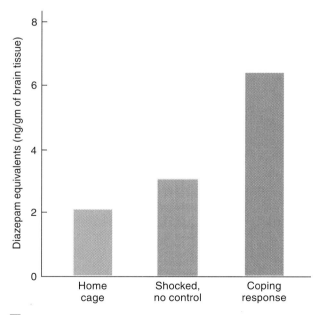

Figure 18.10
Mean levels of endogenous benzodiazepine receptor agonists in normal control rats, rats who were able to make a coping response, and rats who received inescapable shock.
(Adapted from Drugan, R.C., Basile, A.S., Ha, J.-.H., and Ferland, R.J. *Brain Research,* 1994, 661, 127–136.)

● Psychoneuroimmunology

As we have seen, long-term stress can be harmful to one's health and can even result in brain damage. The most important cause of these effects is elevated levels of glucocorticoids, but the high blood pressure caused by epinephrine and norepinephrine also plays a contributing role. In addition, the stress response can impair the functions of the immune system, which protects us from assault from viruses, microbes, fungi, and other types of parasites. Study of the interactions between the immune system and behavior (mediated by the nervous system, of course) is called **psychoneuroimmunology.** This relatively new field is described in the following subsection.

The Immune System

The immune system is one of the most complex systems of the body. Its function is to protect us from infection; and because infectious organisms have developed devious tricks through the process of evolution, our immune system has evolved devious tricks of its own. The description I provide here is abbreviated and simplified, but it presents some of the important elements of the system.

The immune system derives from white blood cells that develop in the bone marrow and in the thymus gland. Some of the cells roam through the blood or lymphatic system; others reside permanently in one place. The immune reaction occurs when the body is invaded by foreign organisms, including bacteria, fungi, and viruses. Two types of reactions occur, *nonspecific* and *specific*. One nonspecific reaction, called the *inflammatory reaction*, occurs early, in response to tissue damage produced by an invading organism. The damaged tissue secretes substances that increase the local blood circulation and make capillaries leak fluids, which causes the region to become inflamed. The secretions also attract phagocytic white blood cells that destroy both the invading cells and the debris produced by the breakdown of the body's own cells. Another nonspecific reaction occurs when a virus infects a cell. The infection causes the cell to release a peptide called *interferon*, which suppresses the ability of viruses to reproduce. In addition, **natural killer cells** continuously prowl through tissue; when they encounter a cell that has been infected by a virus or that has become transformed into a cancer cell,

psychoneuroimmunology The branch of neuroscience involved with interactions between environmental stimuli, the nervous system, and the immune system.

natural killer cell A white blood cell that destroys cancer cells or cells infected by viruses.

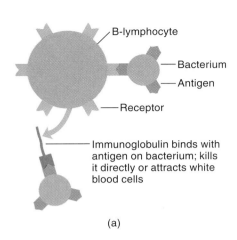

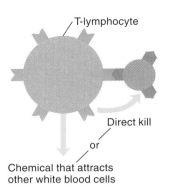

(a)   (b)

Figure 18.11
Immune reactions. (a) Chemically mediated reaction. The B-lymphocyte detects an antigen on a bacterium and releases a specific immunoglobulin. (b) Cell-mediated reaction. The T-lymphocyte detects an antigen on a bacterium and kills it directly or releases a chemical that attracts other white blood cells.

they engulf and destroy it. Thus, natural killer cells constitute one of our first defense against the development of malignant tumors.

The immune system produces two types of specific immune reactions: *chemically mediated* and *cell-mediated.* Chemically mediated immune reactions involve antibodies. Infectious microorganisms have unique proteins on their surfaces, called **antigens.** These proteins serve as the invaders' calling cards, identifying them to the immune system. Through exposure to the microorganisms, the immune system learns to recognize these proteins. (I will not try to explain the mechanism by which this learning takes place.) The result of this learning is the development of special lines of cells that produce specific **antibodies**—proteins that recognize antigens and help kill the invading microorganism. One type of antibody is released into the circulation by **B-lymphocytes,** which receive their name from the fact that they develop in bone marrow. These antibodies, called **immunoglobulins,** are chains of protein. Each type of immunoglobulin (there are five of them) is identical except for one end, which contains a unique receptor. A particular receptor binds with a particular antigen, just as a molecule of a hormone or neurotransmitter binds with its receptor. When the appropriate line of B-lymphocytes detects the presence of an invading bacterium, the cells release their antibodies, which bind with the antigens present on the surface of the invading microorganisms. The antigens either kill the invaders directly or attract other white blood cells, which then destroy them. (See *Figure 18.11a.*)

The other type of defense by the immune system, cell-mediated immune reactions, is produced by **T-lymphocytes,** which originally develop in the thymus gland. These cells also produce antibodies, but the antibodies remain attached to the outside of their membrane. T-lymphocytes primarily defend the body against fungi, viruses, and multicellular parasites. When antigens bind with their surface antibodies, the cells either directly kill the invaders or signal other white blood cells to come and kill them. (See *Figure 18.11b.*)

The reactions illustrated in Figure 18.11 are much simplified; actually, both chemically mediated and cell-mediated immune reactions involve several different types of cells. The communication between these cells is accomplished by **cytokines,** chemicals that stimulate cell division. The cytokines released by certain white blood cells when an invading microorganism is detected (principally *interleukin-1* and *interleukin-2*) cause other white blood

---

antigen A protein present on a microorganism that permits the immune system to recognize it as an invader.

antibody A protein produced by a cell of the immune system that recognizes antigens present on invading microorganisms.

B-lymphocyte A white blood cell that originates in the bone marrow; part of the immune system.

immunoglobulin An antibody released by B-lymphocytes that bind with antigens and help destroy invading microorganisms.

T-lymphocyte A white blood cell that originates in the thymus gland; part of the immune system.

cytokine A category of chemicals released by certain white blood cells when they detect the presence of an invading microorganism; causes other white blood cells to proliferate and mount an attack against the invader.

cells to proliferate and direct an attack against the invader. The primary way in which glucocorticoids suppress specific immune responses is by interfering with the messages conveyed by the cytokines (Sapolsky, 1992).

Neural Control of the Immune System

As we will see in the next subsection, the stress response can increase the likelihood of infectious diseases. It may even affect the growth of cancers. What is the physiological explanation for these effects? One answer, probably the most important one, is that stress increases the secretion of glucocorticoids, and as we saw, these hormones directly suppress the activity of the immune system.

A direct relation between stress and the immune system was demonstrated by Kiecolt-Glaser et al. (1987). These investigators found that caregivers of family members with Alzheimer's disease, who certainly underwent considerable stress, showed weaker immune systems, based on several different laboratory tests. Bereavement, another source of stress, also suppresses the immune system. Schleifer et al. (1983) tested the husbands of women with breast cancer and found that their immune response was lower after their wives died. (See *Figure 18.12.*) Knapp et al. (1992) even found that when healthy subjects imagined themselves reliving unpleasant emotional experiences, the immune response measured in samples of their blood was decreased.

Several studies indicate that the suppression of the immune response by stress is largely mediated by glucocorticoids. For example, in a study with rats, Keller et al. (1983) found that the stress of inescapable shock decreased the number of lymphocytes (B-cells, T-cells, and natural killer cells) found in the blood. This effect was abolished by removal of the adrenal glands; thus, it appears to have been caused by the release of glucocorticoids triggered by the stress response. (See *Figure 18.13a.*) However, the same authors found that adrenalectomy did *not* abolish the effects of stress on another type of immune response: stimulation of lymphocytes by an antigen. (See *Figure 18.13b.*) Thus, not all the effects of stress on the immune system are mediated by glucocorticoids; there must be other mechanisms as well.

Because the secretion of glucocorticoids is controlled by the brain (through its secretion of CRF), the brain is obviously responsible for the suppressing effect of these hormones on the immune system. Neurons in the central nucleus of the amygdala send axons to CRF-secreting neurons in the paraventricular nucleus of the hypothalamus; thus, we can reasonably expect that the mechanism responsible

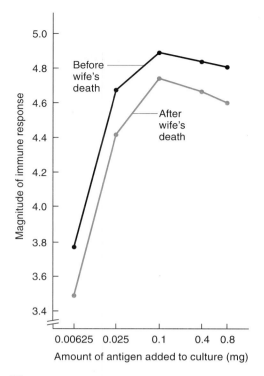

Figure 18.12
Stimulation of white blood cell (lymphocyte) production by an antigen in blood of husbands before and after their wives' death.
(Adapted from Schleifer, S.J., Keller, S.E., Camerino, M., Thornton, J.C., and Stein, M. *Journal of the American Medical Association,* 1983, *250,* 374–377.)

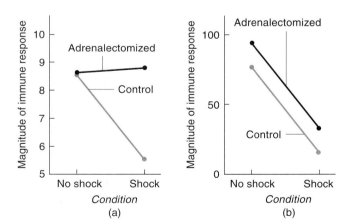

Figure 18.13
Effects of removal of rats' adrenal glands on the suppression of the immune system by inescapable shocks. (a) Number of white blood cells (lymphocytes) found in the blood. (b) Stimulation of lymphocyte production after exposure to an antigen.
(Based on data from Keller, Weiss, Schleifer, Miller, and Stein, 1983.)

for negative emotional responses is also responsible for the stress response and the immunosuppression that accompanies it. Several studies have shown that stress increases the activity of neurons in brain regions that have been shown to play a role in emotional responses, including the central nucleus of the amygdala and the PVN (Sharp et al., 1991; Imaki et al., 1992).

Some of the stress-induced immunosuppression that does not involve the secretion of glucocorticoids may be under direct neural control. The bone marrow, the thymus gland, and the lymph nodes all receive neural input. Although researchers have not yet obtained direct proof that this input modulates immune function, it would be surprising if it did not. In addition, the immune system appears to be sensitive to chemicals produced by the nervous system. The best evidence comes from studies with the opioids produced by the brain. Shavit et al. (1984) found that inescapable intermittent shock produced both analgesia (decreased sensitivity to pain) and suppression of the production of natural killer cells. These effects both seem to have been mediated by endogenous opioids, because both effects were abolished when the experimenters administered a drug that blocks opiate receptors. Shavit et al. (1986) found that natural killer cell activity could be suppressed by injecting morphine directly into the brain; thus, the effect of the opiates appears to take place in the brain. The mechanism by which the brain affects the natural killer cells is not yet known.

Stress and Infectious Diseases

Often when a married person dies, his or her spouse dies soon afterward, frequently of an infection. In fact, a wide variety of stress-producing events in a person's life can increase the susceptibility to illness. For example, Glaser et al. (1987) found that medical students were more likely to contract acute infections and to show evidence of suppression of the immune system during the time that final examinations were given. In addition, autoimmune diseases often get worse when a person is subjected to stress, as Feigenbaum, Masi, and Kaplan (1979) found for rheumatoid arthritis. In a laboratory study, Rogers et al. (1980) found that when rats were stressed by handling them or exposing them to a cat, they developed a more severe case of an artificially induced autoimmune disease. Lehman et al. (1991) found that the incidence of diabetes in a strain of rats that are susceptible to this autoimmune disease was considerably higher when the animals were subjected to moderate chronic stress.

Stone, Reed, and Neale (1987) attempted to see whether stressful events in people's daily lives might predispose them to upper respiratory infection. If a person is exposed to a microorganism that might cause such a disease, the symptoms do not occur for several days; that is, there is an incubation period between exposure and signs of the actual illness. Thus, the authors reasoned that if stressful events suppressed the immune system, one might expect to see a higher likelihood of respiratory infections several days after such stress. To test their hypothesis, they asked volunteers to keep a daily record of desirable and undesirable events in their lives over a twelve-week period. The volunteers also kept a daily record of any discomfort or symptoms of illness.

The results were as predicted: During the three-to-five-day period just before showing symptoms of an upper respiratory infection, people experienced an increased number of undesirable events and a decreased number of desirable events in their lives. (See *Figure 18.14*.) Stone et al. (1987) suggest that the effect is caused by decreased production of a particular immunoglobulin that is present in the secretions of mucous membranes, including those in the nose, mouth, throat, and lungs. This immunoglobulin, IgA, serves as the first defense against infectious microorganisms that enter the nose or mouth. They found

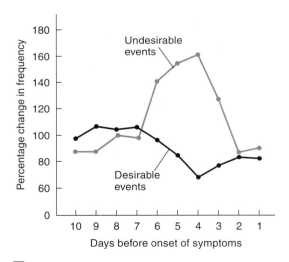

Figure 18.14
Mean percentage change in frequency of undesirable and desirable events during the ten-day period preceding the onset of symptoms of upper respiratory infections.
(Based on data from Stone, A.A., Reed, B.R., and Neale, J.M. *Journal of Human Stress*, 1987, *13*, 70–74.)

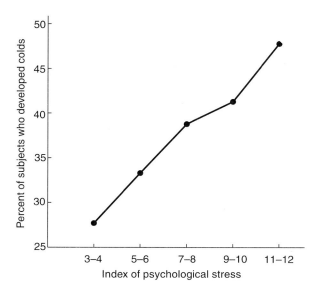

Figure 18.15
Percent of subjects with colds as a function of an index of psychological stress.
(Adapted from Cohen, S., Tyrrell, D.A.J., and Smith, A.P. *New England Journal of Medicine*, 1991, *325*, 606–612.)

that IgA is associated with mood; when a subject is unhappy or depressed, its levels are lower than normal. The results suggest that the stress caused by undesirable events may, by suppressing the production of IgA, lead to a rise in the likelihood of upper respiratory infections.

The results of the study by Stone and his colleagues were confirmed by an experiment by Cohen, Tyrrell, and Smith (1991). The investigators found that subjects who were given nasal drops containing cold viruses were much more likely to develop colds if they reported stressful experiences during the past year and if they said they felt threatened, out of control, or overwhelmed by events. (See *Figure 18.15.*)

Interim Summary

People's emotional reactions to aversive stimuli can harm their health. The stress response, which Cannon called the fight-or-flight response, is useful as a short-term response to threatening stimuli but is harmful in the long term. This response includes increased activity of the sympathetic branch of the autonomic nervous system and increased se-

cretion of hormones by the adrenal gland: epinephrine, norepinephrine, and glucocorticoids.

Although increased levels of epinephrine and norepinephrine can raise blood pressure, most of the harm to health comes from glucocorticoids. Prolonged exposure to high levels of these hormones can increase blood pressure, damage muscle tissue, lead to infertility, inhibit growth, inhibit the inflammatory response, and suppress the immune system. It can also damage the hippocampus. Prenatal exposure to excessive levels of glucocorticoids (caused by maternal stress) causes developmental changes that appear to predispose animals to react more to stressful situations. Exposure to extreme stress can also have long-lasting effects; it can lead to the development of posttraumatic stress disorder.

Because the harm of most forms of stress comes from our own response to it, individual differences in personality variables can alter the effects of stressful situations. Research with twin studies indicates that heredity is one of the factors that determines an individual's response to stress. Another important variable is the ability to perform a coping response; being able to do so considerably reduces the aversive effects of stressful situations. One study suggests that performance of a coping response causes the release of endogenous benzodiazepines by neurons in the brain.

Psychoneuroimmunology is a relatively new field of study that investigates interactions between behavior and the immune system, mediated by the nervous system. The immune system consists of several types of white blood cells that produce both nonspecific and specific responses to invading microorganisms. The nonspecific responses include the inflammatory response, the antiviral effect of interferon, and the action of natural killer cells against viruses and cancer cells. The specific responses include chemically mediated and cell-mediated responses. Chemically mediated responses are carried out by B-lymphocytes, which release antibodies that bind with the antigens on microorganisms and kill them directly or target them for attack by other white blood cells. Cell-mediated responses are carried out by T-lymphocytes, whose antibodies remain attached to their membranes.

A wide variety of stressful situations have been shown to increase people's susceptibility to infectious diseases. The most important mechanism by which stress impairs immune function is the increased blood levels of glucocorticoids. In addition, the neural input to the bone marrow, lymph nodes, and thymus gland may also play a role; and the endogenous opioids appear to suppress the activity of natural killer cells.

SUGGESTED READINGS

Ader, R., Felten, D.L., and Cohen, N. (eds.). *Psychoneuroimmunology,* 2nd ed. San Diego: Academic Press, 1991.

Bauman, M.L., and Kemper, T.L. *The Neurobiology of Autism.* Baltimore: Johns Hopkins University Press, 1994.

Brown, M.R., Koob, G.F., and Rivier, C. (eds.). *Stress: Neurobiology and Neuroendocrinology.* New York: Dekker, 1990.

Gershon, E.S., and Cloninger, C.R. *New Genetic Approaches to Mental Disorders.* Washington, D.C.: American Psychiatric Press, 1994.

Goodwin, D.W., and Guze, S.B. *Psychiatric Diagnosis,* 5th ed. New York: Oxford University Press, 1996.

Hollander, E. *Obsessive-Compulsive Related Disorders.* Washington, D.C.: American Psychiatric Press, 1993.

Yudofsky, S.C., and Hales, R.E. *The American Psychiatric Press Textbook of Neuropsychiatry.* Washington, DC: American Psychiatric Press, 1997.

CHAPTER 19

Drug Abuse

Raw: Like Sushi by Mercedes Nuñez. Courtesy of the artist.

Drug addiction poses a serious problem to our species. Consider the disastrous effects caused by the abuse of one of our oldest drugs, alcohol: automobile accidents, fetal alcohol syndrome, cirrhosis of the liver, Korsakoff's syndrome, increased rate of heart disease, and increased rate of intracerebral hemorrhage. Smoking (addiction to nicotine) greatly increases the chances of dying of lung cancer, heart attack, and stroke; and women who smoke give birth to smaller, less healthy babies. Cocaine addiction can cause psychotic behavior, brain damage, and death from overdose; its use by pregnant women can result in the birth of babies with brain damage and consequent psychological problems; and competition for lucrative markets terrorizes neighborhoods, subverts political and judicial systems, and causes many deaths. The use of "designer drugs" exposes users to unknown dangers of untested and often contaminated products, as several people discovered when they acquired Parkinson's disease after taking a synthetic opiate tainted with a neurotoxin. Addicts who take their drugs intravenously run a serious risk of contracting AIDS. What makes these drugs so attractive to so many people?

The answer, as you may have predicted from what you have learned about the physiology of reinforcement in Chapter 14, is that all of these substances stimulate brain mechanisms responsible for positive reinforcement. In addition, some of them reduce or eliminate unpleasant feelings, some of which are produced by the drugs themselves. The immediate consequences of these drugs are more powerful than the realization that in the long term, bad things will happen.

WHAT IS ADDICTION?

The term *addiction* derives from the Latin word *addicere,* "to sentence." Someone who is addicted to a drug is, in a way, sentenced to a term of involuntary servitude, being obliged to fulfill the demands of his or her drug dependency.

A Little Background

Long ago, people discovered that many substances found in nature—primarily, leaves, seeds, and roots of plants, but also some animal products—had medicinal qualities. They discovered herbs that helped prevent infections, that promoted healing, that calmed an upset stomach, that reduced pain, or that helped provide a night's sleep. They also discovered "recreational drugs"—drugs that produced pleasurable effects when eaten, drunk, or smoked. The most universal recreational drug, and perhaps the first one that our ancestors discovered, is ethyl alcohol. Yeast spores are present everywhere, and these microorganisms can feed on sugar solutions and produce alcohol as a by-product. Undoubtedly, people in many different parts of the world discovered the pleasurable effects of drinking liquids that had been left alone for a while, such as the juice that had accumulated in the bottom of a container of fruit. The juice may have become sour and bad-tasting because of the action of bacteria, but the effects of the alcohol encouraged people to experiment, which led to the development of a wide variety of fermented beverages.

Our ancestors also discovered other recreational drugs. Some of them were consumed only locally; others became so popular that their cultivation as commercial crops spread throughout the world. For example, Asians discovered the effects of the sap of the opium poppy and the beverage made from the leaves of the tea plant, Indians discovered the effects of the smoke of cannabis, South Americans discovered the effects of chewing coca leaves and making a drink from coffee beans, and North Americans discovered the effects of the smoke of the tobacco plant. Many of the drugs they discovered served to protect the plants from animals (primarily insects) that ate them. Although the drugs were toxic in sufficient quantities, our ancestors learned how to take these drugs in quantities that would not make them ill—at least, not right away. The effects of these drugs on their brains kept them coming back for more.

Because most recreational drugs produce significant changes in consciousness, they often became associated with religious rituals. For example, smoking tobacco was part of a ritual of some natives of North America, and the ritual drinking of wine is a part of Judaism and most Christian denominations. In some cases, religious orders took over the cultivation of drug-producing crops and developed rules for their consumption.

Some drugs are associated with unpleasant tastes and aftereffects, and people must learn to tolerate them. Here, social customs can play an important role. For example, most people do not enjoy their first cigarette, but, encouraged by their peers, they persist long enough to experience the pleasurable effects of nicotine. Societies also devote resources to finding ways to extract and purify drugs, eliminating bad-tasting substances or substances that produce undesirable effects. People have learned how to extract morphine from opium, how to distill fermented beverages, and how to develop tobacco plants with high nicotine levels. The motivation for the work that went into these developments was provided by an effect common to all recreational drugs: activation of the brain's reinforcement mechanisms.

● Physical versus Psychological Addiction

Some drugs have very potent reinforcing effects, which lead some people to abuse them or even to become addicted to them. Many people (psychologists, health professionals, and laypeople) believe that "true" addiction is caused by

the unpleasant physiological effects that occur when an addict tries to stop taking the drug. For example, Eddy et al. (1965) defined *physical dependence* as "an adaptive state that manifests itself by intense physical disturbances when the administration of a drug is suspended" (p. 723). In contrast, they defined *psychic dependence* as a condition in which a drug produces "a feeling of satisfaction and a psychic drive that requires periodic or continuous administration of the drug to produce pleasure or to avoid discomfort" (p. 723). Most people regard the latter as less important than the former. But, as we shall see, the *reverse* is true.

For many years, heroin addiction has been considered the prototype for all drug addictions. People who habitually take heroin become physically dependent on the drug; that is, they show *tolerance* and *withdrawal symptoms*. As we saw in Chapter 4, **tolerance** is the decreased sensitivity to a drug that comes from its continued use; the drug user must take larger and larger amounts of the drug for it to be effective. Once a person has taken an opiate regularly enough to develop tolerance, that person will suffer *withdrawal symptoms* if he or she stops taking the drug. **Withdrawal symptoms** are primarily the opposite of the effects of the drug itself. The effects of heroin—euphoria, constipation, and relaxation—lead to the withdrawal effects of dysphoria, cramping and diarrhea, and agitation.

Most investigators believe that tolerance is produced by the body's attempt to compensate for the unusual condition of heroin intoxication. The drug disturbs normal homeostatic mechanisms in the brain, and in reaction these mechanisms begin to produce effects opposite to those of the drug, partially compensating for the disturbance. Because of these compensatory mechanisms, the user must take increasing amounts of heroin to achieve the effects that were produced when he or she first started taking the drug. They also account for the symptoms of withdrawal: When the person stops taking the drug, the compensatory mechanisms make themselves felt, unopposed by the action of the drug. (The neural mechanisms responsible for tolerance and withdrawal symptoms are described later in this chapter.)

---

tolerance   The fact that increasingly large doses of drugs must be taken to achieve a particular effect; caused by compensatory mechanisms that oppose the effect of the drug.

withdrawal symptoms   The appearance of symptoms opposite to those produced by a drug when the drug is suddenly no longer taken; caused by the presence of compensatory mechanisms.

Heroin addiction has provided such a striking example of drug dependence that some authorities have concluded that "real" addiction does not occur unless a drug causes tolerance and withdrawal. Without doubt, withdrawal symptoms make it difficult for a person to stop taking heroin: They help keep the person hooked. But withdrawal symptoms do not explain why a person becomes a heroin addict in the first place; that fact is explained by the drug's reinforcing effect. Certainly, people do not start taking heroin so that they will become physically dependent on it and feel miserable when they go without it. Instead, they begin taking it because it makes them feel good.

Even though the withdrawal effects of heroin make it difficult to stop taking the drug, these effects alone are not the sole reason for remaining addicted. In fact, when the cost of the habit gets too high, some addicts stop taking heroin "cold turkey." Doing so is not as painful as most people believe; withdrawal symptoms have been described as similar to a bad case of the flu—unpleasant, but survivable. After a week or two, when their nervous systems adapt to the absence of the drug, the addicts recommence their habit, which now costs less to sustain. If their only reason for taking the drug was to avoid unpleasant withdrawal symptoms, they would not be able to follow this strategy. The reason that people take and continue to take drugs such as heroin is that the drugs give them a pleasurable "rush"; in other words, the drugs have a reinforcing effect on their behavior.

In the past, the preoccupation with "physical" drug dependence has led to the neglect of the addictive properties of some drugs. For example some very potent drugs, including cocaine, do not produce physical dependency. That is, people who take the drug do not show tolerance; and if they stop, they do not show significant withdrawal symptoms. As a result, experts believed for many years that cocaine was a relatively innocuous drug, not in the same league as heroin. Obviously, they were wrong; cocaine is even more addictive than heroin.

The most important lesson we can learn from the misguided distinction between "physiological" and "psychological" addiction is that we should never underestimate the importance of "psychological" factors. After all, given that behavior is controlled by circuits of neurons in the brain, even "psychological" factors involve physiological

mechanisms. People often pay more attention to physiological symptoms than to psychological ones because they consider them more *real*. But behavioral research indicates that a preoccupation with physiological symptoms can hinder our understanding of the causes of addiction.

● Modern Definitions of Drug Dependence

There is no simple, consistent set of definitions for the problems that may occur when people take psychoactive drugs. The term *addiction* has, for the most part, been replaced with the term *dependence*. The most succinct definition was formulated in 1969 by the World Health Organization: "A state, psychic and sometimes also physical, resulting from the interaction between a living organism and a drug, characterized by behavioural and other responses that always include a compulsion to take a drug on a continuous or periodic basis in order to experience its psychic effects, and sometimes to avoid the discomfort of its absence. Tolerance may or may not be present" (WHO, 1969). A more recent definition is provided by the American Psychiatric Association in its *Diagnostic and Statistical Manual-IV*, which lists a set of criteria for what it refers to as **substance dependence** (avoiding the word "drug"). The person must exhibit three of the following criteria in a twelve-month period: tolerance; withdrawal symptoms; increasing doses; unsuccessful efforts to cut down intake of the substance; a considerable amount of time spent in obtaining the substance or using it; interference with important social, occupational, or recreational activities; and continuation of use of the substance despite recognition of the fact that doing so has causes physical or psychological problems. Note that tolerance and withdrawal symptoms are associated with dependence but are not essential criteria.

Not all people who take drugs become addicted to them. According to the *DSM-IV*, a less serious problem associated with the taking of drugs is **substance abuse,** defined as interference with major role obligations at work, school, or home; recurrent use in potentially hazardous situations (such as driving while impaired); legal problems related to use of the drug; or continued use despite the occurrence of social or interpersonal problems. As you can see, the primary difference between dependence and abuse is that the former is chronic and the latter is acute or episodic.

The definitions found in the *DSM-IV* stress the personal, legal, and social effects of drug taking. The definition given by the World Health Organization is closer to the one I will use in this chapter. It emphasizes the most important aspect of drug dependence: *compulsive drug-tak-*

---

substance dependence   A maladaptive pattern of substance abuse that includes taking increasing doses of the drug or other signs of addiction.

substance abuse   A maladaptive pattern of substance use short of addiction that interferes with a person's health of social situation.

ing behavior. Let me explain why compulsion is the most important factor. Suppose that a physician becomes addicted to morphine. He manages to obtain the drug without getting caught, and because he is habituated to the drug, he is not mentally impaired. Thus, his addiction does not interfere with his professional activities or social life, and he does not have legal problems. As far as I can tell, unless he tries and fails to break his habit, his addiction would not meet the necessary criteria for a diagnosis of substance abuse, according to the *DSM-IV.* Or let's consider a person addicted to nicotine. She smokes two packs of cigarettes each day and cannot go for more than a short time without smoking, but she is able to obtain her cigarettes peacefully and legally. Her addiction does not interfere with her work (let's suppose she works out-of-doors and can smoke whenever she wants), and, being young, she does not exhibit any of the symptoms of ill health that often accompany long-term smoking. Finally, smoking does not produce intoxication that would make it dangerous to drive a car or operate a machine. Does this mean that nicotine is not an addictive drug?

The answer is no; nicotine is, indeed, an addictive drug. As we shall see later in this chapter, people can become just as dependent on nicotine as they can on "hard" drugs that produce intoxication or that have been declared illegal. This book is concerned with the physiology of behavior, not the subtleties of legal definitions. Certainly, dependence on some drugs is much more serious than dependence on others. For example, habitual caffeine-taking is generally innocuous, while chronic alcoholism has serious consequences. But the essential characteristic of an addictive drug is its ability to establish a pattern of compulsive drug-taking behavior.

Interim Summary

Addictive drugs are those whose reinforcing effects are so potent that some people who are exposed to them are unable to go for very long without taking them and whose lives become organized around taking them. Originally, addictive drugs came from plants, which used them as a defense against insects or other animals that otherwise would eat them, but chemists have synthesized many other drugs that have even more potent effects. If a person regularly takes some addictive drugs (most notably, the opiates), the effects of the drug show tolerance, and the person must take increasing doses to achieve the same effect. If the person then stops taking the drug, withdrawal effects, opposite to the primary effects of the drug, will occur. However, withdrawal effects are not the cause of addiction—the

abuse potential of a drug is related to its ability to reinforce drug-taking behavior.

COMMON FEATURES OF ADDICTION

What goes on physiologically to make a person dependent on a drug? This section describes some common features of addictive drugs—drugs that people often become dependent on. A later section describes the details of particular drugs.

Positive Reinforcement

Drugs that lead to dependency must first reinforce people's behavior. As we saw in Chapter 14, positive reinforcement refers to the effect that certain stimuli have on the behaviors that preceded them. If, in a particular situation, a behavior is regularly followed by an appetitive stimulus (one that the organism will tend to approach), then that behavior will become more frequent in that situation. For example, if a hungry rat accidentally bumps into a lever and receives some food, it will eventually learn to press the lever. What actually seems to happen is that the occurrence of an appetitive stimulus activates a reinforcement mechanism in the brain that increases the likelihood of the most recent response (the lever press) in the present situation (the chamber that contains the lever).

Addictive drugs have reinforcing effects. That is, their effects include activation of the reinforcement mechanism. This activation strengthens the response that was just made. If the drug was taken by a fast-acting route such as injection or inhalation, the last response will be the act of taking the drug, so that response will be reinforced. This form of reinforcement is powerful and immediate and works with a wide variety of species. For example, a rat or a monkey will quickly learn to press a lever that controls a device that injects cocaine through a plastic tube inserted into a vein.

Role in Drug Abuse

When appetitive stimuli occur, they usually do so because we just did something to make them happen—and not because an experimenter was controlling the situation. The effectiveness of a reinforcing stimulus is greatest if it occurs immediately after a response occurs. If the reinforcing stimulus is delayed, it becomes considerably less effective. The reason for this fact is found by examining the function of instrumental conditioning: learning about the consequences of our own behavior. Normally, causes and effects are closely related in time; we do something, and something happens, good or bad. The consequences of the actions teach us whether to repeat that action, and events that follow a response by more than a few seconds were probably not caused by that response.

An experiment by Logan (1965) illustrates the importance of the immediacy of reinforcement. Logan trained hungry rats to run through a simple maze in which a single passage led to two corridors. At the end of one corridor the rats would find a small piece of food. At the end of the other corridor they would receive much more food, but it would be delivered only after a delay. Although the most intelligent strategy would be to enter the second corridor and wait for the larger amount of food, the rats chose to take the small amount of food that was delivered right away. Immediacy of reinforcement took precedence over quantity.

This phenomenon explains why the most addictive drugs are those that have immediate effects. As we saw in Chapter 4, drug users prefer heroin to morphine not because heroin has a *different* effect, but because it has a more *rapid* effect. In fact, heroin is converted to morphine as soon as it reaches the brain. But because heroin is more lipid soluble, it passes through the blood–brain barrier more rapidly and its effects on the brain are felt sooner than those of morphine. The most potent reinforcement occurs when drugs produce sudden changes in the activity of the reinforcement mechanism; slow changes are much less reinforcing, and continuous activity may even be aversive. As we saw in Chapter 14, animals will learn to press a lever that delivers a brief burst of electrical stimulation to the reinforcement mechanism through an electrode implanted in the brain. But the animals will also learn to press a lever that will *turn off* the stimulation if the experimenter turns it on. If the apparatus contains two levers, one that turns the stimulation on and the other that turns it off, the animals will shuttle rapidly between the two levers, turning the stimulation on and off. Similarly, a person taking an addictive drug seeks a sudden "rush" produced by a fast-acting drug. (As we will see later, the use of methadone for opiate addiction and nicotine patches for tobacco addiction are based on this phenomenon.)

Earlier, I posed the question of why people would ever expose themselves to the risks associated with dangerous addictive drugs. Who would rationally chose to become addicted to a drug that produced pleasurable effects in the short term but also produced even more powerful aversive effects in the long term: loss of employment and social status, legal problems and possible imprisonment, damage to health, and even premature death? The answer is that, as we saw, our reinforcement mechanism evolved to deal with the *immediate* effects of our behavior. The immediate reinforcing effects of an addictive drug can, for some individuals, overpower the recognition of the long-term aversive effects. Fortunately, most people are able to resist the short-term effects; only a minority of people who try addictive drugs go on to become dependent on them.

If an addictive drug is taken by a slow-acting route, reinforcement can also occur, but the process is somewhat more complicated. If a person takes a pill and several minutes later experiences a feeling of euphoria, he or she will certainly remember swallowing the pill. The recollection of this behavior will activate some of the same neural circuits involved in actually swallowing the pill, and the reinforcement mechanism, now active because of the effects of the drug, will reinforce the behavior. In other words, people's ability to remember having performed a behavior make it possible to reinforce their behavior vicariously. The immediacy is between an imagined act and a reinforcing stimulus—the euphoria produced by the drug. Other cognitive processes contribute to the reinforcement, too, such as the expectation that euphoric effects will occur. Perhaps someone said, "Take one of these pills; you'll get a great high!" But if a nonhuman animal is fed one of these pills, its behavior is unlikely to be reinforced. By the time the euphoric effect occurs, the animal will be doing something other than ingesting the drug. Without the ability to recall an earlier behavior and thus activate circuits involved in the performance of that behavior, the delay between the behavior and the reinforcing effect of the drug prevent the animal from learning to take the drug. As we will see later in this chapter, researchers have developed ways to teach animals to become addicted to drugs that have delayed effects, such as alcohol.

Neural Mechanisms

As we saw in Chapter 14, all natural reinforcers that have been studied so far (such as food for a hungry animal, water for thirsty one, or sexual contact) have one physiological effect in common: They cause the release of dopamine in the nucleus accumbens (White, 1996). This effect is undoubtedly not the *only* effect of reinforcing stimuli, and even aversive stimuli can trigger the release of dopamine (Salamone, 1992). But even though there is much that we do not yet understand about the neural basis of reinforcement, the release of dopamine appears to be a *necessary* (but not *sufficient*) condition for reinforcement to take place.

Addictive drugs—including amphetamine, cocaine, opiates, nicotine, alcohol, PCP, and cannabis—trigger the release of dopamine in the nucleus accumbens, as measured by microdialysis (Di Chiara, 1995). Some drugs do so by increasing the activity of the dopaminergic neurons of the mesolimbic system, which originates in the ventral tegmental area and terminates in the nucleus accumbens (and some other forebrain regions). Other drugs inhibit the reuptake of dopamine by terminal buttons and hence facilitate the postsynaptic effects of dopamine. If the release of dopamine in the nucleus accumbens is prevented by damaging the mesolimbic neurons, most addictive drugs lose their reinforcing effects. The details of the ways in which particular drugs interact with the mesolimbic dopaminergic system are described later.

In recent years, evidence has been accumulating that the endogenous opioids may also be involved in reinforcement. As we shall see, although opiate drugs such as heroin and morphine do activate the dopaminergic neurons of the mesolimbic system, this activation does not appear to be essential for the reinforcing effects of these drugs. Furthermore, the behavioral effects of some natural reinforcers appear to involve the secretion of the endogenous opioids. Whether dopaminergic and opioidergic neurons are parts of a single system of reinforcement or whether they have at least a certain degree of independence is not yet known.

Does Reinforcement Equal Pleasure?

For the most part, events that reinforce behavior also provide pleasure: If we like something, it tends to reinforce our behavior. However, reinforcement and pleasure are not synonymous terms. For one thing, a decrease in the intensity of an aversive stimulus (one that causes pain or discomfort) can reinforce behavior, and although reduction in the intensity of an unpleasant stimulus is certainly desirable, it can hardly be called *pleasurable.* (As we will see in the next section, this phenomenon is called *negative reinforcement.*) But another phenomenon shows even more graphically that reinforcement can occur even when people are unable to detect any subjective effects at all.

Several investigators have noted that long-term heroin addicts often report that the drug no longer gives them pleasure, but they continue to take the drug anyway, even at great financial and social cost to themselves. One possible explanation for this behavior is that the drug is providing negative reinforcement, as described in the next subsection. However, research by Lamb et al. (1991) indicates that *positive* reinforcement may take place without any feelings of pleasure. The experimenters recruited subjects with histories of intravenous heroin addiction. The subjects were not currently dependent on opiates or other drugs; thus, any reinforcing effects that an opiate might have on their behavior could not be attributed to a reduction in unpleasant withdrawal symptoms. (The experimenters observed the subjects for several days in an addic-

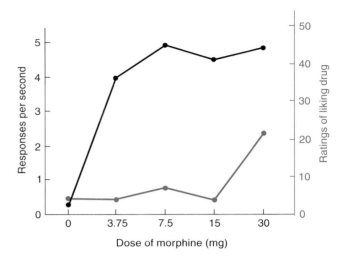

Figure 19.1
Reinforcement without subjective pleasure. Rate of lever pressing and ratings of liking of various doses of morphine.
(Adapted from Lamb, R.J., Preston, K.L., Schindler, C.W., Meisch, R.A., Davis, F., Katz, J.L., Henningfield, J.E., and Goldberg, S.R. *Journal of Pharmacology and Experimental Therapeutics*, 1991, *259,* 1165–1173.)

tion research ward at a hospital to be certain that they did not exhibit withdrawal symptoms.)

Each day, the subjects were given a lever to press. After 100 responses, a light was briefly illuminated; after the light had appeared 30 times (for a total of 3000 responses), the subjects received an intramuscular injection of morphine or a placebo. When the subjects received one of four different doses of morphine, they pressed the lever at a rate of four to five times per second. When they received a placebo instead, they soon stopped responding. So far, the results are what we might expect. The most interesting result was that the subjects reported feelings of pleasure only when they received the highest dose of morphine, 30 mg. They said that, on the average, the dose felt to them like the equivalent of $15 worth of heroin. When the subjects received one of the lower doses (3.75, 7.5, or 15 mg), they said that they felt nothing at all and reported that what they had received was worthless. Nevertheless, they pressed the lever thousands of times for the "worthless" injections. Their behavior distinguished between injections of a placebo and of a low dose of morphine even when their subjective report did not. (See *Figure 19.1.*)

● Negative Reinforcement

You probably have heard the old joke in which someone says that the reason he bangs his head against the wall is that "it feels so good when I stop." Of course, that joke is funny (well, mildly amusing) because we know that although no one would act that way, ceasing to bang our head against the wall is certainly better than continuing to do so. If someone else started hitting us on the head and we were able to do something to get them to stop, whatever it was that we did would certainly be reinforced.

A behavior that turns off (or reduces) an aversive stimulus will be reinforced. This phenomenon is known as **negative reinforcement,** and its usefulness is obvious. For example, consider the following scenario: A woman staying in a rented house cannot get to sleep because of the unpleasant screeching noise that the furnace makes. She goes to the basement to discover the source of the noise and finally kicks the side of the oil burner. The noise ceases. The next time the furnace screeches, she immediately goes to the basement and kicks the side of the oil burner. The unpleasant noise (the aversive stimulus) is terminated when the woman kicks the side of the oil burner (the response), so the response is reinforced.

It is worth pointing out that *negative reinforcement* should not be confused with *punishment*. Both phenomena involve aversive stimuli, but one makes a response more likely, while the other makes it less likely. For negative reinforcement to occur, the response must make the unpleasant stimulus end (or at least decrease). For punishment to occur, the response must *make the unpleasant stimulus occur*. For example, if a little boy touches a mousetrap and hurts his finger, he is unlikely to touch a mousetrap again. The painful stimulus *punishes* the behavior of touching the mousetrap.

As we saw earlier in this chapter, the withdrawal effects, which occur when a habitual user of a drug stops taking the drug, are unpleasant. Although positive reinforcement seems to be what provokes drug taking in the first place, reduction of withdrawal effects could certainly play a role in maintaining someone's drug addiction. The withdrawal effects are unpleasant, but as soon as the person takes some of the drug, these effects go away, producing negative reinforcement.

Negative reinforcement could also explain the acquisition of drug addictions under some conditions. If a person is suffering from some unpleasant feelings and then takes a drug that eliminates these feelings, the person's drug-taking behavior is likely to be reinforced. For example, alcohol can relieve feelings of anxiety. If a person finds himself

in a situation that arouses anxiety, he may find that a drink or two makes him feel much better. In fact, people often anticipate this effect and begin drinking before the situation actually occurs.

● Tolerance and Withdrawal

What neural mechanisms are responsible for tolerance and withdrawal effects? As we saw earlier, most investigators believe that tolerance is produced by the brain's attempt to compensate for the effects of the drug—a hypothesis that was first proposed by Himmelsbach (1943). Research suggests that there are basically two types of compensatory mechanisms. The first mechanism involves a decrease in the effectiveness of the drug. For example, let's consider heroin addiction. Heroin acts like the endogenous opioids, which serve as neurotransmitters and neuromodulators. Overstimulation of opiate receptors causes downregulation—desensitization of opioid receptors or of their effects on physiological processes within the cells on which they are found (Trujillo and Akil, 1991; Zukin et al., 1993). The mechanism responsible for downregulation will be discussed later.

A second effect involves classical conditioning, a form of learning. As we saw in Chapter 14, when a neutral stimulus (a stimulus that has no significant effects on an organism's behavior) regularly occurs just before a behaviorally effective stimulus, the neutral stimulus eventually comes to elicit the behavior controlled by the effective stimulus. For example, Ivan Pavlov discovered that when he repeatedly presented an auditory stimulus just before giving a dog a small amount of food, the sound alone would eventually cause salivation, the natural response to the food.

A similar effect occurs with some drugs. The drug produces its effects, which in turn activate the homeostatic compensatory mechanisms. For example, if we give an injection of insulin to a rat, the primary effect is to lower the animal's blood sugar level. The low blood sugar level then turns on compensatory mechanisms that eventually bring the level back to normal. (The compensatory mechanism involves the secretion of *glucagon*, a hormone that raises the blood sugar level.) If we injected the rat with insulin several times, we would find that its blood sugar level would return to normal more rapidly. Now suppose that we give the rat an injection of a placebo. Normally, the placebo would have no effect on the rat's blood sugar level. Instead, we find that the injection causes the rat's blood sugar level to *rise*.

Here is what happened. Stimuli associated with the administration of the injection—the stimuli produced by

negative reinforcement   The removal or reduction of an aversive stimulus that is contingent on a particular response, with an attendant increase in the frequency of that response.

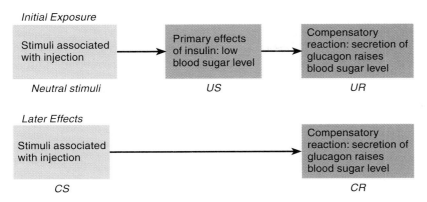

Figure 19.2
A schematic explanation for the way in which the compensatory reaction to a chemical messenger (in this case, insulin) can be classically conditioned to the stimuli involved with its administration.

holding the rat and sticking it with a needle—were paired with the physiological effects of the insulin. The response to the insulin—the secretion of glucagon that returned the blood sugar level back to normal—became conditioned to these stimuli. Then, when we gave the animal an injection of a placebo, the secretion of glucagon increased the animal's blood sugar level because there was no insulin to lower it. (See *Figure 19.2.*)

A similar phenomenon happens to a heroin addict. The stimuli associated with taking the drug—including the paraphernalia involved in preparing the solution of the drug, the syringe, the needle, the feel of the needle in a vein, and even the room in which the drug is taken—act like the auditory stimulus in Pavlov's experiments (Siegel, 1978). The result is that whenever a heroin addict encounters these stimuli, he or she is likely to experience an intense set of withdrawal symptoms, caused by compensatory mechanisms that normally counteract the effects of the drug. (See *Figure 19.3.*)

In the past, agencies that sponsored anti-addiction programs sometimes prepared posters illustrating the dangers of drug abuse that featured drug paraphernalia—syringes, needles, spoons, piles of white powder, and so on. Possibly, these posters did succeed in reminding people who did not use drugs that they should avoid them. But we do know that their effect on people trying to break a drug habit was exactly opposite of what was intended. A former drug addict would see the poster, and the sight of the drug paraphernalia would intensify their urge to take the drug again. For this reason, such posters are no longer used in campaigns against drug addiction.

An experiment by Siegel et al. (1982) graphically illustrates the potency of classical conditioning as a mechanism responsible for drug tolerance. The experimenters gave rats daily doses of heroin—always in the same chamber—long enough for tolerance to develop. Then, on the test day, the experimenters gave the rats a large dose of the drug. Some of the animals received the drug in the familiar chamber, while others received it in a new environment. The investigators predicted that the animals receiving the drug in the familiar environment would have some protection from the drug overdose because the stimuli in that environment would produce a classically conditioned compensatory response. Their prediction was correct; almost all of the rats who received the overdose in the new environment died, compared with slightly more than half of the rats injected

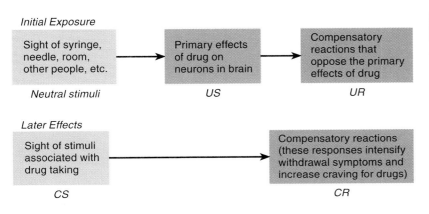

Figure 19.3
The classical conditioning model of drug tolerance proposed by Siegel (1978).

in the familiar environment. Siegel and his colleagues suggest that when human heroin addicts take the drug in an unfamiliar environment, they too run the risk of death from a drug overdose.

● Craving and Relapse

Why do drug addicts crave drugs? Why does this craving occur even after a long period of abstinence? Knowing the answers to these questions might help clinicians devise therapies that will assist people in breaking their drug dependence once and for all.

Robinson and Berridge (1993) suggest that when an addictive drug activates the mesolimbic dopaminergic system, it gives *incentive salience* to stimuli present at that time. By this they mean that the stimuli associated with drug taking become exciting and motivating—a provocation to act. When a person with a history of drug abuse sees or thinks about these stimuli, he or she experiences craving—an impulsion to take the drug. Note that this hypothesis does not imply that the craving is caused solely by an unpleasant feeling, as described in the previous subsection. Hyman (1996b) suggests a similar explanation—that long-term activation of the neural circuitry responsible for reinforcement gives rise to changes that produce unpleasant feelings when the person abstains from the drug and also produces positive emotional memories of stimuli associated with the drug. Both of these changes contribute to craving and relapse.

Evidence obtained from both humans and laboratory animals indicates that long-term drug abuse does, indeed, produce long-term changes. For example, Grant et al. (1996) used a PET scanner to measure regional metabolic activity of the brains of people with and without a history of cocaine abuse. The experimenters presented two types of stimuli, neutral and drug-related. The neutral stimuli included arts and crafts items such as a leather punch, a paint brush, paint bottles, and clay and a videotape of a person handling some sea shells. The drug-related stimuli included a glass pipe, a mirror, a razor blade, a straw, a pile of cocaine (yes, the real stuff), and a videotape of a people handling a white powder and sniffing and smoking it. The people with a history of cocaine abuse were told that after the experiment was over, they could sniff the pile of cocaine in front of them.

The PET scans revealed that the drug-related stimuli increased the activity of the dorsolateral prefrontal cortex, the amygdala, and the cerebellum, but only in subjects with a history of drug abuse. These stimuli also produced self-reports of craving in these subjects. The neutral stimuli had no effects on neural activity of subjects in either of the groups.

Several studies have suggested that long-term cocaine addiction may increase the sensitivity of D_3 dopamine receptors and that this increased sensitivity may be responsible for craving. D_3 receptors are found in brain regions that have been implicated in reinforcement—in particular, in the nucleus accumbens and other projections regions of the mesolimbic dopamine system (Levesque et al., 1992). For example, Nader and Mach (1996) found that the reinforcing value of 7-OH-DPAT, a direct agonist for D_3 receptors, depended on an animal's prior drug-taking experience. Squirrel monkeys that had a long history of intravenous self-administration would readily press a lever that delivered injections of 7-OH-DPAT. However, monkeys that had never received cocaine would not press a lever for the drug. The results suggest that long-term cocaine abuse may increase the sensitivity of D_3 receptors and that their stimulation with 7-OH-DPAT is reinforcing.

These results received support from a study by Staley and Mash (1996), who studied the brains of people who had died of cocaine overdoses. They found an increased density of dopamine D_3 receptors in the nucleus accumbens of these people, compared with the brains of people without a history of drug abuse. (See *Figure 19.4.*)

As everyone knows, a taste of food can provoke hunger, which is why we refer to tidbits we eat before a meal as "appetizers." For a person with a history of drug abuse, a small

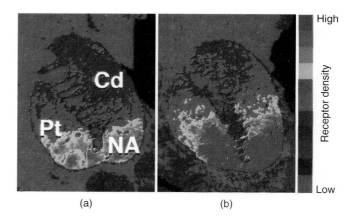

(a)   (b)

Figure 19.4
Concentration of D_3 dopamine receptors in the human ventral striatum, as measured by binding of 7-OH-DPAT. (a) Autoradiogram of the ventral striatum of a control subject. (b) Autoradiogram of the ventral striatum of a subject who died of a cocaine overdose. Cd = caudate nucleus, Pt = putamen, NA = nucleus accumbens. Note the increased concentration of D_3 receptors in the nucleus accumbens of the cocaine addict.
(From Staley, J.K., and Mash, D.C. *Journal of Neuroscience,* 1996, 16, 6100–6106.)

dose of the drug has similar effects: It increases craving, or "appetite," for the drug. The same phenomenon is seen in laboratory animals. If a rat that has been trained to self-administer cocaine is given a small dose of the drug, the animal will immediately seek to perform the behaviors it had previously learned to perform to obtain the drug. Self et al. (1996) found that this *priming effect* is produced by stimulation of D_3 dopamine receptors. The experimenters found that 7-OH-DPAT, the D_3 agonist, induced rats to engage in cocaine-seeking behavior.

Other stimuli can also trigger drug-seeking behavior. For example, clinicians have long observed that stressful situations can cause former drug addicts to relapse. Presumably, the intense, pleasurable effects of the drug help them forget about their current difficulties. These effects have been observed in rats that had previously learned to self-administer cocaine or heroin (Goeders and Goeders, 1994; Shaham and Stewart, 1995). The priming effect of stress may even be caused by the release of dopamine. Shaham and Stewart trained rats to press a lever to receive intravenous injections of heroin and then extinguished the behavior with several sessions in which the rats received nothing but a saline solution. Then the experimenters produced short-term stress by placing the rats in a chamber in which they received intermittent electric shocks through the metal grid floor. Immediately afterward, the animals began vigorously pressing the lever again. Microdialysis probes in the nucleus accumbens revealed that the stress triggered the release of dopamine. Presumably, this release of dopamine is what induced the rats to begin pressing the lever again.

Interim Summary

Positive reinforcement occurs when a behavior is regularly followed by an appetitive stimulus—one that an organism will approach. All addictive drugs produce positive reinforcement; they reinforce drug-taking behavior. Laboratory animals will learn to make responses that result in the delivery of these drugs. The faster a drug produces its effects, the more quickly dependence will be established.

All addictive drugs stimulate the release of dopamine in the nucleus accumbens, a structure that plays an important role in reinforcement. In addition, release of the endogenous opioids in the brain may mediate the reinforcing effects of certain drugs. Although for the most part, stimuli that provide positive reinforcement are perceived as pleasurable, the relation is not perfect. People with long-standing drug dependence remain addicted even though they report that taking the drug no longer gives them pleasure. In addition, doses of morphine that are too small to be de-

tected by the person receiving them can nevertheless reinforce their behavior.

Negative reinforcement occurs when a behavior is followed by the reduction or termination of an aversive stimulus. If, because of a person's social situation or personality characteristics, he or she feels unhappy or anxious, a drug that reduces these feelings can reinforce drug-taking behavior by means of negative reinforcement. Also, the reduction of unpleasant withdrawal symptoms by a dose of the drug undoubtedly plays a role in maintaining drug addictions, but it is not the sole cause of craving.

Tolerance of the effects of a drug is part of a compensatory mechanism by which the brain resists long-term disruption of normal balances in its activity. Tolerance is caused by a decrease in the sensitivity of the receptors for that drug or the intracellular mechanism responsible for the drug's effects. In addition, compensatory activity of neural circuits can be classically conditioned to stimuli associated with taking the drug or the place in which it is regularly taken. These stimuli can intensify an addict's craving for the drug.

Craving—the urge to take a drug to which one has become addicted—cannot completely be explained by withdrawal symptoms, because it can occur even after an addict has refrained from taking the drug for a long time. A PET study found that craving for cocaine increased the activity of the dorsolateral prefrontal cortex, the amygdala, and the cerebellum. Cocaine craving may be associated with increased numbers of D_3 dopamine receptors; only cocaine-dependent monkeys will self-administer a D_3 agonist, and the brains of people with a history of cocaine abuse show increased density of D_3 receptors in the nucleus accumbens. The most effective stimulus for craving is a small dose of the drug to which the person (or laboratory animal) has become addicted, or even stressful stimuli that trigger the release of dopamine in the nucleus accumbens.

COMMONLY ABUSED DRUGS

People have been known to abuse an enormous variety of drugs, including alcohol, barbiturates, opiates, tobacco, amphetamine, cocaine, cannabis, LSD, psilocybin, PCP, volatile solvents such as glues or even gasoline, ether, and nitrous oxide. The pleasure that children often derive from spinning themselves until they become dizzy may even be related to the effects of some of these drugs. Obviously, I cannot hope to discuss all these drugs in any depth and keep the chapter to a reasonable length, so I will restrict my discussion to the most important of them in terms of popularity and potential for addiction. Some drugs, such as caffeine, are both popular and addictive, but because they do not normally cause intoxication, impair health, or interfere with productivity, I will not discuss them here. (Chapter 4 did discuss the behavioral effects and site of action of caffeine.) I will also not discuss the wide variety of hallocinogenic drugs such as LSD or PCP. Although some people enjoy the mind-altering effects of LSD, many people simply find them frightening; and in any event, LSD use does not normally lead to addiction. PCP (phencyclidine) acts as an inverse agonist at the NMDA receptor, which means that its effects overlap with those of alcohol. Rather than devoting space to this drug, I have chosen to say more about alcohol, which is abused far more than any of the hallucinogenic drugs. If you would like to learn more about drugs other than the ones I discuss here, I suggest you consult the books listed among the suggested readings at the end of this chapter.

● Opiates

Opium, derived from a sticky resin produced by the opium poppy, has been eaten and smoked for centuries. Opiate addiction has several high personal and social costs. First, because heroin, the most commonly abused opiate, is an illegal drug, an addict becomes, by definition, a criminal. Second, because of tolerance, a person must take increasing amounts of the drug to achieve a "high." The habit thus becomes more and more expensive, and the person often turns to crime to obtain enough money to support his or her habit. Third, an opiate addict often uses unsanitary needles; at present, a substantial percentage of people who inject illicit drugs have been exposed in this way to hepatitis or the AIDS virus. Fourth, if the addict is a pregnant woman, her infant will also become dependent on the drug, which easily crosses the placental barrier. The infant must be given opiates right after being born and then weaned off the drug with gradually decreasing doses. Fifth, the uncertainty about the strength of a given batch of heroin makes it possible for a user to receive an unusually large dose of the drug, with possibly fatal consequences. In addition, dealers typically dilute pure heroin with various adulterants such as milk sugar, quinine, or talcum powder; and dealers are not known for taking scrupulous care with the quality and sterility of the substances they use. Some heroin-induced deaths have actually been reactions to the adulterants mixed with the drugs.

As we saw in Chapters 4 and 7, opiates are secreted when an animal is performing behaviors important to its survival or the survival of its species. For example, when an animal fights with another animal, the outcome of the bat-

tle is usually very important for that animal. The animal may be fighting with a rival in a dispute over territory or access to a mate, in defense of its offspring, or it may be attacking prey or defending itself against a predator. Fighting usually produces pain, and if an animal were too easily inhibited by pain, it would be less likely to thrive and reproduce—or it might even die. For this reason, the evolutionary process has equipped mammals with circuits of neurons that release endogenous opioids when it is fighting or mating. These chemicals stimulate receptors that produce analgesia that reduce the inhibitory effects of pain and positive reinforcement that encourage the animal to continue what it is doing. The problem is, of course, that when a person takes an artificial opiate, the effects of the drug encourage a person to continue taking that drug.

Neural Basis of Reinforcing Effects

As we saw earlier, laboratory animals will self-administer opiates. When an opiate is administered systemically, it stimulates opiate receptors located on neurons in various parts of the brain and produces a variety of effects, including analgesia, hypothermia (lowering of body temperature), sedation, and reinforcement. Opiate receptors in the periaqueductal gray matter are primarily responsible for the analgesia, those in the preoptic area are responsible for the hypothermia, and those in the mesencephalic reticular formation are responsible for the sedation. As we shall see, opiate receptors in the ventral tegmental area and the nucleus accumbens may play a role in the reinforcing effects of opiates, but other regions appear to be important, too.

As we saw in Chapter 4, there are three major types of opiate receptors: mu, delta, and kappa. Evidence suggests that mu receptors are responsible for reinforcement and analgesia and that stimulation of kappa receptors produces aversive effects. The best evidence for the role of mu receptors comes from a study by Matthes et al. (1996), who performed a targeted mutation ("knockout") of the gene responsible for production of the mu opiate receptor in mice. These animals, when they grew up, were completely insensitive to the reinforcing or analgesic effects of morphine, and they showed no signs of withdrawal symptoms after having been given increasing doses of morphine for 6 days. (See *Figure 19.5.*)

Chemicals that stimulate kappa opiate receptors, including **dynorphin** (an endogenous opioid) and various artificial kappa-receptor agonists, produce aversive effects (Mucha and Herz, 1985; Suzuki et al., 1993). Infusion of

dynorphin An endogenous opioid; the natural ligand for kappa opiate receptors.

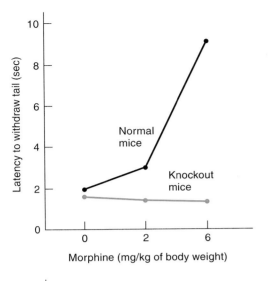

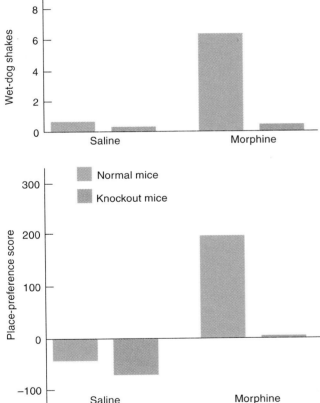

Figure 19.5
Lack of responses to morphine in mice with targeted mutations of the mu opiate receptor. (top) Latency to tail withdrawal from a hot object (a measure of analgesia). (middle) Wet-dog shakes after being withdrawn from long-term morphine administration (a prominent withdrawal symptom in rodents). (bottom) Conditioned place preference for a chamber associated with an injection of morphine (a measure of reinforcement).
(Adapted from Matthes, H.W.D., Maldonado, R., Simonin, F., Valverde, O., Slowe, S., Kitchen, I., Befort, K., Dierich, A., Le Meur, M., Dolle, P., Tzavara, E., Hanoune, J., Roques, B.P., and Kieffer, B.L. *Nature*, 1996, *383*, 819–823.)

tal area and the nucleus accumbens, dramatically reduce the release of dopamine in the nucleus accumbens—a phenomenon that occurs during withdrawal from long-term administration of opiates (Devine et al., 1993).

As we saw earlier, reinforcing stimuli cause the release of dopamine in the nucleus accumbens. Injections of opiates are no exception to this general rule; Wise et al. (1995) found that the level of dopamine in the nucleus accumbens increased by 150 to 300 percent while a rat was pressing a lever that delivered intravenous injections of heroin. Rats will also press a lever that delivers injections of an opiate directly into the ventral tegmental area (Devine and Wise, 1994) or the nucleus accumbens Goeders, Lane, and Smith (1984). In other words, injections of opiates into both ends of the mesolimbic dopaminergic system are reinforcing. Injection of an opiate into the ventral tegmental area activates the dopaminergic neurons located there by decreasing the activity of GABA-secreting neurons that normally inhibit the DA neurons (Johnson and North, 1992). All these findings suggest that the reinforcing effects of opiates are produced by activation of neurons of the mesolimbic system and release of dopamine in the nucleus accumbens.

However, other experimental findings indicate that opiates can reinforce behavior independent of their effects on the mesolimbic dopamine system. Several studies have found that lesions of the nucleus accumbens do not prevent opiates from reinforcing behavior. For example, Gerrits and Vanree (1996) found that 6-HD lesions of the nucleus accumbens, which destroys dopaminergic axons and terminals, disrupted lever pressing of rats for intravenous injections of cocaine but had no effect on lever pressing for IV injections of heroin. Olmstead and Franklin (1996) found that destruction of all the cells of the nucleus accumbens with kainic acid had similar effects. They trained rats on a **conditioned place preference.** A condi-

kappa-receptor agonists into several brain regions, including the periaqueductal gray matter, ventral tegmental area, and nucleus accumbens, has aversive effects (Balskubik et al., 1993; Motta, Penha, and Brandao, 1995). Kappa-receptor agonists, acting on neurons in the ventral tegmen-

conditioned place preference   The learned preference for a location in which an organism encountered a reinforcing stimulus, such as food or a reinforcing drug.

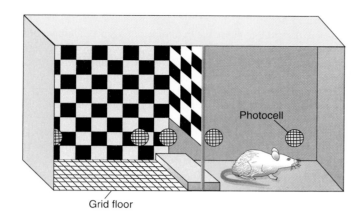

Photocell

Grid floor

Figure 19.6
The conditioned place preference procedure.
(Adapted from Feldman, R.S., Meyer, J.S., and Quenzer, L.F. *Principles of Neuropsychopharmacology.* Sunderland, MA: Sinauer Associates, 1997.)

tioned place preference task is often used in studies investigating the reinforcing or punishing properties of drugs. The apparatus consists of two distinctly different chambers, which the animal can easily distinguish. Photocells automatically keep track of the animal's location. An animal who receives an addictive drug just before being placed in one chamber and an injection of a placebo before being placed in another will learn to prefer the "drug" chamber and will go there if given a choice. If a drug produces an unpleasant aversive effect, the animal will avoid the drug chamber and will show a conditioned place *aversion.* (See *Figure 19.6.*) Olmstead and Franklin found that destruction of the nucleus accumbens blocked development of a conditioned place preference to amphetamine but not to morphine. These studies indicate that unlike other addictive drugs, opiates need not trigger the release of dopamine by neurons of the mesolimbic system to reinforce behavior.

As I mentioned earlier, a considerable amount of evidence suggests that endogenous opioids are involved in the behavioral effects of natural reinforcers. Let's look at some of this evidence. Agmo et al. (1993) used a conditioned place preference task to measure the reinforcing effects of a drink of water for thirsty rats. Rats in the control group, previously given an injection of a placebo, showed a clear preference for the chamber in which they were placed after drinking the water. Rats who were given an injection of **naloxone** (a drug that blocks opiate receptors) or **pimozide** (a drug that blocks dopamine receptors) showed no preference. Thus, the release of both dopamine and the endogenous opioids are essential for the reinforcing effects of a drink of water.

The release of endogenous opioids may even play a role in the reinforcing effects of some addictive drugs. Many studies have shown that naloxone and other drugs that block opiate receptors reduce the reinforcing effects of alcohol in both humans and laboratory animals. Because the use of opiate blockers has recently been approved as a treatment for alcoholism, I will discuss relevant research later in this chapter.

Neural Basis of Withdrawal Effects

Several studies have investigated the neural systems responsible for the withdrawal effects of opiates. Several regions of the brain have been implicated, including the periaqueductal gray matter (PAG), the locus coeruleus, and the amygdala. As we saw in Chapter 7, the PAG contains a high concentration of opiate receptors and is involved in the analgesic effects of opiates. As we saw in Chapters 4 and 9, the locus coeruleus contains noradrenergic neurons whose terminals innervate most regions of the brain. This nucleus plays an excitatory role in vigilance and an inhibitory role in REM sleep. And as we saw in Chapter 11, the amygdala is involved in emotional responses to aversive stimuli.

Maldonado et al. (1992) made rats physically dependent on morphine and then injected naloxone into various regions of the brain to see whether the sudden blocking of opiate receptors would stimulate symptoms of withdrawal. (This technique—administering an opiate for a prolonged interval and then blocking its effects with an antagonist—is referred to as **antagonist-precipitated withdrawal.**) The investigators found that the most sensitive site was the locus coeruleus, followed by the periaqueductal gray matter. Injection of naloxone into the amygdala produced a weak withdrawal syndrome. Using a similar technique (first infusing morphine into various regions of the brain and then precipitating withdrawal by giving the animals an intraperitoneal injection of naloxone), Bozarth (1994) found that injections into the locus coeruleus and the PAG produced withdrawal symptoms.

These studies suggest that opiate receptors in the locus coeruleus and periaqueductal gray matter are involved in withdrawal symptoms. So far, most of the research effort has been directed toward study of the locus coeruleus. A

naloxone   A drug that blocks mu opiate receptors; antagonizes the reinforcing and sedative effects of opiates.
pimozide   A drug that blocks dopamine receptors.
antagonist-precipitated withdrawal   Sudden withdrawal from long-term administration of a drug caused by cessation of the drug and administration of an antagonistic drug.

single dose of an opiate decreases the firing rate of these neurons, but if the drug is administered chronically, the firing rate will return to normal. Then, if an opiate antagonist is administered (to precipitate withdrawal symptoms), the firing rate of neurons in the locus coeruleus increases dramatically, which increases the release of norepinephrine in the projection of this nucleus (Hyman, 1996b; Koob, 1996; Nestler, 1996). In addition, lesions of the locus coeruleus reduce the severity of antagonist-precipitated withdrawal symptoms (Maldonado and Koob, 1993). A microdialysis study by Aghajanian, Kogan, and Moghaddam (1994) found that antagonist-precipitated withdrawal caused an increase in the level of glutamate and aspartate, two excitatory amino acid neurotransmitters, in the locus coeruleus.

The intracellular processes involved in the development of withdrawal symptoms to opiates appear to involve a protein known as **CREB** (cyclic AMP-responsive element-binding protein). As we saw, long-term exposure to opiates causes tolerance—a decreased sensitivity of neurons to opiates. This decreased sensitivity (also known as *downregulation*) occurs even though the number of opiate receptors does not change, which implies that the alteration must be intracellular, in the biochemical steps that link activation of the opiate receptor (a metabotropic receptor) to production of second messengers and the effects they produce (Hyman, 1996a). When mu receptors are activated by an opiate, they cause the production of cyclic AMP within the cell. This second messenger travels to the nucleus, where it binds with CREB. CREB itself plays a role in regulating the activity of some genes. Just what occurs in the nucleus when CREB is activated by cyclic AMP is not yet known.

Maldonado et al. (1996) produced a targeted mutation of the gene responsible for the production of CREB in mice. The animals appeared behaviorally normal, and injections of morphine produced analgesia and increased the animals' activity. (The investigators did not assess morphine's reinforcing effects.) However, the animals' response to antagonist-precipitated withdrawal from morphine was drastically reduced. (See *Figure 19.7.*) This study strongly suggests that CREB plays a critical role in the intracellular events responsible for the withdrawal effects of opioids. It will be interesting to learn whether other drugs that produce withdrawal effects, such as alcohol, also involve this mechanism.

● Cocaine and Amphetamine

Cocaine and amphetamine have similar behavioral effects, because both act as potent dopamine agonists. However, their sites of action are different. Cocaine binds with and deactivates the dopamine transporter proteins, thus block-

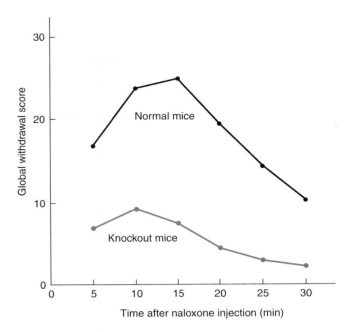

Figure 19.7
Withdrawal symptoms of normal mice and mice with a targeted mutation (knockout) of the gene responsible for the production of CREB.
(Adapted from Maldonado, R., Blendy, J.A., Tzavara, E., Gass, P., Roques, B.P., Hanoune, J., and Schütz, G. *Science,* 1996, *273,* 657–659.)

ing the reuptake of dopamine after it is released by the terminal buttons. Amphetamine also inhibits the reuptake of dopamine, but its most important effect is to directly stimulate the release of dopamine from terminal buttons. Free base cocaine ("crack"), a particularly potent form of the drug, is smoked and thus enters the blood supply of the lungs and reaches the brain very quickly. Because its effects are so potent and so rapid, it is probably the most effective reinforcer of all available drugs.

A recent study confirms that the reinforcing effects of cocaine involve the dopamine transporter molecules. Giros et al. (1996) produced a targeted mutation of the gene responsible for production of the dopamine transporter protein in mice. They found evidence for several compensatory mechanisms in the animals' brains that helped them adapt to the chronically higher level of dopamine. For example, they found a drastic reduction in postsynaptic dopamine receptors, and the level of tyrosine

CREB Cyclic AMP-responsive element-binding protein; a nuclear protein to which cyclic AMP can bind and affect the activity of a gene or set of genes.

hydroxylase, the enzyme required for the synthesis of dopamine, was reduced. Despite these compensatory mechanisms, dopamine that was released by terminal buttons persisted more than 100 times longer in the extracellular space, so even a small amount of dopamine had a profound effect. Because dopamine reuptake no longer occurred, cocaine had no effects on the animal's behavior. Neither did amphetamine. Some investigators believe that amphetamine causes the release of dopamine from terminal buttons by running the dopamine transporters in reverse so that they pump dopamine out of the cell rather than into it. The study by Giros and his colleagues suggests that this may indeed be the case. If the dopamine transporter does not exist, it cannot pump dopamine molecules in *either* direction.

When people take cocaine, they become euphoric, active, and talkative. They say that they feel powerful and alert. Some of them become addicted to the drug, and obtaining it becomes an obsession to which they devote more and more time and money. Laboratory animals, who will quickly learn to self-administer cocaine intravenously, also act excited and show intense exploratory activity. After receiving the drug for a day or two, rats start showing stereotyped movements, such as grooming, head bobbing, and persistent locomotion (Geary, 1987). If rats or monkeys are given continuous access to a lever that permits them to self-administer cocaine, they often self-inject so much cocaine that they die. In fact, Bozarth and Wise (1985) found that rats that self-administered cocaine were almost three times more likely to die than rats that self-administered heroin. (See *Figure 19.8.*)

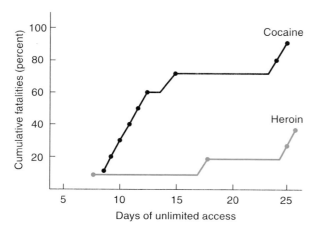

Figure 19.8
Cumulative fatalities in groups of rats self-administering cocaine or heroin.
(Adapted from Bozarth, M.A., and Wise, R.A. *Journal of the American Medical Association,* 1985, 254, 81–83. Reprinted with permission.)

One of the alarming effects of cocaine and amphetamine seen in people who abuse these drugs regularly is psychotic behavior: hallucinations, delusions of persecution, mood disturbances, and repetitive behaviors. These symptoms so closely resemble those of paranoid schizophrenia that even a trained mental health professional cannot distinguish them unless he or she knows about the person's history of drug abuse. As we saw in Chapter 17, the fact that these symptoms are provoked by dopamine agonists and reduced by drugs that block dopamine receptors suggests that overactivity of dopaminergic synapses is one of the causes of schizophrenia.

As we have seen, the mesolimbic dopamine system plays an essential role in all forms of reinforcement except, perhaps, for reinforcement mediated by opiate receptors. Because cocaine and amphetamine are potent dopamine agonists, these drugs activate the mesolimbic system and reinforce drug-taking behavior. Because cocaine is currently the stimulant drug of choice, much more research effort has been devoted to cocaine than to amphetamine.

Several studies have shown that intravenous injections of cocaine and amphetamine increase the concentration of dopamine in the nucleus accumbens, as measured by microdialysis (Petit and Justice, 1989; Di Ciano et al., 1995; Wise et al., 1995). For example, Figure 19.9 shows data collected from rats who learned to press a lever that delivered intravenous injections of cocaine or amphetamine. The colored bars at the base of the graphs indicate the animals' responses, and the line graphs indicate the level of dopamine in the nucleus accumbens. (See *Figure 19.9.*)

Several other lines of research indicate that the nucleus accumbens is a critical site for the reinforcing effects of cocaine and amphetamine. For example, rats will learn to press a lever that causes the injection of a small quantity of amphetamine directly into the nucleus accumbens (Hoebel et al., 1983; Phillips, Robbins, and Everitt, 1994). However, an injection of cocaine into the nucleus accumbens is *not* reinforcing (Goeders and Smith, 1983). A possible explanation for this unexpected result is that cocaine serves as a local anesthetic as well as a dopamine agonist. (Ophthalmologists often use cocaine to anesthetize the eye and the membranes surrounding it.) Thus, when cocaine is injected into the nucleus accumbens, it prevents neural communication by blocking the transmission of action potentials. In support of this suggestion, Carlezon, Devine, and Wise (1995) found that rats would press a lever that delivered injections of *nomifensine* into the nucleus accumbens. Like cocaine, nomifensine inhibits the reuptake of dopamine, but unlike cocaine, it does not act as a local anesthetic.

If drugs that block dopamine receptors are injected into the nucleus accumbens, cocaine loses much of its reinforcing effect (McGregor and Roberts, 1993; Caine et al.,

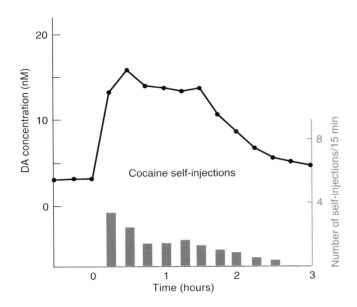

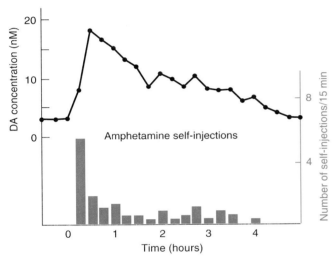

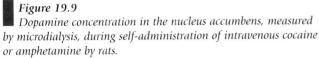

Figure 19.9
Dopamine concentration in the nucleus accumbens, measured by microdialysis, during self-administration of intravenous cocaine or amphetamine by rats.
(Adapted from Di Ciano, P., Coury, A., Depoortere, R.Y., Egilmez, Y., Lane, J.D., Emmett-Oglesby, M.W., Lepiane, F.G., Phillips, A.G., and Blaha, C.D. *Behavioural Pharmacology,* 1995, *6,* 311–322.)

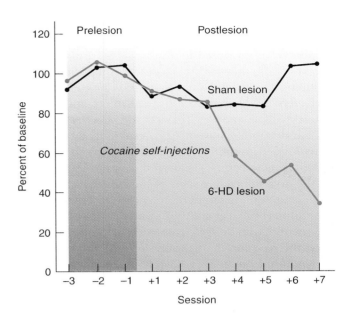

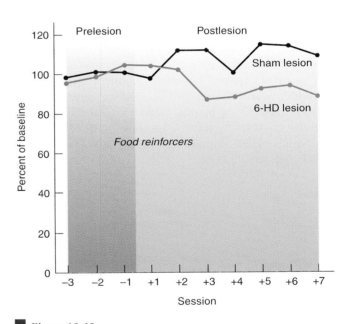

Figure 19.10
Changes in rate of responding for cocaine or food reinforcement by rats with sham lesions or 6-HD lesions of the nucleus accumbens, expressed as percentage of baseline rate.
(Adapted from Caine, S.B., and Koob, G.F. *Journal of the Experimental Analysis of Behavior,* 1994, *61,* 213–221.)

1995). In addition, lesions of the nucleus accumbens or destruction of dopaminergic terminals there with a local injection of 6-HD interferes with the reinforcing effects of both cocaine and amphetamine. For example, Caine and Koob (1994) found that after they injected 6-HD into the nucleus accumbens, rats stopped pressing a lever that produced intravenous injections of cocaine. They did, however, continue pressing the lever when doing so caused the delivery of a small pellet of food. Thus, the damage caused by the 6-HD did not simply interfere with the animals' ability to press the lever. (See *Figure 19.10.*)

As we saw, long-term cocaine or amphetamine use does not produce tolerance and is even likely to produce *sensitization* to the effects of the drug. But although withdrawal from long-term cocaine abuse does not cause physical symptoms, it does cause unpleasant feelings, including dysphoria and decreased ability to experience pleasure. We also saw that withdrawal from a variety of addictive drugs—including cocaine and amphetamine—cause a drastic fall in the level of dopamine in the nucleus accumbens (Rossetti, Hmaidan, and Gessa, 1992). This decrease in extracellular dopamine appears to be caused by an increased secretion of dynorphin, the endogenous opioid that stimulates kappa receptors. Dynorphin seems to act as a brake on the dopaminergic system of the nucleus accumbens. Stimulation of dopamine D_1 receptors increases levels of dynorphin (Engber et al., 1992), and the lack of D_1 receptors (in mice with a targeted mutation in the gene that produces this receptor) dramatically decreases the production of dynorphin (Xu et al., 1994). Kappa receptors serve as heteroreceptors on dopaminergic terminal buttons, where they produce presynaptic inhibition; thus, dynorphin has an inhibitory effect on the release of dopamine and reverses the effects of cocaine (Steiner and Gerfen, 1995).

Hyman (1996a) proposes that chronic, long-term cocaine or amphetamine use sensitizes dynorphin-secreting neurons in the nucleus accumbens. The increased release of dynorphin stimulates presynaptic kappa opiate receptors on dopaminergic terminal buttons, which decreases the release of dopamine. Then, if cocaine or amphetamine is suddenly withdrawn, the continuing activity of the dynorphin-secreting neurons reduces the levels of dopamine in the nucleus accumbens, causing the unpleasant symptoms that accompany discontinuation of these drugs. (See *Figure 19.11*.)

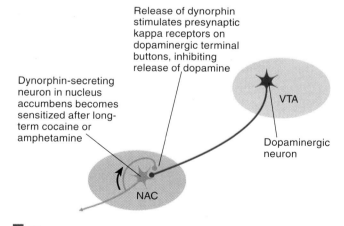

Release of dynorphin stimulates presynaptic kappa receptors on dopaminergic terminal buttons, inhibiting release of dopamine

Dynorphin-secreting neuron in nucleus accumbens becomes sensitized after long-term cocaine or amphetamine

VTA

Dopaminergic neuron

NAC

Figure 19.11
The role of dynorphin secretion in the regulation of dopamine release in the nucleus accumbens.
(Adapted from Hyman, S.E. *Neuron*, 1996, *16*, 901–904.)

● Nicotine

Nicotine may seem rather tame in comparison to opiates, cocaine, and amphetamine. Nevertheless, nicotine is an addictive drug, and it undoubtedly accounts for more deaths than the so-called "hard" drugs. The combination of nicotine and other substances in tobacco smoke is carcinogenic and leads to cancer of the lungs, mouth, throat, and esophagus. The addictive potential of nicotine should not be underestimated; many people continue to smoke even when doing so causes serious health problems. For example, Sigmund Freud, whose theory of psychoanalysis stressed the importance of insight in changing one's behavior, was unable to stop smoking even after most of his jaw had been removed because of the cancer that this habit had caused (Brecher, 1972). He suffered severe pain and, as a physician, realized that he should have stopped smoking. He did not, and his cancer finally killed him.

Although executives of tobacco companies and others whose economic welfare is linked to the production and sale of tobacco products argue that smoking is a "habit" rather than an "addiction," evidence suggests that the behavior of people who regularly use tobacco resembles that of compulsive drug users. In a review of the literature, Stolerman and Jarvis (1995) note that smokers tend to smoke regularly or not at all; few can smoke just a little. Males smoke an average of seventeen cigarettes per day, while females smoke an average of fourteen. Nineteen out of twenty smokers smoke every day, and only 60 out of 3500 smokers questioned smoke fewer than five cigarettes per day. Forty percent of people continue to smoke after having had a laryngectomy (which is usually performed to treat throat cancer), more than 50 percent of heart attack survivors continue to smoke, and about 50 percent of people continue to smoke after submitting to surgery for lung cancer. Of those who attempt to quit smoking by enrolling in a special program, 20 percent manage to abstain for one year. The record is much poorer for those who try to quit on their own: One-third manage to stop for one day, one-fourth for one week, but only 4 percent manage to abstain for six months. It is difficult to reconcile these figures with the assertion that smoking is merely a "habit" that is pursued for the "pleasure" that it produces.

Ours is not the only species willing to self-administer nicotine; so will laboratory animals (Donny et al., 1995). Nicotine stimulates acetylcholine receptors, of course. It also increases the activity of dopaminergic neurons of the mesolimbic system, which contain these receptors (Mereu et al., 1987), and causes dopamine to be released in the nucleus accumbens (Damsma, Day, and Fibiger, 1989).

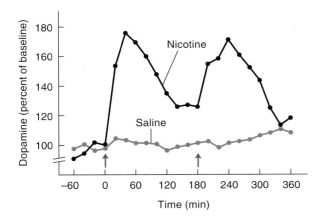

Figure 19.12
Changes in dopamine concentration in the nucleus accumbens, measured by microdialysis, in response to injections of nicotine or saline. The arrows indicate the time of the injections.
(Adapted from Damsma, G., Day, J., and Fibiger, H.C. *European Journal of Pharmacology,* 1989, *168*, 363–368. Reprinted with permission.)

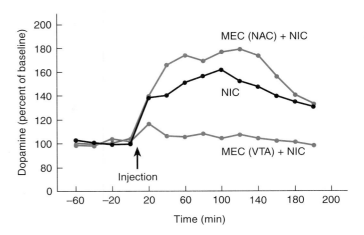

Figure 19.13
Changes in dopamine concentration in the nucleus accumbens, measured by microdialysis, in response to injections of intravenous nicotine alone or in conjunction with an infusion of a nicotinic antagonist in the ventral tegmental area of the nucleus accumbens. Only the injection in the ventral tegmental blocked the secretion of dopamine in the nucleus accumbens.
(Adapted from Nisell, M., Nomikos, G.G., and Svensson, T.H. *Synapse,* 1994, *16*, 36–44.)

Figure 19.12 shows the effects of two injections of nicotine or saline on the extracellular dopamine level of the nucleus accumbens, measured by microdialysis. (See *Figure 19.12.*)

Injection of a nicotinic agonist directly into the ventral tegmental area will reinforce a conditioned place preference (Museo and Wise, 1994). Conversely, injection of a nicotinic antagonist into the VTA will reduce the reinforcing effect of intravenous injections of nicotine (Corrigall, Coen, and Adamson, 1994). But although nicotinic receptors are found in both the ventral tegmental area and the nucleus accumbens (Swanson et al., 1987), Corrigall and his colleagues found that injections of a nicotinic antagonist in the nucleus accumbens has no effect on reinforcement. Corroborating these findings, Nisell, Nomikos, and Svensson (1994) found that infusion of a nicotinic antagonist into the VTA—but not into the nucleus accumbens—will prevent an intravenous injection of nicotine from triggering the release of dopamine in the nucleus accumbens. (See *Figure 19.13.*) Thus, the reinforcing effect of nicotine appears to occur in the ventral tegmental area, on nicotinic receptors located on the dendrites of mesolimbic dopaminergic neurons.

Cessation of smoking after long-term use causes withdrawal symptoms, including anxiety, restlessness, insomnia, and inability to concentrate (Hughes et al., 1989). Like the withdrawal symptoms of other drugs, these symptoms may increase the likelihood of relapse, but they do not explain why people become addicted to the drug in the first place. As we saw earlier, withdrawal from cocaine, amphetamine, or the opiates causes a dramatic decrease in the level of dopamine in the nucleus accumbens. The same phenomenon accompanies withdrawal from nicotine (Fung et al., 1996).

Wise (1988) notes that because nicotine stimulates the tegmentostriatal dopaminergic system, smoking could potentially make it more difficult for a cocaine or heroin addict to stop taking the drug. As several studies with laboratory animals have shown, if self-administration of cocaine or heroin is extinguished through nonreinforcement, an injection of drugs that stimulate dopaminergic neurons can reinstate the responding. A similar "cross-priming" effect from cigarette smoking could potentially contribute to a relapse in people who are trying to abstain. (And because alcohol also stimulates dopaminergic neurons, drinking could present the same problem.)

● Alcohol and Barbiturates

Alcohol has greater costs to society than any other drug. A large percentage of deaths and injuries caused by motor vehicle accidents are related to alcohol use, and alcohol contributes to violence and aggression. Chronic alcoholics often lose their jobs, their homes, and their families; and many die of cirrhosis of the liver, exposure, or diseases

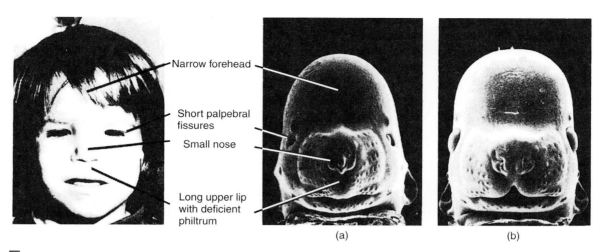

Narrow forehead

Short palpebral fissures

Small nose

Long upper lip with deficient philtrum

(a)   (b)

Figure 19.14
A child with fetal alcohol syndrome, along with magnified views of rat fetuses. (a) Fetus whose mother received alcohol during pregnancy. (b) Normal rat fetus.
(Photograph courtesy of Katherine K. Sulik.)

caused by poor living conditions and abuse of their bodies. Women who drink during pregnancy run the risk of giving birth to babies with the fetal alcohol syndrome, which includes malformation of the head and the brain. Figure 19.14 compares a child and a rat fetus with fetal alcohol syndrome; as you can see, similar malformations are seen in the face and head in both species. More serious, of course, are the malformations in the brain. (See *Figure 19.14.*) The leading cause of mental retardation in the Western world today is alcohol consumption by pregnant women (Abel and Sokol, 1986). Thus, understanding the physiological and behavioral effects of this drug is an important issue.

At low doses, alcohol produces mild euphoria and has an *anxiolytic* effect—that is, it reduces the discomfort of anxiety. At higher doses, it produces incoordination and sedation. In studies with laboratory animals the anxiolytic effects manifest themselves as a release from the punishing effects of aversive stimuli. For example, if an animal is given electric shocks whenever it makes a particular response (say, one that obtains food or water), it will stop doing so. However, if it is then given some alcohol, it will begin making the response again (Koob et al., 1984). This phenomenon explains why people often do things they normally would not when they have had too much to drink; the alcohol removes the inhibitory effect of social controls on their behavior.

Alcohol produces both positive and negative reinforcement. The positive reinforcement manifests itself as mild euphoria. As we saw earlier, *negative* reinforcement is caused by the termination of an aversive stimulus. If a person feels anxious and uncomfortable, then an anxiolytic drug that relieves this discomfort provides at least a temporary escape from an unpleasant situation.

The negative reinforcement provided by the anxiolytic effect of alcohol is probably not enough to explain the drug's addictive potential. Other drugs, such as the benzodiazepines (tranquilizers such as Valium), are even more potent anxiolytics than alcohol, and yet such drugs are rarely abused. It is probably the unique combination of stimulating and anxiolytic effects—of positive and negative reinforcement—that makes alcohol so difficult for some people to resist.

Laboratory animals can be induced to become dependent on alcohol. As I mentioned earlier, the drugs with the strongest abuse potential are those that produce the most rapid effects, such as heroin, cocaine, and nicotine. Because alcohol is ingested orally, its reinforcing effects do not occur for several minutes. Most animals find the flavor of alcohol to be aversive. For example, if rats are offered a 10 percent alcohol solution, they tend not to drink it and hence do not experience its reinforcing effects. However, if some saccharine is mixed with the solution, they begin drinking it. At first, they drink a small amount each day, but after several days, they drink enough to become intoxicated (Reid, 1996). What appears to happen is that they begin to experience the reinforcing effects while drinking, and these effects increase their intake. The sweet taste gets them to sample enough of the alcohol and its reinforcing effects to become dependent on the drug.

Alcohol, like other addictive drugs, increases the activity of the dopaminergic neurons of the mesolimbic system and increases the release of dopamine in the nucleus accumbens as measured by microdialysis (Gessa et al., 1985; Imperato and Di Chiara, 1986). The release of dopamine appears to be related to the positive reinforcement that alcohol can produce. An injection of a dopamine antagonist directly into the nucleus accumbens decreases alcohol intake (Samson et al., 1993), as does the injection of a drug into the ventral tegmental area that decreases the activity of the dopaminergic neurons there (Hodge et al., 1993).

In low to moderate doses, alcohol appears to have two major sites of action in the nervous system, acting as an inverse agonist at NMDA receptors and an indirect agonist at GABA$_A$ receptors. That is, alcohol enhances the action of GABA at GABA$_A$ receptors and interferes with the transmission of glutamate at NMDA receptors. A study by Shelton and Balster (1994) indicated that the perceptual effects of alcohol are mimicked by both GABA agonists and NMDA antagonists. To do this, they employed the **drug discrimination procedure.** This procedure uses the physiological effects of drugs as discriminative stimuli to learn something about the nature of these effects (Schuster and Balster, 1977). An animal is given a drug and then is trained to press one of two levers to receive food. The next day, it receives an injection of saline (or another placebo) and is trained to press the other lever. Each day thereafter, it is injected with either the drug or the saline, and it receives food only if it presses the appropriate lever. Obviously, the presence or absence of feedback from the effects of the drug tells the animal which lever to press. Then on test days the animal is given another drug. If the animal presses the "drug" lever, we can conclude that the feedback feels similar to the first drug; if it presses the "saline" lever, we can conclude that it does not.

Shelton and Balster (1994) trained rats to discriminate between the effects of injections of alcohol and saline and then injected the animals with various drugs on test days. The rats pressed the "alcohol" lever when they received injections of drugs that facilitated GABA transmission (including a benzodiazepine tranquilizer and a barbiturate) or those that interfered with glutamate transmission at NMDA receptors. Thus, the perceptual effects of alcohol include those produced by both of these classes of drugs.

Let's consider the evidence that alcohol acts as an NMDA antagonist. Like alcohol, NMDA antagonists produce sedative, hypnotic, and anxiolytic effects and interfere with cognitive performance (Tabakoff and Hoffman, 1996). Also like alcohol, NMDA antagonists cause the release of dopamine in the nucleus accumbens (Imperato et al., 1990; Loscher, Annies, and Honack, 1991).

As we saw in Chapter 14, NMDA receptors are involved in long-term potentiation, a phenomenon that plays an important role in learning. Thus, it will not surprise you to learn that alcohol, which antagonizes the action of glutamate at NMDA receptors, disrupts long-term potentiation and interferes with the spatial receptive fields of place cells in the hippocampus (Givens and McMahon, 1995; Matthews, Simson, and Best, 1996). Presumably, this effect at least partly accounts for the deleterious effects of alcohol on memory and other cognitive functions.

Withdrawal from long-term alcohol intake (like that of heroin, cocaine, amphetamine, and nicotine) decreases the activity of mesolimbic neurons and their release of dopamine in the nucleus accumbens (Diana et al., 1993). If an inverse agonist for NMDA receptors is then administered, dopamine secretion in the nucleus accumbens recovers. The evidence suggests the following sequence of events: Some of the acute effects of a single dose of alcohol are caused by the antagonistic effect of the drug on NMDA receptors. Long-term suppression of NMDA receptors causes upregulation—a compensatory increase in the sensitivity of the receptors. Then, when alcohol intake suddenly ceases, the increased activity of NMDA receptors inhibits the activity of ventral tegmental neurons and the release of dopamine in the nucleus accumbens.

Although the effects of heroin withdrawal have been exaggerated, those produced by barbiturate or alcohol withdrawal are serious and can even be fatal. Convulsions caused by alcohol withdrawal are considered to be a medical emergency and are usually treated with benzodiazepines. Evidence suggests that activation of NMDA receptors may be responsible for the seizures caused by alcohol withdrawal. For example, Valverius et al. (1990) studied two strains of mice that had been bred for their sensitivity to the effects of alcohol withdrawal (Crabbe et al., 1990). Like humans, mice will develop seizures if they are given large doses of alcohol for several days and are then abruptly withdrawn from the drug. Under these conditions, animals from the withdrawal-seizure prone (WSP) strain are much more likely than those from the withdrawal-seizure resistant (WSR) strain to develop seizures. (Incidentally, the WSP mice do not voluntarily drink alcohol any more than do the WSR mice; thus, the neural mechanisms of seizure susceptibility are different from those of alcohol preference. The genetics of alcohol addiction are discussed later in this chapter.) Valverius and his colleagues found that the WSP mice had a greater number of NMDA receptors in the hippocampus than the WSR

drug discrimination procedure An experimental procedure in which an animal shows, through instrumental conditioning, whether the perceived effects of two drugs are similar.

mice. Confirming these results, Liljequist (1991) found that seizures caused by alcohol withdrawal could be prevented by giving mice a drug that blocks NMDA receptors. These observations strongly suggest that NMDA receptors are responsible for seizures produced by alcohol withdrawal.

The second site of action of alcohol is the GABA$_A$ receptor. Alcohol binds with one of the many binding sites on this receptor and increases the effectiveness of GABA in opening the chloride channel and producing inhibitory postsynaptic potentials. Proctor et al. (1992) used the microiontophoresis technique to record the activity of single neurons in the cerebral cortex of slices of rat brains. They found that the presence of alcohol significantly increased the postsynaptic response produced by the action of GABA at the GABA$_A$ receptor. As we saw in Chapter 4, the anxiolytic effects of the benzodiazepine tranquilizers is caused by their action as indirect agonists at the GABA$_A$ receptor. Because alcohol has this effect also, we can surmise that the anxiolytic effect of alcohol is a result of this action of the drug.

The sedative effect of alcohol also appears to be exerted at the GABA$_A$ receptor. Suzdak et al. (1986) discovered of a drug (Ro15-4513) that reverses alcohol intoxication by blocking the alcohol binding site on this receptor. Figure 19.15 shows two rats who received injections of enough alcohol to make them pass out. The one facing us also received an injection of the alcohol antagonist and appears completely sober. (See *Figure 19.15.*)

This wonder drug is not likely to reach the market soon, if ever. Although the behavioral effects of alcohol are mediated by their action on GABA$_A$ receptors and NMDA receptors, high doses of alcohol have other, potentially fatal

▌ *Figure 19.15*
Effects of Ro15-4513, an alcohol antagonist. Both rats received an injection of alcohol, but the one facing us also received an injection of the alcohol antagonist.
(Photograph courtesy of Steven M. Paul, National Institute of Mental Health, Bethesda, Md.)

effects on all cells of the body, including destabilization of cell membranes. Thus, people taking some of the alcohol antagonist could then go on to drink themselves to death without becoming drunk in the process. Drug companies naturally fear possible liability suits stemming from such occurrences.

Barbiturates have effects very similar to those of alcohol. In fact, both drugs act as indirect agonists on the GABA$_A$ receptor (Maksay and Ticku, 1985). However, the binding sites for alcohol and barbiturates appear to be different; Ro15-4513, the alcohol antagonist, does not reverse the intoxicating effects of barbiturates (Suzdak et al., 1986). But because both drugs act on the same receptor, their effects are additive; if a person takes a moderate dose of alcohol and a moderate dose of a barbiturate, the effect can be fatal.

I mentioned earlier that opiate receptors appear to be involved in a reinforcement mechanism that does not directly involve dopaminergic neurons. The reinforcing effects of alcohol is at least partly caused by its ability to trigger the release of the endogenous opioids. Several studies have shown that the opiate receptor blockers such as naloxone or naltrexone block the reinforcing effects of alcohol in a variety of species, including rats, monkeys, and humans (Altschuler, Phillips, and Feinhandler, 1980; Davidson, Swift, and Fitz, 1996; Reid, 1996). Because naltrexone has become a useful adjunct to treatment of alcoholism, I will discuss this topic further in the last section of this chapter.

● Cannabis

Another drug that people regularly self-administer—almost exclusively by smoking—is THC, the active ingredient in marijuana. As you learned in Chapter 4, THC receptors have been discovered, and their distribution in the brain has been mapped. The endogenous ligand for these receptors, anandamide, is a lipid. But we still do not know what situations trigger the release of anandamide or what functions this chemical serves. Incidentally, di Tomaso, Beltramo, and Piomelli (1996) discovered that chocolate contains three anandamidelike chemicals. Whether the existence of these chemicals is related to the great appeal that chocolate has for many people is not yet known. (I suppose that this is the place for a chocoholic joke.)

One thing we do now know about THC is that it, like other drugs with abuse potential, has an effect on dopaminergic neurons. Chen et al. (1990) injected rats with low doses of THC and measured the release of dopamine in the nucleus accumbens by means of microdialysis. Sure

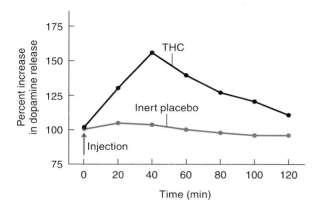

Figure 19.16

Changes in dopamine concentration in the nucleus ac-cumbens, measured by microdialysis, in response to injec-tions of THC or an inert placebo.

(Adapted from Chen, J., Paredes, W., Li, J., Smith, D., Lowin-son, J., and Gardner, E.L. *Psychopharmacology,* 1990, *102,* 156–162. Reprinted with permission.)

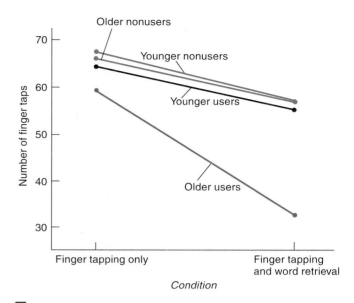

Figure 19.17

Speed of finger tapping alone or while naming words in a particular category of younger and older users and nonusers of cannabis.

(Adapted from Fletcher, J.M., Page, J.B., Francis, D.J., Copeland, K., Naus, M.J., Davis, C.M., Morris, R., Krauskopf, D., and Satz, P. *Archives of General Psychiatry,* 1996, *53,* 1051–1057.)

enough, they found that the injections caused the release of dopamine. (See *Figure 19.16.*) Chen et al. (1993) found that local injections of small amounts of THC into the ven-tral tegmental area had no effect on the release of dopa-mine in the nucleus accumbens. However, injection of THC into the nucleus accumbens *did* cause dopamine re-lease there. Thus, the drug appears to act directly on dopa-minergic terminal buttons—presumably on presynaptic heteroreceptors.

As we saw in Chapter 4, the hippocampus contains a large concentration of THC receptors. Marijuana is known to affect people's memory. Specifically, it impairs their abil-ity to keep track of a particular topic—they frequently lose the thread of a conversation if they are momentarily dis-tracted. Perhaps the drug does so by disrupting the normal functions of the hippocampus, which plays such an im-portant role in memory.

Students often ask me whether researchers have discov-ered any damaging effects of long-term marijuana use. Un-til now, most studies that have shown deleterious effects of cannabis on cognitive abilities have involved people who abused other drugs as well, and more carefully controlled studies have failed to demonstrate any effects. However, a more recent study (Fletcher et al., 1995) examined Costa Rican men with long histories of cannabis use. The users were compared with nonusers who were matched on age, occupational status, education, marital status, and use of alcohol and tobacco. Several measures of cognitive abilities showed small but statistically significant impairments in the cannabis users. A test of the ability to perform two dif-

ferent tasks simultaneously (tapping a finger rapidly while trying to think of words that fit a particular category) was especially sensitive to long-term cannabis use. Men who had used cannabis for eight years showed no deficit on this task, while those who had used it for about 25 years showed a substantial decline. (See *Figure 19.17.*)

Interim Summary

Opiates produce analgesia, hypothermia, sedation, and re-inforcement. Opiate receptors in the periaqueductal gray matter are responsible for the analgesia, those in the pre-optic area for the hypothermia, those in the mesencephalic reticular formation for the sedation, and those in the ven-tral tegmental area and nucleus accumbens at least partly for the reinforcement. A targeted mutation in mice indi-cates that mu receptors are responsible for analgesia, rein-forcement, and withdrawal symptoms. Kappa receptors, normally stimulated by dynorphin, have an inhibitory ef-fect on the release of dopamine in the nucleus accumbens and have an aversive effect. A study using the conditioned place preference procedure found that morphine will rein-force behavior even after the destruction of the nucleus accumbens, so the release of dopamine there is not the only cause of the reinforcing effects of opiates. The release of the endogenous opioids may play a role in the reinforcing effects of natural stimuli such as water or even other addictive drugs such as alcohol.

The symptoms produced by antagonist-precipitated withdrawal from opiates can be elicited by injecting naloxone into the periaqueductal gray matter and the locus coeruleus, which implicate these structures in these symptoms. A targeted mutation of the gene responsible for the production of CREB (cyclic AMP-responsive element-binding protein) drastically reduces the magnitude of withdrawal effects.

Cocaine inhibits the reuptake of dopamine by terminal buttons, and amphetamine causes the dopamine transporters in terminal buttons to run in reverse, releasing dopamine from terminal buttons. A targeted mutation of the gene responsible for the production of the dopamine transporter blocks these effects. Besides producing alertness, activation, and positive reinforcement, cocaine and amphetamine can produce psychotic symptoms that resemble those of paranoid schizophrenia. Long-term use of these drugs leads to sensitization rather than tolerance. The reinforcing effects of cocaine and amphetamine are mediated by an increase in dopamine in the nucleus accumbens. Unpleasant symptoms that accompany withdrawal from these drugs may be mediated by the activity of dynorphin-secreting neurons.

The status of nicotine as a strongly addictive drug (for both humans and laboratory animals) was long ignored, primarily because it does not cause intoxication and because the ready availability of cigarettes and other tobacco products does not make it necessary for addicts to engage in illegal activities. However, the craving for nicotine is extremely motivating. Nicotine stimulates the release of mesolimbic dopaminergic neurons, and injection of nicotine into the ventral tegmental area is reinforcing.

Alcohol and barbiturates have similar (but not identical) effects. Alcohol has positively reinforcing effects and, through its anxiolytic action, has negatively reinforcing effects as well. It serves as an inverse agonist at NMDA receptors and an indirect agonist at $GABA_A$ receptors. It stimulates the release of dopamine in the nucleus accumbens. Withdrawal from long-term alcohol abuse can lead to seizures, an effect that seems to be caused by compensatory upregulation of NMDA receptors. Release of the endogenous opioids also plays a role in the reinforcing effects of alcohol.

The active ingredient in cannabis, THC, stimulates receptors whose natural ligand is anandamide. THC, like other addictive drugs, stimulates the release of dopamine in the nucleus accumbens.

HEREDITY AND DRUG ABUSE

Not everyone is equally likely to become addicted to a drug. Many people manage to drink alcohol moderately, and even many users of potent drugs such as cocaine and heroin use them "recreationally" without becoming dependent on them. There are only two possible sources of individual differences in any characteristic: heredity and environment. Because this book considers the *physiology* of behavior, I will not discuss the role that environment plays in a person's susceptibility to the addicting effects of drugs. Obviously, environmental effects are important; people who are raised in a squalid environment without any real hope for a better life are more likely than other people to turn to drugs for some temporary euphoria and removal from the unpleasant world that surrounds them. But even in a given environment, poor or privileged, some people become addicts and some do not—and some of these behavioral differences are a result of genetic differences, as we will see in the following subsections.

Heritability Studies of Humans

Most of the research on the effects of heredity on addiction have been devoted to alcoholism. One of the reasons for this focus—aside from the importance of the problems caused by alcohol—is that almost everyone is exposed to alcohol. Most people drink alcohol sometime in their lives and thus have firsthand experience with its reinforcing effects. The same is not true for cocaine, heroin, and other drugs that have even more potent effects. In most countries, alcohol is freely and legally available in local shops, whereas cocaine and heroin must often be purchased in dangerous neighborhoods from unsavory dealers. From what we now know about the effects of addictive drugs on the nervous system, it seems likely that the results of studies on the heredity of alcoholism will apply to other types of drug addiction as well.

Before I begin my discussion of the genetics of alcohol abuse, I should mention that some investigators have recently begun studying the abuse of another freely available drug: nicotine (Gilbert and Gilbert, 1995; Heath et al., 1995). In general, studies have found that the heritability of smoking is just as strong as that of alcoholism. Smoking has also been shown to be related to some personal characteristics, including neurosis, social alienation, impulsiveness, sensation seeking, low conscientiousness, low socioeconomic status, and low achievement.

The Evidence

Alcohol consumption is not distributed equally across the population; in the United States, 10 percent of the people drink 50 percent of the alcohol (Heckler, 1983). The best evidence for an effect of heredity on susceptibility to alcoholism comes from two main sources: twin studies and cross-fostering studies. Monozygotic twins tend to resemble each other more closely than dizygotic twins in many ways, including the likelihood of alcohol abuse (Goodwin, 1979).

The second type of heritability study uses children who were adopted by nonrelatives when they were young. A study like this permits the investigator to estimate the effects of family environment as well as genetics. That is, one can examine the effects of being raised by an alcoholic parent, or having a biological parent who is an alcoholic, or both on the probability of becoming alcoholic. Such a study was carried out in Stockholm by Cloninger et al. (1981, 1985) and was replicated in Gothenburg, another Swedish city (Sigvardsson, Bohman, and Cloninger, 1996). Briefly, the studies found that heredity was much more important than family environment. But the story is not quite that simple.

In a review of the literature on alcohol abuse, Cloninger (1987) notes that many investigators have concluded that there are two principal types of alcoholics: those who cannot abstain but drink consistently and those who are able to go without drinking for long periods of time but are unable to control themselves once they start. (For convenience I will refer to these two groups as "steady drinkers" and "bingers.") Steady drinking is associated with antisocial personality disorder, which includes a lifelong history of impulsiveness, fighting, lying, and lack of remorse for antisocial acts. Binge drinking is associated with emotional dependence, behavioral rigidity, perfectionism, introversion, and guilt feelings about one's drinking behavior. Steady drinkers usually begin their alcohol consumption early in life, whereas binge drinkers begin much later. (See Table 19.1.)

Steady drinking is strongly influenced by heredity. The Stockholm adoption study found that men with fathers who were steady drinkers were almost seven times more likely to become steady drinkers themselves than were men whose fathers did not abuse alcohol. Family environment had no measurable effect; the boys began drinking whether or not the members of their adoptive family themselves drank heavily. Very few women become steady drinkers;

Table 19.1
Characteristic Features of Two Types of Alcoholism

Feature	Steady	Binge
Usual age of onset (years)	Before 25	After 25
Spontaneous alcohol seeking (inability to abstain)	Frequent	Infrequent
Fighting and arrests when drinking	Frequent	Infrequent
Psychological dependence (loss of control)	Infrequent	Frequent
Guilt and fear about alcohol dependence	Infrequent	Frequent
Novelty seeking	High	Low
Harm avoidance	Low	High
Reward dependence	Low	High

Source: From Cloninger, C.R. *Science,* 1987, 236, 410–416. Copyright 1987 by the American Association for the Advancement of Science.

the daughters of steady-drinking fathers instead tend to develop *somatization disorder.* People with this disorder chronically complain of symptoms for which no physiological cause can be found, leading them to seek medical care almost continuously. Thus, the genes that predispose a man to become a steady-drinking alcoholic (antisocial type) predispose a woman to develop somatization disorder. The reason for this interaction with gender is not known.

Binge drinking is influenced both by heredity and by environment. The Stockholm adoption study found that having a biological parent who was a binge drinker had little effect on the development of binge drinking unless the child was exposed to a family environment in which there was heavy drinking. The effect was seen in both males and females.

Possible Mechanisms

When we find an effect of heredity on behavior, we have good reason to suspect the existence of a biological difference. That is, genes affect behavior only by affecting the body. A susceptibility to alcoholism could conceivably be caused by differences in the ability to digest or metabolize alcohol or by differences in the structure or biochemistry of the brain. Most investigators believe that differences in brain physiology are more likely to play a role. Cloninger (1987) notes that many studies have shown that people with antisocial tendencies, which includes the group of steady drinkers, show a strong tendency to seek novelty and excitement. These people are disorderly and distractible (many have a history of hyperactivity as children) and show little restraint in their behavior. They tend not to fear dangerous situations or social disapproval. They are easily bored. On the other hand, binge drinkers tend to be anxious, emotionally dependent, sentimental, sensitive to social cues, cautious and apprehensive, fearful of novelty or change, rigid, and attentive to details. Their EEGs show little slow alpha activity, which is characteristic of a relaxed state (Propping, Kruger, and Mark, 1981). When they take alcohol, they report a pleasant relief of tension (Propping, Kruger, and Janah, 1980). Perhaps, as Cloninger suggests, these personality differences are a result of differences in the sensitivity of neural mechanisms involved in reinforcement, exploration, and punishment.

For example, steady drinkers may have an undersensitive punishment mechanism, which makes them unresponsive to danger and to social disapproval. They may also have an undersensitive reinforcement system, which leads them to seek more intense thrills (including those provided by alcohol) to experience pleasurable sensations. Thus, they seek the excitatory (dopamine-stimulating) effect of alcohol. Binge drinkers may have oversensitive punishment systems. Normally, they avoid drinking because of the guilt they experience afterward; but once they begin, and once the sedative effect begins, the alcohol-induced suppression of the punishment system makes it impossible for them to stop.

Recently, investigators have focused on the possibility that susceptibility to addiction may involve differences in dopaminergic mechanisms—for reasons you will understand, having read this chapter. Blum et al. (1990) reported that severe alcoholism was related to the presence of the A1 allele of the gene responsible for the production of the D_2 dopamine receptor, which is found on chromosome 11. (An *allele* is a particular form of a gene.) The idea that susceptibility to addiction is related to genetic differences in receptors known to be involved in the physiology of reinforcement is an intriguing one, and the report of the research was greeted with considerable interest from clinicians and other researchers.

Unfortunately, the issue is still not settled. One review of the literature concluded that an association between the A1 allele and alcoholism had not been established (Gelernter, Goldman, and Risch, 1993). Neiswanger, Kaplan, and Hill (1995) describe complications that make it difficult to decide whether there is a statistically significant cor-

relation. For example, Caucasian nonalcoholics have a lower frequency of the A1 allele than either alcoholics or the general population. Because the issue of appropriate comparison groups is important, we will have to await further research to decide the facts of the matter.

Meanwhile, just to confuse matters further, I should note that some studies suggest that cocaine addiction and smoking may be associated with a higher frequency of the A1 allele (Noble et al., 1993, Noble et al., 1994). And as we saw in Chapter 18, susceptibility to development of posttraumatic stress disorder may be related to the presence of the A1 allele.

● Animal Models of Drug Abuse

Another approach to the study of the physiology of addiction is through the use of animal models. Several different strains of alcohol-preferring rats have been developed through selective breeding, and studies have shown that these animals differ in interesting ways. Alcohol-preferring rats do just what their name implies: If they are given a drinking tube containing a solution of alcohol along with their water and food, they become heavy drinkers. The alcohol-nonpreferring rats abstain (Li, Lumeng, and Doolittle, 1993). Figure 19.18 shows the amount of alcohol consumed by subsequent generations of rats selected for high and low preference for alcohol. (See *Figure 19.18.*)

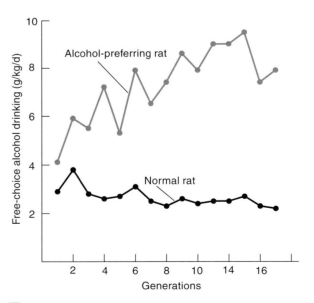

Figure 19.18
Alcohol intake of successive generations of rats selected for alcohol preference and nonpreference.
(Adapted from Li, T.-.K., Lumeng, L., and Doolittle, D.P. *Behavioral Genetics*, 1993, 23, 163–170.)

Alcohol-preferring rats (*P rats*) and alcohol-nonprefer-ring rats (*NP rats*) show interesting behavioral and physio-logical differences. If they are given small doses of alcohol, the alcohol-preferring rats show more behavioral activa-tion. They also are more tolerant of the aversive effects of high doses, and they have lower brain levels of serotonin and dopamine (Gongwer et al., 1989; McBride et al., 1991). Li, Lumeng, and Doolittle (1993) suggest that the mesolimbic dopaminergic system in alcohol-preferring rats may be more sensitive to the effects of alcohol, but so far the evidence is inconclusive. P rats may also be more sensitive to the hedonic value of tastes; they drink more of a tasty sucrose solution and less of an aversive sodium chloride solution than NP rats do (Stewart et al., 1994).

Several studies (for example, Murphy et al., 1987) have found a lower level of dopamine in the nucleus accum-bens of alcohol-preferring rats. Zhou et al (1995) found a smaller number of dopaminergic neurons projecting from the ventral tegmental area to the nucleus accumbens. McBride et al. (1995) studied the offspring of rats of mixed P and NP parentage. They found that heavier drinkers had a lower level of dopamine in the nucleus accumbens, as measured by microdialysis. As we saw, a low level of do-pamine in the NAC correlates with anhedonia and dys-phoria, and Cloninger suggests that at least some forms of alcoholism may be caused by a decreased sensitivity to re-inforcement. Perhaps the NP rats drink more to make up for this insensitivity.

Not all laboratory research on the role of heredity in drug abuse has involved rodents. Higley, Suomi, and Lin-noila (1996) report the results of a long-term study with rhesus monkeys. They found that the cerebrospinal fluid levels of 5-HIAA in monkeys was stable from infancy to adulthood; thus, the levels were probably under the con-trol of genetic factors. The level of 5-HIAA, a metabolite of serotonin (5-HT), is an indirect measure of the activity of serotonergic neurons. (As we saw in Chapter 17, the level of 5-HIAA in the CSF of humans is related to depression and suicide.) Higley and his colleagues made an alcoholic beverage available to the monkeys and found that those with the lowest levels of 5-HIAA had the highest rates of al-cohol intake. They also found evidence for environmental effects: Monkeys that had been deprived of contact with their mothers early in life also tended to drink more.

Interim Summary

Most people who are exposed to addictive drugs—even drugs with a high abuse potential—do not become ad-dicts. Evidence suggests that the likelihood of addiction,

especially to alcohol and nicotine, is strongly affected by heredity. There may be two types of alcoholism, one re-lated to an antisocial, pleasure-seeking personality (steady drinkers) and another related to a repressed, anxiety-rid-den personality (binge drinkers). Alcoholism may be re-lated to the presence of the A1 allele of the D2 dopamine receptor. Some investigators believe that a better under-standing of the physiological basis of reinforcement and punishment will help us understand the effects of hered-ity on susceptibility to addiction. In fact, animal studies have shown that it is possible to selectively breed animals who do or do not prefer alcohol, and physiological stud-ies have found that the level of dopamine release is lower in alcohol-preferring rats. The low level of serotonin may play an important role in alcoholism; a long-term study with monkeys showed that CSF levels of the serotonin metabolite 5-HIAA were stable throughout life and that low levels were associated with higher levels of alcohol intake.

THERAPY FOR DRUG ABUSE

There are many reasons for engaging in research on the physiology of drug abuse, including an academic interest in the nature of reinforcement and the pharmacology of psychoactive drugs. But most researchers entertain the hope that the results of their research will contribute to the development of ways to treat and (better yet) prevent drug abuse in members of our own species. As you well know, the incidence of drug abuse is far too high, so obviously, re-search has not yet solved the problem. However, real progress has been made.

The most common treatment for opiate addiction is methadone maintenance. Methadone is a potent opiate, just like morphine or heroin. If it were available in a form suitable for injection, it would be abused. (In fact, metha-done clinics must control their stock of methadone care-fully to prevent it from being stolen and sold to opiate abusers.) Methadone maintenance programs administer the drug to their patients in the form of a liquid, which they must drink in the presence of the personnel supervis-ing this procedure. Because the oral route of administra-tion increases the opiate level in the brain slowly, the drug does not produce a high, the way an injection of heroin will. In addition, because methadone is long-lasting, the patient's opiate receptors remain occupied for a long time, which means that an injection of heroin has little effect. Of course, a very large dose of heroin will displace methadone from opiate receptors and produce a "rush," so the method is not foolproof.

As we saw, opiate receptor blockers such as naloxone and naltrexone interfere with the action of opiates. Emergency rooms always have one of these drugs available to rescue patients who have taken an overdose of heroin, and many lives have been saved by these means. But although an opiate antagonist will block the effects of heroin, the research reviewed earlier in this chapter suggests that it should *increase* the craving for heroin. Nevertheless, some clinicians have reported that naltrexone treatment during six hours of general anesthesia can be used to withdraw patients from heroin very quickly. After the withdrawal, the patient is kept on maintenance doses of naltrexone to prevent him or her from experiencing reinforcing effects of heroin (Sandler and Freundlich, 1996). So far, this procedure is proprietary and has been used only by clinics licensed by a company that own the rights to it. It has not yet been evaluated by independent researchers.

As we saw earlier, the reinforcing effects of cocaine and amphetamine are primarily a result of the sharply increased levels of dopamine these drugs produce in the nucleus accumbens. Drugs that block dopamine receptors certainly block the reinforcing effects of cocaine and amphetamine, but they also produce dysphoria and anhedonia. People will not tolerate the unpleasant feelings these drugs produce, so they are not useful treatments for cocaine and amphetamine abuse. Drugs that *stimulate* dopamine receptors can reduce a person's dependence on cocaine or amphetamine, but these drugs are just as addictive as the drugs they replace and have the same deleterious effects on health.

You may recall that several studies found that the increased sensitivity of D_3 dopamine receptors produced by chronic exposure to cocaine may be involved in the craving for cocaine experienced by people trying to break their dependency on cocaine. Some investigators suggest that drugs that block D_3 receptors may reduce this craving and thus be a useful adjunct to treatment of cocaine dependency (Staley and Mash, 1996).

An interesting approach to cocaine addiction is suggested by a study by Carrera et al. (1995), who conjugated cocaine to a foreign protein and managed to stimulate rats' immune systems to develop antibodies to cocaine. These "cocaine-immunized" rats were less sensitive to the activating effects of cocaine, and brain levels of cocaine in these animals were lower after an injection of the drug. As Leshner (1996) suggests, it might someday be possible to vaccinate cocaine abusers (or perhaps inject them with an antibody developed by genetic engineering) so that an injection of cocaine will not produce reinforcing effects. This treatment would have many advantages because (theoretically, at least) it would interfere only with the action of cocaine and not with the normal operations of people's reinforcement mechanisms. Thus, the treatment should not decrease their ability to experience normal pleasure.

A treatment similar to methadone maintenance has been used as an adjunct to treatment for nicotine addiction. For several years, chewing gum containing nicotine has been available by prescription, and more recently, transdermal patches that release nicotine through the skin have been marketed. Both methods maintain a sufficiently high level of nicotine in the brain to decrease a person's craving for nicotine. Once the habit of smoking has subsided, the dose of nicotine can be decreased to wean the person from the drug. Carefully controlled studies have shown that nicotine maintenance therapy, and not administration of a placebo, is useful in treatment for nicotine dependence (Stolerman and Jarvis, 1995). However, nicotine maintenance therapy is most effective if it is part of a counseling program. (See *Figure 19.19.*)

As we saw in Chapter 18, serotonin agonists have proved themselves useful in treatment of panic disorder and obsessive compulsive disorder (and related disorders such as hair pulling and nail biting). These drugs also appear to be useful in treating alcoholism; several double-blind studies have found that 5-HT reuptake blockers make it easier for alcoholics to abstain. For example, Naranjo et al. (1992) found that citalopram (a serotonin agonist) "decreased interest, desire, craving, and liking for alcohol" in alcoholics who were receiving treatment for their addiction. It appeared to do so by decreasing the reinforcing effects of alcohol.

As I mentioned earlier, several studies have shown that opiate antagonists decrease the reinforcing value of alcohol in a variety of species, including our own. This finding suggests that the reinforcing effect of alcohol—at least in part—is produced by the secretion of endogenous opioids and the activation of opiate receptors in the brain. A study by Davidson, Swift, and Fitz (1996) clearly illustrates this effect. The investigators arranged a double-blind, placebo-controlled study with sixteen college-age men and women to investigate the effects of naltrexone on social drinkers. None of the participants were alcohol abusers, and pregnancy tests assured that the women were not pregnant. They gathered around a table in a local restaurant/bar for three two-hour drinking sessions, two weeks apart. For several days before the meeting, they swallowed capsules that contained either naltrexone or an inert placebo. The results showed that naltrexone increased the latency to take the first sip and to take a second drink and that the blood alcohol levels of the naltrexone-treated participants were lower at the end of the session. In general, the people who had taken naltrexone found that their drinks did not taste

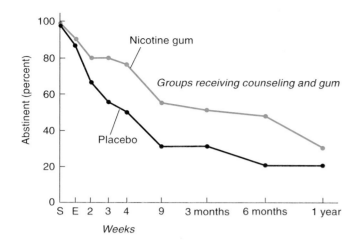

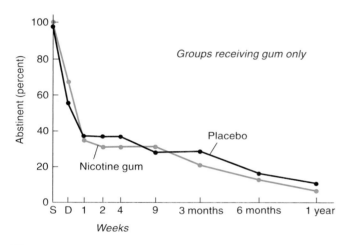

Figure 19.19
Percentage of smokers chewing nicotine gum alone or in conjunction with counseling who abstained from smoking.
(Adapted from Schneider, N.G., and Jarvik, M.E. *NIDA Research Monographs,* 1985, *53,* 83–101.)

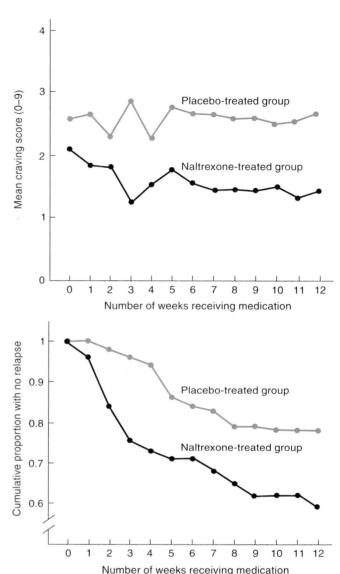

Figure 19.20
Mean craving score and proportion of patients who abstained from drinking while receiving naltrexone or a placebo.
(Adapted from O'Brien, C.P., Volpicelli, L.A., and Volpicelli, J.R. *Alcohol,* 1996, *13,* 35–39.)

very good—and in fact, some of them asked for a different drink after taking the first sip.

These results are consistent with reports of the effectiveness of naltrexone as an adjunct to programs designed to treat alcohol abuse. For example, O'Brien, Volpicelli, and Volpicelli (1996) reported the results of two long-term programs using naltrexone along with more traditional behavioral treatments. Both programs found that administration of naltrexone significantly increased the likelihood of success. As Figure 19.20 shows, naltrexone decreased the participants' craving for alcohol and increased the number of participants who managed to abstain from alcohol. (See **Figure 19.20.**)

Interim Summary

Although drug abuse is difficult to treat, researchers have developed several useful therapies. Methadone maintenance replaces addiction to heroin by addiction to an opiate that does not produce euphoric effects when administered orally. Similarly, nicotine-containing gum and transdermal patches help smokers combat their addiction. Naloxone and naltrexone block opiate receptors, but because they produce unpleasant effects, they are useful only with addicts who are strongly motivated to break their habit. D_3 receptor antagonists show promise of helping people break an addiction to cocaine. The development of antibodies to cocaine in rats holds out the possibility that people may some day be immunized against the drug. Serotonin agonists show promise in decreasing craving for alcohol. However, the most effective pharmacological adjunct to treatment for alcoholism appears to be naltrexone, which blocks some of the drug's reinforcing effects.

A personal note: You are now at the end of the book (as you well know), and you have spent a considerable amount of time reading my words. While working on this book, I have tried to imagine myself talking to someone who is interested in learning something about the physiology of behavior. As I mentioned in the preface, writing is often a lonely activity, and the imaginary audience helped keep me company. If you would like to turn this communication into a two-way conversation, write to me—my address is given at the end of the preface.

SUGGESTED READINGS

Dietrich, R., and Erwin, V.G. *Pharmacological Effects of Ethanol on the Central Nervous System.* Boca Raton, FL: CRC Press, 1996.

Feldman. R.S., Meyer, J.S., and Quenzer, L.F. *Principles of Neuropsychopharmacology.* Sunderland, MA: Sinauer Associates, 1997.

Grilly, D.M. *Drugs and Human Behavior.* 2nd ed. Boston: Allyn and Bacon, 1989.

Winger, G., Hofmann, F.G., and Woods, J.H. *A Handbook on Drug and Alcohol Abuse: The Biomedical Aspects.* New York: Oxford University Press, 1992.

Glossary

absorptive phase   The phase of metabolism during which nutrients are absorbed from the digestive system; glucose and amino acids constitute the principal source of energy for cells during this phase, and excess nutrients are stored in adipose tissue in the form of triglycerides.

accessory olfactory bulb   A neural structure located in the main olfactory bulb that receives information from the vomeronasal organ.

accommodation   Changes in the thickness of the lens of the eye, accomplished by the ciliary muscles, that focus images of near or distant objects on the retina.

acetyl-CoA *(a see tul)*   A cofactor that supplies acetate for the synthesis of acetylcholine.

acetylcholine (ACh) *(a see tul koh leen)*   A neurotransmitter found in the brain, spinal cord, and parts of the peripheral nervous system; responsible for muscular contraction.

acetylcholinesterase (AChE) *(a see tul koh lin ess ter ace)*   The enzyme that destroys acetylcholine soon after it is liberated by the terminal buttons, thus terminating the postsynaptic potential.

achromatopsia *(ay krohm a top see a)*   Inability to discriminate among different hues; caused by damage to the visual association cortex.

actin   One of the proteins (with myosin) that provide the physical basis for muscular contraction.

action potential   The brief electrical impulse that provides the basis for conduction of information along an axon.

activational effect (of hormone)   The effect of a hormone that occurs in the fully developed organism; may depend on the organism's prior exposure to the organizational effects of hormones.

adenosine triphosphate (ATP) *(ah den o seen)*   A molecule of prime importance to cellular energy metabolism; its breakdown liberates energy.

adenosine *(a den oh seen)*   A nucleoside; a combination of ribose and adenine; serves as a neuromodulator in the brain.

adrenal medulla   The inner portion of the adrenal gland, located atop the kidney, controlled by sympathetic nerve fibers; secretes epinephrine and norepinephrine.

adrenocorticotropic hormone (ACTH)   A hormone released by the anterior pituitary gland in response to CRF; stimulates the adrenal cortex to produce glucocorticoids.

afferent axon   An axon directed toward the central nervous system, conveying sensory information.

affinity   The readiness with which two molecules join together.

agonist   1. A drug that facilitates the effects of a particular neurotransmitter on the postsynaptic cell. 2. A muscle whose contraction produces or facilitates a particular movement.

agoraphobia   A fear of being away from home or other protected places.

agouti mouse   A strain of mice whose yellow fur and obesity are caused by a mutation that causes the production of a peptide that blocks MC4 receptors in the brain.

agrammatism   One of the usual symptoms of Broca's aphasia; a difficulty in comprehending or properly employing grammatical devices, such as verb endings and word order.

akinetic mutism   A motor disorder characterized by a relative lack of movement and lack of speech; caused by damage to the cingulate gyrus.

albumin *(al bew min)*   A protein found in the blood; serves to transport free fatty acids and can bind with some lipid-soluble drugs.

aldosterone *(al dahs ter own)*   A hormone of the adrenal cortex that causes the retention of sodium by the kidneys.

all-or-none law   The principle that once an action potential is triggered in an axon, it is propagated, without decrement, to the end of the fiber.

allylglycine   A drug that inhibits the activity of GAD and thus blocks the synthesis of GABA.

alpha activity   Smooth electrical activity of 8–12 Hz recorded from the brain; generally associated with a state of relaxation.

alpha motor neuron   A neuron whose axon forms synapses with extrafusal muscle fibers of a skeletal muscle; activation contracts the muscle fibers.

2,5-AM   A drug that inhibits carbohydrate metabolism in the liver by making phosphate unavailable, thus blocking the production of ATP.

amacrine cell (*amm a krin*)   A neuron in the retina that interconnects adjacent ganglion cells and the inner processes of the bipolar cells.

AMPA receptor   An ionotropic glutamate receptor that controls a sodium channel; stimulated by AMPA and blocked by CNQX.

AMPT   A drug that blocks the activity of tyrosine hydroxylase and thus interferes with the synthesis of the catecholamines.

ampulla (*am pull uh*)   An enlargement in a semicircular canal; contains the cupula and the crista.

amygdala (*a mig da la*)   A structure in the interior of the rostral temporal lobe, containing a set of nuclei; part of the limbic system.

anandamide (*a nan da mide*)   A lipid; the endogenous ligand for receptors that bind with THC, the active ingredient of marijuana.

androgen insensitivity syndrome   A condition caused by a congenital lack of functioning androgen receptors; in a person with XY sex chromosomes, causes the development of a female with testes but no internal sex organs.

androgen (*an dro jen*)   A male sex steroid hormone. Testosterone is the principal mammalian androgen.

angiotensin (*ann gee oh ten sin*)   A peptide hormone that constricts blood vessels, causes the secretion of aldosterone, and produces thirst and a salt appetite.

angiotensinogen (*ann gee oh ten sin oh jen*)   A protein in the blood that can be converted by renin to angiotensin.

anomia   Difficulty in finding (remembering) the appropriate word to describe an object, action, or attribute; one of the symptoms of aphasia.

anorexia nervosa   A disorder that most frequently afflicts young women; exaggerated concern with overweight that leads to excessive dieting and often compulsive exercising; can lead to starvation.

antagonist-precipitated withdrawal   Sudden withdrawal from long-term administration of a drug caused by cessation of the drug and administration of an antagonistic drug.

antagonist   1. A drug that opposes or inhibits the effects of a particular neurotransmitter on the postsynaptic cell. 2. A muscle whose contraction resists or reverses a particular movement.

anterior pituitary gland   The anterior part of the pituitary gland; an endocrine gland whose secretions are controlled by the hypothalamic hormones.

anterior   With respect to the central nervous system, located near or toward the head.

anterograde   In a direction along an axon from the cell body toward the terminal buttons.

anterograde amnesia   Amnesia for events that occur after some disturbance to the brain, such as head injury or certain degenerative brain diseases.

anterograde labeling method (*ann ter oh grade*)   A histological method that labels the axons and terminal buttons of neurons whose cell bodies are located in a particular region.

anti-Müllerian hormone   A peptide secreted by the fetal testes that inhibits the development of the Müllerian system, which would otherwise become the female internal sex organs.

antibody   A protein produced by a cell of the immune system that recognizes antigens present on invading microorganisms.

anticipatory anxiety   A fear of having a panic attack; may lead to the development of agoraphobia.

antigen   A protein present on a microorganism that permits the immune system to recognize it as an invader.

anxiety disorder   A psychological disorder characterized by tension, overactivity of the autonomic nervous system, expectation of an impending disaster, and continuous vigilance for danger.

anxiolytic (*angz ee oh lit ik*)   An anxiety-reducing effect.

AP5   2-amino-5-phosphonopentanoate; a drug that blocks NMDA receptors.

aphasia   Difficulty in producing or comprehending speech not produced by deafness or a simple motor deficit; caused by brain damage.

apomorphine (*ap o more feen*)   A drug that blocks dopamine autoreceptors at low doses; at higher doses blocks postsynaptic receptors as well.

apperceptive visual agnosia   Failure to perceive objects, even though visual acuity is relatively normal.

apraxia   Difficulty in carrying out purposeful movements, in the absence of paralysis or muscular weakness.

apraxia of speech   Impairment in the ability to program movements of the tongue, lips, and throat required to produce the proper sequence of speech sounds.

arachnoid granulation   Small projections of the arachnoid membrane through the dura mater into the superior sagittal sinus; CSF flows through them to be reabsorbed into the blood supply.

arachnoid membrane (*a rak noyd*)   The middle layer of the meninges, between the outer dura mater and inner pia mater. The subarachnoid space beneath the arachnoid membrane is filled with cerebrospinal fluid, which cushions the brain.

arcuate fasciculus   A bundle of axons that connects Wernicke's area with Broca's area; damage causes conduction aphasia.

arcuate nucleus   A nucleus in the base of the hypothalamus that controls secretions of the anterior pituitary gland; contains NPY-secreting neurons involved in feeding and control of metabolism.

area postrema (*poss* **tree** *ma*)   A region of the medulla where the blood–brain barrier is weak; poisons can be detected there and can initiate vomiting.

aromatization (*air* oh mat i **zay** shun)   A chemical reaction catalyzed by an aromatase; the process by which testosterone is transformed into estradiol.

associative long-term potentiation   A long-term potentiation in which concurrent stimulation of weak and strong synapses to a given neuron strengthens the weak ones.

associative visual agnosia   Inability to identify objects that are perceived visually, even though the form of the perceived object can be drawn or matched with similar objects.

astrocyte   A glial cell that provides support for neurons of the central nervous system, provides nutrients and other substances, and regulates the chemical composition of the extracellular fluid.

atrial natriuretic peptide (ANP) (*nay* tree ur **ett** ik)   A peptide secreted by the atria of the heart when blood volume is higher than normal; increases water and sodium excretion, inhibits renin, vasopressin, and aldosterone secretion, and inhibits sodium appetite.

atropine (*a* tro peen)   A drug that blocks muscarinic acetylcholine receptors.

autistic disorder   A chronic disorder whose symptoms include failure to develop normal social relations with other people, impaired development of communicative ability, lack of imaginative ability, and repetitive, stereotyped movements.

autonomic nervous system (ANS)   The portion of the peripheral nervous system that controls the body's vegetative functions.

autoradiography   A procedure that locates radioactive substances in a slice of tissue; the radiation exposes a photographic emulsion or a piece of film that covers the tissue.

autoreceptor   A receptor molecule located on a neuron that responds to the neurotransmitter released by that neuron.

autotopagnosia   Inability to name body parts or to identify body parts that another person names.

axon   The long, thin, cylindrical structure that conveys information from the soma of a neuron to its terminal buttons.

axonal varicosities   Enlarged regions along the length of an axon that contain synaptic vesicles and release a neurotransmitter or neuromodulator.

axoplasmic transport   An active process by which substances are propelled along microtubules that run the length of the axon.

β-CCM   A direct agonist for the benzodiazepine binding site of the $GABA_A$ receptor.

B-lymphocyte   A white blood cell that originates in the bone marrow; part of the immune system.

Balint's syndrome   A syndrome caused by bilateral damage to the parieto-occipital region; includes optic ataxia, ocular apraxia, and simultanagnosia

basal forebrain region   The region at the base of the forebrain rostral to the hypothalamus; involved in thermoregulation and control of sleep.

basal ganglia   A group of subcortical nuclei in the telencephalon, the caudate nucleus, the globus pallidus, and the putamen; important parts of the motor system.

basal nucleus   A group of subnuclei of the amygdala that receives sensory input from the lateral and basolateral nuclei and relays information to other amygdaloid nuclei and to the periaqueductal gray matter.

basic rest–activity cycle (BRAC)   A 90-min cycle (in humans) of waxing and waning alertness, controlled by a biological clock in the caudal brain stem; controls cycles of REM sleep and slow-wave sleep.

basilar membrane (*bazz* i ler)   A membrane in the cochlea of the inner ear; contains the organ of Corti.

benzodiazepine (ben zoe dy **azz** a peen)   A category of anxiolytic drugs; an indirect agonist for the $GABA_A$ receptor.

beta activity   Irregular electrical activity of 13–30 Hz recorded from the brain; generally associated with a state of arousal.

bicuculline (by **kew** kew leen)   A direct antagonist for the GABA binding site on the $GABA_A$ receptor.

binding site   The location on a receptor protein to which a ligand binds.

bipolar cell   A bipolar neuron located in the middle layer of the retina, conveying information from the photoreceptors to the ganglion cells.

bipolar disorder   A serious mood disorder characterized by cyclical periods of mania and depression.

bipolar neuron   A neuron with one axon and one dendrite attached to its soma.

black widow spider venom   A poison produced by the black widow spider that triggers the release of acetylcholine.

blindsight   The ability of a person who cannot see objects in his or her blind field to accurately reach for them while remaining unconscious of perceiving them; caused by damage restricted to the primary visual cortex.

blood–brain barrier A semipermeable barrier produced by the cells in the walls of the capillaries in the brain.

botulinum toxin *(bot you **lin** um)* An acetylcholine antagonist: prevents release by terminal buttons.

brain stem The "stem" of the brain, from the medulla to the diencephalon, excluding the cerebellum.

bregma The junction of the sagittal and coronal sutures of the skull; often used as a reference point for stereotaxic brain surgery.

brightness One of the perceptual dimensions of color; intensity.

Broca's aphasia A form of aphasia characterized by agrammatism, anomia, and extreme difficulty in speech articulation.

Broca's area A region of frontal cortex, located just rostral to the base of the left primary motor cortex, that is necessary for normal speech production.

Bruce effect Termination of pregnancy caused by the odor of a pheromone in the urine of a male other than the one that impregnated the female; first identified in mice.

bulimia nervosa Bouts of excessive hunger and eating, often followed by forced vomiting or purging with laxatives; sometimes seen in people with anorexia nervosa.

cable properties The passive conduction of electrical current, in a decremental fashion, down the length of an axon.

caffeine A drug that blocks adenosine receptors.

calcarine fissure *(**kal** ka rine)* A horizontal fissure located in the medial occipital lobe; contains most of the primary visual cortex.

callosal apraxia An apraxia of the left hand caused by damage to the anterior corpus callosum.

CaM-KII Type II calcium-calmodulin kinase, an enzyme that must be activated by calcium; may play a role in the establishment of long-term potentiation.

capsaicin *(kap **say** sin)* An ingredient in hot peppers that can destroy small, unmyelinated sensory axons that innervate the internal organs.

carbachol *(**car** ba call)* A drug that stimulates acetylcholine receptors.

carbamazepine A drug (trade name: Tegretol) that is used to treat seizures originating from a focus, generally in the medial temporal lobe.

cardiac muscle The muscle responsible for the contraction of the heart.

cataplexy *(**kat** a plex ee)* A symptom of narcolepsy; complete paralysis that occurs during waking.

catecholamine *(cat a **kohl** a meen)* A class of amines that includes the neurotransmitters dopamine, norepinephrine, and epinephrine.

cauda equina *(ee **kwye** na)* A bundle of spinal roots located caudal to the end of the spinal cord.

caudal "Toward the tail"; with respect to the central nervous system, in a direction along the neuraxis away from the front of the face.

caudal block The anesthesia and paralysis of the lower part of the body produced by injection of a local anesthetic into the cerebrospinal fluid surrounding the cauda equina.

caudate nucleus A telencephalic nucleus, one of the input nuclei of basal ganglia; involved with control of voluntary movement.

central nervous system (CNS) The brain and spinal cord.

central nucleus The region of the amygdala that receives information from the basolateral division and sends projections to a wide variety of regions in the brain; involved in emotional responses.

central sulcus *(**sul** kus)* The sulcus that separates the frontal lobe from the parietal lobe.

cerebellar cortex The cortex that covers the surface of the cerebellum.

cerebellar peduncle *(**pee** dun kul)* One of three bundles of axons that attach each cerebellar hemisphere to the dorsal pons.

cerebellum *(sair a **bell** um)* A major part of the brain located dorsal to the pons, containing the two cerebellar hemispheres, covered with the cerebellar cortex; an important component of the motor system.

cerebral aqueduct A narrow tube interconnecting the third and fourth ventricles of the brain, located in the center of the mesencephalon.

cerebral cortex The outermost layer of gray matter of the cerebral hemispheres.

cerebral hemisphere *(sa **ree** brul)* One of the two major portions of the forebrain, covered by the cerebral cortex.

cerebrospinal fluid (CSF) A clear fluid, similar to blood plasma, that fills the ventricular system of the brain and the subarachnoid space surrounding the brain and spinal cord.

cerebrovascular accident A "stroke"; brain damage caused by occlusion or rupture of a blood vessel in the brain.

chlorpromazine *(klor **proh** ma zeen)* A drug that reduces the symptoms of schizophrenia by blocking dopamine D_2 receptors.

cholecystokinin (CCK) *(coal i sis toe **ky** nin)* A hormone secreted by the duodenum that regulates gastric motility and causes the gallbladder (cholecyst) to contract; appears to provide a satiety signal transmitted to the brain through the vagus nerve.

choline acetyltransferase (ChAT) (*koh* leen a see tul *trans fer ace*)   The enzyme that transfers the acetate ion from acetyl coenzyme A to choline, producing the neurotransmitter acetylcholine.

chorda tympani   A branch of the facial nerve that passes beneath the eardrum; conveys taste information from the anterior part of the tongue and controls the secretion of some salivary glands.

choroid plexus   The highly vascular tissue that protrudes into the ventricles and produces cerebrospinal fluid.

chromosome   A strand of DNA, with associated proteins, found in the nucleus; carries genetic information.

cilium   A hairlike appendage of a cell involved in movement or in transducing sensory information; found on the receptors in the auditory and vestibular system.

cingulate gyrus (*sing* yew lett)   A strip of limbic cortex lying along the lateral walls of the groove separating the cerebral hemispheres, just above the corpus callosum.

circadian rhythm (sur *kay* dee un or sur ka *dee* un)   A daily rhythmical change in behavior or physiological process.

circumlocution   A strategy by which people with anomia find alternative ways to say something when they are unable to think of the most appropriate word.

cisterna   A part of the Golgi apparatus; through the process of pinocytosis, it receives portions of the presynaptic membrane and recycles them into synaptic vesicles.

clasp-knife reflex   A reflex that occurs when force is applied to flex or extend the limb of an animal showing decerebrate rigidity; resistance is replaced by sudden relaxation.

classical conditioning   A learning procedure; when a stimulus that initially produces no particular response is followed several times by an unconditional stimulus that produces a defensive or appetitive response (the **unconditional response**), the first stimulus (now called a conditional stimulus) itself evokes the response (now called a conditional response).

clozapine (*kloz* a peen)   A drug that reduces the symptoms of schizophrenia, apparently by blocking dopamine D_4 receptors.

cochlea (*cock* lee uh)   The snail-shaped structure of the inner ear that contains the auditory transducing mechanisms.

cochlear implant   An electronic device surgically implanted in the inner ear that can enable deaf people to hear.

cochlear nerve   The branch of the auditory nerve that transmits auditory information from the cochlea to the brain.

cochlear nucleus   One of a group of nuclei in the medulla that receive auditory information from the cochlea.

colloid (*kalh* oyd)   A soluble, gluelike substance made of large molecules that cannot penetrate cell membranes.

color constancy   The relatively constant appearance of the colors of objects viewed under varying lighting conditions.

commissure (*kahm* i sher)   A fiber bundle that interconnects corresponding regions on each side of the brain.

complementary colors   Colors that make white or gray when mixed together.

complex cell   A neuron in the visual cortex that responds to the presence of a line segment with a particular orientation located within its receptive field, especially when the line moves perpendicularly to its orientation.

compulsion   The feeling that one is obliged to perform a behavior, even if one prefers not to do so.

computerized tomography (CT)   The use of a device that employs a computer to analyze data obtained by a scanning beam of X rays to produce a two-dimensional picture of a "slice" through the body.

conditioned emotional response   A classically conditioned response that occurs when a neutral stimulus is followed by an aversive stimulus; usually includes autonomic, behavioral, and endocrine components such as changes in heart rate, freezing, and secretion of stress-related hormones.

conditioned flavor aversion   The avoidance of a relatively unfamiliar flavor that previously caused (or was followed by) illness.

conditioned place preference   The learned preference for a location in which an organism encountered a reinforcing stimulus, such as food or a reinforcing drug.

conditioned punisher   A previously neutral stimulus that has been followed by an aversive stimulus, which then itself becomes capable of punishing a response.

conditioned reinforcer   A previously neutral stimulus that has been paired with an appetitive stimulus, which then itself becomes capable, of reinforcing a response.

conduction aphasia   An aphasia characterized by inability to repeat words that are heard but normal speech and the ability to comprehend the speech of others.

cone   One of the receptor cells of the retina; maximally sensitive to one of three different wavelengths of light and hence encodes color vision.

confabulation   The reporting of memories of events that did not take place without the intention to deceive; seen in people with Korsakoff's syndrome.

congenital adrenal hyperplasia (CAH) (hy per *play* zha)   A condition characterized by hypersecretion of androgens by the adrenal cortex; in females, causes masculinization of the external genitalia.

consolidation The process by which short-term memories are converted into long-term memories.

constructional apraxia Difficulty in drawing pictures or diagrams or in making geometrical constructions of elements such as building blocks or sticks; caused by damage to the right parietal lobe.

content word A noun, verb, adjective, or adverb that conveys meaning.

contralateral Located on the opposite side of the body.

Coolidge effect The restorative effect of introducing a new female sex partner to a male that has apparently become "exhausted" by sexual activity.

coping response A response through which an organism can avoid, escape from, or minimize an aversive stimulus; reduces the stressful effects of an aversive stimulus.

corpus callosum *(core pus ka low sum)* The largest commissure of the brain, interconnecting the areas of neocortex on each side of the brain.

corpus luteum *(lew tee um)* A cluster of cells that develops from the ovarian follicle after ovulation; secretes estradiol and progesterone.

correctional mechanism In a regulatory process, the mechanism that is capable of changing the value of the system variable.

corticobulbar pathway A bundle of axons from the motor cortex to the fifth, seventh, ninth, tenth, eleventh, and twelfth cranial nerves; controls movements of the face, neck, tongue, and parts of the extraocular eye muscles.

corticorubral tract The system of axons that travels from the motor cortex to the red nucleus.

corticospinal tract The system of axons that originates in the motor cortex and terminates in the ventral gray matter of the spinal cord.

corticotropin-releasing factor (CRF) A hypothalamic hormone that stimulates the anterior pituitary gland to secrete ACTH (adrenocorticotrophic hormone).

cranial nerve A peripheral nerve attached directly to the brain.

CREB Cyclic AMP-responsive element-binding protein; a nuclear protein to which cyclic AMP can bind and affect the activity of a gene or set of genes.

cross section With respect to the central nervous system, a slice taken at right angles to the neuraxis.

cupula *(kew pew luh)* A gelatinous mass found in the ampulla of the semicircular canals; moves in response to the flow of the fluid in the canals.

curare *(kew rahr ee)* A drug that blocks nicotinic acetylcholine receptors.

cutaneous sense *(kew tane ee us)* One of the somatosenses; includes sensitivity to stimuli that involve the skin.

cytochrome oxidase (CO) blob The central region of a module of the primary visual cortex, revealed by a stain for cytochrome oxidase; contains wavelength-sensitive neurons; part of the parvocellular system.

cytokine A category of chemicals released by certain white blood cells when they detect the presence of an invading microorganism; causes other white blood cells to proliferate and mount an attack against the invader.

cytoplasm The viscous, semiliquid substance contained in the interior of a cell.

cytoskeleton Formed of microtubules, neurofilaments, and microfilaments, linked to each other and forming a cohesive mass that gives a cell its shape.

D system A system of serotonergic neurons that originates in the dorsal raphe nucleus; its axonal fibers are thin, with spindle-shaped varicosities that do not appear to form synapses with other neurons.

decerebrate Describes an animal whose brain stem has been transected.

decerebrate rigidity Simultaneous contraction of agonistic and antagonistic muscles; caused by decerebration or damage to the reticular formation.

declarative memory Memory that can be verbally expressed, such as memory for events in a person's past.

deep cerebellar nuclei Nuclei located within the cerebellar hemispheres; receive projections from the cerebellar cortex and send projections out of the cerebellum to other parts of the brain.

defeminizing effect An effect of a hormone present early in development that reduces or prevents the later development of anatomical or behavioral characteristics typical of females.

defensive behavior A species-typical behavior by which an animal defends itself against the threat of another animal.

Deiters's cell *(dye terz)* A supporting cell found in the organ of Corti; sustains the auditory hair cells.

delayed matching-to-sample task A task that requires the subject to indicate which of several stimuli has just been perceived.

delta activity Regular, synchronous electrical activity of approximately 1–4 Hz recorded from the brain; occurs during the deepest stages of slow-wave sleep.

delusion A belief that is clearly in contradiction to reality.

dendrite A branched, treelike structure attached to the soma of a neuron; receives information from the terminal buttons of other neurons.

dendritic spike An action potential that occurs in the dendrite of some types of pyramidal cells.

dendritic spine A small bud on the surface of a dendrite, with which a terminal button from another neuron forms a synapse.

dentate gyrus   Part of the hippocampal formation; receives inputs from the entorhinal cortex and projects to field CA3 of the hippocampus.

dentate nucleus   A deep cerebellar nucleus; involved in the control of rapid, skilled movements by the corticospinal and rubrospinal systems.

2-deoxyglucose (2-DG) *(dee ox ee **gloo** kohss)*   A sugar that enters cells along with glucose but is not metabolized.

deoxyribonucleic acid (DNA) *(dee ox ee **ry** bo new **clay** ik)*   A long, complex macromolecule consisting of two interconnected helical strands; along with associated proteins, strands of DNA constitute the chromosomes.

depolarization   Reduction (toward zero) of the membrane potential of a cell from its normal resting potential.

depot binding   Binding of a drug with various tissues of the body or with proteins in the blood.

deprenyl *(**depp** ra nil)*   A drug that blocks the activity of MAO-B; acts as a dopamine agonist.

desynchrony   Irregular electrical activity recorded from the brain, generally associated with periods of arousal.

detector   In a regulatory process, a mechanism that signals when the system variable deviates from its set point.

deuteranopia *(dew ter an **owe** pee a)*   An inherited form of defective color vision in which red and green hues are confused; "green" cones are filled with "red" cone opsin.

developmental dyslexia   A reading difficulty in a person of normal intelligence and perceptual ability; of genetic origin or caused by prenatal or perinatal factors.

diabetes insipidus *(in **sipp** i duss)*   The loss of excessive amounts of water through the kidneys; caused by lack of secretion of vasopressin.

diencephalon *(dy en **seff** a lahn)*   A region of the forebrain surrounding the third ventricle; includes the thalamus and the hypothalamus.

diffusion   Movement of molecules from regions of high concentration to regions of low concentration.

dihydrotestosterone *(dy hy dro tess **tahss** ter own)*   An androgen, produced from testosterone through the action of the enzyme 5α reductase.

direct agonist   A drug that binds with and activates a receptor.

direct antagonist   A synonym for receptor blocker.

direct dyslexia   A language disorder caused by brain damage in which the person can read words aloud without understanding them.

display rule   A culturally determined rule that modifies the expression of emotion in a particular situation.

doctrine of specific nerve energies   Müller's conclusion that because all nerve fibers carry the same type of message, sensory information must be specified by the particular nerve fibers that are active.

dopamine (DA) *(**dope** a meen)*   A neurotransmitter; one of the catecholamines.

dorsal   "Toward the back"; with respect to the central nervous system, in a direction perpendicular to the neuraxis toward the top of the head or the back.

dorsal lateral geniculate nucleus   A group of cell bodies within the lateral geniculate body of the thalamus; receives inputs from the retina and projects to the primary visual cortex.

dorsal root   The spinal root that contains incoming (afferent) sensory fibers.

dorsal root ganglion   A nodule on a dorsal root that contains cell bodies of afferent spinal nerve neurons.

dose-response curve   A graph of the magnitude of an effect of a drug as a function of the amount of drug administered.

double labeling   Labeling neurons in a particular region by two different means; for example, by using an anterograde tracer and a label for a particular enzyme.

drug dependency insomnia   An insomnia caused by the side effects of ever-increasing doses of sleeping medications.

drug discrimination procedure   An experimental procedure in which an animal shows, through instrumental conditioning, whether the perceived effects of two drugs are similar.

drug effects   The changes a drug produces in an organism's physiological processes and behavior.

dualism   The belief that the body is physical but the mind (or soul) is not.

duodenum *(doo oh **dee** num)*   The portion of the small intestine immediately adjacent to the stomach.

dura mater   The outermost of the meninges; tough, flexible, unstretchable.

dynorphin   An endogenous opioid; the natural ligand for kappa opiate receptors.

efferent axon *(**eff** ur ent)*   An axon directed away from the central nervous system, conveying motor commands to muscles and glands.

electroconvulsive therapy (ECT)   A brief electrical shock, applied to the head, that results in an electrical seizure; used therapeutically to alleviate severe depression.

electrode   A conductive medium that can be used to apply electrical stimulation or to record electrical potentials.

electroencephalogram (EEG)   An electrical brain potential recorded by placing electrodes on in the scalp.

electrolyte   An aqueous solution of a material that ionizes—namely, a soluble acid, base, or salt.

electromyogram (EMG) *(**my** oh gram)*   An electrical potential recorded from an electrode placed on or in a muscle.

electro-oculogram (EOG) (*ah kew loh gram*) An electrical potential from the eyes, recorded by means of electrodes placed on the skin around them; detects eye movements.

electrostatic pressure The attractive force between atomic particles charged with opposite signs, or the repulsive force between atomic particles charged with the same sign.

emotional facial paresis Lack of movement of facial muscles in response to emotions in people who have no difficulty moving these muscles voluntarily; caused by damage to the insular prefrontal cortex, subcortical white matter of the frontal lobe, or parts of the thalamus.

endocrine gland A gland that liberates its secretions into the extracellular fluid around capillaries and hence into the bloodstream.

endogenous opioid (*en dodge en us oh pee oyd*) A class of peptides secreted by the brain that act as opiates.

endoplasmic reticulum Parallel layers of membrane found within the cytoplasm of a cell. Rough endoplasmic reticulum contains ribosomes and is involved with production of proteins that are secreted by the cell. Smooth endoplasmic reticulum is the site of synthesis of lipids and provides channels for the segregation of molecules involved in various cellular processes.

endplate potential The postsynaptic potential that occurs in the motor endplate in response to release of acetylcholine by the terminal button.

enkephalin (*en keff a lin*) One of the endogenous opioids.

entorhinal cortex A region of the limbic cortex that provides the major source of input to the hippocampal formation.

enzymatic deactivation The destruction of a transmitter substance by an enzyme after its release—for example, the destruction of acetylcholine by acetylcholinesterase.

enzyme A molecule that controls a chemical reaction, combining two substances or breaking a substance into two parts.

epidemiology The study of the distribution and causes of diseases in populations.

epinephrine (*epp i neff rin*) One of the catecholamines; a hormone secreted by the adrenal medulla; serves also as a neurotransmitter in the brain.

esophageal fistula (*ee soff a jee ul fiss tew la*) A diversion of the esophagus so that when an animal eats or drinks, the substance does not reach the stomach.

estradiol (*ess tra dye ahl*) The principal estrogen of many mammals, including humans.

estrogen (*ess trow jen*) A class of sex hormones that cause maturation of the female genitalia, growth of breast tissue, and development of other physical features characteristic of females.

estrous cycle The female reproductive cycle of mammals other than primates.

excitotoxic lesion (*ek sigh tow tok sik*) A brain lesion produced by intracerebral injection of an excitatory amino acid, such as kainic acid.

exocytosis (*ex o sy toe sis*) The secretion of a substance by a cell through means of vesicles; the process by which neurotransmitters are secreted.

experimental ablation The research method in which the function of a part of the brain is inferred by observing the behaviors an animal can no longer perform after that part is damaged.

extension A movement of a limb that tends to straighten its joints; the opposite of flexion.

extinction With respect to classical conditioning, the reduction or elimination of a conditional response by repeatedly presenting the conditional stimulus without the unconditional stimulus.

extracellular fluid All body fluids outside cells: interstitial fluid, blood plasma, and cerebrospinal fluid.

extrafusal muscle fiber One of the muscle fibers that are responsible for the force exerted by contraction of a skeletal muscle.

extrastriate cortex A region of visual association cortex; receives fibers from the striate cortex and from the superior colliculi and projects to the inferior temporal cortex.

fastigial nucleus A deep cerebellar nucleus; involved in the control of movement by the reticulospinal and vestibulospinal tracts.

fasting phase The phase of metabolism during which nutrients are not available from the digestive system; glucose, amino acids, and fatty acids are derived from glycogen, protein, and adipose tissue during this phase.

fatal familial insomnia A fatal inherited disorder characterized by progressive insomnia.

fatty acid A substance derived from the breakdown of triglycerides, along with glycerol; can be metabolized by most cells of the body except for the brain.

fenfluramine (FEN) (*fen fluor i meen*) A drug that causes the release of serotonin and inhibits eating.

field CA1 Part of the hippocampus; receives inputs from field CA3 and projects out of hippocampal formation via the subiculum.

field CA3 Part of the hippocampus; receives inputs from the dentate gyrus and projects to field CA1.

fight-or-flight response A species-typical response preparatory to fighting or fleeing; thought to be responsible for some of the deleterious effects of stressful situations on health.

fissure A major groove in the surface of the brain, larger than a sulcus.

fixative A chemical such as formalin; used to prepare and preserve body tissue.

flexion A movement of a limb that tends to bend its joints; opposite of extension.

flocculonodular lobe A region of the cerebellum; involved in control of postural reflexes.

fluorogold (*flew* roh gold) A dye that serves as a retrograde label; taken up by terminal buttons and carried back to the cell bodies.

fluoxetine (floo *ox* i teen) A drug that inhibits the reuptake of 5-HT.

follicle-stimulating hormone (FSH) The hormone of the anterior pituitary gland that causes development of an ovarian follicle and the maturation of its oocyte into an ovum.

forebrain The most rostral of the three major divisions of the brain; includes the telencephalon and diencephalon.

formalin (*for* ma lin) The aqueous solution of formaldehyde gas; the most commonly used tissue fixative.

fornix A fiber bundle that connects the hippocampus with other parts of the brain, including the mammillary bodies of the hypothalamus.

Fos (fahs) A protein produced in the nucleus of a neuron in response to synaptic stimulation.

fourth ventricle The ventricle located between the cerebellum and the dorsal pons, in the center of the metencephalon.

fovea (*foe* vee a) The region of the retina that mediates the most acute vision of birds and higher mammals. Color-sensitive cones constitute the only type of photoreceptor found in the fovea.

fragile X syndrome A genetic disorder caused by a faulty gene on the X chromosome; the leading genetic cause of mental retardation.

frontal lobe The anterior portion of the cerebral cortex, rostral to the parietal lobe and dorsal to the temporal lobe.

frontal section A slice through the brain parallel to the forehead.

function word A preposition, article, or other word that conveys little of the meaning of a sentence but is important in specifying its grammatical structure.

functional MRI (fMRI) A modification of the MRI procedure that permits the measurement of regional metabolism in the brain.

functionalism The principle that the best way to understand a biological phenomenon (a behavior or a physiological structure) is to try to understand its useful functions for the organism.

fundamental frequency The lowest, and usually most intense, frequency of a complex sound; most often perceived as the sound's basic pitch.

furosemide (few *row* se myde) A diuretic; a drug that increases the production of urine.

fusaric acid (few *sahr* ik) A drug that inhibits the activity of the enzyme dopamine-b-hydroxylase and thus blocks the production of norepinephrine.

G protein A protein coupled to a metabotropic receptor; conveys messages to other molecules when a ligand binds with and activates the receptor.

GABA An amino acid; the most important inhibitory transmitter substance in the brain.

galanin (*gal* a nin) A peptide neurotransmitter whose release stimulates ingestion of fats.

gamete (*gamm* eet) A mature reproductive cell; a sperm or ovum.

gamma motor neuron A neuron whose axons form synapses with intrafusal muscle fibers.

ganglion cell A neuron located in the retina that receives visual information from bipolar cells; its axons give rise to the optic nerve.

gap junction A special junction between cells that permits direct communication by means of electrical coupling.

gene The functional unit of the chromosome, which directs synthesis of one or more proteins.

generalization Type of scientific explanation; a general conclusion based on many observations of similar phenomena.

glabrous skin (*glab* russ) Skin that does not contain hair; found on the palms and soles of the feet.

glia (*glee* ah) The supporting cells of the central nervous system.

globus pallidus A telencephalic nucleus; the primary output nucleus of the basal ganglia; involved with control of voluntary movement.

glucagon (*gloo* ka gahn) A pancreatic hormone that promotes the conversion of liver glycogen into glucose.

glucocorticoid One of a group of hormones of the adrenal cortex that are important in protein and carbohydrate metabolism, secreted especially in times of stress.

glucoprivation A dramatic fall in the level of glucose available to cells; can be caused by a fall in the blood level of glucose or by drugs that inhibit glucose metabolism.

glutamate An amino acid; the most important excitatory transmitter substance in the brain.

glycerol (*gliss* er all) A substance (also called glycerine) derived from the breakdown of triglycerides, along with fatty acids; can be converted by the liver into glucose.

glycine (*gly* seen) An amino acid; an important inhibitory transmitter substance in the lower brain stem and spinal cord.

glycogen *(gly ko jen)* A polysaccharide often referred to as *animal starch;* stored in liver and muscle; constitutes the short-term store of nutrients.

Golgi apparatus *(goal jee)* A complex of parallel membranes in the cytoplasm that wraps the products of a secretory cell.

Golgi tendon organ (GTO) The receptor organ at the junction of the tendon and muscle that is sensitive to stretch.

gonad *(rhymes with moan ad)* An ovary or testis.

gonadotropic hormone A hormone of the anterior pituitary gland that has a stimulating effect on cells of the gonads.

gonadotropin-releasing hormone *(go nad oh trow pin)* A hypothalamic hormone that stimulates the anterior pituitary gland to secrete gonadotropic hormone.

granule cell A small, granular cell; those found in the dentate gyrus send axons to field CA3 of the hippocampus.

gustducin *(gust doo sin)* A G protein that plays a vital role in the transduction of sweetness and bitterness.

gyrus (plural: gyri) *(jye russ, jye rye)* A convolution of the cortex of the cerebral hemispheres, separated by sulci or fissures.

hair cell The receptive cell of the auditory apparatus.

hallucination Perception of a nonexistent object or event.

Hebb rule The hypothesis proposed by Donald Hebb that the cellular basis of learning involves strengthening of a synapse that is repeatedly active when the postsynaptic neuron fires.

hemicholinium *(hem ee koh lin um)* A drug that inhibits the uptake of choline.

hepatic portal vein The vein that receives blood from the digestive system and passes it to the liver.

hertz (Hz) Cycles per second.

5-HIAA A breakdown product of the neurotransmitter serotonin (5-HT).

hindbrain The most caudal of the three major divisions of the brain; includes the metencephalon and myelencephalon.

hippocampal formation A forebrain structure of the temporal lobe, constituting an important part of the limbic system; includes the hippocampus proper (Ammon's horn), dentate gyrus, and subiculum.

hippocampus A forebrain structure of the temporal lobe, constituting an important part of the limbic system.

homeostasis *(home ee oh stay sis)* The process by which the body's substances and characteristics (such as temperature and glucose level) are maintained at their optimal level.

horizontal cell A neuron in the retina that interconnects adjacent photoreceptors and the outer processes of the bipolar cells.

horizontal section A slice through the brain parallel to the ground.

hue One of the perceptual dimensions of color; the dominant wavelength.

Huntington's chorea A fatal inherited disorder that causes degeneration of the caudate nucleus and putamen; characterized by uncontrollable jerking movements, writhing movements, and dementia.

6-hydroxydopamine (6-HD) A chemical that is selectively taken up by axons and terminal buttons of noradrenergic or dopaminergic neurons and acts as a poison, damaging or killing them.

hyperpolarization An increase in the membrane potential of a cell, relative to the normal resting potential.

hypertonic The characteristic of a solution that contains enough solute that it will draw water out of a cell placed in it, through the process of osmosis.

hypnagogic hallucination *(hip na gah jik)* A symptom of narcolepsy; vivid dreams that occur just before a person falls asleep; accompanied by sleep paralysis.

hypothalamus The group of nuclei of the diencephalon situated beneath the thalamus; involved in regulation of the autonomic nervous system, control of the anterior and posterior pituitary glands, and integration of species-typical behaviors.

hypotonic The characteristic of a solution that contains so little solute that a cell placed in it will absorb water, through the process of osmosis.

hypovolemia *(hy poh voh lee mee a)* Reduction in the volume of the intravascular fluid.

immunocytochemical method A histological method that uses radioactive antibodies or antibodies bound with a dye molecule to indicate the presence of particular proteins of peptides.

immunoglobulin An antibody released by B-lymphocytes that bind with antigens and help destroy invading microorganisms.

in situ hybridization *(in see too)* The production of DNA complementary to a particular messenger RNA in order to detect the presence of the RNA.

incus The "anvil"; the second of the three ossicles.

indirect agonist A drug that attaches to a binding site on a receptor and facilitates the action of the receptor; does not interfere with the binding site for the principal ligand.

inferior colliculi Protrusions on top of the midbrain; part of the auditory system.

inferior temporal cortex In primates, the highest level of the ventral stream of the visual association cortex; located on the inferior portion of the temporal lobe.

ingestive behavior *(in jess tiv)* Eating or drinking.

inhalation   Administration of a vaporous substance into the lungs.

insertional plaque   The point of attachment of a tip link to a cilium of a hair cell.

instrumental conditioning   A learning procedure whereby the effects of a particular behavior in a particular situation increase (reinforce) or decrease (punish) the probability of the behavior; also called *operant conditioning.*

insulin   A pancreatic hormone that facilitates entry of glucose and amino acids into the cell, conversion of glucose into glycogen, and transport of fats into adipose tissue.

intergeniculate leaflet (IGL)   A part of the lateral geniculate nucleus that receives information from the retina and projects to the SCN.

internal carotid artery   An artery whose branches serve the rostral and lateral portions of the brain.

interneuron   A neuron located entirely within the central nervous system.

interposed nuclei   A set of deep cerebellar nuclei; involved in the control of the rubrospinal system.

interstitial fluid   The fluid that bathes the cells, filling the space between the cells of the body (the "interstices").

intracellular fluid   The fluid contained within cells.

intracerebral administration   Administration of a substance directly into the brain.

intracerebroventricular (ICV) administration   Administration of a substance into one of the cerebral ventricles.

intrafusal muscle fiber   A muscle fiber that functions as a stretch receptor, arranged parallel to the extrafusal muscle fibers, thus detecting changes in muscle length.

intramuscular (IM) injection   Injection of a substance into a muscle.

intraperitoneal (IP) injection *(in tra pair i toe **nee** ul)*   Injection of a substance into the *peritoneal cavity*—the space that surrounds the stomach, intestines, liver, and other abdominal organs.

intrarectal administration   Administration of a substance into the rectum.

intravascular fluid   The fluid found within the blood vessels.

intravenous (IV) injection   Injection of a substance directly into a vein.

inverse agonist   A drug that attaches to a binding site on a receptor and interferes with the action of the receptor; does not interfere with the binding site for the principal ligand.

ion   A charged molecule. *Cations* are positively charged, and *anions* are negatively charged.

ion channel   A specialized protein molecule that permits specific ions to enter or leave cells.

ionotropic receptor *(eye on oh **trow** pik)*   A receptor that contains a binding site for a neurotransmitter and an ion channel that opens when a molecule of the neurotransmitter attaches to the binding site.

ipsilateral   Located on the same side of the body.

isotonic   Equal in osmotic pressure to the contents of a cell. A cell placed in an isotonic solution neither gains nor loses water.

James–Lange theory   A theory of emotion that suggests that behaviors and physiological responses are directly elicited by situations and that feelings of emotions are produced by feedback from these behaviors and responses.

kainate receptor *(**kay** in ate)*   An ionotropic glutamate receptor that controls a sodium channel; stimulated by kainic acid and blocked by CNQX.

kinesthesia   Perception of the body's own movements.

Korsakoff's syndrome   Permanent anterograde amnesia caused by brain damage resulting from chronic alcoholism or malnutrition.

lamella   A layer of membrane containing photopigments; found in rods and cones of the retina.

lateral   Toward the side of the body, in a direction at right angles with the neuraxis and away from it.

lateral/basolateral nuclei   Nuclei of the amygdala that receive sensory information from the neocortex, thalamus, and hippocampus and send projections to the ventral striatum, dorsomedial nucleus of the thalamus, and the central nucleus.

lateral corticospinal tract   The system of axons that originates in the motor cortex and terminates in the contralateral ventral gray matter of the spinal cord; controls movements of the distal limbs.

lateral fissure   The fissure that separates the temporal lobe from the overlying frontal and parietal lobes.

lateral geniculate nucleus   A group of cell bodies within the lateral geniculate body of the thalamus that receives fibers from the retina and projects fibers to the primary visual cortex.

lateral group   The corticospinal tract, the corticobulbar tract, and the rubrospinal tract.

lateral lemniscus   A band of fibers running rostrally through the medulla and pons; carries fibers of the auditory system.

lateral parabrachial nucleus   A nucleus in the pons that receives gustatory information and information from the liver and digestive system and relays it to the forebrain.

lateral ventricle   One of the two ventricles located in the center of the telencephalon.

latitude effect   The increased incidence of schizophrenia in people born far from the equator.

L-DOPA *(ell dope a)*   The levorotatory form of DOPA; the precursor of the catecholamines; often used to treat Parkinson's disease because of its effect as a dopamine agonist.

Lee–Boot effect   The increased incidence of false pregnancies seen in female animals that are housed together; caused by a pheromone in the animals' urine; first observed in mice.

left parietal apraxia   An apraxia caused by damage to the left parietal lobe; characterized by difficulty in producing sequences of movements by verbal request or in imitation of movements made by someone else.

leptin   A hormone secreted by adipose tissue; decreased food intake and increased metabolic rate, primarily by inhibiting NPY-secreting neurons in the arcuate nucleus.

lesion study   A synonym for experimental ablation.

L-ethionine   A drug that inhibits carbohydrate metabolism in the liver by making adenosine unavailable, thus blocking the production of ATP.

ligand *(ligh gand or ligg and)*   A chemical that binds with the binding site of a receptor.

limbic cortex   Phylogenetically old cortex, located at the edge ("limbus") of the cerebral hemispheres; part of the limbic system.

limbic system   A group of brain regions including the anterior thalamic nuclei, amygdala, hippocampus, limbic cortex, and parts of the hypothalamus, as well as their interconnecting fiber bundles.

lipoprivation   A dramatic fall in the level of fatty acids available to cells; usually caused by drugs that inhibit fatty-acid metabolism.

lithium   An element; lithium carbonate is used to treat bipolar disorder.

locus coeruleus *(sa roo lee us)*   A dark-colored group of noradrenergic cell bodies located in the pons near the rostral end of the floor of the fourth ventricle; involved in arousal and vigilance.

long-term depression   A long-term decrease in the excitability of a neuron to a particular synaptic input caused by stimulation of the terminal button while the postsynaptic membrane is hyperpolarized or only slightly depolarized.

long-term memory   Relatively stable memory of events that occurred in the more distant past, as opposed to short-term memory.

long-term potentiation   A long-term increase in the excitability of a neuron to a particular synaptic input caused by repeated high-frequency activity of that input.

lordosis   A spinal sexual reflex seen in many four-legged female mammals; arching of the back in response to approach of a male or to touching the flanks, which elevates the hindquarters.

losartan *(low sar tan)*   A drug that blocks angiotensin receptors.

Loudness   A perceptual dimension of sound; corresponds to intensity.

LSD   A drug that stimulates 5-HT_{2A} receptors.

luteinizing hormone (LH) *(lew tee a nize ing)*   A hormone of the anterior pituitary gland that causes ovulation and development of the ovarian follicle into a corpus luteum.

lysosome *(lye so soam)*   An organelle surrounded by membrane; contains enzymes that break down waste products.

M system   A system of serotonergic neurons that originates in the median raphe nucleus; its axonal fibers are thick and rounded and appear to form conventional synapses with other neurons.

macroelectrode   An electrode used to record the electrical activity of large numbers of neurons in a particular region of the brain; much larger than a microelectrode.

magnetic resonance imaging (MRI)   A technique whereby the interior of the body can be accurately imaged; involves the interaction between radio waves and a strong magnetic field.

magnocellular layer   One of the inner two layers of cells in the dorsal lateral geniculate nucleus; transmits information necessary for the perception of form, movement, depth, and small differences in brightness.

magnocellular nucleus   A nucleus in the medulla; involved in the atonia (muscular paralysis) that accompanies REM sleep.

major affective disorder   A serious mood disorder; includes unipolar depression and bipolar disorder.

malleus   The "hammer"; the first of the three ossicles.

mammillary bodies *(mam i lair ee)*   A protrusion of the bottom of the brain at the posterior end of the hypothalamus, containing some hypothalamic nuclei.

masculinizing effect   An effect of a hormone present early in development that promotes the later development of anatomical or behavioral characteristics typical of males.

medial   Toward the neuraxis, away from the side of the body.

medial forebrain bundle (MFB)   A fiber bundle that runs in a rostral-caudal direction through the basal forebrain and lateral hypothalamus; electrical stimulation of these axons is reinforcing.

medial geniculate nucleus   A group of cell bodies within the medial geniculate body of the thalamus; receives fibers from the auditory system and projects fibers to the primary auditory cortex.

medial nucleus   A group of subnuclei of the amygdala that receives sensory input, including information about the presence of odors and pheromones, and relays it to the medial basal forebrain and hypothalamus.

medial nucleus of the amygdala (*a **mig** da la*)   A nucleus that receives olfactory information from the olfactory bulb and accessory olfactory bulb; involved in the effects of odors and pheromones on reproductive behavior.

medial pontine reticular formation (MPRF)   A region that contains neurons involved in the initiation of REM sleep; activated by acetylcholinergic neurons of the peri-brachial area.

medial preoptic area (MPA)   An area of cell bodies just rostral to the hypothalamus; plays an essential role in male sexual behavior.

median preoptic nucleus   A small nucleus situated around the decussation of the anterior commissure; plays a role in thirst stimulated by angiotensin.

medulla oblongata (*me **doo** la*)   The most caudal portion of the brain; located in the myelencephalon, immediately rostral to the spinal cord.

Meissner's corpuscle   The touch-sensitive end organs located in the papillae, small elevations of the dermis that project up into the epidermis.

melanocortin-4 receptor (MC4-R)   A receptor normally stimulated by the hormone melanocortin; responsible for the production of melanin; also plays a role in control of appetite.

melatonin (*mell a **tone** in*)   A hormone secreted during the night by the pineal body; plays a role in circadian and seasonal rhythms.

membrane   A structure consisting principally of lipid molecules that defines the outer boundaries of a cell and also constitutes many of the cell organelles, such as the Golgi apparatus.

membrane potential   The electrical charge across a cell membrane; the difference in electrical potential inside and outside the cell.

meninges (singular: meninx) (*men **in** jees*)   The three layers of tissue that encase the central nervous system: the dura mater, arachnoid membrane, and pia mater.

menstrual cycle (***men** strew al*)   The female reproductive cycle of most primates, including humans; characterized by growth of the lining of the uterus, ovulation, development of a corpus luteum, and (if pregnancy does not occur), menstruation.

mercaptoacetate (MA)   A drug that inhibits fatty-acid metabolism and produces lipoprivic hunger.

Merkel's disk   The touch-sensitive end organs found at the base of the epidermis, adjacent to sweat ducts.

mesencephalic locomotor region   A region of the reticular formation of the midbrain whose stimulation causes alternating movements of the limbs normally seen during locomotion.

mesencephalon (*mezz en **seff** a lahn*)   The midbrain; a region of the brain that surrounds the cerebral aqueduct; includes the tectum and the tegmentum.

mesocortical system (*mee zo **kor** ti kul*)   A system of dopaminergic neurons whose cell bodies are located in the ventral tegmental area and whose terminal buttons are located in the cerebral cortex and hippocampus.

mesolimbic system (*mee zo **lim** bik*)   A system of dopaminergic neurons whose cell bodies are located in the ventral tegmental area and whose terminal buttons are located in the nucleus accumbens, amygdala, lateral septum, hippocampus, and bed nucleus of the stria terminalis.

messenger ribonucleic acid (mRNA)   A macromolecule that delivers genetic information concerning the synthesis of a protein from a portion of a chromosome to a ribosome.

metabotropic receptor (*meh tab oh **trow** pik*)   A receptor that contains a binding site for a neurotransmitter; activates an enzyme that begins a series of events that opens an ion channel elsewhere in the membrane of the cell when a molecule of the neurotransmitter attaches to the binding site.

methyl palmoxirate (MP)   A drug that inhibits fatty-acid metabolism and produces lipoprivic hunger.

methylphenidate (*meth ul **fen** i date*)   A drug that inhibits the reuptake of dopamine.

MGm   The medial division of the medial geniculate nucleus; transmits auditory and somatosensory information to the lateral nucleus of the amygdala.

microdialysis   A procedure for analyzing chemicals present in the interstitial fluid through a small piece of tubing made of a semipermeable membrane that is implanted in the brain.

microelectrode   A very fine electrode, generally used to record activity of individual neurons.

microfilament   The thinnest of the fibers of the cytoskeleton; forms a meshwork just inside the membrane that holds membrane-bound proteins in place.

microglia   The smallest of glial cells; act as phagocytes and protect the brain from invading microorganisms.

microiontophoresis   A procedure that uses electricity to eject a chemical from a micropipette in order to determine the effects of the chemical on the electrical activity of a cell.

microtome (***my** krow tome*)   An instrument that produces very thin slices of body tissues.

microtubule (*my kro **too** bule*)   A long strand of bundles of protein filaments arranged around a hollow core; part of the cytoskeleton and involved in transporting substances from place to place within the cell.

midbrain The mesencephalon; the central of the three major divisions of the brain.

midsagittal plane The plane through the neuraxis perpendicular to the ground; divides the brain into two symmetrical halves.

mitochondria An organelle responsible for extracting energy from nutrients.

mitral cell A neuron located in the olfactory bulb that receives information from olfactory receptors; axons of mitral cells bring information to the rest of the brain.

moclobemide (*mak low **bem** ide*) A drug that blocks the activity of MAO-A; acts as a noradrenergic agonist.

model A mathematical or physical analogy for a physiological process; for example, computers have been used as models for various functions of the brain.

monism (***mahn*** *ism*) The belief that the world consists only of matter and energy and the mind is part of it.

monoamine (***mahn*** *o a meen*) A class of amines that includes indolamines such as serotonin and catecholamines such as dopamine, norepinephrine, and epinephrine.

monoamine hypothesis A hypothesis that states that depression is caused by a low level of activity of one or more monoaminergic synapses.

monoamine oxidase (MAO) (***mahn*** *o a meen*) A class of enzymes that destroy the monoamines: dopamine, norepinephrine, and serotonin.

monosynaptic stretch reflex A reflex in which a muscle contracts in response to its being quickly stretched; involves a sensory neuron and a motor neuron, with one synapse between them.

motor association cortex The region of the frontal lobe rostral to the primary motor cortex.

motor endplate The postsynaptic membrane of a neuromuscular junction.

motor learning Learning to make a new response.

motor neuron A neuron located within the central nervous system that controls the contraction of a muscle or the secretion of a gland.

motor unit A motor neuron and its associated muscle fibers.

Müllerian system The embryonic precursors of the female internal sex organs.

multibarreled micropipette A group of micropipettes attached together, used to infuse several different substances by means of iontophoresis while recording from a single neuron.

multipolar neuron A neuron with one axon and many dendrites attached to its soma.

muscarinic receptor (*muss ka **rin** ic*) A metabotropic acetylcholine receptor that is stimulated by muscarine and blocked by atropine.

muscimol (***musk*** *i mawl*) A direct agonist for the GABA binding site on the GABA$_A$ receptor.

mutation A change in the genetic information contained in the chromosomes of sperms or eggs, which can be passed on to an organism's offspring; provides genetic variability.

myelin sheath (***my*** *a lin*) A sheath that surrounds axons and insulates them, preventing messages from spreading between adjacent axons.

myofibril An element of muscle fibers that consists of overlapping strands of actin and myosin; responsible for muscular contractions.

myosin One of the proteins (with actin) that provide the physical basis for muscular contraction.

naloxone (*na **lox** own*) A drug that blocks mu opiate receptors; antagonizes the reinforcing and sedative effects of opiates.

narcolepsy (***nahr*** *ko lep see*) A sleep disorder characterized by periods of irresistible sleep, attacks of cataplexy, sleep paralysis, and hypnagogic hallucinations.

natural killer cell A white blood cell that destroys cancer cells or cells infected by viruses.

natural selection The process by which inherited traits that confer a selective advantage (increase an animal's likelihood to live and reproduce) become more prevalent in the population.

negative afterimage The image seen after a portion of the retina is exposed to an intense visual stimulus; consists of colors complementary to those of the physical stimulus.

negative feedback A process whereby the effect produced by an action serves to diminish or terminate that action; a characteristic of regulatory systems.

negative reinforcement The removal or reduction of an aversive stimulus that is contingent on a particular response, with an attendant increase in the frequency of that response.

negative symptom A symptom of schizophrenia characterized by the absence of behaviors that are normally present: social withdrawal, lack of affect, and reduced motivation.

neocortex The phylogenetically newest cortex, including the primary sensory cortex, primary motor cortex, and association cortex.

neostigmine (*nee o **stig** meen*) A drug that inhibits the activity of acetylcholinesterase.

nephron A functional unit of the kidney; extracts fluid from the blood and carries the fluid, through collecting ducts, to the ureter.

neural integration The process by which inhibitory and excitatory postsynaptic potentials summate and control the rate of firing of a neuron.

neuraxis An imaginary line drawn through the center of the length of the central nervous system, from the bottom of the spinal cord to the front of the forebrain.

neurofilament One of the fibers of the cytoskeleton, made of long, continuous strands of protein similar to those found in hair.

neuromodulator A naturally secreted substance that acts like a neurotransmitter except that it is not restricted to the synaptic cleft but diffuses through the extracellular fluid.

neuromuscular junction The synapse between the terminal buttons of an axon and a muscle fiber.

neuropeptide Y (NPY) A peptide neurotransmitter whose release stimulates feeding, insulin and glucocorticoid secretion, decreased breakdown of triglycerides, and a decrease in body temperature.

neuropeptide Y A peptide released by the terminals of the neurons that project from the IGL to the SCN.

neurosecretory cell A neuron that secretes a hormone or hormonelike substance.

neurotransmitter-dependent ion channel An ion channel that opens when a molecule of a neurotransmitter binds with a postsynaptic receptor.

nicotinic receptor An ionotropic acetylcholine receptor that is stimulated by nicotine and blocked by curare.

nigrostriatal system (*nigh grow stry ay tul*) A system of neurons originating in the substantia nigra and terminating in the neostriatum (caudate nucleus and putamen).

nitric oxide (NO) A gas produced by cells in the nervous system; used as a means of communication between cells.

nitric oxide synthase The enzyme responsible for the production of nitric oxide.

NMDA receptor A specialized ionotropic glutamate receptor that controls a calcium channel that is normally blocked by Mg^{2+} ions; involved in long-term potentiation.

node of Ranvier (*raw vee ay*) A naked portion of a myelinated axon, between adjacent oligodendroglia or Schwann cells.

non-REM sleep All stages of sleep except REM sleep.

noncompetitive binding Binding of a drug to a site on a receptor; does not interfere with the binding site for the principal ligand.

nondeclarative memory Memory whose formation does not depend on the hippocampal formation; a collective term for perceptual, stimulus-response, and motor memory.

norepinephrine (NE) (*nor epp i neff rin*) One of the catecholamines; a neurotransmitter found in the brain and in the sympathetic division of the autonomic nervous system.

nucleolus (*new clee o lus*) A structure within the nucleus of a cell that produces the ribosomes.

nucleus 1. A structure in the central region of a cell, containing the nucleolus and chromosomes. 2. An identifiable group of neural cell bodies in the central nervous system.

nucleus accumbens A nucleus of the basal forebrain near the septum; receives dopamine-secreting terminal buttons from neurons of the ventral tegmental area and is thought to be involved in reinforcement and attention.

nucleus basalis A nucleus of the basal forebrain that contains most of the acetylcholine-secreting neurons that send axons to the neocortex; degenerates in patients with Alzheimer's disease.

nucleus of the solitary tract (NST) A nucleus of the medulla that receives information from visceral organs and from the gustatory system.

nucleus raphe magnus A nucleus of the raphe that contains serotonin-secreting neurons that project to the dorsal gray matter of the spinal cord and is involved in analgesia produced by opiates.

ob mouse A strain of mice whose obesity and low metabolic rate is caused by a mutation that prevents the production of leptin.

obsession An unwanted thought or idea with which a person is preoccupied.

obsessive-compulsive disorder A mental disorder characterized by obsessions and compulsions.

obstructive hydrocephalus A condition in which all or some of the brain's ventricles are enlarged; caused by an obstruction that impedes the normal flow of CSF.

occipital lobe (*ok sip i tul*) The region of the cerebral cortex caudal to the parietal and temporal lobes.

ocular apraxia (*ay prak see a*) Difficulty in visual scanning.

ocular dominance The extent to which a particular neuron receives more input from one eye than from the other.

olfactory bulb The protrusion at the end of the olfactory nerve; receives input from the olfactory receptors.

olfactory epithelium The epithelial tissue of the nasal sinus that covers the cribriform plate; contains the cilia of the olfactory receptors.

olfactory glomerulus (*glow mare you luss*) A bundle of dendrites of mitral cells and the associated terminal buttons of the axons of olfactory receptors.

oligodendrocyte (*oh li go den droh site*) A type of glial cell in the central nervous system that forms myelin sheaths.

olivocochlear bundle   A bundle of efferent axons that travel from the olivary complex of the medulla to the auditory hair cells on the cochlea.

opsin (*opp* sin)   A class of protein that, together with retinal, constitutes the photopigments.

optic ataxia (*ay* **tack** see a)   Difficulty in reaching for objects under visual guidance.

optic chiasm (**kye** az' m)   A cross-shaped connection between the optic nerves, located below the base of the brain, just anterior to the pituitary gland.

optic disk   The location of the exit point from the retina of the fibers of the ganglion cells that form the optic nerve; responsible for the blind spot.

oral administration   Administration of a substance into the mouth, so that it is swallowed.

orbitofrontal cortex   The region of the prefrontal cortex at the base of the anterior frontal lobes.

organ of Corti   The sensory organ on the basilar membrane that contains the auditory hair cells.

organic sense   A sense modality that arises from receptors located within the inner organs of the body.

organizational effect (of hormone)   The effect of a hormone on tissue differentiation and development.

orthographic dysgraphia   A writing disorder in which the person can spell regularly spelled words but not irregularly spelled ones.

oscilloscope   A laboratory instrument capable of displaying a graph of voltage as a function of time on the face of a cathode ray tube.

osmometric thirst   Thirst produced by an increase in the osmotic pressure of the interstitial fluid relative to the intracellular fluid, thus producing cellular dehydration.

osmoreceptor   A neuron that detects changes in the solute concentration of the interstitial fluid that surrounds it.

ossicle (*ahss* i kul)   One of the three bones of the middle ear.

oval window   An opening in the bone surrounding the cochlea that reveals a membrane, against which the baseplate of the stapes presses, transmitting sound vibrations into the fluid within the cochlea.

ovarian follicle   A cluster of epithelial cells surrounding an oocyte, which develops into an ovum.

overtone   The frequency of complex tones that occurs at multiples of the fundamental frequency.

OVLT (organum vasculosum of the lamina terminalis)   A circumventricular organ located anterior to the anteroventral portion of the third ventricle; served by fenestrated capillaries and thus lacks a blood–brain barrier.

oxytocin (*ox ee* **tow** sin)   A hormone secreted by the posterior pituitary gland; causes contraction of the smooth muscle of the milk ducts, the uterus, and the male ejac-ulatory system; also serves as a neurotransmitter in the brain.

Pacinian corpuscle (pa **chin** ee un)   A specialized, encapsulated somatosensory nerve ending that detects mechanical stimuli, especially vibrations.

panic disorder   A disorder characterized by episodic periods of symptoms such as shortness of breath, irregularities in heartbeat, and other autonomic symptoms, accompanied by intense fear.

parahippocampal cortex   A region of limbic cortex adjacent to the hippocampal formation that, along with the perirhinal cortex, relays information between the entorhinal cortex and other regions of the brain.

parasympathetic division   The portion of the autonomic nervous system that controls functions that occur during a relaxed state.

paraventricular nucleus   A hypothalamic nucleus that contains cell bodies of neurons that produce vasopressin and oxytocin and transport them through their axons to the posterior pituitary gland.

parietal lobe (pa **rye** i tul)   The region of the cerebral cortex caudal to the frontal lobe and dorsal to the temporal lobe.

Parkinson's disease   A neurological disease characterized by tremors, rigidity of the limbs, poor balance, and difficulty in initiating movements; caused by degeneration of the nigrostriatal system.

parturition (par tew **ri** shun)   The act of giving birth.

parvocellular layer   One of the four outer layers of cells in the dorsal lateral geniculate nucleus; transmits information necessary for perception of color and fine details.

PCP   Phencyclidine; a drug that binds with the PCP binding site of the NMDA receptor and serves as an inverse agonist.

PCPA   A drug that inhibits the activity of tryptophan hydroxylase and thus interferes with the synthesis of 5-HT.

peptide   A chain of amino acids joined together by peptide bonds.

perceptual learning   Learning to recognize a particular stimulus.

perfusion (per **few** zhun)   The process by which an animal's blood is replaced by a fluid such as a saline solution or a fixative in preparing the brain for histological examination.

periaqueductal gray matter (PAG)   The region of the midbrain that surrounds the cerebral aqueduct; plays an essential role in various species-typical behaviors, including female sexual behavior.

peribrachial area (pair ee **bray** kee ul)   The region around the brachium conjunctivum, located in the dorsolateral pons; contains acetylcholinergic neurons involved in the initiation of REM sleep.

peripheral nervous system (PNS) That part of the nervous system outside the brain and spinal cord, including the spinal and cranial nerves and ganglia.

perirhinal cortex A region of limbic cortex adjacent to the hippocampal formation that, along with the parahippocampal cortex, relays information between the entorhinal cortex and other regions of the brain.

persistent Müllerian duct syndrome A condition caused by a congenital lack of functioning anti-Müllerian hormone receptors; in a male, causes development of both male and female internal sex organs.

PGO wave Bursts of phasic electrical activity originating in the pons, followed by activity in the lateral geniculate nucleus and visual cortex; a characteristic of REM sleep.

PHA-L Phaseolus vulgaris leukoagglutinin; a protein derived from lima beans used as an anterograde tracer; taken up by dendrites and cell bodies and carried to the ends of the axons.

phagocytosis *(fagg o sy toe sis)* The process by which cells engulf and digest other cells or debris caused by cellular degeneration.

phantom limb Sensations that appear to originate in a limb that has been amputated.

pharmacokinetics The process by which drugs are absorbed, distributed within the body, metabolized, and excreted.

phase difference The difference in arrival times of sound waves at each of the eardrums.

phenylketonuria A hereditary disorder caused by the absence of an enzyme that converts the amino acid phenylalanine to tyrosine; causes brain damage unless a special diet is implemented soon after birth.

pheromone *(fair oh moan)* A chemical released by one animal that affects the behavior or physiology of another animal; usually smelled or tasted.

phonetic reading Reading by decoding the phonetic significance of letter strings; "sound reading."

phonological dysgraphia A writing disorder in which a person cannot sound out words and write them phonetically.

phonological dyslexia A reading disorder in which a person can read familiar words but has difficulty reading unfamiliar words or pronounceable nonwords.

phosphoinositide system A biochemical pathway that is responsible for the production of several second messengers.

photopigment A protein dye bonded to retinal, a substance derived from vitamin A; responsible for transduction of visual information.

photoreceptor One of the receptor cells of the retina; transduces photic energy into electrical potentials.

phototherapy Treatment of seasonal affective disorder by daily exposure to bright light.

physiological psychologist A scientist who studies the physiology of behavior, primarily by performing physiological and behavioral experiments with laboratory animals.

pia mater The layer of the meninges adjacent to the surface of the brain.

pimozide A drug that blocks dopamine receptors.

pineal gland *(py nee ul)* A gland attached to the dorsal tectum; produces melatonin and plays a role in circadian and seasonal rhythms.

pinocytosis *(pee no sy toh sis)* The pinching off of a bud of cell membrane, which travels to the interior of the cell.

pitch A perceptual dimension of sound; corresponds to the fundamental frequency.

place cell A neuron of the hippocampus that becomes active when the animal is in a particular location in the environment.

place code The system by which information about different frequencies is coded by different locations on the basilar membrane.

placebo *(pla see boh)* An inert substance given to an organism in lieu of a physiologically active drug; used experimentally to control for the effects of mere administration of a drug.

planum temporale A region of the superior temporal lobe; normally larger in the left hemisphere.

POAH The region of the preoptic area and the adjacent anterior hypothalamus, involved in thermoregulation and induction of slow-wave sleep.

pons The region of the metencephalon rostral to the medulla, caudal to the midbrain, and ventral to the cerebellum.

pontine nucleus A large nucleus in the pons that serves as an important source of input to the cerebellum.

population EPSP An evoked potential that represents the EPSPs of a population of neurons.

positive symptom A symptom of schizophrenia evident by its presence: delusions, hallucinations, or thought disorders.

positron emission tomography (PET) The use of a device that reveals the localization of a radioactive tracer in a living brain.

posterior With respect to the central nervous system, located near or toward the tail.

posterior pituitary gland The posterior part of the pituitary gland; an endocrine gland that contains hormone-secreting terminal buttons of axons whose cell bodies lie within the hypothalamus.

postganglionic neuron   Neurons of the autonomic nervous system that form synapses directly with their target organ.

postsynaptic membrane   The cell membrane opposite the terminal button in a synapse; the membrane of the cell that receives the message.

postsynaptic potential   Alterations in the membrane potential of a postsynaptic neuron, produced by liberation of transmitter substance at the synapse.

postsynaptic receptor   A receptor molecule in the postsynaptic membrane of a synapse that contains a binding site for a neurotransmitter.

posttraumatic stress disorder   A psychological disorder caused by exposure to a situation of extreme danger and stress; symptoms include recurrent dreams or recollections; can interfere with social activities and a feeling of hopelessness.

predation   Attack of one animal directed at an individual of another species, on which the attacking animal normally preys.

prefrontal cortex   The neocortex of the frontal lobes rostral to the supplementary motor area and premotor cortex.

preganglionic neuron   The efferent neuron of the autonomic nervous system whose cell body is located in a cranial nerve nucleus or in the intermediate horn of the spinal gray matter and whose terminal buttons synapse on postganglionic neurons in the autonomic ganglia.

premotor cortex   A region of motor association cortex of the lateral frontal lobe, rostral to the primary motor cortex.

presynaptic facilitation   The action of a presynaptic terminal button in an axoaxonic synapse; increases the amount of neurotransmitter released by the postsynaptic terminal button.

presynaptic heteroreceptor   A receptor located in the membrane of a terminal button that receives input from another terminal button by means of an axoaxonic synapse; binds with the neurotransmitter released by the presynaptic terminal button.

presynaptic inhibition   The action of a presynaptic terminal button in an axoaxonic synapse; reduces the amount of neurotransmitter released by the postsynaptic terminal button.

presynaptic membrane   The membrane of a terminal button that lies adjacent to the postsynaptic membrane.

primary auditory cortex   The region of the cerebral cortex whose primary input is from the auditory system.

primary motor cortex   The region of the cerebral cortex that contains neurons that control movements of skeletal muscles.

primary somatosensory cortex   The region of the cerebral cortex whose primary input is from the somatosensory system.

primary visual cortex   The region of the cerebral cortex whose primary input is from the visual system.

priming   A phenomenon in which exposure to a particular stimulus automatically facilitates perception of that stimulus or related stimuli.

progesterone (*pro jess ter own*)   A steroid hormone produced by the ovary that maintains the endometrial lining of the uterus during the later part of the menstrual cycle and during pregnancy; along with estradiol, it promotes receptivity in female mammals with estrous cycles.

projection fiber   An axon of a neuron in one region of the brain whose terminals form synapses with neurons in another region.

prolactin   A hormone of the anterior pituitary gland, necessary for production of milk; has an inhibitory effect on male sexual behavior.

prosody   The use of changes in intonation and emphasis to convey meaning in speech besides that specified by the particular words; an important means of communication of emotion.

prosopagnosia (*prah soh pag no zha*)   Failure to recognize particular people by the sight of their faces.

prostaglandin   A member of a family of fatty acid derivatives that serve as hormones; first discovered in the prostate gland; involved in many physiological processes, including pain perception.

protanopia (*pro tan owe pee a*)   An inherited form of defective color vision in which red and green hues are confused; "red" cones are filled with "green" cone opsin.

protein kinase   An enzyme that attaches a phosphate (PO_4) to a protein and thereby causes it to change its shape.

psychoneuroimmunology   The branch of neuroscience involved with interactions between environmental stimuli, the nervous system, and the immune system.

psychopharmacology   The study of the effects of drugs on the nervous system and on behavior.

pulvinar (*pull vi nar*)   A large thalamic nucleus that projects to the visual association cortex and may play a role in compensating for eye and head movements.

punishing stimulus   An aversive stimulus that follows a particular behavior and thus makes the behavior become less frequent.

pure alexia   Loss of the ability to read without loss of the ability to write; produced by brain damage.

pure word deafness   The ability to hear, to speak, and (usually) to read and write without being able to comprehend the meaning of speech; caused by damage to

Wernicke's area or disruption of auditory input to this region.

pursuit movement   The movement that the eyes make to maintain an image of a moving object on the fovea.

putamen   A telencephalic nucleus; one of the input nuclei of the basal ganglia; involved with control of voluntary movement.

pylorus *(pie lorr us)*   The ring of smooth muscle at the junction of the stomach and duodenum that controls the release of the stomach contents.

pyramidal cell   A category of large neurons with a pyramid shape; found in the cerebral cortex and Ammon's horn of the hippocampal formation.

pyramidal tract   An alternate term for the corticospinal tract.

raphe nuclei *(ruh fay)*   A group of nuclei located in the reticular formation of the medulla, pons, and midbrain, situated along the midline; contain serotonergic neurons.

rate code   The system by which information about different frequencies is coded by the rate of firing of neurons in the auditory system.

rate law   The principle that variations in the intensity of a stimulus or other information being transmitted in an axon are represented by variations in the rate at which that axon fires.

rebound phenomenon   The increased frequency or intensity of a phenomenon after it has been temporarily suppressed; for example, the increase in REM sleep seen after a period of REM sleep deprivation.

receptive field   That portion of the visual field in which the presentation of visual stimuli will produce an alteration in the firing rate of a particular neuron.

receptor blocker   A drug that binds with a receptor but does not activate it; prevents the natural ligand from binding with the receptor.

receptor potential   A slow, graded electrical potential produced by a receptor cell in response to a physical stimulus.

recurrent collateral   A branch of an axon leaving a particular region of the brain that turns back and forms synapses with neurons near the one that gives rise to it.

red nucleus   A large nucleus of the midbrain that receives inputs from the cerebellum and motor cortex and sends axons to motor neurons in the spinal cord.

reduction   Type of scientific explanation; a phenomenon is described in terms of the more elementary processes that underlie it.

reference memory   A form of long-term memory of stable conditions and contingencies in the environment; includes perceptual memory and stimulus-response memory.

reflex   An automatic, stereotyped movement produced as the direct result of a stimulus.

refractory period *(ree frak to ree)*   A period of time after a particular action (for example, an ejaculation by a male) during which that action cannot occur again.

reinforcing stimulus   An appetitive stimulus that follows a particular behavior and thus makes the behavior become more frequent.

release zone   A region of the interior of the postsynaptic membrane of a synapse to which synaptic vesicles attach and release their neurotransmitter into the synaptic cleft.

REM sleep   A period of desynchronized EEG activity during sleep, at which time dreaming, rapid eye movements, and muscular paralysis occur; also called *paradoxical sleep.*

REM without atonia *(ay tone ee a)*   A neurological disorder in which the person does not become paralyzed during REM sleep and thus acts out dreams.

renin *(ree nin)*   A hormone secreted by the kidneys that causes the conversion of angiotensinogen in the blood into angiotensin.

reserpine *(ree sur peen)*   A drug that interferes with the storage of monoamines in synaptic vesicles.

resting potential   The membrane potential of a neuron when it is not being altered by excitatory or inhibitory postsynaptic potentials; approximately –70 mV in the giant squid axon.

reticular formation   A large network of neural tissue located in the central region of the brain stem, from the medulla to the diencephalon.

reticulospinal tract   A bundle of axons that travels from the reticular formation to the gray matter of the spinal cord; controls the muscles responsible for postural movements.

retina   The neural tissue and photoreceptive cells located on the inner surface of the posterior portion of the eye.

retinal *(rett i nahl)*   A chemical synthesized from vitamin A; joins with an opsin to form a photopigment.

retinal disparity   The fact that points on objects located at different distances from the observer will fall on slightly different locations on the two retinas; provides the basis for stereopsis.

retrograde   In a direction along an axon from the terminal buttons toward the cell body.

retrograde amnesia   Amnesia for events that preceded some disturbance to the brain, such as a head injury or electroconvulsive shock.

retrograde labeling method   A histological method that labels cell bodies that give rise to the terminal buttons that form synapses with cells in a particular region.

reuptake The reentry of a transmitter substance just liberated by a terminal button back through its membrane, thus terminating the postsynaptic potential.

rhodopsin (*roh dopp* sin) A particular opsin found in rods.

ribosome (*ry bo soam*) A cytoplasmic structure, made of protein, that serves as the site of production of proteins translated from mRNA.

rod One of the receptor cells of the retina; sensitive to light of low intensity.

rostral "Toward the beak"; with respect to the central nervous system, in a direction along the neuraxis toward the front of the face.

round window An opening in the bone surrounding the cochlea of the inner ear that permits vibrations to be transmitted, via the oval window, into the fluid in the cochlea.

rubrospinal tract The system of axons that travels from the red nucleus to the spinal cord; controls independent limb movements.

Ruffini corpuscle A vibration-sensitive organ located in hairy skin.

saccadic movement (*suh kad* ik) The rapid, jerky movement of the eyes used in scanning a visual scene.

saccule (*sak* yule) One of the vestibular sacs.

sagittal section (*sadj* i tul) A slice through the brain parallel to the neuraxis and perpendicular to the ground.

salt appetite A craving for sodium chloride.

saltatory conduction Conduction of action potentials by myelinated axons. The action potential "jumps" from one node of Ranvier to the next.

saralasin (*sair a lay* sin) A drug that blocks angiotensin receptors.

satiety mechanism A brain mechanism that causes cessation of hunger or thirst, produced by adequate and available supplies of nutrients or water.

saturation One of the perceptual dimensions of color; purity.

scanning electron microscope A microscope that provides three-dimensional information about the shape of the surface of a small object.

schizophrenia A serious mental disorder characterized by disordered thoughts, delusions, hallucinations, and often bizarre behaviors.

Schwann cell A cell in the peripheral nervous system that is wrapped around a myelinated axon, providing one segment of its myelin sheath.

seasonal affective disorder A mood disorder characterized by depression, lethargy, sleep disturbances, and craving for carbohydrates during the winter season when days are short.

seasonality effect The increased incidence of schizophrenia in people born during late winter and early spring.

second messenger A chemical produced when a G protein activates an enzyme; carries a signal that results in the opening of the ion channel or causes other events to occur in the cell.

selective advantage A characteristic of an organism that permits it to produce more than the average number of offspring of its species.

self-stimulation Making a response that causes the electrical stimulation of a particular region of the brain through an implanted electrode.

semicircular canal One of the three ringlike structures of the vestibular apparatus that detect changes in head rotation.

sensitization An increase in the effectiveness of a drug that is administered repeatedly.

sensory association cortex Those regions of the cerebral cortex that receive information from the regions of primary sensory cortex.

sensory neuron A neuron that detects changes in the external or internal environment and sends information about these changes to the central nervous system.

sensory receptor A specialized neuron that detects a particular category of physical events.

sensory-specific satiety Satiety for a specific food that has been ingested recently in the absence of general satiety for all foods.

sensory transduction The process by which sensory stimuli are transduced into slow, graded receptor potentials.

serotonin (5-HT) (*sair a toe* nin) An indolamine transmitter substance; also called 5-hydroxytryptamine.

set point The optimal value of the system variable in a regulatory mechanism.

sex chromosome The X and Y chromosomes, which determine an organism's gender. Normally, XX individuals are female, and XY individuals are male.

sexually dimorphic behavior A behavior that has different forms or that occurs with different probabilities or under different circumstances in males and females.

sexually dimorphic nucleus A nucleus in the preoptic area that is much larger in males than in females; first observed in rats; plays a role in male sexual behavior.

sham feeding Feeding behavior of an animal with an open gastric or esophageal fistula that prevents food from remaining in the stomach.

sham lesion A "placebo" procedure that duplicates all the steps of producing a brain lesion except for the one that actually causes the brain damage.

short-term memory Memory for a stimulus that has just been perceived.

simple cell An orientation-sensitive neuron in the striate cortex whose receptive field is organized in an opponent fashion.

simultanagnosia *(sime ul tane ag **no** zha)* Difficulty in perceiving more than one object at a time.

sine-wave grating A series of straight parallel bands varying continuously in brightness according to a sine-wave function, along a line perpendicular to their lengths.

single-unit recording Recording of the electrical activity of a single neuron.

sites of action The locations at which molecules of drugs interact with molecules located on or in cells of the body, thus affecting some biochemical processes of these cells.

skeletal muscle One of the striated muscles attached to bones.

sleep apnea *(app nee a)* Cessation of breathing while sleeping.

sleep attack A symptom of narcolepsy; an irresistible urge to sleep during the day, after which the person awakes feeling refreshed.

sleep paralysis A symptom of narcolepsy; paralysis occurring just before a person falls asleep.

slow-wave sleep Non-REM sleep, characterized by synchronized EEG activity during its deeper stages.

smooth muscle Nonstriated muscle innervated by the autonomic nervous system, found in the walls of blood vessels, in the reproductive tracts, in sphincters, within the eye, in the digestive system, and around hair follicles.

sodium-potassium transporter A protein found in the membrane of all cells that extrudes sodium ions from and transports potassium ions into the cell.

soma The cell body of a neuron, which contains the nucleus.

somatic nervous system The part of the peripheral nervous system that controls the movement of skeletal muscles or transmits somatosensory information to the central nervous system.

somatotopic organization A topographically organized mapping of parts of the body that are represented in a particular region of the brain.

spatial frequency The relative width of the bands in a sine-wave grating, measured in cycles per degree of visual angle.

specific serotonin reuptake inhibitor (SSRI) A drug that inhibits the reuptake of serotonin without affecting the reuptake of other neurotransmitters.

spelling dyslexia An alternative name for word-form dyslexia.

spinal cord The cord of nervous tissue that extends caudally from the medulla.

spinal nerve A peripheral nerve attached to the spinal cord.

spinal nucleus of the bulbocavernosus (SNB) *(bul bo kav er **no** sis)* A nucleus located in the lower spinal cord; in some species of rodents, present only in males.

spinal root A bundle of axons surrounded by connective tissue that occurs in pairs, which fuse and form a spinal nerve.

spinal sympathetic ganglia Sympathetic ganglia either adjacent to the spinal cord in the sympathetic chain or located in the abdominal cavity.

split-brain operation Brain surgery occasionally performed to treat a form of epilepsy; surgeon cuts the corpus callosum, which connects the two hemispheres of the brain.

stapes *(stay peez)* The "stirrup"; the last of the three ossicles.

stereotaxic apparatus A device that permits a surgeon to position an electrode or cannula into a specific part of the brain.

stereotaxic atlas A collection of drawings of sections of the brain of a particular animal with measurements that provide coordinates for stereotaxic surgery.

stereotaxic surgery *(stair ee oh **tak** sik)* Brain surgery using a stereotaxic apparatus to position an electrode or cannula in a specified position of the brain.

steroid A chemical of low molecular weight, derived from cholesterol. Steroid hormones affect their target cells by attaching to receptors found within the cell.

stimulus-response learning Learning to make a particular response automatically in the presence of a particular stimulus; includes classical and instrumental conditioning.

stress A general, imprecise term that can refer either to a stress response or to a stressor (stressful situation).

stress response A physiological reaction caused by the perception of aversive or threatening situations.

stressor A stimulus (or situation) that produces a stress response.

stria terminalis *(stree a ter mi **nal** is)* A long fiber bundle that connects portions of the amygdala with the hypothalamus.

striate cortex *(stry ate)* The primary visual cortex.

striated muscle Skeletal muscle; muscle that contains striations.

strychnine *(strik neen)* A direct agonist for the glycine receptor.

subarachnoid space The fluid-filled space between the arachnoid membrane and the pia mater.

subcortical region The region located within the brain, beneath the cortical surface.

subcutaneous (SC) injection Injection of a substance into the space beneath the skin.

subfornical organ (SFO) A small organ located in the confluence of the lateral ventricles, attached to the underside of the fornix; contains neurons that detect the presence of angiotensin in the blood and excite neural circuits that initiate drinking.

sublingual administration (*sub ling* wul) Administration of a substance by placing it beneath the tongue.

submissive behavior A stereotypical behavior shown by an animal in response to threat behavior by another animal; serves to prevent an attack.

subsensitivity Decreased sensitivity of neurotransmitter receptors; a compensatory response to their prolonged stimulation.

substance abuse A maladaptive pattern of substance use short of addiction that interferes with a person's health of social situation.

substance dependence A maladaptive pattern of substance abuse that includes taking increasing doses of the drug or other signs of addiction.

substantia nigra A darkly stained region of the tegmentum that contains neurons that communicate with the caudate nucleus and putamen in the basal ganglia.

sulcus (plural: sulci) (*sul* kus, *sul* sigh) A groove in the surface of the cerebral hemisphere, smaller than a fissure.

summer depression A mood disorder characterized by depression, sleep disturbances, and loss of appetite.

superior colliculi (ka *lik* yew lee) Protrusions on top of the midbrain; part of the visual system.

superior olivary complex A group of nuclei in the medulla; involved with auditory functions, including localization of the source of sounds.

superior sagittal sinus A venous sinus located in the midline just dorsal to the brain, between the two cerebral hemispheres.

supersensitivity The increased sensitivity of neurotransmitter receptors; caused by damage to the afferent axons or long-term blockage of neurotransmitter release.

supplementary motor area A region of motor association cortex of the dorsal and dorsomedial frontal lobe, rostral to the primary motor cortex.

suprachiasmatic nucleus (SCN) (*soo* pra ky az *mat* ik) A nucleus situated atop the optic chiasm. It contains a biological clock responsible for organizing many of the body's circadian rhythms.

supraoptic nucleus (*sue* pra *op* tik) A hypothalamic nucleus that contains cell bodies of neurons that produce vasopressin and transport it through their axons to the posterior pituitary gland.

surface dyslexia A reading disorder in which a person can read words phonetically but has difficulty reading irregularly spelled words by the whole-word method.

Sydenham's chorea An autoimmune disease that attacks parts of the brain, including the basal ganglia, and produces involuntary movements and often the symptoms of obsessive-compulsive disorder.

sympathetic apraxia A movement disorder of the left hand caused by damage to the left frontal lobe; similar to callosal apraxia.

sympathetic division The portion of the autonomic nervous system that controls functions that accompany arousal and expenditure of energy.

sympathetic ganglion chain One of a pair of groups of sympathetic ganglia that lie ventrolateral to the vertebral column.

synapse A junction between the terminal button of an axon and the membrane of another neuron.

synaptic cleft The space between the presynaptic membrane and the postsynaptic membrane.

synaptic vesicle (*vess* i kul) A small, hollow, beadlike structure found in terminal buttons; contains molecules of a neurotransmitter.

synchrony High-voltage, low-frequency EEG activity, characteristic of slow-wave sleep or coma, during which neurons fire together in a regular fashion.

system variable A variable that is controlled by a regulatory mechanism; for example, temperature in a heating system.

tardive dyskinesia A movement disorder that can after prolonged treatment with antipsychotic medication, characterized by involuntary movements of the face and neck.

target cell The type of cell that is directly affected by a hormone or nerve fiber.

tectorial membrane (tek *torr* ee ul) A membrane located above the basilar membrane; serves as a shelf against which the cilia of the auditory hair cells move.

tectospinal tract A bundle of axons that travels from the tectum to the spinal cord; coordinates head and trunk movements with eye movements.

tectum The dorsal part of the midbrain; includes the superior and inferior colliculi.

tegmentum The ventral part of the midbrain; includes the periaqueductal gray matter, reticular formation, red nucleus, and substantia nigra.

temporal lobe (*tem* por ul) The region of the cerebral cortex rostral to the occipital lobe and ventral to the parietal and frontal lobes.

terminal button The bud at the end of a branch of an axon; forms synapses with another neuron; sends information to that neuron.

testosterone (tess *tahss* ter own) The principal androgen found in males.

thalamus The largest portion of the diencephalon, located above the hypothalamus; contains nuclei that project information to specific regions of the cerebral cortex and receive information from it.

therapeutic index The ratio between the dose that produces the desired effect in 50 percent of the animals and the dose that produces toxic effects in 50 percent of the animals.

theta activity EEG activity of 5–8 Hz that occurs intermittently during early stages of slow-wave sleep and REM sleep; an important indication of the physiological state of the hippocampus.

third ventricle The ventricle located in the center of the diencephalon.

thought disorder Disorganized, irrational thinking.

threat behavior A species-typical behavior that warns another animal that it may be attacked if it does not flee or show a submissive behavior.

threshold of excitation The value of the membrane potential that must be reached in order to produce an action potential.

timbre (*tim* ber or *tamm* ber) A perceptual dimension of sound; corresponds to complexity.

tip link Elastic filaments that attach the tip of one cilium of a hair cell to the side of the adjacent cilium.

T-lymphocyte A white blood cell that originates in the thymus gland; part of the immune system.

tolerance A decrease in the effectiveness of a drug that is administered repeatedly; caused by compensatory mechanisms that oppose the effect of the drug.

tonotopic representation (*tonn* oh *top* ik) A topographically organized mapping of different frequencies of sound that are represented in a particular region of the brain.

topical administration Administration of a substance directly onto the skin or mucous membrane.

Tourette's syndrome A neurological disorder characterized by tics and involuntary vocalizations and sometimes by compulsive uttering of obscenities and repetition of the utterances of others.

transcortical sensory aphasia A speech disorder in which a person has difficulty comprehending speech and producing meaningful spontaneous speech but can repeat speech; caused by damage to the region of the brain posterior to Wernicke's area.

transcranial magnetic stimulation Stimulation of the cortex by the magnetic field produced by alternating current passing through a coil placed against the skull; disrupts normal activity of the affected brain region.

transducin A G protein that is activated when a photon strikes a photopigment; activates phosphodiesterase molecules, which destroy cyclic GMP and close cation channels in the photoreceptor.

transmitter substance/neurotransmitter A chemical that is released by a terminal button; has an excitatory or inhibitory effect on another neuron.

tricyclic antidepressant A class of drugs used to treat depression; inhibits the reuptake of norepinephrine and serotonin; named for the molecular structure.

triglyceride (*try* **gliss** er ide) The form of fat storage in adipose cells; consists of a molecule of glycerol joined with three fatty acids.

tritanopia (*try tan* **owe** pee a) An inherited form of defective color vision in which hues with short wavelengths are confused; "blue" cones are either lacking or faulty.

tryptophan depletion procedure A procedure involving a low-tryptophan diet and a tryptophan-free amino acid "cocktail" that lowers brain tryptophan and consequently decreases the synthesis of 5-HT.

Turner's syndrome The presence of only one sex chromosome (an X chromosome); characterized by lack of ovaries but otherwise normal female sex organs and genitalia.

tympanic membrane The eardrum.

tyrosine kinase A type of protein kinase that may play a role in the establishment of long-term potentiation.

umami (*oo mah mee*) The taste sensation produced by glutamate.

unipolar depression A serious mood disorder that consists of unremitting depression or periods of depression that do not alternate with periods of mania.

unipolar neuron A neuron with one axon attached to its soma; the axon divides, with one branch receiving sensory information and the other sending the information into the central nervous system.

ureter (*your* eh ter) One of two tubes that carries urine from the kidneys to the bladder.

utricle (*you* trih kul) One of the vestibular sacs.

vagus nerve The largest of the cranial nerves, conveying efferent fibers of the parasympathetic division of the autonomic nervous system to organs of the thoracic and abdominal cavities.

Vandenbergh effect The earlier onset of puberty seen in female animals that are housed with males; caused by a pheromone in the male's urine; first observed in mice.

vasopressin (*vay zo* **press** in) A hormone secreted by the posterior pituitary gland that controls the secretion of urine by the kidneys; also serves as a neurotransmitter in the brain.

ventral "Toward the belly"; with respect to the central nervous system, in a direction perpendicular to the neuraxis toward the bottom of the skull or the front surface of the body.

ventral angular bundle The bundle of axons that conveys information from the hippocampal formation to the basolateral amygdala.

ventral anterior nucleus (of thalamus)   A thalamic nucleus that receives projections from the basal ganglia and sends projections to the motor cortex.

ventral corticospinal tract   The system of axons that originates in the motor cortex and terminates in the ipsilateral ventral gray matter of the spinal cord; controls movements of the upper legs and trunk.

ventral root   The spinal root that contains outgoing (efferent) motor fibers.

ventral tegmental area   A nucleus in the ventral midbrain; plays an essential role in maternal behavior.

ventricle *(ven trik ul)*   One of the hollow spaces within the brain, filled with cerebrospinal fluid.

ventrolateral nucleus (of thalamus)   A thalamic nucleus that receives projections from the cerebellum and basal ganglia and sends projections to the motor cortex.

ventromedial group   The vestibulospinal tract, the tectospinal tract, the reticulospinal tract, and the ventral corticospinal tract.

ventromedial nucleus of the hypothalamus (VMH)   A large nucleus of the hypothalamus located near the walls of the third ventricle; plays an essential role in female sexual behavior.

vergence movement   The cooperative movement of the eyes, which ensures that the image of an object falls on identical portions of both retinas.

vermis   The portion of the cerebellum located at the midline; receives somatosensory information and helps control the vestibulospinal and reticulospinal tracts through its connections with the fastigial nucleus.

vertebral artery *(ver tee brul)*   An artery whose branches serve the posterior region of the brain.

vestibular ganglion   A nodule on the vestibular nerve that contains the cell bodies of the bipolar neurons that convey vestibular information to the brain.

vestibular sac   One of a set of two receptor organs in each inner ear that detect changes in the tilt of the head.

vestibulospinal tract   A bundle of axons that travels from the vestibular nuclei to the gray matter of the spinal cord; controls postural movements in response to information from the vestibular system.

visual agnosia *(ag no zha)*   Deficits in visual perception in the absence of blindness; caused by brain damage.

volitional facial paresis   Difficulty in moving the facial muscles voluntarily; caused by damage to the face region of the primary motor cortex or its subcortical connections.

voltage-dependent ion channel   An ion channel that opens or closes according to the value of the membrane potential.

volumetric thirst   Thirst produced by hypovolemia.

vomeronasal organ *(voah mer oh nay zul)*   A sensory organ that detects the presence of certain chemicals, especially when a liquid is actively sniffed; mediates the effects of some pheromones.

Wada test   A test often performed before brain surgery; verifies the functions of one hemisphere by testing patients while the other hemisphere is anesthetized.

Wernicke's aphasia   A form of aphasia characterized by poor speech comprehension and fluent but meaningless speech.

Wernicke's area   A region of auditory association cortex on the left temporal lobe of humans, which is important in the comprehension of words and the production of meaningful speech.

Whitten effect   The synchronization of the menstrual or estrous cycles of a group of females, which occurs only in the presence of a pheromone in a male's urine.

whole-word reading   Reading by recognizing a word as a whole; "sight reading."

withdrawal symptoms   The appearance of symptoms opposite to those produced by a drug when the drug is suddenly no longer taken; caused by the presence of compensatory mechanisms.

Wolffian system   The embryonic precursors of the male internal sex organs.

word-form dyslexia   A disorder in which a person can read a word only after spelling out the individual letters.

working memory   Memory of what has just been perceived and what is currently being thought about; consists of new information and related information that has recently been "retrieved" from long-term memory.

zeitgeber *(tsite gay ber)*   A stimulus (usually the light of dawn) that resets the biological clock responsible for circadian rhythms.

zona incerta *(in sir ta)*   An oblong extension of the midbrain reticular formation, extending from the midbrain to the medial diencephalon.

References

Abe, H., Rusak, B., and Robertson, H. A. Photic induction of Fos protein in the suprachiasmatic nucleus is inhibited by the NMDA receptor antagonist MK-801. *Neuroscience Letters,* 1991, *127,* 9–12.

Abe, M., Saito, M., and Shimazu, T. Neuropeptide Y and norepinephrine injected into the paraventricular nucleus of the hypothalamus activate endocrine pancreas. *Biomedical Research,* 1989, *10,* 431–436.

Abel, E. L., and Sokol, R. J. Fetal alcohol syndrome is now a leading cause of mental retardation. *Lancet,* 1986, *2,* 1222.

Adams, D. B., Gold, A. R., and Burt, A. D. Rise in female-initiated sexual activity at ovulation and its suppression by oral contraceptives. *New England Journal of Medicine,* 1978, *299,* 1145–1150.

Adams, J. B., Pyke, R. E., Costa, J., Cutler, N. R., Schweizer, E., Wilcox, C. S., Wisselink, P. G., Greiner, M., Pierce, M. W., and Pande, A. C. A double-blind, placebo-controlled study of a CCK-B receptor antagonist, CI-988, in patients with generalized anxiety disorder. *Journal of Clinical Psychopharmacology,* 1995, *15,* 428–434.

Adams, R. D. The anatomy of memory mechanisms in the human brain. In *The Pathology of Memory,* edited by G. A. Talland and N. C. Waugh. New York: Academic Press, 1969.

Adams, R. D., and Victor, M. *Principles of Neurology.* New York: McGraw-Hill, 1981.

Adey, W. R., Bors, E., and Porter, R. W. EEG sleep patterns after high cervical lesions in man. *Archives of Neurology,* 1968, *19,* 377–383.

Adieh, H. B., Mayer, A. D., and Rosenblatt, J. S. Effects of brain antiestrogen implants on maternal behavior and on postpartum estrus in pregnant rats. *Neuroendocrinology,* 1987, *46,* 522–531.

Adolph, E. F. Measurements of water drinking in dogs. *American Journal of Physiology,* 1939, *125,* 75–86.

Adolphs, R., Tranel, D., Damasio, H., and Damasio, A. Impaired recognition of emotion in facial expressions following bilateral damage to the human amygdala. *Nature,* 1994, *372,* 669–672.

Advokat, C., and Kutlesic, V. Pharmacotherapy of the eating disorders: A commentary. *Neuroscience and Biobehavioral Reviews,* 1995, *19,* 59–66.

Aghajanian, G. K., Graham, A. W., and Sheard, M. H. Serotonin-containing neurons in brain: Depression of firing by monoamine oxidase inhibitors. *Science,* 1970, *169,* 1100–1102.

Aghajanian, G. K., Kogan, J. H., and Moghaddam, B. Opiate withdrawal increases glutamate and aspartate efflux in the locus coeruleus: An in vivo microdialysis study. *Brain Research,* 1994, *636,* 126–130.

Agmo, A., Federman, I., Navarro, V., Padua, M., and Velasquez, G. Reward and reinforcement produced by drinking water: Role of opioids and dopamine-receptor subtypes. *Pharmacology, Biochemistry and Behavior,* 1993, *46,* 183–194.

Aguilar-Roblero, R., Morin, L. P., and Moore, R. Y. Morphological correlates of circadian rhythm restoration induced by transplantation of the suprachiasmatic nucleus in hamsters. *Experimental Neurology,* 1994, *130,* 250–260.

Akabayashi, A., Wahlestedt, C., Alexander, J. T., and Leibowitz, S. F. Specific inhibition of endogenous neuropeptide Y synthesis in arcuate nucleus by antisense oligonucleotides suppresses feeding behavior and insulin secretion. *Molecular Brain Research,* 1994, *21,* 55–61.

Akabayashi, A., Zaia, C. T. B. V., Silva, I., Chae, H. J., and Leibowitz, S. F. Neuropeptide Y in the arcuate nucleus is modulated by alterations in glucose utilization. *Brain Research,* 1993, *621,* 343–348.

Akbarian, S., Kim, J. J., Potkin, S. G., Hetrick, W. P., Bunney, W. E., and Jones, E. G. Maldistribution of interstitial neurons in prefrontal white matter of the brains of schizophrenic patients. *Archives of General Psychiatry,* 1996, *53,* 425–436.

Akhtar, S., Wig, N., Pershad, D., and Varma, S. A phenomenological analysis of symptoms in obsessive compulsive disorder. *British Journal of Psychiatry,* 1975, *127,* 342–348.

Alam, M. N., McGinty, D., and Szymusiak, R. Neuronal discharge of preoptic anterior hypothalamic thermosensitive neurons: Relation to NREM sleep. *American Journal of Physiology: Regulatory, Integrative and Comparative Physiology,* 1995b, *269,* R1240–R1249.

Alam, M. N., Szymusiak, R., and McGinty, D. Local preoptic anterior hypothalamic warming alters spontaneous and evoked neuronal activity in the magno-cellular basal forebrain. *Brain Research,* 1995a, *696,* 221–230.

Albers, H. E., and Ferris, C. F. Neuropeptide Y: Role in light-dark cycle entrainment of hamster circadian rhythms. *Neuroscience Letters*, 1984, *50*, 163–168.

Albrecht, D. G. Analysis of visual form. Doctoral dissertation, University of California, Berkeley, 1978.

Albright, T. D., Desimone, R., and Gross, C. G. Columnar organization of directionally selective cells in visual area MT of the macaque. *Journal of Neurophysiology*, 1984, *51*, 16–31.

Aldrich, M. S. Narcolepsy. *Neurology*, 1992, *42*, 34–43.

Alexander, G. M., and Sherwin, B. B. Sex steroids, sexual behavior, and selective attention for erotic stimuli in women using oral contraceptives. *Psychoneuroendocrinology*, 1993, *18*, 91–102.

Alexander, G. M., Sherwin, B. B., Bancroft, J., and Davidson, D. W. Testosterone and sexual behavior in oral contraceptive users and nonusers: A prospective study. *Hormones and Behavior*, 1990, *24*, 388–402.

Alexander, M. P., and Albert, M. L. The anatomical basis of visual agnosia. In *Localization in Neuropsychology*, edited by A. Kertesz. New York: Academic Press, 1983.

Alexander, M. P., Fischer, R. S., and Friedman, R. Lesion localization in apractic agraphia. *Archives of Neurology*, 1992, *49*, 246–251.

Allen, L. S., and Gorski, R. A. Sexual orientation and the size of the anterior commissure in the human brain. *Proceedings of the National Academy of Sciences, USA*, 1992, *89*, 7199–7202.

Allison, D. B., Kaprio, J., Korkeila, M., Koskenvuo, M., Neale, M. C., and Hayakawa, K. The heritability of body mass index among an international sample of monozygotic twins reared apart. *International Journal of Obesity*, 1996, *20*, 501–506.

Almers, W. Exocytosis. *Annual Review of Physiology*, 1990, *52*, 607–624.

Altschuler, H. L., Phillips, P. E., and Feinhandler, D. A. Alterations of ethanol self-administration by naltrexone. *Life Sciences*, 1980, *26*, 679–688.

Amir, S., and Stewart, J. Resetting of the circadian clock by a conditioned stimulus. *Nature*, 1996, *379*, 542–545.

Amyes, E. W., and Nielsen, J. M. Clinicopathologic study of vascular lesions of the anterior cingulate region. *Bulletin of the Los Angeles Neurological Societies*, 1955, *20*, 112–130.

Anand, B. K., and Brobeck, J. R. Hypothalamic control of food intake in rats and cats. *Yale Journal of Biology and Medicine*, 1951, *24*, 123–140.

Anderson, R. H., Fleming, D. E., Rhees, R. W., and Kinghorn, E. Relationships between sexual activity, plasma testosterone, and the volume of the sexually dimorphic nucleus of the preoptic area in prenatally stressed and non-stressed rats. *Brain Research*, 1986, *370*, 1–10.

Andersson, B. The effect of injections of hypertonic NaCl solutions in different parts of the hypothalamus of goats. *Acta Physiologica Scandinavica*, 1953, *28*, 188–201.

Andreasen, N. C. Symptoms, signs, and diagnosis of schizophrenia. *Lancet*, 1995, *346*, 477–481.

Andreasen, N. C., Arndt, S., Swayze, V., Cizadlo, T., Flaum, M., O'Leary, D., Ehrhardt, J. C., and Yuh, W. T. C. Thalamic abnormalities in schizophrenia visualized through magnetic resonance image averaging. *Science*, 1994, *266*, 294–298.

Andrews, K. M., McGowan, M. K., Gallitano, A., and Grossman, S. P. Water intake during chronic preoptic infusions of osmotically active or inert solutions. *Physiology and Behavior*, 1992, *52*, 241–245.

Angrilli, A., Mauri, A., Palomba, D., Flor, H., Birbaumer, N., Sartori, G., and Dipaola, F. Startle reflex and emotion modulation impairment after a right amygdala lesion. *Brain*, 1996, *119*, 1991–2000.

Archer, J. Testosterone and aggression. *Journal of Offender Rehabilitation*, 1994, *5*, 3–25.

Arendt, J., Deacon, S., English, J., Hampton, S., and Morgan, L. Melatonin and adjustment to phase-shift. *Journal of Sleep Research*, 1995, *4*, 74–79.

Argiolas, A., Collu, M., Gessa, G., Melis, M., and Serra, G. The oxytocin antagonist $d(CH_3)_3$ Tyr (Me)-Orn^8-vasotocin inhibits male copulatory performance in rats. *European Journal of Pharmacology*, 1988, *149*, 389–392.

Argiolas, A., and Gessa, G. L. Central functions of oxytocin. *Neuroscience and Biobehavioral Reviews*, 1991, *15*, 217–231.

Arletti, R., Benelli, A., and Bertolini, A. Oxytocin involvement in male and female sexual behavior. *Annals of the New York Academy of Sciences*, 1992, *652*, 180–193.

Arnold, A. P., and Jordan, C. L. Hormonal organization of neural circuits. In *Frontiers in Neuroendocrinology*, Vol. 10, edited by L. Martini and W. F. Ganong. New York: Raven Press, 1988.

Arnold, S. E., Franz, B. R., Gur, R. C., Gur, R. E., Shapiro, R. M., Moberg, P. J., and Trojanowski, J. Q. Smaller neuron size in schizophrenia in hippocampal subfields that mediate cortical-hippocampal interactions. *American Journal of Psychiatry*, 1995, *152*, 738–748.

Aroniadou, V. A., and Teyler, T. J. The role of NMDA receptors in long-term potentiation (LTP) and depression (LTD) in rat visual cortex. *Brain Research*, 1991, *562*, 136–143.

Aronson, B. D., Bell-Pedersen, D., Block, G. D., Bos, N. P. A., Dunlap, J. C., Eskin, A., Garceau, N. Y., Geusz, M. E., Johnson, K. A., Khalsa, S. B. S., Koster-Van Hoffen, G. C., Koumenis, C., Lee, T. M., LeSauter, J., Lindgren, K. M., Liu, Q., Loros, J. J., Michel, S. H., Mirmiran, M., Moore, R. Y., Ruby, N. F., Silver, R., Turek, F. W., and Zatz, M. Circadian rhythms. *Brain Research Reviews*, 1993, *18*, 315–333.

Artigas, F., Perez, V., and Alvarez, E. Pindolol induces a rapid improvement of depressed patients treated with serotonin reuptake inhibitors [letter] [see comments]. *Archives of General Psychiatry*, 1994, *51*, 248–251.

Artigas, F., Romero, L., de Montigny, C., and Blier, P. Acceleration of the effect of selected antidepressant drugs in major depression by 5-HT1A antagonists. *Trends in Neuroscience,* 1996, *19,* 378–383.

Artmann, H., Grau, H., Adelman, M., and Schleiffer, R. Reversible and non-reversible enlargement of cerebrospinal fluid spaces in anorexia nervosa. *Neuroradiology,* 1985, *27,* 103–112.

Asanuma, H., and Rosén, I. Topographical organization of cortical efferent zones projecting to distal forelimb muscles in monkey. *Experimental Brain Research,* 1972, *13,* 243–256.

Aschoff, J. Circadian rhythms: General features and endocrinological aspects. In *Endocrine Rhythms,* edited by D. T. Krieger. New York: Raven Press, 1979.

Assad, J. A., and Corey, D. P. An active motor model for adaptation by vertebrate hair cells. *Journal of Neuroscience,* 1992, *12,* 3291–3309.

Aston-Jones, G., and Bloom, F. E. Activity of norepinephrine-containing locus coeruleus neurons in behaving rats anticipates fluctuations in the sleep-waking cycle. *Journal of Neuroscience,* 1981a, *1,* 876–886.

Aston-Jones, G., and Bloom, F. E. Norepinephrine-containing locus coeruleus neurons in behaving rats exhibit pronounced responses to non-noxious environmental stimuli. *Journal of Neuroscience,* 1981b, *1,* 887–900.

Aston-Jones, G., Rajkowski, J., Kubiak, P., and Alexinsky, T. Locus coeruleus neurons in monkey are selectively activated by attended cues in a vigilance task. *Journal of Neuroscience,* 1994, *14,* 4467–4480.

Atack, J. R., Broughton, H. B., and Pollack, S. J. Inositol monophosphatase: A putative target for Li$^+$ in the treatment of bipolar disorder. *Trends in Neurosciences,* 1995, *18,* 343–349.

Auer, R. N., Jensen, M. L., and Whishaw, I. Q. Neurobehavioral deficit due to ischemic brain damage limited to half of the CA1 section of the hippocampus. *Journal of Neuroscience,* 1989, *9,* 1641–1647.

Avenet, P., and Lindemann, B. Perspectives of taste reception. *Journal of Membrane Biology,* 1989, *112,* 1–8.

Baddeley, A. D. Memory: Verbal and visual subsystems of working memory. *Current Biology,* 1993, *3,* 563–565.

Baer, L., Rauch, S. L., Ballantine, H. T., Martuza, R., Cosgrove, R., Cassem, E., Giriunas, I., Manzo, P. A., Dimino, C., and Jenike, M. A. Cingulotomy for intractable obsessive-compulsive disorder: Prospective long-term follow-up of 18 patients. *Archives of General Psychiatry,* 1995, *52,* 384–392.

Bai, F. L., Yamano, M., Shiotani, Y., Emson, P. C., Smith, A. D., Powell, J. F., and Tohyama, M. An arcuato-paraventricular and dorsomedial hypothalamic neuropeptide Y-containing system which lacks noradrenaline in the rat. *Brain Research,* 1985, *331,* 172–175.

Bailey, A., Le Couteur, A., Gottesman, I., Bolton, P., Simonoff, E., Yuzda, E., and Rutter, M. Autism as a strongly genetic disorder: Evidence from a British twin study. *Psychological Medicine,* 1995, *25,* 63–77.

Bailey, A. J. The biology of autism. *Psychological Medicine,* 1993, *23,* 7–11.

Bailey, J. M., and Pillard, R. C. A genetic study of male sexual orientation. *Archives of General Psychiatry,* 1991, *48,* 1089–1096.

Bailey, J. M., Pillard, R. C., Neale, M. C., and Agyei, Y. Heritable factors influence sexual orientation in women. *Archives of General Psychiatry,* 1993, *50,* 217–223.

Baizer, J. S., Ungerleider, L. G., and Desimone, R. Organization of visual inputs to the inferior temporal and posterior parietal cortex in macaques. *Journal of Neuroscience,* 1991, *11,* 168–190.

Bakin, J. S., and Weinberger, N. M. Classical conditioning induces CS-specific receptive field plasticity in the auditory cortex of the guinea pig. *Brain Research,* 1990, *536,* 271–286.

Bakin, J. S., and Weinberger, N. M. Induction of a physiological memory in the cerebral cortex by stimulation of the nucleus basalis. *Proceedings of the National Academy of Sciences, USA,* 1996, *93,* 11219–11224.

Bakker, J., Van Ophemert, J., and Slob, A. K. Sexual differentiation of odor and partner preference in the rat. *Physiology and Behavior,* 1996, *60,* 489–494.

Baldessarini, R. J. *Chemotherapy in Psychiatry.* Cambridge, Mass.: Harvard University Press, 1977.

Baldessarini, R. J., and Tarsy, D. Dopamine and the pathophysiology of dyskinesias induced by antipsychotic drugs. *Annual Review of Neuroscience,* 1980, *3,* 23–42.

Balint, R. Seelenlahmung des "Schauens", optische Ataxie, raumliche Storung der Aufmerksamkeit. *Monatsschr. Psychiat. Neurol.,* 1909, *25,* 51–81.

Ballantine, H. T., Bouckoms, A. J., Thomas, E. K., and Giriunas, I. E. Treatment of psychiatric illness by stereotactic cingulotomy. *Biological Psychiatry,* 1987, *22,* 807–819.

Balon, R., Jordan, M., Pohl, R., and Yeragani, V. K. Family history of anxiety disorders in control subjects with lactate-induced panic attacks. *American Journal of Psychiatry,* 1989, *146,* 1304–1306.

Balskubik, R., Ableitner, A., Herz, A., and Shippenberg, T. S. Neuroanatomical sites mediating the motivational effects of opioids as mapped by the conditioned place preference paradigm in rats. *Journal of Pharmacology and Experimental Therapeutics,* 1993, *264,* 489–495.

Bamshad, M., Novak, M. A., and De Vries, G. J. Sex and species differences in the vasopressin innervation of sexually naive and parental prairie voles, *Microtus ochrogaster,* and meadow voles, *Microtus Pennsylvanicus. Journal of Neuroendocrinology,* 1993, *5,* 245–255.

Bamshad, M., Novak, M. A., and De Vries, G. J. Cohabitation alters vasopressin innervation and paternal behavior in prairie voles, *Microtus ochrogaster. Physiology and Behavior,* 1994, *56,* 751–758.

Banks, W. A., Kastin, A. J., Huang, W. T., Jaspan, J. B., and Maness, L. M. Leptin enters the brain by a saturable system independent of insulin. *Peptides,* 1996, *17,* 305–311.

Baranyi, A., Szente, M. B., and Woody, C. D. Properties of associative long-lasting potentiation induced by cellular conditioning in the motor cortex of conscious cats. *Neuroscience*, 1991, *42*, 321–334.

Barbazanges, A., Piazza, P. V., Le Moal, M., and Maccari, S. Maternal glucocorticoid secretion mediates long-term effects of prenatal stress. *Journal of Neuroscience*, 1996, *16*, 3943–3949.

Barclay, C. D., Cutting, J. E., and Kozlowski, L. T. Temporal and spatial factors in gait perception that influence gender recognition. *Perception and Psychophysics*, 1978, *23*, 145–152.

Baron-Cohen, S., Leslie, A. M., and Frith, U. Does the autistic child have a "theory of mind"? *Cognition*, 1985, *21*, 37–46.

Barr, L. C., Goodman, W. K., McDougle, C. J., Delgado, P. L., Heninger, G. R., Charney, D. S., and Price, L. H. Tryptophan depletion in patients with obsessive-compulsive disorder who respond to serotonin reuptake inhibitors. *Archives of General Psychiatry*, 1994, *51*, 309–317.

Bartness, T. J., Powers, J. B., Hastings, M. H., Bittman, E. L., and Goldman, B. D. The timed infusion paradigm for melatonin delivery: What has it taught us about the melatonin signal, its reception, and the photoperiodic control of seasonal responses? *Journal of Pineal Research*, 1993, *15*, 161–190.

Basbaum, A. I., and Fields, H. L. Endogenous pain control mechanisms: Review and hypothesis. *Annals of Neurology*, 1978, *4*, 451–462.

Basbaum, A. I., and Fields, H. L. Endogenous pain control systems: Brainstem spinal pathways and endorphin circuitry. *Annual Review of Neuroscience*, 1984, *7*, 309–338.

Bassett, A. S., McGillivray, B. C., Jones, B., and Pantzar, J. T. Partial trisomy chromosome 5 cosegregating with schizophrenia. *Lancet*, 1988, *1*, 799–801.

Bauer, R. H., and Fuster, J. M. Delayed-matching and delayed-response deficit from cooling dorsolateral prefrontal cortex in monkeys. *Journal of Comparative and Physiological Psychology*, 1976, *90*, 293–302.

Baxter, L. R., Schwartz, J. M., Mazziotta, J. C., Phelphs, M. E., Pahl, J. J., and Guze, B. H. Cerebral glucose metabolic rates in non-depressed obsessive compulsives. *American Journal of Psychiatry*, 1989, *145*, 1560–1563.

Baylis, G. C., Rolls, E. T., and Leonard, C. M. Selectivity between faces in the responses of a population of neurons in the cortex in the superior temporal sulcus of the monkey. *Brain Research*, 1985, *342*, 91–102.

Baylor, D. How photons start vision. *Proceedings of the National Academy of Sciences, USA*, 1996, *93*, 560–565.

Bazett, H. C., McGlone, B., Williams, R. G., and Lufkin, H. M. Sensation. I. Depth, distribution, and probable identification in the prepuce of sensory end-organs concerned in sensations of temperature and touch: Thermometric conductivity. *Archives of Neurology and Psychiatry (Chicago)*, 1932, *27*, 489–517.

Beach, F. A. Cerebral and hormonal control of reflexive mechanisms involved in copulatory behavior. *Physiological Review*, 1967, *47*, 289–316.

Bean, N. J. Modulation of agonistic behavior by the dual olfactory system in male mice. *Physiology and Behavior*, 1982, *29*, 433–437.

Bean, N. J., and Conner, R. Central hormonal replacement and home-cage dominance in castrated rats. *Hormones and Behavior*, 1978, *11*, 100–109.

Beauvois, M. F., and Dérouesné, J. Phonological alexia: Three dissociations. *Journal of Neurology, Neurosurgery and Psychiatry*, 1979, *42*, 1115–1124.

Beauvois, M. F., and Dérouesné, J. Lexical or orthographic dysgraphia. *Brain*, 1981, *104*, 21–45.

Bechara, A., Tranel, D., Damasio, H., Adolphs, R., Rockland, C., and Damasio, A. R. Double dissociation of conditioning and declarative knowledge relative to the amygdala and hippocampus in humans. *Science*, 1995, *269*, 1115–1118.

Beckstead, R. M., Morse, J. R., and Norgren, R. The nucleus of the solitary tract in the monkey: Projections to the thalamus and brainstem nuclei. *Journal of Comparative Neurology*, 1980, *190*, 259–282.

Beecher, H. K. *Measurement of Subjective Responses: Quantitative Effects of Drugs.* New York: Oxford University Press, 1959.

Beeman, E. A. The effect of male hormone on aggressive behavior in mice. *Physiological Zoology*, 1947, *20*, 373–405.

Behringer, R. R. The Müllerian inhibitor and mammalian sexual development. *Philosophical Transactions of the Royal Society of London B: Biological Sciences*, 1995, *350*, Biological Sciences, 1995, *350*, 285–288.

Beidler, L. M. Physiological properties of mammalian taste receptors. In *Taste and Smell in Vertebrates*, edited by G. E. W. Wolstenholme. London: J. & A. Churchill, 1970.

Beitz, A. J. The organization of afferent projections to the midbrain periaqueductal gray of the rat. *Neuroscience*, 1982, *7*, 133–159.

Bell, A. P., Weinberg, M. S., and Hammersmith, S. K. *Sexual Preference: Its Development in Men and Women.* Bloomington: Indiana University Press, 1981.

Benington, J. H., and Heller, H. C. Does the function of REM sleep concern non-REM sleep or waking? *Progress in Neurobiology*, 1994, *44*, 433–449.

Benington, J. H., and Heller, H. C. Monoaminergic and cholinergic modulation of REM-sleep timing in rats. *Brain Research*, 1995, *681*, 141–146.

Benington, J. H., Kodali, S. K., and Heller, H. C. Stimulation of A1 adenosine receptors mimics the electroencephalographic effects of sleep deprivation. *Brain Research*, 1995, *692*, 79–85.

Benkelfat, C., Bradwejn, J., Meyer, E., Ellenbogen, M., Milot, S., Gjedde, A., and Evans, A. Functional neuroanatomy of CCK4-induced anxiety in normal healthy volunteers. *American Journal of Psychiatry*, 1995, *152*, 1180–1184.

Benkelfat, C., Ellenbogen, M. A., Dean, P., Palmour, R. M., and Young, S. N. Mood-lowering effect of tryptophan depletion: Enhanced susceptibility in young men at genetic risk for major affective disorders. *Archives of General Psychiatry*, 1994, *51*, 687–697.

Benson, D. F., Djenderedjian, A., Miller, B. L., Pachana, N. A., Chang, L., Itti, L., and Mena, I. Neural basis of confabulation. *Neurology*, 1996, *46*, 1239–1243.

Benson, D. F., and Geschwind, N. The alexias. In *Handbook of Clinical Neurology*, Vol. 4, edited by P. Vinken and G. Bruyn. Amsterdam: North-Holland, 1969.

Benson, D. F., and Geschwind, N. Aphasia and related disorders: A clinical approach. In *Principles of Behavioral Neurology*, edited by M.-M. Mesulam. Philadelphia: F. A. Davis, 1985.

Benson, D. F., and Greenberg, J. Visual form agnosia. *Archives of Neurology*, 1969, *20*, 82–89.

Berger, B., Gaspar, P., and Verney, C. Dopaminergic innervation of the cerebral cortex: Unexpected differences between rodents and primates. *Trends in Neuroscience*, 1991, *14*, 21–27.

Berger, R. J., and Phillips, N. H. Energy conservation and sleep. *Behavioural Brain Research*, 1995, *69*, 65–73.

Bermant, G., and Davidson, J. M. *Biological Bases of Sexual Behavior*. New York: Harper & Row, 1974.

Bernard, C. *Leçons de Physiologie Expérimentale Appliquée à la Médicine Faites au Collège de France*, Vol. 2. Paris: Bailliere, 1856.

Bernstein, I. L. Learned taste aversion in children receiving chemotherapy. *Science*, 1978, *200*, 1302–1303.

Bernstein, I. L. Meal patterns in "free running humans." *Physiology and Behavior*, 1981, *27*, 621–624.

Berthier, M., Kulisevsky, J., Gironell, A., and Heras, J. A. Obsessive-compulsive disorder associated with brain lesions: Clinical phenomenology, cognitive function, and anatomic correlates. *Neurology*, 1996, *47*, 353–361.

Besson, J. M., Guilbaud, G., Abdelmoumene, M., and Chaouch, A. Physiologie de la nociception. *Journal of Physiology (Paris)*, 1982, *78*, 7–107.

Bettelheim, B. *The Empty Fortress*. New York: Free Press, 1967.

Bier, M. J., and McCarley, R. W. REM-enhancing effects of the adrenergic antagonist idazoxan infused into the medial pontine reticular formation of the freely moving cat. *Brain Research*, 1994, *634*, 333–338.

Binder, J. R., Lazar, R. M., Tatemichi, T. K., Mohr, J. P., Desmond, D. W., and Ciecierski, K. A. Left hemiparalexia. *Neurology*, 1992, *42*, 562–569.

Binder, J. R., Rao, S. M., Hammeke, T. A., Yetkin, F. Z., Jesmanowicz, A., Bandettini, P. A., Wong, E. C., Estkowski, L. D., Goldstein, M. D., Haughton, V. M., and Hyde, J. S. Functional magnetic resonance imaging of human auditory cortex. *Annals of Neurology*, 1994, *35*, 662–672.

Bingman, V. P., and Mench, J. A. Homing behavior of hippocampus and parahippocampus lesioned pigeons following short-distance releases. *Behavioural Brain Research*, 1990, *40*, 227–238.

Birch, L. L., McPhee, L., Shoba, B. C., Steinberg, L., and Krehbiel, R. "Clean up your plate": Effects of child feeding prac-

tices on the conditioning of meal size. *Learning and Motivation*, 1987, *18*, 301–317.

Birch, L. L., McPhee, L., Sullivan, S., and Johnson, S. Conditioned meal initiation in young children. *Appetite*, 1989, *13*, 105–113.

Bird, E., Cardone, C. C., and Contreras, R. J. Area postrema lesions disrupt food intake induced by cerebroventricular infusions of 5-thioglucose in the rat. *Brain Research*, 1983, *270*, 193–196.

Blander, D. S., Mark, G. P., Hernandez, L., and Hoebel, B. G. Angiotensin and drinking induce dopamine release in the nucleus accumbens. *Neuroscience Abstracts*, 1988, *14*, 527.

Blasdel, G. G. Differential imaging of ocular dominance and orientation selectivity in monkey striate cortex. *Journal of Neuroscience*, 1992a, *12*, 3115–3138.

Blasdel, G. G. Orientation selectivity, preference, and continuity in monkey striate cortex. *Journal of Neuroscience*, 1992b, *12*, 3139–3161.

Blass, E. M., and Epstein, A. N. A lateral preoptic osmosensitive zone for thirst. *Journal of Comparative and Physiological Psychology*, 1971, *76*, 378–394.

Blaustein, J. D., and Feder, H. H. Cytoplasmic progestin receptors in guinea pig brain: Characteristics and relationship to the induction of sexual behavior. *Brain Research*, 1979, *169*, 481–497.

Blaustein, J. D., and Olster, D. H. Gonadal steroid hormone receptors and social behaviors. In *Advances in Comparative and Environmental Physiology*, Vol. 3, edited by J. Balthazart. Berlin: Springer-Verlag, 1989.

Blest, A. D. The function of eyespot patterns in insects. *Behaviour*, 1957, *11*, 209–256.

Bleuler, E. *Dementia Praecox of the Group of Schizophrenia*, 1911. Translated by J. Zinkin. New York: International Universities Press, 1911/1950.

Blier, P., and Bergeron, R. Effectiveness of pindol with selected antidepressant drugs in the treatment of major depression. *Journal of Clinical Psychopharmacology*, 1995, *15*, 217–222.

Blier, P., de Montigny, C., and Chaput, Y. Modifications of the serotonin system by antidepressant treatments: Implications for the therapeutic response in major depression. *Journal of Clinical Psychopharmacology*, 1987, *6*(Suppl.), 24S–35S.

Bliss, T. V. P., and Lømo, T. Long-lasting potentiation of synaptic transmission in the dentate area of the anaesthetized rabbit following stimulation of the perforant path. *Journal of Physiology (London)*, 1973, *232*, 331–356.

Bloch, V., Hennevin, E., and Leconte, P. Interaction between post-trial reticular stimulation and subsequent paradoxical sleep in memory consolidation processes. In *Neurobiology of Sleep and Memory*, edited by R. R. Drucker-Colín and J. L. McGaugh. New York: Academic Press, 1977.

Blonder, L. X., Bowers, D., and Heilman, K. M. The role of the right hemisphere in emotional communication. *Brain*, 1991, *114*, 1115–1127.

Blum, K., Noble, E. P., Sheridan, P. J., Montgomery, A., Ritchie, T., Jagadeeswaran, P., Nogami, H., Briggs, A. H., and Cohn, J. B. Allelic association of human dopamine D_2 receptor gene in alcoholism. *Journal of the American Medical Association*, 1990, *263*, 2055–2060.

Blumer, D., and Walker, A. E. The neural basis of sexual behavior. In *Psychiatric Aspects of Neurologic Disease*, edited by D. F. Benson and D. Blumer. New York: Grune & Stratton, 1975.

Bodner, M., Kroger, J., and Fuster, J. M. Auditory memory cells in dorsolateral prefrontal cortex. *NeuroReport*, 1996, *7*, 1905–1908.

Bogerts, B., Lieberman, J. A., Ashtari, M., Bilder, R. M., Degreef, G., Lerner, G., Johns, C., and Masiar, S. Hippocampus-amygdala volumes and psychopathology in chronic schizophrenia. *Biological Psychiatry*, 1993, *33*, 236–246.

Boller, F., and Dennis, M. *Auditory Comprehension: Clinical and Experimental Studies with the Token Test*. New York: Academic Press, 1979.

Bolton, R. F., Cornwall, J., and Phillipson, O. R. Collateral axons of cholinergic pontine neurones projecting to midline, mediodorsal and parafascicular thalamic nuclei in the rat. *Journal of Chemical Neuroanatomy*, 1993, *6*, 101–114.

Bon, C., Böhme, G. A., Doble, A., Stutzmann, J.-M., and Blanchard, J.-C. A role for nitric oxide in long-term potentiation. *European Journal of Neuroscience*, 1992, *4*, 420–424.

Bonnet, M. H., and Arand, D. L. We are chronically sleep deprived. *Sleep*, 1995, *18*, 908–911.

Borbély, A. A., and Tobler, I. Endogenous sleep-promoting substances and sleep regulation. *Physiological Reviews*, 1989, *69*, 605–670.

Born, R. T., and Tootell, R. B. H. Spatial frequency tuning of single units in macaque supragranular striate cortex. *Proceedings of the National Academy of Sciences*, 1991, *88*, 7066–7070.

Bornstein, B., Stroka, H., and Munitz, H. Prosopagnosia with animal face agnosia. *Cortex*, 1969, *5*, 164–169.

Bornstein, R. A., Schwarzkopf, S. B., Olson, S. C., and Nasrallah, H. A. Third-ventricle enlargement and neuropsychological deficit in schizophrenia. *Biological Psychiatry*, 1992, *31*, 954–961.

Bottini, G., Corcoran, R., Sterzi, R., Paulesu, E., Schenone, P., Scarpa, P., Frackowiak, R. S. J., and Frith, C. D. The role of the right hemisphere in the interpretation of figurative aspects of language: A positron emission tomography activation study. *Brain*, 1994, *117*, 1241–1253.

Bouchard, C. Genetic factors in obesity. *Medical Clinics of North America*, 1989, *73*, 67–81.

Bouchard, C. Heredity and the path to overweight and obesity. *Medicine and Science of Sports Exercise*, 1991, *23*, 285–291.

Boulos, Z., Campbell, S. S., Lewy, A. J., Terman, M., Dijk, D. J., and Eastman, C. I. Light treatment for sleep disorders: Consensus report. 7: Jet-lag. *Journal of Biological Rhythms*, 1995, *10*, 167–176.

Bouskila, Y., and Dudek, F. E. Neuronal synchronization without calcium-dependent synaptic transmission in the hypothalamus. *Proceedings of the National Academy of Sciences*, 1993, *90*, 3207–3210.

Boussaoud, D., Desimone, R., and Ungerleider, L. G. Visual topography of area TEO in the macaque. *Journal of Comparative Neurology*, 1991, *306*, 554–575.

Bowers, D., Blonder, L. X., Feinberg, T., and Heilman, K. M. Differential impact of right and left hemisphere lesions on facial emotion and object imagery. *Brain*, 1991, *114*, 2593–2609.

Bowers, D., and Heilman, K. M. A dissociation between the processing of affective and nonaffective faces. Paper presented at the meeting of the International Neuropsychological Society, Atlanta, 1981.

Bowers, R. L., Herzog, C. D., Stone, E. H., and Dionne, T. J. Defensive burying following injections of cholecystokinin, bombesin, and LiCl in rats. *Physiology and Behavior*, 1992, *51*, 969–972.

Bowersox, S. S., Kaitin, K. I., and Dement, W. C. EEG spindle activity as a function of age: Relationship to sleep continuity. *Brain Research*, 1985, *63*, 526–539.

Boynton, R. M. *Human Color Vision*. New York: Holt, Rinehart and Winston, 1979.

Bozarth, M. A. Physical dependence produced by central morphine infusions: An anatomical mapping study. *Neuroscience and Biobehavioral Reviews*, 1994, *18*, 373–383.

Bozarth, M. A., and Wise, R. A. Toxicity associated with long-term intravenous heroin and cocaine self-administration in the rat. *Journal of the American Medical Association*, 1985, *254*, 81–83.

Bracha, H. S., Torrey, E. F., Gottesman, I. I., Bigelow, L. B., and Cunniff, C. Second-trimester markers of fetal size in schizophrenia: A study of monozygotic twins. *American Journal of Psychiatry*, 1992, *149*, 1355–1361.

Brackett, N. L., and Edwards, D. A. Medial preoptic connections with the midbrain tegmentum are essential for male sexual behavior. *Physiology and Behavior*, 1984, *32*, 79–84.

Bradbury, M. W. B. *The Concept of a Blood-Brain Barrier*. New York: John Wiley & Sons, 1979.

Bradwejn, J., and Koszycki, D. The cholecystokinin hypothesis of anxiety and panic disorder. *Annals of the New York Academy of Sciences*, 1994, *713*, 273–282.

Bradwejn, J., Koszycki, D., and Meterissian, G. Cholecystokinin-tetrapeptide induced panic attacks in patients with panic disorder. *Canadian Journal of Psychiatry*, 1990, *35*, 83–85.

Bramham, C. R., Bacher-Svendsen, K., and Sarvey, J. M. LTP in the lateral perforant path is α-adrenergic receptor dependent. *Neuroreport*, 1997, *8*, 719–724.

Brand, T., Kroonen, J., Mos, J., and Slob, A. K. Adult partner preference and sexual behavior of male rats affected by perinatal endocrine manipulations. *Hormones and Behavior*, 1991, *25*, 323–341.

Bray, G. A. Drug treatment of obesity. *American Journal of Clinical Nutrition*, 1992, *55*, 538S–544S.

Brecher, E. M. *Licit and Illicit Drugs*. Boston: Little, Brown, 1972.

Breedlove, S. M. Sexual differentiation of the brain and behavior. In *Behavioral Endocrinology*, edited by J. B. Becker, S. M. Breedlove, and D. Crews. Cambridge, Mass.: MIT Press, 1992.

Breedlove, S. M. Sexual differentiation of the human nervous system. *Annual Review of Psychology*, 1994, *45*, 389–418.

Breedlove, S. M., and Arnold, A. Hormone accumulation in a sexually dimorphic motor nucleus of the rat spinal cord. *Science*, 1980, *210*, 564–566.

Breedlove, S. M., and Arnold, A. Sex differences in the pattern of steroid accumulation by motoneurons of the rat lumbar spinal cord. *Journal of Comparative Neurology*, 1983, *215*, 211–216.

Breier, A., Buchanan, R. W., Elkashef, A., Munson, R. C., Kirkpatrick, B., and Gellad, F. Brain morphology and schizophrenia: A magnetic resonance imaging study of limbic, prefrontal cortex, and caudate structures. *Archives of General Psychiatry*, 1992, *49*, 921–926.

Breisch, S. T., Zemlan, F. P., and Hoebel, B. G. Hyperphagia and obesity following serotonin depletion by intraventricular *p*-chlorphenylalanine. *Science*, 1976, *192*, 382–384.

Breiter, H. C., Rauch, S. L., Kwong, K. K., Baker, J. R., Weisskoff, R. M., Kennedy, D. N., Kendrick, A. D., Davis, T. L., Jiang, A. P., Cohen, M. S., Stern, C. E., Belliveau, J. W., Baer, L., O'-Sullivan, R. L., Savage, C. R., Jenike, M. A., and Rosen, B. R. Functional magnetic resonance imaging of symptom provocation in obsessive-compulsive disorder. *Archives of General Psychiatry*, 1996, *53*, 595–606.

Bremner, J. D., Innis, R. B., Salomon, R. M., Staib, L. H., Ng, C. K., Miller, H. L., Bronen, R. A., Krystal, J. H., Duncan, J., Rich, D., Price, L. H., Malison, R., Dey, H., Soufer, R., and Charney, D. S. Positron emission tomography measurement of cerebral metabolic correlates of tryptophan depletion-induced depressive relapse. *Archives of General Psychiatry*, 1997, *54*, 364–374.

Bremner, J. D., Randall, P., Scott, T. M., Bronen, R. A., Seibyl, J. P., Southwick, S. M., Delaney, R. C., McCarthy, G., Charney, D. S., and Innis, R. B. MRI-based measurement of hippocampal volume in patients with combat-related posttraumatic stress disorder. *American Journal of Psychiatry*, 1995, *152*, 973–981.

Brickner, R. M. *The Intellectual Functions of the Frontal Lobe: A Study Based Upon Observations of a Man After Partial Frontal Lobectomy*. New York: Macmillan, 1936.

Bridges, R. S. A quantitative analysis of the roles of dosage, sequence and duration of estradiol and progesterone exposure in the regulation of maternal behavior in the rat. *Endocrinology*, 1984, *114*, 930–940.

Bridges, R. S., and Ronsheim, P. M. Prolactin (PRL) regulation of maternal behavior in rats: Bromocriptine treatment delays and PRL promotes the rapid onset of behavior. *Endocrinology*, 1990, *126*, 837–848.

Britton, D. R., Koob, G. F., Rivier, J., and Vale, W. Intraventricular corticotropin-releasing factor enhances behavioral effects of novelty. *Life Sciences*, 1982, *31*, 363–367.

Broberg, D. J., and Bernstein, I. L. Cephalic insulin release in anorexic women. *Physiology and Behavior*, 1989, *45*, 871–874.

Broca, P. Remarques sur le siège de la faculté du langage articulé, suivies d'une observation d'aphemie (perte de la parole). *Bulletin de la Société Anatomique (Paris)*, 1861, *36*, 330–357.

Broussaud, D., di Pellegrino, G., and Wise, S. P. Frontal lobe mechanisms subserving vision-for-action versus vision-for-perception. *Behavioural Brain Research*, 1996, *72*, 1–15.

Brown, G. L., Ebert, M. H., Goyer, P. F., Jimerson, D.C., Klein, W. J., Bunney, W. E., and Goodwin, F. W. Aggression, suicide, and serotonin: Relationships to CSF amine metabolites. *American Journal of Psychiatry*, 1982, *139*, 741–746.

Brown, G. L., Goodwin, F. K., Ballenger, J. C., Goyer, P. F., and Major, L. F. Aggression in humans correlates with cerebrospinal fluid amine metabolites. *Psychiatry Research*, 1979, *1*, 131–139.

Brown, T. H., Ganong, A. H., Kairiss, E. W., Keenan, C. L., and Kelso, S. R. Long-term potentiation in two synaptic systems of the hippocampal brain slice. In *Neural Models of Plasticity: Experimental and Theoretical Approaches*, edited by J. H. Byrne and W. O. Berry. San Diego: Academic Press, 1989.

Brownell, H. H., Michel, D., Powelson, J., and Gardner, H. Surprise but not coherence: Sensitivity to verbal humor in right-hemisphere patients. *Brain and Language*, 1983, *18*, 20–27.

Brownell, H. H., Simpson, T. L., Bihrle, A. M., Potter, H. H., and Gardner, H. Appreciation of metaphoric alternative word meanings by left and right brain-damaged patients. *Neuropsychologia*, 1990, *28*, 173–184.

Brownell, W. E., Bader, C. R., Bertrand, D., and de-Ribaupierre, Y. Evoked mechanical responses of isolated cochlear outer hair cells. *Science*, 1985, *227*, 194–196.

Brozowski, T. J., Brown, R. M., Rosvold, H. E., and Goldman, P. S. Cognitive deficit caused by regional depletion of dopamine in prefrontal cortex of rhesus monkey. *Science*, 1979, *205*, 929–932.

Bruce, H. M. A block to pregnancy in the mouse caused by proximity of strange males. *Journal of Reproduction and Fertility*, 1960a, *1*, 96–103.

Bruce, H. M. Further observations of pregnancy block in mice caused by proximity of strange males. *Journal of Reproduction and Fertility*, 1960b, *2*, 311–312.

Brunner, H. G., Nelen, M., Breakefield, X. O., Ropers, H. H., and van Oost, B. A. Abnormal behavior associated with a point mutation in the structural gene for monoamine oxidase A. *Science*, 1993, *262*, 578–580.

Bryden, M. P., and Ley, R. G. Right-hemispheric involvement in the perception and expression of emotion in normal humans. In *Neuropsychology of Human Emotion*, edited by K. M. Heilman and P. Satz. New York: Guilford Press, 1983.

Buchs, P. A., and Muller, D. Induction of long-term potentiation is associated with major ultrastructural changes of activated synapses. *Proceedings of the National Academy of Sciences, USA,* 1996, *93,* 8040–8045.

Buchsbaum, M. S., Gillin, J. C., Wu, J., Hazlett, E., Sicotte, N., Dupont, R. M., and Bunney, W. E. Regional cerebral glucose metabolic rate in human sleep assessed by positron emission tomography. *Life Sciences,* 1989, *45,* 1349–1356.

Buck, L. B. Information coding in the vertebrate olfactory system. *Annual Review of Neuroscience,* 1996, *19,* 517–544.

Buck, L., and Axel, R. A novel multigene family may encode odorant receptors: A molecular basis for odor recognition. *Cell,* 1991, *65,* 175–187.

Buckley, P., Stack, J. P., Madigan, C., O'Callaghan, E., Larkin, C., Redmond, O., Ennis, J. T., and Waddington, J. L. Magnetic resonance imaging of schizophrenia-like psychoses associated with cerebral trauma: Clinicopathological correlates. *American Journal of Psychiatry,* 1993, *150,* 146–148.

Buggy, J., Hoffman, W. E., Phillips, M. I., Fisher, A. E., and Johnson, A. K. Osmosensitivity of rat third ventricle and interactions with angiotensin. *American Journal of Physiology,* 1979, *236,* R75–R82.

Burt, D. R., Creese, I., and Snyder, S. H. Antischizophrenic drugs: Chronic treatment elevated dopamine receptor binding in brain. *Science,* 1977, *196,* 326–328.

Burton, M. J., Rolls, E. T., and Mora, F. Effects of hunger on the responses of neurons in the lateral hypothalamus to the sight and taste of food. *Experimental Neurology,* 1976, *51,* 668–677.

Buzsáki, G. Two-stage model of memory trace formation: A role for "noisy" brain states. *Neuroscience,* 1989, *31,* 551–570.

Buzsáki, G. The hippocampo-neocortical dialogue. *Cerebral Cortex,* 1996, *6,* 81–92.

Buzsáki, G., Gage, F. H., Czopf, J., and Björklund, A. Restoration of rhythmic slow activity (theta) in the subcortically denervated hippocampus by fetal CNS transplants. *Brain Research,* 1987, *400,* 334–347.

Cabanac, M., and Lafrance, L. Facial consummatory responses in rats support the ponderostat hypothesis. *Physiology and Behavior,* 1991, *50,* 179–183.

Cador, M., Robbins, T. W., and Everitt, B. J. Involvement of the amygdala in stimulus-reward associations: Interaction with the ventral striatum. *Neuroscience,* 1989, *30,* 77–86.

Cahill, L., Babinsky, R., Markowitsch, H. J., and McGaugh, J. L. The amygdala and emotional memory. *Nature,* 1995, *377,* 295–296.

Cahill, L., Haier, R. J., Fallon, J., Alkire, M. T., Tang, C., Keator, D., Wu, J., and McGaugh, J. L. Amygdala activity at encoding correlated with long-term, free recall of emotional information. *Proceedings of the National Academy of Sciences, USA,* 1996, *93,* 8016–8021.

Cain, W. S. Olfaction. In *Stevens' Handbook of Experimental Psychology.* Vol. 1. *Perception and Motivation,* edited by R. C. Atkinson, R. J. Herrnstein, G. Lindzey, and R. D. Luce. New York: John Wiley & Sons, 1988.

Caine, S. B., Heinrichs, S. C., Coffin, V. L., and Koob, G. F. Effects of the dopamine D-1 antagonist SCH 23390 microinjected into the accumbens, amygdala or striatum on cocaine self-administration in the rat. *Brain Res,* 1995, *692,* 47–56.

Caine, S. B., and Koob, G. F. Effects of mesolimbic dopamine depletion on responding maintained by cocaine and food. *Journal of the Experimental Analysis of Behavior,* 1994, *61,* 213–221.

Calabrese, P., Markowitsch, H. J., Harders, A. G., Scholz, M., and Gehlen, W. Fornix damage and memory: A case report. *Cortex,* 1995, *31,* 555–564.

Calder, A. J., Young, A. W., Rowland, D., Perrett, D. I., Hodges, J. R., and Etcoff, N. L. Facial emotion recognition after bilateral amygdala damage: Differentially severe impairment of fear. *Cognitive Neuropsychology,* 1996, *13,* 699–745.

Calhoun, J. Population density and social pathology. *Scientific American,* 1962, *206,* 139–148.

Calingasan, N. Y., and Ritter, S. Lateral parabrachial subnucleus lesions abolish feeding induced by mercaptoacetate but not by 2-deoxy-D-glucose. *American Journal of Physiology,* 1993, *265,* R1168–R1178.

Callaway, C. W., Lydic, R., Baghdoyan, H. A., and Hobson, J. A. Pontogeniculoccipital waves: Spontaneous visual system activity during rapid eye movement sleep. *Cellular and Molecular Neurobiology,* 1987, *2,* 105–149.

Calles-Escandon, J., and Horton, E. S. The thermogenic role of exercise in the treatment of morbid obesity: A critical evaluation. *American Journal of Clinical Nutrition,* 1992, *55,* 533S–537S.

Calvert, G. A., Bullmore, E. T., Brammer, M. J., Campbell, R., Williams, S. C. R., McGuire, P. K., Woodruff, P. W. R., Iversen, S. D., and David, A. S. Activation of auditory cortex during silent lipreading. *Science,* 1997, *276,* 593–596.

Campbell, R., De Gelder, B., and De Haan, E. The lateralization of lip-reading: A second look. *Neuropsychologia,* 1996, *34,* 1235–1240.

Campbell, R., Heywood, C. A., Cower, A., Regard, M., and Landis, T. Sensitivity to eye gaze in prosopagnosic patients and monkeys with superior temporal sulcus ablation. *Neuropsychologia,* 1990, *28,* 1123–1142.

Campeau, S., Hayward, M. D., Hope, B. T., Rosen, J. B., Nestler, E. J., and Davis, M. Induction of the c-fos proto-oncogene in rat amygdala during unconditioned and conditioned fear. *Brain Research,* 1991, *565,* 349–352.

Campeau, S., Miserendino, M. J. D., and Davis, M. Intra-amygdala infusion of the N-methyl-D-aspartate receptor antagonist AP5 blocks acquisition but not expression of fear-potentiated startle to an auditory conditioned stimulus. *Behavioral Neuroscience,* 1992, *106,* 569–574.

Campfield, L. A., Smith, F. J., Guisez, Y., Devos, R., and Burn, P. Recombinant mouse ob protein: Evidence for a peripheral signal linking adiposity and central neural networks. *Science,* 1995, *269,* 546–549.

Cannon, W. B. The James-Lange theory of emotions: A critical examination and an alternative. *American Journal of Psychology,* 1927, *39,* 106–124.

Canteras, N. S., Simerly, R. B., and Swanson, L. W. Organization of projections from the medial nucleus of the amygdala: A PHA-L study in the rat. *Journal of Comparative Neurology,* 1995, *360,* 213–245.

Card, J. P., Riley, J. N., and Moore, R. Y. The suprachiasmatic hypothalamic nucleus: Ultrastructure of relations to optic chiasm. *Neuroscience Abstracts,* 1980, *6,* 758.

Carew, T. J. Development assembly of learning in Aplysia. *Trends in Neuroscience,* 1989, *12,* 389–394.

Carlezon, W. A., Devine, D. P., and Wise, R. A. Habit-forming actions of nomifensine in nucleus accumbens. *Psychopharmacology,* 1995, *122,* 194–197.

Carmichael, M. S., Humbert, R., Dixen, J., Palmisano, G., Greenleaf, W., and Davidson, J. M. Plasma oxytocin increases in the human sexual response. *Journal of Clinical Endocrinology and Metabolism,* 1987, *64,* 27–31.

Caro, J. F., Kolaczynski, J. W., Nyce, M. R., Ohannesian, J. P., Opentanova, I., Goldman, W. H., Lynn, R. B., Zhang, P. L., Sinha, M. K., and Considine, R. V. Decreased cerebrospinal fluid/serum leptin ration in obesity: A possible mechanism for leptin resistance. *Lancet,* 1996, *348,* 159–161.

Carpenter, C. R. Sexual behavior of free ranging rhesus monkeys (*Macaca mulatta*). I. Specimens, procedures and behavioral characteristics of estrus. *Journal of Comparative Psychology,* 1942, *33,* 113–142.

Carr, C. E., and Konishi, M. Axonal delay lines for time measurement in the owl's brainstem. *Proceedings of the National Academy of Sciences, USA,* 1989, *85,* 8311–8315.

Carr, C. E., and Konishi, M. A circuit for detection of interaural time differences in the brain stem of the barn owl. *Journal of Neuroscience,* 1990, *10,* 3227–3246.

Carrera, M. R., Ashley, J. A., Parsons, L. H., Wirsching, P., Koob, G. F., and Janda, K. D. Suppression of psychoactive effects of cocaine by active immunization. *Nature,* 1995, *378,* 727–730.

Carter, C. S. Hormonal influences on human sexual behavior. In *Behavioral Endocrinology,* edited by J. B. Becker, S. M. Breedlove, and D. Crews. Cambridge, Mass.: MIT Press, 1992.

Cases, O., Seif, I., Grimsby, J., Gaspar, P., Chen, K., Pournin, S., Muller, U., Aguet, M., Babinet, C., Shih, J. C., and Demaeyer, E. Aggressive behavior and altered amounts of brain serotonin and norepinephrine in mice lacking MAO-A. *Science,* 1995, *268,* 1763–1766.

Castles, A., and Coltheart, M. Varieties of developmental dyslexia. *Cognition,* 1993, *47,* 149–180.

Cavada, C., and Goldman-Rakic, P. S. Posterior parietal cortex in rhesus monkey. II. Evidence for segregated corticocortical networks linking sensory and limbic areas with the frontal lobe. *Journal of Comparative Neurology,* 1989, *287,* 422–445.

Cenci, M. A., Kalen, P., Mandel, R. J., and Bjoerklund, A. Regional differences in the regulation of dopamine and noradrenaline release in medial frontal cortex, nucleus accumbens and caudate-putamen: A microdialysis study in the rat. *Brain Research,* 1992, *581,* 217–228.

Chang, F.-L. F., and Greenough, W. T. Lateralized effects of monocular training on dendritic branching in adult split-brain rats. *Brain Research,* 1982, *232,* 283–292.

Chang, V. C., Mark, G. P., Hernandez, L., and Hoebel, B. G. Extracellular dopamine increases in the nucleus accumbens following rehydration or sodium repletion. *Society for Neuroscience Abstracts,* 1988, *14,* 527.

Chaudhari, N., Yang, H., Lamp, C., Delay, E., Cartford, C., Than, T., and Roper, S. The taste of monosodium glutamate: Membrane receptors in taste buds. *Journal of Neuroscience,* 1996, *16,* 3817–3826.

Chen, C., Rainnie, D. G., Greene, R. W., and Tonegawa, S. Abnormal fear response and aggressive behavior in mutant mice deficient for α-calcium-calmodulin kinase II. *Science,* 1994, *266,* 291–294.

Chen, J., Marmer, R., Pulles, A., Paredes, W., and Gardner, E. L. Ventral tegmental microinjection of delta⁹-tetrahydrocannabinol enhances ventral tegmental somatodendritic dopamine levels but not forebrain dopamine levels: Evidence for local neural action by marijuana's psychoactive ingredient. *Brain Research,* 1993, *621,* 65–70.

Chen, J., Paredes, W., Li, J., Smith, D., Lowinson, J., and Gardner, E. L. Delta⁹-tetrahydrocannabinol produces naloxone-blockable enhancement of presynaptic basal dopamine efflux in nucleus accumbens of conscious, freely-moving rats as measured by intracerebral microdialysis. *Psychopharmacology,* 1990, *102,* 156–162.

Chen, W. R., Lee, S. H., Kato, K., Spencer, D. D., Shepherd, G. M., and Williamson, A. Long-term modifications of synaptic efficacy in the human inferior and middle temporal cortex. *Proceedings of the National Academy of Sciences, USA,* 1996, *93,* 8011–8015.

Chen, Y.-C., Thaler, D., Nixon, P. D., Stern, C. E., and Passingham, R. E. The functions of the medial premotor cortex. II. The timing and selection of learned movements. *Experimental Brain Research,* 1995, *102,* 461–473.

Chen, Y. W., and Dilsaver, S. C. Lifetime rates of suicide attempts among subjects with bipolar and unipolar disorders relative to subjects with other axis I disorders. *Biological Psychiatry,* 1996, *39,* 896–899.

Chess, S., Fernandez, F., and Korn, S. J. *Psychiatric Disorders of Children with Congenital Rubella.* New York: Brunner-Mazel, 1971.

Chi, J. G., Dooling, E. C., and Gilles, F. H. Gyral development of the human brain. *Annals of Neurology,* 1977, *1,* 86–93.

Cipolotti, L., and Warrington, E. K. Does recognizing orally spelled words depend on reading? An investigation into a case of better written than oral spelling. *Neuropsychologia,* 1996, *34,* 427–440.

Clark, J. R., Kalra, P. S., and Kalra, S. P. Neuropeptide Y stimulates feeding but inhibits sexual behavior in rats. *Endocrinology,* 1985, *117,* 2435–2442.

Clark, J. T., Gist, R. S., Kalra, S. P., and Kalra, P. S. α_2-adrenoreceptor blockade attenuates feeding behavior induced by neuropeptide Y and epinephrine. *Physiology and Behavior,* 1988, *42,* 417–422.

Clark, J. T., Kalra, P. S., Crowley, W. R., and Kalra, S. P. Neuropeptide Y and human pancreatic polypeptide stimulates feeding behavior in rats. *Endocrinology,* 1984, *115,* 427–429.

Clément, K., Vaisse, C., St. J. Manning, B., Basdevant, A., Guy-Grand, B., Ruiz, J., Silver, K. D., Shuldiner, A. R., Froguel, P., and Strosberg, A. D. Genetic variation in the beta3-adrenergic receptor and an increased capacity to gain weight in patients with morbid obesity. *New England Journal of Medicine,* 1995, *333,* 352–354.

Cloninger, C. R. Neurogenetic adaptive mechanisms in alcoholism. *Science,* 1987, *236,* 410–416.

Cloninger, C. R., Bohman, M., and Sigvardsson, S. Inheritance of alcohol abuse: Cross-fostering analysis of adopted men. *Archives of General Psychiatry,* 1981, *38,* 861–868.

Cloninger, C. R., Bohman, M., Sigvardsson, S., and von Knorring, A.-L. Psychopathology in adopted-out children of alcoholics: The Stockholm Adoption Study. *Recent Developments in Alcoholism,* 1985, *3,* 37–51.

Clugnet, M.-C., and LeDoux, J. E. Synaptic plasticity in fear conditioning circuits: Induction of LTP in the lateral nucleus of the amygdala by stimulation of the medial geniculate body. *Journal of Neuroscience,* 1990, *10,* 2818–2824.

Cobb, S., and Rose, R. M. Hypertension, peptic ulcer, and diabetes in air traffic controllers. *Journal of the American Medical Association,* 1973, *224,* 489–492.

Coble, P. A., Scher, M. S., Reynolds, C. F., Day, N. L., and Kupfer, D. J. Preliminary findings on the neonatal sleep of offspring of women with and without a prior history of affective disorder. *Sleep Research,* 1988, *16,* 120.

Coburn, P. C., and Stricker, E. M. Osmoregulatory thirst in rats after lateral preoptic lesions. *Journal of Comparative and Physiological Psychology,* 1978, *92,* 350–361.

Coccaro, E. F. Neurotransmitter correlates of impulsive aggression in humans. *Annals of the New York Academy of Sciences,* 1996, *794,* 82–89.

Cohen, E. A. *Human Behavior in the Concentration Camp.* New York: W. W. Norton, 1953.

Cohen, S., Tyrrell, D. A. J., and Smith, A. P. Psychological stress and susceptibility to the common cold. *New England Journal of Medicine,* 1991, *325,* 606–612.

Coirini, H., Magarinos, A. M., DeNicola, A. F., Rainbow, T. C., and McEwen, B. S. Further studies of brain aldosterone binding sites employing new mineralocorticoid and glucocorticoid receptor markers in vitro. *Brain Research,* 1985, *12,* 212–216.

Colditz, G. A. Economic costs of obesity. *American Journal of Clinical Nutrition,* 1992, *55,* 503S–507S.

Cole, B. J., and Koob, G. F. Propranalol antagonizes the enhanced conditioned fear produced by corticotropin releasing factor. *Journal of Pharmacology and Experimental Therapeutics,* 1988, *247,* 901–910.

Comarr, A. E. Sexual function among patients with spinal cord injury. *Urologia Internationalis,* 1970, *25,* 134–168.

Comings, D. E., and Comings, B. G. Clinical and genetic relationships between autism-pervasive developmental disorder and Tourette syndrome: A study of 19 cases. *American Journal of Medical Genetics,* 1991, *39,* 180–191.

Comings, D. E., Muhleman, D., and Gysin, R. Dopamine D2 receptor (DRD2) gene and susceptibility to posttraumatic stress disorder: A study and replication. *Biological Psychiatry,* 1996, *40,* 368–372.

Constantinidis, C., and Steinmetz, M. A. Neuronal activity in posterior parietal area 7a during the delay periods of a spatial memory task. *Journal of Neurophysiology,* 1996, *76,* 1352–1355.

Coon, H., Byerley, W., Holik, J., Hoff, M., Myles-Worsley, M., Lannfelt, L., Sokoloff, P., Schwartz, J.-C., Waldo, M., Freedman, R., and Plaetke, R. Linkage analysis of schizophrenia with five dopamine receptor genes in nine pedigrees. *American Journal of Human Genetics,* 1993, *52,* 327–334.

Coover, G. D., Murison, R., and Jellestad, F. K. Subtotal lesions of the amygdala: The rostral central nucleus in passive avoidance and ulceration. *Physiology and Behavior,* 1992, *51,* 795–803.

Coplan, J. D., Gorman, J. M., and Klein, D. F. Serotonin related functions in panic-anxiety: A critical overview. *Neuropsychopharmacology,* 1992, *6,* 189–200.

Corkin, S., Sullivan, E. V., Twitchell, T. E., and Grove, E. The amnesic patient H. M.: Clinical observations and test performance 28 years after operation. *Society for Neuroscience Abstracts,* 1981, *7,* 235.

Cornelissen, P., Bradley, L., Fowler, S., and Stein, J. What children see affects how they read. *Developmental Medicine and Child Neurology,* 1991, *33,* 755–762.

Cornwall, J., Cooper, J. D., and Phillipson, O. T. Afferent and efferent connections of the laterodorsal tegmental nucleus in the rat. *Brain Research Bulletin,* 1990, *25,* 271–284.

Corrigall, W. A., Coen, K. M., and Adamson, K. L. Self-administered nicotine activates the mesolimbic dopamine system through the ventral tegmental area. *Brain Research,* 1994, *653,* 278–284.

Corwin, J. T., and Warchol, M. E. Auditory hair cells: Structure, function, development, and regeneration. *Annual Review of Neuroscience,* 1991, *14,* 301–333.

Courchesne, E. Neuroanatomic imaging in autism. *Pediatrics,* 1991, *87,* 781–790.

Cousins, M. S., Atherton, A., Turner, L., and Salamone, J. D. Nucleus accumbens dopamine depletions alter relative response allocation in a T-maze cost/benefit task. *Behavioural Brain Research*, 1996, 74, 189–197.

Cowey, A., and Stoerig, P. The neurobiology of blindsight. *Trends in Neuroscience*, 1991, 14, 140–145.

Cowley, J. J., and Brooksbank, B. W. L. Human exposure to putative pheromones and changes in aspects of social behaviour. *Journal of Steroid Biochemistry and Molecular Biololgy*, 1991, 39, 647–659.

Cox, A., Rutter, M., Newman, S., and Bartak, L. A comparative study of infantile autism and specific developmental language disorders. I. Parental characteristics. *British Journal of Psychiatry*, 1975, 126, 146–159.

Crabbe, J. C., Merrill, C. M., Kim, D., and Belknap, J. K. Alcohol dependence and withdrawal: A genetic animal model. *Annals of Medicine*, 1990, 22, 259–263.

Crane, G. E. Iproniazid (Marsilid) phosphate, a therapeutic agent for mental disorders and debilitating diseases. *Psychiatry Research Reports*, 1957, 8, 142–152.

Creese, I., Burt, D. R., and Snyder, S. H. Dopamine receptor binding predicts clinical and pharmacological potencies of antischizophrenic drugs. *Science*, 1976, 192, 481–483.

Crick, F., and Mitchison, G. The function of dream sleep. *Nature*, 1983, 304, 111–114.

Crow, T. J. A map of the rat mesencephalon for electrical self-stimulation. *Brain Research*, 1972, 36, 265–273.

Crow, T. J. Positive and negative schizophrenic symptoms and the role of dopamine. *British Journal of Psychiatry*, 1980, 137, 383–386.

Crowe, R. R., Noyes, R., Pauls, D. L., and Slymen, D. A family study of panic disorder. *Archives of General Psychiatry*, 1983, 40, 1065–1069.

Crowe, R. R., Noyes, R., Wilson, A. F., Elston, R. C., and Ward, L. J. A linkage study of panic disorder. *Archives of General Psychiatry*, 1987, 44, 933–937.

Crowley, W. R., Nock, B., and Feder, H. H. Facilitation of lordosis behavior by clinidine in female guinea pigs. *Pharmacology, Biochemistry, and Behavior*, 1978, 8, 207–209.

Crowley, W. R., Rodriguez-Sierra, J. F., and Komisaruk, B. R. Monoaminergic mediation of the antinociceptive effect of vaginal stimulation in rats. *Brain Research*, 1977, 137, 67–84.

Cruikshank, S. J., and Weinberger, N. M. Receptive-field plasticity in the adult auditory cortex induced by Hebbian covariance. *Journal of Neuroscience*, 1996, 16, 861–875.

Csonka, E., Fekete, M., Nagy, G., Sxanto-Fekete, M., Feledgy, G., Penke, B., and Kovaks, K. Anxiogenic effect of cholecystokinin in rats. In *Peptides*, edited by B. Penke and A. Torok. New York: Walter de Gruyter & Co., 1988.

Cubelli, R. A selective deficit for writing vowels in acquired dysgraphia. *Nature*, 1991, 353, 258–260.

Culebras, A., and Moore, J. T. Magnetic resonance findings in REM sleep behavior disorder. *Neurology*, 1989, 39, 1519–1523.

Culotta, E., and Koshland, D. E. NO news is good news. *Science*, 1992, 258, 1862–1865.

Cummings, J. L., and Cunningham, K. Obsessive-compulsive disorder in Huntington's disease. *Biological Psychiatry*, 1992, 31, 263–270.

Cunningham, J. T., Beltz, T., Johnson, R. F., and Johnson, A. K. The effects of ibotenate lesions of the median preoptic nucleus on experimentally-induced and circadian drinking behavior in rats. *Brain Research*, 1992, 580, 325–330.

Currie, P. J., and Coscina, D. V. Regional hypothalamic differences in neuropeptide Y-induced feeding and energy substrate utilization. *Brain Research*, 1996, 737, 238–242.

Czech, D. A., and Stein, E. A. Effect of drinking on angiotensin-II-induced shifts in regional cerebral blood flow in the rat. *Brain Research Bulletin*, 1992, 28, 529–535.

Dabbs, J. M., Frady, R. L., Carr, T. S., and Besch, N. F. Saliva testosterone and criminal violence in young adult prison inmates. *Psychosomatic Medicine*, 1987, 49, 174–182.

Dabbs, J. M., and Morris, R. Testosterone, social class, and antisocial behavior in a sample of 4,462 men. *Psychological Science*, 1990, 1, 209–211.

Dabbs, J. M., Ruback, J. M., Frady, R. L., and Hopper, C. H. Saliva testosterone and criminal violence among women. *Personality and Individual Differences*, 1988, 9, 269–275.

Dacey, D. M. Circuitry for color coding in the primate retina. *Proceedings of the National Academy of Sciences, USA*, 1996, 93, 582–588.

Dacey, D. M., Lee, B. B., Stafford, D. K., Pokorny, J., and Smith, V. C. Horizontal cells of the primate retina: Cone specificity without spectral opponency. *Science*, 1996, 271, 656–659.

Dahl, D., and Sarvey, J. M. Norepinephrine induces pathway-specific long-lasting potentiation and depression in the hippocampal dentate gyrus. *Proceedings of the National Academy of Science, USA*, 1989, 86, 4775–4780.

Dalen, P. Month of birth and schizophrenia. *Acta Psychiatrica Scandanivica*, 1968, 44(Suppl.), 55–60.

Dallos, P. The active cochlea. *Journal of Neuroscience*, 1992, 12, 4575–4585.

Damasio, A. Aphasia. *New England Journal of Medicine*, 1992, 326, 531–539.

Damasio, A. R. Disorders of complex visual processing: Agnosias, achromatopsia, Balint's syndrome, and related difficulties of orientation and construction. In *Principles of Behavioral Neurology*, edited by M.-M. Mesulam. Philadelphia: F. A. Davis, 1985.

Damasio, A. R., Brandt, J. P., Tranel, D., and Damasio, H. Name dropping: Retrieval of proper or common nouns depends on different systems in left temporal cortex. *Society for Neuroscience Abstracts*, 1991, 17, 4.

Damasio, A. R., and Damasio, H. The anatomic basis of pure alexia. *Neurology*, 1983, 33, 1573–1583.

Damasio, A. R., and Damasio, H. Hemianopia, hemiachromatopsia, and the mechanisms of alexia. *Cortex,* 1986, *22,* 161–169.

Damasio, A. R., Damasio, H., and Van Hoesen, G. W. Prosopagnosia: Anatomic basis and behavioral mechanisms. *Neurology,* 1982, *32,* 331–341.

Damasio, A. R., and Tranel, D. Knowing that "Colorado" goes with "Denver" does not imply knowledge that "Denver" *is* in "Colorado." *Behavioural Brain Research,* 1990, *40,* 193–200.

Damasio, A. R., and Tranel, D. Nouns and verbs are retrieved with differentially distributed neural systems. *Proceedings of the National Academy of Sciences, USA,* 1993, *90,* 4957–4960.

Damasio, A. R., Yamada, T., Damasio, H., Corbett, J., and McKee, J. Central achromatopsia: Behavioral, anatomic, and physiologic aspects. *Neurology,* 1980, *30,* 1064–1071.

Damasio, H. Neuroimaging contributions to the understanding of aphasia. In *Handbook of Neuropsychology,* Vol. 2, edited by F. Boller and J. Grafman. Amsterdam: Elsevier, 1989.

Damasio, H., Eslinger, P., and Adams, H. P. Aphasia following basal ganglia lesions: New evidence. *Seminars in Neurology,* 1984, *4,* 151–161.

Damasio, H, Grabowski, T., Frank, R., Galaburda, A. M., and Damasio, A. R. The return of Phineas Gage: Clues about the brain from the skull of a famous patient. *Science,* 1994, *264,* 1102–1105.

D'Amato, T., Rochet, T., Dalery, J., Laurent, A., Chauchat, J.-H., Terra, J.-L., and Marie-Cardine, M. Relationship between symptoms rated with the Positive and Negative Syndrome Scale and brain measures in schizophrenia. *Psychiatry Research,* 1992, *44,* 55–62.

Damsma, G., Day, J., and Fibiger, H. C. Lack of tolerance to nicotine-induced dopamine release in the nucleus accumbens. *European Journal of Pharmacology,* 1989, *168,* 363–368.

Damsma, G., Pfaus, J. G., Wenkstern, D., Phillips, A. G., and Fibiger, H. C. Sexual behavior increases dopamine transmission in the nucleus accumbens and striatum of male rats: Comparison with novelty and locomotion. *Behavioral Neuroscience,* 1992, *106,* 181–191.

Daniel, D. G., Weinberger, D. R., Jones, D. W., Zigon, J. R., Cippola, R., Handel, S., Bigelow, L. B., Goldberg, T. E., Berman, K. F., and Kleinman, J. E. The effect of amphetamine on regional cerebral blood flow during cognitive activation in schizophrenia. *Journal of Neuroscience,* 1991, *11,* 1907–1917.

Daniele, A., Giustolisi, L., Silveri, M. C., Colosimo, C., and Gainotti, G. Evidence for a possible neuroanatomical basis for lexical processing of nouns and verbs. *Neuropsychologia,* 1994, *32,* 1325–1341.

Darwin, C. *The Expression of the Emotions in Man and Animals.* Chicago: University of Chicago Press, 1872/1965.

Davidson, D., Swift, R., and Fitz, E. Naltrexone increases the latency to drink alcohol in social drinkers. *Alcoholism: Clinical and Experimental Research,* 1996, *20,* 732–739.

Davidson, J. M. Hormones and sexual behavior in the male. In *Neuroendocrinology,* edited by D. T. Krieger and J. C. Hughes. Sunderland, Mass.: Sinauer Associates, 1980.

Davis, J. D., and Campbell, C. S. Peripheral control of meal size in the rat: Effect of sham feeding on meal size and drinking rate. *Journal of Comparative and Physiological Psychology,* 1973, *83,* 379–387.

Davis, J. O., and Bracha, H. S. Famine and schizophrenia: First-trimester malnutrition or second-trimester beriberi? *Biological Psychiatry,* 1996a, *40,* 1–3.

Davis, J. O., Phelps, J. A., and Bracha, H. S. Prenatal development of monozygotic twins and concordance for schizophrenia. *Schizophrenia Bulletin,* 1995, *21,* 357–366.

Davis, K. L., Kahn, R. S., Ko, G., and Davidson, M. Dopamine in schizophrenia: A review and reconceptualization. *American Journal of Psychiatry,* 1991, *148,* 1474–1486.

Davis, M. The role of the amygdala in fear and anxiety. *Annual Review of Neuroscience,* 1992a, *15,* 353–375.

Davis, M. The role of the amygdala in fear-potentiated startle: Implications for animal models of anxiety. *Trends in Pharmacological Sciences,* 1992b, *13,* 35–41.

Davis, M., Rainnie, D., and Cassell, M. Neurotransmission in the rat amygdala related to fear and anxiety. *Trends in Neuroscience,* 1994, *17,* 208–214.

Davison, G. C., and Neale, J. M. *Abnormal Psychology: An Experimental Clinical Approach.* New York: John Wiley & Sons, 1974.

Daw, N. W. Colour-coded ganglion cells in the goldfish retina: Extension of their receptive fields by means of new stimuli. *Journal of Physiology (London),* 1968, *197,* 567–592.

Dawson, E., and Murray, R. Schizophrenia: A gene at 6p? *Current Biology,* 1996, *6,* 268–271.

Dawson, V. L., Dawson, T. M., Bartley, D. A., Uhl, G. R., and Snyder, S. H. Mechanisms of nitric oxide mediated neurotoxicity in primary brain cultures. *Journal of Neuroscience,* 1993, *13,* 2651–2661.

Day, J., Damsma, G., and Fibiger, H. C. Cholinergic activity in the rat hippocampus, cortex and striatum correlates with locomotor activity: An in vivo microdialysis study. *Pharmacology, Biochemistry, and Behavior,* 1991, *38,* 723–729.

D'Cruz, O. F., Vaughn, B. V., Gold, S. H., and Greenwood, R. S. Symptomatic cataplexy in pontomedullary lesions. *Neurology,* 1994, *44,* 2189–2191.

Deacon, S., and Arendt, J. Adapting to phase shifts. I. An experimental model for jet lag and shift work. *Physiology and Behavior,* 1996, *59,* 665–673.

Dean, P. Effects of inferotemporal lesions on the behavior of monkeys. *Psychological Bulletin,* 1976, *83,* 41–71.

Dean, P. Visual behavior in monkeys with inferotemporal lesions. In *Analysis of Visual Behavior,* edited by D. J. Ingle, M. A. Goodale, and R. J. W. Mansfield. Cambridge, Mass.: MIT Press, 1982.

Debanne, D., Gähwiler, B. H., and Thompson, S. M. Asynchronous pre- and postsynaptic activity induces associative long-term depression in area CA1 of the rat hippocampus in vitro. *Proceedings of the National Academy of Sciences, USA,* 1994, *91,* 1148–1152.

De Bold, A. J. Atrial natriuretic factor: A hormone produced by the heart. *Science,* 1985, *230,* 767–770.

De Bold, A. J., Borenstein, H. B., Veres, A. T., and Sonnenberg, H. A rapid and potent natriuretic response to intravenous injection of atrial myocardial extracts in rats. *Life Science,* 1981, *28,* 89–94.

de Castro, J. M. A microregulatory analysis of spontaneous fluid intake by humans: Evidence that the amount of liquid ingested and its timing is mainly governed by feeding. *Physiology and Behavior,* 1988, *43,* 705–714.

de Castro, J. M. Genetic influences on daily intake and meal patterns of humans. *Physiology and Behavior,* 1993, *53,* 777–782.

de Castro, J. M., and de Castro, E. S. Spontaneous meal patterns of humans: Influence of the presence of other people. *American Journal of Clinical Nutrition,* 1989, *50,* 237–247.

de Castro, J. M., McCormick, J., Pedersen, M., and Kreitzman, S. N. Spontaneous human meal patterns are related to preprandial factors regardless of natural environmental constraints. *Physiology and Behavior,* 1986, *38,* 25–29.

Dechant, K. L., and Clissold, S. P. Paroxetine: A review of its pharmacodynamic and pharmacokinetic properties, and therapeutic potential in depressive illness. *Drugs,* 1991, *41,* 225–253.

Degreef, G., Ashtari, M., Bogerts, B., Bilder, R. M., Jody, D. N., Alvir, J. M. J., and Lieberman, J. A. Volumes of ventricular system subdivisions measured from magnetic resonance images in first-episode schizophrenic patients. *Archives of General Psychiatry,* 1992, *49,* 531–537.

Dejerine, J. Contribution à l'étude anatomo-pathologique et clinique des différentes variétés de cécité verbale. *Comptes Rendus des Séances de la Société de Biologie et de Ses Filiales,* 1892, *4,* 61–90.

De Jonge, F. H., Louwerse, A. L., Ooms, M. P., Evers, P., Endert, E., and van de Poll, N. E. Lesions of the SDN-POA inhibit sexual behavior of male Wistar rats. *Brain Research Bulletin,* 1989, *23,* 483–492.

De Jonge, F. H., Oldenburger, W. P., Louwerse, A. L., and van de Poll, N. E. Changes in male copulatory behavior after sexual exciting stimuli: Effects of medial amygdala lesions. *Physiology and Behavior,* 1992, *52,* 327–332.

Delay, J., and Deniker, P. Le traitement des psychoses par une methode neurolytique derivée d'hibernothérapie; le 4560 RP utilisée seul une cure prolongée et continuée. *Comptes Rendus Congrès des Médecins Aliénistes et Neurologistes de France et des Pays de Langue Française,* 1952a, *50,* 497–502.

Del Cerro, M. C. R., Izquierdo, M. A. P., Rosenblatt, J. S., Johnson, B. M., Pacheco, P., and Komisaruk, B. R. Brain 2-deoxyglucose levels related to maternal behavior-inducing stimuli in the rat. *Brain Research,* 1995, *696,* 213–220.

De Lecea, L., Criado, J. R., Prospero-Garcia, O., Gautvik, K. M., Schweitzer, P., Danielson, P. E., Dunlop, C. L. M., Siggins, G. R., Henriksen, S. J., and Sutcliffe, J. G. A cortical neuropeptide with neuronal depressant and sleep-modulating properties. *Nature,* 1996, *381,* 242–245.

Delgado, P. L., Charney, D. S., Price, L. H., Aghajanian, G. K., Landis, H., and Heninger, G. R. Serotonin function and the mechanism of antidepressant action: Reversal of antidepressant induced remission by rapid depletion of plasma tryptophan. *Archives of General Psychiatry,* 1990, *47,* 411–418.

DeLong, G. R. Autism, amnesia, hippocampus, and learning. *Neuroscience and Biobehavioral Reviews,* 1992, *16,* 63–70.

Dement, W. C. The effect of dream deprivation. *Science,* 1960, *131,* 1705–1707.

Denk, W., Holt, J. R., Shepherd, G. M. G., and Corey, D. P. Calcium imaging of single stereocilia in hair cells: Localization of transduction channels at both ends of tip links. *Neuron,* 1995, *15,* 1311–1321.

Deol, M. S., and Gluecksohn-Waelsch, S. The role of inner hair cells in hearing. *Nature,* 1979, *278,* 250–252.

De Renzi, E., Perani, D., Carlesimo, G. A., Silveri, M. C., and Fazio, F. Prosopagnosia can be associated with damage confined to the right hemisphere: An MRI and PET study and a review of the literature. *Neuropsychologia,* 1994, *32,* 893–902.

Dérousné, J., and Beauvois, M.-F. Phonological processing in reading: Data from alexia. *Journal of Neurology, Neurosurgery, and Psychiatry,* 1979, *42,* 1125–1132.

Desimone, R., Albright, T. D., Gross, C. G., and Bruce, D. Stimulus-selective properties of inferior temporal neurons in the macaque. *Journal of Neuroscience,* 1984, *8,* 2051–2062.

D'Esposito, M., Verfaellie, M., Alexander, M. P., and Katz, D. I. Amnesia following traumatic bilateral fornix transection. *Neurology,* 1995, *45,* 1546–1550.

Detera-Wadleigh, S. D., Yoon, S. W., Berrettini, W. H., Goldin, L. R., Turner, G., Yoshikawa, T., Rollins, D. Y., Muniec, D., Nurnberger, J. I., and Gershon, E. S. Adrenocorticotropin receptor/melanocortin receptor-2 maps within a reported susceptibility region for bipolar illness on chromosome 18. *American Journal of Medical Genetics,* 1995, *60,* 317–321.

Deutsch, J. A. The cholinergic synapse and the site of memory. In *The Physiological Basis of Memory,* edited by J. A. Deutsch. New York: Academic Press, 1983.

Deutsch, J. A., and Gonzalez, M. F. Gastric nutrient content signals satiety. *Behavioral and Neural Biology,* 1980, *30,* 113–116.

Deutsch, J. A., and Hardy, W. T. Cholecystokinin produces bait shyness in rats. *Nature,* 1977, *266,* 196.

De Valois, R. L., Albrecht, D. G., and Thorell, L. Cortical cells: Bar detectors or spatial frequency filters? In *Frontiers in Visual Science,* edited by S. J. Cool and E. L. Smith. Berlin: Springer-Verlag, 1978.

De Valois, R. L., and De Valois, K. K. *Spatial Vision.* New York: Oxford University Press, 1988.

De Valois, R. L., Thorell, L. G., and Albrecht, D. G. Periodicity of striate-cortex-cell receptive fields. *Journal of the Optical Society of America*, 1985 2, 1115–1123.

Devane, W. A., Hanus, L., Breuer, A., Pertwee, R. G., Stevenson, L. A., Griffin, G., Gibson, D., Mandelbaum, A., Etinger, A., and Mechoulam, R. Isolation and structure of a brain constituent that binds to the cannabinoid receptor. *Science*, 1992, *258*, 1946–1949.

Devine, D. P., Leone, P., Pocock, D., and Wise, R. A. Differential involvement of ventral tegmental mu, delta, and kappa opioid receptors in modulation of basal mesolimbic dopamine release: *In vivo* microdialysis studies. *Journal of Pharmacology and Experimental Therapeutics*, 1993, *266*, 1236–1246.

Devine, D. P., and Wise, R. A. Self-administration of morphine, DAMGO, and DPDPE into the ventral tegmental area of rats. *Journal of Neuroscience*, 1994, *14*, 1978–1984.

Devinsky, O., Perrine, K., Llinas, R., Luciano, D. J., and Dogali, M. Anterior temporal language areas in patients with early onset of temporal lobe epilepsy. *Annals of Neurology*, 1993, *34*, 727–732.

DeVries, G. J. Sex differences in neurotransmitter systems. *Journal of Neuroendocrinology*, 1990, *2*, 1–13.

Diana, M., Pistis, M., Carboni, S., Gessa, G. L., and Rossetti, Z. L. Profound decrement of mesolimbic dopaminergic neuronal activity during ethanol withdrawal syndrome in rats: Electrophysiological and biochemical evidence. *Proceedings of the National Academy of Sciences, USA*, 1993, *90*, 7966–7969.

Di Chiara, G. The role of dopamine in drug abuse viewed from the perspective of its role in motivation. *Drug and Alcohol Dependency*, 1995, *38*, 95–137.

Di Ciano, P., Coury, A., Depoortere, R. Y., Egilmez, Y., Lane, J. D., Emmett-Oglesby, M. W., Lepiane, F. G., Phillips, A. G., and Blaha, C. D. Comparison of changes in extracellular dopamine concentrations in the nucleus accumbens during intravenous self-administration of cocaine or d-amphetamine. *Behavioural Pharmacology*, 1995, *6*, 311–322.

Digiovanni, M., Dalessandro, G., Baldini, S., Cantalupi, D., and Bottacchi, E. Clinical and neuroradiological findings in a case of pure word deafness. *Italian Journal of Neurological Sciences*, 1992, *13*, 507–510.

Dijk, D. J., Boulos, Z., Eastman, C. I., Lewy, A. J., Campbell, S. S., and Terman, M. Light treatment for sleep disorders: Consensus report. 2: Basic properties of circadian physiology and sleep regulation. *Journal of Biological Rhythms*, 1995, *10*, 113–125.

di Tomaso, E., Beltramo, M., and Piomelli, D. Brain cannabinoids in chocolate. *Nature*, 1996, *382*, 677–678.

Divac, I., Rosvold, H. E., and Szcwarcbart, M. K. Behavioral effects of selective ablation of the caudate nucleus. *Journal of Comparative and Physiological Psychology*, 1967, *63*, 184–190.

Dixon, A. K. The effect of olfactory stimuli upon the social behaviour of laboratory mice (*Mus musculus L*). Doctoral dissertation, Birmingham University, Birmingham, England, 1973.

Dixon, A. K., and Mackintosh, J. H. Effects of female urine upon the social behaviour of adult male mice. *Animal Behaviour*, 1971, *19*, 138–140.

Doherty, P. C., Baum, M. J., and Todd, R. B. Effects of chronic hyperprolactinemia on sexual arousal and erectile function in male rats. *Neuroendocrinology*, 1986, *42*, 368–375.

Dolan, R. P., and Schiller, P. H. Evidence for only depolarizing rod bipolar cells in the primate retina. *Visual Neuroscience*, 1989, *2*, 421–424.

Donny, E. C., Caggiula, A. R., Knopf, S., and Brown, C. Nicotine self-administration in rats. *Psychopharmacology*, 1995, *122*, 390–394.

Doty, R. L., Ford, M., Preti, G., and Huggins, G. R. Changes in the intensity and pleasantness of human vaginal odors during the menstrual cycle. *Science*, 1975, *190*, 1316.

Drevets, W. C., Videen, T. O., Price, J. L., Preskorn, S. H., Carmichael, S. T., and Raichle, M. E. A functional anatomical study of unipolar depression. *Journal of Neuroscience*, 1992, *12*, 3628–3641.

Dronkers, N. F. A new brain region for coordinating speech articulation. *Nature*, 1996, *384*, 159–161.

Drugan, R. C., Basile, A. S., Ha, J.-H., and Ferland, R. J. The protective effects of stress control may be mediated by increased brain levels of benzodiazepine receptor agonists. *Brain Research*, 1994, *661*, 127–136.

Dryden, S., Wang, Q., Frankish, H. M., Pickavance, L., and Williams, G. The serotonin (5-HT) antagonist methysergide increases neuropeptide-Y (NPY) synthesis and secretion in the hypothalamus of the rat. *Brain Research*, 1995, *699*, 12–18.

Duchenne, G.-B. *The Mechanism of Human Facial Expression* (translated by R. A. Cuthbertson). Cambridge, England: Cambridge University Press, 1990. (Original work published 1862.)

Dudek, S. M., and Bear, M. F. Homosynaptic long-term depression in area CA1 of hippocampus and effects of N-methyl-D-aspartate receptor blockade. *Proceedings of the National Academy of Sciences, USA*, 1992, *89*, 4363–4367.

Dujardin, K., Guerrien, A., and Leconte, P. Sleep, brain activation and cognition. *Physiology and Behavior*, 1990, *47*, 1271–1278.

Dunnett, S. B., Lane, D. M., and Winn, P. Ibotenic acid lesions of the lateral hypothalamus: Comparison with 6-hydroxy-dopamine-induced sensorimotor deficits. *Neuroscience*, 1985, *14*, 509–518.

Durie, D. J. Sleep in animals. In *Psychopharmacology of Sleep*, edited by D. Wheatley. New York: Raven Press, 1981.

Duvauchelle, C. L., and Ettenberg, A. Haloperidol attenuates conditioned place preferences produced by electrical stimulation of the medial prefrontal cortex. *Pharmacology, Biochemistry, and Behavior*, 1991, *38*, 645–650.

Dykes, R. W. Parallel processing of somatosensory information: A theory. *Brain Research Reviews*, 1983, *6*, 47–115.

East, S. J., and Garthwaite, J. NMDA receptor activation in rat hippocampus induces cyclic GMP formation through the L-arginine-nitric oxide pathway. *Neuroscience Letters,* 1991, *123,* 17–19.

Eastman, C. I., Boulos, Z., Terman, M., Campbell, S. S., Dijk, D. J., and Lewy, A. J. Light treatment for sleep disorders: Consensus report. 6: Shift work. *Journal of Biological Rhythms,* 1995, *10,* 157–164.

Eddy, N. B., Halbach, H., Isbell, H., and Seevers, M. H. Drug dependence: Its significance and characteristics. *Bulletin of the World Health Organization,* 1965, *32,* 721–733.

Edeline, J.-M., and Weinberger, N. M. Subcortical adaptive filtering in the auditory system: Associative receptive field plasticity in the dorsal medial geniculate body. *Behavioral Neuroscience,* 1991a, *105,* 154–175.

Edeline, J.-M., and Weinberger, N. M. Thalamic short-term plasticity in the auditory system: Associative retuning of receptive fields in the ventral medial geniculate body. *Behavioral Neuroscience,* 1991b, *105,* 618–639.

Edeline, J.-M., and Weinberger, N. M. Associative retuning in the thalamic source of input to the amygdala and auditory cortex: Receptive field plasticity in the medial division of the medial geniculate body. *Behavioral Neuroscience,* 1992, *106,* 81–105.

Eden, G. F., VanMeter, J. W., Rumsey, J. M., Maisog, J. M., Woods, R. P., and Zeffiro, T. A. Abnormal processing of visual motion in dyslexia revealed by functional brain imaging. *Nature,* 1996, *382,* 66–69.

Edwards, D. P., Purpura, K. P., and Kaplan, E. Contrast sensitivity and spatial-frequency response of primate cortical neurons in and around the cytochrome oxidase blobs. *Vision Research,* 1995, *35,* 1501–1523.

Egawa, M., Yoshimatsu, H., and Bray, G. A. Neuropeptide Y (NPY) suppresses sympathetic activity to interscapular brown adipose tissue in rats. *American Journal of Physiology,* 1991, *260,* R328–R334.

Egeland, J. A., Gerhard, D. S., Pauls, D. L., Sussex, J. N., Kidd, K. K., Allen, C. R., Hostetter, A. M., and Housman, D. E. Bipolar affective disorders linked to DNA markers on chromosome 11. *Nature,* 1987, *325,* 783–787.

Ehrhardt, A. A., and Meyer-Bahlburg, H. F. L. Effects of prenatal sex hormones on gender-related behavior. *Science,* 1981, *211,* 1312–1318.

Ehrlich, K. J., and Fitts, D. A. Atrial natriuretic peptide in the subfornical organ reduces drinking induced by angiotensin or in response to water deprivation. *Behavioral Neuroscience,* 1990, *104,* 365–372.

Eichenbaum, H., Otto, T., and Cohen, N. J. The hippocampus: What does it do? *Behavioral and Neural Biology,* 1992, *57,* 2–36.

Eichenbaum, H., Steward, C., and Morris, R. G. M. Hippocampal representation in spatial learning. *Journal of Neuroscience,* 1990, *10,* 331–339.

Eilam, R., Malach, R., Bergmann, F., and Segal, M. Hypertension induced by hypothalamic transplantation from genetically hypertensive to normotensive rats. *Journal of Neuroscience,* 1991, *11,* 401–411.

Ekman, P. *The Face of Man: Expressions of Universal Emotions in a New Guinea Village.* New York: Garland STPM Press, 1980.

Ekman, P. Facial expressions of emotion: An old controversy and new findings. *Philosophical Transactions of the Royal Society of London [B],* 1992, *335,* 63–69.

Ekman, P., and Davidson, R. J. Voluntary smiling changes regional brain activity. *Psychological Science,* 1993, *4,* 342–345.

Ekman, P., and Friesen, W. V. Constants across cultures in the face and emotion. *Journal of Personality and Social Psychology,* 1971, *17,* 124–129.

Ekman, P., and Friesen, W. V. *Unmasking the Face.* Englewood Cliffs, N.J.: Prentice-Hall, 1975.

Ekman, P., Friesen, W. V., and Ellsworth, P. *Emotion in the Human Face: Guidelines for Research and a Review of Findings.* New York: Pergamon Press, 1972.

Ekman, P., Levenson, R. W., and Friesen, W. V. Autonomic nervous system activity distinguished between emotions. *Science,* 1983, *221,* 1208–1210.

Elias, M. Serum cortisol, testosterone and testosterone binding globulin responses to competitive fighting in human males. *Aggressive Behavior,* 1981, *7,* 215–224.

Elkis, H., Friedman, L., Buckley, P. F., Lee, H. S., Lys, C., Kaufman, B., and Meltzer, H. Y. Increased prefrontal sulcal prominence in relatively young patients with unipolar major depression. *Psychiatry Research: Neuroimaging,* 1996, *67,* 123–134.

El Mansari, M., Sakai, K., and Jouvet, M. Unitary characteristics of presumptive cholinergic tegmental neurons during the sleep-waking cycle in freely moving cats. *Experimental Brain Research,* 1989, *76,* 519–529.

Endoh, M., Maiese, K., and Wagner, J. A. Expression of the neural form of nitric oxide synthase by CA1 hippocampal neurons and other central nervous system neurons. *Neuroscience,* 1994, *63,* 679–689.

Engber, T. M., Boldry, R. C., Kuo, S., and Chase, T. N. Dopaminergic modulation of striatal neuropeptides: Differential effects of D_1 and D_2 receptor stimulation on somatostatin, neuropeptide Y, neurotensin, dynorphin and enkephalin. *Brain Research,* 1992, *581,* 261–268.

Epstein, A. N. Epilogue: Retrospect and prognosis. In *The Neuropsychology of Thirst: New Findings and Advances in Concepts,* edited by A. N. Epstein, H. R. Kissileff, and E. Stellar. New York: John Wiley & Sons, 1973.

Erickson, J. C., Hollopeter, G., and Palmiter, R. D. Attenuation of the obesity syndrome of ob/ob mice by the loss of neuropeptide Y. *Science,* 1996, *274,* 1704–1707.

Ernulf, K. E., Innala, S. M., and Whitam, F. L. Biological explanation, psychological explanation, and tolerance of homosexuals: A cross-national analysis of beliefs and attitudes. *Psychological Reports,* 1989, *248,* 183–188.

Eslinger, P. J., and Damasio, A. R. Severe disturbance of higher cognition after bilateral frontal lobe ablation: Patient EVR. *Neurology,* 1985, *35,* 1731–1741.

Evans, E. F. Auditory processing of complex sounds: An overview. *Philosophical Transactions of the Royal Society of London [B],* 1992, *336,* 295–306.

Evans, J. J., Heggs, A. J., Antoun, N., and Hodges, J. R. Progressive prosopagnosia associated with selective right temporal lobe atrophy: A new syndrome? *Brain,* 1995, *118,* 1–13.

Evarts, E. V. Sensorimotor cortex activity associated with movements triggered by visual as compared to somesthetic inputs. In *The Neurosciences: Third Study Program,* edited by F. O. Schmitt and F. G. Worden. Cambridge, Mass.: MIT Press, 1974.

Everitt, B. J., Cador, M., and Robbins, T. W. Interactions between the amygdala and ventral striatum in stimulus-reward associations: Studies using a second-order schedule of sexual reinforcement. *Neuroscience,* 1989, *30,* 63–75.

Everson, C. A. Functional consequences of sustained sleep deprivation in the rat. *Behavioural Brain Research,* 1995, *69,* 43–54.

Everson, C. A., and Wehr, T. A. Nutritional and metabolic adaptations to prolonged sleep deprivation in the rat. *American Journal of Physiology,* 1993, *264,* R376–R387.

Fallon, J. H. Topographic organization of ascending dopaminergic projections. *Annals of the New York Academy of Sciences,* 1988, *537,* 1–9.

Falls, W. A., Miserendino, M. J. D., and Davis, M. Extinction of fear-potentiated startle: Blockade by infusion of an NMDA antagonist into the amygdala. *Journal of Neuroscience,* 1992, *12,* 854–863.

Fan, W., Boston, B. A., Kesterson, R. A., Hruby, V. J., and Cone, R. D. Role of melanocortinergic neurons in feeding and the agouti obesity syndrome. *Nature,* 1997, *385,* 165–168.

Fanselow, M. S., and Kim, J. J. Acquisition of contextual Pavlovian fear conditioning is blocked by application of an NMDA receptor antagonist, D,L-2-amino-5-phosphonovaleric acid to the basolateral amygdala. *Behavioral Neuroscience,* 1994, *108,* 210–212.

Farde, L., Wiesel, F.-A., Stone-Elander, S., Halldin, C., Nördstrom, A.-L., Hall, H., and Sedvall, G. D_2 dopamine receptors in neuroleptic-naive schizophrenic patients: A positron emission tomography study with [^{11}C]raclopride. *Archives of General Psychiatry,* 1990, *47,* 213–219.

Fava, M., Copeland, P. M., Schweiger, U., and Herzog, M. D. Neurochemical abnormalities of anorexia nervosa and bulimia nervosa. *American Journal of Psychiatry,* 1989, *146,* 963–971.

Feder, H. H. Estrous cyclicity in mammals. In *Neuroendocrinology of Reproduction,* edited by N. T. Adler. New York: Plenum Press, 1981.

Feigenbaum, S. L., Masi, A. T., and Kaplan, S. B. Prognosis in rheumatoid arthritis: A longitudinal study of newly diagnosed younger adult patients. *American Journal of Medicine,* 1979, *66,* 377–384.

Feigin, M. B., Sclafani, A., and Sunday, S. R. Species differences in polysaccharide and sugar taste preferences. *Neuroscience and Biobehavioral Reviews,* 1987, *11,* 231–240.

Feldman, R. S., Meyer, J. S., and Quenzer, L. F. *Principles of Neuropsychopharmacology.* Sunderland, Mass.: Sinauer Associates, 1997.

Ferguson, N. B. L., and Keesey, R. E. Effect of a quinine-adulterated diet upon body weight maintenance in male rats with ventromedial hypothalamic lesions. *Journal of Comparative and Physiological Psychology,* 1975, *89,* 478–488.

Fernandez-Guasti, A., Larsson, K., and Beyer, C. Potentiative action of α- and ß-adrenergic receptor stimulation in inducing lordosis behavior. *Pharmacology, Biochemistry, and Behavior,* 1985, *22,* 613–617.

Fernell, E., Gillberg, C., and Von Wendt, L. Autistic symptoms in children with infantile hydrocephalus. *Acta Paediatrica Scandinavica,* 1991, *80,* 451–457.

Fibiger, H. C. The dopamine hypothesis of schizophrenia and mood disorders: Contradictions and speculations. In *The Mesolimbic Dopamine System: From Motivation to Action,* edited by P. Willner and J. Scheel-Krüger. Chichester, England: John Wiley & Sons, 1991.

Field, T., Woodson, R., Greenberg, R., and Cohen, D. Discrimination and imitation of facial expressions in neonates. *Science,* 1982, *218,* 179–181.

Fieve, R. R. The clinical effects of lithium treatment. *Trends in Neurosciences,* 1979, *2,* 66–68.

Fiez, J. A. Cerebellar contributions to cognition. *Neuron,* 1996, *16,* 13–15.

Filipek, P. A. Neurobiologic correlates of developmental dyslexia: How do dyslexics' brains differ from those of normal readers? *Journal of Child Neurology,* 1995, *10,* S62–S69.

Firestein, S., Zufall, F., and Shepherd, G. M. Single odor-sensitive channels in olfactory receptor neurons are also gated by cyclic nucleotides. *Journal of Neuroscience,* 1991, *11,* 3565–3572.

Fisch, G. S. Is autism associated with the fragile X syndrome? *American Journal of Medical Genetics,* 1992, *43,* 47–55.

Fisher, C., Byrne, J., Edwards, A., and Kahn, E. A psychophysiological study of nightmares. *Journal of the American Psychoanalytic Association,* 1970, *18,* 747–782.

Fisher, C., Gross, J., and Zuch, J. Cycle of penile erection synchronous with dreaming (REM) sleep: Preliminary report. *Archives of General Psychiatry,* 1965, *12,* 29–45.

Fiske, A. P., and Haslam, N. Is obsessive-compulsive disorder a pathology of the human disposition to perform socially meaningful rituals? Evidence of similar content. *Journal of Nervous and Mental Disease,* 1997, *185,* 211–222.

Fitts, D. A., and Masson, D. B. Preoptic angiotensin and salt appetite. *Behavioral Neuroscience,* 1990, *104,* 643–650.

Fitts, D. A., Tjepkes, D. S., and Bright, R. O. Salt appetite and lesions of the ventral part of the ventral median preoptic nucleus. *Behavioral Neuroscience*, 1990, *104*, 818–827.

Fitzpatrick, D., Itoh, K., and Diamond, I. T. The laminar organization of the lateral geniculate body and the striate cortex in the squirrel monkey *(Saimiri sciureus)*. *Journal of Neuroscience*, 1983, *3*, 673–702.

Fitzsimons, J. T. Drinking by rats depleted of body fluid without increase in osmotic pressure. *Journal of Physiology (London)*, 1961, *159*, 297–309.

Fitzsimons, J. T. Thirst. *Physiological Reviews*, 1972, *52*, 468–561.

Fitzsimons, J. T., and Le Magnen, J. Eating as a regulatory control of drinking in the rat. *Journal of Comparative and Physiological Psychology*, 1969, *3*, 273–283.

Fitzsimons, J. T., and Moore-Gillon, M. J. Drinking and antidiuresis in response to reductions in venous return in the dog: Neural and endocrine mechanisms. *Journal of Physiology (London)*, 1980, *308*, 403–416.

Flaum, M., and Andreasen, N. C. Diagnostic criteria for schizophrenia and related disorders: Options for DNS-IV. *Schizophrenia Bulletin*, 1990, *17*, 27–49.

Fleming, A., and Rosenblatt, J. S. Olfactory regulation of maternal behavior in rats. II. Effects of peripherally induced anosmia and lesions of the lateral olfactory tract in pup-induced virgins. *Journal of Comparative and Physiological Psychology*, 1974, *86*, 233–246.

Fleming, A., Vaccarino, F., and Luebke, C. Amygdaloid inhibition of maternal behavior in the nulliparous female rat. *Physiology and Behavior*, 1980, *25*, 731–745.

Fleming, A., Vaccarino, F., Tambosso, L., and Chee, P. Vomeronasal and olfactory system modulation of maternal behavior in the rat. *Science*, 1979, *203*, 372–374.

Fleming, A. S., Cheung, U., Myhal, N., and Kessler, Z. Effects of maternal hormones on "timidity" and attraction to pup-related odors in female rats. *Physiology and Behavior*, 1989, *46*, 449–453.

Fleming, A. S., and Sarker, J. Experience-hormone interactions and maternal behavior in rats. *Physiology and Behavior*, 1990, *47*, 1165–1173.

Fletcher, J. M., Page, J. B., Francis, D. J., Copeland, K., Naus, M. J., Davis, C. M., Morris, R., Krauskopf, D., and Satz, P. Cognitive correlates of long-term cannabis use in Costa Rican men. *Archives of General Psychiatry*, 1996, *53*, 1051–1057.

Fletcher, P. J., Currie, P. J., Chambers, J. W., and Coscina, D. V. Radiofrequency lesions of the PVN fail to modify the effects of serotonergic drugs on food intake. *Brain Research*, 1993, *630*, 1–9.

Flock, A. Physiological properties of sensory hairs in the ear. In *Psychophysics and Physiology of Hearing*, edited by E. F. Evans and J. P. Wilson. London: Academic Press, 1977.

Flood, J. F., and Morley, J. E. Increased food intake by neuropeptide Y is due to an increased motivation to eat. *Peptides*, 1991, *12*, 1329–1332.

Floody, O. R. Hormones and aggression in female mammals. In *Hormones and Aggressive Behavior*, edited by B. B. Svare. New York: Plenum Press, 1983.

Folstein, S. E., and Piven, J. Etiology of autism: Genetic influences. *Pediatrics*, 1991, *87*, 767–773.

Folstein, S. E., and Rutter, M. L. Autism: Familiar aggregation and genetic implications. *Journal of Autism and Developmental Disorders*, 1988, *18*, 3–30.

Foltin, R. W., Fischman, M. W., Moran, T. H., Rolls, B. J., and Kelly, T. H. Caloric compensation for lunches varying in fat and carbohydrate content by humans in a residential laboratory. *American Journal of Clinical Nutrition*, 1990, *52*, 969–980.

Fort, P., Luppi, P.-H., Wenthold, R., and Jouvet, M. Neurones immunoréactifs à la glycine dans le bulbe rachidien du chat. *Comptes Rendus de l'Académie des Sciences (Paris)*, 1990, *311*, 205–212.

Foster, R. G., Provencio, I., Hudson, D., Fiske, S., De Grip, W., and Menaker, M. Circadian photoreception in the retinally degenerate mouse *(rd/rd)*. *Journal of Comparative Physiology*, 1991, *169*, 39–50.

Foster, R. S., Mulcahy, J. J., Callaghan, J. T., Crabtree, R., and Brashear, D. Role of serum prolactin determination in evaluation of impotent patient. *Urology*, 1990, *36*, 499–501.

Foundas, A. L., Leonard, C. M., Gilmore, R. L., Fennell, E. B., and Heilman, K. M. Pars triangularis asymmetry and language dominance. *Proceedings of the National Academy of Sciences, USA*, 1996, *93*, 719–722.

Frankland, P. W., Josselyn, S. A., Bradwejn, J., Vaccarino, F. J., and Yeomans, J. S. Activation of amygdala cholecystokinin$_B$ receptors potentiates the acoustic startle response in the rat. *Journal of Neuroscience*, 1997, *17*, 1838–1847.

Franzek, E., and Beckmann, H. Gene-environment interaction in schizophrenia: Season-of-birth effect reveals etiologically different subgroups. *Psychopathology*, 1996, *29*, 14–26.

Frey, U., Krug, M., Reymann, K. G., and Matthies, H. Anisomycin, an inhibitor of protein synthesis, blocks late phases of LTP phenomena in the hippocampal CA1 region in vitro. *Brain Research*, 1988, *452*, 57–65.

Friedman, M. I., and Bruno, J. P. Exchange of water during lactation. *Science*, 1976, *191*, 409–410.

Friedman, M. I., Tordoff, M. G., and Ramirez, I. Integrated metabolic control of food intake. *Brain Research Bulletin*, 1986, *17*, 855–859.

Friesen, W. V. Cultural differences in facial expression in a social situation: An experimental test of the concept of display rules. Doctoral dissertation, University of California, San Francisco, 1972.

Frith, U., Morton, J., and Leslie, A. M. The cognitive basis of a biological disorder: Autism. *Trends in Neuroscience*, 1991, *14*, 433–438.

Fulton, J. F. *Functional Localization in Relation to Frontal Lobotomy*. New York: Oxford University Press, 1949.

Fung, Y. K., Schmid, M. J., Anderson, T. M., and Lau, Y. S. Effects of nicotine withdrawal on central dopaminergic systems. *Pharmacology, Biochemistry and Behavior,* 1996, *53,* 635–640.

Fuster, J. M., and Jervey, J. P. Inferotemporal neurons distinguish and retain behaviorally relevant features of visual stimuli. *Science,* 1981, *212,* 952–955.

Gabrieli, J. D. E., Cohen, N. J., and Corkin, S. The impaired learning of semantic knowledge following bilateral medial temporal-lobe resection. *Brain and Cognition,* 1988, *7,* 157–177.

Gabrieli, J. D. E., Milberg, W., Keane, M. M., and Corkin, S. Intact priming of patterns despite impaired memory. *Neuropsychologia,* 1990, *28,* 417–427.

Gaffan, D., and Eacott, M. J. Visual learning for an auditory secondary reinforcer by macaques is intact after uncinate fascicle section: Indirect evidence for the involvement of the corpus striatum. *European Journal of Neuroscience,* 1995, *7,* 1866–1871.

Gaffan, D., Gaffan, E. A., and Harrison, S. Disconnection of the amygdala from visual association cortex impairs visual reward-association learning in monkeys. *Journal of Neuroscience,* 1988, *9,* 3144–3150.

Gaffan, D., and Harrison, S. Amygdalectomy and disconnection in visual learning for auditory secondary reinforcement by monkeys. *Journal of Neuroscience,* 1987, *7,* 2285–2292.

Gage, F. H., Björklund, A., Stenevi, U., Dunnett, S. B., and Kelly, P. A. T. Intrahippocampal septal grafts ameliorate learning impairments in aged rats. *Science,* 1984, *225,* 533–536.

Galaburda, A. M. The pathogenesis of childhood dyslexia. In *Language, Communication, and the Brain,* edited by F. Plum. New York: Raven Press, 1988.

Galaburda, A. M., and Livingstone, M. Evidence for a magnocellular defect in developmental dyslexia. *Annals of the New York Academy of Science,* 1993, *682,* 70–82.

Galaburda, A. M., Rosen, G. D., and Sherman, G. F. Cerebrocortical asymmetry. In *Cerebral Cortex,* edited by A. Peters and E. G. Jones. New York: Plenum Press, 1991.

Galaburda, A. M., Sherman, G. F., Rosen, G. D., Aboitiz, F., and Geschwind, N. Developmental dyslexia: Four consecutive patients with cortical anomalies. *Annals of Neurology,* 1985, *18,* 222–233.

Gallassi, R., Morreale, A., Montagna, P., Cortelli, P., Avoni, P., Castellani, R., Gambetti, P., and Lugaresi, E. Fatal familial insomnia: Behavioral and cognitive features. *Neurology,* 1996, *46,* 935–939.

Gandelman, R., and Simon, N. G. Spontaneous pup-killing by mice in response to large litters. *Developmental Psychobiology,* 1978, *11,* 235–241.

Gandelman, R., and Simon, N. G. Postpartum fighting in the rat: Nipple development and the presence of young. *Behavioral and Neural Biology,* 1980, *28,* 350–360.

Garcia, J., and Koelling, R. A. Relation of cue to consequence in avoidance learning. *Psychonomic Science,* 1966, *4,* 123–124.

Garcia-Velasco, J., and Mondragon, M. The incidence of the vomeronasal organ in 1000 human subjects and its possible clinical significance. *Journal of Steroid Biochemistry and Molecular Biololgy,* 1991, *39,* 561–563.

Gardner, H., Brownell, H. H., Wapner, W., and Michelow, D. Missing the point: The role of the right hemisphere in the processing of complex linguistic materials. In *Cognitive Processing in the Right Hemisphere,* edited by E. Pericman. New York: Academic Press, 1983.

Gariano, R. F., and Groves, P. M. Burst firing induced in midbrain dopamine neurons by stimulation of the medial prefrontal and anterior cingulate cortices. *Brain Research,* 1988, *462,* 194–198.

Gasbarri, A., Sulli, A., Innocenzi, R., Pacitti, C., and Brioni, J. D. Spatial memory impairment induced by lesion of the mesohippocampal dopaminergic system in the rat. *Neuroscience,* 1996, *74,* 1037–1044.

Gatchel, R. J., Baum, A., and Krantz, D. S. *An Introduction to Health Psychology,* 2nd ed. New York: Newbery Award Records, 1989.

Gaw, A. C., Chang, L. W., and Shaw, L.-C. Efficacy of acupuncture on osteoarthritic pain. *New England Journal of Medicine,* 1975, *293,* 375–378.

Gazzaniga, M. S. *The Bisected Brain.* New York: Appleton-Century-Crofts, 1970.

Gazzaniga, M. S., and LeDoux, J. E. *The Integrated Mind.* New York: Plenum Press, 1978.

Geary, N. Cocaine: Animal research studies. In *Cocaine Abuse: New Directions in Treatment and Research,* edited by H. I. Spitz and J. S. Rosecan. New York: Brunner-Mazel, 1987.

Geinisman, Y., DeToledo-Morrell, L., and Morrell, F. Induction of long-term potentiation is associated with an increase in the number of axospinous synapses with segmented postsynaptic densities. *Brain Research,* 1991, *566,* 77–88.

Geinisman, Y., DeToledo-Morrell, L., Morrell, F., Persina, I. S., and Beatty, M. A. Synapse restructuring associated with the maintenance phase of hippocampal long-term potentiation. *Journal of Comparative Neurology,* 1996, *368,* 413–423.

Gelernter, J., Goldman, D., and Risch, N. The A1 allele at the D_2 dopamine receptor gene and alcoholism: A reappraisal. *Journal of the American Medical Association,* 1993, *269,* 1673–1677.

Gentil, C. G., Mogenson, G., and Stevenson, J. A. F. Electrical stimulation of septum, hypothalamus and amygdala and saline preference. *American Journal of Physiology,* 1971, *220,* 1172–1177.

Gentilucci, M., and Rizzolatti, G. In *Vision and Action: The Control of Grasping,* edited by M. A. Goodale. Norwood, N. J.: Ablex, 1990.

George, M. S., Parekh, P. I., Rosinsky, N., Ketter, T. A., Kimbrell, T. A., Heilman, K. M., Herscovitch, P., and Post, R. M. Understanding emotional prosody activates right hemisphere regions. *Archives of Neurology,* 1996, *53,* 665–670.

Gerbino, L., Oleshansky, M., and Gershon, S. Clinical use and mode of action of lithium. In *Psychopharmacology: A Generation of Progress*, edited by M. A. Lipton, A. DiMascio, and K. F. Killam. New York: Raven Press, 1978.

Gerren, R., and Weinberger, N. M. Long term potentiation in the magnocellular medial geniculate nucleus of the anesthetized cat. *Brain Research*, 1983, *265*, 138–142.

Gerrits, M. A. F. M., and Vanree, J. M. Effects of nucleus accumbens dopamine depletion on motivational aspects involved in initiation of cocaine and heroin self-administration in rats. *Brain Research*, 1996, *713*, 114–124.

Gershon, E. S., Bunney, W. E., Leckman, J., Van Eerdewegh, M., and DeBauche, B. The inheritance of affective disorders: A review of data and hypotheses. *Behavior Genetics*, 1976, *6*, 227–261.

Geschwind, N., Quadfasel, F. A., and Segarra, J. M. Isolation of the speech area. *Neuropsychologia*, 1968, *6*, 327–340.

Geschwind, N. A., and Behan, P. O. Laterality, hormones, and immunity. In *Cerebral Dominance: The Biological Foundations*, edited by N. Geschwind and A. M. Galaburda. Cambridge, Mass.: Harvard University Press, 1984.

Gessa, G. L., Muntoni, F., Collu, M., Vargiu, L., and Mereu, G. Low doses of ethanol activate dopaminergic neurons in the ventral tegmental area. *Brain Research*, 1985, *348*, 201–204.

Ghiraldi, L., and Svare, B. Unpublished observations cited in Svare, B. Recent advances in the study of female aggressive behavior in mice. In *House Mouse Aggression: A Model for Understanding the Evolution of Social Behavior*, edited by S. Parmigiani, D. Mainardi, and P. Brain. London: Gordon and Breach, 1989.

Gibbs, J., Young, R. C., and Smith, G. P. Cholecystokinin decreases food intake in rats. *Journal of Comparative and Physiological Psychology*, 1973, *84*, 488–495.

Gibbs, W. W. Gaining on fat. *Scientific American*, 1996, *275*, 88–94.

Giedd, J. N., Rapoport, J. L., Kruesi, M. J. P., Parker, C., Schapiro, M. B., Allen, A. J., Leonard, H. L., Kaysen, D., Dickstein, D. P., Marsh, W. L., Kozuch, P. L., Vaituzis, A. C., Hamburger, S. D., and Swedo, S. E. Sydenham's chorea: Magnetic resonance imaging of the basal ganglia. *Neurology*, 1995, *45*, 2199–2202.

Gilbert, D. G., and Gilbert, B. O. Personality, psychopathology, and nicotine response as mediators of the genetics of smoking. *Behavioral Genetics*, 1995, *25*, 133–148.

Giles, D. E., Biggs, M. M., Rush, A. J., and Roffwarg, H. P. Risk factors in families of unipolar depression. I. Psychiatric illness and reduced REM latency. *Journal of Affective Disorders*, 1988, *14*, 51–59.

Giles, D. E., Roffwarg, H. P., and Rush, A. J. REM latency concordance in depressed family members. *Biological Psychiatry*, 1987, *22*, 910–924.

Gillespie, P. G. Molecular machinery of auditory and vestibular transduction. *Current Opinion in Neurobiology*, 1995, *5*, 449–455.

Gillette, M. U., and McArthur, A. J. Circadian actions of melatonin at the suprachiasmatic nucleus. *Behavioural Brain Research*, 1995, *73*, 135–139.

Giordano, A. L., Siegel, H. I., and Rosenblatt, J. S. Nuclear estrogen receptor binding in the preoptic area and hypothalamus of pregnancy-terminated rats: Correlation with the onset of maternal behavior. *Neuroendocrinology*, 1989, *50*, 248–258.

Giros, B., Jaber, M., Jones, S. R., Wightman, R. M., and Caron, M. G. Hyperlocomotion and indifference to cocaine and amphetamine in mice lacking the dopamine transporter. *Nature*, 1996, *379*, 606–612.

Givens, B. Low doses of ethanol impair spatial working memory and reduce hippocampal theta activity. *Alcohol: Clinical and Experimental Research*, 1995, *19*, 763–767.

Givens, B., and McMahon, K. Ethanol suppresses the induction of long-term potentiation in vivo. *Brain Research*, 1995, *688*, 27–33.

Givens, B. S., and Olton, D. S. Cholinergic and GABAergic modulation of medial septal area: Effect on working memory. *Behavioral Neuroscience*, 1990, *104*, 849–855.

Giza, B. K., Scott, T. R., and Vanderweele, D. A. Administration of satiety factors and gustatory responsiveness in the nucleus tractus solitarius of the rat. *Brain Research Bulletin*, 1992, *28*, 637–639.

Glaser, R., Rice, J., Sheridan, J., Post, A., Fertel, R., Stout, J., Speicher, C. E., Kotur, M., and Kiecolt-Glaser, J. K. Stress-related immune suppression: Health implications. *Brain, Behavior, and Immunity*, 1987, *1*, 7–20.

Glaum, S. R., Hara, M., Bindokas, V. P., Lee, C. C., Polonsky, K. S., Bell, G. I., and Miller, R. J. Leptin, the obese gene product, rapidly modulates synaptic transmission in the hypothalamus. *Molecular Pharmacology*, 1996, *50*, 230–235.

Gloor, P., Olivier, A., Quesney, L. F., Andermann, F., and Horowitz, S. The role of the limbic system in experiential phenomena of temporal lobe epilepsy. *Annals of Neurology*, 1982, *12*, 129–144.

Goddard, A. W., Sholomskas, D. E., Walton, K. E., Augeri, F. M., Charney, D. S., Heninger, G. R., Goodman, W. K., and Price, L. H. Effects of tryptophan depletion in panic disorder. *Biological Psychiatry*, 1994, *36*, 775–777.

Goeders, N. E., and Guerin, G. F. Non-contingent electric footshock facilitates the acquisition of intravenous cocaine self-administration in rats. *Psychopharmacology (Berlin)*, 1994, *114*, 63–70.

Goeders, N. E., Lane, J. D., and Smith, J. E. Self-administration of methionine enkephalin into the nucleus accumbens. *Pharmacology, Biochemistry, and Behavior*, 1984, *20*, 451–455.

Goeders, N. E., and Smith, J. E. Cortical dopaminergic involvement in cocaine reinforcement. *Science*, 1983, *221*, 773–775.

Golden, P. L., MacCagnan, T. J., and Pardridge, W. M. Human blood-brain barrier leptin receptor: Binding and endocytosis in isolated human brain microvessels. *Journal of Clinical Investigation*, 1997, *99*, 14–18.

Golgi, C. *Opera Omnia*, Vols. I and II. Milan: Hoepli, 1903.

Gongwer, M. A., Murphy, J. M., McBride, W. J., Lumeng, L., and Li, R.-K. Regional brain contents of serotonin, dopamine and their metabolites in the selectively bred high- and low-alcohol drinking lines of rats. *Alcohol*, 1989, *6*, 317–320.

Goodale, M. A., Meenan, J. P., Bülthoff, H. H., Nicolle, D. A., Murphy, K. H., and Racicot, C. I. Separate neural pathways for the visual analysis of object shape in perception and prehension. *Current Biology*, 1994, *4*, 604–610.

Goodale, M. A., and Milner, A. D. Separate visual pathways for perception and action. *Trends in Neuroscience*, 1992, *15*, 20–25.

Goodglass, H. Agrammatism. In *Studies of Neurolinguistics*, edited by H. Whitaker and H. A. Whitaker. New York: Academic Press, 1976.

Goodglass, H., and Kaplan, E. *Assessment of Aphasia and Related Disorders*. Philadelphia: Lea & Febiger, 1972.

Goodwin, D. W. Alcoholism and heredity: A review and hypothesis. *Archives of General Psychiatry*, 1979, *36*, 57–61.

Gordon, H. W., and Sperry, R. Lateralization of olfactory perception in the surgically separated hemispheres in man. *Neuropsychologia*, 1969, *7*, 111–120.

Gorski, R. A., Gordon, J. H., Shryne, J. E., and Southam, A. M. Evidence for a morphological sex difference within the medial preoptic area of the rat brain. *Brain Research*, 1978, *148*, 333–346.

Gottesman, I. I., and Bertelsen, A. Confirming unexpressed genotypes for schizophrenia. *Archives of General Psychiatry*, 1989, *46*, 867–872.

Gottesman, I. I., and Shields, J. *Schizophrenia: The Epigenetic Puzzle*. New York: Cambridge University Press, 1982.

Gouras, P. Identification of cone mechanisms in monkey ganglion cells. *Journal of Physiology (London)*, 1968, *199*, 533–538.

Goy, R. W., Bercovitch, F. B., and McBrair, M. C. Behavioral masculinization is independent of genital masculinization in prenatally androgenized female rhesus macaques. *Hormones and Behavior*, 1988, *22*, 552–571.

Graber, G. C., and Kristal, M. B. Uterine distention facilitates the onset of maternal behavior in pseudopregnant but not in cycling rats. *Physiology and Behavior*, 1977, *19*, 133–137.

Grace, A. A. Phasic versus tonic dopamine release and the modulation of dopamine system responsivity: A hypothesis for the etiology of schizophrenia. *Neuroscience*, 1991, *41*, 1–24.

Graf, P., Squire, L. R., and Mandler, G. The information that amnesic patients do not forget. *Journal of Experimental Psychology: Learning, Memory, and Cognition*, 1984, *10*, 164–178.

Grafton, S. T., Waters, C., Sutton, J., Lew, M. F., and Couldwell, W. Pallidotomy increases activity of motor association cortex in Parkinson's disease: A positron emission tomographic study. *Annals of Neurology*, 1995, *37*, 776–783.

Grant, S., London, E. D., Newlin, D. B., Villemagne, V. L., Liu, X., Contoreggi, C., Phillips, R. L., Kimes, A. S., and Margolin, A. Activation of memory circuits during cue-elicited cocaine craving. *Proceedings of the National Academy of Sciences, USA*, 1996, *93*, 12040–12045.

Grant, S. G. N., O'Dell, T. J., Karl, K. A., Stein, P. L., Soriano, P., and Kandel, E. R. Impaired long-term potentiation, spatial learning, and hippocampal development in *fyn* mutant mice. *Science*, 1992, *258*, 1903–1910.

Gray, C., Freeman, W. J., and Skinner, J. E. Chemical dependencies of learning in the rabbit olfactory bulb: Acquisition of the transient and spatial pattern change depends on norepinephrine. *Behavioral Neuroscience*, 1986, *100*, 585–596.

Graybiel, A. M. Basal ganglia: New therapeutic approaches to Parkinson's disease. *Current Biology*, 1996, *6*, 368–371.

Green, E. J., and Greenough, W. T. Altered synaptic transmission in dentate gyrus of rats reared in complex environments: Evidence from hippocampal slices maintained in vitro. *Journal of Neurophysiology*, 1986, *55*, 739–750.

Greenberg, D., Kava, R., Lewis, D. R., and Greenwood, M. R. C. Satiation following intraduodenal Intralipid preceded appearance of [^{14}C]-Intralipid in hepatic portal blood. *FASEB Journal*, 1991, *5*, A1451.

Greenberg, D., Smith, G. P., and Gibbs, J. Intraduodenal infusions of fats elicit satiety in the sham feeding rat. *American Journal of Physiology*, 1990, *259*, R110–R118.

Greenberg, R., and Pearlman, C. A. Cutting the REM nerve: An approach to the adaptive role of REM sleep. *Perspectives in Biology and Medicine*, 1974, *17*, 513–521.

Greenough, W. T., Juraska, J. M., and Volkmar, F. R. Maze training effects on dendritic branching in occipital cortex of adult rats. *Behavioral and Neural Biology*, 1979, *26*, 287–297.

Griffith, J. D., Cavanaugh, J., Held, N. N., and Oates, J. A. Dextroamphetamine: Evaluation of psychotomimetic properties in man. *Archives of General Psychiatry*, 1972, *26*, 97–100.

Grigorenko, E. L., Wood, F. B., Meyer, M. S., Hart, L. A., Speed, W. C., Shuster, A., and Pauls, D. L. Susceptibility loci for distinct components of developmental dyslexia on chromosomes 6 and 15. *American Journal of Human Genetics*, 1997, *60*, 27–39.

Grijalva, C. V., Levin, E. D., Morgan, M., Roland, B., and Martin, F. C. Contrasting effects of centromedial and basolateral amygdaloid lesions on stress-related responses in the rat. *Physiology and Behavior*, 1990, *48*, 495–500.

Grill, H. J., Friedman, M. I., Norgren, R., Scalera, G., and Seeley, R. Parabrachial nucleus lesions impair feeding response elicited by 2,5-anhydro-D-mannitol. *American Journal of Physiology*, 1995, *268*, R676–R682.

Grill, H. J., and Kaplan, J. M. Caudal brainstem participates in the distributed neural control of feeding. In *Handbook of Behavioral Neurobiology*. Vol. 10. *Neurobiology of Food and Fluid Intake*, edited by E. Stricker. New York: Plenum Press, 1990.

Gross, C. G. Visual functions of inferotemporal cortex. In *Handbook of Sensory Physiology*. Vol. 7. *Central Processing of Visual Information,* edited by R. Jung. Berlin: Springer-Verlag, 1973.

Grossman, S. P., and Grossman, L. Parametric study of the regulatory capabilities of rats with rostromedial zona incerta lesions: Responsiveness to hypertonic saline and polyethylene glycol. *Physiology and Behavior,* 1978, *21,* 431–440.

Guerin, G. F., Goeders, N. E., Dworkin, S. I., and Smith, J. E. Intracranial self-administration of dopamine into the nucleus accumbens. *Society for Neuroscience Abstracts,* 1984, *10,* 1072.

Guilleminault, C., Wilson, R. A., and Dement, W. C. A study on cataplexy. *Archives of Neurology,* 1974, *31,* 255–261.

Gulevich, G., Dement, W. C., and Johnson, L. Psychiatric and EEG observations on a case of prolonged (264 hours) wakefulness. *Archives of General Psychiatry,* 1966, *15,* 29–35.

Gura, T. Obesity sheds its secrets. *Science,* 1997, *275,* 751–753.

Gurd, J. M., and Marshall, J. C. Cognition: Righting reading. *Current Biology,* 1993, *3,* 593–595.

Gurevich, E. V., Bordelon, Y., Shapiro, R. M., Arnold, S. E., Gur, R. E., and Joyce, J. N. Mesolimbic dopamine D_3 receptors and use of antipsychotics in patients with schizophrenia: A postmortem study. *Archives of General Psychiatry,* 1997, *54,* 225–232.

Gurvits, T. V., Shenton, M. E., Hokama, H., Ohta, H., Lasko, N. B., Gilbertson, M. W., Orr, S. P., Kikinis, R., Jolesz, F. A., McCarley, R. W., and Pitman, R. K. Magnetic resonance imaging study of hippocampal volume in chronic, combat-related posttraumatic stress disorder. *Biological Psychiatry,* 1996, *40,* 1091–1099.

Haas, R. H. Thiamin and the brain. *Annual Review of Nutrition,* 1988, *8,* 483–515.

Haas, R. H., Townsend, J., Courchesne, E., Lincoln, A. J., Schreibman, L., and Yeung-Courchesne, R. Neurologic abnormalities in infantile autism. *Journal of Child Neurology,* 1996, *11,* 84–92.

Hajak, G., Clarenbach, P., Fischer, W., Haase, W., Bandelow, B., Adler, L., and Ruther, E. Effects of hypnotics on sleep quality and daytime well-being: Data from a comparative multicentre study in outpatients with insomnia. *European Psychiatry,* 1995, *10*(Suppl. 3), 173S–179S.

Hakansson, M. L., Hulting, A. L., and Meister, B. Expression of leptin receptor messenger RNA in the hypothalamic arcuate nucleus: Relationship with NPY neurons. *Neuroreport,* 1996, *7,* 3087–3092.

Halaas, J. L., Gajiwala, K. D., Maffei, M., Cohen, S. L., Chait, B. T., Rabinowitz, D., Lallone, R. L., Burley, S. K., and Friedman, J. M. Weight-reducing effects of the plasma protein encoded by the obese gene. *Science,* 1995, *269,* 543–546.

Haley, J. E., Wilcox, G. L., and Chapman, P. F. The role of nitric oxide in hippocampal long-term potentiation. *Neuron,* 1992, *8,* 211–216.

Halgren, E. Walter, R. D., Cherlow, D. G., and Crandall, P. E. Mental phenomena evoked by electrical stimulation of the human hippocampal formation and amygdala. *Brain,* 1978, *101,* 83–117.

Hall, W. G. A remote stomach clamp to evaluate oral and gastric controls of drinking in the rat. *Physiology and Behavior,* 1973, *11,* 897–901.

Hall, W. G., and Blass, E. M. Orogastric determinants of drinking in rats: Interaction between absorptive and peripheral controls. *Journal of Comparative and Physiological Psychology,* 1977, *91,* 365–373.

Hallmayer, J., Hebert, J. M., Spiker, D., Lotspeich, L., McMahon, W. M., Petersen, P. B., Nicholas, P., Pingree, C., Lin, A. A., Cavalli-Sforza, L. L., Risch, N., and Ciaranello, R. D. Autism and the X chromosome: Multipoint sib-pair analysis. *Archives of General Psychiatry,* 1996, *53,* 985–989.

Halmi, K. A. Anorexia nervosa: Recent investigations. *Annual Review of Medicine,* 1978, *29,* 137–148.

Halmi, K. A., Eckert, E., LaDu, T. J., and Cohen, J. Anorexia nervosa: Treatment efficacy of cyproheptadine and amitriptyline. *Archives of General Psychiatry,* 1986, *43,* 177–181.

Halpern, M. The organization and function of the vomeronasal system. *Annual Review of Neuroscience,* 1987, *10,* 325–362.

Han, Y. C., Shaikh, M. B., and Siegel, A. Medial amygdaloid suppression of predatory attack behavior in the cat. 1. Role of a substance P pathway from the medial amygdala to the medial hypothalamus. *Brain Research,* 1996a, *716,* 59–71.

Han, Y. C., Shaikh, M. B., and Siegel, A. Medial amygdaloid suppression of predatory attack behavior in the cat. 2. Role of a GABAergic pathway from the medial to the lateral hypothalamus. *Brain Research,* 1996b, *716,* 72–83.

Hansen, S., and Ross, S. B. Role of descending monoaminergic neurons in the control of sexual behavior: Effects of intrathecal infusion of 6-hydroxydopamine and 5,7-dihydroxytryptamine. *Brain Research,* 1983, *268,* 285–290.

Hansen, S., Stanfield, E. J., and Everitt, B. J. The role of ventral bundle noradrenergic neurones in sensory components of sexual behaviours and coitus-induced pseudopregnancy. *Nature,* 1980, *286,* 152–154.

Happé, F., and Frith, U. The neuropsychology of autism. *Brain,* 1996, *119,* 1377–1400.

Harmon, L. D., and Julesz, B. Masking in visual recognition: Effects of two-dimensional filtered noise. *Science,* 1973, *180,* 1194–1197.

Harries, M. H., and Perrett, D. I. Visual processing of faces in the temporal cortex: Physiological evidence for a modular organization and possible anatomical correlates. *Journal of Cognitive Science,* 1991, *3,* 9–24.

Harrington, M. E., and Rusak, B. Lesions of the thalamic intergeniculate leaflet alter hamster circadian rhythms. *Journal of Biological Rhythms,* 1986, *1,* 309–325.

Harris, G. W., and Jacobsohn, D. Functional grafts of the anterior pituitary gland. *Proceedings of the Royal Society of London [B],* 1951–1952, *139,* 263–267.

Hart, B. Sexual reflexes and mating behavior in the male dog. *Journal of Comparative and Physiological Psychology,* 1967, *66,* 388–399.

Hart, B. Gonadal hormones and sexual reflexes in the female rat. *Hormones and Behavior,* 1969, *1,* 65–71.

Hart, B. L. Hormones, spinal reflexes, and sexual behaviour. In *Determinants of Sexual Behaviour,* edited by J. B. Hutchinson. Chichester, England: John Wiley & Sons, 1978.

Hartline, H. K. The response of single optic nerve fibers of the vertebrate eye to illumination of the retina. *American Journal of Physiology,* 1938, *121,* 400–415.

Hashimoto, T., Tayama, M., Murakawa, K., Yoshimoto, T., Miyazaki, M., Harada, M., and Kuroda, Y. Development of the brainstem and cerebellum in autistic patients. *Journal of Autism and Developmental Disorders,* 1995, *25,* 1–18.

Haug, H.-J. Prediction of sleep deprivation outcome by diurnal variation of mood. *Biological Psychiatry,* 1992, *31,* 271–278.

Hauser, M. D. Right hemisphere dominance for the production of facial expression in monkeys. *Science,* 1993, *261,* 475–477.

Hawke, C. Castration and sex crimes. *American Journal of Mental Deficiency,* 1951, *55,* 220–226.

Haxby, J. V., Horwitz, B., Ungerleider, L. G., Maisog, J. M., Pietrini, P., and Grady, C. L. The functional organization of human extrastriate cortex: A PET-rCBF study of selective attention to faces and locations. *Journal of Neuroscience,* 1994, *14,* 6336–6353.

Hayaishi, O. Sleep-wake regulation by prostaglandins D2 and E2. *Journal of Biological Chemistry,* 1988, *263,* 14593–14596.

Hayes, T. L., and Lewis, D. A. Hemispheric differences in layer III pyramidal neurons of the anterior language area. *Archives of Neurology,* 1993, *50,* 501–505.

Heath, A. C., Madden, P. A. F., Slutske, W. S., and Martin, N. G. Personality and the inheritance of smoking behavior: A genetic perspective. *Behavioral Genetics,* 1995, *25,* 103–118.

Hebb, D. O. *The Organization of Behaviour.* New York: Wiley-Interscience, 1949.

Heckler, M. M. *Fifth Special Report to the U.S. Congress on Alcohol and Health.* Washington, D.C.: U.S. Government Printing Office, 1983.

Heffner, H. E., and Heffner, R. S. Role of primate auditory cortex in hearing. In *Comparative Perception.* Vol. II. *Complex Signals,* edited by W. C. Stebbins and M. A. Berkley. New York: John Wiley & Sons, 1990.

Heilman, K. M., Rothi, L., and Kertesz, A. Localization of apraxia-producing lesions. In *Localization in Neuropsychology,* edited by A. Kertesz. New York: Academic Press, 1983.

Heilman, K. M., Scholes, R., and Watson, R. T. Auditory affective agnosia: Disturbed comprehension of affective speech. *Journal of Neurology, Neurosurgery, and Psychiatry,* 1975, *38,* 69–72.

Heilman, K. M., Watson, R. T., and Bowers, D. Affective disorders associated with hemispheric disease. In *Neuropsychology of Human Emotion,* edited by K. M. Heilman and P. Satz. New York: Guilford Press, 1983.

Heimer, L., and Larsson, K. Impairment of mating behavior in male rats following lesions in the preoptic-anterior hypothalamic continuum. *Brain Research,* 1966–1967, *3,* 248–263.

Heinrichs, S. C., Menzaghi, F., Pich, E. M., Baldwin, H. A., Rassnick, S., Britton, K. T., and Koob, G. F. Anti-stress action of a corticotropin-releasing factor antagonist on behavioral reactivity to stressors of varying type and intensity. *Neuropsychopharmacology,* 1994, *11,* 179–186.

Hellhammer, D. H., Hubert, W., and Schurmeyer, T. Changes in saliva testosterone after psychological stimulation in men. *Psychoneuroendocrinology,* 1985, *10,* 77–81.

Hendrickson, A. E., Wagoner, N., and Cowan, W. M. Autoradiographic and electron microscopic study of retino-hypothalamic connections. *Zeitschrift für Zellforschung und Mikroskopische Anatomie,* 1972, *125,* 1–26.

Hendrie, C. A. The calls of murine predators activate endogenous analgesia mechanisms in laboratory mice. *Physiology and Behavior,* 1991, *49,* 569–573.

Heninger, G. R., Delgado, P. L., and Charney, D. S. The revised monoamine theory of depression: A modulatory role for monoamines, based on new findings from monoamine depletion experiments in humans. *Pharmacopsychiatry,* 1996, *29,* 2–11.

Henke, P. G. The telencephalic limbic system and experimental gastric pathology: A review. *Neuroscience and Biobehavioral Reviews,* 1982, *6,* 381–390.

Hennessey, A. C., Camak, L., Gordon, F., and Edwards, D. A. Connections between the pontine central gray and the ventromedial hypothalamus are essential for lordosis in female rats. *Behavioral Neuroscience,* 1990, *104,* 477–488.

Herholz, K. Neuroimaging in anorexia nervosa. *Psychiatry Research,* 1996, *62,* 105–110.

Hering, E. *Outlines of a Theory of the Light Sense,* 1905. Translated by L. M. Hurvich and D. Jameson. Cambridge, Mass.: Harvard University Press, 1965.

Hernandez, L., and Hoebel, B. G. Food reward and cocaine increase extracellular dopamine in the nucleus accumbens as measured by microdialysis. *Life Sciences,* 1988, *42,* 1705–1712.

Hernandez, L., and Hoebel, B. G. Feeding can enhance dopamine turnover in the prefrontal cortex. *Brain Research Bulletin,* 1990, *25,* 975–979.

Hetherington, A. W., and Ranson, S. W. Hypothalamic lesions and adiposity in the rat. *Anatomical Record,* 1942, *78,* 149–172.

Heuser, J. E. Synaptic vesicle exocytosis revealed in quick-frozen frog neuromuscular junctions treated with 4-aminopyridine and given a single electrical shock. In *Society for Neuroscience Symposia,* Vol. II, edited by W. M. Cowan and J. A. Ferrendelli. Bethesda, Md.: Society for Neuroscience, 1977.

Heuser, J. E., and Reese, T. S. Evidence for recycling of synaptic vesicle membrane during transmitter release at the frog neuromuscular function. *Journal of Cell Biology*, 1973, *57*, 315–344.

Heuser, J. E., Reese, T. S., Dennis, M. J., Jan, Y., Jan, L., and Evans, L. Synaptic vesicle exocytosis captured by quick freezing and correlated with quantal transmitter release. *Journal of Cell Biology*, 1979, *81*, 275–300.

Heywood, C. A., and Cowey, A. The role of the "face-cell" area in the discrimination and recognition of faces by monkeys. *Philosophical Transactions of the Royal Society of London [B]*, 1992, *335*, 31–38.

Heywood, C. A., Gaffan, D., and Cowey, A. Cerebral achromatopsia in monkeys. *European Journal of Neuroscience*, 1995, *7*, 1064–1073.

Hickok, G., Bellugi, U., and Klima, E. S. The neurobiology of sign language and its implications for the neural basis of language. *Nature*, 1996, *381*, 699–702.

Hickok, G., Klima, E., Kritchevsky, M., and Bellugi, U. A case of sign blindness' following left occipital damage in a deaf signer. *Neuropsychologia*, 1995, *33*, 1597–1601.

Higley, J. D., Mehlman, P. T., Poland, R. E., Taub, D. M., Vickers, J., Suomi, S. J., and Linnoila, M. CSF testosterone and 5-HIAA correlate with different types of aggressive behaviors. *Biological Psychiatry*, 1996a, *40*, 1067–1082.

Higley, J. D., Mehlman, P. T., Higley, S. B., Fernald, B., Vickers, J., Lindell, S. G., Taub, D. M., Suomi, S. J., and Linnoila, M. Excessive mortality in young free-ranging male nonhuman primates with low cerebrospinal fluid 5-hydroxyindoleacetic acid concentrations. *Archives of General Psychiatry*, 1996b, *53*, 537–543.

Hikosaka, O., Sakai, K., Miyauchi, S., Takino, R., Sasaki, Y., and Puetz, B. Activation of human presupplementary motor area in learning of sequential procedures: A functional MRI study. *Journal of Neurophysiology*, 1996, *76*, 617–621.

Hill, A. J., and Best, P. J. Effects of deafness and blindness on the spatial correlates of hippocampal unit activity in the rat. *Experimental Neurology*, 1981, *74*, 204–217.

Himmelsbach, C. K. Can the euphoric analgetic and physical dependence effects of drugs be separated? With reference to physical dependence. *Federation Proceedings*, 1943, *2*, 201–203.

Hines, M., Allen, L. S., and Gorski, R. A. Sex differences in subregions of the medial nucleus of the amygdala and the bed nucleus of the stria terminalis of the rat. *Brain Research*, 1992, *579*, 321–326.

Hinjo, S., Hirano, C., Murase, S., Kaneko, T., Sugiyama, T., Ohtaka, K., Aoyama, T., Takei, Y., Inoko, K., and Wakbayshai, S. Obsessive-compulsive symptoms in childhood and adolescence. *Acta Psychiatrica Scandanivica*, 1989, *80*, 83–91.

Hitchcock, J., and Davis, M. Lesions of the amygdala, but not of the cerebellum or red nucleus, block conditioned fear as measured with the potentiated startle paradigm. *Behavioral Neuroscience*, 1986, *100*, 11–22.

Hobson, J. A. *The Dreaming Brain*. New York: Basic Books, 1988.

Hodge, C. W., Haraguchi, M., Erickson, H., and Samson, H. H. Ventral tegmental microinjections of quinpirole decrease ethanol and sucrose-reinforced responding. *Alcohol: Clinical and Experimental Research*, 1993, *17*, 370–375.

Hodges, J. R., Patterson, K., Oxbury, S., and Funnell, E. Semantic dementia: Progressive fluent aphasia with temporal lobe atrophy. *Brain*, 1992, *115*, 1783–1806.

Hoebel, B. G., Monaco, A. P., Hernandez, L., Aulisi, E. F., Stanley, B. G., and Lenard, L. Self-injection of amphetamine directly into the brain. *Psychopharmacology*, 1983, *81*, 158–163.

Hoebel, B. G., and Teitelbaum, P. Weight regulation in normal and hypothalamic hyperphagic rats. *Journal of Comparative and Physiological Psychology*, 1966, *61*, 189–193.

Hofer, M. A., and Shair, H. N. Ultrasonic vocalization, laryngeal braking, and thermogenesis in rat pups: A reappraisal. *Behavioral Neuroscience*, 1993, *107*, 354–362.

Hohman, G. W. Some effects of spinal cord lesions on experienced emotional feelings. *Psychophysiology*, 1966, *3*, 143–156.

Hollander, E., DeCaria, C. M., Nitescu, A., Gully, R., Suckow, R. F., Cooper, T. B., Gorman, J. M., Klein, D. F., and Liebowitz, M. R. Serotonergic function in obsessive-compulsive disorder: Behavioral and neuroendocrine responses to oral m-chlorophenylpiperazine and fenfluramine in patients and healthy volunteers. *Archives of General Psychiatry*, 1992, *49*, 21–28.

Hollander, E., Schiffman, E., Cohen, B., Rivera-Stein, M. A., Rosen, W., Gorman, J. M., Fyer, A. J., Papp, L., and Liebowitz, M. R. Signs of central nervous system dysfunction in obsessive-compulsive disorder. *Archives of General Psychiatry*, 1990, *47*, 27–32.

Holmes, G. The cerebellum of man. *Brain*, 1939, *62*, 21–30.

Holroyd, S., Reiss, A. L., and Bryan, R. N. Autistic features in Joubert syndrome: A genetic disorder with agenesis of the cerebellar vermis. *Biological Psychiatry*, 1991, *29*, 287–294.

Honda, T., and Semba, K. Serotonergic synaptic input to cholinergic neurons in the rat mesopontine tegmentum. *Brain Research*, 1994, *647*, 299–306.

Hong, C. C. H., Jin, Y., Potkin, S. G., Buchsbaum, M. S., Wu, J., Callaghan, G. M., Nudelman, K. L., and Gillin, J. C. Language in dreaming and regional EEG alpha-power. *Sleep*, 1996, *19*, 232–235.

Hopf, H. C., Mueller-Forell, W., and Hopf, N. J. Localization of emotional and volitional facial paresis. *Neurology*, 1992, *42*, 1918–1923.

Horne, J. Human slow wave sleep: A review and appraisal of recent findings, with implications for sleep functions, and psychiatric illness. *Experientia*, 1992, *48*, 941–954.

Horne, J. A. A review of the biological effects of total sleep deprivation in man. *Biological Psychology*, 1978, *7*, 55–102.

Horne, J. A. The effects of exercise on sleep. *Biological Psychology*, 1981, *12*, 241–291.

Horne, J. A. *Why We Sleep: The Functions of Sleep in Humans and Other Mammals.* Oxford, England: Oxford University Press, 1988.

Horne, J. A., and Harley, L. J. Human SWS following selective head heating during wakefulness. In *Sleep '88,* edited by J. Horne. New York: Gustav Fischer Verlag, 1989.

Horne, J. A., and Minard, A. Sleep and sleepiness following a behaviourally "active" day. *Ergonomics,* 1985, *28,* 567–575.

Horne, J. A., and Reid, A. J. Night-time sleep EEG changes following body heating in a warm bath. *Electroencephalography and Clinical Neurophysiology,* 1985, *60,* 154–157.

Horowitz, R. M., and Gentili, B. Dihydrochalcone sweeteners. In *Symposium: Sweeteners,* edited by G. E. Inglett. Westport, Conn.: Avi Publishing, 1974.

Horton, J. C., and Hubel, D. H. Cytochrome oxidase stain preferentially labels intersection of ocular dominance and vertical orientation columns in macaque striate cortex. *Society for Neuroscience Abstracts,* 1980, *6,* 315.

Horvath, T. L., Naftolin, F., Leranth, C., Sahu, A., and Kalra, S. P. Morphological and pharmacological evidence for neuropeptide Y-galanin interaction in the rat hypothalamus. *Endocrinology,* 1996, *137,* 3069–3077.

Hosokawa, T., Rusakov, D. A., Bliss, T. V. P., and Fine, A. Repeated confocal imaging of individual dendritic spines in the living hippocampal slice: Evidence for changes in length and orientation associated with chemically induced LTP. *Journal of Neuroscience,* 1995, *15,* 5560–5573.

Houpt, T. A., Boulos, Z., and Moore-Ede, M. C. MidnightSun: Software for determining light exposure and phase-shifting schedules during global travel. *Physiology and Behavior,* 1996, *59,* 561–568.

Houtsmuller, E. J., Brand, T., De Jonge, F. H., Joosten, R. N. J. M. A., Van de Poll, N. E., and Slob, A. K. SDN-POA volume, sexual behavior, and partner preference of male rats affected by perinatal treatment with ATD. *Physiology and Behavior,* 1994, *56,* 535–541.

Hrdy, S. B. Infanticide as a primate reproductive strategy. *American Scientist,* 1977, *65,* 38–47.

Huang, Y. H., and Mogenson, G. J. Neural pathways mediating drinking and feeding in rats. *Experimental Neurology,* 1972, *37,* 269–286.

Hubel, D. H., and Wiesel, T. N. Functional architecture of macaque monkey visual cortex. *Proceedings of the Royal Society of London,* 1977, *198,* 1–59.

Hubel, D. H., and Wiesel, T. N. Brain mechanisms of vision. *Scientific American,* 1979, *241,* 150–162.

Hublin, C. Narcolepsy: Current drug-treatment options. *CNS Drugs,* 1996, *5,* 426–436.

Hudspeth, A. J. Mechanoelectrical transduction by hair cells in the acousticolateralis sensory system. *Annual Review of Neuroscience,* 1983, *6,* 187–215.

Hudspeth, A. J., and Gillespie, P. G. Pulling springs to tune transduction: Adaptation by hair cells. *Neuron,* 1994, *12,* 1–9.

Huerta, P. T., and Lisman, J. E. Synaptic plasticity during the cholinergic theta-frequency oscillation in vitro. *Hippocampus,* 1996, *6,* 58–61.

Hughes, J., Smith, T. W., Kosterlitz, H. W., Fothergill, L. A., Morgan, B. A., and Moris, H. R. Identification of two related pentapeptides from the brain with potent opiate agonist activity. *Nature,* 1975, *258,* 577–579.

Hughes, J. R., Gust, S. W., Skoog, K., Keenan, R. M., and Fenwick, J. W. Symptoms of tobacco withdrawal: A replication and extension. *Archives of General Psychiatry,* 1989, *14,* 577–580.

Hull, E. M., Bitran, D., Pehek, E. A., Warner, R. K., Band, L. C., and Holmes, G. M. Dopaminergic control of male sex behavior in rats: Effects of an intracerebrally infused agonist. *Brain Research,* 1986, *370,* 73–81.

Hull, E. M., Du, J. F., Lorrain, D. S., and Matuszewich, L. Extracellular dopamine in the medial preoptic area: Implications for sexual motivation and hormonal control of copulation. *Journal of Neuroscience,* 1995, *15,* 7465–7471.

Humm, J. L., Lambert, K. G., and Kinsley, C. H. Paucity of c-fos expression in the medial preoptic area of prenatally stressed male rats following exposure to sexually receptive females. *Brain Research Bulletin,* 1995, *37,* 363–368.

Humphrey, A. L., and Hendrickson, A. E. Radial zones of high metabolic activity in squirrel monkey striate cortex. *Society for Neuroscience Abstracts,* 1980, *6,* 315.

Humphreys, G. W., Donnelly, N., and Riddoch, M. J. Expression is computed separately from facial identity, and it is computed separately for moving and static faces: Neuropsychological evidence. *Neuropsychologia,* 1993, *31,* 173–181.

Humphreys, P., Kaufmann, W. E., and Galaburda, A. M. Developmental dyslexia in women: Neuropathological findings in three patients. *Annals of Neurology,* 1990, *28,* 727–738.

Hunterensor, M., Ousley, A., and Sehgal, A. Regulation of the *Drosophila* protein *Timeless* suggests a mechanism for resetting the circadian clock by light. *Cell,* 1996, *84,* 677–685.

Husby, G., Van De Rign, I., Zabriskie, J. B., Abdin, A. H., and Williams, R. C. Antibodies reacting with cytoplasm of subthalamic and caudate nuclei neurons in chorea and acute rheumatic fever. *Journal of Experimental Medicine,* 1976, *144,* 1094–1110.

Huszar, D., Lynch, C. A., Fairchild-Huntress, V., Dunmore, J. H., Fang, Q., Berkemeier, L. R., Gu, W., Kesterson, R. A., Boston, B. A., Cone, R. D., Smith, F. J., Campfield, L. A., Burn, P., and Lee, F. *Cell,* 1997, *88,* 131–141.

Huttunen, M. O., and Niskanen, P. Prenatal loss of father and psychiatric disorders. *Archives of General Psychiatry,* 1978, *35,* 429–431.

Hyman, S. E. Addiction to cocaine and amphetamine. *Neuron,* 1996a, *16,* 901–904.

Hyman, S. E. Shaking out the cause of addiction. *Science,* 1996b, *273,* 611–612.

Ibuka, N., and Kawamura, H. Loss of circadian rhythm in sleep-wakefulness cycle in the rat by suprachiasmatic nucleus lesions. *Brain Research,* 1975, *96,* 76–81.

Iggo, A., and Andres, K. H. Morphology of cutaneous receptors. *Annual Review of Neuroscience,* 1982, *5,* 1–32.

Ihnat, R., White, N. R., and Barfield, R. J. Pup's broadband vocalizations and maternal behavior in the rat. *Behavioral Processes,* 1995, *33,* 257–272.

Imaki, T., Shibasaki, T., Hotta, M., and Demura, H. Early induction of c-fos precedes increased expression of corticotropin-releasing factor messenger ribonucleic acid in the paraventricular nucleus after immobilization stress. *Endocrinology,* 1992, *131,* 240–246.

Imbeaud, S., Faure, E., Lamarre, I., Mattéi, M. G., di Clemente, N., Tizard, R., Carré-Eusèbe, D., Belville, C., Tragethon, L., Tonkin, C., et al. Insensitivity to anti-Müllerian hormone due to a mutation in the human anti-Müllerian hormone receptor. *Nature Genetics,* 1995, *11,* 382–388.

Imperato, A., and Di Chiara, G. Preferential stimulation of dopamine-release in the accumbens of freely moving rats by ethanol. *Journal of Pharmacology and Experimental Therapeutics,* 1986, *239,* 219–228.

Imperato, A., Scrocco, M. G., Bacchi, S., and Angelucci, L. NMDA receptors and in vivo dopamine release in the nucleus accumbens and caudatus. *European Journal of Pharmacology,* 1990, *187,* 555–556.

Ingelfinger, F. J. The late effects of total and subtotal gastrectomy. *New England Journal of Medicine,* 1944, *231,* 321–327.

Ingram, S. M., Krause, R. G., Baldino, F., Skeen, L. C., and Lewis, M. E. Neuronal localization of cholecystokinin mRNA in the rat brain by using in situ hybridization histochemistry. *Journal of Comparative Neurology,* 1989, *287,* 260–272.

Inoue, M., Koyanagi, T., Nakahara, H., Hara, K., Hori, E., and Nakano, H. Functional development of human eye movement in utero assessed quantitatively with real time ultrasound. *American Journal of Obstetrics and Gynecology,* 1986, *155,* 170–174.

Invernizzi, R., Belli, S., and Samanin, R. Citalopram's ability to increase the extracellular concentrations of serotonin in the dorsal raphe prevents the drug's effect in the frontal cortex. *Brain Research,* 1992, *584,* 322–324.

Iwai, E., and Mishkin, M. Further evidence of the locus of the visual area in the temporal lobe of the monkey. *Experimental Neurology,* 1969, *25,* 585–594.

Iwata, J., LeDoux, J. E., Meeley, M. P., Arneric, S., and Reis, D. J. Intrinsic neurons in the amygdaloid field projected to by the medial geniculate body mediate emotional responses conditioned to acoustic stimuli. *Brain Research,* 1986, *383,* 195–214.

Iwata, M. Kanji versus Kana: Neuropsychological correlates of the Japanese writing system. *Trends in Neurosciences,* 1984, *7,* 290–293.

Izard, C. E. *The Face of Emotion.* New York: Appleton-Century-Crofts, 1971.

Jacobs, B. L., and Fornal, C. A. 5-HT and motor control: A hypothesis. *Trends in Neuroscience,* 1993, *16,* 346–352.

Jacobs, B. L., and McGinty, D. J. Participation of the amygdala in complex stimulus recognition and behavioral inhibition: Evidence from unit studies. *Brain Research,* 1972, *36,* 431–436.

Jacobs, B. L., Wilkinson, L. O., and Fornal, C. A. The role of brain serotonin: A neurophysiologic perspective. *Neuropsychopharmacology,* 1990, *3,* 473–479.

Jacobs, G. H. Primate photopigments and primate color vision. *Proceedings of the National Academy of Sciences, USA,* 1996, *93,* 577–581.

Jacobsen, C. F., Wolfe, J. B., and Jackson, T. A. An experimental analysis of the functions of the frontal association areas in primates. *Journal of Nervous and Mental Disorders,* 1935, *82,* 1–14.

Jakobson, L. S., Archibald, Y. M., Carey, D., and Goodale, M. A. A kinematic analysis of reaching and grasping movements in a patient recovering from optic ataxia. *Neuropsychologia,* 1991, *29,* 803–809.

James, W. What is an emotion? *Mind,* 1884, *9,* 188–205.

James, W. P. T., and Trayhurn, P. Thermogenesis and obesity. *British Medical Bulletin,* 1981, *27,* 43–48.

Jaramillo, F. Signal transduction in hair cells and its regulation by calcium. *Neuron,* 1995, *15,* 1227–1230.

Jaskiw, G., and Kleinman, J. Postmortem neurochemistry studies in schizophrenia. In *Schizophrenia: A Scientific Focus,* edited by S. C. Schulz and C. A. Tamminga. New York: Oxford University Press, 1988.

Jasper, J. H., and Tessier, J. Acetylcholine liberation from cerebral cortex during paradoxical (REM) sleep. *Science,* 1969, *172,* 601–602.

Jaynes, J. The problem of animate motion in the seventeenth century. *Journal of the History of Ideas,* 1970, *6,* 219–234.

Jeffcoate, W. J., Lincoln, N. B., Selby, C., and Herbert, M. Correlations between anxiety and serum prolactin in humans. *Journal of Psychosomatic Research,* 1986, *30,* 217–222.

Jeffress, L. A. A place theory of sound localization. *Journal of Comparative and Physiological Psychology,* 1948, *41,* 35–39.

Jensen, T., Genefke, I., and Hyldebrandt, N. Cerebral atrophy in young torture victims. *New England Journal of Medicine,* 1982, *307,* 1341.

Jeste, D. V., Del Carmen, R., Lohr, J. B., and Wyatt, R. J. Did schizophrenia exist before the eighteenth century? *Comprehensive Psychiatry,* 1985, *26,* 493–503.

Jewett, D. C., Cleary, J., Levine, A. S., Schaal, D. W., and Thompson, T. Effects of neuropeptide Y on food-reinforced behavior in satiated rats. *Pharmacology, Biochemistry, and Behavior,* 1992, *42,* 207–212.

Jiang, C. L., and Hunt, J. N. The relation between freely chosen meals and body habitus. *American Journal of Clinical Nutrition,* 1983, *38,* 32–40.

Jiminez, A. J., Garcia-Fernandez, J. M., Gonzalez, B., and Foster, R. G. The spatiotemporal pattern of photoreceptor degeneration in the aged *rd/rd* mouse retina. *Cell and Tissue Research,* 1996, *284,* 193–202.

Johansson, G. Visual perception of biological motion and a model for its analysis. *Perception and Psychophysics,* 1973, *14,* 201–211.

Johnson, A. K., and Cunningham, J. T. Brain mechanisms and drinking: The role of lamina terminalis-associated systems in extracellular thirst. *Kidney International,* 1987, *32,* S35–S42.

Johnson, A. K., and Edwards, G. L. The neuroendocrinology of thirst: Afferent signaling and mechanisms of central integration. *Current Topics in Neuroendocrinology,* 1990, *10,* 149–190.

Johnson, M. K., Kim, J. K., and Risse, G. Do alcoholic Korsakoff's syndrome patients acquire affective reactions? *Journal of Experimental Psychology: Learning, Memory, and Cognition,* 1985, *11,* 22–36.

Johnson, S. W., and North, R. A. Opioids excite dopamine neurons by hyperpolarization of local interneurons. *Journal of Neuroscience,* 1992, *12,* 483–488.

Jones, B. E. Influence of the brainstem reticular formation, including intrinsic monoaminergic and cholinergic neurons, on forebrain mechanisms of sleep and waking. In *The Diencephalon and Sleep,* edited by M. Mancia and G. Marini. New York: Raven Press, 1990.

Jones, B. E., and Beaudet, A. Distribution of acetylcholine and catecholamine neurons in the cat brain stem studied by choline acetyltransferase and tyrosine hydroxylase immunohistochemistry. *Journal of Comparative Neurology,* 1987, *261,* 15–32.

Jones, D. T., and Reed, R. R. G$_{olf}$: An olfactory neuron specific-G protein involved in odorant signal transduction. *Science,* 1989, *244,* 790–795.

Jones, M. B., and Szatmari, P. Stoppage rules and genetic studies of autism. *Journal of Autism and Developmental Disorders,* 1988, *18,* 31–40.

Jones, S. S., Collins, K., and Hong, H.-W. An audience effect on smile production in 10-month-old infants. *Psychological Science,* 1991, *2,* 45–49.

Jope, R. S., Song, L., Li, P. P., Young, L. T., Kish, S. J., Pacheco, M. A., and Warsh, J. J. The phosphoinositide signal transduction system is impaired in bipolar affective disorder brain. *Journal of Neurochemistry,* 1996, *66,* 2402–2409.

Josso, N., Boussin, L., Knebelmann, B., Nihoul-Fekete, C., and Picard, J.-Y. Anti-Muellerian hormone and intersex states. *Trends in Endocrinology and Metabolism,* 1991, *2,* 227–233.

Jouvet, M. The role of monoamines and acetylcholine-containing neurons in the regulation of the sleep-waking cycle. *Ergebnisse der Physiologie,* 1972, *64,* 166–307.

Jouvet, M. Biochemical regulation of states of vigilance. *International Journal of Neurology,* 1975, *10,* 1–4, 141–157, 252–258.

Jouvet, M. Paradoxical sleep and the nature-nurture controversy. *Progress in Brain Research,* 1980, *53,* 331–346.

Kadekaro, M., Cohen, S., Terrell, M. L., Lekan, H., Gary, H., and Eisenberg, H. M. Independent activation of subfornical organ and hypothalamo-neurohypophysial system during administration of angiotensin II. *Peptides,* 1989, *10,* 423–429.

Kales, A., Scharf, M. B., Kales, J. D., and Soldatos, C. R. Rebound insomnia: A potential hazard following withdrawal of certain benzodiazepines. *Journal of the American Medical Association,* 1979, *241,* 1692–1695.

Kales, A., Tan, T.-L., Kollar, E. J., Naitoh, P., Preston, T. A., and Malmstrom, E. J. Sleep patterns following 205 hours of sleep deprivation. *Psychosomatic Medicine,* 1970, *32,* 189–200.

Kalin, N. H., Sherman, J. E., and Takahashi, L. K. Antagonism of endogenous CRG systems attenuates stress-induced freezing behavior in rats. *Brain Research,* 1988, *457,* 130–135.

Kanamori, N., Sakai, K., and Jouvet, M. Neuronal activity specific to paradoxical sleep in the ventromedial medullary reticular formation of unrestrained cats. *Brain Research,* 1980, *189,* 251–255.

Kanner, L. Autistic disturbances of affective contact. *The Nervous Child,* 1943, *2,* 217–250.

Kapp, B. S., Gallagher, M., Applegate, C. D., and Frysinger, R. C. The amygdala central nucleus: Contributions to conditioned cardiovascular responding during aversive Pavlovian conditioning in the rabbit. In *Conditioning: Representation of Involved Neural Functions,* edited by C. D. Woody. New York: Plenum Press, 1982.

Kapur, N., Thompson, S., Cook, P., Lang, D., and Brice, J. Anterograde but not retrograde memory loss following combined mammillary body and medial thalamic lesions. *Neuropsychologia,* 1996, *34,* 1–8.

Karacan, I., Salis, P. J., and Williams, R. L. The role of the sleep laboratory in diagnosis and treatment of impotence. In *Sleep Disorders: Diagnosis and Treatment,* edited by R. J. Williams and I. Karacan. New York: John Wiley & Sons, 1978.

Karacan, I., Williams, R. L., Finley, W. W., and Hursch, C. J. The effects of naps on nocturnal sleep: Influence on the need for stage 1 REM and stage 4 sleep. *Biological Psychiatry,* 1970, *2,* 391–399.

Karlson, P., and Luscher, M. "Pheromones": A new term for a class of biologically active substances. *Nature,* 1959, *183,* 55–56.

Karreman, M., and Moghaddam, B. The prefrontal cortex regulates the basal release of dopamine in the limbic striatum: An effect mediated by ventral tegmental area. *Journal of Neurochemistry,* 1996, *66,* 589–598.

Kartsounis, L. D., Rudge, P., and Stevens, J. M. Bilateral lesions of CA1 and CA2 fields of the hippocampus are sufficient to cause a severe amnesic syndrome in humans. *Journal of Neurology, Neurosurgery and Psychiatry,* 1995, *59,* 95–98.

Kasper, S., Rogers, S. L. B., Yancey, A., Schulz, P. M., Skwerer, R. G., and Rosenthal, N. E. Phototherapy in individuals with and without subsyndromal seasonal affective disorder. *Archives of General Psychiatry*, 1989a, *46*, 837–844.

Kasper, S., Wehr, T. A., Bartko, J. J., Gaist, P. A., and Rosenthal, N. E. Epidemiological findings of seasonal changes in mood and behavior: A telephone survey of Montgomery County, Maryland. *Archives of General Psychiatry*, 1989b, *46*, 823–833.

Katayama, Y., DeWitt, D. S., Becker, D. P., and Hayes, R. L. Behavioral evidence for cholinoceptive pontine inhibitory area: Descending control of spinal motor output and sensory input. *Brain Research*, 1986, *296*, 241–262.

Kattler, H., Dijk, D. J., and Borbély, A. A. Effect of unilateral somatosensory stimulation prior to sleep on the sleep EEG in humans. *Journal of Sleep Research*, 1994, *3*, 159–164.

Kavaliers, M. Brief exposure to a natural predator, the short-tailed weasel, induces benzodiazepine-sensitive analgesia in white-footed mice. *Physiology and Behavior*, 1985, *43*, 187–193.

Kawamura, M., Hirayama, K., and Yamamoto, H. Different interhemispheric transfer of kanji and kana writing evidenced by a case with left unilateral agraphia without apraxia. *Brain*, 1989, *112*, 1011–1018.

Kayama, Y., Ohta, M., and Jodo, E. Firing of "possibly" cholinergic neurons in the rat laterodorsal tegmental nucleus during sleep and wakefulness. *Brain Research*, 1992, *569*, 210–220.

Kaye, W. H. Neuropeptide abnormalities in anorexia nervosa. *Psychiatry Research*, 1996, *62*, 65–74.

Kaye, W. H., Berrettini, W., Gwirtsman, H., and George, D. T. Altered cerebrospinal fluid neuropeptide Y and peptide YY immunoreactivity in anorexia and bulimia nervosa. *Archives of General Psychiatry*, 1990, *47*, 548–556.

Keller, S. E., Weiss, J. M., Schleifer, S. J., Miller, N. E., and Stein, M. Stress-induced suppression of immunity in adrenalectomized rats. *Science*, 1983, *221*, 1301–1304.

Kelso, S. R., and Brown, T. H. Differential conditioning of associative synaptic enhancement in hippocampal brain slices. *Science*, 1986, *232*, 85–87.

Kelso, S. R., Ganong, A. H., and Brown, T. H. Hebbian synapses in hippocampus. *Proceedings of the National Academy of Sciences, USA*, 1986, *83*, 5326–5330.

Kelsoe, J. R., Ginns, E. I., Egeland, J. A., Gerhard, D. S., Goldstein, A. M., Bale, S. J., Pauls, D. L., Long, R. T., Kidd, K. K., Conte, G., Housman, D. E., and Paul, S. M. Re-evaluation of the linkage relationship between chromosome 11p loci and the gene for bipolar affective disorder in the Old Order Amish. *Nature*, 1989, *342*, 238–243.

Kelsoe, J. R., Sadovnick, A. D., Kristbjarnarson, H., Bergesh, P., Mroczkowski-Parker, Z., Drennan, M., Rapaport, M. H., Flodman, P., Spence, M. A., and Remick, R. A. Possible locus for bipolar disorder near the dopamine transporter on chromosome 5. *American Journal of Medical Genetics*, 1996, *67*, 533–540.

Kemp, D. T. Stimulated acoustic emissions from within the human auditory system. *Journal of the Acoustical Society of America*, 1978, *64*, 1386–1391.

Kemperman, G., Kuhn, H. G., and Gage, F. H. More hippocampal neurons in adult mice living in an enriched environment. *Nature*, 1997, *386*, 493–495.

Kendell, R. E., and Adams, W. Unexplained fluctuations in the risk for schizophrenia by month and year of birth. *British Journal of Psychiatry*, 1991, *158*, 758–763.

Kennard, C., Lawden, M., Morland, A. B., and Ruddock, K. H. Colour identification and colour constancy are impaired in a patient with incomplete achromatopsia associated with prestriate cortical lesions. *Proceedings of the Royal Society of London [B]*, 1995, *260*, 169–175.

Kennedy, J. L., Giuffra, L. A., Moises, H. W., Cavalli-Sforza, L. L., Pakstis, A. J., Kidd, J. R., Castiglione, C. M., Sjögren, B., Wetterberg, L., and Kidd, K. K. Evidence against linkage of schizophrenia to markers on chromosome 5 in a northern Swedish pedigree. *Nature*, 1988, *336*, 167–170.

Kennedy, S. H., and Goldbloom, D. S. Current perspectives on drug therapies for anorexia nervosa and bulimia nervosa. *Drugs*, 1991, *41*, 367–377.

Kertesz, A. Anatomy of jargon. In *Jargonaphasia*, edited by J. Brown. New York: Academic Press, 1981.

Kety, S. S., Rosenthal, D., Wender, P. H., and Schulsinger, K. F. The types and prevalence of mental illness in the biological and adoptive families of adopted schizophrenics. In *The Transmission of Schizophrenia*, edited by D. Rosenthal and S. S. Kety. New York: Pergamon Press, 1968.

Kety, S. S., Wender, P. H., Jacobsen, B., Ingraham, L. J., Jansson, L., Faber, B., and Kinney, D. K. Mental illness in the biological and adoptive relatives of schizophrenic adoptees: Replication of the Copenhagen Study in the rest of Denmark. *Archives of General Psychiatry*, 1994, *51*, 442–455.

Keverne, E. B., and de la Riva, C. Pheromones in mice: Reciprocal interactions between the nose and brain. *Nature*, 1982, *296*, 148–150.

Khanna, S., and Channabasavanna, S. Toward a classification of compulsions in obsessive compulsive neurosis. *Psychopathology*, 1987, *20*, 23–28.

Kiang, N. Y.-S. *Discharge Patterns of Single Fibers in the Cat's Auditory Nerve*. Cambridge, Mass.: MIT Press, 1965.

Kiecolt-Glaser, J. K., Glaser, R., Shuttleworth, E. C., Dyer, C. S., Ogrocki, P., and Speicher, C. E. Chronic stress and immunity in family caregivers of Alzheimer's disease victims. *Psychosomatic Medicine*, 1987, *49*, 523–535.

Kiecolt-Glaser, J. K., Marucha, P. T., Malarkey, W. B., Mercado, A. M., and Glaser, R. Slowing of wound healing by psychological stress. *Lancet*, 1995, *346*, 1194–1196.

Kingston, K., Szmukler, G., Andrewes, D., Tress, B., and Desmond, P. Neuropsychological and structural brain changes in anorexia nervosa before and after refeeding. *Psychological Medicine*, 1996, *26*, 15–28.

Kinnamon, J. C., and Roper, S. D. Evidence for a role of voltage-sensitive apical K$^+$ channels in sour and salt taste transduction. *Chemical Senses*, 1988, *13*, 115–121.

Kinnamon, S. C., and Cummings, T. A. Chemosensory transduction mechanisms in taste. *Annual Review of Physiology*, 1992, *54*, 715–731.

Kinnamon, S. C., Dionne, V. E., and Beam, K. G. Apical localization of K$^+$ channels in taste cells provides the basis for sour taste transduction. *Proceedings of the National Academy of Sciences, USA*, 1988, *85*, 7023–7027.

Kinney, D. K., Yurgelun-Todd, D. A., Levy, D. L., Medoff, D., Lajonchere, C. M., and Radford-Paregol, M. Obstetrical complications in patients with bipolar disorder and their siblings. *Psychiatry Research*, 1993, *48*, 47–56.

Kinon, B. J., and Lieberman, J. A. Mechanisms of action of atypical antipsychotic drugs: A critical analysis. *Psychopharmacology*, 1996, *124*, 2–34.

Kinsey, A. C., Pomeroy, W. B., Martin, C. E., and Gebhard, P. H. *Sexual Behavior in the Human Female.* Philadelphia: Saunders, 1943.

Kinsley, C., and Svare, B. Prenatal stress reduces intermale aggression in mice. *Physiology and Behavior*, 1986, *36*, 783–785.

Kinsley, C. H., Konen, C. M., Miele, L., Ghiraldi, L., and Svare, B. Intrauterine position modulates maternal behaviors in female mice. *Physiology and Behavior*, 1986, *36*, 793–799.

Kirchgessner, A. L., and Sclafani, A. PVN-hindbrain pathway involved in the hypothalamic hyperphagia-obesity syndrome. *Physiology and Behavior*, 1988, *42*, 517–528.

Kirkpatrick, B., Kim, J. W., and Insel, T. R. Limbic system fos expression associated with paternal behavior. *Brain Research*, 1994, *658*, 112–118.

Klausner, J. D., Sweeney, J. A., Deck, M. D. F., Haas, G. L., and Kelly, A. B. Clinical correlates of cerebral ventricular enlargement in schizophrenia. Further evidence for frontal lobe disease. *Journal of Nervous and Mental Disorders*, 1992, *180*, 407–412.

Kleitman, N. The nature of dreaming. In *The Nature of Sleep*, edited by G. E. W. Wolstenholme and M. O'Connor. London: J.&A. Churchill, 1961.

Kleitman, N. Basic rest-activity cycle—22 years later. *Sleep*, 1982, *4*, 311–317.

Klukowski, G., and Harley, C. W. Locus coeruleus activation induces perforant path-evoked population spike potentiation in the dentate gyrus of awake rat. *Experimental Brain Research*, 1994, *102*, 165–170.

Knapp, P. H., Levy, E. M., Giorgi, R. G., Black, P. H., Fox, B. H., and Heeren, T. C. Short-term immunological effects of induced emotion. *Psychosomatic Medicine*, 1992, *54*, 133–148.

Knebelmann, B., Boussin, L., Guerrier, D., Legeai, L., Kahn, A., Josso, N., and Picard, J.-Y. Anti-Muellerian hormone Bruxelles: A nonsense mutation associated with the persistent Muellerian duct syndrome. *Proceedings of the National Academy of Sciences, USA*, 1991, *88*, 3767–3771.

Knefati, M., Somogyi, C., Kapas, L., Bourcier, T., and Krueger, J. M. Acidic fibroblast growth factor (FGF) but not basic FGF induces sleep and fever in rabbits. *American Journal of Physiology*, 1995, *269*, R87–R91.

Knowlton, B. J., Mangels, J. A., and Squire, L. R. A neostriatal habit learning system in humans. *Science*, 1996, *273*, 1399–1402.

Kobashi, M., and Adachi, A. Effect of hepatic portal infusion of water on water intake by water-deprived rats. *Physiology and Behavior*, 1992, *52*, 885–888.

Kobatake, E., Tanaka, K., and Tamori, Y. Long-term learning changes the stimulus selectivity of cells in the inferotemporal cortex of adult monkeys. *Neuroscience Research*, 1992, *S17*, S237.

Kolvalzon, V. M., and Mukhametov, L. M. Temperature fluctuations of the dolphin brain corresponding to unihemispheric slow-wave sleep. *Journal of Evolutionary Biochemistry and Physiology*, 1982, *18*, 307–309.

Komisaruk, B. R., and Larsson, K. Suppression of a spinal and a cranial nerve reflex by vaginal or rectal probing in rats. *Brain Research*, 1971, *35*, 231–235.

Komisaruk, B. R., and Steinman, J. L. Genital stimulation as a trigger for neuroendocrine and behavioral control of reproduction. *Annals of the New York Academy of Sciences*, 1987, *474*, 64–75.

Koob, G. F. Drug addiction: The yin and yang of hedonic homeostasis. *Neuron*, 1996, *16*, 893–896.

Koob, G. F., Thatcher-Britton, K., Britton, D., Roberts, D.C. S., and Bloom, F. E. Destruction of the locus coeruleus or the dorsal NE bundle does not alter the release of punished responding by ethanol and chlordiazepoxide. *Physiology and Behavior*, 1984, *33*, 479–485.

Koopman, P., Gubbay, J., Vivian, N., Goodfellow, P. N., and Lovell-Badge, R. Male development of chromosomally female mice transgenic for Sry. *Nature*, 1991, *351*, 117–121.

Koopmans, H. S. Internal signals cause large changes in food intake in one-way crossed intestines rats. *Brain Research Bulletin*, 1985, *14*, 595–603.

Kopelman, M. D. The Korsakoff syndrome. *British Journal of Psychiatry*, 1995, *166*, 154–173.

Kornhuber, H. H. Cerebral cortex, cerebellum, and basal ganglia: An introduction to their motor functions. In *The Neurosciences: Third Study Program*, edited by F. O. Schmitt and F. G. Worden. Cambridge, Mass.: MIT Press, 1974.

Kovács, G., Vogels, R., and Orban, G. A. Selectivity of macaque inferior temporal neurons for partially occluded shapes. *Journal of Neuroscience*, 1995, *15*, 1984–1997.

Kovner, R., and Stamm, J. S. Disruption of short-term visual memory by electrical stimulation of inferotemporal cortex in the monkey. *Journal of Comparative and Physiological Psychology*, 1972, *81*, 163–172.

Kozlowski, L. T., and Cutting, J. E. Recognizing the sex of a walker from a dynamic point-light display. *Perception and Psychophysics*, 1977, *21*, 575–580.

Kozlowski, S., and Drzewiecki, K. The role of osmoreception in portal circulation in control of water intake in dogs. *Acta Physiologica Polonica*, 1973, *24*, 325–330.

Kral, J. G. Surgical treatment of obesity. *Medical Clinics of North America*, 1989, *73*, 251–264.

Kraly, F. S. Drinking elicited by eating. In *Progress in Psychobiology and Physiological Psychology*, Vol. 14, edited by A. N. Epstein and A. Morrison. New York: Academic Press, 1990.

Kraly, F. S., and Corneilson, R. Angiotensin II mediates drinking elicited by eating in the rat. *American Journal of Physiology*, 1990, *258*, R436–R442.

Kraly, F. S., and June, K. R. A vagally mediated histaminergic component of food-related drinking in the rat. *Journal of Comparative and Physiological Psychology*, 1982, *96*, 89–104.

Kraly, F. S., Kim, Y.-M., and Tribuzio, R. A. Renal nerve transection inhibits drinking elicited by eating and by intragastric osmotic loads in rats. *Physiology and Behavior*, 1995, *58*, 1129–1136.

Kraly, F. S., and Specht, S. M. Histamine plays a major role for drinking elicited by spontaneous eating in rats. *Physiology and Behavior*, 1984, *33*, 611–614.

Kramer, F. M., Jeffery, R. W., Forster, J. L., and Snell, M. K. Long-term follow-up of behavioral treatment for obesity: Patterns of weight regain among men and women. *International Journal of Obesity*, 1989, *13*, 123–136.

Kraut, R. E., and Johnston, R. Social and emotional messages of smiling: An ethological approach. *Journal of Personality and Social Psychology*, 1979, *37*, 1539–1553.

Krueger, J. M., and Majde, J. A. Cytokines and sleep. *International Archives of Allergy and Immunology*, 1995, *106*, 97–100.

Kuczmarski, R. J. Prevalence of overweight and weight gain in the United States. *American Journal of Clinical Nutrition*, 1992, *55*, 495S–502S.

Kuffler, S. W. Neurons in the retina: Organization, inhibition and excitation problems. *Cold Spring Harbor Symposium on Quantitative Biology*, 1952, *17*, 281–292.

Kuffler, S. W. Discharge patterns and functional organization of mammalian retina. *Journal of Neurophysiology*, 1953, *16*, 37–68.

Kulka, R. A., Schlenger, W. E., Fairbank, J. A., Hough, R. L., Jordan, B. K., Marmar, C. R., and Weiss, D. S. *Trauma and the Vietnam War Generation: Report of Findings from the National Vietnam Veterans Readjustment Study.* New York: Brunner/Mazel, 1990.

Kumar, K., Wyant, G. M., and Nath, R. Deep brain stimulation for control of intractable pain in humans, present and future: A ten-year follow-up. *Neurosurgery*, 1990, *26*, 774–782.

Kupfer, D. J. REM latency: A psychobiologic marker for primary depressive disease. *Biological Psychiatry*, 1976, *11*, 159–174.

Kupfer, D. J., Ehlers, C. L., Frank, E., Grochocinski, V. J., McEachran, A. B., and Buhari, A. Persistent effects of antidepressants: EEG sleep studies in depressed patients during maintenance treatment. *Biological Psychiatry*, 1994, *35*, 781–793.

Kurihara, K. Recent progress in taste receptor mechanisms. In *Umami: A Basic Taste*, edited by Y. Kawamura and M. R. Kare. New York: Dekker, 1987.

Kurihara, K., Katsuragi, Y., Matsuoka, I., Kashiwayanagi, M., Kumazawa, T., and Shoji, T. Receptor mechanisms of bitter substances. *Physiology and Behavior*, 1994, *56*, 1125–1132.

LaBar, K. S., LeDoux, J. E., Spencer, D. D., and Phelps, E. A. Impaired fear conditioning following unilateral temporal lobectomy in humans. *Journal of Neuroscience*, 1995, *15*, 6846–6855.

Laborit, H. La thérapeutique neuro-végétate du choc et de la maladie post-traumatique. *Presse Medicale*, 1950, *58*, 138–140. Cited by Snyder, 1974.

Laitinen, L. V., Bergenheim, A. T., and Hariz, M. I. Leksell's posteroventral pallidotomy in the treatment of Parkinson's disease. *Journal of Neurosurgery*, 1992, *76*, 53–61.

Lamb, R. J., Preston, K. L., Schindler, C. W., Meisch, R. A., Davis, F., Katz, J. L., Henningfield, J. E., and Goldberg, S. R. The reinforcing and subjective effects of morphine in post-addicts: A dose-response study. *Journal of Pharmacology and Experimental Therapeutics*, 1991, *259*, 1165–1173.

Land, E. H. The retinex theory of colour vision. *Proceedings of the Royal Institute of Great Britain*, 1974, *47*, 23–57.

Lange, C. G. *Über Gemüthsbewegungen.* Leipzig, East Germany: T. Thomas, 1887.

Langston, J. W., Ballard, P., Tetrud, J., and Irwin, I. Chronic parkinsonism in humans due to a product of meperidine-analog synthesis. *Science*, 1983, *219*, 979–980.

Langston, J. W., Irwin, I., Langston, E. B., and Forno, L. S. Pargyline prevents MPTP-induced parkinsonism in primates. *Science*, 1984, *225*, 1480–1482.

Laruelle, M., Abi-Dargham, A., Van Dyck, C. H., Gil, R., D'-Souza, C. D., Erdos, J., McCance, E., Rosenblatt, W., Fingado, C., Zoghbi, S. S., Baldwin, R. M., Seibyl, J. P., Krystal, J. H., Charney, D. S., and Innis, R. B. Single photon emission computerized tomography imaging of amphetamine-induced dopamine release in drug-free schizophrenic subjects. *Proceedings of the National Academy of Sciences, USA*, 1996, *93*, 9235–9240.

Laschet, U. Antiandrogen in the treatment of sex offenders: Mode of action and therapeutic outcome. In *Contemporary Sexual Behavior: Critical Issues in the 1970's*, edited by J. Zubin and J. Money. Baltimore: Johns Hopkins University Press, 1973.

Lavie, P., Pratt, H., Scharf, B., Peled, R., and Brown, J. Localized pontine lesion: Nearly total absence of REM sleep. *Neurology*, 1984, *34*, 1118–1120.

Lavond, D. G., Kim, J. J., and Thompson, R. F. Mammalian brain substrates of aversive classical conditioning. *Annual Review of Psychology*, 1993, *44*, 317–342.

Lawrence, D. G., and Kuypers, G. J. M. The functional organization of the motor system in the monkey. I. The effects of bilateral pyramidal lesions. *Brain*, 1968a, *91*, 1–14.

Lawrence, D. G., and Kuypers, G. J. M. The functional organization of the motor system in the monkey. II. The effects of lesions of the descending brain-stem pathways. *Brain,* 1968b, *91,* 15–36.

Leblanc, R., Meyer, E., Bub, D., Zatorre, R. J., and Evans, A. C. Language localization with activation positron emission tomography scanning. *Neurosurgery,* 1992, *31,* 369–373.

LeDoux, J. E. Brain mechanisms of emotion and emotional learning. *Current Opinion in Neurobiology,* 1992, *2,* 191–197.

LeDoux, J. E. Emotion: Clues from the brain. *Annual Review of Psychology,* 1995, *46,* 209–235.

LeDoux, J. E., Iwata, J., Cicchetti, P., and Reis, D. J. Different projections of the central amygdaloid nucleus mediate autonomic and behavioral correlates of conditioned fear. *Journal of Neuroscience,* 1988, *8,* 2517–2529.

LeDoux, J. E., Iwata, J., Pearl, D., and Reis, D. J. Disruption of auditory but not visual learning by destruction of intrinsic neurons in the rat medial geniculate body. *Brain Research,* 1986, *371,* 395–399.

LeDoux, J. E., Sakaguchi, A., and Reis, D. J. Subcortical efferent projections of the medial geniculate nucleus mediate emotional responses conditioned to acoustic stimuli. *Journal of Neuroscience,* 1984, *4,* 683–698.

Lee, C., Parikh, V., Itsukaichi, T., Bae, K., and Edery, I. Resetting the *Drosophila* clock by photic regulation of PER and a PER-TIM complex. *Science,* 1996, *271,* 1740–1744.

Lee, J.-H., and Beitz, A. J. Electroacupuncture modifies the expression of c-fos in the spinal cord induced by noxious stimulation. *Brain Research,* 1992, *577,* 80–91.

Lehman, C. D., Rodin, J., McEwen, B., and Brinton, R. Impact of environmental stress on the expression of insulin-dependent diabetes mellitus. *Behavioral Neuroscience,* 1991, *105,* 241–245.

Lehman, M. N., Silver, R., Gladstone, W. R., Kahn, R. M., Gibson, M., and Bittman, E. L. Circadian rhythmicity restored by neural transplant: Immunocytochemical characterization with the host brain. *Journal of Neuroscience,* 1987, *7,* 1626–1638.

Lehman, M. N., and Winans, S. S. Vomeronasal and olfactory pathways to the amygdala controlling male hamster sexual behavior: Autoradiographic and behavioral analyses. *Brain Research,* 1982, *240,* 27–41.

Leibenluft, E., and Wehr, T. A. Is sleep deprivation useful in the treatment of depression? *American Journal of Psychiatry,* 1992, *149,* 159–168.

Leibowitz, S. F., Weiss, G. F., and Shor-Posner, G. Hypothalamic serotonin: Pharmacological, biochemical and behavioral analyses of its feeding-suppressive action. *Clinical Neuropharmacology,* 1988, *11,* 551–571.

Leibowitz, S. F., Weiss, G. F., and Suh, J. S. Medial hypothalamic nuclei mediate serotonin's inhibitory effect on feeding behavior. *Pharmacology, Biochemistry, and Behavior,* 1990, *37,* 735–742.

Leibowitz, S. F., Weiss, G. F., Yee, F., and Tretter, J. B. Noradrenergic innervation of the paraventricular nucleus: Specific role in control of carbohydrate ingestions. *Brain Research Bulletin,* 1985, *14,* 561–567.

Le Magnen, J. Hyperphagie provoquée chez le rat blanc par l'altération du méchanisme de satiéte périphérique. *Comptes Rendus de la Société de Biologie,* 1956, *147,* 1753–1757.

Le Magnen, J., and Tallon, S. Enregistrement et analyse préliminaire de la "périodicité alimentaire spontanée" chez le rat blanc. *Journal of Physiology (Paris),* 1963, *55,* 286–297.

Le Magnen, J., and Tallon, S. La périodicité spontanée de la prise d'aliments *ad libitum* du rat blanc. *Journal of Physiology (Paris),* 1966, *58,* 323–349.

Leon, M. Plasticity of olfactory output circuits related to early olfactory learning. *Trends in Neurosciences,* 1987, *10,* 434–438.

Leonard, C. M., Rolls, E. T., Wilson, F. A. W., and Baylis, G. C. Neurons in the amygdala of the monkey with responses selective for faces. *Behavioral Brain Research,* 1985, *15,* 159–176.

Leonard, C. S., Kerman, I., Blaha, G., Taveras, E., and Taylor, B. Interdigitation of nitric oxide synthase-, tyrosine hydroxylase-, and serotonin-containing neurons in and around the laterodorsal and pedunculopontine tegmental nuclei of the guinea pig. *Journal of Comparative Neurology,* 1995, *362,* 411–432.

Leonard, H. L., Lenane, M. C., Swedo, S. E., Rettew, D. C., and Rapoport, J. L. A double-blind comparison of clomipramine and desipramine treatment of severe onychophagia (nail biting). *Archives of General Psychiatry,* 1992, *48,* 821–827.

Leonard, H. L., Swedo, S. E., Rapoport, J. L., Koby, E. V., Lenane, M. C., Cheslow, D. L., and Hamburger, S. D. Treatment of obsessive-compulsive disorder with clomipramine and desipramine in children and adolescents: A double-blind crossover comparison. *Archives of General Psychiatry,* 1989, *46,* 1088–1092.

Lepkovsky, S., Lyman, R., Fleming, D., Nagumo, M., and Dimick, M. Gastrointestinal regulation of water and its effect on food intake and rate of digestion. *American Journal of Physiology,* 1957, *188,* 327–331.

Leshner, A. I. Molecular mechanisms of cocaine addiction. *The New England Journal of Medicine,* 1996, *335,* 128–129.

Lesser, R. Selective preservation of oral spelling without semantics in a case of multi-infarct dementia. *Cortex,* 1989, *25,* 239–250.

Lester, L. S., and Fanselow, M. S. Exposure to a cat produces opioid analgesia in rats. *Behavioral Neuroscience,* 1985, *99,* 756–759.

LeVay, S. A difference in hypothalamic structure between heterosexual and homosexual men. *Science,* 1991, *253,* 1034–1037.

Levenson, R. W., Ekman, P., and Friesen, W. V. Voluntary facial action generates emotion-specific autonomic nervous system activity. *Psychophysiology,* 1990, *27,* 363–384.

Levesque, D., Diaz, J., Pilon, C., Martres, M. P., Giros, B., Souil, E., Schott, D., Morgat, J. L., Schwartz, J. C., and Sokoloff, P. Identification, characterization, and localization of the dopamine-D$_3$ receptor in rat brain using 7-(H-3)hydroxy-N,N-di-normal-propyl-2-aminotetralin. *Proceedings of the National Academy of Sciences, USA*, 1992, *89*, 8155–8159.

Levine, J. D., Gordon, N. C., and Fields, H. L. The role of endorphins in placebo analgesia. In *Advances in Pain Research and Therapy*, Vol. 3, edited by J. J. Bonica, J. C. Liebeskind, and D. Albe-Fessard. New York: Raven Press, 1979.

Li, B.-H., and Rowland, N. E. Effects of vagotomy on cholecystokinin- and dexfenfluramine-induced fos-like immunoreactivity in the rat brain. *Brain Research Bulletin*, 1995, *37*, 589–593.

Li, B.-H., Spector, A. C., and Rowland, N. E. Reversal of dexfenfluramine-induced anorexia and c-Fos/c-Jun expression by lesion in the lateral parabrachial nucleus. *Brain Research*, 1994, *640*, 255–267.

Li, T.-K., Lumeng, L., and Doolittle, D. P. Selective breeding for alcohol preference and associated responses. *Behavioral Genetics*, 1993, *23*, 163–170.

Li, X.-J., Li, S. H., Sharp, A. H., Nucifora, F. C., Schilling, G., Lanahan, A., Worley, P., Snyder, S. H., and Ross, C. A. A huntingtin-associated protein enriched in brain with implications for pathology. *Nature*, 1995, *378*, 392–402.

Li, X.-J., Sharp, A. H., Li, S.-H., Dawson, T. M., Snyder, S. H., and Ross, C. A. Huntingtin-associated protein (HAP1): Discrete neuronal localizations in the brain resemble those of neuronal nitric oxide synthase. *Proceedings of the National Academy of Sciences, USA*, 1996, *93*, 4839–4844.

Liao, D., Hessler, N. A., and Malinow, R. Activation of postsynaptically silent synapses during pairing-induced LTP in CA1 region of hippocampal slice. *Nature*, 1995, *375*, 400–404.

Lichtman, S. W., Pisarska, K., Berman, E. R., Pestone, M., Dowling, H., Offenbacher, E., Weisel, H., Heshka, S., Matthews, D. E., and Heymsfield, S. B. Discrepancy between self-reported and actual caloric intake and exercise in obese subjects. *New England Journal of Medicine*, 1992, *327*, 1893–1898.

Liljequist, S. The competitive NMDA receptor antagonist, CGP 39551, inhibits ethanol withdrawal seizures. *European Journal of Pharmacology*, 1991, *192*, 197–198.

Lind, R. W., and Johnson, A. K. Central and peripheral mechanisms mediating angiotensin-induced thirst. In *The Renin Angiotensin System in the Brain*, edited by D. Ganten, M. Printz, M. I. Phillips, and B. A. Schölkens. Berlin: Springer-Verlag, 1982.

Lind, R. W., Thunhorst, R. L., and Johnson, A. K. The subfornical organ and the integration of multiple factors in thirst. *Physiology and Behavior*, 1984, *32*, 69–74.

Lindemann, B. Taste reception. *Physiological Reviews*, 1996, *76*, 719–766.

Lindvall, O. Dopamine pathways in the rat brain. In *The Neurobiology of Dopamine*, edited by A. S. Horn, J. Korb, and B. H. C. Westerink. New York: Academic Press, 1979.

Lisk, R. D., Pretlow, R. A., and Friedman, S. Hormonal stimulation necessary for elicitation of maternal nest-building in the mouse (*Mus musculus*). *Animal Behaviour*, 1969, *17*, 730–737.

Liuzzi, F. J., and Lasek, R. J. Astrocytes block axonal regeneration in mammals by activating the physiological stop pathway. *Science*, 1987, *237*, 642–645.

Livingstone, M. S., and Hubel, D. H. Anatomy and physiology of a color system in the primate visual cortex. *Journal of Neuroscience*, 1984, *4*, 309–356.

Livingstone, M. S., and Hubel, D. H. Psychophysical evidence for separate channels for the perception of form, color, movement, and depth. *Journal of Neuroscience*, 1987, *7*, 3416–3468.

Livingstone, M. S., and Hubel, D. Segregation of form, color, movement, and depth: Anatomy, physiology, and perception. *Science*, 1988, *240*, 740–749.

Ljungberg, T., Apicella, P., and Schultz, W. Responses of monkey dopamine neurons during learning of behavioral reactions. *Journal of Neurophysiology*, 1992, *67*, 145–163.

Loeb, G. E. Cochlear prosthetics. *Annual Review of Neuroscience*, 1990, *13*, 357–371.

Loewenstein, W. R., and Mendelson, M. Components of receptor adaptation in a Pacinian corpuscle. *Journal of Physiology (London)*, 1965, *177*, 377–397.

Logan, F. A. Decision making by rats: Delay versus amount of reward. *Journal of Comparative and Physiological Psychology*, 1965, *59*, 1–12.

Logothetis, N. K., Pauls, J., and Poggio, T. Shape representation in the inferior temporal cortex of monkeys. *Current Biology*, 1995, *5*, 552–563.

Lømo, T. Frequency potentiation of excitatory synaptic activity in the dentate area of the hippocampal formation. *Acta Physiologica Scandinavica*, 1966, *68*(Suppl. 227), 128.

Loscher, W., Annies, R., and Honack, D. The N-methyl-D-aspartate receptor antagonist MK-801 induces increases in dopamine and serotonin metabolism in several brain regions of rats. *Neuroscience Letters*, 1991, *128*, 191–194.

Lowe, T. L., Tanaka, K., Seashore, M. R., Young, J. G., and Cohen, D. J. Detection of phenylketonuria in autistic and psychotic children. *Journal of the American Medical Association*, 1980, *243*, 126–128.

Lu, E., Willard, D., Patel, I. R., Kadwell, S., Overton, L., Kost, T., Luther, M., Chen, W., Woychik, R. P., and Wilkison, W. O. Agouti protein is an antagonist of the melanocyte-stimulating-hormone receptor. *Nature*, 1994, *371*, 799–802.

Lucey, J. V., Costa, D. C., Busatto, G., Pilowsky, L. S., Marks, I. M., Ell, P. J., and Kerwin, R. W. Caudate regional cerebral blood flow in obsessive-compulsive disorder, panic disorder and healthy controls on single photon emission computerised tomography. *Psychiatry Research: Neuroimaging,* 1997, *74,* 25–33.

Lupien, S., Lecours, A. R., Schwartz, G., Sharma, S., Hauger, R. L., Meaney, M. J., and Nair, N. P. V. Longitudinal study of basal cortixol levels in healthy elderly subjects: Evidence for subgroups. *Neurobiology of Aging,* 1996, *17,* 95–105.

Luppino, G., Matelli, M., Camarda, R., and Rizzolatti, G. Corticocortical connections of area F3 (SMA proper) and area F6 (pre-SMA) in the macaque monkey. *Journal of Comparative Neurology,* 1993, *228,* 114–140.

Lydic, R., Baghdoyan, H. A., Hibbard, L., Bonyak, E. V., DeJoseph, M. R., and Hawkins, R. A. Regional brain glucose metabolism is altered during rapid eye movement sleep in the cat: A preliminary study. *Journal of Comparative Neurology,* 1991, *304,* 517–529.

Lydic, R., McCarley, R. W., and Hobson, J. A. The time-course of dorsal raphe discharge, PGO waves and muscle tone averaged across multiple sleep cycles. *Brain Research,* 1983, *274,* 365–370.

Lynch, G., Larson, J., Kelso, S., Barrionuevo, G., and Schottler, F. Intracellular injections of EGTA block induction of long-term potentiation. *Nature,* 1984, *305,* 719–721.

Lynch, G., Larson, J., Staubli, U., and Granger, R. Variants of synaptic potentiation and different types of memory operations in hippocampus and related structures. In *Memory: Organization and Locus of Change,* edited by L. R. Squire, N. M. Weinberger, G. Lynch, and J. L. McGaugh. New York: Oxford University Press, 1991.

Lytton, W. W., and Brust, J. C. M. Direct dyslexia: Preserved oral reading of real words in Wernicke's aphasia. *Brain,* 1989, *112,* 583–594.

MacLean, H. E., Warne, G. L., and Zajac, J. D. Defects of androgen receptor function: From sex reversal to motor-neuron disease. *Molecular and Cellular Endocrinology,* 1995, *112,* 133–141.

MacLean, P. D. Psychosomatic disease and the "visceral brain": Recent developments bearing on the Papez theory of emotion. *Psychosomatic Medicine,* 1949, *11,* 338–353.

Madden, P. A. F., Heath, A. C., Rosenthal, N. E., and Martin, N. G. Seasonal changes in mood and behavior: The role of genetic factors. *Archives of General Psychiatry,* 1996, *53,* 47–55.

Madsen, P. L., Holm, S., Vorstrup, S., Friberg, L., Lassen, N. A., and Wildschiodtz, G. Human regional cerebral blood flow during rapid-eye-movement sleep. *Journal of Cerebral Blood Flow and Metabolism,* 1991, *11,* 502–507.

Magee, J. C., and Johnston, D. A synaptically controlled, associative signal for Hebbian plasticity in hippocampal neurons. *Science,* 1997, *275,* 209–213.

Maier, S. F., Drugan, R. C., and Grau, J. W. Controllability, coping behavior, and stress-induced analgesia in the rat. *Pain,* 1982, *12,* 47–56.

Maksay, G., and Ticku, M. K. Dissociation of [^{35}S]t-butylbicyclophosphorothionate binding differentiates convulsant and depressant drugs that modulate GABAergic transmission. *Journal of Neurochemistry,* 1985, *44,* 480–486.

Malach, R., Reppas, J. B., Benson, R. R., Kwong, K. K., Jiang, H., Kennedy, W. A., Ledden, P. J., Brady, T. J., Rosen, B. R., and Tootell, R. B. H. Object-related activity revealed by functional magnetic resonance imaging in human occipital cortex. *Proceedings of the National Academy of Sciences, USA,* 1995, *92,* 8135–8139.

Malamut, B. L., Graff-Radford, N., Chawluk, J., Grossman, R. I., and Gur, R. C. Memory in a case of bilateral thalamic infarction. *Neurology,* 1992, *42,* 163–169.

Maldonado, R., Blendy, J. A., Tzavara, E., Gass, P., Roques, B. P., Hanoune, J., and Schütz, G. Reduction of morphine abstinence in mice with a mutation in the gene encoding CREB. *Science,* 1996, *273,* 657–659.

Maldonado, R., Stinus, L., Gold, L. H., and Koob, G. F. Role of different brain structures in the expression of the physical morphine-withdrawal syndrome. *Journal of Pharmacology and Experimental Therapeutics,* 1992, *261,* 669–677.

Malenka, R. C., Kauer, J. A., Zucker, R. S., and Nicoll, R. A. Postsynaptic calcium is sufficient for potentiation of hippocampal synaptic transmission. *Science,* 1988, *242,* 81–84.

Mallick, B. N., Siegel, J. M., and Fahringer, H. Changes in pontine unit activity with REM sleep deprivation. *Brain Research,* 1989, *515,* 94–98.

Mallow, G. K. The relationship between aggression and cycle stage in adult female rhesus monkeys (*Macaca mulatta*). *Dissertation Abstracts,* 1979, *39,* 3194.

Malsbury, C. W. Facilitation of male rat copulatory behavior by electrical stimulation of the medial preoptic area. *Physiology and Behavior,* 1971, *7,* 797–805.

Mann, F., Bowsher, D., Mumford, J., Lipton, S., and Miles, J. Treatment of intractable pain by acupuncture. *Lancet,* 1973, *2,* 57–60.

Mann, M. A., Konen, C., and Svare, B. The role of progesterone in pregnancy-induced aggression in mice. *Hormones and Behavior,* 1984, *18,* 140–160.

Manning, L., and Campbell, R. Optic aphasia with spared action naming: A description and possible loci of impairment. *Neuropsychologia,* 1992, *30,* 587–592.

Mantyh, P. W. Connections of midbrain periaqueductal gray in the monkey. II. Descending efferent projections. *Journal of Neurophysiology,* 1983, *49,* 582–594.

Manuck, S. B., Kaplan, J. R., and Clarkson, T. B. Behaviorally-induced heart rate reactivity and atherosclerosis in cynomolgous monkeys. *Psychosomatic Medicine,* 1983, *45,* 95–108.

Manuck, S. B., Kaplan, J. R., and Matthews, K. A. Behavioral antecedents of coronary heart disease and atherosclerosis. *Arteriosclerosis,* 1986, *6,* 1–14.

Maquet, P. Sleep function(s) and cerebral metabolism. *Behavioural Brain Research,* 1995, *69,* 75–83.

Maquet, P., Dive, D., Salmon, E., Sadzot, B., Franco, G., Poirrier, R., Von Frenckell, R., and Franck, G. Cerebral glucose utilization during sleep-wake cycle in man determined by positron emission tomography and [18F]2-fluoro-2-deoxy-D-glucose method. *Brain Research*, 1990, *513*, 136–143.

Marczynski, T. J., and Urbancic, M. Animal models of chronic anxiety and "fearlessness." *Brain Research Bulletin*, 1988, *21*, 483–490.

Maren, S., and Fanselow, M. S. Synaptic plasticity in the basolateral amygdala induced by hippocampal formation stimulation in vivo. *Journal of Neuroscience*, 1995, *15*, 7548–7564.

Margolin, D. I., and Goodman-Schulman, R. Oral and written spelling impairments. In *Cognitive Neuropsychology in Clinical Practice*, edited by D. I. Margolin. New York: Oxford University Press, 1992.

Margolin, D. I., Marcel, A. J., and Carlson, N. R. Common mechanisms in dysnomia and post-semantic surface dyslexia: Processing deficits and selective attention. In *Surface Dyslexia: Neuropsychological and Cognitive Studies of Phonological Reading*, edited by M. Coltheart. London: Lawrence Erlbaum Associates, 1985.

Margolin, D. I., and Walker, J. A. Personal communication, 1981.

Mark, G. P., Blander, D. S., Hernandez, L., and Hoebel, B. G. Effects of salt intake, rehydration and conditioned taste aversion (CTA) development on dopamine output in the rat nucleus accumbens. *Appetite*, 1989, *12*, 224.

Marks, G. A., Shaffery, J. P., Oksenberg, A., Speciale, S. G., and Roffwarg, H. P. A functional role for REM sleep in brain maturation. *Behavioural Brain Research*, 1995, *69*, 1–11.

Marrocco, R. T., Witte, E. A., and Davidson, M. C. Arousal systems. *Current Opinion in Neurobiology*, 1994, *4*, 166–170.

Marshall, J. C., and Newcombe, F. Patterns of paralexia: A psycholinguistic approach. *Journal of Psycholinguistic Research*, 1973, *2*, 175–199.

Martinot, J.-L., Peron-Magnan, P., Huret, J.-D., Mazoyer, B., Baron, J.-C., Boulenger, J. P., Loc'h, C., Maziere, B., Caillard, V., Loo, H., and Syrota, A. Striatal D_2 dopaminergic receptors assessed with positron emission tomography and [^{76}Br]bromospiperone in untreated schizophrenic patients. *American Journal of Psychiatry*, 1990, *147*, 44–50.

Mas, M. Neurobiological correlates of masculine sexual behavior. *Neuroscience and Biobehavioral Reviews*, 1995, *19*, 261–277.

Mather, P., Nicolaïdis, S., and Booth, D. A. Compensatory and conditioned feeding responses to scheduled glucose infusions in the rat. *Nature*, 1978, *273*, 461–463.

Matsuda, L. A., Lolait, S. J., Brownstein, M. J., Young, A. C., and Bonner, T. I. Structure of a cannabinoid receptor and functional expression of the cloned cDNA. *Nature*, 1990, *346*, 561–564.

Matsuyama, S., Nei, K., and Tanaka, C. Regulation of glutamate release via NMDA and 5-HT$_1$ receptors in guinea pig dentate gyrus. *Brain Research*, 1996, *728*, 175–180.

Matteo, S., and Rissman, E. F. Increased sexual activity during the midcycle portion of the human menstrual cycle. *Hormones and Behavior*, 1984, *18*, 249–255.

Matthes, H. W. D., Maldonado, R., Simonin, F., Valverde, O., Slowe, S., Kitchen, I., Befort, K., Dierich, A., Le Meur, M., Dolle, P., Tzavara, E., Hanoune, J., Roques, B. P., and Kieffer, B. L. Loss of morphine-induced analgesia, reward effect and withdrawal symptoms in mice lacking the Mu-opioid-receptor gene. *Nature*, 1996, *383*, 819–823.

Matthews, D. B., Simson, P. E., and Best, P. J. Ethanol alters spatial processing of hippocampal place cells: A mechanism for impaired navigation when intoxicated. *Alcoholism—Clinical and Experimental Research*, 1996, *20*, 404–407.

Maunsell, J. H. R. Functional visual streams. *Current Opinion in Neurobiology*, 1992, *2*, 506–510.

Mawson, A. R. Anorexia nervosa and the regulation of intake: A review. *Psychological Medicine*, 1974, *4*, 289–308.

Mayer, D. J., and Liebeskind, J. C. Pain reduction by focal electrical stimulation of the brain: An anatomical and behavioral analysis. *Brain Research*, 1974, *68*, 73–93.

Mayer, D. J., Price, D. D., Rafii, A., and Barber, J. Acupuncture hypalgesia: Evidence for activation of a central control system as a mechanism of action. In *Advances in Pain Research and Therapy*, Vol. 1, edited by J. J. Bonica and D. Albe-Fessard. New York: Raven Press, 1976.

Mazur, A. Hormones, aggression, and dominance in humans. In *Hormones and Aggressive Behavior*, edited by B. B. Svare. New York: Plenum Press, 1983.

Mazur, A., and Lamb, T. Testosterone, status, and mood in human males. *Hormones and Behavior*, 1980, *14*, 236–246.

McBride, W. J., Bodart, B., Lumeng, L., and Li, T. K. Association between low contents of dopamine and serotonin in the nucleus accumbens and high alcohol preference. *Alcoholism: Clinical and Experimental Research*, 1995, *19*, 1420–1422.

McBride, W. J., Murphy, J. M., Gatto, G. J., Levy, A. D., Lumeng, L., and Li, T.-K. Serotonin and dopamine systems regulating alcohol self-administration. *Alcohol and Alcoholism*, 1991, *1*(Suppl.), 411–416.

McCann, M. J., Verbalis, J. G., and Stricker, E. M. LiCl and CCK inhibit gastric emptying and feeding and stimulate OT secretion in rats. *American Journal of Physiology*, 1989, *256*, R463–R468.

McCarley, R. W., and Hobson, J. A. The form of dreams and the biology of sleep. In *Handbook of Dreams: Research, Theory, and Applications*, edited by B. Wolman. New York: Van Nostrand Reinhold, 1979.

McCarthy, G., Blamire, A. M., Rothman, D. L., Gruetter, R., and Shulman, R. G. Echo-planat magnetic resonance imaging studies of frontal cortex activation during word generation in humans. *Proceedings of the National Academy of Sciences, USA*, 1993, *90*, 4952–4956.

McCarthy, M. M., Kleopoulos, S. P., Mobbs, C. V., and Pfaff, D. W. Infusion of antisense oligodeoxynucleotides to the oxytocin receptor in the ventromedial hypothalamus reduces estrogen-induced sexual receptivity and oxytocin receptor binding in the female rat. *Neuroendocrinology,* 1994, *59,* 432–440.

McCarthy, R. A., and Warrington, E. K. Evidence for modality-specific meaning systems in the brain. *Nature,* 1988, *334,* 428–435.

McCarthy, R. A., and Warrington, E. K. *Cognitive Neuropsychology: A Clinical Introduction.* San Diego: Academic Press, 1990.

McCaul, K. D., Gladue, B. A., and Joppa, M. Winning, losing, mood, and testosterone. *Hormones and Behavior,* 1992, *26,* 486–504.

McClintock, M. K. Menstrual synchrony and suppression. *Nature,* 1971, *229,* 244–245.

McClintock, M. K., and Adler, N. T. The role of the female during copulation in wild and domestic Norway rats (*Rattus norvegicus*). *Behaviour,* 1978, *67,* 67–96.

McDonald, R. J., and White, N. M. A triple dissociation of memory systems: Hippocampus, amygdala, and dorsal striatum. *Behavioral Neuroscience,* 1993, *107,* 3–22.

McGinty, D., Szymusiak, R., and Thomson, D. Preoptic/anterior hypothalamic warming increases EEG delta frequency activity within non-rapid eye movement sleep. *Brain Research,* 1994, *667,* 273–277.

McGinty, D. J., and Sterman, M. B. Sleep suppression after basal forebrain lesions in the cat. *Science,* 1968, *160,* 1253–1255.

McGrath, J., Welham, J., and Pemberton, M. Month of birth, hemisphere of birth and schizophrenia. *British Journal of Psychiatry,* 1995, *167,* 783–785.

McGrath, M. J., and Cohen, D. B. REM sleep facilitation of adaptive waking behavior: A review of the literature. *Psychological Bulletin,* 1978, *85,* 24–57.

McGregor, A., and Roberts, D.C. S. Dopaminergic antagonism within the nucleus accumbens or the amygdala produces differential effects on intravenous cocaine self-administration under fixed and progressive ratio schedules of reinforcement. *Brain Research,* 1993, *624,* 245–252.

McHugh, T. J., Blum, K. I., Tsien, J. Z., Tonegawa, S., and Wilson, M. A. Impaired hippocampal representation of space in CA1-specific NMDAR1 knockout mice. *Cell,* 1996, *87,* 1339–1349.

McIver, B., Connacher, A., Whittle, I., Baylis, P., and Thompson, C. Adipsic hypothalamic diabetes insipidus after clipping of anterior communicating artery aneurysm. *British Medical Journal,* 1991, *303,* 1465–1467.

McKenna, T. M., Weinberger, N. M., and Diamond, D. M. Responses of single auditory cortical neurons to tone sequences. *Brain Research,* 1989, *481,* 142–153.

McLaughlin, S. K., McKinnon, P. J., Robichon, A., Spickofsky, N., and Margolskee, R. F. Gustducin and transducin: A tale of 2 G-proteins. *CIBA Foundation Symposia,* 1993, *179,* 186–200.

McMackin, D., Cockburn, J., Anslow, P., and Gaffan, D. Correlation of fornix damage with memory impairment in 6 cases of colloid cyst removal. *Acta Neurochirurigica,* 1995, *135,* 12–18.

McNaughton, B. L., Leonard, B., and Chen, L. Cortical-hippocampal interactions and cognitive mapping: A hypothesis based on reintegration of the parietal and inferotemporal pathways for visual processing. *Psychobiology,* 1989, *17,* 230–235.

Meddis, R., Pearson, A., and Langford, G. An extreme case of healthy insomnia. *Electroencephalography and Clinical Neurophysiology,* 1973, *35,* 213–214.

Mednick, S. A., Machon, R. A., and Huttunen, M. O. An update on the Helsinki influenza project. *Archives of General Psychiatry,* 1990, *47,* 292.

Meesters, Y., Jansen, J. H. C., Beersma, D. G. M., Bouhuys, A. L., and Van den Hoofdakker, R. H. Light therapy for seasonal affective disorder. The effects of timing. *British Journal of Psychiatry,* 1995, *166,* 607–612.

Mehlman, P. T., Higley, J. D., Faucher, I., Lilly, A. A., Taub, D. M., Vickers, J., Suomi, S. J., and Linnoila, M. Correlation of CSF 5-HIAA concentration with sociality and the timing of emigration in free-ranging primates. *American Journal of Psychiatry,* 1995, *152,* 907–913.

Meijer, J. H., and Rietveld, W. J. Neurophysiology of the suprachiasmatic circadian pacemaker in rodents. *Physiological Reviews,* 1989, *69,* 671–707.

Melander, T., Fuxe, K., Harfstrand, A., Eneroth, P., and Hökfelt, T. Effects of intraventricular injections of galanin on neuroendocrine functions in the male rat: Possible involvement of hypothalamic catecholamine neuronal systems. *Acta Physiologica Scandanavica,* 1987, *131,* 25–32.

Melges, F. T. *Time and the Inner Future: A Temporal Approach to Psychiatric Disorders.* New York: John Wiley & Sons, 1982.

Meltzer, H. Y. Treatment of the neuroleptic-nonresponsive schizophrenic patient. *Schizophrenia Bulletin,* 1992, *18,* 515–542.

Melzak, R. Phantom limbs. *Scientific American,* 1992, *266*(4), 120–126.

Menco, B. P. M., Bruch, R. C., Dau, B., and Danho, W. Ultrastructural localization of olfactory transduction components: The G protein subunit G_{olf} and type III adenylyl cyclase. *Neuron,* 1992, *8,* 441–453.

Mercer, J. G., Hoggard, N., Williams, L. M., Lawrence, C. B., Hannah, L. T., Morgan, P. J., and Trayhurn, P. Coexpression of leptin receptor and preproneuropeptide Y mRNA in arcuate nucleus of mouse hypothalamus. *Journal of Neuroendocrinology,* 1996, *8,* 733–735.

Meredith, M. Chronic recording of vomeronasal pump activation in awake behaving hamsters. *Physiology and Behavior,* 1994, *56,* 345–354.

Meredith, M., and O'Connell, R. J. Efferent control of stimulus access to the hamster vomeronasal organ. *Journal of Physiology,* 1979, *286,* 301–316.

Mereu, G., Yoon, K.-W. P., Boi, V., Gessa, G. L., Naes, L., and Westfall, T. C. Preferential stimulation of ventral tegmental area dopaminergic neurons by nicotine. *European Journal of Pharmacology*, 1987, *141*, 395–400.

Mesulam, M.-M. Frontal cortex and behavior. *Annals of Neurology*, 1986, *19*, 320–325.

Metter, E. J. Brain-behavior relationships in aphasia studied by positron emission tomography. *Annals of the New York Academy of Sciences*, 1991, *620*, 153–164.

Meyer-Bahlburg, H. F. L. Psychoendocrine research on sexual orientation: Current status and future options. *Progress in Brain Research*, 1984, *63*, 375–398.

Mikulincer, M., and Solomon, Z. Attributional style and combat-related posttraumatic stress disorder. *Journal of Abnormal Psychology*, 1988, *97*, 308–313.

Miller, E. K., Erickson, C. A., and Desimone, R. Neural mechanisms of visual working memory in prefrontal cortex of the macaque. *Journal of Neuroscience*, 1996, *16*, 5154–5167.

Miller, M. T., and Strömland, K. Thalidomide embryopathy: An insight into autism. *Teratology*, 1993, *47*, 387–388.

Miller, N. E. Understanding the use of animals in behavioral research: Some critical issues. *Annals of the New York Academy of Sciences*, 1983, *406*, 113–118.

Miller, N. E., Sampliner, R. I., and Woodrow, P. Thirst reducing effects of water by stomach fistula versus water by mouth, measured by both a consummatory and an instrumental response. *Journal of Comparative and Physiological Psychology*, 1957, *50*, 1–5.

Miller, V. M., and Best, P. J. Spatial correlates of hippocampal unit activity are altered by lesions of the fornix and entorhinal cortex. *Brain Research*, 1980, *194*, 311–323.

Milner, A. D., Perrett, D. I., Johnston, R. S., and Benson, P. J. Perception and action in "visual form agnosia." *Brain*, 1991, *114*, 405–428.

Milner, B. Memory disturbance after bilateral hippocampal lesions. In *Cognitive Processes and the Brain*, edited by P. Milner and S. Glickman. Princeton, N.J.: Van Nostrand, 1965.

Milner, B. Memory and the temporal regions of the brain. In *Biology of Memory*, edited by K. H. Pribram and D. E. Broadbent. New York: Academic Press, 1970.

Milner, B., Corkin, S., and Teuber, H.-L. Further analysis of the hippocampal amnesic syndrome: 14-year follow-up study of H. M. *Neuropsychologia*, 1968, *6*, 317–338.

Minami, S., Kamegai, J., Sugihara, H., Suzuki, N., Higuchi, H., and Wakabayashi, I. Central glucoprivation evoked by administration of 2-deoxy-D-glucose induces expression of the c-fos gene in a subpopulation of neuropeptide Y neurons in the rat hypothalamus. *Molecular Brain Research*, 1995, *33*, 305–310.

Mindus, P., Rasmussen, S. A., and Lindquist, C. Neurosurgical treatment for refractory obsessive-compulsive disorder: Implications for understanding frontal lobe function. *Journal of Neuropsychiatry and Clinical Neurosciences*, 1994, *6*, 467–477.

Mirmiran, M. The function of fetal/neonatal rapid eye movement sleep. *Behavioural Brain Research*, 1995, *69*, 13–22.

Miselis, R. R., Weiss, M. L., and Shapiro, R. E. Modulation of the visceral neuraxis. In *Circumventricular Organs and Body Fluids*, edited by P. M. Gross. Boca Raton, Fla.: CRC Press, 1987.

Mishkin, M. Visual mechanisms beyond the striate cortex. In *Frontiers in Physiological Psychology*, edited by R. W. Russell. New York: Academic Press, 1966.

Mishkin, M., Ungerleider, L. G., and Macko, K. Object vision and spatial vision: Two cortical pathways. *Trends in Neuroscience*, 1983, *6*, 414–417.

Mitchell, J. E. Psychopharmacology of eating disorders. *Annals of the New York Academy of Sciences*, 1989, *575*, 41–49.

Mitler, M. M. Evaluation of treatment with stimulants in narcolepsy. *Sleep*, 1994, *17*, S103–S106.

Mitsuno, K., Sasa, M., Ishihara, I., Ishikawa, M., and Kikuchi, H. LTP of mossy fiber-stimulated potentials in CA3 during learning in rats. *Physiology and Behavior*, 1994, *55*, 633–638.

Miyauchi, S., Takino, R., and Azakami, M. Evoked potentials during REM sleep reflect dreaming. *Electroencephalography and Clinical Neurophysiology*, 1990, *76*, 19–28.

Moghaddam, B., and Bunney, B. S. Differential effect of cocaine on extracellular dopamine levels in rat medial prefrontal cortex and nucleus accumbens: Comparison to amphetamine. *Synapse*, 1989, *4*, 156–161.

Mok, D., and Mogenson, G. J. Contribution of zona incerta to osmotically induced drinking in rats. *American Journal of Physiology*, 1986, *251*, R823–R832.

Moldin, S. O., Reich, T., and Rice, J. P. Current perspectives on the genetics of unipolar depression. *Behavioral Genetics*, 1991, *21*, 211–242.

Mollon, J. D. "Tho' she kneel'd in that place where they grew . . . ": The uses and origins of primate colour vision. *Journal of Experimental Biology*, 1989, *146*, 21–38.

Moltz, H., Lubin, M., Leon, M., and Numan, M. Hormonal induction of maternal behavior in the ovariectomized nulliparous rat. *Physiology and Behavior*, 1970, *5*, 1373–1377.

Monaghan, D. T., and Cotman, C. W. Distribution of NMDA-sensitive L-^{3}H-glutamate binding sites in rat brain as determined by quantitative autoradiography. *Journal of Neuroscience*, 1985, *5*, 2909–2919.

Money, J. Components of eroticism in man: Cognitional rehearsals. In *Recent Advances in Biological Psychiatry*, edited by J. Wortis. New York: Grune & Stratton, 1960.

Money, J., and Ehrhardt, A. *Man & Woman, Boy & Girl*. Baltimore: Johns Hopkins University Press, 1972.

Money, J., Schwartz, M., and Lewis, V. G. Adult erotosexual status and fetal hormonal masculinization and demasculinization: 46,XX congenital virilizing adrenal hyperplasia and 46,XY androgen-insensitivity syndrome compared. *Psychoneuroendocrinology*, 1984, *9*, 405–414.

Montero, S., Fuentes, J. A., and Fernandez-Tome, P. Lesions of the ventral noradrenergic bundle prevent the rise in blood pressure induced by social deprivation stress in the rat. *Cellular and Molecular Neurobiology*, 1990, *10*, 497–505.

Monti-Bloch, L., Jennings-White, C., Dolberg, D. S., and Berliner, D. L. The human vomeronasal system. *Psychoneuroendocrinology*, 1994, *19*, 673–686.

Mook, D. Some determinants of preference and aversion in the rat. *Annals of the New York Academy of Sciences*, 1969, *157*, 1158–1170.

Moore, B. O., and Deutsch, J. A. An antiemetic is antidotal to the satiety effects of cholecystokinin. *Nature*, 1985, *315*, 321–322.

Moore, C. L. Interaction of species-typical environmental and hormonal factors in sexual differentiation of behavior. *Annals of the New York Academy of Sciences*, 1986, *474*, 108–119.

Moore, C. L., Dou, H., and Juraska, J. M. Maternal stimulation affects the number of motor neurons in a sexually dimorphic nucleus of the lumbar spinal cord. *Brain Research*, 1992, *572*, 52–56.

Moore, R. Y. Neural control of the pineal gland. *Behavioural Brain Research*, 1995, *73*, 125–130.

Moore, R. Y., and Bernstein, M. E. Synaptogenesis in the rat suprachiasmatic nucleus demonstrated by electron microscopy and synapsin I immunoreactivity. *Journal of Neuroscience*, 1989, *9*, 2161–2162.

Moore, R. Y., and Card, J. P. Intergeniculate leaflet: An anatomically and functionally distinct subdivision of the lateral geniculate complex. *Journal of Comparative Neurology*, 1994, *344*, 403–430.

Moore, R. Y., Card, J. P., and Riley, J. N. The suprachiasmatic hypothalamic nucleus: Neuronal ultrastructure. *Neuroscience Abstracts*, 1980, *6*, 758.

Moore, R. Y., and Eichler, V. B. Loss of a circadian adrenal corticosterone rhythm following suprachiasmatic lesions in the rat. *Brain Research*, 1972, *42*, 201–206.

Moore-Gillon, M. J., and Fitzsimons, J. T. Pulmonary vein-atrial junction stretch receptors and the inhibition of drinking. *American Journal of Physiology*, 1982, *242*, R452–R457.

Morairty, S. R., Szymusiak, R., Thomson, D., and McGinty, D. J. Selective increases in non-rapid eye movement sleep following whole body heating in rats. *Brain Research*, 1993, *617*, 10–16.

Morales, F. R., Boxer, P. A., and Chase, M. H. Behavioral state-specific inhibitory postsynaptic potentials impinge on cat lumbar motoneurons during active sleep. *Experimental Neurology*, 1987, *98*, 418–435.

Moran, T. H., Shnayder, L., Hostetler, A. M., and McHugh, P. R. Pylorectomy reduces the satiety action of cholecystokinin. *American Journal of Physiology*, 1989, *255*, R1059–R1063.

Morin, L. P., Blanchard, J., and Moore, R. Y. Intergeniculate leaflet and suprachiasmatic nucleus organization and connections in the golden hamster. *Visual Neuroscience*, 1992, *8*, 219–230.

Morrell, M. J. Sexual dysfunction in epilepsy. *Epilepsia*, 1991, *32*, S38–S45.

Morrell, M. J., Sperling, M. R., Stecker, M., and Dichter, M. A. Sexual dysfunction in partial epilepsy: A deficit in physiologic sexual arousal. *Neurology*, 1994, *44*, 243–247.

Morris, G. O., Williams, H. L., and Lubin, A. Misperception and disorientation during sleep deprivation. *Archives of General Psychiatry*, 1960, *2*, 247–254.

Morris, J. S., Frith, C. D., Perrett, D. I., Rowland, D., Young, A. W., Calder, A. J., and Dolan, R. J. A differential neural response in the human amygdala to fearful and happy facial expressions. *Nature*, 1996, *383*, 812–815.

Morris, N. M., Udry, J. R., Khan-Dawood, F., and Dawood, M. Y. Marital sex frequency and midcycle female testosterone. *Archives of Sexual Behavior*, 1987, *16*, 27–37.

Morris, R. G. M., Garrud, P., Rawlins, J. N. P., and O'Keefe, J. Place navigation impaired in rats with hippocampal lesions. *Nature*, 1982, *297*, 681–683.

Moscovitch, M., Kapur, S., Koehler, S., and Houle, S. Distinct neural correlates of visual long-term memory for spatial location and object identity: A positron emission tomography study in humans. *Proceedings of the National Academy of Sciences, USA*, 1995, *92*, 3721–3725.

Moscovitch, M., and Olds, J. Asymmetries in emotional facial expressions and their possible relation to hemispheric specialization. *Neuropsychologia*, 1982, *20*, 71–81.

Motta, V., Penha, K., and Brandao, M. L. Effects of microinjections of mu-receptor and kappa-receptor agonists into the dorsal periaqueductal gray of rats submitted to the plus-maze test. *Psychopharmacology*, 1995, *120*, 470–474.

Mountcastle, V. B. Modality and topographic properties of single neurons of cat's somatic sensory cortex. *Journal of Neurophysiology*, 1957, *20*, 408–434.

Mountcastle, V. B., Lynch, J. C., Georgopoulos, A., Sakata, H., and Acuna, C. Posterior parietal association cortex: Command functions for operations within extra-personal space. *Journal of Neurophysiology*, 1975, *38*, 871–908.

Mountjoy, K. G., Mortrud, M. T., Low, M. J., Simerly, R. B., and Cone, R. D. Localization of the melanocortin-r receptor (MC4-R) in neuroendocrine and autonomic control circuits in the brain. *Molecular Endocrinology*, 1994, *8*, 1298–1308.

Mucha, R. F., and Herz, A. Motivational properties of kappa and mu opioid receptor agonists studied with place and taste preference conditioning. *Psychopharmacology*, 1985, *86*, 274–280.

Mukhametov, L. M. Sleep in marine mammals. In *Sleep Mechanisms*, edited by A. A. Borbély and J. L. Valatx. Munich: Springer-Verlag, 1984.

Muller, R. U., and Kubie, J. L. The effects of changes in the environment on the spatial firing of hippocampal complex-spike cells. *Journal of Neuroscience*, 1987, *7*, 1935–1950.

Munro, J. F., Stewart, I. C., Seidelin, P. H., Mackenzie, H. S., and Dewhurst, N. E. Mechanical treatment for obesity. *Annals of the New York Academy of Sciences*, 1987, *499*, 305–312.

Murphy, J. M., McBride, W. J., Lumeng, L., and Li, T.-K. Contents of monoamines in forebrain regions of alcohol-preferring

(P) and -nonpreferring (NP) lines of rats. *Pharmacology, Biochemistry and Behavior*, 1987, *26*, 389–392.

Murphy, P. J., Badia, P., Myers, B. L., Boecker, M. R., and Wright, K. P. Nonsteroidal anti-inflammatory drugs affect normal sleep patterns in humans. *Physiology and Behavior*, 1994, *55*, 1063–1066.

Murray, A. M., Hyde, T. M., Knable, M. B., Herman, M. M., Bigelow, L. B., Carter, J. M., Weinberger, D. R., and Kleinman, J. E. Distribution of putative D4 dopamine receptors in postmortem striatum from patients with schizophrenia. *Journal of Neuroscience*, 1995, *15*, 2186–2191.

Murray, A. M., Ryoo, H., Gurevich, E., and Joyce, J. N. Localization of dopamine D_3 receptors to mesolimbic and D_2 receptors to mesostriatal regions of human forebrain. *Proceedings of the National Academy of Sciences, USA*, 1994, *91*, 11271–11275.

Museo, G., and Wise, R. A. Place preference conditioning with ventral tegmental injections of cystine. *Life Sciences*, 1994, *55*, 1179–1186.

Mushiake, H., Inase, M., and Tanji, J. Neuronal activity in the primate premotor, supplementary, and precentral motor cortex during visually guided and internally determined sequential movements. *Journal of Neurophysiology*, 1991, *66*, 705–718.

Myers, M. P., Wagner-Smith, K., Rotherfluh-Hilfiker, A., and Young, M. W. Light-induced degradation of TIMELESS and entrainment of the *Drosophila* circadian clock. *Science*, 1996, *271*, 1736–1740.

Myers, R. D., Wooten, M. H., Ames, C. D., and Nyce, J. W. Anorexic action of a new potential neuropeptide Y antagonist [D-Tyr27,36,D-Thr32]-NPY (27–36) infused into the hypothalamus of the rat. *Brain Research Bulletin*, 1995, *37*, 237–245.

Nadeau, S. E. Impaired grammar with normal fluency and phonology. *Brain*, 1988, *111*, 1111–1137.

Nader, M. A., and Mach, R. H. Self-administration of the dopamine D_3 agonist 7-OH-DPAT in rhesus monkeys is modified by prior cocaine exposure. *Psychopharmacology*, 1996, *125*, 13–22.

Naeser, M. A., Palumbo, C. L., Helm-Estabrooks, N., Stiassny-Eder, D., and Albert, M. L. Severe nonfluency in aphasia: Role of the medial subcallosal fasciculus and other white matter pathways in recovery of spontaneous speech. *Brain*, 1989, *112*, 1–38.

Nafe, J. P., and Wagoner, K. S. The nature of pressure adaptation. *Journal of General Psychology*, 1941, *25*, 323–351.

Naito, K., Osama, H., Ueno, R., Hayaishi, O., Honda, K., and Inoue, S. Suppression of sleep by prostaglandin synthesis inhibitors in unrestrained rats. *Brain Research*, 1988, *453*, 329–336.

Nakahara, D., Ozaki, N., Miura, Y., Miura, H., and Nagatsu, T. Increased dopamine and serotonin metabolism in rat nucleus accumbens produced by intracranial self-stimulation of medial forebrain bundle as measured by in vivo microdialysis. *Brain Research*, 1989, *495*, 178–181.

Nakamura, T., and Gold, G. A cyclic nucleotide-gated conductance in olfactory receptor cilia. *Nature*, 1987, *325*, 442–444.

Nakano, I., and Hirano, A. Loss of large neurons of the medial septal nucleus in an autopsy case of Alzheimer's disease. *Journal of Neuropathology and Experimental Neurology.* 1982, *41*, 341.

Naranjo, C. A., Poulos, C. X., Bremner, K. E., and Lanctot, K. L. Citalopram decreases desirability, liking, and consumption of alcohol in alcohol-dependent drinkers. *Clinical Pharmacology and Therapeutics*, 1992, *51*, 729–739.

Nathans, J., Piantanida, T. P., Eddy, R. L., Shows, T. B., and Hogness, D. S. Molecular genetics of inherited variation in human color vision. *Science*, 1986, *232*, 203–210.

Nauta, W. J. H. Hypothalamic regulation of sleep in rats: Experimental study. *Journal of Neurophysiology*, 1946, *9*, 285–316.

Nauta, W. J. H. Some efferent connections of the prefrontal cortex in the monkey. In *The Frontal Granular Cortex and Behavior*, edited by J. M. Warren and K. Akert. New York: McGraw-Hill, 1964.

Nef, P., Hermansborgmeyer, I., Artierespin, H., Beasley, L., Dionne, V. E., and Heinemann, S. F. Spatial pattern of receptor expression in the olfactory epithelium. *Proceedings of the National Academy of Sciences, USA*, 1992, *89*, 8948–8952.

Neiswanger, K., Kaplan, B. B., and Hill, S. Y. What can the DRD2/alcoholism story teach us about association studies in psychiatric genetics? *American Journal of Medical Genetics*, 1995, *60*, 272–275.

Nermo-Lindquist, E., Kadekaro, M., Terrell, M. L., Nassar, J., Lekan, H., and Freeman, S. Atriopeptin prevents angiotensin II-stimulated glucose utilization in the subfornical organ. *Peptides*, 1990, *11*, 837–842.

Nestler, E. J. Under siege: The brain on opiates. *Neuron*, 1996, *16*, 897–900.

Neumeister, A., Goessler, R., Lucht, M., Kapitany, T., Bamas, C., and Kasper, S. Bright light therapy stabilizes the antidepressant effect of partial sleep deprivation. *Biological Psychiatry*, 1996, *39*, 16–21.

Nichelli, P., Grafman, J., Pietrini, P., Clark, K., Lee, K. Y., and Miletich, R. Where the brain appreciates the moral of a story. *NeuroReport*, 1995, *6*, 2309–2313.

Nicholl, C. S., and Russell, R. M. Analysis of animal rights literature reveals the underlying motives of the movement: Ammunition for counter offensive by scientists. *Endocrinology*, 1990, *127*, 985–989.

Nicolaïdis, S. Short-term and long-term regulation of energy balance. *Proceedings of the International Congress of Physiological Sciences*, 1974, *10*, 122–123.

Nicolaïdis, S. What determines food intake? The ischymetric theory. *NIPS*, 1987, *2*, 104–107.

Nicoll, R. A., Alger, B. E., and Nicoll, R. A. Enkephalin blocks inhibitory pathways in the vertebrate CNS. *Nature*, 1980, *287*, 22–25.

Niiyama, Y., Fushimi, M., Sekine, A., and Hishikawa, Y. K-complex evoked in nrem sleep is accompanied by a slow negative potential related to cognitive process. *Electroencephalography and Clinical Neurophysiology*, 1995, *95*, 27–33.

Niiyama, Y., Satoh, N., Kutsuzawa, O., and Hishikawa, Y. Electrophysiological evidence suggesting that sensory stimuli of unknown origin induces spontaneous K-complexes. *Electroencephalography and Clinical Neurophysiology*, 1996, *98*, 394–400.

Nilsson, O. G., Shapiro, M. L., Gage, F. H., Olton, D. S., and Björklund, A. Spatial learning and memory following fimbria-fornix transection and grafting of fetal septal neurons to the hippocampus. *Experimental Brain Research*, 1987, *67*, 195–215.

Nisell, M., Nomikos, G. G., and Svensson, T. H. Systemic nicotine-induced dopamine release in the rat nucleus accumbens is regulated by nicotinic receptors in the ventral tegmental area. *Synapse*, 1994, *16*, 36–44.

Nishino, S., Reid, M. S., Dement, W. C., and Mignot, E. Neuropharmacology and neurochemistry of canine narcolepsy. *Sleep*, 1994, *17*, S84–S92.

Nishino, S., Tafti, M., Reid, M. S., Shelton, J., Siegel, J. M., Dement, W. C., and Mignot, E. Muscle atonia is triggered by cholinergic stimulation of the basal forebrain: Implication for the pathophysiology of canine narcolepsy. *Journal of Neuroscience*, 1995, *15*, 4806–4814.

Nitz, D., Andersen, A., Fahringer, H., Nienhuis, R., Mignot, E., and Siegel, J. Altered distribution of cholinergic cells in the narcoleptic dog. *NeuroReport*, 1995, *6*, 1521–1524.

Noble, E. P. The D2 dopamine receptor gene: A review of association studies in alcoholism. *Behavioral Genetics*, 1993, *23*, 119–129.

Noble, E. P., Blum, K., Khalsa, M. E., Ritchie, T., Montgomery, A., Wood, R. C., Fitch, R. J., Ozkaragoz, T., Sheridan, P. J., Anglin, M. D., Paredes, A., Treiman, L. J., and Sparkes, R. S. Allelic association of the D2 dopamine receptor gene with cocaine dependence. *Drug and Alcohol Dependency*, 1993, *33*, 271–285.

Noble, E. P., St. Jeor, S. T., Ritchie, T., Syndulko, K., St. Jeor, S. C., Fitch, R. J., Brunner, R. L., and Sparkes, R. S. D2 dopamine receptor gene and cigarette smoking: A reward gene? *Medical Hypotheses*, 1994, *42*, 257–260.

Nobler, M. S., Sackeim, H. A., Prohovnik, I., Moeller, J. R., Mukherjee, S., Schnur, D. B., Prudic, J., and Devanand, D. P. Regional cerebral blood flow in mood disorders. III. Treatment and clinical response. *Archives of General Psychiatry*, 1994, *51*, 884–897.

Noirot, E. Selective priming of maternal responses by auditory and olfactory cues from mouse pups. *Developmental Psychobiology*, 1972, *5*, 371–387.

Norgren, R., and Grill, H. Brain-stem control of ingestive behavior. In *The Physiological Mechanisms of Motivation*, edited by D. W. Pfaff. New York: Springer-Verlag, 1982.

Nose, H., Morita, M., Yawata, T., and Morimoto, T. Continuous determination of blood volume on conscious rats during water and food intake. *Japanese Journal of Physiology*, 1986, *36*, 215–218.

Novin, D., Robinson, B. A., Culbreth, L. A., and Tordoff, M. G. Is there a role for the liver in the control of food intake? *American Journal of Clinical Nutrition*, 1983, *9*, 233–246.

Novin, D., VanderWeele, D. A., and Rezek, M. Hepatic-portal 2-deoxy-D-glucose infusion causes eating: Evidence for peripheral glucoreceptors. *Science*, 1973, *181*, 858–860.

Nowlis, G. H., and Frank, M. Qualities in hamster taste: Behavioral and neural evidence. In *Olfaction and Taste*, Vol. 6, edited by J. LeMagnen and P. MacLeod. Washington, D.C.: Information Retrieval, 1977.

Numan, M. Medial preoptic area and maternal behavior in the female rat. *Journal of Comparative and Physiological Psychology*, 1974, *87*, 746–759.

Numan, M., and Numan, M. J. Preoptic-brainstem connections and maternal behavior in rats. *Behavioral Neuroscience*, 1991, *105*, 1013–1029.

Numan, M., Rosenblatt, J. S., and Komisaruk, B. R. Medial preoptic area and onset of maternal behavior in the rat. *Journal of Comparative and Physiological Psychology*, 1977, *91*, 146–164.

Numan, M., and Smith, H. G. Maternal behavior in rats: Evidence for the involvement of preoptic projections to the ventral tegmental area. *Behavioral Neuroscience*, 1984, *98*, 712–727.

Nyby, J., Matochik, J. A., and Barfield, R. J. Intracranial androgenic and estrogenic stimulation of male-typical behaviors in house mice (*Mus domesticus*). *Hormones and Behavior*, 1992, *26*, 24–45.

Oaknin, S., Rodriguez del Castillo, A., Guerra, M., Battaner, E., and Mas, M. Change in forebrain Na,K-ATPase activity and serum hormone levels during sexual behavior in male rats. *Physiology and Behavior*, 1989, *45*, 407–410.

O'Brien, C. P., Volpicelli, L. A., and Volpicelli, J. R. Naltrexone in the treatment of alcoholism: A clinical review. *Alcohol*, 1996, *13*, 35–39.

O'Callaghan, E. Obstetric complications, the putative familial-sporadic distinction, and tardive dyskinesia in schizophrenia. *British Journal of Psychiatry*, 1990, *157*, 578–584.

O'Callaghan, E., Gibson, T., Colohan, H. A., Buckley, P., Walshe, D. G., Larkin, C., and Waddington, J. L. Risk of schizophrenia in adults born after obstetric complications and their association with early onset of illness: A controlled study. *British Medical Journal*, 1992, *305*, 1256–1259.

O'Carroll, R., Shapiro, C., and Bancroft, J. Androgens, behavior and nocturnal erection in hypogonadal men: The effects of varying the replacement dose. *Clinical Endocrinology*, 1985, *23*, 527–538.

O'Connor, H. T., Richman, R. M., Steinbeck, K. S., and Caterson, I. D. Dexfenfluramine treatment of obesity: A double blind trial with post trial follow up. *International Journal of Obesity,* 1995, *19,* 181–189.

O'Dell, T. J., Hawkins, R. D., Kandel, E. R., and Arancio, O. Tests of the roles of two diffusible substances in long-term potentiation: Evidence for nitric oxide as a possible early retrograde messenger. *Proceedings of the National Academy of Sciences, USA,* 1991, *88,* 11285–11289.

Ogawa, S., Olazabal, U. E., Parhar, I. S., and Pfaff, D. W. Effects of intrahypothalamic administration of antisense DNA for progesterone receptor mRNA on reproductive behavior and progesterone receptor immunoreactivity in female rat. *Journal of Neuroscience,* 1994, *14,* 1766–1774.

O'Keefe, J., and Bouma, H. Complex sensory properties of certain amygadala units in the freely moving cat. *Experimental Neurology,* 1969, *23,* 384–398.

O'Keefe, J., and Dostrovsky, T. The hippocampus as a spatial map: Preliminary evidence from unit activity in the freely moving rat. *Brain Research,* 1971, *34,* 171–175.

Olds, J. Commentary. In *Brain Stimulation and Motivation,* edited by E. S. Valenstein. Glenview, Ill.: Scott, Foresman, 1973.

Olds, J., and Milner, P. Positive reinforcement produced by electrical stimulation of septal area and other regions of rat brain. *Journal of Comparative and Physiological Psychology,* 1954, *47,* 419–427.

Olds, M. E., and Fobes, J. L. The central basis of motivation: Intracranial self-stimulation studies. *Annual Review of Psychology,* 1981, *32,* 523–574.

Olmstead, M. C., and Franklin, K. B. J. Differential effects of ventral striatal lesions on the conditioned place preference induced by morphine or amphetamine. *Neuroscience,* 1996, *71,* 701–708.

Olton, D. S. Memory functions and the hippocampus. In *Neurobiology of the Hippocampus,* edited by W. Siefert. New York: Academic Press, 1983.

Olton, D. S., Collison, C., and Werz, M. A. Spatial memory and radial arm maze performance in rats. *Learning and Motivation,* 1977, *8,* 289–314.

Olton, D. S., Givens, B. S., Markowska, A. L., Shapiro, M., and Golski, S. Mnemonic functions of the cholinergic septohippocampal system. In *Memory: Organization and Locus of Change,* edited by L. R. Squire, N. M. Weinberger, G. Lynch, and J. L. McGaugh. New York: Oxford University Press, 1991.

Olton, D. S., and Papas, B. C. Spatial memory and hippocampal function. *Neuropsychologia,* 1979, *17,* 669–682.

Olton, D. S., and Samuelson, R. J. Remembrance of places past: Spatial memory in rats. *Journal of Experimental Psychology: Animal Behavior Processes,* 1976, *2,* 97–116.

O'Mara, S. M., Rolls, E. T., Berthoz, A., and Kesner, R. P. Neurons responding to whole-body motion in the primate hippocampus. *Journal of Neuroscience,* 1994, *14,* 6511–6523.

Owen, A. M., James, M., Leigh, P. N., Summers, B. A., Marsden, C. D., Quinn, N. P., Lange, K. W., and Robbins, T. W. Frontostriatal cognitive deficits at different stages of Parkinson's disease. *Brain,* 1992, *115,* 1727–1751.

Owen, A. M., Milner, B., Petrides, M., and Evans, A. C. Memory for object features versus memory for object location: A positron-emission tomography study of encoding and retrieval processes. *Proceedings of the National Academy of Sciences, USA,* 1996, *93,* 9212–9217.

Oyachi, H., and Ohtsuka, K. Transcranial magnetic stimulation of the posterior parietal cortex degrades accuracy of memory-guided saccades in humans. *Investigative Ophthalmology and Visual Science,* 1995, *36,* 1441–1449.

Pallast, E. G. M., Jongbloet, P. H., Straatman, H. M., and Zeilhuis, G. A. Excess of seasonality of births among patients with schizophrenia and seasonal ovopathy. *Schizophrenia Bulletin,* 1994, *20,* 269–276.

Panksepp, J. Aggression elicited by electrical stimulation of the hypothalamus in albino rats. *Physiology and Behavior,* 1971, *6,* 321–329.

Papadimitriou, G. N., Christodoulou, G. N., Katsouyanni, K., and Stefanis, C. N. Therapy and prevention of affective illness by total sleep deprivation. *Journal of the Affective Disorders,* 1993, *27,* 107–116.

Papez, J. W. A proposed mechanism of emotion. *Archives of Neurology and Psychiatry,* 1937, *38,* 725–744.

Pascoe, J. P., and Kapp, B. S. Electrophysiological characteristics of amygdaloid central nucleus neurons during Pavlovian fear conditioning in the rabbit. *Behavioural Brain Research,* 1985, *16,* 117–133.

Passingham, R. Delayed matching after selective prefrontal lesions in monkeys (*Macaca mulatta*). *Brain Research,* 1975, *92,* 89–102.

Pattatucci, A. M. L., and Hamer, D. H. Development and familiality of sexual orientation in females. *Behavior Genetics,* 1995, *25,* 407–420.

Patterson, K., and Kay, J. A. How word-form dyslexics form words. Paper presented at the meeting of the British Psychological Society Conference on Reading, Exeter, England, 1980.

Paulesu, E., Frith, C. D., and Frackowiak, R. S. J. The neural correlates of the verbal component of working memory. *Nature,* 1993, *362,* 342–345.

Pauls, D. L., and Leckman, J. F. The inheritance of Gilles de la Tourette's syndrome and associated behaviors. *New England Journal of Medicine,* 1986, *315,* 993–997.

Pavlasevic, S., Bednar, I., Qureshi, G. A., and Soderste, P. Brain cholecystokinin tetrapeptide levels are increased in a rat model of anxiety. *NeuroReport,* 1993, *5,* 225–228.

Pavlides, C., Greenstein, Y. J., Grudman, M., and Winson, J. Long-term potentiation in the dentate gyrus is induced preferentially on the positive phase of theta rhythms. *Brain Research,* 1988, *439,* 383–387.

Peck, B. K., and Vanderwolf, C. H. Effects of raphe stimulation on hippocampal and neocortical activity and behaviour. *Brain Research*, 1991, *568*, 244–252.

Peck, J. W., and Blass, E. M. Localization of thirst and antidiuretic osmoreceptors by intracranial injections in rats. *American Journal of Physiology*, 1975, *5*, 1501–1509.

Pelleymounter, M. A., Cullen, M. J., Baker, M. B., Hecht, R., Winters, D., Boone, T., and Collins, F. Effects of the obese gene product on body weight regulation in ob/ob mice. *Science*, 1995, *269*, 540–543.

Penfield, W., and Jasper, H. *Epilepsy and the Functional Anatomy of the Human Brain*. Boston: Little, Brown, 1954.

Penfield, W., and Milner, B. Memory deficit produced by bilateral lesions in the hippocampal zone. *American Medical Association Archives of Neurological Psychiatry*, 1958, *79*, 475–497.

Penfield, W., and Rasmussen, T. *The Cerebral Cortex of Man: A Clinical Study of Localization*. Boston: Little, Brown, 1950.

Pennington, B. F., Gilger, J. W., Pauls, D., Smith, S. A., Smith, S. D., and DeFries, J. C. Evidence for major gene transmission of developmental dyslexia. *Journal of the American Medical Association*, 1991, *266*, 1527–1534.

Perrett, D. I., Hietanen, J. K., Oram, M. W., and Benson, P. J. Organization and functions of cells responsive to faces in the temporal cortex. *Philosophical Transactions of the Royal Society of London [B]*, 1992, *335*, 23–30.

Persky, H. Reproductive hormones, moods, and the menstrual cycle. In *Sex Differences in Behavior*, edited by R. C. Friedman, R. M. Richart, and R. L. Vande Wiele. New York: John Wiley & Sons, 1974.

Persky, H., Lief, H. I., Strauss, D., Miller, W. R., and O'Brien, C. P. Plasma testosterone level and sexual behavior of couples. *Archives of Sexual Behavior*, 1978, *7*, 157–173.

Pert, C. B., Snowman, A. M., and Snyder, S. H. Localization of opiate receptor binding in presynaptic membranes of rat brain. *Brain Research*, 1974, *70*, 184–188.

Petersen, S. E., Fox, P. T., Posner, M. I., Mintun, M., and Raichle, M. W. Positron emission tomographic studies of the cortical anatomy of single-word processing. *Nature*, 1988, *331*, 585–589.

Petersen, S. E., Fox, P. T., Snyder, A. Z., and Raichle, M. E. Activation of extrastriate and frontal cortical areas by visual words and word-like stimuli. *Science*, 1990, *249*, 1041–1044.

Petit, H. O., and Justice, J. B. Dopamine in the nucleus accumbens during cocaine self-administration as studied by in vivo microdialysis. *Pharmacology, Biochemistry and Behavior*, 1989, *23*, 899–904.

Petre-Quadens, O., and De Lee, C. Eye movement frequencies and related paradoxical sleep cycles: Developmental changes. *Chronobiologia*, 1974, *1*, 347–355.

Pfaff, D. W., and Keiner, M. Atlas of estradiol-concentrating cells in the central nervous system of the female rat. *Journal of Comparative Neurology*, 1973, *151*, 121–158.

Pfaff, D. W., and Sakuma, Y. Deficit in the lordosis reflex of female rats caused by lesions in the ventromedial nucleus of the hypothalamus. *Journal of Physiology*, 1979, *288*, 203–210.

Pfaus, J. G., Damsma, G., Nomikos, G. G., Wenkstern, D. G., Blaha, C. D., Phillips, A. G., and Fibiger, H. C. Sexual behavior enhances central dopamine transmission in the male rat. *Brain Research*, 1990, *530*, 345–348.

Pfaus, J. G., Kleopoulos, S. P., Mobbs, C. V., Gibbs, R. B., and Pfaff, D. W. Sexual stimulation activates c-fos within estrogen-concentrating regions of the female rat forebrain. *Brain Research*, 1993, *624*, 253–267.

Phillips, D. P., and Farmer, M. E. Acquired word deafness, and the temporal grain of sound representation in the primary auditory cortex. *Behavioural Brain Research*, 1990, *40*, 85–94.

Phillips, G. D., Robbins, T. W., and Everitt, B. J. Bilateral intra-accumbens self-administration of d-amphetamine: Antagonism with intra-accumbens SCH-23390 and sulpiride. *Psychopharmacology*, 1994, *114*, 477–485.

Phillips, M. I., and Felix, D. Specific angiotensin II receptive neurons in the cat subfornical organ. *Brain Research*, 1976, *109*, 531–540.

Phillips, R. G., and LeDoux, J. E. Differential contribution of amygdala and hippocampus to cued and contextual fear conditioning. *Behavioral Neuroscience*, 1992, *106*, 274–285.

Pickar, D. Prospects for pharmacotherapy of schizophrenia. *Lancet*, 1995, *345*, 557–562.

Pickar, D., Breier, A., Hsiao, J. K., Doran, A. R., Wolkowitz, O. M., Pato, C. N., Konicki, P. E., and Potter, W. Z. Cerebrospinal fluid and plasma monoamine metabolites and their relation to psychosis: Implications for regional brain dysfunction in schziophrenia. *Archives of General Psychiatry*, 1990, *47*, 641–648.

Pickles, J. O., and Corey, D. P. Mechanoelectrical transduction by hair cells. *Trends in Neuroscience*, 1992, *15*, 254–259.

Pijl, S., and Schwarz, D. W. F. Intonation of musical intervals by deaf subjects stimulated with single bipolar cochlear implant electrodes. *Hearing Research*, 1995a, *89*, 203–211.

Pijl, S., and Schwartz, D. W. F. Melody recognition and musical interval perception by deaf subjects stimulated with electrical pulse trains through single cochlear implant electrodes. *Journal of the Acoustical Society of America*, 1995b, *98*, 886–895.

Pilcher, J. J., and Huffcutt, A. I. Effects of sleep deprivation on performance: A meta-analysis. *Sleep*, 1996, *19*, 318–326.

Pilleri, G. The blind Indus dolphin, *Platanista indi*. *Endeavours*, 1979, *3*, 48–56.

Pi-Sunyer, F. X. Health implications of obesity. *American Journal of Clinical Nutrition*, 1991, *53*, 1595S-1603S.

Pitkaenen, A., Stefanacci, L., Farb, C. R., Go, G.-G., LeDoux, J. E., and Amaral, D. G. Intrinsic connections of the rat amygdaloid complex: Projections originating in the lateral nucleus. *Journal of Comparative Neurology*, 1995, *356*, 288–310.

Pleim, E. T., and Barfield, R. J. Progesterone versus estrogen facilitation of female sexual behavior by intracranial administration to female rats. *Hormones and Behavior*, 1988, *22*, 150–159.

Poggio, G. F., and Poggio, T. The analysis of stereopsis. *Annual Review of Neuroscience*, 1984, *7*, 379–412.

Portas, C. M., Thakkar, M., Rainnie, D., and McCarley, R. W. Microdialysis perfusion of 8-hydroxy-2-(di-n-propylamino) tetralin (8-OH-DPAT) in the dorsal raphe nucleus decreases serotonin release and increases rapid eye movement sleep in the freely moving cat. *Journal of Neuroscience*, 1996, *16*, 2820–2828.

Post, R. M., Ballenger, J. C., Uhde, T., and Bunney, W. Efficacy of carbamazepine in manic-depressive illness: Implications for underlying mechanisms. In *Neurobiology of Mood Disorders*, edited by R. M. Post and C. Ballenger. Baltimore: Williams and Wilkins, 1984.

Post, R. M., Leverich, G. S., Altshuler, L., and Mikalauskas, K. Lithium-discontinuation-induced refractoriness: Preliminary observations. *Americal Journal of Psychiatry*, 1992, *149*, 1727–1729.

Post, R. M., Weiss, S. R. B., and Chuang, D.-M. Mechanisms of action of anticonvulsants in affective disorders: Comparison with lithium. *Journal of Clinical Psychopharmacology*, 1992, *12*, 23s-35s.

Powers, J. B., and Winans, S. S. Vomeronasal organ: Critical role in mediating sexual behavior of the male hamster. *Science*, 1975, *187*, 961–963.

Pratt, J. A., and Brett, R. R. The benzodiazepine receptor inverse agonist FG7142 induces cholecystokinin gene expression in the rat brain. *Neuroscience Letters*, 1995, *184*, 197–200.

Preyer, S., Hemmert, W., Zenner, H. P., and Gummer, A. W. Abolition of the receptor potential response of isolated mammalian outer hair cells by hair-bundle treatment with elastase: A test of the tip-link hypothesis. *Hearing Research*, 1995, *89*, 187–193.

Price, J. The genetics of depressive behavior. *British Journal of Psychiatry*, 1968, *2*, 37–45.

Price, L. H., and Heninger, G. R. Drug therapy: Lithium in the treatment of mood disorders. *New England Journal of Medicine*, 1994, *331*, 591–598.

Price, R. A., and Gottesman, I. I. Body fat in identical twins reared apart: Roles for genes and environment. *Behavioral Genetics*, 1991, *21*, 1–7.

Pritchard, T. C., Hamilton, R. B., Morse, J. R., and Norgren, R. Projections of thalamic gustatory and lingual areas in the monkey, *Macaca fascicularis*. *Journal of Comparative Neurology*, 1986, *244*, 213–228.

Proctor, W. R., Soldo, B. L., Allan, A. M., and Dunwiddie, T. V. Ethanol enhances synaptically evoked GABAA receptor-mediated responses in cerebral cortical neurons in rat brain slices. *Brain Research*, 1992, *595*, 220–227.

Propping, P., Kruger, J., and Janah, A. Effect of alcohol on genetically determined variants of the normal electroencephalogram. *Psychiatry Research*, 1980, *2*, 85–98.

Propping, P., Kruger, J., and Mark, N. Genetic disposition to alcoholism: An EEG study in alcoholics and their relatives. *Human Genetics*, 1981, *59*, 51–59.

Quattrochi, J. J., Mamelak, A. N., Madison, R. D., Macklis, J. D., and Hobson, J. A. Mapping neuronal inputs to REM sleep induction sites with carbachol-fluorescent microspheres. *Science*, 1989, *245*, 984–986.

Quillen, E. W., Keil, L. C., and Reid, I. A. Effects of baroreceptor denervation on endocrine and drinking responses to caval constriction in dogs. *American Journal of Physiology*, 1990, *259*, R618–R626.

Quintana, J., and Fuster, J. M. Mnemonic and predictive functions of cortical neurons in a memory task. *NeuroReport*, 1992, *3*, 721–724.

Quirion, R. Receptor sites for atrial natriuretic factors in brain and associated structures: An overview. *Cellular and Molecular Neurobiology*, 1989, *9*, 45–55.

Quirion, R., Dalpe, M., De Lean, A., Gutkowska, J., Cantin, M., and Genest, J. Atrial natriuretic factor (ANF) binding sites in brain and related structures. *Peptides*, 1984, *5*, 1167–1172.

Quirk, G. J., Muller, R. U., Kubie, J. L., and Ranck, J. B. The positional firing properties of medial entorhinal neurons: Description and comparison with hippocampal place cells. *Journal of Neuroscience*, 1992, *12*, 1945–1963.

Quirk, G. J., Repa, J. C., and LeDoux, J. E. Fear conditioning enhances short-latency auditory responses of lateral amygdala neurons: Parallel recordings in the freely behaving rat. *Neuron*, 1995, *15*, 1029–1039.

Radke, K. J., Willis, L. R., Zimmerman, G. W., Weinberger, M. H., and Selkurt, E. E. Effects of histamine-receptor antagonists on histamine-stimulated renin secretion. *European Journal of Pharmacology*, 1986, *123*, 421–426.

Raffaele, K. C., and Olton, D. S. Hippocampal and amygdala involvement in working memory for nonspatial stimuli. *Behavioral Neuroscience*, 1988, *102*, 349–355.

Raiguel, S., Van Hulle, M. M., Xiao, D.-K., Marcar, V. L., and Orban, G. A. Shape and spatial distribution of receptive fields and antagonistic motion surrounds in the middle temporal area (V5) of the macaque. *European Journal of Neuroscience*, 1995, *7*, 2064–2082.

Raine, A., Lencz, T., Reynolds, G. P., Harrison, G., Sheard, C., Medley, I., Reynolds, L. M., and Cooper, J. E. An evaluation of structural and functional prefrontal deficits in schizophrenia: MRI and neuropsychological measures. *Psychiatry Research Neuroimaging*, 1992, *45*, 123–137.

Rajendren, G., Dudley, C. A., and Moss, R. L. Role of the vomeronasal organ in the male-induced enhancement of sexual receptivity in female rats. *Neuroendocrinology*, 1990, *52*, 368–372.

Raleigh, M. J., McGuire, M. T., Brammer, G. L., Pollack, D. B., and Yuwiler, A. Serotonergic mechanisms promote dominance acquisition in adult male vervet monkeys. *Brain Research,* 1991, *559,* 181–190.

Ralph, M. R., and Lehman, M. N. Transplantation: A new tool in the analysis of the mammalian hypothalamic circadian pacemaker. *Trends in Neuroscience,* 1991, *14,* 362–366.

Ramirez, I. Why do sugars taste good? *Neuroscience and Biobehavioral Reviews,* 1990, *14,* 125–134.

Ramsay, D. J., Rolls, B. J., and Wood, R. J. Thirst following water deprivation in dogs. *American Journal of Physiology,* 1977, *232,* R93–R100.

Rapoport, J. L. Recent advances in obsessive-compulsive disorder. *Neuropsychopharmacology,* 1991, *5,* 1–10.

Rapoport, J. L., Ryland, D. H., and Kriete, M. Drug treatment of canine acral lick: An animal model of obsessive-compulsive disorder. *Archives of General Psychiatry,* 1992, *49,* 517–521.

Rasmusson, D. D., Clow, K., and Szerb, J. C. Modification of neocortical acetylcholine release and electroencephalogram desynchronization due to brain stem stimulation by drugs applied to the basal forebrain. *Neuroscience,* 1994, *60,* 665–677.

Ratcliff, G., and Newcombe, F. Object recognition: Some deductions from the clinical evidence. In *Normality and Pathology in Cognitive Functions,* edited by A. W. Ellis. London: Academic Press, 1982.

Ratnasuriya, R. H., Eisler, I., Szmukler, G. I., and Russell, G. F. M. Anorexia nervosa: Outcome and prognostic factors after 20 years. *British Journal of Psychiatry,* 1991, *158,* 495–502.

Rauhofer, E. A., Smith, G. P., and Gibbs, J. Acute blockade of gastric emptying and meal size in rats. *Physiology and Behavior,* 1993, *54,* 881–884.

Rauschecker, J. P., Tian, B., and Hauser, M. Processing of complex sounds in the macaque nonprimary auditory cortex. *Science,* 1995, *268,* 111–114.

Ravussin, E., Pratley, R. E., Maffei, M., Wang, H., Friedman, J. M., Bennett, P. H., and Bogardus, C. Relatively low plasma leptin concentrations precede weight gain in Pima Indians. *Nature Medicine,* 1997, *3,* 238–240.

Ravussin, E., Valencia, M. E., Esparza, J., Bennett, P. H., and Schulz, L. O. Effects of a traditional lifestyle on obesity in Pima Indians. *Diabetes Care,* 1994, *17,* 1067–1074.

Rawson, N. E., Ulrich, P. M., and Friedman, M. I. L-Ethionine, an amino acid analogue, stimulates eating in rats. *American Journal of Physiology,* 1994, *267,* R612–R615.

Rawson, N. E., Ulrich, P. M., and Friedman, M. I. Fatty acid oxidation modulates the eating response to the fructose analogue 2,5-anhydro-D-mannitol. *American Journal of Physiology: Regulatory, Integrative and Comparative Physiology,* 1996, *271,* R144–R148.

Raybin, J. B., and Detre, T. P. Sleep disorder and symptomatology among medical and nursing students. *Comprehensive Psychiatry,* 1969, *10,* 452–467.

Rechtschaffen, A., and Bergmann, B. M. Sleep deprivation in the rat by the disk-over-water method. *Behavioural Brain Research,* 1995, *69,* 55–63.

Rechtschaffen, A., Bergmann, B. M., Everson, C. A., Kushida, C. A., and Gilliland, M. A. Sleep deprivation in the rat: X. Integration and discussion of the findings. *Sleep,* 1989, *12,* 68–87.

Rechtschaffen, A., Gilliland, M. A., Bergmann, B. M., and Winter, J. B. Physiological correlates of prolonged sleep deprivation in rats. *Science,* 1983, *221,* 182–184.

Rechtschaffen, A., Wolpert, E. A., Dement, W. C., Mitchell, S. A., and Fisher, C. Nocturnal sleep of narcoleptics. *Electroencephalography and Clinical Neurophysiology,* 1963, *15,* 599–609.

Reebs, S., and Mrosovsky, N. Effects of induced wheel running on the circadian activity rhythms of the Syrian hamster: Entrainment and phase response curve. *Journal of Biological Rhythms,* 1989, *4,* 39–48.

Rehkämper, G., Haase, E., and Frahm, H. D. Allometric comparison of brain weight and brain structure volumes in different breeds of the domestic pigeon, *Columbia livia f.d.* (fantails, homing pigeons, strassers). *Brain, Behavior and Evolution,* 1988, *31,* 141–149.

Reid, L. D. Endogenous opioids and alcohol dependence: Opioid alkaloids and the propensity to drink alcoholic beverages. *Alcohol,* 1996, *13,* 5–11.

Reinink, E., Bouhuys, N., Wirz-Justice, A., and van den Hoofdakker, R. Prediction of the antidepressant response to total sleep deprivation by diurnal variation of mood. *Psychiatry Research,* 1990, *32,* 113–124.

Reinoso-Suarez, F., De Andres, I., Rodrigo-Angulo, M. L., and Rodriguez-Veiga, E. Location and anatomical connections of a paradoxical sleep induction site in the cat ventral pontine tegmentum. *European Journal of Neuroscience,* 1994, *6,* 1829–1836.

Reiss, A. L., and Freund, L. Behavioral phenotype of fragile X syndrome: DSM-III-R autistic behavior in male children. *American Journal of Medical Genetics,* 1992, *43,* 35–46.

Rempel-Clower, N. L., Zola, S. M., Squire, L. R., and Amaral, D. G. Three cases of enduring memory impairment after bilateral damage limited to the hippocampal formation. *Journal of Neuroscience,* 1996, *16,* 5233–5255.

Reppert, S. M., and Schwartz, W. J. The suprachiasmatic nuclei of the fetal rat: Characterization of a functional circadian clock using ^{14}C-labeled deoxyglucose. *Journal of Neuroscience,* 1984, *4,* 1677–1682.

Ressler, K. J., Sullivan, S. L., and Buck, L. A molecular dissection of spatial patterning in the olfactory system. *Current Opinion in Neurobiology,* 1994a, *4,* 588–596.

Ressler, K. J., Sullivan, S. L., and Buck, L. Information coding in the olfactory system: Evidence for a stereotyped and highly organized epitope map in the olfactory bulb. *Cell,* 1994b, *79,* 1245–1255.

Reynecke, L., Allin, R., Russell, V. A., and Taljaard, J. J. F. Lack of effect of chronic desipramine treatment on dopaminergic activity in the nucleus accumbens of the rat. *Neurochemical Research,* 1989, *14,* 661–665.

Reynolds, D. V. Surgery in the rat during electrical analgesia induced by focal brain stimulation. *Science,* 1969, *164,* 444–445.

Reynolds, G. P. Beyond the dopamine hypothesis: The neurochemical pathology of schizophrenia. *British Journal of Psychiatry,* 1989, *155,* 315–316.

Reznic, J., and Stäubli, U. Effects of 5-HT₃ receptor antagonism on hippocampal cellular activity in the freely moving rat. *Journal of Neurophysiology,* 1997, *77,* 517–521.

Rhees, R. W., Shryne, J. E., and Gorski, R. A. Termination of the hormone-sensitive period for differentiation of the sexually dimorphic nucleus of the preoptic area in male and female rats. *Developmental Brain Research,* 1990, *52,* 17–23.

Ricardo, J. A. Efferent connections of the subthalamic region in the rat. II. The zona incerta. *Brain Research,* 1981, *214,* 43–60.

Ridley, R. M., Thornley, H. D., Baker, H. F., and Fine, A. Cholinergic neural transplants into hippocampus restore learning ability in monkeys with fornix transections. *Experimental Brain Research,* 1991, *83,* 533–538.

Riege, W. H. Environmental influences on brain and behavior of old rats. *Developmental Psychobiology,* 1971, *4,* 157–167.

Riemann, D., Hohagen, F., Koenig, A., Schwarz, B., Gomille, J., Voderholzer, U., and Berger, M. Advanced vs normal sleep timing: Effects on depressed mood after response to sleep deprivation in patients with a major depressive disorder. *Journal of Affective Disorders,* 1996, *37,* 121–128.

Riemann, D., Wiegand, M., and Berger, M. Are there predictors for sleep deprivation response in depressive patients? *Biological Psychiatry,* 1991, *29,* 707–710.

Ritter, R. C., Brenner, L., and Yox, D. P. Participation of vagal sensory neurons in putative satiety signals from the upper gastrointestinal tract. In *Neuroanatomy and Physiology of Abdominal Vagal Afferents,* edited by S. Ritter, R. C. Ritter, and C. D. Barnes. Boca Raton, Fla.: CRC Press, 1992.

Ritter, R. C., Slusser, P. G., and Stone, S. Glucoreceptors controlling feeding and blood glucose: Location in the hindbrain. *Science,* 1981, *213,* 451–453.

Ritter, S., Dinh, T. T., and Friedman, M. I. Induction of Fos-like immunoreactivity (Fos-li) and stimulation of feeding by 2,5-anhydro-D-mannitol (2,5-AM) require the vagus nerve. *Brain Research,* 1994, *646,* 53–64.

Ritter, S., and Taylor, J. S. Capsaicin abolishes lipoprivic but not glucoprivic feeding in rats. *American Journal of Physiology,* 1989, *256,* R1232–R1239.

Ritter, S., and Taylor, J. S. Vagal sensory neurons are required for lipoprivic but not glucoprivic feeding in rats. *American Journal of Physiology,* 1990, *258,* R1395–R1401.

Ritvo, E. R., Mason-Brothers, A., Freeman, B. J., Pingree, C., Jenson, W. R., McMahon, W. M., Petersen, P. B., and Jorde, L. B. The UCLA-University of Utah epidemiologic survey of autism: The etiologic role of rare diseases. *American Journal of Psychiatry,* 1990, *147,* 1614–1621.

Rizzo, M., and Robin, D. A. Simultanagnosia: A defect of sustained attention yields insights on visual information processing. *Neurology,* 1990, *40,* 447–455.

Robbins, L. N., Helzer, J. E., Weissman, M. M., Orvaschel, H., Gruenberg, E., Burke, J. D., and Regier, D. A. Lifetime prevalence of specific psychiatric disorders in three sites. *Archives of General Psychiatry,* 1984, *41,* 949–958.

Roberts, S. B., and Greenberg, A. S. The new obesity genes. *Nutrition Reviews,* 1996, *54,* 41–49.

Roberts, W. W., and Kiess, H. O. Motivational properties of hypothalamic aggression in cats. *Journal of Comparative and Physiological Psychology,* 1964, *58,* 187–193.

Robertson, G. S., Pfaus, J. G., Atkinson, L. J., Matsumura, H., Phillips, A. G., and Fibiger, H. C. Sexual behavior increases c-fos expression in the forebrain of the male rat. *Brain Research,* 1991, *564,* 352–357.

Robinson, D. L., McClurkin, J. W., Kurtzman, C., and Petersen, S. E. Visual responses of pulvinar and collicular neurons during eye movements of awake, trained macaques. *Journal of Neurophysiology,* 1991, *66,* 485–496.

Robinson, D. L., and Petersen, S. E. The pulvinar and visual salience. *Trends in Neuroscience,* 1992, *15,* 127–132.

Robinson, F. R. Role of the cerebellum in movement control and adaptation. *Current Opinion in Neurobiology,* 1995, *5,* 755–762.

Robinson, T. E., and Berridge, K. C. The neural basis of drug craving: An incentive-sensitization theory of addiction. *Brain Research Reviews,* 1993, *18,* 247–291.

Rodier, P. M., Ingram, J. L., Tisdale, B., Nelson, S., and Romano, J. Embryological origin for autism: Developmental anomalies of the cranial nerve motor nuclei. *Journal of Comparative Neurology,* 1996, *370,* 247–261.

Rodin, J., Schank, D., and Striegel-Moore, R. Psychological features of obesity. *Medical Clinics of North America,* 1989, *73,* 47–66.

Rodman, H. R., Gross, C. G., and Albright, T. D. Afferent basis of visual response properties in area MT of the macaque. I. Effects of striate cortex removal. *Journal of Neuroscience,* 1989, *9,* 2033–2050.

Rodman, H. R., Gross, C. G., and Albright, T. D. Afferent basis of visual response properties in area MT of the macaque. II. Effects of superior colliculus removal. *Journal of Neuroscience,* 1990, *10,* 1154–1164.

Roeltgen, D. P., Rothi, L. H., and Heilman, K. M. Linguistic semantic apraphia: A dissociation of the lexical spelling system from semantics. *Brain and Language,* 1986, *27,* 257–280.

Roffwarg, H. P., Dement, W. C., Muzio, J. N., and Fisher, C. Dream imagery: Relation to rapid eye movements of sleep. *Archives of General Psychiatry,* 1962, *7,* 235–258.

Roffwarg, H. P., Muzio, J. N., and Dement, W. C. Ontogenetic development of human sleep-dream cycle. *Science,* 1966, *152,* 604–619.

Rogan, M. T., and LeDoux, J. E. LTP is accompanied by commensurate enhancement of auditory-evoked responses in a fear conditioning circuit. *Neuron*, 1995, *15*, 127–136.

Rogers, M. P., Trentham, D. E., McCune, W. J., Ginsberg, B. I., Rennke, H. G., Reike, P., and David, J. R. Effect of psychological stress on the induction of arthritis in rats. *Arthritis and Rheumatology*, 1980, *23*, 1337–1342.

Roland, P. E. Metabolic measurements of the working frontal cortex in man. *Trends in Neurosciences*, 1984, *7*, 430–435.

Rolls, B. J., Rowe, E. A., Rolls, E. T., Kingston, B., Megson, A., and Gunary, R. Variety in a meal enhances food intake in man. *Physiology and Behavior*, 1981, *26*, 215–221.

Rolls, E. T. Feeding and reward. In *The Neural Basis of Feeding and Reward*, edited by B. G. Hobel and D. Novin. Brunswick, Maine: Haer Institute, 1982.

Rolls, E. T. Neuronal activity related to the control of feeding. In *Neural and Humoral Controls of Food Intake*, edited by R. Ritter and S. Ritter. New York: Academic Press, 1986.

Rolls, E. T. Functions of the primate hippocampus in spatial processing and memory. In *Neurobiology of Comparative Cognition*, edited by D. S. Olton and R. P. Kesner. Hillsdale, N.J.: Lawrence Erlbaum Associates, 1989.

Rolls, E. T. Learning mechanisms in the temporal lobe visual cortex. *Behavioural Brain Research*, 1995a, *66*, 177–185.

Rolls, E. T. Central taste anatomy and neurophysiology. In *Handbook of Olfaction and Gustation*, edited by R. L. Doty. New York: Dekker, 1995b.

Rolls, E. T. A theory of hippocampal function in memory. *Hippocampus*, 1996, *6*, 601–620.

Rolls, E. T., and Baylis, G. C. Size and contrast have only small effects on the responses to faces of neurons in the cortex of the superior temporal sulcus of the monkey. *Experimental Brain Research*, 1986, *65*, 38–48.

Rolls, E. T., Yaxley, S., and Sienkiewicz, Z. J. Gustatory responses of single neurons in the orbitofrontal cortex of the macaque monkey. *Journal of Neurophysiology*, 1990, *64*, 1055–1066.

Romero, P. R., Beltramino, C. A., and Carrer, H. F. Participation of the olfactory system in the control of approach behavior of the female rat to the male. *Physiology and Behavior*, 1990, *47*, 685–690.

Rose, G. Physiological and behavioral characteristics of dentate granule cells. In *Neurobiology of the Hippocampus*, edited by W. Seifert. London: Academic Press, 1983.

Rose, G. A., and Williams, R. T. Metabolic studies of large and small eaters. *British Journal of Nutrition*, 1961, *15*, 1–9.

Rose, J. D. Changes in hypothalamic neuronal function related to hormonal induction of lordosis in behaving hamsters. *Physiology and Behavior*, 1990, *47*, 1201–1212.

Roselli, C. E., Handa, R. J., and Resko, J. A. Quantitative distribution of nuclear androgen receptors in microdissected areas of the rat brain. *Neuroendocrinology*, 1989, *49*, 449–453.

Rosenblatt, J. S., and Aronson, L. R. The decline of sexual behavior in male cats after castration with special reference to the role of prior sexual experience. *Behaviour*, 1958a, *12*, 285–338.

Rosenblatt, J. S., and Aronson, L. R. The influence of experience on the behavioural effects of androgen in prepuberally castrated male cats. *Animal Behaviour*, 1958b, *6*, 171–182.

Rosenthal, D. A program of research on heredity in schizophrenia. *Behavioral Science*, 1971, *16*, 191–201.

Rosenthal, N. E., Sack, D. A., Gillin, C., Lewy, A. J., Goodwin, F. K., Davenport, Y., Mueller, P. S., Newsome, D. A., and Wehr, T. A. Seasonal affective disorder: A description of the syndrome and preliminary findings with light therapy. *Archives of General Psychiatry*, 1984, *41*, 72–80.

Rosenthal, N. E., Sack, D. A., James, S. P., Parry, B. L., Mendelson, W. B., Tamarkin, L., and Wehr, T. A. Seasonal affective disorder and phototherapy. *Annals of the New York Academy of Sciences*, 1985, *453*, 260–269.

Rosenzweig, M. R., and Bennett, E. L. Psychobiology of plasticity: Effects of training and experience on brain and behavior. *Behavioural Brain Research*, 1996, *78*, 57–65.

Rosewell, K. L., Siwicki, K. K., and Wise, P. M. A period (per)-like protein exhibits daily rhythmicity in the suprachiasmatic nuclei of the rat. *Brain Research*, 1994, *659*, 231–236.

Rosén, I., and Asanuma, H. Peripheral inputs to the forelimb area of the monkey motor cortex: Input-output relations. *Experimental Brain Research*, 1972, *14*, 257–273.

Ross, E. D., Homan, R. W., and Buck, R. Differential hemispheric lateralization of primary and social emotions. *Neuropsychiatry, Neuropsychology, and Behavioral Neurology*, 1994, *7*, 1–19.

Rosser, A. E., and Keverne, E. B. The importance of central noradrenergic neurons in the formation of an olfactory memory in the prevention of pregnancy block. *Neuroscience*, 1985, *16*, 1141–1147.

Rossetti, A. L., Hmaidan, Y., and Gessa, G. L. Marked inhibition of mesolimbic dopamine release: A common feature of ethanol, morphine, cocaine and amphetamine abstinence in rats. *European Journal of Pharmacology*, 1992, *221*, 227–234.

Roth, W. T., Margraf, J., Ehlers, A., Taylor, C. B., Maddock, R. J., Davies, S., and Agras, W. S. Stress test reactivity in panic disorder. *Archives of General Psychiatry*, 1992, *49*, 301–310.

Rothman, S. M., and Olney, J. W. Excitotoxicity and the NMDA receptor. *Trends in Neurosciences*, 1987, *10*, 299–302.

Routtenberg, A. "Self-starvation" of rats living in activity wheels: Adaptation effects. *Journal of Comparative Psychology*, 1968, *66*, 234–238.

Routtenberg, A., and Malsbury, C. Brainstem pathways of reward. *Journal of Comparative and Physiological Psychology*, 1969, *68*, 22–30.

Rowland, N. E. Neural activity and meal-associated drinking in rats. *Neuroscience Letters*, 1995, *189*, 125–127.

Roy, A., De Jong, J., and Linnoila, M. Cerebrospinal fluid monoamine metabolites and suicidal behavior in depressed patients. *Archives of General Psychiatry*, 1989, *46*, 609–612.

Rozin, P., and Kalat, J. W. Specific hungers and poison avoidance as adaptive specializations of learning. *Psychological Review,* 1971, *78,* 459–486.

Rubin, B. S., and Barfield, R. J. Priming of estrous responsiveness by implants of 17B-estradiol in the ventromedial hypothalamic nucleus of female rats. *Endocrinology,* 1980, *106,* 504–509.

Rubin, R. T., Ananth, J., Villanueva-Meyer, J., Trajmar, P. G., and Mena, I. Regional [133]Xenon cerebral blood flow and cerebral ^{99m}Tc-HMPAO uptake in patients with obsessive-compulsive disorder before and during treatment. *Biological Psychiatry,* 1995, *38,* 429–437.

Rubin, R. T., Villanueva-Meyer, J., Ananth, J., Trajmar, P. G., and Mena, I. Regional xenon 133 cerebral blood flow and cerebral technetium 99m HMPAO uptake in unmedicated patients with obsessive-compulsive disorder and matched normal control subjects: Determination by high-resolution single-photon emission computed tomography. *Archives of General Psychiatry,* 1992, *49,* 695–702.

Rudy, J. W., and Sutherland, R. J. Configural association theory and the hippocampal formation: An appraisal and reconfiguration. *Hippocampus,* 1995, *5,* 375–389.

Ruggero, M. A. Responses to sound of the basilar membrane of the mammalian cochlea. *Current Opinion in Neurobiology,* 1992, *2,* 449–456.

Rusak, B., McNaughton, L., Robertson, H. A., and Hunt, S. P. Circadian variation in photic regulation of immediate-early gene mRNAs in rat suprachiasmatic nucleus cells. *Molecular Brain Research,* 1992, *14,* 124–130.

Rusak, B., Meijer, J. H., and Harrington, M. E. Hamster circadian rhythms are phase-shifted by electrical stimulation of the geniculohypothalamic tract. *Brain Research,* 1989, *493,* 283–291.

Rusak, B., and Morin, L. P. Testicular responses to photoperiod are blocked by lesions of the suprachiasmatic nuclei in golden hamsters. *Biology of Reproduction,* 1976, *15,* 366–374.

Rusak, B., Robertson, H. A., Wisden, W., and Hunt, S. P. Light pulses that shift rhythms induce gene expression in the suprachiasmatic nucleus. *Science,* 1990, *248,* 1237–1240.

Russchen, F. T., Amaral, D. G., and Price, J. L. The afferent connections of the substantia innominata in the monkey, *Macaca fascicularis. Journal of Comparative Neurology,* 1986, *242,* 1–27.

Russek, M. Hepatic receptors and the neurophysiological mechanisms controlling feeding behavior. In *Neurosciences Research,* Vol. 4, edited by S. Ehrenpreis. New York: Academic Press, 1971.

Russell, G. F. M., and Treasure, J. The modern history of anorexia nervosa: An interpretation of why the illness has changed. *Annals of the New York Academy of Sciences,* 1989, *575,* 13–30.

Russell, M. J. Human olfactory communication. *Nature,* 1976, *260,* 520–522.

Russell, M. J., Switz, G. M., and Thompson, K. Olfactory influences on the human menstrual cycle. Paper presented at the meeting of the American Association for the Advancement of Science, San Francisco, June 1977.

Rutter, M. Cognitive deficits in the pathogenesis of autism. *Journal of Child Psychology and Psychiatry,* 1983, *24,* 513–531.

Ryback, R. S., and Lewis, O. F. Effects of prolonged bed rest on EEG sleep patterns in young, healthy volunteers. *Electroencephalography and Clinical Neurophysiology,* 1971, *31,* 395–399.

Saad, W. A., Luiz, A. C., Camargo, L. A. D., Renzi, A., and Manani, J. V. The lateral preoptic area plays a dual role in the regulation of thirst in the rat. *Brain Research Bulletin,* 1996, *39,* 171–176.

Saayman, G. S. Aggressive behaviour in free-ranging chacma baboons (*Papio ursinus*). *Journal of Behavioral Science,* 1971, *1,* 77–83.

Sachar, E. J., and Baron, M. The biology of affective disorders. *Annual Review of Neuroscience,* 1979, *2,* 505–518.

Sachdev, P., and Hay, P. Does neurosurgery for obsessive-compulsive disorder produce personality change? *Journal of Nervous and Mental Disease,* 1995, *183,* 408–413.

Sackheim, H. A., and Gur, R. C. Lateral asymmetry in intensity of emotional expression. *Neuropsychologia,* 1978, *16,* 473–482.

Saffran, E. M., Marin, O. S. M., and Yeni-Komshian, G. H. An analysis of speech perception in word deafness. *Brain and Language,* 1976, *3,* 209–228.

Saffran, E. M., Schwartz, M. F., and Marin, O. S. M. Evidence from aphasia: Isolating the components of a production model. In *Language Production,* edited by B. Butterworth. London: Academic Press, 1980.

Sahu, A., Kalra, P. S., and Kalra, S. P. Food deprivation and ingestion induce reciprocal changes in neuropeptide Y concentrations in the paraventricular nucleus. *Peptides,* 1988, *9,* 83–86.

Saitoh, K., Maruyama, N., and Kudoh, M. Sustained response of auditory cortex units in the cat. In *Brain Mechanisms of Sensation,* edited by Y. Katsuki, R. Norgren, and M. Sato. New York: John Wiley & Sons, 1981.

Sakai, F., Meyer, J. S., Karacan, I., Derman, S., and Yamamoto, M. Normal human sleep: Regional cerebral haemodynamics. *Annals of Neurology,* 1979, *7,* 471–478.

Sakai, K. Some anatomical and physiological properties of pontomesencephalic tegmental neurons with special reference to the PGO waves and postural atonia during paradoxical sleep in the cat. In *The Reticular Formation Revisited,* edited by J. A. Hobson and M. A. Brazier. New York: Raven Press, 1980.

Sakai, K., and Jouvet, M. Brain stem PGO-on cells projecting directly to the cat dorsal lateral geniculate nucleus. *Brain Research,* 1980, *194,* 500–505.

Sakai, R. R., Chow, S. Y., and Epstein, A. N. Peripheral angiotensin II is not the cause of sodium appetite in the rat. *Appetite,* 1990 *15,* 161–170.

Sakuma, Y., and Pfaff, D. W. Facilitation of female reproductive behavior from mesencephalic central grey in the rat. *American Journal of Physiology,* 1979a, *237,* R278–R284.

Sakuma, Y., and Pfaff, D. W. Mesencephalic mechanisms for integration of female reproductive behavior in the rat. *American Journal of Physiology,* 1979b, *237,* R285–R290.

Sakuma, Y., and Pfaff, D. W. Convergent effects of lordosis-relevant somatosensory and hypothalamic influences on central gray cells in the rat mesencephalon. *Experimental Neurology,* 1980a, *70,* 269–281.

Sakuma, Y., and Pfaff, D. W. Excitability of female rat central gray cells with medullary projections: Changes produced by hypothalamic stimulation and estrogen treatment. *Journal of Neurophysiology,* 1980b, *44,* 1012–1023.

Sakurai, Y., Sakai, K., Sakuta, M., and Iwata, M. Naming difficulties in alexia with agraphia for kanji after a left posterior inferior temporal lesion. *Journal of Neurology, Neurosurgery, and Psychiatry,* 1994, *57,* 609–613.

Salamone, J. D. Complex motor and sensorimotor function of striatal and accumbens dopamine: Involvement in instrumental behavior processes. *Psychopharmacology,* 1992, *107,* 160–174.

Salamone, J. D., Steinpreis, R. E., McCullough, L. D., Smith, P., Grebel, D., and Mahan, K. Haloperidol and nucleus accumbens dopamine depletion suppress lever pressing for food but increase free food consumption in a novel food choice procedure. *Psychopharmacology (Berlin),* 1991, *104,* 515–521.

Saller, C. F., and Stricker, E. M. Hyperphagia and increased growth in rats after intraventricular injection of 5,7-dihydroxytryptamine. *Science,* 1976, *192,* 385–387.

Salzman, C. D., Murasugi, C. M., Britten, K. H., and Newsome, W. T. Microstimulation in visual area MT: Effects on direction discrimination performance. *Journal of Neuroscience,* 1992, *12,* 2331–2355.

Samson, H. H., Hodge, C. W., Tolliver, G. A., and Haraguchi, M. Effect of dopamine agonists and antagonists on ethanol reinforced behavior: The involvement of the nucleus accumbens. *Brain Research Bulletin,* 1993, *30,* 133–141.

Sananes, C. B., and Campbell, B. A. Role of the central nucleus of the amygdala in olfactory heart rate conditioning. *Behavioral Neuroscience,* 1989, *103,* 519–525.

Sananes, C. B., and Davis, M. N-methyl-D-aspartate lesions of the lateral and basolateral nuclei of the amygdala block fear-potentiated startle and shock sensitization of startle. *Behavioral Neuroscience,* 1992, *106,* 72–80.

Sanders, S. K., and Shekhar, A. Anxiolytic effects of chlordiazepoxide blocked by injection of GABA$_A$ and benzodiazepine receptor antagonists in the region of the anterior basolateral amygdala of rats. *Biological Psychiatry,* 1995, *37,* 473–476.

Sandler, N., and Freundlich, N. A magic bullet for heroin addiction? *Business Week,* Dec. 9, 1996, 48.

Sapolsky, R. Glucocorticoid toxicity in the hippocampus: Reversal by supplementation with brain fuels. *Journal of Neuroscience,* 1986, *6,* 2240–2244.

Sapolsky, R. M. Neuroendocrinology of the stress-response. In *Behavioral Endocrinology,* edited by J. B. Becker, S. M. Breedlove, and D. Crews. Cambridge, Mass.: MIT Press, 1992.

Sapolsky, R. M., Krey, L. C., and McEwen, B. S. The adrenocortical axis in the aged rat: impaired sensitivity to both fast and delayed feedback inhibition. *Neurobiology of Aging,* 1986 *7,* 331–335.

Sassenrath, E. N., Powell, T. E., and Hendrickx, A. G. Perimenstrual aggression in groups of female rhesus monkeys. *Journal of Reproduction and Fertility,* 1973, *34,* 509–511.

Saudou, F., Amara, D. A., Dierich, A., Lemeur, M., Ramboz, S., Segu, L., Buhot, M. C., and Hen, R. Enhanced aggressive behavior in mice lacking 5-HT$_{1B}$ receptor. *Science,* 1994, *265,* 1875–1878.

Savander, V., Go, C. G., LeDoux, J. E., and Pitkaenen, A. Intrinsic connections of the rat amygdaloid complex: Projections originating in the basal nucleus. *Journal of Comparative Neurology,* 1995, *361,* 345–368.

Sawchenko, P. E., Gold, R. M., and Leibowitz, S. F. Evidence for vagal involvement in the eating elicited by adrenergic stimulation of the paraventricular nucleus. *Brain Research,* 1981, *225,* 249–269.

Sawchenko, P. E., Swanson, L. W., Grzanna, R., Howe, P. R. C., Bloom, S. R., and Polak, J. M. Colocalization of neuropeptide Y immunoreactivity in brain stem catecholaminergic neurons that project to the paraventricular nucleus of the hypothalamus. *Journal of Comparative Neurology,* 1985, *241,* 138–153.

Scammell, T. E., Price, K. J., and Sagar, S. M. Hyperthermia induces c-fos expression in the preoptic area. *Brain Research,* 1993, *618,* 303–307.

Schacter, D. L., Alpert, N. M., Savage, C. R., Rauch, S. L., and Albert, M. S. Conscious recollection and the human hippocampal formation: Evidence from positron emission tomography. *Proceedings of the National Academy of Sciences, USA,* 1996, *93,* 321–325.

Scheel-Krüger, J., and Willner, P. The mesolimbic system: Principles of operation. In *The Mesolimbic Dopamine System: From Motivation to Action,* edited by P. Willner and J. Scheel-Krüger. Chichester, England: John Wiley & Sons, 1991.

Schein, S. J., and Desimone, R. Spectral properties of V4 neurons in the macaque. *Journal of Neuroscience,* 1990, *10,* 3369–3389.

Schenck, C. H., Bundlie, S. R., Ettinger, M. G., and Mahowald, M. W. Chronic behavioral disorders of human REM sleep: A new category of parasomnia. *Sleep,* 1986, *9,* 293–308.

Schenck, C. H., Garciarill, E., Segall, M., Noreen, H., and Mahowald, M. W. HLA class-II genes associated with REM-sleep behavior disorder. *Annals of Neurology,* 1996, *39,* 261–263.

Schenck, C. H., Hurwitz, T. D., and Mahowald, M. W. REM-sleep behavior disorder: An update on a series of 96 patients and a review of the world literature. *Journal of Sleep Research,* 1993, *2,* 224–231.

Schenck, C. H., and Mahowald, M. W. Motor dyscontrol in narcolepsy: Rapid-eye-movement (REM) sleep without atonia and REM sleep behavior disorder. *Annals of Neurology,* 1992, *32,* 3–10.

Schenkel, E., and Siegel, J. M. REM sleep without atonia after lesions of the medial medulla. *Neuroscience Letters,* 1989, *98,* 159–165.

Scherschlicht, R., Polc, P., Schneeberger, J., Steiner, M., and Haefely, W. Selective suppression of rapid eye movement sleep (REMS) in cats by typical and atypical antidepressants. In *Typical and Atypical Antidepressants: Molecular Mechanisms,* edited by E. Costa and G. Racagni. New York: Raven Press, 1982.

Schiffmann, S. N., and Vanderhaeghen, J. J. Distribution of cells containing mRNA encoding cholecystokinin in the rat central nervous system. *Journal of Comparative Neurology,* 1991, *304,* 219–233.

Schiffman, S. S., Lockhead, E., and Maes, F. W. Amiloride reduces the taste intensity of Na^+ and Li^+ salts and sweeteners. *Proceedings of the National Academy of Sciences, USA,* 1983, *80,* 6136–6140.

Schiller, P. H. The ON and OFF channels of the visual system. *Trends in Neuroscience,* 1992, *15,* 86–92.

Schiller, P. H., and Malpeli, J. G. Properties and tectal projections of monkey retinal ganglion cells. *Journal of Neurophysiology,* 1977, *40,* 428–445.

Schiller, P. H., Sandell, J. H., and Maunsell, J. H. R. Functions of the ON and OFF channels of the visual system. *Nature,* 1986, *322,* 824–825.

Schleifer, S. J., Keller, S. E., Camerino, M., Thornton, J. C., and Stein, M. Suppression of lymphocyte stimulation following bereavement. *Journal of the American Medical Association,* 1983, *15,* 374–377.

Schmitz, F., and Drenckhahn, D. Influence of Ca^{2+} on synaptic morphology of fish cone photoreceptors. *Brain Research,* 1991, *546,* 341–344.

Schneider, F., Gur, R. E., Alavi, A., Seligman, M. E. P., Mozley, L. H., Smith, R. J., Mozley, P. D., and Gur, R. C. Cerebral blood flow changes in limbic regions induced by unsolvable anagram tasks. *American Journal of Psychiatry,* 1996, *153,* 206–212.

Schubert, K., Shaikh, M. B., and Siegel, A. NMDA receptors in the midbrain periaqueductal gray mediate hypothalamically evoked hissing behavior in the cat. *Brain Research,* 1996, *726,* 80–90.

Schulkin, J., Marini, J., and Epstein, A. N. A role for the medial region of the amygdala in mineralocorticoid-induced salt hunger. *Behavioral Neuroscience,* 1989, *103,* 178–185.

Schumacher, M., Coirini, H., Frankfurt, M., and McEwen, B. S. Localized actions of progesterone in hypothalamus involve oxytocin. *Proceedings of the National Academy of Sciences, USA,* 1989, *86,* 6798–6801.

Schumacher, M., Coirini, H., Pfaff, D. W., and McEwen, B. S. Behavioral effects of progesterone associated with rapid modulation of oxytocin receptors. *Science,* 1990, *250,* 691–694.

Schuman, E. R., and Madison, D. V. A requirement for the intercellular messenger nitric oxide in long-term potentiation. *Science,* 1991, *254,* 1503–1506.

Schuster, C. R., and Balster, R. L. The discriminative stimulus properties of drugs. *Advances in Behavioral Pharmacology,* 1977, *1,* 85–138.

Schwartz, M. F., Marin, O. S. M., and Saffran, E. M. Dissociations of language function in dementia: A case study. *Brain and Language,* 1979, *7,* 277–306.

Schwartz, M. F., Saffran, E. M., and Marin, O. S. M. The word order problem in agrammatism. I. Comprehension. *Brain and Language,* 1980, *10,* 249–262.

Schwartz, M. W., Peskind, E., Raskind, M., Boyko, E. J., and Porte, D. Cerebrospinal fluid leptin levels: Relationship to plasma levels and to adiposity in humans. *Nature Medicine,* 1996, *2,* 589–593.

Schwartz, W. J., and Gainer, H. Suprachiasmatic nucleus: Use of ^{14}C-labelled deoxyglucose uptake as a functional marker. *Science,* 1977, *197,* 1089–1091.

Schwartz, W. J., Gross, R. A., and Morton, M. T. The suprachiasmatic nuclei contain a tetrodotoxin-resistant circadian pacemaker. *Proceedings of the National Academy of Sciences, USA,* 1987, *84,* 1694–1698.

Schwartz, W. J., Reppert, S. M., Eagan, S. M., and Moore-Ede, M. C. In vivo metabolic activity of the suprachiasmatic nuclei: A comparative study. *Brain Research,* 1983, *274,* 184–187.

Schwartzman, R. J., Alexander, G. M., Grothusen, J. R., and Stahl, S. CNS glucose metabolic changes in the stages of the MPTP primate model of Parkinson's disease. *Neurology,* 1987, *37,* 338.

Schwarzkopf, S. B., Nasrallah, H. A., Olson, S. C., Coffman, J. A., and McLaughlin, J. A. Perinatal complications and genetic loading in schizophrenia: Preliminary findings. *Psychiatry Research,* 1989, *27,* 233–239.

Sclafani, A., and Aravich, P. F. Macronutrient self-selection in three forms of hypothalamic obesity. *American Journal of Physiology,* 1983, *244,* R686–R694.

Sclafani, A., and Nissenbaum, J. W. Robust conditioned flavor preference produced by intragastric starch infusions in rats. *American Journal of Physiology,* 1988, *255,* R672–R675.

Scott, S. K., Young, A. W., Calder, A. J., Hellawell, D. J., Aggleton, J. P., and Johnson, M. Impaired auditory recognition of fear and anger following bilateral amygdala lesions. *Nature,* 1997, *385,* 254–257.

Scott, T. R., and Plata-Salaman, C. R. Coding of taste quality. In *Smell and Taste in Health and Disease,* edited by T. N. Getchell. New York: Raven Press, 1991.

Scott, T. R., Plata-Salaman, C. R., Smith, V. L., and Giza, B. K. Gustatory neural coding in the monkey cortex: Stimulus intensity. *Journal of Neurophysiology,* 1991, *65,* 76–86.

Scott, T. R., Yaxley, S., Sienkiewicz, Z. J., and Rolls, E. T. Gustatory responses in the nucleus tractus solitarius of the alert cynomolgus monkey. *Journal of Neurophysiology,* 1986, *55,* 182–200.

Scoville, W. B., and Milner, B. Loss of recent memory after bilateral hippocampal lesions. *Journal of Neurology, Neurosurgery and Psychiatry,* 1957, *20,* 11–21.

Seagraves, M. A., Goldberg, M. E., Deny, S., Bruce, C. J., Ungerleider, L. G., and Mishkin, M. The role of striate cortex in the guidance of eye movements in the monkey. *The Journal of Neuroscience,* 1987, *7,* 3040–3058.

Sedvall, G., Fyrö, B., Gullberg, B., Nybäck, H., Wiesel, F.-A., and Wode-Helgodt, B. Relationship in healthy volunteers between concentrations of monoamine metabolites in cerebrospinal fluid and family history of psychiatric morbidity. *British Journal of Psychiatry,* 1980, *136,* 366–374.

Seeley, R. J., Kaplan, J. M., and Grill, H. J. Effect of occluding the pylorus on intraoral intake: A test of the gastric hypothesis of meal termination. *Physiology and Behavior,* 1995, *58,* 245–249.

Seifritz, E., Müller, M. J., Schoenenberger, G. A., Trachsel, L., Hemmeter, U., Hatzinger, M., Ernst, A., Moore, P., and Holsboer-Trachsler, E. Human plasma DSIP decreases at the initiation of sleep at different circadian times. *Peptides,* 1995, *16,* 1475–1481.

Self, D. W., Barnhart, W. J., Lehman, D. A., and Nestler, E. J. Opposite modulation of cocaine-seeking behavior by D$_1$-like and D$_2$-like dopamine receptor agonists. *Science,* 1996, *271,* 1586–1589.

Selye, H. *The Stress of Life.* New York: McGraw-Hill, 1976.

Semba, K. Aminergic and cholinergic afferents to REM sleep induction regions of the pontine reticular formation of the rat. *Journal of Comparative Neurology,* 1993, *330,* 543–556.

Semenza, C., Cipolotti, L., and Denes, G. Reading aloud in jargonaphasia: An unusual dissociation in speech output. *Journal of Neurology, Neurosurgery, and Psychiatry,* 1992, *55,* 205–208.

Semenza, C., and Zettin, M. Evidence from aphasia for the role of proper names as pure referring expressions. *Nature,* 1989, *342,* 678–679.

Sergent, J., Ohta, S., and MacDonald, B. Functional neuroanatomy of face and object processing: A positron emission tomography study. *Brain,* 1992, *115,* 15–36.

Sergent, J., and Signoret, J.-L. Functional and anatomical decomposition of face processing: Evidence from prosopagnosia and PET study of normal subjects. *Philosophical Transactions of the Royal Society of London [B],* 1992, *335,* 55–62.

Sergent, J., and Villemure, J.-G. Prosopagnosia in a right hemispherectomized patient. *Brain,* 1989, *112,* 975–995.

Sesack, S. R., and Pickel, V. M. Prefrontal cortical efferents in the rat synapse on unlabeled neuronal targets of catecholamine terminals in the nucleus accumbens septi and on dopamine neurons in the ventral tegmental area. *Journal of Comparative Neurology,* 1992, *320,* 145–160.

Sforza, E., Montagna, P., Tinuper, P., Cortelli, P., Avoni, P., Ferrillo, F., Petersen, R., Gambetti, P., and Lagaresi, E. Sleep-wake cycle abnormalities in fatal familial insomnia: Evidence of the role of the thalamus in sleep regulation. *Electroencephalography and Clinical Neurophysiology,* 1995, *94,* 398–405.

Shaham, Y., and Stewart, J. Stress reinstates heroin-seeking in drug-free animals: An effect mimicking heroin, not withdrawal. *Psychopharmacology,* 1995, *119,* 334–341.

Shaikh, M. B., Schubert, K., and Siegel, A. Basal amygdaloid facilitation of midbrain periaqueductal gray elicited defensive rage behavior in the cat is mediated through NMDA receptors. *Brain Research,* 1994, *635,* 187–195.

Shaikh, M. B., and Siegel, A. Naloxone-induced modulation of feline aggression elicited from midbrain periaqueductal gray. *Pharmacology, Biochemistry, and Behavior,* 1989, *31,* 791–796.

Shaikh, M. B., Steinberg, A., and Siegel, A. Evidence that substance P is utilized in medial amygdaloid facilitation of defensive rage behavior in the cat. *Brain Research,* 1993, *625,* 283–294.

Shallice, T. Phonological agraphia and the lexical route in writing. *Brain,* 1981, *104,* 413–429.

Sham, P. C., O'Callaghan, E., Takei, N., Murray, G. K., Hare, E. H., and Murray, R. M. Schizophrenia following pre-natal exposure to influenza epidemics between 1939 and 1960. *British Journal of Psychiatry,* 1992, *160,* 461–466.

Shannon, R. V., Zeng, F. G., Kamath, V., Wygonski, J., and Ekelid, M. Speech recognition with primarily temporal cues. *Science,* 1995, *270,* 303–304.

Shapiro, L. E., Leonard, C. M., Sessions, C. E., Dewsbury, D. A., and Insel, T. R. Comparative neuroanatomy of the sexually dimorphic hypothalamus in monogamous and polygamous voles. *Brain Research,* 1991, *541,* 232–240.

Shapiro, M. L., Simon, D. K., Olton, D. S., Gage, F. H., Nilsson, O., and Björklund, A. Intrahippocampal grafts of fetal basal forebrain tissue alter place fields in the hippocampus of rats with fimbria-fornix lesions. *Neuroscience,* 1989, *32,* 1–18.

Sharp, F. R., Sagar, S. M., Hicks, K., Lowenstein, D., and Hisanaga, K. C-fos mRNA, Fos, and Fos-related antigen induction by hypertonic saline and stress. *Journal of Neuroscience,* 1991, *11,* 2321–2331.

Shavit, Y., Depaulis, A., Martin, F. C., Terman, G. W., Pechnick, R. N., Zane, C. J., Gale, P. P., and Liebeskind, J. C. Involvement of brain opiate receptors in the immune-suppressive effect of morphine. *Proceedings of the National Academy of Sciences, USA,* 1986, *83,* 7114–7117.

Shavit, Y., Lewis, J. W., Terman, G. W., Gale, R. P., and Liebeskind, J. C. Opioid peptides mediate the suppressive effect of stress on natural killer cell cytotoxicity. *Science*, 1984, *223*, 188–190.

Shelton, K. L., and Balster, R. L. Ethanol drug discrimination in rats: Substitution with GABA agonists and NMDA antagonists. *Behavioural Pharmacology*, 1994, *5*, 441–450.

Shepherd, G. M. Discrimination of molecular signals by the olfactory receptor neuron. *Neuron*, 1994, *13*, 771–790.

Sher, A. E. Surgery for obstructive sleep apnea. *Progress in Clinical Biology Research*, 1990, *345*, 407–415.

Sherrington, R., Brynjolfsson, J., Petursson, H., Potter, M., Dudleston, K., Barraclough, B., Wasmuth, J., Dobbs, M., and Gurling, H. Localization of a susceptibility locus for schizophrenia on chromosome 5. *Nature*, 1988, *336*, 164–167.

Sherry, D. F., Jacobs, L. F., and Gaulin, S. J. C. Spatial memory and adaptive specialization of the hippocampus. *Trends in Neuroscience*, 1992, *15*, 298–303.

Sherwin, B. B. Sex hormones and psychological functioning in postmenopausal women. *Experimental Gerontology*, 1994, *29*, 423–430.

Sherwin, B. B., Gelfand, M. M., and Brender, W. Androgen enhances sexual motivation in females: A prospective, crossover study of sex steroid administration in the surgical menopause. *Psychosomatic Medicine*, 1985, *47*, 339–351.

Shik, M. L., and Orlovsky, G. N. Neurophysiology of locomotor automatism. *Physiological Review*, 1976, *56*, 465–501.

Shimura, T., and Shimokochi, M. Involvement of the lateral mesencephalic tegmentum in copulatory behavior of male rats: Neuron activity in freely moving animals. *Neuroscience Research*, 1990, *9*, 173–183.

Shimura, T., Yamamoto, T., and Shimokochi, M. The medial preoptic area is involved in both sexual arousal and performance in male rats: Re-evaluation of neuron activity in freely moving animals. *Brain Research*, 1994, *640*, 215–222.

Shin, L. M., Kosslyn, S. M., McNally, R. J., Alpert, N. M., Thompson, W. L., Rauch, S. L., Macklin, M. L., and Pitman, R. K. Visual imagery and perception in posttraumatic stress disorder. *Archives of General Psychiatry*, 1997, *54*, 233–241.

Shindy, W. W., Posley, K. A., and Fuster, J. M. Reversible deficit in haptic delay tasks from cooling prefrontal cortex. *Cerebral Cortex*, 1994, *4*, 443–450.

Shipley, M. T., and Ennis, M. Functional organization of the olfactory system. *Journal of Neurobiology*, 1996, *30*, 123–176.

Shiromani, P. J., Malik, M., Winston, S., and McCarley, R. W. Time course of Fos-like immunoreactivity associated with cholinergically induced REM sleep. *Journal of Neuroscience*, 1995, *15*, 3500–3508.

Shor-Posner, G., Azar, A. P., Jhanwar-Uniyal, M., Filart, R., and Leibowitz, S. F. Destruction of noradrenergic innervation to the paraventricular nucleus: Deficits in food intake, macronutrient selection, and compensatory eating after food deprivation. *Pharmacology, Biochemistry, and Behavior*, 1986, *25*, 381–392.

Shouse, M. N., and Siegel, J. M. Pontine regulation of REM sleep components in cats: Integrity of the pedunculopontine tegmentum (PPT) is important for phasic events but unnecessary for atonia during REM sleep. *Brain Research*, 1992, *571*, 50–63.

Sicard, G., and Holley, A. Receptor cell responses to odorants: Similarities and differences among odorants. *Brain Research*, 1984, *292*, 282–296.

Sidman, M., Stoddard, L. T., and Mohr, J. P. Some additional quantitative observations of immediate memory in a patient with bilateral hippocampal lesions. *Neuropsychologia*, 1968, *6*, 245–254.

Siegel, A., Schubert, K., and Shaikh, M. B. Neurochemical mechanisms underlying amygdaloid modulation of aggressive behavior in the cat. *Aggressive Behavior*, 1995, *21*, 49–62.

Siegel, J. M. Brainstem mechanisms generating REM sleep. In *Principles and Practice of Sleep Medicine*, edited by M. H. Kryger, T. Roth, and W. C. Dement. Philadelphia: W. B. Saunders, 1989.

Siegel, J. M., and McGinty, D. J. Pontine reticular formation neurons: Relationship of discharge to motor activity. *Science*, 1977, *196*, 678–680.

Siegel, R. M., and Andersen, R. A. Motion perceptual deficits following ibotenic acid lesions of the middle temporal area (MT) in the behaving monkey. *Society for Neuroscience Abstracts*, 1986, *12*, 1183.

Siegel, S. A Pavlovian conditioning analysis of morphine tolerance. In *Behavioral Tolerance: Research and Treatment Implications*, edited by N. A. Krasnegor. Washington, D.C.: NIDA Research Monographs, 1978.

Siegel, S., Hinson, R. E., Krank, M. D., and McCully, J. Heroin "overdose" death: Contribution of drug-associated environmental cues. *Science*, 1982, *216*, 436–437.

Siever, L. J., Kahn, R. S., Lawlor, B. A., Trestman, R. L., Lawrence, T. L., and Coccaro, E. F. Critical issues in defining the role of serotonin in psychiatric disorders. *Pharmacological Reviews*, 1991, *43*, 509–526.

Sigvardsson, S., Bohman, M., and Cloninger, R. Replication of the Stockholm adoption study of alcoholism. *Archives of General Psychiatry*, 1996, *53*, 681–687.

Silva, A. J., Stevens, C. F., Tonegawa, S., and Wang, Y. Deficient hippocampal long-term potentiation in α-calcium-calmodulin kinase II mutant mice. *Science*, 1992, *257*, 201–206.

Silver, R., LeSauter, J., Tresco, P. A., and Lehman, M. N. A diffusible coupling signal from the transplanted suprachiasmatic nucleus controlling circadian locomotor rhythms. *Nature*, 1996, *382*, 810–813.

Silveri, M. C. Peripheral aspects of writing can be differentially affected by sensorial and attentional defect: Evidence from a patient with afferent dysgraphia and case dissociation. *Cortex*, 1996, *32*, 155–172.

Silveri, M. C., Leggio, M. G., and Molinari, M. The cerebellum contributes to linguistic production: A case of agrammatic speech following a right cerebellar lesion. *Neurology*, 1994, *44*, 2047–2050.

Silverman, J. M., Greenberg, D. A., Altstiel, L. D., Siever, L. J., Mohs, R. C., Smith, C. J., Zhou, G. L., Hollander, T. E., Yang, X. P., Kedache, M., Li, G., Zaccario, M. L., and Davis, K. L. Evidence of a locus for schizophrenia and related disorders on the short arm of chromosome 5 in a large pedigree. *American Journal of Medical Genetics*, 1996, *67*, 162–171.

Simpson, J. B., Epstein, A. N., and Camardo, J. S. The localization of dipsogenic receptors for angiotensin II in the subfornical organ. *Journal of Comparative and Physiological Psychology*, 1978, *92*, 581–608.

Sims, E. A. H., and Horton, E. S. Endocrine metabolic adaptation to obesity and starvation. *American Journal of Clinical Nutrition*, 1968, *21*, 1455–1470.

Sinclair, D. *Mechanisms of Cutaneous Sensation*. Oxford, England: Oxford University Press, 1981.

Singer, A. G. A chemistry of mammalian pheromones. *Journal of Steroid Biochemistry and Molecular Biology*, 1991, *39*, 627–632.

Singer, A. G., Macrides, F., Clancy, A. N., and Agosta, W. C. Purification and analysis of a proteinaceous aphrodisiac pheromone from hamster vaginal discharge. *Journal of Biological Chemistry*, 1986, *261*, 13323–13326.

Singer, C., and Weiner, W. J. Male sexual dysfunction. *Neurologist*, 1996, *2*, 119–129.

Singer, F., and Zumoff, B. Subnormal serum testosterone levels in male internal medicine residents. *Steroids*, 1992, *57*, 86–89.

Sirigu, A., Duhamel, J.-R., and Poncet, M. The role of sensorimotor experience in object recognition: A case of multimodal agnosia. *Brain*, 1991, *114*, 2555–2573.

Sitaram, N., Moore, A. M., and Gillin, J. C. Experimental acceleration and slowing of REM ultradian rhythm by cholinergic agonist and antagonist. *Nature*, 1978, *274*, 490–492.

Skakkebaek, N. E., Bancroft, J., Davidson, D. W., and Warner, P. Androgen replacement with oral testosterone undecanoate in hypogonadal men: A double blind controlled study. *Clinical Endocrinology*, 1981, *14*, 49–61.

Skene, D. J., Deacon, S., and Arendt, J. Use of melatonin in circadian-rhythm, disorders and following phase-shifts. *Acta Neurobiologiae Experimentalis*, 1996, *56*, 359–362.

Skutella, T., Criswell, H., Moy, S., Probst, J. C., Breese, G. R., Jirikowski, G. F., and Holsboer, F. Corticotropin-releasing hormone (CRH) antisense oligodeoxynucleotide induces anxiolytic effects in rat. *NeuroReport*, 1994, *5*, 2181–2185.

Slater, B., and Shields, J. Genetical aspects of anxiety. In *British Journal of Psychiatry Special Publication No. 3: Studies of Anxiety*. Ashford, Kent: Headley Bros., 1969.

Slawski, B. A., and Buntin, J. D. Preoptic area lesions disrupt prolactin-induced parental feeding behavior in ring doves. *Hormones and Behavior*, 1995, *29*, 248–266.

Slimp, J. C., Hart, B. L., and Goy, R. W. Heterosexual, autosexual, and social behavior of adult male rhesus monkeys with medial preoptic-anterior hypothalamic lesions. *Brain Research*, 1975, *142*, 105–122.

Smith, C. Sleep states and learning: A review of the animal literature. *Neuroscience and Biobehavioral Reviews*, 1985, *9*, 157–168.

Smith, C. Sleep states, memory processes and synaptic plasticity. *Behavioural Brain Research*, 1996, *78*, 49–56.

Smith, C., and Lapp, L. Increased number of REMs following an intensive learning. *Sleep*, 1991, *14*, 325–330.

Smith, G. P., Gibbs, J., and Kulkosky, P. J. Relationships between brain-gut peptides and neurons in the control of food intake. In *The Neural Basis of Feeding and Reward*, edited by B. G. Hoebel and D. Novin. Brunswick, Maine: Haer Institute, 1982.

Smith, M. J. Sex determination: Turning on sex. *Current Biology*, 1994, *4*, 1003–1005.

Smith, P. M., Beninger, R. J., and Ferguson, A. V. Subfornical organ stimulation elicits drinking. *Brain Research Bulletin*, 1995, *38*, 209–213.

Smith-Swintosky, V. L., Plata-Salaman, C. R., and Scott, T. R. Gustatory neural coding in the monkey cortex: Stimulus quality. *Journal of Neurophysiology*, 1991, *66*, 1156–1165.

Smulders, T. V., Sasson, A. D., and DeVoogd, T. J. Seasonal variation in hippocampal volume in a food-storing bird, the black-capped chickadee. *Journal of Neurobiology*, 1995, *27*, 15–25.

Snyder, F. Towards an evolutionary theory of dreaming. *American Journal of Psychiatry*, 1966, *123*, 121–136.

Snyder, S. H. *Madness and the Brain*. New York: McGraw-Hill, 1974.

Soares, J. C., and Mann, J. J. The anatomy of mood disorders: Review of structural neuroimaging studies. *Biological Psychiatry*, 1997, *42*, 86–106.

Solyom, L., Turnbull, I. M., and Wilensky, M. A case of self-inflicted leucotomy. *British Journal of Psychiatry*, 1987, *151*, 855–857.

Sørensen, T. I. A., Price, R. A., Stunkard, A. J., and Schulsinger, F. Genetics of obesity in adult adoptees and their biological siblings. *British Medical Journal*, 1989, *298*, 87–90.

Spence, M. A., Flodman, P. L., Sadovnick, A. D., Bailey-Wilson, J. E., Ameli, H., and Remick, R. A. Bipolar disorder: Evidence for a major locus. *American Journal of Medical Genetics*, 1995, *60*, 370–376.

Sperry, R. W. Brain bisection and consciousness. In *Brain and Conscious Experience*, edited by J. Eccles. New York: Springer-Verlag, 1966.

Spiegler, B. J., and Mishkin, M. Evidence for the sequential participation of inferior temporal cortex and amygdala in the acquisition of stimulus-reward associations. *Behavioural Brain Research*, 1981, *3*, 303–317.

Spitzer, M., Kwong, K. K., Kennedy, W., Rosen, B. R., and Belliveau, J. W. Category-specific brain activation in fMRI during picture naming. *NeuroReport*, 1995, *6*, 2109–2112.

Squire, L. R. Stable impairment in remote memory following electroconvulsive therapy. *Neuropsychologia*, 1974, *13*, 51–58.

Squire, L. R. Memory and the hippocampus: A synthesis from findings with rats, monkeys, and humans. *Psychological Review*, 1992, *99*, 195–231.

Squire, L. R., Haist, F., and Shimamura, A. P. The neurology of memory: Quantitative assessment of retrograde amnesia in two groups of amnesia patients. *Journal of Neuroscience*, 1989, *9*, 828–839.

Squire, L. R., Shimamura, A. P., and Amaral, D. G. Memory and the hippocampus. In *Neural Models of Plasticity: Experimental and Theoretical Approaches*, edited by J. H. Byrne and W. O. Berry. San Diego: Academic Press, 1989.

Squires, R. F. How a poliovirus might cause schizophrenia: A commentary on Eagles' hypothesis. *Neurochemical Research*, 1997, *22*, 647–656.

Staley, J. K., and Mash, D. C. Adaptive increase in D3 dopamine receptors in the brain reward circuits of human cocaine fatalities. *Journal of Neuroscience*, 1996, *16*, 6100–6106.

Stallone, D., and Nicolaïdis, S. Increased food intake and carbohydrate preference in the rat following treatment with the serotonin antagonist metergoline. *Neuroscience Letters*, 1989, *102*, 319–324.

Standing, L. Learning 10,000 pictures. *Quarterly Journal of Experimental Psychology*, 1973, *25*, 207–222.

Stanley, B. G., Magdalin, W., and Leibowitz, S. F. A critical site for neuropeptide Y-induced eating lies in the caudolateral paraventricular/perifornical region of the hypothalamus. *Society for Neuroscience Abstracts*, 1989, *15*, 894.

Stanley, B. G., Magdalin, W., Seirafi, A., Thomas, W. J., and Leibowitz, S. F. The perifornical area: The major focus of (a) patchily distributed hypothalamic neuropeptide Y-sensitive feeding system(s). *Brain Research*, 1993b, *604*, 304–317.

Stanley, B. G., Willett, V. L., Donias, H. W., Dee, M. G., and Duva, M. A. Lateral hypothalamic NMDA receptors and glutamate as physiological mediators of eating and weight control. *American Journal of Physiology: Regulatory, Integrative and Comparative Physiology*, 1996, *270*, R443–R449.

Stanton, P. K., and Sejnowski, T. J. Associative long-term depression in the hippocampus induced by Hebbian covariance. *Nature*, 1989, *339*, 215–218.

Starkey, S. J., Walker, M. P., Beresford, I. J. M., and Hagan, R. M. Modulation of the rat suprachiasmatic circadian clock by melatonin in-vitro. *NeuroReport*, 1995, *6*, 1947–1951.

St. Clair, D. M., Blackwood, D., Muir, W., Baillie, D., Hubbard, A., Wright, A., and Evans, H. J. No linkage of chromosome 5q11-q13 markers to schizophrenia in Scottish families. *Nature*, 1989, *339*, 305–309.

Stebbins, W. C., Miller, J. M., Johnsson, L.-G., and Hawkins, J. E. Ototoxic hearing loss and cochlear pathology in the monkey. *Annals of Otology, Rhinology and Laryngology*, 1969, *78*, 1007–1026.

Steffens, A. B. Influence of reversible obesity on eating behavior, blood glucose and insulin in the rat. *American Journal of Physiology*, 1975, *228*, 1738–1744.

Stein, J., and Walsh, V. To see but not to read: The magnocellular theory of dyslexia. *Trends in Neuroscience*, 1997, *20*, 147–152.

Stein, L., and Belluzzi, J. D. Cellular investigations of behavioral reinforcement. *Neuroscience and Biobehavioral Reviews*, 1989, *13*, 69–80.

Stein, M. B., and Uhde, T. W. The biology of anxiety disorders. In *American Psychiatric Press Textbook of Psychopharmacology*. Washington, D.C.: American Psychiatric Press, 1995.

Steiner, H., and Gerfen, C. R. Dynorphin opioid inhibition of cocaine-induced, D_1 dopamine receptor-mediated immediate-early gene expression in the striatum. *Journal of Comparative Neurology*, 1995, *353*, 200–212.

Stellar, J. R., Kelley, A. E., and Corbett, D. Effects of peripheral and central dopamine blockade on lateral hypothalamic self-stimulation: Evidence for both reward and motor deficits. *Pharmacology, Biochemistry, and Behavior*, 1983, *18*, 433–442.

Stephan, F. K., and Nuñez, A. A. Elimination of circadian rhythms in drinking activity, sleep, and temperature by isolation of the suprachiasmatic nuclei. *Behavioral Biology*, 1977, *20*, 1–16.

Stephan, F. K., and Zucker, I. Circadian rhythms in drinking behavior and locomotor activity of rats are eliminated by hypothalamic lesion. *Proceedings of the National Academy of Sciences, USA*, 1972, *69*, 1583–1586.

Steriade, M. Basic mechanisms of sleep generation. *Neurology*, 1992, *42*(Suppl. 6), 9–18.

Steriade, M. Arousal: Revisiting the reticular activating system. *Science*, 1996, *272*, 225–226.

Steriade, M., Paré, D., Datta, S., Oakson, G., and Curró Dossi, R. Different cellular types in mesopontine cholinergic nuclei related to ponto-geniculo-occipital waves. *Journal of Neuroscience*, 1990, *8*, 2560–2579.

Sterman, M. B., and Clemente, C. D. Forebrain inhibitory mechanisms: Cortical synchronization induced by basal forebrain stimulation. *Experimental Neurology*, 1962a, *6*, 91–102.

Sterman, M. B., and Clemente, C. D. Forebrain inhibitory mechanisms: Sleep patterns induced by basal forebrain stimulation in the behaving cat. *Experimental Neurology*, 1962b, *6*, 103–117.

Stern, J. M. A revised view of the multisensory control of maternal behaviour in rats: Critical role of tactile inputs. *Ethoexperimental Approaches to the Study of Behavior*, edited by R. J. Blanchard, D.C. Blanchard, S. Parmigiani, and P. F. Brain. The Hague: Nijhoff, 1989a.

Stern, J. M. Maternal behavior: Sensory, hormonal, and neural determinants. In *Psychoendocrinology*, edited by S. Levine and F. R. Brush. New York: Academic Press, 1989b.

Sternbach, R. A. *Pain: A Psychophysiological Analysis.* New York: Academic Press, 1968.

Stevens, J. R. Neurology and neuropathology of schizophrenia. In *Schizophrenia as a Brain Disease,* edited by F. A. Henn and H. A. Nasrallah. New York: Oxford University Press, 1982.

Stevens, J. R. Schizophrenia and multiple sclerosis. *Schizophrenia Bulletin,* 1988, *14,* 231–241.

Stevens, S. S., and Newman, E. B. Localization of actual sources of sound. *American Journal of Psychology,* 1936, *48,* 297–306.

Stewart, M., and Fox, S. E. Do septal neurons pace the hippocampal theta rhythm? *Trends in Neuroscience,* 1990, *13,* 163–168.

Stewart, R. B., Russell, R. N., Lumeng, L., Li, T.-K., and Murphy, J. M. Consumption of sweet, salty, sour, and bitter solutions by selectively bred alcohol-preferring and alcohol-nonpreferring lines of rats. *Alcoholism: Clinical and Experimental Research,* 1994, *18,* 375–381.

Stine, O. C., Xu, J. F., Koskela, R., McMahon, F. J., Gschwend, M., Friddle, C., Clark, C. D., McInnis, M. G., Simpson, S. G., Breschel, T. S., Vishio, E., Riskin, K., Feilotter, H., Chen, E., Shen, S., Folstein, S., Meyers, D. A., Botstein, D., Marr, T. G., and DePaulo, J. R. Evidence for linkage of bipolar disorder to chromosome 18 with a parent-of-origin effect. *American Journal of Human Genetics,* 1995, *57,* 1384–1394.

Stinson, D., and Thompson, C. Clinical experience with phototherapy. *Journal of the Affective Disorders,* 1990, *18,* 129–135.

Stolerman, I. P., and Jarvis, M. J. The scientific case that nicotine is addictive. *Psychopharmacology,* 1995, *117,* 2–10.

Stone, A. A., Reed, B. R., and Neale, J. M. Changes in daily event frequency precede episodes of physical symptoms. *Journal of Human Stress,* 1987, *13,* 70–74.

Stoyva, J., and Metcalf, D. Sleep patterns following chronic exposure to cholinesterase-inhibiting organophosphate compounds. *Psychophysiology,* 1968, *5,* 206.

Stricker, E. M., Swerdloff, A. F., and Zigmond, M. J. Intrahypothalamic injections of kainic acid produces feeding and drinking deficits in rats. *Brain Research,* 1978, *158,* 470–473.

Stricker, E. M., and Verbalis, J. G. Caloric and noncaloric controls of food intake. *Brain Research Bulletin,* 1991, *27,* 299–303.

Stricker, E. M., and Zigmond, M. J. Recovery of function after damage to central catecholamine-containing neurons: A neurochemical model for the lateral hypothalamic syndrome. *Progress in Psychobiology and Physiological Psychology,* 1976, *6,* 121–188.

Strömland, K., Nordin, V., Miller, M., Akerstrom, B., and Gillberg, C. Autism in thalidomide embryopathy: A population study. *Developmental Medicine and Child Neurology,* 1994, *36,* 351–356.

Stromswold, K., Kaplan, D., Alpert, N., and Rauch, S. Localization of syntactic comprehension by positron emission tomography. *Brain and Language,* 1996, *52,* 452–473.

Stäubli, U., and Otaky, N. Serotonin controls the magnitude of LTP induced by theta bursts via an action on NMDA receptor-mediated responses. *Brain Research,* 1994, *643,* 10–16.

Stunkard, A. J., Sørensen, T. I. A., Harris, C., Teasdale, T. W., Chakraborty, R., Schull, W. J., and Schulsinger, F. An adoption study of human obesity. *New England Journal of Medicine,* 1986, *314,* 193–198.

Sturup, G. K. Correctional treatment and the criminal sexual offender. *Canadian Journal of Correction,* 1961, *3,* 250–265.

Su, T.-P., Pagliaro, M., Schmidt, P. J., Pickar, D., Wolkowitz, O., and Rubinow, D. R. Neuropsychiatric effects of anabolic steroids in male normal volunteers. *Journal of the American Medical Association,* 1993, *269,* 2760–2764.

Suddath, R. L., Christison, G. W., Torrey, E. F., Casanova, M. F., and Weinberger, D. R. Anatomical abnormalities in the brains of monozygotic twins discordant for schizophrenia. *The New England Journal of Medicine,* 1990, *322,* 789–794.

Sulser, F., and Sanders-Bush, E. From neurochemical to molecular pharmacology of antidepressants. In *Tribute to B. B. Brodie,* edited by E. Costa. New York: Raven Press, 1989.

Sunderland, G. S., and Sclafani, A. Taste preferences of squirrel monkeys and bonnet macaques for polycose, maltose, and sucrose. *Physiology and Behavior,* 1988, *43,* 685–690.

Suppes, T., Baldessarini, R. J., Faedda, G. L., and Tohen, M. Risk of recurrence following discontinuation of lithium treatment in bipolar disorder. *Archives of General Psychiatry,* 1991, *48,* 1082–1088.

Susser, E., Neugebauer, R., Hoek, H. W., Brown, A. S., Lin, S., Labovitz, D., and Gorman, J. M. Schizophrenia after prenatal famine: Further evidence. *Archives of General Psychiatry,* 1996, *53,* 25–31.

Susser, E. S., and Lin, S. P. Schizophrenia after prenatal exposure to the Dutch Hunger Winter of 1944–1945. *Archives of General Psychiatry,* 1992, *49,* 983–988.

Sutherland, R. J., and Rudy, J. W. Configural association theory: The role of the hippocampal formation in learning, memory, and amnesia. *Psychobiology,* 1989, *17,* 129–144.

Suzdak, P. D., Glowa, J. R., Crawley, J. N., Schwartz, R. D., Skolnick, P., and Paul, S. M. A selective imidazobenzodiazepine antagonist of ethanol in the rat. *Science,* 1986, *234,* 1243–1247.

Suzuki, T., Funada, M., Narita, M., Misawa, M., and Nagase, H. Morphine-induced place preference in the CXBK mouse: Characteristics of mu-opioid receptor subtypes. *Brain Research,* 1993, *602,* 45–52.

Svare, B. Psychobiological determinants of maternal aggressive behavior. In *Aggressive Behavior: Genetic and Neural Approaches,* edited by E. C. Simmel, M. E. Hahn, and J. K. Walters. Hillsdale, N.J.: Lawrence Erlbaum Associates, 1983.

Svare, B. Recent advances in the study of female aggressive behavior in mice. In *House Mouse Aggression: A Model for Understanding the Evolution of Social Behavior,* edited by S. Parmigiani, D. Mainardi, and P. Brain. London: Gordon and Breach, 1989.

Svare, B., Betteridge, C., Katz, D., and Samuels, O. Some situational and experiential determinants of maternal aggression in mice. *Physiology and Behavior*, 1981, *26*, 253–258.

Svare, B., and Gandelman, R. Postpartum aggression in mice: The influence of suckling stimulation. *Hormones and Behavior*, 1976, *7*, 407–416.

Svare, B., Mann, M. A., Broida, J., and Michael, S. Maternal aggression exhibited by hypophysectomized parturient mice. *Hormones and Behavior*, 1982, *16*, 455–461.

Svennilson, E., Torvik, A., Lowe, R., and Leksell, L. Treatment of Parkinsonism by stereotactic thermolesions in the pallidal region. *Neurologica Scandanavica*, 1960, *35*, 358–377.

Sverd, J. Tourette syndrome and autistic disorder: A significant relationship. *American Journal of Medical Genetics*, 1991, *39*, 173–179.

Swaab, D. F., Gooren, L. J. G., and Hofman, M. A. Brain research, gender, and sexual orientation. *Journal of Homosexuality*, 1995, *28*, 283–301.

Swaab, D. F., and Hofman, M. A. An enlarged suprachiasmatic nucleus in homosexual men. *Brain Research*, 1990, *537*, 141–148.

Swaab, D. F., and Hofman, M. A. Sexual differentiation of the human hypothalamus in relation to gender and sexual orientation. *Trends in Neuroscience*, 1995, *18*, 264–270.

Swanson, L. W., Köhler, C., and Björklund, A. The limbic region. I. The septohippocampal system. In *Handbook of Chemical Neuroanatomy. Vol. 5. Integrated Systems of the CNS, Part I*, edited by A. Björklund, T. Hökfelt, and L. W. Swanson. Amsterdam: Elsevier, 1987.

Swanson, R. A. Physiologic coupling of glial glycogen metabolism to neuronal activity in brain. *Canadian Journal of Physiology and Pharmacology*, 1992, *70*, S138–S144.

Swedo, S., Rapoport, J., Cheslow, D., Leonard, H., Ayoub, E., Hosier, D., and Wald, E. High prevalence of obsessive compulsive symptoms in patients with Sydenham's chorea. *American Journal of Psychiatry*, 1989a, *146*, 246–249.

Swedo, S. E., Pietrini, P., Leonard, H. L., Schapiro, M. B., Rettew, D.C., Goldberger, E. L., Rapoport, S. I., Rapoport, J. L., and Grady, C. L. Cerebral glucose metabolism in childhood-onset obsessive-compulsive disorder: Revisualization during pharmacotherapy. *Archives of General Psychiatry*, 1992, *49*, 690–694.

Swedo, S. E., Schapiro, M. B., Grady, C. L., Cheslow, D. L., Leonard, H. L., Kumarn, A., Friedland, R., Rapoport, S. I., and Rapoport, J. L. Cerebral glucose metabolism in childhood-onset obsessive-compulsive disorder. *Archives of General Psychiatry*, 1989b, *46*, 518–523.

Sweet, W. H. Participant in brain stimulation in behaving subjects. Neurosciences Research Program Workshop, 1966.

Swerdlow, N. R., Geyer, M. A., Vale, W. W., and Koob, G. F. Corticotropin-releasing factor potentiates acoustic startle in rats: Blockade by chlordiazepoxide. *Psychopharmacology*, 1986, *88*, 147–152.

Szuba, M. P., Baxter, L. R., and Fairbanks, L. A. Effects of partial sleep deprivation on the diurnal variation of mood and motor activity in major depression. *Biological Psychiatry*, 1991, *30*, 817–829.

Szymusiak, R., and McGinty, D. Sleep-related neuronal discharge in the basal forebrain of cats. *Brain Research*, 1986a, *370*, 82–92.

Szymusiak, R., and McGinty, D. Sleep suppression following kainic acid-induced lesions of the basal forebrain. *Experimental Neurology*, 1986b, *94*, 598–614.

Tabakoff, B., and Hoffman, P. L. Alcohol addiction: An enigma among us. *Neuron*, 1996, *16*, 909–912.

Takahashi, L. K. Hormonal regulation of sociosexual behavior in female mammals. *Neuroscience and Biobehavioral Reviews*, 1990, *14*, 403–413.

Takahashi, L. K., Turner, J. G., and Kalin, N. H. Prenatal stress alters brain catecholaminergic activity and potentiates stress-induced behavior in adult rats. *Brain Research*, 1992, *574*, 131–137.

Takahashi, N., Kawamura, M., Shinotou, H., Hirayama, K., Kaga, K., and Shindo, M. Pure word deafness due to left hemisphere damage. *Cortex*, 1992, *28*, 295–303.

Takei, N., Sham, P. C., O'Callaghan, E., Glover, G., and Murray, R. M. Early risk factors in schizophrenia: Place and season of birth. *European Psychiatry*, 1995, *10*, 165–170.

Talairach, J., Bancaud, J., Geier, S., Bordas-Ferrer, M., Bonis, Z., Szikla, G., and Rusu, M. The cingulate gyrus and human behaviour. *Electroencephalography and Clinical Neurophysiology*, 1973, *34*, 45–52.

Tam, W.-C. C., and Sewell, K. W. Seasonality of birth in schizophrenia in Taiwan. *Schizophrenia Bulletin*, 1995, *21*, 117–127.

Tamminga, C. A., Burrows, G. H., Chase, T. N., Alphs, L. D., and Thaker, G. K. Dopamine neuronal tracts in schizophrenia: Their pharmacology and *in vivo* glucose metabolism. *Annals of the New York Academy of Sciences*, 1988, *537*, 443–450.

Tan, S. E., and Liang, K. C. Spatial learning alters hippocampal calcium calmodulin-dependent protein kinase II activity in rats. *Brain Research*, 1996, *711*, 234–240.

Tanabe, T., Iino, M., Ooshima, Y., and Takagi, S. F. An olfactory area in the prefrontal lobe. *Brain Research*, 1974, *80*, 127–130.

Tanabe, T., Iino, M., and Takagi, S. G. Discrimination of odors in olfactory bulb, pyriform-amygdaloid areas, and orbitofrontal cortex of the monkey. *Journal of Neurophysiology*, 1975, *38*, 1284–1296.

Tanaka, J., and Nomura, M. Involvement of neurons sensitive to angiotensin II in the median preoptic nucleus in the drinking response induced by angiotensin II activation of the subfornical organ in rats. *Experimental Neurology*, 1993, *119*, 235–239.

Tanaka, K. Inferotemporal cortex and object vision. *Annual Review of Neuroscience*, 1996, *19*, 109–139.

Tarjan, E., Denton, D. A., and Weisinger, R. S. Atrial natriuretic peptide inhibits water and sodium intake in rabbits. *Regulatory Peptides,* 1988, *23,* 63–75.

Taylor, S. F. Cerebral blood flow activation and functional lesions in schizophrenia. *Schizophrenia Research,* 1996, *19,* 129–140.

Tei, H., Soma, Y., and Maruyama, S. Right unilateral agraphia following callosal infarction in a left-hander. *European Neurology,* 1994, *34,* 168–172.

Teitelbaum, P., and Epstein, A. N. The lateral hypothalamic syndrome: Recovery of feeding and drinking after lateral hypothalamic lesions. *Psychological Review,* 1962, *69,* 74–90.

Teitelbaum, P., and Stellar, E. Recovery from the failure to eat produced by hypothalamic lesions. *Science,* 1954, *120,* 894–895.

Tempel, D. L., Leibowitz, K. J., and Leibowitz, S. F. Effects of PVN galanin on macronutrient selection. *Peptides,* 1988, *9,* 309–314.

Tempel, D. L., and Leibowitz, S. F. Galanin inhibits insulin and corticosterone release after injection into the PVN. *Brain Research,* 1990, *536,* 353–357.

Terenius, L., and Wahlström, A. Morphine-like ligand for opiate receptors in human CSF. *Life Sciences,* 1975, *16,* 1759–1764.

Tetel, M. J., Celentano, D.C., and Blaustein, J. D. Intraneuronal convergence of tactile and hormonal stimuli associated with female reproduction in rats. *Journal of Neuroendocrinology,* 1994, *6,* 211–216.

Tetel, M. J., Getzinger, M. J., and Blaustein, J. D. Fos expression in the rat brain following vaginal-cervical stimulation by mating and manual probing. *Journal of Neuroendocrinology,* 1993, *5,* 397–404.

Tetrud, J. W., and Langston, J. W. The effect of deprenyl (Selegiline) on the natural history of Parkinson's disease. *Science,* 1989, *245,* 519–522.

Thach, W. T. Correlation of neural discharge with pattern and force of muscular activity, joint position, and direction of intended movement in motor cortex and cerebellum. *Journal of Neurophysiology,* 1978, *41,* 654–676.

Thaler, D., Chen, Y.-C., Nixon, P. D., Stern, C. E., and Passingham, R. E. The functions of the medial premotor cortex. I. Simple learned movements. *Experimental Brain Research,* 1995, *102,* 445–460.

Theorell, T., Leymann, H., Jodko, M., Konarski, K., Norbeck, H. E., and Eneroth, P. "Person under train" incidents: Medical consequences for subway drivers. *Psychosomatic Medicine,* 1992, *54,* 480–488.

Thiels, E., Xie, X. P., Yeckel, M. F., Barrionuevo, G., and Berger, T. W. NMDA receptor-dependent LTD in different subfields of hippocampus in vivo and in vitro. *Hippocampus,* 1996, *6,* 43–51.

Thompson, L. T., and Best, P. J. Long-term stability of the place-field activity of single units recorded from the dorsal hippocampus of freely behaving rats. *Brain Research,* 1990, *509,* 299–308.

Thornton, S. N., de Beaurepaire, R., and Nicolaïdis, S. Electrophysiological investigation of cells in the region of the anterior hypothalamus firing in relation to blood pressure and volaemic changes. *Brain Research,* 1984, *299,* 1–7.

Thornton, S. N., Sanchez, A., and Nicolaïdis, S. An angiotensin-independent, hypotension-induced, sodium appetite in the rat. *Physiology and Behavior,* 1994, *57,* 555–561.

Thrasher, T. N. Role of forebrain circumventricular organs in body fluid balance. *Acta Physiologica Scandanavica,* 1989, *136*(Suppl. 583), 141–150.

Thrasher, T. N., and Keil, L. C. Regulation of drinking and vasopressin secretion: Role of organum vasculosum laminae terminalis. *American Journal of Physiology,* 1987, *253,* R108–R120.

Thunhorst, R. L., and Fitts, D. A. Peripheral angiotensin causes salt appetite in the rat. *American Journal of Physiology,* 1994, *267,* R171–R177.

Tiedge, H., and Brosius, J. Translational machinery in dendrites of hippocampal neurons in culture. *Journal of Neuroscience,* 1996, *16,* 7171–7181.

Tocco, G., Maren, S., Shors, T. J., Baudry, M., and Thompson, R. F. Long-term potentiation is associated with increased [^{3}H]AMPA binding in rat hippocampus. *Brain Research,* 1992, *573,* 228–234.

Tordoff, M. G., and Friedman, M. I. Hepatic portal glucose infusions decrease food intake and increase food preference. *American Journal of Physiology,* 1986, *251,* R192–R196.

Tordoff, M. G., and Friedman, M. I. Hepatic control of feeding: Effect of glucose, fructose, and mannitol. *American Journal of Physiology,* 1988, *254,* R969–R976.

Tordoff, M. G., Hopfenbeck, J., and Novin, D. Hepatic vagotomy (partial hepatic denervation) does not alter ingestive responses to metabolic challenges. *Physiology and Behavior,* 1982, *28,* 417–424.

Tordoff, M. G., Rawson, N., and Friedman, M. I. 2,5-Anhydro-D-mannitol acts in liver to initiate feeding. *American Journal of Physiology,* 1991, *261,* R283–R288.

Tordoff, M. G., Schulkin, J., and Friedman, M. I. Further evidence for hepatic control of salt intake in rats. *American Journal of Physiology,* 1987, *253,* R444–R449.

Torrey, E. F. A viral-anatomical explanation of schizophrenia. *Schizophrenia Bulletin,* 1991, *17,* 15–18.

Torrey, E. F., Torrey, B. B., and Peterson, M. R. Seasonality of schizophrenic births in the United States. *Archives of General Psychiatry,* 1979, *34,* 1065–1070.

Träskmann, L., Åsberg, M., Bertilsson, L., and Sjöstrand, L. Monoamine metabolites in CSF and suicidal behavior. *Archives of General Psychiatry,* 1981, *38,* 631–636.

True, W. R., Rice, J., Eisen, S. A., Heath, A. C., Goldberg, J., Lyons, M. J., and Nowak, J. A twin study of genetic and environmental contributions to liability for posttraumatic stress symptoms. *Archives of General Psychiatry*, 1993, *50*, 257–264.

Trujillo, K. A., and Akil, H. Opiate tolerance and dependence: Recent findings and synthesis. *New Biologist*, 1991, *3*, 915–923.

Trulson, M. E., and Jacobs, B. L. Raphe unit activity in freely moving cats: Correlation with level of behavioral arousal. *Brain Research*, 1979, *163*, 135–150.

Tsacopoulos, M., and Magistretti, P. J. Metabolic coupling between glia and neurons. *Journal of Neuroscience*, 1996, *16*, 877–885.

Tsien, J. Z., Huerta, P. T., and Tonegawa, S. The essential role of hippocampal CA1 NMDA receptor-dependent synaptic plasticity in spatial memory. *Cell*, 1996, *87*, 1327–1338.

Tsuang, M. T., Gilbertson, M. W., and Faraone, S. V. The genetics of schizophrenia: Current knowledge and future directions. *Schizophrenia Research*, 1991, *4*, 157–171.

Turetsky, B., Cowell, P. E., Gur, R. C., Grossman, R. I., Shtasel, D. L., and Gur, R. E. Frontal and temporal lobe brain volumes in schizophrenia: Relationship to symptoms and clinical subtype. *Archives of General Psychiatry*, 1995, *52*, 1061–1070.

Turner, A. M., and Greenough, W. T. Differential rearing effects on rat visual cortex synapses. I. Synaptic and neuronal density and synapses per neuron. *Brain Research*, 1985, *329*, 195–203.

Turner, S. M., Beidel, D.C., and Nathan, R. S. Biological factors in obsessive-compulsive disorders. *Psychological Bulletin*, 1985, *97*, 430–450.

Tyrell, J. B., and Baxter, J. D. Glucocorticoid therapy. In *Endocrinology and Metabolism*, edited by P. Felig, J. D. Baxter, A. E. Broadus, and L. A. Frohman. New York: McGraw-Hill, 1981.

Ungerleider, L. G., and Mishkin, M. Two cortical visual systems. In *Analysis of Visual Behavior*, edited by D. J. Ingle, M. A. Goodale, and R. J. W. Mansfield. Cambridge, Mass.: MIT Press, 1982.

Uno, H., Tarara, R., Else, J. G., Suleman, M. A., and Sapolsky, R. M. Hippocampal damage associated with prolonged and fatal stress in primates. *Journal of Neuroscience*, 1989, *9*, 1705–1711.

Valenstein, E. S. *Great and Desperate Cures: The Rise and Decline of Psychosurgery and Other Radical Treatments for Mental Illness.* New York: Basic Books, 1986.

Valverius, P., Crabbe, J. C., Hoffman, P. L., and Tabakoff, B. NMDA receptors in mice bred to be prone or resistant to ethanol withdrawal seizures. *European Journal of Pharmacology*, 1990, *184*, 185–189.

Vandenbergh, J. G., Whitsett, J. M., and Lombardi, J. R. Partial isolation of a pheromone accelerating puberty in female mice. *Journal of Reproductive Fertility*, 1975, *43*, 515–523.

van de Poll, N. E., Taminiau, M. S., Endert, E., and Louwerse, A. L. Gonadal steroid influence upon sexual and aggressive behavior of female rats. *International Journal of Neuroscience*, 1988, *41*, 271–286.

van der Lee, S., and Boot, L. M. Spontaneous pseudopregnancy in mice. *Acta Physiologica et Pharmacologica Néerlandica*, 1955, *4*, 442–444.

Van der Zee, E. A., Compaan, J. C., De Boer, M., and Luiten, P. G. M. Changes in PKC-gamma immunoreactivity in mouse hippocampus induced by spatial discrimination learning. *Journal of Neuroscience*, 1992, *12*, 4808–4815.

Vanderwolf, C. H. Hippocampal electrical activity and voluntary movement in the rat. *Electroencephalography and Clinical Neurophysiology*, 1969, *26*, 407–418.

Vanderwolf, C. H. The electrocorticogram in relation to physiology and behavior: A new analysis. *Electroencephalography and Clinical Neurophysiology*, 1992, *82*, 165–175.

Vanderwolf, C. H., Kramis, R., Gillespie, L. A., and Bland, B. G. Hippocampal rhythmical slow activity and neocortical low voltage fast activity: Relations to behavior. In *The Hippocampus*. Vol. 2. *Neurophysiology and Behavior*, edited by R. L. Isaacson and K. H. Pribram. New York: Plenum Press, 1975.

Van Essen, D.C., Anderson, C. H., and Felleman, D. J. Information processing in the primate visual system: An integrated systems perspective. *Science*, 1992, *255*, 419–423.

Van Tol, H. H. M., Bunzow, J. R., Hong-Chang, G., Sunahara, R. K., Seeman, P., Niznik, H. B., and Civelli, O. Cloning of the gene for a human dopamine D4 receptor with high affinity for the antipsychotic clozapine. *Nature*, 1991, *350*, 614–619.

Vassar, R., Ngai, J., and Axel, R. Spatial segregation of odorant receptor expression in the mammalian olfactory epithelium. *Cell*, 1993, *74*, 309–318.

Vathy, I. U., and Etgen, A. M. Hormonal activation of female sexual behavior is accompanied by hypothalamic norepinephrine release. *Journal of Neuroendocrinology*, 1989, *1*, 383–388.

Vergnes, M., Depaulis, A., Boehrer, A., and Kempf, E. Selective increase of offensive behavior in the rat following intrahypothalamic 5,7-DHT-induced serotonin depletion. *Brain Research*, 1988, *29*, 85–91.

Verney, E. B. The antidiuretic hormone and the factors which determine its release. *Proceedings of the Royal Society of London [B]*, 1947, *135*, 25–106.

Victor, M., and Agamanolis, J. Amnesia due to lesions confined to the hippocampus: A clinical-pathological study. *Journal of Cognitive Neuroscience*, 1990, *2*, 246–257.

Vindlacheruvu, R. R., Ebling, F. J. P., Maywood, E. S., and Hastings, M. H. Blockade of glutamatergic neurotransmission in the suprachiasmatic nucleus prevents cellular and behavioural responses of the circadian system to light. *European Journal of Neuroscience*, 1992, *4*, 673–679.

Voci, V. E., and Carlson, N. R. Enhancement of maternal behavior and nest behavior following systemic and diencephalic administration of prolactin and progesterone in the mouse. *Journal of Comparative and Physiological Psychology*, 1973, *83*, 388–393.

Vogel, G. W., Buffenstein, A., Minter, K., and Hennessey, A. Drug effects on REM sleep and on endogenous depression. *Neuroscience and Biobehavioral Reviews*, 1990, *14*, 49–63.

Vogel, G. W., Thurmond, A., Gibbons, P., Sloan, K., Boyd, M., and Walker, M. REM sleep reduction effects on depression syndromes. *Archives of General Psychiatry*, 1975, *32*, 765–777.

Vogel, G. W., Vogel, F., McAbee, R. S., and Thurmond, A. J. Improvement of depression by REM sleep deprivation: New findings and a theory. *Archives of General Psychiatry*, 1980, *37*, 247–253.

vom Saal, F. S. Models of early hormonal effects on intrasex aggression in mice. In *Hormones and Aggressive Behavior*, edited by B. B. Svare. New York: Plenum Press, 1983.

vom Saal, F. S. Time-contingent change in infanticide and parental behavior induced by ejaculation in male mice. *Physiology and Behavior*, 1985, *34*, 7–15.

vom Saal, F. S., and Bronson, F. H. *In utero* proximity of female mouse fetuses to males: Effect on reproductive performance during later life. *Biology of Reproduction*, 1980, *22*, 777–780.

von Békésy, G. *Experiments in Hearing*. New York: McGraw-Hill, 1960.

von der Heydt, R., Peterhans, E., and Duersteler, M. R. Periodic-pattern-selective cells in monkey visual cortex. *Journal of Neuroscience*, 1992, *12*, 1416–1434.

Wada, J., and Rasmussen, T. Intracarotid injection of sodium amytal for the lateralization of cerebral speech dominance. *Journal of Neurosurgery*, 1960, *17*, 266–282.

Wade, G. N., Schneider, J. E., and Li, H.-Y. Control of fertility by metabolic cues. *American Journal of Physiology*, 1996, *270*, E1–E19.

Wagner, H. J. Light-dependent plasticity of the morphology of horizontal cell terminals in cone pedicles of fish retinas. *Journal of Neurocytology*, 1980, *9*, 573–590.

Wahlestedt, C., Skagerberg, G., Edman, R., Heilig, M., Sundler, F., and Hakanson, R. Neuropeptide Y (NPY) in the area of the paraventricular nucleus activates the pituitary-adrenocortical axis in the rat. *Brain Research*, 1987, *417*, 33–38.

Walker, E. F., Lewine, R. R. J., and Neumann, C. Childhood behavioral characteristics and adult brain morphology in schizophrenia. *Schizophrenia Research*, 1996, *22*, 93–101.

Walker, E. F., Savoie, T., and Davis, D. Neuromotor precursors of schizophrenia. *Schizophrenia Bulletin*, 1994, *20*, 441–451.

Walker, P. A., and Meyer, W. J. Medroxyprogesterone acetate for paraphiliac sex offender. In *Violence and the Violent Individ-* ual, edited by J. R. Hays, T. K. Roberts, and T. S. Solway. New York: SP Medical and Scientific Books, 1981.

Wallace, D. M., Magnuson, D. J., and Gray, T. S. Organization of amygdaloid projections to brainstem dopaminergic, noradrenergic, and adrenergic cell groups in the rat. *Brain Research Bulletin*, 1992, *28*, 447–454.

Wallen, K. Desire and ability: Hormones and the regulation of female sexual behavior. *Neuroscience and Biobehavioral Reviews*, 1990, *14*, 233–241.

Wallen, K., Mann, D. R., Davis-DaSilva, M., Gaventa, S., Lovejoy, J. C., and Collins, D.C. Chronic gonadotropin-releasing hormone agonist treatment suppresses ovulation and sexual behavior in group-living female rhesus monkeys (*Macaca mulatta*). *Animal Behaviour*, 1986, *36*, 369–375.

Walsh, L. L., and Grossman, S. P. Dissociation of responses to extracellular thirst stimuli following zona incerta lesions. *Pharmacology, Biochemistry, and Behavior*, 1978, *8*, 409–415.

Walsh, V., and Butler, S. R. The effects of visual cortex lesions on the perception of rotated shapes. *Behavioural Brain Research*, 1996, *76*, 127–142.

Walsh, V., Carden, D., Butler, S. R., and Kulikowski, J. J. The effects of V4 lesions on the visual abilities of macaques: Hue discrimination and color constancy. *Behavioural Brain Research*, 1993, *53*, 51–62.

Walters, E. E., and Kendler, K. S. Anorexia nervosa and anorexic-like syndromes in a population-based female twin sample. *American Journal of Psychiatry*, 1995, *152*, 64–71.

Wang, G., Tanaka, K., and Tanifuji, M. Optical imaging of functional organization in the monkey inferotemporal cortex. *Science*, 1996, *272*, 1665–1668.

Wang, Z. X., and De Vries, G. J. Androgen and estrogen effects on vasopressin messenger RNA expression in the medial amygdaloid nucleus in male and female rats. *Journal of Neuroendocrinology*, 1995, *7*, 827–831.

Wang, Z. X., Ferris, C. F., and De Vries, G. J. Role of septal vasopressin innervation in paternal behavior in prairie voles (*Microtus ochrogaster*). *Proceedings of the National Academy of Sciences, USA*, 1994, *91*, 400–404.

Wang, Z. X., Smith, W., Major, D. E., and De Vries, G. J. Sex and species differences in the effects of cohabitation on vasopressin messenger RNA expression in the bed nucleus of the stria terminalis in prairie voles (*Microtus ochrogaster*) and meadow voles (*Microtus pennsylvanicus*). *Brain Research*, 1994, *650*, 212–218.

Ward, I. Prenatal stress feminizes and demasculinizes the behavior of males. *Science*, 1972, *175*, 82–84.

Ward, I. L., and Stehm, K. E. Prenatal stress feminizes juvenile play patterns in male rats. *Physiology and Behavior*, 1991, *50*, 601–605.

Warner, R. K., Thompson, J. T., Markowski, V. P., Loucks, J. A., Bazzett, T. J., Eaton, R. C., and Hull, E. M. Microinjection of the dopamine antagonist cis-flupenthixol into the MPOA impairs copulation, penile reflexes and sexual motivation in male rats. *Brain Research*, 1991, *540*, 177–182.

Warrington, E. K., and Duchen, L. W. A re-appraisal of a case of persistent global amnesia following right temporal lobectomy: A clinico-pathological study. *Neuropsychologia*, 1992, *30*, 437–450.

Warrington, E. K., and James, M. Visual apperceptive agnosia: A clinico-anatomical study of three cases. *Cortex*, 1988, *24*, 1–32.

Warrington, E. K., and Shallice, T. Word-form dyslexia. *Brain*, 1980, *103*, 99–112.

Wauquier, A., Aloe, L., and Declerck, A. K-complexes: Are they signs of arousal or sleep protective? *Journal of Sleep Research*, 1995, *4*, 138–143.

Webb, W. B. *Sleep: The Gentle Tyrant.* Englewood Cliffs, N.J.: Prentice-Hall, 1975.

Webb, W. B. Some theories about sleep and their clinical implications. *Psychiatric Annals*, 1982, *11*, 415–422.

Webster, H. H., and Jones, B. E. Neurotoxic lesions of the dorsolateral pontomesencephalic tegmentum-cholinergic cell area in the cat. II. Effects upon sleep-waking states. *Brain Research*, 1988, *458*, 285–302.

Wehr, T. A. Improvement of depression and triggering of mania by sleep deprivation. *Journal of the American Medical Association*, 1992, *267*, 548–551.

Wehr, T. A., Giesen, H. A., Schulz, P. M., Anderson, J. L., Joseph-Vanderpool, J. R., Kelly, K., Kasper, S., and Rosenthal, N. E. Contrasts between symptoms of summer depression and winter depression. *Journal of the Affective Disorders*, 1991, *23*, 173–183.

Wehr, T. A., Sack, D. A., and Rosenthal, N. E. Seasonal affective disorder with summer depression and winter hypomania. *American Journal of Psychiatry*, 1987, *114*, 1602–1603.

Weiler, I. J., Hawrylak, N., and Greenough, W. T. Morphogenesis in memory formation: Synaptic and cellular mechanisms. *Behavioural Brain Research*, 1995, *66*, 1–6.

Weinberger, D. R. Schizophrenia and the frontal lobe. *Trends in Neurosciences*, 1988, *11*, 367–370.

Weinberger, D. R., Berman, K. F., Suddath, R., and Torrey, E. F. Evidence of dysfunction of a prefrontal-limbic network in schizophrenia: A magnetic resonance imaging and regional cerebral blood flow study of discordant monozygotic twins. *American Journal of Psychiatry*, 1992, *149*, 890–897.

Weinberger, D. R., Berman, K. F., and Zec, R. F. Physiologic dysfunction of dorsolateral prefrontal cortex in schizophrenia. I. Regional cerebral blood flow evidence. *Archives of General Psychiatry*, 1986, *43*, 114–124.

Weinberger, D. R., and Wyatt, R. J. Brain morphology in schizophrenia: *In vivo* studies. In *Schizophrenia as a Brain Disease*, edited by F. A. Henn and H. A. Nasrallah. New York: Oxford University Press, 1982.

Weiner, R. D., and Krystal, A. D. The present use of electroconvulsive therapy. *Annual Review of Medicine*, 1994, *45*, 273–281.

Weingarten, H. P. Conditioned cues elicit feeding in sated rats: A role for learning in meal initiation. *Science*, 1983, *220*, 431–432.

Weingarten, J. P., Chang, P. K., and McDonald, T. J. Comparison of the metabolic and behavioral disturbances following paraventricular- and ventromedial-hypothalamic lesions. *Brain Research Bulletin*, 1985, *14*, 551–559.

Weintraub, S., Mesulam, M.-M., and Kramer, L. Disturbances in prosody: A right-hemisphere contribution to language. *Archives of Neurology*, 1981, *38*, 742–744.

Weisinger, R. S., Blair-West, J. R., Burns, P., Denton, D. A., McKinley, M. J., and Tarjan, E. The role of angiotensin II in ingestive behaviour: A brief review of angiotensin II, thirst and Na appetite. *Regulatory Peptides*, 1996, *66*, 73–81.

Weisinger, R. S., Denton, D. A., Di Nicolantonio, R., Hards, D. K., McKinley, M. J., Oldfield, B., and Osborne, P. G. Subfornical organ lesion decreases sodium appetite in the sodium-depleted rat. *Brain Research*, 1990, *526*, 23–30.

Weiskrantz, L. Residual vision in a scotoma: A follow-up study of "form" discrimination. *Brain*, 1987, *110*, 77–92.

Weiskrantz, L., Warrington, E. K., Sanders, M. D., and Marshall, J. Visual capacity in the hemianopic field following a restricted occipital ablation. *Brain*, 1974, *97*, 709–728.

Weiss, J. M. Effects of coping response on stress. *Journal of Comparative and Physiological Psychology*, 1968, *65*, 251–260.

Weissman, M. M., Canino, G. J., Greenwald, S., Joyce, P. R., Karam, E. G., Lee, C. K., Rubio-Stipec, M., Wells, J. E., Wickramaratne, P. J., and Wittchen, H. U. Current rates and symptom profiles of panic disorder in six cross-national studies. *Clinical Neuropharmacology*, 1995, *18*(Suppl. 2), S1–S6.

Weitzman, E. D. Sleep and its disorders. *Annual Review of Neuroscience*, 1981, *4*, 381–418.

Welsh, D. K., Logothetis, D. E., Meister, M., and Reppert, S. M. Individual neurons dissociated from rat suprachiasmatic nucleus express independently phased circadian firing rhythms. *Neuron*, 1995, *14*, 697–706.

Weltzin, T. E., Hsu, L. K. G., Pollice, C., and Kaye, W. H. Feeding patterns in bulimia nervosa. *Biological Psychiatry*, 1991, *30*, 1093–1110.

Wernicke, C. *Der Aphasische Symptomenkomplex.* Breslau, Poland: Cohn & Weigert, 1874.

Westbrook, P. R. Treatment of sleep disordered breathing: Nasal continuous positive airway pressure (CPAP). *Progress in Clinical Biology Research*, 1990, *345*, 387–394.

Whipple, B., and Komisaruk, B. R. Analgesia produced in women by genital self-stimulation. *Journal of Sex Research*, 1988, *24*, 130–140.

White, F. J. Synaptic regulation of mesocorticolimbic dopamine neurons. *Annual Review of Neuroscience*, 1996, *19*, 405–436.

White, J. Autonomic discharge from stimulation of the hypothalamus in man. *Association for Research in Nervous and Mental Disorders*, 1940, *20*, 854–863.

Whitehouse, P. J., Price, D. L., Struble, R. G., Clark, A. W., Coyle, J. T., and DeLong, M. R. Alzheimer's disease and senile dementia: Loss of neurons in the basal forebrain. *Science*, 1982, *215*, 1237–1239.

Whitfield, I. C., and Evans, E. F. Responses of auditory cortical neurons to stimuli of changing frequency. *Journal of Neurophysiology*, 1965, *28*, 655–672.

Whitten, W. K. Occurrence of anestrus in mice caged in groups. *Journal of Endocrinology*, 1959, *18*, 102–107.

Wickland, C., and Turek, F. W. Lesions of the thalamic intergeniculate leaflet block activity-induced phase shifts in the circadian activity rhythm of the golden hamster. *Brain Research*, 1994, *660*, 293–300.

Wickland, C. R., and Turek, F. W. Phase-shifting effects of acute increases in activity on circadian locomotor rhythms in hamsters. *American Journal of Physiology*, 1991, *261*, R1109–R1117.

Wiener, S. I., Korshunov, V. A., Garcia, R., and Berthoz, A. Inertial, substratal and landmark cue control of hippocampal CA1 place cell activity. *European Journal of Neuroscience*, 1995, *7*, 2206–2219.

Wiener, S. I., Paul, C. A., and Eichenbaum, H. Spatial and behavioral correlates of hippocampal neuronal activity. *Journal of Neuroscience*, 1989, *9*, 2737–2763.

Wiesner, B. P., and Sheard, N. *Maternal Behaviour in the Rat*. London: Oliver and Brody, 1933.

Wilckens, T., Schweiger, U., and Pirke, K. M. Activation of 5-HT1C-receptors suppresses excessive wheel running induced by semi-starvation in the rat. *Psychopharmacology (Berlin)*, 1992, *109*, 77–84.

Wilska, A. Eine Methode zur Bestimmung der Horschwellenamplituden der Tromenfells bei verscheideden Frequenzen. *Skandinavisches Archiv für Physiologie*, 1935, *72*, 161–165.

Wilson, B. E., Meyer, G. E., Cleveland, J. C., and Weigle, D. S. Identification of candidate genes for a factor regulating body weight in primates. *American Journal of Physiology*, 1990, *259*, R1148–R1155.

Wilson, F. A. W., Scalaidhe, S. P. O., and Goldman-Rakic, P. S. Dissociation of object and spatial processing domains in primate prefrontal cortex. *Science*, 1993, *260*, 1955–1958.

Winans, S. S., and Powers, J. B. Olfactory and vomeronasal deafferentation of male hamsters: Histological and behavioral analyses. *Brain Research*, 1977, *126*, 325–344.

Winslow, J. T., Ellingoe, J., and Miczek, J. A. Effects of alcohol on aggressive behavior in squirrel monkeys: Influence of testosterone and social context. *Psychopharmacology*, 1988, *95*, 356–363.

Winslow, J. T., and Miczek, J. A. Social status as determinants of alcohol effects on aggressive behavior in squirrel monkeys *(Saimiri sciureus)*. *Psychopharmacology*, 1985, *85*, 167–172.

Winter, P., and Funkenstein, H. The auditory cortex of the squirrel monkey: Neuronal discharge patterns to auditory stimuli. *Proceedings of the 3rd Congress of Primatology, Zurich*, 1971, *2*, 24–28.

Wirz-Justice, A., Graw, P., Kraeuchi, K., Gisin, B., Jochum, A., Arendt, J., Fisch, H.-U., Buddeberg, C., and Poeldinger, W. Light therapy in seasonal affective disorder is independent of time of day or circadian phase. *Archives of General Psychiatry*, 1993, *50*, 929–937.

Wirz-Justice, A., Graw, P., Kraeuchi, K., Sarrafzadeh, A., English, J., Arendt, J., and Sand, L. 'Natural' light treatment of seasonal affective disorder. *Journal of Affective Disorders*, 1996, *37*, 109–120.

Wise, R., Chollet, F., Hadar, U., Friston, K., Hoffner, E., and Frackowiak, R. Distribution of cortical neural networks involved in word comprehension and word retrieval. *Brain*, 1991, *114*, 1803–1817.

Wise, R. A. Psychomotor stimulant properties of addictive drugs. *Annals of the New York Academy of Sciences*, 1988, *537*, 228–234.

Wise, R. A., Leone, P., Rivest, R., and Leeb, K. Elevations of nucleus accumbens dopamine and DOPAC levels during intravenous heroin self-administration. *Synapse*, 1995, *21*, 140–148.

Wise, S. P., and Rapoport, J. L. Obsessive compulsive disorder: Is it a basal ganglia dysfunction? *Psychopharmacology Bulletin*, 1988, *24*, 380–384.

Wolf, G., Schulkin, J., and Simson, P. E. Multiple factors in the satiation of salt appetite. *Behavioral Neuroscience*, 1984, *98*, 661–673.

Wolff, P. H., and Melngailis, I. Family patterns of developmental dyslexia: Clinical findings. *American Journal of Medical Genetics*, 1994, *54*, 122–131.

Wong, D. F., Wagner, H. N., Tune, L. E., Dannals, R. F., Pearlson, G. D., Links, J. M., Tamminga, C. A., Broussolle, E. P., Ravert, H. T., Wilson, A. A., Toung, J. K. T., Malat, J., Williams, J. A., O'Tuama, L. A., Snyder, S. H., Kuhar, M. J., and Gjedde, A. Positron emission tomography reveals elevated D_2 dopamine receptors in drug-naive schizophrenics. *Science*, 1986, *234*, 1558–1563.

Wong, G. T., Gannon, K. S., and Margolskee, R. F. Transduction of bitter and sweet taste by gustducin. *Nature*, 1996, *381*, 796–800.

Wong-Riley, M. Personal communication, 1978. Cited by Livingstone, M. S., and Hubel, D. H. Thalamic inputs to cytochrome oxidase-rich regions in monkey visual cortex. *Proceedings of the National Academy of Sciences, USA*, 1982, *79*, 6098–6101.

Wood, D. L., Sheps, S. G., Elveback, L. R., and Schirder, A. Cold pressor test as a predictor of hypertension. *Hypertension*, 1984, *6*, 301–306.

Wood, R. I., and Newman, S. W. Mating activates androgen receptor-containing neurons in chemosensory pathways of the male Syrian hamster brain. *Brain Research*, 1993, *614*, 65–77.

Woodruff-Pak, D. S. Eyeblink classical conditioning in H. M.: Delay and trace paradigms. *Behavioral Neuroscience*, 1993, *107*, 911–925.

Woodruff, R. A., Guze, S. B., and Clayton, P. J. Anxiety neurosis among psychiatric outpatients. *Comprehensive Psychiatry*, 1972, *13*, 165–170.

Woodworth, R. S., and Schlosberg, H. *Experimental Psychology*. New York: Holt, Rinehart and Winston, 1954.

Wooley, S. C., and Garner, D. M. Controversies in management: Should obesity be treated? Dietary treatments for obesity are ineffective. *British Medical Journal*, 1994, *309*, 655–656.

Wu, J. C., and Bunney, W. E. The biological basis of an antidepressant response to sleep deprivation and relapse: Review and hypothesis. *American Journal of Psychiatry*, 1990, *147*, 14–21.

Wu, J. C., Gillin, J. C., Buchsbaum, M. S., Hershey, T., Johnson, J. C., and Bunney, W. E. Effect of sleep deprivation on brain metabolism of depressed patients. *American Journal of Psychiatry*, 1992, *149*, 538–543.

Wyatt, R. J., Kirch, D. G., and DeLisi, L. E. Biochemical, endocrine, and immunologic studies of schizophrenia. In *Comprehensive Textbook of Psychiatry*, 5th ed., edited by H. I. Kaplan and B. J. Sadock. Baltimore: Williams and Wilkins, 1988.

Wysocki, C. J. Neurobehavioral evidence for the involvement of the vomeronasal system in mammalian reproduction. *Neuroscience and Biobehavioral Reviews*, 1979, *3*, 301–341.

Xu, M., Moratalla, R., Gold, L. H., Hiroi, N., Koob, G. F., Graybiel, A. M., and Tonegawa, S. Dopamine D_1 receptor mutant mice are deficient in striatal expression of dynorphin and in dopamine-mediated behavioral responses. *Cell*, 1994, *79*, 729–742.

Yadin, E., Thomas, E., Strickland, C. E., and Grishkat, H. L. Anxiolytic effects of benzodiazepines in amygdala-lesioned rats. *Psychopharmacology*, 1991, *103*, 473–479.

Yates, W. R., Perry, P., and Murray, S. Aggression and hostility in anabolic steroid users. *Biological Psychiatry*, 1992, *31*, 1232–1234.

Yavari, P., Vogel, G. W., and Neill, D. B. Decreased raphe unit acivity in a rat model of endogenous depression. *Brain Research*, 1993, *611*, 31–36.

Yee, F., MacLow, C., Chan, I. N., and Leibowitz, S. F. Effects of chronic paraventricular nucleus infusion of clonidine and α-methyl-*para*-tyrosine on macronutrient intake. *Appetite*, 1987, *9*, 127–138.

Yeo, J. A. G., and Keverne, E. B. The importance of vaginal-cervical stimulation for maternal behaviour in the rat. *Physiology and Behavior*, 1986, *37*, 23–26.

Yettefti, K., Orsini, J. C., and Perrin, J. Characteristics of glycemia-sensitive neurons in the nucleus tractus solitarii: Possible involvement in nutritional regulation. *Physiology and Behavior*, 1997, *61*, 93–100.

Yokoo, H., Tanaka, M., Yoshida, M., Tsuda, A., Tanaka, T., and Mizoguchi, K. Direct evidence of conditioned fear-elicited enhancement of noradrenaline release in the rat hypothalamus assessed by intracranial microdialysis. *Brain Research*, 1990, *536*, 305–308.

Yokota, T., Ishiai, S., Furukawa, T., and Tsukagoshi, H. Pure agraphia of kanji due to thrombosis of the Labbe vein. *Journal of Neurology, Neurosurgery, and Psychiatry*, 1990, *53*, 335–338.

Yost, W. A. Auditory image perception and analysis: The basis for hearing. *Hearing Research*, 1991, *56*, 8–18.

Young, A. W., Aggleton, J. P., Hellawell, D. J., Johnson, M., Broks, P., and Hanley, J. R. Face processing impairments after amygdalotomy. *Brain*, 1995, *118*, 15–24.

Young, B. J., Fox, G. D., and Eichenbaum, H. Correlates of hippocampal complex-spike cell activity in rats performing a nonspatial radial maze task. *Journal of Neuroscience*, 1994, *14*, 6553–6563.

Yuste, R., and Denk, W. Dendritic spines as basic functional units of neuronal integration. *Nature*, 1995, *375*, 682–684.

Zeki, S. The visual image in mind and brain. *Scientific American*, 1992, *267(3)*, 69–76.

Zeki, S., and Shipp, S. The functional logic of cortical connections. *Nature*, 1988, *335*, 311–317.

Zeki, S., Watson, J. D. G., Lueck, C. J., Friston, K. J., Kennard, C., and Frackowiak, R. S. A direct demonstration of functional specialization in human visual cortex. *Journal of Neuroscience*, 1991, *11*, 641–649.

Zeki, S. M. The representation of colours in the cerebral cortex. *Nature*, 1980, *284*, 412–418.

Zeng, H. K., Qian, Z. W., Myers, M. P., and Rosbach, M. A light-entrainment mechanism for the *Drosophila* circadian clock. *Nature*, 1996, *380*, 129–135.

Zenner, H.-P., Zimmermann, U., and Schmitt, U. Reversible contraction of isolated mammalian cochlear hair cells. *Hearing Research*, 1985, *18*, 127–133.

Zhang, C. Y., and Wong-Riley, M. T. T. Do nitric oxide synthase, NMDA receptor subunit R1 and cytochrome oxidase co-localize in the rat central nervous system? *Brain Research*, 1996, *729*, 205–215.

Zhou, F. C., Zhang, J. K., Lumeng, L., and Li, T. K. Mesolimbic dopamine system in alcohol-preferring rats. *Alcohol*, 1995, *12*, 403–412.

Zihl, J., Von Cramon, D., Mai, N., and Schmid, C. Disturbance of movement vision after bilateral posterior brain damage.

Further evidence and follow up observations. *Brain,* 1991, *114,* 2235–2252.

Zola-Morgan, S., Squire, L., Clower, R. P., and Rempel, N. L. Damage to the perirhinal cortex exacerbates memory impairment following lesions to the hippocampal formation. *Journal of Neuroscience,* 1993, *13,* 251–265.

Zola-Morgan, S., Squire, L., Rempel, N. L., Clower, R. P., and Amaral, D. G. Enduring memory impairment in monkeys after ischemic damage to the hippocampus. *Journal of Neuroscience,* 1992, *12,* 2582–2596.

Zola-Morgan, S., Squire, L. R., and Amaral, D. G. Human amnesia and the medial temporal region: Enduring memory impairment following a bilateral lesion limited to field CA1 of the hippocampus. *Journal of Neuroscience,* 1986, *6,* 2950–2967.

Zola-Morgan, S., Squire, L. R., and Amaral, D. G. Lesions of the hippocampal formation but not lesions of the fornix or the mammillary nuclei produce long-lasting memory impairment in monkeys. *Journal of Neuroscience,* 1989, *9,* 898–913.

Zukin, S. R., Pellegrini-Giampietro, D. E., Knapp, C. M., and Tempel, A. Opioid receptor regulation. *Handbook of Experimental Pharmacology,* 1993, *104,* 107–123.

Zumpe, D., Bonsall, R. W., and Michael, R. P. Effects of the nonsteroidal aromatase inhibitor, fadrozole, on the sexual behavior of male cynomolgus monkeys (*Macaca fascicularis*). *Hormones and Behavior,* 1993, *27,* 200–215.

Name Index

Subject Index